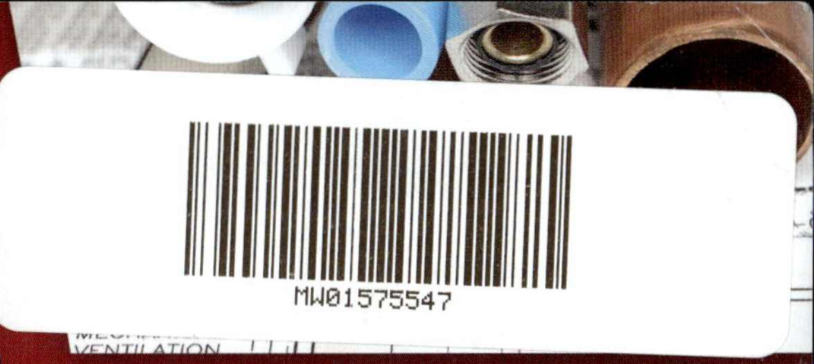

A Practical Guide to

HOME INSPECTION

4th Edition

Detailed information on performing home inspections including:

Structure, Exterior, Roofing, Plumbing, Electrical, Heating, Cooling, Interior, Insulation, Ventilation, Fireplaces & Solid Fuel Burning Appliances.

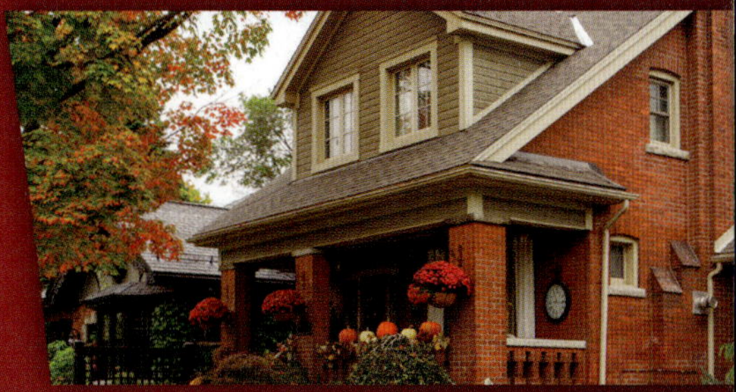

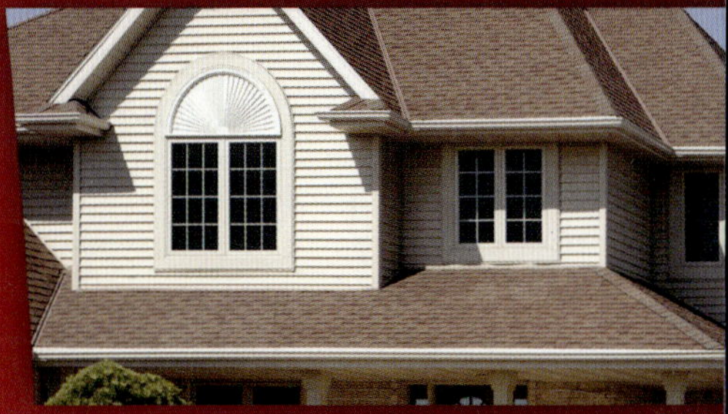

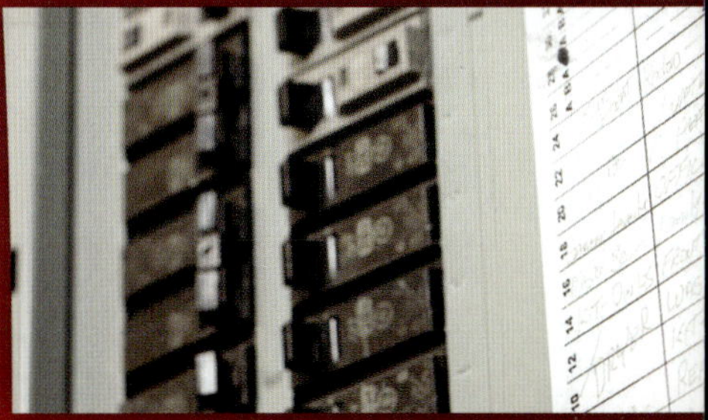

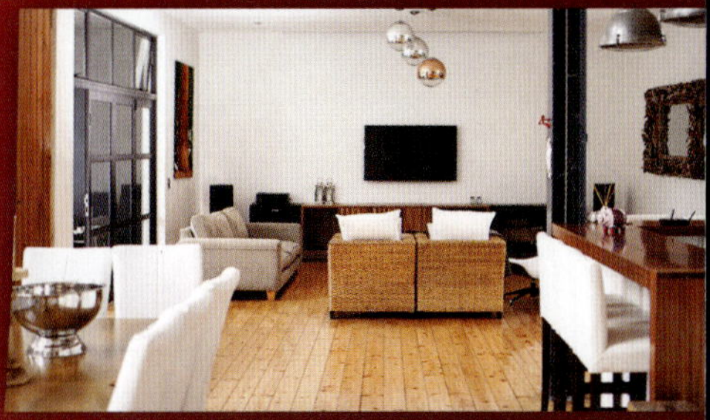

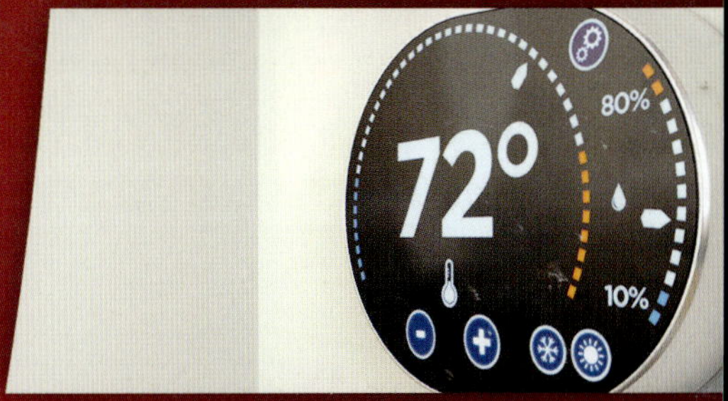

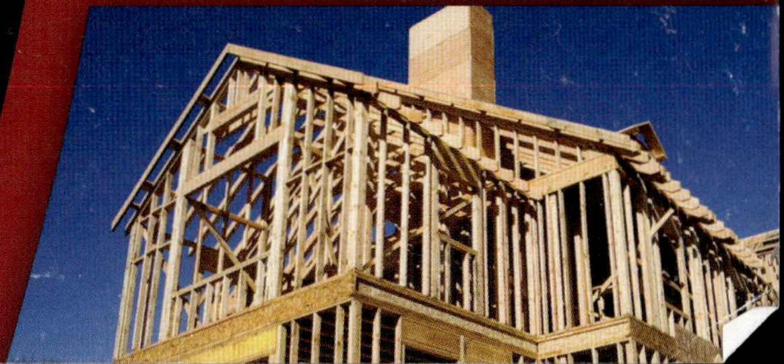

A Practical Guide to Home Inspection, 4th Edition

Vice President, Real Estate Product Management: Eric Solecki

Product Manager: Chris Chirafisi

Executive Editor: Sara Glassmeyer

Subject Matter Expert: Steven R O'Donnell

Project Manager: Arlin Kauffman, LEAP Publishing Services

Product Specialist: Abby Franklin

Director of Channel Marketing: Brad Tusing

Channel Marketing Manager: Jared Schulze

Cover Composition: Chris Dailey and Julianna Szamlewski

Illustrations by Paddy Morrissey ©2015 Code Check

Copyrighted Illustrations are for informational usage only and may not be copied or reproduced without the express written permission of Code Check. Inquiries shall be sent to paddy@codecheck.com

© 2016 American Home Inspectors Training

ALL RIGHTS RESERVED. No part of this work covered by the copyright herein may be reproduced, transmitted, stored, or used in any form or by any means graphic, electronic, or mechanical, including but not limited to photocopying, recording, scanning, digitizing, taping, web distribution, information networks, or information storage and retrieval systems, except as permitted under Section 107 or 108 of the 1976 United States Copyright Act, without the prior written permission of the publisher.

> For product information and technology assistance, contact us at
> **American Home Inspectors Training Institute Sales Support,**
> **1-800-441-9411**
> For permission to use material from this text or product.

Library of Congress Control Number: 2015955322
ISBN-13: 978-1-62980-054-7
ISBN-10: 1-62980-054-6

American Home Inspectors Training
20225 Water Tower Blvd., 4th Floor
Brookfield, WI 53045

Visit us at **www.ahit.com**

Printed in the United States of America
1 2 3 4 5 6 7 20 19 18 17 16

CONTENTS

INTRODUCTION vi

Chapter One
THE STRUCTURAL INSPECTION 1
    1.1 The Structural Inspection 1
    1.2 Foundation Construction 10
    1.3 Footings 10
    1.4 Stone Masonry 18
    1.5 Slab Construction 23
    1.6 Inspecting Foundations 24
    1.7 Let's Review 32
    1.8 Inspecting the Basement 35
    1.9 Inspecting Crawl Spaces 53
    1.10 Inspecting the Floor 54
    1.11 Structural Concerns 58
    1.12 Inspecting Slabs 60
    1.13 Above-Grade Construction 62
    1.14 Log Homes 68
    1.15 Brick Veneer over Wood Framing 69
    1.16 Reporting 74
    1.17 Interior Framing 74
    1.18 Other Framing Concerns 78
    1.19 Inspecting Roof Structure 80

Chapter Two
THE EXTERIOR INSPECTION 91
    2.1 Inspection Guidelines and Overview 91
    2.2 Inspecting the Siding 94
    2.3 Trim, Windows, Doors 118
    2.4 Around the House 128
    2.5 Landscaping and Grading 136
    2.6 Retaining Walls 138
    2.7 Inspecting the Garage and Carport 140

Chapter Three

THE ROOF INSPECTION ·················· **151**

    3.1 General Information 160
    3.2 Natural Enemies 162
    3.3 Structure from the Exterior 165
    3.4 Inspecting the Roof Covering 166
    3.5 Flashings 189
    3.6 Inspecting the Chimney 198
    3.7 Inspecting Roof Drainage 207

Chapter Four

THE PLUMBING INSPECTION ·················· **213**

    4.1 Water Service Entrance 218
    4.2 Water Distribution Piping 234
    4.3 Drain, Waste, and Vent System 251
    4.4 Hot Water System 271
    4.5 Fixtures and Faucets 289
    4.6 Gas Piping 296

Chapter Five

THE ELECTRICAL INSPECTION ·················· **301**

    5.1 Inspection Guidelines and Overview 304
    5.2 Basic Electricity 310
    5.3 Section Review 316
    5.4 Inspecting the Service Entrance 316
    5.5 Main Power 326
    5.6 Grounding System 328
    5.7 Inspecting the Main Panel 339
    5.8 Inspecting Branch Circuit Wiring 355
    5.9 Types of Branch Wiring 355
    5.10 Inspecting Fixtures, Switches, and Receptacles 367

Chapter Six

THE HEATING INSPECTION ·················· **393**

    6.1 Inspection Guidelines and Overview 395
    6.2 General Information 403
    6.3 Gas-Fired Systems 416
    6.4 Oil-Fired Systems 434
    6.5 Gravity Furnaces 447
    6.6 Forced-Air Furnaces 451

6.7 Hot Water Boilers 475
6.8 Steam Boilers 493
6.9 Other Heating Systems 500
6.10 The Cooling Inspection... 503
6.11 Air-Cooled Air-Conditioning 510
6.12 Other Cooling Systems 529
6.13 The Heat Pump.. 534

Chapter Seven
THE INTERIOR INSPECTION — 541
7.1 Inspection Guidelines and Overview 541
7.2 Walls and Ceilings 549
7.3 Floors.. 559
7.4 Windows and Doors 567
7.5 Stairs and Balconies... 578
7.6 Fireplaces and Fuel-Burning Appliances 584
7.7 Room-By-Room Inspection 595
7.8 The Insulation and Ventilation Inspection.................... 613
7.9 Insulation... 617
7.10 Ventilation 632
7.11 Inspecting the Attic 643

GLOSSARY — 651
INDEX — 679

INTRODUCTION

Until the 1990s, home inspection companies had to rely on training their own staff of inspectors. Home inspections had already been around for a number of years, but virtually all of the people performing them had no formal training. Most were contractors or tradespeople earning extra money on the side inspecting properties for friends and family. There was a need for a more formal training program with uniform goals and standards.

In 1993 the American Home Inspectors Training Institute, Ltd. (AHIT) was started to meet this need. Originally holding home inspection seminars across the country and developing study courses, books, and videos for home inspectors, American Home Inspectors Training Institute, Ltd. was founded as a result of the desire to share experience and knowledge in the industry and to promote excellence in home inspection.

A Practical Guide to Home Inspection, 4th Edition is intended for both beginning and experienced home inspectors. Whether you're studying home inspection for the first time or are using the materials as a refresher, this guide should be of assistance to you.

This book includes all aspects of home inspection. The text not only provides a broad technical background in home systems, but also includes the other things you need to know in order to perform a thorough inspection of those systems. We lay out technical information, provide industry accepted standards of practice (SOP) or guidelines for the inspection, explain instructions for inspecting system components, and point out the defects, deficiencies, and problems you'll be looking for during the inspection. This guide also includes some advice on how to report your findings to the home inspection customer.

We encourage you to follow the standards of the organization to which you might belong, or any state regulation or licensing that might take precedent over the standards used here. Use the standards in this book as a general guide for study and apply the standard or state regulation that applies to you. The inspection standards or guidelines presented here are an attempt to meet or exceed standards and regulations as they exist at the time of this book's publication.

There's a lot to learn about home inspection and this practical guide is just the starting point. For beginning inspectors, there are some hands-on exercises in this guide that should be done. We're great believers in learning by doing, and we hope you'll try them. There are also some inspection stories to let you know what it's really like out there.

Be sure to watch for the Don't Ever Miss lists. We've included them to alert home inspectors to report those defects (if found during the inspection) in the inspection report. If missed, these items are often the cause for unhappy customers or lawsuits later.

A Practical Guide to Home Inspection covers all aspects of the general home inspection and each chapter focuses on a major aspect of the inspection so you can quickly become an expert on all the parts of a home.

HOME INSPECTION

CHAPTER 1
THE STRUCTURAL INSPECTION

1.1 THE STRUCTURAL INSPECTION

The structure of a home is its *skeleton*, including the foundation and footings, the roof, and the framework—the floor, wall, and ceiling structures. Think of the home stripped of its exterior and interior finishings, standing naked without its siding and roofing materials and the interior wall, floor, and ceiling coverings. You would see exposed studs, beams, rafters, trusses, joists, and other structural components of the home.

The structure of a home is not seen in its entirety except during the construction process. Once the home is finished, much of its structure is **buried below the ground** or **hidden behind the coverings**. The home inspector learns to inspect these hidden structural components by looking at clues to what is going on under the surface. Surface cracks may indicate that the structure is moving or breaking apart. Sagging and buckling can indicate failing structural members. Staining on surface finishes may signal water penetration or condensation in the unseen components of the structure. The home inspector learns to read the visible signs. But even with excellent training and structural knowledge, the home inspector is not always able to determine whether structural defects are present. Sometimes, there are no external signs of what's going on behind the scene. Exterior and interior finishes as well as repair and the homeowner's patchwork can conceal problems with the actual structure of the house. Sometimes, the identification of problems is not possible. When there are indications or signs of problems, the home inspector may recommend that a structural engineer or contractor be consulted.

Inspecting the structure of the home is the **most important step** in the home inspection process. The general usefulness of the home depends on the soundness of its structure. And in cases of extreme structural

> **Chapter Note**
>
> *Pages 1–10 lay out the content and scope of the inspection of the structural components. It's an overview of the inspection of the home's structure, including what to observe, what to describe, and what specific actions to take. Now's the time to study these requirements in depth.*

> **Definition**
>
> *The <u>structure</u> of a home is its skeleton, including the foundation and footings, the roof, and the framework.*

INSPECTING STRUCTURE

- Foundation
- Floor structure
- Wall structure
- Columns
- Ceiling structure
- Roof structure

defects, the safety of the occupants may be at risk. The home inspector observes all aspects of the home's structure that are available for inspection, describes the type of construction and the materials used in the structural components, and reports any problems or defects found. At the same time, the inspector is dealing with major questions about the home's structural integrity, such as the failure and collapse of any structural component.

Inspection SOP

Read and study these guidelines and Standards of Practice (SOPs) or **state requirements** carefully. Pay attention to the stated objective of the structural inspection.

Not every detail of what is to be inspected and reported is stated in these standards. This is just an outline of the structural inspection. You'll learn many other details in this chapter. But for now, an overview of the inspection for each of the major structural components is listed in the table below.

Observe and/or Report: The act of making a visual examination of a system or component and reporting on its condition.	• Render a written opinion as to the performance of the foundation • The vantage point from which the attic and/or crawl space was inspected • Evidence of water penetration (attics, slabs, crawl spaces, basements) • The condition and serviceability of visible, exposed areas of foundation walls, grade slab, bearing walls, posts, piers, beams, joists, trusses, subfloors, chimney foundations, stairs, and other similar structural components • Foundations for indications of flooding, moisture, or water penetration • Probe structural components where deterioration is suspected or where clear indications of possible deterioration exist. Probing is NOT required when doing so would damage any finished surface or where no deterioration is visible or is presumed to exist. • Foundation anchoring and cripple wall bracing (related to seismic requirements) • Access attics and crawl spaces that are readily accessible, as determined by inspector
Describe: Report in writing a system or component by its type or other observed characteristics to distinguish it from other components used for the same purpose.	• The foundation • The floor structure • The wall structure • The ceiling structure • The roof structure • The location of access to the underfloor and attic spaces

Report as deficient deficiencies in:	• Deteriorated materials • Deficiencies in foundation components such as beams, joists, bridging, blocking, piers, posts, pilings, columns, sills, or subfloor • Deficiencies in retaining walls related to foundation performance • Exposed or damaged reinforcement • Crawl space drainage that is not performing • Deflections or depressions in the roof surface as related to adverse performance of the framing and decking • Deficiencies in installed framing members and decking • Attic access ladders and access openings • Deficiencies related to structural performance or water penetration (past or current) • When applicable, in attics, a floored passageway (catwalk) and service platform that would allow access for equipment inspection, service, repair, or replacement • Grade slab, floor slab, post-tension slab, etc. • Observed indications of wood in contact with or near soil • Observed indications of possible foundation movement, such as sheetrock cracks, masonry cracks, out-of-square door frames, and unlevel floors • Observed cutting, notching, and boring of framing members that may, in the inspector's opinion, present a structural or safety concern

Foundations

The home inspector examines the foundation walls from outside and inside where possible. The inspector is required to describe the **materials** and **types of foundation construction**. Examples of materials used in foundations are stone masonry, brick, poured concrete, concrete block, insulated concrete forms (ICFs), precast concrete, structural insulated panels (SIPs), and wood. Examples of foundation structures are basements, crawl spaces, slab-on-grade (including floating, monolithic, and post-tension), and pier and beam.

> ### *Definitions*
>
> *Footings are the bases on which the foundation rests. Footings support and distribute the weight of the structure to the soil.*
>
> *The foundation is that part of a structure that supports it, transmits the weight of the structure from above-grade walls to the footings, and protects the structure from the effects of soil pressure upon it.*

*The inspector examines the **condition** of the foundation and reports any visible **defects** found—deteriorating materials, cracking, movement, bowing, and water penetration, for example. The inspector is also looking for any indications of defects in the foundation **footings**, which are usually below the ground and not visible. Footing movement or failure may evidence itself above ground in the cracking or displacement of the foundation wall and the exterior walls.*

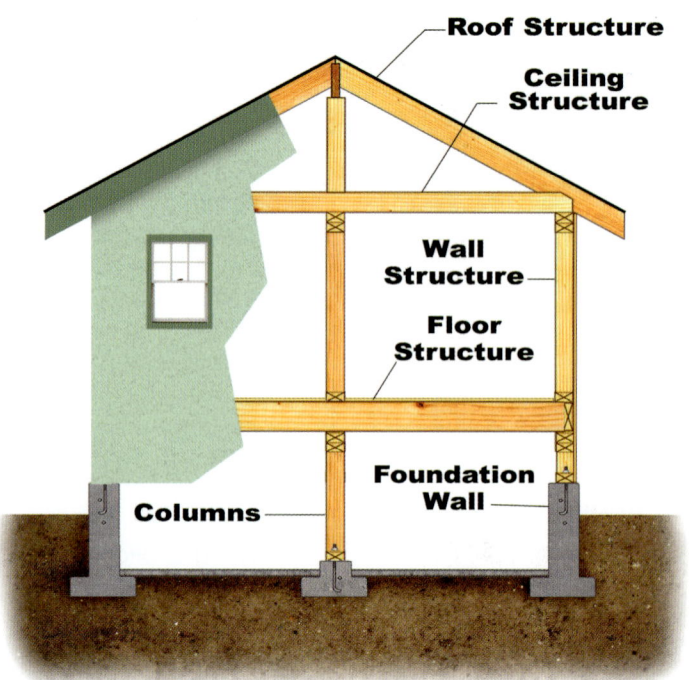

Illustration by Paddy Morrissey

Definitions

<u>Columns and Piers</u> are vertical supports that carry the weight of the structure from the girders (or beams) to the ground. Columns transmit weight to footings.

<u>Girders</u> (or beams) are horizontal load-bearing members of a floor system that carry the weight of the floor and wall loads to the foundation and columns.

<u>Joists</u> are horizontal members of a floor system that carry the weight of the floor to the foundation, girders, or load-bearing walls.

The <u>subflooring</u> transfers the load of the home's furnishings and people to the floor joists.

Basements and crawl spaces

The foundation walls are also inspected from inside the basement or crawl space. The inspector is required to report signs of **water penetration or condensation** into the building and pays attention to moisture and provisions for drainage.

Note that the inspector is required to **enter the under-floor crawl space** whenever possible and to report the methods used to observe it. The inspector should make every effort to get into the crawl space. The more difficult the access,

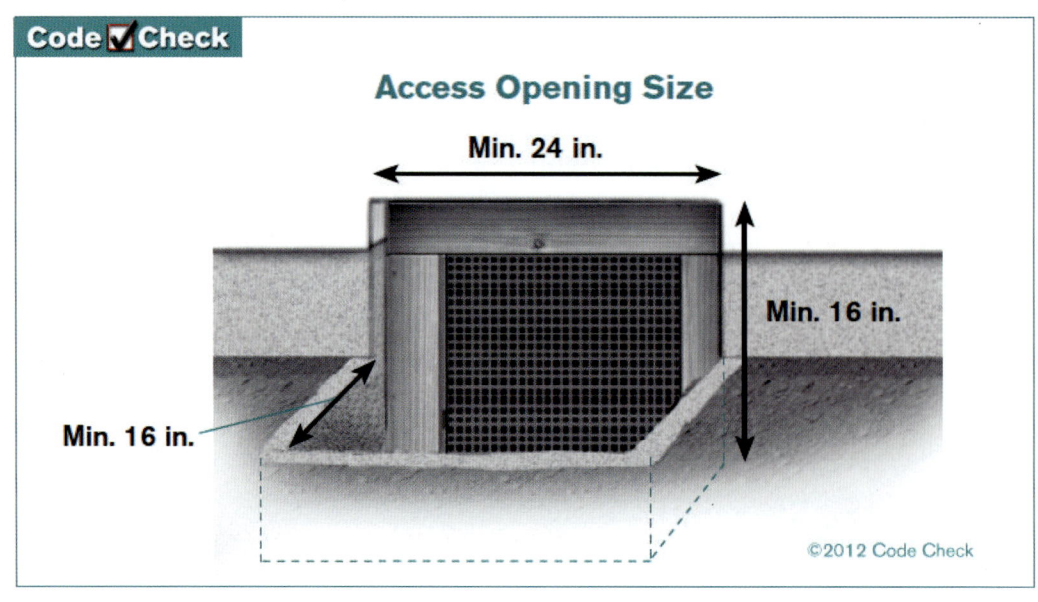

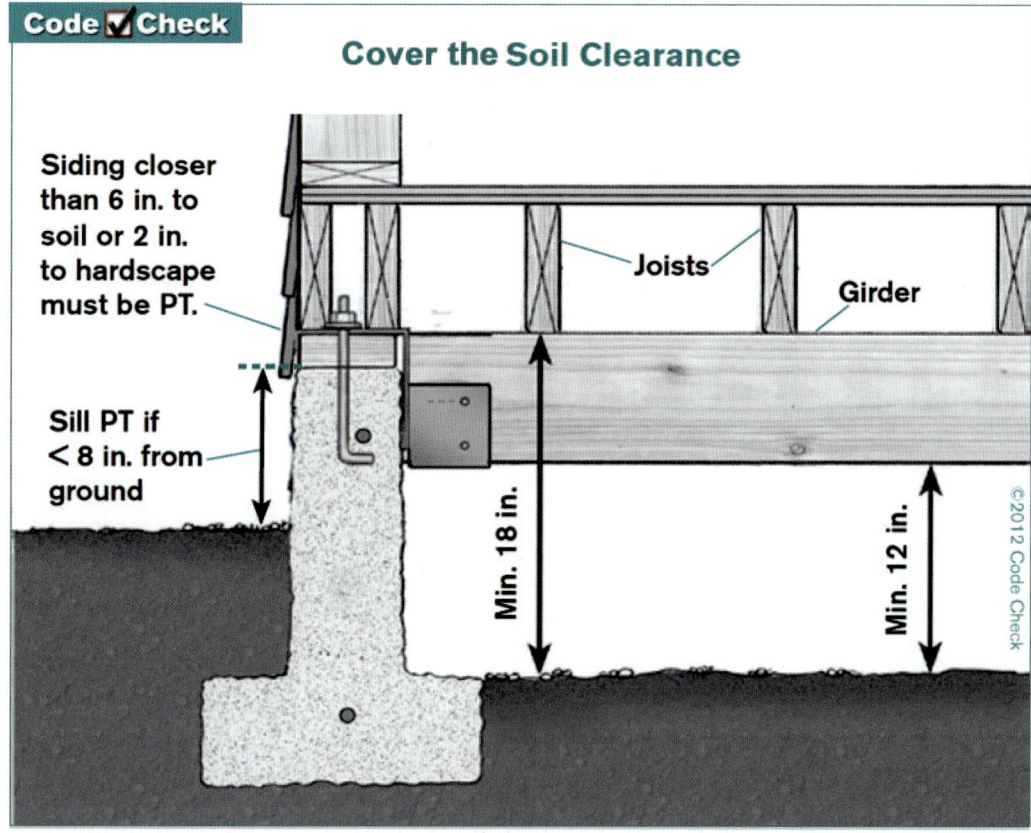

the more likely that problems are present or have not been addressed. Reporting from where the crawl space was viewed and/or whether the crawl space was not observed is for the inspector's protection.

Columns

The inspector examines the supports (columns or piers and posts) inside the foundation. Columns and piers are generally inspected from the basement or crawl space. The inspector describes the type of materials used and inspects for any deterioration in these materials such as corrosion on metal, cracking or spalling of concrete, and damage in wood posts. Note that wooden structural members are **probed** only when deterioration is observed or suspected. The inspector uses the tip of a screwdriver, an ice pick, or a knife to test the extent of wood damage or rot.

Floors

The inspector describes the materials and condition of the floor in the basement or crawl space. The floor of most basements is made from concrete, although dirt floors were common over 100 years ago. Crawl spaces often have dirt or gravel floors. Some parts of the country have wood floors for the basement. An example is in the Denver area where expansive soils are a problem. More on this will be discussed later.

Walls

In the inspection of the structural components of the house, the inspector identifies the wall construction—whether solid masonry walls, wood or steel frame, log, SIPs, ICFs, or post and beam. The wall finishes in the interior of the home are not part of the inspection of structure. Here, the inspector is concerned with the type of construction and the condition of the visible aspects of exterior wall construction and gross cracking or displacement (offset) of interior walls.

Ceilings

The floor system of the above-grade part of the structure is usually visible only from underneath—from the basement or crawl space. The inspector describes the materials and condition of girders/beams, joists, and the subfloor visible from below. The inspector inspects the junctions of the members for structural integrity—where girders (beams) rest on the foundation and/or columns and where joists meet above girders or where joists are hung from girders as with joist hangers—and checks the floor joists for visible deflection or sagging. The topmost ceiling in the structure may be visible for inspection from the attic depending on the amount of insulation present.

> **Section Note**
>
> *Ceiling, wall, and floor finishes are not part of the structural inspection. That's presented in Chapter 7: Interiors.*

> **Chapter Note**
>
> *Pages 6–10 present a discussion of the forces that act on the structure of a building.*

Roofs

If possible, the inspector gets in the attic to observe the roof structure. Again, as with crawl spaces, it's required that the inspector record the method of observation—whether viewing the roof structure from inside the attic, viewing the roof structure through an access panel while standing on a ladder, or viewing the roof structure while standing on pull-down stairs. The inspector describes the type of roof structure, whether rafters, SIPs, logs, or trusses, and inspects structural members for condition and structural integrity.

The structure of a house is more than its foundation, framework, and roof. It's a dynamic system designed to protect and preserve itself and the interior spaces it encloses from the forces working against it. Think of the structure as a fortress holding back the enemy. You might think that the structure is constructed, the finishing coverings are added, people move in, and that's that. Not so. The structure of a home is in a continual battle with elemental forces.

Weight

A structure is expected to stand up. The force of **gravity** is constantly working to bring it down. A structure must be designed to resist gravity. It must support its own weight, which is called the **dead load** of the structure. It must also support the **live load** of the structure, which includes the people inside, the furniture, and other weight such as snow on the roof. A structure *does* transfer its weight to the soil—as gravity would have it—but in a well-designed way. If the skeleton of the structure is weak, it cannot support the dead and live loads of the home, and the structure can collapse.

> **Definitions**
>
> *The <u>dead load</u> of a structure is the weight of the structure and its sheathing and wall coverings and other integral components.*
>
> *The <u>live load</u> is the weight of the home's occupants, the furnishings, and other weight the structure must support.*

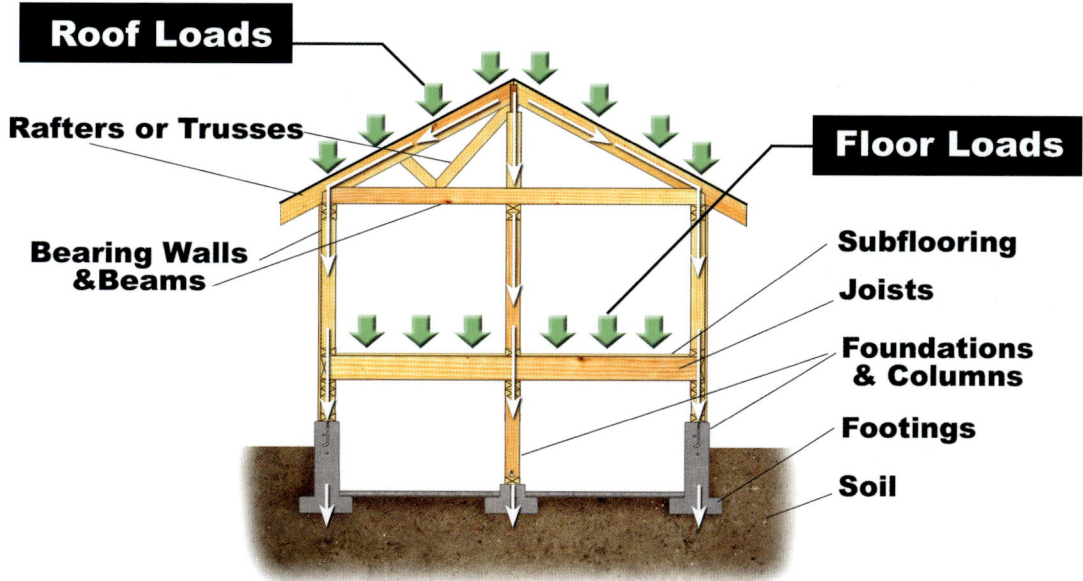

Illustration by Paddy Morrissey

Movement

A structure is expected not only to stand *up*, but also to stand *still*. Whether a structure moves is partially determined by the condition of the soil underneath and around it. The house must be sitting on soil that is strong enough to support it. When the ground below the house fails, the house sinks. Picking a good site is an important step in construction. Soil is a dynamic system. Soil

FORCES

- Gravity and weight
- Movement of soil
- Wind and water
- Internal stresses

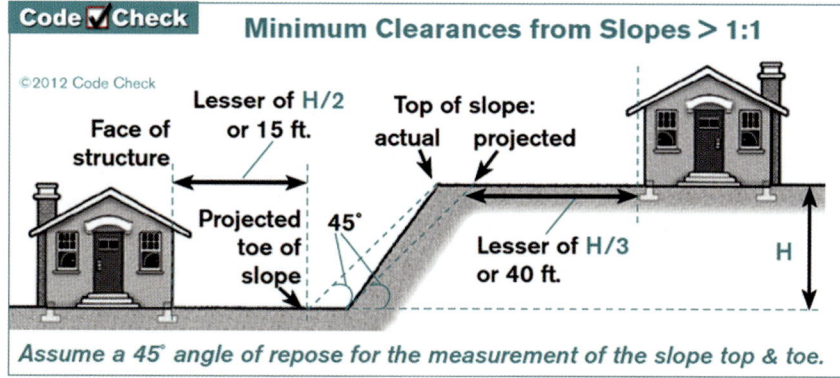

Assume a 45° angle of repose for the measurement of the slope top & toe.

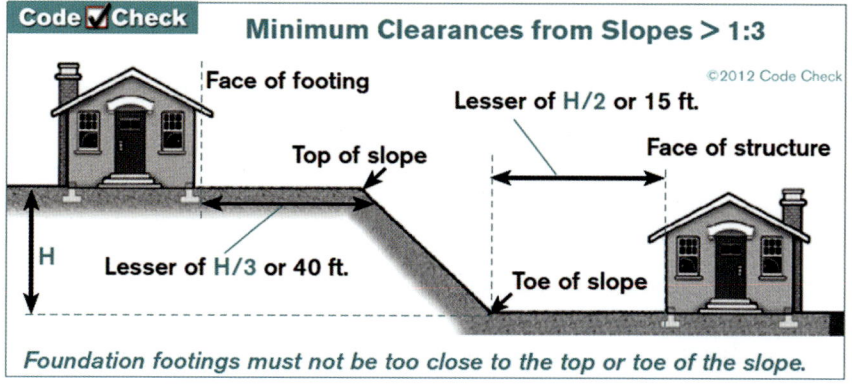

Foundation footings must not be too close to the top or toe of the slope.

THE STRUCTURAL INSPECTION 7

moves. Soil can be both expansive and subsidive—that is, it swells and shrinks depending on the water content. A house at the bottom of a hill can have soil moving toward it over time, exerting more and more pressure against the foundation. Such a house may be pushed from its original position. And a house built at the edge of a bank may begin moving toward the edge of the bank as soil erodes away.

The foundation resists the **pressure of the soil** against the structure, even in homes built on a proper site. The foundation must be built strong enough to resist this natural pressure. In earthquake zones, structures must follow local building codes to resist violent earth movement, and in areas with expansive soils, they also must be built appropriately.

Wind and Water

A structure is expected to *hold together* under the forces that act upon it. Wind acts on the structure from time to time and in varying degrees—from balmy breezes to hurricane forces. Wind can push and pull at a building and try to lift it. Structures must be strong enough to resist this pressure. Those who work in hurricane areas have the opportunity to perform wind mitigation inspections. They also may perform four-point inspections, which are also insurance-related inspections. Both inspections generally give clients a discount on their homeowners insurance if they meet certain criteria set by their insurance carrier. These inspections are making their way across the country from hurricane areas such as Florida and the Gulf Coast to areas prone to tornadoes. You might want to look into your local market for additional revenue opportunities.

Although water doesn't appear to have the power of other forces such as strong winds, it poses a big challenge to structures. Water plays a large role in the action of the soil on the foundation of the structure. Increasing the water content of the soil increases its pressure against the foundation. Then as the soil dries, it can shrink away from the foundation. Frozen water in the soil also causes the soil to expand and exert increased pressure against the foundation from the sides and from below. Underground water can move soil away, creating voids under a structure, causing the structure to settle. It will also try to enter the structure. The materials used in construction must be able to protect the structure against water penetration and the resulting deterioration of those materials. The structure must provide the proper drainage systems to deal with underground water.

> ### *Definitions*
>
> *Compression is a stress that pushes on a structural member, tending to make the member smaller in size.*
>
> *Tension is a stress that pulls at a structural member, tending to make the member larger in size.*
>
> *Shear is a stress resulting from forces being applied on a structural member from opposite directions. Shearing can cause the structural member to crack or split or completely separate.*
>
> *Bending, in terms of structure, refers to the movement of a structural member out of its original position without shearing as a result of forces applied to the member.*

Internal Stresses

The integrity of a structure depends on each of its structural members. A structure can be in a constant state of stress as individual members exert forces on each other.

For example, floor joists spanning the structure would sag without the restraint and support provided by the girders or beams, which in turn push on supporting columns and foundation walls. These members must work in concert with each other without damaging each other.

Two forces that individual structural members experience are **compression** and **tension**. Compression pushes at building components; tension pulls at them.

Structural members under compression tend to get shorter; those under tension, longer. Some members may be under both stresses. For example, collar ties withstand compression loads **along the grain** of the wood from the weight of the roof pushing the rafters inward. They could also experience tension loads from the outward push of the rafters. Trusses are another example of multiple forces at work simultaneously. The chords and webs may be in tension or compression depending on what part of the truss they make up. Girders withstand compression **against the grain** from joists above and columns below.

Two other stresses the structure must be able to withstand are **shearing** and **bending**. Individual structural members may fail under these stresses. Shearing occurs when nonaligned forces are applied against a member from opposite directions, causing the material to tear.

Movement of a structural member out of its original position without shearing is called bending. Such members can sag and buckle from the forces applied to them.

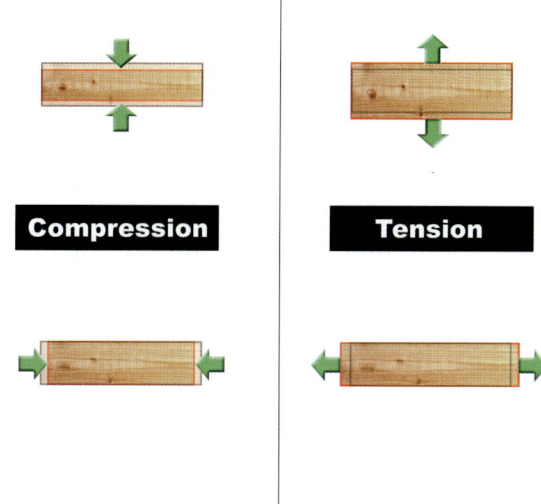

Illustration by Paddy Morrissey

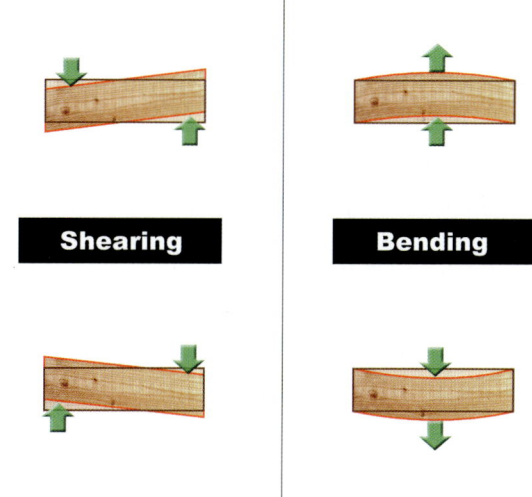

Illustration by Paddy Morrissey

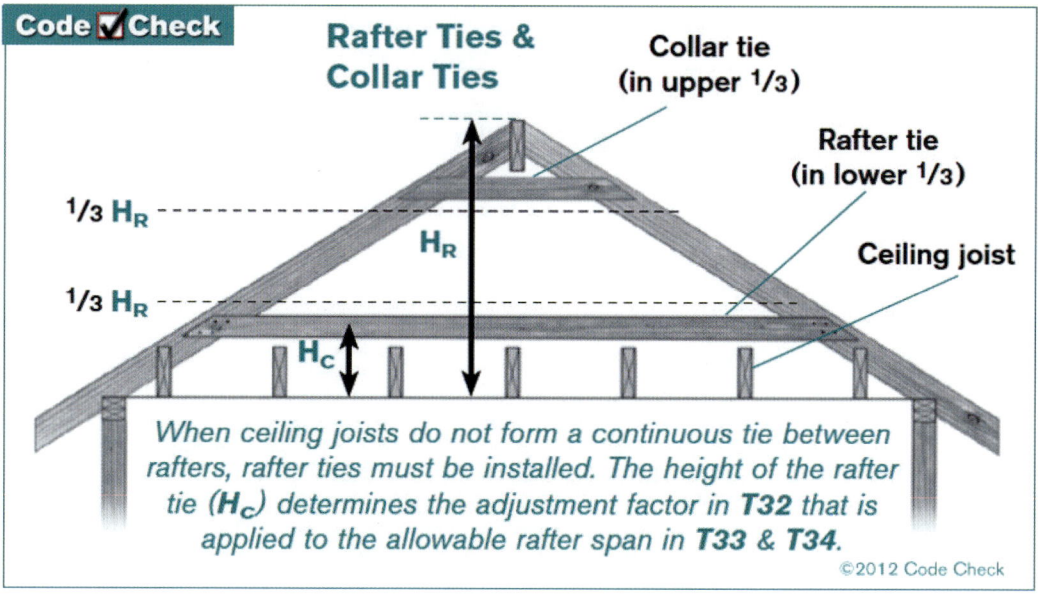

When ceiling joists do not form a continuous tie between rafters, rafter ties must be installed. The height of the rafter tie (H_C) determines the adjustment factor in **T32** that is applied to the allowable rafter span in **T33 & T34**.

©2012 Code Check

Materials used in a structure are chosen for their ability to withstand the internal stresses of the structure. Some materials do well; others don't.

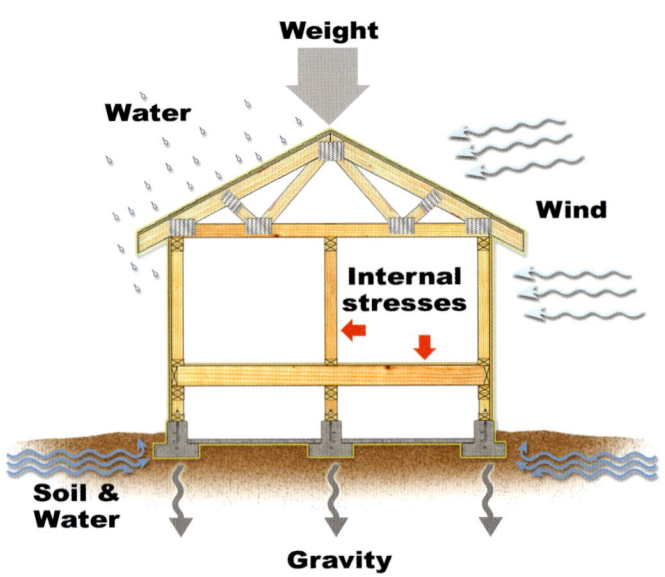

Illustration by Paddy Morrissey

Thinking about Structure

The home inspector must understand the dynamics of structure and should be thinking about the forces acting both against and within the structure. The image of the **fortress** standing firm against and doing battle with these "enemies" may be an overstated dramatic image, but it's not far from the truth. The structural integrity of a home must be sound and strong.

The home inspector, viewing a house from the structural standpoint, should be thinking about gravity and weight, the soil, water and wind, and the actions of individual members on each other. These are the **causes** of what can go wrong with the structure. Understanding these causes helps the home inspector recognize and understand their **effects** on the structure.

- Movement of the entire structure or parts of it

- Distortions of the structure such as leaning, bowing, sagging, and buckling

- Failure or defects of any structural components as evidenced by cracking and splitting

- Water penetration

- Deterioration of building materials

Chapter Note

Pages 10–24 present a discussion on foundation construction, stone masonry, and slab construction

Definitions

Grade is the slope of the land at the building site. Below grade means "below the surface of the ground."

The frost line marks the depth of penetration of frost into the ground. In cold climates, the frost line is normally about 4' below the grade.

NOTE: Not to be forgotten in the discussion of structural dynamics is the use of the **right building materials** for each structural member and the **proper construction methods**. One without the other will damage the structure. The lack of both can be a disaster. This section will address both issues.

1.2 FOUNDATION CONSTRUCTION

This section will present the various types of foundation construction.

1.3 FOOTINGS

Footings support and transmit the **dead load** (weight of the structure) and the structure's **live load** (weight of its occupants and furnishings) to the soil.

Footings are found below foundation walls and under columns, piers, or posts. In the case of monolithic slabs, the footing is part of the slab, where the thickness

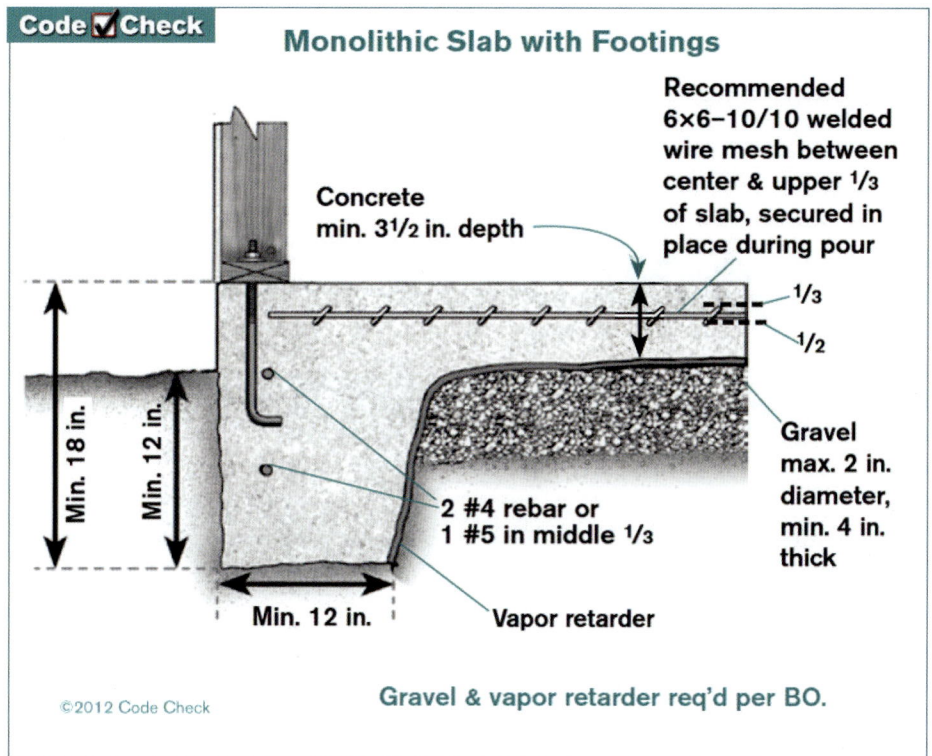

is much greater around the perimeter. Their purpose is to spread these dead and live weights over a large area and prevent the structure from sinking into the soil.

Footings should be built **below grade** on undisturbed soil and be wide enough so that the loading per square foot is less than the bearing capacity of the soil. Footings in cold climates are laid **below the frost line** to keep the foundation and columns from heaving if moisture in the ground freezes. Because footings are laid below grade, they are not usually visible.

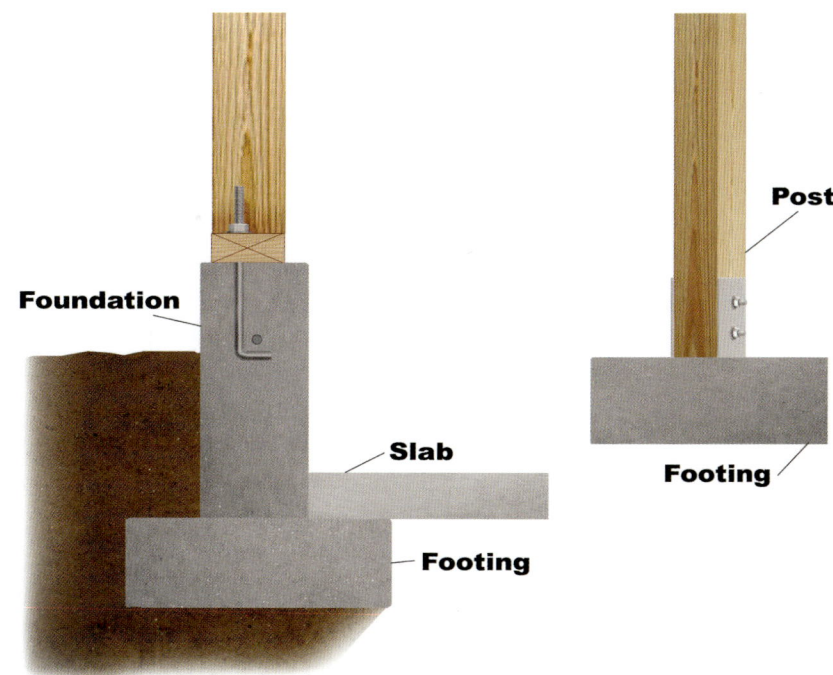

Illustration by Paddy Morrissey

THE STRUCTURAL INSPECTION

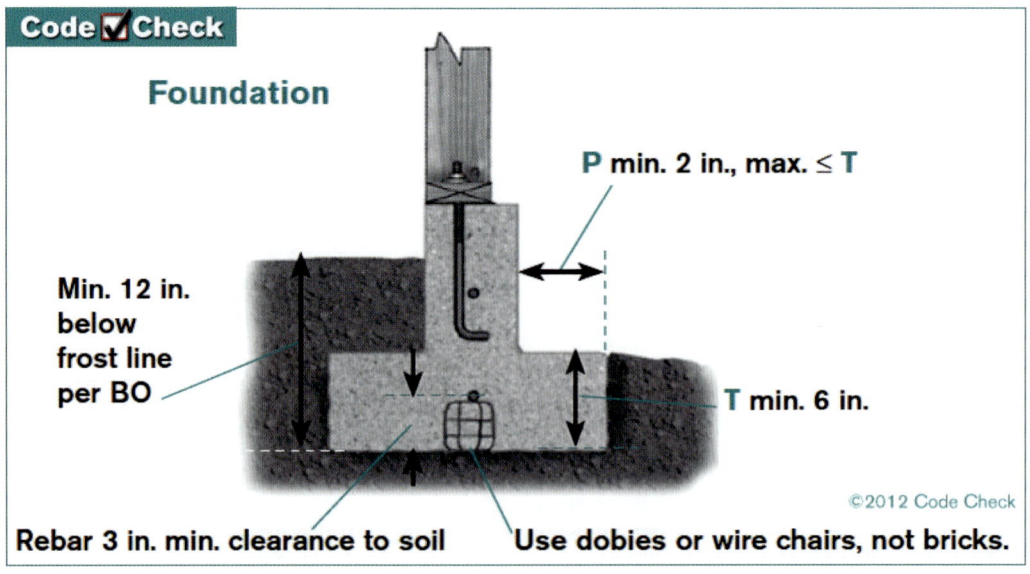

Footing materials can be stone, brick, or concrete. Today, however, almost all footings are **poured concrete**. They are normally from 16–24″ wide and from 6–16″ thick.

In those areas where soil conditions prevent the use of footings, pilings or grade beams and post-tension slabs may be used instead of conventional footings.

Footing Drains

Footing drains are used to collect and drain water away from the foundation, where it can cause damage. It is managing the water that may collect along the foundation walls and footings. **Drain tile** is laid around the perimeter of the foundation next to the footing and below the level of the floor slab. The use of perimeter drainage systems started after World War I, and at that time, the drain tile was 4″ clay tile pipe that came in sections. Today, a flexible and perforated plastic piping is used. The drain tile is laid, perforations down, around the perimeter (both inside and outside) of the foundation at the footing level. The pipe is covered with permeable fabric, known as a sock, to prevent the drain tile from clogging with fine soil particles and silt. Then the pipe is covered with at least 6″ of gravel or crushed stone. Most areas of the country require both **exterior** and **interior** drain tile. Some areas require only exterior drain tile. The requirements vary based on soil types and water table levels.

The drainage system collects water and drains it away from the house (if the slope permits). In older homes, the water often drained into a sanitary sewer or storm drain. Draining into a sanitary sewer is now prohibited. The water may also drain into a dry well or an underground gravel pit at least 15′ from the building or inside the

> **Definitions**
>
> A *footing drain*, a drainage system laid around the perimeter of a foundation below the level of the slab, drains water from the soil to another location. The *drain tile* used in footing drains today is made of flexible, perforated plastic piping.
>
> A *sump* is a pit located under the basement floor that contains an electric pump. The pit collects water from the footing drains, and the *sump pump* pumps it away from the house

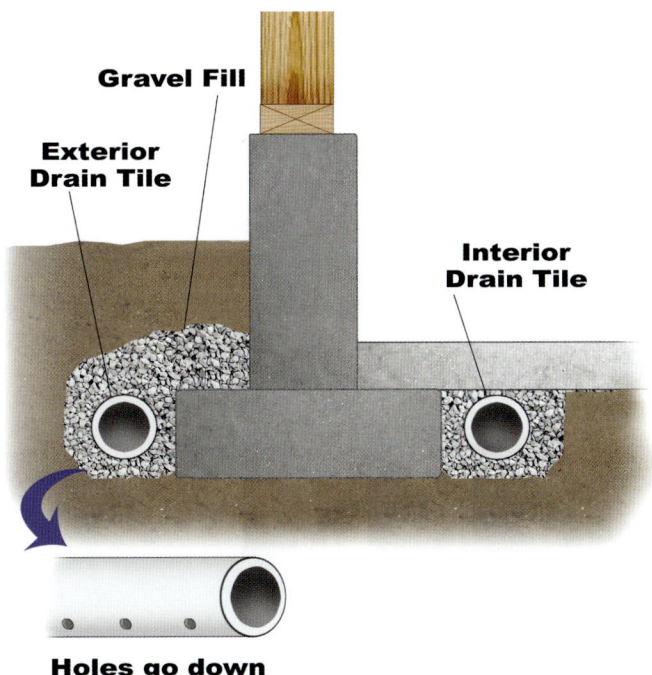

Illustration by Paddy Morrissey

foundation perimeter to a **sump**, which pumps the water away from the house. A sump is a pit located below the basement floor. In older homes, it may have concrete or earth floors and walls. Plastic or fiberglass liners are used in new construction. An electric **sump pump** is located in the pit to pump water that is coming from the perimeter drainage system away from the house. A **bleeder** runs from the exterior drain tile through the footings to interior tile, if present, and ultimately to the sump.

Interior footing drains may be added later underneath the basement floor to deal with a water problem—perhaps after the exterior drain tile has failed. Putting in interior drains to solve the problem is less expensive than doing exterior work. A concrete saw is used to cut through the concrete floor slab around the inside of the foundation wall, and a trench is dug. Drain tile (pipe) and gravel fill is laid so that water can run to a sump. Concrete may be poured to cover the drains, but you may also see an open trench or a slit left in the basement floor. You will find that the trench is not always continuous with sections of the slab left in place to provide lateral support to the walls to prevent the soil from pushing the walls in. If the trench is continuous all the way around the basement floor, look for possible foundation wall movement.

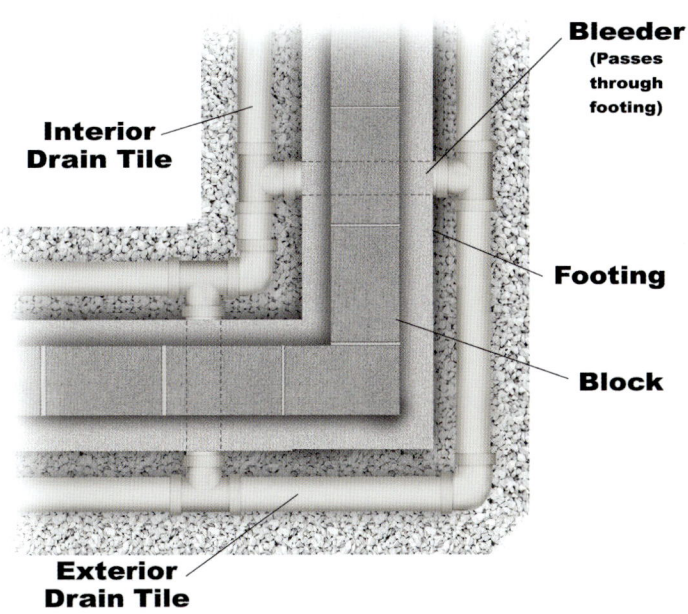

Illustration by Paddy Morrissey

THE STRUCTURAL INSPECTION 13

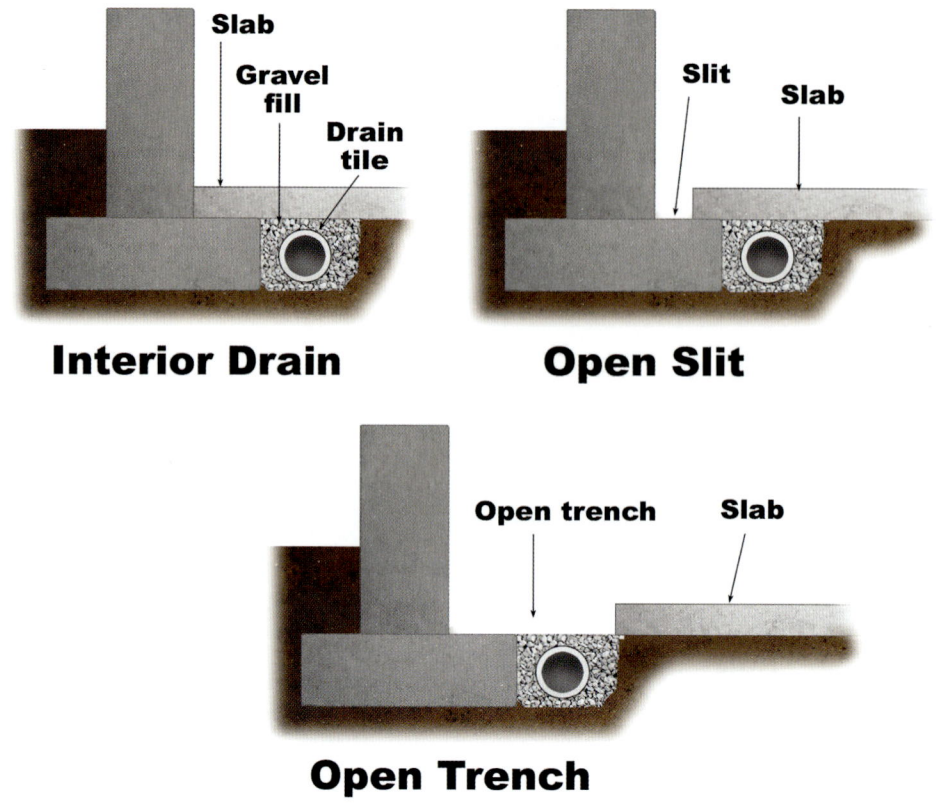

Illustration by Paddy Morrissey

Foundation Walls
The foundation supports the structure, transmits the weight of the structure from above-grade walls to the footings, and protects the structure from the effects of soil pressure on it. The foundation wall, which carries this weight below the frost line, sits on top of the footing. Because soil pressure increases with depth, a foundation wall that is below grade must be stronger (thicker) the deeper it goes. Local codes and regulations set the proper thickness for various types of foundations at

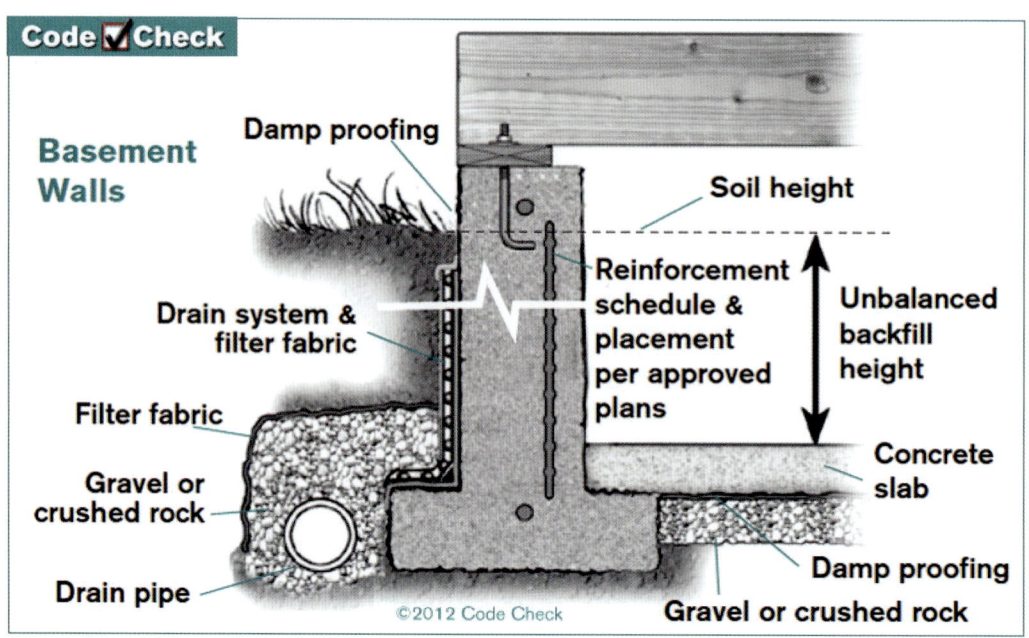

various depths. For example, concrete block walls need to be 8″ thick at a depth of 5′ but 12″ thick at a depth of 7′, whereas poured concrete foundations need to be only 6″ and 8″ thick at those same depths.

The Block Foundation

The **concrete masonry unit** (CMU) describes various kinds of hollow-core blocks used in foundation construction. **Cinder block** is made from slag from steel making or cinders from the railroad. Cinders and slag are no longer widely used as components; however, they enjoyed a long history in home construction and generally did well. However, both types of cinder blocks can deteriorate over time. Both can retain moisture and break from freezing and thawing. The iron particles in slag can expand when they rust and cause spalling and staining on the face of the block.

Concrete block is made from crushed stone, Portland cement, builder's sand, and water. Many foundation walls were made with concrete block. Concrete blocks are **mortared together** and can be reinforced with wire mesh laid in the mortar every three or four courses and/or with vertical steel bars (rebar) held in place inside the block cavity with **grout**. Rebar is steel-reinforcing bar. It is measured in 1/8″ increments. So #4 rebar is 4 eighths, or 1/2″, thick. Grout is essentially a soupy concrete with small aggregate (rock) to allow it to flow into the block cells and past the rebar. In modern construction, some form of damp proofing or waterproofing is applied to foundation walls. Black tar is a common bituminous damp-proofing material.

It retards moisture from damp soil, but it does not keep out water that pushes against the foundation. True waterproofing may consist of a liquid that is applied by a roller or brush, sheets of self-adhesive rubberized asphalt or plastic film,

> **FOUNDATION TYPES**
> - Concrete masonry unit
> - Poured concrete
> - Stone masonry
> - Brick
> - Wood foundation
> - Piles, piers, and grade beams

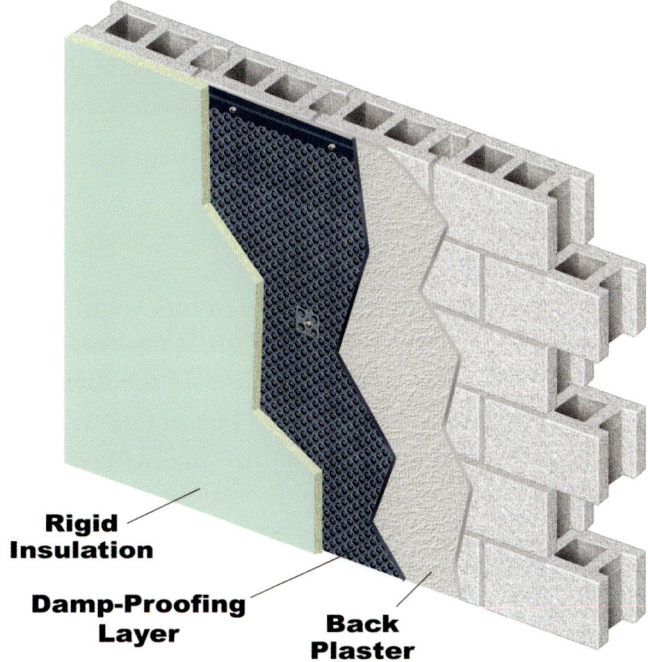

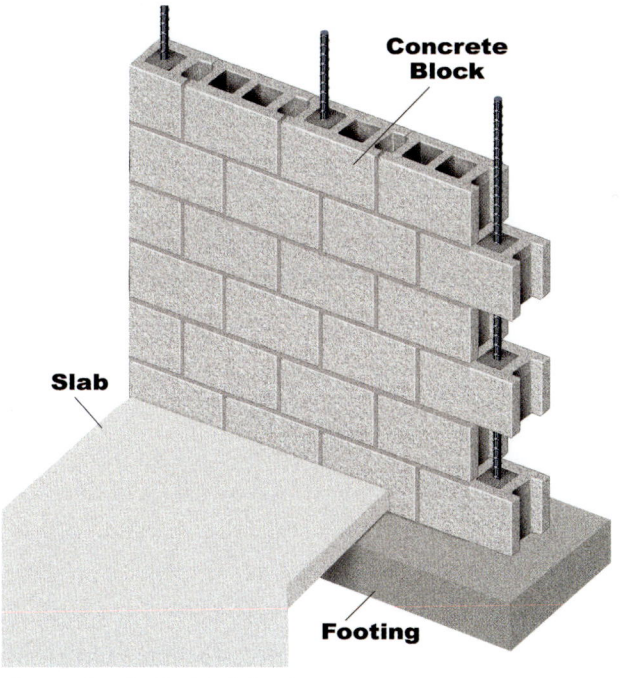

Illustration by Paddy Morrissey   Illustration by Paddy Morrissey

THE STRUCTURAL INSPECTION   15

layers of hot tar and felt, bentonite (a highly absorbent clay) panels, or cementitious (cement-based) products. The use of plaster or cement on foundation walls as a form of waterproofing is known as parging or back plastering. Parging is essentially mortar or stucco applied to the exterior of block walls. It can also be found on the inside of masonry chimneys.

Photo #1 WATERPROOFING MATERIAL

This is an example of waterproofing. The dimpled material provides an air-space that allows water to drain to the drain tile below.

For Beginning Inspectors

If you haven't seen a new foundation being laid, take a ride to a development where houses are going up. It's a good idea to do this when the construction crew is around so that you can ask questions about what you're seeing. You should find these craftsmen more than willing to explain their craft.

Poured Concrete

In the poured concrete foundation wall, **forms** are set up on the footings and concrete is poured into them. Rebar and sometimes wire reinforcing are set in the forms before the concrete is poured. To hold the forms apart and support them, wire or metal bar ties (or wall ties) may be run from side to side within the forms and left in the concrete after it has cured. Sometimes, metal clips are used to tie the forms together where they meet. The exposed parts are removed after the pour. The clips leave vertical indentations, or seams, in the surface of the wall. If the wall ties are not properly sealed, they can be a source of leakage.

A poured concrete foundation, using high-quality concrete and poured and left to cure properly, provides a very strong wall. However, the job can be botched. Failures of the wall can result from using the wrong formulation of chemical additives in the concrete, pouring in temperatures that are too hot or below freezing, or removing the forms as soon as the concrete sets. Concrete needs time to cure. Poorly cured concrete can be soft and powdery. When this happens, there can be **spalling** on the exterior and interior faces of the wall. This is where the surface of the concrete crumbles, exposing the stone or aggregate within (known as honeycombing). A really bad job can cause the wall to collapse. Letting one section set up before another is poured can cause cold joints in the surface. A cold joint is formed when the initial pour is allowed to partially or fully cure before the remainder of the pour is completed. It will create a weak spot in the wall and will be prone to leaking.

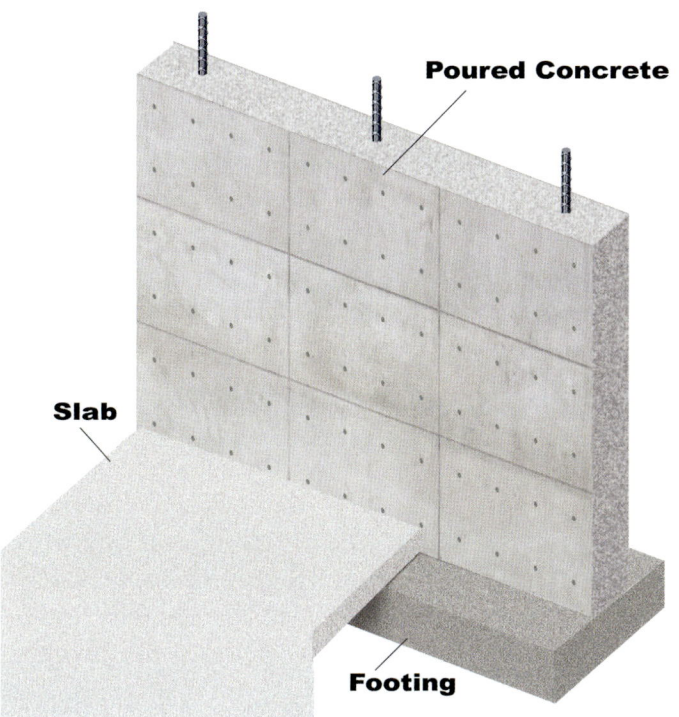

Illustration by Paddy Morrissey

Insulated Concrete Forms

A newer type of poured concrete foundation uses insulated concrete forms (ICFs). The forms consist of lightweight foam blocks or panels that are stacked and glued to the desired height. Rebar is placed vertically and horizontally per design, and the concrete is then poured into the forms. The concrete is pumped into the forms in short "lifts" so as not to blow out the foam forms. The foam forms are not removed when the concrete cures. They insulate the basement or walls of

Photo #2 INSULATED CONCRETE FORMS

These insulated concrete forms can be used for the foundation or complete exterior walls.

the house (they can be up to two stories above grade), making insulated concrete forms a good choice when there are plans to finish the basement for living space. Drywall or paneling can be attached with screws directly to the ICFs. The plastic ties that hold the inner and outer form together have a flat piece into which screws can be driven for finish materials both inside and outside.

Precast Concrete Walls

Precast concrete walls are poured at a factory and brought to the house site, where they are lowered into place by a crane. The preformed walls have several inches of foam insulation built into them. Insulation values currently range from R-5 to R-20+. They incorporate strips of treated lumber, called nailers, which are attached to the face of the concrete studs. Nailers make it easy to finish the interior of the basement without having to fasten strips of wood (furring strips) to the wall after it is set. The concrete studs also have holes cast into them so that wiring and plumbing can be run. The precast walls are set on a bed of crushed and compacted gravel instead of concrete footings. The crushed gravel has a very high load-bearing capacity and offers improved drainage. Because they are made in a factory under controlled conditions, precast walls are more uniform than poured concrete or CMU walls. Precast walls are poured square, so the finished foundation will be plumb (perfectly vertical), level (perfectly horizontal), and square (corners with perfect right angles).

Photo #3 *This is an example of a precast concrete wall. Note the concrete ribs with nailers for attachment of interior finishes.*

1.4 STONE MASONRY

A stone masonry foundation can be either **dry-laid** or **laid in mortar**. A dry-laid stone wall is built with no mortar and no footings. Gravity holds the piled stones together. The loads these walls support are distributed from stone to stone, from point to point. Smaller stones may have been inserted into gaps. These stones are usually nonstructural and are not load-bearing. They may even fall out without damaging the structural integrity of the stone foundation. Rubble stone foundations that are currently installed must be at least 16" thick and have less than 8' of backfill. In older homes, these walls may be 2' thick or more. Field stone and rubble stone are sometimes dry-laid.

> **Definitions**
>
> The <u>dry-laid</u> stone foundation is a wall constructed of stone piled on stone without mortar and with no footings.
>
> <u>Mortar</u> is a mixture of a binder (lime, masonry cement, Portland cement), an aggregate (sand), and water in many variations. It is used to bond together masonry units such as concrete blocks, stones, and bricks.

Dry-laid masonry walls, without the mortar seal, can let in water, soil, and air. Sometimes, these old foundations have been treated in some way to eliminate water problems. Concrete grout can be poured between and around the stones to absorb the external soil pressure. Depending on how this is done, it may have little effect or may even be detrimental to the integrity of the walls. Mixing modern fixes with old practices doesn't always work well. Sealing the interior of the wall by repointing or waterproofing is not usually helpful because water still enters the wall and pushes against the finish. It may also compromise the integrity of the wall by preventing it from flexing, drying out, and breathing in response to changing pressure from water and soil. If water is already present when the sealant is applied, the water will be trapped inside the wall and cause the problems the sealing is designed to prevent.

Photo #4 *This is an example of a rubble-stone wall. Note the absence of mortar.*

A stone foundation is usually very thick and can last forever. It can be constructed with fieldstone, limestone, or other types of stone used over 200 years ago.

Stone foundations laid in mortar have loads transmitted through both the mortar and the stones. In good condition, these walls are solid and waterproof. However, the lime mortar used by masons in earlier times can deteriorate over time due to humidity, soil moisture, and condensation. The mortar actually turns into sand and falls out. Because the mortar that was originally used strengthened the wall, the mason may have used a lower-quality stone than might have been used in a dry-laid foundation. Without the support of the mortar, the wall acts as though it's dry-laid and the lower-quality stones can crack and crush. The problem that many repaired walls have is that the new mortar is Portland cement–based instead of lime-based. Lime-based mortar is softer than Portland cement, which is too hard and inflexible. Again, this mixing of old practices and newer products doesn't always work well. Coastal areas of the country often used beach sand, which had a high salt content, mixed with the mortar. This leads to deterioration decades later.

> **For Beginning Inspectors**
>
> *If stone foundation walls are common in your area, you might want to visit a mason who's repaired some of them. Ask what particular problems the mason has seen in walls of this type.*

Photo #5 BRICK FOUNDATIONS

Note the orientation of the bricks. Some bricks present their sides while others their ends. This ties the brick wythes together in a wall that may be up to a couple of feet thick.

Brick Foundations

A brick foundation is less common than other types and is quite uncommon in many parts of the country. Some very old brick foundations may still be in very good condition depending on the soil and moisture content of the ground. However, a great variety of bricks were put into these foundations, made from different clays and additives. Today, bricks are made of shale, not clay. Some bricks are appropriate for below grade; most others are not.

Bricks are strong under compression but weak and brittle under tension. A brick foundation may be up to a foot thick and consist of several wythes (vertical sections of masonry, each 1 unit thick). Bricks are also porous; they actually pull water from the soil into themselves, a process known as rising damp. This process can hasten the deterioration of the mortar in any foundation as well as the brick itself. Salts in the ground water may cause the brick to deteriorate.

On the outside of the house where the brick foundation is above grade, rain and roof runoff may wash or splash against the brick. Mortar can be washed away, allowing bricks to fall out. Water/moisture inside the bricks can cause spalling, where the surface of the brick crumbles away. Where water has frozen inside the brick, you may see the surface of the brick coming off in thin sheets.

Wood Foundations

A permanent wood foundation (PWF) is made of load-bearing lumber-framed walls sheathed with pressure-treated wood using the same framing techniques as main floor exterior walls. The basement walls and floor rest on a bed of compacted gravel as mentioned above during the discussion of the precast walls, with more gravel backfilled around the foundation. The theory is that it offers a superior drainage system and wood stud interior walls that can be insulated and finished off like other interior walls. The foundation is built with **pressure-treated wood** that is impregnated with much higher concentrations of, or different types of, chemical preservatives than traditional above-grade pressure-treated wood, protecting the wood against fungi that cause rot. Some environmental groups have expressed concern that certain chemicals can leech into the soil and contaminate the groundwater. PWFs are advertised as reducing dampness in the basement because the wood can be insulated. However, a properly constructed concrete foundation is less vulnerable to moisture than wood and will last far longer.

It isn't always easy to recognize a wood foundation because the interior is likely to be covered with drywall or other coverings. One clue is that the floor slab is poured against the wood foundation wall plates to hold them in place against the pressure of the backfill, although this can only be seen when the walls are unfinished in places such as the mechanical or laundry room.

From the exterior, you'll usually find some sort of protective and decorative covering, such as Hardie™ Board or other cementitious material, applied over the portion of the foundation at grade. The portion of the wall where the soil, moisture, and air meet is the most likely place for deterioration or rot.

A basement slab floor with cracks, tilting, humps, or hollows can be a sign that the wood foundation wall is failing or that the drainage system isn't working. The smell of decaying wood is a very bad sign. When inspecting the wood foundation, look under stairwells or other unfinished areas where walls may not be covered. If you suspect problems that aren't visible, you might advise the homeowner to call in a qualified professional who can remove the covering and get a better look at the foundation itself.

Piles, Piers, and Grade Beams

A foundation doesn't have to be a continuous form or wall. Piles (or pilings) and piers are columns that serve the same purpose as the foundation wall and/or footing by supporting the rest of the structure and transmitting the weight of the structure to the footings or directly to the soil.

Piles are generally steel, treated wood, or concrete. They're used when the soil can't support the load of the structure due to poor soil quality or bearing. This is fairly common near lakes, rivers, and marshy/swampy soil. Piles are driven into the ground by a machine to reach a soil of bearing strength or until friction prevents any further movement. The top of each pile, which is just above grade, may be topped with a concrete cap. This cap acts as a footing upon which the rest of the structure is built. In coastal areas, you see the pilings sticking several feet out of the ground with the house built on top to allow for tidal and storm surges. Places such as New Orleans, which are below sea level, must build their homes on pilings, or "stilts" as they are commonly called.

Piers are columns of stone, brick, poured concrete, concrete block, cinder block, or wood. Piers can be 12″ or more in diameter and from 6–30′ in length. They're installed in a hole that is then filled in around them. Piers should sit on footings below the frost line. Piers may also be topped with a concrete cap. A crawl space usually has a pier and beam system on which the house is built. The crawl space may be enclosed or left open, as is commonly seen in the South.

Grade beams are poured reinforced concrete beams that rest on the caps of the pilings or piers and in certain unique systems using void forms. This concept is very common in Denver, for example. That area has expansive soil and can't build directly on the soil. Pilings are installed with a grade beam poured between them. The void form (basically a cardboard box) supports

Photo #6 FOUNDATION WALL

This is a foundation wall utilizing void forms, which is typically found in areas with expansive soils. Note that the cardboard form supports the concrete during the pour. The weight of the wall rests on the caisson, piers, or pilings.

the concrete between pilings until it cures. Over time, the form disintegrates, thereby disconnecting the beam from the ground; then if the soil expands, it doesn't affect the foundation. Some garages are built on grade beams supported by piles.

Structural insulated panels (SIPs) are a relatively recent addition to the foundation line-up (1980s). SIPs have been around for years (late 1960s) as above-grade construction. Their installation is similar to that of PWFs, as that is essentially what they are. They can be placed on standard concrete footings or compacted gravel as previously discussed.

Photo #7 STRUCTURAL INSULATED PANELS

This photo shows structural insulated panels being used for the foundation of this home.

1.5 SLAB CONSTRUCTION

Slab-on-grade construction has no basement or crawl space, although it can be used in conjunction with either one or both. A poured concrete floor (slab), often reinforced with steel (rebar or welded-wire mesh), rests directly on the ground. The slab is usually 4″ thick and is laid over several inches of gravel, a moisture barrier, and possibly insulation. Slab-on-grade is less expensive than building on a basement or crawl space. It is often used in warmer southern or western climates and on level lots. It can be used in any climate if it is constructed properly. In northern climates, it is often found in less expensive homes and in the main floor of condominiums and townhouses.

There are four types of slab-on-grade construction. A **monolithic slab** is a concrete floor, footing, and foundation poured all at once. The slab is basically one piece that is thicker around the edges. It is sometimes referred to as a turndown slab.

A **floating slab** is constructed by pouring the footing and foundation or stem wall first and then the slab so that the slab is not connected to the foundation walls.

A **post-tension slab** is stronger than an ordinary slab and is widely used in parts of the country with expansive soil, such as the South and Southwest. Tendons (cables) are placed at regular intervals running perpendicular to each other. They resemble a checkerboard and are stretched with hydraulic jacks after the concrete is poured but before it's fully cured (typically 4-10 days). The tendons keep the concrete compressed, forming a stronger foundation without the use of typical rebar. This process results in fewer cracks, which in turn protects the finish flooring above, which in the South is typically stone or ceramic tile.

Slab-on-Grade

- Monolithic
- Resting on foundation
- Supported by the foundation
- Floating and pinned to foundation
- Post-tensioned

Definitions

<u>Slab-on-grade</u> *construction consists of a poured concrete slab that rests directly on the ground.*

In the <u>monolithic slab-on-grade</u>*, the slab, foundation, and footing are poured as one piece.*

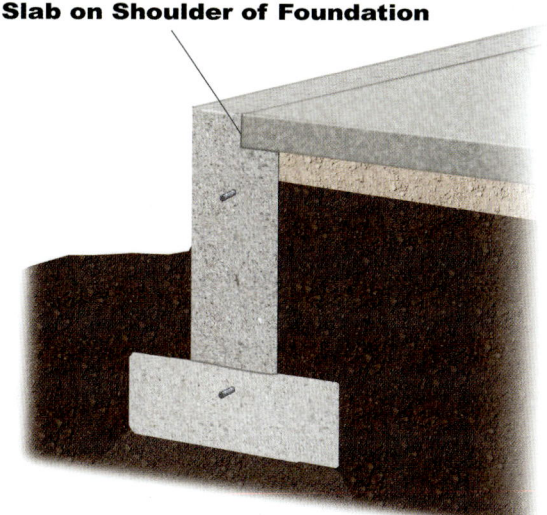

Illustration by Paddy Morrissey

Illustration by Paddy Morrissey

THE STRUCTURAL INSPECTION

A **supported or shoulder slab** is poured separately from the rest of the foundation, but rests on foundation walls typically made of concrete blocks. The top block, known as an FHA block, has a 4″ ledge. Insulation or an expansion joint may be placed between the slab and the foundation wall. An expansion joint is a gap between adjacent parts, which allows the components to move without causing damage.

It is often difficult to inspect slab-on-grade construction. Unlike basements and crawl spaces, the foundation is only visible from the exterior around the house below the siding and above the soil, grass, and/or landscaping materials.

The top of the foundation and the floor slab should be at least 6–8″ above grade. Grade refers to the surface of the ground. However, this is not always the case. If a slab is at or below grade, the floor and wall studs may become wet due to water draining toward the building, leading to insect and/or moisture damage. In many cases, sewer lines, electrical lines, plumbing, gas piping, radiant heating pipes, or forced-air heating ducts are installed below or in the slab. It is difficult or impossible to inspect these systems, and problems may go undetected until they are very serious. For example, water leakage from plumbing or radiant heating pipes may cause sub-slab erosion. In time, the slab may settle and cause serious damage.

1.6 INSPECTING FOUNDATIONS

The home inspector starts the inspection of the foundation from the **outside** of the house, looking for signs of footing and foundation failure on the exterior. The inspector looks for **settlement or movement** of the house and their effect on the rest of the structure. While some conditions signal obvious problems, other signs may only indicate that the inspector must continue to investigate to find the cause of the exterior sign. The inspector focuses on the following:

- The ridge line of the roof
- Racking, twisting, or leaning of the house
- The chimney pulling away from the house
- Twisted or cracked siding
- Movement of foundation wall
- Corners of the building settling
- Cracks in exterior foundation walls
- Displacement of windows and doors in bearing walls

The inspector also inspects the foundation from **inside**, from the basement or crawl space, paying attention to the following:

- Cracks in foundation walls
- Bowing or leaning of foundation walls

> **Chapter Note**
>
> *Pages 24–35 present the procedures for foundation inspections.*

- Window and door displacement
- Deterioration of materials in the walls, piers, and supports
- Evidence of water penetration or efflorescence

Cracks

Wall cracks appear as the result of shrinkage or overloading or because of settlement or heaving. The location and pattern of the cracks can be a clue to what is going on with a foundation.

Vertical cracks are most often caused by settlement of the structure, soil compacting, or soil washing away under the footings. Vertical cracks may appear when there is an upward overload force adjacent to a downward overload force. They can also occur after remodeling, when new dead loads are added to the structure (such as a second story) or when very heavy live loads are added (such as a hot tub or piano).

Vertical cracks that extend to the footing may be serious and should be investigated carefully. These cracks could be caused by uneven settlement of the building and could indicate that the wall is separating—one part settling more on one side of the crack than the other. A crack extending to the footing could also indicate a failure of materials such as deteriorating block, decayed mortar, or weak concrete.

This diagram shows the results of settling due to soil weakness at one side of the house. Note that cracking on the exterior and the foundation wall is an indication of settlement. In this case, one part of the house is pulling away from the other part.

Angled cracks appear when the upload and download offset each other. They can appear when there is a major difference in the soil under the house from one location to another, heaving of the soil, and

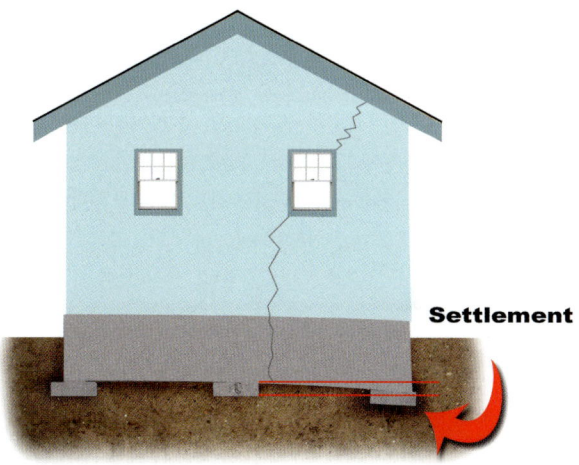

FOUNDATION CRACKS
- Vertical cracks
- Angled cracks
- Horizontal cracks
- Shrinkage cracks

Illustration by Paddy Morrissey

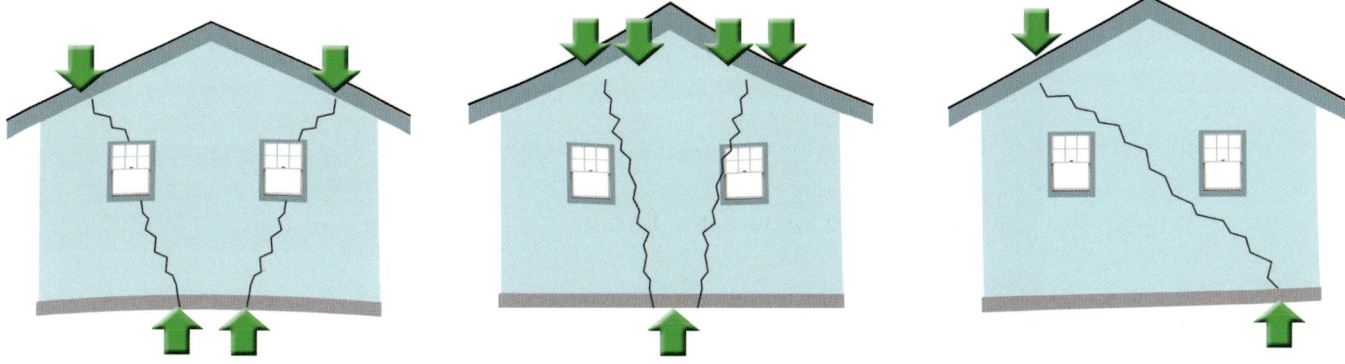

Illustration by Paddy Morrissey

THE STRUCTURAL INSPECTION 25

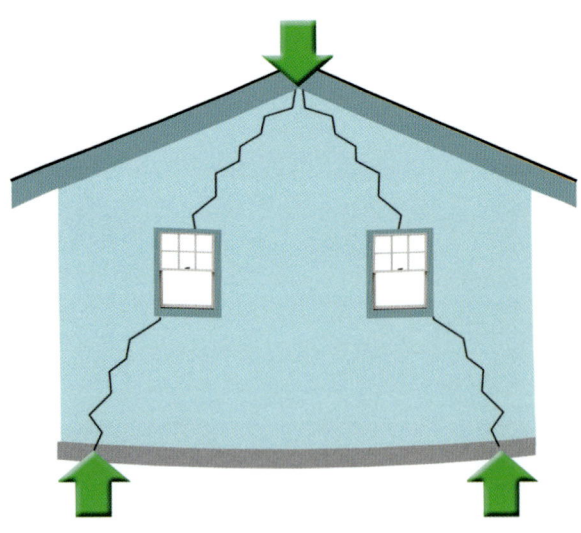

Illustration by Paddy Morrissey

V-CRACKS

When a crack increases in width along its path, this is called a V-crack. A vertical V-crack, wider at the top, indicates that the wall is settling at the ends of the wall more than in the middle of the wall. A horizontal V-crack indicates that the wall is moving out from the middle more than from the top and bottom. Watch out for V-cracks!

resulting footing failure. This type of crack points down to the location of the upload. In block construction, the angled crack may appear along the mortar block joints in an angled direction. This is called a **step crack**. Angled cracks can appear in pairs, where a load in one direction is offset by a pair of loads from the other direction.

The house diagram shows the result of settlement, where the stress is borne at one corner of the house. Here, the angled step crack is likely to have a companion crack on the adjacent wall at that corner, indicating that the corner is breaking away entirely from the rest of the house and sinking. A crack at a single corner of the house can indicate a broken footing because of the condition of the soil underneath, expansive clay soils, or even the uplift from heavy tree roots in that location.

A **horizontal crack** on the foundation wall can be an indication of pressure being applied from outside. The cause may be soil pressure against the wall, improper backfilling, or surface problems such as inadequate downspouts that increase the amount of water pushing against the wall. The wall will bow inward and crack horizontally. If the wall is **displaced**—when the surface of the wall is out of alignment—and the crack is wider on the inside face of the wall, serious problems or even complete failure can result. Concrete block and masonry walls usually show the horizontal crack along the mortar joint.

There are other causes for horizontal cracks in foundation walls. There could be a vertical overload on the wall. The weight of a second-story addition could cause the wall to "fold." The crack could be caused by settlement, where the wall has dropped as the soil underneath has settled or eroded away. In this case, the home inspector would probably not see any lateral displacement. Cracks may also be caused by heavy equipment during backfilling.

Photo #8
Horizontal and step cracks in a concrete masonry wall.

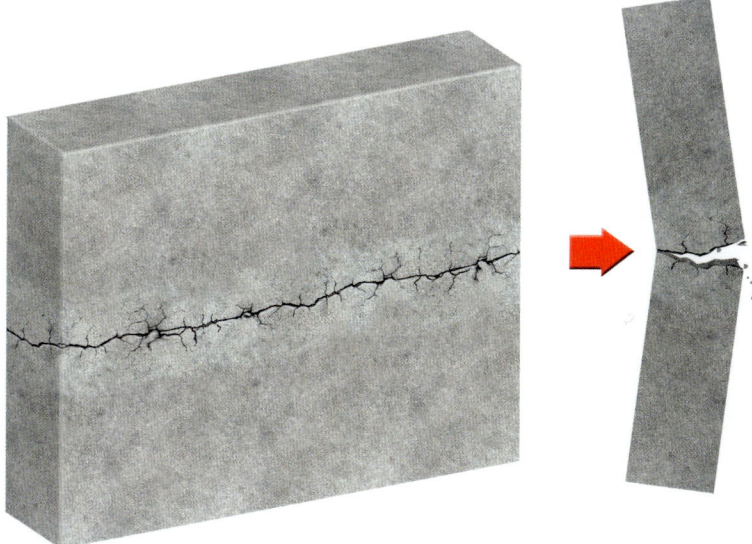

Illustration by Paddy Morrissey

The home inspector may see **pilasters**—masonry or block columns against the interior foundation wall—built to support the wall and help absorb the lateral load and prevent further movement. Pilasters may be part of the original construction or erected later as a corrective measure. In many cases, such as the photo below, they are not installed correctly and are a temporary fix at best.

Shrinkage cracks can appear in foundation walls as part of the curing process. In the concrete block wall, you may see symmetrical step cracks that indicate block shrinkage. If the cracks appear around each block, this could be an indication of block shrinkage due to excess moisture in the blocks when they were set. It could also be the result of mortar that was placed in cold weather and later froze and expanded before curing. The home inspector may see a vertical shrinkage crack in the middle of a concrete block wall. The crack may be wider at the top, indicating shrinkage during curing, while the bottom of the wall is held firm by the footings.

In a poured concrete foundation wall, shrinkage usually occurs naturally in the first few months. Some poured concrete walls are designed to have control areas, such as seams, where cracking can be localized. If these areas are not provided, cracking is likely to be random over the surface of the wall. In addition, if control joints are provided, they need to be sealed properly to prevent water entry or seepage.

> ### Definition
>
> A _pilaster_ is a masonry column built against a wall to help absorb the horizontal load and stiffen the wall.

> ### Section Note
>
> "I urge you to realize how complicated the diagnosis of foundation cracks can be. Unless you're a structural engineer, you should constantly remind yourself that you don't know everything. And be extremely careful about suggesting solutions to customers. You'll probably give uneducated advice only once. Then after the lawsuit, you'll learn to keep your mouth shut when you're not sure. What you do need to know is when to tell customers to monitor a crack and when to advise them to call in a structural engineer to assess the problem."

Using Your Judgment

Reading cracks as a clue to what is happening to the structure of a home requires judgment on the part of the home inspector. Cracks may indicate anything from

Photo #9 PILASTERS

This is sort of a Pilaster. A steel pipe has been placed against the failing wall and then braced. The red screw-jack is applying pressure to straighten the wall. In all likelihood, the wall will still need to be replaced.

serious structural problems to merely cosmetic or surface damage. The home inspector must learn when cracks are serious enough to suggest that customers monitor the cracks or seek advice from a structural engineer or contractor. Here are some general guidelines to follow:

- Surface cracks that don't pierce the wall and show no displacement in any direction are not typically structural in nature.

- Cracks less than 1/4" wide, with or without displacement in any direction, are not likely signs of serious failure unless they are active.

- Cracks over 3/8" wide should be examined carefully as an indication of a potentially serious problem.

- Cracks that are still active should be noted as major defects. Active cracks have sharp edges and will break a new painted surface or mortar repair. They indicate a failure in progress and a situation that can grow worse. Probe the repair to see if it is mortar or just caulking, which would be a sign of a homeowner having made a repair or possibly hiding the crack.

- Don't come to a conclusion based on a single crack. Investigate further. A crack in one area of the foundation often has a corresponding crack in another area.

Section Note

Take a drive through several neighborhoods and pay attention to the general outline of the structure. On various homes, see if you can spot sagging ridge lines, racking walls, chimneys pulling away, and settling portions.

Inspecting from the Outside

The home inspector begins the inspection of the foundation from the outside of the house. Let's go through the list of what to watch for on the exterior:

- **The ridge line of the roof:** The home inspector should sight the ridge line of the roof to make sure it is a straight line. Sags and distortions in the ridge line can be an indication of the failure of the structural members of the roof. But they may, along with other indications, be an indication of problems stemming from the foundation.

- **Racking of the house:** Racking refers to a structure that is leaning in such a way that the angles it forms with the foundation are no longer 90°. Think of twisting a cardboard box out of square. Racking generally indicates a failure of the wall structure, such as poorly braced walls. If you notice racking, keep it in mind as you examine cracking and other signs that something may be amiss with the foundation as well.

- **The chimney pulling away from the house:** Part of your inspection of the foundation involves checking the foundation of the masonry chimney. A chimney sits on its own footing, which can experience the same settlement problems as the main foundation. Footings can fail due to soil weakness below.

- **Twisted siding:** In framed houses, siding sometimes hides damage to the inner wall due to the foundation settling. But often the damage can be seen in siding that is twisted, bent, or cracked from the settling.

- **Movement of foundation walls and cracks:** The home inspector should walk around the entire exterior of the house to check the foundation. With **stone and brick masonry** foundations, the exterior and visible portion of the foundation should be checked for movement and cracks as well as the condition of the **mortar**. Use the tip of your screwdriver or a knife to probe the mortar. With brickwork that has water splashing against it from faulty or missing downspouts or lack of gutters, enough mortar can wash away to cause bricks to become loose or fall out. If water has been absorbed into the bricks, the face surface may **spall**, or crumble away.

- **Corners of the building settling:** Pay particular attention to the cracks in the foundation and exterior walls at the corners of the house. Often, footings fail at the corners due to soil weakness or expansive soils.

- **Cracks in exterior walls:** Check for crack patterns in the exterior walls. Some cracks are cosmetic cracks or an indication of a problem with the wall itself, but others may indicate a settling problem. Cracks starting at windows and doors and ending a short distance away can be a result

Illustration by Paddy Morrissey

EXTERIOR INSPECTION

- The ridge line
- Racking of the house
- Chimney pulling away
- Twisted siding
- Cracks and movement in foundation
- Settling corners
- Cracks in exterior walls
- Displacement of windows

Definition

Spalling is the crumbling and falling away of the surface of bricks, blocks, or concrete.

BRICK OR VENEER?

How can you tell if an exterior wall is solid brick or brick veneer? Header rows of bricks (with the short end of the brick facing out) typically appear at every sixth row in a solid brick wall.

of overloading the header (wood framing or beam above an opening in an exterior bearing wall) or lintel (steel spanning an opening in an exterior veneer wall) at the opening. Here are some examples of cracks that are most likely cosmetic in nature, unless the cracks are large and active.

Other exterior wall cracks should be inspected carefully.

> **Section Note**
>
> *Examine as many foundations up close as often as you can while you study this chapter. Bother your friends. Look at their foundations from the exterior and ask to see the basements.*

- **Displacement of windows:** Another sign to check for is distortion of the window framing, especially in bearing walls, which can also indicate settling of the house. Displacement of windows is often accompanied by other signs of settlement (exterior wall cracks, for example).

Signs of footing or foundation problems noted on the exterior require further investigation. Don't come to a conclusion without inspecting the foundation from the inside. The home inspector should point out cracks or other exterior signs to the customer while viewing them and explain that the situation must be investigated inside the basement or crawl space.

One additional thing to look for when inspecting the foundation from the exterior is to make note of where the **ground slopes away** from the house, exposing much of the foundation at the lower side. This is typical of a hillside lot or a home with a walkout basement. The uphill portion of the foundation and footing are well below grade, but the downhill portion is sometimes too close to the surface. Obviously the frost line is lower on the low side of the slope, and the footings should be stepped down in this area. Check this portion of the foundation once you get inside.

Inspecting from the Inside

The home inspector continues the inspection of the foundation from inside the basement or crawl space. It's important to remember the findings from the exterior of the house and to search for answers for them.

> **INTERIOR INSPECTION**
>
> - Wall cracks
> - Bowing or leaning of foundation walls
> - Displacement of windows
> - Deterioration of materials
> - Water penetration

- **Cracks in foundation walls:** The inspector should inspect *all* interior foundation walls, piers, columns, beams, and piles. First let's talk about visibility and access—crawl spaces can be inaccessible, and basement finishes and storage can hide portions of the foundation wall. Home sellers can be clever about stacking mattresses and boxes in front of walls they don't want the home inspector to see. The home inspector is not required to move any items that obstruct such access. However, it pays to look behind storage as much as possible to see if anything is hidden. In case questions arise later about the condition of the foundation, it's also a good idea to take photos of areas where access is blocked to document the fact that you were unable to inspect those areas.

- The home inspector must be careful to report what can and can't be seen. Reporting is discussed later in this chapter.

NOTE: Most of the examples shown here are rather bad and require a structural engineer to evaluate them. We aren't suggesting that you recommend an evaluation by an engineer *every time* you see a crack. Don't raise this alarm when you don't need to. You won't get any more referrals from real estate agents if they believe you're going to suggest an engineer for every house. When to recommend further evaluation by a qualified professional is discussed later in the chapter.

- **Bowing or leaning in foundation walls:** A foundation wall can have an inward or outward curve or lean inward. A **bow** is a vertical curve in a wall, a **sweep** is a horizontal curve, and a **bulge** is a combination of the two. They can be caused by the load from behind the wall, such as a boulder in the backfill, or from a narrow load from above. When a wall shows these distortions, cracks may or may not be associated with them. The danger is that the wall's center of gravity could move beyond its base, causing the wall to collapse.

> **Definitions**
>
> A <u>bow</u> in a wall is a vertical curve, where the wall has an outward curve from top to bottom.
>
> A <u>sweep</u> is a horizontal curve in a wall, where the wall has an outward curve from side to side.
>
> A <u>bulge</u> in a wall is a combination of both a bow and a sweep.

Photo #10 *The level is plumb and touching the wall at the bottom. You can see that the top of the wall is leaning to the right about an inch or so.*

THE STRUCTURAL INSPECTION

Section Note

"I once inspected a concrete block foundation with a steep step crack coming down from a window in the corner of the basement. There was some movement in the wall, and the paint was coming off the wall in sheets in that area. It looked very serious to me, so I recommended someone come to evaluate the situation. I went back to the house with the engineer to see what was up. The house had been built on foundry sand and had settled about 12 years ago. But the engineer thought that the crack had not opened for years and that all movement was done. He said it was nothing to worry about. It turns out the wall had been spray painted with some kind of coating that wasn't adhering to the wall—a paint problem having nothing to do with structure or water penetration. It was one of the worst basements I'd ever seen, yet the engineer gave it a clean bill of health. Of course, I'm not sorry that I recommended him. It's better to be sure."

The center of gravity is at the midpoint of the mass of an object. The object will overturn when the center of gravity moves outside its base. In a wall, if the center of gravity has moved more than one-third from the center of its base, the wall may collapse.

The home inspector can stand along a wall and sight down the wall to spot bows and leans. A 4′ level or a plumb bob can be used to measure any displacement in the wall. Shining a flashlight parallel along the wall while sighting can sometimes help the inspector see bows in the wall.

- **Window displacement:** When inspecting a foundation wall from the interior, always take note of the basement windows and check them for displacement. This is a clue that the wall is moving. Basements now require egress windows. Please see diagram below.

- **Deterioration of materials:** The home inspector should identify the materials used in the foundation construction and inspect them for any decay or deterioration.

- **Water penetration:** The home inspector should inspect the foundation for water penetration into the interior. This is an important part of the foundation inspection.

Inspecting for water penetration and drainage problems is discussed later in this section.

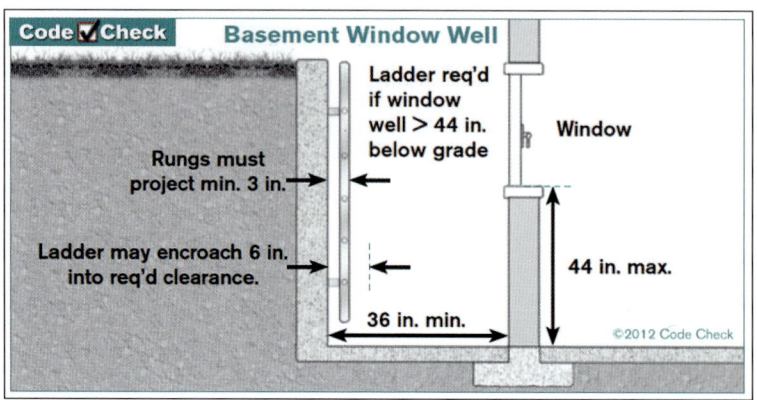

1.7 LET'S REVIEW

Use your judgment. Know what you've found and what constitutes a foundation in good condition and one with defects. These guidelines discuss settlement and movement of the foundation and cracking of the foundation walls.

Water penetration and its effects on the foundation are discussed later in this chapter.

- **When to give the foundation an okay:** You find nothing wrong with the foundation, with no indication of movement, settlement, or wall cracks. There may be minor surface cracking that doesn't pierce the wall and no displacement in any direction. Remember, you never say that the foundation is "structurally sound" or anything similar as that is rendering an engineering opinion. What you should do is comment on defects or issues. If none are present, there is nothing to note.

- **When to have the customer monitor the situation:** You find cracks with displacement in the foundation wall that indicate that some settlement has taken place, but all signs point to the cracks no longer being active. For example, an old basement with an old paint job may have a crack but the crack has not broken the paint seal or recracked the mortar joint or previous repair. This indicates that no more movement has taken place. To be on the safe side, you should suggest that the crack be monitored.

> **Section Note**
>
> *"If you do recommend a structural engineer be called in to investigate a foundation, go back to the house when the engineer comes. Find out what the engineer thinks of the situation. It's a great learning experience for you and will contribute to your skills. It will also let you know if you're overreacting and raising a red flag when you don't need to."*

There may also be cracks less than 1/4″ wide that appear to be active but are showing little or no movement. Suggest that these be monitored, but mention that a structural engineer should be consulted if the cracks become wider or displaced.

- **When to recommend a structural engineer:** The problem is potentially serious when you find active cracks over 3/8″ wide indicating ongoing movement or settlement, horizontal cracks with movement, step cracks indicating footing failure, excessive bowing or leaning of the wall with or without cracks, and shearing in the foundation. These are indications of a structural failure in progress and should be investigated by an expert. Recommend that a structural engineer be brought in now.

A NOTE ABOUT MONITORING: The home inspector's initial suggestion should be for the customer to have the cracks patched with mortar, epoxy, or a similar material (not caulk) and then monitor the walls for further movement. The homeowner can make marks on each side of a crack, measure the distance with an accurate measuring device (steel ruler, screw adjustment dividers, etc.), and re-measure the crack every three to six months. Another method is to glue a microscope slide across the crack. If there is further movement, the glass slide will shatter or break away. Stiff paper or plastic can be glued across the crack. These materials will twist or deform if there is further movement.

> **IMPORTANT POINT**
>
> *The more the customer understands during the inspection, the better off the home inspector is after the inspection.*

Reporting Your Findings
When you're inspecting the foundation, you should have your customer present. When the client comes with you, you have an opportunity to explain the inspection fully and point out findings. Client knowledge is a big step toward the prevention of complaint calls later.

Keep a running dialogue going with the client. Not everyone is familiar with foundation construction and problems, and your client may not understand what you're doing and what you're finding. Because some foundation problems can represent a major repair to the home, you want to make sure the client understands what you're saying. So **keep it simple** but do talk about it. Pay attention to whether the customer understands. During the inspection, explain the following as you go along:

- **What you're inspecting**—the foundation.

- **What you're looking for**—cracks, deterioration of materials, evidence of movement and settlement, etc.

- **What you're doing**—probing the mortar, observing wall displacement, sighting the wall, etc.

- **What you're finding**—footing failure, cracks indicating wall movement, etc.

- **Suggestions about dealing with the findings**—monitoring a wall; calling in a structural engineer, contractor, or mason; etc. Don't make uneducated guesses about how foundation repairs should be made.

Filling in Your Report
Every home inspector needs an inspection report. A **written report** is the work product of the home inspection, and every home inspector is expected to deliver one to the customer after the inspection. Inspection reports vary a great deal in the industry. Some home inspection companies develop their own version; others use state required formats (Texas), home inspection software, apps, or formats provided by training companies such as AHIT. Some are considered to be excellent, while others are not very good. A workable and easy-to-use inspection report is important for a home inspector. Of greater importance are its thoroughness, accuracy, and helpfulness to the customer. Whatever reporting format you choose, make sure it presents your findings in a clear, professional manner such that it reduces your liability and client dissatisfaction.

The **Don't Ever Miss** list is a reminder of those specific findings you should include in your inspection report. We list these items based on years of experience performing home inspections. Missing them can result in complaint calls and possible lawsuits. Here is an overview of what to report on during the inspection of the foundation:

- **Type:** Identify the type of foundation walls present, such as poured concrete, concrete block, SIPs, or ICFs.

- **Wall condition:** In the report, take time to report accurately on the condition of the foundation walls. For your own protection, if some areas are not visible for inspection, note that in your report and take pictures of the areas. This is a protective measure in case a complaint comes in later about something that was missed during the inspection.

  If cracks or movement of the walls are found, record the precise location and clearly define what you've found. This helps a structural engineer who may be called to evaluate the condition.

- **Recommending monitoring:** If your finding is that a crack condition should be monitored, mention that fact in your inspection report.

- **Recommending a structural engineer:** Be sure to indicate clearly when a problem is serious enough to call for an evaluation by a structural engineer. Any foundation condition requiring a structural engineer's evaluation should be classified as a **major concern** in your report. It's a good idea to report this major concern both on the foundation page and a summary page of the report.

> **DON'T EVER MISS**
> - Horizontal cracks in the foundation wall
> - Step cracks indicating footing settlement
> - Unstable bowing or leaning walls with or without cracks
> - Shearing action in the foundation

1.8 INSPECTING THE BASEMENT

The home inspector inspects the entire interior of the basement, including the foundation walls, which we've already discussed. The basement inspection includes the following:

- Basement moisture and water penetration
- Basement drainage
- Basement stairs and/or hatchway
- Wall penetrations
- Basement floor
- Supporting structures—columns, sills, girders, joists
- Seismic bolts and cripple walls, where applicable

> **Chapter Note**
>
> *Pages 35–53 present the procedures for a basement inspection.*

Inspecting for Water Penetration

Water is the enemy of a home's foundation. Even small amounts that penetrate the foundation may cause moisture problems such as mold and mildew, heaving,

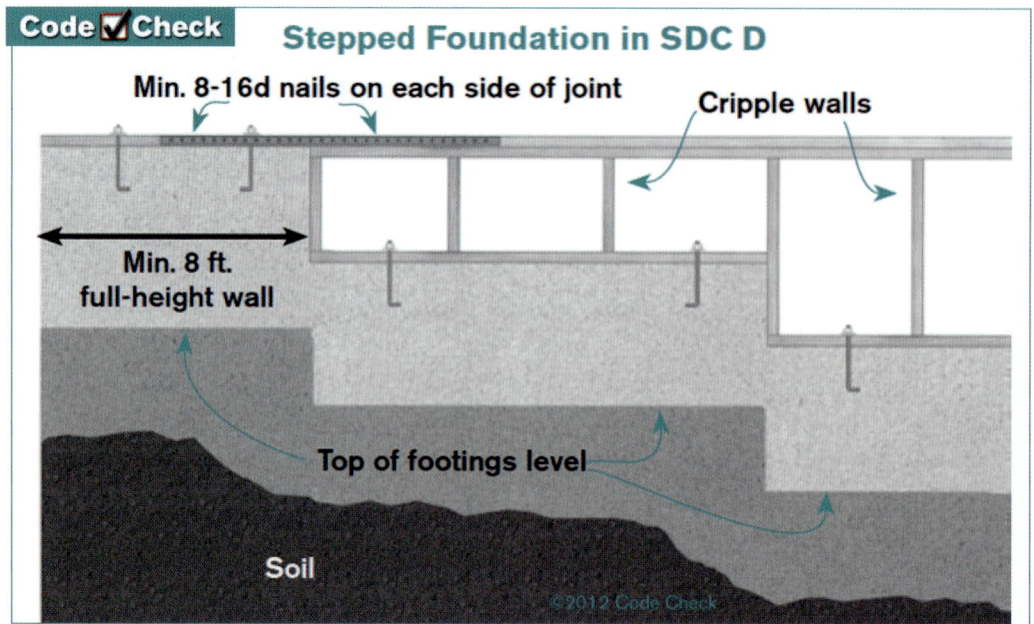

and cracking. **Hydrostatic pressure**, which is the push of water against a surface, can exert tremendous force. Over time, small problems may grow, leading to serious foundation damage.

Leaking basements are a common problem. Generally, water problems in the basement are not dangerous to the home's occupants. However, water and excessive moisture in the basement are nasty and interfere with the use of the space. It's predicted that almost all basements will leak at some time. Leaks can be categorized as occurring:

Photo #11 *This is a total horror story. This basement had too many issues to note in the inspection report: leaks, structural problems, insulation issues, and so on.*

- During a **catastrophic event** such as a flood, a hurricane, or an incident of broken plumbing.

- **Periodically** such as during the spring thaw or an unusually heavy rain when the ground water rises.

- **Constantly**, that is, with every rainfall or in an area with an abnormally high water table or where an underground spring is present.

About 90% of leaking basements are caused by **surface water**—rain and snow collecting on/in the soil around the home and getting into the basement through the foundation walls and floor. Surface water should be made to flow away from the house and not be allowed to collect in the soil around the foundation. Constant leaking problems can be caused by the following:

— A faulty gutter and downspout system, improper grading of the land around the house, nonfunctioning or broken drain tiles due to silt buildup in the tiles

— Patios, drives, and walkways tilted toward the house (negative grade)

— Another major cause of leaky basements is **groundwater**. Groundwater is water beneath the surface of the earth. The highest level to which groundwater rises is known as the water table. This level varies tremendously from one location to another, and it may change over time depending on drought or rainfall conditions. If the water table is higher than the foundation footing, water may exert hydrostatic pressure on the floor slab, causing flooding or, in extreme cases, buckling of the slab.

— Basements can also have water or excessive moisture due to problems other than leaking. Rainwater leaking through the roof can make its way to the basement through the interior of the house. The plumbing system, air-conditioning condensate, or appliances can leak; the sewer can back up; and there can be condensation.

> **MOISTURE INSPECTION**
> - Standing water
> - Staining
> - Efflorescence
> - Rust
> - Ceiling damage
> - Damage to finishings and contents

When entering the basement, use your senses to get an overall opinion about moisture being present. Does the basement smell damp, musty, moldy, or mildewy? Does the air feel damp and cold? Can you see other signs of leakage? Watch for these signs:

- **Standing water:** This is the most obvious sign, and the home inspector should investigate the source of this water.

- **Staining:** This is evidence of there being water in the basement previously. Stains on foundation walls and the basement floor can be old stains or recent stains, possibly indicating when the problem occurred. Some stains are wet, and some are dry. Use a moisture meter to determine if the staining is "current," meaning that it is wet.

- **Efflorescence:** This is a whitish mineral "salt" deposit often seen on foundation walls.

> *Definition*
>
> *Efflorescence is the white mineral deposit left after water passes through the foundation wall, having dissolved salts from the materials of the wall. It appears on the interior of the foundation after the water has evaporated.*

The crystals are left on the wall after water has seeped through the wall, bringing with it dissolved salts from the masonry or concrete. The crystals are left on the interior wall as the water evaporates.

- **Rust:** Even if stains have been cosmetically covered, the home inspector can often see evidence of water problems by inspecting the base of steel supporting columns for rust. Other items that can rust are nails in baseboards and paneling, electrical outlets, or the metal feet on appliances. The worst cases of rusting may be visible where the steel rebar imbedded in the walls or floor has rusted, expanded, and broken through, exposing the rebar itself.

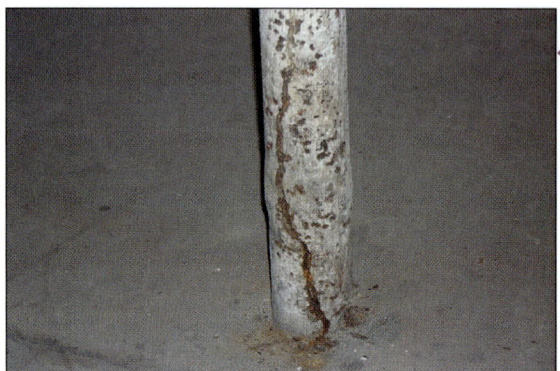

Photo #12 *This rusty column is a sure sign of long-term moisture issues.*

- **Damage to the ceiling:** Water penetration into the basement from the house can usually be seen in the condition of the structural members in the floor (wood deck) above. The home inspector may find evidence of leaking in rotted subflooring and joists under bathrooms and kitchens.

- **Damage to basement finishes and contents:** Look for warped paneling, crumbling drywall, moldy carpeting, warped floor tiles, and soggy storage boxes or storage placed on pallets.

Section Note

"One of my inspectors was looking at a basement that had a counter-high cabinet built along one wall. The tiniest evidence of water stain appeared on the wall at the top of the cabinet. He opened its door to find water flowing out of a crack down the wall behind the cabinet. He could so easily have walked right by that cabinet without looking further. The point I'm making is to keep your eyes open and to investigate. Look behind storage as much as possible. And open doors to cabinets and storage areas to see what's inside."

It isn't always possible to determine the situation with the wet basement or the source of the problem. During a single visit to the property, it's difficult to get a fix on the severity and frequency of the problem. It isn't always possible to know if stains are present because of a one-time occurrence, an ongoing problem, or a problem that has since been remedied. But that doesn't get the inspector off the hook. Every effort should be made to figure out why the problem occurred.

Sometimes, water penetrates into the basement through cracks in the foundation wall. Often, you'll see patches on cracks with evidence of previous water staining on the wall or the floor below. If everything is dry at the time of the inspection, it isn't always possible to tell if the patch is working and the problem is solved. The cracking may have occurred initially from excess water in the soil outside the foundation. So unless the problem is corrected properly from the outside, interior patches will only cause the water to break through somewhere else.

Basement Drainage

The home inspector should note the presence or absence of a **floor drain** in the basement, which isn't always visible. In some areas of the country, the floor drain will have a **palmer valve** in it, which is not very common. You can see this valve by shining your flashlight down the drain. A little cover inside the drain on hinges opens and closes to allow the water in the drain tile system to flow through and out to the city sewer while preventing sewage backflow from entering the drain. This valve should be functioning. Sometimes, what appears to be a drain tile problem turns out to be a malfunction with the palmer valve, a much less expensive problem to fix.

If palmer valves are widely used in your area and you've seen evidence of a drain tile problem, check the floor drain to see if it has a valve. Suggest that your customer check with a plumber to determine if the valve is causing the problem. You'll be a hero if a malfunctioning valve, not faulty drain tile, is the cause of the basement leakage.

If the basement has a **sump pump**, the home inspector should check to see if it's operating. As described earlier, a sump is a pit (crock) below the basement floor; it is made of concrete, plastic, fiberglass, or earth walls and floor. Water enters the sump from the perimeter drainage system, which can be inside, outside, or both depending on the age of the home. Bleeders allow water to pass through the footing from the outside drain tile to the inside. An electric sump pump in the pit pumps water away from the house.

The pump can be a **pedestal-style pump**, which has the motor mounted on a shaft where it sits above the water level. A rod will stick out of the crock. To test the operation of the pump, pull up on this rod. The sump pump may be the **submersible** type, sitting below the water level. For this type of pump, use a wooden stick or broom handle to lift the float in the crock. Another way to test each kind of sump pump is to run water into the crock with a hose (not required).

The sump pump motor should run quietly and should discharge water. It shouldn't run all the time. The pump should have its own dedicated electrical

Section Note

"I once found rust on the bottom of a steel column and immediately suspected prior basement leakage. However, the column stood right next to the chimney clean out. I opened the door to find that water was coming down the inside of the chimney. Water had leaked out here and puddled at the base of the column. It pays to look."

Definition

A palmer valve is a hinged valve in the floor drain that allows water from the drain tile system to flow through the floor drain out to the sewer. They are not used everywhere in the country.

For Your Information

Ask a plumber whether palmer valves are used in your area. Find out as much as you can about them.

CAUTION!

Don't ever put your hands in the sump when the sump pump is plugged in. And don't use a metal rod to start the submersible pump. Use a wooden stick.

Photo #13 *This is a typical sump pump crock with a submersible pump. On a side note, the rusty tabs sticking out of the walls are the wall ties from the forms noted earlier.*

circuit (it is generally not GFCI-protected, however new sump pumps are required to have GFCI protection as required by their manufacturer and current electrical code) so that it continues working even if some other equipment malfunctions. A backup system is recommended in case the primary pump fails due to a power outage, mechanical failure, or inability of the pump to keep up with a high volume of water. The backup system should be completely redundant, consisting of a second pump, float switch, and power source (rarely the case). Backup systems may be battery-powered or water-powered. In a **water-powered sump pump**, when water rises higher than normal, the float in the sump is lifted and hydraulically activates the water-powered pump through a pressurized tube. As municipal water rushes through the ejector, it creates a powerful suction force that causes the suction pipe to act like a giant soda straw, drawing water up from the sump and ejecting it outdoors. As the water level falls, the float drops and a preset timing control keeps the ejector running for 30–45 seconds before shutting off the system. This allows a full pump-down of the sump, like an electric sump pump. As noted above, you must be connected to a municipal (city) water system. If there was a power failure, the well pump would not operate, just as the sump pump wouldn't.

The crock should be covered and kept free of silt buildup and debris. If water drains from the basement floor into the sump, a perforated cover may sometimes be used. The cover need not be sealed unless testing reveals high levels of radon. Sealing the sump cover does not totally prevent radon from entering the home, but it does drastically reduce radon exposure. If a radon

Photo #14 *This is a water-powered sump pump as described above.*

mitigation system has been installed, the sump pump lid would be completely sealed.

Stairways, Floors, and Penetrations

Part of the inspection of the basement is to inspect the entryways into the basement (interior stairway or exterior hatchway); the basement floor; and penetrations through the foundation wall such as electrical, gas, and plumbing lines.

- **Stairways:** Interior or exterior stairways to the basement should be inspected for safety. The home inspector should check for proper lighting so that people going down the stairs can see their way to the bottom. If the basement is unfinished, a switch at the top of the stairs usually suffices. If the basement is finished, a switch at the top and bottom of the stairs with an overhead light is required. Handrails should be present and securely fastened. Steps should have risers of equal height and should be level, uncracked, unworn, and stable. The stairway should be examined at the points of contact with the basement floor. Sometimes, the feet of the stairway (stringers) sit within the slab (when the stairway is built before the slab is poured) and may be in contact with damp soil. Check this area for wood rot or insect damage.

> **MORE INSPECTION**
> - Stairways and exterior hatchways
> - Basement floor
> - Penetrations through the foundation wall

The home inspector will find the most interesting stairways in old houses. The stairs can be dangerously steep and uneven, headroom can be insufficient, and handrails may be missing or loose. These conditions may not bother the client who expects some quaintness in an old house, but these findings should be noted in the report nonetheless.

- **Exterior hatchways:** When there is an entry to the basement from the outside, the home inspector should check the covers (called cellar doors,

Photo #15 *This is a typical set of basement stairs, which are not at all proper. Note the lack of a handrail and that the risers are open, unequal, and tilted to the right.*

THE STRUCTURAL INSPECTION

bulkheads, Bilco doors, or hatch covers) for rust, deterioration, and water penetration. The inspector should check the steps for safety, and the condition of the sidewalls.

- **The basement floor:** Although basement floors are usually not structural, the concrete slab plays a role in supporting the base of the foundation wall against lateral pressure of the soil. This is especially true with a PWF (wood foundation) where the slab contributes to the support of the wall. The home inspector should note whether the floor is concrete or dirt or wood and whether it is covered with carpeting, tile, or another material.

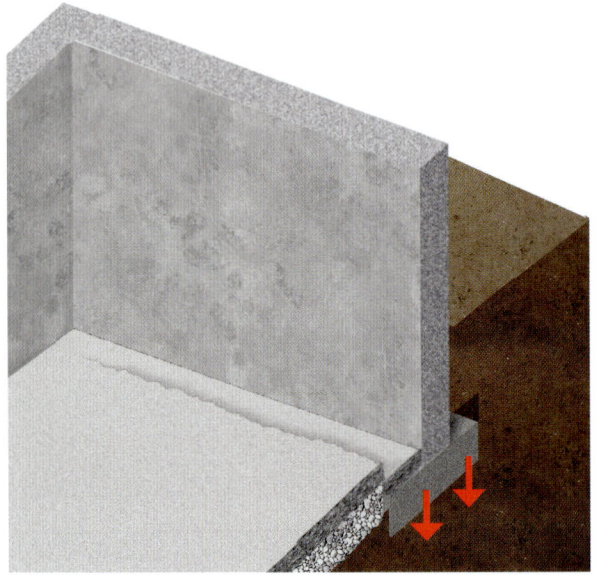

Illustration by Paddy Morrissey

The concrete floor can have **shrinkage cracks**, which occur during the cure of the concrete. The floor can also heave, sink, or crack in areas due to the action of the soil below. When footings fail, the home inspector may see **shear cracks** where the concrete slab is displaced. The diagram shows the footing and foundation settling, causing a shear crack at the perimeter of the slab.

- **Penetrations through the wall:** The home inspector should check all areas in the foundation wall where there are penetrations to the outside, looking for water and/or soil coming in and for cracks around the penetrations.

The home inspector must watch for any evidence that the property has an old **underground oil tank**. It is more likely that you will run across the vent and fill pipes and not the actual tank. This is discussed in more detail in both the plumbing and heating chapters. In some areas, it used to be acceptable for these old tanks to be filled in with gravel or sand. The term *abandoning* was used to describe a tank that was properly taken out of service (filled with sand) but left in place. Under new regulations, they must be removed entirely. Evidence that the home used to have an oil-fired appliance can be seen if there are two penetrations in the basement wall. You'll see two holes where 1/2" or 3/4" copper tubing is sticking out, or you'll see two patches over the holes. The tubing may be bent in or up, a poor way of terminating the piping. There could have been an above- or below-ground tank. If you see two corresponding holes in the floor (near the wall penetration), that's where the tubing came through the wall into the floor and up out of the floor to the oil-fired appliance. Those holes indicate that there was or still is an underground tank. However, when the use of oil was discontinued (usually switched to propane or gas due to expense), the new furnace, water heater, or boiler was often installed over the floor holes, in which case, you may not be able to see this clue.

> **UNDERGROUND OIL TANKS**
>
> *Watch for evidence of an old underground oil tank and alert your customer to the possibility.*

Photo #16
Abandoned fuel oil lines are evidence of a previous tank installation.

If evidence suggests there may be an underground oil tank but you are unable to confirm it, the customer should still be alerted to the possibility. The owner may have paperwork showing that the oil tank was filled with gravel or sand or removed at some earlier date. Even underground storage tanks that don't leak can cause environmental issues that cost thousands of dollars.

Section Note

Find out what the situation is for old underground oil tanks in your area. Can they be filled in? Must they be removed?

Supporting Structures

From the basement, the home inspector will report on the condition of supporting structures such as columns, piers, pilings, beams or girders, and the visible framing overhead.

BASEMENT STRUCTURES

- Columns
- Sills and headers
- Girders and joists

- **Columns:** Posts and columns are vertical supports that carry the weight of the structure from the girders (or beams) to the footing and ultimately to the ground. Columns transmit the weight to footings below the slab. Often, you'll find columns or posts put in to support an unusually heavy load from above, such as a piano or whirlpool tub or an added second story. The home inspector must identify the materials used in column construction—typically steel, wood, or masonry. Columns should be inspected for their condition and ability to support the structure above. In **steel columns**, look for rust throughout the length of the column. Rusting at the bottom shows that water was or is present at the floor level. Rusting higher up may indicate water from above running down the column or an unusually high moisture content in the air or condensation. In **wood posts**, look for and report evidence of wood rot and possible insect damage, especially in dirt floors. **Masonry columns** should be inspected for the condition of the mortar and in most cases should be grouted solid.

The inspector should determine if the column or post is doing a proper job of supporting the structure above. First look for footing problems (or the

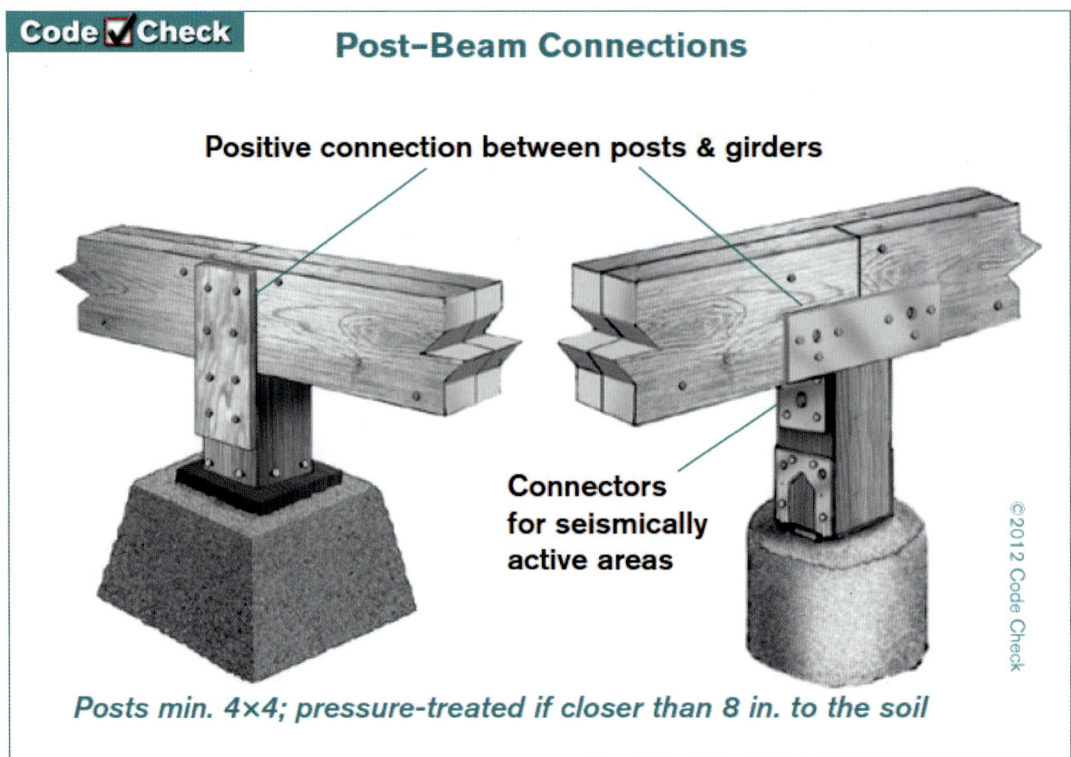

absence of footings altogether). Because you can't see the footing (it's under the slab), you look for cracking in the slab around the base of the column or sagging of the beam above. If the column is sitting directly on the slab, that may be an indication that there is no footing beneath. You can't rest a column on the 3–4″ slab when the footing should be a foot or so thick. Columns and posts should **sit on their own footings** and be **secured to the beam** overhead. They should be plumb. A column or post that is out of plumb by more than one-third its thickness may no longer have its structural integrity.

You may see a **shim** of metal or hardwood inserted between the beam and column. The shim should be large enough to cover the interface between the beam and column. If it's too small, the beam or top of the column may be crushed. Report on damaged or crushed shims.

The bottom on any new column should be inspected carefully. Is the column simply sitting on the slab? Does it have a footing of its own? An easy way to tell if the builders put in a footing after the slab was poured is evidence of saw cuts in the floor where the repair was made. In this case, the new column was free-standing, which is reported. The base of all columns must be secured to resist lateral movement (sliding out sideways). This is typically accomplished by pouring the slab around the base of the column.

Section Note

Try to view as many basements as you can. There's nothing as helpful to the learning process as seeing these things for yourself. Pay particular attention to the girders and joists. Make note of the different building methods you find.

Sills and headers: The **sill**, sometimes called the sill plate or mud sill, is the portion of the framework that sits directly on the foundation and provides a pad for the bottom of the framing system. Sills today are pressure-treated 2 × 4s to 2 × 10s laid flat on the foundation and anchored in place with bolts (or Simpson Strong-Tie mudsill anchors, which are common in new construction). The sill in older construction may be an 8 × 8 wood beam. Wood sills support wood framing members, which sit directly on the foundation, but not masonry. The **rim joist**, also called box beam, header, or band/ribbon joist, is nailed to the sill.

> **Definitions**
>
> The sill, mudsill, or sill plate, is a 2 × 4 or 2 × 6 laid flat on and anchored to the foundation, providing a pad for the framing system.
>
> The header, or rim joist, is one of the framing members and is the perimeter joist nailed to the sill.

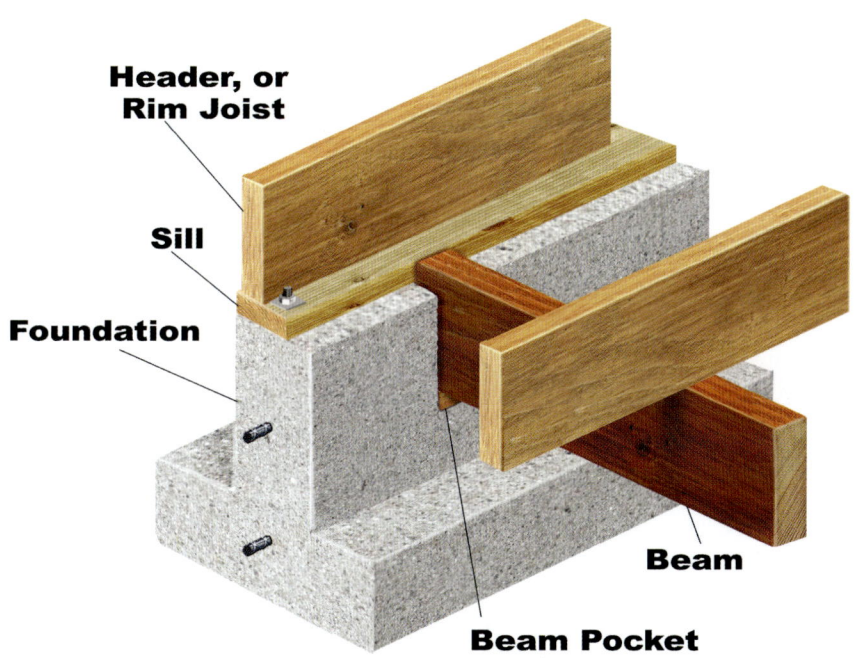

Illustration by Paddy Morrissey

The home inspector should inspect the sill and rim joist for rot. Rot can be caused by water penetration due to a defect in the siding, soil piled too high around the exterior of the house, or water wicking up through the foundation. Suspicious wood should be probed with a screwdriver, as required by most Standards of Practice. Sometimes in cold climates, you'll find a pad under the sill or mortar packed against the sill. Check the condition of the mortar. The home inspector often finds insulation around the top of the basement wall in each "bay," in which case the sill and rim joist will not be visible.

A sill over a window or door opening may sag or break from stress without a lintel or header having been installed. This should be pointed out to the client.

THE STRUCTURAL INSPECTION

INSPECTING BEAMS

- Watch for deterioration, sags, cracks, and crushing.
- Be sure beams are secured to supporting columns and have proper end support.
- Check for improper notches, holes, and missing portions of the beam.

Section Note

"You simply won't believe the sorts of things I've run into when looking up into basement ceilings. Be especially careful where new heating runs or plumbing lines have been installed. Take the time to think it through. For example, they've cut through this beam. Does it still function? What does that do to the joists? What's supporting the wall above?

Watch out too when you see repairs. Don't automatically accept the repair as successful. Think it through. A lot of handyman work is incredibly inept."

RULES

- Mid-notches one-sixth of depth on top only and not in middle one-third of beam.
- End notches one-quarter of depth with 3" to 4" of overhang.
- Holes one-third of depth and not within 2" of edges.
- Trusses not cut or any parts removed.

- **Girders:** Girders (or beams) are horizontal load-bearing members of a floor system, walls, or roof that carry the weight of the roof, floor, and wall loads to the foundation and columns. Girders usually run parallel to the long side of the house, but there may be others—shorter ones running elsewhere. Types of girders include large wood timbers, steel I-beams, spiked together 2× lumber, flitch plates, lengths of engineered lumber, or Glulams. Another option is the prefabricated floor truss.

  Girders rest in pockets of the foundation wall, shown in the diagram on page 45 on the sill, or on pilasters attached to the foundation. There should be a minimum of 3" of girder resting on end supports and 1/2" of clear space for ventilation around a wooden beam where it rests at the foundation in a pocket. Wooden beams should also have a waterproof material such as metal or polyethylene film between the beams and the foundation to prevent rot and deterioration.

- **Built-up beams** (a three-piece 2 × 8 or a three-piece 2 × 10 or a three-piece 2 × 12) should have their butted ends staggered along the length and be located over support columns and posts. The joint should be within 6" of the quarter point of the span of the beam. That is, if the beam is 12', the joint should occur 3' from either end, give or take 6" on either side.

There are no simple rules to tell if wood girders are properly **spanned**, center to center on their supports. It depends on the type and grade of the lumber. A three-piece 2 × 10 beam should be able to span up to 10' in most two-story homes; a three-piece 2 × 8 can span up to 8' in a one-story home.

Rules

There are, however, specific rules about what notches and holes can be cut into beams.

Rule #1: Mid-notches—where a notch is cut into a beam along its length—should be no deeper than one-sixth the depth of the beam. A mid-notch is allowable only at the top of the beam, not at its bottom. The notch shouldn't be cut in the middle one-third of the beam's length.

Rule #2: End notches cut into beams—where the end of the beam rests on the foundation, sill, or pier—can be no more than one-quarter the depth of the beam. And as mentioned previously, the beam resting on the foundation wall or pier should have 3″ of beam resting on the end supports.

Rule #3: Holes cut into beams should be no more than one-third the depth of the beam. Holes should not be cut into the top or bottom 2″ of the beam.

Rule #4: Trusses should not be cut into at all or have any parts of the chords or webs removed. The strength of the truss depends on the relationship of *all* of its parts to each other, and integrity can be lost by cutting or removing *any* part. Inspect trusses for loose or rusted gusset plates.

Girders should be carefully inspected for *any* violation of these rules. Often, heating contractors, plumbers, and electricians, who come in to do remodel work on finished houses, are the worst culprits. The home inspector may see evidence of their work.

- **Joists:** Joists are horizontal members of a floor system that carry the weight of the floor to the foundation, girders, or load-bearing walls. Joists are supported by beams as shown on page 45. They meet the foundation wall by resting on and being nailed to the sill and rim joist. Less common would be joists attached with metal hangers to a ledger board bolted to the foundation wall. Joists are generally wood—or more recently metal, engineered wood I-joists, or wood trusses placed 16–24″ apart.

Photo #17 WOOD JOIST

This is an example of a wood floor truss with glued finger jointing.

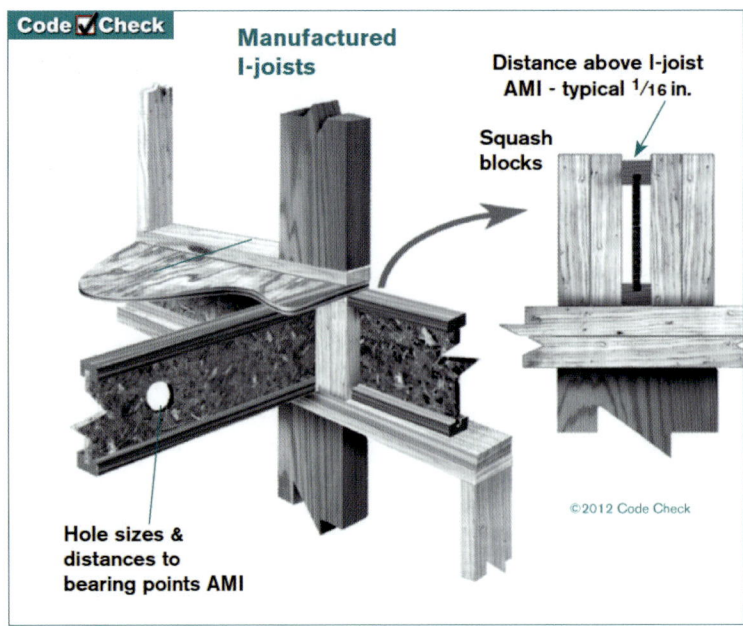

The allowable span for joists can vary considerably depending on the material used. For example, a 2 × 8 joist of Douglas fir or yellow pine can safely span further than one made of spruce, redwood, or white fir. The inspector is usually unable to determine proper span without knowing the species of wood and is limited instead to determining the condition of the joist. Watch for deterioration and wood rot, cracking, twisting, sags, and loss of bearing.

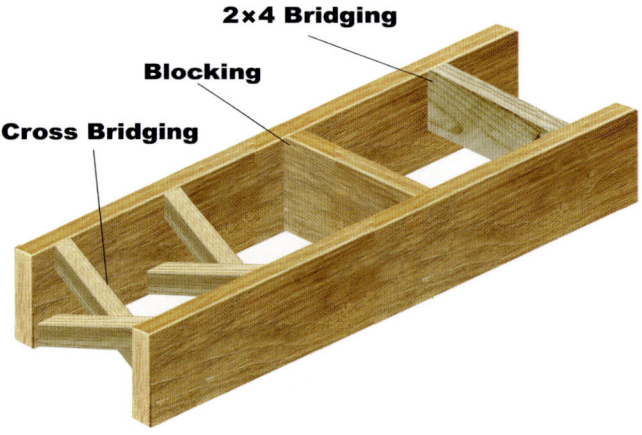

Illustration by Paddy Morrissey

Floor joists should be reinforced (doubled or tripled) under a partition wall above. Other areas such as stairway openings are reinforced with double or triple headers running perpendicular to the joist; for wide openings, the joists themselves are doubled.

You'll often see a **bracing system** used between joists to add stiffness to the joists and keep them from twisting. Building codes on how bracing may be done vary from area to area. You may see **blocking**, where the board nailed between joists is the same depth as the joists. Or **bridging** methods may be used in combination where 1 × 3s are used diagonally in cross bridging and 2 × 4s are nailed between the joists. Also, metal strapping and squash blocks on engineered lumber may be used for added stiffness.

> **Definition**
>
> *Blocking between joists is the use of a brace of wood the same depth as the joist, which gives stiffness to the joists. Bridging is a bracing method between joists where diagonal 1 × 3s (cross bridging) and/or perpendicular 2 × 4s are used.*

> **Photo #18 BRACING SYSTEM**
>
> *Cross-bracing or bridging is just one of many common applications used to stiffen the floor assembly.*

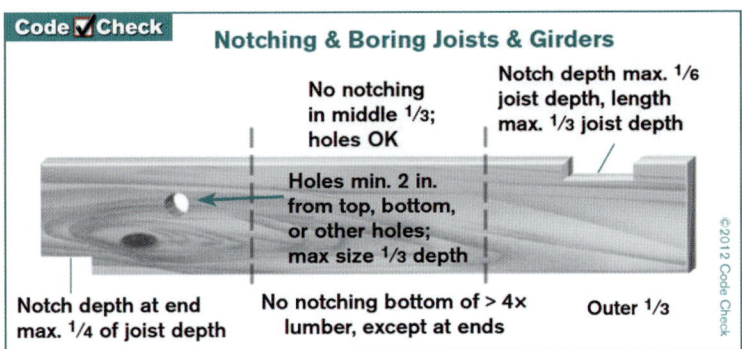

The same rules that apply to girders regarding notches and holes also apply to joists. Joists can be seriously weakened by improper notching, cutting, or drilling. Any violation should be reported.

- **Girder/joist connections:** There are several ways in which joists and girders can be joined. The joists can be **end nailed**, **face nailed**,

THE STRUCTURAL INSPECTION 49

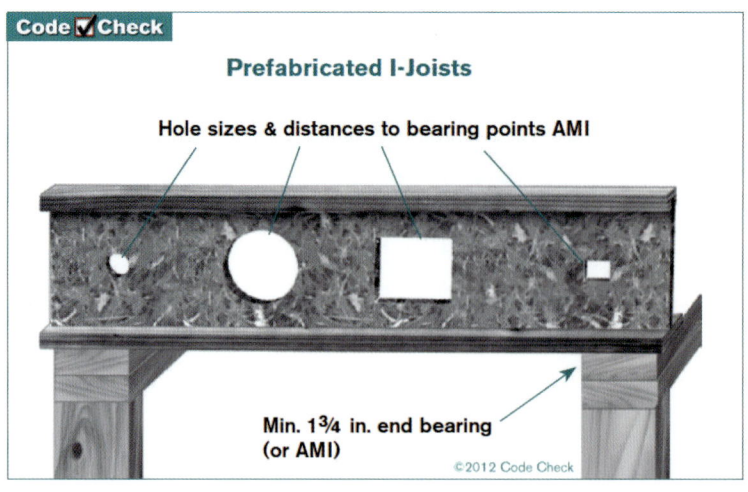

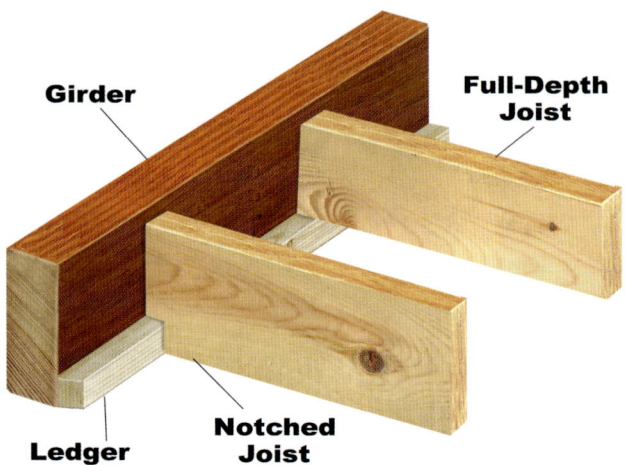

Illustration by Paddy Morrissey

Definitions

Ledger strips are lengths of wood nailed along the bottom edge of a beam to provide support for joists.

A *mortise* is the hole or slot in a wooden beam that accepts the tenon, which is the projecting end of the joist.

A *gusset plate* is a piece of wood placed over partial bearing joists and nailed into the joists to hold them in place.

or **toe nailed** directly into the girder (not pictured here). In those cases, the home inspector should watch for nails pulling out.

Ledger strips are strips of wood nailed along the bottom edge of the beam. They may be supporting a notched joist or full-depth joist. These are weak connections between beam and joist. Watch for nails pulling out. The ledger strip itself may be broken, cracked, or sagging.

The home inspector may find **mortise and tenon connections** in older homes. These type of connection are more common with post and beam style construction. The members are more substantial than what is used for conventional home framing. The mortise is the hole or slot in the girder; the tenon is the projecting end of the joist. The mortises can be back-to-back with the center portion of the girder remaining or with the entire center section removed. This older method is weak, and you should look carefully for joist cracks at the tenons following or along the grain.

Joists can be **full bearing** on the girder or can be **partial bearing**. Full bearing can be done with or without overhang, as shown here. In the partial bearing method, joists can meet above the girder and be nailed in place with the use of a gusset plate or be notched or end-lapped over the girder.

Another method used in joist/girder connections is the **metal hanger** approach, also called joist hangers (see Photo #19 Metal Hanger Approach). Metal hangers are

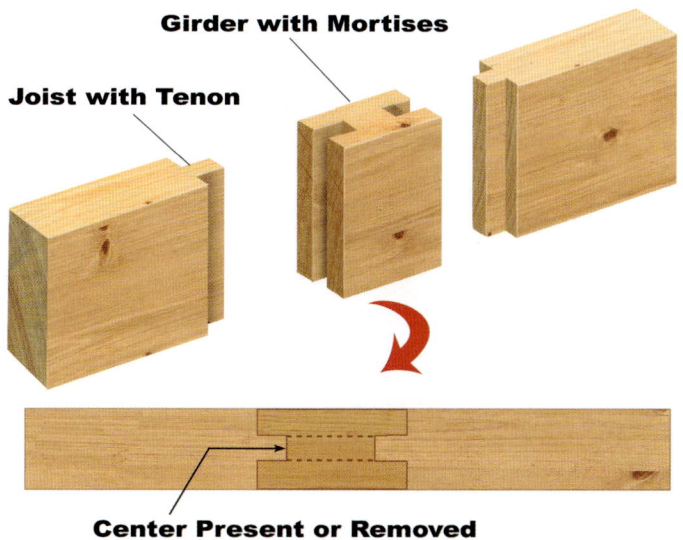

Illustration by Paddy Morrissey

now required and are therefore the most common method seen in newer construction. Some older construction have metal straps or hangars supporting the joists. Newer methods are the use of sheet metal hangars, screws, clips, or fasteners nailed to both girders and joists. These methods make for very strong connections, but are only as strong as the fasteners holding them in place. Any of these methods should be inspected carefully for

JOIST/GIRDER CONNECTIONS

- Butt, toe, or face nailed
- Ledger strips
- Mortise and tenon
- Full or partial bearing
- Metal hangers or straps

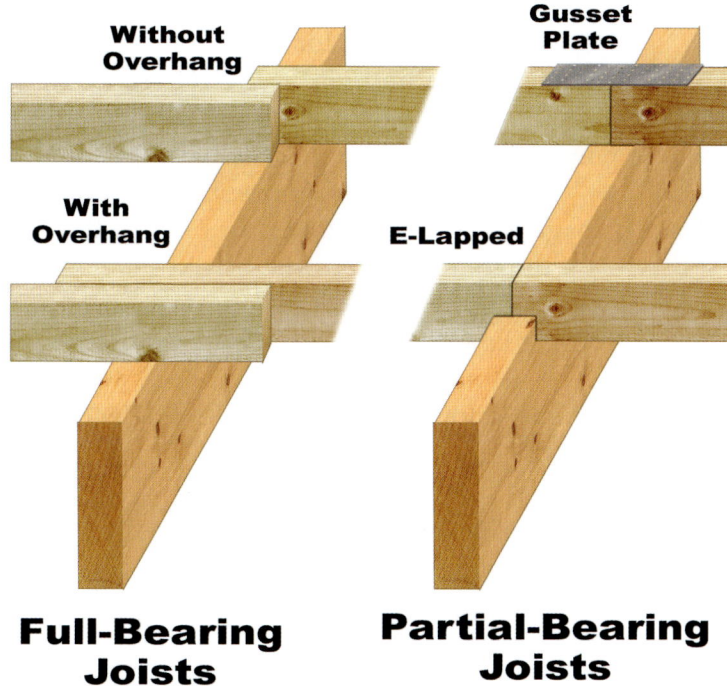

Illustration by Paddy Morrissey

THE STRUCTURAL INSPECTION

Photo #19 METAL HANGER APPROACH

This is a typical metal joist hanger fastened to both the beam and joist or truss with appropriate nails.

proper size and loose or missing nails or screws and for any damage to the metal parts.

Reporting Your Findings

We've covered a lot of ground in this section. The basement inspection includes many items and is detailed. Talk to your client while you're inspecting the basement. Be sure to explain what you were inspecting and what you found in each case. Take time to answer questions. Clients may not understand the consequences of your findings and are counting on you to make sense of it for them. Show them where you've recorded the findings in the report. Suggest that they review the report again on their own after the inspection.

Your inspection report should include a basement page if your state allows for one, with room to report on the items listed in the box at the left. For a start, be sure to record **access**—that is, whether you were able to gain access to the basement and to inspect it. Always make a note if your access was limited and let clients know that you can't find defects if you can't see them.

- **Basement moisture:** Indicate whether you found moisture or evidence of past staining in the basement. Indicate whether there's standing water, fresh stains (must use a moisture meter) or old stains, and signs of leaking. And record where you found it—on the walls, floor, or ceiling, for example.

BASEMENT INSPECTION

- Stairways
- Foundation wall cracks and penetrations
- Basement floor
- Girders and joists
- Water penetration, moisture, and drainage

DON'T EVER MISS

- Old stains indicating water penetration
- Cracked floor joists
- Improperly cut or removed structural members

- **Floor:** Identify the type of flooring. Indicate if the floor is covered with carpeting, hardwood, laminate, tile, etc., and therefore not visible for inspection. Record if cracks were found in the slab.

- **Girders and columns:** Identify the materials used in girders and columns and report on their condition. Make a note of any that are stained or rusted, damaged, or in need of repair.

- **Joists:** Identify the type of joists present—whether trusses, conventional wood, or metal. It's a good idea to record their size as well. Note any defects such as cracking, improper notching, and so on.

- **Sump pump:** For sumps, note whether one is present, whether it's been tested, and whether it's operating. Note any defects you found. If the sump pump is not operating and needs replacement, you might want to include it in a **major concern** category on the summary page of your report.

> **SUMP PUMP LIFETIME**
>
> Since sump pumps have a relatively short lifetime, it's a good idea to list them as <u>items needing replacement within the next five years</u>. Do this for your protection.

- **Stairs:** Report on the condition of the basement stairway. Stress safety factors such as uneven risers, missing handrails, and the lack of balusters if the situation calls for them.

1.9 INSPECTING CRAWL SPACES

When it's possible, the home inspector must inspect the crawl space. We already covered the inspection of **foundation walls** starting on page 24. And starting on page 35, we discussed how to inspect the basement for **leakage** and to inspect the **supporting structures**. When inspecting a crawl space, do it last! The reason for this has more to do with plumbing issues than getting the house dirty. If the house is vacant and the access panel is outside, you might be tempted to inspect the crawl space while you are outside. But the plumbing in that vacant house may not have been run for weeks or even months. You may inspect the crawl space and find that it is completely dry. But after you test all of the plumbing fixtures in the house, the crawl space may be a swimming pool and you will never know because you already inspected it. These items are also part of the crawl space inspection:

> **Chapter Note**
>
> *Pages 53–59 present procedures on the crawl space inspection.*

- The crawl space floor/ground

- Ventilation

- Insulation

- Seismic (earthquake) bolts and cripple walls, where applicable

Access

When the foundation is put in and the earth beneath the house is not removed, a crawl space is created. You can also have what is called a raised foundation (pier and beam), which is a crawl space, but above grade. Building codes have varied regarding the allowable height of the crawl space. In some areas, it was as much as 36″, but the height was only 12″ in others. Some crawl spaces are inaccessible. Some SOPs provide guidelines for entering crawl spaces. You will see minimum access panel sizes ranging from 24″ × 18″ to 16″ × 24″ in various SOPs.

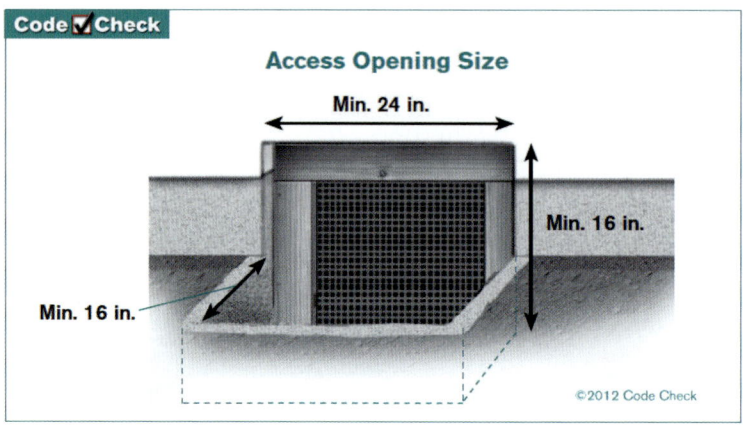

The more difficulty the home inspector has getting into a crawl space, the more likelihood he or she will find problems there that have been ignored. The home inspector should make every effort to get into the crawl space and inspect it thoroughly. Yes, it can be a nasty job. Most standards state the following:

- Required to enter under floor crawl spaces except when entry could damage property or when dangerous or adverse situations are suspected.

- Required to report the methods used to observe under floor crawl spaces.

Perhaps the most important point for the home inspector's protection against liability is reporting the **methods used** to access to the crawl space. Because serious defects may be present in the crawl space, the home inspector must let the customer know if he or she was able to gain access to find those defects. The customer must understand that the inspector cannot be responsible for reporting these defects if access is impossible or limited.

1.10 INSPECTING THE FLOOR

The floor of the crawl space may be dirt, gravel, or concrete. One of the most common problems with crawl spaces is deterioration of piping, insulation, and the framing members above due to moisture in the crawl space. There is some debate as to whether the moisture often found in a crawl space is due to moisture released from the soil or moisture in the air from the wall vents. This is especially true if a dirt or gravel floor is left uncovered (no vapor barrier) and if there is no proper venting of the space. Wait until you inspect a crawl space that is covered with mushrooms. You can bet there is a moisture problem. We are not just talking about mushrooms in the soil as you would think. Mushrooms growing out of the framing is not an uncommon sight in certain parts of the country with very humid weather.

A dirt or gravel crawl space floor should typically be covered with a **vapor barrier** to prevent moisture from the soil from being released into the crawl space. Vapor barriers, or more accurately vapor retarders, may be polyethylene sheeting, roofing paper, asphalt, or concrete. These vapor retarders, if present, should be in good condition. They should be free of holes and tears and should be sealed together at seams. If they are not covering the soil area "completely," write them up as being inadequate or in need of repair or replacement.

Ventilation

Proper ventilation in crawl spaces is a subject of controversy. Traditionally crawl spaces have been vented, and most building codes required ventilation. In recent years, some researchers have found that crawl space vents may not be necessary, especially in southern climates where vents can introduce hot, humid (outside) air into the crawl space. It was previously thought that moisture in a crawl space came from damp soil. In fact, the relative humidity in a crawl space is directly correlated with the relative humidity outside. Building codes have changed crawl space requirements to reflect this new information.

The amount of ventilation required by code varies depending on the use of a vapor barrier, such as plastic that is spread over the ground to prevent moisture from entering. With a vapor barrier, the code calls for 1 square foot of net venting for every 1500 square feet of area, with one vent opening located within 3′ of each corner. Without a vapor barrier, 1 square foot of net vent is needed for every 150 square feet of floor area. The minimum opening size is 1 square foot with mesh or screening not larger than 1/4″. The term *net venting* has to do with the louvers, screening, and hardware that may block the vent opening. You may have a vent that is 12″ × 12″, for example, but only has a net venting area of 0.67 square feet due to obstructions. This varies

TOOLS TO USE

- A jumpsuit to protect your clothes
- Screwdriver or knife to probe mortar and wood
- Strong flashlight for dark areas
- Tape measure for cracks and displacement
- Level for determining lean (plumb)

Section Note

"One of my inspectors once inspected a house that was six years old. The code inspectors had passed the house on all aspects. But the house happened to have a crawl space that my inspector inspected thoroughly. On the farthest side from the crawl space entrance, he found a long span of foundation wall sagging, indicating a serious footing failure. He suspected that the entire wall would eventually fail because of it.

This raised quite a stink with the code inspectors, but upon further investigation, they discovered that someone had dug underneath the wall and no footing existed at all. The inspector was right. What's the point? Investigate the entire crawl space carefully."

Section Note

Obviously it would be good for you to see crawl spaces for yourself. Get yourself a jumpsuit, locate some friends with crawl spaces, and go to it.

greatly depending on the material. Most vents have stamped or molded vent area labels on them.

Heated and cooled (conditioned) crawl spaces should not be vented. Some structures have both a crawl space and a basement. A heated/cooled crawl space may be connected to a basement. According to some recent research, the best way to avoid moisture trouble may be to seal completely the crawl space floor (soil) and the foundation walls as well as insulate the foundation walls. In a sealed crawl space, moisture may be kept to an acceptable level and damage avoided. If this is done as a retrofit, foundation vents must be eliminated.

Photo #20 *This is an example of a completely sealed and conditioned crawl space. The foundation walls are insulated instead of the underside of the floor above.*

A crawl space, when sealed (unvented), must be done according to very strict requirements. The floor must be sealed with poly, seams sealed, that runs up the walls. The walls must be insulated, and in areas prone to termites, there must be an inspection strip. A small HVAC supply register and return are installed in the crawl space to maintain a slight positive pressure relative to the exterior. A very good study was conducted in 2009 by Advanced Energy and is available at www.crawlspaces.org.

On a separate note, there are requirements for "flood openings" in areas prone to flooding. Openings are to allow for the automatic entry and exit of floodwaters to minimize hydrostatic pressure that can cause structural damage. The requirement is to have 1 square inch of opening for every 1 square foot of enclosed space. If the crawl space was 2000 square feet, you would need 2000 square inches (almost 14 square feet). If typical air vents rated at 60 square inches per unit were used, you would need 33 vents total. In alternatives such as the "Smart Vent," only 10 vents would be required for the same size crawl space.

Insulation

Mistakes are often made when insulation is installed in a crawl space. If the insulation is installed in the **ceiling** of the crawl space, the vapor retarder should be located up against the floor above, with the batting facing "fuzzy

Photo #21 SMART VENT

These are vents that open and close with water movement. This allows water to move in or out of the crawl space to prevent build-up of hydrostatic pressure that could damage foundation walls.

side" down toward the crawl space. The home inspector may find damaged, damp, or even wet insulation because of this mistake. When the insulation is installed upside down with the paper flanges stapled to the ends of the floor joists, the moisture from the crawl space condenses in the batting, rotting the floor joists and causing the insulation to fall down. Another problem with insulation that is installed incorrectly is that it does not fill the full depth of the floor joists, leaving a space between the top of the insulation and the wood deck. A typical configuration is an R-19 batt (5.5″) installed in a 2′ × 10′ (9.25″) joist bay. The space allows for condensation to form as well. The home inspector should suggest that such insulation be replaced—this time with the moisture barrier *up*, facing the warm side as it should or possibly not at all depending on where in the country the house may be. The insulation should also be tightly attached to the underside of the deck. It is often improperly installed flush with the bottom of the joists as described above. If the insulation does not touch the surface it is insulating, it is basically worthless.

Photo #22 *This photo shows properly installed insulation between the floor joists.*

THE STRUCTURAL INSPECTION

In the unconditioned crawl space with insulation installed "underfloor" (most common configuration) at the deck; ducts and piping should be insulated to prevent freezing of pipes and to increase efficiency for ductwork.

1.11 STRUCTURAL CONCERNS

We're not going to review everything previously discussed about sills, columns, girders, and joists. But they are part of the inspection of the crawl space and should be given the same attention as described in the basement inspection starting on page 35. Materials should be probed for deterioration if there are visible signs. Girders and joists should be examined for condition and structural integrity. Nothing should be overlooked. In a crawl space that we inspected, the joists shrunk and were slipping off the foundation walls.

Photo #23 *This is a screw-jack that is improperly installed. Note that the screw is missing a plate at the top and that it is not fastened to the beam. On a side note, you can see that the insulation is installed upside-down.*

The homeowner's solution was to insert a beam, supported by jacks, under the joists. What do you do when you see a situation such as this? Although steel columns or wood posts with proper footings would have been the best solution to support the new beam, jacks can be acceptable under certain conditions. First examine the jacks. The jacks must be the proper kind of **screw jack** used for these purposes. Under no circumstances should car jacks be used. Next, determine if they're attached to the beam. They should be securely attached. Next, determine if footings have been put in. Here, a concrete footing was visible, but we dug around these footings to see if they were roughly the right depth, which is not required. Sometimes, you'll find that only an inch or two of concrete has been poured, and that's not enough. One more thing—shims were inserted between the jack and the beam. This needs to be looked at. Determine if the shim was inserted because the weight of the beam has pushed the jack down, causing it to sink, or the shim was inserted to maintain proper height upon initial installation. If it's the former, this is not a good solution.

Reporting Your Findings

The home inspector *must* investigate the crawl space if it's possible to get in and move around in it. Of course, the customer is probably not going to get in the crawl space with you. So take plenty of photos, and when you come out, communicate your findings with the customer. Talk about what you were looking for, showing and explaining what you found.

NOTE: Sometimes, a house has a partial basement and a crawl space. Each area should be inspected, and each should be reported in your inspection report, typically on separate pages.

Here's an overview on what to report on the crawl space inspection:

> **DON'T EVER MISS**
> - Cracks in the foundation wall
> - Unstable bowing or leaning of the foundation wall
> - Shearing action in the foundation
> - Signs of water penetration
> - Cracked floor joists
> - Deterioration or improper cuts in structural members

- **Access:** Explain whether your access to the crawl space was complete, partial, or impossible. If some areas were not visible during the inspection (once you got in there), make a note of that and take a photo of the inaccessible area(s).

- **Foundation condition:** As stated on page 34 for foundation inspection, report the type of foundation walls, piers, or pilings present and note cracks, movements, settlement, and water penetration found. If the condition warrants, include a recommendation to monitor cracks or call in a structural engineer for an evaluation.

- **Floor:** Identify the type of floor in the crawl space as concrete, gravel, or dirt. Note the presence or absence of a vapor barrier and, if present, its condition. You may want to recommend that a vapor barrier be added if a gravel or dirt floor is uncovered and there is an indication of moisture with the framing above. Report on any evidence you've found on water seepage through the floor or walls.

- **Structures:** As described on page 53 for basement inspection, write your findings on the materials used for girders, joists, piers, pilings, and columns and report their condition. Report any signs of deterioration in these framing members and in the subfloor caused by excessive moisture in the crawl space.

- **Insulation and ventilation:** Note if pipes are properly insulated in the unconditioned crawl space and whether underfloor (deck) insulation is properly installed. For ventilation, note whether vents are found and whether there are moisture issues.

We recommend that you spend a little time after the inspection reviewing the inspection report with the client. Especially with the crawl space, which the client didn't see, it's important to stress any findings you may have. Show the client the page on which you've written your findings. Often, clients will forget what you said during the inspection, and this short review can remind them.

> **Chapter Note**
>
> *Pages 60–62 discuss inspecting slab construction. Before reading this short chapter, you may want to go back to pages 23–24 to review slab-on-grade construction techniques.*

1.12 INSPECTING SLABS

Slab-on-grade construction can be almost invisible to the home inspector. What may appear to be the slab when viewed from the exterior is actually the stem wall or foundation. The outside edge of the slab should never be visible. The slab is behind (inside) the foundation wall and should not be visible regardless of the siding type. The surface of the slab (inside) is normally covered with a finish flooring material such as tile, wood, or carpeting. You may find a home with "stained" concrete, which is the slab itself and is fully visible. These types of slabs are usually saw-cut to minimize unwanted cracking. In some applications, you may have a wood deck on a slab, but this is not typical. Sleepers or 2 × 4 lumber is laid on the slab and insulated, with a plywood or OSB deck laid on top of it and then finish flooring on top of that. This creates a much warmer floor than just the concrete slab would provide.

First, the home inspector should make sure the construction method *is* slab-on-grade. Rarely, you may find that what appears to be a slab-on-grade is actually a concrete floor resting on piers and beams or simply grade beams. There are instances of this in New Orleans, where concrete slabs were elevated several feet above grade following Hurricane Katrina. Ask the homeowner if there is some doubt on this point.

Even though the slab is not typically visible, there are signs that the home inspector can look for when determining the condition of the slab.

- **Settlement:** The home inspector should try to determine if the foundation wall that surrounds the slab has settled. Improperly placed downspouts and splash blocks may cause water to pool or erode soil near the foundation. Heaving soil due to freeze/thaw and expansive soils under the slab can cause the slab to tilt or sink, even twist and skew. Settlement can be caused by a leak in the plumbing or heating system embedded in the slab, which undermines the soil below.

Watch for **cracks** in the exterior foundation (stem) wall and the slab itself. Noticeable cracks on the interior floor can indicate settlement but are not

Photo #24 *This is spalling as a result of the rebar being too close to the surface, rusting, expanding, and then breaking through the concrete.*

typically structural in nature. This is not the case with monolithic or post-tension slabs. Cracks in the slab are not likely to be visible. But even when the floor is covered, cracks can sometimes be felt underfoot or seen when a flashlight is used to side-light the floor.

- **Shifting:** Slabs can shrink and pull away from the outer wall if they are not properly installed during construction. The slab can crack along the perimeter of the foundation wall. As a result, shreds of slab may be left on the wall where the slab has become separated. The home inspector may find cracking along the floor edge.

- **Moisture:** The home inspector should report evidence of water penetration through the slab. Moisture can come up into the house through cracks in the slab or through the openings or utility penetrations in the slab. During the inspection, the home inspector should pay attention to these openings, such as plumbing lines coming up under the sink. These openings are where moisture and insects can come up from the soil into the home. Moisture along the edge of the slab can indicate that the slab has broken away from the foundation. When the slab and foundation sink and settle, water penetration can be a problem. You may find older homes where the water lines and sometimes even the gas line are embedded within the slab, which is no longer allowed. If the piping fails, you can have water issues or, worse yet, a gas leak beneath the house. Modern houses sometimes have radiant floor heating, which is typically plastic PEX piping embedded within the concrete to heat the home.

- **Post-tension slabs:** Post-tension cable ends can rust if they are exposed to the weather. It is not always easy to determine what type of slab you are looking at. There are three key clues you can look for in determining whether the slab is a post-tension slab. First, look for the faint circles of the cable end patches on two of the four side stem walls of the house. This is where the cable ends ran through the wall, were tensioned, and then were cut off and the

DON'T EVER MISS

- Cracked, shifting, or settling slabs
- Moisture penetration

Photo #25 *This is one way to tell if you are dealing with a post-tension slab. This imprint may be located in an obvious place, such as a garage or patio floor that will not be covered by finish materials.*

ends patched. The other ends of these cables are embedded in the concrete. Second, look for a stamp in the concrete somewhere prominent, such as in the floor of the garage or on an attached patio slab. Third, investigate local construction practices in your area. As of the printing of this book, post-tension slabs are being used across the southern United States and moving northward. Verify that the concrete plugs over the cable ends are intact. If the cable ends are visible or rust is present, note it in your inspection report and recommend repair. If the slab is visible, check to see if the floor is flat. Overtensioning the cables can cause the floor to dish or cup.

Photo #26 POST-TENSION SLAB CABLE END

These should always be sealed. This is new construction and they just tensioned the cable and it will be patched soon. Also, note the poor concrete work; honeycombing is what the exposed aggregate is called.

Reporting Your Findings
Clients should understand that visual inspection of the slab is not usually possible. Explain that you're looking for *evidence* that something may be wrong with the slab but that situations could be developing that are not yet apparent.

- **Not visible:** When you're reporting on slab inspection, it's a good idea to check off every "not-visible" box, unless the floor is just stained concrete and completely visible.

- **Slab condition:** Note if you've found signs of settlement, cracks in the floor tile and most likely the slab, and the presence of moisture or water penetration.

1.13 ABOVE-GRADE CONSTRUCTION
The home inspector should be familiar with various types of framing and construction methods and

Chapter Note

Pages 62–74 present information on wall construction. Interior framing is presented in Chapter 07; roof structures will be covered in Chapter 03.

materials, including metal, wood, and masonry. This and the following sections will give you an overview.

Wood Framing

The most common wood framing construction method used for the last hundred years is the **platform framing** method. With platform framing, one story is constructed at a time, using studs one story high.

Photo #27 PLATFORM FRAMING METHOD

Foundation wall, foam sill-sealer, sill plate, and rim joist of platform construction.

Photo #28 PLATFORM FRAMING

Photo #29 PLATFORM FRAMING

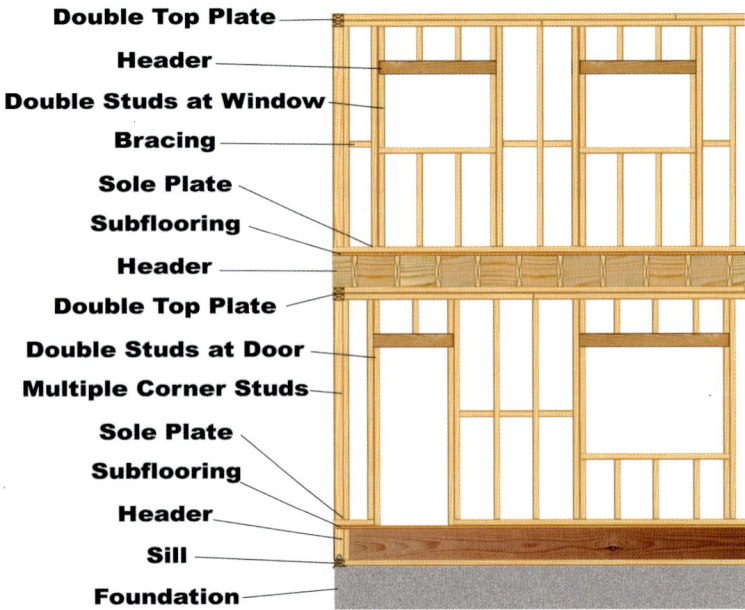

Illustration by Paddy Morrissey

The first story is constructed by installing the mudsill or sill plate on top of the foundation wall (which may have a foam sill seal); this is bolted or fastened to the foundation. Next, the floor joists are set on the sill plate at one end and on a beam or girder at the other end (middle of the house) and fastened. Then the rim joist is installed along the ends of the floor joists at the edge of the sill plate and fastened to both. With the advent of engineered lumber such as I-joists, the joists may span across the entire basement or crawl space from foundation wall to foundation wall. Next, the deck is created, where plywood or OSB is laid over the floor joists spanning the basement or crawl space. If the foundation is slab-on-grade, the wall construction is started directly on the slab. The exterior walls are created laying down on the deck or the slab. The **sole plate** or bottom plate, studs (typically 16″ on center), and **top plate** are assembled and end-nailed together, and the wall is stood up at the edge of the deck or slab. Once all perimeter (exterior) walls are stood up and braced, the second top plate is installed along the top of the exterior wall.

A special type of framing called advanced framing techniques or Optimum Value Engineering (OVE) employs a different method of wall construction. Walls are constructed similarly, but at 24″ on center and with single top plates. The wall, deck, and roof framing components must line up directly above one another. Double studs are used at openings in the walls; multiple studs are used at corners (one less with OVE walls). Usually, a double **top plate** is end-nailed to the wall studs. Then the process begins again. Joists or trusses are laid for the second story, with an outer band or ribbon joist followed by the subflooring, the sole plate, studs, and the top plate(s) and repeated as necessary per floor.

At one time, the norm was to use 2 × 4 studs placed at 16–24″ intervals, although today, 2 × 6s have become common in energy-efficient homes because they provide more space for insulation. However, 2 × 4 walls are still widely used by production builders, but they employ the use of 2–4″ exterior foam insulation beneath the siding to gain the necessary R-values needed by current building

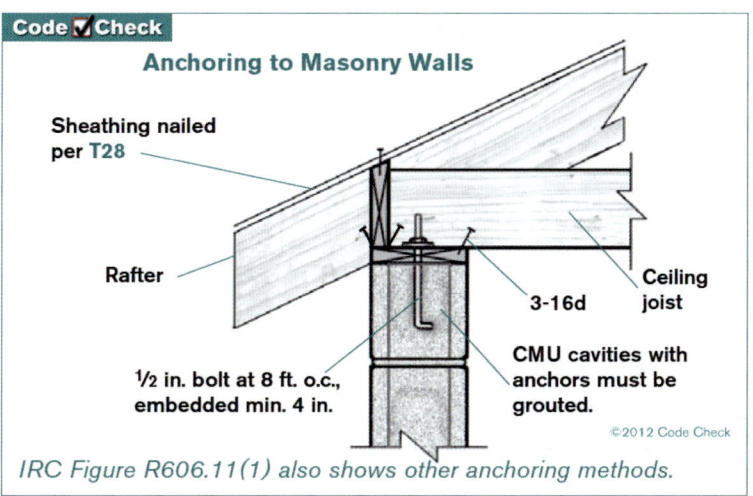

IRC Figure R606.11(1) also shows other anchoring methods.

code. In ultra-high efficiency homes, double walls and other complex arrangements allow the wall assembly to have insulation values up to R-40. The exterior wood frame walls are typically load-bearing walls that carry the weight of the roof and floors down to the foundation. Metal studs are sometimes used as load-bearing or interior partition walls, although they are not that common in residential construction.

Another construction technique home inspectors will find, which was commonly used in the late 1800s and early 1900s, is called **balloon framing**. This method used very long, uncut vertical studs and corner posts that ran from foundation to roof in two-story structures. Here, the studs and corner posts were erected first, sitting directly on the sill plate or mudsill on top of the

> **Definitions**
>
> In _platform framing_, the stories of the house are constructed one on top of each other. The story-high wall _studs_ are vertical framing members connected at the bottom to the horizontal _sole plate_ and at the top to the horizontal _top plate_. _Girts_ are horizontal bracing members used between adjacent studs as blocking. The _header_, a horizontal framing member, carries the load above a window or door opening. In _balloon framing_, long vertical studs and corner posts run from the foundation to the roof and the floors are hung on the wall frame. A horizontal _ledger_ attached to the wall studs supports the second-story joists.

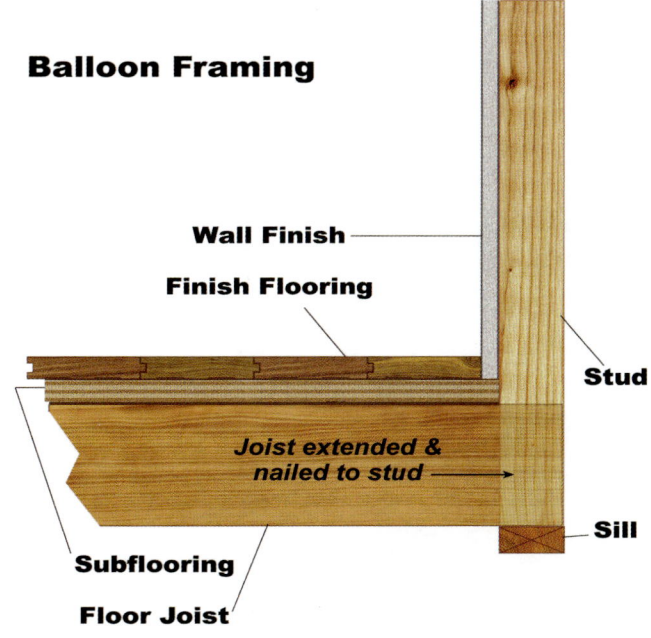

Illustration by Paddy Morrissey

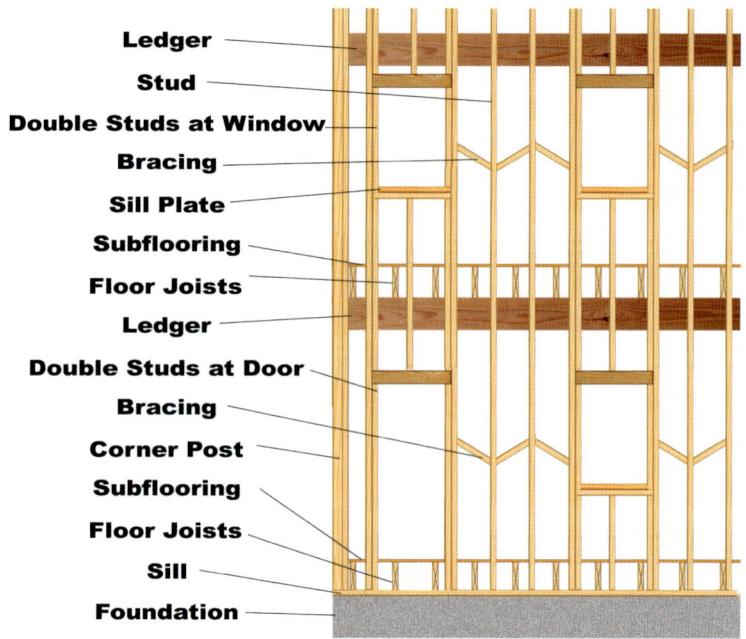

foundation walls. The first-floor joists rested on the sill beside the studs, and the second floor was basically hung on the wall studs. A **ledger** was attached to the studs to support the second-story joists.

Both platform and balloon framing are equally stable when properly constructed. Platform framing replaced balloon framing as the predominant method in the early 20th century due to the ease of construction and the savings in materials cost. Another significant factor leading to the adoption of platform construction was the lack of fire blocking in the wall cavities of a

Photo #30 EXTERIOR BALLOON FRAME WALLS

balloon-framed house. Without fire blocking, flames can easily shoot up through the wall and spread quickly from the basement to the second-floor ceiling cavity, and attic, which are all connected like little chimney stacks. In the diagram of platform framing (page 64) and balloon framing (page 65), you can see that the wall cavities in balloon framing are open from the basement to under the second floor deck and all the way to the attic.

Of course, the home inspector can't see the framing of a home because it is covered on both the exterior and interior. There can be problems with the framing that are not always visible upon inspection, although their effects can be seen elsewhere.

- **Faulty construction:** A home may be constructed with overspaced studs. Door and window openings may not be adequately supported, and the inspector may be able to spot sagging above large doors or windows if not supported with the appropriate header. Nailing maybe insufficient.

  Wall studs may buckle from overloading, especially if they're not properly spaced or lack blocking to brace them. Often, you'll see framing that was originally adequate to bear their loads, but a second- or third-story addition was added that increased the load beyond the capacity of the studs and the foundation to support it.

- **Inadequate lumber:** Poor-quality lumber used in some wood framing can result in warped or bowed studs. Lumber that is too wet when it is installed can shrink excessively after construction, resulting in warping, bowing, and cracking of the interior finishes. Both of these situations will probably be evident in the condition of the interior walls.

- **Deterioration of wood:** Wood framing can rot if there is water penetration into the structure, and can suffer insect damage. Condensation can also occur when insulation is upgraded and vapor retarders are not properly installed on the warm (in winter) side of the wall. During the cold months, warm moist air entering the wall from the house cools in the insulation and condenses, trapping water in the walls. Patches of peeling exterior paint can be a sign of condensation in the walls.

> **CONSTRUCTION**
>
> - Platform framing
> - Balloon framing
> - Logs
> - Post and beam
> - Wood with brick veneer
> - Solid masonry

Structural Insulated Panels (SIPs)

Structural insulated panels (SIPs) are a high-performance building system for residential and light commercial construction. The panels consist of an insulating foam core sandwiched between two structural facings, typically oriented strand board (OSB). SIPs are manufactured under factory-controlled conditions and can be fabricated to fit nearly any building design.

SIPs combine minimal air infiltration (draftiness) and high levels of insulation to make them one of the most energy-efficient methods currently available. They can be used for walls, floors, foundations, and roof decks.

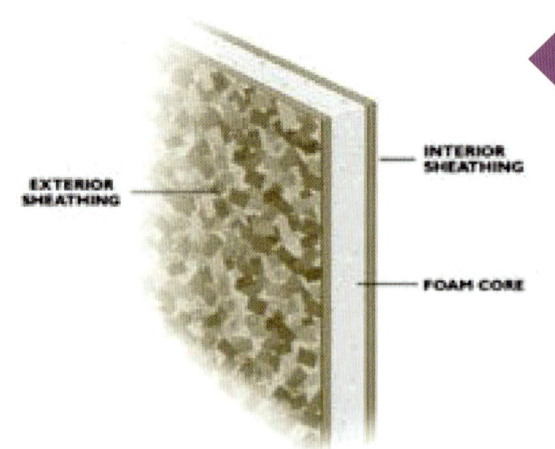

Photo #31 STRUCTURAL INSULATED PANEL

Post and Beam

Another type of wood framing construction is **post and beam**. Some prefabricated kits available today use this type of construction, but by and large, post and beam construction isn't commonly used in homes. You're more likely to see it in barns and large buildings such as churches and old mills.

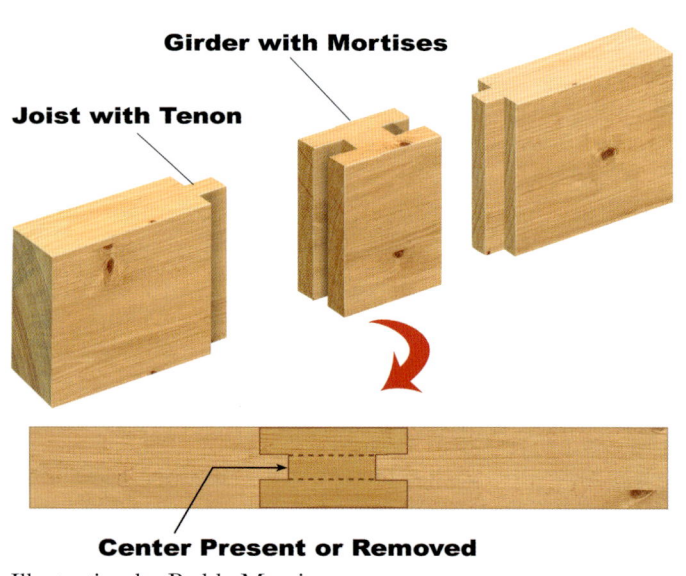

Illustration by Paddy Morrissey

The post and beam method uses framing members that are larger and fewer in number than the studs used in platform or balloon framing. A combination of posts and beams carries the weight of the structure down to the foundation.

In post and beam framing, 2″ thick floor planks are typically laid. Some older floor planks can be up to 12″ wide. The walls may simply be heavy plank that is installed horizontally or vertically and are typically not load-bearing. A stud framework can be introduced between the posts to form the framework for a finished wall. In post and beam construction, fewer roof rafters are used, one at the top of each post, and planks are used to form the surface of the roof.

These types of structures usually have a variety of connecting methods between the posts and beams—mortise and tenon, dovetail joints, and wooden dowels—and many used no nails.

There are problems associated with post and beam construction. There can be a lack of rigidity to the structure when the exterior wall finish doesn't provide a stabilizing function. Because the load of the structure is concentrated at the posts, the foundation may be weak at these points. And the large timbers used in the structure may shrink and expand, causing the whole structure to shift with each changing season.

1.14 LOG HOMES

Log construction is not always visible. In the old days, people often covered a log home with stucco or clapboard on the outside and finished the interior walls. If that's the case, it's hard for the home inspector to know about the logs or to assess any deterioration of the wall.

Photo #32 *This chinking was applied too thin, and the wrong foam backer was used. The chinking should have been 3/8" to 1/2" thick to span the 4" gap between logs.*

In traditional log homes, **chinking**—a mortar made of clay, sand, and other binders such as animal hair—was used to fill the gaps between the logs. Today, urethane products are used for that purpose. Chinking needs annual maintenance, and some parts will have to be redone each year. Also in the traditional log home, the logs will shrink and expand across the grain of the log. That is, a log wall will get shorter and taller, causing gaps around windows and doors and pulling the floor up and down with it.

Modern log construction makes use of tooled logs with insulation between the faces. These logs are usually well dried before construction to minimize shrinkage. A plastic sealant is used instead of chinking. We recommend significant additional training before inspecting log homes as they are so different from wood-framed homes.

1.15 BRICK VENEER OVER WOOD FRAMING

Brick houses built today—and since the early 1970s—are generally brick veneer over wood framing. A brick veneer wall does not carry the load of the structure; it is essentially siding. It is included in this structure section to clarify its use and to explain how it is different from solid masonry homes, described below.

The brick veneer is constructed from the foundation up and is attached to the wall sheathing with **brick ties**. These ties are usually galvanized steel crimped accordion-style to allow them to expand and contract with the wooden frame and keep them from cracking the brick veneer.

The wall sheathing, if present or framing is covered with a water or weather-resistant barrier (WRB), typically called house wrap. An air space of about 1" is left behind the brick veneer to allow water passing through the brick to run down the wall. The water exits just above the foundation wall, typically through the bottom

> **Definition**
>
> *Chinking was a mortar made of clay, sand, and other binders such as animal hair that is used to fill the gaps between logs in a log home.*

> **POINT TO REMEMBER**
>
> *Wood shrinks more across the grain than along the grain. That's why a log wall shrinks more vertically than does a wall made with studs.*

> **Chapter Note**
>
> *Chapter 2 will present more information about the inspection of brick veneer and other exterior sidings. This chapter is to be used to learn about construction techniques more than about the actual inspection of the exterior walls.*

Photo #33 BRICK TIES

This is new construction in Texas. The green foam is the sheathing. You can see the corrugated metal ties between the framing and the brick.

row of brick through **weep holes**, which are openings about every 2–3′ along the bricks. Some areas require weep holes be provided at the top of the veneer as well as the bottom for air circulation.

Flashing (a thin sheet of material, usually corrosion-resistant metal or plastic) is placed at the base of the wall and above all openings, such as windows and doors, to divert water away from within the walls and foundation.

With brick veneer, the inspector is able to see signs of problems. Weep holes can become blocked and not allow water to exit from behind the bricks, leading to deterioration of the brick and the mortar as well as the framing. Brick ties can be improperly installed or loosened over time, and the veneer can separate from the wall.

Photo #34 BRICK VENEER WALL

This is a brick veneer wall with weep holes at the bottom just above the foundation wall. These weep holes have not yet been filled with something that will prevent insects from entering. The holes may be filled with many products that prevent insect entry, but allow water to drain from the wall cavity.

Chapter 1

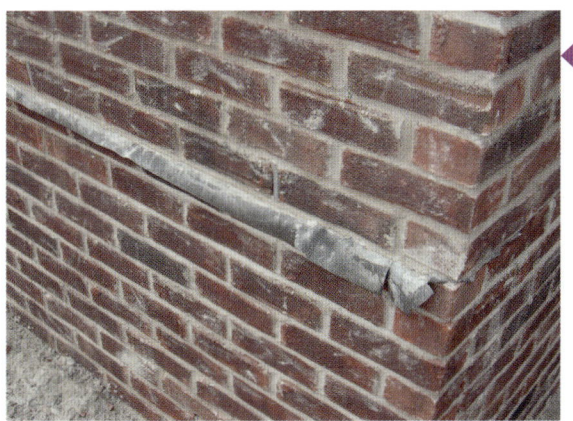

Photo #35 BRICK VENEER WALL

This photo shows another brick veneer wall with the weep holes filled with a piece of plastic with small holes in it. They are the vertical gray pieces just above the black plastic flashing hanging out of the mortar joint. This black plastic is typical of flashing used in modern brick veneer construction.

Solid Masonry Walls

The walls of a home can be made of solid masonry. Usually, there are two thicknesses (wythes) of masonry. The interior wall may be left exposed, plastered over, or furred out and covered with drywall. The masonry wall can be made of one or a combination of materials such as brick, stone, and concrete block.

A **solid brick wall** can usually be identified by the **header rows or bonding courses**, where the brick is turned with its small end facing out. The header rows serve as ties to hold the two or more wythes of bricks together. (Header rows are not necessary in brick veneer walls but are sometimes used for decorative purposes.) The thickness of brick walls has declined over the centuries from 20″ thick to 12–16″ and finally to 8″ thick. Most brick homes built since the early 1970s are brick veneer (siding) over a wood framework.

The solid masonry wall may be built of two materials—an inner and outer layer. Each layer (wall) is called a wythe. Courses are horizontal rows, and wythes are vertical walls. This is called a **compound wall**. Metal ties are sometimes used to connect the two walls together and give strength to the wall.

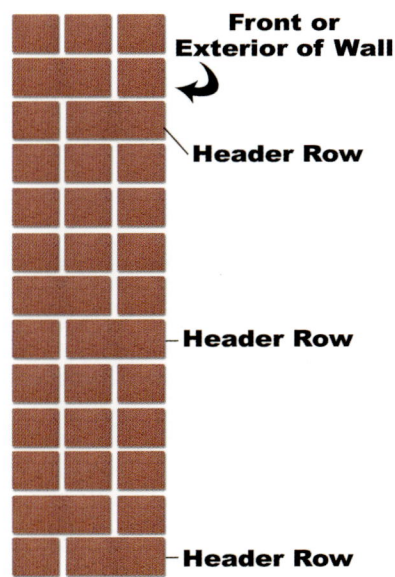

Solid Brick Wall

Illustration by Paddy Morrissey

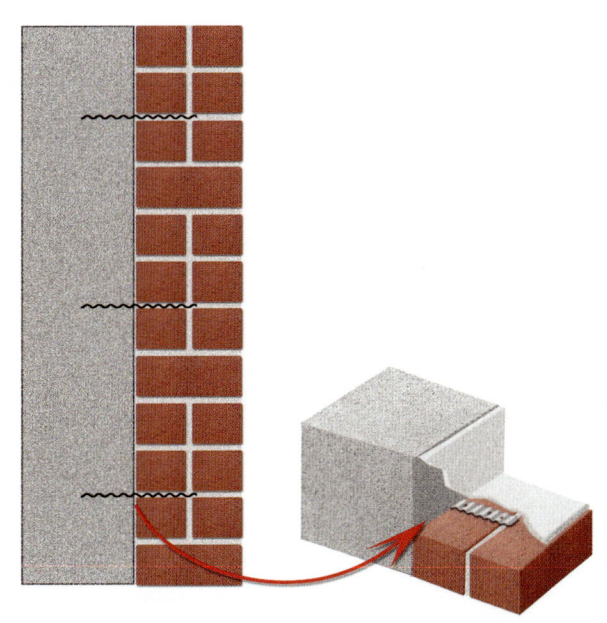

Illustration by Paddy Morrissey

Definitions

In a brick veneer house, an outer layer of bricks is attached to the wood framework of the house using brick ties, which are accordion-style metal fasteners. Weep holes are openings in the bottom row of brick that provide an exit for water accumulating behind the brick veneer. A flashing placed at the foundation is sheet metal that prevents water leaks into the foundation.

In a solid brick house, three layers, or wythes, of brick are used to construct a solid wall with no wood framing. Header rows are rows of bricks turned small end out to act as ties to hold the wall together.

A compound wall is a solid masonry wall built of two different materials. A cavity wall is a masonry wall with dead air space left between layers.

MASONRY WALLS

- Solid brick wall
- Compound wall
- Cavity wall

The positioning of header rows in the brick outer layer can be random, not necessarily every five to seven rows.

A masonry wall with an air space left between the inner and outer layers of the wall is called a **cavity wall**. In older construction, both inner and outer layers were often brick. A header row of bricks laid with the small end out traversed the cavity and held the wythes together. In more modern construction, the inner layer could be stone or concrete block. In the **compound cavity wall**, where you find different inner and outer materials, the brick could be attached to the inner layer with metal ties or with header rows.

The home inspector will note the following problems that may be seen with solid masonry walls.

- **Cracking:** Cracks can appear in a masonry wall for a variety of reasons. Some cracks are the result of foundation settling and movement. Refer back to pages 25–28 for the discussion on cracking involving the foundation.

Other types of cracks appear because of a problem with the above-grade construction of the home. **Step cracks** above doors and windows indicate a problem with the steel lintel or brick arches. A rusting lintel, which expands as it rusts, can lift the masonry above it, causing step cracks to move upward from the top of the window or door. A sagging lintel may cause step cracks in an inverted V shape over the top of the opening or a **horizontal crack** at the top. There can be lower horizontal cracks and sagging above an opening in the foundation, such as a hatchway.

- **Deterioration of brick and mortar:** Both brick and mortar can deteriorate if the right materials were

Photo #36 STRUCTURAL BRICK WALL WITH HEADER ROWS

not used in the original construction. It's possible that mortar could have been mixed with too much sand, making it weak, or with too little sand, making it brittle. And bricks can have a surface that is too soft to keep out water.

- **Water** is the enemy of brick and mortar. Depending on how the mortar was finished off, rain may be allowed to enter into the wall and into the interior of the brick. Deteriorating mortar will wash away. The surface face of deteriorating brick will crumble and fall away if water is absorbed into the bricks and freezes. This is called **spalling**. Deterioration may be present at the bottom of the wall where rain has been allowed to splash against the masonry. Both brick and mortar can be damaged from condensation inside the wall.

- **Bowing or leaning:** The masonry wall should be plumb, but for a number of reasons, there can be distortions such as **bowing** (vertical outward curve), **sweeping** (horizontal outward curve), **bulging** (a combination of bow and sweep), and leaning. Common causes are deterioration of the mortar and expansion and contraction of the wall.

> **Section Note**
>
> *If masonry walls are common in your area and you can expect to be inspecting many of them, it's a good idea to invest in books on the subject. Look for titles that will educate you further in problems with masonry walls and appropriate repair work.*

Photo #37 BOWING

Old and new: the new construction on the left shows a plumb wall next to a structural brick wall over 100 years old.

Masonry walls can be affected by the **interior framing**. Expanding or warping joists can cause the wall to bulge outward and even crack. Spreading roof rafters can push out the tops of walls. And, of course, foundation problems and movement can cause the masonry wall to distort.

> **Chapter Note**
>
> *Pages 74–80 present information about the interior framing of a home. The inspection and reporting of interior walls, ceilings, and floors is covered in Chapter 7, Interior Inspection. Use these pages to learn about construction techniques.*

1.16 REPORTING

When reporting on wall structure in your inspection report, identify the walls as framing or masonry. If you can't determine the wall structure in the home, make a note that the interior wall structure was not visible. (The inspection and reporting of findings for exterior walls is presented in more detail in *Chapter 2.*)

1.17 INTERIOR FRAMING

The inspector should be familiar with the interior framing in a home. Even with solid masonry outer walls, the home has interior framing defining walls, ceilings, and floors.

Floors

Most homes have a **two-layer floor** consisting of a subfloor and a finish floor above it. In balloon framing, the subfloor goes to the inner edge of the wall stud. In platform framing, the subfloor goes under the sole plate to the exterior (edge).

The subfloor today is normally **plywood, OSB, or particle board sheets 5/8–3/4″ thick** that are laid perpendicular or diagonally to the joists. If the subfloor is laid on the perpendicular, the finish floor is then laid parallel to the joists. If the subfloor is on the diagonal, then the finish floor is laid perpendicular or parallel to the joists.

The meeting edges of the plywood or particle board sheets are nailed to the joists. A structural adhesive may be applied to the joists to reduce squeaks and add strength to the connection with the sheathing.

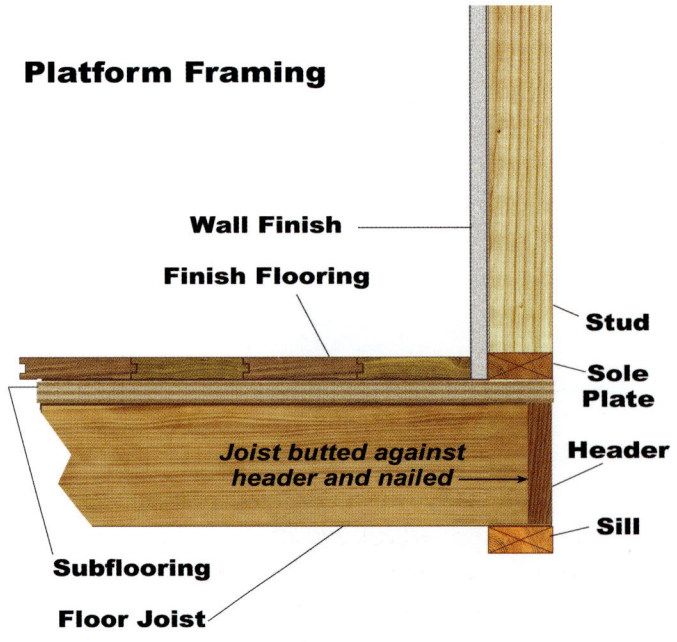

Illustration by Paddy Morrissey

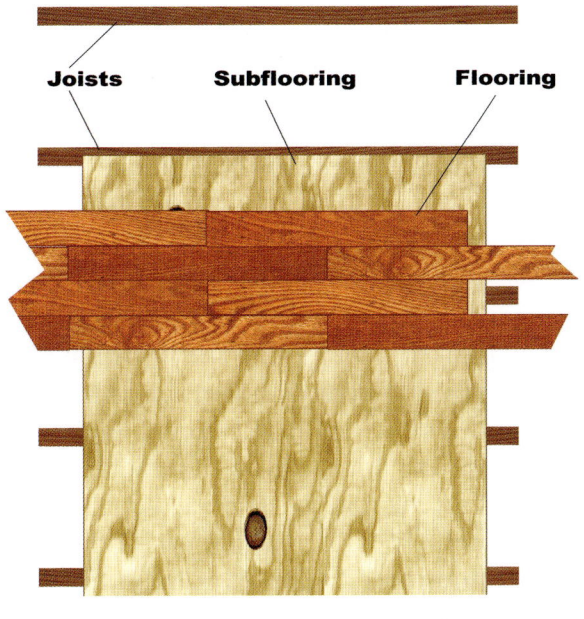

Subflooring Perpendicular, Finish Flooring Parallel

Illustration by Paddy Morrissey

Subflooring Diagonal, Finish Flooring Perpendicular or Parallel

Illustration by Paddy Morrissey

Some older subfloors are made with **tongue and groove planking**. The home inspector can determine whether this is true by examining the subfloor from the basement or crawl space. In some cases, you may find that there is no subfloor under a hardwood finish floor. This is common in older buildings where the builder didn't install a subfloor under a hardwood floor.

The top layer of flooring may be one of the following:

- **Hardwood:** Tongue and groove strips from 1 3/4–2 1/4" wide, usually made of oak, but birch, beech, chestnut, maple, pecan, walnut, or hard pine can be used. Strip flooring is usually nailed. If no subfloor is installed, the strips should be at least 1 1/2" thick.

- **Softwood:** 1 × 4 tongue and groove strips, usually pine, although fir and cedar may be used.

- **Underlayment:** 1/4" plywood or particle board sheets are often used over the subfloor when the floor is expected to be finished with carpeting or resilient coverings such as linoleum or sheet vinyl.

- **Ceramic, stone, marble, slate:** When tiles are used, they are laid in a bed of mortar or adhesive on the subfloor or on a plywood underlayment. If no underlayment is used, the subfloor should be 3/4" thick to reduce flexing, which could cause the tiles and/or grout to crack.

NOTE: Finish flooring may be applied directly to the concrete floor in slab on grade construction. Decorative concrete floors are also popular. Concrete may be stained or colored and stamped with designs.

THE STRUCTURAL INSPECTION

The problems we've discussed regarding beams and joists (pages 46–52) can have a detrimental effect on the floor. Deterioration of girders and joists, cracking, sagging, twisting, rot, improper notches or cuts in these members, and loss of connection and/or support can all contribute to defects in the floor. Here is an overview of signs the inspector may encounter in floors that indicate structural problems:

> **PROBLEM SIGNS**
> - Uneven floors
> - Unlevel floors
> - Sagging floors
> - Deflecting floors
> - Noisy floors

- **Uneven floors:** A floor can have highs and lows in it. A **hollow** can be caused by the failure of a single joist. When a hollow is present in the floor along a partition, it may be that the partition is built between the joists. When the hollow appears on either side of a doorway, it's an indication of poor support for the studs on either side of the opening. A **ridge** in an upstairs floor may be caused by a downstairs partition built parallel to a joist. There may be a **bulge** in the floor over a support column, indicating that the column is moving up or the house is moving down. Another cause of a bulge can be from an overloaded cantilevered joist, where the joist's interior end is being forced upward.

- **Unlevel floors:** Unlike uneven floors, an unlevel floor has a continuous slope in one direction. This can be caused by foundation settlement pulling the floor lower at the outer edges. The condition can also be caused by shrinkage of wood members, where interior walls shrink more than the outer wood framing. In this case, floors are likely to tilt inward toward partitions.

> *Section Note*
>
> *In slab on grade construction, the floor can indicate problems with the slab (see pages 60–62 of this chapter).*

- **Sagging floors:** This is where there is a low area in the middle of a room. This is largely due to overloading the floor without the proper supports being added to prevent the sag. Waterbeds, refrigerators, pianos, and other heavy objects can cause floor sag. More support is needed.

- **Deflecting floors:** These floors have upward and downward movement. **Bouncy floors** are usually due to weakness in the joists or a lack of proper bridging. **Soft** or **springy floors** can indicate a problem between the subfloor and joists—poor support of the subfloor by the joists because of poor nailing or loss of connection. Improper spanning can also result in similar defects.

> *Definitions*
>
> *A <u>floor truss</u> is an engineered, prefabricated rectangular floor framing component. The <u>chord</u> is a horizontal member of the truss. The <u>web</u> is one of the interior members of the truss. <u>Gusset</u> plates are metal connectors that hold members of the truss together.*

- **Noisy floors: Squeaks** in flooring are caused by a poor connection between the subfloor and the joists. Weight on the floor pushes the subfloor down to the joist, and the resulting squeak is caused by friction, nails sliding in and out of the joists. The home inspector may notice **drumming** and **rattling sounds** from the floor. These sounds are associated with the joists, not the subfloor. Low-frequency sounds can be caused by weak, flexible floor joists. Higher frequencies are the result of stiffness in the joists.

A Word about Trusses

The home inspector may find floor trusses in a home. The floor truss is essentially an engineered floor joist, usually made of 2 × 4s. The truss can span a space twice as long as a regular wood joist. The horizontal (outer) members of the truss are called **chords**; the inner members are called **webs**. Gusset plates, usually metal, although glued finger-jointed applications can be found, act as connectors between the chords and webs. Vertical members appear in the truss at the ends, where the truss rests on the foundation wall, for example, and in interior spots such as above or below partitions for extra strength. For additional support, blocks supplied by the truss manufacturer may be inserted in the truss at particular points.

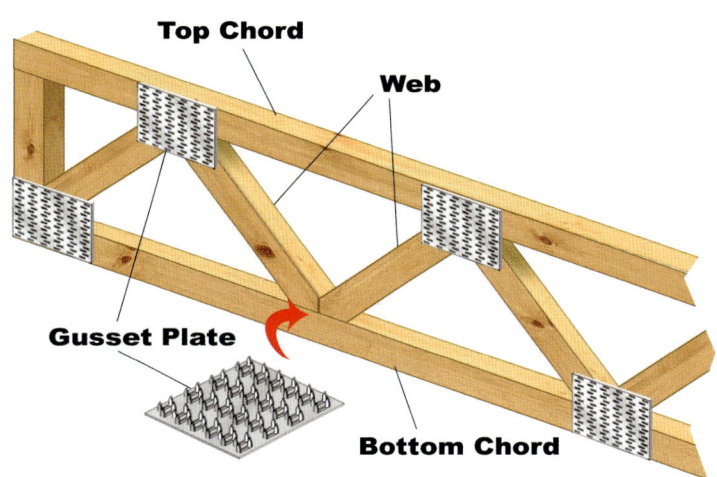

Illustration by Paddy Morrissey

Some trusses are designed so that the top chord rests on the foundation wall. Others are designed for the bottom chord to rest on the wall. In these cases, installing the trusses wrong side up can seriously weaken their ability to carry the load for which they were intended. A tag should be present on the truss, indicating it's *up* position.

The truss remains strong as long as it is properly installed, its connectors are securely attached to the members, no members of the truss are cut or removed, and the wood is not subjected to cracking or water and insect damage. As with

Photo #38 ENGINEERED FLOOR TRUSS

This is an engineered floor truss. This truss does not have true gusset plates. The webs have fingers which are glued into slots in the chords.

> **Definition**
>
> A <u>cantilever</u> is an extension of the floor structure that depends on the strength of the unsupported portion of the girder or joists to carry the load of the structure. A cantilever can be an interior balcony or an exterior balcony or deck.

wooden joists, problems with trusses can manifest themselves in the floor above. Floors can become uneven, sag, or deflect for the same reasons.

Cantilevers

Joists or girders can be extended out to provide support for a deck or balcony inside or outside the house without a support at the farthest end. This is called a **cantilever**.

A cantilevered structure can be springy if the joists or girders are not able to carry the load properly. This may be the case in older homes where no restrictions were placed on how much of the joist could extend beyond the bearing wall. Today, it's recommended that only one-sixth of the length of the joist be unsupported.

With an **interior balcony**, as shown here, the downward load at the unsupported end of the joist is reflected by an upward load on the joist that is an equal distance from the support point. If the joist is overloaded at its cantilevered end and is pushed downward, there can be a bulge in the floor at the other end of the joist. Or the joist can crush or crack where it is supported by the partition below. Sometimes, the un-cantilevered portion of the room can be overloaded, causing the cantilevered area to rise.

With the cantilever that extends through the wall of the house to form an **outside deck or balcony**, these same problems can occur. When the cantilever is outside and exposed to the elements, the interface between the floor of the structure and the wall should be examined carefully for wood rot. This is an area that is particularly susceptible to leakage. In many cases, this penetration is caulked and not properly flashed as a roof penetration would be.

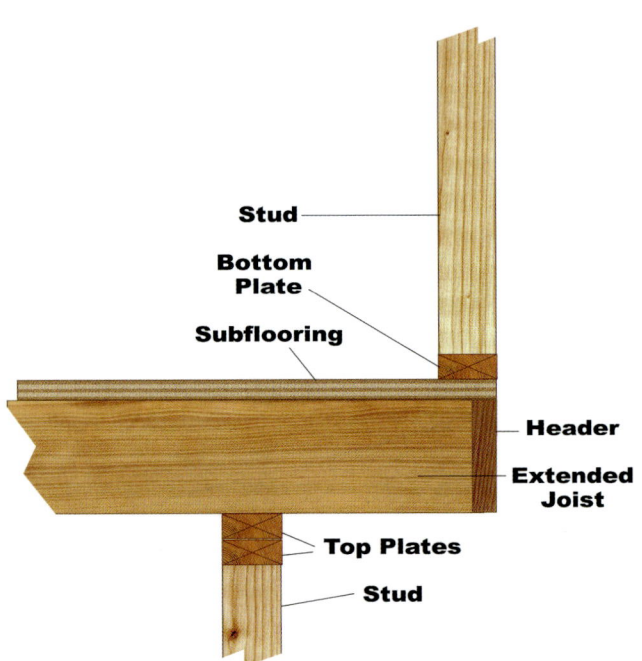

Illustration by Paddy Morrissey

1.18 OTHER FRAMING CONCERNS

The home inspector needs to be aware of other structural framing concerns:

- **Load-bearing walls:** Some of the interior walls of a structure are load-bearing whereas others are not. Ideally, a first-floor load-bearing wall should be constructed above the supporting beam in the basement and the second-floor load-bearing wall directly above so that the load from the roof is transferred vertically downward. But more often, the load-bearing walls are offset on either side of this vertical line. Generally a 3′ offset is allowed if the load-bearing wall does not support a floor above it; otherwise, only a 2′ offset is allowed. An offset wall can cause the joists supporting it to be deflected, with a resulting low spot in the floor at the wall and a hump over the beam or bearing wall below.

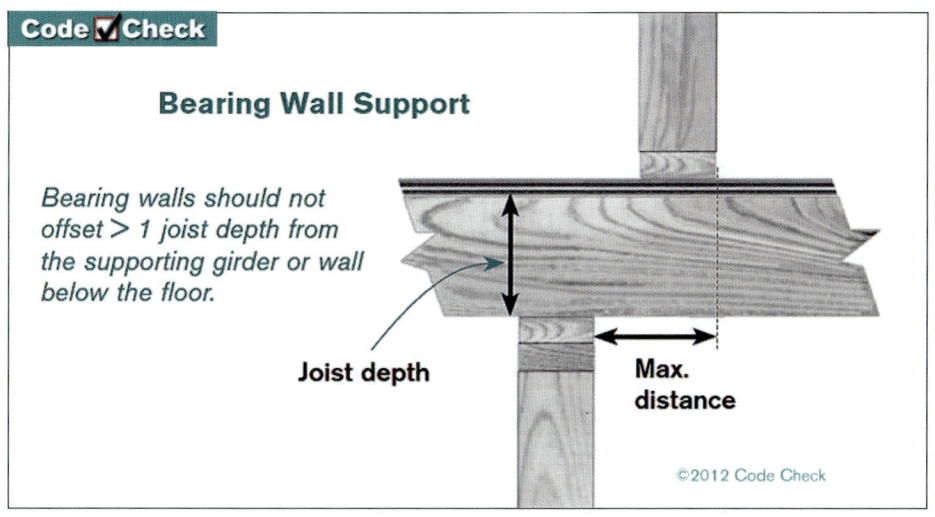

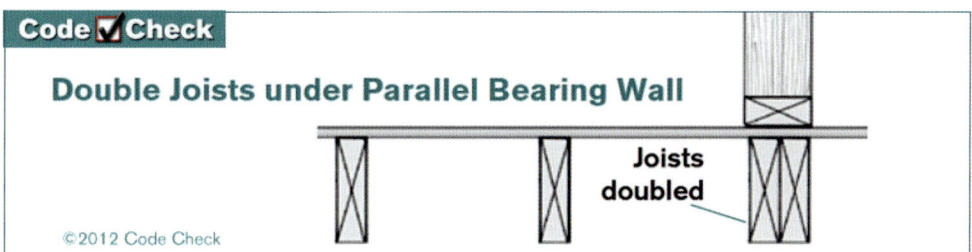

- **Double joists:** Joists that are subjected to concentrated loads may not be strong enough. Therefore, joists are doubled under non-load-bearing partitions to support this concentrated load. Joists should also be doubled where expected to support heavy live loads such as pianos, bookcases, and waterbeds.

NOTE: Load-bearing partitions should not rest on joists, but should be supported by beams.

- **Framing around stairs:** When an opening in the floor is needed, as around the opening for a stairway, joists are interrupted. These joists are secured to a header running perpendicular to the joists. The header carries the load from the joists over to the trimmer joists. When an opening is wide enough, the headers and trimmer joists are doubled for stability. Generally, if the opening is wider than 32", the trimmers are doubled. When the opening is 48" or more, the headers should also be doubled.

> **PAY ATTENTION TO**
> - Problems in floors indicating structural failure
> - Failing cantilevers
> - Inadequate joists under concentrated loads
> - Support around stairway openings

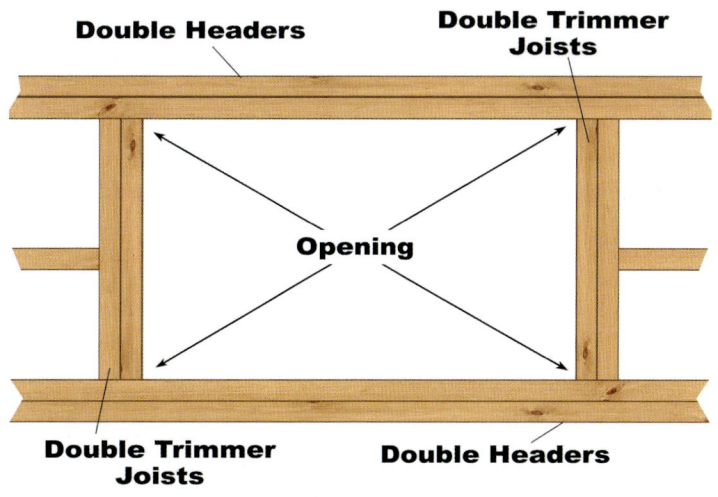

Illustration by Paddy Morrissey

THE STRUCTURAL INSPECTION

Headers and trimmers must be securely fastened to each other. Evidence of failing connections can be seen in the walls and ceiling around the stairway, where the members are pulling apart.

1.19 INSPECTING ROOF STRUCTURE

This section covers the inspection of the roof structure. The home inspector inspects the roof structure from the underside, using any information that was gathered from viewing the external roof. The inspection includes the following:

- Rafters, collar ties, purlins, and knee walls
- Trusses
- Roof sheathing
- Ceiling structure
- Attic leakage and condensation
- Insulation
- Ventilation

Chapter Note

Pages 80–90 present the procedures on inspecting the roof structure. The inspection of the roof's coverings and other external aspects of the roof is covered in Chapter 3.

Most standards of practice require the inspector to indicate the methods used to observe the attic (for example, whether the inspector entered the attic or stood on the ladder and looked around without entering). The inspector should enter the attic space except when access is blocked, property damage may occur, or dangerous or adverse conditions may be present.

As with the crawl space, it's sometimes difficult to get into the attic to view the structural members. And sometimes it's not possible to walk through the attic and inspect the roof structure completely. So it's important for the home inspector to report the **methods used** to access the attic, letting customers know that there may be defects in the attic that he or she was unable to find due to limited access. Sometimes, the attic may be finished and structural members may not be visible or the members may be covered by insulation.

Section Note

A beginning home inspector will walk on a ceiling only once in his or her career. After putting your foot through the ceiling, you'll never try it again. Some attics have only the ceiling joists—no actual floor or walking surface. You definitely don't want to step between the joists to get a look at the rafters. That's how you break through the ceiling below. Other attics may have a plank walkway laid over the joists. You'll want to be careful about stepping on loose planks too. "Be careful up there."

Framing Members

From the attic, the home inspector reports on the condition of the roof structures, including rafters, collar ties, purlins, knee walls, and ceiling joists.

Rafters

Rafters are structural members of the pitched roof that are designed to support the roof sheathing and transmit the roof load to bearing walls and beams below. Rafters are made of wood, 2 × 6s, 2 × 8s, or 2 × 10s occurring every 16–24″ along the length of the roof. In a flat roof, rafters are called roof joists (**roof** rafters and ceiling **joists**, as they are one and the same with a flat roof).

Rafters are placed on edge, their narrow dimension up for nailing. The deeper dimension is on the vertical to provide strength. They are connected to the outer walls of the house in various ways.

In **balloon framing**, rafters are notched and connected to a top plate that sits on top of the wall studs.

In **platform framing**, rafters are attached to the single or double top plate or a special rafter plate. Rafters are nailed to the plate and in newer homes are securely attached with metal ties, known as hurricane ties because they were first used in hurricane-prone parts of the country. Rafters can be notched or end cut to sit flush on the plate. In roof framing, there is a rafter for every ceiling joist. The rafter can be nailed to the ceiling joist or not depending on the design of the roof.

> **INSPECTING RAFTERS**
> - Report any cracked or cut rafters.
> - Watch for sagging, waviness, and rafter spread.
> - Be sure rafters are securely fastened to all other framing members.
> - Check for deterioration.
> - When rafters support roof equipment, check for reinforcement.

Rafters that are overloaded from several layers of roof covering or ice and snow will **sag** or even crack. They can be supported with collar ties, purlins, or knee walls (see page 82), which absorb some of the roof load. Rafters have a natural curve or warp, known as a **crown**. During construction, carpenters make sure that rafters will be installed with the crown facing upward. If rafters are installed with crowns facing both up and down, the result can be a **wavy** roof surface. The roof can also appear wavy if rafters are cut to unequal lengths. The home inspector can usually see sag and waviness from the exterior roof surface.

Rafters should be checked for **cracks**, cuts, warping, and sagging. All **rafter fastenings** should be secure and, if visible, carefully examined at ridge, top plate, and joist connections and with supporting structures.

Rafters experience a phenomenon called **rafter spread**, where the roof load bearing on the rafters forces them outward. This condition can be so bad that the soffit and the upper walls of the structure are pushed outward along with the rafters. Secure connections to all framing members and collar ties, purlins, and/or knee walls help prevent this problem.

Rafters should be inspected carefully for **water** and **condensation damage** and should be probed where wood deterioration is suspected. Rafters should not be cut through, although you will find homeowner modifications for numerous reasons. These cuts or modifications must be noted in your report.

When equipment such as roof-top HVAC units, solar photovoltaic (PV) panels, or solar hot water collectors are mounted on the roof, the rafters below might have to be reinforced. This may be done with doubled or tripled rafters, a knee wall, or a vertical

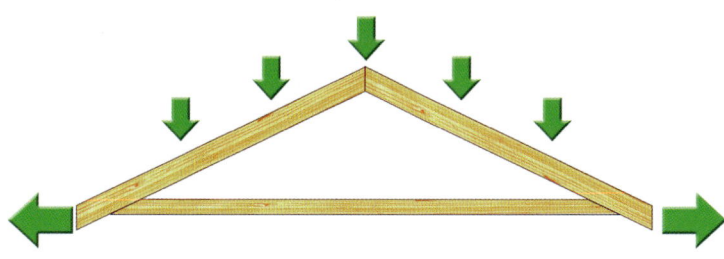

Illustration by Paddy Morrissey

column. Where the supports rest on joists, the joists also should have the proper added support.

- **Ridge:** Rafters can be attached to each other where they meet at the peak of the roof or attached to a ridge board. In the conventional roof, the ridge is not a structural part of the framework. However, the ridge should not be twisted or cracked, and rafters should remain securely fastened to the ridge. Although the ridge is most likely not a *structural* member of the roof framework, its condition can tell you what's going on elsewhere.

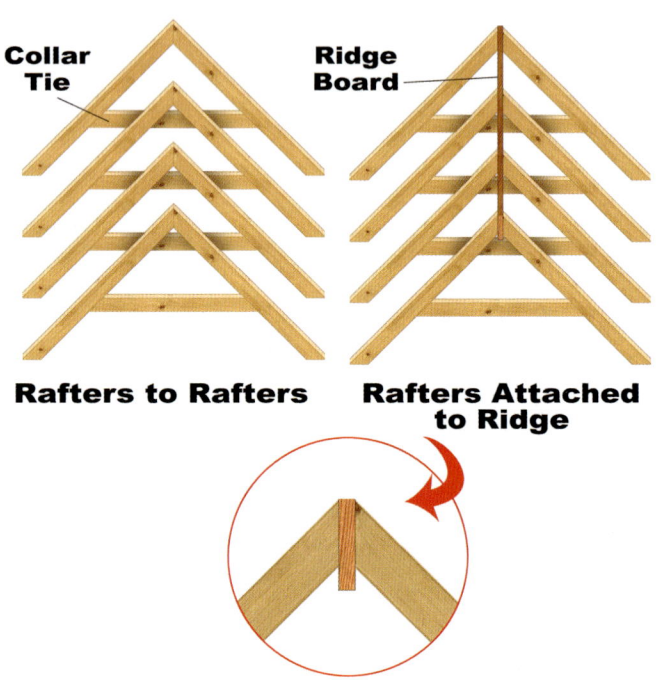

Illustration by Paddy Morrissey

- **Collar ties:** These are horizontal structural members of the roof framing system that prevent the rafters from sagging and spreading. They are most often present in a steep sloped roof. They may form the framework for a finished ceiling in a converted attic room.

Collar ties are 2 × 4s, 2 × 6s, or 1 × 8s and 1 × 10s attached securely to each pair of rafters about one-third to one-half of the way down from the peak of the roof. The lower the ties, the more support they provide. There should be a collar tie for each pair of rafters, but you might see attics where there's a collar tie for every two or three pairs. Sometimes, if the roof load has increased since the house was constructed by several layers of roofing being added (remember, two layers max), one collar tie for every two or three rafter pairs is no longer enough, and the extra layers of roofing should be removed.

Collar ties are under **compression** from the weight of the roof pushing down on the rafters and are under **tension** from the natural tendency of the rafters to spread outward. These forces can cause the collar ties to buckle, especially if the ties are 1 × 8's instead of 2 × 4's. **Lateral bracing** is usually used if collar ties are 8' or longer. This is framing that is installed perpendicular to the rafters to prevent sideways or lateral movement. It is much more common on trusses than rafters.

When inspecting collar ties, the home inspector should look for missing pieces, buckling or deterioration of the wood, and for secure nailing to the rafters.

- **Knee walls:** Knee walls are used with a low-sloped roof to prevent the rafters from sagging. They are small walls typically made of 2 × 4s that run from the attic floor (ceiling joists) to the rafters near their midpoint. Knee walls may form the framework for side walls in a finished attic room. Knee walls must be properly secured to the rafters and ceiling joists to prevent movement. Ceiling joists must be strong enough to support the wall. Deflection of the joists beneath knee walls can be seen in damage to the ceiling finish in the rooms below.

In some cases, where the roof has a very long, low slope, there may be both a knee wall at the lower ends of the rafters and collar ties on the higher ends.

- **Purlins:** Purlins are horizontal (perpendicular to the rafters) structural members of the roof. Purlins support the loads from the roof deck or sheathing and are supported by the principal rafters. As with other roof framing members, purlins should be securely nailed to the rafters and should not be warped, bent, or sagging. The purlins are supported by struts, which extend from the purlin to a bearing wall below.

- **Ceiling joists:** The joists in the attic support the attic floor and the ceiling of the rooms below. In some cases, the home inspector may find 2 × 4 or 2 × 6 joists that were intended only to support the ceiling finish, not to provide an attic floor to be used as storage or worse yet a living area. Joists must be securely fastened. If overlapped or butted, they should be reinforced with a gusset plate to keep them from pulling apart at these junctions from the stress of rafter spread.

Definitions

Rafters are the main structural members of the roof that support the roof covering and transmit roof loads to bearing walls or beams below.

The *ridge* is a horizontal framing board at the peak of the roof to which the rafters are attached.

Collar ties are horizontal structural members of the roof that connect opposite pairs of rafters together to prevent rafter sag and rafter spread.

Knee walls are supporting walls running from ceiling joists to rafters, preventing rafter sag.

Photo #39 *This photo shows both collar ties and purlins. The collar ties are the horizontal boards running from rafter to rafter near the ridge. The purlins are the boards running perpendicular to and on the underside of the rafters. They are supported by the angled boards, called purlin struts, running to a bearing wall below. The purlins must be at least the same size as the rafters they support.*

Section Note

It's time to bother your friends again. This time ask to see the attic and take a look at rafter or truss construction. The more variations you see, the more you'll learn about roof structure and defects that may be present. However, you should refrain from scaring your friends about situations you're not sure about. During this learning process, it's best to let them know that you're not an expert yet. Of course, if you spot a situation that appears to be serious, you might suggest that someone else take a look at it.

Photo #40 KNEE WALLS

This is a typical attic space converted to a living area. You can see the short knee walls on either side of the room. The long sloping sections are the underside of the roof rafters.

Roof Trusses

A roof truss is an engineered geometric construction whose members perform the same function as rafters, collar ties, knee walls, purlins, and ceiling joists. Roof trusses used in residential homes are typically made of 2 × 4s or 2 × 6s, but 2 × 3 trusses may be found and all are attached with wood or metal gusset plates nailed or glued together. The bottom chord of the truss is used as the framework that supports the ceiling finish below. Trusses are normally placed every 24″ along the length of the roof.

Two commonly used trusses in residential construction are the **Fink truss** and the **Howe truss**; they incorporate different geometries in their web configurations.

There are many other truss designs with variations on the inner members, or webs, of the truss. Some are designed for heavy top chord loading or heavy bottom chord support. Some of the chords may be 2 × 5s or 2 × 6s. The **scissors truss**, as shown here, is used in vaulted or cathedral ceiling structures.

Trusses may require that **permanent lateral bracing** be added at the midpoint of some of the webs to keep them from buckling. Directions for

INSPECTING TRUSSES

- Watch for any cracked, cut, or missing truss members.
- Be sure bracing is present if it's required.
- Inspect gussets for corrosion or looseness.
- Check for deterioration.
- Look for truss uplift.
- Look for bowing and warping.

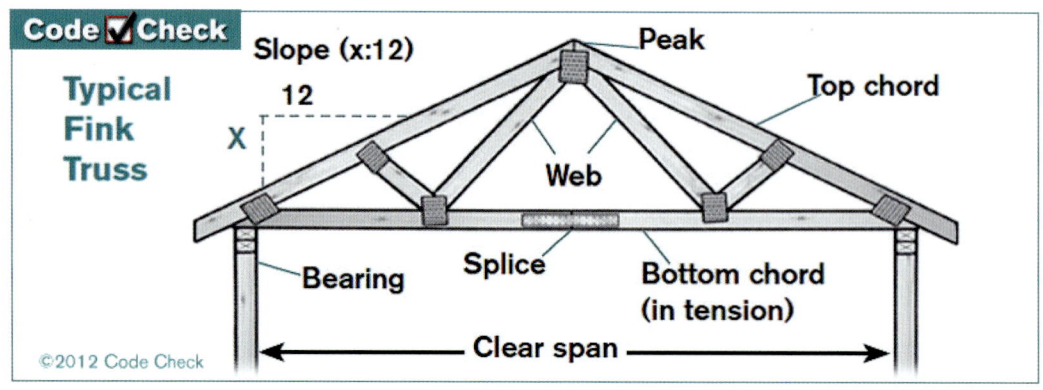

84 Chapter 1

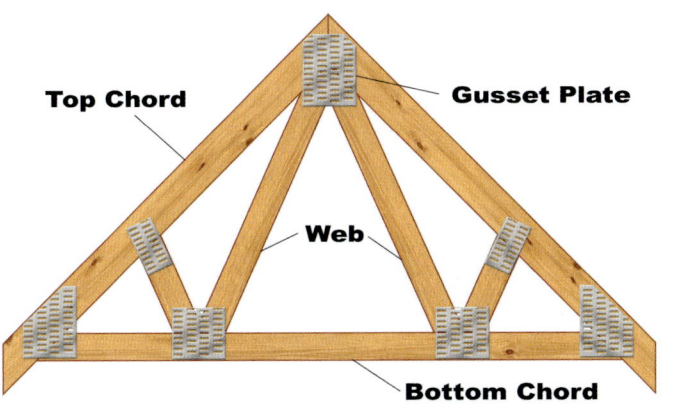

Fink Truss
Illustration by Paddy Morrissey

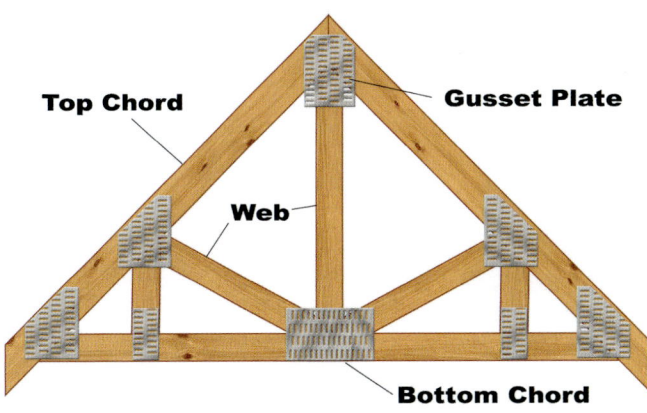

Howe Truss
Illustration by Paddy Morrissey

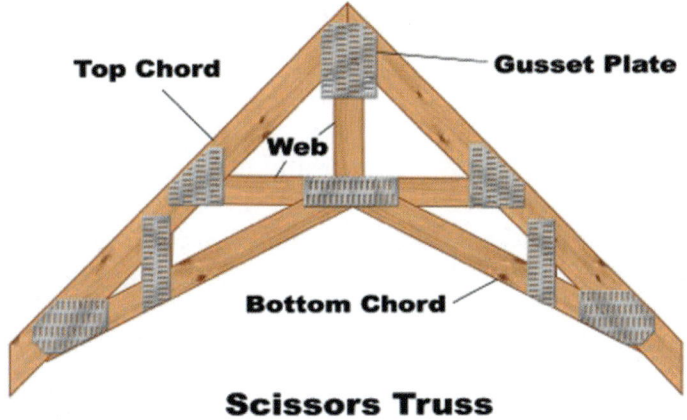

Scissors Truss
Illustration by Paddy Morrissey

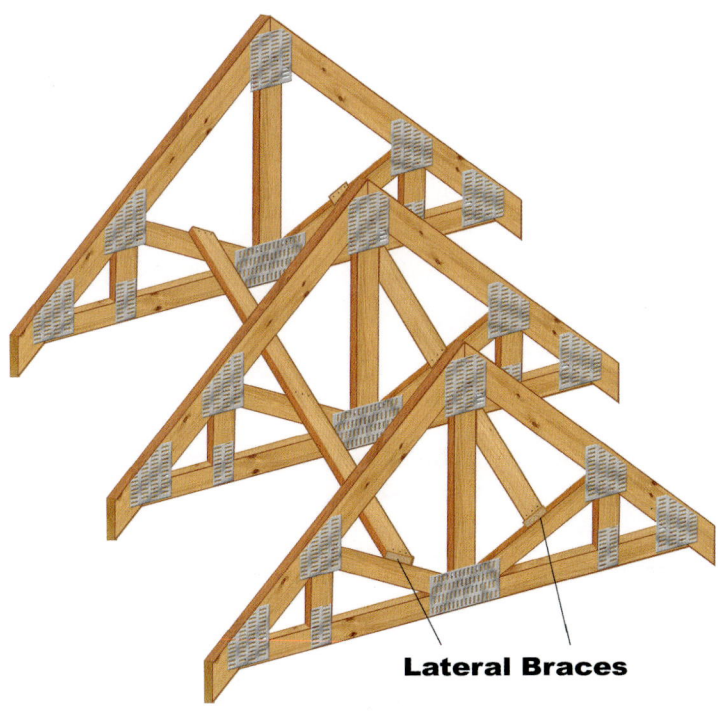

Illustration by Paddy Morrissey

THE STRUCTURAL INSPECTION

> **Definitions**
>
> A <u>roof truss</u> is an engineered, prefabricated geometric roof framing component. A <u>chord</u> is an outer member of the truss, either horizontal or diagonal. A <u>web</u> is one of the interior members of the truss, either vertical or diagonal. <u>Gusset plates</u> are metal or wood connectors that hold members of the truss together.
>
> <u>Truss uplift</u> is a phenomenon where the bottom chord of a roof truss bows upward during the cold months and returns to its normal position during the warmer months.

installing the trusses may suggest that 2 × 4s be used for bracing. (Brightly colored tags are typically stapled to the webs or under the gusset plates where permanent lateral bracing is required.) If the tags are present, the lateral bracing must be installed per design. Be sure to note in your report the absence of lateral bracing where required. When inspecting trusses, the home inspector should check a representative number of gusset plates to make sure they are securely fastened. Look for loose nails (on wood gussets), hammer marks on metal gussets (this is to re-secure a gusset plate that came off or is loose), splitting of members at these connections, corrosion of the gusset plates, or broken plates. If the connections fail, the truss fails. These members are engineered, and they must be in their original configuration to work. Any modifications must be approved by an engineer.

It is not always easy to get through an attic filled with insulation-covered chords and all the truss webbing, but the home inspector should make every effort to get down the length of the attic for a look. Watch for any water damage or deterioration of truss members and for any cut or removed members of trusses. Trusses with missing members are not working trusses.

When the bottom chords of trusses are covered with insulation, especially in cold climates, a phenomenon called **truss uplift** can occur. In truss uplift, the bottom chords of the trusses deflect upward as much as an inch or two during the winter weather. When the uplift is extreme, the truss can pick up the ceiling finish below, even separating the ceiling from the walls of the room. In some cases, all of the walls of the rooms below can be lifted, leaving a separation between the walls and the floor. If truss uplift is suspected, the home inspector should check the rooms below for these signs.

The experts believe that truss uplift is caused by changes in temperature and humidity in the attic during the cold months. The bottom chord, buried in insulation and retaining more heat, reacts differently from the upper truss members. The bottom chord bows upward as a result. During the warmer months, the bottom chord moves downward again.

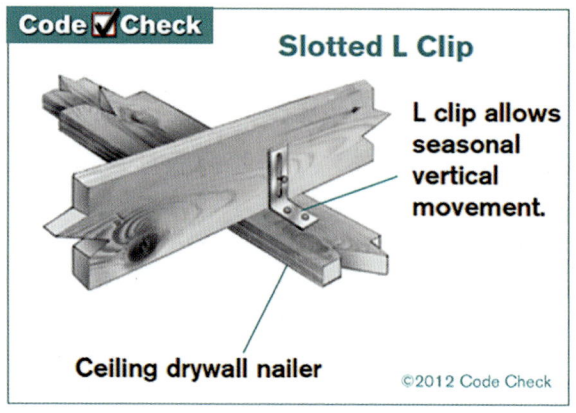

©2012 Code Check

Truss uplift is not considered to be a structural problem, although it can cause cracks in the junction between the ceiling and wall below. One solution is to attach crown molding in this room, where the molding is secured to the ceiling but not to the wall. Then when the ceiling moves up and down, the separation is not visible. Another solution is to disconnect the ceiling drywall from the truss and provide alternative ceiling support.

Roof Sheathing

Roof sheathing, or roof decking, supports the roof covering and transmits its weight, as well as live loads such as snow and ice, to the rafters or trusses. It also serves to stabilize the roof structure by holding the rafters in position.

Roof sheathing used before the 1960s was usually 1× **planking**. Spaced planking (a 3" gap between planks) is best for wood shingles and shakes and in some cases rigid roofing such as slate or tile, the spaces allowing for moisture exchange and drying of the wood roofing material from both sides. Planking can also be butted or tongue and groove. Enough nails should be used to keep planks from warping and buckling. You'll notice warped or buckled planking from the outside because of the visible waviness in the roof's surface.

Plywood panels for sheathing were introduced in the 1950s to 1960s. **Wafer board**, also known as flake board panels or, more correctly, **oriented strand board (OSB)**, have been around since the 1960s. Panels, generally 4' × 8' in size, are installed perpendicular to the rafters. The 4' edges should be nailed to the rafters, leaving 1/16" to 1/8" for swelling of the panel. The 8' edges are nailed to rafters and are typically secured to each other with metal H-clips between rafters. Plywood and OSB used today may be as thin as 15/32" or 7/16" or may be 1/2" to 3/4" thick over rafters spaced at 24".

> **INSPECTING ROOF SHEATHING**
> - Look for delamination in plywood or OSB panels.
> - Watch for sags, warping, and buckling in the sheathing.
> - Check that nails and clips are in place.

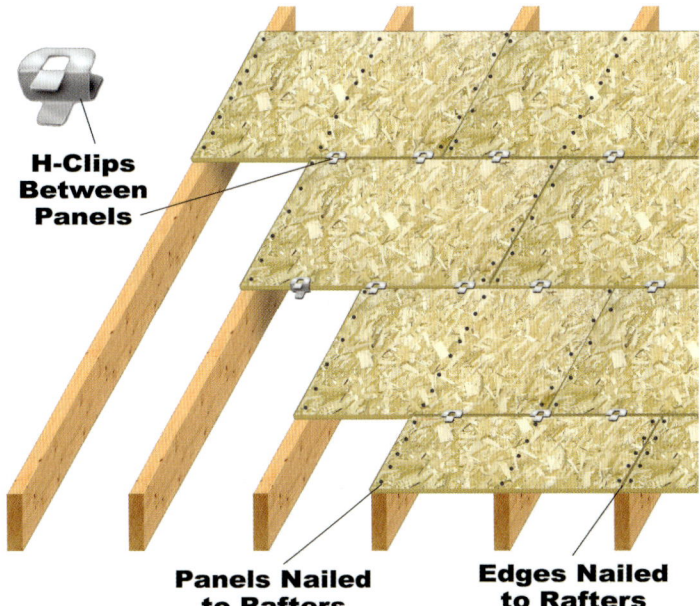

Illustration by Paddy Morrissey

If the sheathing is too thin, it can sag under the roof load. Waviness in panel sheathing can be a sign that H-clips haven't been used (not required in all areas).

Panel sheathing should be inspected carefully for deterioration. Too much moisture and condensation in the attic can cause sheathing to delaminate. **Delamination** is a deterioration process in which the laminated, bonded (glued) layers in the sheathing begin to separate. Most often, delaminated sheathing can be spotted by its color—it turns darker or **black**, although this is not always the case. Delaminated plywood no longer holds nails and can be dangerous to walk on and sounds like walking on potato chips. OSB doesn't

> **Definition**
>
> *Delamination is a deterioration process during which the layers in the laminated plywood panel begin to separate.*

delaminate because it is small pieces of wood glued and pressed together; it just turns to mulch!

Water Penetration

The home inspector should examine the attic for evidence of water leaking into the house. Examine the sheathing and rafters for any signs of deterioration from water penetrating through the roof surface. Inspect the chimney to see if there is any deterioration in the mortar and bricks from leaking flashings. Check carefully around other roof penetrations such as vents and piping to make sure they are watertight.

Attic Moisture

Many homeowners misunderstand the principles behind attic insulation and ventilation and the effects they can have on the roof structure of a home. As a consequence of that misunderstanding, the home inspector may find insulation and ventilation in such a state that they actually promote attic moisture, resulting in damage to the structural components. When there is unlimited moisture in the attic air and no proper venting of the attic space, the wood deck of the roof structure absorbs this moisture and becomes saturated. Wood rot, mildew, and plywood delamination is the result. When moisture condenses inside the insulation, insulation falls apart and wood members next to the insulation fall victim to rot and decay and provide conditions conducive to termite activity. Here is an overview of the principles on insulation and ventilation:

> **Section Note**
>
> *The inspection of attic insulation and ventilation will be presented in Chapter 7. Our discussion on these pages is an overview that is intended to explain the effects of insulation and ventilation on the roof structure.*

- **Principle #1: The goal in the unfinished and vented attic is to have the temperature roughly the same as the outdoors.** Therefore, insulation should be laid on the attic floor, not between the rafters. When insulation is placed between the rafters, the attic is part of the heated area of the house. This is an acceptable practice if insulation is done correctly, as is the case in new energy-efficient homes with the underside of the roof deck sprayed with foam insulation. Usually, the homeowner does not want warm air from the house to enter the attic space at all. Insulation laid between the ceiling joists is the norm and acts as a heat retarder.

- **Principle #2: Warm air from the house brings moisture into the attic.** All attempts should be made to keep moisture and humidity from entering the attic space. In the past, a **vapor retarder** (a sheet of plastic such as polyethylene) was laid beneath the attic floor insulation to enhance its ability to keep warm air from entering the attic space. Today, this is done only in extremely cold climates. If insulation has a **moisture retarder side** (most likely Kraft paper), it should be placed with this side down, toward the warm (in winter) house below. Because warm air trapped in the insulation condenses as it cools, these barriers also protect the ceiling structure from the moisture that collects in the insulation.

Another way moisture can enter the attic is if household fans exhaust into the attic. The attic could be properly insulated and have a vapor retarder and then have plumbing vents and exhaust fan ducts pouring warm air into the attic where it doesn't belong. This would undo whatever good the insulation and barrier are doing. Plumbing vents and fan ducts *must* be vented directly to the outside and not to the soffit.

- **Principle #3: The attic space must be vented to eliminate any moisture in the air.** It's not possible to completely prevent warm moist air from entering the attic from the house below due to the biggest culprit—recessed lights.

> **ATTIC CONDITIONS**
> - The temperature in the unfinished attic should be the same as outdoors.
> - Warm air should be prevented from entering the attic space from the house.
> - Moist air in the attic should be vented to the outside.
> - Plumbing vents and exhaust fans should vent to the outside, not into the attic.

The cold side of the insulation needs to be ventilated to remove the moist air that does get through. The goal is to move this air to the outside.

Homes are designed with various kinds of **attic venting systems**— gable vents, soffit vents, ridge vents, and/or vent fans in the roof surface or gables. Sometimes, homeowners will tape plastic over the vents in winter to "retain the heat." That's a serious mistake. Vents should be in operating condition at all times, especially in the winter in cold climates. Vent screens should not be blocked with debris, animal nests, or paint. And vents should not be covered with insulation. The purpose is to remove moist air from the attic, and this can't happen if the vents are obstructed.

The home inspector may find no signs of leaking in the roof and yet find rotting sheathing, rusting nails and gusset plates on trusses, and delaminating plywood sheathing. This is the result of inadequate insulation and/or the lack of ventilation, which allow the attic air to become warm and moisture laden. This also promotes ice damming in the winter. The home inspector finding these conditions should carefully investigate the cause of the problem.

The **finished attic** is a different story, however. When collar ties and knee walls define a heated attic room, the *attic space* becomes the area between the rafters and the finished room. There, the same principles apply. This space between the rafters and the room should be kept at the outside temperature. A vapor retarder should be laid up the outer side of the knee wall and across the ceiling. Insulation should be installed along this same path with its moisture retarder side facing the room. A mistake often made is installing insulation between the rafters in this type of attic space. It should be on the ceiling and against the warm inner room. This type of attic space must also be ventilated to provide an escape for moist air collecting in the space.

Reporting Your Findings

You'll probably have a page reserved for attic findings in your inspection report. That's where you report on the roof's structure. Ideally, there should be sections on the page for reporting the following:

> **DON'T EVER MISS**
>
> - Cracked, bowing, or twisting rafters
> - Rafter spread and sidewall separation
> - Sags in the roof
> - Delaminated plywood
> - Loose truss fastenings; bowing trusses; cracked, cut, or missing members
> - Deterioration of structural members
> - Water penetration

- **Access:** Don't forget to report on how the attic was observed, whether from the scuttle hole or from its interior. Note whether access was partial, complete, or not possible. Remind customers that you can't find defects in areas you were not able to access. You should report where attic access is located—in the upper hallway, above the bedroom closet, and so on.

- **Rafters and trusses:** Identify the type of roof structure. For rafters, note their size as 2×6, 2×8, or more. Then note their condition, not forgetting to note items from the Don't Ever Miss list at the right.

- **Sheathing:** Identify the type of sheathing as plywood, solid planking, and so on. Be sure to record delamination in the sheathing, noting a ventilation condition as the cause if that's the case. Note other defects such as sagging and deterioration.

- **Ceiling structure (attic floor):** Note if trusses or wood joists are present and whether they are visible due to insulation. If the floor is finished, note that the underlying structure was not visible.

- **Water penetration:** Record any evidence of leaking into the attic and water stains on structural members or around the chimney and other places. Identify the location of such evidence. Don't ever miss reporting this!

- **Major repairs:** You may find roof structural problems that are serious enough to classify as major repairs in your inspection report. Certainly, **cracked rafters** and **delaminated plywood** fall into that category. If you've noted these problems on the attic page of your report, list them again as major repairs on a summary page.

CHAPTER 2: THE EXTERIOR INSPECTION

2.1 INSPECTION GUIDELINES AND OVERVIEW

These are the standards of practice that govern the inspection of the exterior components of the property.

Observe and/or Report: The act of making a visual examination of a system or component and reporting on its condition.	• Grading, drainage, and vegetation that may adversely affect the structure or its components • Framing or frieze board separations • Rotating, buckling, cracking, or deflecting masonry cladding • Inspect flatwork (walks, drives, patios, etc.) or detention/retention ponds (especially related to slope and drainage) • Flashing, trim, wall cladding/siding, doors, and windows • Attached and adjacent balconies, carports, and porches • Stairs, steps, stoops, stairways, and ramps • Abutting porches, decks, and balconies • Eaves, soffits, and fascia • Visible structural components • Vehicle doors for type, general condition, and intended function by manual operation and by the use of permanently affixed opener(s)
Describe: Report in writing a system or component by its type, or other observed characteristics, to distinguish it from other components used for the same purpose.	• Wall cladding/siding and trim materials • Driveways, walkways, grade steps, patios, and other items contiguous with the inspected structure • Visible exterior portions of chimney(s) • Windows and doors • Decks, balconies, steps, stairs, and railings

> **Chapter Note**
>
> *Pages 91–94 lay out the content and scope of the exterior inspection, which includes the exterior components of the property, excluding the roof. It's an overview of the inspection, including what to observe, what to describe, and what specific actions to take during the inspection.*

Not every detail of what is to be inspected and reported is listed in these standards. However, they do present a good overview of the exterior inspection.

Note that the standards of practice for inspecting the exterior of a house explicitly list a number of items that the home inspector is not required to observe and report on. For clarity, the standards define the inspection by listing both what to do and what not to do. We are going to suggest a few deviations from the standards in that we like to inspect and report on the condition of fences, storm windows, and screens. We suggest the home inspector identify the materials used and report on their general condition.

Here is an overview of the exterior inspection:

> **Definitions**
>
> *Wall cladding, or siding, is a covering for the exterior of the house that protects the framework of the structure.*
>
> *The eave, or overhang, is the lower portion of the roof that extends beyond the outer wall. It is made up of the fascia, which is the outer board laid vertical at the edge of the eave, and the soffit, which is the underside of the eave. Frieze board is the portion of the top of the exterior wall that fills in the spaces between the ends of the ceiling joists or bottom truss chords.*

- **Siding:** The home inspector examines the wall cladding, or siding, covering the exterior of the house. The inspector is required to describe the materials used as siding. Examples of siding materials are wood clapboard, fiberboard, composite materials, wood shingles and shakes, asbestos shingles (cement and asphalt), brick, stone, aluminum, steel, stucco, EIFS (explained in detail later), and vinyl.

   The home inspector is also required to report on the condition of the siding and report any defects found. Sidings can warp, rust, crack, twist, leak, and come loose from the walls and outright fail. The inspector looks for deterioration of materials such as rotting wood and spalling brick, peeling paint, cracking stucco, and so on. Missing trim and caulking in need of replacement are also reported.

- **Trim:** The home inspector examines the trim on the house, including the window and door casing, brick mold/mould, eaves, frieze boards, soffits, and fascia. The materials used for trim are reported as well as their condition. The home inspector pays close attention to wood damage from rot or insects. The tip of a screwdriver, ice pick, or knife should be used to probe the trim when deterioration is visible or suspected. The inspector also looks at materials such as composite and PVC, which may shrink in cold weather and leave gaps or expand in hot weather and bow if installed too tightly.

- **Doors and windows:** The inspector is required to inspect and operate all entryway (exterior) doors and inspect all windows. On the interior portion of the inspection, a representative number of windows means enough to have a fairly accurate idea of their condition for each type present (refer to **state standards** for all vs. representative). The inspector identifies the materials used in window construction and reports on the condition of these materials. Particular attention is paid to whether wood damage or rot is present, caulking needs replacing, and a new paint job is needed. All doors should be opened and inspected for ease of operation and condition, along with the presence and condition of weather stripping, threshold, and door sweep. The home inspector is not typically required to inspect (although some SOPs require it) or report on safety glazing, although it is a good practice to do so.

NOTE: We also advise the home inspector to inspect the storm windows and screens. Notice that most standards of practice state that the home inspector is not required to observe storm windows, storm doors, screening, shutters, awnings, and similar seasonal accessories. We find an exception in storm windows and screens because it's an easy and quick process to observe and report torn, bent, or missing screens and cracked or missing storm windows and uninstalled storm doors, especially with regard to storms/screens when one is installed and the other is in the basement or garage for the off season.

- **Attached structures:** The home inspector carefully inspects all attached and adjacent structures such as balconies, decks, porches, stoops, and stairs. The structural integrity of these attachments is one issue the inspector pays attention to, examining ledger boards, support posts and beams, flooring, and railings. Because these structures are exposed to the elements, care is taken to probe them for wood damage or rot and deterioration. Safety aspects of steps and stoops are examined, such as treads, risers, handrails, guardrails, and balusters.

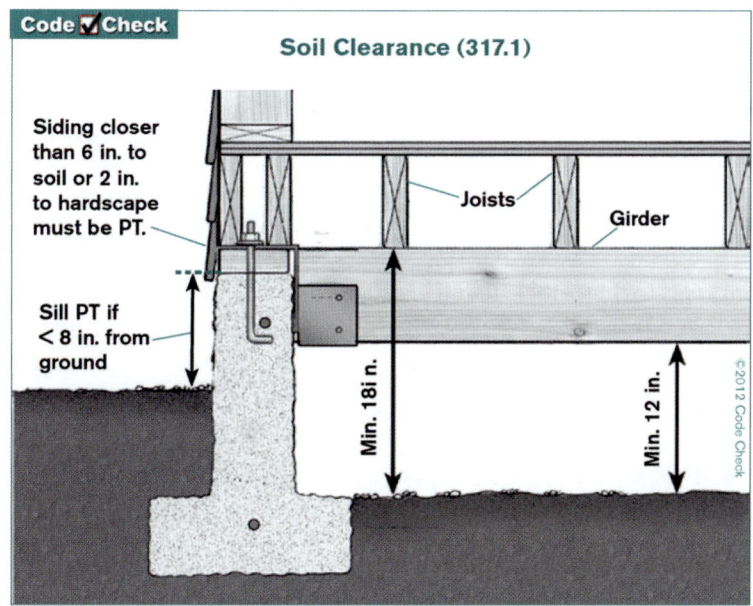

- **Drives, walkways, and patios:** When the home inspector inspects these areas, attention is paid to their relation to the house—whether drives, sidewalks, or patios slope toward the house or show gaps at the junction of the house and are likely to send or allow water toward the structure. This is especially problematic in freezing climates and areas with expansive soils. They're also examined for materials and condition. Cracks and gaps in these surfaces are noted as potential trip hazards. The general home inspection and most SOPs do not include recreational facilities such as barbecues, fire pits, tennis courts, play structures, exercise equipment, and pools/spas.

- **Grading and vegetation:** The home inspector is not a landscape designer passing judgment on the pleasing effects of grading and vegetation. But the inspector determines if the slope of the land around the house and trees and bushes near the house have a detrimental effect on the foundation, siding, or roofing. The inspector does not have to inspect or report on soil type or other geological conditions.

- **The garage:** The garage is also described and inspected. The outside siding and trim are inspected along with the rest of the house. Attention is paid to windows and doors, especially the overhead garage door. The home inspector is required to test the operation of the safety reverse feature(s) of the automatic door and report its malfunction or lack of adjustment as a safety hazard. The home inspector does not have to test the remote control for the garage door opener (as it is usually in the homeowner's car). Inside the garage, the home inspector identifies the floor materials and reports their condition. The home inspector also inspects the structure of the garage and reports on its general or visible condition. Other outbuildings such as gardening sheds and barns are not considered to be a part of the general home inspection. They may be inspected upon request for an additional fee, but are excluded by most standards of practice.

- **Retaining walls:** The home inspector observes the condition of retaining walls that are close to the house and may have an effect on the structure or foundation of the building. For example, a retaining wall holding back soil next to or near the house is inspected. A wall at the back of the property, which has no potential effect on the structure, is not inspected. The exception is if the wall is a safety issue and in imminent danger of collapsing regardless of where it is located. The home inspector inspects the wall for movement and stability, checking the wall's ability to drain water.

Chapter Note

Pages 94–118 present procedures for the inspection of the siding.

2.2 INSPECTING THE SIDING

An important aspect of the exterior inspection is the inspection of the wall cladding or siding. The home inspector identifies the **type** of wall cladding(s) used and reports on its **condition**. Siding should be inspected from all sides of the home and from both directions, not just selected views. The inspection of the siding includes:

- Condition of siding materials

- Loose or missing components

- Siding fastenings/fasteners
- Condition of the joints and interfaces with other materials
- Finish coatings, paints, and stains
- Distance from the ground

Under the Siding

The purpose of the siding is to protect the framework and the interior of the structure from the elements. In some cases, the siding also contributes to bracing the structure and enhancing its rigidity. With solid masonry walls, the exterior walls are also structural members of the building structure.

In old balloon frame homes, the wood clapboard siding may have stabilized the structure without the help of any **wall sheathing** beneath it. But more recent construction includes wall sheathing to brace the framework (shear walls) and provide some insulation and weather resistance. A shear wall is a series of panels, typically plywood or OSB attached to the wall framing that prevents the structure from twisting or racking.

In older platform frame homes, wall sheathing was **tongue and groove planking** nailed on the diagonal to the wall studs. **Building paper** was applied over the planking to act as a water repellent. It also acted as a lubricating layer between wood surfaces. The siding was nailed to the planking through the building paper. The cavities between the studs may or may not have been filled with insulation. Today, a weather-resistive barrier (WRB), commonly known as house wrap or by the common brand name Tyvek, has replaced building paper in many parts of the country. When properly taped, it is both water resistant and seals out air and drafts.

Most recent platform frame structures make use of oriented strand board OSB, an engineered wood panel or board or **plywood sheathing** that serves to brace the home. If the house is well braced through some other bracing method, **fibrous sheathing or foam sheathing** may be used. But with fibrous sheathing, the siding should add stiffness to the framing. Today in many parts of the country, instead of building paper, a **synthetic plastic fabric (Tyvek)** that comes in large rolls is likely to be used to protect against water and air penetration. Foam board is now very common and serves as combination air barrier and insulation, when properly taped and sealed. If a vapor retarder is used, it should be inside the wall studs and against the drywall or plaster, not outside (always towards the warm in winter side). Plank, plywood, and fibrous sheathing are permeable materials as are the building papers and house wrap fabrics used to repel water and air infiltration.

> **WALL SHEATHING**
> - Diagonal planking
> - Plywood/OSB
> - Fibrous sheathing
> - Foam board
> - Sometimes none

> **WATER AND AIR REPELLENT LAYER**
> - Building paper
> - Housewrap, a type of non-woven plastic fabric
> - Foam board

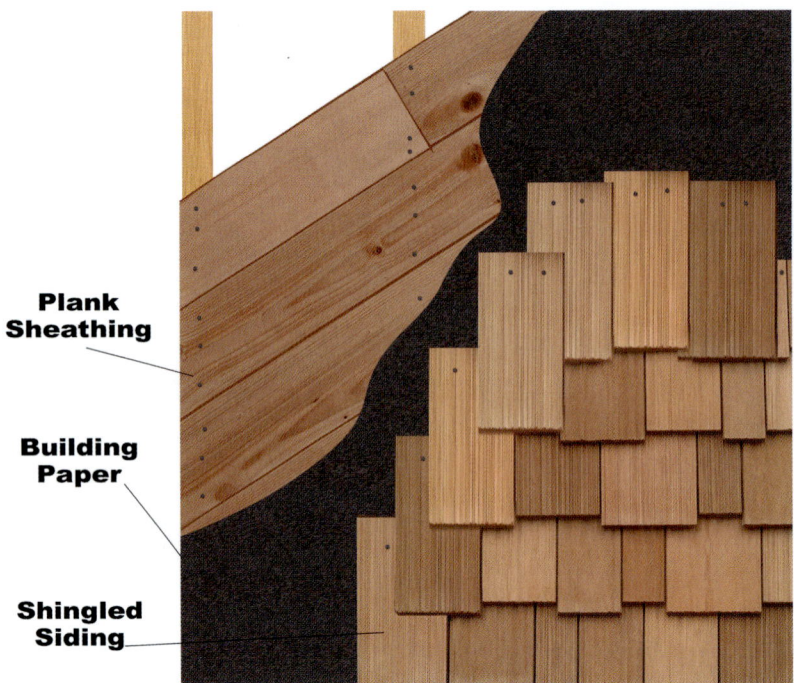

Illustration by Paddy Morrissey

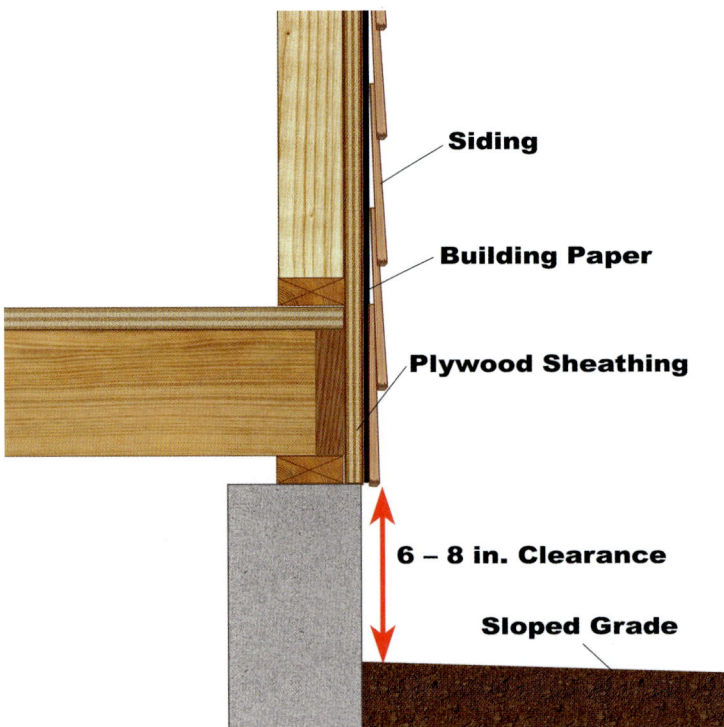

Illustration by Paddy Morrissey

Foam insulation sheathing is sometimes used, with or without conventional wood sheathing. Foam sheathing is a rigid plastic product that is cut to the same size as standard wood sheathing (4 × 8, 4 × 10 or 4 × 12). It may be applied over plywood, OSB sheathing, or open framing (studs) as some varieties are intended to replace wood sheathing. A WRB is not required with certain foam sheathing installations, although it typically is used. Foam sheathing must be sealed with a special kind of tape to maximize air and water resistance. Another advantage of foam board is that when properly installed, it protects against condensation on the inside wall by keeping the interior of the wall warmer.

Flashings are used under the siding to prevent water penetration. They are generally used at the interfaces between the siding and other building components where water can easily leak in, such as around windows, doors, and penetrations. Flashings are commonly made of sheet metal but plastic, liquid-applied, or self-adhesive materials may be seen in newer construction.

One example of where flashings are found under the exterior siding is at the top of the foundation to keep water from entering and running down the foundation wall. For example, with a brick veneer wall, a flashing runs over the foundation beneath the brick and up the wall behind the WRB behind the brick to provide protection.

Where the exterior wall of the house's upper story meets a roof, flashing should be used to prevent water from entering at this interface. Ideally, flashings should be used over the top of window and door trim, projecting out from the siding (drip caps) unless positioned under an overhang.

Wood Plank Siding

Wood plank siding can be installed either horizontally or vertically. These planks can be cut perfectly rectangular, can be tapered, or can be made with special milled cuts.

> ### Definitions
>
> *Wall sheathing is planking, foam, OSB, or plywood sheets used to cover the wall framework of a structure.*
>
> *When a surface is moisture permeable it allows moisture to pass through it.*
>
> *Flashings are a type of sheet metal or plastic used at interfaces between building components to prevent water penetration. Flashings are used around chimneys and vents in the roof, above doors and windows in exterior walls to protect the top of the foundation, and so on.*

> ### Wood Sidings
>
> - Plank
> - Clapboard
> - Shingles and shakes
> - Plywood panels
> - Composition board or hardboard

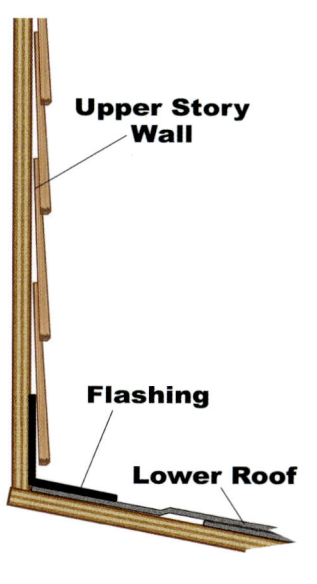
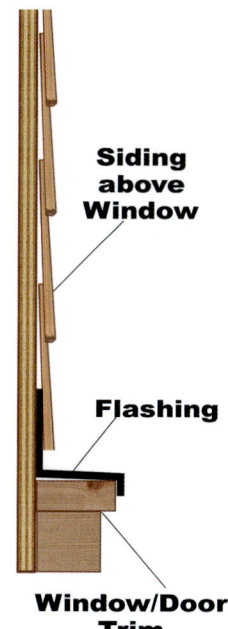

Illustration by Paddy Morrissey

THE EXTERIOR INSPECTION

Rectangular planks are perfect rectangular cuts that can be laid flat with their ends butted for a smooth exterior surface. These butted planks are usually installed vertically as siding. Vertical joints may be protected with **battens**. When rectangular boards are laid horizontally and overlapped, the style is called **clapboard**. This name comes from clamping or clapping the horizontal planks together with nails. Clapboard has a softer line if the planks are tapered or **beveled** instead of perfectly rectangular.

Various **milled planks**, are used for plank siding, including tongue and groove siding. **Shiplap** style planking is laid close enough that it appears to the eye to be butted.

The home inspector should carefully inspect wood plank siding for:

> **Definitions**
>
> <u>Battens</u> are narrow strips of wood placed over joints in vertical wall siding. They serve to seal the joint.
>
> <u>Clapboard</u> is overlapping, horizontal wood plank siding made from either rectangular planks or <u>beveled</u> or tapered planks.

- **Fastenings:** Proper nailing plays an important role in the life of the siding. Too many nails can limit the wood siding's ability to expand and contract with moisture and temperature changes. Nails too close to the edges can result in splitting the wood. When face nailing is done as with clapboard, rabbeted bevel, and channel siding, nails should be properly set and puttied. Proper nailing decreases warping, checking (cracking), cupping, and the tendency of nails to pull out. Watch for the following problems with the nails themselves:

    — Nails too short and not holding

    — Nails too long and sticking out

    — Nails too thick that are splitting the siding

    — Corroded nails that are discoloring or damaging the wood

    — Un-puttied nails that leave rusty streaks on paint

    — Nails that don't seem to grip

    The last item in the list—nails that don't seem to grip—can signal another problem in vertical plank siding. The nailing base may not be properly installed or may not be adequate. When vertical siding is installed, there should be horizontal blocking between the studs every 24″ for the vertical planks to be nailed into. The wall sheathing is usually not strong enough or thick enough to hold the nails.

- **Deterioration and finishes:** Wood siding should be painted or stained to form a protective seal on the wood. Even cedar and redwood are improved by staining. The coating should be free of peeling, blisters, bubbles, dirt, and worn areas. If it isn't, the condition should be reported and the exposed siding inspected for wood damage. Wood rot can be hidden under newly painted surfaces. Sometimes, you can see slight surface irregularities or waviness in the paint, which are characteristic of hidden or concealed decay. In any case, if you suspect wood rot, you should probe the siding to make sure without obviously damaging the new paint job. Blistering or peeling paint in a localized area should be explored for its cause. It may be from an obvious cause such as a leaking gutter or water that is splashing against the house at a corner. It can also be an indication that water or excess moisture is penetrating into the siding from the interior of the house. An example is where water from a roof leak is running down the rafters and into the wall.

Broken or split plank siding and pulled out nails can be caused by improper nailing (see pages 97–98). When plank siding absorbs and retains too much moisture, cupping and checking of the planks can result. Any cracks appearing in wood allow additional moisture to enter the wall.

Distortions: Warping and buckling of plank siding can be an indication of deterioration of the siding or a problem with the framework. You might see humps, bulges, and low places in the siding that can be the result of the movement of the framing or foundation. It could also be the result of warped or crooked studs pushing on the exterior siding, or warped sheathing.

When vertical siding bulges and nails are loose, this may indicate the absence of a proper nailing base. Distortions or displacements of planks make openings for water to penetrate behind the siding, and wood rot as well as insects can be expected.

- **Distance from the ground:** Wood siding should end 6" to 8" above the soil. Check the bottom edge of the siding to see if it touches the ground. Wood rot and insect problems will be present if it does. You will find many homes with sidings of all types too close to the ground. Then, to make it worse, the homeowner adds several inches of landscape mulch to completely bury the siding.

- **Joints and interfaces:** Always inspect the joints in wood plank siding for water penetration and wood rot. Where battens are used to cover joints in vertical planking, check the top surface of the batten for deterioration. Problem areas include horizontal joints in vertical planking. Caulking may be used to seal joints between planks or cracks in the wood. If that is the case, be sure to inspect it to make sure it's

---

INSPECTING WOOD SIDING

- Nail problems
- Decay and wood rot
- Blistering and peeling paint
- Warping, buckling, and cupping
- Water penetration at interfaces
- Broken, loose, or missing components
- Distance from the ground

Definitions

<u>Cupping</u> *in wood plank siding is a warp across the grain of the board.*

<u>Checking</u> *in wood plank siding is a crack or split along the grain of the board as a result of cupping.*

Section Note

The best way to prepare yourself for inspecting wood and other types of siding is to look at some homes. Before you focus on finding defects, concentrate on being able to identify the types of siding you see. Identification of the type of siding is an important part of the home inspection.

For Beginning Inspectors

Make some stops at siding suppliers to see firsthand the variety of siding material available—in wood, aluminum, vinyl, and fiber cement (HardiePlank). It also is helpful to visit suppliers who carry stone and brick facings.

Photo #1 *This siding is too close to the walk and has deteriorated significantly as a result. A minimum of a 2" space is required at pavement.*

in good condition. Check interfaces at corners, where siding abuts a roof, and so on. Be sure these areas are water tight and free of deterioration.

- **Loose or missing components:** Get close enough to check the siding. Push against it to test its tightness to the framework. Wood plank siding should always be checked for any missing parts. Watch for any missing battens and report them.

Plywood Siding

Plywood sheets with weather-resistant glue are used as exterior siding. T-111 is a very common product. They must be securely nailed in place with a sufficient number of nails in order to contribute to the stiffness of the framework. The backing for plywood siding should be sturdy. Where plywood sheets meet horizontally, there should be extra horizontal blocking between the studs to provide a proper nailing base.

The outer ply of plywood siding can be disguised in a variety of ways. A common approach is to groove the outer ply to look like vertical planking and to sandblast it for a grainy or rough appearance.

The home inspector should check the joints—both vertical and horizontal—for tightness. Horizontal joints are particularly vulnerable to water penetration and should have flashing behind them or be **scarfed** (see illustration) rather than butted to prevent water from getting in. Vertical joints may have battens for extra protection that makes the siding look even more like vertical wood planking.

Exterior plywood can expand and contract at different rates than the framing, causing joints to be pulled apart from the movement. Nails can be pulled out and panels can actually fall off. Relief joints may be provided to counteract this problem.

Plywood siding has low permeability for water vapor and can absorb a great deal of moisture into the siding. The siding can easily warp if surface finishes are allowed to deteriorate.

Plywood siding should be inspected as plank siding—finish, condition, distortion, joints, and distance from the ground—as well as for delamination.

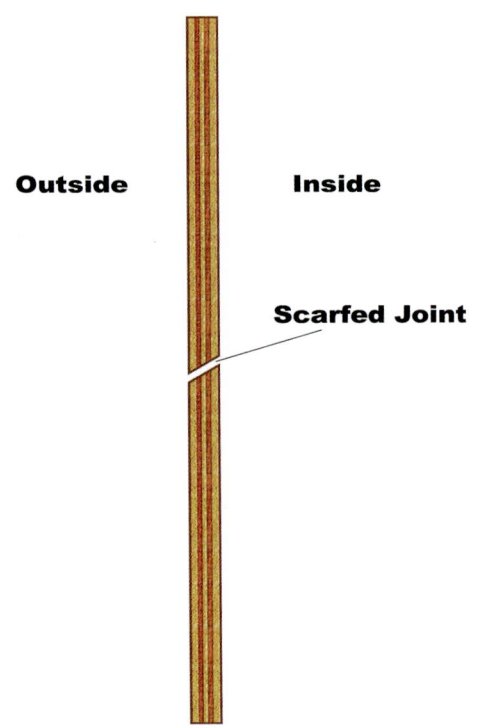

Illustration by Paddy Morrissey

Photo #2 PLYWOOD SIDING

T-111 siding must be well painted or it will deteriorate. Even though it's made with waterproof glue, it can only get wet for so long before it fails.

Composition Board

Composition board, also called fiberboard or hardboard, is made of **compressed wood fibers** with weather-resistant binders. It can be made into planks or sheets for exterior siding purposes. However, boards and sheets made with wood chips or ground wood are usually intended for the inside of the house.

Long runs of siding without joints, up to as much as 16′ without interruption, is commonly composition board. But when made to imitate planks and installed horizontally, this fabricated siding can look like clapboard.

The home inspector should pay particular attention to the condition of composition board, fiberboard, and hardboard, as they are likely to absorb moisture if not properly protected. Boards can expand and bow out, causing a wavy appearance in the wall. They may be swollen at the edges and bottom from moisture absorption. The boards can swell, warp, and disintegrate. Hardboard siding needs to be repainted more often than wood siding due to the material's lesser ability to hold paint. The home inspector may notice watery-looking, thinning, or fading paint on composition board and hardboard.

Section Note

"I want to emphasize the importance of inspecting the siding from all sides of the house. Don't inspect one wall and make assumptions about the others. Inspect the entire structure.

One of my inspectors was inspecting a ranch-style home with extensions outward and expansion upward. The inspector walked around the entire house to review the siding and discovered that four different sidings had been used—concrete block, brick, wood, and vinyl. It turns out the owner was a construction laborer who had brought materials home from building sites and then went nuts building additions. It took the inspector some time to thoroughly inspect the interfaces between these sidings."

Wood Shingles

Wood shingles are usually redwood, cedar, or cypress. Shingles are rough or smooth sawn; **wood shakes** are hand-split. They can be installed in a variety of ways. When laid **single course**, each shingle is exposed to the weather. With **double course** shingles or shakes, an undercourse lies completely behind and is covered by a top course.

> **Definitions**
>
> A _shake_ is a type of wood shingle that is hand-split instead of rough or smooth sawn. A _single course_ of shingles or shakes is where each course is exposed to the weather. In a _double course_ of shingles or shakes, an undercourse, covered completely by a top course, is not exposed to the weather.

In one type of single coursing, the shingles can be laid one-half or one-third of their length to the weather. This results in three layers of shingles.

Another approach to single coursing is to use a tapered shingle, where the top end is very thin. This end is pinched under a **nailing strip**, and the butt edge of the next course is then nailed to the strip. A much longer portion of the shingle is exposed with this approach.

In double coursing, two layers of shingles are laid for each row. They may be even at the butt end, or the top course may extend an inch or more beyond the undercourse. This is done for decorative reasons to enhance the shadow line at the bottom of each course.

Shingling can vary from rough, uneven-looking patterns using different sizes of shakes, all the way to uniform sizes of shingles, which when painted, look similar to clapboard. Shingles with fancy cuts at the butt end, either pointed or rounded, were common in Victorian times. In the 1920s, a popular style was to lay alternating courses at different exposures for a more interesting pattern.

Cedar, redwood, and cypress will weather naturally, but different exposures to sunlight and moisture causes uneven aging and coloring. Discoloration is not a problem, although some homeowners may be concerned about uneven coloring. But shingles and shakes can be stained for a uniform look and should be renewed

Photo #3 *This is an example of a wood shingle home. As you can see they are laying flat and in very good condition.*

periodically. They can be painted, although once that's done, the homeowner must keep up with the painting…forever!

The home inspector should be on the lookout for the following:

- Warping and cracking from age. Shingles also cup and split when they're not allowed to dry out.

- Buckling shingles caused by joints too tightly spaced, leaving no room for shingles to expand when wet.

- Joints that are not staggered from course to course and split shingles that create new joints directly below the joints above. This creates a vertical alignment that promotes the flow of water behind the shingles.

- Missing shingles and shakes.

- Loose shingles or shakes. They should fit tightly (to the wall). You shouldn't be able to lift them up.

- As with other sidings, distortions such as bowing or sagging of an exterior wall of shingles can indicate a problem with foundation settlement or warped framework.

Metal Siding

Exterior metal siding may be made of either aluminum or steel. Neither type requires much maintenance, and both come in smooth or embossed surfaces. Aluminum is the more popular metal siding these days, although steel is still used.

Aluminum siding has a baked-on enamel surface that stands up over time. It can fade over the years, and some homeowners paint the siding. If the siding has been painted, it will require repainting on a regular basis.

> **INSPECTING METAL AND VINYL**
> - Loose and missing planks
> - Courses not level
> - Bad trim installation
> - Missing caulking
> - Mechanical damage
> - Interference with moisture release

Photo #4 *An older home with aluminum siding. It was falling off in spots exposing the old wooden clapboard siding beneath.*

TYPES OF SIDING

- Wood siding
- Metal siding
- Vinyl siding
- Asphalt composition
- Asbestos cement
- Stucco
- Brick veneer
- Clay or slate shingles
- Brick and stone facings

For Your Information

It would be a good idea to get your hands on your local building codes and spend some time studying them. Bonding of metal siding is only one requirement that varies from area to area. Although you're not required to inspect for code compliance, it's important to know what to look for in certain instances. And it's helpful to your customers when you can point out some problem with code.

Metal siding wears well, although it can become dented. It also can be noisy. Because of expansion, it is not uncommon to hear it bang and pop when sunlight warms a side of the house.

Most of the problems with metal siding are the result of **defective installation procedures**. The siding should be securely and tightly fastened to the wall. When joined lengthwise, metal planks should be overlapped. The home inspector will want to check that these overlaps are big enough to prevent water penetration. The proper trim and moldings at corners and around doors and windows should be installed and securely fastened. At the corners, be sure each corner molding is overlapped by the one above. It's not unusual to have installers reverse them with the lower molding overlapping the one above.

The home inspector might find aluminum siding installed with **no sheathing** or house wrap under it. This is not a problem if the framework is properly braced. But if installers removed old siding and sheathing when installing replacement aluminum siding, the framework can be severely weakened. The lack of house wrap or building paper can result in moisture getting into the walls.

Caulking is sometimes used with aluminum siding—often in the corners around windows and perhaps at overlaps or corners. The home inspector should inspect caulking and determine whether it's still doing its job. Caulking is a maintenance item and must be periodically replaced.

Another thing to watch for is the siding's inability to allow **moisture to escape** through the wall to the outside.

Metal planking is waterproof, which is good, but it should not be a moisture barrier. To keep it from becoming a moisture barrier, small drainage/ventilation holes are punched along the bottom of each plank. If there aren't enough holes or if the holes are blocked, the siding can trap moisture inside the wall. The home inspector should check for these tiny holes and look for rot behind the siding by examining the header or rim joists in the basement and along the outer floor edge in the living areas.

Building codes require metal sidings to be **bonded**. Sometimes incorrectly referred to as grounding, bonding refers to connecting non-electrical devices/materials together so that a circuit is tripped (by taking current to ground) if an ungrounded conductor touches the surface associated with the system. Bonding will be discussed at length in the electrical section. There has been a difference of opinion nationwide over the years about whether bonding is needed. However, if your local codes require bonding, you should look for it.

Twisted, buckled, and bent aluminum siding may be an indication of structural problems. Always investigate further. One inspector noticed twisted aluminum siding. On further investigation, he discovered that the corner of the house had settled, leading to the twisted siding.

Vinyl Siding

Siding made of polyvinyl chloride (PVC) acts very much like aluminum siding. One difference is that older vinyl siding can be easily damaged. It becomes brittle in temperatures at or below freezing and can break or crack on impact. If inspecting under these conditions, be careful about putting your ladder against the siding or banging anything against it. You may see vinyl siding that has melted (sagged) due to sunlight reflected off low-emissivity (low-E) windows.

> **Section Note**
>
> *"In one house with twisted siding, I discovered that the sill had entirely rotted out and the house had settled down to the foundation wall. The foundation itself was in good condition."*

Low-E windows allow light into a room while reflecting heat and UV rays. While this is good news for the homeowner's air-conditioning bill, the reflected heat may melt the neighbor's vinyl siding. Most problems with vinyl siding are the result of defective installation. Because vinyl siding has less strength than aluminum, sheathing should be present. Inspect vinyl siding for the same defects as you would metal sidings.

Photo #5 *Vinyl siding significantly damaged, probably due to hail.*

The home inspector can tell the difference between metal and vinyl siding using a scratch test. A knife is used to make a small surface scratch at the end of a panel or joint. Vinyl siding is colored all the way through; metal siding has only surface color (paint). You can also use a magnet to differentiate between steel and aluminum. A magnet will stick to steel and not to aluminum.

Asphalt Composition

Asphalt composition shingles used in siding are essentially the same as those used for roofing. They were popular in the 1930s through the 1950s, often placed over the original wood siding.

This siding consists of strips of shingles laid in courses with the higher courses overlapping the lower. Asphalt shingles manufactured before 1970 may (probably) contain asbestos. Today, asphalt shingles come with an adhesive on the upper portion of the strip that bonds to the lower portion of the strip above.

This adhesive doesn't always work as well as it should, and shingles can lift, curl, and be damaged when blown by the wind.

Photo #6 *This asphalt shingle siding looks like brick from the street, but it is definitely not. You can see that every five courses is a seam for the next sheet.*

Asbestos Cement

Asbestos cement siding is a material made of asbestos and Portland cement, is fireproof, and is weather resistant. It was widely used in the 1950s. The asbestos present in the siding poses no health danger as long as the siding is intact. Asbestos that can be damaged or crumbled due to hand pressure (described as friable) is dangerous because the asbestos fibers are released into the air. Asbestos cement siding is considered non-friable.

However, fibers can be released when the siding is scraped in preparation for painting or when the siding is removed, cut, or drilled through. Under EPA regulations, asbestos cement siding can only be removed by qualified asbestos remediation specialists and disposed of in an approved landfill. If you find asbestos cement siding, your report should include this information. Unfortunately, in real life, many municipalities do not enforce the EPA removal and disposal requirements. Be sure to check local enforcement.

Asbestos cement siding is durable. However, it is brittle and can be cracked or broken on impact. (Be careful not to bang tools against asbestos siding, breaking it.) The color of the shingles or planks can dull over the years. The home inspector may find that the siding has been painted. The finish paint should be inspected like other paint jobs.

When inspecting asbestos cement siding, report cracked, chipped, missing, loose, or displaced shingles. Check to see that nails are not loose or backed out. Report excessively soiled or stained patches and moss growth, which this siding seems to attract. The biggest problem with this type of siding is the lack of

Photo #7 *Every once in a while you find a home with pristine original asbestos cement siding. This is one of those homes.*

replacement pieces that match. You may see sections replaced that look different and are probably the material described below.

Fiber Cement Siding

Fiber cement siding is sold under several trade names, including HardiePlank and WeatherBoards. Portland cement, ground sand, cellulose fiber, and select additives are mixed with water and formed into siding pieces and panels. It can be finished with a wood-grain look, a smooth finish, or a rough-sawn texture and is available in almost any color (it can be painted as well). Properly installed, the look of fiber cement siding is almost indistinguishable from wood. Unlike wood, it is not subject to rot or insect infestation, and its manufacturers claim that it is less likely to fade under UV light. It is also rated as Class 1 fire resistant, meaning it will not burn and produces virtually no smoke. Few problems or defects are found with fiber cement siding.

> **INSPECTING STUCCO**
> - Detachment from wall
> - Water penetration
> - Exposed lath or chicken wire
> - Cracks that hold water
> - Offset cracks and breaks
> - Cracks that go through all layers

The siding should be examined to see that it is in generally good condition, without cracks, chips, splits, or gaps between sections. Check for overdriven or countersunk nail heads that can pull through the thin fiber cement material. The manufacturer's installation instructions should be consulted for specific installation requirements. There have been several versions since the products inception.

Photo #8 *New fiber cement siding installed on an old home. HardiePlank brand siding is very commonly used.*

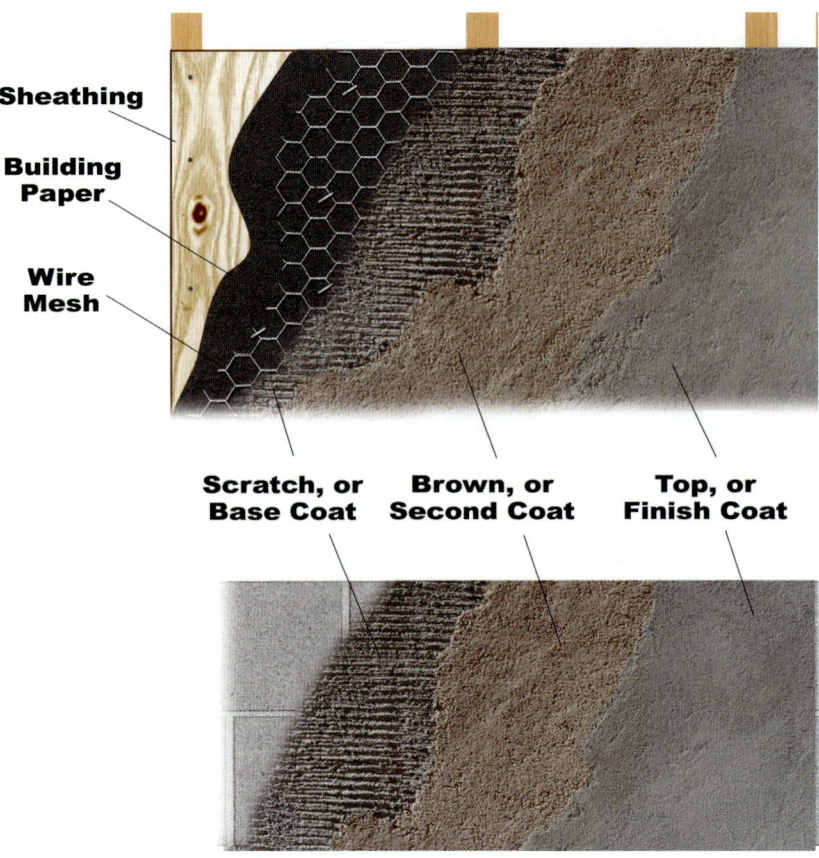

Illustration by Paddy Morrissey

Stucco

Stucco is a cement plaster used to cover exterior wall surfaces, usually applied over a base of metal lath or chicken wire. There are three basic systems: traditional three-coat stucco, new proprietary one-coat systems, and exterior insulation and finish systems (EIFS) that use synthetic stucco in a system. With traditional stucco over wood framework, a wire mesh is attached to the sheathing and studs with building paper between the two (framing and wire). Stucco can be applied over masonry walls as well. In this case, the wall provides enough stiffening to bypass the wire mesh layer. The stucco itself is a mixture of Portland cement, sand, water, and sometimes lime. Traditionally three coats were applied: a 3/8″ scratch coat, a second 3/8″ brown coat, and a 1/8″ thin topcoat. The topcoat may contain colored powder or pigment and polymer additives to protect the finish. Stucco may also be painted, which is most common. You also have newer applications, which are common in the South and Southwest, where a single 3/8″ coat of fiber-reinforced stucco is applied over chicken wire type lath. A common brand is Western 1-Kote. You may also encounter stucco applications with a Portland cement base coat and a synthetic topcoat or finish coat. This topcoat, commonly known as the color coat, comes in whatever color the homeowner desires and does not need to be painted (comes in 5-gallon pails).

    Portland cement stucco, like all cement products, is a porous material. Inevitably, water will penetrate it, which could cause the underlying wood framing to deteriorate and rot. That is what the building paper (or now more commonly house wrap) is for. To prevent water from becoming trapped behind the stucco,

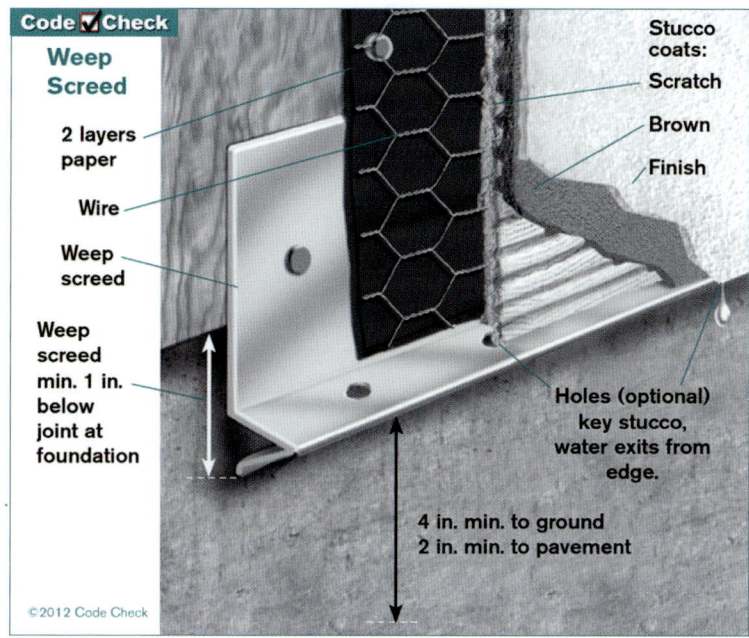

a weep screed (also known as a drip screed) is installed at the bottom edge of the wall. The weep screed is a type of perforated flashing or trim piece at the bottom of the wall that the building paper or WRB drains onto and allows the water out of the wall assembly. It should end at least 8″ above grade. Watch for defects in gutters and downspouts, flashings, and drip edges that cause water to leak down behind the stucco.

Inspect stucco walls carefully for **cracking**, and if possible, try to find the cause of it. Cracks that go through all layers, cracks that hold water, and offset cracks and breaks in the stucco should be reported to the customer and immediate repair recommended. Cracks can appear in stucco over wood framework when the **framing members shrink**, especially at the floor levels where the most shrinkage tends to occur. Vertical and horizontal cracking can take place when there is **foundation settlement**. Cracks in random directions can appear during the **curing** of the stucco. These types of cracks may be hairline cracks in the outer surface only, or they may be deeper, involving the undercoats as well. One of the primary causes of stucco cracks is too large of a panel/section without any breaks or expansion joints. It shrinks as it cures, and if it is a huge sheet, it will crack. Think of your driveway: control joints or saw cuts give the concrete a place to crack. This is another reason synthetic stucco is used as the color coat as it cracks much less than painted Portland cement stucco.

Stucco can become **detached** from the wall due to trapped moisture, expansion/contraction, and wetting/drying. Bulging and sagging can be a sign of trapped moisture. Often, homeowners paint stucco after repairs are made, using an impermeable paint. Stucco paint should be a permeable masonry paint, which allows moisture to escape. The home inspector can tap the wall with a screwdriver handle and listen for signs of detachment just like plaster on the interior. Areas in the wall coming loose will make a dull thud sound when tapped.

Stucco is sometimes combined with wood in Tudor or half-timbered exterior walls. In modern Tudors, painted wood trim pieces are nailed to the sheathing

Photo #9 *This is traditional stucco that has been damaged. Damaged corners like this allow moisture into the wall assembly and must be repaired.*

and surrounding panels of stucco. When inspecting this type of exterior wall covering, pay special attention to wood rot in the wooden members, especially in the horizontal ones.

EIFS

Exterior Insulation and Finish System (EIFS) is a non-loadbearing, exterior wall cladding **system** that consists of an insulation board attached adhesively or mechanically (or both) to the substrate (usually OSB), an integrally reinforced base coat, and a textured protective finish coat. EIFS was first introduced in the United States in the late 1960s and was first used on commercial buildings (and later on homes). EIFS typically consists of the following components:

- An optional water-resistive barrier (WRB) that covers the substrate

- A drainage plane between the WRB and the insulation board that is most commonly achieved with vertical ribbons of adhesive applied over the WRB

- Insulation board typically made of expanded polystyrene (EPS) that is secured with an adhesive or is secured mechanically to the substrate

- Glass-fiber reinforcing mesh embedded in the base coat

- A water-resistant base coat that is applied on top of the insulation to serve as a weather barrier

- A finish coat that typically uses colorfast and crack-resistant acrylic co-polymer technology

EIFS today is one of the most-tested and well-researched claddings in the construction industry. Research, conducted by the Oak Ridge National Laboratory and supported by the Department of Energy, has validated that EIFS is the "best performing cladding" in relation to thermal and moisture control when compared with brick, stucco, and cementitious fiberboard siding. The problem, as with most materials, is with its installation. Poor workmanship and corner cutting caused huge problems with EIFS installations. In addition, EIFS is in full compliance with modern building codes that emphasize energy conservation through the use of CI (continuous insulation) and a continuous air barrier. Both these components are built into today's EIFS products to provide maximum energy savings, reduced environmental impact over the life of the structure, and improved Indoor Air Quality.

Solid Masonry Walls

The walls of a home can be made of solid masonry (discussed in Chapter 1). Usually, there are two to four thicknesses (wythes) of masonry. The interior wall may be left exposed, plastered over, or furred out and covered with drywall. The masonry wall can be made of materials such as brick, stone, and concrete block.

A **solid brick wall** can usually be identified by the **header rows or bonding courses**, where the brick is turned with its small end facing out. The header rows serve as ties to hold the wythes of bricks together. (Header rows are not required in brick veneer walls, although you may see them as a decorative pattern.) The thickness of brick walls has declined over the centuries from 20″ to 16″ to 12″ and finally to 8″ thick. Most brick homes built since the early 1970s are, in fact, brick veneer over a wood framework.

The solid masonry wall may be built of two materials—an inner and an outer wythe. This is called a **compound wall**. Metal ties are used to attach the two wythes together and give strength to the wall. The positioning of header rows in the brick outer layer can be random, not necessarily every five to seven rows.

> **MASONRY WALLS**
> - Solid brick wall
> - Compound wall
> - Cavity wall
> - Brick veneer over wood framing

> **Definitions**
>
> In a *solid brick house*, three layers or wythes of brick are used to construct a solid wall with no wood framing. *Header rows* are rows of bricks turned small end out to act as ties to hold the wall together. A *compound wall* is a solid masonry wall built of two different materials. A *cavity wall* is a masonry wall with a dead air space left between wythes.

Photo #10 *This is an example of a solid brick wall. Note the header rows where the end of the bricks are seen.*

A masonry wall with an air space left between the inner and outer wythes of the wall is called a **cavity wall**.

In older construction, both inner and outer wythes were often brick. A header row of bricks laid with the small end out traversed the cavity and held the wall together. In more modern construction, the inner layer could be stone or concrete block. In the compound cavity wall, where you find different inner and outer materials, the brick could be attached to the inner layer with metal ties or header rows.

Walk around the house slowly, paying attention to the entire surface of the wall and its condition at each window and door opening. Here is a list of the items you should watch for when inspecting a solid brick, stone, or concrete block wall.

Cracking in the wall indicating foundation settlement and movement. Step cracks on adjacent walls at a corner is a sign of footing failure at that corner due to soil weakness or erosion. Vertical cracks that run down to the foundation often signal settlement. Jagged, sharp-edged cracks are an indication that movement is active. Distortion of the window framing can also indicate settlement of the structure.

> *Definitions*
>
> In a brick veneer house, an outer wythe of bricks is attached to the wood framework of the house using brick ties, which are accordion-style metal fasteners. Weep holes are openings in the bottom row of brick providing an exit for water accumulating behind the brick veneer. A flashing placed at the foundation is sheet metal or plastic in modern construction that prevents water leaks into the foundation. Spalling is the crumbling and falling away of the surface of bricks, blocks, or concrete.

- **Cracking** above openings indicating a rotted header or rusted lintel or failed arches.
- **Spalling** or **deteriorating** wall material.
- **Deterioration of mortar.** Use the tip of your screwdriver or a knife to probe mortar, testing it for its condition.
- **Bowing, leaning, or distortions** in the wall caused by mortar deterioration, interior framing problems, rafter spread, and foundation movement.

We haven't said much about **concrete block walls**. Concrete block left as the exterior wall is most often seen in commercial buildings. Although used in home construction, they're not often left uncovered. Generally, residential concrete block walls are finished with stucco, painted, or left natural and sealed as is the case with "slump block."

Brick Veneer

Brick houses built today (and since the early 1970s) are generally brick veneer over wood framing. A brick veneer wall does not carry the load of the structure; it is just siding.

The brick veneer is constructed from the foundation up and is attached to the wall framing with **brick ties**. These ties are usually crimped, accordion-style, to allow them to expand and contract with the wood frame and keep them from cracking the brick veneer.

An air space of about 1″ is left behind the brick veneer to allow moisture/water passing through the brick to run down the back side of the wall. This water exits through the bottom of the wall at the foundation through **weep holes** (shown below), which are openings approximately every 2–3′ along the bricks. A **flashing** runs beneath the brick and up the wall to prevent this water from entering the building at the foundation.

With brick veneer, the inspector can see signs of problems. Weep holes can become blocked and not allow water to exit from behind the bricks, leading to deterioration of the brick and the mortar and, in a worst-case scenario, damaging the interior finish materials, especially with slab-on-grade. Brick ties can be improperly installed or loosened over time, and the veneer can separate from the wall.

When inspecting brick veneer, the most important thing to look for is **detachment or separation of the veneer** from the house. The brick ties can be improperly installed or can come loose. Sight along window and door openings or trim or door casings where

Section Note

"We've come across other veneer detachment problems. Recently, one of my inspectors inspected a house where the brick veneer was in place. However, there was a considerable bow along one wall and marked displacement of the veneer around the windows and doors in that wall. He discovered that the veneer was held in place by the fascia board at the top. One push and the whole wall would have come down. I should say that it's better to caution customers about problems like these and not be the person who actually causes the wall to fall. It's hard to convince people that you didn't do something wrong."

Illustration by Paddy Morrissey

you might see the lean of detached veneer framing—more brick shows at the top than the bottom. A detaching veneer may have a decided bow to it or can show signs of cracking as it pulls loose and separates from the house.

VENEER PROBLEM

Watch carefully for the separation of brick veneer from a house. Don't be the one to cause it to fall off.

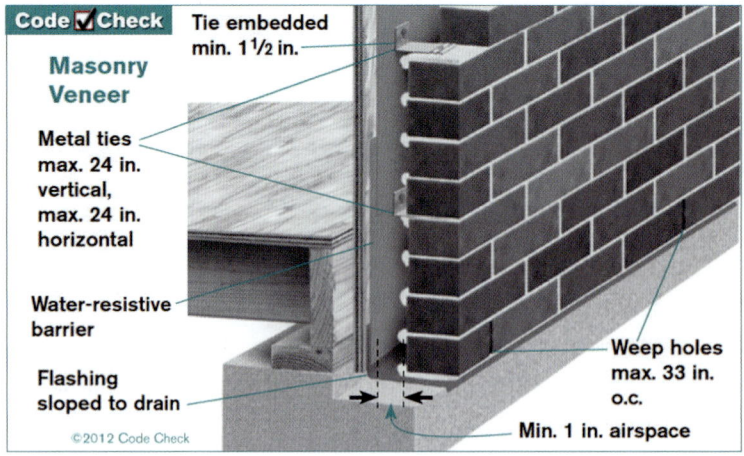

As with solid brick walls, the home inspector should examine the wall for **cracking** in the brick, which can indicate structural problems. Check for **deterioration** of brick and mortar. Examine the **weep holes** in the lower course of bricks in the veneer to make sure they are open and functioning. Water behind the wall cannot escape if weep holes are blocked or missing.

Often, there is brick veneer on only a portion of the house. Be sure to check areas where the veneer meets other surfaces.

Other Sidings

A home may have other less common wall coverings as listed here:

- **Slate shingles:** You may find slate shingles (slates) in small areas such as gables or dormers on late 1800 and early 1900 homes. Slate shingles have a very long life. However, nails can rust or corrode, causing the shingles to slip out of position and fall off the building.

- **Brick and stone facings:** You may find thin (less than 1/2" thick) facings on all or part of the exterior of the house. Other materials include Novabrik (a system of interlocking bricks that do not require mortar) and Cultured Stone or Adhered Manufactured Stone Veneer (an aggregate material that can be made to resemble any kind of natural stone). Many of these fake stone siding materials were improperly installed over inadequate bases and leak tremendously. They are essentially stuck or glued onto a stucco wall. Class action suits have begun over improper installation of these materials, much like or even worse than the EIFS issues mentioned above. Check the National Concrete Masonry Association website for current issues and pending litigation. Problems with facings include detachment and significant water penetration.

A Word about Paint

The home inspector should be familiar with defects in the exterior paint surface and should know why the paint failed. You will find that the common denominator in all of these issues is improper prepping of the surfaces to be painted.

The three components of house paints are the **pigment**, or color particles; the **vehicle**, or film-forming compound; and the **thinner** or **solvent**, which evaporates from the pigment and vehicle after the paint is applied.

The following problems may be found with a paint surface:

- **Chalking:** This is a process in which ultraviolet radiation causes the vehicle to break down and pigment particles to be released. Rain washes oxidized vehicle and pigment particles away until the underlying siding material is exposed. Any chalking left on the surface should be cleaned off before repainting.

- **Alligatoring:** Wrinkling or cracking in the exterior paint surface is called alligatoring. It looks like the hide of an alligator. This condition is caused when the solvent evaporates too quickly upon application, preventing the rest of the solvent in the paint from escaping. It can happen when paint with quick evaporating solvents is applied in the sun. It can also occur if the paint is applied too thickly.

- **Cracking and crazing:** Cracks appear in the paint surface when the outer layer of paint can't respond to the expansion of the old layers of paint or the siding beneath. Cracks often appear in the paint on window sills where wet wood expands. Crazing is a network of crossing cracks all over the surface, occurring when the outer layer of paint shrinks while it is drying.

- **Peeling:** Paint peels when layers of paint and primer separate due to painting without removing chalking, painting over grease left on the surface, or applying new paint that won't adhere to the old. When the finish separates from the wood beneath, suspect moisture buildup in the wood. Peeling paint often indicates a leak into or behind the siding.

- **Excessive layers of paint:** Older homes may have so many layers of paint that the layers separate from the siding entirely and stand on their own. Moisture can get under the layers and into the siding. The home inspector can check for this defect, especially at corners.

- **Staining:** There are many causes of staining on paint, including a type of air pollution that causes a chemical reaction with the paint, rust

> **Definition**
>
> *Pigment* in paint is the color particles. The *vehicle* in paint is the film-forming compound. The *solvent or thinner* is the third constituent in paint, which evaporates after the paint is applied.
>
> *Chalking* is a process in which ultraviolet radiation causes the vehicle in exterior house paint to break down and pigment particles to be released.
>
> *Alligatoring* is a process in which the solvent evaporates too quickly, leaving residual solvent in the paint and causing wrinkling or cracking in the surface.
>
> *Crazing* of a paint surface is a condition of net-like patterns of cross cracking caused when a new layer of paint shrinks while drying.

> **PAINT PROBLEMS**
>
> - Chalking
> - Alligatoring
> - Cracks and crazing
> - Peeling
> - Excessive layers of paint
> - Staining
> - Mildew

from nails, rusting gutters and downspouts, resin or sap from the siding that bleeds through the paint, airborne grease and soot, and insect eggs.

- **Mildew:** Mildew is not a stain. It's fungi that live on and in the paint, usually on the north face of the house or under shady areas where the sun can't dry it. The home inspector can test for mildew with bleach, which will kill the mildew but will not clean other types of staining. This is not required by any SOP.

Reporting Your Findings

Some home inspectors like to arrive early to give themselves time to take a walk around the house alone to get an overall view of the place, the general layout, and any obvious problems. Once the customer arrives, have him or her come with you as you start the exterior inspection. Having the customer come with you as you conduct the inspection may be the number one rule in home inspection. This is for protection against lawsuits. If the customer is fully informed during the inspection, the chances are much lower that you'll get a complaint call later.

It's important to be systematic about the exterior inspection. If trying to do everything in a single trip around the house with the customer causes you to miss something, plan two or three trips. It's all right to tell the customer that you'll only be looking at the foundation on the first trip, for example. You also can explain that you do this to be sure not to miss anything. The customer will appreciate it.

When inspecting the siding, keep a running dialogue going with the customer, explaining:

> **IMPORTANT POINT**
>
> *The home inspector takes responsibility for the customer's understanding. Don't give technical lectures to people with glassy eyes who don't understand what you're talking about. Speak in simple terms. Your job is to educate the customer.*

- **What you're inspecting**—siding, corner moldings, fastenings, joints, paint surface, weep holes, and so on.

- **What you're looking for**—deterioration, improper installation, warping, buckling, and so on.

- **What you're doing**—probing for wood rot, probing the mortar, testing for mildew, listening for loose stucco, and so on.

- **What you're finding**—chalking paint, wood rot, missing moldings, detached stucco, and so on.

- **Suggestions about dealing with the findings**—calling a mason to evaluate a mortar condition, replacing a window sill, caulking joints, repainting, and so on. But be cautious, don't make uneducated guesses about how repairs should be made.

Communication with the customer is such a major point in home inspection that some inspectors fail because they can't communicate properly.

Communication entails both output and input. The home inspector must be sensitive to the customer's attention span and his or her level of understanding. There's nothing worse than the home inspector who goes on and on without noticing a bored customer or a customer who doesn't under what the inspector is saying. There's no need to explain the chemistry of paint; it's enough to explain in simple terms that the paint has broken down and needs to be redone.

Filling in Your Report

Every home inspector needs an inspection report. A **written report** is the work product of the home inspection, and every home inspector is expected to deliver one to the customer after the inspection. Inspection reports vary a great deal in the industry. Some home inspection companies develop their own version; others use state required formats (Texas), home inspection software, apps, or formats provided by training companies such as AHIT. Some are considered to be excellent, while others are not very good. A workable and easy-to-use inspection report is important for a home inspector in terms of being able to fill it in. Of greater importance are its thoroughness, accuracy, and helpfulness to the customer. Whatever reporting format you choose, make sure it presents your findings in a clear, professional manner such that it reduces your liability and client dissatisfaction.

> **DON'T EVER MISS**
> - Rotted wood
> - Loose face brick
> - Detached stucco
> - Water penetration

The Don't Ever Miss list presented to the right is a reminder of those specific findings you should be sure to include in your inspection report. We list these items after years of experience performing home inspections. Missing them can result in complaint calls and lawsuits later.

When you're filling in your inspection report, be sure to put in enough detail so that your customer knows what your findings were, even if the report is read at a later date.

Here is an overview of what to report on during the inspection of the siding:

- **Siding information:** Identify the type of siding present on the house, noting materials such as stone, stucco, aluminum, vinyl, and so on. You may find more than one type of siding on the house. If you do, be sure to identify each type and note its location on the house.

- **Siding condition:** In general, an inspection report should have categories of satisfactory, marginal, and poor regarding the condition of the siding. If you use the rating marginal or poor, be sure to explain further what you found troubling about the siding. It pays to put as much into the writing as you can. Here are some examples: "Stucco cracked and leaking at back of house, needs repair." "Veneer loose on east wall, needs immediate attention." "Siding should not be touching ground, need 6″ clearance." "Rotted planks on north wall." "Siding needs to be repainted." "Caulk at southeast corner to prevent leaking."

> **Report Available**
>
> *The American Home Inspectors Training Institute offers both manual and computerized reports. These reports include an inspection agreement, complete reporting pages, and helpful customer information. If you're interested in purchasing the Home Inspection Report, please contact us at 1-800-441-9411.*

> **Chapter Note**
>
> *Pages 118–128 present the study and inspection of exterior trim, windows, and doors.*

> **Definitions**
>
> *The <u>cornice</u> consists of the trim and moldings at the eave line. At the gable end of the roof, it may have only a vertical board called the <u>rake-board or barge rafter</u>. A <u>closed cornice</u> has both a vertical fascia board and a horizontal <u>soffit</u> on the underside of the eave.*

- **Major repair or replacement:** Only in extreme circumstances will the home inspector need to classify siding as a major concern. Use this classification if siding needs to be replaced or undergo major repairs to bring it up to an acceptable level. Serious veneer detachment or asbestos cement siding in poor condition would qualify as major repairs. It's a good idea to report this situation on the exterior page of your report and then list the major repair or replacement again on a summary page of your report.

- **Safety hazard:** A brick veneer wall about to fall down is probably the only example of a safety hazard as far as siding is concerned. If, as in the case of our example, a simple push would bring the wall of veneer down, call it a safety hazard in your inspection report.

2.3 TRIM, WINDOWS, DOORS

Another aspect of the exterior inspection is to inspect the trim, the windows, and the exterior doors of the house. The home inspector may include the inspection of these items while inspecting the siding or make a separate trip around the house.

Inspecting the Trim

The exterior trim includes all pieces added to the siding that serve to protect the framework and the interior of the structure from the elements. The trim seals and protects the joints where the siding ends. Trim includes casings around windows and doors, corner boards, skirt boards at the bottom of the siding, and the **fascias** and **soffits** that make up the side and under part of the eaves. The eave trim is also called the **cornice**. Shutters and window boxes should be examined for their condition and for their possible damaging effect on the siding behind them.

- **Wooden trim** is likely to be pine, which needs regular painting and maintenance. Look for the following:

- **Wood rot:** The home inspector can use a probing tool attached to a long pole for reaching and probing any first-floor fascia and soffits from the ground. Test-probe all areas where wood rot is suspected. If rot is found in the trim, examine the area beneath, where the siding, sheathing, and framing may also be rotting. Rot can spread when rotted trim has been painted over. It's difficult to discover that condition without probing areas showing evidence of, or an indication of, damage or staining.

- **Condition:** Look for warping, split, and broken trim pieces. Watch for insect damage. Soffits and fascia can be damaged by small animals such as squirrels and birds trying to get into the attic.

- **Loose or missing trim:** Check to see that all trim pieces are present and securely attached. If missing or loose, there is probably water leakage into the wall. Check seams and joints in the trim pieces. Watch for nails coming loose.

- **Painting and caulking:** The condition of surface paint should be inspected. Let the customer know that he or she should expect to maintain trim on a regular, perhaps annual, basis. Point out areas that need repainting as a part of regular maintenance, distinguishing them from peeling areas that indicate serious water penetration into the trim. Check caulking at seams and joints in the trim and at interfaces around windows and doors. Inform the customer that caulking is also part of routine maintenance and should be examined on a regular basis.

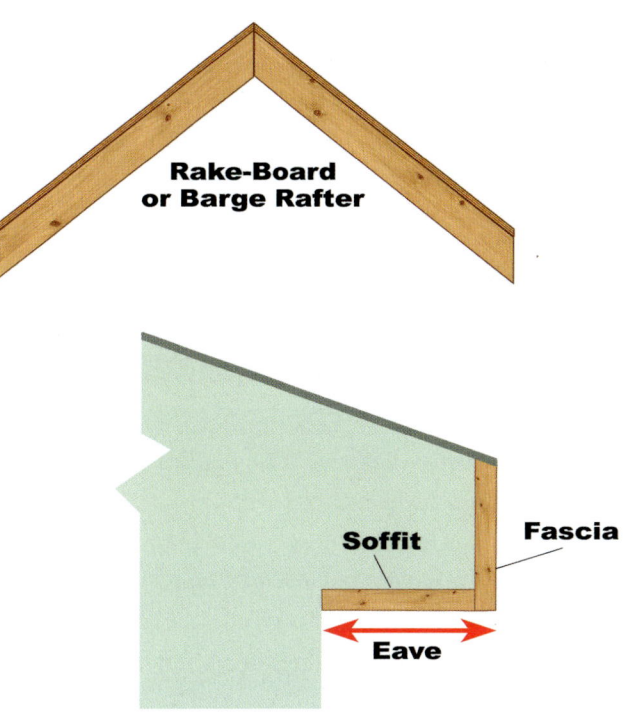

Illustration by Paddy Morrissey

Aluminum and **vinyl trim** are, for the most part, maintenance-free. The home inspector should examine it to make sure that the pieces are properly installed, no pieces are broken or missing, and the trim is still securely fastened. Solid vinyl trim is relatively new and not typically installed correctly. It shrinks in the winter and gaps may appear. In the summer, it expands and if installed too tightly will warp or bow.

If exterior **wooden shutters** are present, examine them and tell the customer about the presence of wood rot or other deterioration. Try to assess what is going on with the siding behind deteriorating shutters. Sometimes the condition of the shutters can have a damaging effect on the siding they cover. When looking behind shutters, be careful—wasps like to build nest in places like this. Most shutters are decorative and nonfunctional and are not part of the inspection. Vinyl shutters, especially those painted a dark color, may fade or warp in the sun. These are cosmetic problems. Keep in mind that shutters in certain parts of the country prone to hurricanes are functional. You may see studs sticking out of the walls around windows and doors. You may also see threaded holes, which accept bolts for securing shutters too. If you run across these studs or threaded holes, make mention of the fact that the shutters may be stored until the next hurricane.

Check window boxes and planters for condition and examine their hangers and supports for decay. Many are designed to hold potted plants, not to be filled with soil and plants directly.

INSPECTING TRIM

- Wood rot
- Broken or split pieces
- Loose or missing pieces
- Loose nails
- Painting and caulking
- Proper installation

Miscellaneous structures may be attached to the outer wall, such as decorative boxes holding lighting fixtures and niches in the wall. Examine each for deterioration. Boxes holding any electrical work must be waterproof, so check weatherproofing and make sure the box is firmly attached to the wall. Check caulking around these structures.

Window Construction

All exterior window components are inspected during the exterior inspection. Although **most** standards of practice state that a representative number of windows must be checked for operation, that's done after the home inspector goes inside the house.

The components showing on the exterior of the window are the **sashes** (upper and lower in the traditional single-hung or double-hung window), the **head** and **jambs**, the **sill** and **subsill**, and the **casings** around the window.

For a weatherproof opening in the exterior wall, building paper and/or adhesive flashing is applied around the window's nailing flange. Ideally, flashings or drip caps are present at the top of the window. Vinyl and aluminum siding may be installed with **J channels** around openings that the siding fits into, forming a channel to direct the water away from the building. If not, caulking is required around windows as it is with other siding materials.

> ### Definitions
>
> A <u>window sash</u> is the frame-work that holds the glass or other material. The <u>window frame</u>, which surrounds and holds the sash, is made up of a top piece called the <u>head</u>, side pieces or <u>jambs</u>, and a bottom piece or <u>sill</u>. The window <u>casing</u> covers the edge of the window frame where it meets the wall covering.
>
> A <u>J channel</u> is a manufactured component of an aluminum or vinyl siding system that has a curved channel that the planks fit into. J channels are used around window and door openings to make a weather-tight seal.

Illustration by Paddy Morrissey

There are many styles of windows. One of the most common is the **double-hung window** with two sashes that move. The upper sash is on the outside; the lower, on the inside. Windows may be **single-hung** where only the lower sash moves. A **slider window** has a sash that moves horizontally.

Sashes can be hinged into window framing to open in a variety of ways. The **awning window** is hinged at the top and opens outward. A **hopper window**, often found in basements, is hinged at the bottom and opens inward.

The **casement window** is hinged at the side to open outward. The **pivot window** pivots from a center hinge or pin. The **jalousie window** contains narrow strips of glass in a device that allows the strips to move together, lifting out from the bottom.

A **fixed-pane window** does not open or close. A **picture window** is basically a large fixed-pane window. **Combination windows** can be made up of a large fixed-pane window in the center between two smaller casement windows. Another configuration might be a fixed-pane window in the center with a slider at each end. Fixed-pane windows may have snap-in **muntin**

> **WINDOWS**
>
> SLIDING WINDOWS
> • Single hung
> • Double hung
> • Horizontal sliders
>
> HINGED WINDOWS
> • Awning
> • Casement
> • Hopper
> • Jalousie
> • Pivot
>
> MULTIPLE WINDOWS
> • Combination
> • Bays and box bays
> • Bow windows

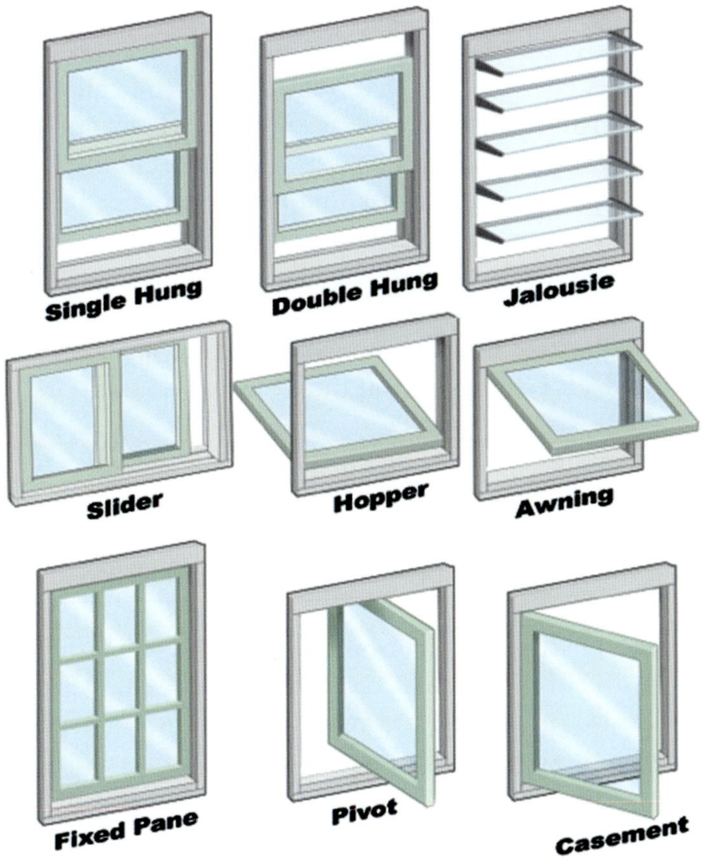

Illustration by Paddy Morrissey

bars (a grid of crossed pieces of wood, metal, or plastic creating a simulated divided-light window) that fit into the window. A true **divided-light window** has small individual pieces of glass set into wood or lead muntins, as in many historic homes. The reason for this was their limited ability to only make small pieces of glass hundreds of years ago and therefore numerous small windows instead of one large pane like today.

> **Definition**
>
> *Muntins are a grid of crosspieces of wood, plastic, or lead that hold small panes of glass in a divided-light window. Snap-in muntins made of wood or plastic can be applied to imitate a true divided-light window.*

Bay windows are made up of three windows set at angles to each other in a bay that is cantilevered from the structure. There is usually a larger fixed-pane window on the length of the bay with standard-size opening windows at each side. In a **box bay**, the windows are at right angles. A **bow window** is similar to a bay, but has more than three windows, each at an angle from the others.

Glazing is a term that refers to a window pane made of glass or another material. Each piece of glass is called a **light**. You can have one or more pieces of glass in a window. If you had six pieces of glass in the upper sash and a single piece in the lower sash, the window would be called a six over one window. You can also have multiple thicknesses of glass as in a double or triple pane window.

Insulated glass is the generic term for multi-paned windows. It has a space between the panes, which, in cold climates, may be filled with an inert gas such as argon. Triple panes may be three layers of glass or two outer layers of glass with a Mylar layer in between. A type of glass that reflects heat while allowing light into the room is called low-emissivity (low-E) glass, which is made by applying an ultra-thin metallic coating to the glass. Hard-coat low-E glass is made by applying tin directly to the molten glass during the manufacturing process. It is designed for storm windows and is not commonly used on traditional insulated glass windows. It is applied to the exterior surface of the glass, while soft coat is applied to the inner surface of the glass between the panes. Soft-coat low-E glass is produced by coating the glass with silver in a vacuum. Because the silver coating on soft-coat low-E glass is fragile, it is used only on the inside of double- or triple-pane windows.

> **Definition**
>
> *Glazing refers to the glass or other material that sits in the window framework or sash. Each pane of glass is called a light.*

In some windows, manufacturers used a layer of low-E plastic film between two panes of glass, effectively adding a third "pane" to the window. However, over time, the film tends to pull loose from the edge, leaving wrinkles in the plastic between the glass panes and forcing homeowners to replace the windows as they are no longer transparent.

Soft-coat low-E glass is prone to oxidation (tarnishing that results when the silver coating is exposed to air) most commonly as a result of a failed seal. Argon gas prevents this oxidation, while also preventing a convection loop from forming in the air space between the panes, thereby greatly increasing its efficiency.

All new windows come with a label from the National Fenestration Rating Council (NFRC) so that potential buyers can compare different brands. The efficiency of windows is determined by the U-value or U-factor and solar heat gain coefficient (SHGC). The lower the U-value and SHGC, the more energy-efficient the windows. Typical Energy Star windows in a cold climate have a U-value of 0.30 or lower, while homes in sunny warm climates may have an SHGC in the 0.23 range. The U-value and SHGC vary greatly depending on the climate in which they are installed.

When multiple-pane windows are cracked or the seal is broken between layers of glass, air and water vapor leak into the space. Condensation may be seen between the panes. Leaking multi-pane windows discolor. This is primarily a cosmetic problem because the loss of energy efficiency is negligible, with the exception of argon-filled windows, which do lose efficiency with a broken/leaking seal. Although this is not typically an efficiency issue, replacing many unsightly windows may prove costly to the homebuyer.

Glazing can be **transparent** (clear) or **translucent** (semi-opaque) by design. Shower doors, for example, are often translucent (obscured glass). The home inspector may come across plastic, acrylic, and polycarbonate glazing as well as glass.

The home inspector is not required to report on the effectiveness of **safety glazing**. However, for your information, safety features include the following:

- **Tempered or safety glass:** This type of glass is difficult to break. When it does break, the pane shatters into small, smooth-edged cubes. Tempered glass is required for certain applications, including shower doors, shower/tub windows, entry doors, low windows, and patio doors.

- **Laminated glass:** A plastic inner layer between panes holds broken pieces together if the pane cracks or shatters. This type of glass is mostly used in areas prone to hurricanes, to prevent penetration of the building envelope and pressurization of the house, which may cause the roof to blow off the building.

- **Wire mesh:** The common misperception is that the embedded wires reinforce impact strength, when they do just the opposite. The wires actually weaken the glass and substantially reduce its impact resistance, so wired glass is only half as strong as ordinary tempered glass. When it breaks, wired glass is more dangerous than regular glass because the exposed wires are razor-sharp and catch a victim's body, thereby increasing the severity of the injury. This should be written up as a potential safety hazard.

> **INSPECTING WINDOWS**
> - Sagging header, rusted or rotting lintel
> - Missing flashings
> - Rotted framing
> - Broken or discolored glazing
> - Loose or missing caulking
> - Level and plumb
> - Storms and screens

Inspecting Windows

When inspecting windows, remember that the window is an interruption in the wall structure and an opening in the siding system. The interruption to the framed structure must be supported by a header between the studs. As an opening to the siding, the opening must be properly sealed and weatherproofed.

The home inspector should pay attention to the following aspects of windows during the exterior inspection:

- **Header:** Watch for sagging headers above large windows. Rusted lintels can cause cracking above the window and allow water to leak into the window flange and frame. Probe wood at the top of windows for wood rot.

- **Flashings:** Check for the presence of flashings above windows. Flashing is not always there. Instead, there may be a wood drip cap molding over the top of the window casing. These moldings can rot easily. They're often unpainted on the back, and water, instead of being deflected off the edge of the molding, seeps behind the back of the molding. Probe them for wood rot. Windows under overhangs should be protected from these problems.

Code Check

Window Flashing

The window flashing essentially extends the window flange. WRB is integrated shingle fashion to the flange. Numbers indicate flashing & caulking sequence.

©2012 Code Check

> **Section Note**
>
> *"For a house with wood shingles, I get up on the ladder to check out the windows to see if the casings and frames are rotted out too. If they are, I would have to inspect every window on the house."*

- **Framing:** Inspect wood casings, frames, and sashes for wood rot. The sill is especially vulnerable to rot and should be probed even if a new layer of paint covers it completely. Note other damage such as loose or detached framing pieces, loose nails, deteriorating paint, rust or corrosion on metal framing, and insect damage.

- **Glazing:** Inspect glass and report broken, cracked, or foggy window panes that may indicate a broken or failed seal. Check that the putty or glazing compound holding the glass into the sash is not loose, cracked, or missing.

- **Caulking:** Examine caulking around the casings to make sure the window is sealed where it meets the siding. Caulking should not be loose, missing, cracked, or broken. When J channels are present, check to see that they form a seal with the window opening.

- **Level and plumb:** If window frames are distorted and no longer form right angles at the corners, there may be defects in the structure. Windows pulled out of square can be the result of more serious structural problems such as foundation settlement. Try to find the cause of any distortion you see.

- **Storms and screens:** Where weather is cold, storm windows are used to protect older homes against heat loss. With many types of windows, such as double-hung, storms are attached to the outside of the window. Hinged windows opening outward have storms for the inside. Examples are casement, pivot, and jalousie windows. In older homes, you may see triple-track or self-storing windows. These windows consist of two panes of glass, each operating along its own track, with a screen or storm window on a third track in between. The screens and storms can be switched out when the seasons change. Self-storing storm windows have both a glass storm window and a screen that remain in place year-round and can be adjusted (switched) depending on the outside temperature.

> **Section Note**
>
> *"Remember the construction worker I mentioned who brought home different siding materials for building his own additions? Well, this same fellow got his windows from the job too. The inspector had to inspect each one, not just a representative number of them, because every single window in the house was different."*

The inspection of storm windows, although not required by most standards of practice, should describe both the materials used in construction and their condition. Report storms with cracked or broken glazing and deterioration of materials or putty. If storms are present on the house, make a note if any windows are missing them. Keep in mind that storms and screens are swapped out seasonally. The screens may be piled up in the garage or basement during the winter; the storms likewise in the summer. If condensation appears between the storm and primary window, the home inspector can tell which of the two windows is leaking. If moisture appears on the storm, the inner window is leaking air from the house. If moisture appears on the inner window, the storm is leaking air from the outside. Make sure that the bottom of storm windows have openings, or weep holes, for drainage. If they are not present, the bottom of the sash can rot.

> **BASEMENT WINDOWS**
>
> *Don't forget to inspect basement windows. Homeowners often forget about them. Watch for leaking, rot and rust, broken glass, and missing putty.*

If screens are present, check them quickly for general condition, paying attention to those that are bent, broken, or torn.

Inspecting Doors

All outside doors should be inspected and operated during the home inspection. Entry doors can be single-hinged doors, French doors, or sliders such as a patio door and fixed window combination. Some doors are solid wood, vinyl, fiberglass, or steel, while others have partial windows or large lights set in a frame. The entryway may have side lights (small windows on one or both sides of the door) and a transom (small window above the door). There may be only a single door or the addition of a screen or storm door.

NOTE: Any entry door should be fire resistant. Some codes require a fire rating on these doors. There may be a manufacturer's metal label on one edge of the door, usually on the hinged side, indicating the rating.

> **INSPECTING DOORS**
> - Condition
> - Door operation
> - Framing
> - Caulking
> - Header
> - Level and plumb
> - Storm and screen doors

The inspection of exterior entry doors includes the following:

- **Condition:** Pay attention to the door itself, noting whether it's solid, paneled, made of wood, fiberglass, or metal, or is partially or completely glazed. Make note of damage to the surface of the door, warping, cracked or broken panels, and deteriorating finishes. When glazing is present, inspect for broken glass and discoloration, indicating a leak in the seal. Check the condition of the seals, putty, or glazing compound.

- **Operation:** Open each entry door and check its operation. Inspect hinges on hinged doors. They should be tight and large enough to support the weight of the door. If the door rubs the frame, loose or too short hinge screws can be the cause. Many heavy doors are only screwed into the jamb and not the framing behind, causing the door to sag or tilt away from the hinge side and rub on the jamb or drag on the threshold. Swing the door open and watch for easy movement. If weather stripping is present, inspect it to be sure it is firmly attached. If not, recommend that it be repaired or installed if missing or painted over. Check the lock hardware to be sure it works. Make note of double cylinder locks (keyed both inside and outside) as a potential safety hazard. You must have the key to exit, and it may not be readily accessible in an emergency or fire.

  With **patio doors (sliders)**, slide the door open and check that the bearings or rollers are running smoothly on the metal or vinyl tracks. Sliders that stop halfway along the track may have dirty or worn tracks and bearings that don't work. Movement can also be impeded by distortions of the frame and by a sagging header or lintel bearing down on the door. Check that the lock hardware is working. Be sure that the door is not installed backwards. This is a security/safety issue. The operable side should be inside the fixed side.

> **ABOUT SECURITY**
>
> *It's best that the home inspector refrain from commenting on how secure a house is. Report malfunctioning locks and door hardware, but don't comment on how good you think the locks are. Security and level of risk is a personal attitude.*

- **Framing:** Inspect casings and door framing for wood rot. A door has, in addition to its head and jamb framing, additional framing pieces called stop moldings that restrict the movement of the door. At the foot of the door is the threshold that keeps out the rain. Around this additional framing is the casing or brick mold. All of these pieces should be inspected for wood rot and for broken, loose, or missing pieces. The threshold acts like the window sill and is particularly susceptible to wood rot. Also make sure the bottom edge of the door is equipped with a sweep that fits tightly against the threshold.

- **Caulking:** Door openings should be caulked the same as windows. Inspect the caulking and make sure it's secure, not cracked, not broken, and not missing in any areas. Check J channels too, if present.

- **Header:** Watch for sagging headers, especially double doors and wide openings such as sliding door and window combinations. French doors are a likely candidate for issues. Rusted lintels and rotted and broken headers can cause the door frame to distort and door operation to be impeded.

- **Level and plumb:** As with windows, distortions of the door frame can indicate structural problems with the house. Use a 4′ level above large expanses of doors and windows to check that the line is level.

- **Storm and screen doors:** Depending on the season, a storm door or screen door or combination storm/screen door may be present. Storms and screen doors are installed on the outside of the stop moldings and open outward. They can be made of fiberglass, metal, or wood. Although not required, we advise the inspector to examine storm doors and screens and make note of any defects. A new issue that has become problematic is the installation of storm doors in front of fiberglass or composite doors. Many manufacturers prohibit the use of storms in front of their doors to prevent overheating and warping of the primary door. Many manufacturers also prohibit painting the doors dark colors, which may also cause distortions in the doors or plastic trim. Note the presence or absence of safety glass. Slide open outer screen doors that accompany sliders and point out to the customer any faulty operation. Report if screening is missing, torn, or loose.

> **DON'T EVER MISS**
> - Rotted wood on trim and on windows and doors
> - Broken, loose, and missing pieces

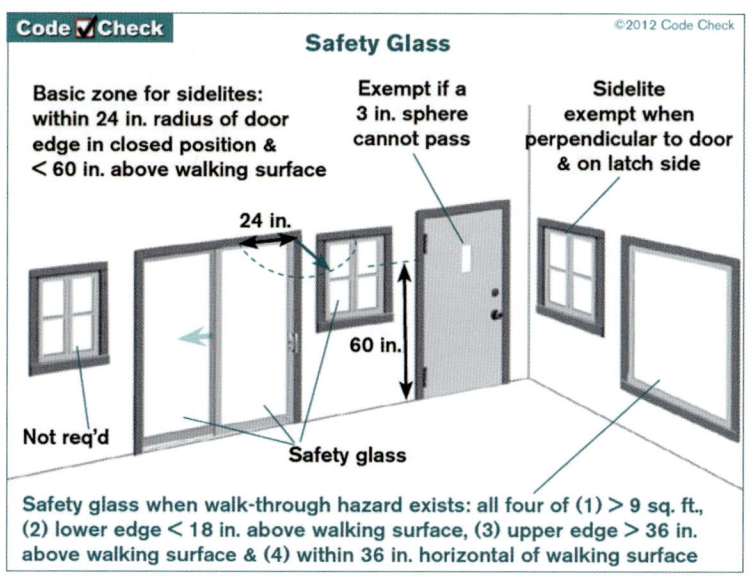

Reporting Your Findings

Sometimes it seems as if you can't possibly write everything in the inspection report except the important findings. Yet you'll be seeing many small details when you're inspecting the windows and doors. You should at least *talk about* these minor points with the customer during the inspection. You see how important communication is.

As you record your findings of the trim, window, and door inspection, be sure to record the following:

- **Trim:** Identify the materials used in trim, soffits, and fascia boards. Then report on their condition, noting defects such as wood rot.

- **Caulking:** Your report should have room to record your findings on the condition of the caulking. Identify its general condition as satisfactory, marginal, or poor.

- **Windows:** Identify the type of windows and the materials used in the window framing. Rate the general condition of the windows and be sure to record your comments on specific defects you've found, such as rotted sills, cracked glazing, and so on. Also, we suggest that you identify the type of storms and screens and their condition.

- **Doors:** Take the time to list each exterior door (front entry, patio door, and so on) and write your findings for each one. For example, the front entry door may be in perfect condition, but the back door may have a serious defect. A general rating applied to all doors is not detailed enough.

> **Section Note**
>
> *"Sometimes the little things you notice make a good impression on the customer. Pointing out a torn screen, trying the doorbell for operation, and testing door locks convinces them that you're paying attention to every little detail. That's why we suggest some items beyond the normal standards of practice. Let's say it's because of salesmanship.*
>
> *It's not that you have to write up these details, but that they become part of your ongoing conversation with the customer."*

2.4 AROUND THE HOUSE

In addition to the siding, trim, windows, and doors, many other items are part of the exterior inspection of the house. The following other exterior items will be studied in this section:

- Attached or adjacent structures such as steps, porches, balconies, and decks

- Driveways, walks, and patios

- Grading that affects the foundation

- Retaining walls

> **Chapter Note**
>
> *Pages 128–140 present procedures for the inspection of the many other exterior elements that must be inspected.*

Steps and Stoops

The home inspector should inspect all exterior stairs and stoops to patios, balconies, decks, and entryways. Codes vary across the country and over time regarding handrail/guardrail requirements, dimensions of risers and treads, and other regulations. The home inspector would be well advised to check with local building codes for information.

All **risers**, the vertical portion of the steps, should be the same height. Heights allowed are generally from 7–8″. Some steps are constructed with open risers, that is,

Definitions

The <u>riser</u> is the vertical portion of a step. The <u>tread</u> is the horizontal portion of the step.

The <u>stringer</u> is the side supporting member that supports the stairway. <u>Balusters</u> are the vertical poles that support the railing of a staircase.

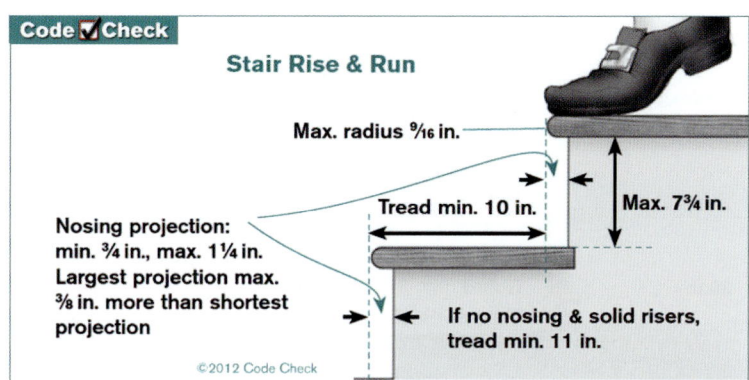

with the vertical area below each step left open. Codes in most areas forbid open risers due to the safety hazard of a child falling through to the floor below. The **treads** are the horizontal portions of the steps that you walk on. They should be of even depth, generally from 9–11″. The treads (nosing) are allowed to extend over the riser 1 1/4″. Codes also vary about **handrails**. Generally, when there are more than three risers or the height is greater than 30″ from the ground, a handrail/guardrail is required. Where steps are very wide, a handrail may be required on each side or down the middle.

When inspecting exterior steps, the home inspector should check the following items:

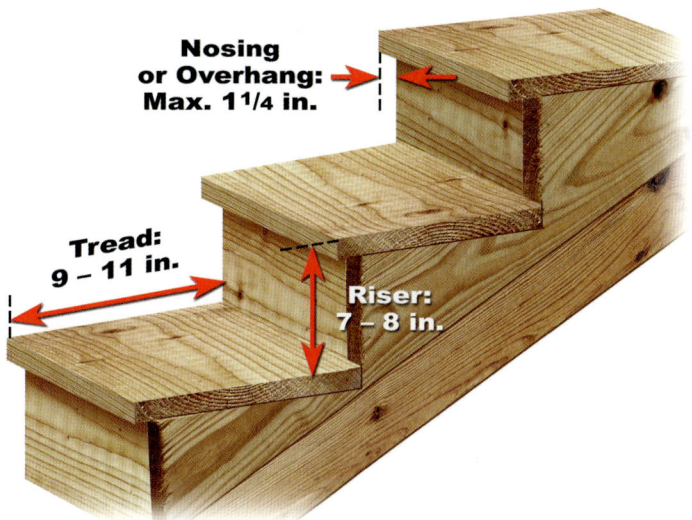

Illustration by Paddy Morrissey

- **Landing at the top:** When steps lead to an entry door, the platform at the top should be large enough to stand on (3′ minimum) while opening an outward swinging storm door or screen door. When the platform is too small or you have to stand on the steps, this should be reported as a safety hazard.

- **Condition of materials:** With wooden steps, the first requirement is that the steps must be sturdy enough to support

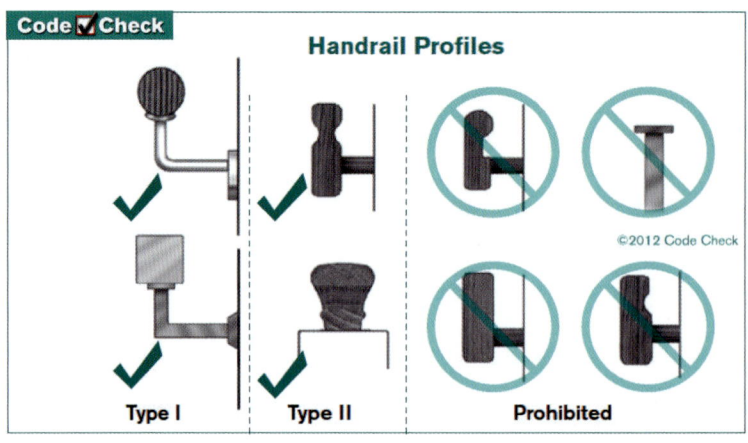

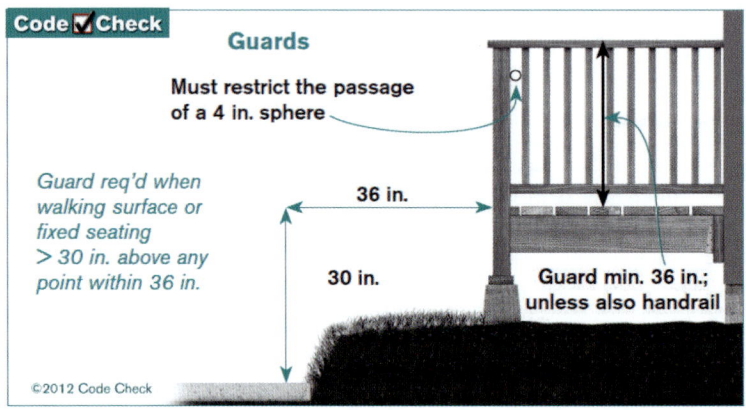

SAFETY HAZARDS

- Platform/landing too small
- Rotting boards
- Loose stone, brick, or mortar
- Uneven risers and treads
- Loose or missing handrails
- Balusters too far apart
- Cracking or tilting stoops

the weight of a person. Steps should not be too flexible or springy. Inspect for damage, especially at the base of the stringers and any area where wood may be in contact with the soil. The home inspector may want to advise the customer to remove outdoor carpeting from wooden steps or decks because it holds moisture and promotes decay. Make sure all fastenings are tight. Report any dangerous conditions such as rotting boards or protruding nails as a safety hazard. If composite materials are used, note that they are typically slippery when wet.

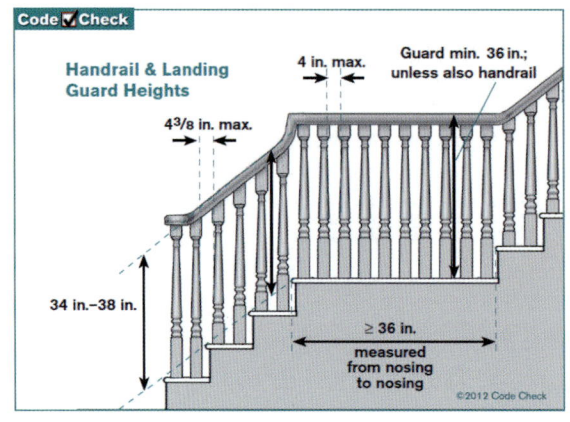

Steps may be made of concrete, stone, or brick. Inspect for loose stones and bricks and check to see that the mortar is in good condition. Loose stones or bricks should be reported as a safety hazard.

- **Risers and treads:** Inspect risers and treads for appropriate dimensions and pay attention to whether risers are of uniform height and treads are of uniform depth. Unexpected differences from one step to another can pose a trip hazard and should be reported as a safety hazard.

- **Handrails:** Inspect handrails carefully. Know your local code as to when handrails are required. Handrails should be of the proper height—roughly 34–38″ high, but vary according to local codes. Balusters or spindles, which are the vertical poles in the railing, should have gaps of no more than 4″ to prevent children from falling through. Check that handrails are securely fastened at the bottom and where they connect to the house. Missing and/or loose railings and balusters should be reported as a safety hazard.

For Your Information

Find out what your local code is regarding exterior steps and stoops. We've seen areas of the country that require a guardrail for landings and decks that are as low as 18″ above the ground.

Photo #11 *These steps and the concrete stoop at the top have been patched and painted numerous times. Unfortunately, in a freezing climate patches don't fare too well.*

Stoops can be made from brick, stone, concrete block, or poured concrete. Precast concrete stoops are available, brought to the site, and mounted on concrete piers that extend below the frost line. The home inspector should inspect stoops for cracking, which can present a trip hazard. Check to see if mortar on masonry installations is in good condition.

The soil below a stoop can settle, causing the stoop to settle or tilt as well. If the stoop tilts toward the house, it can drain water toward the house and press against and damage the foundation. A stoop tilting significantly away from the house can be dangerous to walk on, especially in freezing climates. Customers should be advised that either of these situations should be fixed.

Porches

A porch is a roofed extension of the house that is built as part of the house, as opposed to a deck, which is a separate attached structure. When inspecting a porch, inspect the porch stairs for the conditions and hazards outlined on the preceding pages. Also inspect for the following:

Photo #12 *Porches can be very complex structures such as this or a simple extension of the house roof over an entry.*

INSPECTING PORCHES

- Deteriorating supports
- Sagging and leaking in roof and ceiling
- Decaying floors
- Safety hazards in steps and railings

- **Supports:** Porch columns and posts support the roof above and below the floor system. They may be wood, metal, poured concrete, brick, or stone. Columns and posts should have their own footings to prevent settling and heaving. The home inspector should look under the porch to determine if the support materials are in good condition, inspecting for wood rot, mortar deterioration, settling, and so on. The floor joists and beams should be inspected from underneath to determine whether they're properly installed to support the dead and live loads on the porch floor, whether they're in good condition, and whether they're properly supported at their ends.

- **Roof structure:** The home inspector should eye the roof of a porch to spot sagging. The ceiling of the porch will most likely be covered with finishes such as plastering, stucco, drywall, or wood. But the inspector should look for sagging in the ceiling, indicating leaking into the roof structure or beams that have warped or lost their bearing on the support columns. Be sure to probe ceilings, trim, and fascia for wood rot.

- **Floors:** Open porches are built with a floor that tilts away from the house to allow rain to drain away. Porches that are later enclosed often keep the same pitched floor. Examine floors for wood rot. As with wooden steps, a wooden porch floor should not be covered with outdoor carpeting because it holds moisture and promotes decay.

- **Railings:** Porch railings are required for porches that are more than 30″ above the ground. Baluster requirements vary also, but their spacing should be 4″ or less as mentioned above. Be sure to report any variation from these requirements as safety hazards. This may seem like a minor detail. However, toddlers can squeeze their bodies through openings of less than 5″, and there are tragic stories about children getting their bodies through balusters and hanging themselves. So be serious about reporting safety hazards.

Decks

A deck is basically a platform that is attached to a house, but is an independent structure. Decks can be attached, adjacent, freestanding, and completely open to the weather, as is most common, or roofed and partially or completely walled or screened. The key to identifying if a deck is part of the house structure or is independent is in the supports. A deck is not built on the house foundation; it is usually mounted on columns and posts and attached to the house with a ledger board.

With decks, inspect the following items as described for porches in the preceding text:

> **INSPECTING DECKS**
> - Deteriorating supports
> - Floorboard spacing
> - Finish stain and treatments
> - Wood rot
> - Loose fastenings to house
> - Safety hazards on steps and railings

Photo #13 *Not only is this deck in bad shape, but it's also about 10′ above the ground. Note the cracked rim joist, the direction of the floor joists, and their spacing.*

- Steps
- Supports
- Floors
- Railings

A special aspect the home inspector should pay attention to with regard to **deck supports** is that wooden support posts should have their feet above the

THE EXTERIOR INSPECTION   133

ground on piers. Probe the wood below the ground for wood rot and insect damage if you find them buried, which is quite common. If possible, check beneath the deck for the presence of wood rot in the joists. Some decks are built so close to the ground or are entirely closed in that ventilation is poor and decay is promoted and access limited.

The wood used for decking is often pressure-treated, protecting the wood from termites and rot, but staining and the use of water repellents are suggested to make it truly weather resistant. Staining and treatment is usually done only for redwood and cedar decks. Most pressure-treated decks are left natural. Point out decks that need to be restained and that need water-repellent treatments. Some decks with expensive and exotic woods such as Ipe (eepay) last a very long time without any type of finish or stain.

Floorboards that are not properly maintained can cup and check, holding more water as the process progresses. Space also should be left between the floorboards when they are laid so that water can drain and evaporate at the seams. Check carefully for wood rot in flooring and at the header joists at the perimeter of the deck.

The **fastenings** by which the deck is secured to the house should be inspected. Fastenings should be secure so that the deck doesn't separate from the house. There may be nails, metal hangers, bolts, or lag screws (lag bolts should be recommended if not present). Structural deck screws also are now available as well. These special screws are used instead of lag bolts and through bolts. Lateral load connectors are also required. Simpson Strong-Tie is a useful resource for products such as these. Inspect the area for wood rot and corroded fastenings. If certain types of pressure-treated wood are used, double hot-dipped galvanized or stainless fasteners and specially treated joist hangers are required because the chemicals used to treat the wood can quickly corrode certain metals.

INSPECTING BALCONIES
• Safety hazards on railings and balusters
• Water penetration at junction with house
• Wood rot
• Shaking, sagging, and tilting

Balconies
A balcony is defined as a platform protruding from the house that may or may not be supported by the ground. Balconies can be built on cantilevered joists extending to the exterior or on joists fastened to the interior framing with supports on the ground. Some balconies have exterior supports such as cables or wood that support the balcony from above. All framing members on balconies should be inspected for **wood rot**—supports, joists, flooring, railings, and balusters.

Problems are common where the balcony meets the wall of the house. Beams and joists cantilevered out can protrude through and be crushed from the weight of the balcony at this point. Check for joist-to-wall flashing—where it's absent, water often penetrates into the intersection and promotes decay within the wall.

Be cautious when stepping onto a balcony. Balconies often aren't used and can be neglected. Test the balcony first for **stability**. In general, if you notice shaking, sagging, or tilting of the balcony when stepping onto it, report the condition as a safety hazard. Be especially suspicious if it's covered with carpeting, as the balcony may be rotted underneath, which isn't visible.

Patios

A patio is a flat, paved area abutting the house, made of stones, concrete pavers, bricks, or a poured concrete slab. A patio should **slope slightly away** from the house to prevent water from running toward the foundation. Inspect stone and brick patios for **trip hazards**—pieces tilting up with a raised edge, pieces missing, and surfaces deteriorating. In concrete patios, there shouldn't be any unplanned cracks. Offset/raised cracks in the surface should be reported as a trip hazard. If patios have railings, fencing, or side walls of brick or stone, inspect them for their condition.

> **PATIO SLOPE**
>
> *A patio should slope away from the house so as not to send water flowing toward the foundation.*

Photo #14 *Someone added terracotta tile to a patio slab that was already too high. Look at the tile height compared to the threshold of the French doors. Where do you think the rain will go on a windy day?*

Walks and Driveways

Walkways can be made of concrete, bricks, pavers, gravel, or flagstones. Sidewalks on the property should be inspected for their condition and whether they pose a **trip hazard**. Always report trip hazards. The sidewalks can have cracking or uneven settlement that can easily trip people.

Sidewalks near the house should not slope toward the house, especially those that abut the foundation, for obvious reasons. Water should flow away from the foundation.

Driveways may be dirt or gravel or be paved with brick, pavers, asphalt, or concrete. Driveways should be inspected and the following types of problems noted:

> **INSPECTING WALKS AND DRIVEWAYS**
>
> - Trip hazards
> - Negative slope
> - Pitting, upheaval, and sunken areas

- **Pitting** can occur as a result of poor-quality materials, poor installation, acid spills, or the use of salt as a deicer. Extensive salting in cold climates can deteriorate an old or inferior concrete surface.

- **Upheaval** can be caused from poor construction, an insufficient base, tree roots, and even stones that move to the surface after years of frost heaving. If the condition is extensive, a complete replacement may be called for, especially if a construction deficiency is the cause. If tree roots are causing the upheaval, removing the tree will eventually halt the process, but the damage to the drive or walk must still be repaired or the drive or walk replaced.

Photo #15 *This is a typical walk with a trip hazard. It could be due to settling, frost heave, or tree roots. Safety hazards should always be noted in your inspection report.*

- **Sunken areas with cracks and breaks** are caused by uneven soil settlement. If the damage is not too severe, mud-jacking the paved area may solve the problem. Mud-jacking is a method of leveling a concrete surface by pumping grout or foam through the concrete from below to raise the surface.

2.5 LANDSCAPING AND GRADING

During the exterior inspection of the house, the home inspector should pay attention to the **vegetation** and the **grading**, or slope of the land, around the house. The basic concern during the home inspection is to determine whether landscaping and grading cause damage to the exterior and the foundation. The principles are simple:

AT THE FOUNDATION

- No reverse slope of ground sending water toward house
- No potentially damaging vegetation too close to house
- Window wells in good condition

- **Principle #1:** Vegetation and grading should not encourage water to flow toward the house.

- **Principle #2:** Vegetation should not be allowed to damage siding, trim, screens, and roofing or pose the potential of doing so.

As you inspect the exterior of the house, take note of the slope of the land at the foundation. The land should slope away from the house. A proper slope is 6″ within the first 10′ from the house. Land with a reverse (negative) slope sends excess water toward the foundation and eventually ends up in the basement or may damage the foundation in areas with expansive soils.

In some cases, adding additional backfill to slope the land away from the house solves the problem. That may pose an additional problem at basement windows, which would then be below grade. **Window wells** may be recommended to prevent water penetration through the windows.

Photo #16 *This is what happens when the grade is so bad that the only solution is to dig a moat around your house.*

If window wells are already in place, they should be inspected for drainage, for the presence of a good gravel base, for corrosion of the metal well siding or rot if constructed of wood, and for absence of debris buildup. If there's a water line (stain) on the basement window, you'll know that drainage is poor. Some window wells have plastic domes to deflect rain away. Inspect the domes for cracking, breakage, and debris. If metal grills appear over an egress window well, inspect them for corrosion and breakage. Some window wells are installed for the purpose of emergency egress (exit). Recent construction practices call for the installation of at least one window well for the basement. Additional window wells are required if bedrooms are present in the basement. Report egress window well grills/grates that are fastened or bolted in place, as they must be removable without tools. Report grills with sharp cutting points and those that are significantly corroded as safety hazards.

Make one trip around the house just to look at grading and vegetation. Note the presence of **trees** close to the house. These trees can lead to root problems with the foundation and sewer lines, messy gutters, and falling overhanging branches. Where areas are too shady, siding may not have the chance to dry out and moss, mildew, rot, and algae can thrive. Point this out to the

Section Note

"We were asked to inspect a house when the owners brought a lawsuit against the builder. I don't think I've ever felt quite so sorry for a young couple as much as this one. The builder had messed up so badly and resisted the only workable solution because of the expense. He had suggested digging out the land around the house, which would have had the result of this house sitting in a hole with an elevated driveway and garage. What a jerk."

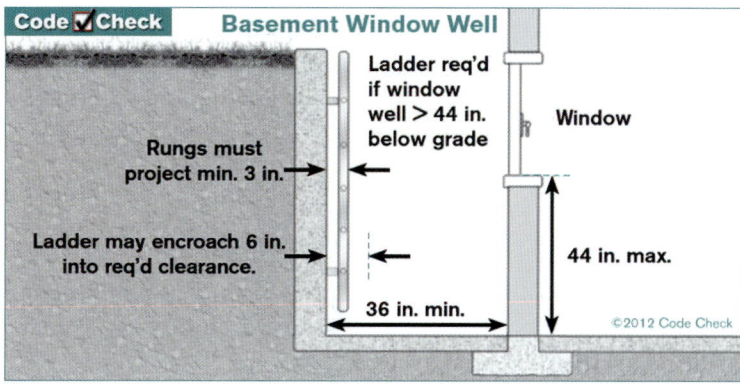

THE EXTERIOR INSPECTION

> **Section Note**
>
> *"Keep your eyes open when walking around the house looking at vegetation. One inspector I'm acquainted with stepped into a pile of leaves only to discover that the leaves were hiding a tarp lying over a 6′ deep hole. He broke his leg as a result."*

customer and suggest that trees be trimmed back or removed if they present a danger.

Vines on the house may be pretty and cozy, but it's not a good idea. They can hold moisture and promote insect damage. English ivy has a very strong grip and can puncture paint surfaces, grow behind siding and loosen it, damage mortar joints, and even grow under sills. Vines keep the siding from drying out. The home inspector should inspect the siding for damage and note the lack of access or visibility of the underlying siding. If there is none, it should be recommended that the customer monitor the situation.

Shrubbery near the house should be trimmed back so that there is about a one foot clearance from the house to prevent moisture retention and allow access for maintenance, such as painting, caulking, and window washing. Loose and mulched soil in **flower beds** should not touch wood siding or cover the top of the foundation. Leaves and plant debris should be raked away from the house.

2.6 RETAINING WALLS

The home inspector should inspect retaining walls on the property that **affect the foundation or structure of the house and/or garage**. This includes those that are close to the house or present an imminent safety hazard. Other retaining walls, according to most SOPs, do not have to be inspected.

> **Definitions**
>
> *A <u>tieback</u> is used to anchor a wooden retaining wall to the soil behind it. Each tieback has an <u>anchor post</u> that connects to the wall and extends back into the soil. A <u>deadman</u> is a crosspiece spiked to the anchor post at the end in the soil.*

- **Wooden retaining walls:** Horizontal walls of wood are fairly common in residential construction. The walls are usually built to lean back toward the high side. Wood members are connected to each wall with metal spikes. Gravel fill is often added behind the wall; the soil above meets the wall to allow water to run over. Weep holes are present, or the wood joints allow water to drain through the wall.

  The wall may be professionally anchored to the soil through the use of **tiebacks** with an **anchor post** and a **deadman** crosspiece. The tiebacks are staggered between every second or third vertical pier. Vertical anchors are used with walls over 30″ high. These anchors are placed about every 10′ along the wall and extend about 4′ into the soil. You can tell if tiebacks are used if you see the end of the member between the horizontally stacked members (much like the header course in a solid brick wall).

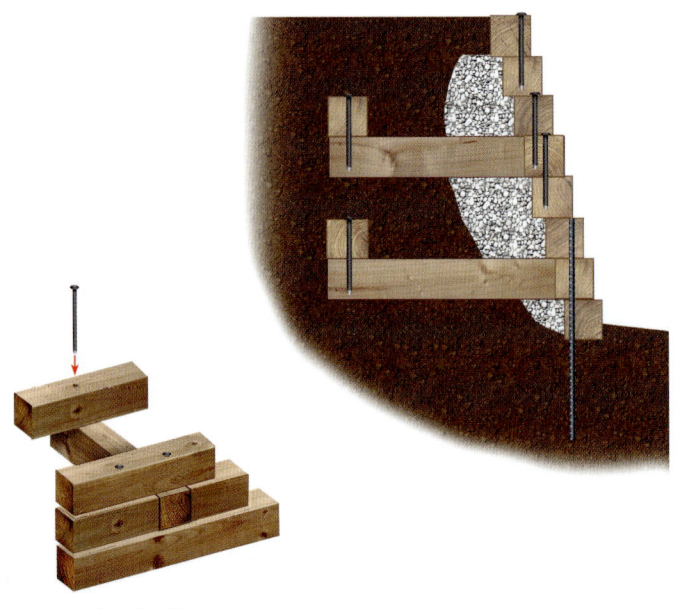

Illustration by Paddy Morrissey

- **Precast concrete:** New wall systems on the market are made of interlocking concrete sections that also make use of tiebacks. These blocks come in various sizes and shapes with decorative stone-like faces.

- **Poured concrete:** A retaining wall made of poured concrete reinforced with steel can be like an inverted T, where the crosspiece is buried below the soil to prevent the wall from tilting forward. Such a wall has its footing below the frost line to prevent heaving and is equipped with drain holes near the bottom.

- **Masonry walls:** The home inspector will find masonry retaining walls too. Often, these types of walls, especially those of stone, are dry-laid and move out of position rather easily.

- **Pile walls:** Normally, vertical steel members are driven into the ground until they resist the pressure of the soil beneath them. Wood pile walls can work in sandy soil or gravel.

> **INSPECTING RETAINING WALLS**
> - Soil too low behind wall
> - Poor drainage
> - Tilting or bowing
> - Cracking or deterioration

Water is the main cause of **retaining wall problems**. When inspecting retaining walls, first look behind the wall for holes or depressions in the soil where water can pool. The soil should come to the top of the wall to allow the water to go over the top. Water-saturated soil pushes against a wall, causing movement and bowing. Sight down the wall and use a level to determine the lean of the wall and to inspect it for **bowing**. Most walls are tilted back into the hillside, so a plumb wall can be an indication of a developing problem.

Look for **drainage holes** toward the bottom of the wall and for evidence that the drainage holes are working. Wood and block or stacked stone walls have natural openings, so weep holes won't be present.

Report **cracking** in poured concrete walls and suggest that they be patched/repaired and monitored for ongoing movement.

Reporting Your Findings

During the exterior inspection, be sure to communicate with your customer continually as you inspect attached structures, the walks and driveway, the grading and vegetation, and the retaining walls and fencing. Talk about what you're inspecting and what you're finding. Here's an overview on how to record your findings of the exterior inspection:

- **Walks and driveway:** Identify the types of sidewalks present and state their general condition. Note if walks are pitched toward the house and if any trip hazards are present. Identify the type of driveway material and report on its condition. Again, note any trip hazards.

> **DON'T EVER MISS**
> - Missing handrails and railings
> - Balusters too far apart
> - Unstable railings and supports
> - Trip hazards
> - Rotted wood
> - Reverse grading
> - Poor retaining walls

- **Patio:** Identify the patio material and report its condition. Don't miss reporting if the patio is sloped toward the house or has trip hazards.

- **Balcony:** Record any safety hazards with balconies. Remember, any missing balusters or railings, any balusters too far apart, loose railings, rotted wood, or instability in the balcony constitute potential safety hazards. Note the general condition of the balcony.

- **Deck:** Note the deck materials and their general condition. You might want to record whether wood decks are treated, painted, or stained, and comment on the condition of the finish.

- **Stoops and stairs:** Identify the materials used in construction and note the general condition of the stoops and stairs. Be sure not to miss any trip hazards.

- **Porch:** If the home has a porch, identify the construction materials and state the general condition of the porch and note defects with the structure. Be sure to identify the type of support piers present, noting that they're not visible if you can't see them. Make a special note if the porch is missing a railing that is needed for safety.

- **Retaining wall:** Identify the type of retaining wall present and record any defects you find with it.

- **Landscaping affecting the foundation:** It's important to indicate the location (east, west, north, or south side of the house) of any reverse (negative) grading found during the inspection and to suggest additional backfill or window wells if that's a viable solution. The situation may be such that you recommend that a soil engineer be called to look at the grading.

- **Safety hazards:** When you find safety hazards during your exterior inspection, it's a good idea to record them on the page for that part of the inspection and on a summary page at the back of your report. Don't miss them. Pay attention to balusters that are too far apart, missing handrails, loose railings, and dangerous balcony conditions.

> **Chapter Note**
>
> *Pages 140–149 present procedures for the inspection of the garage. This inspection normally includes the garage roof and electrical work. These two aspects of the garage inspection are presented.*

2.7 INSPECTING THE GARAGE AND CARPORT

The final item we're going to study on exteriors is the garage and/or carport, whether attached or detached. The complete inspection of the garage or carport includes the following:

- Siding and trim

- Windows and doors

- Structure

- Floors
- Vehicle door and automatic opener
- Electrical

This chapter won't emphasize the roofing, drainage, or electrical systems. These items are presented in other chapters.

Siding and Trim

Garages may be separate structures completely **detached** from the home. Detached garages may have been constructed at a different time than the house and may be built with different materials, siding, roofing, etc. Other garages may be **attached**, sharing a common wall or walls with the living area of the house. Attached or interior garages may also have rooms above them, a type of garage known as a tuck-under garage. Tuck-under garages are particularly problematic from a fire separation and safety perspective, as will be discussed later.

Photo #17 *Tuck-under garages have special problems when it comes to fire-separation. The ceiling of the garage is usually just open framing and often with the kraft-facing on the insulation facing the wrong way. Since there is living area above, car exhaust and potentially fire can get into the house.*

Inspect the **siding of the garage** with the same diligence you did the house. Identify the type of siding present and report on its condition. Pay attention to the following as described on pages 94–118 in this chapter:

- Deterioration of siding
- Joints and interfaces
- Loose or missing components
- Fastenings
- Warping, cracking, buckling, and detachment
- Caulking
- Water penetration

Next, inspect the **exterior trim** on the garage. Check the trim as you did with the house as described on pages 118–120. Be particularly careful when you examine a detached garage, which may have had less attention paid to it than the house.

Sometimes, homeowners paint the house more frequently than the detached garage, haven't caulked as often, or replace trim on the house but not the garage. When you inspect the garage trim, pay attention to the following:

> **INSPECTING THE GARAGE**
>
> - Siding and trim
> - Windows and doors
> - Structure
> - Fire separation
> - Floors
> - Vehicle door and automatic opener

- Wood rot
- Broken or split trim pieces
- Loose or missing pieces
- Loose nails
- Paint and caulking condition
- Proper trim installation

Windows and Doors

The home inspector should inspect windows and doors to the garage as stated in pages 120–128. Be sure to operate all "people" doors and inspect them as you would other exterior doors. (We'll talk about the vehicle door starting on page 146.) Examine **doors** for the following:

- General condition
- Door operation
- Framing
- Caulking
- Header
- Level and plumb
- Any storm or screen doors

There should be no direct opening between the garage and a bedroom. In other words, you can't walk directly into a bedroom from the garage. If you can, this is a safety issue and must be recorded in your report.

The **passage door** from the garage into the house should be fire rated. Fire rating is expressed as the number of minutes the door will resist the spread of fire. A door between a garage and the residence must be rated at least 20 minutes (the rating will appear on a tag on the hinge edge of the door). Under most local codes, a 1 3/8″ thick solid wood or steel door may also meet fire rating requirements. The door should have self-closing hinges (or mechanism) and be weather-stripped too including a threshold and door sweep. The door or walls of the garage that open to or are adjacent to the living area may not have windows installed in them. You will find many carports that have been converted improperly (without a permit) to a garage. Improper passage doors and the presence of windows should be reported as a **safety hazard**.

Photo #18 *This is a label from a "fire door." As you can see it's only a 20-minute rating, which is why wood or metal doors also qualify without an actual rating label.*

Inspect **windows** from the exterior and the interior, of the garage. Garage windows may be fixed-pane windows or an opening variety. Windows in the garage should be examined just as carefully as those on the house. At this time in the inspection, garage windows should be opened and tested for smooth operation. In many cases, these windows are never used and may not work very well. They even may be painted or nailed shut, which should be pointed out to the customer. Inspect all garage windows for the following:

- Framing
- Glazing (broken glass)
- Caulking and putty
- Level and plumb
- Operation - latches/locks

Inspecting the Structure

Garages, particularly the structure of the garage, can be neglected from the start. Builders may supply less than adequate bracing. Often, detached garages are built without proper foundations and footings, with the wood frame (sill plate) sitting directly on the slab. Homeowners often pay less attention to the condition of the garage than they do to the house. Don't make any assumptions about garage structure after viewing the house. Conditions may vary considerably, especially in detached garages.

> **Section Note**
>
> "One of my inspectors was inspecting a one-car detached garage and found the sill entirely rotted out. He was curious, I guess, to see how bad the problem was and gave the side of the garage a nudge. He held his breath as the side of the garage tilted, lifting about 3" up at his side, hung there, and finally settled back down. A stiff wind could take that garage down. The inspector was extremely thankful that he wasn't the one to do it."

When you begin the inspection of the garage, look it over **from the outside**. Pay attention to any evidence of racking, twisting, tilting, or sagging. Eye the line of the roof for evidence of structural failure.

Once on the inside of the garage, check the visible structure, as they are often not finished (dry walled). Don't overlook the **ceiling joists or truss cords**. Often, garage ceiling joists are only intended to prevent rafter spread and to keep the walls from spreading and are not intended to support storage or to be used for attaching engine hoists. Homeowners often store equipment on top of the joists. Although it is not within the standards of practice to determine the structural strength of a framing member, however, any damage or sagging should be noted.

Note the condition of the visible framing. Be sure to check at the base of walls for a **rotted or insect-damaged sill plate**. If wood framing is sitting on the slab, the sill is likely to have some damage to it. Inspect the rest of the garage structure for the following:

- Warping, twisting, and sagging
- Cracked, rotted, and cut members
- Loose fastenings
- Water penetration
- Delamination of sheathing
- Proper supports in place and secured

Distortion of the garage framing can be noticed by the fit of the doors, especially the vehicle door. If the framing is racking or twisting, the doors may not fit their frames, rub, be hard to operate, or have gaps.

Safety Concerns

There are two main safety concerns with the garage. One is being **fire resistant**, and the other is protecting the living area of the house from **car exhaust fumes** and **gasoline vapors**.

> **SAFETY HAZARDS**
> - Absence of fire separation
> - Passage door not fire rated
> - Exposed flammable or combustible insulation
> - Sources of ignition (heating system, water heater, or dryer) less than 18" above garage floor

Any surface of the garage interior that abuts the house—abutting walls and the garage ceiling—should be fire resistant and sealed against exhaust fumes. Wood frame walls between the garage and living area should have drywall on both sides of the studs with finished (mudded and taped) joints. Of course, the passage door should be fire-rated, solid-core wood, or metal (as mentioned above), and self-closing.

These abutting walls and ceiling (if living space present above) should be **insulated** to the same degree as the exterior walls of the home. Insulation may not be visible to the home inspector, may be seen in holes or gaps in the wall facings, or may be exposed. Combustible insulation such as polystyrene and polyurethane foam should have a fire-resistant covering. You may also find plastic or kraft-faced fiberglass insulation left exposed, which is also combustible. If the insulation is exposed and is combustible, it should be reported as a **safety hazard**. Exposed combustible insulation is quite common in garages.

Gasoline leaking from the car, lawn mower, or other sources poses a danger. Gasoline vapors are potentially explosive and can ignite easily. These vapors are heavier than air and tend to hug the floor. Any source of ignition in the garage

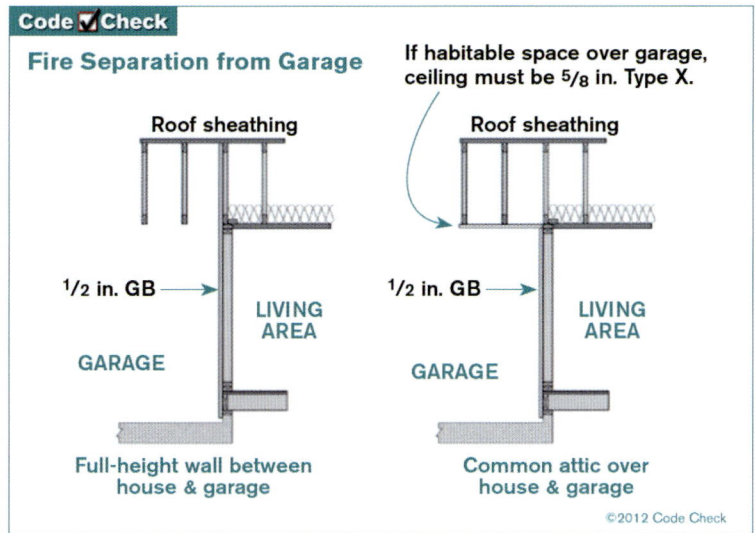

should be at **least 18″ from the floor**. Undiluted gasoline vapors could ignite when they hit the open flame of an oil or gas burner or electric switch. At the recommended height, gasoline vapor is diluted enough for safety. An exception to this rule is if flammable vapor ignition resistant (FVIR) water heater is in use. FVIR water heaters do not have an exposed flame, and they may be installed directly on the floor. Report any deviations from these standards as **safety hazards**. It is common in southern parts of the United States to have the washer and dryer in the garage. This violates the 18″ rule and should be written up as a **safety hazard**.

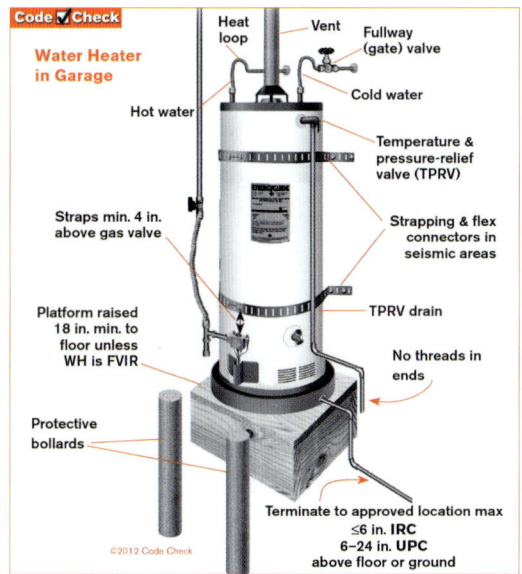

The Floor

The home inspector first identifies the type of floor in the garage. It could be dirt, gravel, asphalt, or wood, but is most commonly a concrete slab. An asphalt floor that is an extension of an asphalt driveway may be seen in carports but should not be present in an enclosed garage.

> **Section Note**
>
> It's time to visit some garages. After studying this section, you'll notice things in them you haven't noticed before. Pay attention to the structural members of the garages. See if you can find storage over joists not meant to support the weight. Check the garages for firewall, for proper passage door, and for flammable insulation.

The **concrete slab floor** in the garage can be laid too thin—it should be at least 3 1/2″ thick—with or without steel reinforcement. Inspect the floor for the following defects:

- **Settling fill:** Concrete slabs are generally laid on grade on fill. Some may not have a layer of gravel for drainage or a moisture barrier. Later, the fill settles or washes away, causing the concrete slab to settle, twist, or fall. The home inspector can tap the floor in suspect areas. A hollow sound indicates voids under the slab. If the floor has settled, there may be a line of concrete still adhering to the walls where the slab once sat.

- **Cracking:** Minor cracks in the slab are quite common and may not indicate any structural problem with the garage, but they should still be reported. Serious cracking is another story. Cracks that run from wall to wall may indicate that the foundation has settled or that footings have failed. They should be investigated for causes. Cracks around sunken or hollow areas will indicate that the slab is settling.

- **Spalling:** The surface of the slab may crumble away. This can result from salts (snow with road salt melting from vehicles) that penetrate the floor.

- **Drainage:** The garage floor should have a slope to it or a floor drain to allow water to flow/drain away. The home inspector should check any garage drains for condition. Often, these drains are neglected and become plugged or broken. If the slab is settling or low in places, water may not be able to flow from the garage or toward the drain.

The home inspector may come across a situation where the **garage is built** over **a room**. In this case, the floor may be constructed of heavy timbers or of steel-reinforced concrete. The suspended wooden floor can rot. The suspended slab can experience rusting in its steel structural members, causing spalling of the concrete. The floor system may be weak, but this situation is very difficult to assess during the general home inspection. The home inspector should inform the customer of this and recommend that a **structural engineer** be called in to determine the condition of the suspended garage floor. You may also find the tuck-under garage with open framing overhead and insulation and ductwork fully exposed. This should always be written up as a safety hazard.

Vehicle Door

The vehicle door to the garage may be made of wood, aluminum, steel (most common), Masonite, or fiberglass. The home inspector should identify the door's materials and condition, noting broken panels, loose joints, deteriorating paint, unpainted surfaces, and so on.

Hinged doors: The home inspector should open these doors and test for smooth operation. With these heavy doors, rubbing can indicate a problem with the hinges, which should be strong enough and tightly secured. The doors may sag from their own weight unless properly braced to lift the outer edge up. When you open hinged doors, notice if there is the right amount of clearance for them to swing open freely. Do the doors bang into a wall of the house? Has vegetation grown up to restrict their movement?

> **VEHICLE DOORS**
> - Hinged
> - Swinging
> - Manual overhead
> - Automatic overhead

Swinging doors: This type of door swings up to open. Lifted manually, the entire door swings overhead without "bending." It is assisted by a mechanical system of counterweights and/or springs. The door should be tested for smooth operation and its hardware inspected.

- **Manual overhead doors:** Overhead doors are made of hinged horizontal sections that "bend" along overhead tracks as they are opened. The home inspector should operate this type of door. The movement should be smooth. Manually operated overhead doors should hold their position when raised about one-third of the way up. They should rise by themselves above that point and lower themselves below that point. Make sure the springs are properly tensioned. The door's weight should be counterbalanced by the spring tension. It should be noted if the doors close with too much force. Doors with exposed springs must have a safety cable run within them to contain them if the springs were to break. If movement is difficult, check for dented or twisted tracks, loose bolts, rusted rollers, and so on. Note if door panels are cracked or broken.

  NOTE: We often find wood overhead doors, both manual and automatic, painted on only the exterior side. Usually, a manufacturer's sticker or stencil is still on the inner side of the door saying that the entire door should be painted. Be sure to point this out to your customer if the inside isn't painted. When the door has paint on only one face, it can warp and rot.

- **Automatic overhead doors:** Always test the operation of automatic doors. First, run them up and down while noting how freely they move. There should be no noise such as squeaks and no halting or jerking movements. Noise and halting indicates a maladjustment in the motorized mechanism or in the hardware.

The home inspector must check the automatic door for **safety**. There should be two **safety reverse features** on a modern door, which will automatically reverse the movement of the door if it encounters an obstacle upon closing. This feature is especially important to families with pets or small children. Do not attempt to stop the door with your hands. You can hurt your back. Place a block of wood at the door opening and close the door. Testing of the electric eye feature can be performed by blocking the beam, which should be mounted within 6″

> **DON'T EVER MISS**
>
> - Rotting siding or trim
> - Rotted sill
> - Structural problems
> - Missing firewall
> - Passage door not fire-rated
> - Exposed flammable insulation
> - Improper heights of passage door and mechanical equipment
> - Springs without safety cables
> - No safety reverse on vehicle door

of the floor. The door should reverse when the block of wood is touched or the beam is blocked. A malfunctioning safety reverse feature must be reported as a **safety hazard**.

As with the manually operated overhead door, check the automatic door and its hardware for condition. Again, you might find the inside of the wood door unpainted.

Reporting Your Findings

Be sure to continue your ongoing conversation with the customer as you inspect the garage. Although the garage is a relatively small structure, there are so many features of the garage to discuss—from both the exterior and inside of the garage. Point out what you're inspecting and what your findings are. Be sure to discuss any safety hazards you find in the garage, such as a missing fire separation, dangers from exhaust fumes, a malfunctioning safety reverse feature on the automatic door, and so on.

Your inspection report should have a separate page or portion of a page for reporting on the garage. Don't skimp on reporting space for the garage. There's a lot to report. Here's an overview of what to report:

- **Garage information and structure:** Define the type of garage you inspected with terms such as attached, detached, two-car, and so on. Note the condition of the garage structure, giving its overall structure a rating of satisfactory, marginal, or poor. Note defects such as racking, problems with ceiling joists, rotted sills, inadequate support columns, and so on. We suggest that you write a recommendation to call a structural engineer to evaluate a suspended slab when the garage is built over a room.

- **Fire issues:** Be sure to report on the presence or absence of a properly rated passage door to the house. Record whether the proper firewall separation is present. Make a note of the type of insulation present and identify exposed polystyrene or polyurethane insulation and kraft paper as a **safety hazard**. Keep in mind that these fire safety issues only apply to enclosed garages and not to carports.

- **Siding and trim:** As described earlier in this section, record the type and condition of the garage's siding and trim. Pay attention to the caulking job on the garage and rate the caulking as to condition.

- **Vehicle door:** Identify the type of door present and report on its condition.

- **Automatic opener:** Indicate whether an automatic opener is present, whether it operates, and whether the safety reverses operate. Be sure to report a **safety hazard** if either safety reverse feature is not functioning.

- **Floors:** Describe the type of floor in the garage and write your findings on its condition. Make note of both typical cracking and large cracks that may be present.

- **Safety hazards:** For those safety hazards listed here, report them on the garage page of your report and repeat them again on a summary page. That way, customers can look over a single page to be reminded of any safety hazards found on the property.

  — Improper passage doors to the house
  — Sources of ignition within 18″ of the floor
  — Absence of firewall
  — Exposed combustible insulation
  — Safety reverses on automatic openers not operating
  — Absence of safety cables at exposed springs

> **SAFETY REVERSE FEATURE**
>
> *The home inspector is required to report whether or not any garage door operator will automatically reverse or stop when meeting reasonable resistance during closing.*

CHAPTER 3
THE ROOF INSPECTION

While the structure of the house ranks number one in importance to the home inspector when judging how sound a home is, a wet basement and a leaky roof tie for first place in customer concerns. The customer will concentrate on the roof covering, wanting to know if it needs to be replaced. The home inspector inspects the roof for the condition of the covering, the soundness of the structure, water penetration, the condition of the chimney and flashings, and the effectiveness of drainage.

Inspection SOP

These are the standards of practice that guide the inspection of the roofing system. Please read them carefully.

> **Chapter Note**
>
> *Pages 151–160 outline the content and scope of the roof inspection. It's an overview of the inspection, including what to observe, what to describe, and what specific actions to take during the inspection. Study these guidelines carefully.*
>
> *These pages also present cautions about inspecting the roof. Please read them and take heed of the potential of injuring yourself or damaging the roof during the roof inspection.*

ROOFING SYSTEM

Observe and/or Report: The act of making a visual examination of a system or component and reporting on its condition.	• The inspector *should* inspect the roof covering materials from the surface of the roof • Type of roof coverings • Vantage point from where the roof was inspected • Evidence of active or previous water penetration or abnormal condensation on/in building components • Evidence of previous repairs to the roof covering material, flashing details, skylights, and other roof penetrations • Roof drainage systems; gutters, downspouts, roof drains, and scuppers
Describe: Report in writing a system or component by its type (or other observed characteristics) to distinguish it from other components used for the same purpose.	• Roof covering material(s) • Roof ventilation system(s) • Roof drainage systems; gutters, downspouts, roof drains, and scuppers
Report as deficient deficiencies in:	• Fasteners, if accessible and/or visible • Adhesion • Roof covering materials • Flashing details • Skylights and other roof penetrations

INSPECTING THE ROOF
• Roof coverings
• Roof drainage systems
• Flashings
• Chimneys
• Roof penetrations
• Water penetration and condensation

Not every detail on what to inspect and what to report is given in these SOPs. But they do serve as a good outline of what is expected from the home inspector during the inspection of the roof.

The **main purpose** of the roof is to protect the house from the elements—wind, snow, rain, and sun. The home inspector must determine how well the roof can do its job. The roof also provides *some* protection from falling objects, although not enough to protect the house from falling trees. Contrary to popular belief, the roof does *not* serve as an insulator to keep out the cold, with the exception of new state-of-the-art homes with unvented attics and insulated roof decks.

This section presents information on the **exterior roof inspection**. This inspection goes hand in hand with the inspection of the roof's structure and deck or sheathing. The home inspector cannot separate the structural inspection from the exterior inspection of the roof.

When you're on the roof, you need to be conscious of what's going on underneath. When you're inside the attic, you need to remember the indicators (sags, bulges, soft spots, etc.) you saw on the outside.

Here is an overview of the exterior roofing inspection as stated in the SOPs:

> **Chapter Note**
>
> *This chapter presents the exterior roof inspection, not the inspection of the roof's structure.*

- **Access:** Probably the most important information the home inspector can record in the inspection report is how much of the roof was visible and from what vantage point the roof was inspected. In fact, the SOPs state that the home inspector is **required to report methods used to inspect the roof**. This is to protect the home inspector from later lawsuits. New homeowners with a leaking roof want to blame someone, and that blame usually initially falls on the home inspector. If the report clearly states that only 30% of the roof was visible due to snow coverage (documented with a photo) and that the roof had to be inspected from the ladder at the roof's edge, the inspector is probably legally covered.

We'll talk more about when it is and isn't safe to get on a roof. Note that the SOPs say that the home inspector is **not required to walk on the roof** when walking could damage the roof covering or could be unsafe.

> **REMEMBER**
>
> *The inspection of the roofing system includes the garage roof too, even if it's a detached garage.*

- **Roof coverings:** The home inspector examines the roof of the house and garage(s) to determine their approximate age and identifies the style—gable, mansard, flat, and so on. The **type of roof covering** is described. Examples are asphalt shingles, wood shingles and wood shakes, modified bitumen (often called roll roofing), built-up roofing or tar & gravel roofing, metal, slate, foam, TPO, EPDM, PVC, and

Photo #1 TPO ROOFING

Thermoplastic polyolefin or TPO is a single-ply membrane type roof covering. It is not likely that you will find it in residential applications, with the exception of condominiums.

clay or concrete tile. The home inspector inspects the **condition** of the roofing, looking for defects such as improper installation, curling, cracking, cupping, missing pieces, moss buildup, nail pops, water ponding—and the list goes on.

Although not required, customers also expect the home inspector to estimate the roof covering's remaining **useful lifetime**. We use a simple system of reporting expected lifetime in our inspection reporting App or software. A report of **satisfactory** means that the roof covering will last more than five years, **marginal** is used to indicate that the roof covering will have to be replaced within the next five years, and **poor** is used when we determine that the roof covering needs to be replaced now or very soon

Photo #2 EPDM ROOFING

This is another flat roofing material, ethylene propylene diene monomer or EPDM for short, that is used on commercial roofs. This too is not typically found on residential buildings; although you may run across it once or twice in your career.

THE ROOF INSPECTION

Photo #3 PVC

Poly vinly chloride, PVC, roofs have been around for quite a long time. Yes, it's the same material as your drain piping with a UV coating. They use heat-welded seams.

Illustration by Paddy Morrissey

Definitions

Flashings are a type of sheet metal or plastic used at joints between building components to prevent water penetration. Flashings in the roofing system are used in valleys and at hips and ridges where roof and walls meet, and around chimneys and penetrations through the roof, such as vents.

The *ridge* is the horizontal intersection of two sloping roof surfaces. A *valley* is the trough formed by the junction of two sloping sides of the roof.

A *dormer* is a structure built out from the roof slope, having its own roof and walls.

(at most, within the next year). (That's explained to the customer in the report.)

- **Flashings:** The home inspector examines the flashings used in the roofing system. Flashings are necessary to protect the roof in **valleys** where different roof sections meet, where roof and walls meet at a lower roof or a **dormer**, around chimneys and other penetrations through the roof, and at the edge of the roof. The inspector is required to identify the **materials** used, such as copper, aluminum, plastic, rubber, or galvanized steel. The inspector must report the **condition** of flashings and whether the flashing is rusted, UV-damaged, bent, loose, leaking, improperly installed, or missing.

  Where flashings are covered with tar, they should be reported as not visible (or possibly not present) beneath the tar for inspection.

- **Chimneys:** The home inspector inspects the chimney(s), noting the location on the roof. For the home inspector's protection, it is a good idea to record from where the chimney(s) were viewed. The material of the **chase** (the structure through which the chimney flue is run) is identified and its condition noted. The inspector checks for rust, deteriorating mortar, and leaning. The **chimney cap or crown** over the chase is inspected to see if it is rusted, cracked, broken, or missing. The **flue material** is identified and the flue checked for condition. (There may be a spark arrestor and/or rain cap that restricts visible access to the flue.) The home inspector may recommend that the flue be cleaned and evaluated. Of course, chimney flashings are inspected.

- **Roof penetrations:** Whenever a vent or skylight is penetrating the roof, the home inspector examines the flashings around that penetration for water tightness. Skylights are inspected for physical condition. The home inspector may note cracked or broken glazing (plastic or glass) or condensation between the panes or bubbles.

NOTE: The SOPs state that the home inspector is not required to observe attached accessories such as antennae, satellite dishes, solar panels, etc. But, if these accessories have a detrimental effect on the roof, it should be reported. It is also potentially an issue with regard to access or visibility if these accessories block the roof covering.

The home inspector examines the attachments of such accessories to the roof surface to see if they are securely attached, have proper flashings, or are the cause of leaks. Some homeowners have an antenna or satellite dish strapped to the chimney or a vent, which can result in damage to the chimney or vent. When heavy accessories such as rooftop package HVAC units are present, the home inspector checks the attic to see if the roof's structural members can support this additional weight or if there is evidence of failure of the framing components.

- **Water penetration:** Leaks through the roof are not always discovered from the exterior. The home inspector should enter the attic to see what damage has been done. But from the surface, the home inspector watches for signs of leakage in the roof coverings and through areas where flashings are present. Roofs leak where the roof starts, stops, or changes direction. They rarely leak in the middle.

> **Definitions**
>
> The <u>chimney chase</u> is the outer construction (box) that encloses the flue. The <u>chimney flue</u> is the tube that carries gases, fumes, and smoke from furnaces and fireplaces. The <u>chimney cap</u> is a concrete, stone, or metal covering for the top of the chase.

> **Photo #4 ROOF PENETRATION**
>
> *Here we have a chimney and three attic vents all of which penetrate the roof. These should all be "flashed" to prevent water entry into the building.*

THE ROOF INSPECTION

- **Drainage system (gutters and scuppers):** Water should drain off the roof, but it also must drain in such a way that it doesn't collect around the foundation and cause water penetration into the basement or undermine the foundation. This is especially true in areas with expansive soils. Gutters and downspouts are inspected carefully to make sure they're not rusted or rotted, disconnected, or full of debris (the most common cause of failure). The home inspector also checks extensions to downspouts, visible portions of underground drainage systems, and splash blocks to make sure water isn't draining/flowing against the foundation.

- **Structure:** Although the roof's structure is examined from the attic, the home inspector watches for any signs of structural problems while examining the roof from the outside. A wavy surface to the roof can indicate that rafters were improperly installed, sheathing is too thin, or there are too many layers of roofing.

Soffits that pull away from the wall with gaps at the frieze boards are an indication of rafter spread. A sagging or broken ridge line can be a sign of other structural problems. Falling through the roof, although very unlikely, is a definite sign of deterioration of some of the roof's structural members (usually the decking). Many first-time inspectors are afraid of falling through the roof. If there is going to be any failure of the roof structure, it is usually to the sheathing and not the rafters or trusses. That being the case, the worst-case scenario is that you put a foot through the roof, but it will not collapse beneath you.

INSPECTION TOOLS

- Solid and safe ladder
- Binoculars
- Probe
- Proper shoes
- Possibly a drone

Inspection Equipment
When inspecting the roof from the exterior, the home inspector needs the following:

- A ladder to get on the roof (typically a 17-foot Little Giant ladder)

- Binoculars for inspecting the roof from below

- A probe such as a screwdriver or an awl

- Soft rubber-soled shoes or boots that grip the roof surface

- Some inspectors now use drones with cameras to evaluate roofs. This is by no means required; it is also possibly illegal. Be sure to comply with all FAA regulations. However, many options are available.

A home inspector travels fairly lightly, without a large number of tools and without tools that take up too much space. The ladder is the only exception. Most home inspectors use their personal vehicles (a truck is not necessary and good gas mileage is essential) to get to the inspection site. You must have a long enough ladder, but you don't want that to dictate what sort of vehicle you drive.

We recommend a compact **extension ladder** called the Little Giant, which can also be used as a stepladder, perfect when inspecting soffits and fascia boards around the house. For getting on the roof of a single story home, you'll need at least 17′ of ladder, which the Little Giant gives you. This ladder will allow you to access the roof of a typical suburban house. If you are working in the city with older two- and three-story homes, you may want to invest in an extension ladder. Local market conditions and Client/Realtor expectations will dictate what type of ladder you need to perform your inspections.

No matter what brand or type of ladder you buy, make sure it fits safely in or on your vehicle, gives you the necessary extension, and is solid and safe.

Inspection Concerns

The best home inspection is conducted when the customer is present throughout the inspection, following the home inspector through each step of the inspection. In fact, we consider having the customer present to be the number one rule of home inspection.

Communication after the inspection is never as good as talking to the customer during the inspection. The educational process works best when the customer is present to see what is being inspected and what the findings are.

One obvious exception to that rule should be stated up front: *never, never, never* allow the customer to get on your ladder or get on the roof. You must consider yourself responsible for your customer's safety. There are too many horror stories that home inspectors tell when they get together. Inspectors fall off roofs. Some fall through roofs into the attic. Inspecting the roof is the most dangerous part of the inspection.

There are two other concerns the home inspector should keep in mind when inspecting the roof:

- The inspector's own safety
- Damage to the roof

Standards of practice explicitly state that the inspector is *not required to walk on the roofing when walking could damage the property or be unsafe to the inspector.* Take heed of these instructions. You don't want to hurt yourself or do any damage to the roof. The following list briefly discusses instances where the home inspector should exercise caution. Some are regarding the inspector's safety; others are listed because walking on the roof can damage the roof covering. (We'll talk about specific examples of roof coverings again on pages 166–189.)

> **Section Note**
>
> #1 RULE
>
> *The home inspector takes the customer along on the inspection . . .*
>
> #2 RULE . . .
>
> *but <u>never</u> up the ladder or on the roof.*

> **Section Note**
>
> *"One of my inspectors was inspecting a property on a frosty morning. He got on the roof from the south side where the frost had melted off. As he was inspecting the chimney, he stepped over the ridge to the north side without paying attention to the roof surface.*
>
> *You guessed it. The north side was still covered with frost and was very slick. The inspector slid down the roof and rolled off into a snow bank—unhurt, thank goodness.*
>
> *The inspector walked around to the south side again, where the ladder was. The Realtor smiled and asked, 'Did you get off the roof the way I think you got off?'*
>
> *We still tease him about it."*

- **Too steep:** Some roofs are too steep to walk on safely. You'll have to decide what you can navigate safely. Getting on a roof that is too steep may also cause damage by sliding and scraping granules off the shingles, especially on a hot sunny day, and the seller will expect you to fix the damage. Remember, walking *up* a steep roof is easier than walking *down* a steep roof. Before you get on the roof, make a decision about what's too steep. That's better than getting into trouble when you want off the roof.

- **Snow-/frost-covered:** Do not walk on a snow-covered roof. They can be very slippery, and home inspectors have been known to slide off. Snow covers up defects the inspector can't see. A heavy **frost** on a roof can also pose a dangerous slippery roof surface. Keep in mind that frost or snow may only cover the shady side of the roof and the other side may be perfectly accessible. Inspect and note what you can and can't inspect.

- **Wet wood shingles or shakes:** A wood roof becomes slippery in the rain. Even after a shower, when the shingles or shakes are thoroughly saturated with water, they're slippery. The home inspector also should exercise caution when walking on a dry wood roof. Usually, there's no problem, but some dry roofs can be slippery. The home inspector should not step onto deteriorated curled and cupped wood shingles and shakes because of the potential of breaking them.

- **Moss-covered:** Moss creates a slippery surface. You'll often find mossy roofs on the north side of a house or in areas under overhanging trees. Don't get on a roof that is covered entirely with moss. The sheathing may be damaged or rotted. If there are small patches of moss, be careful not to step on them.

- **Tile roof:** A tile roof is typically not meant to be walked on. You can't walk on clay tiles without damaging them. Inspect a tile roof from the ladder at several places around the house. Be sure to check local practices as there are certain parts of the country (for example, the Southwest) where **concrete** tile roofs are usually walked on during an inspection. You should be properly trained on how to walk on concrete tile roofs if you decide to inspect them from the roof's surface instead of a ladder.

- **Slate roof:** Never walk on a slate roof during the inspection because of the possibility of damaging it. Slate is a brittle roof covering that can crack and break if you walk on it. These roofs are also very expensive to have repaired, and they are slippery.

DON'T GET ON THE ROOF

- Too steep
- Covered with snow
- Wet wood shingles or shakes
- Covered with moss
- Tile roof
- Slate roof
- Asbestos cement shingles
- Curled asphalt shingles
- Corrugated plastic
- Soft or spongy
- And be cautious over cathedral ceilings!

Section Note

"One of my inspectors walked up a steep roof with no problem.

When it was time to get down, he began sliding and grabbed the chimney to stop himself. There was no way he could get off the roof without sliding off.

A neighbor finally noticed him and threw him a hose to wrap around the chimney, enabling him to work his way down safely—but not before the real estate agent snapped his picture! He made the broker's monthly newsletter—'Home Inspector Stranded on Roof.' Of course, when he visits this broker, they don't let him forget it."

Photo #5 *This is a sand-cast or pinto clay tile roof and is too fragile to walk on. You would destroy the roof if you walked on it. View it only from a ladder or from the ground.*

- **Asbestos cement shingles:** This roof covering is similar to slate in its brittle quality. Don't walk on this type of roof either. You can damage it, and you won't find replacement shingles because they haven't been made since the late fifties to early sixties.

- **Curled asphalt shingles:** When asphalt shingles curl at their tabs, it's a sign that the roofing material is at or beyond its useful lifetime. (The shingles curl up at the edges of the tabs. Cupping is where the shingles curl over and pucker in the middle.) Don't get on such a roof. You already know that the condition is poor. Shingles in this condition will only crack and break under your weight. It is better to point out the condition to the customer than to explain why you destroyed the shingles.

- **Corrugated plastic:** Some homes have a translucent corrugated plastic roof over patios or carports. This material is not meant to support the weight of someone walking on it. Its purpose is more for shade than water protection.

- **Soft and spongy:** If you're on a roof and the surface feels soft or spongy, get off the roof immediately. Go to the attic and investigate the situation from below. Only if you confirm a solid roof structure from the attic should you consider getting back on the roof. Keep in mind that certain parts of the country at different times in the past have allowed 3/8″ sheathing, which feels quite flimsy underfoot.

- **Cathedral or vaulted ceilings:** Use special caution on a roof over a cathedral or vaulted ceiling. Often, they're improperly insulated and ventilation is so bad under the roof that the plywood sheathing delaminates and is considerably weakened. We've had the experience of our home inspection staff stepping boldly around a roof over a cathedral ceiling and putting a foot right through

> **Section Note**
>
> *Different types of roof covering are defined and discussed in pages 166–189. Warnings about whether to walk on a particular type of roof are repeated in these pages.*

> **Chapter Note**
>
> *Pages 160–162 present some roofing terms and types of roofs.*

it. It's better to test each step before using your full weight. Walking close to the ridge (but not on it) and close to the valleys (but not in them) will help. Take photos to document conditions, access, and snow coverage.

3.1 GENERAL INFORMATION

The home inspector should be familiar with different types of roof styles and some of the terms used when referring to roofs.

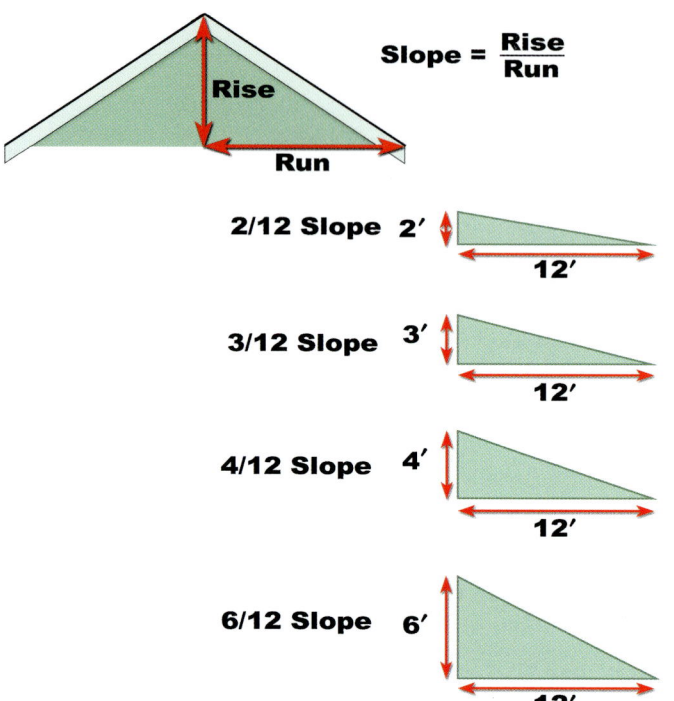

Illustration by Paddy Morrissey

Terms

The **slope** of a roof is also called the pitch. The slope is defined as the ratio of the **rise** of the roof to the **run** of the roof. The rise is the vertical height of the roof; the run is the horizontal length to the center of the roof (half of the whole span). The angle, or pitch, of a roof is calculated by the number of inches it rises vertically for every 12 inches it extends horizontally. For example, a roof that rises 6 inches for every 12 inches of horizontal run has a 6-in-12 pitch.

Roofs that have a slope of less than 2/12 are considered to be **flat roofs**. Flat roofs, of course, should not be perfectly flat. They should have a slight pitch for drainage purposes. Roofs with a slope between 2/12 and 4/12 are considered to have a **low slope**. What would be considered **conventional** roofing systems are those with a slope of 4/12 or greater. Various roof coverings are not appropriate for certain slopes. Wood shingles should not be used on roofs with a slope less than 3/12. A greater slope can add years to the life of most coverings; that is, the steeper the roof is, the longer the roofing will last. Again, wood shingles may last 20 years on a 3/12 roof and 30+ years on a 6/12 roof. That's because water moves off a steeper roof faster and the lower-sloped roof is more likely to leak. The flat roof, for which no kind of shingles are appropriate, must use a sealed roofing material such as a single-ply membrane, built-up or roll roofing.

Roofers use the term **square** as a shortcut to mean the amount of roofing material used to cover 100 square feet of a roof's surface. They may talk about so many squares needed to cover the roof. When determining how much weight the roof structure must support, engineers and architects think in terms of how much a square of a particular roof covering weighs. This becomes important when additional layers of roofing are added over the original. A roof built to

> ### Definitions
>
> The <u>slope</u> of a roof is the ratio of its rise to its run, where the <u>rise</u> is the vertical height of the roof and the <u>run</u> is the horizontal length of the roof to the center point. The slope is normally expressed with the measure of the rise over a run of 12″. A slope of 3/12 is stated as "three in twelve."
>
> The term <u>square</u> is used to indicate the amount of roofing material used to cover 100 square feet of roof surface.
>
> A <u>dormer</u> is a gabled extension built out from a sloping roof to accommodate a vertical window.

Illustration by Paddy Morrissey

support so many pounds per square may not be able to support a second layer of roofing (there should never be more than two layers of asphalt or wood shingles on a roof).

Types of Roofs

The home inspector should be able to name the basic style(s) of roof(s) present on the property. There are many styles and almost endless variations.

One of the most common roof styles is the **gable roof**. This roof style is made up of two equal (and opposite) slopes that meet to form a ridge. The term *gable* refers to the triangular areas at each end of the roof. Gable roof homes often have dormers in them, which have gable roofs of their own.

The **gambrel roof** has a double slope on each side, where the bottommost slope is typically the steepest. This type of roof isn't very common in residential homes, although you'll recognize it as a familiar barn shape.

The **hip roof** has a slope on all four sides. Each side may meet in a peak at the top of the roof. If a hip roof has a ridge line, the ridge won't extend the length of the house. Note that the gable roof runs the entire length/width of the house. A hip roof is named for the hips where adjacent sides meet. A home may have hip or gable roofs that intersect each other or both.

The **mansard roof** is a variation of the hip roof. The mansard roof is most often nearly flat on top with steeply sloping nearly vertical sides, although you'll find

SOME ROOF STYLES

- Gable
- Gambrel (Barn)
- Hip
- Mansard
- Shed
- Flat

Section Note

It's time to get in the car and take a ride around town looking at roofs. Look for interesting variations of the basic styles presented on this page. You may find the saltbox, which is a gable roof with one side having a longer run than the other. Or you might see a hip roof with a gabled section along the ridge line.

NATURAL ENEMIES

- Sun
- Rain
- Wind
- Trees
- Moss
- Snow and Ice
- Time

most mansard roofs with the top portion sloped up to a ridge line or to a center peak.

The **shed roof** is a single slope roof slanting in one direction (essentially half a gable). You may find a shed roof over an addition. Sometimes, dormers will have a shed roof instead of a gable.

The **flat roof**, as mentioned earlier, is most likely not really flat. It's actually a shed roof with a very small slope—less than 2/12.

3.2 NATURAL ENEMIES

Roof coverings don't last forever. Natural enemies work against them over time to wear them out.

- **Sun:** The constant exposure to ultraviolet radiation degrades organic materials in roof coverings. The covering continues to heat up and cool down. Too much sun on wood roofs dehydrates the shingles, causing them to become brittle. Thermal expansion and contraction can destroy adhesive materials in asphalt shingles, for example, and cause cracking in other roofing materials. The southern or southwestern exposure on a home often wears out faster than the northern or eastern, clearly showing that sun is the enemy.

- **Rain:** Although roof covering systems are designed to protect the roof's structure from water penetration, rain eventually takes a toll on any roof covering. Some materials used in roof coverings are soluble and will dissolve over time. Rain washes away granular or gravel finishes that have lost adhesion in roofing such as asphalt shingles and built-up roofing. Constant wetting of wood shingles can cause them to rot. Metal roofs are susceptible to rust.

- **Wind:** Strong winds can lift shingles off a building. Wind blows rain against a roof and can drive water under the edges of flashing, shingles, slates, and tiles. Wind can also blow sand against the roof's surface, causing erosion of the covering. Wind may also cause leaks that will only happen once due to the direction and velocity of the wind.

Photo #6 *Sun is the natural enemy of asphalt roofing shingles. As the granules loose adhesion, the sun degrades the tar and causes the roof to deteriorate.*

- **Hail:** Depending on where you live in the country, hail may be a serious concern. Hail can significantly damage a roof covering. Parts of the country prone to hail damage, such as "tornado alley" in the central United States, are limited to only one layer of roofing by building code.

- **Trees:** Homeowners may enjoy the cozy effect of trees overhanging their house, but those trees can do a great deal of damage to a roof. Branches that scrape back and forth over the roof's surface can remove the granules from an asphalt shingle roof or dislodge other types of roofing. Trees can provide too much shade and, as a consequence, can keep a roof from drying out after a rain. Wood shingles that are not allowed to dry out properly become rotten. Leaves clog drainage systems, causing water damage. Falling branches are an obvious problem to any roof.

- **Moss:** Moss reacts with the organic materials in wood and hastens its breakdown. Wood and built-up roofs are especially vulnerable to the decaying effects of moss. Its "root system" penetrates the surfaces and creates paths for water to get into and under the roof surface. On other roofing systems, moss rusts nails and impedes water runoff. It's also just plain slippery.

- **Snow and ice:** A phenomenon called **ice damming** can occur in northern climates when melting snow on the roof refreezes at the roof's eave. This causes an ice dam, or ridge of ice, to form. Water from melting snow higher on the roof becomes blocked by the ice dam and cannot escape to the gutters. This water backs up under shingles and seeps into the interior.

Illustration by Paddy Morrissey

Ice dams occur when heat from the attic (from inside the house) melts snow on the roof and the water flows down the roof and refreezes at the eaves. The water freezes because the gutters and eaves (overhangs) are not heated. As the ice

Section Note

Ice damming is caused by the temperature differential between the eave, where the temperature is below 32°, and the upper part of the roof (attic area), where the temperature is above 32° due to heat from the house.

Photo #7 *This is what happens when you have improper and/or inadequate ventilation and insulation.*

builds up, melting and refreezing water backs up under the shingles and seeps into the structure through seams in the roof sheathing, gaps around plumbing stacks, and nail holes. This ice buildup settles in the gutters and under roof shingles, causing roof damage. As the ice dams melt, water leaks into the house, damaging the walls and ceilings along the eave side of the house.

Proper attic insulation and ventilation as well as a waterproof underlayment applied to the roof deck can prevent ice dams from forming. Better attic insulation and ventilation can typically remedy this situation.

- **Time:** No roof covering lasts forever. This chart shows the estimated natural lifetime of various types of roof coverings.

ROOF COVERING	LIFE EXPECTANCY
Asphalt three-tab shingles	15 to 20 years
Architectural grade	20 years to lifetime guarantee
Architectural interlocking shingles	15 to 25 years
Roll roofing (modified bitumen)	8 to 15 years
Built-up roofing (tar and gravel)	15 to 25 years
Wood shingles/shakes	10 to 50+ years
Clay tiles	30 to 50 years
Concrete tiles	30 to 50 years
Slates	30 to 100+ years
Asbestos-cement shingles	30 to 75 years
Metal roofing	15 to 40+ years
Single-ply membrane (EPDM, TPO, PVC)	15 to 25 years
Polyurethane with Elastomeric Coating (depending on coating thickness)	5 to 10 years

3.3 STRUCTURE FROM THE EXTERIOR

The first step of the exterior roof inspection should be to make a **complete tour around the house**, viewing the roof/building from all sides. Don't take any shortcuts. Circle the house (and garage) completely and view the roof(s) from all angles. You may need to go into the neighbor's yard (always ask permission first) or across the street to get a complete view. And don't make any assumptions about what the roof looks like at the back of the house or over additions or porches. We've seen houses where the south slope of the roof is in good condition and the north slope is completely covered with moss. We've also seen houses where the slope at the front of the house has a new roof covering but the back doesn't.

The home inspector starts the exterior roof inspection by paying attention to the structure of the roof, looking for any exterior signs of structural problems with the roof or the house. This should be done from the ground and from the ladder or the roof's surface. The home inspector should concentrate on the following:

- **The ridge line:** Eye the ridge line(s) on the ground from all angles as you circle the house. A **cracked or broken ridge** can be an indication of structural damage to the roof structure or of structural problems all the way down to the footings. A cracked or broken ridge needs to be investigated further. Sight along the ridge line (from the roof) to see if there is a sag or a hump. A **sagging ridge** in an old house may not indicate any other problems. The sagging ridge could be because of age or its original design (although not very common), but it needs to be investigated later from the underside. The sag could be caused by warped rafters pulling the ridge board down. A **hump** shows that the underlying structure is pushing the ridge board up. The home inspector should make note of any problems and search for the cause when the roof's structure is inspected. Keep in mind that you are there to identify the problems, not necessarily identify their causes.

> **Section Note**
>
> *"I came across a house where I noticed a definite slope in the ridge going down toward each side from a center point in the ridge. From the attic, I could see that the ridge board was cracked in the middle. The house was actually breaking in half and sinking at each end due to settlement problems."*

- **The planes of the roof:** As you walk around the house, look for any distortions in the planes (faces) of the roof. Look at each slope from several angles. Watch for **waviness** across the surface, **sunken areas**, and **raised areas**. Distortions along the roof's surface can be caused by the following problems:

  — Wet, rotted, and/or delaminated sheathing

  — Sheathing that is too thin to support the roof covering

  — Buckling sheathing that was too closely butted during installation

  — Rafters at too wide a span

  — Cuts or modifications made in rafters or trusses

  — Overloaded rafters that are sagging under the weight

  — Too many layers or excessive snow load

— Rafters installed with crowns facing both up *and* down. The crown of a piece of dimensional rough lumber is the upward arching curvature you see when you look down its narrowest dimensional edge. Framing to be installed and put under load should be installed "crown" up.

— Warped, cracked, or twisted rafters or truss chords

The home inspector should make note of any distortions of the planes of the roof and investigate further from inside the attic to find the cause of the problem.

- **The soffits/eaves:** The home inspector should look for breaks in the joints between the main house and the roof at the soffits/eaves. Breaks or cracks at these joints can indicate:

    — **Rafter spread.** This is a phenomenon where the roof load forces the rafters down and outward. The soffit and sometimes the exterior walls can be pushed outward along with the rafters, actually separating from the house.

    — **Truss uplift.** The bottom chords of roof trusses can bow and deflect upward during the winter months, pulling ceilings and walls below with them and cracking the interior finishes. In extreme cases, stresses can cause cracking of the soffits as the bottom chords pull them inward.

> **Definitions**
>
> *Rafter spread occurs when the roof load bearing on the rafters forces them outward.*
>
> *Truss uplift occurs when the bottom chord of a roof truss bows upward during the cold months and returns to its normal position during the warmer months.*

Make a mental note while on the roof to investigate any signs of structural damage when you get to the attic. Also note any signs that it is dangerous for you to walk on the roof, particularly with distortions that may indicate rotten or delaminated sheathing.

3.4 INSPECTING THE ROOF COVERING

A very important aspect of the exterior inspection is the inspection of the roof covering. The home inspector should **determine the approximate age** of the roof covering. This can be done by checking with the homeowner, if possible, as to when the roofing was last replaced. In places subject to hurricanes, such as Florida, you may be able to find when permits were pulled, especially if you are also doing a wind mitigation inspection. Of course, homeowners aren't always honest, so you should use your own judgment as to whether to double-check. If the homeowner has documentation, you should determine the age and condition prior to looking at the records to see how close you came on your own. The home inspector should also estimate **how many layers** of roofing are present and estimate its **remaining useful lifetime**. The home inspector identifies the **type** of roofing present and reports on its **condition**. The inspection of the roof covering includes the following:

> **INSPECTING ROOF COVERING**
>
> - Approximate age
> - Number of layers
> - Remaining useful lifetime
> - Type of roof covering
> - Condition of roof covering

> **Chapter Note**
>
> *Pages 166–189 present procedures for the inspection of the roof covering.*

- Condition of roofing materials
- Condition at ridge, valleys, and interfaces
- Loose or missing components
- Roofing fastenings
- Proper installation
- Water penetration
- Repaired areas
- Improper or incompatible materials

The purpose of the roof covering is to protect the roof framework and the interior from the elements. The roof covering must be able to shed water and protect the house from the sun.

The home inspector should look over the roof covering while making **an initial tour** around the house, perhaps when looking at the structural aspects of the roof from the ground. The inspector should look at the roof covering from all sides of the house. He or she should determine the type of roofing, ball-park its age and wear, and make note of areas that look damaged or look as though they were repaired recently. During this tour, the home inspector may be able to determine whether walking on the roof is possible and where the ladder may be put for access. As a general rule, don't put the ladder right on the front of the house, just in case you scratch or dent the gutter. If you place your ladder properly, neither should be an issue.

The inspector should be creating a **mental plan** of the roof during this tour—various intersecting planes of the roof, dormer areas, lower roofs over additions and porches, and so on. That way the inspector can inspect all areas once he or she is on the ladder at the edge of the roof or on the roof's surface. It is possible to lose track of things you noticed from below once you're on the roof. A mental layout and photos help you remember.

Asphalt Shingles

Asphalt shingles are made of an asphalt-impregnated mat of cellulose or glass fibers that may be coated with another asphalt formulation and covered with a granular material. If glass fibers are used, they are **fiberglass shingles**. If the core is organic felt, they are **organic shingles**. Of the two, fiberglass shingles are by far more commonly used today.

Asphalt shingles are the most commonly used roof covering today (about 80% of roof coverings). They come in strips with three tabs, multilayered or multi-thickness, or they can be individual shingles in various shapes—square butted, hexagonal, or interlocking.

Asphalt shingles used to be graded according to weight. They run anywhere from 210 pounds per square (100 square feet) to 400 pounds per square.

> **Section Note**
>
> *Take the time to visit roofing suppliers and see what types of roof coverings are available. The home inspector must identify the type of covering on the roof with each inspection, and this is a good way to learn how to recognize different types.*

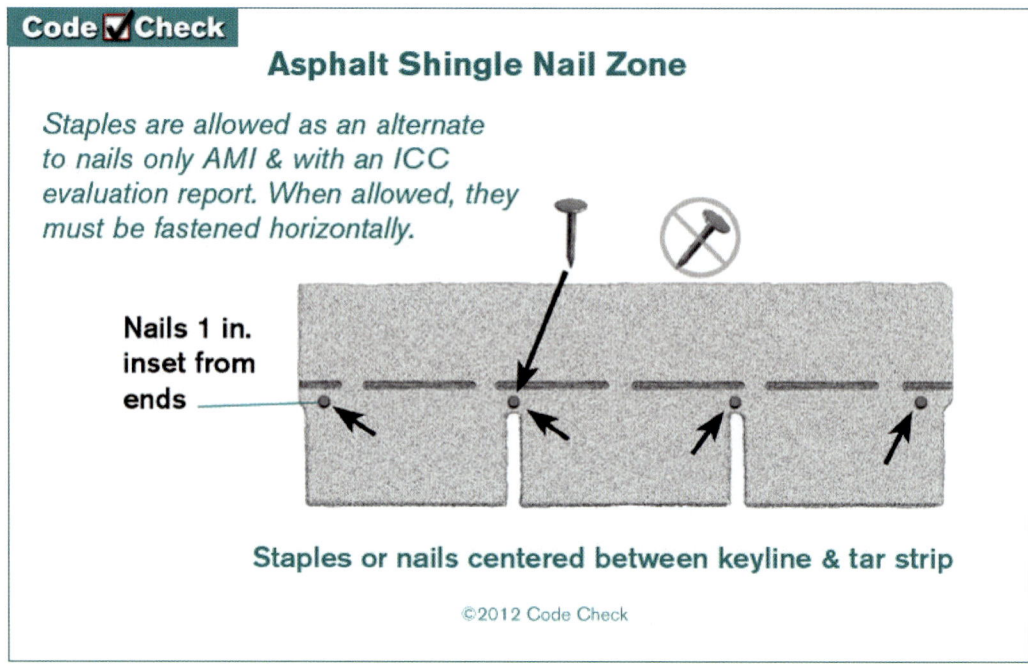

The heavier the shingle, the longer its life. The packaging has changed so that consumers understand the life expectancy from weight per square to warranty period. A 225 lb shingle may last 15 to 20 years; a 400 lb, more than 45 years. Today, it's more common to grade these shingles by lifetime or warranty—a manufacturer may offer 20-, 25-, or 45-year or even lifetime warranty shingles.

Today, most asphalt shingles come with a self-seal strip on the surface. The tar lies under the tabs, or edge, of the next course of shingles. When warmed by the sun, the two courses seal together and are prevented from being blown up by the wind. When roofing is laid in cold weather, the sealing won't take place until the weather warms up again, making the roof susceptible to wind damage.

Asphalt shingles can be used on a roof with a slope of 4/12 or more using the normal installment techniques. **Felt paper** or new breathable membranes such as GAF's DeckArmor™ or USP's RoofTopGuard II™, are laid over the roof sheathing as an underlayment. These products keep water out and allow moisture from the attic side of the sheathing to dry. At the eave, a double layer of roofing is laid. The **starter course**, laid under the first course of shingles, is a solid strip of asphalt roll roofing or a layer with the tabs cut off or a roll of starter course material. The shingles are laid with an offset. Nails are covered by the course above. To prevent water penetration due to ice dams, the roofer may install a self-adhered bituminous membrane known as an ice and water shield under the shingles at the eaves, up to a point 24" inside the exterior wall.

An asphalt shingle roof should have a **drip edge** or metal flashing at the lower edge of the roof. This flashing may direct the water into the gutters. A similar piece of metal flashing is installed along the rake of the roof at the gable ends.

INSPECTING ASPHALT SHINGLES

- Loss of granules
- Curling tabs
- Cracking and buckling
- Fish-mouthing
- Nail pops
- Loose or missing tabs
- Damaged areas
- Improper installation

A roof with a slope of less than 4/12 (down to 2/12) may use a special **low slope asphalt shingle installation**. The shingles are the same, but the installation is different. When installed, a double layer of special felt paper should be used. This is rarely done correctly, so if you find shingles on a 2/12 or 3/12 pitch, recommend that a roofer evaluate the installation.

When inspecting the asphalt shingle roof, the home inspector should estimate the **number of layers** of shingles at the eave. When the roofing wears out, the new shingles may be laid over the old (keep in mind regional requirements like tornado alley where only one layer is allowed, ever). Codes put a limit on the number of layers of shingles that can be present—only two layers. You can understand why. Doubling or tripling the weight per square can put an overload on the roof's structure, especially in areas with large annual snowfalls.

The home inspector should look for the following when inspecting the asphalt shingle roof:

- **Loss of granules:** The granules on the asphalt shingle are what protect the shingle from the ultraviolet rays of the sun. The sun, in fact, is what is responsible for the aging of the shingle. As time goes by, these granules lose adhesion and wear off. As the granules are lost, the shingles dry out and become brittle. Granules are washed away by the rain, thereby exposing the underlying tar to the sun and elements and allowing further decay. The home inspector can look for granule deposits in the gutters and at the bottom of downspouts to confirm that the roof is losing them.

- **Curling/cupping tabs:** After the granules are lost from the asphalt shingle, water and sun can enter the mat (core) and lead to rapid breakdown. The shingle at the end of its useful lifetime will begin to curl under or up at the tab edges. This same condition may be caused by poor ventilation in the attic, although the jury is still out on this subject. But basically, when an asphalt shingle roof has curling tabs, it's about time to replace the roof. New shingles cannot be installed over a roof that's gone that far.

> **CAUTION**
>
> *Don't walk on an asphalt shingled roof when the <u>shingles are curling/cupping at the tabs</u>. They'll break. Walk on the roof only in areas that aren't curling.*

Photo #8 *This roof has significant wear and loss of granules with limited remaining life.*

Section Note

"Sometimes there's no clue that something is wrong with a roof. One of my inspectors was on a shingle roof that was only two years old.

Everything looked fine. Suddenly, he went right through the roof, catching himself on the rafters by the armpits.

The homeowner had patched certain areas of sheathing with 1/4" waferboard, which doesn't meet code. It can't support a person walking on it.

I don't mean to scare you. Instead, I'd like you <u>always to be prepared</u> for the unexpected. Don't get too cocky up there."

CAUTION

<u>Moss on a roof is like ice</u>, and the sheathing is probably damaged or rotten. Don't walk on areas that are covered with moss. If the roof is completely covered with moss, stay off.

- **Cracking and buckling:** Fiberglass shingles—shingles with a fiberglass mat—don't respond well if the roof sheathing moves while expanding and contracting. The less common organic asphalt shingle can handle the movement better, but the lighter, thinner fiberglass shingle sometimes cracks. Single shingles or a small area of shingles that are buckled may be the result of warped sheathing.

- **Fish-mouthing:** A condition called fish-mouthing can occur with asphalt shingles, and it is caused by excessive overheating from either multiple layers of shingles or heat buildup in the attic. Shingles can expand so much that they separate from the mat/core. As a result, the center portion of the tabs curls upward. As you look up the roof, each shingle looks like a fish's mouth.

- **Nail pops:** The nails or staples holding asphalt shingles in place are under the tabs of the next course. These nails can pop out. The condition is very easy to see. The nails break the seal between courses, pushing up the tabs or shingles. You'll see space that puckers or bulges where they should be lying perfectly flat. The nail holes leave paths where water can enter. The condition needs to be fixed. One or two nail pops on a roof is not a big deal. A lot of nail pops indicate a possible nailing issue or nails that are too short. This is especially true for the overlay or second layer. Be sure to check local requirements as some states prohibit the use of staples as fasteners. Nails must be used in those areas even though the manufacturer says staples are acceptable.

- **Loose or missing tabs/shingles:** You may find a perfectly good roof that is missing one or two tabs. This can happen when the seal between the

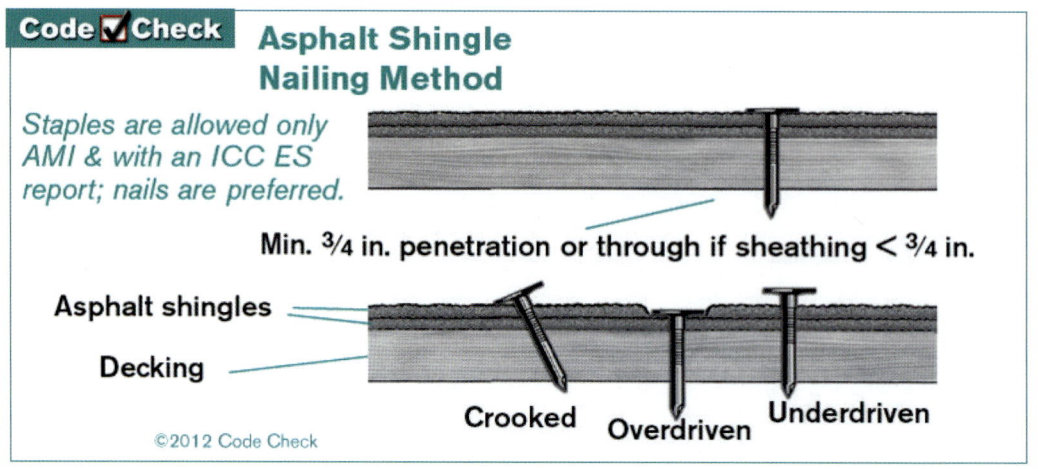

Photo #9 *Significant damage at eave with half of the asphalt shingle tab missing.*

courses didn't take and they've blown off. Obviously, the shingles need to be replaced. The home inspector should look at other areas on the roof to see if other shingles are loose.

- **Damaged areas:** Roofing can wear unevenly due to problems with water runoff or the roof's underlying structure. The home inspector should investigate the causes of these problems. Be cautious about stepping on these areas.

- **Improper installation:** Shingles should be installed so that the slots don't line up, and they should run parallel to the roof line. Nailing must be done properly. This is not possible to determine in most applications without potentially damaging the roof covering. Some materials such as tile can be reasonably checked for proper nailing. The correct length/amount of the shingle should be exposed to the weather. Any deviations from perfect installation should be reported to the customer. "Not professionally installed" is a good way to describe a poor installation. The homeowner may have installed the roof.

Section Note

"Home inspectors sometimes run into people with peculiar ideas. One of my inspectors came across a <u>painted</u> asphalt shingled roof. Sorry, that just doesn't work.

Roll Roofing

Roll roofing, also known as modified bituminous torch-down, peel and stick, and cold-lap process, usually comes in 36″-wide rolls and is made of the same or very similar material as asphalt shingles—an asphalt-impregnated felted or a fiberglass mat coated with asphalt formulations and covered with a granular material. It may also be made without a mineral surface. Roll roofing is available with complete granular coverage for single-ply application or with 50% coverage for double layers.

INSPECTING ROLL ROOFING

- Loss of granules
- Buckling and wrinkling
- Lifting laps
- Tearing
- Repaired areas

Roll roofing is available in any of three materials: cold-lap process, torch-down-modified bitumen, or peel and stick. Cold-lap process is the least expensive; it is found in home improvement stores and is often

Photo #10 *This is roll roofing and the edge was not properly sealed to the drip edge flashing. Wind-driven rain will get under the roof covering and cause damage to the deck and interior of home.*

Definition

The word ply as it applies to roof coverings means a layer of covering. A single-ply roof covering has one layer.

used by homeowners for do-it-yourself jobs on sheds or garages. Cold-lap process roofing usually only lasts about 8 years. Torch-down and peel and stick are professionally applied and are found mostly on flat-roofed commercial buildings, although they are also seen on flat-roofed residential buildings such as apartment buildings and condominiums. Torch-down is the longest lasting of the three, with an expected life of approximately 15 years. It is applied by heating the back side of the roofing material with a propane torch as the roofing is rolled out. Peel and stick roofing is often used to repair or replace torch-down roofing. It is nearly as durable as torch-down, lasting about 12 to 15 years.

Flashing is installed first. A fiberglass mat is laid down and nailed to the sheathing, followed by strips of roofing laid parallel to the edge of the roof, with overlapping beginning at the eave and extending to the top edge. To complete installation, the roofer pulls back the strips part way and applies the torch to the underside of the material, laying it back in place, pressing down on it to get good adhesion, and rolling over it with a heavy roller to seal the seams.

The home inspector should inspect the condition of roll roofing for the following:

- **Loss of granules:** As with asphalt shingles, asphalt roll roofing loses its granules over time. Moisture and sun entering the mat causes further breakdown. The surface becomes dull and begins to deteriorate.

- **Buckling and wrinkling:** These conditions occur from ongoing expansion and contraction. The buckled and wrinkled areas wear out faster because granules are lost at the wrinkles.

- **Lifting laps:** If you see the edges of the seams or strips of roll roofing lifting up, the seal isn't working. It's likely that water (especially wind-driven rain) is leaking into these places. Check the roof from underneath (if possible) to find water penetration through the roof.

- **Tearing:** When roll roofing is torn, it's an indication of movement or warping in the roof sheathing or structure. This condition should be investigated further.

- **Repaired areas:** Homeowners are more likely to try their hand at repairing roll roofing than other kinds. Repairs indicate that the homeowner has a problem. Either the strips have been lifting up or there's been leaking into the house. Repaired areas should be reported to the customer. They are rarely done correct and exposed tar is a very good sign of an improper repair.

Built-Up Roofing

A flat or slightly sloping roof up to 3/12 can be covered with a covering known as a built-up roof, also known as tar and gravel or hot-mop roofing. The built-up roof consists of alternating layers of impregnated **roofing felts and bitumen**. Bitumen is petroleum asphalt or coal tar, although coal tar is seldom used anymore. Each ply is a layer of felt mopped with a layer of asphalt. Built-up roofs can be 2-ply to 5-ply, meaning from two to five layers of felt and asphalt. The built-up roof is finished with a layer of asphalt formulated for weather resistance or a layer of **slag or gravel** may be applied to the top. (These roofs may be referred to as tar and gravel roofs.) Some built-up roofs have a finish layer of roll roofing instead of gravel on them.

The 2-ply built-up roof will last 5 to 10 years; the 4-ply will last 20 to 25 years. This depends, of course, on periodic maintenance and geographic location of the surface.

Definitions

A <u>built-up roof</u> is made of alternating layers of impregnated felt and hot bitumen and topped with a weather-resistant coat of bitumen. It may be topped with slag, gravel, or a layer of roll roofing or aluminized silver paint. <u>Bitumen</u> is petroleum asphalt or coal tar.

INSPECTING BUILT-UP ROOFING

- Alligatoring
- Blisters and bubbles
- Water ponding

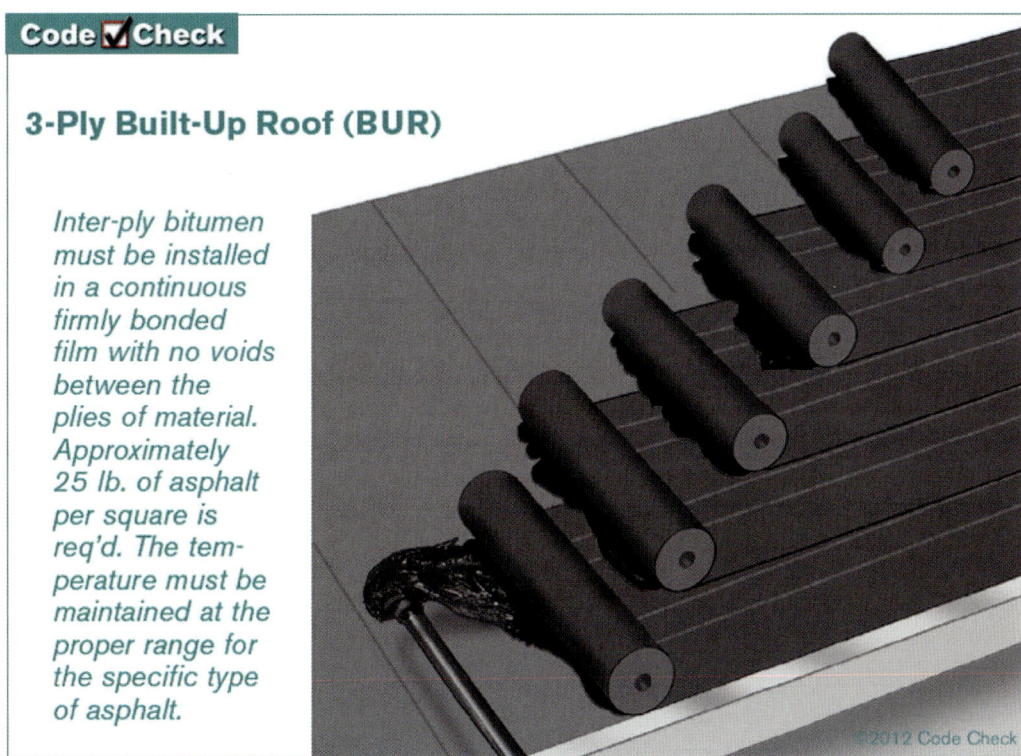

Code Check

3-Ply Built-Up Roof (BUR)

Inter-ply bitumen must be installed in a continuous firmly bonded film with no voids between the plies of material. Approximately 25 lb. of asphalt per square is req'd. The temperature must be maintained at the proper range for the specific type of asphalt.

©2012 Code Check

Photo #11 *Significantly deteriorated tar and gravel roof. Gravel is missing and has exposed the underlying tar, which has degraded in the sun.*

Built-up roofs should be examined for the following problems:

> **Section Note**
>
> *"I came across built-up bitumen and gravel roofing on a roof. I suggested that a roofing contractor look at it. The contractor evaluated the roof using an infrared camera to detect areas of heat loss. He informed me, 'It's not heat loss you see, it is the cool spots where the water is trapped and evaporating.' He could tell where the bitumen was pulling loose from the plywood sheathing."*

- **Alligatoring:** As the surface of the built-up roof ages and the roofing breaks down, you'll see a network of cracks called alligatoring. The action of the sun causes the surface to expand/contract and heat/cool until these cracks form. The cracks let moisture in to the layers below. A roof with alligatoring needs to be recovered with another layer of asphalt, which is typically not cost-effective and is not done, or as is more likely, needs to be replaced.

  When the built-up roof leaks, it's very difficult to tell where the leak is coming from. Water can seep into the roofing at one area and run along the plies or decking/framing to emerge to the interior in a different place. The only definitive way to check them is with infrared cameras.

- **Blistering and bubbling:** When moisture is trapped between the plies through leakage, dew, or rain or during installation, blisters or bubbles form. The plies become delaminated, pulling away from each other and from the roof. This reduces the life expectancy of the roofing. Some roofers cut the blisters open, let them dry out, and reseal them. Others leave them alone.

- **Water ponding:** Because built-up roofs are usually flat or gently sloping, water ponding is a problem. The home inspector should report any standing water. If the roof is dry at the time of the inspection, look for a pattern of dried-up ponds left in the dust on the surface. In general, water should not stand or pond on a flat roof for more than 48 hours.

  Water ponding may indicate a structural problem on the flat roof that could be related to age or poor workmanship. The roof already has to be sagging under the weight of the roofing for the water to pond there. The additional weight of the water will cause more sag. (One inch of water over 385 square feet weighs one ton!) The roof may have to be restructured or roof drains installed to drain the water from this area.

CAUTION: It isn't always easy to tell what is going on with a built-up roof. And with the tar and gravel roof, you can't see what's going on beneath the gravel. When a built-up roof is topped with gravel, the home inspector should report it as *not visible* in the inspection report. The correct way to inspect the roof is with infrared thermography.

Wood Shingles and Shakes

Wood shingles are sawn, lie flat on one another, and are thinner and more uniform than shakes. **Wood shakes** are thicker with an uneven surface and uneven thickness. Shakes are hand-split, split on one side and sawn on the other, or sawn on both sides. It gets confusing. Shingles and shakes are usually Western Red Cedar, although some are made from redwood and pressure-treated southern yellow pine. They come in lengths of 16″, 18″, and 24″ and vary in thickness. Most are tapered.

Shingles and shakes are recommended for 3/12 or greater pitched roofs. The greater the slope, the longer they'll last. The lifetime can be up to 50 years, but low-grade shingles may last only 15 to 20 years.

Shingles and shakes are sold according to grade. Most codes allow number 1 or number 2 grade only as the top layer; lesser grades are used for undercoursing. A quality number 1 grade shingle or shake is cut from **heartwood** (the inner core of the wood), not from sapwood (the outer rings); it's cut from the **edge grain** (at right angles to the rings); and it's **clear** without knots and wormholes. Shingles are almost always installed over spaced sheathing where shakes are installed over either. Both are acceptable per current code. Shakes and shingles are laid with a **starter course** under the first course of shakes at

Definitions

Wood shingles are sawn and are of even thickness. *Wood shakes* are generally thicker with an uneven thickness and rough surface and can be hand-split, both hand-split and sawn, or sawn.

Heartwood is the wood taken from the inner core of the tree.

Edge grain is a cut taken at right angles to the rings of the tree. *Clear* means that the shingle or shake has no knots or wormholes.

Interlayment refers to the practice of installing roofing felt between each course of shakes. *Underlayment* refers to a single layer of roofing felt laid over the roof sheathing.

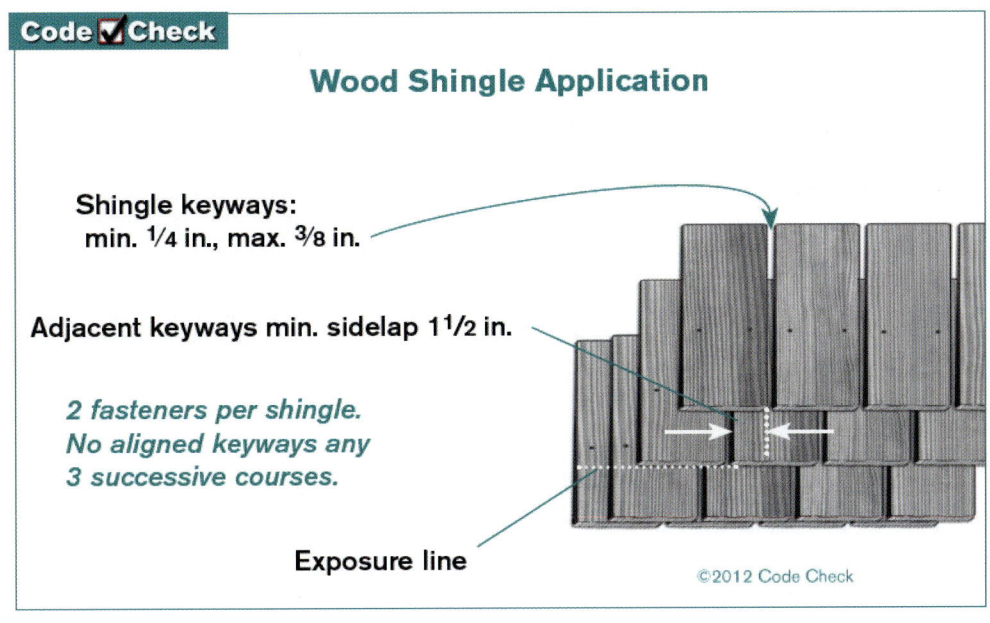

THE ROOF INSPECTION

Illustration by Paddy Morrissey

> **CAUTION**
>
> *Do not walk on a wood shingle or wood shake roof if the roofing is <u>wet, moss-covered, or mildewed</u>. If the shingles or shakes are badly deteriorated, stay off them. They'll break.*

> **Section Note**
>
> *There's quite a bit to learn about wood shingle and shake roofs. We recommend that you do some additional reading on the subject. Go to the library or check the Internet. Study grading, installation, and chemical treatments applied to wood roofs. If you know a roofer who works with wood roofs, take advantage of the acquaintance to learn more.*

the roof's edge with a 1 1/2" overhang as a drip edge. An **interlayment** of roofing felt is laid between each course of **shakes.** With shingles, the interlayment is not used. Instead, shingles may be laid over an **underlayment** or more typically without the use of any roofing felt at all. If underlayment is used, a product called "Cedar Breather" or something similar is typically used to create a space between courses to allow for quicker and complete drying of the shingles.

Shingles are laid from 1/4–3/8" apart; shakes, 3/8–5/8" apart. This spacing allows the shingles and shakes to expand when wet. If the proper spacing isn't observed during installation, shingles and shakes can buckle, split, and cup when they expand. Gaps between shingles and shakes should be staggered from course to course. Each shingle and shake is fastened in place with two fasteners hidden under the next course. Flashings should be galvanized steel or aluminum; copper is not recommended due to the tannins in the wood, which will corrode the copper. We'll talk more about flashings on pages 189–198.

When inspecting the wood shingle or wood shake roof, the first thing you should do is determine whether to walk on the roof. Shingles and shakes that are wet, covered with moss, or mildewed are very slippery. *Do not walk on the roof if any of these conditions are present.* If the shingles or shakes are badly deteriorated, you'll break them if you walk on the roof. Avoid getting on the roof if its condition is bad or unsafe.

If you do get on the roof, try to walk *across* the roof, not directly up and down from eave to ridge. But be careful, even dry wood roofs in good condition can be tricky.

Start inspecting the wood shingle or shake roof **from the ground**. Looking at the roof from this low vantage point can help you spot areas that are excessively buckled, curled, cupped, or deteriorated. If the weather is dry, you may notice some curling and lifted shingles or shakes. That's normal. When it rains, they swell up and lay back down and flatten out.

With the wood roofing, the inspection of the roof **from the attic** is very important. The home inspector should check the type of roof sheathing and determine if it's appropriate. Remember, wood shingles and shakes should have spaced plank sheathing. Spaced sheathing allows the wood to dry out faster from both sides.

It may surprise the home inspector looking at the roof from underneath to find that space planking has been used. In dry weather, you may see light coming through from the outside (indirect light, not straight in). When it rains and the roofing swells, these spaces close up. This is fairly common, although the home inspector should look carefully for evidence of water leakage in the attic to make sure the roof isn't leaking. Matted or stained insulation is a good clue.

During the exterior inspection, the home inspector should inspect the condition of the wood shingle and shake roof for the following:

- **Improper installation:** In dry weather, shingles should not be butted tightly against each other and certainly should not be tight or buckled, split, and cupped. Such shingles are laid without proper spacing. Note that the gaps between shingles and shakes are staggered. Check the overhang at the eaves.

- **Softness and rot:** When the wood roof is not allowed to dry out, shingles and shakes can rot. In dry weather, you may see shingles that remain damp or you may see shingles where the butt ends are breaking up, splitting, and cracking. They should be probed for softness and rot at the butt ends and underneath these areas.

- **Damaged and weathered:** Over time, sunlight can dehydrate and degrade shingles and shakes, causing them to become brittle and to split and cup. Wind-blown sand can erode the shingles and wear them down. Watch for splits that lie directly under the gap in the course above, making a pathway for water to enter the roof. Watch for mechanical damage that can occur from rubbing or falling tree branches. You may see evidence of someone else being on the roof. Some roof and gutter cleaners wear spiked shoes or boots on a wood roof for traction. These distinctive holes allow water to get into the shingle. You should wear rubber-soled shoes. A popular type of shoe called "Cougar Paws" is specifically designed for walking on roofing materials.

- **Loose or missing:** Check the fastenings on the shingles and shakes. There should be two nails or fasteners for each one shingle or shake. When fasteners pull loose, the shingle or shake may slip out of position. If the shingles or shakes are loose, they can be refastened. Look for any shingles or

> **INSPECTING WOOD SHINGLES AND SHAKES**
>
> - Improper installation
> - Softness and rot
> - Damaged and weathered
> - Loose or missing
> - Moss and mildew
> - Water penetration

> *Section Note*
>
> *"This is our favorite roofing story. One of my inspectors was on a flat roof with roll roofing. The house was newly remodeled and everything seemed okay. He took a step, and his leg went right through the roofing. The good news was that his other foot was firm and kept him from falling through. The bad news was that a swarm of wasps flew out the hole at him, some right up his pants leg. Investigating from the attic revealed a 6′ by 8′ wasp nest. There was no sheathing above the nest. (Of course not; the homeowner didn't want to bother the wasps either.) The pest inspector called to deal with the nest froze it, cut it in fourths, and removed it. It now stands on display as the largest wasp nest ever found in our area. Our inspector actually finished the inspection, although he said that he felt rather dizzy by the time it was over. He decided to stop at the emergency room on the way home. He had 47 wasp stings!"*

Photo #12 *Worn wood shake roof. Note the missing ridge shingles. There are also a great many cracks and curled shakes.*

shakes that have loosened and blown away, typically along the ridge line. These should be replaced.

- **Moss and mildew:** Moss present on the wood or any roof should be reported. The most common cause of shingle and shake deterioration is the buildup of moss. If you see moss or algae, be careful, but probe these areas for wood rot. Also, check the roof framing below mossy areas, as it can also be damaged from the moss. Moss should be removed from the roof. Environmentally safe chemical treatments are available to kill moss. Preservative treatments also are available that will retard the growth of moss. Another popular method is to use strips of zinc along the ridge. When it rains, the zinc slowly dissolves and prevents growth on the roof. You may have already seen this and not noticed the effect. Look at a shingle roof with gray or black streaks (algae) and then look at the lead or galvanized flashing at penetrations. You will see that the shingles downhill from the flashing is clean or free of staining from the metals dissolving and running down the roof.

  Mildew can also be present. Be careful. Mildew is also slippery. Red Cedar normally lightens as it ages. If shingles and shakes are very dark or black, that's a sign of mildew. Mildew can be scraped off but seldom without damaging the shingle. There are chemical treatments that can kill mildew too.

- **Water penetration:** The home inspector should inspect the wood roofing carefully for water penetration. Make note of rotted areas on the exterior and inspect the roof framing from the attic for any evidence of leaking.

Perhaps the most difficult part of inspecting the wood roof is determining its remaining useful life. A roof that is in good condition and has a long life ahead of it and a roof that is totally shot are both easy to identify. It's the in-between ones that can be difficult to verify. Start by asking the homeowner how old the roof is. A 10-year-old roof in bad condition has serious problems and is aging too fast. Don't estimate 10 more years for it. In general, when about 15% of the roof requires repair, you should recommend that the roof be replaced soon.

SOME ADVICE: We suggest that homeowners have a sealant/preservative applied to wood roofing—a water-resistant stain that includes a mildecide and moss retarder. It prolongs the life of the roof considerably. Some of the better treatments include naphthenic and paraffinic oils.

CAUTION: There is so much to learn about wood roofs. We suggest that you do further studying on the subject. When commenting on a wood shingle or shake roof, you should not make *uneducated guesses* about the cause of its condition or suggest repairs or treatments you're not sure of.

> **CAUTION**
>
> *Do not walk on <u>concrete or clay tile roofing</u>. Walking on the tiles will break them.*

Tile Roofs

Tiles are made from concrete or clay and can be flat, curved, or corrugated. They are becoming more common across the country, even in northern climates. You should become familiar with their applications. Special pieces are made for ridges and rakes. Tiles are suitable for a 4/12 sloped roof or steeper using standard installation practices. Tile can be installed on slopes as low as 2 1/2 in 12 when double lapped tar paper is used as described earlier. The tile roof may require an underlayment. ALL concrete tile needs at least 30# tar paper. Clay tiles in very old installations may have no tar paper at all. MOST new clay tile installations have a completely watertight torch-down roof beneath them.

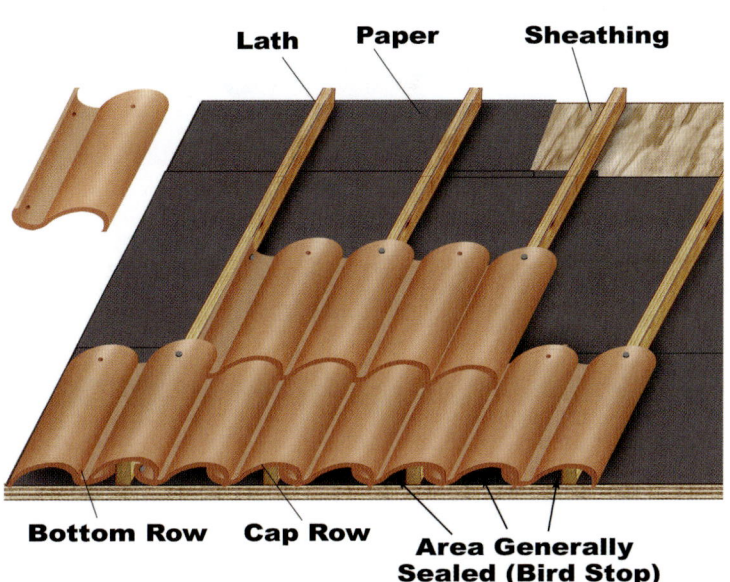

Illustration by Paddy Morrissey

The tile roof is heavy, long-lasting, fireproof, and weather-resistant. It can be up to 4 or 5 times heavier (about 1,000 lbs/square average) than a roof with asphalt shingles, and the underlying roof structure must be strong enough to the support the tiles. A tile roof can last from 35 to 50 years with average installation and upward of 100 years with good workmanship.

Traditional 2-piece barrel clay tile in the Spanish style are shown above. Support battens are nailed in place over the plank or plywood roof sheathing. (Most clay tile roofs don't use battens; this applies to concrete, which always uses battens or counter battens.) A bottom row of inverted tiles is laid between a cap row of tiles. Tiles are overlapped. The fastenings vary. Some tiles are nailed in place, while others have special clips, screws, or wire ties. Some tiles are mortared in place. The eaves may be sealed with concrete mortar to keep out birds and wind-driven rain.

The home inspector should not attempt to walk on a **clay** tile roof. Walking on the tiles will damage them. Local inspectors may or may not walk on concrete tiles; it is dictated by what the local practice is.

Clay and concrete tile roofs should be inspected for the following:

> **INSPECTING TILE ROOFING**
>
> - Loose, slipped, or missing tiles
> - Broken tiles
> - Prior repairs
> - Paint job if present

- **Loose, slipped, or missing tiles:** Fasteners can come loose or were never installed on tile roofing, and many tiles that should have been

THE ROOF INSPECTION 179

Photo #13 *This is a very common site with tile roofs. These clay (terracotta) tiles are not properly fastened to the rake board and are about to fall off. This is also a safety issue.]*

nailed are not or become loose and slip out of place. Slipped tiles are easy to spot and should be reported. They should be repaired (or more likely replaced) as they usually break when they hit the ground. Test other tiles to make sure fastenings are secure (give them a tug). Any tiles that are missing or broken should be replaced as you can't fix broken tiles.

When suggesting repairs or tile replacement to customers, we like to warn them not to call in just any roofer in areas where tiles are not common. The homeowner should locate an expert in tile roofs and get an evaluation of the situation before having any repairs done.

- **Broken tiles:** Be sure to point out any tiles that are broken or cracked. Also, note improper repairs of tiles. They can't be glued back together. They must be replaced. Damaged tiles can let water through the roof and into the building.

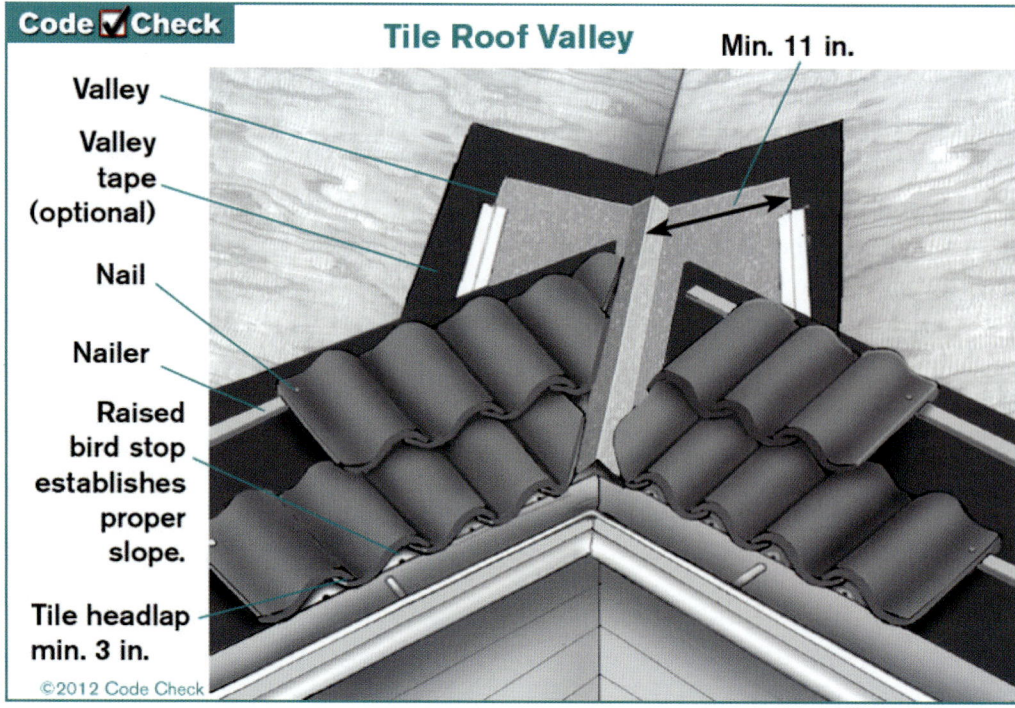

180 Chapter 3

Tiles can be broken by mechanical damage, the satellite guy, or a chimney sweep. Watch for evidence of tree damage.

- **Prior repairs:** Keep an eye out for previously made repairs. You may see areas where concrete mortar has been applied. This is not an acceptable repair, it's like putting tar on a shingle roof. If possible, try to determine if the repairs are working. Always report any repairs you see. It's an indication that something went wrong. Repairs may not have been done by a reliable or expert roofer. If you can tell that the roof was repaired, the work wasn't done correctly. The one exception to this is in a tile re-roof. When a roof is redone the tiles are reused. There will be breakage in the process. The new and most likely mismatched tiles will be installed on the backside of the roof so the street side looks more uniform. Customers should monitor a roof with previous repairs. It can be a sign that the roofing will need more repairs or will need to be replaced in the near future. Also, they should monitor whether the repair is still working.

- **Paint job:** If concrete tiles have been painted (not a common or good thing), inspect the condition of the paint job. Painting tiles serves no purpose and is a cover-up or a temporary fix at best. We have seen thousands of tile roofs but never saw one that was painted for other than cosmetic reasons.

Slate and Asbestos Cement Shingles

Slate is sedimentary rock, a natural material, and it should make a long-lasting roof. Depending on its quality and thickness (from 3/16" to 2"), slate can last from 30 to over 100 years. One exception is **ribbon slate**, which has a ribbon of color in it. This slate is of lower quality and can crack along the ribbons, lasting only 10 or 15 years. Slate is up to about 5 times heavier per square than an asphalt shingle roof and must have a strong roof structure to support it. A proper slope for slate is 4/12 or greater.

> **CAUTION**
>
> *Do not walk on a slate roof, on clay tile, or on asbestos cement shingles. They are brittle and can break.*

Photo #14 *This is a new slate installation using battens with counter battens. The counter battens run vertically up and down the roof and the battens are installed horizontally. This is also commonly used with tile roofs in northern climates.*

Slate shingles may have a rectangular exposure or may be laid in diamond patterns.

Traditionally slate was laid over spaced sheathing, and this still may be seen in homes built prior to the 1960s. It now must be laid over solid sheathing. Special copper slating nails (or nowadays, stainless steel nails) should be used. In the north, where snow and ice can slide off slate too easily, you'll find snow shovels, also called ice-guards and **snow-birds**. These are metal finger-like claws that hold the snow in place until it melts. Snow shovels are installed in a band 1′ to 4′ wide starting about a foot above the eaves.

Asbestos cement shingles are becoming more rare. They were last made in the late 1950s and early 1960s. They're made from a mixture of Portland cement and asbestos fibers and can last from 30 to 75+ years. The homeowner needs to be careful during repair or replacement because of the asbestos content in the shingle. Although the material is considered non-friable, the EPA requires that these shingles be disposed of according to their standards.

Asbestos cement shingles are brittle and may look like slate. These shingles often confuse home inspectors and at times have been improperly identified as slate. Here's one sure way to tell the difference. **Moss cannot grow on slate.** If you think you have a slate roof but it's got moss on it, then you've got asbestos cement shingles.

Both slate and asbestos cement shingles are too brittle to walk on. Don't try to walk on either type of roofing. You'll only damage the roof material. Instead, inspect the roofing from a ladder at several points around the house.

The home inspector should inspect the condition of slate and asbestos cement shingles for the following:

> *Definition*
>
> Snow shovels, ice-guards, and snow-birds are metal finger-like claws installed with slate, tile, and metal roofing to hold snow and ice in place until it melts.

> **IMPORTANT POINT**
>
> If you think you've found slate shingles and they have moss on them, they're really asbestos cement shingles. Moss will not grow on slate.

- **Loose, slipped, or missing shingles:** Fasteners holding the slates or shingles in place can become loose, causing them to slip out of place. Slipped pieces should be reported so that the customer can have them

Photo #15 *This is an asbestos cement shingle. The bottom edge of each shingle has a wire or clip holding it down so the wind doesn't lift them up and crack them. They are very brittle and inflexible.*

replaced and/or put back in place and refastened. If some shingles have slipped, test other shingles for looseness. Report any missing shingles. Check nails, connectors, and clips to make sure they are in place and secure.

- **Broken or flaking shingles:** Because both slate and asbestos cement shingles are brittle, they can be broken or cracked from mechanical damage such as someone walking on them or a falling tree branch or hail. Damaged shingles should be replaced. Low-quality slate can **delaminate**, flaking or sloughing off thin layers. When this process continues, the entire exposed portion of the slate can be reduced to tiny bits. A slate roof in that condition would have to be replaced. Tell customers to find a qualified and reputable roofer to repair or replace slate. In some states, the roofer may have to be licensed to work with slate.

> **INSPECTING SLATE AND ASBESTOS CEMENT SHINGLES**
>
> - Loose, slipped, or missing shingles
> - Broken or flaking shingles
> - Prior repairs

- **Prior repairs:** Watch for repairs. Where repairs have been made, try to determine if the repair was done correctly and if it's working. Report any repairs you find. Customers should be told to monitor a roof with previous repairs.

Metal Roofing

Metal roofing may come in sheets, which is appropriate for flat (as low as 2% slope) or sloped roofs, and as shingles for use on sloped roofs only (slope of 3/12). The metal used may be one of the following:

- Copper
- Stainless steel
- Aluminum
- Galvanized steel in which sheets are covered with zinc
- Coated steel, which is coated with tin, antimony, lead, or nickel alloys. There also are "steel" roofs that are painted or coated.
- Terne was a copper-containing steel alloy sheet covered with an 80% lead/20% tin plating. Modern terne roofing is 50/50 zinc and tin.

> **INSPECTING METAL ROOFING**
>
> - Rusting and corrosion
> - Secure seams
> - Loose sections
> - Paint job
> - Prior repairs

> *Definition*
>
> *Terne metal was a copper-containing steel alloy sheet covered with an 80% lead/20% tin plating. Modern terne roofing is 50/50 zinc and tin.*

Metal roofs vary in their expected lifetime of a minimum of 15 years up to 40 to 50 years. But even with a coating, terne and other steel-based roofing **eventually needs to be painted** to prevent corrosion and rusting if they are to last their lifetime.

Corrugated galvanized steel is a common metal roofing material. Adjacent sheets are overlapped by one corrugation. Overlapping sheets are laid over the lower course. Each sheet is nailed at the top, not the bottom. There are many different types of metal roofs. Some of them are fastened with exposed screws. These screws typically have a rubber washer beneath them. The problem is that over time, the washers deteriorate from UV damage and allow leakage at the screws.

Alloy coated steel sheets are overlapped and can be **soldered** at the seams. Expansion joints must be provided so that these seams don't pull apart. Adjacent sheets can also be **folded and crimped** together to form a flat or standing seam. Clips nailed to the roof deck hold the sheets in place. In this case, the lower ends are lapped over and either soldered or waterproofed with roofing cement. Many metal roofs now start out as coil stock like gutters. They are formed onsite with cold-roll forming equipment, which makes one piece from ridge to eaves.

The home inspector may find **metal shingles**. Older homes in the south may have tin plated steel shingles. There are new metal shingles that are formed and colored to resemble wood shakes, tiles, and slates which should be installed over plywood or OSB sheathing with a felt underlay.

Because metal roofs are very tight, a good attic system is needed. The home inspector should carefully inspect the roof framing from the attic for any signs of rot.

The condition of metal roofing should be inspected for the following:

Section Note

Travel with a ladder when you visit friends and ask to take a look at the roof. The more experience you have with real roofs, the better off you'll be. We don't have to warn you to be careful, do we?

- **Rusting and corrosion:** Inspect for rusting. The lack of paint on steel-based and terne roofing is the most likely reason for these roofs to deteriorate. For some reason, it's not common knowledge that they should be painted. Copper roofing can undergo a chemical reaction with some pollutants in the air (typically sulfuric acid rain), resulting in fine pinholes in the copper, which can cause leaks through the roof.

- **Secure seams:** Inspect metal roofing at the seams, looking for seams that are open, split, or distorted. Check the condition of the solder, if present.

Photo #16 *Believe it or not, this is a metal roof. They are not just your standard corrugated or standing seam variety anymore.*

- **Loose sections:** Metal roofing can come loose when seams open or fasteners pop out. Report any loose sections and those that are torn, bent, or punctured.

- **Paint job:** Examine the condition of the coating or paint job on terne and steel-based roofing. Terne roofs should be recoated every few years. Report on the absence of paint on those surfaces/materials that require it.

- **Prior repairs:** People may be tempted to use tar (asphalt roofing compound or mastic) to repair open seams or breaks and punctures in a metal roof. But tar should not be used on a metal roof for any reason. The tar traps moisture, which leads to more rusting. The home inspector may even find an entire roof that's been tarred over. This is a short-lived repair job and should be reported as such.

Sprayed Polyurethane Foam

Spray applied polyurethane foam should be installed on roofs with a slope of at least 1/4 in 12 (2% slope). The foam is typically applied directly to the wood decking. It can be overlaid directly onto an existing roof if the roof is still watertight. The foam must be coated with a UV-protective coating, typically elastomeric paint, within 72 hours of application of the foam. Polyurethane foam is very susceptible to UV damage, and the elastomeric coating must be recoated approximately every 5 to 10 years for a typical application. The longevity of the elastomeric is based on the thickness of its original application. Coatings of 30 mils will last about 12 years. Blisters are common with foam roofing. This happens when water was introduced into the application process as dew or rain. As the sun heats up the assembly, blisters will form. They eventually crack and allow the sun to damage the underlying foam. All blisters should be repaired. Use caution on foam roofs when wearing hard-soled shoes or shoes with large heels, as you can puncture the foam covering. As the elastomeric coating deteriorates over time, it will start to allow UV penetration and damage the foam beneath. Look for an orange hue to the typically white

Photo #17 *This is a completely destroyed foam roof. It should be a white elastomeric coating over a cream colored foam. As you can see the elastomeric coating is missing and the foam is UV damaged, causing it to turn an orange color. This is a remove and replace scenario now. It should just require repainting every 7-10 years indefinitely if properly maintained.*

elastomeric coating to tell you that the coating is wearing or worn thin and is due for recoating.

Single-Ply Membranes

A relatively recent development in roofing is the single-ply membrane, which is made of plastics, or synthetic rubber. The most common types are polyvinyl chloride (PVC), ethylene propylene diene monomer (EPDM), and Thermoplastic PolyOlefin (TPO). These are flexible membranes that cover and seal the entire roof.

PVC and TPO, roofs typically white in color (although many colors are available), are generally installed using "heat welding" techniques. You can usually see the printing from the manufacturer right on the roofing material. It will tell you the type of material (TPO or PVC) and its thickness in mils. EPDM roofs, which may be black or white in color, are glued together with adhesives. Luckily, none of these single-ply roofs are very common on residential structures. If you do find them, they would typically be on a condominium complex or an apartment building with a flat roof.

> **INSPECTING SINGLE-PLY MEMBRANES**
>
> - Poor installation
> - Tearing and punctures
> - Joints broken
> - Brittleness

The home inspector should inspect the condition of a single-ply membrane roof for the following:

- **Poor installation:** Check the membrane to make sure it is securely fastened to the roof to prevent liftoff. It may be covered with smooth stone, like pea gravel to ballast the covering. Seams should be bonded; the surface, if glued down, should not be overly wrinkled or bubbled; tar should not be used with PVC or EPDM; proper venting should be present; and fasteners should not be exposed.

- **Tearing and punctures:** The home inspector should report any tears or punctures in the membrane itself. Because this is a *single-ply* roofing material, any break in the membrane will result in leaking into insulation and/or the roof framing.

Photo #18 *This is an EPDM roof with a terribly installed pair of skylights. The roofing itself was well installed, but whoever installed the skylights didn't use the proper materials to seal the flashing at the roof's surface.*

- **Joints broken:** Sometimes, bonded joints in membrane roofs will break open (due to shrinkage or poor workmanship). Again, any opening in the surface will cause leaking. This condition should be repaired.

- **Brittleness:** The single-ply membrane is a soft, flexible material, and it should remain flexible. The home inspector should report any evidence that the membrane is becoming brittle.

Reporting Your Findings

As we said, the number 1 rule of home inspection is to take the customer along on the inspection. The number 2 rule is **never take the customer up the ladder or on the roof**. How then does the home inspector manage to communicate his or her findings on the inspection of the roof covering? Whether you decide to walk on the roof or inspect it from a ladder, it's important to take plenty of pictures of defects or areas of concern, particularly those the client cannot see from the ground.

Some home inspectors choose to arrive early at the inspection site and begin the roof inspection before the customer arrives. It doesn't hurt to have the customer see you on the roof hard at work when he or she gets there. That may even be better than asking the client to stand by and wait while you inspect the roof.

However you manage the inspection of the roof, you still must talk to the client about your inspection. First, tell the client why you walked on the roof or inspected it from the ladder. If you didn't get on the roof, explain that the roof was too dangerous or that you would have damaged the roofing if you walked on it. Explain how old you estimate the roof covering to be. Then walk around the house with the customer, pointing out the roof from various views and highlighting defective areas as you answer any questions and explain the following:

> **IMPORTANT POINT**
>
> *A roof in poor condition is one of the greatest concerns a customer has. Be patient in answering questions and explaining your findings. Be calm when reporting good and bad news.*

> **WHEN YOU REPORT**
>
> *If you're not certain of the roof's age or the number of layers of shingles, use ranges in the written report. For example, use 10 to 15 years and 2 or 3 layers.*

- **What you were inspecting**—the roof covering (and other aspects of the roof).

- **What you were looking for**—any deterioration of the roof covering, loose fastenings, missing pieces, improper installation, evidence of water penetration, and so on.

- **What you were doing**—probing wood shingles/shakes for rot, checking repaired areas, and so on.

- **What you found**—curled asphalt shingles, wood rot, broken tiles, missing slates, improper repairs, and so on.

- **Suggestions about dealing with the findings**—replacing missing shingles, applying moss or mildew treatments, repainting a metal terne roof, and so on, but with this caution—don't make uneducated guesses about how repairs should be made.

Chapter Note

The American Home Inspectors Training Institute offers both paper and computerized reports. These reports include an inspection agreement, complete reporting pages, and helpful customer information pages.

If you're interested in purchasing the Home Inspection Report, please contact us at 1-800-441-9411.

- **Estimate of remaining useful lifetime:** With the inspection of the roof covering, clients expect to be told when it will have to be replaced. We suggest that you stick with three general categories—immediate replacement, replacement within 5 years, and replacement after 5 years. This estimate should be based on the age of the current roof covering *and* your examination.

  Be patient with clients when you discuss the roof and show them defective areas as best you can so they can see for themselves what you're talking about. This is where good photos can be very helpful. Be calm and don't blow minor problems out of proportion. A few shingles that need replacing is not a disaster. Help the client to understand that.

Filling in Your Report

Every home inspector needs an inspection report. A **written report** is the work product of the home inspection, and every home inspector is expected to deliver one to the customer after the inspection. Inspection reports vary a great deal in the industry. Some home inspection companies develop their own version; others use state required formats (Texas), home inspection software, apps, or formats provided by training companies such as AHIT. Some are considered to be excellent, while others are not very good. A workable and easy-to-use inspection report is important for a home inspector. Of greater importance are its thoroughness, accuracy, and helpfulness to the customer. Whatever reporting format you choose, make sure it presents your findings in a clear, professional manner such that it reduces your liability and client dissatisfaction.

The **Don't Ever Miss** list is a reminder of those specific findings you should include in your inspection report. We list these items based on years of experience performing home inspections. Missing them can result in complaint calls and possible lawsuits. Here is an overview of what to report on during the inspection of the foundation:

DON'T EVER MISS

- Missing components
- Loose fastenings
- Wood rot
- Improper installation
- Water penetration
- Repaired areas
- Sag in the ridge or rafters

- **Roof information:** First identify the style of the roof and the type of roof covering. Then write the approximate age of the roof and the estimated number of layers. Also, make a note of roof visibility. You may want to give a percentage of visibility or note particular areas of the roof that couldn't be inspected. (We suggest that you report a tar and gravel roof as *not visible*.) And if appropriate, recommend an infrared scan to identify possible leaks that are not visible with the naked eye. It's also a good idea to record from where the roof was viewed—from the roof, the ladder, or the ground.

- **Roof condition:** Write your findings of the condition of the roof covering. We suggest that you use a rating in your report (as mentioned earlier), such as the following:
  - **Satisfactory** indicates that the roof covering will last 5 or more years.
  - **Marginal** indicates that the roof covering will have to be replaced within the next 5 years. If this is your rating, emphasize this **replacement within the next 5 years** on a summary page of your report as well as on the roof page.
  - **Poor** indicates that the roof covering needs to be repaired or replaced now or very soon. If this is your finding, you should note this fact as a **major concern** on a summary page of your report as well as on the roof page.
- **Note defects:** Record other findings, such as structural defects, found in the roof and other problems found in the covering as listed in the Don't Ever Miss list.

> **GARAGE ROOFING**
>
> *Don't forget to report the type and condition of the roof covering on the detached garage.*

3.5 FLASHINGS

The roof has a number of vulnerable areas that require more protection than just the roof covering. These areas include:

- At ridges and hips, junctions where planes of the roof slope away from each other
- In valleys, junctions where planes of the roof slope toward each other
- At junctions where a sloping roof meets a flat roof
- At junctions where roof and wall meet
- Around chimneys and other roof penetrations
- At the edges of the roof

> *Chapter Note*
>
> *Pages 189–198 present procedures for inspecting the flashings found on the roof.*

Flashings are designed to keep water out of these vulnerable areas. Flashings can be metal—galvanized steel, tin, terne, aluminum, copper, plastic, or rubber—or roll roofing, or the roof covering itself can be used. Flashings must be fastened in place but be free to expand and contract.

Ridge and Hip Flashing

Ridge and hip flashings are rarely visible. Metal or tar paper is applied to the sheathing across the ridge or hip, and the roof covering is applied over it. Finishes are then applied over the top. On the asphalt shingle roof, shingles are cut or specific premade shingles are installed and placed across the ridge and nailed.

> **CAUTION**
>
> *Do not walk on valley flashings. You can easily damage (tear) them.*

Photo #19 *There are just too many things to note in this photo. Obvious repairs by the mismatched shingles, the chimney flashing is a mess, no visible flashing at the siding, and the skylights we described earlier.*

With the wood shingle or shake roof, special bevel-cut shingles or shakes are used at ridges and hips for a watertight seal. Pieces are laid with alternate overlaps. Nails are concealed, except for the last one and its nail heads should be sealed. The home inspector should make sure shingles and shakes in these areas are tight and free of distortion, splits, or cracks.

Slate and asbestos cement shingle roofs may use shingles as was described for wood roofs or have metal flashings capping the ridge. Metal roofs are capped with metal. With roll roofing, a strip of roll roofing is laid across the ridge, glued down with adhesives or heat-welded, and nailed. With built-up roofs, the plies are carried right across the ridge if there is one. Tile roofs have special cap pieces for ridges, hips, and gables (rakes).

The home inspector should check ridges and hips to make sure the material used is watertight. Hips and ridges on tile roofs may be mortared or make use of pre-molded plastic flashing to prevent wind-driven rain from blowing under caps. Metal flashings should be inspected to look for rust and to make sure they are securely fastened.

Valley Flashing

A valley is a trough formed by the junction of two sloping faces of the roof. In an **open valley**, the roof covering stops short of this trough and the flashing is visible. This is common with rigid roofing materials such as wood shingles, tile, and slates, as well as asphalt shingles. In a **closed valley**, the roof covering passes from one face of the roof to the other without a break and the flashing underneath is not visible. Shingles across a closed valley may be interwoven or closed-cut.

When roll roofing is used as valley flashing, two layers are used. An 18" strip is laid facedown, and a 36" strip is laid face up on top. Flashings should be cemented to the shingles and nailed to the roof deck.

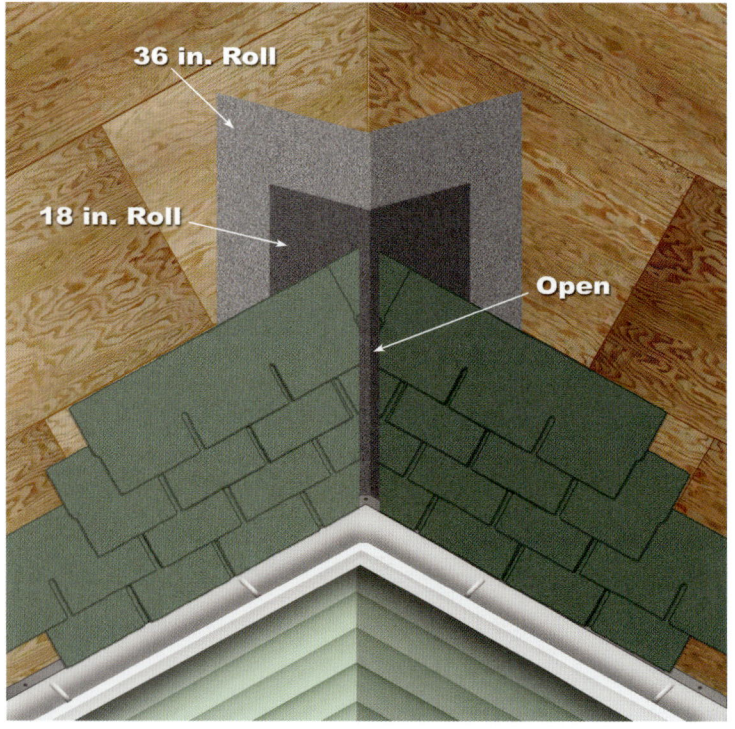

Illustration by Paddy Morrissey

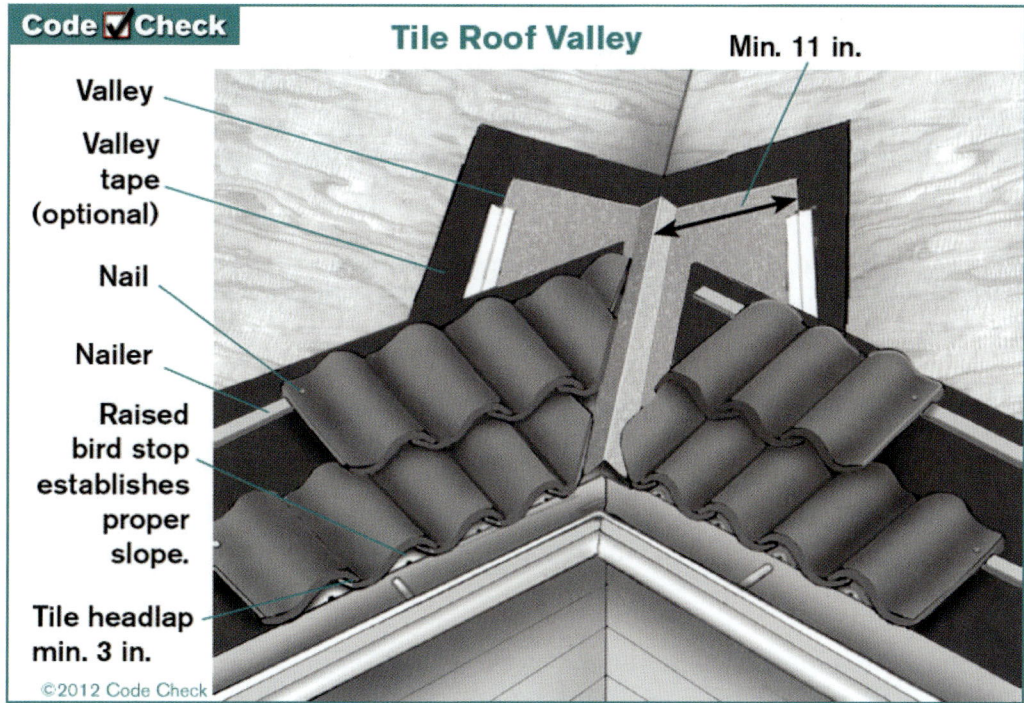

Metal valley flashing is a minimum of 24" wide. Materials consist of galvanized steel or aluminum with wood roofs, not copper. Copper flashings can be found with slate and most other roofing materials, generally on higher-end installations. Some metal valley flashings are crimped up along the center line to form a rib (also called a "W" flashing); this reduces the tendency for water to wash from side to side along the valley. This type of flashing is required on tile and metal roofing.

The home inspector may see special valley flashings when water from a steep slope flashing flows into the flashing on a lower slope. These are constructed to keep water from overshooting the lower flashing and going under the roof covering on the other side.

The home inspector should inspect the condition of valley flashings for the following:

> **INSPECTING VALLEY FLASHINGS**
>
> - Poor installation
> - Deterioration
> - Damaged
> - Repairs
> - Water penetration
> - Debris

- **Poor installation:** Valley flashings should extend to the edge (eave) of the roof. If they are too short, water can seep into the eaves/soffit. If lengths of flashing are overlapped along the valley, check to see that there is a sufficient overlap (minimum of 4 inches). Flashings should lie flat for smooth water flow.

- **Deterioration:** Inspect the flashing materials for corrosion, rust, and abnormal wear. Note if the paint job on painted metals is in good condition.

- **Damaged:** Torn or split valley flashings can be an indication that they are nailed too tightly. Valley flashings can be dented or bent if someone has walked on them. The home inspector should be careful not to damage them further by stepping on them.

- **Repairs:** Note where homeowners have repaired valley flashings, indicating a problem area. Try to determine if the repair is working.

  NOTE: Sometimes the home inspector may find valleys that are completely tarred over. In your inspection report, be sure to report tarred valley flashings as *not visible* as well as an improper repair.

- **Water penetration:** Always check for signs of leaking at valleys. Suspected areas should be noted for further evaluation once you are inside the attic.

- **Debris:** Report the presence of debris and leaves in valleys. Suggest that valleys be kept clean so that water isn't diverted under the roofing.

Roof-to-Wall Flashing

Flashings are required where second-story walls meet first-story roofs. A flashing (headwall or sidewall flashing) is nailed to the framing at least 4″ up under the siding material and must extend onto the shingles at least 4″ too. The home inspector should make sure the flashing is securely fastened beneath the siding. This is where leaking commonly occurs.

A **counter flashing** can be used to cover the lower continuous or step flashing. The counter flashing is nailed to the wall under the siding or can be embedded into masonry siding. See the diagram below. Many builders currently use the siding as the counter flashing, which is not a good practice (although technically it is allowed) because it makes replacing the roofing material very difficult at the flashing transition. In many cases, the roofer tars over the shingles up against the siding, which is not acceptable. You will also see J channel for vinyl siding resting directly on the roofing material. This is not acceptable and is incorrect based on the siding manufacturers' installation instructions. The J channel must be held off the roof at least 1/2″ to be properly installed.

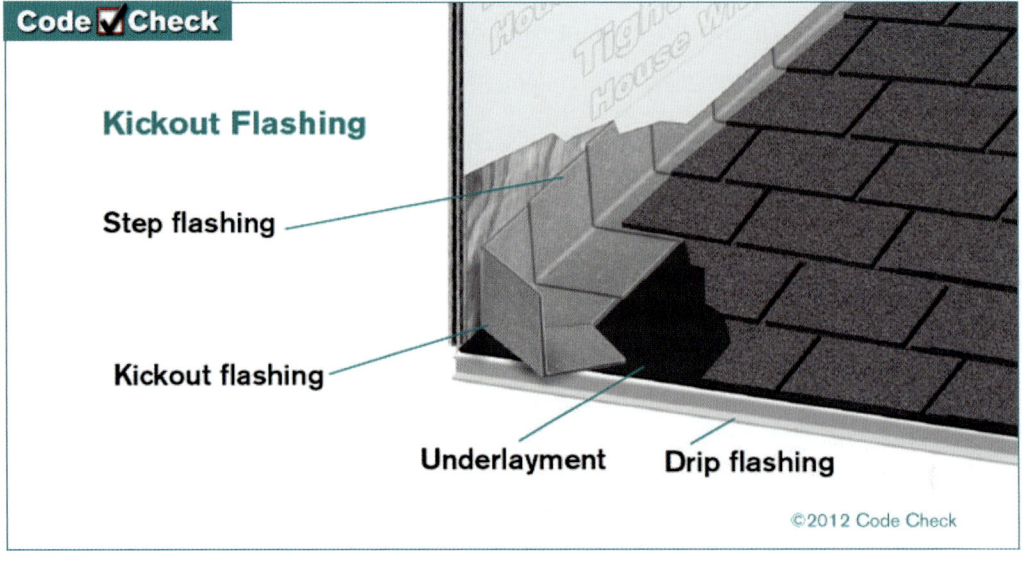

When the bottom of the wall is on a sloping roof, as at the side of a dormer, then **step or continuous flashing** and counter flashing (again siding can be used as the counter flashing) are required. Step flashing consists of short metal "L-shaped" flashings that lie under the roof covering and bend up the wall behind the siding or counter flashing. Step flashings are overlapped at least 4" to form a continuous sloping flashing. A counter flashing is installed over the top of the step flashing and under the siding or the siding itself is used as the counter flashing. A common type of flashing used with rigid roofing materials, like tile, is "Z" flashing. It is called this due to the shape of the bent metal pieces. It is nailed to the framing then a piece of continuous "pan" flashing is installed beneath and behind the Z flashing (see photo below). The siding is then installed along the top edge. This directs the water off the siding onto the Z flashing and into the pan flashing which carries the water to the eave or back onto the tile depending on the location on the roof.

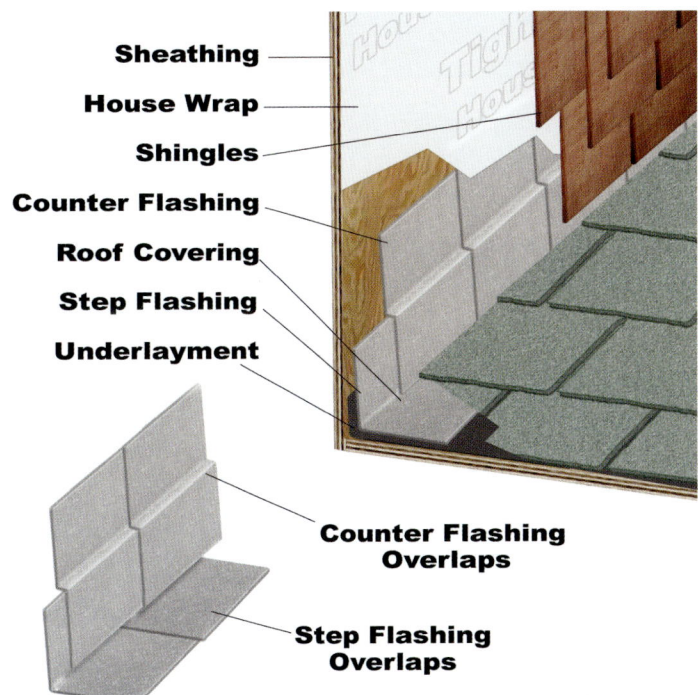

Illustration by Paddy Morrissey

The home inspector should inspect roof-to-wall flashings for the following:

- Poor installation
- Deterioration
- Damage
- Repairs
- Water penetration

Photo #20 Z FLASHING

This is an example of "Z" flashing. The Z portion being the top piece that will be covered up by the siding. The bottom "pan" tucks behind the Z and has a lip on it to prevent water from drifting back under the tile.

Definitions

The rake is the overhang at the gable end of the roof. A drip edge is a metal flashing used at the eaves and rakes to prevent water from damaging the roof deck and fascia boards and rake. It directs water flow into the gutter and off the gable end.

Sloped Roof-to-Flat Roof Flashing

Flashings are needed where a sloping roof meets a flat roof. The roof covering of the flat roof—such as roll roofing or built-up roofing—should extend up under the roof covering on the sloped roof. A flashing is then applied at this junction to reduce erosion of the roofing material. The home inspector should inspect this flashing for any breaks, corrosion, erosion, or tearing, as movement and settlement of the structure often damages these joints.

Joints between a sloped roof and a single-ply membrane roof should have metal flashings. The joint should not be tarred. Asphalt (tar) is not compatible with plastic roofing materials such as PVC and EPDM.

Drip Edge Flashing

Flashing at the edge of the roof serves to prevent water from getting to the roof sheathing, backing up behind the roof covering and gutters, and seeping into the fascia board. With some roof coverings such as asphalt shingles, drip edges are required at the eave and the **rake**. The rake is the overhang at the gable end of the roof.

Edge flashing is nailed to the sheathing under the tar paper and roof covering and extends down to cover the joint between the roof deck and the fascia board. The underlayment is to run over the top of the drip edge at the eave and should be beneath the drip edge at a gable end. The eave drains by gravity, so the tar paper is on top. The drip edge is on top of the tar paper at the rakes to prevent wind-driven rain from blowing in under the tar paper directly to the sheathing. The lower edge is bent out (lip) to allow water to drip off into the gutter or away from the fascia board.

Not all roofing systems have drip edge flashing. If it is not present, the home inspector should check at eaves and rakes for water damage, rot, and fungus.

INSPECTING CHIMNEY FLASHINGS

- Missing or incomplete
- Loose, torn, or damaged
- Rusted or corroded
- Prior repairs
- Water penetration

Photo #21 *Metal drip edge flashing is required and is obviously missing here.*

The home inspector should inspect the drip edge for proper installation and function. Check to see that water is not seeping into the roof deck or into the fascia or rake board.

Chimney Flashing

Another vulnerable area on the roof is the junction between the roof and chimney. Flashings are required on all sides of the chimney abutting the roof. They are most often metal, although roll roofing was sometimes used. Metal flashings are now required.

The **sloping sides** of the chimney normally have a two-part system of step flashings and counter flashings as described on page 192. The top of the counter flashing is embedded in the mortar joints on the masonry chimney or under the siding if "Z" flashing is used, or a flat piece of metal is caulked to the chimney chase (least desirable). The **low side** of the chimney has typical roof-to-wall flashings as described earlier. For chimneys sitting below the ridge, the **high side** of the chimney may also have typical roof-to-wall flashing. In this case, flashing should extend up at least 4″.

> **Definition**
>
> A <u>cricket</u> is a small peaked roof perpendicular to the main roof slope that is constructed at the high side of the chimney.

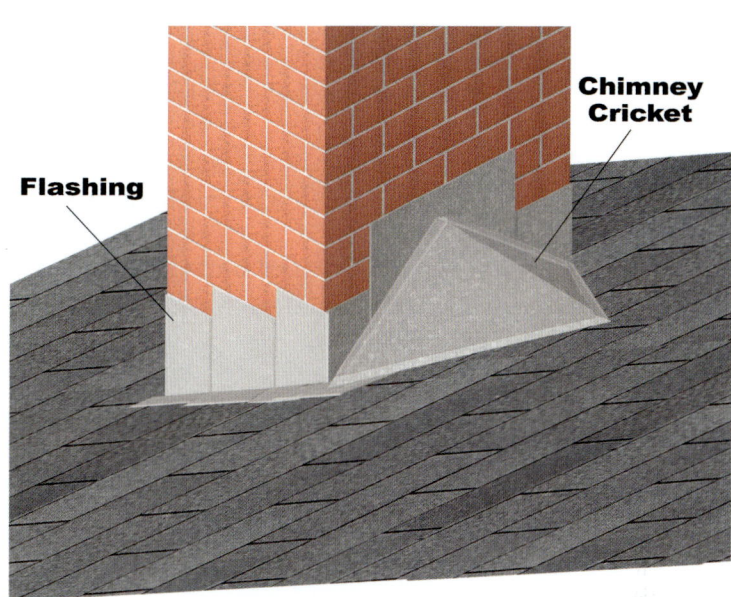

Illustration by Paddy Morrissey

When the chimney is wider than 30″, a **cricket or saddle** should be installed. A cricket is a small peaked roof perpendicular to the main roof slope and as wide as the chimney that is constructed on the high ridge side of the chimney to direct water and debris around the chimney. The height of the cricket should be between one-eighth and one-half the width of the chimney depending on the pitch of the roof. The cricket must have valley flashings on its roof sides and flashings where it meets the chimney. Check the condition of the roof covering on the cricket. Check valley flashings and flashings against the chimney side(s). Flashings should be in good condition, secure, and watertight.

The home inspector should inspect the condition of chimney flashings for the following:

- **Missing or incomplete:** Report any missing, incomplete, or inadequate chimney flashings.

- **Loose, torn, or damaged:** There may be movement of the structure while the chimney stays in place, and flashings can pull away from the chimney.

- **Rust or corrosion:** Check the condition of the flashing material for rusting and corrosion.

- **Prior repairs:** Look for repairs done to chimney flashings. Roofing cement (tar) can be used to repair chimney flashing leaks, but it should be

Photo #22 *It's never a good sign to see tar gooped onto the chimney flashing and surrounding roofing materials. This chimney is also wide enough to require a cricket.*

considered a temporary solution. Tar is not a proper flashing or long-term repair. Try to determine if the repair was done properly and whether it is working. Note that the repair is temporary at best and must be replaced with a permanent solution.

- **Water penetration:** As with other flashing areas, check around the chimney for leaks in the flashing from underneath in the attic.

Penetration Flashing

Areas around piping, vents, fans, and skylights must also have flashing to protect the roof.

ROOF PENETRATIONS
- Piping and vents
- Ventilators and fans
- Skylights

- **Pipe and vent flashing:** This type of flashing has a flat part that is laid on the deck and a cylindrical part that extends up and is crimped into or placed around the piping. The flat part lies under the roofing on the high side and over the roofing on the low side. Tar should not be used around vents and other penetrations. Aluminum, galvanized steel, plastic, and rubber flashing are

Photo #23 *You have to give them an A for effort. Not sure if the plumber made the vent pipe too long or the roofer used lead flashing that was too short? Either way it is improperly installed.*

Chapter 3

available off the shelf for various pipe sizes and roof slopes. These flashings may also be made of lead, a flexible material. If a rubber or plastic flashing is present, the home inspector should feel it to make sure it hasn't become brittle with age or UV damage.

The home inspector may come across a **pitch pocket**. This is a box placed around a plumbing stack or other small penetration, an old method not typically used anymore. The box was filled with a plaster of Paris material and covered with bitumen, pitch, or tar. If you find a pitch pocket, examine it carefully to see if the metal box has corroded, if the "pitch" is loose to the box and pipe, and if the filling has shrunk so much that water is ponding in the box. One or all of these conditions can result in leaking.

> **Definition**
>
> A <u>pitch pocket</u> is an old method used to flash a plumbing stack on the roof. It is a circular metal box surrounding the plumbing stack that is filled with a plaster of paris material and topped with tar, pitch, or bitumen.

- **Ventilators and fans:** These items usually come with flanges that serve as flashings, although the flanges are often not wide enough and may have to be extended or counter-flashed. On a sloping roof, the high side of the flange is cemented and nailed under the roof covering while the lower side lies over it. On a flat roof, the flanges should lie under the roof covering on all sides.

- **Skylights:** Many skylights come with a flashing assembly. Higher-end products such as Velux skylights have their own engineered flashings and work very well.

  In some cases, a skylight is a plastic bubble with no flashing (poor quality). The bubble flange is simply laid under the roofing on the high side and extends over the roofing on the low side. Ideally, skylights should have a curb (raised framing above the plane of the roof deck) and be flashed in a manner similar to chimneys. The home inspector should check skylights for leaking, but note that condensation on the interior of the skylight is not necessarily a sign of water penetration. In single and double bubble plastic skylights, the condensation you see often is trapped between the bubbles just like a dual-pane window seal that has failed.

The Cricket

If the chimney has a cricket, it should be inspected thoroughly. Check the condition of the roof covering on the cricket. Check valley flashings and flashings against the chimney side. Flashings should be in good condition and watertight.

Roof Structures

Any structure such as dormers, hatchways, bulkheads, and cupolas on the roof should be properly flashed.

- **Dormers:** Dormer roofs form valleys with the main slope of the roof and should have proper valley flashings as described earlier. The side walls of dormers should have step flashing and counter-flashing. The low side of the dormer should have typical roof-to-wall flashing.

> **Definition**
>
> A <u>cupola</u> is a small, rounded structure built on top of a roof; it is normally used to ventilate attics.

> **Definition**
>
> A <u>parapet</u> is a low wall running above the edge of a flat roof.

> **DON'T EVER MISS**
>
> - Loose or missing flashings
> - Flashing deterioration
> - Water penetration
> - Prior repairs

- **Parapets:** The low wall that runs above the edge of a flat roof is called a parapet. Parapets need flashing at the junction of the roof and the wall of the parapet and at the top of the parapet. The flashing at the roof is usually typical roof-to-wall flashing or "Z" flashing. The top of the wall should have cap flashing or coping to prevent water penetration. This cap may be asphalt composition, formed metal, brick, cast concrete, or stone.

Flashings on the parapet are often in bad condition. They may be loose, deteriorated, or missing completely. The caps should be checked to make sure they're not allowing water to seep into the wall. This is especially true for stucco walls, which crack over time, and from maintenance activities such as placing a ladder against the wall.

Reporting Your Findings

After you've finished the roof inspection and are communicating your findings to the customer, point out areas where you've found problems with the flashing. Show the customer tarred-over flashings and valleys and emphasize that you couldn't inspect or verify the presence of the flashings underneath the tar. It's important that customers understand what you've found to be in both good and not good condition and what can't be inspected.

You'll probably be reporting flashings on the same page of your report that discusses roof coverings. Here's an overview of what you should record in your inspection report:

- **Valley flashings:** It's helpful to have a separate section in your report for valley flashings. Identify the type of valley flashings present, such as galvanized, aluminum, copper, or asphalt. Then note their condition. Don't report on the condition of valley flashings if you can't see them. (We suggest that you report tarred valleys and flashings as *not visible*.)

- **Chimney flashings:** Identify the type of flashing used around the chimney as above and note its condition.

- **Other flashings:** Again, identify the other types of flashing materials present on the roof and note their condition. Your report may itemize each type of flashing present and allow you to check off satisfactory, marginal, and poor to note the condition of each. In any case, be sure defects, problems, and your recommendations are noted.

> **Chapter Note**
>
> *Pages 198–207 present procedures for chimney inspection.*

3.6 INSPECTING THE CHIMNEY

A property being inspected may have more than one chimney. The home inspector reports the **location** and **condition** of each chimney. Then the inspector records the **methods used** to inspect the chimney—from the ground with binoculars, from the ladder at the eaves, or from the roof. The inspection of the chimney is conducted not only from the exterior, but also from the attic and elsewhere in the house where it is visible. The chimney inspection includes the following:

- Chimney location and clearances
- Chimney foundation
- The material and condition of the chase
- The presence and condition of the chimney cap
- The material and condition of the flue
- Chimney flashings (see pages 195–196)
- Condition of the cricket or saddle
- The presence or absence of a rain cap/spark arrestor

Chimney Construction

Masonry chimneys should be self-supporting structures. Their footings and foundations exist separately from the house and must be deep enough to maintain chimney stability. In cold climates, they should extend well below the frost line.

The **chimney chase** is the outer "box" of the chimney. It may be constructed of brick, concrete block, stone, metal, or framed with siding. The **chimney flue** is the channel or tube that carries gases, fumes, and smoke from furnaces, fireplaces, and wood burning stoves. It can be made from clay tile, metal, or asbestos cement pipe (Transite™). The **chimney cap or crown**, made of concrete, stone, or sheet metal, covers the top of the chase and prevents water and small animals from entering. A **rain cap** may be present over the top of the flue.

Chimneys built before World War II were often **unlined**, meaning that the outer masonry chase (box) served as the flue. An unlined chimney with its masonry exposed to gases, fumes, water vapor, and smoke worked well enough then for fireplaces and oil furnaces, but gas furnaces today usually require a separate flue or flue liner as it is sometimes called. This is due primarily to the lower flue gas temperatures as compared with those of oil or wood-fired appliances or fireplaces.

There are also **metal chimneys**, which are metal from top to bottom. They require special handling, such as being isolated from the roof framing, being covered with approved fittings, and meeting safety clearance standards on the interior of the house.

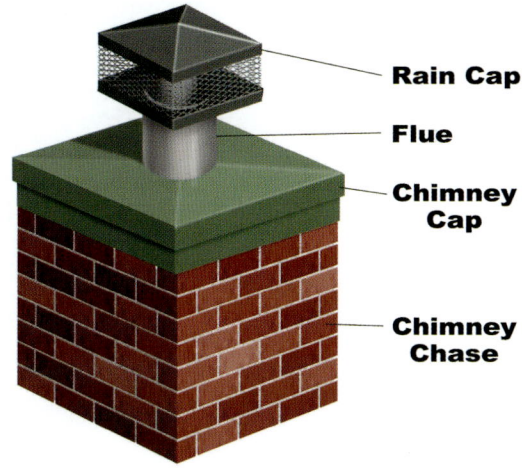

Illustration by Paddy Morrissey

CHIMNEY HEIGHT

- At least 3' higher than point of roof penetration
- At least 2' higher than anything within 10' of it

Local building codes generally include regulations regarding the following:

- Height in relation to roof line and neighboring roofs
- Horizontal distance from parapets and other components
- Construction material and thickness
- Type and construction of flues
- Separate flues for each type of heating system
- Number of flues per chimney
- Construction and depth of chimney footings
- Installation of prefabricated chimneys

Photo #24 CHIMNEY CLEARANCES

As you can see this home was originally constructed with a chimney that was the proper height. Unfortunately, someone built-out the attic and constructed a dormer right next to the existing chimney.

Clearances

The home inspector should begin the chimney inspection by making note of the location of each chimney. Chimneys may be located in the slope of the roof, through the ridge, or on the end of the roof inside or outside the exterior wall. The location of the chimney must relate to roof lines for both safety and the efficient draft of the chimneys.

A chimney must extend at least 3′ from the point of penetration through the roof. The top of a chimney must be at least 2′ higher than anything within 10′ of it, including the ridge, dormers, and parapets. This is known as the 2-foot/10-foot rule. If a new addition or dormer is constructed higher than an existing chimney (see photo), the chimney must be extended to meet these rules.

Chimneys not constructed to these standards can experience back drafting problems. Required clearances vary for other types of vents. Gas appliance "B" vents are used for gas water heaters, gas furnaces/boilers, and gas fireplace logs. They must be at least 1″ away from combustible materials and terminate at least 1′ above the roof, although the vent may need to be higher depending on the pitch of the roof. Oil appliance "L" vents must terminate at least 2′ above the roof. Clearance is usually not an issue because they typically vent into a masonry chimney. However, if they vent directly to the exterior in an "L" vent, they must have a clearance of 6–9″ depending on the type of appliance they are connected to.

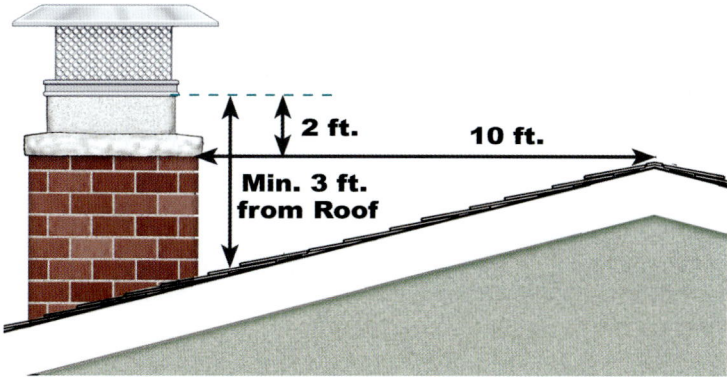

Illustration by Paddy Morrissey

Inspecting the Chase

The best place to inspect the chimney is from the roof and later from the attic if it penetrates the roof from the middle of the house. It's difficult to know what's happening on the back side of the chimney if you can only see the front. Be sure to record whether you viewed the chimney from the ground, from the ladder, or from the roof. If you haven't been able to view it from all sides, let your customer know that.

Another point to make is that old, unused chimneys may be only **partially removed**. The chimney may be merely capped off, torn down to below roof level and covered with roofing, or removed entirely. In one case, we found an unused chimney that had been removed *except* for the portion on the roof. The home inspector should determine whether a chimney is no longer in use.

As was stated earlier, the chimney chase may be masonry, may be made of brick, stone, or concrete block, or may be framed. In newer construction, the chimney chase may be wood framing covered with siding. The home inspector must identify the chase construction material. Then the chimney should be inspected for the following:

> **INSPECTING CHIMNEY CHASES**
>
> - Settling or leaning
> - Unlined flue
> - Loose, missing, cracked, or spalling masonry
> - Deteriorating mortar
> - Cracked or missing chimney cap
> - Improper or damaged flashing

- **Settling or leaning:** The home inspector should inspect the chimney to see if it is settling, pulling away from the house, or leaning. The chimney should be plumb (vertical). A chimney sits on its own footing and foundation, which can experience the same settlement problems as the house. Chimney footings can fail due to soil weakness below. In some cases, you may discover that the chimney has no foundation. Chimney settlement or movement should be reported to the client. Deteriorating mortar and masonry can cause a chimney to lean, the causes of which are varied and many. Here are a few:

  — **Erosion of mortar and settlement of joints:** Moisture from condensation in addition to sulphates from flue gases turn into weak acids that attack the parging or mortar joints. Excessive condensation in the flue is due to improper fuel or poor draft.

- **Unlined chimney:** One of the first things to check in the chimney is if it is unlined—that is, there is no separate interior flue (tube) and the chase (box) acts as the flue. This condition should be reported to the customer. In this case, the bricks and mortar are the only barrier preventing the escape of flue gases into the interior of the home or attic.

  CAUTION: If you find an unlined chimney, take great care when inspecting the chase **in the attic**. It's of extreme importance. Any cracked or missing bricks or missing mortar means that carbon monoxide gases, soot, creosote, smoke, and potentially sparks and embers are escaping into the attic or wall cavities. This should be reported as a **safety hazard**. When you point out a safety hazard such as carbon monoxide escaping into the house, your clients will give a sigh of relief for having hired you. All of a sudden, they've gotten their money's worth.

- **Loose, missing, cracked, or spalling masonry:** Inspect the condition of the chase from the roof *and* from the attic. The chimney takes a lot of abuse and is expected to deteriorate over time. Without the proper protection of a chimney cap or crown, rain constantly wets the interior as well as the exterior. Freeze/thaw cycles exaggerated by heating cycles cause masonry to spall. It is a result of water entering brick, concrete, or natural stone and forcing the surface to peel, pop out, or flake off often during freeze/thaw cycles. In the absence of a separate flue (unlined chimney), the chase also collects condensation from the exhaust as it cools near the top of the chimney. Inspect the chase material for any loose or missing masonry pieces, for cracking masonry, and for spalling on the face of the masonry. With metal chases, look for corrosion and rusting. Creosote and mineral deposits from moisture condense within the flue. Inspect framed chases as you would the rest of the building and siding.

UNLINED CHIMNEY

When you find an unlined chimney, <u>check the condition of the chase in the attic</u>. Cracks in the chase or missing bricks permit carbon monoxide to escape into the attic.

Photo #25 *This is a chimney showing its age. Tuck-pointing or just pointing is needed as some of the mortar is cracking and the bricks deteriorating.*

- **Deteriorating mortar:** The same circumstances that cause the masonry to deteriorate have a detrimental effect on the mortar. Mortar should be solid. The home inspector should note any mortar that is loose, broken, missing, or deteriorating. Missing or damaged mortar can be repaired/replaced using a technique called pointing, repointing, or tuckpointing.

- **Cracked or missing chimney cap:** A chimney chase with interior and separate flues should have a chimney cap to keep the rain out. A chimney cap prevents moisture deterioration of the masonry and the mortar. On framed chases, the cap keeps the rain from entering the chase, which is generally made of wood. The cap should go over the chimney top and fit snugly around the flues. The joint between the flue and the masonry cap should be caulked, not mortared, to allow for thermal expansion. A concrete chimney cap should be at least 2″ thick. Sometimes, mortar is substituted for concrete, but it usually cracks in a short time. A precast concrete, stone, or metal flashing cap may be used to replace a deteriorated or damaged cap. The home inspector should inspect the chimney cap for cracks. A missing cap should be reported to the customer and a suggestion made to have one installed.

- **Improper or damaged flashing:** Chimney flashing should be inspected.

Let's talk about a number of examples of chimneys. If a chimney has loose and missing mortar or the mortar is lying on the roof and all the joints are missing mortar a mason should definitely be recommended. If the bricks are farther apart at the top than at the bottom of the chimney, this is a sign of movement and probably failure of the chimney. You will also sometimes see metal straps where TV antennas were previously installed. TV antennas will destroy a chimney over time due to the flexing of the chase with the antenna blowing in the wind.

Cracks in a chimney cap where rain has been getting in and freezing during the winter can also destroy a chimney. It is likely that a chimney in this condition will be taken down to the roof line and be rebuilt. A chimney that has deteriorating flashing and needs a cricket on the high side is a common problem. Crickets will prevent damaged due to freeze thaw and decay of organic materials.

> **Section Note**
>
> *"One of my inspectors was on the roof of an old Victorian that had been remodeled extensively. As he walked past the chimney and rested his hand on it, the chimney swayed slightly. When he turned his back, he heard a horrendous crash. He turned around to find the chimney gone! Only a hole was left. The chimney had fallen three stories to the basement.*
>
> *When the home was remodeled, the chimney was no longer needed. The homeowners had left the roof portion of the chimney in place while removing the rest of it. However, they hadn't made allowances for supporting the remaining portion on the roof.*
>
> *You never quite know what to expect."*

> **Section Note**
>
> *"An instructor here at American Home Inspectors Training Institute (and a very experienced home inspector) told me about a particular chimney he was inspecting.*
>
> *The chimney was outside the exterior wall of the house. While on the roof, the home inspector noted that the chimney wasn't in very good shape. He gave it a light push (a little tap, he says), and to his surprise, the chimney fell over into the yard like a falling tree.*
>
> *Believe it or not, it's not that unusual with an exterior chimney in bad repair. Try not to be the one who topples it over."*

SOME ADVICE: Don't push or lean on a masonry chimney that's in poor condition. With mortar deteriorating and missing, you're likely to topple it over or knock down portions of it.

INSPECTING THE FLUE

- Requirements
- Cracked, joints open, loose mortar
- Rain cap condition
- Interior soot covered
- Metal chimneys
- Unlined flue

Inspecting the Flue

The flue is the channel or tube that carries gases, fumes, and smoke from furnaces, fireplaces, and wood burning stoves. When the chimney chase is unlined, the chase serves as the flue. Obviously, the home inspector who cannot get on the roof is not going to be able to inspect the chimney flue. The customer should be informed that the flue was *not accessible and not evaluated*.

If possible, the home inspector identifies the material the flue is made of. The home inspector should inspect the condition of the chimney flue for the following:

- **Requirements:** There should be a 4″ separation between multiple flues within the same chase. If not, the flues should be at different heights so as not to interfere with each other's drafts. In general, an unlined chase is not appropriate for a gas furnace, and the home inspector should confirm the presence of an interior flue for a gas furnace. Many older chimneys have metal flue liners installed for gas and oil appliances.

- **Cracked, joints open, loose mortar:** The flue should be inspected for its condition. Check the joints in clay tile flues for loose or missing mortar and cracks in the tiles. In metal flues, joints should be securely closed. A metal flue should be checked for rust and corrosion. It should also be sleeved/installed correctly. Many are installed upside down.

- **Rain cap condition:** The rain cap should be high enough above the flue to allow gases to escape, about four times the free air space of the flue

Photo #26 *The flue in this chimney is not properly aligned. You can see that the flue tile sections are offset with gaps present.*

it is protecting. Inspect the rain cap for its condition. It should be firmly attached to the flue and free of cracks, rusting, and corrosion. A spark arrestor should also be present for any solid fuel burning fireplace or stove to prevent catching the roof on fire.

- **Interior soot covered:** Most standards do not require the home inspector to inspect the interior of the flue that is not accessible, but we suggest that you do if you can see into the flue. Shine your flashlight into the flue. If it is covered entirely with soot and creosote, report the condition as **not visible**. You should let the customer know that the interior of the flue was **not evaluated** and recommend that a chimney technician be called to clean the flue and **reevaluate its condition**.

- **Metal chimneys:** With a metal chimney where the chimney is also essentially the flue, inspect it to make sure all sections are tight and securely fastened to each other. Lower sections should be fitted inside upper sections. Watch for rusting and corrosion. Where possible, check the metal chimney as it passes through the attic and the house. Any breaks in the joints will cause the release of carbon monoxide into the house. Metal chimneys must be isolated from the roof covering. On the interior, certain clearances must be maintained near combustible surfaces, generally much more than an inch depending on the device and type of flue. Be careful as you can have a metal flue for a gas or oil appliance or for a solid fuel appliance (stove or fireplace), but they have different clearance and height requirements. You may not know what the flue/chimney is for until you go inside the house. Be sure to correlate what it's for and apply proper rules once you go inside.

> **Personal Note**
>
> *"I once inspected a home with a metal chimney. I found that the chimney passed through a bedroom closet. Although the chimney was the proper distance from the walls, the homeowner had clothes pushed up against it. That's a safety hazard. Customers should be warned about dangerous situations such as this."*

- **Unlined chimney:** With the unlined chimney, note the interior of the chase for material and mortar deterioration. Any time you find an unlined chimney, you should recommend that a chimney technician be called to **reevaluate** it. If you find the interior covered with soot or creosote, report the condition as **not visible**. Again, carefully check the unlined chimney in the attic for cracks, missing masonry, and broken or missing mortar.

Other Roof Items

The home inspector will find other items on the roof. Here is an overview of what should be inspected and what does not need to be inspected in the general home inspection.

- **Structures:** Structures on the roof's surface such as dormers and cupolas should be inspected for framing, roof covering, and siding condition just like other parts of the home's structure. Watch for decay, especially with cupolas, which are often neglected. Check the condition of the flashings (see pages 189–198).

- **Skylights:** Check skylight glazing for cracks, breaks, and discoloration. Many skylights are plastic bubbles, not glass, and these may become brittle in the sun and crack. There should be no condensation between lights. Frames should be free of rot and corrosion. Check for signs of leaking on the interior.

- **Lightning rods, electric service masts, antennae, and satellite dishes:** Standards do not require the inspection of these attached accessories although electrical masts must be inspected as part of the electrical system. However, the home inspector should check that the lightning rods and ground cables are securely fastened to the roof. Electric service masts and antennae should sit on pads or protective mountings. Sometimes, the antenna may be strapped to the chimney. Wind vibration can loosen mortar joints in the chimney.

- **Solar systems:** This is not a requirement of the home inspector. But mountings should be tight, and they should be properly flashed and waterproofed. If debris is trapped by the collectors, examine the condition of the roof covering in this area for deterioration. Be sure to disclaim the areas of the roof that are not visible due to the equipment mounted on the roof.

Reporting Your Findings

Talk to your customer about your findings from the chimney inspection. After you come down from the roof, point out those defects from the ground the customer may be able to see. Here's an overview of how you should report the chimney inspection in your inspection report:

- **Chimney information:** First, record where you viewed the chimney, such as from the roof, a ladder, or the ground. Many homes have more than one chimney. Include the location of each one in the inspection report. You can locate them by describing them, for example, as on the ridge, on the exterior at the north wall, or on the southern slope. If you viewed each chimney from a different place, record that too.

- **The chimney chase:** Identify the chase material and record its condition, noting defects such as loose bricks, deteriorating mortar, and a cracked or missing chimney cap. Be sure to record your findings of the inspection of the chase from the attic. Note that a chimney in such poor condition that it needs replacement should be noted in your report as a *major concern*

- **The flue:** If you haven't been able to get on the roof, mark the flue as *not visible and/or not accessible and not evaluated*. Identify the flue material and note any defects you've found. Be sure to note if the flue is missing (unlined). We suggest that you recommend having an unlined chimney cleaned and evaluated by a technician and possibly relined if the buyer

---

DON'T EVER MISS

- Loose bricks or stones
- Deteriorating mortar
- Cracked or missing chimney cap
- Unlined chimneys
- Loose or missing flashings
- Cracked flues or open flue joints
- Condition in attic

will be using it in the future. The same is true for a flue covered with soot and creosote. You should recommend cleaning and evaluation.

- **Safety hazard:** If you find an unlined chimney from which flue gases are escaping into the attic, list the condition as a safety hazard. It's a good idea to pull out any safety hazards you've mentioned in your inspection report and list them on a summary page at the back of the report. This makes it easy for the customer to find them.

3.7 INSPECTING ROOF DRAINAGE

The purpose of the roof drainage system is to allow water to drain off the roof in such a way as to prevent damage to the grade or vegetation and house and to the foundation. Roofs should be pitched so that water runs to the lower edges. Gutter and downspout systems are a common way to divert water away from the roof and house. Flat roofs may have internal drains or scuppers that carry away water.

> **Chapter Note**
>
> *Pages 207–212 present the study and inspection of the roof drainage system.*

The home inspector should inspect the following components of the roof drainage system:

- Edge flashings (see page 194)

- Gutters (internal and external)

- Downspouts

- Roof drains and overflows

- Scuppers

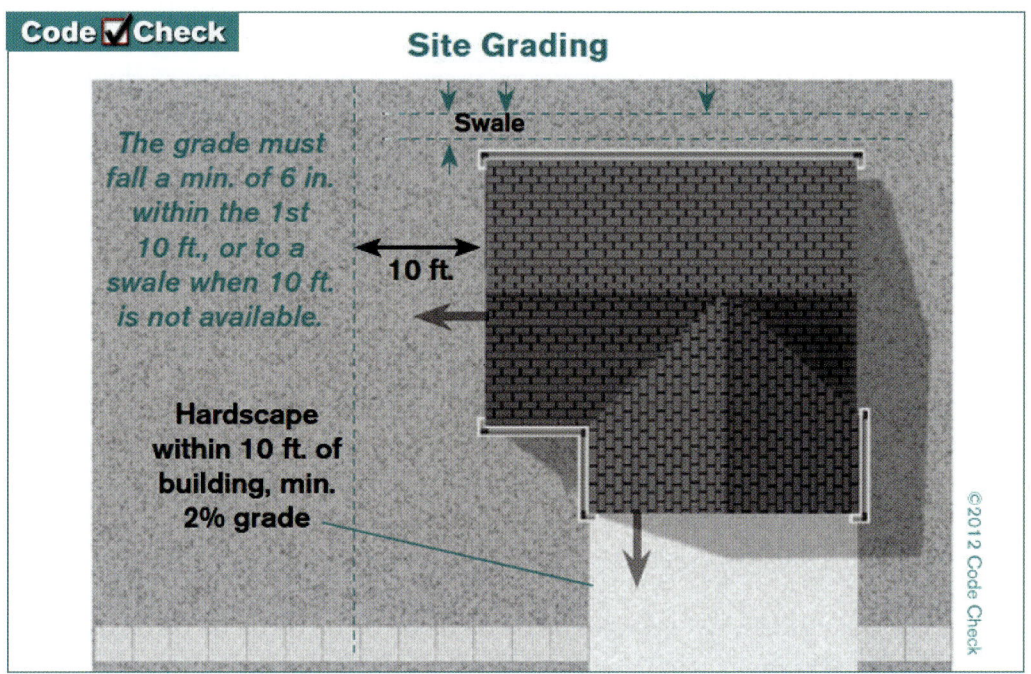

THE ROOF INSPECTION

Inspecting Gutters

Most homes have external gutters attached to the fascia board or rafter tails at the edge of the eaves, some homes have built-in or internal gutter systems, and many other homes have no gutters. Gutters are made from copper, aluminum, galvanized steel, lead, vinyl, or wood.

- **Metal gutters:** These gutters may be flat-bottomed or half-rounds. They may be hung from brackets, nailed to the fascia board, or spiked to the ends of the rafters.

- **Copper gutters** are the longest lasting—50 to 100 years—but they are expensive and not very common. Sections of gutter are soldered together. Copper is vulnerable to pitting and deterioration from air pollution (acid rain); copper also is prone to problems when it is used with a cedar roof due to tannins from the wood. The home inspector should look for stains on the copper and for broken joints. Orange spots in the metal and rings on the underside will show where water is dripping through.

- **Aluminum gutters** are by far the most common type. They are available in long lengths, so there are few joints, if any, to worry about. They don't rust but can be dented when ladders are placed against them. Special end and corner pieces are used. Joints are usually riveted or screwed together and sealed. You should inspect them for leaking at these joints. Aluminum gutters usually last 25+ years.

- **Galvanized steel gutters** must be painted to prevent rusting. Some come prefinished. Joints are usually soldered. Rust is a clue to problems.

- **Vinyl gutters:** Gutters made of vinyl are available. One problem with vinyl gutters is that they become brittle in cold weather. The home inspector should never place a ladder against them. These gutters vary in life expectancy because of the quality of the types available. They are often installed by the homeowner and generally are too small to be effective in most applications.

- **Wood gutters:** Generally found on historic homes. Planked troughs were once used, but now wood gutters are made from clear milled lumber chosen for its straight, tight grain. They can last up to 20 years, although once they begin to decay, their life is limited. Wood gutters may be lined with copper, aluminum, galvanized steel, or lead lined with roofing compound or roofing fabric, or they may be painted on the inside with boiled linseed oil to fill the pores. They should be probed carefully with a screwdriver for rot, especially at joints and ends where water can enter the end grain. Metal linings deteriorate over time and let water through.

- **Built-in or internal gutters** are constructed as part of the roof. A trough lined with copper, terne, or galvanized steel is made at the rafter ends.

GUTTER TYPES

- Copper, galvanized steel, aluminum
- Plastic
- Wood lined with metal or roofing fabric
- Ground-level gutters

The metal lining may be replaced with asphalt composition roofing or roofing felt and hot tar. Built-ins can be hard to inspect. There may be leaking into the walls of the house depending on the overhang at the eaves. The home inspector should examine them carefully for corrosion of the liner and wood rot.

- **Yankee gutters**, also called flush or Philadelphia gutters, were once very common. They divert water to the edge of the roof and prevent it from running over the eaves at entrances and doorways. Planks are laid against shaped blocks which are nailed to the roof surface. The fastenings to the roof must be waterproof. The home inspector may find short runs of Yankee gutters over doorways or at the ends of valleys. These gutters may be lined with metal or roofing fabric.

- **No gutters:** Many homes were designed without gutters because of the dry climate or in an attempt to solve water runoff without the use of gutters, as was tried in the 1950s when some homes were designed with extra wide overhangs. The ground around the house should be examined for a trench or erosion showing where the roof water drips off. A determination can be made as to whether the system is depositing water too close to the foundation. Often, the home inspector will find short runs of gutters or diverters that have been added to such homes to solve runoff problems. Don't confuse a home designed to work without gutters with a home where the owner has taken down failed gutters and never replaced them. Although not required to know from an inspection standpoint, areas of the country with expansive soils are required to have gutters regardless of the type of foundation present.

    Some homes without gutters may have ground-level gutters. In this case, a concrete trough in the ground catches the runoff and diverts it away from the house.

The home inspector should inspect the condition of gutters for the following:

- **Corrosion, rust, and rot:** Inspect gutter material and any linings for deterioration. Check for corrosion, rust, and wood rot at joints and ends where soldering and sealing may break down. Probe wood gutters for wood rot in stained areas and in apparently "good" areas where rot may be present but not visible. For best drainage, gutters should be placed so that the slope of the roof clears the edge of the gutter by 1/4" to 1". The exact distance depends on the slope of the roof, but in general, the steeper the pitch, the less clearance that is required. Proper slope allows snow and ice to slide off the roof and clear the gutter rather than sliding into the gutter and possibly creating an ice dam.

- **Leakage:** Leaks are most likely to occur at joints and at deteriorated areas. Check along the roof edge and fascia for any evidence of leaking and wood rot. Trenches and holes in the ground around the house will show where water is leaking

> *Section Note*
>
> *"I've found gutters so filled with organic matter from leaf breakdown that there are tree saplings growing in them. Of course, the gutters can no longer function. I always stress the importance of keeping gutters cleaned out. Most people don't recognize clogged gutters as a cause of a wet basement."*

> **Definitions**
>
> The <u>shoe</u> of a downspout is a curved section at its bottom that directs water away from the house.
>
> A <u>drywell</u> is a rock-filled cavity in the ground near the house. Water is directed from the downspout through piping to a drywell.

through the gutters. Look for improper repairs to holes and joints and try to determine if those repairs are working.

- **Loose fastenings:** Make sure gutters are not sagging due to loose fastenings. Check to see that brackets and spikes/ferrules are in place and tightly secured. When fastenings loosen up, gutters can change their pitch and may pond water rather than direct it toward the downspout. Water can pour over the edge of the gutter.

- **Damaged:** Gutters can become damaged when trees and ladders lean against them. Watch for breaks in the gutters and dents or distortions that can restrict or alter the flow of water.

- **Debris filled:** Gutters should be cleaned regularly. Debris and leaves can block the flow of water. Gutters can also be damaged by ice accumulation and the weight of ice or icicles.

Photo #27 *The number one issue with gutters is lack of maintenance" that causes them to become full of debris.*

- **Gutter covers:** Wire mesh or screens can be installed over gutters to prevent leaves and other debris from entering the gutter. These types of covers usually do not perform as they should. Smaller items may still get through the screening and block the gutters. They also make it more difficult to see into the gutters and to clean them. Inspect the covers to see if they are in place and are not damaged. Check to see if gutters are blocked anyway.

Inspecting Downspouts

Downspouts connect to the gutters and carry water to the ground or to drains designed for the purpose of disposing of the water. They may be made of the same material as the gutters, although this is not always the case. The bottom end of the downspout may have a shoe and/or a splash block to divert water away from the foundation. Extensions up to 6′ in length should be present when the grading is poor around the house.

> **INSPECTING DOWNSPOUTS**
>
> - Corrosion and rust
> - Leaking
> - Disconnections
> - Missing sections
> - Clogged with debris

Some downspouts go into the ground. Water may be directed through buried piping to an outlet some distance from the house. Water could be discharged into the waste disposal system or into basement floor drains. It could be diverted to a **drywell**, which is a rock-filled cavity in the ground near the house. In some cases, piping channels water directly into the ground away from the house. It may also run to the storm sewer or street at the curb. Piping can become clogged with debris and begin to malfunction. The home inspector is not required to inspect downspout underground piping, but it is a good idea to determine which method is being used and whether it is functioning, if possible.

The home inspector should inspect the condition of downspouts for the following:

- **Corrosion and rust:** Inspect the condition of the downspout material for deterioration.

- **Leaking:** Look for leaking at the back of the downspout where a broken seam may send water down the siding. Check at connections between sections of the downspout.

- **Disconnections:** It's not unusual to find loose connections between sections of the downspout or to find the shoe disconnected entirely and lying on the ground. When downspouts come apart and are put back together, homeowners often reconnect them incorrectly. The upper section should fit *inside* the lower section.

- **Missing sections:** Often, shoes and extensions to the downspout are crushed or are missing entirely. Sometimes, vertical sections are missing too, and the downspout simply ends a few feet from the ground. There may be a hole in the ground as a result of the water being dumped in one spot. Suggest that any missing sections be replaced.

- **Clogged with debris:** Check both the top and bottom of downspouts for evidence of debris blocking the downspout. Remind customers that downspouts should be cleaned regularly.

The Flat Roof

A perfectly flat roof will not drain. But in most instances, the so-called flat roof is slightly pitched to allow water to drain off.

In the drawing on the previous page, the flat roof is constructed with a slight pitch. The flashed parapet along three sides of the roof prevents water from escaping. Water is diverted to the roof's edge. A typical gutter and downspout system may be present to catch and carry water away from the roof. If all four sides of the roof have parapet walls, **scuppers** will typically be installed through the walls. If parapets are on all four sides of the building and scuppers are the primary source or drainage, then roof drains must also be present as a backup, described below.

When inspecting a flat roof such as that shown on the previous page, the home inspector should look for evidence of ponding water. Water ponds on the roof when the roof is sagging. If there is no standing water, look for evidence of dried-up ponds leaving a dirt stain or small pile of dirt and debris.

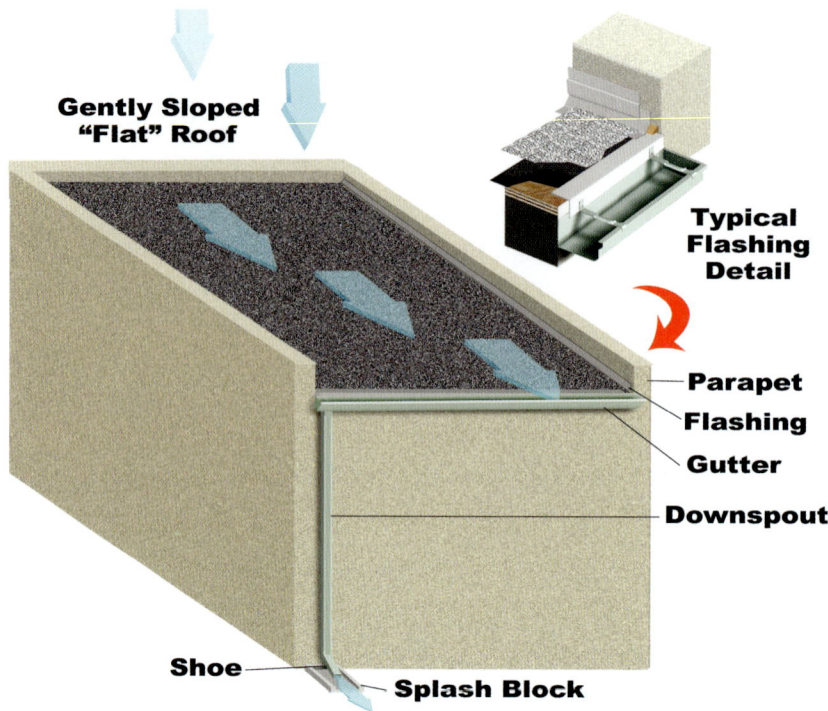

Illustration by Paddy Morrissey

Flat roofs may be built with reverse slopes to direct the water to a central area for draining or collection and storage. The butterfly roof is an example. When roof drains are present, they must have overflows or scuppers that are no more than 2″ above the lowest point of the roof. This prevents the roof from becoming a "swimming pool" if the main drains or scuppers become clogged. Cleanout traps, grills, and drain covers should be kept free of debris. Look for evidence that water has been ponding around the drain.

DON'T EVER MISS

- Leaking gutters or downspouts
- Corrosion, rust, or wood rot
- Loose fastenings or connections
- Missing sections
- Debris-filled or clogged

Reporting Your Findings

Talk to your customer about what you find when you inspect the roof drainage system. Point out areas in gutters where you find leaking, rusting, or sagging so that the customer can see them. When you report on the gutters and downspouts in your inspection report, identify the materials they're made of. Also, report their condition. Note defects such as those mentioned in the Don't Ever Miss list. If you find gutters clogged with debris, write the suggestion that gutters should be cleaned. Don't overlook reporting on extensions.

The home inspector should also report the condition of gutters and downspouts on the garage, especially if it is detached as it may or may not have the same configuration as the house.

CHAPTER 4
THE PLUMBING INSPECTION

As with the electrical system, much of the plumbing system is hidden behind the walls of the home. The home inspector performs a **visual inspection** of the exposed supply and waste distribution piping and fixtures, reporting any defects found in the system and helping clients to understand those defects.

Inspection SOP

These are the Standards of Practice that apply to the plumbing system. The chart provides a good outline of the SOP to govern the plumbing inspection. Not every detail is presented in the table, but there is enough of an overview to give you a good idea of what is and is not to be inspected. Here is a layout of what the plumbing inspection entails:

> **Chapter Note**
>
> *Pages 213–218 outline the content and scope of the plumbing inspection. It's an overview of the inspection, including what to observe, what to describe, and what specific actions to take during the inspection. Study these guidelines well.*

OBSERVE AND/OR REPORT

Observe: The act of making a visual examination of a system or component and reporting on its condition.	• Static water pressure • Condition of the gas distribution system • Interior water supply and distribution systems including all fixtures and faucets • Interior drain, waste, and vent systems including fixtures • Water heating equipment and hot water supply systems • Vent systems, flues, and chimneys • Fuel storage and fuel distribution systems • Sewage ejectors, sump pumps, and related piping
Describe: Report in writing a system or component by its type or other observed characteristics to distinguish it from other components used for the same purpose.	• Location of water meter • Location of homeowner's main water supply shut-off valve and hose bibs • Interior water supply, drain, waste, and vent piping materials • Water heating equipment including, capacity and energy source(s) • Location of main fuel shut-off valve(s) • Location of any observed fuel storage system(s)

Report as deficient deficiencies in:	• Presence of active leaks
	• Lack of a pressure-reducing valve when the water pressure exceeds 80 psi
	• Lack of an expansion tank at the water heater(s) when a pressure-reducing valve is in place at the water supply line/system
	• Absence of:
	  • fixture shut-off valves
	  • dielectric unions, when applicable
	  • backflow devices, anti-siphon devices, or air gaps at the flow end of fixtures
	• Water supply pipes and waste pipes
	• Installation and termination of the vent system
	• Performance of fixtures and faucets not connected to an appliance
	• Water supply, as determined by viewing functional flow in two fixtures operated simultaneously
	• Fixture drain performance
	• Orientation of hot and cold faucet controls
	• Installed mechanical drain stops (pop-ups)
	• Commodes/water closets, fixtures, showers, tubs, and enclosures
	• Commodes/water closets that were damaged, had loose connections to the floor, were leaking, or had tank components that did not operate
	• Water heating unit(s)
	  • Leaking or corroded fittings or tanks
	  • Damaged or missing components
	  • Absence of a cold water shut-off valve
	  • If applicable, absence of a pan or pan drain system that does not terminate over a waste receptor or to the exterior of the building above the ground surface
	  • Inappropriate locations
	  • Lack of protection from physical damage (bollards)
	  • Burners, burner ignition devices, or heating elements, switches, or thermostats (sources of ignition) that are not a minimum of 18″ above the lowest garage floor elevation, unless the unit is listed for garage floor installation (FVIR type)
	  • Absence of an opening that allows access to equipment for inspection, service, repair, or replacement without removing permanent construction or building finish
	  • When applicable, a floored passageway and service platform that allows access for equipment inspection, service, repair, or replacement
	  • Absence of or deficiencies in the temperature and pressure relief valve and discharge piping, Watts 210 valves, and seismic bracing (required in seismic areas)

- Temperature and pressure relief valve that failed to operate when tested manually (Texas only)
- Deficiencies in performance of electric heating elements
- Condition of conductors
- Gas leaks
- Flame impingement, uplifting flame, improper flame color, or excessive scale buildup
- Absence of a gas shut-off valve within 6′ of the appliance
- Absence of a gas appliance connector or one that exceeds 6′ in length (varies by local requirements)
- Gas appliance connectors that are concealed within or extended through walls, floors, partitions, ceilings, or appliance housings
- Combustion and dilution air
- Gas shut-off valves
- Access to gas shut-off valves that prohibit full operation
- Gas appliance connector materials
- Vent pipe, draft hood, draft, proximity to combustibles, and vent termination point and clearances
- Hydromassage therapy equipment
  - Inoperative units
  - Presence of active leaks
  - Deficiencies in components and performance
  - Missing and damaged components
  - Absence of an opening that allows access to equipment for inspection, service, repair, or replacement without removing permanent construction or building finish
  - Absence or failure of operation of ground-fault circuit interrupter protection devices

Note that the home inspector is **not required to inspect water conditioning systems (softeners or filters)** and is not required to test or report on the **quantity or quality** of the water supply.

- **Water service entrance:** Although most Standards of Practice state that the home inspector is not required to determine if the water supply is public or private, we suggest that you do. The home inspector should identify the service piping and inform the client if this piping is lead, which typically occurs in homes built prior to 1950 and in urban areas. The inspector should describe the location of the water meter and main shut-off valve. The inspector doesn't test the main shut-off valve. In fact, the home inspector is **not required to operate any valve except toilet flush valves, hose bibs, fixtures, and faucets**.

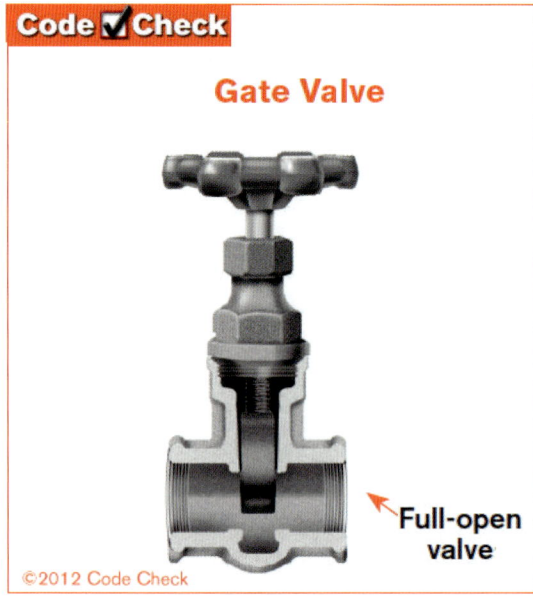

Code ✓ Check

Gate Valve

Full-open valve

©2012 Code Check

Code ✓ Check

Ball Valve

Full-open valve

©2012 Code Check

PLUMBING INSPECTION

- Water supply entrance
- Supply distribution piping
- Fixtures and faucets
- Drain, waste, and vent system
- Hot water system
- Fuel storage and distribution piping
- Sump pumps

For a private service, the home inspector should locate the source of water supply and determine the type of well, if possible, and the condition of its well equipment. The inspector checks the pressure gauge and listens for a waterlogged tank.

- **Water distribution piping:** The home inspector identifies the materials used in distribution piping. All visible interior hot and cold water (domestic) piping is inspected for leaking and deterioration. The home inspector looks for evidence of leaking throughout the house and looks for any repairs to the distribution system. The home inspector watches for and reports all visible safety hazards such as cross connections and the presence of asbestos-like insulation on piping.

The home inspector is **not required to inspect fire and lawn sprinkler systems** or **hydro-massage therapy equipment**, except for functional flow and drainage (check your state SOP to be sure). Also, the inspector is not required to determine the **effectiveness of anti-siphon devices, but should comment on their presence or absence as required**.

- **Fixtures and faucets:** The home inspector operates all fixtures and faucets in the supply system (not shut-off valves), paying attention to the functional flow of water

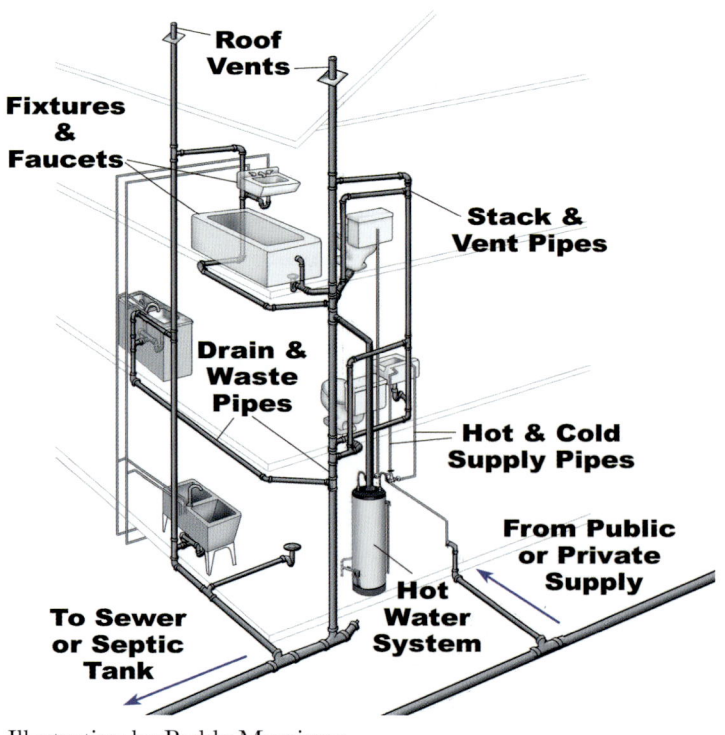

Illustration by Paddy Morrissey

and or leakage. This includes sinks, bidets, toilets, tubs and showers, hose bibs, and utility room tubs.

- **Drain, waste, and vent system (DWV):**
  The home inspector identifies the piping material in this system and inspects it for leaks and deterioration. The inspector determines if the proper traps are used in the system and checks the visible piping for support and insulation as necessary. Drains are checked for functional drainage. The home inspector verifies the existence of the vent system and its emergence to the exterior, most typically through the roof. Any indication of leaking sewer gas odor is reported.

  > **NOT REQUIRED TO**
  > - State the effectiveness of anti-siphon devices
  > - Operate automatic safety controls
  > - Operate any valve except toilet flush valves and faucets
  > - Observe water conditioning systems
  > - Observe fire and lawn sprinkler systems
  > - Observe water supply quantity or quality
  > - Observe hydro-massage therapy equipment, except for flow and drainage

  The inspection of a private waste disposal (septic) system is beyond the scope of the general home inspection. Numerous types of waste systems (septics) are available now, and you should be familiar with them even though you don't evaluate their performance. The home inspector is **not required to inspect the septic system** or to report on it other than to mention its existence (if determined) and to advise clients to have the tank pumped out on a regular basis. Some state or county health departments require a septic certificate from the seller to verify that it was pumped out and inspected prior to the sale.

- **Hot water system:** The home inspector always inspects the water heater during the plumbing inspection. The inspector describes the **type** of water heater as gas, propane, electric, geothermal, heat pump, oil, or other type, noting its **brand name, capacity, and approximate age**. Most inspectors describe the remaining useful life of the water heater, though this is not required. The home inspector checks for the presence and proper installation of a pressure/temperature safety relief valve and extension and possibly a Watts 210 valve. The Watts 210 valve will shut off the gas supply and therefore the water heater if the temperature in the water heater exceeds 210°F. This is installed **in conjunction with,** *not* **instead of** the standard TPR valve. The purpose of the valve is to allow for locations where the standard TPR valve may not be able to drain by gravity. Note again that the inspector is **not required to operate any valves or operate automatic safety controls (with the exception of Texas)**. The tank itself is inspected

Watts 210 Gas Shut-off Valve

©2012 Code Check

for condition. The water heater (combustion type only) is turned up, and the home inspector listens to its operation. If the water heater is an older model (pre-FVIR) gas or propane heater, the burner cover is removed to observe the flame. You have to look at the burner on oil-fired units too, using the porthole and/or site glass. With newer Flammable Vapor Ignition Resistant (FVIR) water heaters, the inspector should not open the burner (the burner compartment is sealed with a gasket). FVIR water heaters have a site glass window through which the flame can be observed. The home inspector checks for proper venting (flue) and the presence of combustion air venting (fresh air).

- **Fuel storage and distribution:** The inspection of interior gas piping as part of the plumbing inspection is included here because it's convenient to check gas piping while inspecting the water piping. The inspection includes the location of the gas meter or propane or oil storage tank depending on what is present at the home. The location of the main fuel shut-off valve should be identified, typically at the tank or meter. The most important part of this inspection is noticing the odor of a gas/propane leak, which must be reported as a safety hazard. You should also look for the presence of fuel oil leakage/staining near the storage tank and oil-fired appliances.

- **Sanitary pumps:** In this chapter, we're going to be studying "gray water" **sanitary pumps** that may be used to pump water from clothes washers into the waste disposal system. We will also study "black water" pumps, which are known by several names, which will be discussed later. The home inspector will inspect both types of these pumps. (The inspection of sump pumps is also presented in Chapter 1 referring to fresh water sumps that pump ground water from the foundation drainage system.)

INSPECTING WATER SUPPLY ENTRANCE

- Public or private water source
- Service pipe material
- Meter location
- Location of main shut-off valve
- Condition of private pump and well tank and operation of pressure gauge

4.1 WATER SERVICE ENTRANCE

The first component of the plumbing system to be studied is the water service entrance, although it isn't necessarily the first to be inspected during a real home inspection. We'll look at the components one by one before talking about inspection order. The inspection of the water service begins at the pipe that brings water into the house. This pipe is called the **service pipe** or the **house main**, and the inspector describes the material it is made of. The inspector also checks for the presence of a **main shut-off valve** on the service pipe. (Actually, there should be two shut-off valves for many installations, one on each side of the meter). The inspector should determine (if possible and *don't* guess!) whether the water supply comes from a **public service or private source** such as a well, spring, or storage tank on the property. The inspection of the water supply entrance includes the following:

- **Public or private** water source (as indicated by the state's Standards of Practice)

- The **service pipe** material

- **Meter location** if public supply (which is usually your best indicator that it is a public supply)

- The presence of **main shut-off valve** and its location

- The **pump and well tank** condition and the operation of the **pressure gauge** if private supply

> **Chapter Note**
>
> *Pages 218–234 present the study and inspection of the water supply entrance portion of the plumbing system.*

Public Water Supply

A service line carries water from the city water main at the street or alley to the house. The **minimum service pipe size** for bringing water into a house from a public water service is typically 3/4″ nominal size although the size depends on the material. As of the 2012 IRC, 18 different types/materials are approved for service piping, many of which are not commonly used. The most common materials are copper, galvanized, CPVC (chlorinated polyvinyl chloride), PE (polyethylene), PEX (cross-linked polyethylene), PVC (polyvinyl chloride), or PP (polypropylene)—but the home inspector may see 1″ and larger pipes in old installations, especially in old inner city areas, and in new construction of large homes. The service pipe should be buried far below grade to prevent freezing in cold climates and interference with surface plantings in warmer climates. In warmer climates with no frost lines, it may be as close as 12″ from the surface. It may enter into the house through the foundation wall or the basement floor or the exterior wall of the house in warmer climates. City water is usually provided at a **pressure** of 40 (minimum) to 80 psi (pounds per square inch), whereas wells provide water at about 40–60 psi. Higher pressures put stress on the household water system, whereas lower pressures do not provide enough pressure to the house.

The public service line may be made of one of the following materials:

- **Copper:** This was the most commonly used material for service pipes for decades. When copper prices spiked in 2005–2010, plastics became more popular for most of the country. Since about 1970, pipes are required to be 3/4″ nominal, although 1/2″ nominal was also used in the 20 years before 1970. Types M, L, and K are approved for such underground installations and last for many years.

- **Brass:** Red brass piping is still an approved material, but you rarely find it today. At a field

> **Definitions**
>
> *The <u>house main</u> or service pipe is the pipe that brings water from its public or private source into the house.*
>
> *The <u>main shut-off</u> valve turns off the water supply to the house.*
>
> *The use of the abbreviation <u>ID</u> with pipe measurements refers to the inside diameter of the pipe.*
>
> *The abbreviation <u>psi</u> is a measurement of water pressure and means pounds per square inch.*

inspection during class in suburban Indianapolis, the 1969 home being inspected had red brass piping. It was still in use and in visibly good condition.

- **Galvanized steel:** Galvanized steel is steel-coated with a corrosion-resistant layer of zinc. Galvanized steel (which was very common throughout the country through about 1970) is not used very often as service lines, and those communities that used it may have required pipe of at least 1 1/4″ nominal. These pipes can last 30 to 60 years, depending on the acidity of the water, before the zinc is lost and the steel begins to rust. The problem with galvanized piping over time is that it corrodes from the inside out and ultimately becomes completely blocked with calcification and corrosion. This greatly diminishes the flow (volume) at the fixtures.

- **Lead:** Lead piping was used between the street and the house up until the 1950s in most of the country's urban areas. It was, however, used much later than that in certain parts of the country. At a class in suburban Chicago at one of the field inspections, lead service piping was found in a home constructed in 1965. This is much later than expected and in a suburban, not urban, location. Many of these lines are still in use, although fewer every year. There is concern over the safety of these lead service lines because of the lead, which can contaminate the water. As evidenced by the 2015 Flint, MI water crisis, this is especially problematic for young children under the age of 6. It causes neurological and developmental issues to their immature central nervous system.

- **Plastic:** Public water service lines are more frequently becoming plastic, although plastic piping has historically been used more often in private water systems. Today, PVC, CPVC, and more commonly PEX are being used instead, with good results. **Polybutylene (PB)**, which is a blue color in exterior service piping (interior piping is gray), was used. But PB shrinks in cold weather and can pull loose from fittings, split from temperature changes, or become brittle from the chlorination of the city water. PB has a history of failure and has been the subject of a number of class action settlements, the last of which ended in May 2009.

With public water services, a **water meter** may be present inside or outside the house. In some communities, there are unmetered services and no meter may be found, although this is not common (the customer pays a flat monthly fee for their water usage regardless of how much they use). You will need to determine the local practices in your area. When street pressure is too high for home use, there may be a **pressure-reducing valve** (PRV) on the service pipe near the meter or at the house main shut-off. The location of the PRV varies depending on the geographic area. In homes with basements, the PRV is typically at the meter. In southern homes, the PRV may be at the exterior of the building where the piping enters the building.

NOTE: In rare cases where water pressure from city service is too low, a **booster pump and pressure tank** may be installed. This setup looks like a shallow well system, but the presence of a meter should indicate that the water

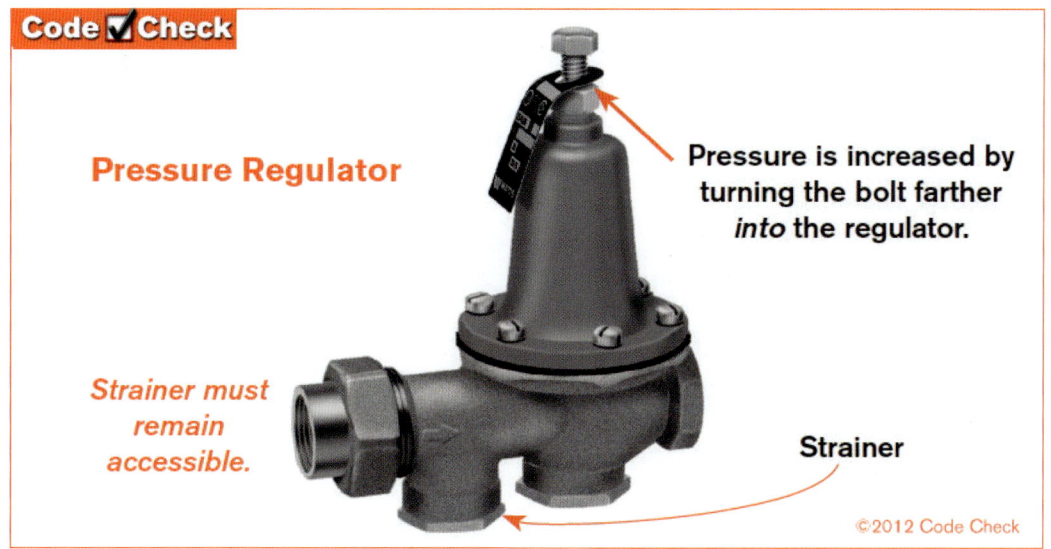

supply is public. Don't be fooled by the presence of a meter and public water supply. In rural areas, you may find a "shared well" where several homeowners use the same well. They all have meters, but only to measure usage for shared maintenance expenses.

Each house should have a **main shut-off valve**, typically on the house side of the meter, which is used to turn off the water supply to the house. Again, homes in various parts of the country have shut-off valves located outside the building in the front or rear yard or at the exterior wall of the house. Record it in your report as required by your Standards of Practice. This valve should be operable by hand, not by wrench, so that anyone can turn it off. Inspectors should tag the main shut-off to let everyone in the house know where it is located so that it can be turned off in case of a catastrophic plumbing leak. This is also good from a marketing standpoint because the tag will have your company information for future referrals.

When inspecting the water service entrance, first locate the incoming service pipe. Identify the service as public or private based on the presence of a water meter and lack of well equipment, but don't guess if you're not sure. You can always record "not determined" or "unknown." During the inspection, watch for the following:

- **Lead service pipes:** Both lead and galvanized steel pipes are gray in color. To determine if the service piping is lead, use your screwdriver to make a scratch in the pipe. Lead is soft, and the scratch can be made easily. The scratch line will be shiny (scraping away the oxidation, leaving bare lead exposed). Galvanized steel is very hard to scratch, and the resulting scratch line is not as shiny as lead. Lead pipes can easily be bent and are usually not straight. Galvanized pipe is much harder to bend and usually runs in straight lengths. Some home inspectors carry a magnet to help with this identification. Galvanized steel is magnetic, but lead isn't.

LEAD vs. GALVANIZED STEEL

	Lead	Steel
• Joints	Bulb	Threaded
• Magnetic	No	Yes
• Scratch	Easy, Shiny	Harder, Dull
• Bends	Easy	Harder

Photo #1 *Lead service piping has a tulip shaped connection to the house piping or water meter.*

Another difference is that galvanized steel pipes are threaded, whereas lead pipes have a distinctive tulip bulb–shaped joint.

The home inspector should let the client know when lead pipes have been identified, and it should be noted in the inspection report. Because of health concerns, clients may want to have the water tested for lead contamination. The standard recommendation is to have lead pipes replaced because they are a health hazard or when the pipes are more than 60 years old, at best. The inspector can suggest that the clients run the water for 2 or 3 minutes before drinking it, install a filtration system such as reverse osmosis (RO), or use bottled water for drinking and cooking.

INSPECTING PUBLIC SUPPLY

- Lead service pipe
- Pipe too small
- Missing, damaged, or leaking main shut-off valve

For Beginning Inspectors

Locate the service pipe into your own home. Perform the inspection as described in these pages. First determine whether the source of water is public or private. Note the pipe material and use the scratch test if necessary to identify lead piping. Locate the main shut-off valve. You might want to tag this valve and show your family where it is in case of an emergency.

- **Pipe too small:** Check out the size of the service pipe. Copper pipe should be 3/4″, and if you find 1/2″ pipe, it should be pointed out to the client as it can cause water flow (volume) problems. Remember, the reason we use 3/4″ service piping (0.44 square inches) minimum is because that is more than twice the area of 1/2″ piping (0.2 square inches). When a house is plumbed with 3/4″ piping, you can feed two 1/2″ fixtures with no drop in flow. If you start with 1/2″ and feed two fixtures simultaneously, you will have a considerable drop in flow (volume).

- **Missing, damaged, or leaking main shut-off valve:** Check for a main shut-off valve *where the piping enters the building* and report a missing valve. Even if the water meter is outside, the main shut-off may be inside the house—and in many cases outside the building. Inspect the valve for damage or leaking. It should be operational by hand (by the homeowner) in case of an emergency.

Do not test the main shut-off valve by turning it on or off. Too often, a home inspector operates a main shut-off valve only to find that it can't be turned back to its original position or a valve that hasn't been operated for a long time becomes damaged or begins leaking after the test. If you damage it, you'll pay to have a plumber to fix it. Your job is to let the client know where the valve is located, what its function is, and how it *would be* operated. If the valve is already damaged or leaking, suggest that it be repaired or, more likely, replaced.

There may be another shut-off on the street side of the meter, which allows water to be turned off by the water service provider (city) to work on the meter. This valve may have to be operated with a wrench, known as a curb key or T-bar, which is available at most large home improvement stores. It's not intended to serve as the homeowner's shut-off.

NOTE: It's when you're inspecting the water supply entrance in the basement (or outside or in the crawl space or wherever it is located) that you'll be looking for the electrical grounding or bonding conductor (see Chapter 2). The grounding or bonding conductor should be connected to the street side of the water meter (and main shut-off if it's in the basement), and there should be a jumper across the meter to the house side of the shut-off, if present, for effective grounding or bonding. Of course, a plastic service pipe cannot be used for electrical grounding or be bonded. Be careful in older houses that have been re-plumbed with plastic; the house may no longer have a ground if it was originally connected to the incoming metal water pipe.

Photo #2 *A properly grounded and bonded water line with jumper across meter.*

Private Water Supply

This section contains a great deal of detail for items in the house that we are not required to inspect or evaluate. The reason for the level of detail is that you will eventually (or maybe frequently) inspect homes with wells. Even though you may not be required to inspect them, your client will typically ask questions about the well and its components. You will need to have at least a conversational understanding of how the system and its components work. If you don't, your client may think you are not qualified to be inspecting his or her home. It is an unfair assessment, but that is the way people think during the inspection. You are the hired expert, and as far as the client is concerned, you should know something about anything in the house.

WELL COMPONENTS

- The well
- Well pump
- Pressure tank
- Pressure switch and pressure gauge
- Service pipe and main shut-off valve

The private service line may be made from the same materials as public water service. However, most private (wells) use PVC and PE for their main service line into the house.

A private water supply system typically provides water to the home from a **well**, although water may also be obtained from a storage tank, pond, stream, or spring. The components of a private system are as follows:

- The **water source** (well, spring, tank, etc.)
- The **pump** that moves the water
- The **service pipe** between the source and the pressure tank or house
- A **main shut-off valve** between the source and the pressure tank or house
- A **pressure or storage tank** (typically interior) that holds a supply of water
- A **pressure switch** that activates the pump when water pressure in the tank falls and deactivates the pump when pressure resumes at an acceptable level
- A **pressure gauge** that gives a readout of the water pressure within the tank

The home inspector can generally identify a water supply as private by the presence of the pressure tank in the home (or pump house) *and* the absence of a water meter. (See the note on page 220 about the use of a booster pump and pressure tank in rare cases with a public water service.)

A private water supply is usually provided from an underground stream or **aquifer** (an underground lake of sorts) as opposed to surface water. Surface water seeps into the ground until it reaches an impermeable layer of rock; then it flows underground along this rock strata until it reaches a river or the ocean. This layer of permeable water-containing rock is the aquifer. Wells are dug or driven to reach the aquifer, which in some areas may be less than 25′ below grade and up to several hundred feet below grade. Wells in certain parts of the country are required to be at least 450′ deep, but depths of 1100′ are not uncommon. In an **artesian well or spring**, the aquifer is under enough natural pressure to force water from the ground without a pump.

Wells up to 25′ deep are called **shallow wells**. Wells more than 25′ deep are called **deep wells**. Although rules regarding the location of a private well on a property vary from community to community, the well is usually required to be at least 75′ from a private waste disposal system or septic tank (some areas require up to 200′), should be located uphill of a potential contaminating source, and

---

Chapter Note

Inspecting the home for proper grounding is presented in Chapter 5, Electrical Inspection.

Definitions

An <u>aquifer</u> is a water-bearing strata of permeable rock, sand, or gravel.

An <u>artesian well</u> is a well whose aquifer has enough internal pressure to bring water to the surface without a pump.

The use of the abbreviation <u>gpm</u> is a measurement of water flow and means gallons per minute.

WELL LOCATION

- 75′ from septic
- 30′ from house
- 18″ above ground
- First 50′ in casing

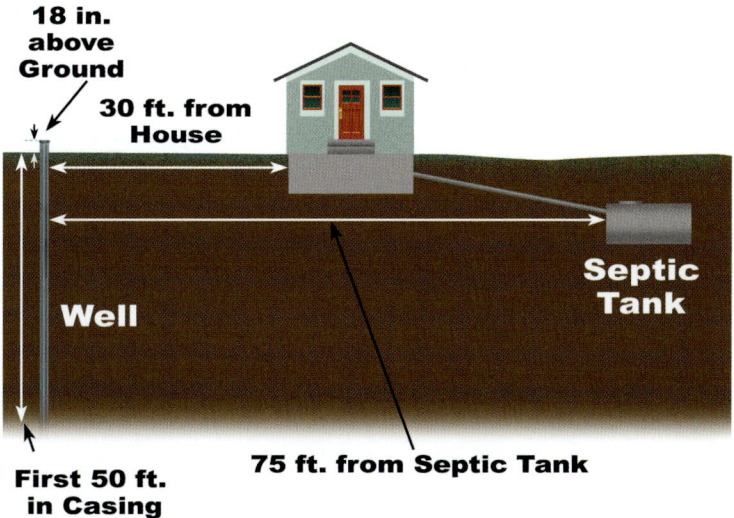

Illustration by Paddy Morrissey

must be a required distance from a stream or pond. Typically the first 50′ of the well must be protected by an impervious casing that is sealed at its lower end. Its upper end should be 12–18″ above the ground to prevent groundwater from entering, although in some areas, the upper end may be flush with the ground. A distance of 30′ from the house is considered safe if chlordane (a very potent and long-lived pesticide that was banned in 1983, except for termite control, and was finally banned for all uses in 1988) had been applied. These standards vary from one locality to another and are usually regulated by the county or state health department. The illustration below shows one possible configuration.

The purpose of a **well pump** is to draw water from the well and push and/or pull it through the house piping system with enough force to provide an adequate flow. A flow rate of 5 to 7 gpm (gallons per minute) is considered adequate in most areas of the country. A peak flow rate of 10 gpm is the optimum flow rate for a modern home with two bathrooms. The following types of well pumps are used:

- **Piston pump:** This type of pump is used in older systems and is no longer installed today, although you may still run across one in the field. It is a **reciprocating pump**, which is a motorized version of the old hand pump. A motor drives a series of pistons that lift water higher and higher, discharging it on every other stroke. The piston pump may be used with shallow wells, where both the motor and piston assembly will be above the ground. When used with deep wells, the motor is above the ground and the piston assembly is in the well.

- **Jet pump:** The jet pump consists of a **centrifugal pump** and a jet assembly. The centrifugal pump can be thought of as a small paddle wheel driven by a motor. The pump recirculates pressurized water into the well,

Section Note

"One of the instructors at AHIT was conducting an inspection and was checking the distance between the well riser in the front yard and the septic tank in the back. He noticed that the neighbor had reversed the locations with his well in the backyard and the septic in the front. The well under inspection was the correct distance from its own septic system, but was only 20′ from the neighbor's.

Either the homeowner or the neighbor would have to switch the systems so that distances were correct in all directions."

WELL PUMPS

- Piston pump (reciprocal)
- Jet pump (centrifugal)
- Submersible pump (centrifugal)

creating a suction that draws more well water into the jet assembly and pushes this water up to the pump. Some of the water enters the house distribution piping, and the rest is diverted back to the jet assembly.

When the jet pump is used with a **shallow well**, the home inspector will see **only one pipe** extending to the well. In this case, the jet assembly is above ground with the centrifugal pump. When the jet pump is used with a **deep well**, two pipes will extend to the well. That's how you can tell if the jet pump is used with a shallow or deep well.

To operate properly, the deep well jet pump needs to be filled with water and have about 15 to 20 pounds of back pressure. When the water in the casing falls below the level of the jet (when the well is pumped dry), it must be re-primed and pressurized before it operates again. Once it is primed, it should operate normally.

- **Submersible pump:** The submersible pump consists of a motor and an electrically driven **centrifugal pump**, both of which are designed to operate under water. With the submersible pump, both the motor and pump are within the well (bottom of the hole). Although the submersible pump can be used with shallow wells, silt, sand, algae, and other contaminants can shorten the pump's life.

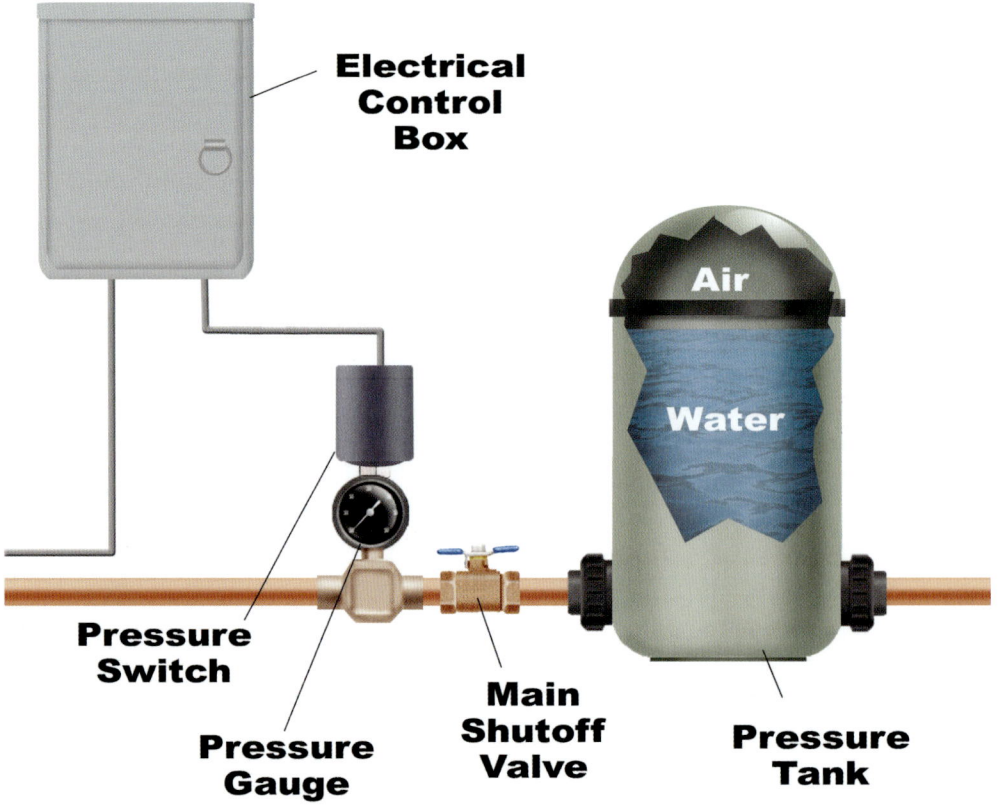

Submersible Pump Setup

Illustration by Paddy Morrissey

Water is drawn into the unit through screened openings between the pump and the motor. The submersible pump delivers water to a storage tank through a single pipe and needs no priming.

The following table summarizes the information about the piston, jet, and submersible pumps. Take the time to sort out this information. It's important to know.

The life expectancy of a well pump may be as little as 7 to 10 years, although many pumps last from 20 to 30 years. Submersible pumps generally last about 20 years. In many cases, the electrical box for the pump will have a date code on it that may indicate when the pump was installed.

> **Section Note**
>
> *It would be well worth your time to locate a friend with a private well. Take a look at the visible equipment and learn what you can about the type of well pump, the depth of the well, and whatever else you can. Study the motor if it is above ground, take a look at the pressure tank, and locate the pressure gauge. The more experience you have with the various types of private water systems, the better your inspections will be.*

PUMP	TYPE	LOCATION	USE
Piston	Reciprocal	With shallow wells, motor and piston above well. With deep wells, motor above and piston in well.	In older homes for both shallow and deep wells, but generally no longer in use.
Jet	Centrifugal	With shallow wells, pump and jet assembly above well. With deep wells, pump above and jet assembly in well.	With both shallow and deep wells. Only 1 pipe to well indicates shallow well; 2 pipes to well indicate deep well.
Submersible	Centrifugal	Both motor and pump located in well.	With both shallow and deep wells, but most often deep.

In the days when pumps were noisy and pressure tanks were large, well equipment was often placed outside the house in a separate **pump house** or in an underground **well pit**. The well pit is a masonry chamber with a hatch cover and a floor below the frost line. If it is accessible, the home inspector should inspect the well equipment even if it is located in the pump house or a well pit.

The other main components of a private well system are as follows:

- **Pressure tank:** This storage tank holds water from the well and is usually located on the lower level of the house or the basement. Other methods of storing water for homes, especially in homes with low-producing wells, include the use of an inside reservoir called a **cistern**, often located

> **Definitions**
>
> *A well pit is an underground chamber, usually made of masonry, that houses the well equipment.*
>
> *A pump house is a separate building built for the purpose of housing well equipment.*
>
> *A vault is an elevated indoor water reservoir, often located in the attic, from which water flows by gravity. A standpipe is an outdoor elevated water reservoir.*

Photo #3 *Pressure tank installed outdoors. Be sure to check if all electrical components are proper exterior type.*

in the basement, underground, or beneath the house or in an outside reservoir or poly tank.

These days, the home inspector is most likely to find water stored in a pressure tank with a capacity of only a few gallons. The water in the tank is under pressure, and the tank must be partially filled with **air** to maintain this pressure. Normally, the tank is maintained between one-half and two-thirds full of water. In a modern system, the pressure tank has a bladder inside to separate the air from the water. Older style tanks are open inside such that the water and air touch. If the tank becomes filled with water, due to the bladder failing or the absorption of the air into the water over time, the tank becomes **waterlogged**. This causes the pump to cycle rapidly and repeatedly or to run continuously.

The pressure tank may be wrapped or insulated due to the cold water in the tank to prevent corrosion caused by condensation on the outside of the tank.

- **Pressure switch and gauge:** A private well system must have a pressure switch that automatically starts and stops the pump at predetermined pressures. Typical low and high limit settings for water in the pressure tank may be 20 and 40 psi, 30 and 50 psi, or even 40 and 60 psi. If, for example, the low and high are set at 30 psi and 50 psi, respectively, then the pressure switch turns the pump on when pressure levels fall below 30 psi and turns the pump off when levels reach 50 psi. When the pressure tank becomes waterlogged, the pressure switch can make a continuous clicking sound, trying to bring water pressure into the acceptable range.

  For a jet pump, the pressure switch is located in the pump assembly. For the submersible pump, the switch is above ground near the pressure tank. A **pressure gauge**, which shows the pressure reading of the tank, may be located near the tank or on the tank itself.

- **Constant pressure systems:** A constant pressure system operates with a variable frequency drive controller that automatically monitors household demand. Like the cruise control on a car, the variable frequency drive speeds up or slows down the pump depending on household water requirements. The result is reliable, constant pressure where and when it is needed. It supports high-volume needs, reduces stress on the pump, is more energy efficient, and uses a smaller pressure tank than the systems described above.

- **Water storage systems:** Many areas of the country, particularly the Southwest, have water storage tanks on their properties. This may be due to an extremely deep water table or because it is more cost effective to buy water. The tanks are typically metal or plastic and range in size from 1,000 to 12,500 gallons for the average home. A booster pump is then installed to pressurize the water from the holding tank to the point of use.

Inspecting Private Water Supply

When inspecting the private water service entrance, the home inspector should identify the **source** of the water, if possible. When there is well equipment, it should be inspected whether it is located in the basement, in a pump house, or in a well pit. The inspector should report the **location** of the well equipment in the report. The **type of well pump** should be identified and, if possible, the well itself as shallow or deep. The home inspector should, if possible, determine the **age of the well pump** and report whether it may have to be replaced within the next 5 years.

> **TESTING WELL EQUIPMENT**
> - Turn on the water.
> - Watch pressure gauge fall.
> - Listen to the pump kick on.
> - Turn off the water.
> - Watch pressure gauge as pressure returns.

NOTE: The home inspector should always suggest that the client **have well water tested** for bacterial and other possible contamination (potability) by a reliable laboratory. Testing the quality of well water is outside the scope of the home inspector. Clients can also have a **yield or draw-down test** performed to test the pumping capacity of the well. The home inspector may want to suggest this as a means of testing whether the available water volume will be appropriate for the client. If he or she is qualified, an inspector can offer to perform both of these tests for an additional fee.

It's necessary to test the well equipment to inspect it properly. Follow these steps to do so:

1. **Run water:** Turn on a faucet, perhaps at a laundry tub in the basement. Let the water run.

2. **Watch the pressure gauge:** As the water is running, locate the pressure gauge and watch the pressure drop until the pump is activated by the low limit. You'll be able to tell if the pressure gauge is working. And you'll be able to note other problems if the pump is *not* activated when pressure reaches the low limit. Keep in mind that you have no idea what the pressure switch is set to and your observations are whether the well pump is cycling on and off.

3. **Listen to the pump:** As the pump is running, listen to it and note any problems. For the submersible pump, put the tip of your screwdriver against the pressure tank and your ear against the other end of the screwdriver. Excessive noise or vibration can indicate problems, which will be discussed below. Also, note if the pump is turning on and off several times each minute, commonly called short cycling, which should be noted as an item in need of attention.

> **Section Note**
>
> *"One of my inspectors had judged a private water system to have good pressure and flow and the well equipment to be in good operation. But then he was asked to let the water run to pull a clean sample for testing. After the water ran an hour, the well went dry. When questioned, the owner said, 'Oh, yeah, the well often goes dry.' The customer was not happy to hear that.*
>
> *You are not required to report on the quantity of water supply and should let your customers know that testing the well equipment for 10 to 20 minutes does not confirm an adequate supply."*

4. **Turn off the water:** Turn off the faucet that's been running or have the client do it so that you can continue to watch the pressure gauge.

5. **Watch the pressure gauge:** Again, watch the pressure gauge as pressure returns. See if the pump stops when pressure returns to the high limit. If the pump doesn't stop or it stops after bringing the tank past the high pressure limit, problems are likely.

During the inspection of the well equipment, the home inspector should watch for the following conditions:

- **Inoperable pump:** When you conduct your test with the well equipment, the pump may not kick in as the pressure falls to or below the low limit. Be sure to report if the pump doesn't work at all. It's possible that there is no power to the pump caused by a blown fuse or poor electrical connections or the pressure switch may have been shut off. If you can't determine why the pump has no power, an electrician should explore the situation. The pump also may not work due to the motor being burned out or to bearings being shot, a faulty pressure switch, or a seized or frozen pump. A waterlogged pump can run hot and appear to be burned out. A well technician should be called to deal with those problems.

- **Constantly running pump:** If the well pump is constantly running before and/or during the tests you perform, the pressure tank is waterlogged, there may be a faulty pressure switch, or there may be a leak in the pump piping. With the jet pump, the pump may have lost its prime. Be sure to report this situation. Feel the side of an uninsulated tank for a marked temperature difference, indicating how much water is in the tank. You can often tell in this way if the tank is short on air and is waterlogged. A waterlogged condition can cause excessive wear and damage to the pump and pressure switch. In some cases, a waterlogged tank can easily be fixed by adding more air to the tank. Because other conditions may be causing the problem, it's best to advise the client to consult a well technician.

- **Excessive noise or vibration in pump:** Listen to the pump equipment as the pump runs. Jet pumps that squeak and squeal probably have defective motor bearings. With submersible pumps, listen to the pump with your screwdriver against the tank. It should run smoothly and quietly. If it sounds noisy, the bearings are probably going out as well. This should be reported and the suggestion made to have a well technician look at the pump.

> **INSPECTING WELL EQUIPMENT**
>
> - Inoperable, noisy, vibrating, or constantly running pump
> - Loose or leaking pump equipment
> - Rusted, corroded, or leaking pressure tank
> - Tank under or over pressure limit
> - Missing or inoperable pressure gauge
> - Missing, damaged, or leaking main shut-off valve
> - Pipe too small
> - Problems with well pit

Photo #4 *The pressure tank is significantly corroded and leaking. Recommend replacement.*

- **Pump equipment loose or leaking:** Inspect any motor and pump assemblies aboveground. They should be solidly secured and not leaking.

- **Rusted, corroded, or leaking pressure tank:** Examine the pressure tank for any evidence of rusting, corrosion, or leaking. Sometimes, it isn't easy to tell the difference between water stains from condensation and leaking on an uninsulated tank. Always check the bottom of the pressure tank to see if it's leaking and/or rusting out.

- **Under or over pressure limit:** If the well system is **below the low pressure limit** or does not come up to this limit while you're performing your test, there may be a faulty pressure switch, the pump piping may be leaking, or the well casing could be cracked. With the jet pump, the jet could be clogged. After your test, if the pressure comes up **over the high pressure limit**, there could be a faulty pressure switch. The pressure tank may have a **relief valve** for excessive pressure buildup. The situation of the well system being under or over the pressure limits should be reported and a recommendation made to have the problem evaluated and corrected by a qualified service provider.

- **Missing or inoperable pressure gauge:** Check to see if a pressure gauge is present; if not, report it as missing. Often, these gauges no longer work. This should also be reported.

- **Missing, damaged, or leaking main shut-off valve:** There should be a main shut-off valve between the entry of the well piping and the pressure tank. Point out its location to your client and suggest that any damage or leaking be fixed.

- **Operation of the main shut-off valve:** If you operate the main shut-off valve, you may find that you can't turn it back on or that the valve starts to leak after you touch it.

- **Incoming pipe too small:** Plastic piping is used quite often with private water supply systems. Plastic pipe from the well should be a minimum of 3/4" to provide an adequate flow of water.

A NOTE

The home inspector is not required to inspect the well itself. The condition of the well casing, pump operation, water quality, and adequate water flow is best left to qualified technicians.

- **Problems with well pit:** The home inspector should inspect the pump equipment located in a well pit. Inspect the pit too. Well pits should be covered and locked so that children cannot fall into them. Report any unlocked or otherwise unprotected well pits as a **safety hazard**. Inspect the cover and report it if it is damaged or rotted out. Take a look at drainage in the well pit, which should be good enough to protect the pump equipment in the pit. Often, a sump pump in the pit pumps out groundwater or rain that seeps in. Test this sump pump for operation, as well as any other sumps in the basement.

Reporting Your Findings

When you're inspecting the plumbing system, ask your client to be present. It's a smart practice. When the client comes with you, you have an opportunity to fully explain the inspection and to point out findings. Client knowledge is a big step toward the prevention of complaint calls later.

With some of the home's mechanical systems, it's important for the home inspector to remind the client *during the inspection* what can and cannot be inspected. That's the case with the plumbing system. Help your client understand that you are performing **a visual inspection** of the plumbing system and will not be able to inspect items hidden from your view—pipes behind walls, for example. Remind them of the **scope and the limits** of your inspection.

Be patient and take time to discuss what you will and will not be inspecting. Clients may not understand that you can't pass judgment on the well casing or the submersible pump, although you'll be on the lookout for symptoms of problems. Remind them that you will not be testing the quality of water supply or adequate quantity and suggest the appropriate technicians who can. Your inspection agreement, which is signed by the client before you begin work, should describe the major limitations of the inspection.

If you get calls several months later about new leaks or well problems, you can remind the client that you discussed how you would not be able to inspect particular aspects of the plumbing system.

As you are performing the inspection of the entrance to the water supply, whether a public service or private well, explain the following patiently and in simple terms the client can understand:

> **Section Note**
>
> *"One of my inspectors lifted the lid of a well pit to find that a family of raccoons had moved into the pit. The mother raccoon was a bit touchy about a home inspector wanting to get into the pit. The inspector was not about to scrap with a mad raccoon and reported that he was unable to inspect the well pit. The customer was very understanding."*

> **REMEMBER**
>
> *During the inspection, remind the customer of the scope of the inspection. You can only inspect visible plumbing. You can inspect the pressure tank, but you cannot inspect the well itself. That's beyond the scope of the inspection.*

- **What you're inspecting**—the service pipe, the main shut-off valve, the pump motor, the pressure tank, and so on.

- **What you're looking for**—proper size piping, leaking, noisy well pump, rusted pressure tank, damaged shut-off valve.

- **What you're doing**—checking the service pipe to see if it's lead, running water to test pump operation, watching the pressure gauge, going into the well pit.

- **What you're finding**—a waterlogged pressure tank, missing main shut-off valve, leaking pump equipment, system that is under or over pressure limits, rotted well pit cover, and so on.

- **Suggestions about dealing with the findings**—calling a well technician to investigate a pump with probable defective bearings, replacing a rusted pressure tank, having a plumber install or repair a faulty main shut-off, and so on. But with this, use caution: don't make uneducated guesses about how repairs should be made. It's best to recommend that the issue be evaluated and corrected by a qualified professional.

Filling in Your Report

Every home inspector needs an inspection report. A **written report** is the work product of the home inspection, and every home inspector is expected to deliver one to the client after the inspection. Inspection reports vary a great deal in the industry. Some home inspection companies develop their own version; others use state required formats (Texas), home inspection software, apps, or formats provided by training companies such as AHIT. Some are considered to be excellent, while others are not very good. A workable and easy-to-use inspection report is important for a home inspector in terms of being able to fill it in. Of greater importance are its thoroughness, accuracy, and helpfulness to the customer. Whatever reporting format you choose, make sure it presents your findings in a clear, professional manner such that it reduces your liability and client dissatisfaction.

The **Don't Ever Miss** list is a reminder of those specific findings you should be sure to include in your inspection report. We list these items after years of experience performing home inspections. Missing them can result in complaint calls and lawsuits later. Here is an overview of what to report on during the inspection of the water supply entrance:

- **Entrance information:** First, if possible, identify the water service as public or private, writing this in the inspection report. Next, identify the type of piping material. If you've found a lead service pipe, note that fact as a safety concern and suggest in writing that a qualified party perform a water contamination test.

- **Main shut-off:** Note whether a main shut-off exists on the service entrance pipe and report on defects such as damage and leaking. Another requirement is that you note the **location** of the main shut-off in the report. This is a helpful bit of information for the client.

> **Report Available**
>
> *The American Home Inspectors Training Institute offers both manual and computerized reports. These reports include an inspection agreement, complete reporting pages, and helpful customer information. If you're interested in purchasing the Home Inspection Report, please contact us at 1-800-441-9411.*

> **DON'T EVER MISS**
>
> - Lead service pipe
> - Missing, damaged, or leaking main shut-off valve
> - Inoperable, noisy, leaking, or constantly running pump
> - Rusted, corroded, or leaking pressure tank
> - Tank under or over pressure limit
> - Missing or inoperable pressure gauge
> - Unlocked well pit cover

- **Well equipment:** If a service is private, include more information about the type of well pump present and where it's located. Note the presence or absence of a pressure gauge and whether it's operating. If you couldn't test the gauge, it's best to report that fact. Record defects such as a waterlogged tank, a rusted or leaking tank, and noisy pump conditions. If the pump bearings sound bad, you may want to include a suggestion about having a well technician examine the pump.

- **Major repair or replacement:** If you've found a well pump that is not operating, list it on the plumbing page of your report and on a summary page as a major concern.

> **OLDER PUMPS**
>
> *For well pumps over 13 years old, note them in your inspection report as items requiring replacement within the next 5 years. The pump will be reaching the end of its life in 5 years.*

4.2 WATER DISTRIBUTION PIPING

The water distribution system is the complete piping system from the source of the water supply to all of the home's fixtures and faucets. The system includes **house mains**, which are the principal pipes to which all branches are connected. **Risers** carry hot and cold water vertically through one or more stories of the house. Branch lines carry water to the fixtures and faucets. Shorter lengths of rigid or flexible tubing connect piping to the fixtures and faucets.

The inspection of distribution piping includes the inspection of the following aspects of the system:

- The **type** of piping material

- The piping **installation**—locations and supports

- The **condition** of the pipes, fittings, and connections

- The presence of **temporary** and/or **improvised plumbing**

- Functional **water flow**

- Branch lines to **outdoor faucets**

> **INSPECTING WATER SUPPLY**
>
> - Piping material
> - Installation
> - Piping condition
> - Temporary or handyman plumbing
> - Functional water flow
> - Outdoor faucets

> *Chapter Note*
>
> *Pages 234–251 present the study and inspection of the water supply distribution piping.*

Corrosion

Before we discuss distribution piping, let's talk about corrosion. Corrosion is the physical or chemical change by which a material is degraded. In metal piping, corrosion leads to alterations in physical form and strength of the piping material.

Two types of corrosion affect metal plumbing pipes.

- **Electrolytic or galvanic corrosion:** This process takes place when there are two **dissimilar metals** (most commonly copper and steel) **connected to each other in water** containing dissolved salts, creating charged ions and tiny electric currents. The currents pick up ions from the metals, eventually destroying the pipes with leaks and failures in the walls of the pipes.

   Galvanic corrosion often happens **from the inside** at the joints where dissimilar metals meet. An example is at a joint with a galvanized steel plug in a copper fitting. It also happens **on the outside** of the pipes where dissimilar metals meet and water from condensation is present. An example is where copper pipes are hung with steel hangers (which is not allowed) in a damp place.

   The important thing to remember is that for galvanic corrosion to take place, two dissimilar metals must be touching each other *and* water or dampness must be present. For this reason, supply piping should not have dissimilar metals in metal-to-metal contact. Professional plumbers use special couplings such as plastic, dielectric connectors, and brass fittings to prevent the flow of current across a joint. Amateurs tend to join copper to galvanized steel piping without any protection, or think Teflon tape will suffice.

   The box above lists dissimilar metals. The metals higher on the list ionize (corrode) first. Sometimes, dissimilar metals are used together intentionally so that one metal will be sacrificed first. An example is a magnesium or aluminum rod in a steel water heater that will give up ions (corrode) first, thereby protecting the steel tank.

- **Chemical corrosion:** This process depends on the presence of oxygen, carbon dioxide, or salts in the water that react with the metal. A chemical reaction takes place, using up some of the metal particles. The product of the chemical reaction becomes soluble and washes away, or it builds up in or on the pipes. An example is rusting in cast iron pipes—the iron reacts with oxygen in the water to become iron oxide, or rust. Another example is what happens in lead pipes where lead salts are released into the water supply.

DISSIMILAR METALS GALVANIC SERIES

- Magnesium
- Zinc
- Aluminum
- Cadmium
- Steel
- Lead
- Tin
- Nickel
- Brass
- Bronze
- Copper
- Stainless steel
- Silver
- Gold
- Platinum

Definitions

<u>Electrolytic or galvanic</u> *corrosion occurs when two dissimilar metals are connected to each other in water containing dissolved salts. The process releases metal ions, causing a current to flow.*

<u>Chemical corrosion</u> *occurs when metals react with oxygen, carbon dioxide, or salts in water. The process uses metal atoms to form new compounds.*

DISTRIBUTION PIPING

- Brass—red and yellow
- Lead
- Galvanized steel
- Copper
- Plastic—PB, CPVC, and PEX

Types of Supply Piping

Water supply piping is generally larger at the supply end and smaller at the faucet end of the system. Copper supply piping is typically a minimum 3/4″ nominal for the cold and hot water mains in the house. Most branch lines use 1/2″ nominal piping to their termination at faucets and fixtures. With regard to size, plastic piping is different from what many people are used to. You will find 3/8″ tubing very commonly for a PEX system, especially with manifolds. These newer pipes are used in combination with low-flow fixtures so the 3/8″ tubing is adequate for today's homes.

The home inspector will find the following types of supply distribution piping used in homes:

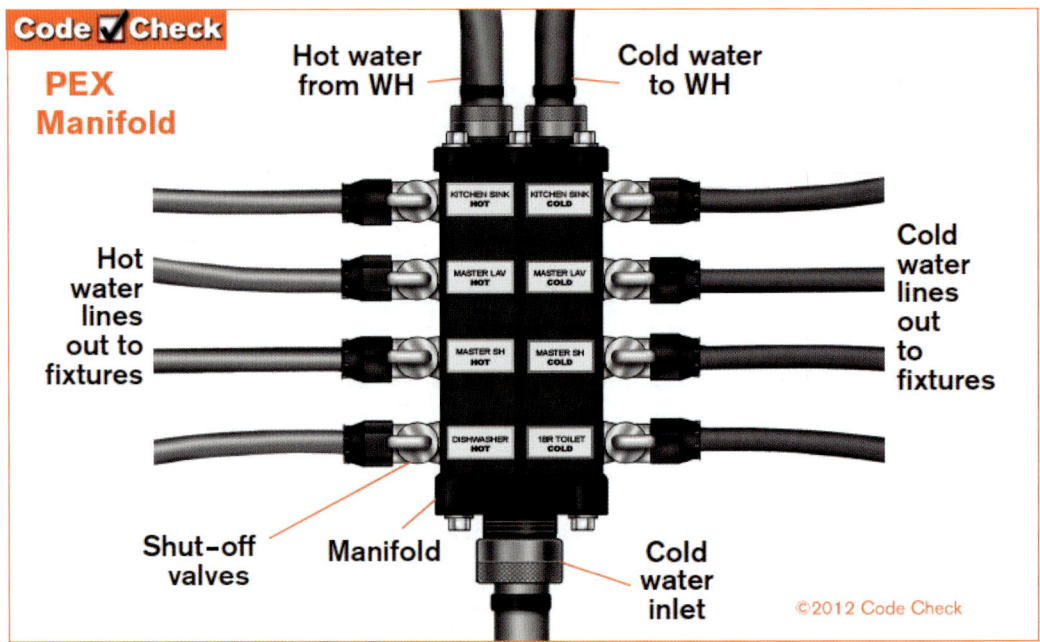

- **Brass:** Brass is an alloy of copper and zinc. It was used as supply piping in better homes in the early 1900s and in areas where water quality was bad for galvanized steel pipes, but it was not used extensively. It hasn't been used in new construction for over 50 years. Brass pipes are threaded. Brass, like copper, is not magnetic, therefore, does not attract a magnet.

  Two kinds of brass pipes were used. Yellow brass is 67% copper and 33% zinc and lasts only 20 to 40 years, being more vulnerable to corrosion. Red brass (actually a yellowish-brown color) is 85% copper and 15% zinc and lasts longer—generally 50 to 60 years but for as long as 75 years. As mentioned earlier, red brass is still an approved material but is rarely used today. Any brass pipes found today are likely to be near the end of their useful life.

  Brass pipes can get pinhole leaks as they age. This happens when chemical components in the water cause the zinc to dissolve from the brass, leaving tiny holes. Water can drip from the pipe, and over time, zinc salts can be left as the water evaporates. These **whitish mineral deposits** can self-heal the pinholes. However, the holes underneath the deposits will continue to grow. When the home inspector sees brass pipes with mineral deposits along their length, the client should be told that the pipes probably need to be replaced.

Similar signs of corrosion may be spotted at the threads, which can become paper thin. The joints become so weak that applying a wrench can rupture the joint. If you see encrusted joints in brass piping, **don't lean against or push at them; don't even touch them!** Some are so weak that any pressure can rupture them. These sections must be replaced.

- **Lead:** In rare cases, the home inspector may find lead pipes that were installed over 50 years ago. Lead was once available for distribution piping, although for safety reasons, its use has long been prohibited. (It was also used in drain and waste piping, but that was prohibited in 1989.) Lead pipes are gray in color and can be identified by their distinctive tulip-shaped joints. These joints were made by a process called wiping, where two lengths of pipe were inserted into each other and molten lead was smeared around the junction, forming the bulb. Lead pipes are not magnetic.

  Chemical corrosion causes lead salts to be released into the water supply. Corroded areas with white deposits of lead salts are very brittle. Watch out! Touching them can cause even further damage to the pipes. The home inspector should **always report the presence of lead pipes** in the distribution system with the recommendation to have the water tested and to have these pipes replaced.

- **Galvanized steel:** These pipes are steel, coated inside and out with corrosion-resistant zinc. The home inspector will find galvanized steel pipes used for both service and distribution piping in homes built up to around 1970. These pipes are gray in color. Joints are threaded, and pipe dope, pastes, or Teflon tape were used to lubricate and seal the threads at the joint when it was tightened. Galvanized steel pipes are magnetic.

  Over time, the zinc coating is lost due to galvanic corrosion; then the steel pipe begins to rust from the inside. Rust and calcification can choke up the pipes, reducing water flow. Eventually the pipes begin to leak, much like brass, when rusting becomes excessive, usually at the joints first. Exposed steel also rusts on the outside of the pipe due to water on the pipe or condensation. Galvanized steel pipes generally last about 40 to 60 years depending on the water quality.

- **Copper:** Copper was the most common service and distribution piping material used since about 1950. Despite its high cost, it is used because of its durability. Copper pipes have varying wall thicknesses:

> *Section Note*
>
> *Inspect the visible supply distribution piping in your own home. Trace pipes in the basement from the service pipe and water heater and notice where risers branch up to the house. Identify the types of pipes used. If you find dissimilar metals, check the joints and look for galvanic corrosion.*

— **Type M**, lighter and thinner (0.28″), is used for indoor piping. Type M can fail in 10 years if the water is too acidic, commonly called aggressive water.

— **Type L**, medium thickness (0.40″), is preferred for distribution; it also is used underground.

— **Type K**, the thickest (0.49″), is used underground.

> **CAUTION**
>
> *Corroded and rusted pipes indicate physical changes in the pipe and loss of strength. Do not push at or lean against corroded and rusted pipes and joints. The home inspector does not want to be the cause of a rupture or break.*

Copper pipes are too thin to be threaded. Instead, they are soldered or brazed at the joints. With **soldering**, the end of the copper pipe and the interior of the fittings are covered with flux, which eliminates chemical contamination. Then the components are heated, and a soft solder or brazing rod is applied. These joints may be broken by mechanical damage from stress, excessive pressure, or poor supports. Since 1988, the use of lead solder is prohibited. It was found that lead can leach into the water supply from soldered joints in copper piping.

In rare instances, copper pipes may have joints that are **brazed**, where so-called silver solder is applied. These joints are stronger than those with soft solder. Brazing is commonly performed on refrigeration (Freon) lines and in slab or under slab piping.

Copper can take on a greenish cast, particularly around the fittings. This is usually the result of excess flux left during the soldering process. Leaks can cause a greenish corrosion of copper pipes. When you see white mineral deposits at fittings, you need to be concerned that the fittings are leaking. In cases where the water is highly acidic, copper may experience corrosion, releasing copper ions into the water supply. A sign of this is greenish stains in sinks and other fixtures. If these signs are found, the water should be tested for the presence of copper, which is a potential health hazard.

- **Plastic piping:** Plastic piping has been around since the 1950s. Codes vary in the use of plastic piping in homes. In some areas, it may be forbidden entirely, but these are local requirements. Many types of plastic piping have been approved by national building codes for decades. Splices and repairs done with plastic piping used to indicate improvised work. A common repair that often indicates non-professional work is the use of PVC in distribution work on water heaters, for instance, or the replacement of failed or rusted out galvanized steel. PVC piping **cannot** be used for distribution piping within the home. PVC **is** approved for service piping into the building from the public or private water supply.

  Compared with metal piping, plastic piping needs more supports. Plastic pipe such PEX and PB must be supported every 32″ and CPVC every 36″

to prevent sagging between hangers. On combustion water heaters (gas, propane, etc.), plastic piping should not be used within 6″ of water heater vent piping and should not run too close to recessed lighting fixtures and heat ducts.

- **PB (polybutylene)** piping comes in gray (for distribution work) and blue (for service piping) and uses crimped-on fittings. It was used as both service and distribution pipe. It's fairly flexible and less likely than copper piping to burst under freezing conditions, but it does not hold up well. PB piping has had a history of failure from chemical reaction with the chlorine in public water systems as well as fitting failure.

- **CPVC (chlorinated polyvinyl chloride)** is a cream or beige plastic piping typically with a gold or yellow stripe down its length that is solvent-welded (glued) at the joints. CPVC is more rigid than PB and usually will split if frozen. CPVC is a very popular choice for homeowner repairs because the lengths of piping are glued together instead of soldered as with copper. Some repairs are done with PEX, but these are generally limited to professionals as a fairly expensive crimping tool is needed to secure the fittings.

There are many types of plastic piping, some of which were mentioned above, but there are others that are less well known. There is ABS, or acrylonitrile butadiene styrene, which uses glued joints and is typically used for waste or drain piping although it is approved for water service piping. PE-AL-PE and PEX-AL-PEX are combinations of polyethylene and aluminum and PEX and aluminum, respectively. Finally, PP, or polypropylene, also is approved for both service and distribution piping. PEX is now very popular, but it took a long time to catch on after the fiasco and class action lawsuits with PB piping. PEX has been used in Europe since the 1960s, originally for radiant heating and then potable water, and in the United States since the 1980s for radiant heating and since the late 1990s for potable water. There have been several lawsuits regarding PEX (chemical leaching and chlorine damage) and the brass fittings (dezincification) used with PEX. It would be wise to research your local market regarding these types of class action lawsuits.

> **Section Note**
>
> *"I wish I could say that I've never caused a plumbing problem during an inspection. But it just ain't so. It only takes a split second to get curious and take a poke at a corroded joint, causing a major break or leak in the system. It's your job to point out problems, not to cause them. Paying for a plumber to correct the damage will teach you not to do it again."*

> **For Your Information**
>
> *You should be aware of local codes on plumbing practices in your area. Find and visit with a plumber who can fill you in on the requirements. Ask questions about the public water service and other concerns.*

The chart on the next page summarizes the important points made about various types of supply piping.

PIPING	COLOR	JOINTS	CORROSION
Copper	Copper turning brown with age	Soldered, brazed	Green corrosion on leaking pipes or from flux at joints
Red brass Yellow brass	Brownish Yellowish	Threaded Threaded	Loses zinc and gets pinhole leaks with white salt deposits
Galvanized steel	Gray	Threaded	Loses zinc and steel rusts out from inside
Lead	Gray	Wiped	Lead salts released into water supply
PB plastic	Blue-gray	Press-on fittings	Not applicable
CPVC plastic	White or beige	Solvent welded	
PEX	Clear, red, or blue	Press-on or expanded	

Inspecting Water Service Piping

During the inspection of water service piping, the home inspector should watch for the following conditions:

- **Presence of lead pipes:** Always be on the lookout for lead service piping and be sure to report it to the client. Inform the client that the water supply must be tested and that pipes will have to be replaced.

- **Corroded or rusted pipes:** Look for corrosion in the piping and at the joints. Watch for mineral deposits on brass and lead pipes, rusting on galvanized steel, and greenish deposits from copper. (Refer to pages 234–240 for corrosion on various kinds of pipes.) Pipes that are corroded are near or at the end of their useful life and will eventually begin leaking. Clients should be told that these pipes will probably need replacement in the near future.

Photo #5 Another improper repair using a hose clamp and electrical tape. Also note the green corrosion on the fitting from the leftover flux.

Be especially alert when you find **dissimilar metals** in lengths of piping such as the use of galvanized steel piping with copper piping. Often,

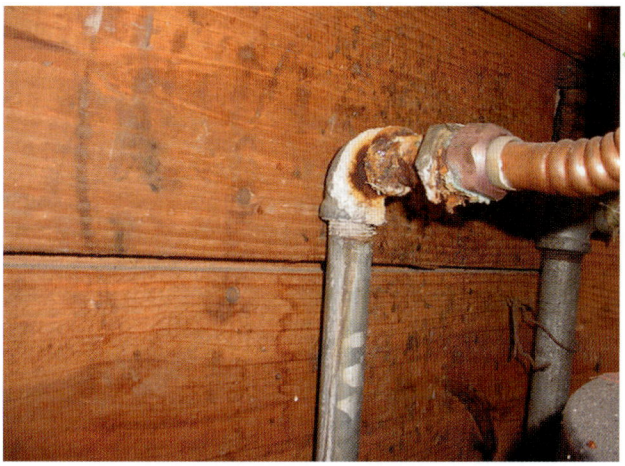

Photo #6 *Flexible copper piping connected to galvanized steel piping almost always results in corrosion. Even if it's not corroded yet, you still need to recommend a dielectric union.*

deteriorated lengths of galvanized steel piping are replaced with copper piping, and the proper dielectric unions or brass fittings may not be used.

- **Drips and leaks:** Watch for dripping and leaking from visible piping and for water stains on ceilings, walls, and floors that indicate leaking. When you see water stains, try to find out where leaks are coming from. The source could be the pipes, their connections to fixtures, or the fixtures themselves. Be sure to report any leaks you find. It's a high-liability issue for home inspectors.

- **Noisy pipes:** Pipes that are not very secure within the walls and are not properly supported with hangers can vibrate, rattle, and bang as water moves through them and comes to a stop. When hangers are too tight or holes are drilled too tightly, pipes rubbing against them can cause a squeaking sound. Whistling and chattering can be a sign of loose or worn-out washers in the faucets.

- **Water hammer** happens when water flow is shut off suddenly and a shock wave is sent back toward the supply end. It happens because flowing water has momentum. When the faucet is turned off quickly, the water slams into the valve with great pressure, creating a vacuum as it bounces back. The vacuum pulls the water against the valve again, repeating the process in smaller and smaller shock waves until they finally stop. These shock waves cause loose pipes to move and make banging noises. Over time, the repeated shock waves can damage connections. The most likely place to have water hammer occur is at electrically actuated valves on appliances such as ice makers, dishwashers, and washing machines. The following

> **INSPECTING SUPPLY PIPING**
> - Presence of lead pipes
> - Corroded, rusted, damaged, leaking, noisy, or improperly installed piping
> - Lack of insulation
> - Missing valves, inoperable hose bibs
> - Handyman plumbing or temporary repairs
> - Poor functional flow
> - Cross connections

> **CAUTION**
>
> *Do not operate any valves in supply piping. It's far too common for unused valves to start leaking, and it may be impossible to turn them back on. You don't want to be the cause of plumbing problems.*

> **Section Note**
>
> *"One of my inspectors was inspecting a home for an old man who was just recovering from heart surgery. The customer wanted the inspector to see if the bypass valve to the water softener system worked.*
>
> *The inspector said no, but the customer virtually begged him to try it. Well, the inspector is a nice guy and couldn't refuse this sick old man, so he did.*
>
> *Water started shooting out, and it wouldn't stop when the valve was turned off. Both the inspector and the old man were soaked to the skin. We paid to have a plumber repair the valve. I suppose we were fortunate not to have to pay hospital bills too."*

suggestions can be made to clients for the cure of water hammer:

— Turning faucets off slowly

— Tightening up supports for loose pipes

— Installing an additional pipe, called an air chamber, past the takeoff for the faucet. When water is cut off quickly, the momentum of the water is carried into the air chamber, which acts like a shock absorber and not backward into the pipes.

— Installing water hammer arrestors. They are basically like small expansion tanks with a bladder that absorbs the shock wave from the moving water. They are now required near appliances with quick-closing valves as mentioned above. Air chambers, although found on older installations, are not allowed on new installations. The reason is that over time, the air in the chambers is absorbed into the water, much like the pressure tank in an older well system.

- **Improper installation:** All piping must be properly supported along its length. Each size and type of pipe has its own requirements for what type of hangers should be used and where supports should be. Watch for the use of steel hangers (plumber's tape) with copper pipes and the resulting galvanic corrosion that can occur. Hangers that are not installed at proper distances or are loose or broken can put strain on fittings and damage piping. Copper tubing must be supported horizontally every 6′, copper piping every 12′, and steel piping every 12′. Keep in mind that we don't actually measure these dimensions; we're look for sagging or poorly supported piping.

Hot and cold distribution pipes should be separated by a few inches.

Photo #7 *These are water hammer arrestors installed at the washing machine connections.*

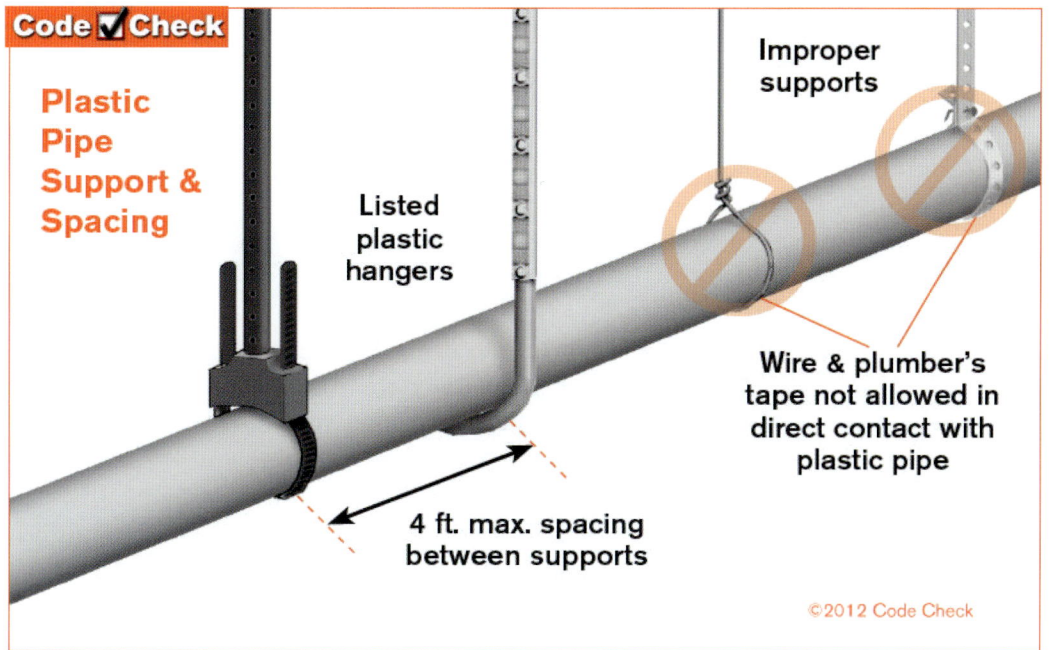

- **Insulation problems:** In certain circumstances, pipes should be insulated. Pipes in unheated areas such as crawl spaces, attics, basements, and garages should be insulated in cold climates to prevent them from freezing and bursting. In some homes, where cold water pipes sweat extensively, they should be insulated to prevent them from sweating and damaging the pipes. Finish materials below the pipes may become damaged, another reason to insulate sweating water piping.

  You may find pipes already insulated with materials such as asbestos, oakum, felt, or sphagnum moss in canvas jackets or newer materials such as mineral wool and glass fibers, rubber, or plastic foam. Asbestos insulation

ASBESTOS INSULATION

Be careful when you are inspecting insulated pipes. Don't disturb what you believe to be asbestos insulation. It's dangerous when particles are released into the air and breathed in.

Photo #8 *Most of the supply pipes in this photo are insulated (black rubber), but some are not. In a freezing climate these pipes may freeze and burst.*

THE PLUMBING INSPECTION

poses a danger to people when it is disturbed and asbestos particles are released into the air and breathed in. The home inspector isn't trained to determine whether piping insulation is asbestos. But if asbestos insulation is suspected, the inspector should indicate in the report that an asbestos-like product is used in the insulation and that it can be tested by a qualified laboratory to confirm or deny its asbestos content.

- **Missing valves:** In the distribution system, there should be a number of shut-off valves to allow work to be done on the system. There must be a shut-off valve on the cold water line to the water heater; one on the hot water line is desirable too. Most toilets have their own shut-off valves, and they're usually found under every sink. They are required at all fixtures except tubs and showers. With the newest construction, shut-off valves are not being put in at the fixtures; they are located at a manifold. If a manifold is used, all of the shut-offs must be properly labeled. A manifold distributes the water to the entire house much like an electrical panel does for electricity. Missing valves are not a serious problem, but they should be written up in the report and their absence pointed out to the client during the inspection. Don't forget—don't operate these valves.

- **Inoperable hose bibs:** Hose bibs, sillcocks, or spigots are outdoor faucets. The home inspector **should test hose bibs for operation**. The **conventional hose bib** setup consists of a regular faucet outside with a hose bib shut-off valve inside the basement or crawl space. In winter, the valve should be closed and drained and the faucet left open to prevent freezing. A special **frost-proof hose bib** is available with a long stem that turns off the water supply inside the house each time the faucet is used. The frost-proof hose bib does not need to be shut off during the winter.

> **HOSE BIBS**
>
> *The home inspector is required to operate all hose bibs but not when they are winterized in cold climates.*

Record whether hose bibs are present outside the house and test each one for operation. If it's winter and you are in a cold climate, it may not be possible to test them because they are turned off inside. The home inspector should report whether hose bibs were tested as well as whether they worked.

- **Anti-siphon protection:** Exterior hose bibs must be equipped with anti-siphon protection. This can be integral to the faucet or added after the hose bib is installed. The integral devices are not as obvious, and you will need to look at the faucet closely for writing indicating that it is anti-siphon–equipped. The added anti-siphon device is a brass fitting screwed on the end of the standard hose bib. In either case, an anti-siphon device prevents the backflow of potentially contaminated water from entering the house's drinking water, potentially causing a health hazard.

- **Temporary repairs:** Watch for and report any repairs to the plumbing system that are temporary. Some homeowners may use rubber tubing or PVC piping to replace a section of piping. The use of rags, tape, putty, clamps, or wood plugs to repair leaks should be reported and fixed by a professional.

Photo #9 *This is the house trap that has been improperly repaired at least twice with the rubber cap and the spray foam sealer.*

- **Handyman or amateur plumbing:** Inspect the distribution lines closely for evidence of handyman plumbing. Signs of handyman or amateur work may be use of PVC pipes, poorly made connections, use of dissimilar metals next to each other without proper fittings, and inadequate supports. Report any handyman or amateur work you find.

Photo #10 *This is another example of handy work by a homeowner. They couldn't figure out if they wanted to be a plumber or an electrician. You can't mix trades when repairing plumbing.*

Functional Flow

Supply piping should also be tested for functional flow during the inspection.
The home inspector should be able to report if the functional flow is satisfactory or poor.

There are two aspects to water flow. The first is **adequate flow**, whether there is enough water volume flowing, which is measured in gallons per minute (gpm). The second is **water pressure**, that is, whether there is enough push behind the flow. Water pressure is measured in pounds per square inch (psi). In general, these two aspects of water flow mean the same thing to homeowners. It's true that when water pressure is low, the water flow is low. But when the water flow is low, it doesn't

Section Note

"One of my inspectors came upon a home with handyman plumbing. In this house, the homeowner had used flexible copper piping to replace corroded pipes. The flexible copper piping went every which way.

The inspector had young children and must have spent a lot of time reading to them because he said the plumbing looked like a drawing in a Dr. Seuss book."

FUNCTIONAL FLOW

Water flow is functional when <u>enough water</u> comes out of a faucet <u>fast enough</u>. The home inspector determines whether flow is okay based on his or her opinion and common sense. Let your customers watch and decide if they agree.

necessarily mean low water pressure. There can be other problems with the plumbing system.

The question for the purpose of the home inspection is whether the water at faucets is **functional**. Is there enough water coming out of the faucet fast enough to be functional? We all know when the flow isn't functional. That's when water trickles out and takes a long time to fill a sink or tub.

Public water systems usually deliver water to homes at a pressure between 40 and 80 psi. Private wells may maintain a water pressure anywhere between 40 and 60 psi, depending on the pressure switch settings. When no water is running in the house, the water sits in the plumbing at this static pressure. When a faucet is turned on, pressure drops as water moves through the pipes. It might drop 2 psi for every 10′ of pipe, depending on several factors. Pressure also drops about 8 psi as it rises from the basement to the second floor of the house, due to the force of gravity acting on it. This is natural. Water pressure at the faucet is expected to be lower than the static pressure. When additional faucets are turned on, water pressure drops again. But taking these conditions into consideration, water flow should still be adequate at faucets.

The home inspector should perform the following tests and determine whether water flow is functional based on his or her opinion of what functional flow means:

1. Run the water at the kitchen sink and note whether water flow is satisfactory.

2. In the bathroom, turn on both the sink and tub faucets and then flush the toilet. You can expect water pressure and flow to drop some but not entirely. Judge whether water flow is still functional. For example, if water to the tub stops completely, water flow should **not be** reported as Satisfactory, but would be noted as Poor.

3. Test other faucets in the home and garage and outside as you did in the kitchen.

The key is whether it is a single fixture with poor flow or the entire plumbing system. A single fixture may be the result of a local issue. If the entire house has flow issues, it becomes a system problem, which can mean that it is more difficult to determine the cause and is more costly to repair. The home inspector does not have to find the cause of poor water flow in the home. However, it helps to be able to tell the client what the possible causes are. A plumber should determine the exact cause. Here are some possible causes of poor water flow:

Section Note

"One of my inspectors turned the faucets on in the bathroom sink and plugged the sink to check flow and drainage. However, while the sink was filling up, he was distracted by the customer and left the bathroom to look at something in the hall.

A few minutes later, he was shocked to see water flowing out of the bathroom into the hall.

He'd forgotten about the sink. I don't have to tell you not to do that, do I? Keep your attention focused on what you're doing at all times."

- **Restricted pipes:** Water supply pipes can become restricted due to corrosion, clogging, or damage, which crimps the pipes. Galvanized steel supply piping rusts out from the inside as it ages, reducing the diameter of the pipe. There may be an adequate flow of water under enough pressure, but a constricted pipe moves less water than normal.

- **Partially closed valve:** If the main shut-off valve or any other valve between the source and the faucet is partially closed, water flow will be reduced.

- **Wrong pipe size:** If a section of pipe with a smaller diameter than is required is inserted in the water distribution piping, the water flow will be reduced.

- **Too many changes in directions of the pipes:** Excessive bends and fittings in the piping slow down the water flow due to friction.

- **Low water volume:** A flow rate of 5 to 7 gpm is considered adequate in most parts of the country. A peak flow rate of 10 gpm is the optimum flow rate for a modern home with two bathrooms. It's possible for a public water service to provide water at an unacceptable flow rate to service the house. The problem could be a clogged service pipe to the house. With private systems, the well may not have enough yield to provide enough water to the house or there could be a problem with the pump itself.

- **Low water pressure:** The city may provide water at a pressure that is too low for functional use in the home. The installation of a booster pump and pressure tank in the home may solve this problem. With private wells, the pressure switch could be broken or out of adjustment.

- **Faucet issues:** Very often, a problem within the faucet, such as a blocked or calcified aerator, is the cause of low flow.

Cross Connections

The last deficiency in the water distribution system to look for during the inspection is the presence of cross connections between water distribution piping and the drain and waste piping or any other source of contamination. A cross connection exists where water from the drain and waste system, the lawn sprinkler, or another source can be siphoned back into the distribution system. Waste being introduced into the water supply system can contaminate the water. Any cross connection presents a **safety hazard**.

    A cross connection can occur when a faucet spout extends lower than the water level in a basin such as a laundry tub (which is very common when people install a short length of garden hose to the end of the faucet and it lays in the bottom of the tub). If water pressure was lowered suddenly, the water in the basin could be sucked back into the distribution pipe. The solution is to raise the faucet

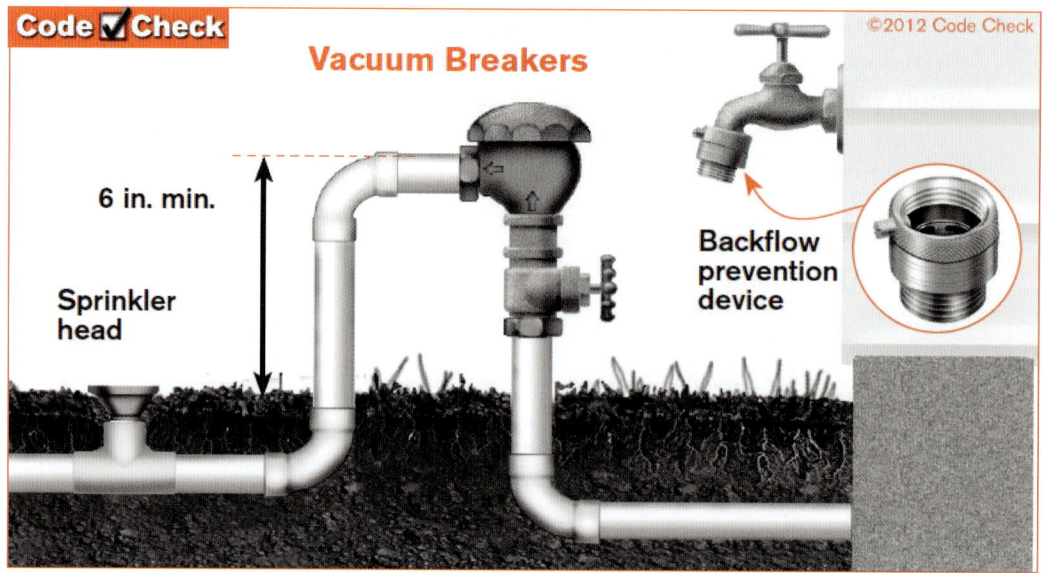

so that the spout can't reach the water level of the basin or install an anti-siphon device on the end of the faucet spout. A cross connection could also occur if a hose is left in a bucket of water outside, in a mud puddle, or in a swimming pool. Again, a lowering water pressure can siphon water back into the water distribution system.

Photo #11 *This is another type of back-flow prevention device called a vacuum breaker.*

There are many other possible sources of cross connections. Without a vacuum breaker, a bidet, which is actually a sink, can allow rinse water from a user to be introduced into the distribution system. Similarly, old tubs that fill from below the tub rim can allow used tub water back into the distribution system.

Photo #12 *This tub is in a 1930s house in Oakland, California. As you can see, it fills from the side, not from above as is the norm now. A cross connection is very possible.*

Cross connections at some equipment and fixtures are prevented through the use of **anti-siphon devices, vacuum breakers, and air gaps**. An air gap is simply a "gap of air" between the fixture and the sink or tub it is filling or draining to. Another location where an air gap may be found is at a dishwasher drain line. The issue the air gap is trying to prevent is that of draining the contents of the sink and possibly the garbage disposal into the dishwasher. Installing either the looped drain line or the actual air-gap device will prevent this from happening. The home inspector is not required to determine the effectiveness of these backflow prevention devices.

> **DON'T EVER MISS**
> - Presence of lead pipes
> - Corroded or rusted pipes
> - Leaks, old or new
> - Inoperable hose bibs
> - Handyman plumbing
> - Temporary plumbing
> - Poor functional flow
> - Cross connections

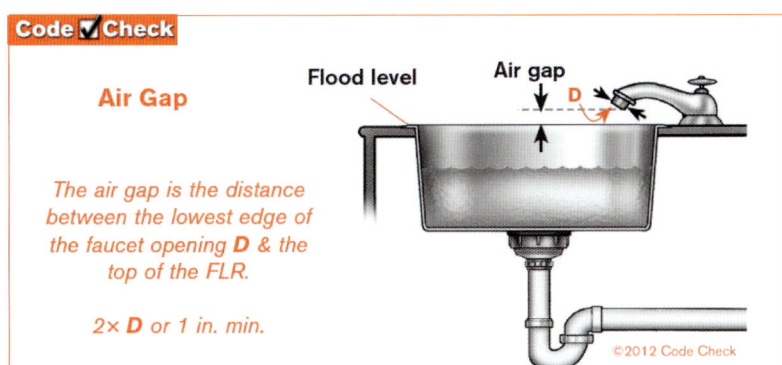

During the inspection of the water distribution piping, the home inspector should watch for the possibility of cross connections and to report any that are found as a safety hazard.

THE PLUMBING INSPECTION

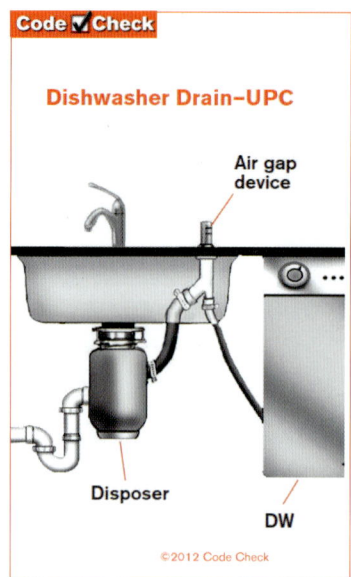
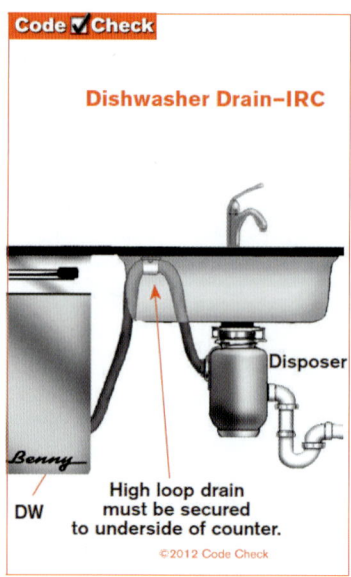

Reporting Your Findings

Depending on how your inspection report is laid out, you may be reporting your findings from the inspection of water distribution piping on a general plumbing page or on several pages. Distribution piping is checked in the kitchen and bathroom as well as any place it's visible in the basement, crawl space, attic, or other areas in the home.

- **Kitchen:** After you test for **functional flow** of water at the kitchen sink, rate the flow as adequate or poor and record that fact in your inspection report. (You should report this on the kitchen page of your report.) Sometimes, it's better to talk about functional flow as water pressure even though that's incorrect. That is a term clients will understand.

- **Bathroom:** Rate the functional flow of water in the bathroom as suggested above. Note that for now, we're concerned only with the water distribution. Drain piping, vents, faucets, toilets, and so on, are presented later in this chapter.

- **Distribution piping:** On the plumbing page of your inspection report, identify the distribution piping material(s) used in the home. If you've found lead supply pipes, highlight that information and suggest that a water contamination test be performed by a professional. Note in the report that lead supply piping should be replaced. Record the defects found in the supply piping, such as those listed here, and suggest when a plumber should be called in to make repairs:

    — Corroded, rusting, damaged, noisy, and leaking pipes

    — Improperly supported or uninsulated pipes

    — Handyman or temporary fixes

- **Hose bibs:** Note whether hose bibs are present, whether you've tested them, and whether they're operating. Note the presence or absence of anti-siphon valves or vacuum breakers.

- **Water stains and leaking:** Report water stains on ceilings, walls, and floors wherever you find them. Remember, a stain is a stain. Don't call it a leak until you verify with a moisture meter as to whether or not it is currently **wet**. The source of the leak may not be water piping, but you don't want to miss them. It's a good idea to report stains/leaks on the page of the report dealing with the location—for example, kitchen, bathroom, and bedroom pages or other locations in the home.

- **Safety hazards:** Never miss reporting any safety hazards you've found. For the plumbing system, a **cross connection** represents a safety hazard. Report a cross connection on your plumbing page and repeat it on a summary page of your report. It's a good idea to list all safety hazards found in the home, not only those for the plumbing system, on a summary page.

- **Major repairs:** Take it easy on defining plumbing problems as major repairs. Some repairs are minor and only require a few hours of a plumber's time to fix. Save the category of major repairs for serious plumbing problems.

4.3 DRAIN, WASTE, AND VENT SYSTEM

The drain, waste, and venting (DWV) system consists of all the piping that carries water and waste from drains and fixtures to the public sewer or private septic system. Any discharge pipes in the DWV system are called **drain pipes**. Some drain pipes carry rainwater or foundation groundwater. The drain pipes that carry water away from fixtures are called **waste pipes**. Waste pipes that carry waste from toilets are called **soil pipes**. Vertical pipes in the system are called **stacks**. **Vent pipes** serve to release gases and equalize pressures in the system. The **vent system** typically exhausts above or through the roof.

The inspection of the DWV system includes the inspection of the following aspects:

- The **type and size** of piping material

- The DWV piping **installation**—location and supports

- The **condition** of visible pipes, connections, and traps

DWV INSPECTION

- Piping material
- Installation
- Piping condition
- Temporary or handyman work
- Functional drainage

Chapter Note

Pages 251–271 present the study and inspection of the drain, waste, and venting system.

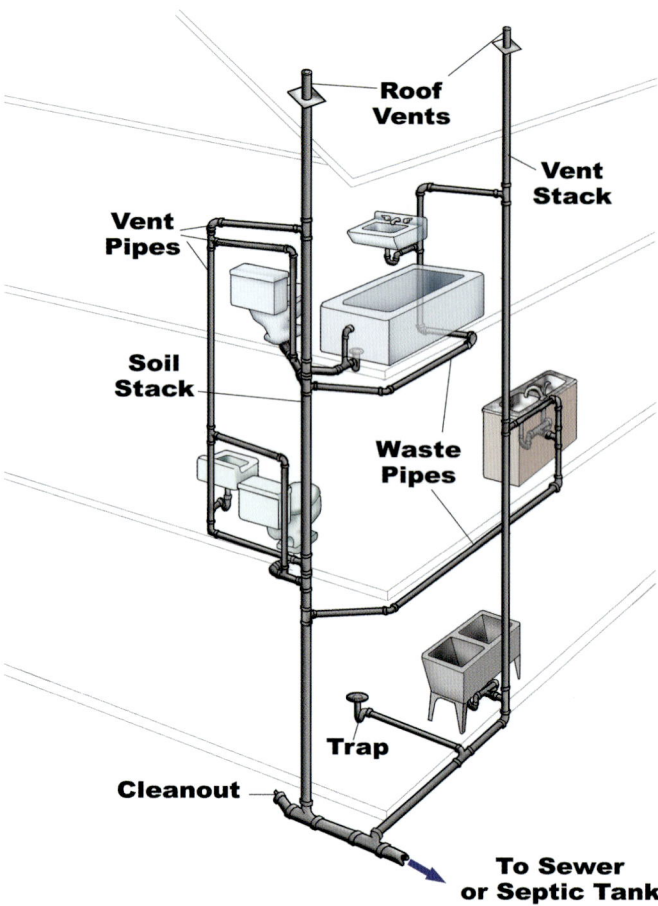

Illustration by Paddy Morrissey

> ### Definitions
>
> A <u>cesspool</u> is a masonry-lined hole used to hold and break down solid materials from the home's waste system before releasing them into the ground through the porous masonry. A <u>septic tank</u> is a watertight underground tank of concrete, steel, or fiberglass into which household waste is held and broken down for release to a seepage field. <u>Aerobic</u> bacteria thrive in an oxygen-rich environment, while <u>anaerobic</u> bacteria live in an oxygen-free environment. Both types of bacteria break down solid waste matter.

> ### SEPTIC SYSTEMS
>
> The home inspector does not have to inspect the septic system. It is beyond the scope of the general home inspection.

- Functional **waste drainage**

- The presence of **temporary** or **handyman work**

Waste Disposal

A home may be connected to a public or private waste disposal system. Public systems in older neighborhoods may have combination waste and storm sewers, which when overloaded with storm water, can back up through the basement's floor drains. New neighborhoods have separate waste sewers and storm sewers. In this case, waste pipes and basement floor drains from the home exit into the city waste sewer while runoff from gutters and downspouts exits through a separate system into the storm sewer.

A private waste disposal system is most often a septic tank and a seepage/leach system, although cesspools were previously allowed and some may still be in use.

A **cesspool** is a hole in the ground lined with masonry that was laid to be porous. Liquids in the waste system passed directly through the masonry into the ground. Solid waste was held back by the masonry and was broken down or digested by bacteria. Oxygen is available in a cesspool to feed the **aerobic bacteria**, which live in the presence of oxygen. Cesspools can become clogged with too much solid waste if they're not porous enough, or they pass solid waste into the soil too easily if they're too porous. Most communities no longer allow cesspools. Be careful, as certain parts of the country use the term cesspool when they are actually talking about a modern septic system.

A **septic tank** is an oxygen-free environment that depends on **anaerobic bacteria** to break down wastes. The tank can be made of concrete, steel, or fiberglass. The entering waste from the house separates with lighter materials rising and solid matter dropping to the bottom of the tank. Bacteria then change solids into simple chemicals that dissolve. Baffles prevent anything but liquid from being discharged from the tank.

The liquid discharged from the septic tank, which is still being worked on by bacteria, flows to a distribution

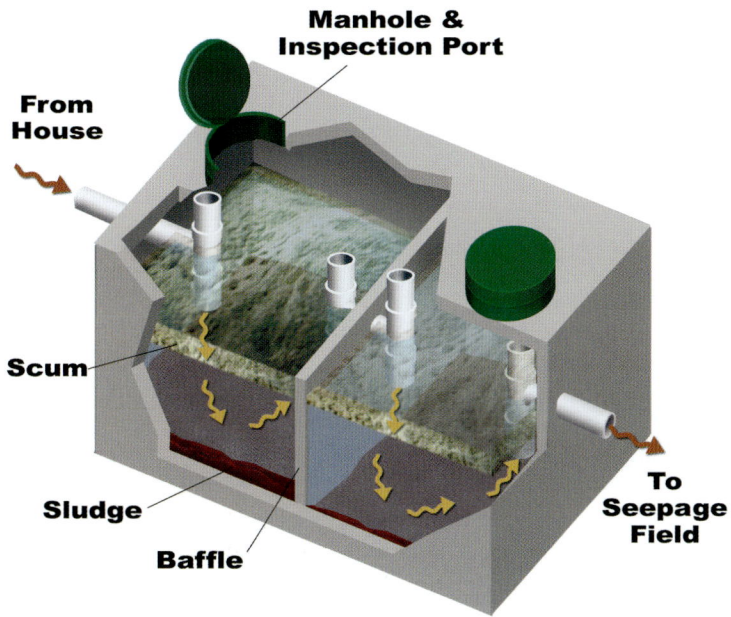

Illustration by Paddy Morrissey

box and into one of many porous drain tiles in a **seepage or leach field or pit**. There, the liquid is further purified as it makes its way down to the water table. The tank, distribution box, and tiles in the leach field must meet local distance requirements from the house and the private well. These distances vary from community to community but approximate those shown here.

> **SEPTIC LOCATION**
> - 15′ from tank to house
> - 75′ from tank to well
> - 100′ from field to well

The inspection of the septic system is beyond the scope of the general home inspection, and the home inspector is **not required to inspect it**. The most a home inspector can be expected to check is whether correct distances are met for local codes (if septic tank can be located) and whether mushy ground or pooled water appears above the leach field or an odor is coming from the field.

Septic contractors can be called in to locate and examine the tank and the leach field. Such an inspection includes running dye through the system and checking for leaks at the tank or leach field and inspecting the interior of the tank, its contents, and the condition of all its components. A word of caution regarding the use of dye testing: keep in mind the current occupancy or use of the home. If the home is vacant or occupied by only one person, a dye test may not yield usable information. What if the buyers have five children? The septic system may not be rated for that occupancy. The contractor

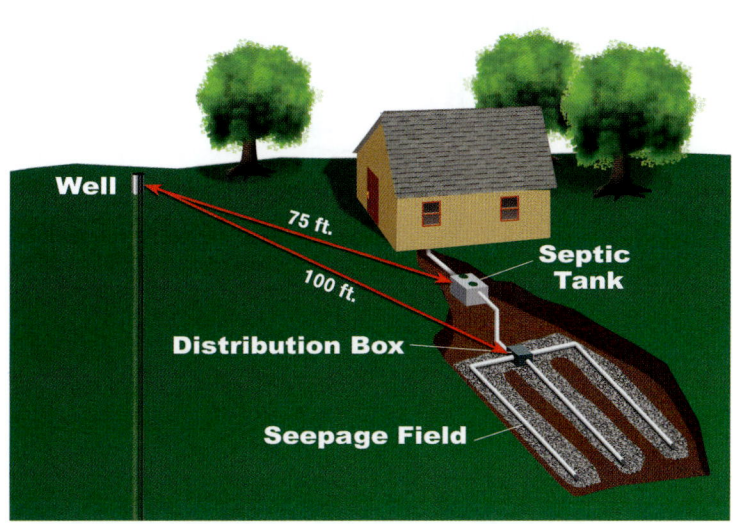

Illustration by Paddy Morrissey

THE PLUMBING INSPECTION 253

Section Note

Check your local codes for regulations regarding septic systems in your area. Local distances can vary from those given here. Check your codes for requirements regarding waste piping and venting as well.

Definitions

A dry vent in a home's DWV system carries only air and water vapor. A wet vent combines both the venting of air and water vapor and the carrying of waste matter.

A trap holds water in the plumbing system and prevents backflow of gases. Different kinds of traps include the P trap, which is shaped like the letter P, the S-trap, shaped like the letter S, and the drum trap.

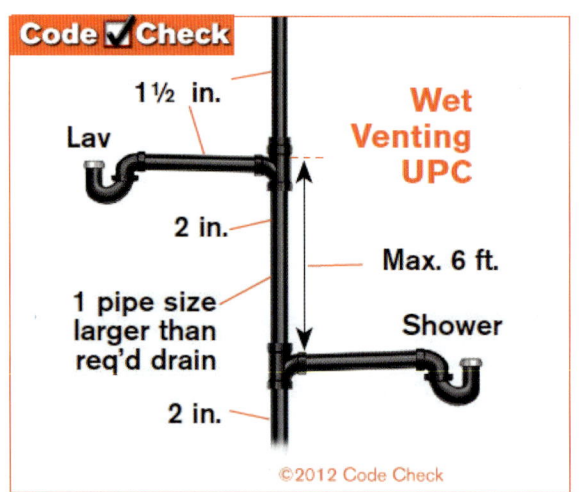

may find problems such as an overloaded tank or field, broken or damaged components, clogged tiles, and soil breakdown at the leach field. Such problems can cause a septic system to fail and require that the system be replaced. With the many new requirements for aerobic septic systems, the replacement costs can be several thousands of dollars.

If a private septic system is present on a property being inspected, the home inspector can inform the client that the septic tank needs to be pumped out every few years. The inspector may also recommend that a septic system specialist come in to inspect the entire system. Most county health departments require this when a home is sold.

The Venting System

The part of the DWV system in a house that is least understood is the venting system. Venting maintains all parts of the DWV system at atmospheric pressure so that gravity can clear the waste pipes. It also serves these three functions:

- It allows air in front of the water going through the pipes to be pushed out of the way.

- It allows air to be reintroduced into the piping after the water has passed.

- It allows sewer gases to escape from the system.

Vent piping from each fixture joins a **main vent or soil stack** above the waste line (see drawing on page 252). The main vent stack extends through the roof, ending 6″ or more above the roof. The roof vent must also be 12″ away from any wall or vertical surface and 10′ from any window, because sewer gases will be expelled through the vent. In ranch-style homes with a bathroom at one end and a kitchen at the other end, two vent stacks typically extend through the roof.

Most vents are **dry vents**, meaning they carry air and water vapor only, not waste. A **wet vent** provides ventilation from two fixtures on the same floor where the upper fixture (a sink) shares the same pipe as a lower fixture (a shower). The sink uses that pipe as a drain and the shower uses it as a vent, combining venting and drainage. The wet vent should be a larger size, but this often is not done, especially when bathrooms are added during remodeling. Wet vents were not allowed in some communities. Vent piping is usually hidden in the walls, and very little can be seen upon inspection.

Every fixture drain has a **trap** to hold water in the plumbing system and to prevent the backflow of gases from the venting system. The amount of water held by the trap is called the trap seal.

The **P-trap** is commonly used today below plumbing fixtures and in basement floor drains where the trap is under the slab. Some plumbing installations do not allow for proper venting, such as an island sink in a kitchen. There are three ways this can be performed. One way is with a loop vent; the second way is with an air admittance valve. You will also see a drain pipe configuration where the sink is installed on an exterior wall with a window above the sink. The vent pipe would be difficult to run in the wall as usual. The third method and a way around this is to use what looks somewhat like an S-trap, but is really a combination waste line and vent. In increasing the size of the pipe, it allows water/waste to flow and enough air for proper drainage.

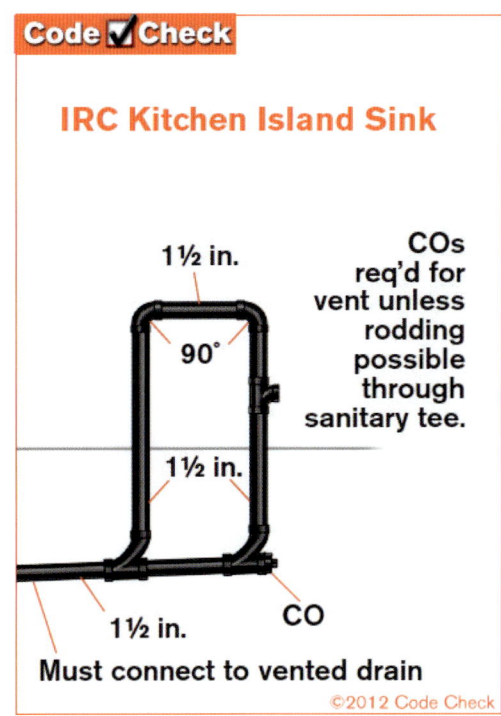

Photo #13 This is a loop vent that will be within an island for the kitchen sink.

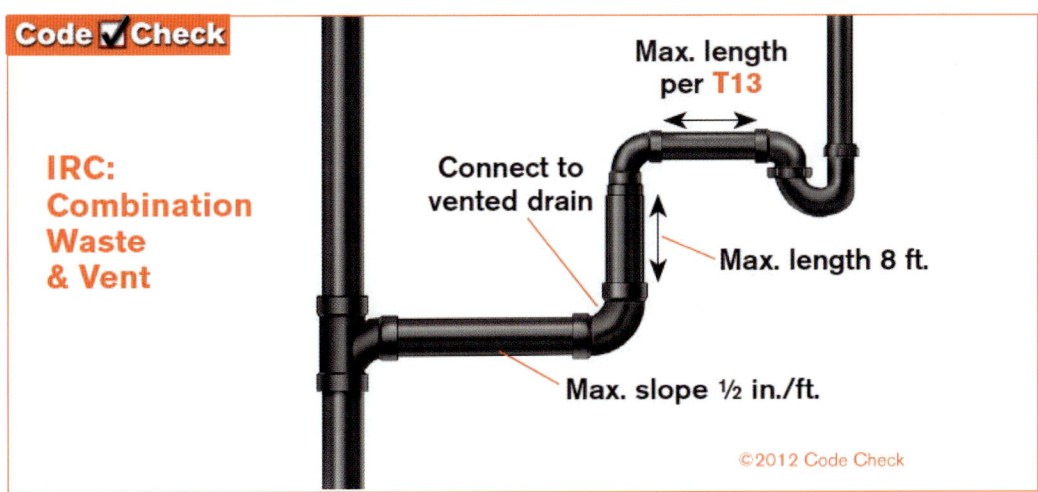

THE PLUMBING INSPECTION 255

It isn't possible for the home inspector to know for sure if a P-trap is, in fact, vented. However, any drain that gurgles and belches as it drains is not at atmospheric pressure, which indicates the absence of proper venting or some obstruction in the vent piping. The **S-trap**, although no longer permitted in modern plumbing work, was once used and is still commonly found. The S-trap is an unvented trap. S-traps can lose their trap seals during a discharge elsewhere on the system, permitting gases to escape into the home. The best solution for old S-traps is to replace them with vented P-traps or P-traps in conjunction with air admittance valves.

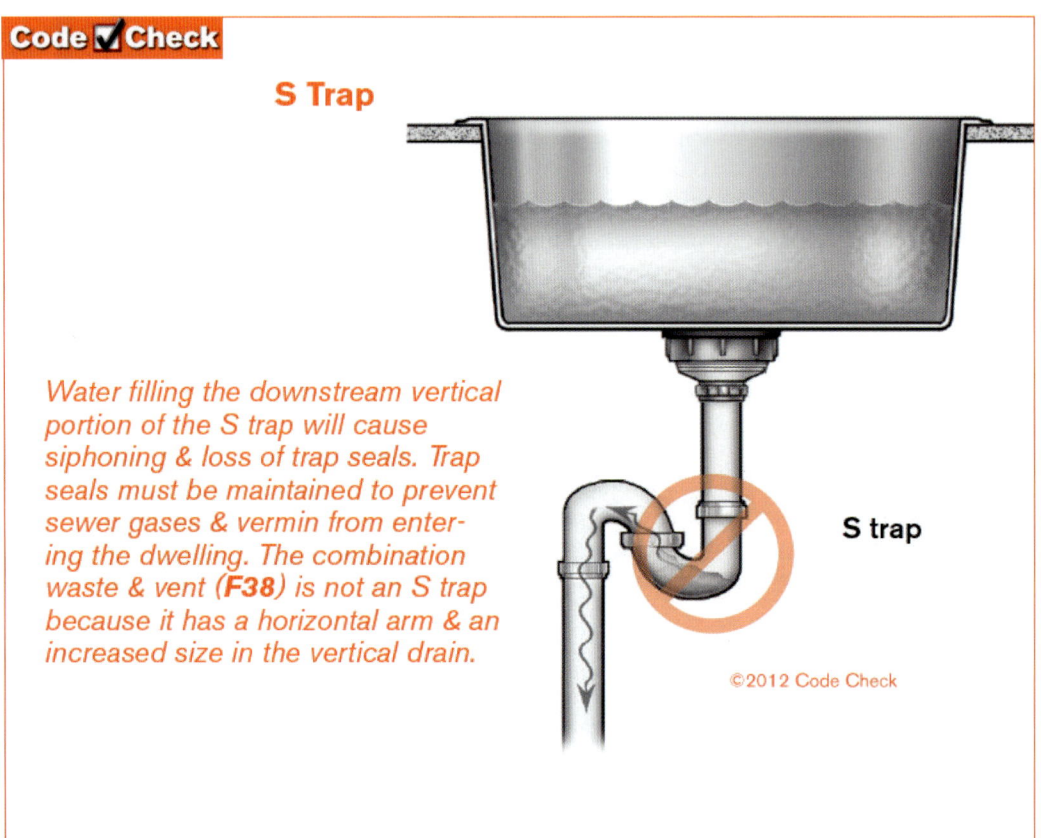

TYPES OF TRAPS

- P-trap
- S-trap
- Drum trap

Another type of trap that was used in the home is the **drum trap**, which can still be found with fixtures such as bathtubs and laundry sinks. The drum trap is not a vented trap either. The old drum traps can leak and should be inspected carefully if they are visible. Often, the drum trap from a first-floor bathroom can be seen from the basement ceiling. As a general rule, they should be replaced because they are a maintenance headache and they typically leak.

Amateur plumbers often ignore the venting system, and it is not unusual to find new fixtures installed that are not connected to the venting systems. Amateurs often omit traps under sinks and other fixtures.

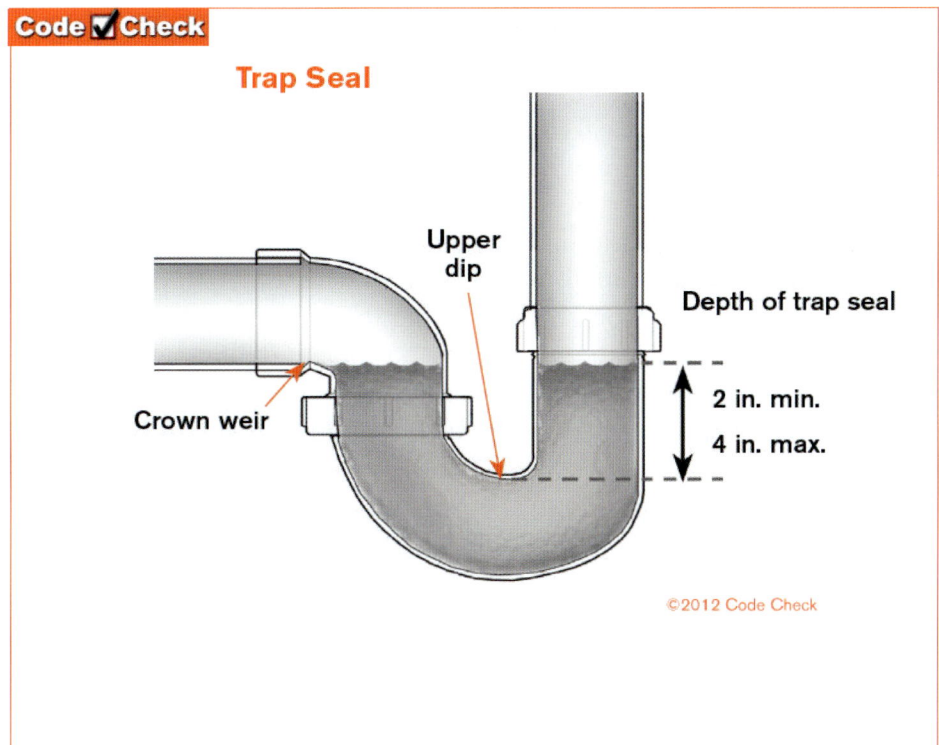

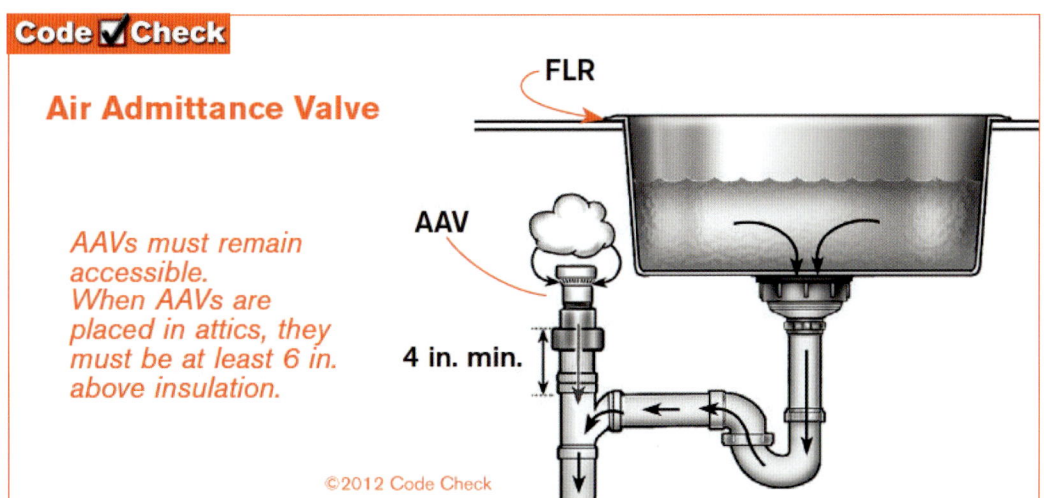

DWV Piping Materials

The size of DWV pipes used in the house varies depending on their location and purpose. Common sizes are shown in the chart at the right. Older homes may have DWV piping that doesn't conform to current requirements. In general, lines carrying solid waste are larger than those carrying liquids. The home inspector will find the following types of DWV piping used in homes:

- **Cast iron:** Up until the 1960s, cast iron pipes at least 3″ in diameter were commonly used for the waste and soil piping, especially for the main stack and large horizontal runs. It should be noted that in DWV

DWV PIPES

	Sizes
Building drain	4"
Soil stack	3" or 4"
Sinks	1 1/2"
Toilet	3" or 4"
Clothes washer	2"
Vent stacks	
No toilet	2"
Over toilet	3" or 4"

HORIZONTAL DWV PIPES

"Horizontal" pipes in the DWV system are not really horizontal. They must have a slight slope to carry away wastes.

Section Note

It's time to look at DWV piping in your own home. Of course, most of it will be hidden in the walls, but there is something to be seen in the unfinished basement, under the sinks, and in the attic. Start in the basement, locating the main stack and identifying the type of piping used. Trace lines into the basement ceiling and notice any signs of leaking. Identify the types of traps found under the sinks. Take a look in the attic to check that the vent stack is present and exhausts through the roof.

piping, the term *horizontal* is not entirely accurate—so-called horizontal piping must have a **slight slope** to allow wastes to flow downward. If the slope is too steep, the water will drain leaving the solids; if the slope is too flat, the pipe will be prone to clogging.

Cast iron piping is black and is, of course, magnetic. A cast iron pipe is manufactured with a **hub** at one end. Pipes are joined by inserting the hubless end into a hub, packing with oakum (hemp rope), and filling with molten lead. Another method is the no-hub joint where hubless lengths of pipe are joined with **slip joints** and neoprene sleeves (known as no-hub bands) are clamped on. Fernco is a common brand of connector. Slip joints are used when cast iron is connected to copper, galvanized steel, or plastic piping.

Cast iron can last 70 years or more. Over time, it will rust from the inside. Rust can self-heal the pinholes for a time, but the pipes eventually leak. Although DWV lines don't hold water all the time as supply lines do, horizontal runs of cast iron are vulnerable to corrosive sewer gas, which eats through the top of the pipe first. Horizontal runs will corrode before the vertical runs. Impurities in the metal can cause rusting or even splitting lengthwise along a seam.

- **Galvanized steel:** Galvanized steel may be used in DWV piping for both drains and vents. In some areas, it's used only for venting, where it lasts 50 or more years because it is not in contact with water. However, sewer gases can even eat at galvanized steel, leaving large holes. Galvanized steel has a shorter life expectancy when used for drain and waste lines. (See page 237 for more information.)

- **Chrome-plated brass:** Used almost exclusively for traps under sinks, chrome-plated brass is usually connected under the floor or behind the wall to other metal or plastic pipes. These traps do leak after a time. Watch for salt deposit corrosion on the underside of the traps. Be careful with chrome-plated brass because many times the only thing left is the chrome plating and the trap itself is paper-thin. Don't touch it; just write it up for replacement. (See pages 236–237 for more information.)

NOTE: It was quite common for homes to use cast iron stacks, galvanized steel smaller-diameter lines, and chrome-plated brass traps together. If you see cast iron stacks and chrome-plated traps, it's a good guess that galvanized DWV lines are hidden in the walls.

- **Copper:** The use of copper DWV lines is relatively rare, although it was used for a while from the 1940s to the 1980s. If used, they may be type M, the thinnest (wall) available, but a grade of copper pipe called DWV was more widely used.

- **Lead:** Lead piping was used up to the 1950s to connect fixtures to the main stack or drain, especially for lead bends under toilets and drum traps under tubs. Today, these lead pipes are likely to be leaking at the connections. These waste lines are likely candidates for being replaced during major plumbing work.

  The lead used in DWV piping does not pose the same danger to people in the home as it does when lead supply piping is used. However, the use of lead even in DWV piping has been prohibited since 1989.

- **Plastic:** For the last 40 years or so, rigid plastic piping has been used almost exclusively for DWV piping. **PVC** (polyvinyl chloride) piping is common in many parts of the United States. It's white in color. Black **ABS** (acrylonitrile butadiene styrene) is also used. ABS is also widely used in various parts of the country and is very common in the Southwest. You will be in either a PVC or ABS use area. It is usually one or the other in any given part of the country.

  Both PVC and ABS are joined to dissimilar materials (for example, cast iron to PVC) with **no-hub joints** as described earlier for cast iron. Both PVC and ABS use solvent cementing (also called chemical welding) to join the pipe and fittings together. You can glue PVC only to PVC and ABS to ABS in a home. The only place you are allowed to glue PVC to ABS is to the sewer piping leaving the building with an approved transition solvent. Drawbacks of plastic piping are that they are noisier than metal pipes and water can be heard rushing through them, they may burst if unprotected in freezing areas (not usually an issue because they are not typically full of water), and they throw off noxious fumes during a house fire (dioxins in the case of PVC).

The following chart summarizes information about DWV piping. We haven't repeated all the information about copper, galvanized steel, and lead piping that was presented earlier. See the chart on page 240 for more information on other metal piping used in the DWV system.

PIPING	COLOR	JOINTS	CORROSION
Cast iron	Black	Hub caulked with lead or no-hub with slip joints	Rusts, the horizontals rust out at top first.
Chrome-plated brass	Shiny silver	Threaded	Loses zinc and gets pinhole leaks with white salt deposits
ABS plastic PVC plastic	Black White or beige	Mechanical no-hub joints	Not applicable

Inspecting DWV Piping

During the inspection of the DWV piping, the home inspector should watch for the following conditions:

> **REMINDER**
>
> *Be sure to report if you've found lead pipes in the DWV system. Customers should be told that lead pipes will most likely require replacement soon.*

- **Corroded, rusty, or leaking pipes:** Check all visible DWV piping for corrosion, rust, and leaks. Remember that horizontal runs of cast iron are likely to develop problems on the top of the pipe first. Check connections for corrosion, especially if two dissimilar metals are connected. Corrosion stops leaks for a while, but eventually the leaks will start. The home inspector should report corroded and rusted pipes and let clients know that leaking will follow. The pipes will ultimately have to be replaced.

Photo #14 *Leaks are usually a bit more subtle than this. This was the result of failed drain piping above. You can actually see the falling water.*

When inspecting the DWV system **always look for water stains** on the walls, floors, and ceilings that may indicate a plumbing leak and record it in your inspection report. This is a **high-liability** area. You may not be able to tell the client the cause of the leak, but you better point out the stain to the client and then put it in writing to protect yourself against any later plumbing catastrophe.

- **Improper installation:** When inspecting DWV lines, be sure to make note of horizontal lines. There should be a downward slope to these lines. Make sure the pipes are properly supported and hangers are in good condition so that lines run straight and no low spots develop in the lines. Waste can get hung up in the pipes if they sag. Much like copper piping being improperly supported with wire or plumber's tape (galvanized strapping with holes in it), it is similarly prohibited from supporting plastic piping. As the piping moves/sways when water runs through it, the metal strapping can cut through the plastic piping, causing it to fail. Listed plastic hangers are required, commonly called J-hooks.

- **Lack of insulation:** (See comments on page 243.) Insulation is common on waste piping beneath mobile and manufactured homes. Some will even have electric heat tape wrapped around them to prevent freezing in cold climates.

- **Prohibited or leaking traps:** Always check for traps at plumbing fixtures. Older **P-traps** under sinks are commonly rusted out and have loose joints, causing drips and leaks. Test the trap by gently grabbing hold of it and moving it

> **Section Note**
>
> *"Try not to be too rough when testing traps. A gentle move back and forth will tell you if the joints are loose.*
>
> *One of my inspectors was inspecting a galvanized steel trap under a sink and gave it a vigorous shake. The result was not good. He actually crushed part of the trap, rendering it useless. We had to pay to have a new trap put in."*

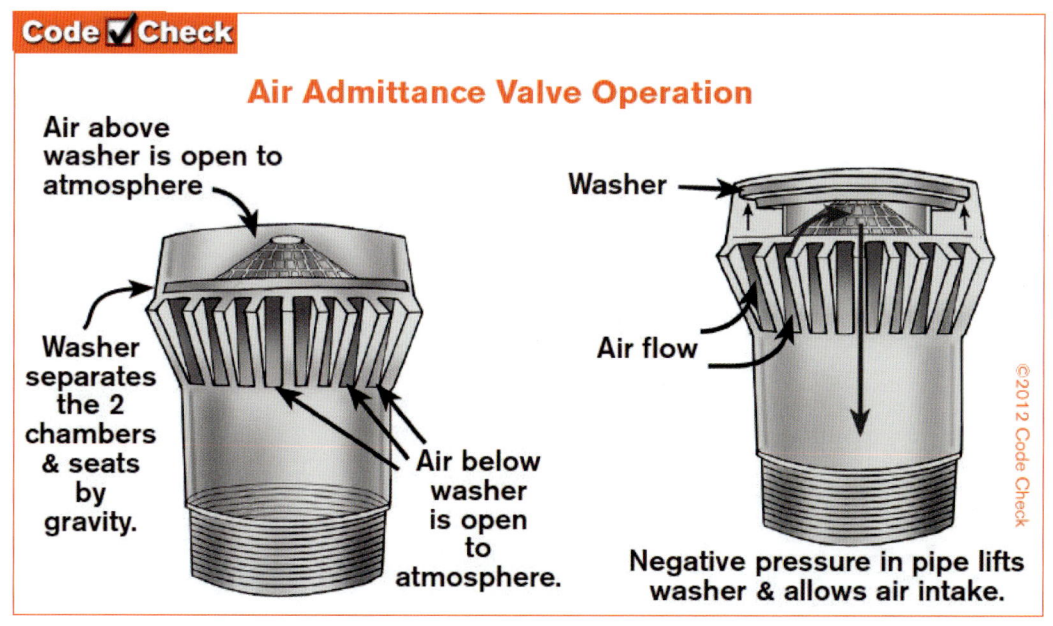

slightly back and forth. (Remember, don't do this with a chrome-plated trap!) But be careful not to be too rough with it. Rusted traps can fall apart if handled too roughly. Report the use of **air admittance valves (commonly called Studor vents)** if local codes do not permit them.

Don't miss reporting **S-traps** and let clients know that an S-trap isn't vented. Water can be sucked out of the trap, letting sewer gas into the house. If an odor of sewer gas is present, suggest that the trap be refilled with water to create the water seal. S-traps also are prone to siphoning by momentum.

The way an S-trap can be converted to a vented P-trap is through the use of an air admittance valve. The trap assembly is reconfigured, and the air admittance valve is installed to provide venting for the fixture.

> **INSPECTING DWV PIPING**
>
> - Corroded, rusted, damaged, leaking, or improperly installed or insulated piping
> - Illegal or leaking traps
> - Missing or improper venting, presence of sewer odor
> - Handyman plumbing or temporary repairs
> - Cross connections
> - Poor functional drainage

Also, check visible **drum traps,** described earlier, for rusting and leaking and inform clients about their unvented condition and propensity for clogging.

When a home is served by a public water supply, there may be a **house trap** where the home waste lines join the public sewer. The house trap is a large U-shaped fitting with capped heads at the top of each arm. There may also be a fresh air vent on the side of the trap. The sewer outlet fitting must have a **cleanout** sealed with a plug that can be removed if any work needs to be done on the sewer lines. This plug should be kept in place and sealed. Sometimes, the home inspector will find rubber patches, wooden bungs, or rags stuck in the cleanout. Improperly sealed cleanouts should be reported.

House (Building) Trap

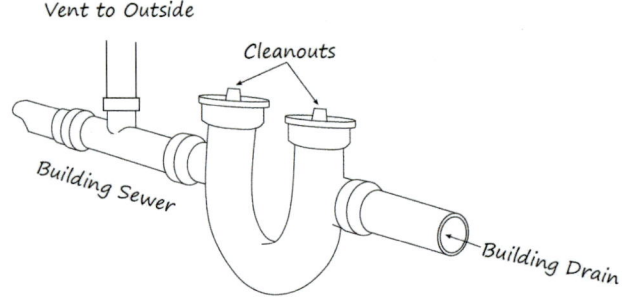

Illustration by Paddy Morrissey

- **Backwater valve:** A backwater valve is required if the fixtures or their drains are below the manhole cover. Sewage could back up to the fixtures when the sewer is blocked. Backup can be prevented by installing backwater valves on the drain lines below the manhole cover.

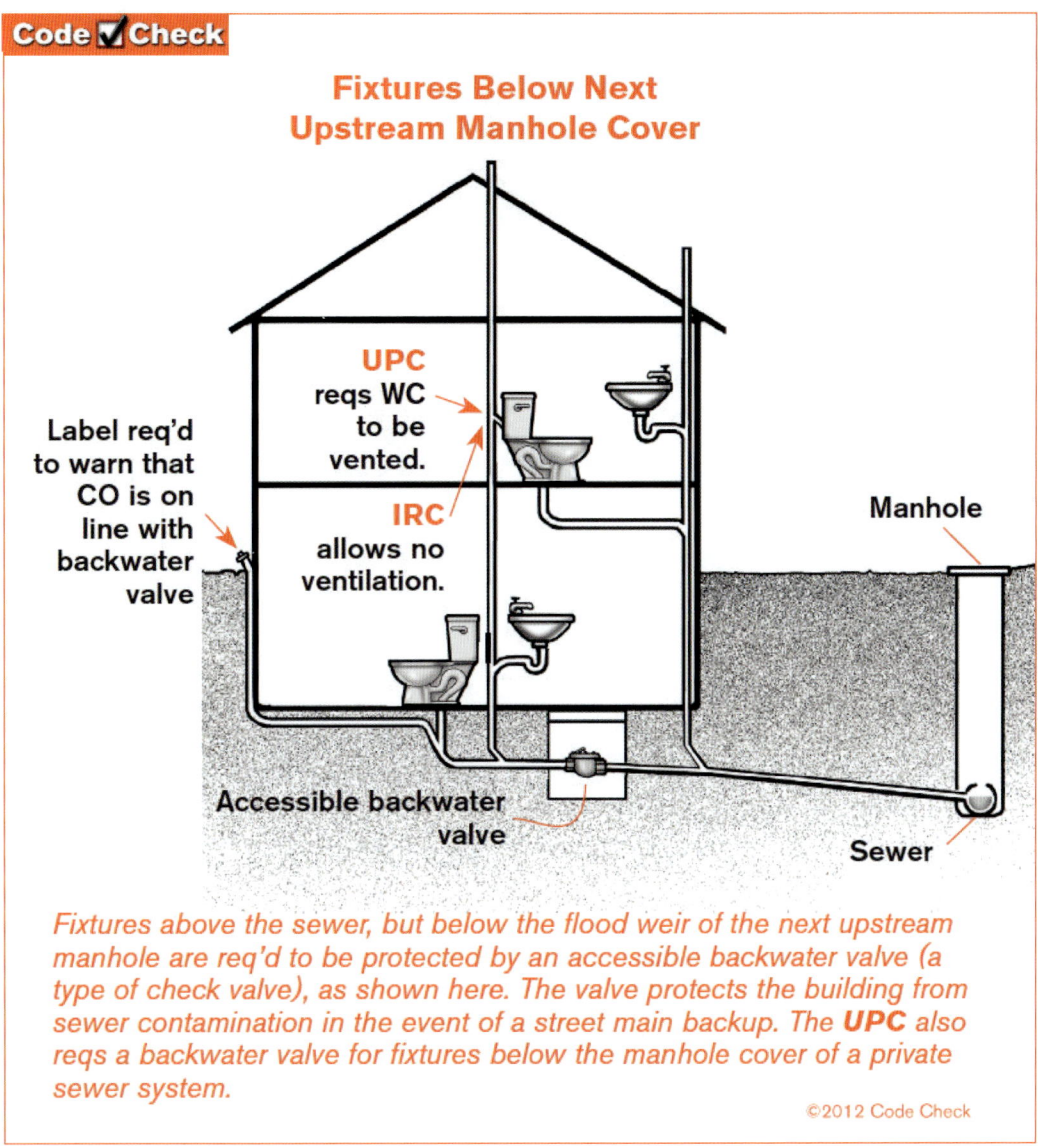

- **Missing or improper venting:** Most vent piping is hidden from view, so the home inspector won't actually see too much of it. However, there are some things to look for. Unvented traps should be reported. Remember that S-traps and drum traps are not vented, nor are they a good idea. Even P-traps can be installed and not connected to a venting system. A sign that a fixture is not vented is a gurgling or belching noise when the fixture drains. If you suspect that a P-trap is not vented, mention it to the client and record it in your inspection report. Improperly installed vent pipes should be reported as a **safety hazard**.

Photo #15 *Don't want to put another hole in the roof? Then just vent your plumbing to the attic. Be sure not to miss things like this.*

If you notice the **odor of sewer gas** anywhere in the house, point it out to the client and report it. Sewer odors can indicate missing, blocked, or damaged venting. Check the roof to see if there are any vent stacks.

Be sure to check the **vent stack(s) in the attic** and from the roof for proper extension and distances. The vent penetration should be checked for proper flashing and for leaking. Look at the vent for corrosion as it passes through the attic. Remember, older cast iron and galvanized piping corrodes from the inside out due to sewer gases. Leaking through the roof and high attic condensation can also damage vent piping here.

- **Temporary repairs:** Watch for repairs to the DWV line and to traps. The use of rags, tape, putty, JB-Weld, and plugs in piping to repair leaks should be reported and fixed or more likely replaced professionally.

- **Improvised plumbing:** New plastic S-traps inserted into the plumbing runs are a signal to watch for other amateur work in the system. Homeowners often put plastic piping in the waste line but don't pay attention to proper configuration, traps, or supports. As a result, the waste line may sag, causing waste to clog the system. Report any handyman work you find.

- **Cross connections:** Watch for possible cross connections where water from the drain and waste system can be siphoned back into the distribution system. (See pages 247–250.) Remember to report any cross connections found as a **safety hazard**.

Inspecting Drainage

The question home inspectors must answer for the inspection of drainage is whether water drainage at fixtures and drains is **functional**. Does all the water drain from a fixture?

Does it drain fast enough? Does one fixture drain and fill an adjacent fixture? The inspector should determine if drainage is satisfactory based on his or her opinion and common sense. Drainage is adequate if the water drains fast enough and completely. If a sink takes a long time to drain or if water doesn't drain completely, then drainage is poor.

The home inspector can test water drainage the same time he or she tests water flow. This can be done in these ways:

1. As each faucet is run, watch as water drains from the fixture. It should not fill with water without plugging the drain.

2. Plug the fixture as water is running to fill the fixture with 3–4″ of water; then pull the plug to watch the water drain.

3. Fill all fixtures, sink(s), and tub in the room with 3–4″ of water; flush the toilet at the same time; and then drain them all at the same time while flushing the toilet again.

The home inspector may find different kinds of pumps in the home, usually in the basement or crawl space, that are considered part of the drainage system:

- A **sewage ejector pump** consists of an electric pump along with its sump or crock. A sewage ejector pump is also known as a solid waste pump or an ejector pump or a lift pump because it can pass solids up to 2″ in diameter through the pump.

> **Section Note**
>
> *"Yes, I've ruined traps under sinks too. I can remember checking out a P-trap that was so rusted that I put my hand right through it.*
>
> *It can be embarrassing. It doesn't matter if the trap was in incredibly poor shape to begin with. You end up having to pay for a new one to be installed."*

Code Check

Sewage Ejector Pump

- Vent min. 1¼ in. **IRC**
- 1½ in. **UPC**
- Electrical cord
- Tight-fitting grommet
- Discharge pipe
- Discharge pipe min. 2 in. diameter
- Full-open valve
- Backwater or check valve
- Bolted & gasketed cover
- Sump min. 18 in. wide, 24 in. deep **IRC**

©2012 Code Check

THE PLUMBING INSPECTION

Grinder pumps and macerating pumps are similar in that they have blades to cut up or grind the solids, much like a garbage disposal, before passing the waste on. Sewage pumps are used for removal of both solid waste "black water" and "gray water" (household wastewater that does not contain human waste). The receiver (crock) should be tightly covered and sealed to prevent sewer odors from escaping.

A vent pipe must be connected to the top of the tank. Some communities don't allow the use of sewage pumps. The home inspector should be aware of local codes regarding their use. You may find one of these tanks in the yard even if the house is on a city sewer. The reason may be due to the elevation of the house's waste piping in relation to the city sewer in the street. It may not be possible for the waste to drain to the street by gravity, and it must be "lifted" or pumped to the street to then drain by gravity to the wastewater processing plant at the city.

- **Macerating toilets** are often used in basements due to their ability to pump waste (liquids and solids) straight up. They are also seen in remodeling projects and additions, where the sewer line may not extend to or may not be located where the homeowner wants to put a bathroom. When inspecting a sewage pump, you should check for leaks and flush the toilet and run water in the sink, tub, and/or shower to get the system to come on. Also, look for a visible check valve or backwater valve, a

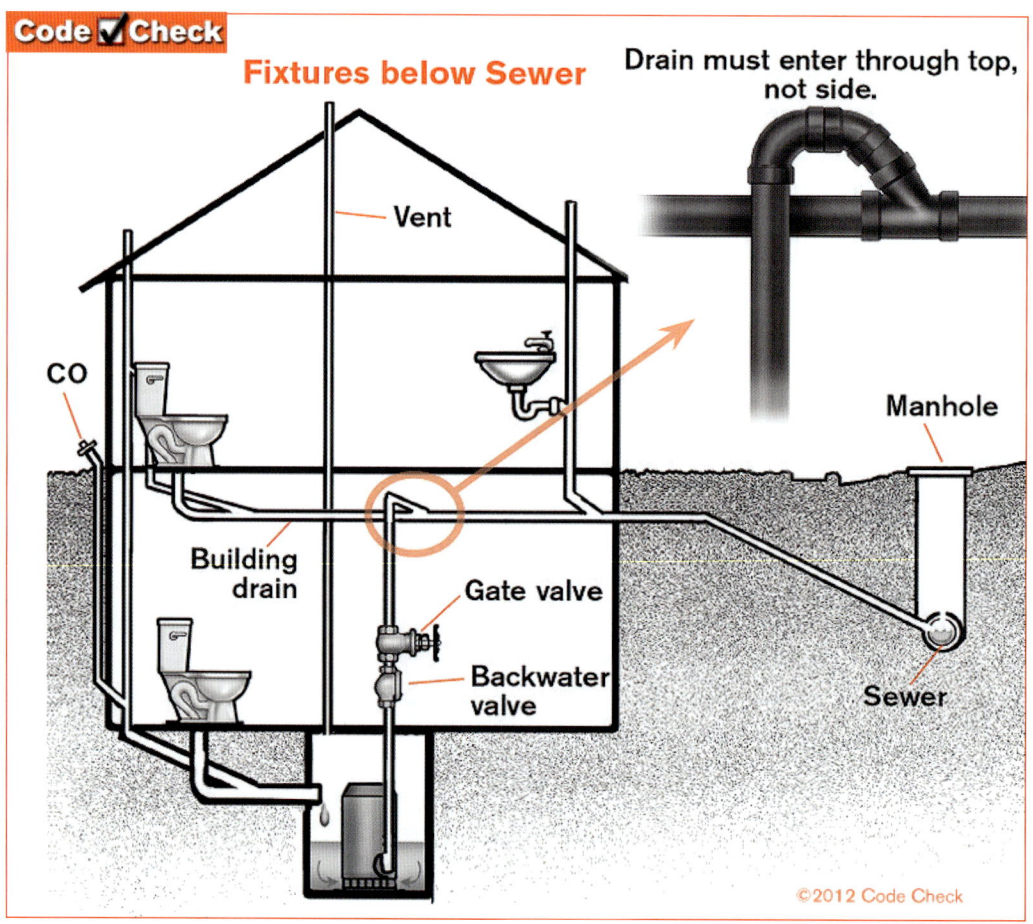

shut-off valve, and a vent. If you hear water rushing back into the tank, causing the pump to cycle on again, it may indicate the absence of a check valve or one that is not operating properly. Short cycling can burn out the pump.

- A **sump pump** is a freshwater pump that moves groundwater and storm water away from the home. A conventional sump pump system is installed in a pit (sump) or crock located below the basement floor level or in a crawl. The sump pump pumps the water into the yard away from the house or into the storm drain. Some homes have a separate gray water installation, which is essentially a sump pump used strictly for wastewater from washing machines, showers, tubs, and other fixtures (except toilets). They pump gray water to a sewer or septic system or into a drywell. A **drywell** is a buried gravel pit that accumulates water and allows it to seep into the ground slowly.

> **FUNCTIONAL DRAINAGE**
>
> *Drainage is functional when all the water in the fixture drains fast enough and completely. The home inspector determines whether drainage is okay based on his or her opinion and common sense. Let customers watch and decide if they agree.*

Photo #16 *This is a typical sump pump crock with a submersible pump.*

- **Sanitary pump:** The sanitary pump is like a sump pump in that it is a pit with a pump. However, water flowing into the sanitary pump is **gray water**, or drainage from the clothes washer or laundry tub and sometimes from the floor drain. When the sewer or septic line from the house is above the floor level, the sanitary pump is needed to pump this waste water up to the sewer line level. A sanitary pump may discharge to an outside drywell instead of to the sewer or septic system, which is acceptable. However, pumping this gray water out onto the surface of the yard is not an accepted practice. Organic waste can rot and cause odors.

The sanitary pump crock should be covered and **sealed**. Some communities require the receptacle to be **vented**. There should be a **check valve** or another type of backflow preventer valve in the discharge pipe. This valve prevents waste from the sewer line from backing up into the receptacle. The valve is usually blue or green and has an arrow on it that points up, showing the proper installation of the valve. The home inspector should determine if the check valve is present.

Test the operation of the sanitary pump, if possible. You should be able to run water into the laundry tubs that will drain into the crock. Listen for the pump to kick on.

The pump may also pump the gray water to a recycling or purification system for reuse in applications such as plant irrigation or in toilet tanks to flush toilets or urinals. If the water is used to flush toilets and urinals, it must be disinfected and dyed blue or green before use. In addition, backflow prevention devices must be installed to prevent cross connections between the gray water and potable water systems.

The home inspector should test the pump for operation. Sump pumps can be a **pedestal-style pump**, which has the motor mounted on a shaft sitting above the water level. A rod sticks out of the receiver tank connected to a switch. To test the operation of the pump, use a pen or pencil to pull up on this rod at the switch to be sure there's not a short at the pump. The sump pump may be the **submersible** type, sitting below the water level in the bottom of the sump. To test this type of sump pump, use a wooden stick or broom handle to lift up on the float in the receiver tank. Another way to test each kind of sump pump is to run water into the receiver tank with a hose (not required). If it's dry, do not test it and record that in your report. Do not turn the "motor" on by lifting the float when empty or dry. This only tells you that the motor, not necessarily the pump, is working.

The sump pump motor should run quietly and should discharge water. It shouldn't run all the time. The pump should have its own dedicated circuit so that it continues working even if other equipment malfunctions. In the past these circuits were **not** GFCI protected for fear of it tripping and being left without a pump when needed. New requirements for manufacturers as well as the NEC now **require** GFCI protected circuits for sump pumps. The receiver tank should be covered and kept free of silt buildup and debris.

> **Section Note**
>
> "One of my inspectors was inspecting an inner city property. While checking drainage at the kitchen sink, he found it to be extremely good. Water went out as fast as it flowed. The owner stood by and watched as the water ran.
>
> Finally, the inspector turned the water off and then bent down to inspect the trap and pipes under the sink. There were no drainage pipes!
>
> Instead, he found a large pail filled to the top. The pail had to be emptied elsewhere every time the sink was used.
>
> The owner shook her head and said, 'I wondered if you were going to let that overflow.' As if the inspector should have known."

> **CAUTION**
>
> Don't put your hands in the sump pump when it's plugged in. And don't use a metal rod to start the submersible pump. Use a wooden stick.

Reporting Your Findings

As you're inspecting the DWV system, talk to your client and let him or her know what you're doing. Be sure to explain what you're inspecting and what your findings are. Take time to answer questions. Remember that clients may not understand what they see in the mass of piping and are counting on you to make sense of it.

Review the inspection report with your client after the inspection. Even though you've been careful to communicate during the inspection, the client will often forget some or all of what you've said. Go through the report page by page, pointing out where you've noted certain findings. This is especially important with technical systems such as plumbing, which the client may not understand thoroughly. The review gives you another chance to test the client's understanding. Spend time pointing out where you included major repairs, safety hazards, and items requiring replacement in the near future.

We've covered quite a bit of information about the DWV inspection, including waste disposal, venting, inspection of DWV lines, and drainage issues. These items should be reported on various pages in your inspection report. Again, it depends on the layout of the report you're using.

> **DON'T EVER MISS**
> - Corroded or rusted DWV pipes
> - Leaks, old or new
> - Missing or improper plumbing vents
> - Illegal or leaking traps
> - Handyman plumbing
> - Temporary plumbing
> - Cross connections
> - Poor functional drainage

- **Kitchen:** After you test for **functional drainage** at the kitchen sink(s), rate the drainage as adequate or poor and record that fact in the inspection report. Note the condition of DWV piping under the sink and report defects such as leaking or corrosion. Watch for any unsafe S-traps or improperly installed or located air admittance valves or mechanical vents. Be on the lookout for homeowner installations, especially garbage disposals. These should be recorded. When reporting these defects, you can write your suggestions about remedying the situation. For example, if S-traps are present, you can suggest replacing them with P-traps and vents or air admittance valves if allowed. Report any odor of sewer gas in this location.

Code Check — Tailpiece Lengths

- IRC max. 24 in.
- UPC max. 24 in.
- IRC max. 30 in.
- Max. 1 slip joint
- Directional fitting

©2012 Code Check

THE PLUMBING INSPECTION

- **Bathroom:** Report functional drainage in the bathroom on the bathroom page in the report. Again, rate it as adequate or poor. Report leaking, illegal traps, and so on, as mentioned above.

- **DWV piping:** On the plumbing page of your report, identify the DWV piping material(s) used throughout the home. Note if you found lead pipe and possibly an attached drum trap somewhere in the DWV line. Because lead DWV pipes don't pose the same hazard that lead supply pipes do, don't record it as a health hazard. Record the defects you found, such as those listed below, and suggest that a plumber repair or replace the piping if your findings warrant it.

    — Corroded, rusting, damaged, and leaking pipes

    — Improperly supported or insulated pipes

    — Handyman or amateur or temporary fixes

    — Unsealed or open cleanouts

    — Unsafe traps or venting

    NOTE: If you find DWV venting exhausting into the attic, leaks around the plumbing vent in the roof, or holes in vent pipes in the attic, report the conditions on the attic page of your inspection report. Sometimes, clients miss these details if they're reported on a general plumbing page.

- **Sumps, sanitary pumps, and solid waste pumps:** For sumps, note whether one is present, whether it's been tested, and whether it's operating. For sanitary pumps, note if the receptacle or crock is sealed, whether a check valve is present, whether you've tested the pump, and whether it's operating. Similar observations should be made about sewage ejector pumps, macerating pumps, and any other solid waste pumps inside or outside the home. Note any other defects you found.

- **Safety hazards:** Always note safety hazards on the page of the report dealing with their location and again on a summary page in the report. Record the following as safety hazards with DWV piping:

    — Cross connections between DWV and supply piping

    — Holes in vent pipes

    — Improperly installed vent pipes

SUMP PUMP LIFETIME

Because sumps have a relatively short lifetime, it's a good idea to list them as items needing replacement within the next 5 years—just for your protection.

Section Note

"Here's another example of improper waste discharge. One of my inspectors flushed a toilet in a remodeled basement and thought it sounded weird. He put toilet paper in it and flushed it again. Then he looked into the freshwater sump pump. Sure enough, he found the toilet paper in there.

Watch out when you find a new bathroom in a remodeled basement. Homeowners sometimes foolishly take these shortcuts for waste discharge."

- **Major repair and replacement:** You can classify **serious problems** with the DWV piping system, indicating immediate and expensive replacement as major. But be careful not to highlight every little finding as a major repair or replacement. Sump pumps and sanitary pumps that are not operating and need replacement should be put in this category.

4.4 HOT WATER SYSTEM

The hot water system in most homes is the common **water heater**, although some homes have systems associated with home heating equipment such as a boiler or heat pump. During the inspection of the water heater, the home inspector identifies the **brand** of water heater, its **type** (gas, oil, or electric, including heat pump type), and its **capacity** in gallons. The inspector also estimates its **approximate age** (date of manufacture is usually stated on the data tag or encoded in the serial number). The inspection includes the following:

- The condition of the water heater tank
- Proper piping, venting, location, and access
- Operating and safety controls
- Safety devices—TPR and Watts 210 valves
- Presence of an expansion tank
- Presence of a catch pan
- Operation of the water heater

> **INSPECTING HOT WATER SYSTEM**
> - Brand and type
> - Capacity
> - Approximate age
> - Condition and operation

> **Chapter Note**
>
> *Pages 271–288 present the study and inspection of the hot water system.*

Water Heaters

A water heater is a tank that is usually steel, lined on the inside with glass, porcelain, or cement and wrapped on the outside with insulation and an enameled metal jacket. Water heaters vary in size. Some standards suggest up to an 80-gallon tank for a family of four with a clothes washer and dishwasher, although a 40-gallon gas (propane or natural gas) or oil water heater or a 50-gallon electric one are common. An electric water heater has a slower recovery rate than oil and gas. A gas water heater has an hourly recovery rate about the same as the tank volume. Oil water heaters recover even faster.

Older homes typically had neither meters with check valves nor pressure regulators. In a modern or updated home, you may have one or both of these devices. The reason for concern is that they both have a check-valve built into them to prevent potentially contaminated house water from going back into the city main. These check-valves isolate the house's distribution piping from the public water supply. When the water heater is first turned on, the water heats up, expands, and increases the pressure within the house's distribution piping.

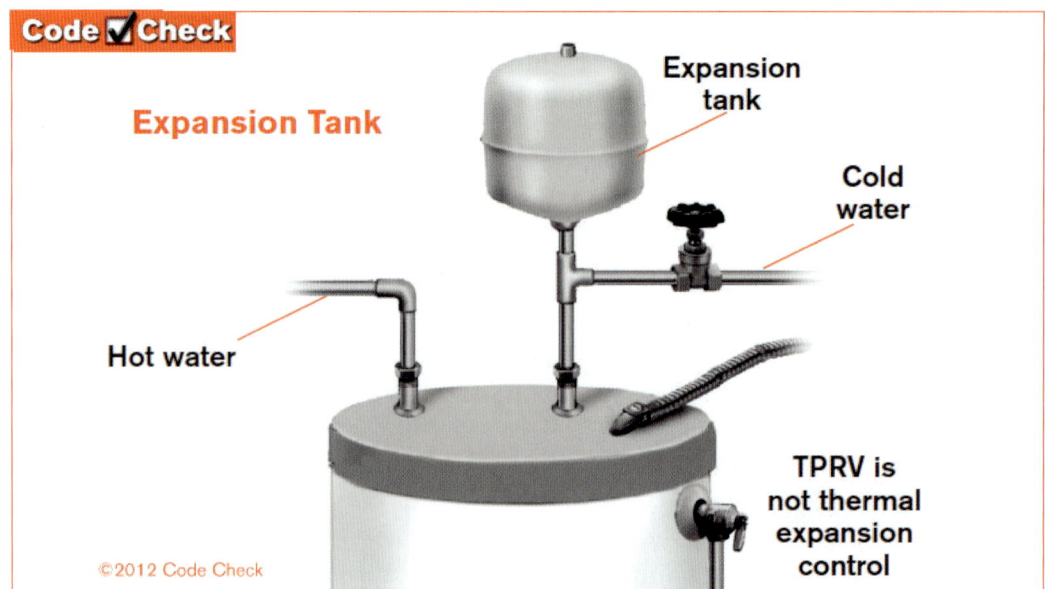

This excess pressure needs to go someplace. That place is the expansion tank. It is typically installed on the piping at the water heater. As the water heats and is used, the pressure increases are absorbed into the expansion tank. If a pressure regulator is on the house service piping, an expansion tank **must** be installed. Your client should be informed if one is not present.

Whether fueled by gas, oil, or electricity, water heaters have the following components in common:

- **Magnesium or aluminum anode rod(s):** Most tanks have one or two magnesium or aluminum anode rods inside to protect exposed steel by giving up ions. (See page 235 on electrolytic corrosion.) In general, a tank with a 6-year guarantee has one rod; a tank with a 10- to 12-year guarantee has two rods. Replacing the rods every two to four years will greatly extend the life of the tank.

    A water heater tank can become contaminated with **Desulfovibrio bacteria**, which thrives in hot water in the presence of magnesium. The bacteria cause the hot water supply (not the cold) to smell like rotten eggs. If this smell is noticed, the water can be tested for contamination. The solution to the problem is to chlorinate the tank and/or replace the anode with an aluminum rod.

- **Cold water turn-off valve:** The incoming water supply pipe to the water heater may come from a water softener or conditioning system, a whole house filtration system, or the service line. There should be a cold water turn-off valve on the supply side near the water heater so that the water can be turned off in case of repair or replacement. (Do not operate this valve during the inspection.) The hot and cold water piping connected to the water heater should be installed with unions for removal and replacement.

HEATER COMPONENTS

- Anode rods
- Cold water turn-off valve
- Inlet, dip tube, and outlet
- Relief valve and extension
- Operating controls and thermostat
- Drain valve

- **Inlet, dip tube, and outlet:** The **inlet** on the top of the tank sends cold water to the bottom of the tank through a **dip tube**. That keeps the cold water from cooling down the hot water, which rises to the top of the tank. Hot water exits the tank from the outlet at the top. Sometimes, you'll find that the inlet and outlet pipes are reversed. Then cold water enters into the top of the tank because it isn't going through a dip tube. Someone who takes a shower is going to start off with a blast of cold water.

- **Relief valve and extension:** All water heaters must be protected with a relief valve, also called a temperature and pressure relief valve (TPR). This valve lets water escape from the tank if the temperature or pressure becomes too high. The valve should be mounted on the top of the tank or on the side within the top 6' of water within the tank. This will most accurately represent the temperature and pressure of the water in the tank. You may find older installations where the relief valves are mounted on the hot water pipe above the tank, but this practice is no longer acceptable and is not considered safe. A leaking relief valve must be replaced. (Do not test this valve during the inspection.) According to the Texas SOP, inspectors must test the TPR valve if they deem it safe and it will not damage person or property. Other corrective measures may be required if the relief valve continues to drip after testing.

The relief valve should have an approved extension or discharge tube that extends down the side of the tank to within 6″ of the floor so that hot water and steam won't spray and potentially scald anyone who is nearby. The discharge tube/pipe can be made of galvanized steel, copper, CPVC, or any listed device. The extension may not be threaded at the bottom or have a shut-off valve. This is to prevent anyone from capping or plugging

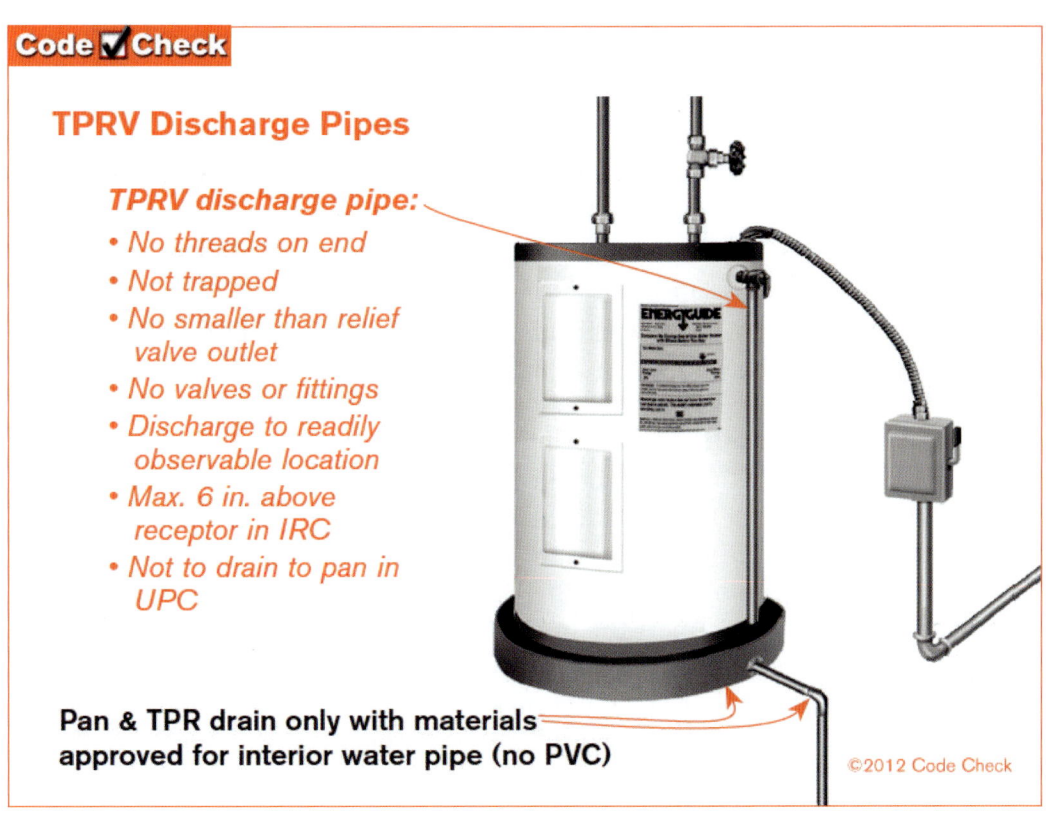

Code ✓ Check

TPRV Discharge Pipes

TPRV discharge pipe:
- No threads on end
- Not trapped
- No smaller than relief valve outlet
- No valves or fittings
- Discharge to readily observable location
- Max. 6 in. above receptor in IRC
- Not to drain to pan in UPC

Pan & TPR drain only with materials approved for interior water pipe (no PVC)

©2012 Code Check

THE PLUMBING INSPECTION 273

the extension. It must also run downhill from the TPR valve to its point of termination and not create a trap in any way.

- **Operating controls and thermostat:** Water heaters are designed to output water at 120° to 140° and can be set to individual preferences with the thermostat. Dishwashers may require a temperature of 140°, but a range from about 115° to 120° is safer and more efficient. This used to be the main reason for the high water heater setting. But with modern dishwashers having their own heating elements to boost the temperature to the necessary levels, water heaters can be set to 115° to 120°F. Gas water heaters have a dial- or knob-type thermostat at the control unit, which is also known as the gas valve. The thermostats on electric heaters are adjusted by removing access covers using a screwdriver. This is not something that is checked, nor is the access cover on electric water heaters removed during a home inspection, except, you guessed it, in Texas. Oil-fired water heaters are similar in the way they are controlled with a dial-type thermostat.

> **NOTE**
>
> *The home inspector does not have to inspect a <u>water softener or conditioning system</u>. Just confirm that it's hooked up, whether or not it's leaking, and that salt is in it.*

> **ANOTHER NOTE**
>
> *Check the BTU reading on the relief valve tag. It must <u>exceed</u> the BTU reading on the water heater data plate.*

- **Drain valve:** Every water heater should have a drain valve at the base of the tank. A few gallons of water should be drained out several times a year to get rid of any calcification or sediment buildup in the tank.

The following rules apply to the installation of water heaters in the home:

- **Location:** If the water heater is located **outside**, it should sit on a concrete pad with its base at least 3″ above adjacent grade and be protected from the weather. If a gas- or oil-fueled water heater is located in the **garage**, it should sit at least 18″ above the garage floor to prevent ignition of gasoline vapors in the garage. Strictly speaking, it is the source of ignition that must be 18″ off the ground, as you will find some installations where the base of the water heater is not 18″ but the source of ignition is the correct height. Flammable Vapor Ignition Resistant (FVIR) water heaters are excluded from this requirement. By design, FVIR-type water heaters will not ignite flammable vapors. If located inside the **living area** of the home on a wooden floor or such that finished materials can be damaged, the water heater should be installed with a drip or catch pan under it, which is plumbed to a safe location so as not to damage finish materials. Sometimes, there is not an appropriate place for the pan to drain. In these cases, you may find a float sensor with an audible alarm to alert the homeowner that the water heater is leaking. Although not technically an approved installation, there may be no better solution. Inform your client about the potentially problematic installation. If the tank is installed in an attic, a crawl space, a cabinet, or a closet, the

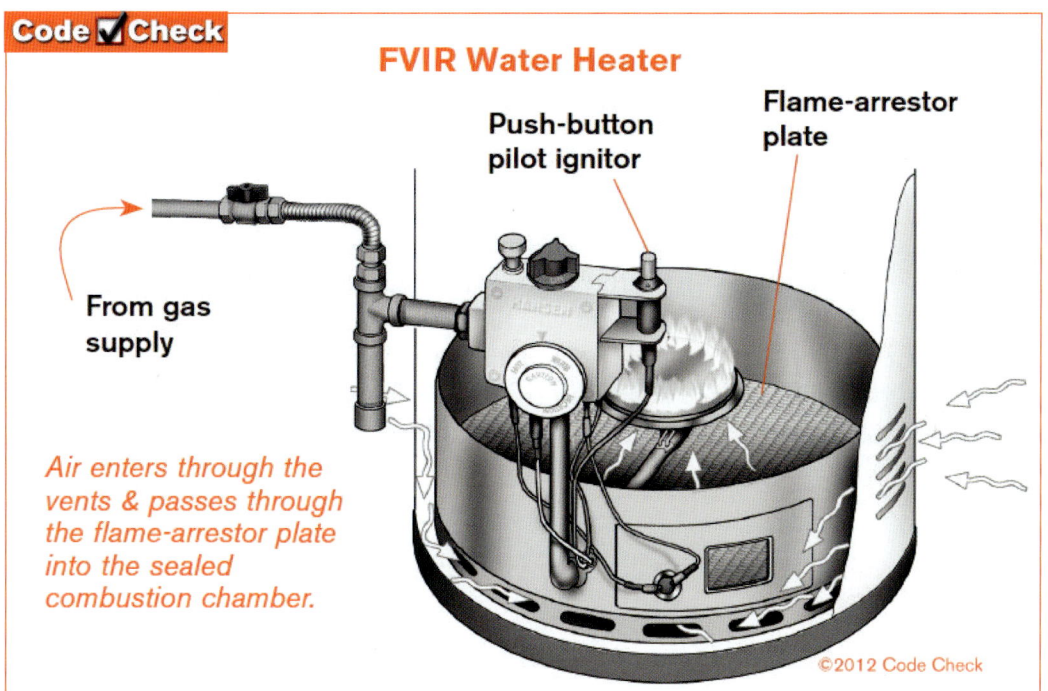

Code ✓ Check
FVIR Water Heater
- Push-button pilot ignitor
- Flame-arrestor plate
- From gas supply

Air enters through the vents & passes through the flame-arrestor plate into the sealed combustion chamber.

©2012 Code Check

doorway must be sufficiently sized to allow for removal of the old water heater and the installation of a new one without having to substantially disassemble the home. Access to the tank from a catwalk in the attic should be at least 24″ wide and should be equipped with a platform on the control side of the unit, an overhead light, and an electrical receptacle. Gas- and oil-fueled water heaters generally should not be installed in storage closets, bedrooms, or bathrooms or their closets. These types of fossil fuel heaters need to have an adequate and continuous supply of air for proper combustion. However, some localities have allowed installation in closets that open to a bedroom or bathroom, providing the closet is used for the equipment only, has a weather-stripped door with an approved self-closing device, and brings in all combustion air from outdoors. Check with your local authorities.

- **Exhaust:** Fossil fuel water heaters must be exhausted to the outdoors, usually through the flue or chimney, although some are designed to vent directly through the wall to the outside. Carbon monoxide is a life-threatening by-product of combustion and must be safely exhausted.

  Gas and oil water heaters must have a **flue pipe or smoke pipe or a vent connector pipe** from the tank to the chimney, requiring an upward slope of 1/4″ for every foot of pipe. If the flue pipe is a single-wall pipe, it should be installed at least 6–9″ from combustibles. The double-walled flue should vent above the roof a minimum of 1′ or higher depending on the fuel used and the slope of the roof. A **draft hood** is required at the top of a natural draft gas water heater to prevent backdrafts from the chimney sending carbon monoxide back into the home. Oil-fired water heaters are equipped with a barometric damper.

THE PLUMBING INSPECTION

In general, gas and electric water heaters last only about 8 to 12 years with oil-fired units lasting a little longer, and possibly longer than that depending on their size, maintenance, water quality, and use. Faulty valves and controls can be repaired, but any water heater that leaks must be replaced.

Seismic bracing is required in certain areas of the country. Most people think of California when it comes to earthquakes, but many more areas qualify—for example, Alaska, Hawaii, the Pacific Northwest, southeastern Arkansas, and western Tennessee. All of these areas and more require seismic bracing on combustion-type water heaters. However, you will find that the requirement is not always enforced. Check your local building practices to see what is required in your area.

Combustion appliances (water heaters, boilers, furnaces, etc.) must be protected from possible vehicular damage. This can be through the use of physical barriers, typically concrete-filled steel pipes called bollards.

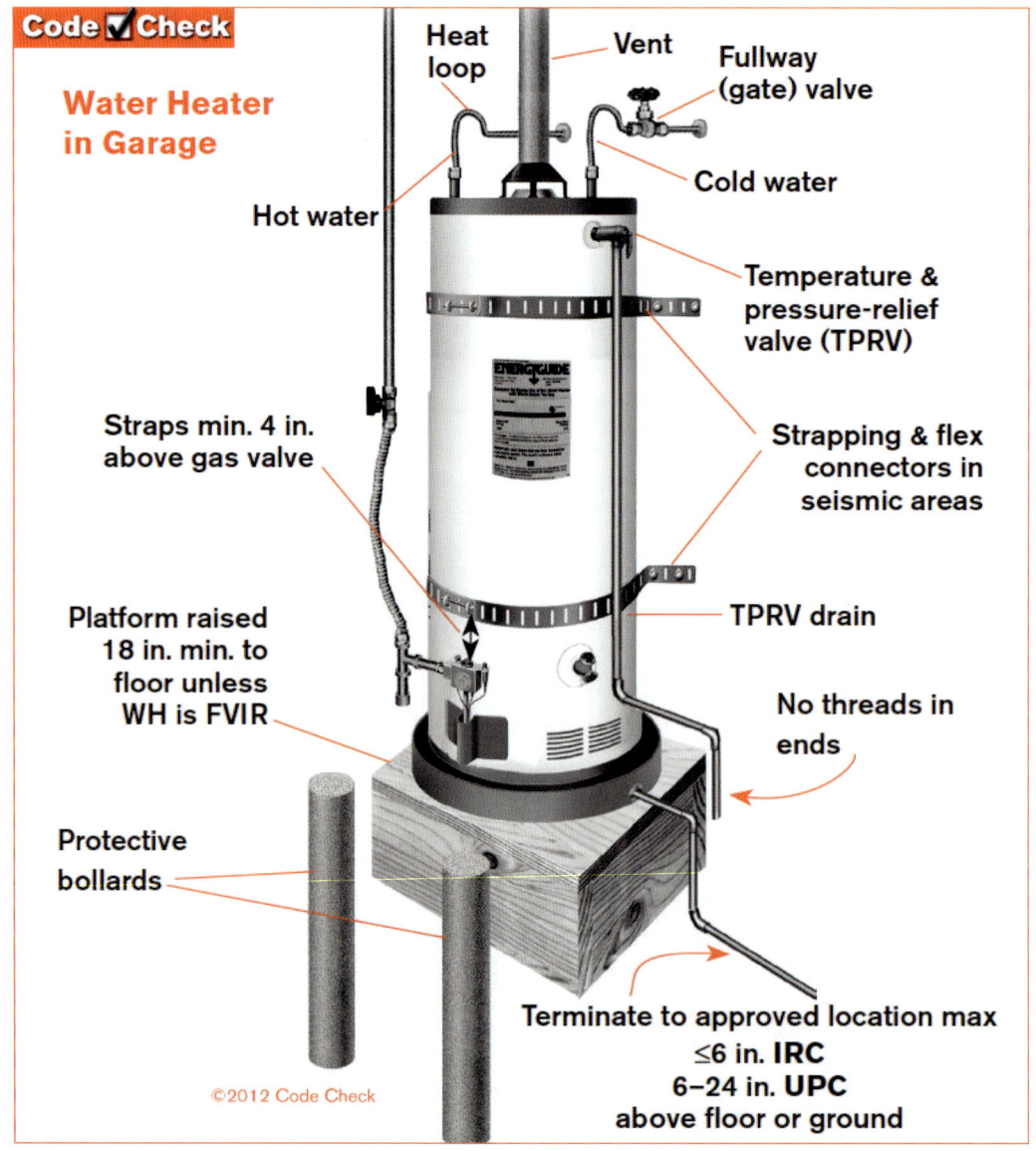

Gas Water Heaters

The following procedures should be followed when inspecting a natural gas or propane water heater:

1. **Examine the manufacturer's plate** to find the brand name and capacity of the water heater. Most new water heaters give the date of manufacture. If not, look at the serial number, which typically gives an indication of the year of manufacture. If the serial number doesn't provide the age of the heater, ask the owner when the water heater was purchased. Because you may not get a truthful answer, record the age in your inspection report as *approximate*. You can also use the American National Standards Institute (ANSI) number on the data tag as an indicator of the age. The ANSI number will read something like "ANSI Z21.10.1A -1991," where 1991 indicates the year of the standard. Combustion appliances are usually made within 3 to 4 years of this date forward. In other words, it was most likely made between 1991 and 1994/95. Although not exact, it is very helpful. There are no ANSI numbers on electric water heaters.

2. **Notice installation** and report any infractions of the rules. Combustion-type water heaters should not be closed off in closets or located in bedrooms or bathrooms. They must have good air circulation and not be in areas that can endanger occupants of the home.

3. **Check inlet and outlet pipes.** Run the water at a fixture for a minute or so and then feel the hot and cold pipes on top of the water heater to confirm that supply pipes are connected to the marked cold inlet and hot water pipes are connected to the outlet. If you find the pipes reversed, make a note in the inspection report. Explain to the client what the implications of the reversal are (pulling cold water out of the bottom of the tank when the hot water is turned on).

4. **Turn down the thermostat** located at the bottom of the tank on the control unit in order to turn down the flame. This is for your own protection when you remove the burner plates. CAUTION: Make a

---

INSPECTING GAS HEATERS

- Brand name, capacity, and age
- Improper installation
- Reversed inlet and outlet pipes
- Leaking, rusting, corrosion, and sediment buildup
- Yellow flame and flame rollout
- Thumping or rumbling noise from the tank
- Gas leaks
- Missing or improper relief valve and extension
- Improper or poor venting

REQUIREMENTS

- Inspect water heating equipment, normal operating and safety controls, and flues
- Describe equipment—brand, capacity, and age are optional
- Not required to operate any valve or safety control

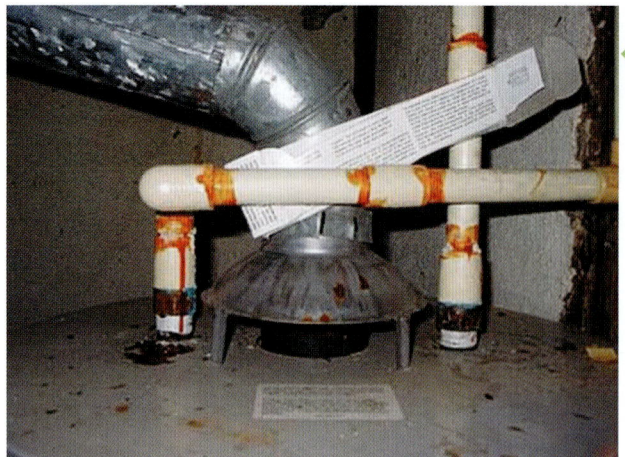

Photo #17 *Plastic piping may not come directly off the water heater tank nipples when it's a gas water heater. The piping must be at least 6" away from the flue as plastic is a combustible material.*

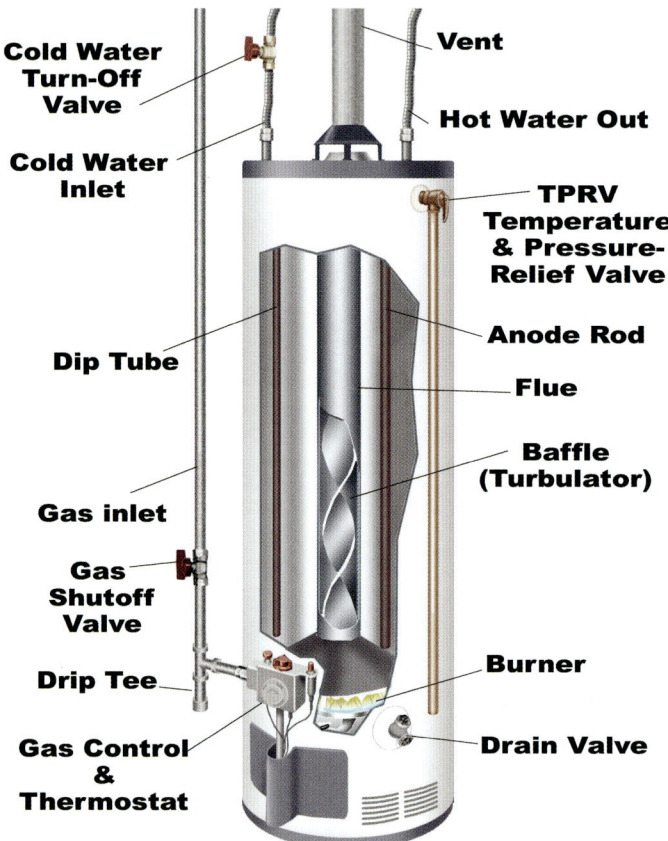

Illustration by Paddy Morrissey

Section Note

If you have a gas water heater, take this book with you and inspect the water heater as laid out on these pages. Follow each step carefully for your own protection.

mental note of the thermostat setting (or mark it with your pen) before you turn it down. You'll have to return it to this same setting after the inspection.

5. **Remove both burner plates** (access panel and interior burner cover) located below the control unit *only* if the water heater is a non-FVIR model. The interior burner plate of an FVIR water heater is screwed in place and has a gasket to seal

278 Chapter 4

it airtight. Observe the flame through the site glass on FVIR-type water heaters.

6. **Inspect for rust, corrosion, signs of leaking, and buildup.** Be sure to check inside the heating chamber and watch for rusting, corrosion, and any buildup that can impede the efficient operation of the flame. Then inspect the bottom of the tank and the area around the access panel for rust, corrosion, and leaking. Also, feel along the bottom of the tank for leaks. If you find water dripping from the tank, try to determine if the tank is indeed leaking or whether you've got leaks from the drain valve or some other connection. If the tank is leaking, it's shot and must be replaced.

7. **Turn up the thermostat** so that the burner kicks on. You may also want to run some hot water at a fixture to make sure the flame ignites. **Evaluate the flame**, which should burn mostly **blue** or blue with some orange tips. Flames that burn **yellow** and **flame rollout** are serious problems. Flame rollout is when the flame burns out from behind the burner plate to the outside of the tank into the room. If you find these conditions, recommend that a specialist be called to fix the situation.

> **Chapter Note**
>
> *The home inspector checks and reports on adequate hot water flow at the faucets. Although this is directly related to the hot water system, we'll be discussing this on page 290 of this chapter.*

8. **Listen to the tank** as the burner is firing. A **thumping, rumbling, or percolating noise** is an indication of sediment buildup inside the tank. You can suggest to the client that sediment and calcification be drained off through the drain valve, which you should point out. Recommend that a few gallons of water be drained from the tank several times a year to help prevent this buildup.

9. **Replace the burner plates and reset the thermostat.** CAUTION: Be sure to reset the thermostat to the **same temperature** setting at which you found it. Forgetting to do this is a high liability for home inspectors. You don't want to be the cause of scalding occupants of the home by leaving the water temperature too high.

> **Section Note**
>
> *"I inspected a gas water heater that was in excellent condition—no corrosion, good flame, proper relief valve extension and all—except in one important way. There was no flue pipe! The draft hood was there, but it was open to the basement without any venting from the house. The carbon monoxide was pouring into the basement. Now that's a safety hazard if I've ever seen one."*

10. **Smell for gas leaks** around the gas control valve and at unions and connections to gas lines near the water heater. Electronic testers are available that detect the presence of natural gas or propane in the air. To alleviate any false positive indications, use a bubble solution to confirm any

THE PLUMBING INSPECTION

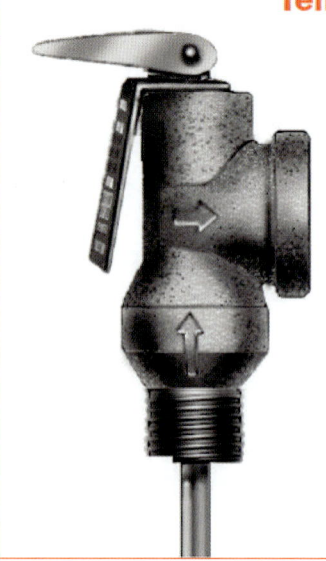

Code Check — Temperature & Pressure-Relief Valve

*When the WH is in a basement or below grade, it may not be possible to arrange for a gravity drain of the TPRV valve. A Watts 210 valve (**F57**) might be an allowable option. The temperature-sensing bulb of the valve goes in the upper portion of the tank & the gas piping runs through the valve. The Watts 210 shuts off the gas if the temperature is excessive. In addition, a separate water pressure–relief valve (**F58**) must be installed in the piping & must drain by gravity to an approved location. Check with the local AHJ to see if this method is accepted in your area.*

leaks identified with an electronic tester. These testers often detect minute quantities of gas that gas company inspectors may consider a safe level. The home inspector should inform the client of any faint gas odor, and if the odor is *extremely* strong, the inspector should tell the people in the house to leave immediately and call the gas company to come and fix the problem. Gas leaks should be reported as a **safety hazard**.

11. **Inspect the relief valve and extension.** The water heater may have separate pressure-relief and temperature-relief valves or more commonly will have a combination temperature and pressure relief (TPR) valve. This TPR valve is set to discharge if the temperature exceeds 210°F or 150 psi. The relief valve(s) should be mounted in the tank, either on

Photo #18 *TPR valve extension piping may not be made out of PVC and may not be installed so as to create a trap. This piping is both made of PVC and installed improperly.*

the top of the tank or at the side within 6″ of the top. The valve should be free of corrosion and should not leak or drip. Missing or improperly installed relief valves should be reported as a **safety hazard**. Leaking or corroded valves should be replaced.

Check that extensions are present and properly installed. The extension piping should not be downsized as it leaves the TPR valve. It must be full-size, typically 3/4″ all the way to its termination. Check that the extension ends within 6″ from the floor or ground and is not threaded or capped at the end.

12. **Inspect the venting.** First, check for the presence of the **draft hood**. Making sure the water heater is fired, light a match or use a smoke stick and hold it next to the draft hood. Move it around the hood, watching to see which way the flame leans. If the flame leans toward the hood, that's good. But if the flame leans outward from the hood, there may be a down-drafting condition, indicating that carbon monoxide is being released from the hood into the room. This should be reported as a **safety hazard**. An inspection mirror can be used to test for down-drafting too. Hold the mirror close to the hood. A fogged-up mirror indicates down-drafting. An electronic tester may also be used to check for the presence of carbon monoxide.

Inspect the **flue pipe** for proper installation and clearances and to note any rusting or corrosion on the pipe. Any holes in the flue pipe should be reported as a **safety hazard**. Corrosion or mineral deposits, especially at seams, may indicate a drafting issue where the flue gases are condensing inside the pipe before they reach the exterior.

Photo #19 *The flue piping must run uphill at least 1/4″ per foot. Note the level on top of the horizontal section. The bubble is to the far right. If properly sloped at the minimum required pitch, the bubble would just touch the left line in the middle of the float. That's what those lines in the float are for, 1/4″ per foot pitch.*

Electric Water Heaters

Electric water heaters typically have two **heating elements**, one at the top of the tank and one at the bottom. They don't come on at the same time. The top unit comes on when the tank is cold or to maintain the temperature while standing by. When cold water enters the tank, the lower element comes on to heat the cold water. The heating elements are connected as a series. That is, if the top element is burned out, the bottom element won't function. However, if the bottom element is burned out, the top one still functions. If there's no hot water, the top element is blown. If there's limited hot water, it could mean that the bottom element is shot. A thermostat is connected to each heating element. To prevent overheating of the water, the thermostat has a safety high limit switch, which is set at the factory to 160° to 190°F. If the thermostat fails, the high limit switch cuts electricity to the water heater. The switch must be manually reset (typically a red button) for the heater to start working again. The manual reset alerts the homeowner to the fact that something is wrong. If the high limit switch also fails, the TPR valve prevents the tank from exploding.

The inspector should examine the electrical connection and wiring at the main electrical service panel. The tank should be equipped with a 30-amp circuit breaker. An electric water heater tank can be installed to receive 120 or 240 volts of electricity, with 240 being the most energy-efficient, economical, and widely used.

A 120-volt connection can typically be found on smaller tanks in bathrooms or kitchens. The average residential water heater uses two 240-volt, 4500-watt elements.

The inspection of the electric water heater is similar in some ways to that of the gas heater. Follow these procedures during the inspection:

1. **Examine the manufacturer's plate** for information about the tank, size, age, etc.

2. **Notice installation.** Does an electric heater on a wooden floor in the living area have a drip pan and drain piping?

3. **Check the inlet and outlet pipes** and report reversed pipes. Is there a cold water supply turn-off valve?

4. **Inspect the tank for rust, corrosion, and leaking.**

> **Section Note**
>
> "An instructor here at the American Home Inspectors Training Institute mentioned to me that he once came across an electric water heater that was 47 years old. It was an old 120 gallon Westinghouse without any significant problems. It was still going fine."

> **HEATING ELEMENTS**
>
> If the upper heating element is burned out, the lower one won't function. There won't be <u>any</u> hot water available at the faucets. If the lower element is burned out, the upper one will still function, but the hot water supply will be limited.

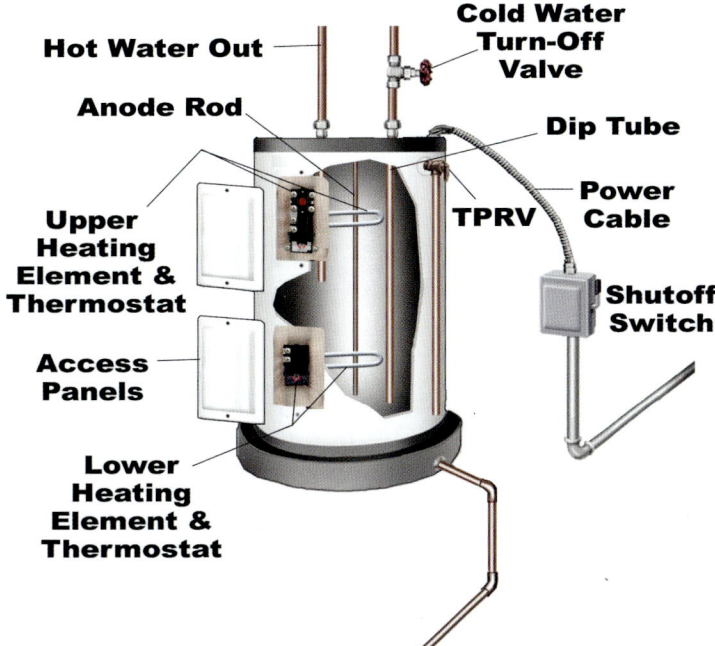

Illustration by Paddy Morrissey

5. **Remove upper and lower access panels (consult SOP for requirements).**

6. **Inspect for any wiring problems or rust and corrosion** on the heating element (if you took the covers off). Wiring problems in the heating element may include conditions such as overheating or corroded wires, but this is uncommon.

7. **Feel the tank at the heating elements.** You don't have to adjust the thermostat to test whether the heating elements are working. Just put your thumb against the tank at each heating element to see if the tank is hot. If the tank is cold at the top, the upper element is burned out and the bottom is not working. If the tank is cold only at the bottom, the lower heating element may be burned out.

8. **Turn on a hot water faucet** and let it run for a while. This is to activate the heating elements.

9. **Listen to the tank.** When the heating elements come on, listen for a hissing, gurgling, or percolating sound that indicates the presence of sediment buildup in the tank.

10. **Inspect the TPR valve and extension.** The valve should be installed within the top 6″ of the tank, usually on the side of the tank. It should be installed in the water tank itself, not in the hot water piping, a defect sometimes seen in older homes.

Oil-Fired Water Heaters

The following procedures should be followed when inspecting an oil-fired water heater:

1. **Examine the manufacturer's plate** to find the brand name and capacity of the water heater. Most new water heaters give the date of manufacture. If not, look at the serial number, which typically gives an indication of the year of manufacture. If the serial number doesn't provide the age of the heater, ask the owner when the water heater was purchased. Because you may not get a truthful answer, record the age in your inspection report as *approximate*. You can also use the American National Standards Institute (ANSI) number on the data tag as an indicator of the age. The ANSI number will read something like "ANSI Z21.10.1A -1991," where 1991 indicates the year of the standard. Combustion appliances are usually made within 3 to 4 years of this date forward. In other words, it was most likely made between 1991 and 1994/95. Although, it is not exact, it is very helpful. There are no ANSI numbers on electric water heaters.

2. **Notice installation** and report any infractions of the rules. Combustion-type water heaters should not be closed off in closets or located in bedrooms or bathrooms. They must have good air circulation and not be in areas that can endanger occupants of the home.

3. **Check inlet and outlet pipes.** Run the water at a fixture for a minute or so and then feel the hot and cold pipes on top of the water heater to confirm that supply pipes are connected to the marked cold inlet and hot water pipes are connected to the outlet. This is the same for all water heaters.

4. **Turn down the thermostat** located at the bottom of the tank on or adjacent to the control unit in order to turn down the flame. This is for your own protection when you open the porthole. CAUTION: Make a mental note of the thermostat setting (or mark it with your pen) before you turn it down. You'll have to return it to this same setting after the inspection.

5. **Inspect for rust, corrosion, signs of leaking, and buildup.** Be sure to check inside the heating chamber and watch for deteriorating fire brick or refractory and any buildup that can impede the efficient operation of the flame. Then inspect the bottom of the tank and the area around the access panel for rust, corrosion, and leaking. Also, feel along the bottom of the tank for leaks. If you find water dripping from the tank, try to determine if the tank is indeed leaking or whether you've got leaks from the drain valve or some other connection. If the tank is leaking, it's shot and must be replaced.

6. **Turn up the thermostat** so that the burner kicks on. You may also want to run some hot water at a fixture to make sure the flame

ignites. **Evaluate the flame**, which should burn mostly orange and white. Flames that burn red, blue, or sooty are serious problems. If you find these conditions, recommend that a specialist be called to fix the situation.

7. **Listen to the tank** as the burner is firing. A **thumping, rumbling, or percolating noise** is an indication of sediment buildup inside the tank. You can suggest to the client that sediment and calcification be drained off through the drain valve, which you should point out. Recommend that a few gallons of water be drained from the tank several times a year to help prevent this buildup.

8. **Close the porthole and reset the thermostat.** CAUTION: Be sure to reset the thermostat to the same **temperature setting** at which you found it. Forgetting to do this is a high liability for home inspectors. You don't want to be the cause of scalding any occupants of the home by leaving the water temperature too high.

9. **Look for oil leaks** at connections to oil lines near the water heater. Oil leaks should be reported as a **safety hazard**.

10. **Inspect the relief valve and extension.** The water heater may have separate pressure-relief and temperature-relief valves or more commonly will have a combination temperature and pressure relief (TPR) valve. This TPR valve is set to discharge if the temperature exceeds 210°F or 150 psi. The relief valve(s) should be mounted directly in the tank, either on the top of the tank or at the side within 6″ of the top. The valve should be free of corrosion and should not leak or drip. Missing or improperly installed relief valves should be reported as a safety hazard. Leaking or corroded valves should be replaced.

    Check that extensions are present and properly installed. The extension piping should not be downsized as it leaves the TPR valve. It must be full-size, typically 3/4″ all the way to its termination. Check that the extension ends within 6″ from the floor or ground and is not threaded or capped at the end.

11. **Inspect the venting.** First, check for the presence of the barometric damper. Making sure the water heater is fired, light a match or use a smoke stick and hold it next to the damper. Move it around the hood, watching to see which way the flame leans. If the flame leans toward the damper, that's good. But if the flame leans outward from the damper, there may be a down-drafting condition, indicating that carbon monoxide is being released from the damper into the room. This should be reported as a **safety hazard**. An inspection mirror can be used to test for down-drafting too. Hold the mirror close to the damper. A fogged-up mirror indicates down-drafting. An electronic tester may also be used to check for the presence of carbon monoxide.

Inspect the smoke pipe for proper installation and clearances and to note any rusting or corrosion on the pipe. Any holes in the smoke pipe should be reported as a **safety hazard**. Corrosion or mineral deposits, especially at seams, may indicate a drafting issue where the flue gases are condensing inside the pipe before they reach the exterior.

Other Hot Water Systems

Some homes may have other types of hot water systems. One example is the **tankless coil** associated with the heating boiler or a stand-alone model. The tankless coil may be located inside the boiler or adjacent to it. One disadvantage with tankless coils is that the boiler (typically with a much larger burner than a standard water heater) must be kept running all summer. These systems may supply too little hot water, or the coils can become clogged with silt and salts from the water. Water inside the boiler can be heated up to 190°, which is very dangerous at faucets, so a mixing valve should be present to mix cold water with the hot water, thereby lowering the temperature to an acceptable range (115° to 120°F at the faucets).

Another type of water heater is a combination system or hydro system, which was marketed under the Apollo brand name.

> **Section Note**
>
> *"Here's an interesting story. A home had been closed up for the winter and the water heater emptied. The homeowner came back to dewinterize the home. He fired up the electric water heater before it had a chance to completely refill with water—it still had a lot of air in it. When he turned it on, the top element exploded and blew right out of the tank."*

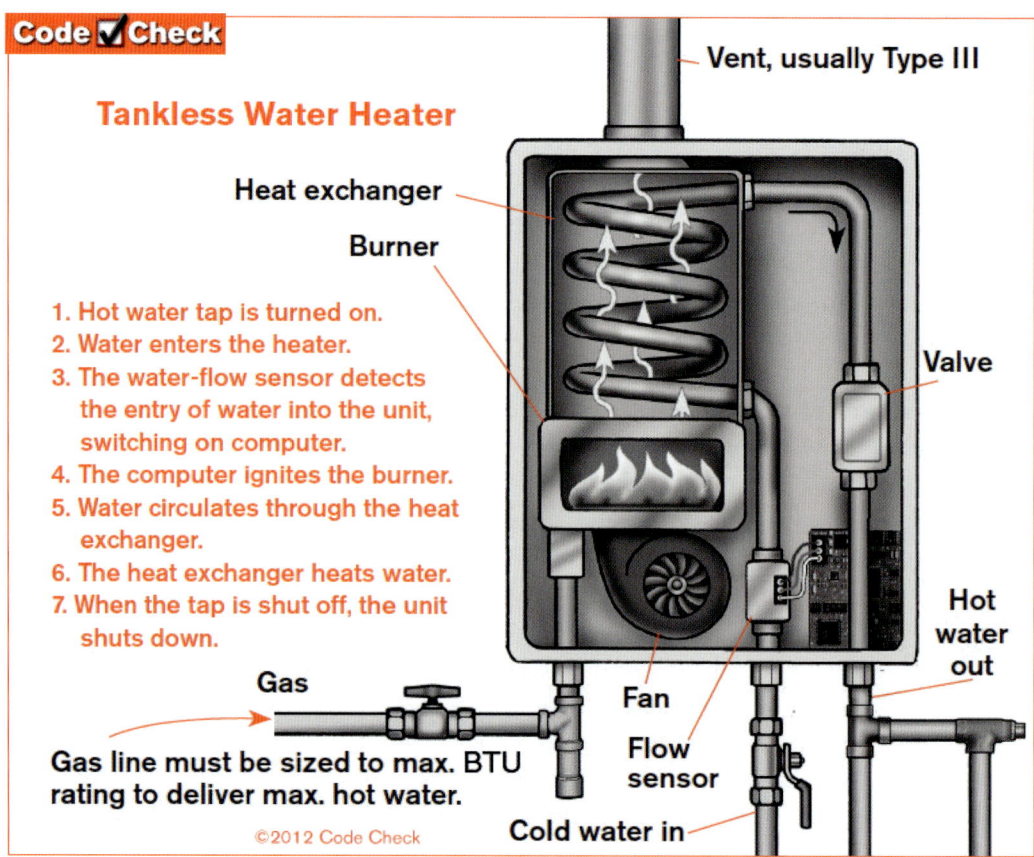

Like the tankless coil, the water heater and house heating system are integrated. But instead of using a boiler, the hydro system produces hot water using a high-output gas water heater. These systems did not fare well over time, and the company no longer exists.

"Demand" water heaters, also called instantaneous or tankless water heaters, are activated only when a hot water fixture is turned on. Cold water travels through pipes, turns on the flow switch and burner, and is heated by a gas burner or electric element. Hot water is not exactly "instantaneous"—it may take time for the hot water to travel from the water heater to the fixture. Units are sometimes installed at the point of use, such as a bathroom, and serve only that location. The biggest issue with these types of water heaters is that they need to be de-scaled annually. Another issue is that they are a nuisance with regard to the way they work. The tankless water heater creates what is often called a "cold water sandwich," which describes the fluctuations in water temperature that owners of tankless water heaters experience when they momentarily close and then re-open a hot water fixture. You can Google this issue and see a visual representation of how it happens.

An indirect water heater system is similar to a tankless coil in that water is heated by the boiler that heats the house, but it has a separate storage tank. Hot water from the boiler circulates through a coil submerged in the storage tank, heating the potable water.

A newer, more energy-efficient system is known as a heat pump water heater (HPWH). A heat pump water heater works like a refrigerator in reverse, drawing heat from the room and transferring it to the water in the tank. Heat from the air evaporates a refrigerant in the evaporator and releases cooler air into the room. Meanwhile, the refrigerant vapor is pumped through a compressor, where it condenses back into liquid form and releases the stored heat into the water. There are two main types of HPWHs—the drop-in or complete unit, which resembles an electric storage tank water heater with a heat pump unit mounted on top, and the add-on, which is like a window heat pump unit connected to the existing water heater. They should be installed away from walls, ceilings, ducts, and other obstacles. Also, they must be in an area with a large enough volume to promote efficiency, usually a minimum of 700 to 1000 cubic feet. In a small space, a louvered door can provide adequate ventilation (for heat distribution, not combustion air as they are electric), but some manufacturers prohibit installation in a closet or another confined space. They are like a normal house heat pump unit in that the filter must be cleaned periodically and they have a condensate drain line that must be run to an appropriate location. They operate in one of several modes. The most efficient mode and the mode used most of the time is the "heat pump" mode, where the compressor is providing the heat to the water in the tank. The second mode is "hybrid," which uses the compressor and the heating elements all of the time. The third mode is "high demand/boost," where only the electric elements are used for faster recovery rates during high-demand periods. The compressor is used during periods of low demand. The last mode is the "electric/standard," which is like a standard electric water heater and, as you would imagine, is the least efficient mode.

Desuperheaters, also known as heat recovery units (HRUs), are connected to the water heater or storage tank and the house's heat pump (in cooling mode) or air-conditioning unit. They take the waste heat put out by the air conditioner or heat pump's refrigerant lines and use it to preheat the domestic hot water. Naturally, this only works when the heat pump or air conditioner is running, which is why they are more commonly found in hot climates such as the South, the Southwest, and Florida.

Solar hot water is becoming popular and more common in all parts of the country. Solar systems, whether for heating water or generating electricity, are not part of the SOP. The information provided here is for informational purposes only in case you run across one in the field. Many people think you have to live in Arizona for solar to be practical. That is not the case.

There are basically two types of collectors for solar hot water. The first one, which is most common, is the "flat plate" collector. This type of collector is generally used in sunny portions of the country. It is basically a black box with copper tubing and a tempered glass top. The sun heats up the box and therefore the water circulating through the copper tubing. These can be active (uses a pump) or passive (uses the house's water pressure). The second kind is the "evacuated tube" collector. This is a fairly high-tech system and is used in northern climates or for high-temperature applications anywhere. It doesn't have to be warm outside for this type of system to work, just sunny. They consist of evacuated glass tubes under a vacuum inside. As you may know, a vacuum is a near perfect insulator. That is why these collectors work in cold climates. Inside the glass tube is a copper tube filled with water. The water in the tube is heated to boiling by the sun and rises in the tube to the header pipe in the manifold, where it transfers its heat to the circulating house water.

DON'T EVER MISS

- Rusted, corroded, or leaking tanks and sediment buildup
- Reversed inlet and outlet pipes
- Missing or improper relief valve or extension
- Gas heaters: yellow flame, flame rollout, gas leaks, improper or poor venting
- Electric heaters: burned-out heating elements, corroded wiring

OLDER WATER HEATERS

For any water heater over 5 years old, list it as an item needing replacement within the next 5 to 7 years. It will be reaching the end of its life in that time.

Reporting Your Findings

Turn to the appropriate page of the inspection report to record your findings on the water heater(s).

Water heater information: Record the brand name of the water heater from the manufacturer's plate, the serial number, and its capacity. Identify the fuel source too (gas, oil, geothermal, HPWH, or electric). Next, write the approximate age of the water heater as best as you can determine (refer to the first two numbers in the serial number or use the ANSI number for combustion units). We suggest that you caution your client that the water heater may have to be replaced within 5 years if it's older than 5 to 7 years.

Water heater condition: Note defects found on the water heater, such as a rusted or leaking tank, a burned-out heating element, reversed water lines, sediment buildup, and improper operation or venting.

Safety hazards: Note safety hazards such as vent problems (down-drafting at draft hood or barometric damper and missing or corroded flue pipes), gas or oil leaks, a missing relief valve, and a missing or improper extension.

4.5 FIXTURES AND FAUCETS

The home inspector inspects each fixture for its **condition** and runs every faucet in the home, testing for **drips and leaks**. Functional flow and drainage and traps are also checked, which were discussed earlier in this chapter.

Inspecting Faucets

The traditional washer type faucet has a washer attached to a threaded stem that is turned down and forms a seal against a mechanical seat. This type of faucet supplies either cold or hot water. Washerless faucets are commonly single-lever faucets that supply a mix of cold and hot water. They have a cartridge, valve, or ball, with or without an O-ring seal, which moves up and down for volume and left and right for hot and cold, respectively.

> **Chapter Note**
>
> Pages 289–296 present the study and inspection of fixtures and faucets.

More sophisticated **shower faucets** maintain a constant temperature even if there are pressure changes in the system. If cold water flow drops, a pressure-sensitive mixing diaphragm or piston in the faucet will adjust hot water flow to maintain the same temperature. These tempering and/or pressure balancing faucets have become commonplace. They can protect the user from scalding or thermal shock injury.

The home inspector should **operate all faucets** in the home, including exterior hose bibs, during the plumbing inspection. The inspector should watch for the following conditions:

- **Leaks and drips:** Notice any leaking or dripping at each faucet before you turn it on. Sometimes, stains in the fixture or around the faucet stem can indicate a leak. Watch for leaking when the faucet is running.

  — **Leaks and drips out of the faucet:** In the washer-type faucet, this usually indicates a deteriorated washer, which is inexpensive to replace. But it could be a damaged seat. For other faucets, it could be a deteriorated O-ring.

  — **Leaks from the faucet handle or stem:** In the washer-type faucet, this condition can be caused by a worn or bent stem, a deteriorated stem packing, or a loose stem packing nut. In other faucets, this indicates faulty valves or cartridges, which will have to be replaced.

  — **Leaking behind or under the faucet:** If the faucet is not tightly secured to the fixture, countertop, or wall, splashed water can run under or behind it, causing staining and damage to walls, cabinets, and floors.

> **INSPECTING FAUCETS**
>
> - Leaking and dripping
> - Noisy faucets
> - Damaged or corroded
> - Loose faucets
> - Cross connections
> - Poor functional flow

  Leaky faucets should be pointed out to the client and reported in your inspection report.

- **Noisy faucets:** Faucets should run smoothly and quietly. **Whistles** while the water is running indicate a faulty interior design in the faucet and are hard to fix. **Chatter and banging** while water is flowing is probably a loose washer. **Water hammer**, which occurs in the pipes just as the faucet is turned off, is not a faucet problem, it's a piping problem. Noisy faucets should be pointed out to the client during the inspection.

> *Chapter Note*
>
> *Outdoor faucets or hose bibs must also be checked during the plumbing inspection, if not in a winterized condition. This was discussed earlier in the chapter. See page 244.*

- **Damaged or corroded faucets:** Check each faucet for damage or corrosion. Ceramic faucet handles can become cracked, and the sharp edges can cut hands. Be sure to report any you find. Corroded faucets may be so damaged that the home inspector should recommend replacement.

- **Loose faucets:** Check faucets to see if they are properly tight at fixtures, countertops, and walls to prevent leaking into the wall or floor structure.

- **Cross connections:** Always check the relation of the faucet to the sink or tub and make sure that it's located above the fill level rim to avoid a possible cross connection. Be sure to record potential cross connections in your inspection report and indicate each as a **safety hazard**.

- **Poor functional flow and lack of hot water:** See the discussion on pages 245–247 for testing the plumbing system at the faucets for functional flow. When running faucets, use your own judgment on the adequacy of water flow. It's possible that the flow of water at only a single faucet in the house is not good. Many new faucets have built-in pressure reducers allowing only a 0.5 to 1.5 gpm flow. But there may be an internal problem with the faucet—the spout could be clogged with corrosion or mineral deposits. Aerators on faucets, which add air to the water flow, can become clogged with mineral deposits. Suggest to the client that aerators be removed and cleaned or replaced.

> **INSPECTING FIXTURES**
>
> - Broken, damaged, or rusted
> - Missing overflow
> - Loose mountings
> - Poor functional drainage
> - Any leaks, old or new
> - Improper traps or venting

Check each hot water faucet or combined faucet for the **presence of hot water**. Make sure it is on the left-hand side. Pay attention to the temperature of the water. If the water is too hot, you may want to suggest to the client that the thermostat on the water heater be set at a lower temperature to prevent accidental scalding. A safe setting is between 115° and 120°F at the faucet. Report the absence of hot water at any hot water faucet.

Inspecting Sinks, Tubs, and Showers

Sinks, basins, and bathtubs can be made of enameled steel or cast iron, stone, plastic, or fiberglass. Those made of fired clay include porcelain, ceramic, and china. A bidet, which is really a type of sink, is usually made of china. Showers may be tiled enclosures with tile floors over metal shower pans, mud set, hot mop tar, PVC, or any number of high-tech systems. Less expensive and more maintenance-free surrounds are made of multiple pieces of molded plastic or fiberglass.

Each fixture should be inspected during the plumbing inspection. The home inspector should watch for the following conditions:

- **Broken, damaged, or rusted fixtures:** Any fixture that is broken or cracked completely through should be reported to the client. Ceramic fixtures can become nicked or chipped. Porcelain can get a network of hairline cracks, called crazing, over time. Enameled finishes can get nicks, spalled spots, or damaged finishes from harsh scouring cleaners. Plastics can crack, distort from poor installation, or become abraded. Fiberglass and acrylic can craze over time, especially in corners and stress points. Any fixture may become stained from rust or copper in the water. Point out these conditions to your client as you inspect the fixtures and note them in your inspection report.

  Always look under sinks during the plumbing inspection even if they are enclosed in cabinets. Look at the overflow hole and the bottom of enameled steel sinks for any signs of rusting. They can rust out at the spot-welded steel overflow on the underside and will eventually leak.

- **Missing overflow:** Kitchen sinks and laundry tubs don't generally have overflows, but bathroom basins and tubs typically do, even though they are no longer required.

- **Loose mountings:** Check that sinks and basins are properly secured to the walls or to supporting columns or countertops. Loose fixtures can damage both the fixtures and the supply and drain piping. Tubs are supported by the house framework and may shift if the structure moves or settles. Report such conditions.

- **Poor functional drainage:** The home inspector should run water at each fixture and observe functional drainage (see pages 265–266). Check the drain fittings (stoppers) at this time to see if they're operating properly. Plug the fixture and let it hold water for a time to see if the stopper holds water.

- **Leaks at and around fixtures:** Always check under sinks for any evidence of leaking from the fixture or faucets, from the distribution piping, at the drain fitting, at the traps, and in the DWV piping. One problem to watch for is the spray hose connection at the kitchen sink, which often leaks.

Carefully check the floor around the bathtub and be sure to report evidence of wood rot or delamination of the decking from leaking. Tubs can leak at the tub overflow/vent and drain fitting, which would be noticeable only from a stained ceiling underneath or in the basement

> **Section Note**
>
> *"I want to stress the importance of noticing evidence of prior leaking around fixtures. I once missed reporting a 1" by 3" soft spot next to a bathtub. That customer called me on it, and, boy, was he irritated. You would have thought the whole floor was rotted out. Anyway, I went back in and personally patched the floor."*

under a first-floor tub. Bathtubs with tile surrounds are vulnerable to leaking at the tub-tile intersection where caulking may be inadequate. Watch for leaking in the tile surround itself and note whether grouting is in good condition.

Check for leaking at showers too, especially those with tiled walls, which may have the same caulking and grouting problems as tubs do.

> **Section Note**
>
> *"Never miss the presence of an old tin or lead shower pan. Even if you don't see leaking now, you can be assured it's going to happen. Warn customers that they don't last very long and can cause problems."*

- **Metal shower pans** are a special problem. Although modern plastic, PVC, and fiberglass molded shower pans are fairly good, the old metal pans are notorious for leaking. These shower pans were made of lead or tin and covered with a finishing layer of ceramic tile. In fact, you should suspect a metal shower pan if the floor of the shower in an older home is finished with small 1″ ceramic tile. The shower begins leaking through the tile grout around the drain, water gets into the metal pan, and the pan rusts through. They usually fail completely in 15 to 25 years. Never miss reporting the **presence of a metal shower pan** and pointing out the potential problems to the client.

If you're not sure the shower pan is leaking, cover the shower drain and let water fill the bottom of the shower. Then uncover the drain and try to observe leaking, if possible, from underneath. Special stoppers designed for testing shower pans are available. They are by no means required, but they are very helpful and will prevent you from accidently overflowing a client's shower.

- **Hydro-massage massage therapy equipment type tubs** are outside of the scope of the SOP, except for Texas. That doesn't mean we just ignore them. We still evaluate them as a "bathtub," but we are not obligated to test the motor and jets. Why not? If you read the other portions of the SOP, you will see that we do have to verify that they are GFCI-protected, that the motor is bonded, and that there is an access panel to service/replace the pump/motor assembly. Looking into the access panel also gives us a view of the drain piping, which usually is not present for a standard tub. If the tub drain/overflow assembly uses slip joints, there must be an access panel. Because we have to do all of the other items, why not push the button to turn on the motor and jets?

- **Improper traps or venting:** When you look under sinks, inspect the traps as described on page 263 (see pages 255 and 256 for additional information).

NOTE: Bidets should be inspected too. Bidets, because water supply is below the fill level, should have a vacuum breaker preventing wastewater from flowing into the supply line. China bidets can crack and leak. The

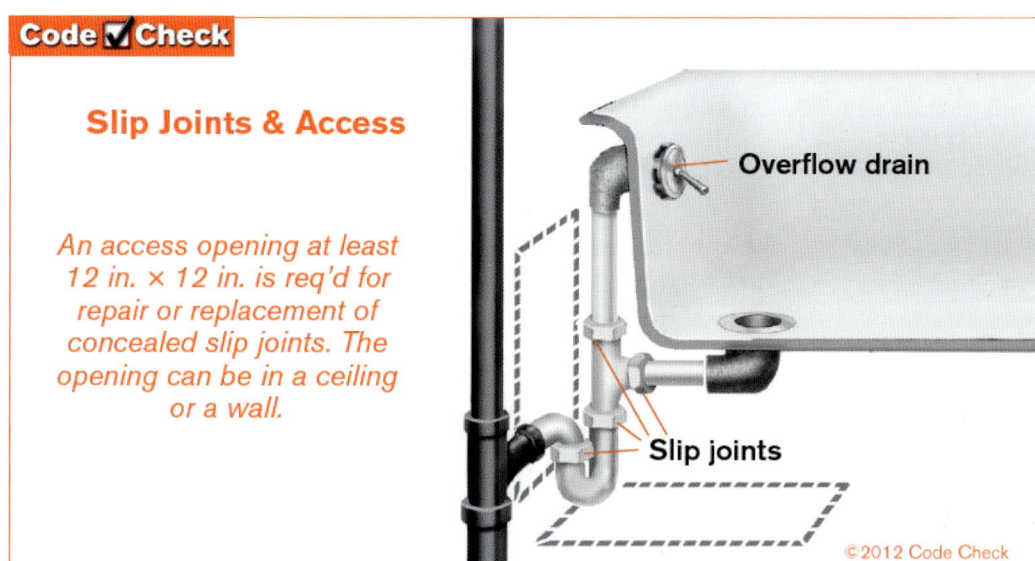

Slip Joints & Access

An access opening at least 12 in. × 12 in. is req'd for repair or replacement of concealed slip joints. The opening can be in a ceiling or a wall.

small jets can become clogged. Run water into the bidet and observe functional flow and drainage. Also, make sure they are tight to the floor like a toilet.

Inspecting Toilets

Toilets are normally made of porcelain enamel (also called vitreous china). There are five common types. The old **washdown toilet** is identified by the large bulge in front of the bowl and a relatively small wetted area in the bowl. It's no longer commonly used, and some local codes don't allow them at all. The **reverse trap** is a better two-piece toilet (tank and bowl) with a larger wetted area. The **siphon jet** is an improved type of reverse trap toilet with a quieter flush. The one-piece **siphon vortex**, or silent flush, toilet is very quiet, and almost all of the whole bowl area is covered with water.

> **INSPECTING TOILETS**
>
> - Damaged, cracked, or leaking
> - Poor operation
> - Loose on floor

There also power flush toilets. The *FLUSHMATE* Pressure-Assist system is a component inside a specially designed toilet that harnesses the pressure from the water supply line to provide the energy needed to complete the flush. **The *FLUSHMATE* Pressure-Assist technology cannot be retrofitted into a standard gravity-fed toilet.** Every leading toilet manufacturer offers a toilet with a *FLUSHMATE* inside.

The home inspector should **flush all toilets** in the home during the inspection. If an unused toilet is found, such as one in the basement, note if the water supply is turned off. Toilets should not be left sitting without water in the bowl (either evaporated or turned off) as this would let sewer gas escape into the house. Report any unused toilets and suggest that water or some other liquid (mineral oil works well) be kept in the bowl at all times. Watch for the following conditions while inspecting each toilet in the home:

- **Damaged, cracked, or leaking:** Inspect the toilet carefully for cracks in the bowl or tank. Report even those cracks on the interior of the bowl

> **Section Note**
>
> *"One of my inspectors was inspecting an old house with lead supply piping throughout.*
>
> *At the toilet, he was checking the bolts that hold the tank. He touched one to discover that the bolt was missing and the hole was self-healed with corrosion.*
>
> *Of course, his touching it caused the corrosion to break through and the tank sprung a vigorous leak that couldn't be stopped. I can still hear him saying, 'All I did was touch it.'"*

> **AGE OF THE HOME**
>
> *The date of manufacture is usually imprinted on the underside of the toilet tank lid or tank back. This gives a clue as to how old the house is if it still has the original toilets.*

and tank lid that aren't the cause of any leaking. Cracked toilets can fail at any time and replacement of the cracked component is usually warranted. Report chips and nicks, crazing or hairline cracks, and any discoloration or serious staining.

As to leaking, toilets can leak from the supply line, at the storage tank, at the connection between the tank and the bowl, at the bowl itself, and at the connection between the bottom of the toilet and the drain pipe (wax ring). Look in each area for any evidence of leaking. Toilets that leak through a crack must be replaced.

Be sure to look for and report any evidence of **wood rot** around the base of the toilet. Get down on your hands and knees or lunge with your foot on the floor around the toilet to see if there are soft spots or a "crunchy" sound. It's not unusual to find rotted or delaminated floor boards. The toilet could have experienced prior leaking and been repaired but left considerable damage to the subflooring. Be sure to report the presence of any damaged wood or rot.

- **Poor operation:** A toilet that won't flush should be reported as not operating. This may be because the water is off or the chain to the flush lever is broken. It is not required, but is a good idea, to lift the lid on the tank to see if water is present and if the chain is intact. Several times, we removed the lid to find that the chain was made from a string of paper clips. Often, the toilet has what is called a **weak flush**, where waste is carried away in a sluggish manner or not all the waste is carried away before the end of the flush. This condition may have one of many causes. One cause is that there is too little water volume in the bowl due to a problem with the ballcock mechanism in the tank or the holes around the bowl rim are blocked with sediment. We have also seen a weak flush in an older-style, large-volume toilet (bowl) where the tank was replaced with a low-volume tank. Weak flush may also be caused by downstream problems such as blockage of the toilet trap, vent stoppage, an improper slope of a waste pipe, or a clogged waste pipe.

Another operational problem is a **running tank**, which continuously sends water into the bowl. This problem is in the tank, and repairs should be made to the component of the flush mechanism (flapper valve) causing the problem.

Mention both conditions—weak flush and running tank—to your client and report them in your inspection report.

- **Loose toilet:** During the toilet inspection, check to see if the bowl is tightly secured to the floor (closet flange). First, straddle the toilet bowl. Then either hold the bowl between your knees and gently rock it back and forth or grab it with your arms and gently nudge or lift the bowl—but not too hard! The reasons a toilet is loose can be improper fastening to the closet flange, rotten subflooring, or sunken joists underneath. A loose bowl can damage the wax ring between the porcelain and the closet flange, which will then cause leaking. Explain to the client that the closet bolts on each side of the toilet bowl should be kept tightened so that the seal doesn't break. Be sure to report any loose toilets that you find.

Putting It All Together

In this chapter, we've presented the inspection of the plumbing system by components, not by the flow of how the plumbing inspection really happens. Let's review how the inspection is performed in proper order:

- **Exterior plumbing:** While inspecting the exterior of the house and the garage, operate all outside faucets. Check for the proper location, extension, and flashing for the plumbing vent when you're on the roof. Notice the evidence of a private well and/or septic system and check for proper distances.

- **Interior living area plumbing:** Starting in the kitchen, run the water at the kitchen sink, checking the condition of the faucets, the sink, the sink traps, and pipes under the sink. Note the presence of hot water, water flow, and drainage. In the bathroom(s), run water at more than one faucet simultaneously to determine if water flow is adequate. Check faucets and fixtures for damage, corrosion, the presence of hot water, and proper drainage. Always watch for signs of leaking, especially around tubs, showers, and toilets. Test the toilet for operation. Report the presence of a metal shower pan if it is accessible or visible. Watch for any signs of leaking or water stains.

- **Attic area:** While you are inspecting the attic, check that the plumbing vent is exhausted through the roof and is in good condition. If air admittance valves are present make sure they are at least 6" above the insulation level.

- **Basement or crawl space:** Here's where you'll be able to get a good look at the underside of the main floor plumbing. You will have run

---

> **Section Note**
>
> *"Nothing ever surprised me more than when I pulled up on a toilet and found myself standing there holding it in my arms. You don't have to nudge or pull on it very hard to tell if it's loose."*

INSPECTION ORDER

- Exterior faucets, roof vent, location of well and septic
- Kitchen and bathroom faucets, fixtures, traps, piping, water pressure, and drainage
- Living area signs of leaking
- Attic plumbing vent
- Basement supply entrance and piping, DWV piping, well equipment, sump and sanitary pumps, water heater

enough water through the drain and waste pipes earlier in the inspection to see any *active* leaks, but look for old leaks (stains) too. Now you'll inspect the water supply entrance, distribution piping, DWV piping, well equipment, sump and sanitary pumps, and water heater.

> **DON'T EVER MISS**
> - Damaged, loose, corroded, or leaking fixtures and faucets
> - Poor functional flow or drainage and no hot water
> - Damaged, loose, leaking, or poorly operating toilets
> - Metal shower pans

Reporting Your Findings

Don't bypass plumbing fixtures and faucets as being too insignificant to report on. These are the details you'll want to emphasize in your report. Now let's get back to reporting on your inspection of the plumbing fixtures and faucets. New homeowners often call us when a faucet is leaking, thinking we're responsible. If you've reported the leaking faucet, you're not responsible. But if you've missed it, you may be. It's as simple as that.

- **Kitchen and laundry room:** Report on faucet and sink conditions and functional flow and drainage and the presence of hot water.

- **Bathroom:** Report on faucet conditions in the bathroom, including functional flow and drainage and the presence of hot water. Record any evidence of leaking or water damage in bathroom ceilings and floors. Your report should have distinct lines for reporting on the condition of the toilet, tub, and shower. Be sure to note if the toilet bowl is loose and whether the toilet operates. If you've found a metal shower pan, write a special note with a warning that if it's not leaking now, it will most likely do so in the future and will need to be replaced.

4.6 GAS PIPING

Some standards include the inspection of fuel storage and distribution piping in the plumbing inspection. For the most part, that means natural gas lines in the home and the storage of bottled propane gas and possibly fuel oil. Traditionally, rigid iron or steel pipe (black iron or galvanized) is used. Plastic should not be used for gas lines inside a home. Many contractors now use alternative piping materials to save money on installation. The most common are copper tubing and corrugated stainless steel tubing (CSST). Copper is not as popular as it used to be due to the rise in copper prices.

> **INSPECTING GAS LINES**
> - Gas leaks
> - Improper piping materials or support
> - Missing shut-off valves
> - Improper tank location

> *Chapter Note*
>
> *Pages 296–300 present the study and inspection of gas piping.*

Copper tubing is semi-flexible and lighter than conventional steel piping, but some studies show that it is vulnerable to corrosion if the gas supply has a high level of hydrogen sulfide. Copper should not be used if the concentration of hydrogen sulfide is greater than 0.3 grains per 100 cubic feet, and it is banned completely under some local codes, as is often the case in the Southwest. Other areas permit its use as a connector between metal pipes and appliances, such as gas stoves. Copper tubing installed away from gas equipment must be labeled to differentiate it from other copper tubes, such as water lines. Unlabeled copper gas tubing should be noted, since cutting a gas line by mistake could have dangerous consequences.

Corrugated stainless steel tubing (CSST) was introduced in the 1980s. This thin, semi-flexible tubing can be identified by its bright yellow or black plastic wrapping. CSST is approved under most major codes. There have been some issues with CSST, including at least one class-action lawsuit. The issue with the CSST had to do with failure of the piping due to lightning strikes. The hope was to properly bond the CSST to the house electrical system as many other items typically are. The other alternative was to install a lightning protection system. Unfortunately, this has not proven to be a good solution. Municipalities in Texas and Missouri have chosen to outright ban the use of CSST. A new CSST product called FlashShield™ is proving to be a possible solution. Be sure to check for current use restrictions in your area.

Photo #20 *CSST piping is becoming very common in new homes. This is a manifold with a regulator supplying several gas appliances.*

Rubber tubing is prohibited in all permanent gas lines. You will however see rubber lines used for things like BBQ grills on decks and patios, which are personal property and not part of our inspection SOP. Check with your local authorities.

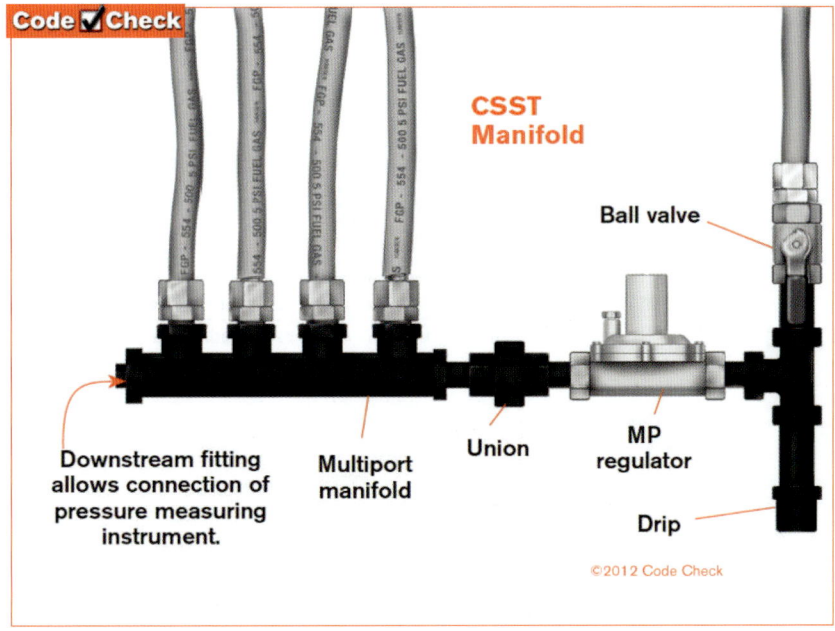

THE PLUMBING INSPECTION

Gas piping may be run beneath a slab in a slab-on-grade home, but not within the slab itself. If the gas piping is run beneath the slab to an island cooktop for example, the potential for a gas leak must be addressed. The way this is performed is by sleeving the gas line within another sealed pipe.

Photo #21 *This is the stub for the gas line that will connect to the gas meter. It is the most common place to find the gas bond.*

The home inspector should pay particular attention for the following conditions:

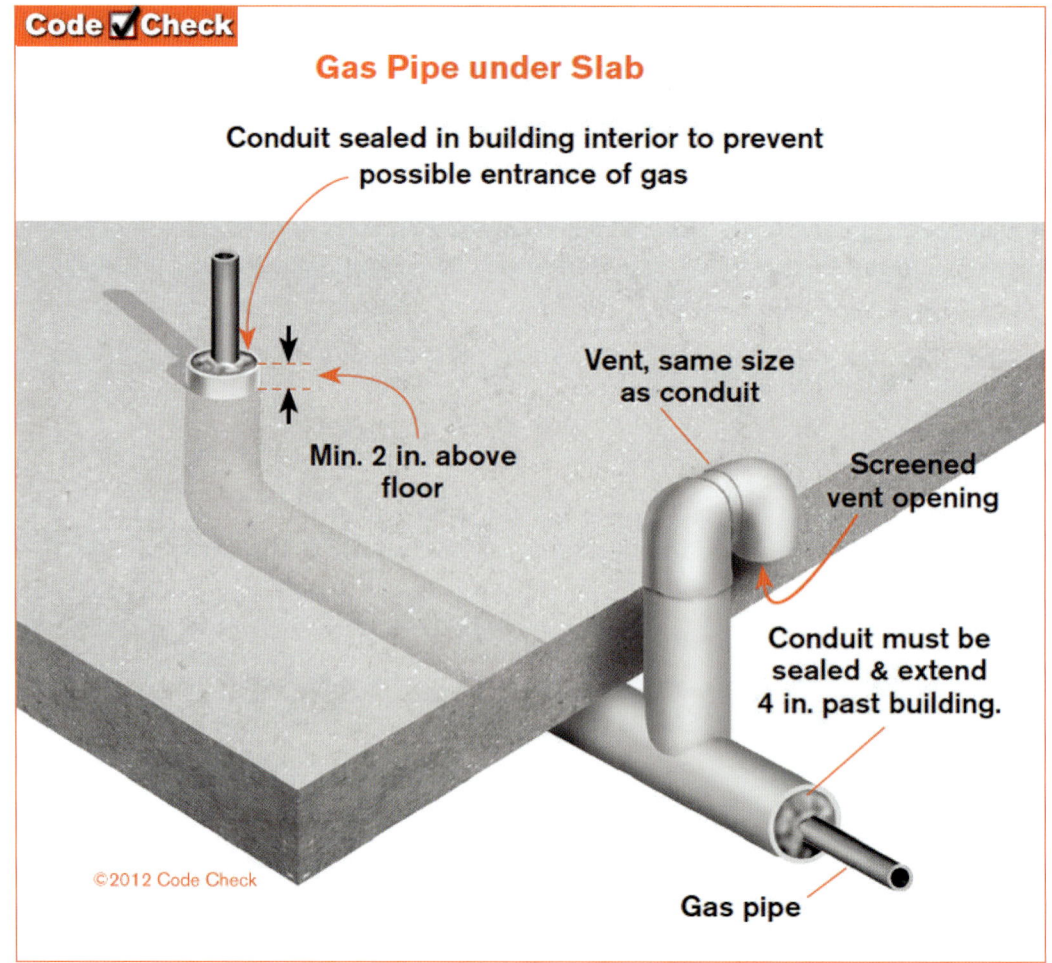

298   Chapter 4

- **Gas leaks:** Any *strong* gas odor in the house should be dealt with immediately. Call the gas company for assistance right away and have the client, homeowner, and others present at the inspection leave the house. Don't take any chances in a serious situation, but don't push the panic button unnecessarily. A faint odor of gas at pilot lights, especially at old stoves, is common and isn't a gas

> **Update**
>
> *Corrugated stainless steel tubing (CSST) is allowed in interior and underground locations in accordance with manufacturer's instruction.*

> **Photo #22** *This is an actual installation of what the Code Check diagram depicts. The most likely place for this is when there is an island in the kitchen with a gas cook-top.*

leak. However, the faint odor of gas along piping runs or at connections to appliances such as the stove, dryer, or water heater is an indication of a gas leak. This should be reported as a **safety hazard** with the

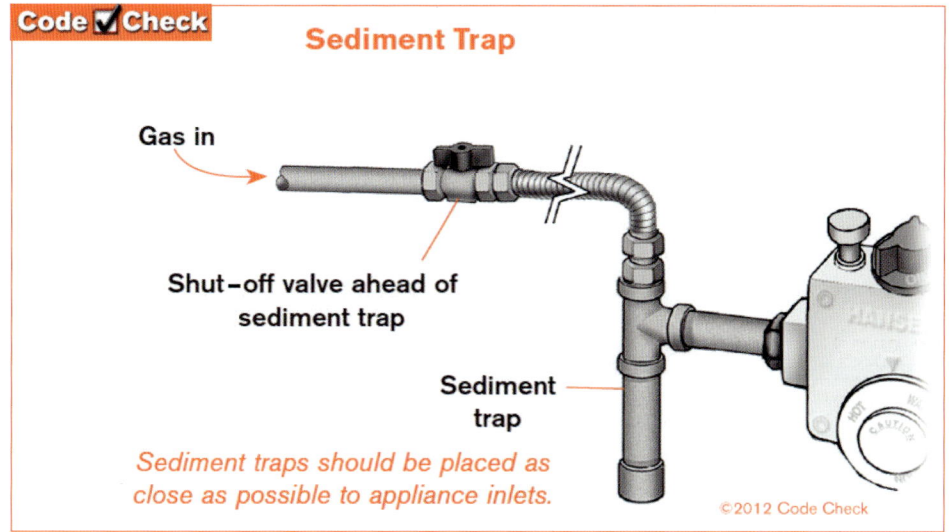

Code Check — Sediment Trap

Gas in

Shut-off valve ahead of sediment trap

Sediment trap

Sediment traps should be placed as close as possible to appliance inlets.

©2012 Code Check

> **Section Note**
>
> *Find out what your local codes require for bottled or natural gas piping so that you can advise customers of violations.*

> **GAS ODOR**
>
> *If the home inspector detects a strong odor of gas in a home, he or she should have people leave the house immediately.*
>
> *Call the gas company for help.*

recommendation that the proper personnel be called to correct the situation. Many parts of the country require a sediment trap, commonly called a drip leg, at water heaters, furnaces, and boilers. That depends on whether you have "wet gas" as determined by your local gas utility.

- **Improper materials:** Note any gas piping materials used in violation of local codes.

- **Poor piping support:** It's important that gas piping be properly supported and that it not experience any strain against the piping.

- **Missing shut-off valves:** All gas-fired appliances should have shut-off valves, and the valves should be located in the same room as the appliance.

- **Appliance connectors:** The connections between appliances and the permanent gas lines (stubs) need to of the correct type. Appliance connectors may be a maximum of 6' in length. They may not pass through a wall, a floor, a ceiling, a partition, or an appliance panel.

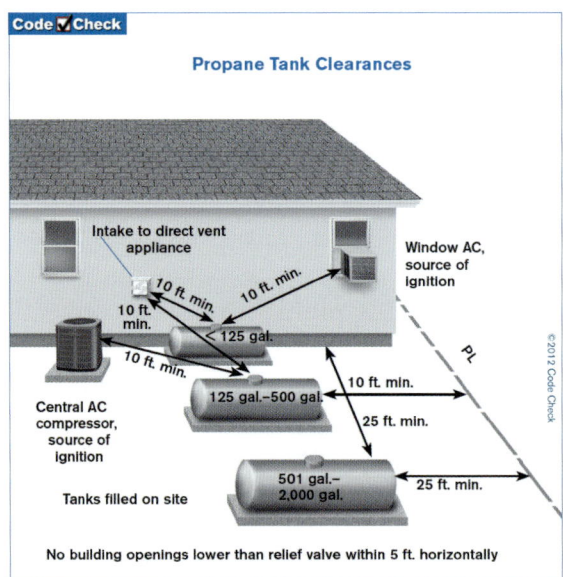

- **Improper tank location:** There are specific requirements for the location of LP gas tanks. Because of their explosive nature, LP gas tanks must not be located in the house, basement, crawl space, or garage. They shouldn't be near an outside window and, in general, are required to be a minimum of 10' from the house depending on the size of the tank. Violations should be reported as a **safety hazard**.

CHAPTER 5
THE ELECTRICAL INSPECTION

The electrical inspection of the home includes the following components:

- The service entrance cables from the masthead and meter box to the main panel
- The main panels and subpanels
- Branch circuit wiring
- Junction boxes, receptacles, switches, and fixtures

All visible components of the electrical system listed above are evaluated during the inspection. We stress the word *visible*. The home inspector removes the cover to the main panel and subpanels to view the inside but is not expected to determine what is behind walls or inside the ceilings or floors. All Standards of Practice state that the electrical inspection is a **visual inspection, not a code compliance inspection**.

Solar photovoltaic systems are not part of a home inspection. However, you may run into them and need to know the basic components. The panels on the roof or in the yard are called the array. The device that converts the DC power created by the panels to AC power that is used by the homeowner or to the grid is called an inverter. There is also typically a dedicated panel for connection of the solar system to the house electrical system. The solar system must have a disconnect to disengage it from the house panel.

Chapter Note

Pages 301–310 outline the content and scope of the electrical inspection according to most states' Standards of Practice. They serve as an overview of the inspection, including what to observe, what to describe, and what specific actions to take during the inspection.

Study these guidelines carefully and know your own Standards of Practice, as they define your career.

The pages also present some special cautions about inspecting the electrical system. Read these carefully too and be aware of the potential for harming yourself or interrupting the flow of power to the house.

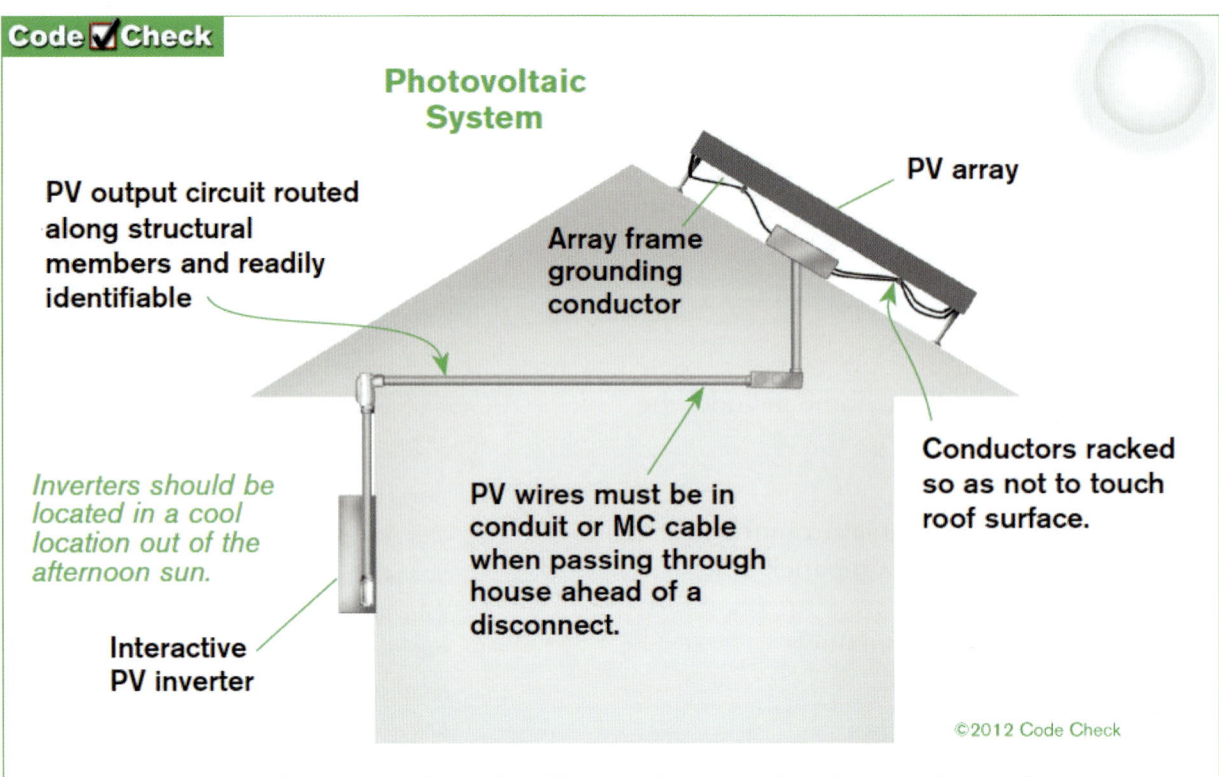

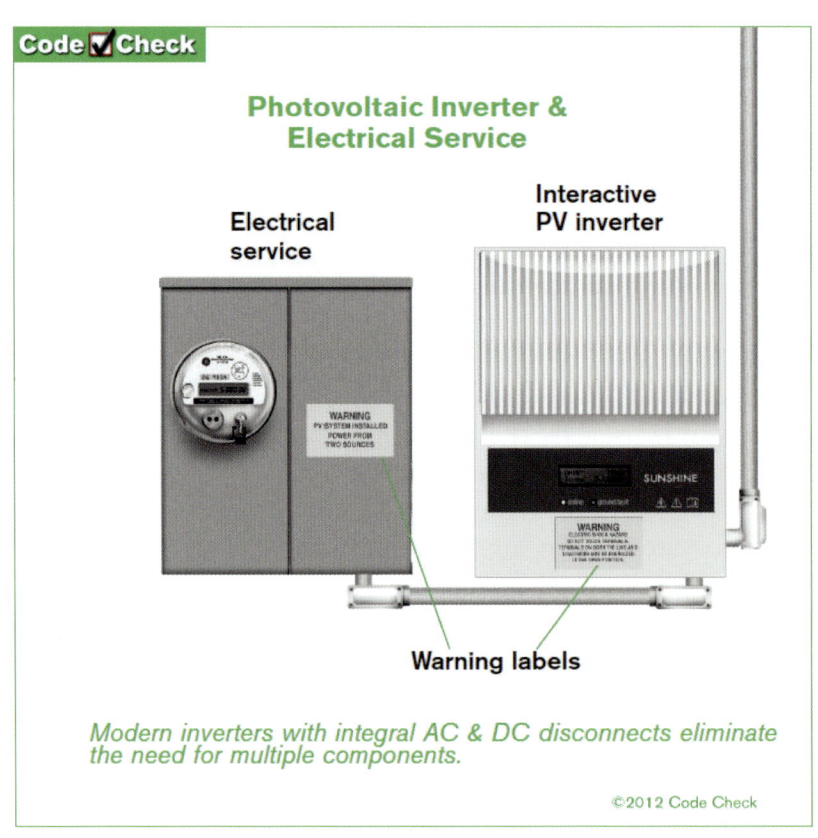

Another device you may encounter is an emergency or backup generator. These too are not part of the inspection. The system will have a generator, a transfer switch, and a subpanel for standby power loads. You **do** need to evaluate the subpanel, but not the other equipment.

Electrical installations for homes and commercial buildings are governed by the **National Electrical Code** (NEC). The NEC, which has been around for decades with revisions every three years (2008, 2011, 2014, etc.), is the authority on safe electrical and wiring practices. Requirements differ for residential and commercial properties and generally are less strict for residences than for buildings meant for public occupancy. States and local communities are not required to adopt the NEC as their standard, although most follow it to some extent. Some locations may adopt each new NEC update, whereas others may follow an earlier or much older version.

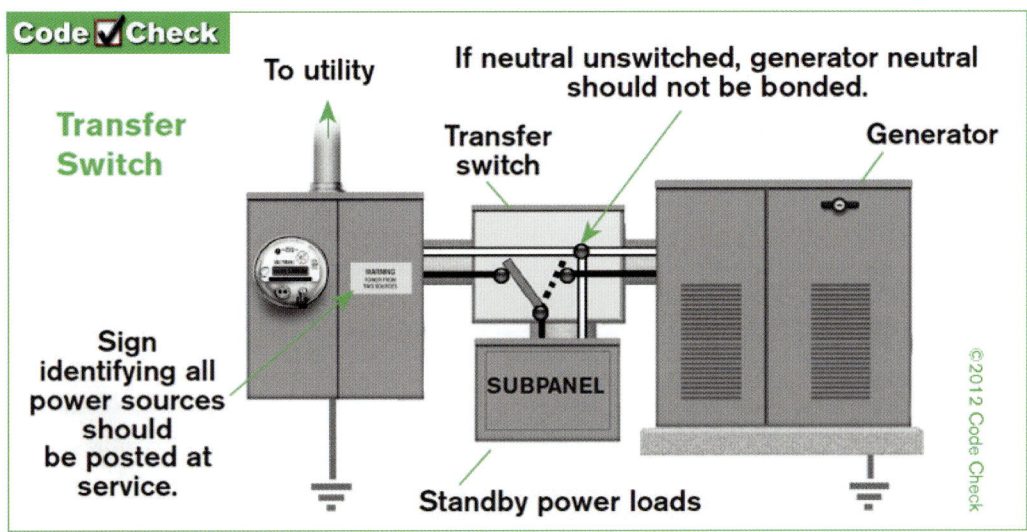

The NEC doesn't require electrical systems in older homes to be updated with each new revision of the code, with a few exceptions. The home inspector may see remodeled buildings wired under both old and revised sections of the code.

Although the home inspector performs only a visual examination of the electrical system and not a code inspection, he or she should be familiar the NEC. Other chapters have mentioned that we do not perform a code inspection. A quality home inspector is familiar with code only to determine implications of conditions and whether a system or component is serving its intended purpose. In the case of electrical, however, a home inspector can afford to be more legalistic than with other systems as improper installations, modifications, and damage are usually safety hazards.

The most important aspect of the electrical inspection is to be on the alert for **safety hazards**. Many house fires are the result of faulty electrical systems, which is why the National Fire Protection Association (NFPA) writes the NEC. The home inspector can play an important role in protecting new homeowners from such dangers.

> **For Your Library**
>
> *Having a copy of the NEC can be helpful, as many home inspectors have found. Procure a copy of Code Check Complete, current edition, for reference. You'll be glad you did!*

ELECTRICAL INSPECTION

- Service entrance from masthead to main panel
- Main panels and subpanels
- Branch circuit wiring
- Junction boxes, receptacles, fixtures

5.1 INSPECTION GUIDELINES AND OVERVIEW

These are representative of the various standards of practice and state standards that govern the inspection of the electrical components of the property.

Most standards of practice provide an outline of what is to be inspected and what is to be reported during the inspection of the home's electrical system. If licensing, registration, or certification is required in your state, you should follow the state's standards of practice. But, of course, not all the details are included in the SOP. There are many other details that will be presented in this chapter.

ELECTRICAL SYSTEM

Observe and/or Report: The act of making a visual examination of a system or component and reporting on its condition.	• Testing of installed and accessible smoke and carbon monoxide alarms • Service drop, goosenecks, and drip loops • Service entrance conductors, cables, and raceways • Service equipment and main disconnects • Service grounding and bonding • Interior components of service panels and subpanels • Conductors • Overcurrent protection devices • Ground-fault circuit interrupters and arc-fault circuit interrupters • Testing of polarity and grounding of a receptacles
Describe: Report in writing a system or component by its type or other observed characteristics to distinguish it from other components used for the same purpose.	• Amperage rating of the service • Location of main disconnect(s), panels, and subpanels • Presence or absence of smoke alarms and carbon monoxide alarms • The predominant branch circuit wiring method(s)

Section Note

There are many electrical terms used on this page and the next. Don't worry about them at this time. They'll all be defined when the topics are discussed in detail later in this book.

The table above provides a good outline of the guidelines that govern the inspection of the electrical system. Not every detail is presented in the table, but there is enough of an overview to give you a good idea of what is inspected and what is not required to be inspected. Here is an overview of the electrical inspection as stated in most Standards of Practice.

- **Service entrance:** The home inspector determines if the electrical service coming to the house is overhead or underground. If overhead, the home inspector observes overhead wires for the proper height above the driveway, proper height above the ground near pedestrian areas, and, if attached to the masthead above the roof, proper height above the roof. The masthead, outside conduit or cable running to the meter, and the meter itself are inspected for secure attachment to the house, water tightness, and rust. The inspector may find, for example, that these items are not securely attached, rusting, bent or broken, or not watertight.

The home inspector identifies the service entrance conductor material used as copper, aluminum, tinned-copper, or copper-clad aluminum and determines the amperage of the service supplied to the home (for example, 60-amp, 100-amp, or 200-amp service) and its voltage rating (for example, 120 volts or 240 volts). The home inspector locates the main overcurrent device (the main disconnect, which may be next to the meter or part of the meter socket assembly or inside the main panel) and determines the compatibility of wiring.

The inspector also determines if the electrical system is grounded by noting the presence of the grounding conductor in the main panel and its termination to a water pipe, foundation footing (Ufer, or concrete-encased electrode), or driven rod grounds. It may also be attached to the well casing if the pipe (casing) is metal.

- **Main panel and subpanels:** The home inspector is required to locate the main panel and all subpanels if present and, if conditions are safe, to remove the panel "dead-fronts" (covers) to inspect their interiors. However, the inspector is not required to dismantle other electrical devices or controls in the electrical system other than removing these covers. Be sure to check your state SOP as with Texas, many things are different and it is in this case too. Also, note that the inspector is not required to insert any tool, probe, or testing device inside the panels.

The home inspector again checks for compatibility of components—of cables to the main disconnect and of fuses or breakers along with incoming and outgoing wire sizes. The home inspector trips the test button on **GFCI (ground-fault circuit interrupter) and AFCI** (arc fault circuit interrupter) breakers in the main panel if they are present.

However, the inspector is **not required to test or operate any overcurrent device (main disconnect, fuse, or breaker) except GFCIs and AFCIs**. Operating circuit breakers in a main panel or subpanel is risky. When a breaker is shut off, the home inspector has no way to verify in many cases **why** it's shut off. Although it may be "obvious" that the breaker to the water heater and AC are turned off because the

> **NOT REQUIRED TO**
>
> - Insert any tool, probe, or testing device inside the panels.
> - Test or operate any overcurrent devices except GFCIs or AFCIs.
> - Dismantle any electrical device or control other than to remove panel covers.
> - Observe low voltage systems.
> - Observe telephone, security, cable TV, intercom, or other ancillary wiring.

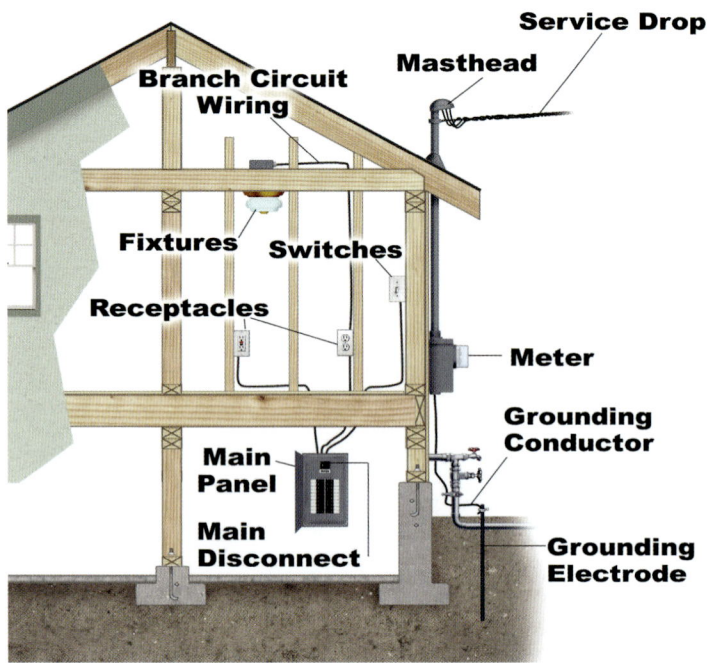

Illustration by Paddy Morrissey

house is vacant, we have no way to verify that completely. The breaker may be shut off due to a safety issue elsewhere in the house. In other words, it is **not** obvious, and the shutdown breaker needs to be noted in the report. A bad day is when the home inspector thinks he or she knows better and arbitrarily resets a shut-off breaker, starting a fire in the attic.

Some of the defects noted in the main panel can include oversized fuses or breakers; the installation of two wires beneath a single screw, an unsafe practice called double-tapping; melted insulation; corrosion; arcing; rusting inside the box, indicating the presence of liquid water or condensation; and damage to the panel box such as a missing cover or a loose attachment to the wall.

NOTE: The home inspector is **not required to inspect low voltage devices or systems**. Low voltage systems, popular in the 1950s, are systems that feature boxes of relays, unusual switches, and one or more switching panels from which all the lights in the house can be controlled. They allow unusual lighting effects and operating flexibility. These relay boxes are usually tucked away in remote corners and can be hard to reach or find. The home inspector should, however, test to see if wall switches work. He or she can identify these systems when operating the switches as there is an unusual click and buzz sound.

> ### For Beginning Inspectors
>
> *Take a tour around your own home to identify the main components of the electrical system. Look at the service entrance components from outside the house. Locate the main panel. From the main panel, trace the branch wiring, noting junction boxes, receptacles, ceiling fixtures, where wiring goes up into the house, and so on. Try to visualize a map of wiring for the house. Don't touch the main panel or any wiring at this time.*

- **Branch circuit wiring:** This is the wiring that carries electricity from the main panel to the fixtures and appliances in the house. The home inspector identifies the type of branch circuit wiring as copper or aluminum and cabling as armored cable, Romex, conduit, or knob-and-tube wiring.

The condition of the wiring and its proper installation are inspected where accessible/visible throughout the living area of the house, basement, crawl space, attic, and garage; any exterior wiring also is inspected.

Findings may be poorly secured wiring, damaged insulation on wiring, installation too close to heating sources and hot water piping, handyman or extension cord wiring, and wire that is undersized for the device it serves.

The home inspector **is required to report any observed solid conductor aluminum branch circuit wiring**. This is because of fire safety concerns with aluminum wiring, which was installed during the mid-1960s to late-1970s. The home inspector should recommend that an electrician inspect any knob-and-tube wiring, which was installed during the 1920s through the 1940s.

NOTE: The home inspector is not required to inspect telephone, data cabling, security, cable TV, intercoms, or other ancillary wiring in the house that is low voltage or not part of the primary electrical distribution system.

- **Junction boxes, receptacles, and fixtures:** The home inspector inspects all accessible receptacles (as in the kitchen and the bathroom) for **polarity and grounding**. Just a quick note on terminology; everyone calls receptacles, outlets. This is incorrect. An outlet is actually the box the receptacle is installed into. Using the **GFCI tester**, the inspector tests and trips all accessible GFCIs in the house, garage, and kitchen and on the exterior of the house, etc., as they can be anywhere. All accessible wall switches and receptacles in each room, hall, and stairway area in the house should be operated/tested. The home inspector inspects **junction boxes** in exposed areas such as the garage, the attic, crawl

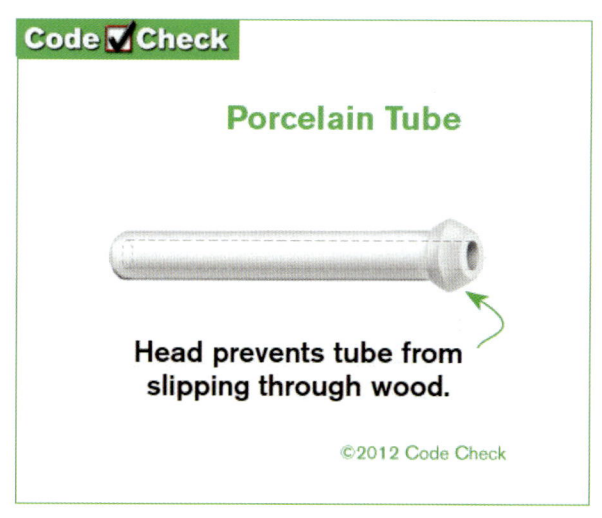

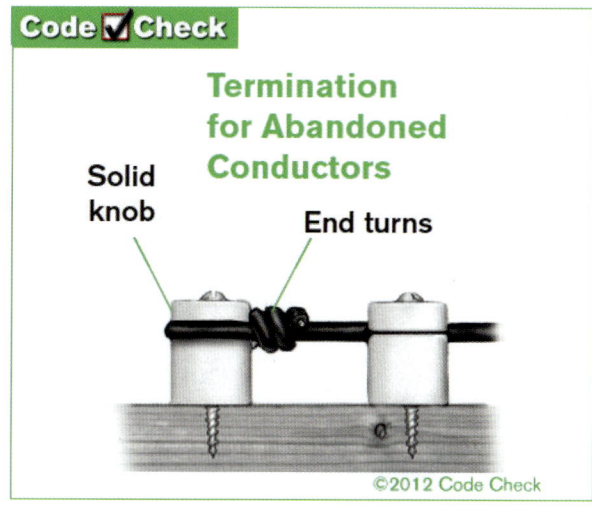

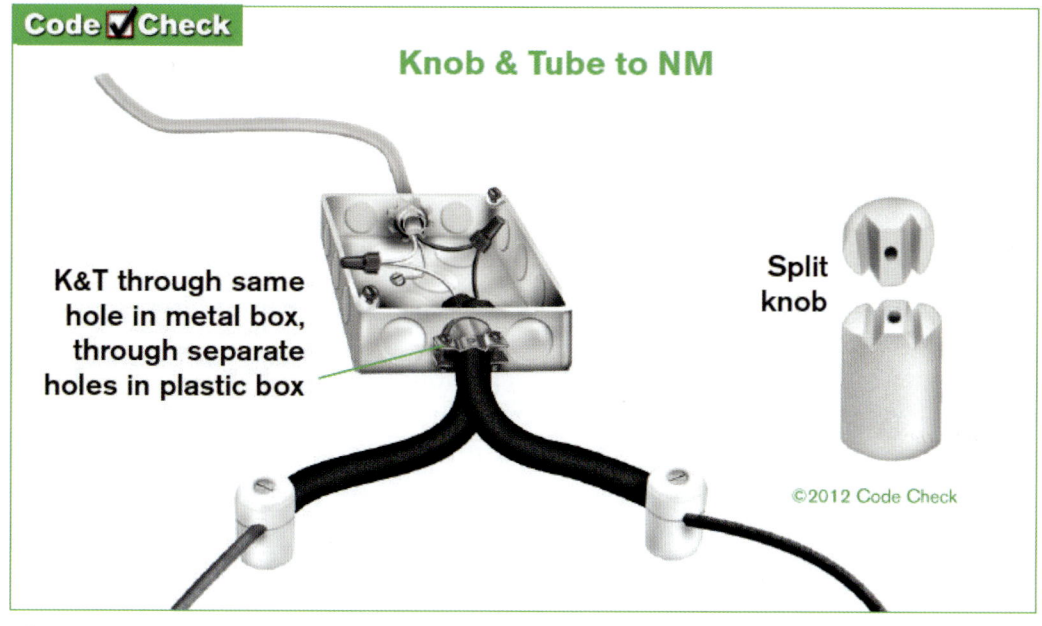

THE ELECTRICAL INSPECTION 307

INSPECTION TOOLS

- GFCI tester
- Neon bulb tester
- Flashlight
- Screwdrivers
- Binoculars
- Sample wire and cable sizes
- Voltmeter and ammeter, if desired

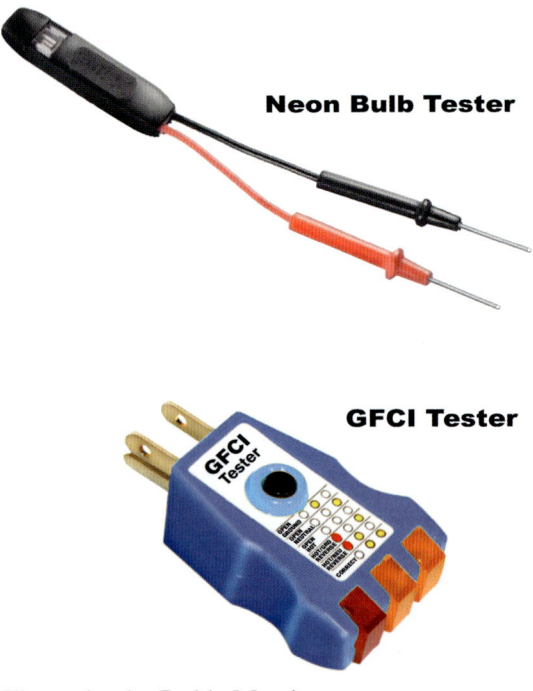

Illustration by Paddy Morrissey

spaces, and the basement, looking for boxes that are not secured, improperly made splices, and other unsafe wiring practices.

Inspection Equipment

The two most important tools you'll need for the electrical inspection are a GFCI receptacle tester and the neon bulb tester. The GFCI tester is a little three-pronged device with three lights typically on its edge or face. It's used to test GFCI and modern grounded receptacles.

The **neon bulb tester** is designed specifically for testing two-slot receptacles. But both testers can be used to test three-slot receptacles for power, grounding, and polarity (if the box is grounded). We'll explain how to use these tools later.

For the electrical inspection, the home inspector should also have a high-power flashlight for inspecting wiring in dark areas and screw or nut drivers for removing the panel cover. Binoculars are useful when inspecting the overhead service and the masthead from the ground. Some inspectors purchase other devices, such as the voltmeter and the ammeter (commonly called a volt-ohm or multi-meter), which can be helpful but are not required for the general home inspection (required in Texas to test for proper bonding).

A skilled electrician can usually identify the various sizes of wires found throughout the home simply by looking at them. This comes from experience in handling the wires during the course of their work. The beginning home inspector may want to purchase short lengths of electrical wires and cables to have on hand for identification purposes—typically one 12″ length of each size wire (copper or aluminum) from 14 American Wire Gauge (AWG) up to 4/0 (4 ought/naught) AWG. We will discuss this in more detail later, including suggestions for bundling the wires and how to use them.

Inspection Concerns

We all know that electricity can be dangerous. We know that water and electricity make a deadly combination. And we know that because wiring generates heat and potentially sparks, we shouldn't grab hold of it. Well, home inspectors can get careless, and getting shocked and thrown across the room is not unheard of. Always keep in mind the dangers present in an electrical system. Have the proper respect for the power that's present and for its ability to harm you. Be smart.

These are some general rules about the electrical inspection the home inspector should follow.

- **Keep your customer safe.** Of greatest concern during the electrical inspection is the customer's safety. The home inspector is responsible for the well-being of the customer. Good home inspection practice is to have the customer present during the home inspection, and that means during the inspection of the electrical system too.

  However, we suggest that the home inspector ask the **customer to stand back a safe distance, preferably behind you**, during this part of the inspection—especially at the main panel, where more things can go wrong. Put yourself between the main panel and the customer. People can touch things they shouldn't or bump into things accidentally. As you perform each step in the electrical inspection, be aware of where the customer is and take measures to protect his or her safety. Explain to your customer that you want him or her to stand back for safety reasons.

- **Protect yourself from harm.** The home inspector should exercise caution when performing all steps in the electrical inspection. Working at the **main** or **subpanel** can be especially dangerous. There are times when the panel cover should not be removed and the panel should be left uninspected:

  — **Water is on the floor** or on the ground (as many are outside) under the panel box.

  — The panel box is **warm** (temperature) **to the touch**.

  — The home inspector **can hear arcing** inside the panel.

  — There is **water leaking** into or onto the panel.

  — The panel is installed directly above grounded appliances (washer, dryer, freezer, etc.) or is in an awkward or inaccessible location where you need to lean across or over something.

  In these cases, stay away and inform the customer that a licensed electrician will need to inspect the panel.

> **Personal Note**
>
> "One of my inspectors removed the main panel cover and was inspecting the wiring. His customer, standing close by, asked, 'What's this?' and suddenly reached up and pointed into the panel, touching a breaker. The customer received a shock that threw him back a few feet.
>
> Although the inspector was not the cause of the problem, I consider it his fault that the customer received the shock. The inspector should have had the customer stand far enough away so that he couldn't reach the panel."

> **IMPORTANT RULES**
>
> - Keep your customer safe.
> - Protect yourself from harm.
> - Don't perform any electrical work.
> - Don't turn off the power.

> **Personal Note**
>
> "This is a case of not thinking and not putting 2 and 2 together. Electricity plus water equals danger. One of my inspectors-in-training actually put his hand into a sump pump to test its operation. He got shocked and thrown over onto his back. Fortunately, it only happened that one time. What a way to learn a lesson."

- **Don't do any electrical work.** The home inspector reports deficiencies in the electrical system; he or she does not perform electrical work. The home inspector does not change fuses or fix reverse polarity in receptacles. The safest thing to do is stick to the standards of practice and nothing more.

  AHIT has had seasoned, experienced electricians attend its classes, and more often than not, they agree wholeheartedly with the above statement for many reasons—not the least of which is that there is no protection from liability should things go wrong. Once a homeowner, REALTOR®, or buyer see the home inspector performing repair work, he or she is likely to point a finger at the inspector if future problems arise with the electrical system.

- **Don't turn off the power.** The electrical inspection does not include turning off the main disconnect or testing the breakers or fuses. An interruption to the power flow to the house can cause all sorts of problems. Circuit breakers may not reset or may malfunction. Appliances or equipment in the house can be affected by momentary loss of power. Clocks have to be reset, burglar alarms may be triggered, and computer data can be lost.

- **Check with the owner before interrupting power.** If a home has a 60-amp panel with fused pull-out blocks, the home inspector will have to pull out the block to read fuse size. This will interrupt power. The home inspector should check with the owner first to see if interrupting the power will cause any problems. This is actually **not necessary** as the standard 60-amp panel has a fuse holder that will only hold a maximum of 60-amp fuses.

  Testing GFCIs also interrupts power at some receptacles on a circuit, but it's unusual and incorrect to have the kitchen or bathrooms on the same circuit with other rooms where sensitive equipment may be plugged in. Some newer kitchen appliances are equipped with programmable features, however, and it is in the inspector's best interest to look for them prior to testing GFCIs. Look for appliances in operation too, such as bread machines, coffeemakers, and answering machines. There are similar potential problems when testing AFCIs too. The AFCIs are typically in bedrooms (although now could be anywhere in the house), many of which are used for offices and have computers, printers, etc. that could be affected. It is a general rule that in an occupied home you do NOT test AFCIs. Make a note of their presence and that they were not tested.

5.2 BASIC ELECTRICITY

As a home inspector, it's important to understand the basic principles of electricity. With regard to the electrical system, an inspector's liability is very high and very expensive. House fires can start and personal injury can occur from a fault in the system. The home inspector wants to point out safety hazards during the inspection.

Volts, Ohms, Amps, and Watts

Electricity is supplied to homes from a power plant in an **alternating current** (AC). It doesn't flow in one direction like water through a pipe to a house. An alternating current means that electrons are made to move back and forth at a frequency of 60 cycles per second, or 60 Hz. An alternator at the power plant creates the movement of electrons, and this back-and-forth movement is what travels along power lines to the lights and appliances in the home and then back to the source.

> *Chapter Note*
>
> *Pages 310–316 present an overview of electrical concepts important to the understanding of every home inspector. The application of these concepts to the practical matter of inspecting electrical systems will be studied later, beginning on page 316.*

- **Resistance:** The alternating current of electricity is channeled through **conductors** such as copper and aluminum wires. As the current alternates back and forth through conductors, it experiences **resistance** (opposition or something like friction) that makes heat. *Resistance is expressed in ohms.*

Good electrical conductors have low resistance. Silver and copper have low resistance and, as a result, make good conductors. Aluminum is also a good conductor, but it has a higher resistance than copper. Therefore, a **larger size aluminum wire would be needed** to carry the same current as a smaller size copper wire. See the wire chart on page 315. Conductors are used to channel electricity where it's supposed to go. By the way, water is an excellent conductor of electricity, which is why water and electricity are so dangerous together.

Materials with a high resistance are poor conductors of electricity. They're called insulators and include materials such as wood, rubber, ceramic, and most plastics. Insulators are used to keep electricity from going where we don't want it to go. Air is an excellent insulator.

While they are operating, lamps, light fixtures, and appliances such as a stoves and refrigerators are called loads. Each load has its own resistance.

- **Electromotive force:** The electromotive force (pressure), or the voltage, is the potential energy of the electrical system. The electromotive

> *Definitions*
>
> *Current is the flow of electricity and is expressed in amps. In an alternating current, electrons move back and forth at a frequency of 60 cycles per second. Ampacity refers to the amount of current that can safely pass through a conductor. Resistance is the opposition offered by a material when a current passes through it. Resistance is expressed in ohms.*
>
> *A good conductor is a material that offers a low resistance to an electric current flowing through it. An insulator is a material that offers a high resistance.*
>
> *The electromotive force, or voltage, is what drives the current of electrons through a given resistance. It is expressed in volts.*
>
> *Power is the heat produced by the flow of current through a given resistance. Power is expressed in watts, kilowatts, or British thermal units (BTUs).*

THE ELECTRICAL INSPECTION

force is **expressed in volts**. This force is what drives a current of electrons through a given resistance. Homes today are supplied with a 120/240 volt electrical system, which can provide 240 or 120 volts. That is, in the house, the voltage is broken down for most appliances to 120 volts and is available for other appliances (for example, central air conditioners) as 240 volts. Houses received 110/220 volts in the 1950s and 115/230 volts in the 1970s. The change over the years is an improvement of the electrical service available to homeowners.

- **Current:** The current is the flow (volume) of electricity that results when the electromotive force is applied across a given resistance. Current is expressed in **amps**, or amperes. This unit of measure refers to the number of electrons flowing past any given point in the circuit during a given time.

  The flow of electricity generates heat. The more amps flowing through a wire, the hotter the wire. If a wire gets too hot, it is no longer safe. Therefore, different-sized wires are required for different amp ratings.

  The term **ampacity** refers to the number of amps that can be pushed through a conductor safely. An ampacity rating is given to wire according to the temperature rating of its insulation, the size of the wire, and the metal it's made from.

  Electrical current, or amps, is what electrocutes people, not the voltage or wattage. A current of less than 1 amp is capable of killing someone. In fact, it is generally accepted throughout the industry that only 6 milliamps (.006 amp) are required to stop the human heart. Considering that the lowest amp circuit in the house is capable of carrying 15 amps, it is safe to assume that every circuit in the house is potentially lethal. For that to happen, however, we must complete the circuit, and there's more on that later.

  Older homes (pre-1940s and 1960s) were provided with a 30-amp or 60-amp service. Most homes today are typically constructed with 100- to 200-amp service, with larger homes having 300- to 400-amp service.

- **Power:** Power can be defined as the output of the electrical system or its ability to do work. Power is the amount of heat produced when the current moves through the resistance of a light filament or an appliance—when electrical energy is changed into heat energy. Power is expressed in watts, and 1000 watts is called a kilowatt. One watt is equal to 3.4 BTUs (British thermal units) or 3412 BTUs per kilowatt (kW).

The units of measure of electromotive force, resistance, current, and power are basically defined in terms of each other.

MEASURE		LETTER	DEFINITION
Electromotive force	Volts	E	Force that drives current through a given resistance
Resistance	Ohms	R	Opposition of a material to the flow of electricity through it
Current	Amps	I	Flow of electricity
Power	Watts Kilowatts BTUs	W KW BTU	Heat produced by flow of electricity through a given resistance

An electromotive force of 1 volt will push a current of 1 amp through a resistance of 1 ohm. This relationship is expressed in the following formula:

$$E = I \times R$$
Electromotive force = Current × Resistance

Or you can say that volts equal amps multiplied by ohms. Using the formula above, you can calculate the force it takes to push 2 amps of current through 60 ohms of resistance. The force equals 2 × 60, or 120 volts. You can manipulate the formula to find the resistance ($R = E/I$) or to calculate the current ($I = E/R$).

The power of 1 watt is produced by a current of 1 amp pushed by an electromotive force of 1 volt. This relationship is expressed in another formula:

$$W = E \times I$$
Power = Electromotive force × Current

This can be thought of as watts equals volts multiplied by amps. You can use the formula to calculate the power available with a 240-volt service and a 100-amp main (breakers/fuses). The power equals 240 × 100, or 24,000 watts. You can find force ($E = W/I$) or current ($I = W/E$) by changing around the formula. For example, a 1200 watt hair dryer uses 10 amps or 120v × 10 amps = 1200 watts.

Circuits

A circuit is a complete path of an electric current. Electricity doesn't flow like water through a pipe that ends at a faucet, and it doesn't get used up like the water coming out of the faucet. Electrons flow in that back-and-forth movement through a light or an appliance and back to its source. The circuit is actually a circular path or a loop.

For electricity to flow, or the electrons to move from the utility company to a flat-screen TV, it needs a path **back to source or ground**. Without one of these paths added to the hot wires, electrons have no place to go. Here's how it works:

> **HOUSEHOLD CIRCUITS**
>
> - A 120-volt circuit is when a load is connected between a neutral wire and a hot wire charged with 120 volts.
> - A 240-volt circuit is when a load is connected between two hot wires, each charged with 120 volts.

THE ELECTRICAL INSPECTION

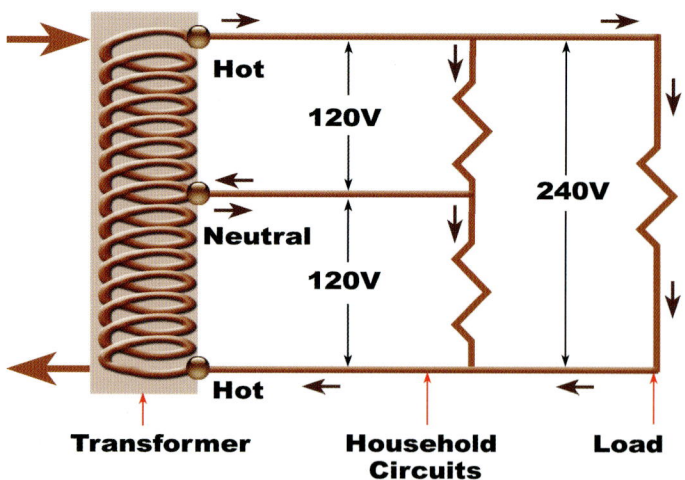

Illustration by Paddy Morrissey

Definitions

An <u>electrical circuit</u> is a complete path of an electric current. An <u>overload protection device</u> is a fuse or breaker that will break the circuit when it overloads.

The <u>neutral wire</u>, for purposes of our discussions, is the grounded center line coming into the house from the power company. Each of the two <u>ungrounded hot wires</u> coming from the power company is charged with 120 volts.

POWER AND CURRENT FOR APPLIANCES

	Watts	Amps
Stove	9600	40.0
Microwave	1500	12.5
Iron	1020	8.5
Color TV	360	3.0
Stereo	120	1.0

The alternator at the power company generates the flow of electricity over high voltage power lines. A transformer on a utility pole reduces the voltage to its appropriate level for home use and provides a third line.

This third line is the **primary path back to the source** and is called the **neutral** or grounded conductor. The outer two lines remain hot or energized, the ungrounded conductor, each with a charge of 120 volts.

These three lines provide the home with both 120-volt and 240-volt circuits. Loads such as lights and small appliances connected between a hot wire and the neutral complete a 120-volt circuit. Loads such as central air conditioners or a kitchen stove connected between the two hot wires complete a 240-volt circuit.

Think of the larger appliances as multiple appliances in one. For example, an electric clothes dryer has multiple appliances located within it and all are necessary for the dryer to dry a load of clothing. It has a blower, a drum motor, a light, a heating element, and a circuit board to control everything. With so many appliances working together to accomplish one function, an electric dryer requires more electrical pressure than one 120-volt hot phase (hot wire) can provide. As a result, we provide **two** 120-volt phases to the appliance.

In a 240-volt main electrical panel in the house, these three wires (two hots and a neutral) make up the main service wires. They can complete as many **branch circuits** as desired for household use, provided each circuit is properly protected with a fuse or breaker (overcurrent protection devices). Electrical wire that can safely carry the current is used. Short circuits and overload protection devices such as fuses and breakers can shut off power by breaking the circuit when more amps flow through the circuit than the wire can handle.

Each 120-volt household **circuit**, for example, may have a 15-amp fuse or breaker. This means that the circuit is capable of supplying 1800 watts of power ($W = E \times I$, or 120×15).

For example, If a 1200-watt toaster is connected to the circuit, a current of only 10 amps would flow ($I = W/E$, or $1200 \div 120$). However, if another 1200-watt appliance were added, a current of 20 amps would be drawn through the circuit ($I = W/E$, $2400 \div 120$). The 15-amp fuse would blow or the breaker would trip and shut off the circuit. If the protection devices were not there, the wires would overheat, melt and possibly cause a fire.

SERVICE CONDUCTORS WIRE SIZES		
FUSE OR BREAKER	COPPER WIRE	ALUMINUM WIRE
100	4	2
110	3	1
125	2	1/0
150	1	2/0
175	1/0	3/0
200	2/0	4/0

The amount of current a wire can carry depends on its gauge or AWG size. The larger its diameter, the more current a wire can safely carry. Because aluminum is not as good a conductor as copper, an aluminum wire must be larger to safely carry the same current as a copper wire. Household circuits, designed to carry 15 amps of current, can safely be wired with #14 copper wire, as the following table shows.

FOLLOWING TABLE IS FOR BRANCH CIRCUITS AND FEEDER WIRE SIZE:	MAXIMUM AMPERAGE ALLOWED	
WIRE GAUGE	COPPER WIRE	ALUMINUM OR COPPER-CLAD ALUMINUM WIRE
#14	15 amps	–
#12	20 amps	15 amps
#10	30 amps	20 amps
#8	40 amps	30 amps
#6	60 amps	40 amps
#6	50 amps	40 amps
#4	70 amps	50 amps
#3	80 amps	60 amps
#2	90-100 amps	70 amps
#1	110 amps	80 amps

NOTE: Copper-clad aluminum wire is an aluminum wire with an outer cladding, or covering, of copper. The wire, viewed from the side, appears to be copper. The home inspector must look at the tips of the wire to see its aluminum center.

Incoming service conductors may be copper-clad aluminum. This also applies to be tinned copper mentioned earlier. It is just the opposite; it is a copper wire coated with tin. It looks like aluminum (silver) from the side and copper from the end. It is rated as a copper wire would be. It is easily identified by the cloth covering and, in most cases, a cellophane covering. It was used primarily in the 1950s and 1960s.

5.3 SECTION REVIEW

- Ohms is **resistance**
- Voltage is force, or **pressure**
- Amperage is **volume**
- For electricity to flow, we need to **complete the circuit** with a path back to **source** or **ground**
- **Neutral** goes back to source
- **Conductors** (wires) must be **appropriately sized** for the **amperage**

INSPECTING SERVICE ENTRANCE

- Overhead or underground
- Clearances
- Amperage and voltage rating of service
- Type of conductors
- Condition of components
- Compatibility of components

Chapter Note

Pages 316–339 present information about inspecting the service entrance.

5.4 INSPECTING THE SERVICE ENTRANCE

Inspection of the service entrance portion of the electrical system begins outside where the home inspector determines whether the service is **overhead** or **underground**. For overhead services, the inspector checks that clearances above drives and walkways (pedestrian areas) are the proper heights. During the inspection, the home inspector observes the various components of the service entrance and is required to **determine** the **amperage** and **voltage rating** of the service. The types of service conductors are identified. All components are inspected for their **condition** and their **compatibility** with each other.

The service entrance inspection includes inspecting the condition of the following components:

- The **service drop** from the utility pole to the building (masthead)

- The **conduit or cable** from the masthead to the meter and from the meter to the main panel

- The **service entrance conductors** at the main disconnect

- The **main disconnect** whether housed separately in a meter box or as part of the main panel

- The **grounding conductor** and grounding system in general

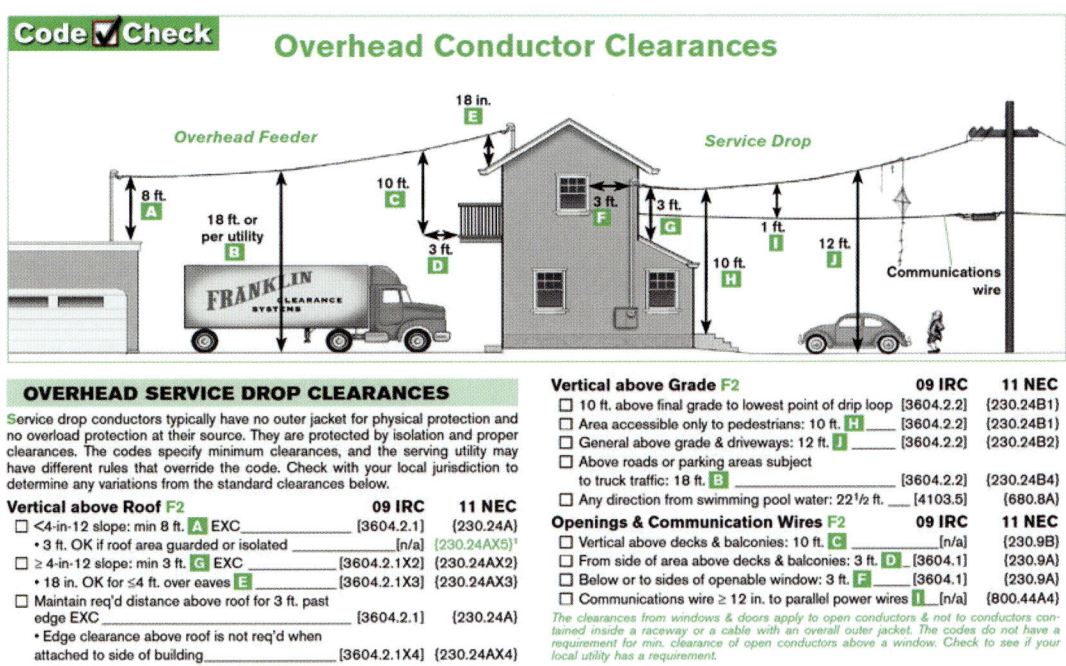

Service Drop

When overhead wires from a utility pole bring power to a house, it's called a **service drop**. If power is supplied underground, it's called a **service lateral**. Normally, a transformer is on the pole or outside in a pit. The service supplied to modern residential homes is usually 200 amps or less. For larger services, up to 600 amps, a transformer may be present inside the building. But that would most likely be a commercial building.

Using binoculars, the home inspector can sight along the overhead service drop from the ground. He or she will notice any obvious frayed wires or tree branches that may be scraping on or weighing down the wires.

When pointing out any problems (minor or major) to customers, remind them that the utility company *may* be responsible for them. Customers should start repairs by calling the local utility company. Many utility companies throughout the United States maintain ownership of the overhead main service wires from the transformer to where they splice before they connect at the meter. Some utility companies require the homeowner to take ownership beginning at the transformer. Be sure you know how things work in your area or the neighborhood before telling the customer this.

Overhead wires must meet certain clearances according to the NEC. The reason for these clearance requirements is to prevent anyone from touching the wires and to prevent vehicles from touching them. The illustration shown above indicates the minimum requirements.

- At least **10'** above the pedestrian areas **and walkways**

- **12'** above the **driveway**

- **3'** above the **roof** (with exceptions)

- At least **3'** from **windows, doors, balconies, and decks**

THE ELECTRICAL INSPECTION

- Wires should clear any **roof ridge** by **3'**

- With a flat roof (less than 4/12 pitch), the clearance should be a minimum of **8'** above the roof surface.

Any deviation from these NEC clearance requirements should be reported as a safety hazard. Instruct your customers to call the utility company to fix problems, although the responsibility may be the homeowner's.

Determining Voltage

Earlier we learned how the utility company provides 120 volts of electricity on each phase, or hot wire, coming to the home from the transformer at the utility pole. We also learned that it provides a neutral from the transformer as a path back to the source. So the number of conductors (wires or cables) going into the masthead is an indication of the voltage rating of the service. If only two wires enter the masthead, the service is 120 volts (1 hot and 1 neutral).

There may be three conductors on the service drop with only two wires entering the masthead and the third tied back to the utility pole as a tension cable (not very common). If three cables are entering, it indicates 120/240-volt service (2 hots and 1 neutral), by far the most common in residential homes today.

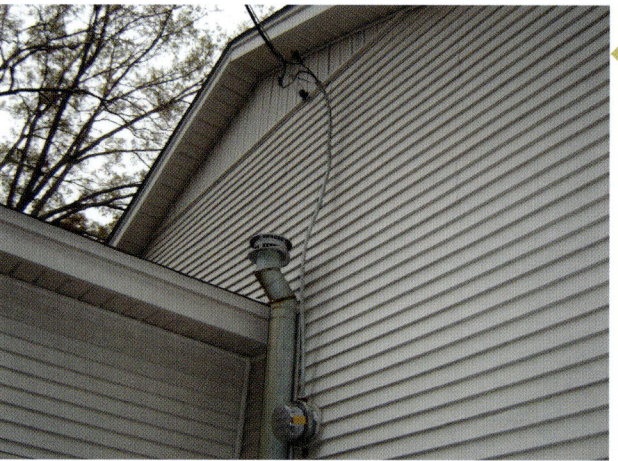

Photo #1 *Overhead service with SE cable not properly secured to house. Gooseneck (drip loop) not present at splice.*

NOTE: Often, the main neutral is a bare wire attached to the mast or the home's structure, spliced, and run into the masthead. This way, the neutral can provide the tension between the transformer and the mast, relieving tension from the splices.

NOTE: On rare occasions, you may see four conductors entering a home. This is a **three-phase** 120/240-volt service. Single-phase power is generated at 60 cycles a second. A three-phase service is also generated at 60 cycles, but with three power peaks in each cycle, and is usually used in industrial, commercial, and farm and ranch operations. If the home happens to have three-phase service, it is not good or bad and you aren't even required to note it, although we recommend that you mention it to your client.

We've seen mastheads in unsafe locations. One example was where a deck had been added to the house without moving the masthead. The masthead was attached to the house at about shoulder height from the surface of the new deck. An adult standing on that deck could easily reach up and touch those wires. It was an extremely dangerous situation, and we reported it as a **safety hazard**.

Conduit or Cable

The overhead conductors coming from the utility pole enter the **masthead** at the front, rear, or side of the house or on the roof. If the masthead is through the roof, the bracket must be raised on a **mast** standing at least 18″ above the roof's surface (see box on page 317).

The mast must be supported so that it will not bend or break. It may be attached to the roof by guy wires or other supports. The home inspector should inspect the mast and any supports for secure attachment and for any rust or corrosion. He or she should inspect the masthead for secure fit over the conduit carrying the incoming conductors. The masthead should be firmly attached and should make watertight the service entrance conduit or cable.

The conductors coming down the outside of the house to the meter and from the meter into the house may be encased in one of the following:

- **Conduit:** Some local codes may require rigid conduit.
- **Plastic-sheathed cable** (SE cabling).

Conduit or cable should be securely fastened to the siding or underlying sheathing in the case of something like vinyl siding with the appropriate brackets. The first bracket should be within a foot of the masthead. Other straps should be at intervals of up to about 3′ down the side of the house. The conduit or cable should not be loose enough to swing back and forth. No vegetation should be touching the conduit or cable.

The home inspector should sight along SE cable to make sure it isn't worn or frayed at any point. Wear or fraying can allow water to enter the cable, causing rusting and corrosion in the meter socket. Water in any panel is obviously a safety hazard.

The home inspector should inspect the roof and siding where conduit or cable passes through. This hole should be properly flashed and sealed to prevent water or pests and air (dust) from entering.

The Meter

The electrical meter may be outside or inside the house, most likely on the exterior in modern construction. It registers electrical use in kilowatts, digitally or on a series of analog dials.

INSPECTING SERVICE DROP

- Frayed or damaged overhead wires
- Improper clearances
- Voltage rating

IMPORTANT POINT

The amperage of the electrical service cannot be determined by the size or type of the conduit bringing the conductors into the house.

INSPECTING THE EXTERIOR RUN

- Bent, broken, or loose mast
- Masthead loose and leaking
- Loose, unstrapped, worn, or frayed conduit or cable
- Broken meter seal
- Tapping before the meter

> **Personal Note**
>
> *"I once inspected a house and noticed where the owner had cut the wires coming from the utility pole right at the edge of the roof. He wired them together and ran them down to the ground and into the basement window. He was stealing electricity.*
>
> *If you ever notice any tapping of wires between the pole and the meter, that means someone is cheating the utility company. That should be pointed out to your customer."*

> **Personal Note**
>
> *"I was teaching a home inspection class to a group of gas company employees. As we were talking about tapping before the meter, one employee innocently pointed out that her air conditioner compressor ran from a tap above the meter. I told her that she was stealing power, and I laughed, suggesting that she may not want to let the electric company know about that. Well, I shouldn't have laughed. Gas company employees are very sensitive about stealing from any utility, gas or electric."*

> **SERVICE CONDUCTOR INFORMATION**
>
> - Note the number of conductors.
> - Identify as copper or aluminum.
> - Note wire size.

The meter should be connected to its pan, base, or socket by a ring sealed by the utility company. Inform the customer if the seal is broken.

When you inspect the electrical meter, look for any tapping (splicing) into the incoming service wires before the meter. You might see someone drawing power before the meter, stealing power from the utility company. It doesn't happen often, but it has been found during inspections. Tapping lines off the incoming service drop at the roof or side of the house and tapping into the conduit or cable before the meter is unsafe and illegal. This should be brought to the attention of your customer.

The shape of the meter base **used to help** the home inspector determine the amperage rating of the electrical service. **That is no longer the case.** You may still see these typical shapes and ratings:

- **Rectangular-base meters:** This type of meter has been installed in the last 20 years. They're usually compatible with 200-amp services, although there are exceptions. In 1976, an Underwriter's Laboratory ruling required that all new meter bases be "continuous rated for 200 amps." Otherwise, only 80% of the actual rating would be considered. That is, a 200-amp meter base that was not continuous rated could only be used on a 160-amp service or smaller. In general, it can be assumed that a rectangular-base meter is compatible with the system it's serving unless a major change or new panel has been installed.

- **Round-base meters:** These meters were installed 50 or more years ago. They were originally rated for 60 amps. Later generations of round-base meters were rated at 100 amps.

- **Square-base meters:** These meters were installed 40 or more years ago. They were normally rated at 100 amps, with later generations sometimes rated at 125 amps.

The shape of the meter base might be a **consideration** in determining the amperage rating of the service. Most modern meters for single-family homes have the designation CL200 or 200CL somewhere on their face, indicating they are rated for *up to* a 200-amp service. The home inspector may find a CL10 meter, which is a transformer-rated meter for large houses with larger electrical systems or two separate main panels.

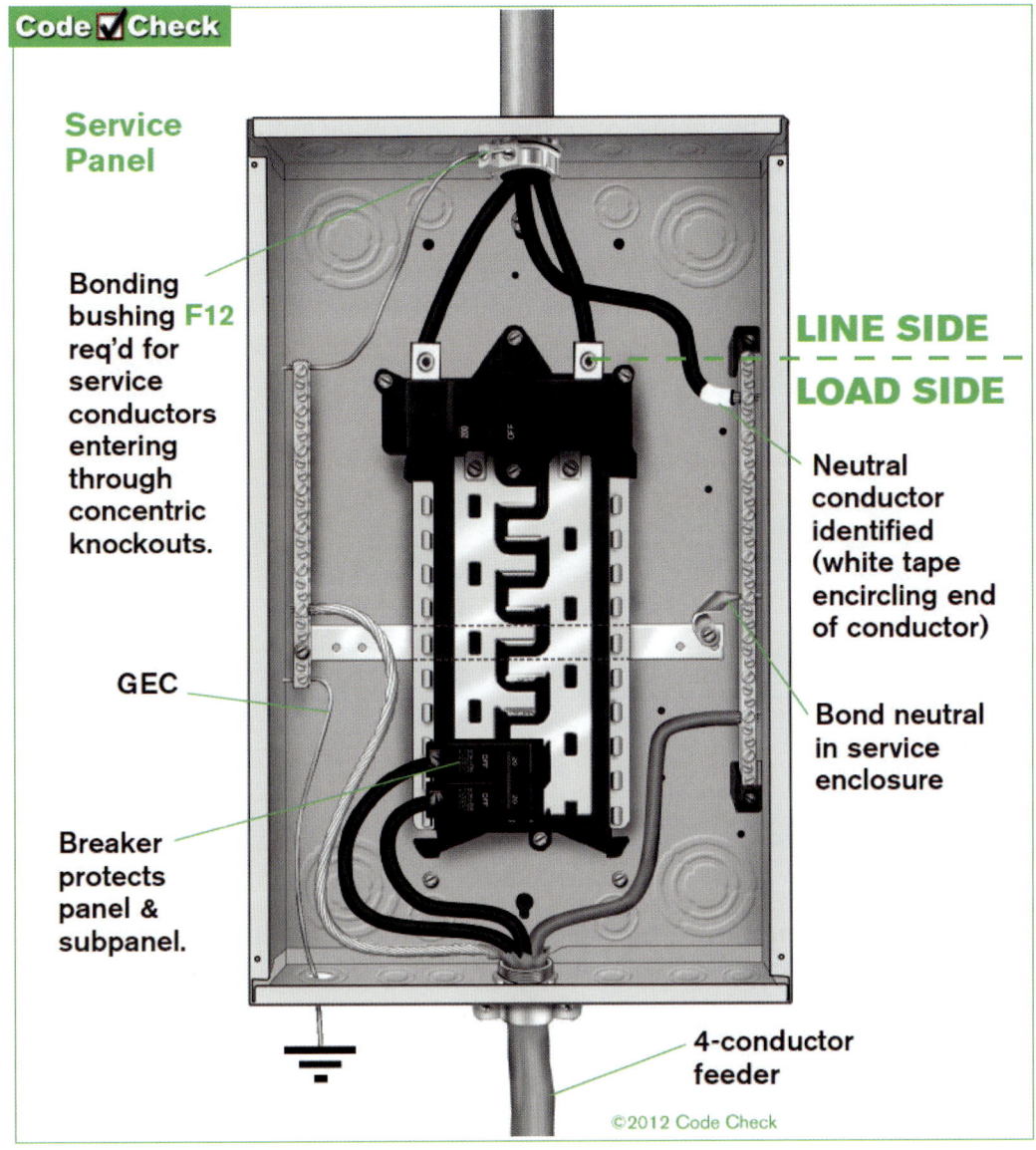

Some older meters have other designations, such as 15 amps, on their faces. This was their test rating. These meters are only usable on systems up to 100 amps. Occasionally, a home inspector will find an upgraded 200-amp service that still has an old 15-amp meter plugged into a new meter base.

REMINDER: You cannot determine amperage rating on the basis of the shape of the meter base alone. As you can see, there are too many what-ifs when using a meter base for determining service size.

Determining Amperage

The service conductors are the wires coming into the home from the utility company's meter. The home inspector is **required to identify** these conductors as copper, aluminum, or copper-clad aluminum. The materials vary from community to community.

Determining amperage of the main service requires three clues the home inspector must try to find. Some of these may not be visible or even accessible, in which case, the clues that are identified should be used and noted.

THE ELECTRICAL INSPECTION

Currently, a minimum of 100 amps are required as main service to residential homes in modern construction.

- The **first** clue a home inspector uses to determine amperage is the **size of the incoming service conductors**.

  This is where the sampling of wires comes in handy. New home inspectors should go to the hardware store or home center and buy a 1-foot length of each wire size (individual wires not Romex; they can be copper or aluminum) from 14 AWG to 4/0 AWG. They can be bundled and taped together like a bouquet of flowers.

AMPERAGE RATING	COPPER WIRE SIZE	ALUMINUM WIRE SIZE
30 amps	#10	#8
60 amps	#6	#4
100 amps	#4	#2
125 amps	#2	#1/0
150 amps	#1	#2/0
200 amps	#2/0	#4/0

  More importantly, the home inspector should trim the insulation from the wire (about an inch), exposing the metal inner wire at the ends to reveal the wire thickness, and label each by size and amperage rating. The inspector trims the wires so that he or she can compare the actual wire and not just the thickness of the insulation.

  Even though all of the electrical wires have labels from the manufacturer indicating their size, it doesn't mean every wire label in every panel will be visible. With the sample wires, the home inspector can compare them to the service conductors at the main disconnect, main panel, and branch circuits without touching live wires.

  Aluminum and copper-clad aluminum wires require the same gauge for various amperage ratings (see chart above). Copper and tinned copper are the same.

- The **second** clue used to determine the amperage rating of the main service is the **rating of the main panel box**. Every modern box is labeled by the manufacturer with a Maximum Service Rating for both voltage and amperage. This is the maximum amperage a panel can carry before one or more individual components (lugs, bus bars, etc.) begin to fail.

  The label can be located in one of a few places:

  - **Outside** the **panel** box (rare)

- **Inside** the panel **door**

- Inside the panel box **behind the cover** (dead-front or one of the sides in the panel box)

- The **third** clue a home inspector uses to determine amperage rating of the main service is the **rating of the main disconnect** (breaker or fuses).

  The main disconnect, an overcurrent protection device, is usually a breaker or fuse and is rated for the maximum amperage allowed before tripping or blowing. By itself, it only informs the inspector at what amperage the panel shuts down. Added to the other clues, however, it is the final information needed to assess the maximum amperage rating of the electrical service into the home.

Remember not to pull main fuses out of the panel without the permission of the homeowner. Sometimes, a small gap or hole in the fuse holder allows a limited view of the fuses, and the inspector may be able to determine the size of the fuses just by looking through the hole. As mentioned earlier, the holder of a typical fuse panel only holds 60 amp cartridge fuses.

The home inspector **should not determine** amperage rating on the **basis of just one** of these clues *unless* it is the only visible clue. In an ideal situation, the wires, panel, and main disconnect are all rated for the same amperage. What new inspectors quickly learn, however, is that ideal often differs from reality. New home inspectors need to remember to document the lowest rating of the three as the service amperage.

The reason for choosing the lowest-rated component is that the least of the three (wire size, panel, and disconnect) is the most amperage that a home will ever draw safely. The hope is that the main disconnect is the lowest of the three; otherwise, a safety hazard is present and an electrician should be called to evaluate and repair the service.

Example 1:

- The main wires are #2/0 copper (200 amps)

- The main disconnect is a circuit breaker rated for 200 amps

- The Maximum Service Rating of the panel (label) is 200 amps

In the above example, should a load of more than 200 amps be drawn through the panel at any given time, the main circuit breaker will trip, shutting down all the power to the house before any component fails. This is safe and is an "ideal" installation.

Example 2:

- The main wires are #1 copper (150 amps)

- The main disconnect is a circuit breaker rated for 200 amps

- The Maximum Service Rating of the panel is 150 amps

In this example, when a load of more than 150 amps is drawn through the box, the wire or the component(s) in the panel are likely to fail before the breaker is tripped. Because the purpose of the overcurrent protection device is to shut down the power before other components fail, Example 2 is a safety hazard.

REPORTING TIP: Be careful not to make a diagnostic statement such as "oversized breaker" or "undersized panel/wires." While either or both may be true, what ultimately determines the repair is the client or current homeowner choosing the best option provided by an electrician. Instead of the possibility of losing credibility by diagnosing the situation, you should document in the report the apparent ratings of the components, call it a safety hazard, and recommend an electrician.

The home inspector is required to report the service amperage. Take your time and examine several components of the service entrance system before coming to a conclusion. Don't report a 100-amp service if two components are rated at 100 amps and one is rated at 60 amps. If you do and you're wrong, you might have to pay to have the service upgraded to 100 amps. You should report it at 60 amps because that is the lesser of the three.

Photo #2 *Main wires (240v) from meter socket. Note the antioxidant grease on the aluminum conductors.*

COPPER-CLAD ALUMINUM

Look at the cut tips of the service conductors to see if what looks like copper wire from the side has an aluminum center.

For Beginning Inspectors

If you're going to locate and examine your own main disconnect, read page 339–340 on safety precautions before opening the service box or main panel.

Of least concern is the meter itself. Sometimes, the utility company will use an old meter in a new meter base when upgrading a service.

As the power enters the house, the service conductors go into a service box or the main panel. The hot wires are red and black (or black and black) and are connected to the lugs (screws) at the main fuses or circuit breaker. The third (neutral or white) wire does not connect to an overcurrent device such as a fuse or a breaker; it's connected to a neutral busbar.

Main Disconnect

The incoming electrical service should have a main disconnect and main overload protection devices, which can be the same thing in most cases (fuses or breakers). This allows the power to be turned off to the house in a single movement. If the main panel is not immediately inside the building from the meter socket, below in the basement, or on the other side of the wall on the interior, there must be a separate disconnect at the meter itself outside.

However, not every home has a main disconnect. A service does not need a single disconnect to be considered safe, but the NEC requires a maximum of six hand movements to disconnect all power to the house. These switches must be close enough together for all of them to be operated using no more than six hand movements. We'll discuss how and when the inspector may encounter this type of configuration later in the text under **split bus-panels**.

The main disconnect may be located in one of the following places:

- In a service box outside at the meter (very common for condos and townhouses)

- In a separate service box inside the house

- Incorporated into the main panel

If the service box is outside, it should be inspected to see if it is watertight, is rusted, and is securely fastened or damaged.

In areas where panels are normally outside, like in Arizona, people lock their panels. It is NOT a good idea, even if the owner knows where the key or combination is.

Whenever a locked service panel is encountered, the inspector should immediately ask agents, homeowners, or clients for the key or combination. If there is any one area of the home clients *don't* want skipped, it's the electric panel.

The electrical service panel inside should also be inspected for rust and corrosion, as this could indicate moisture coming from a leaking or damaged masthead, meter box, or damp basement.

Mention a broken seal in your inspection report. It is never a good idea to open one, but the homeowner owns the meter socket and the utility installs the meter into the socket and the homeowner rents the meter from the utility. It can be dangerous to the inspector, and it exposes the inspector to greater liability.

The main disconnect may consist of one or more of the following types of housings and overload protection devices:

- **Knife switches** are turned off by means of a lever-type handle and protected by **cartridge fuses**, only found in very old installations. Note that where there are two 60-amp fuses in the service box as shown at the right, the house has a 60-amp service (if service conductors and other

> **MAIN POWER**
>
> *The home inspector does not have to turn off the main disconnect or test the main fuses or breakers. As a rule, do not turn off power during the inspection. The only exception is pulling a fuse block to read the fuses. But before you do, ask the owner if that will cause any problems.*

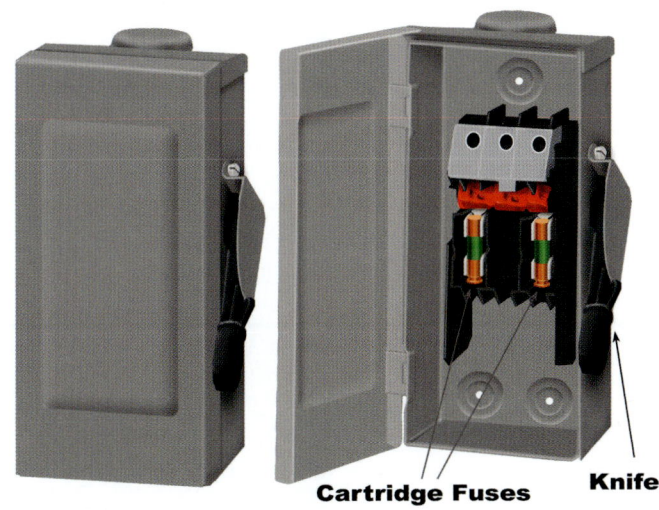

Service Box Covered & Open

Illustration by Paddy Morrissey

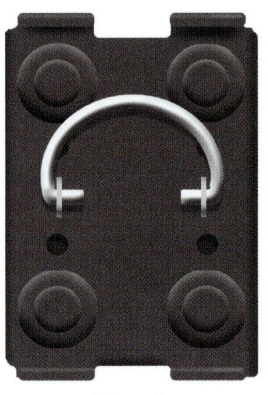 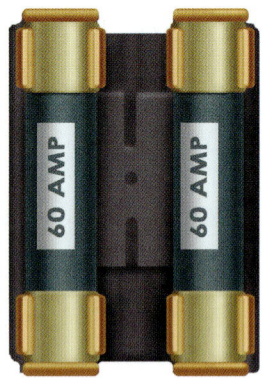

Front   **Back**

Pullout Fuse Block

Illustration by Paddy Morrissey

> **CAUTION**
>
> Do not remove the main panel cover if:
>
> - There is water on the floor/ground below the panel.
> - There is water leaking into the panel.
> - You hear arcing inside the panel.
> - You get a shock when you touch it.
> - It's warm to the touch.

components are compatible). Don't add the two fuse ratings together to get the amperage. We never add amperages for anything during a home inspection.

- **Pull-out fuse blocks** disconnect by means of a handle that allows the block to be pulled out of the box.

5.5 MAIN POWER

The home inspector does not have to turn off the main disconnect or test the main fuses or breakers. As a rule, do not turn off power during the inspection. Whenever possible, read the fuses without pulling the block and cutting power to the house or by using their physical size (60-amps max in standard pull-out fuse block) as previously mentioned.

Main Fuses

As described earlier, it isn't necessary to pull fuses from a fuse block to read them and determine their amperage rating. Just read the fuse block size.

An old 60-amp panel often has two pull-out fuse blocks together. Usually, the one on the left is the main disconnect; the other is commonly for the kitchen stove. They are typically labeled main and range molded into the plastic of the fuse pullout or holder. That is, if you pulled the one on the left, the one on the right would lose power too.

Photo #3 This is a 60-amp service with several issues. The left side says "main lights" and the right side says "main range." So, the left is the "main" for the panel and the right is for the range only. The four green 30-amp, screw-in fuses in the bottom are oversized. The panel should have had four 15-amp circuits. Note the double tapping at the top right for the range circuit.

- **Circuit breakers** are turned off like a wall switch. The main disconnect may be two or more breakers or levers connected by a handle so that they can be turned off at the same time.

Photo #4 *This is a Pushmatic panel. They were a bit problematic and should be referred to an electrician for evaluation or replacement. Note the breaker in the top center labeled Main Lighting. This is the main in this panel. You can see the blank spaces above them where more beakers can be installed up to the maximum of 6 as is dictated by the NEC rule. Always good to look at the label (back right) to see how the panel could be filled.*

- **Screw-in fuses:** Only the oldest electrical systems have screw-in fuses as the sole means of disconnecting the service. If this is the only panel in the house and it has screw-in fuses it is 30-amp service as that is the largest screw-in fuse made.

NOTE ON FUSES: **Type D fuses** are typically used for electrical devices such as an AC unit. They allow more than the rated current to flow through them for a short time before blowing. A **Type P fuse** has an added safety feature in that it is also sensitive to heat buildup between the fuse and the fuse holder. **Type S and C fuses** are not interchangeable, and the wrong size fuse does not fit into the fuse holder. It's a good idea to go to your local home center and look at the fuses and breakers so that you can see the different types, shapes, and sizes.

Photo #5 *These are screw in fuses and essentially a "sub-panel." Again, note the use of 20-, 25-, and 30-amp fuses feeding wires rated for 15-amps.*

THE ELECTRICAL INSPECTION

When inspecting the main disconnect, the home inspector should note these important problems:

- **More than six hand movements:** In cases where there is no single main disconnect but many, count them to make sure the power to the home can be turned off using six or fewer hand movements. Report more than six as a **safety hazard**.

- **Incompatibility of components:** The home inspector may find that the service entrance conductors are rated at a smaller amperage than the main fuses or breakers. This is not allowed and should be reported as a **safety hazard**. Allowing too much current to flow through underrated wires can cause excessive heat and may lead to a fire. This also applies to wire types—if the panel or breaker says copper or aluminum you can use either. If it says copper only, that's it.

> **INSPECTING MAIN DISCONNECT**
>
> - Rusted, corroded, loose, or broken service box
> - More than six hand movements to disconnect
> - Use of incompatible components
> - Tapping before the main disconnect
> - Overheating, arcing, and burned wiring
> - Inspect fuses or breakers for amperage

- **Tapping before the main:** Overcurrent protection devices protect the circuits, receptacles, switches, and appliances **downstream**. When the conductors are spliced before the main disconnect or double tapping is present at the main lugs, the tapped circuit will continue to be live when the main disconnect is off. In other words, all power would **not** be turned off to the house by pulling or switching off the main. This should be reported as a **safety hazard** and repairs should be recommended. Otherwise, the homeowner will have every reason to believe that when he or she disconnects the main, all the power **will** be off.

- **Overheating, arcing, and burned wiring:** The home inspector should note the condition of the service conductors coming to the main breaker and inspect them for any evidence of overheating and arcing.

Loose connections at this point can be dangerous, especially if there is tapping before the main disconnect. Since nothing is touched within the panel box, look for things like arcing, scorching, melted insulation. An up-and-coming practice is to use an infrared camera to detect loose connections in the main panel. If you choose to do this, be sure to get the proper training to perform the evaluation properly!

5.6 GROUNDING SYSTEM

Grounding means connecting the electrical system to the earth, and it is required as a means of disposing of unwanted electricity and energy from lightning strikes to a safe path outside the home. Think of the ground as a **safe alternate path out of the main panel** for the electricity to go should the main neutral be overloaded, bypassed, or disconnected. Before 1960, only the service panel required grounding, but since then, all branch circuits, lights, and electrical receptacles require grounding. This also applies to lightning strikes. Some houses have lightning arrestors installed as part of a lightning protection system. Most houses do not have these systems installed and must rely on a properly installed grounding electrode conductor (GEC).

A term used throughout the rest of this text is *bonding*. Bonding means electrically connecting conductive items together. Just about anything made of metal can conduct electricity, and we must assume that metallic components such as the main panel box (not the circuits, the actual *box*) will at some time become energized. As a result, the **main panel**, the **main neutral**, and the **main ground must be connected, or bonded**, to one another. What is actually happening with bonding is you are bringing the potential to ground equal across all items that could become energized so that you don't become the path of least resistance and get electrocuted.

At the main panel, the incoming main neutral and ground wires share the same neutral busbar (or busbars) with the ground and neutral wires from each branch circuit. A separate conductor must connect (bond) the neutral busbar to the actual panel box. It is designed to bring the potential to ground the same for all components like metal gas piping, CSST, metal water piping, your pool pump housing, pool lights, pool structure, etc.

> ### For Beginning Inspectors
>
> *Locate the main disconnect in your home. Is it located in an outside or inside service box? Is it located in the main panel? (Read pages 339–340 on safety precautions before opening any boxes or panels.) Use the sample wires you purchased and try to identify the gauge of your service entrance conductors. What is their amperage rating? Identify the type of main disconnect if there's one present. What is the amperage rating of the main fuses or breakers? What does that indicate about the service amperage rating? Find an amperage rating on the service box or main panel. Take a look at your meter and meter base. What is its amperage rating? Finally, what is the service amperage rating for your house?*

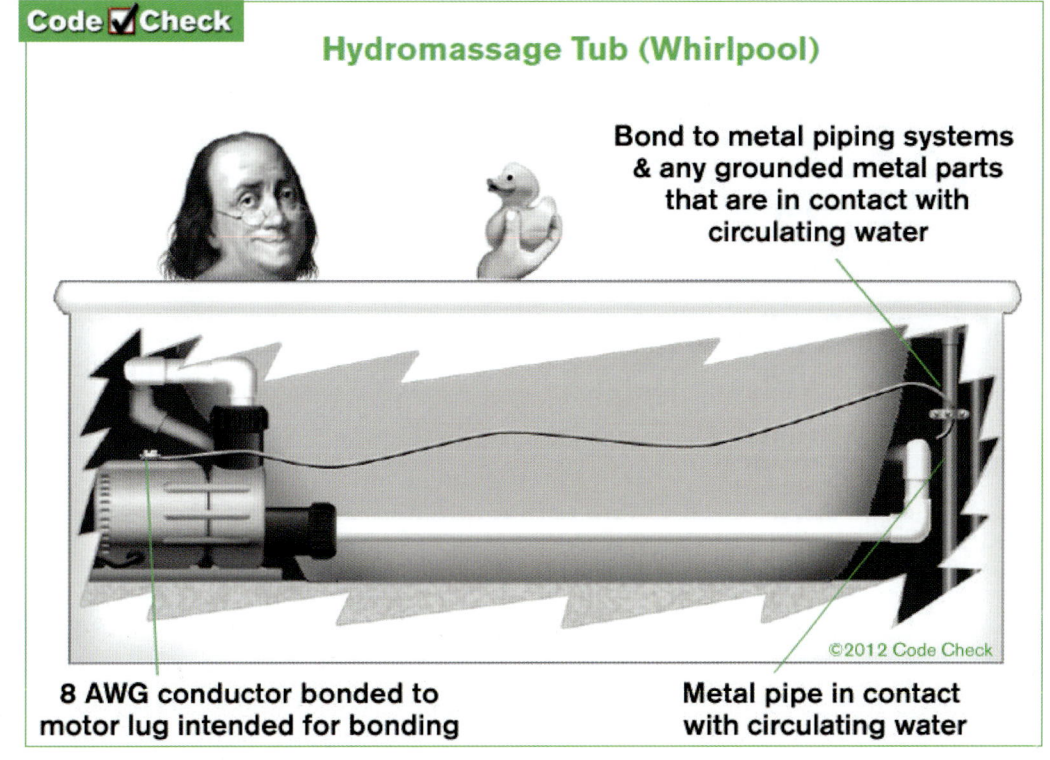

Code Check
Hydromassage Tub (Whirlpool)

Bond to metal piping systems & any grounded metal parts that are in contact with circulating water

8 AWG conductor bonded to motor lug intended for bonding

Metal pipe in contact with circulating water

©2012 Code Check

THE ELECTRICAL INSPECTION

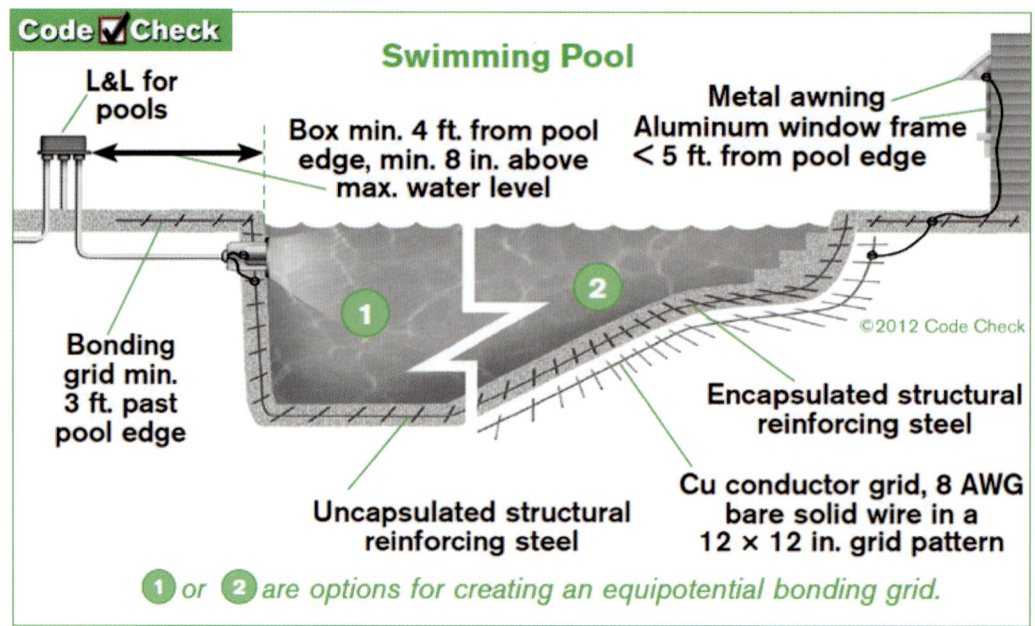

Definitions

Grounding is the process of electrically connecting any electrically conductive item to the earth. Bonding means electrically connecting two or more conductive items together and to the grounding system.

Panelboard

Grounding Electrode Conductor

Neutral Service Conductor

Neutral Bus Bar

Bonding to Main Panel

Branch Circuit Ground Wire

Illustration by Paddy Morrissey

The **electrical system** is grounded by means of a grounding electrode conductor (wire) that runs from the neutral busbar to (depending on the age of the home) the grounding electrode, which may be the plumbing system, the concrete encased electrode (Ufer), and/or a rod or rods driven into the earth, or a metal well casing.

Many students wonder how the electricity flows through the grounding conductor when there is a problem with the main neutral. The answer is simple: electrons always **follow the path of least resistance**. If we want the electricity to flow out on the grounding conductor only in the event of a failed neutral or a lightning strike, the main neutral should be the least resistant path out of the main panel and the main ground should be the second least resistant path out of the box. Again this is only part of the issue. There is also the potential for errant electricity to energize things that aren't supposed to be carrying electricity like the panel box/housing, or the plumbing, or pump housing, etc, as noted above.

Making the ground the second least resistant path is usually accomplished by connecting a bare stranded or solid wire of the appropriate size (usually #4 or #6 copper) from the neutral busbar in the main panel directly to the grounding electrode.

The grounding electrode system could be at the meter enclosure or at the main disconnect

330   Chapter 5

Photo #6 *This is a very typical, incorrect, installation. ALL 8' of the ground rod must be in contact with the earth. Since it's only 8' long, that means none of it can protrude from the soil. You can see the wire passing through the clamp, which is correct as the wire is coming from the first ground rod and then on to the electrical panel. If properly installed all you will see is a wire coming out of the ground at the foundation wall.*

located in a separate service box. In the second case, there should be a ground conductor between them and the main panel (in addition to the two hot conductors and the neutral). All components of the system (meter socket, main panel, separate disconnect, etc.) must be **bonded** together and ultimately connected to the grounding electrode.

Regardless of its source, the grounding conductor should not be spliced. For grounding purposes, a #8 copper conductor can be used for up to 125 amps, #6 for up to 175 amps, and #4 for up to 200 amps. But when grounded to a driven rod, #6 copper is the largest required and #4 copper is largest needed when using a concrete encased electrode (Ufer). Aluminum would require a larger size in each case. Aluminum will corrode when exposed to moisture and concrete, so when it is used as a grounding conductor, its connection should be at least 18″ above grade.

The exception is that separate buildings with more than one branch circuit require their own grounding system.

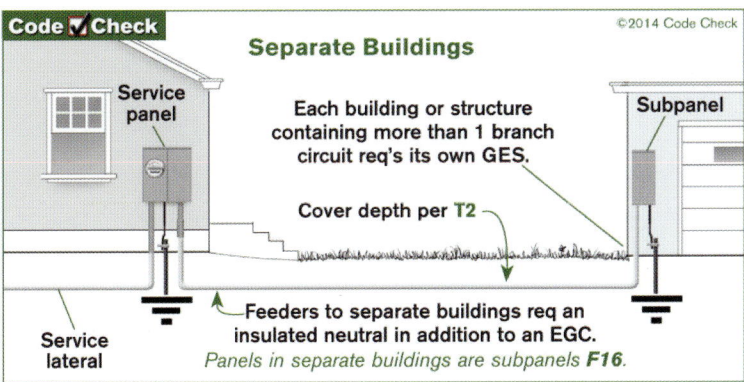

Grounding with Plumbing System

The grounding conductor may be connected to the plumbing system within 5′ of entering the house. When the ground is connected at the house side of the water meter (no longer allowed for new construction because tens of thousands of older homes are grounded this way and it's fine), a jumper wire should be provided across the water meter, whole house filter, etc. The jumper makes use of the broken bond in the water pipes (dielectric connector) at the meter. The grounding conductor may not be connected to plastic water pipes—metal only, for obvious reasons.

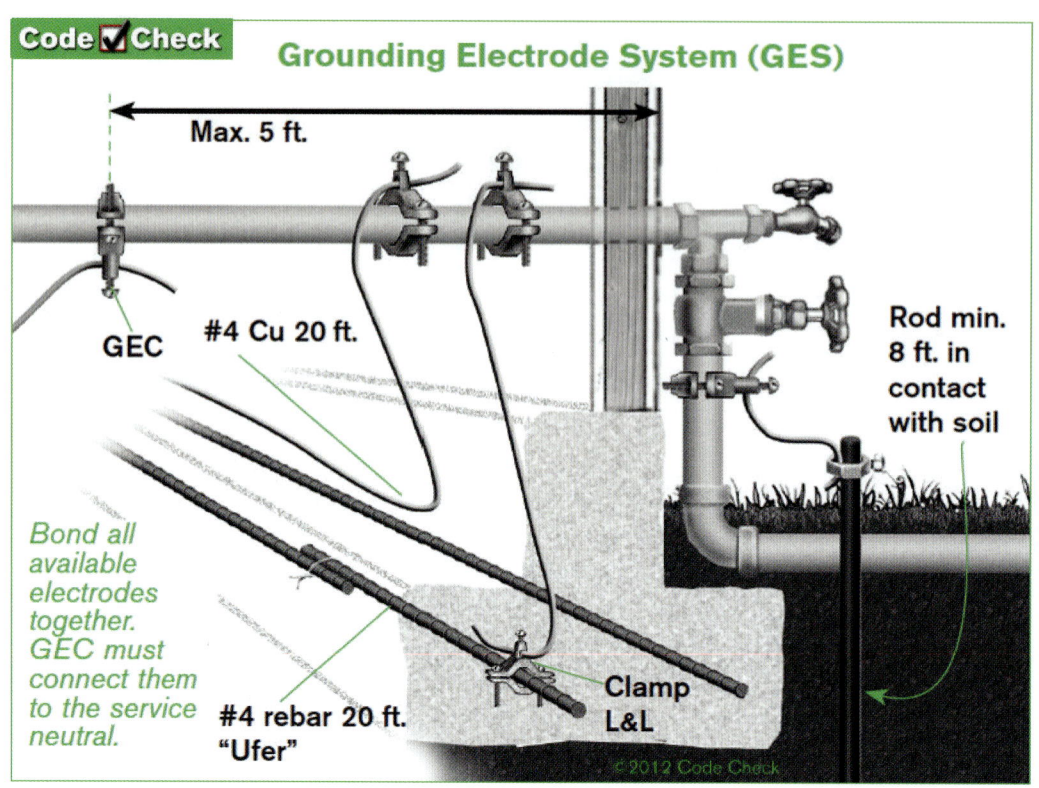

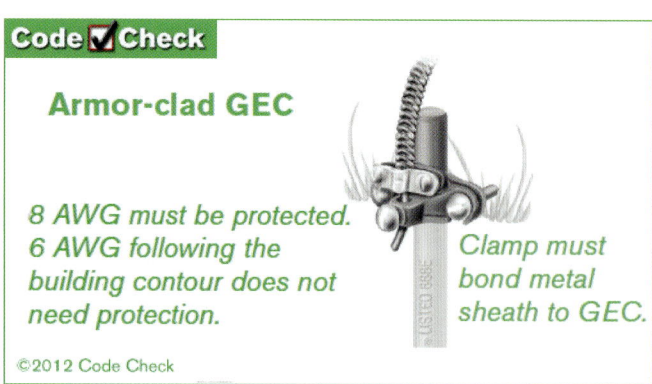

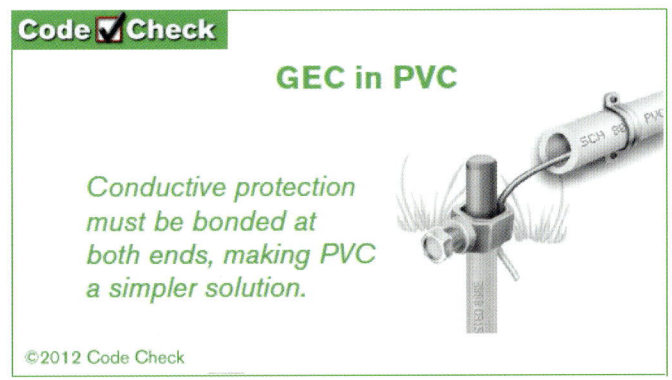

Grounding Rods

Since 1987, the NEC has also required a copper or stainless steel rod driven 8′ into the earth in addition to the plumbing ground. The latest requirement is two driven ground rods spaced a minimum of 6′ apart and bonded together. The entire length of the rod must be in contact with the earth, none of it should be visible or sticking out of the ground. So older installations may have a driven ground rod, a water ground, or both.

Footing Ground

The foundation or Ufer Ground, a concrete-encased electrode, is a more modern installation. It employs the use of copper cables or rebar at the footing to connect the grounding electrode to the earth. Unlike the plumbing or ground rod methods, this encases the electrode in concrete and prevents the accidental or

Photo #7 *This is the end of the 20′ length of #4 rebar embedded in the concrete footing of the house. The mud-ring, as it's called, will allow for a blank cover plate to be installed after they install the drywall. For inspection, there must be access to the location where the ground wire is clamped to the rebar coming out of the foundation wall.*

THE ELECTRICAL INSPECTION 333

inadvertent disconnection of the electrical system's safe alternate path for electricity to follow.

Bonding Metallic Systems

The NEC now requires the metallic water and gas supply piping to be bonded to the neutral busbar at the main panel. As discussed earlier, we must assume that all metallic materials can become energized and should be protected. In addition, the definition of bonding is an electrical connection of metallic components. For safety, newer homes require metal plumbing and gas piping bonds. This is especially true for newer CSST gas piping and potential lighting strike issues.

Imagine a homeowner accidentally connecting a hot wire to a galvanized or copper water pipe in the basement or attic. The connection may trip the breaker or blow a fuse. If not, it may continue to use the water pipes throughout the house while seeking a path back to the ground. This could cause an electrical shock or electrocute someone touching a metal plumbing fixture in the house.

The risk of electrical shock is reduced when a proper plumbing bond connects the water pipes to the neutral busbar in the main panel. The bond provides an instant, easy path for the electricity to find source or ground without using anything else, such as the occupants of the home, as a way out. A typical configuration is to clamp a bare wire (typically the main grounding electrode conductor) to three visible locations in the home:

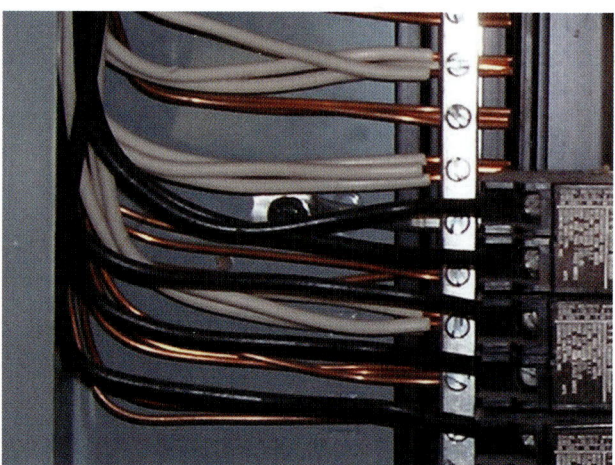

Photo #8 *Note the silver metal part with the screw through it. This is the bonding connection from the panel to the bus bar that protects the panel (cabinet/box) from accidental energizing.*

1. The house side of the main water shutoff where the water supply pipe enters the home.

2. Just upstream from the cold water shutoff at the water heater and again at the exiting hot water pipe. The reason for both is the use of dielectric fittings on the water heater. These connections must be visible and not enclosed in a wall cavity.

3. On the house side of the main gas supply coming off the gas meter. This is, again, especially important with the use of CSST.

Inspection of the grounding system is fairly minimal, as the home inspector is not required to determine the impedance (effectiveness) of the grounding system.

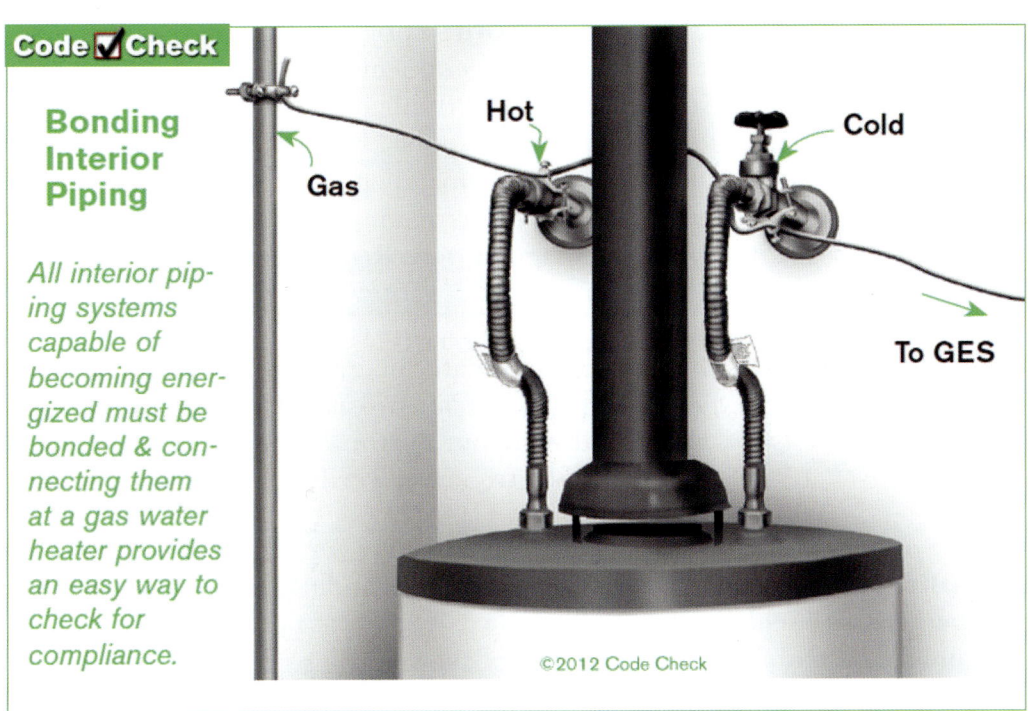

Code ✓ Check

Bonding Interior Piping

All interior piping systems capable of becoming energized must be bonded & connecting them at a gas water heater provides an easy way to check for compliance.

©2012 Code Check

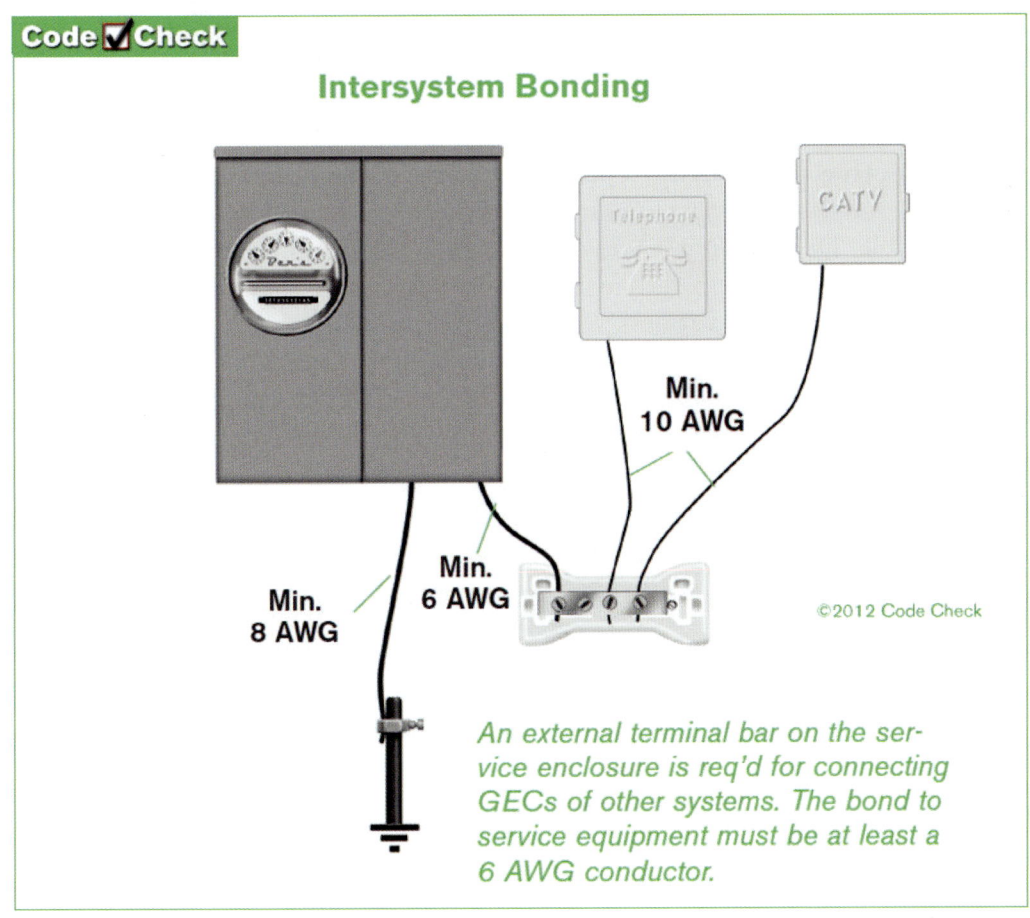

Code ✓ Check

Intersystem Bonding

Min. 10 AWG

Min. 6 AWG

Min. 8 AWG

An external terminal bar on the service enclosure is req'd for connecting GECs of other systems. The bond to service equipment must be at least a 6 AWG conductor.

©2012 Code Check

The inspector is required by most standards to determine whether the system *appears* to be grounded and whether the visible components appear to be proper and connected. Check for the following:

THE ELECTRICAL INSPECTION

> **INSPECTING GROUNDING SYSTEM**
>
> - Missing ground
> - Spliced grounding conductor
> - Lack of bonding
> - Loose, broken, rusted, or corroded clamps
> - Plastic plumbing or dielectric pipe connectors

- **Missing ground:** Look for the presence of an appropriately connected grounding conductor in the main panel (typically bare solid #6 or stranded #4 copper). Sometimes when a new panel box is installed as an upgrade, the grounding conductor may not have been moved from the original box. Recommend that an electrician install a grounding system or reconnect one. As a reminder, this can't be spliced. You may not be able to locate the grounding system, and you don't know if it's missing. In that case, you should inform your customer and tell him or her to call an electrician to verify whether a grounding system exists.

- **Splices in grounding conductor:** The grounding conductor requires special tools (welder) or devices to splice. A splice is a potentially weak connection and for the most part is *not* allowed.

- **Lack of bonding:** As discussed on pages 328–329, the neutral conductor, the branch circuit ground wires, the grounding conductor, and the main panel itself should be bonded at a neutral busbar. Note any loose or missing bonding or defects or corrosion with the busbar. You should recommend an electrician to fix this problem.

- **Ineffective grounding:** Check the clamp that connects the grounding conductor to a water pipe, concrete-encased electrode rebar, or rod if it's visible. Don't worry if you don't see the rods, because they should be buried in the ground, all 8′ feet of them. Make sure it's not loose (clamp), broken, rusted, or corroded, which will break the electrical connection. Follow the plumbing pipe after the grounding connection to see if any portions have been replaced with plastic or dielectric unions and no longer provide continuity for the rest of the system. Also, notice if the electrical system is grounded to old, abandoned water pipes. Sometimes, new piping is installed but the ground is not relocated to the new pipes as it should be (except for plastic re-pipes, which require a new source of ground).

Another problem that can appear with metal water pipes is the use of a **dielectric connector** between two different metals, typically copper and galvanized water pipes. This type of connector removes the metal-to-metal contact between lengths of pipe to prevent corrosion. The grounding conductor should be reconnected with a jumper wire after this type of connection.

Reporting Your Findings

As you begin the inspection of the service entrance, have your customer come with you. But as cautioned, don't allow the customer to get too close to what you're inspecting. Always see to your customer's safety with regard to the electrical service.

One important aspect of the home inspection is the **education** of the customer about the home. Nowhere is that job as important as when you are inspecting the electrical system. So few people know how electrical systems work. Actually, few people want to know. However, the home inspector is still responsible for educating the customer.

The home inspector walks a fine line. You must communicate your findings, and you must put those findings into words that the customer will understand. Some people have a high resistance, pun intended. In some cases, we pointed out electrical safety hazards only to have new homeowners ignore the warnings and lose their home to fire. So use simple terms and work with customers to **help them understand what you're telling them**. Be patient. Explain things clearly without giving a boring technical lecture. And take time to answer any questions the customer may have.

As you are performing the inspection of the service entrance components, explain the following patiently:

- **What you're inspecting**—the service drop, the exterior conduit, service entrance conductors, the main disconnect, the grounding system.

- **What you're looking for**—frayed wires, loose, masthead, leaking, bent mast, overheating, or arcing, spliced grounding conductors, and so on.

- **What you're doing**—comparing wire gauges to your samples, counting hand movements required to turn off the power, following the water pipe to see if any plastic sections or dielectric unions have been added, and so on.

- **What you're finding**—improper clearances, broken meter seal, tapping before the main disconnect, improper fuse sizes, and so on.

- **Suggestions about dealing with the findings**—calling the utility company to fix frayed overhead wires, calling an electrician to fix ineffective grounding, and so on. But, don't make uneducated guesses about how repairs should be made.

> **REMEMBER**
>
> *The home inspector is an educator. Help the customer learn about the electrical system in the home. Make sure the customer understands any safety hazards you find.*

> **Definition**
>
> *A <u>dielectric connector</u> is used between two dissimilar metal pipes that prevents metal-to-metal contact between the pipes and stops the flow of electricity along the pipes.*

> **For Beginning Inspectors**
>
> *See if you can locate the grounding system in your own home. Notice if any of the problems we've discussed are present.*

Filling in Your Report

Every home inspector needs an inspection report. A **written report** is the work product of the home inspection, and every home inspector is expected to deliver one to the customer after the inspection. Inspection reports vary a great deal in the industry. Some home inspection companies develop their own version; others use state required formats (Texas), home inspection software, apps, or formats

> **DON'T EVER MISS**
>
> - Missing components
> - Loose fastenings
> - Wood rot
> - Improper installation
> - Water penetration
> - Repaired areas
> - Sag in the ridge or rafters

provided by training companies such as AHIT. Some are considered to be excellent, while others are not very good. A workable and easy-to-use inspection report is important for a home inspector. Of greater importance are its thoroughness, accuracy, and helpfulness to the customer. Whatever reporting format you choose, make sure it presents your findings in a clear, professional manner such that it reduces your liability and client dissatisfaction.

The **Don't Ever Miss** list is a reminder of those specific findings you should be sure to include in your inspection report. We list these items after years of experience performing home inspections. Missing them can result in complaint calls and lawsuits later.

When you're filling in your inspection report, be sure to put in enough detail so that your customer knows what your findings were, even if the report is read at a later date.

Here is an overview of what to report in your inspection report regarding the electric service entrance inspection:

> **DON'T EVER MISS**
>
> - Improper service drop clearances
> - Unsupported mast, conduit or cable, or meter
> - Tapping before meter or before main disconnect
> - Oversized fuses or breakers for wire size
> - System not grounded
> - Lack of bonding
> - More than six hand movements to turn off power
> - Never guess at amperage size!

- **Exterior service drop:** Report whether the service is overhead or underground and whether it's adequately supported. Report any deficiencies such as improper clearances and tapping before the meter. Make note of whether you have advised the customer to call the utility company to remedy any situations.

- **Main disconnect:** Identify the type of service conductors (copper, aluminum, etc.) present.

    — Report what you've determined to be the service's amperage and voltage ratings.

    — Note whether fuses, breakers, or both are present.

    — Report deficiencies such as inadequate 30-amp or 60-amp services and oversized fuses. Note whether you recommend an evaluation by a licensed electrician because of some existing condition.

- **Grounding:** Report on whether the system is grounded. Report deficiencies on the grounding systems, such as grounding conductors not connected to new water pipes.

- **Safety hazards:** Report any safety hazards you've found. It's a good idea to report them on the page of your report that deals with the subject and then summarize them on a summary page. For the inspection of the service entrance, don't miss these safety hazards:

— Masthead or service drop (wires) within reach of occupants

— Frayed cable on house exterior

— Tapping before the main disconnect

— Oversized fuses or breakers in main disconnect

— System not grounded

— More than six hand movements to turn off power

5.7 INSPECTING THE MAIN PANEL

The home inspector gets a good idea of the condition of the electrical system when inspecting the main panel and subpanels. By doing a professional job here, the inspector can reassure the client that the system is safe and properly installed.

Safety Precautions

Home inspectors should think about customers' and their own safety before approaching the main panel. Here are the steps you should take before you remove the cover to the panel and begin to inspect it:

- **Have your customer stand back**, preferably a few feet behind you and to the side. If you get a shock from the main panel and are thrown back, you won't crash into the customer. Never let the customer approach the main panel first or at your side.

- **Note the presence of water.** If there's standing water on the floor or ground beneath the panel, do not stand in it to inspect the main panel. If there's so much water that you can't get close to the panel, don't inspect it. Make a note in your inspection report that the panel was inaccessible and was not inspected. If you can see water leaking into the panel from above, do not inspect the panel. Report that the panel was not inspected due to water in it. If you work in an area where the panels are located outside, be cautious of thorny plants. You may end up shoving your hand into the live panel if you get stuck by a thorn.

- **Listen for arcing.** If you can hear the buzz of arcing in the panel, do not remove the panel cover and inspect the panel. Report the condition and explain that it was unsafe to inspect the panel.

- **Test for current.** Put any rings or bracelets you're wearing in your pocket before you approach the main panel and leave your screwdriver in your pocket until you've tested the box for current. Put the back of your

> **ANOTHER CAUTION**
>
> Do not remove the main panel cover if:
>
> - There is water on the floor/ground below the panel.
> - There is water leaking into the panel.
> - You hear arcing inside the panel.
> - You get a shock when you touch it.
> - It's warm to the touch.

> *Chapter Note*
>
> *Pages 339–355 present procedures on inspecting the main panel and subpanels.*

SAFETY ALERT

If you find a potentially dangerous safety hazard, be sure to inform the real estate agent and the homeowner as well as your customer.

right hand, your knuckles, against the main panel. If it's live with current, you'll receive a shock and your hand will fly back against your body. You may hit yourself in the face, but at least your arm won't be wrenched outward as it would if you touched the panel with the palm of your hand.

It's also a good idea to develop the practice of keeping your left hand behind you when you touch the panel the first time. If your right hand receives a shock, the current will pass down the right side of your body, not the left side where the heart is. If you do receive a shock, do not approach the main panel again. Leave it uninspected. Write it up in your inspection report as unsafe to inspect because of live current at the main panel and leave a note for the seller/homeowner.

- **Feel the box for heat.** After you're sure there's no live current flowing in the panel box, touch it again to see if it is hot or warm to the touch. A warm panel means that wires inside are overheating due to loose connections or that there are too many wires inside the panel. Such a panel is dangerous. Again, do not open or inspect the panel but be sure to report why you didn't inspect it.

Panel Locations

The home inspector should note the **location** of all panels and subpanels in the inspection report and should check for the proper clearance around the panels. The NEC requires any panels to be located at least 5′6″ above the floor with 6′6″ of headroom. The highest disconnect in the panel should not be more than 6′7″ above the floor. The wall below the panel should be clear to the floor. The panel should be in a clear space that is at least 30″ wide with

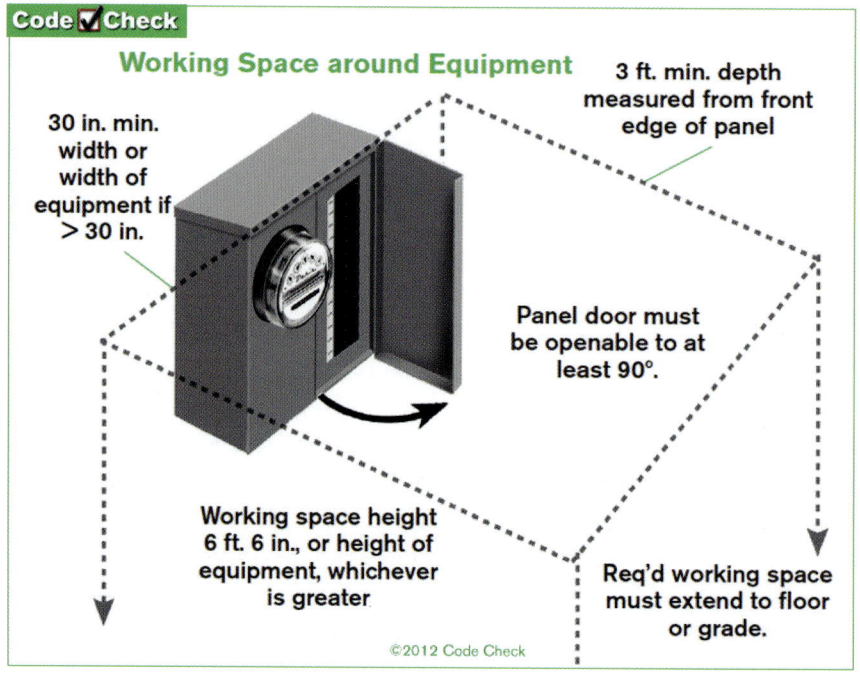

340 Chapter 5

at least 3′ of unobstructed space in front of the panel. There should also be illumination for all indoor panels.

Panels cannot be located in enclosures such as closets, bathrooms, and cabinets or placed near flammable liquids. However, you'll often find that many

Photo #9 *This is an obvious bad location for the main panel (or any panel for that matter).*

multifamily homes or condos have panels in closets. Check with your local building/municipal inspector for local requirements.

SAFETY TIP: If the only way to reach the panel and remove the cover requires leaning on a grounded appliance (washer, dryer, freezer, etc.), do not inspect the panel. Consider asking the homeowner to move the appliances temporarily to create safer access. Move on with your inspection in the meantime.

Main Panel Layouts

The **main panel** is a metal box that includes overload protection devices and/or disconnects for circuits for the home's electrical service. The main panel has **busbars** that provide connections for fuses or breakers. (The term *bus* is a contraction of the Latin *omnibus*, "for all.")

The **single bus panel** has a pair of busbars that provide power to fuses or breakers for 120-volt or 240-volt circuits. The live or hot service entrance is usually connected to a **main disconnect**, either a fuse block or main breaker, and 120 volts is provided for each side or half of the busbar.

Breakers for 120-volt circuits (one-pole breakers) and breakers for 240-volt circuits (two-pole breakers) can be arranged anywhere on the busbar. The 120-volt circuits use only one leg (side) of the busbar, whereas 240-volt circuits use both legs (sides). The 120-volt circuit is provided power between one hot wire and the neutral wire, which

MAIN PANELS

- Single bus panel
- Split bus panel

Definitions

The <u>main panel</u> is a metal box that carries overload protection devices and/or disconnects for household circuits.

A <u>busbar</u> is a conductor bar that provides connections and power for fuses or breakers.

A <u>single bus panel</u> is a panel with a single pair of busbars.

A <u>split bus panel</u> is a panel with two or more pairs of busbars. The <u>upper busbar</u> usually provides connections for up to six 240-volt circuits, one of which provides power to another busbar. The <u>lower busbar</u> provides connections for all 120-volt circuits in the house.

THE ELECTRICAL INSPECTION

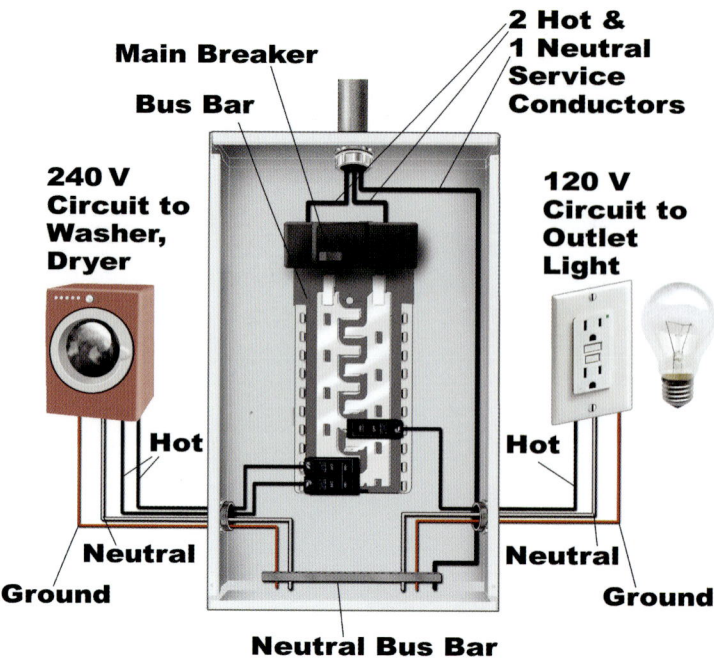

Single Bus Panel

Illustration by Paddy Morrissey

is connected to a neutral busbar in the panel. (See page 313 for an explanation of household circuits and page 328 for grounding procedures.) The 240-volt circuit is provided power between two hot wires, and in some cases, the neutral and ground wires (as is the case for a new electric dryer) may also run to the appliance on the circuit. Both types of circuits have a ground wire that bonds the receptacle to the grounding system.

The two breakers (or fuses) used for 240-volt circuits should be the same size and linked together so that if one is pulled or turned off, the other must also be pulled or turned off. There should be a handle connecting two individual breakers (actually a 2-pole breaker, it just looks like two individual breakers), or a single two-pole breaker should be used.

A **split bus panel** has two or more pairs of busbars providing power to fuses or breakers. In split bus panels there is no single main disconnect. The upper busbar usually provides room for up to six breakers for 240-volt circuits—five for major appliances and a sixth as the main overload device commonly labeled as

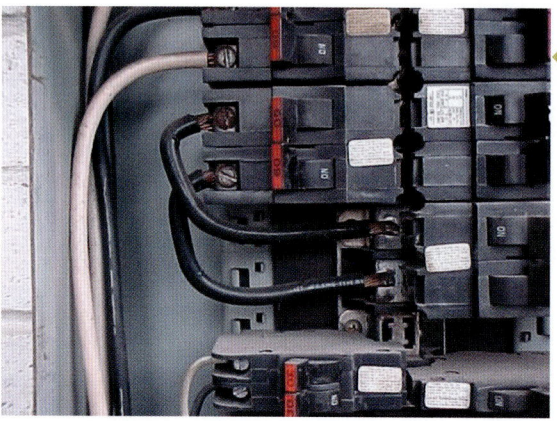

Photo #10 *This is a split bus panel. You can see the connection of the breaker in the top half connecting to the lower half of the bus bar. Hence the term split bus. This breaker is the "main" for the lower half of the panel and anything connected to it.*

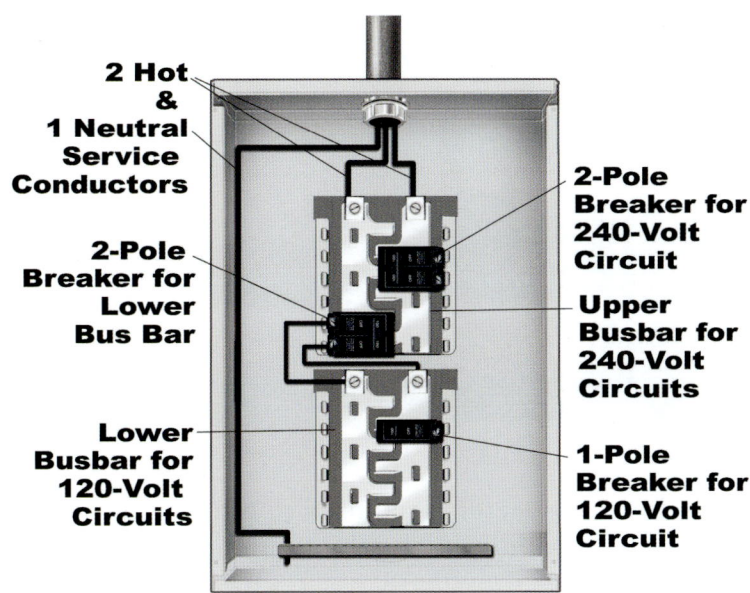

Split Bus Panel

Illustration by Paddy Morrissey

the lighting main or sub-main in older panels. Note how this complies with NEC requirements for turning off all power to the panel using six hand movements. This is actually where the six hand movements comes from as there are still thousands of these panels in use.

The lower busbar, fed by the two-pole breaker from above, provides power for all 120-volt circuits in the house. This two-pole breaker may be labeled lighting main or sub-main. Turning off this breaker turns off the power to all 120-volt circuits in the lower busbar.

Split bus panels have not been allowed by the NEC since 1989. Often, local code authorities require upgrading such a system.

Subpanels

Electrical systems can be upgraded over time. When more power is added to the system, more panels may be added or the main panel may be upgraded. In this case, power is increased service to the house and new circuits are added to distribute it. A trough or gutter may be added that feeds power to multiple panels. When there is more than one panel, there still must be only six hand movements to turn off all power to the house and all disconnects should be within reach of each other.

Sometimes, other panels are added to existing systems not for the purpose of increasing power, but to provide more circuits and better distribution. In that case, the additional panels or boxes are called

SUBPANEL WIRING

- Feed from one of the 240-volt breakers in the main panel.
- Feed from special lugs in the main panel.
- <u>Not allowed</u>: Tapping off the main disconnect in the main panel.
- The neutral wire must be isolated for the subpanel. (Wire cannot come in contact with the panel.)
- The neutral wire (white) and the grounding wire must be on separate grounding bars.
- The grounding wire must be in contact with the panel.

Photo #11 *This is a trough or gutter that feeds power to multiple panels or disconnects. We are not required to take the covers off of gutters as it may be unsafe.*

subpanels. The home inspector is required to remove the covers of all subpanels, if it is safe to do so, and inspect the components and conditions inside them.

The home inspector should find the following wiring techniques between the main panel and subpanel:

- One of the **240-volt circuit breakers** in the main panel supplies power to the circuits in the subpanel. It's like a third busbar at a remote location. This is an acceptable practice if both wire gauges and fuse or breaker sizes are rated correctly. For example, #4 copper or #2 aluminum wire would be needed for a 100-amp fuse or breaker running to a subpanel.

- **Special lugs** (screws) may be provided in the main panel to which feeder wires are attached that feed power to a main overload device in the subpanel. Tapping before the main disconnect in the main panel to feed the subpanel is **not allowed**, although the home inspector may see examples of this. If the main disconnect in the main panel was turned off, the subpanel circuits would still be live. This is a dangerous situation and should be reported as a **safety hazard**. In addition, the wire size feeding the subpanel is most likely undersized and would melt if the subpanel drew more current than it was rated for, which is quite possible.

The keys to proper subpanel wiring are as follows:

- Feed from main panel 240-volt breaker

- Neutrals and grounds are on physically separated busbars

- Neutrals are isolated from the panel

- Panel is bonded with ground from main panel

NOTE: The subpanel should be bonded to the grounding system in the main panel box. But in the subpanel, individual circuit ground wires and the neutral wires should not be bonded to each other and the neutral wires must not be bonded to the box itself.

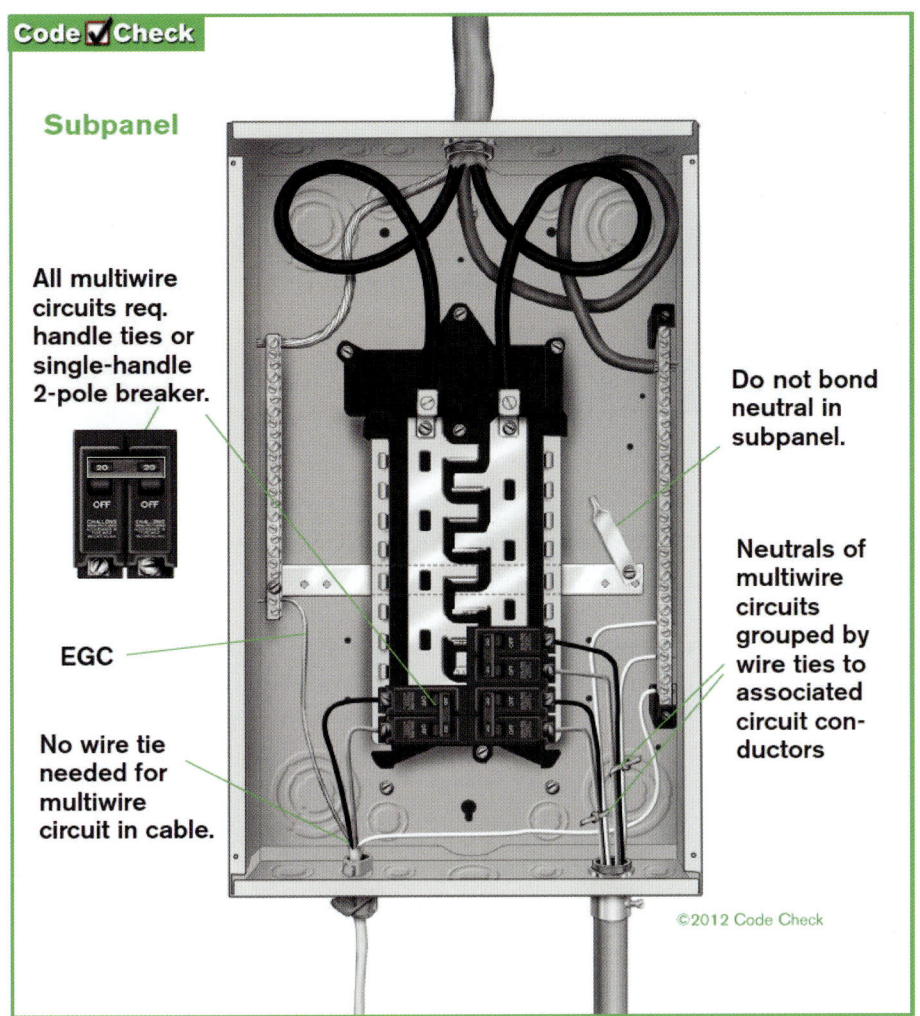

Inspecting the Panels

The home inspector should inspect each main panel and subpanel present, if safe and possible. Watch for the following conditions:

- **Loose, rusted, wet, or uncovered (cover missing) panels:** The home inspector should inspect each panel present. Follow the safety precautions as outlined on pages 339–340 when approaching each panel. Note if there is a cover present on the panel. Often, covers are missing and panels are left open with the wiring exposed. This should be noted in your inspection report as a **safety hazard**.

Check the general condition of each panel. Is it secured to the wall? It should be isolated from a masonry wall, typically on a sheet of plywood or something similar. Are there any signs of rusting? Is there water leaking onto or into the panel?

INSPECTING PANELS

- Loose, rusted, wet, or uncovered panel boxes
- Undersized panel
- Missing grounding conductor
- Undersized main disconnect
- Wear at entry fittings
- Tapping before the main
- Arcing, burned wiring, and melted insulation

THE ELECTRICAL INSPECTION

Photo #12 *This panel was outside without a cover and in use at the time of the inspection. Every single component in the panel was rusted or corroded: a clear candidate for panel replacement.*

Are there proper clearances? Report these conditions in the inspection report.

- **Undersized panel:** Locate the rating label on all boxes and confirm that each box is rated at the proper amperage for the service. Panels my not be sufficient for the house's or homeowner's needs and may need to be upgraded.

- **Missing grounding conductor:** Look for the presence of a grounding conductor in the main panel and subpanel(s). See pages 328–336 for the inspection of the grounding system.

- **Undersized main disconnect:** The fuses or breakers at the main disconnect must be compatible with the service amperage rating. Refer to pages 324–328 for information.

- **Damage where service conductors enter:** Look at the bushings at the back, side, or top of the box where the service conductors enter. The fittings should protect the conductors from chafing or skinning of the insulation as they are pulled into the box.

- **Tapping before the main:** Again, notice the connections of the service conductors to the main disconnect. Are other wires tapped to the main lugs? If so, report the situation as a **safety hazard**.

- **Burned wiring and melted insulation:** Watch for overheating at the main disconnect, burned back wires, and melted insulation.

- **More than six hand movements:** As you inspect the main panel, be sure to count the number of levers required to turn off the power. More than six turnoffs to disconnect all power to the panel should be written up in your inspection report as a problem.

> **Chapter Note**
>
> *At the main panel, the home inspector would also be inspecting the main disconnect and the grounding system. See pages 324–336 for a review of that portion of the inspection.*

> **NOTE THIS**
>
> *Splicing of the main conductors and the main ground is not allowed.*

Photo #13 *We have multiple panels here. You must be sure that there are no more than six hand movements to shut off all power to the house. See how many you count. There are ten total. Note the gutter across the top feeds each main panel separately and each panel has five disconnects.*

Inspecting the Fuses or Breakers

The next step in inspecting the main panel and subpanels is to look at the rest of the fuses and breakers in the panel. The home inspector does not have to test fuses and breakers, except to test for the operation of GFCIs and possibly the AFCIs. And remember, the inspection of the panel is a visual inspection. You don't need to stick your fingers or any tools in the panel to notice the following defects:

- **Overfusing:** With some types of fuses, it's possible to replace the proper size fuse with another incorrect or oversized fuse. The typical household circuit is a 15-amp circuit requiring a 15-amp fuse and #14 copper or #12 aluminum wire. A homeowner can put a 20- or 30-amp fuse into the same fuse holder, potentially causing the wire to overheat and creating a safety hazard. Appliances such as clothes dryers need a 30-amp circuit and larger wiring; kitchen stoves may require a 40-, 50-, or 60-amp circuit with compatible wiring. Check the fuse sizes against the wire sizes (see charts on page 315).

> **INSPECTING FUSES AND BREAKERS**
>
> - Overfusing
> - Scorched cartridge fuses
> - Broken or cracked fuse holders
> - Pennies or foil present
> - Open knockouts
> - Double tapping
> - Inoperable GFCIs and AFCIs
> - Nonapproved breakers for aluminum branch wiring
> - Unlinked breakers

Code Check

Ceramic Fuse Holder

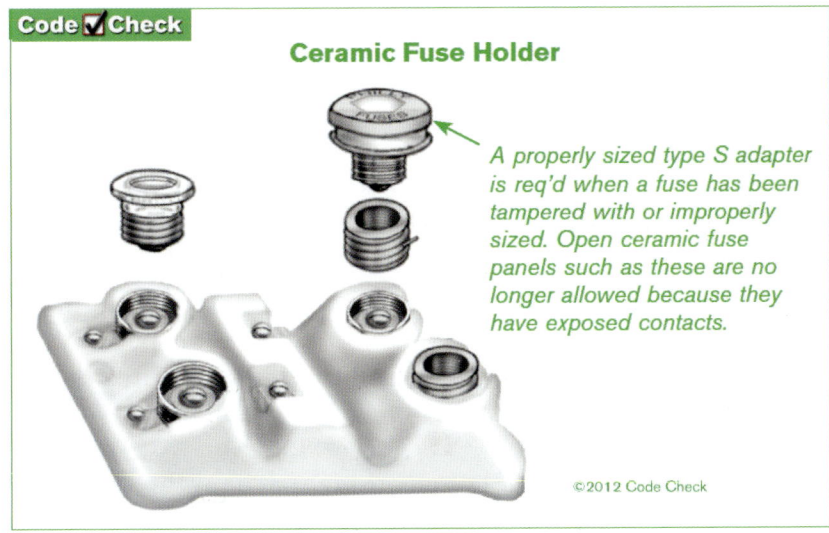

A properly sized type S adapter is req'd when a fuse has been tampered with or improperly sized. Open ceramic fuse panels such as these are no longer allowed because they have exposed contacts.

©2012 Code Check

THE ELECTRICAL INSPECTION

Inform the customer that oversized fuses should be replaced. However, there is a problem with just telling the customer to put the correct size fuses in the panel. The reason they are the wrong size is there is not enough power to the house and the panel needs to be upgraded. Telling them to put the correct size fuses in solves the safety issue, but not the underlying problem of the panel being too small. Type-S adapters can be purchased to fit into the fuse holder that will reject any wrong-sized fuses. However, in most cases, these adapters have been removed and the wrong size fuses installed.

> **Personal Note**
>
> *"Just when you think you've seen everything, something new comes along.*
>
> *One of my inspectors had removed a panel cover not noticing that there was an odd screw among the original ones. When he was replacing the cover, he screwed in the odd screw. The screw was too long and as he tightened it, the screw hit the main lug. Well, the screw shot out of the panel like a bullet and zoomed all the way across the basement, hitting the far wall.*
>
> *I still shudder to think what could have happened if the inspector or the customer had been in the path of the screw."*

- **Scorched cartridge fuses:** If cartridge fuses have scorch marks on them, it's an indication of long-term overheating. If you find any signs of overheating in the panel, suggest that the customer call an electrician.

- **Broken, cracked fuse holders:** In an old box, the porcelain holders or Bakelite can crack or break, causing poor connections, loose fittings, and corrosion. If you see this condition, suspect overheating too.

- **Pennies, copper tubing, or foil present:** People sometimes wrap blown fuses with foil or insert a penny in a screw-in type fuse block. Worse yet is the use of 1/2" copper pipe instead of cartridge fuses. These are dangerous practices and a safety hazard. Suggest that fuses be replaced and any foil and pennies be removed, but upgrading the panel is probably the ultimate solution.

Photo #14 *This is a pull-out fuse holder with 1/2" copper tubing instead of a fuse.*

- **Unused knockouts:** If a circuit is no longer used for some reason, the fuse holder or knockout may remain empty. Any open holes or spaces should be sealed or covered because power is still flowing to the area and touching it could cause a severe shock.

- **Double tapping (120 volts):** People often add more circuits to the house by tapping another wire at the fuse or breaker lug (or screw). With breakers, it is allowed only if the breaker is approved for that purpose, Square D brand breakers are the exception. But in general, only one wire should be present at the fuse or breaker lug. When double tapping is present, it's an indication that a new larger panel or subpanel may need to be added for the additional circuits installed.

It's best to check with your local electrical inspector on how to handle this. Double tapping of circuits is written up as a **safety hazard** because when two wires are jammed into a lug designed for only one wire, the expansion and contraction of the wires at different times prohibit a safe, secure connection. The unsafe connection causes overheating or arcing or allows for corrosion and could lead to a fire.

- **Inoperable AFCIs and GFCIs:** For an in-depth description of the purpose of an AFCI and a GFCI and how they work, refer to page 374. For now, we'll simply discuss how to test an AFCI and GFCI breaker in a panel box.

    The home inspector should note the presence of **ground-fault circuit interrupter and arc-fault circuit interrupter** breakers in the panel boxes and test them for operation. AFCIs were first required in bedrooms and now the rest of the receptacles throughout the house depending on its age. This is a relatively new requirement and not all municipalities have required their installation. Testing AFCIs is a potential problem as many rooms may contain computers or electronics to which the power should not be cut. The common practice is that AFCIs are only tested in vacant homes. The majority of SOPs do not currently require them to be tested, except for Texas in unoccupied homes.

> **Definition**
>
> A *GFCI* is a ground-fault circuit interrupter. It's a monitoring device that will trip in 1/40 second after a ground fault of only .005 amp is detected, interrupting the flow of electricity to the circuit.

Although most GFCIs are for circuits near water, outside, and in the garage, it's a good idea to check with the owner before interrupting the power on these circuits too. To test the GFCI or AFCI breaker, press the test button. The first test is whether the breaker switches off. Next, turn the breaker back on.

The second test is if the breaker will go back on. To reset the breaker, turn it off completely, move the lever away from the on position until it "grabs," and then reset it. If the breaker won't engage, the GFCI or AFCI breaker is defective. If it's defective, you just turned off power to that circuit, so be sure to tell or leave a note for the owner about the defective GFCI or AFCI. You don't use a GFCI tester at the main panel, and AFCIs can only be tested using the test button on the breaker in the panel. As with GFCIs, we'll discuss in greater detail how AFCI breakers protect and operate. They may look like a GFCI breaker and even appear to perform the same way, so you need to read the manufacturer's label (very tiny print) on the breaker to make sure you know what you are testing.

When you press the AFCI test button as you did on a GFCI, the breaker should trip. Reset the breaker and leave a note for the homeowner that he or she may need to reset bedroom clocks and alarms. Just to complicate things, there are now combination GFCI/AFCI breakers that are required for various circuits. There will certainly be more additions as time goes on.

- **Non-approved breakers for aluminum wiring:** We're going to be talking more about aluminum branch circuit wiring starting on page 364. For now, note that if the branch wiring is aluminum, then the breakers must be marked **Al** (aluminum) or Cu/Al for both copper and aluminum. Any other breaker type is a safety hazard.

- **Unlinked breakers:** Where 240-volt or multi-wire circuits are protected by two breakers, those breakers should be linked with a handle so that turning off or tripping one breaker turns off the other (half) breaker. A piece of wire or a nail can not be used as a substitute for the factory handle.

INSPECTING WIRING

- Incompatible wiring
- Damaged wiring
- Overheating, arcing, and melted insulation
- Unprotected splices or abandoned wires
- Missing anti-oxidant on aluminum wiring
- Handyman wiring
- Open knockouts

Inspecting the Wiring

The final step in inspecting the panel boxes is to examine the **branch wiring**—the wiring at the fuses or breakers for the household circuits. (Pages 355–367 will present more detail on branch wiring.) At the panels, identify the type of wire as aluminum or copper and then look for the following conditions:

- **Incompatible wiring:** Wiring from fuses and breakers should be the appropriate gauge and material (Cu/Al) for the amperage rating of the fuse or breaker. Too much current is what causes the heat to flow through underrated wires, causing excessive heat and possibly a fire. This should be reported as a **safety hazard**.

- **Damaged wiring:** Make note of any nicks in the insulation in the panels. Sometimes, wires can get pinched when the panel cover (deadfront) is put back on. Any insulation that is nicked cannot carry its rated amperage and can be overloaded or short directly to the panel. This is why we bond the panel as described earlier.

Photo #15 *This panel has certainly had issues in the past. Even if you can't see a current cause for the scorch mark, you still need to recommend an electrician to verify proper and safe operation of the panel.*

- **Overheating, arcing, and melted insulation:** Check the branch wiring connections to the fuses or breakers and report any evidence of overheating, arcing, and melted insulation. These conditions are usually the result of loose connections at the lugs. An electrician should assess the situation and fix it.

- **Unprotected splices, abandoned wires:** Splices of branch wiring in the panel are allowed when a longer length of wire is needed for a subpanel or replacement panel in the case of upgraded service, although the splices must be properly protected. However, splicing wires for two circuits (pigtails) so that they can use the same breaker is not allowed. This is a common practice in old panels that are over capacity, and a recommendation for replacement or upgrading should be made. Any wires that are abandoned in the panel should be appropriately terminated or removed so that there is no chance of them touching a live component.

> **Definition**
>
> *An <u>anti-oxidant compound</u> is a grayish paste applied to aluminum wiring connections to prevent aluminum oxide from forming on the surface of the wire.*

Pigtails are typically not allowed in the main panel to avoid double tapping. A pigtail is when two separate circuits are wire-nutted to a third wire so that only a single wire is attached to the lug on the breaker.

- **Missing anti-oxidant on aluminum wiring:** All aluminum wiring connections, including the connection to the fuse or breaker lug, should have an anti-oxidant applied. The requirement is dictated by the product manufacturers and therefore is not something that can be verified on-site. The **anti-oxidant or anti-corrosion compound** looks like grease. Without it, aluminum wiring may oxidize, and aluminum oxide is a good insulator. Therefore, oxidation may cause a poor connection and become overheated, perhaps enough to cause a fire.

Photo #16 *This rats' nest of wires is not acceptable and obviously was is not the work of a licensed electrician. Repair is definitely needed.*

The appearance of anti-oxidant paste or gel is either a brownish- or gray-colored paste applied directly to the exposed, trimmed wires at the breaker and lug connections. It should be recommended to be applied whenever you see aluminum wires without it at the main panel or subpanels.

- **Handyman wiring:** Any evidence of handyman (nonprofessional) or amateur wiring at the main panel should put the home inspector on notice that all might not be right with the rest of the service. Whenever you see bizarre and obviously illegal wiring practices, let the customer know that an electrician should be called examine the home's entire electrical system.

Now that you've seen some examples, it should be clear as to why you do not to touch anything inside the main panel and subpanels. Because many dangerous situations can be present, you must be careful when inspecting the panels.

> **Personal Note**
>
> *"Mice can get into everything. I opened a panel and found a mouse nest right in the box. That's not good. Mice can nibble at insulation and make a mess of the box. I'm not sure why more mice aren't electrocuted in the process."*

> **For Beginning Inspectors**
>
> *It's time to get some experience in viewing main panels. Start with your own and move on to your friends' homes to take a look at theirs. Again, take heed of the safety precautions you've learned in these pages. Inform your friends of any safety hazards found.*

Reporting Your Findings

Talk to your customer during the main panel inspection, but have him or her stand back and to the side, out of harm's way. Don't let your customer touch anything in the main panel. Consider yourself responsible for the customer's welfare.

Describe for your customers what you are inspecting at the main panel and subpanels and your findings. Take time to answer questions. Remember that customers may not understand what they see at the main panel and are depending on you to make sense of it for them. Be sure to stress any **safety hazards** you find and tell the customers that you will indicate safety hazards in the inspection report. Suggest that customers review the inspection report again on their own.

When reporting on your inspection of the main panel and subpanels, be sure to report on the following:

- **Panels:** Record the **location** of each panel you find, usually just one. Indicate **whether you were able to evaluate** the panel. For example, you might write "Panel not evaluated due to live current" or "Panel not evaluated due to water present on floor." Report defects such as improper clearances for the panel, rusted box, or undersized panel and safety hazards (see pages 353–354). Defer defects or improper installations to an electrician for repair, and whenever you are uncertain as to whether an installation method is acceptable, recommend that an electrician reevaluate the panel and possibly the entire service.

- **Fuses and breakers:** Report whether fuses and breakers are present and any deficiencies you find as noted in the Don't Ever Miss list. Also, indicate when you find AFCI or GFCI breakers in panels and report whether they were operating or tested.

- **Wiring:** The home inspector should identify the material and type of branch circuit wiring (copper, aluminum, Romex, BX, conduit, knob and tube, etc.) in the panels as well as throughout the house and report on their condition at the panel connections. Don't miss multiple tapping, arcing, burned wiring, and melted insulation. Look for undersized wires, aluminum wiring on breakers rated for copper only, and solid conductor aluminum wiring on 15- and 20-amp circuits (most visible at the neutral busbar).

Photo #17 WIRING

This is the neutral/ground bus bar. As you can see there are a variety of connections. Most are incorrect. Note the copper and aluminum wires under the same screw, different sized wires under same screw, and neutrals and grounds under same screw, all of which are incorrect.

- **Recommending an electrician:** The home inspector should always suggest that the new homeowner have a professional electrician evaluate the main panel and subpanel, if present, when serious conditions are found. This should be noted in the inspection report to help your customer remember your recommendation. Keep in mind that any recommended repairs should be accompanied by a recommendation for a licensed electrician to do the work. Clients and Realtors often ask whether a handyman can do the work. Without knowing the handyman, the home inspector does not know how to answer that question. The best and most appropriate recommendation is the proper specialist.

> **DON'T EVER MISS**
>
> - Loose, rusted, wet, or uncovered, and undersize panels
> - Double tapping at the main lug or fuses or breakers
> - Arcing, burned or damaged wiring, melted insulation
> - Incompatible fuses and wiring, overfusing
> - Cracked fuse holders, open knockouts, abandoned wires
> - Inoperable GFCIs or AFCIs
> - Unlinked or nonapproved breakers
> - Handyman wiring

Don't suggest an electrician when one isn't needed. However, the list of safety hazards below and the following conditions are cause to have an electrician involved:

— Multiple tapping

— Multiple boxes (excessive number of panels) and too many shut-offs

— Wires overheated, burned, damaged

— Melted insulation

— Live current in the cabinet itself (energized)

— Double tapping of fuses or breakers—handyman wiring

- **Safety hazards:** All safety hazards found during the inspection of the main panel and the subpanels should be noted in the inspection report.

— Live current in main cabinet itself (energized)

— Uncovered panel with wires exposed

— Oversized fuses or breakers

— Undersized wires for fuses or breakers

— Supplemental wires tapped into main lug

— Unlinked breakers

— System not grounded

— More than six hand movements needed to turn off all of the power at the panel(s)

NOTE: We stress the importance of accurate and detailed reporting because of the liability the home inspector has regarding the electrical system. If you miss reporting findings in the Don't Ever Miss list, you'll hear about it later in the form of a complaint call. The home inspector who misses these details in the inspection report will have to pay for electrical work later.

Develop Your Flow

Just like other systems in the inspection, develop a flow for inspecting panels. A good place to start is at the main wires where they enter the panel. This is due primarily to the need to determine the amperage and voltage rating of the service. Then compare the size of the wires to the rating of the panel and main disconnect. From there, scan down the center of the panel to inspect the breakers or fuses and compare them to wire sizes while looking for incompatibility issues and proper linking of 240-volt breakers. Next, inspect all of the wires as they travel through the box and around the busbars and overcurrent protection devices. Inspect the condition of the wires and their connections and observe where and how they enter the box.

After the previous steps are completed, it's a good idea to inspect the neutral busbar(s). Observe where the main neutral connects to the busbar and identify the grounding system. Don't forget to look for a method of bonding (connecting) the neutral busbar to the main panel box and a method for separating and isolating the neutrals from the grounds in subpanels. Finally, inspect the panel box for defects such as rust corrosion, open knockouts, and other items on the Don't Ever Miss list.

Consider leaving the panel open as you document your findings in the report. If there is an item or a component that you forgot to look at, having the panel open is a time-saving alternative to opening it up again. Take photos and insert them in your inspection report as needed.

5.8 INSPECTING BRANCH CIRCUIT WIRING

Branch circuit wiring (120 volts) runs from the main panel to the receptacles, fixtures, and devices in the house. While inspecting the branch circuit wiring, the home inspector will identify the type of conductor material (copper or aluminum) and the type of cabling or conduit carrying the wiring. The inspector compares branch wiring for compatibility of its amperage rating to fuses or breakers. The inspector is required to report any **solid conductor aluminum** branch circuit wiring that he or she observes. The branch circuit wiring inspection includes inspecting the following in the house, garage, and exterior:

> **Chapter Note**
>
> *Pages 355–367 present information on the study and inspection of branch circuit wiring.*

- Condition of the cable and the wires
- Proper size wiring for circuits
- Connections at the main panel
- Installation in unfinished areas
- Splices in the circuits
- Presence of handyman wiring

5.9 TYPES OF BRANCH WIRING

Before we get too far into the inspection process, it is important to note that home inspectors need to be somewhat color blind when inspecting wiring. The color of the wires **may** indicate the function of the wire, but only when the proper color was used for the application.

Black = hot
White = neutral
Bare = ground or bonding
Green = ground
Red = second hot on 240-volt circuits

> **Definitions**
>
> <u>Branch circuit wiring</u> is that portion of the electrical system that runs from the electrical panel to outlets, switches, and fixtures in the home. <u>Knob-and-tube wiring</u> is branch circuit wiring using ceramic knobs to secure wire to surfaces and tubes to pass wires through framing members.

A quality home inspector does not rely only on the color of the wire insulation to determine the function or purpose of a wire. He or she follows the wire to a connection. **What the wire is connected to determines its function, not the color.** Just a note about colors. Any color other than white or green should be considered live or energized by default!

In branch circuit wiring, the conductors or wires are typically copper, but the home inspector may find aluminum wiring in homes built in the 1960s to late 1970s. Wires are wrapped in insulation. Today, wires are installed in homes in non-metallic sheathed cable (commonly called Romex, which is a brand name of one manufacturer). A typical 15-amp household circuit today has an insulated hot wire, the insulated neutral wire, and an uninsulated ground wire sheathed in a single cable. Certain parts of the country do not allow the use of Romex. Electrical metallic tubing (EMT), better known as conduit is used. Flexible metal conduit or armored cable, better known as Greenfield and BX respectively (trade names), can also be used in those areas. Special circuit wiring for some 240-volt appliances will have four-wire cables—two hot wires, the neutral, and the ground wire. An example would be a new electric dryer. Older dryers would have only had three wires, not four as is required today.

CIRCUIT WIRING

- Knob-and-tube
- BX cable
- Romex cable
- Rigid conduit

The oldest type of wiring is **knob-and-tube wiring**, which was used through the 1920s to late 1940s. Ceramic knobs secured wire to structural surfaces; ceramic tubes passed wires through wood framing members such as floor joists and studs.

Knob-and-tube wiring used rubber and cloth insulation around the wiring. Only two wires were used—a hot and a neutral—and they were strung separately, not encased together in a cable. No ground wire was used, so receptacles used in knob-and-tube wiring have no grounding connection.

Photo #18
Typical knob and tube wiring with original splices.

Splices in knob and tube were made by twisting the wiring together, soldering the wires, and wrapping them in a rubber tape-like material. With modern wiring, connections must be made in closed junction boxes secured to a structural or framing component of the house.

After knob-and-tube wiring went out of style, a metal armored cable (a type of flexible conduit), such as BX cable was used. The wires were pulled through the conduit during installation.

When connected to a three-slot grounded receptacle, the armored cable served as the grounding conductor. The receptacle was bonded to a metal box, and the metal box was bonded to the metallic armored cable. This provided a continuous metallic path (continuity) back to the panel (source).

When MC cable (MC cable never served as the ground) is used, the NEC requires that a ground wire be included. Almost all modern houses today use non-metallic sheathed cable, or Romex. The exception is in the City of Chicago and some of its suburbs. Romex is a solid plastic sheathing that typically carries three conductors: hot, neutral, and ground for most household circuits. Most of the earliest versions of Romex (cloth covered) were two-conductor and didn't have the ground wire (just the hot and neutral).

Older Romex also came in two colors of plastic sheathing: gray and cream. The cream was used for indoor wiring; the gray, for outdoor applications. Determining the wire size for older Romex requires reading the label (molded into the sheathing) or determining individual wire size using a reference such as your bundled wires.

Modern Romex (since the early 2000s) is color-coded by size when used for indoor applications. Cream is 14 AWG copper, yellow is 12 AWG copper, and orange is 10 AWG copper. The gray color is still used for outdoor purposes and is not an indication of size.

This is where the inspector's selective color blindness comes into play. Depending on the age of the home, the color of the Romex sheathing **may** or **may not** indicate the size of the wire. Reading the visible labels or imprints on the wiring is the best clue.

Often, three conductors and a ground wire were carried to a kitchen to create a split receptacle with two 120-volt circuits at the same receptacle. This is called a **multi-wire circuit**. This was an old practice that made the top and bottom half of the receptacle on two different circuits with the neutral being shared. This circuit must be protected with a 240-volt breaker. Since the neutral is shared, if one circuit were to trip it must kill the other one too. This alleviates a safety issue on the other circuit. This way if two appliances (a blender and toaster, for example) were plugged into the same duplex receptacle, it would not trip the breaker because it is actually two separate circuits. The requirement for two 20-amp circuits is still the case, but the splitting of the receptacles is no longer a common practice due to the extra labor and material needed to run two sets of wiring around the room. The home inspector should identify the types of cabling found in the home. The inspector may find combinations of BX, Romex, and conduit due to upgrading of the electrical service.

Wiring Practices

The NEC has a list of rules governing the installation of branch circuit wiring. The following list covers many of the NEC requirements:

- **Bushings:** Where wires enter metal panels and boxes, there should be special bushings, grommets, or cable clamps to protect the wires from damage (chafing or skinning). The sharp edge of BX cable or the panel

NEC WIRING RULES

- Proper bushings
- Enclosed surface wiring
- Protected by passing through wood framing members
- Stapled at boxes and secured over distance
- Covered junction boxes for connections
- Power to every room and area
- No extension cord wiring
- Proper exterior cable
- GFCI/AFCI protection

box knockouts can cut through the wire insulation unless it is protected with an approved bushing.

- **Surface wiring:** Where wiring exists on the outer surface of a wall or ceiling, it should be encased in conduit to prevent physical damage. Surface wiring is most often seen in the basement and garage or outside at the eaves.

- **Wood framing members:** Wiring should be installed so that wires cannot be mechanically damaged. When wiring runs perpendicular to the floor joists, it should be run through holes drilled in the joists, not strung underneath the joists. Wiring parallel to a joist should be secured to the side of the joist and not attached on the underside of the joist. There are exceptions to this, but these are safe assumptions when inspecting.

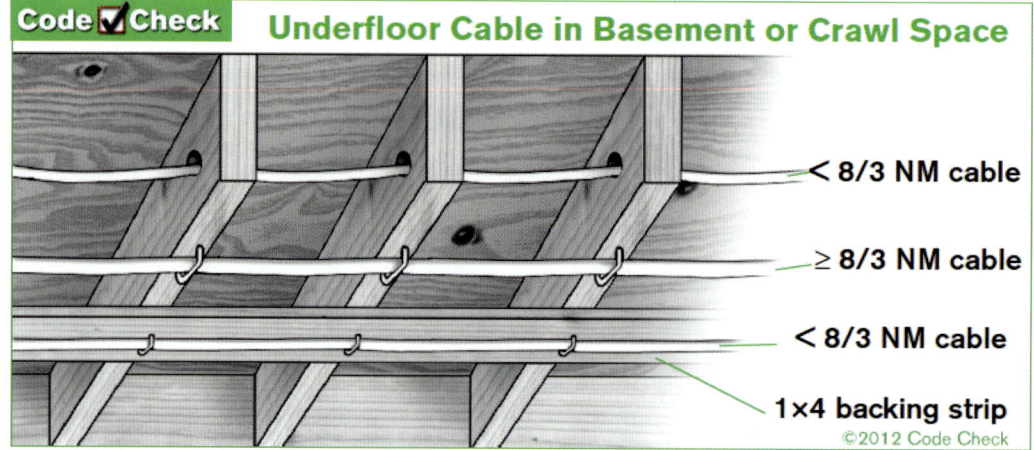

Chapter Note

Pages 355–367 don't cover all of the NEC required wiring practices. They don't discuss proper wiring for outlets, fixtures, and switches, which will be covered in pages 367–391. Also, refer to pages 364–367 for information on particular requirements for aluminum branch wiring.

Ideally, wiring should pass through ceiling joists in the attic, although the home inspector may see cable secured to the top of the joists, trusses, or rafters. Protection should be provided in the form of wood strips on either side of the cabling when:

1. The wires are within 6′ of a standard attic scuttlehole or access hatch.

2. The attic access is a permanent stair or ladder access and the wires are within 7′ of the top of the ceiling joists or the top of the bottom truss cords.

3. The wires run across the face (narrow dimension) of rafters, trusses or studs.

In some areas, it is a common if not acceptable practice to run the cables without protection. When this is observed, the home inspector should document how the wires are secured, look for damaged wiring throughout all accessible areas of the attic, and recommend that an electrician repair any damaged wires.

Holes should be drilled through wall studs, top plates, and bottom plates with the wires passed through the holes for protection.

Metal plates should be used at the outer edge of wall studs where protection is needed.

Wiring should be stapled to wood framing members or secured with hangers within 12″ on both sides of all enclosures—panels, junction boxes, and switches This is true around ceiling fixtures as well. Wiring (Romex) beyond the first secured point next to enclosures should be stapled at 12″ and stapled or secured every 4′6″ along the length of the circuit.

- **Covered junction boxes:** All connections made in the branch circuit wiring should be done properly and enclosed inside covered junction

Photo #19 METAL PLATES AT THE OUTER EDGE OF WALL STUDS

*You can see the wiring running through the studs on the right side. The nailing plates are used to prevent piercing the wiring, plumbing, or gas lines in the wall spaces.***ome**

Photo #20 SPLICES OUTSIDE OF JUNCTION BOXES

These are UL-approved splice connectors for 120v circuits that do NOT require a junction box. We will see how they perform over time.

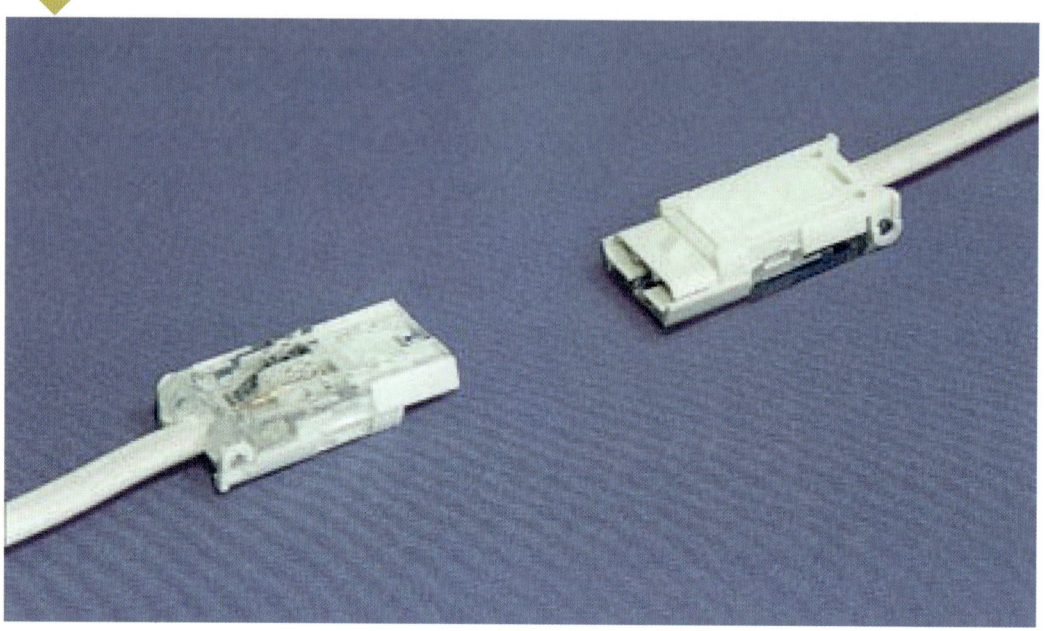

For Beginning Inspectors

Take time to observe the wiring in exposed areas in your home. Start in the basement at the main panel and observe the cable leaving the box. See if you can tell which cables go to which areas of the house. Are some basement circuits in conduit? Can you tell which circuits are dedicated to large appliances and the furnace? Notice how the wiring is secured at junction boxes, switches, and outlets. Can you find any practices of which the NEC would not approve?

boxes. (Note that this was not the practice with knob-and-tube wiring. See page 356.) Any abandoned wires must be terminated correctly in covered junction boxes as well. The junction box should be secured to a structural or framing component such as a wall stud or floor or ceiling joist. As is often the case, a new product violates what used to be the rule. You now can have splices outside junction boxes for 120-volt circuits if the proper connectors are used. Tyco is just one manufacturer that makes NM splice devices for Romex (no junction box required).

- **Power available in each room and area:** Every room or usable space in the home, including stairwells and basements, must have a power source. Crawl spaces and attics must have a power source only if mechanical equipment is present.

- **No extension cord wiring:** The NEC forbids the use of extension or lamp cords as permanent wiring. Extension cords should never be stapled to walls or floors or pass through walls, floors, or ceilings.

Their use is commonly seen in homes that don't have enough receptacles providing power. It's common to see extension cords set up in basements or garages where not enough receptacles are available.

- **Exterior cable:** Romex cable, type **Underground Feed (UF)**, is generally used underground. It should pass through conduit where it exits the ground (susceptible to physical damage) and is attached to the structure. The NEC requires cable traveling horizontally to be buried, not left on the surface, and to be protected by being buried 24″ or less if in concrete or conduit. Exterior connections require that splices be watertight and enclosed in proper covered junction boxes.

- **GFCI protection:** NEC updates from the late 1970s require the presence of GFCIs on all receptacles in the bathroom and kitchen, on exterior receptacles, garage receptacles, unfinished basements, and several other areas of the home. More information will be provided about receptacles, fixtures, and switches on pages 367 to 391.

Inspecting Knob-and-Tube Wiring

When the home inspector finds knob-and-tube wiring in a home, it should be recorded in the inspection report. The inspector should **always recommend that an electrician evaluate the wiring**, even if the inspector can't find obvious fault with it. This wiring is too old to accept as being reliable without a professional opinion. The NEC allows knob-and-tube wiring to remain in place while proper extensions to the service are made, although many electricians bypass it or remove it entirely. Generally, a home with this type of wiring will not have enough receptacles for modern living. Customers should be told that the wiring, even if in good condition now, will eventually have to be replaced. Just because you see it doesn't mean it's in use. Test for live wires. The opposite is true—just because the REALTOR said that the electrical wiring has been updated doesn't mean the knob and tube was disconnected or abandoned.

During the inspection of knob-and-tube branch circuit wiring, the home inspector should look for the following conditions:

- **Damaged or brittle covering:** The old rubber or cloth insulation (not really insulation) can be damaged over time in exposed areas. In the attic, squirrels and mice can chew away the insulation and leave the wires bare. The cloth covering can become brittle from years of overheating or poor connections. Old copper wire can become brittle too. **Knob and tube wires should not be buried under thermal insulation in the attic or walls per NEC and it's a safety issue.**

INSPECTING KNOB-AND-TUBE

- Damaged or brittle insulation
- Covered by thermal insulation
- Poor connections
- Amateur work
- Extension cord wiring
- Use of "grounded" outlets
- Two-fuse circuits

Personal Note

"One of my inspectors was in the attic of an old home with knob-and-tube wiring. The attic was insulated with old cellulose paper insulation. He actually saw sparks from the wiring falling into the insulation. He wanted to get out of there right away!

The inspector left a very prominent note for the owners, warning them of the extremely dangerous situation in the attic and telling them that an electrician must be called today. I'm not sure why anyone would ignore a warning like that, but a week later the home burned down. It's not unusual for the home inspector to discover safety hazards of this magnitude, but it is rare for people not to pay attention to them."

- **Poor connections:** As was discussed on page 356, any original connections in knob-and-tube wiring were made by twisting, soldering, and wrapping the wires in rubber tape. Check any visible connections for their condition. And look for recent extensions, upgrades, or repairs to the service. New connections should be made properly and encased in covered junction boxes. Some people believe that because the original connections weren't done in junction boxes, the new ones don't have to be either. Wrong!

  Connections can be especially poor at light fixtures. Many still require the use of a pull chain to switch them on and off. After years of pulling, the wires can come loose. We suggest to customers that these fixtures be replaced. These are still found in attics, basements, and closets, which is why a plastic spacer or a string on the chain insulates the chain from the user if there happens to be an issue.

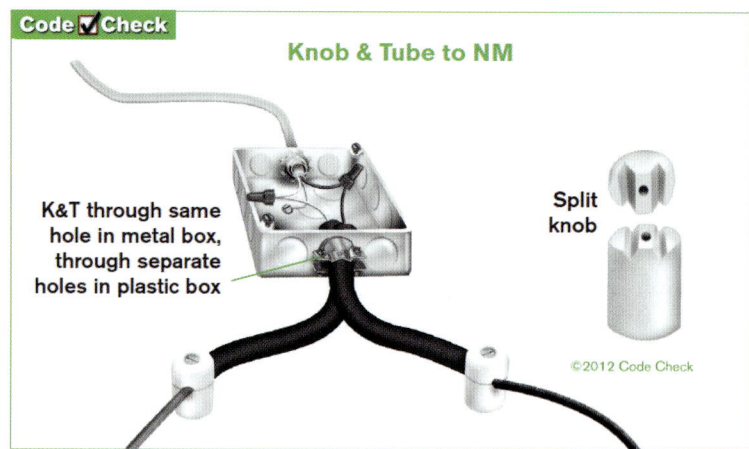

- **Amateur work:** A home with knob-and-tube wiring is rarely adequate for the needs of today's families. At some time, someone will have extended the service in some way. Be on the lookout for improper extensions to the service.

- **Use of "grounded" receptacles:** The NEC prohibits the use of three-slot (grounded) receptacles when they aren't connected to the grounding conductor. And in knob-and-tube wiring, the switches, fixtures, and receptacles are not grounded unless a separate ground wire was installed for each circuit during an upgrade to the service, which is not likely.

- **Two-fuse circuits:** The home inspector may find two fuses on a single circuit, where both the hot wire and the neutral wire are fused at the main panel. If the neutral fuse blows, the circuit (device) won't work, but the hot wire remains live with current. This is a **safety hazard**.

Inspecting Modern Wiring

When inspecting branch circuit wiring, the home inspector should pay attention to its source at the main panel and then observe all visible wiring in exposed areas in the basement, crawl space, garage, attic, and exterior of the home. Watch for the following conditions:

> **INSPECTING BRANCH CIRCUIT WIRING**
>
> - Undersized wiring
> - Improper installation, loose or drooping wires
> - Damaged or worn wires and insulation
> - Uncovered or missing junction boxes
> - Handyman wiring
> - Extension cord wiring

- **Undersized wiring:** Always check that wiring is the appropriate gauge for the amperage of the fuse or breaker.

- **Improper installation, loose or drooping wiring:** As you trace wiring in exposed areas such as the basement, attic, or crawl space, note whether proper installation requirements are met. Note any wires (less than #8 NM cable) stapled to the underside of joists, fixtures, and boxes that are not securely attached on both sides, droops in long runs of cable, and the lack of conduit on surface wiring.

- **Damaged or worn wires and insulation:** Note where wires have been nicked, reducing their ability to carry current and causing overheating. Watch for any evidence of overheating and melted insulation. Report areas where rodents have nibbled on insulation, causing exposed wires. BX cable can become corroded and worn. This should be reported. On the exterior, report any frayed, brittle, or worn insulation.

- **Uncovered or missing junction boxes:** Report any unprotected traditional wire-nut type splices in the circuit as a **safety hazard**. Splices should be properly executed and then enclosed in covered junction boxes. Uncovered boxes are also a safety hazard and should be reported as such. Be sure to inspect the junction boxes in the basement, attic, crawl space, and garage for missing covers and exposed wires.

- **Handyman wiring:** Look for any amateur work in the branch circuit wiring. If the main panel looks like a spaghetti dinner, a warning alarm should sound. Unsafe practices at the main panel can signal more amateur work on the circuits. Handymen can do so many inventive things that it's hard to list them all. Just be sure to watch for anything unusual and to report any amateur wiring you find.

   This doesn't mean, however, that when the panel is in such disarray that the home inspector can simply recommend an electrician because the panel looks bad. Recommending an electrician will usually get the home inspector off the hook for risk, but that falls short of the requirement that the inspector report the deficiencies in the electrical system.

- **Extension cord wiring:** The home inspector often finds the use of extension cords as permanent wiring. This is most common in basement and garage workplaces, but it can be seen in the house as well. Point this out to your customer and suggest that these extension cords be removed. If more circuits or receptacles are needed, an electrician should be called to do a professional job.

> **#1 RULE FOR ALUMINUM WIRING**
>
> *<u>Always</u> recommend an electrician be called to evaluate aluminum branch circuit wiring.*

> **Personal Note**
>
> *"One of my inspectors found a ceiling junction box with a loose cover in the basement. Thinking he'd be helpful, he started to screw the cover down tight. However, the box was not securely attached, and the box and wiring started to fall. He instinctively reached out to catch the falling box—with the screwdriver! The screwdriver connected with the current and delivered a good shock, throwing him about 5' backward.*
>
> *Don't do any electrical work during the inspection. Even the smallest and most helpful gestures can hurt you or damage equipment. It's much safer to point out the problem and leave it at that."*

Aluminum Wiring

Beginning in about 1965 and continuing through the late 1970s, aluminum was often used in branch circuit wiring as a replacement for scarce and expensive copper due to the ongoing Vietnam War. However, serious fires were reported as a result. "A national survey conducted by Franklin Research Institute for CPSC showed that homes built before 1972, and wired with aluminum, are 55 times more likely to have one or more wire connections at outlets reach 'Fire Hazard Conditions' than homes wired with copper."

Problems occur where small-gauge (#14 and #12 AWG) solid aluminum is used in 120-volt circuits (**stranded aluminum in larger gauges is considered safe and is still installed in new construction**). The solid aluminum wires tend to expand/contract and move out from under traditional terminal screws and can corrode at the connections. Both of these conditions create poor connections and serious overheating problems at receptacles, switches, and appliances.

A house with aluminum branch circuit wiring can be made **safer** by fixing **every** connection to or splicing between aluminum wiring in the home. The home inspector will find the following methods used to remedy the problem:

- **COPALUM (copper-aluminum) crimp connectors:** The recommended method of repairing an aluminum-wired home is to bond copper wire to the aluminum wire at each receptacle, switch, and junction. Here, a copper wire is attached to the existing aluminum branch wiring with a specially-designed metal sleeve and a powered crimping tool. The copper wire is then connected to the receptacle or switch.

- **AlumiConn connectors:** Based on an evaluation that was, in part, CPSC-supported, consumers are advised that if the COPALUM repair is not available, the UL-approved AlumiConn connector may be considered the next best alternative for a permanent repair. This repair involves pigtailing using a set screw-type connector instead of the COPALUM crimp connector used in the repaired connections.

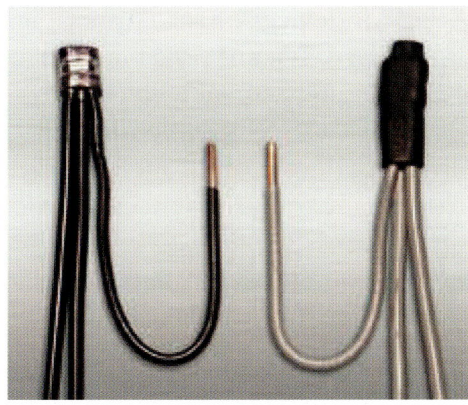

Photo #21 COPALUM CRIMP CONNECTORS

The COPALUM crimp is one of the approved splice connectors for solid core aluminum branch circuit wiring for 120v circuits. This method must be installed by an approved electrician. Consult the www.CPSC.gov website for possible other approved methods.

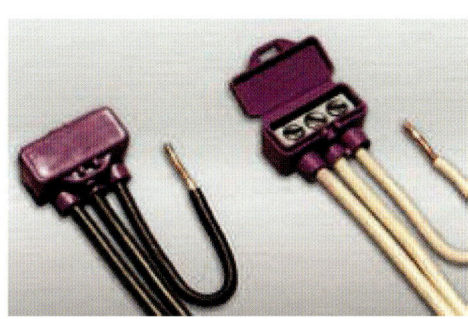

Photo #22 ALUMICONN CONNECTORS

The AlumiConn connector is another UL listed and readily available method for splicing solid core aluminum wiring. They are available at your local Home Improvement Store.

- **CO/ALR (copper-aluminum revised) switches and receptacles:** Another repair method is to replace all switches and receptacles in the home with those labeled CO/ALR, which are designed to work better and safer with aluminum branch circuit wiring. This repair may be less than satisfactory because specialty connectors are not available for all parts of the electrical system—for example, ceiling fixtures and permanently wired appliances. Therefore, only part of the problem may be fixed. "In the opinion of CPSC staff, CO/ALR devices must be considered, at best, an incomplete repair." Identifying them is rare, however, because the label is usually not visible.

- **Copper pigtailing:** Electricians will sometimes attach copper wires between the aluminum branch wiring and receptacles and switches using a method called pigtailing. This is a connection made by twisting the wires together and covering them with a twist-on connector (wire nut). This method is not considered acceptable and is not as good as the COPALUM crimp or AlumiConn methods; the feeling is that the pigtailing can fail just as easily as the original aluminum connection. "It is possible that some pigtailing 'repairs' made with twist-on connectors may be prone to even more failures than the original aluminum wire connectors. Accordingly, CPSC staff believes that this method of repair does not solve the problem of overheating present in aluminum-wired branch circuits."

When the home inspector finds aluminum branch circuit wiring, he or she should recommend that an electrician evaluate the wiring. The inspector may

> **For Beginning Inspectors**
>
> *If you have friends living in homes built from the mid-1960s to the mid-1970s, stop in to examine the electrical service. Start at the main panel and note whether aluminum branch circuit wiring was used. Trace some 120-volt circuits. Feel switches and outlets on these circuits for heat. In exposed areas, see if you can find evidence of copper pigtailing, the use of COPALUM connections, and/or outlets/switches labeled CO/ALR.*

find the presence of CU/AL devices or see copper pigtailing repairs to such a service. It's not possible for the home inspector to judge the safety of such electrical service, and it's not a good idea to lead the customer to believe that the condition of aluminum branch circuit is safe when it might not be. The consequences are too severe.

Follow these steps when you find aluminum branch wiring in a home:

1. Always be sure to **report** the presence of aluminum branch circuit wiring in your inspection report.

2. Explain the history of aluminum wiring to the customer and explain why it may be a safety hazard. Inform the customer that repairs may have been made to the wiring but that you can't determine if all connections have been repaired or if repairs have been made properly.

3. Recommend that an electrician be called to evaluate the wiring completely and note this recommendation in the inspection report.

Reporting Your Findings

Branch circuit wiring should be inspected where it is visible—on the exterior, in the garage, in the basement, crawl space, and in the attic. Depending on the design of your inspection report, you may be reporting your findings on an electrical page or on separate pages for exteriors, garages, attics, and so on. In any case, you want to include those items listed in the Don't Ever Miss list.

> **DON'T EVER MISS**
>
> - Knob-and-tube wiring
> - Aluminum branch circuit wiring
> - Damaged, worn, or overheated wires and insulation
> - Undersized wiring
> - Improper installation
> - Uncovered or missing junction boxes
> - Handyman wiring
> - Extension cord wiring

- **Branch wiring:** Identify the type of branch circuit wiring found in the home (copper or aluminum) and the type of cabling found (knob-and-tube, BX, Romex, etc.). Report on as many types as you find. For example, a home may have old knob-and-tube wiring with upgrades using Romex cable. Note any damage, problems, and improper installation such as drooping wires in the basement.

- **Junction boxes:** Report any deficiencies in visible junction boxes that you find, especially if they're uncovered, not secured, or missing.

- **Recommending an electrician:** The conditions below are cause for recommending that your customer have an electrician evaluate the situation. Again, be sure to note this recommendation in your inspection report.

- Knob-and-tube wiring
- Aluminum branch circuit wiring
- Wiring overheated, burned, damaged
- Handyman wiring

• **Safety hazards:** The hazards listed below can be reported in the inspection report and then summarized on a summary page if your report has one. Make sure customers understand what you're telling them about safety hazards. Show them where you've indicated the hazards in the report.

- Undersized wires for circuit
- Uncovered junction boxes with exposed wires
- Wiring overheated, burned, damaged
- Extension cord or handyman wiring

Exposed Romex or other wires in livable spaces (i.e., Romex running through a kitchen cabinet) are susceptible to physical damage.

5.10 INSPECTING FIXTURES, SWITCHES, AND RECEPTACLES

Most standards of practice state the following requirements for the inspection of switches, fixtures, and receptacles inside and on the exterior of the home. Let's start with proper terminology. A receptacle and an outlet are not the same thing. They are often used interchangeably, but they are different components. An outlet is simply the junction box. The receptacle is installed in the junction box, and an appliance is plugged into a receptacle.

> **Chapter Note**
>
> *Pages 367–391 present information about the inspection of electrical fixtures, switches, and outlets.*

- The inspector is required to observe **polarity and grounding** of all tested receptacles in the inspected structures.

- The inspector should **operate all accessible installed lighting fixtures, switches, and receptacles** located in the house, garage, and exterior.

- The inspector is required to **operate all GFCIs**.

- The inspector is required to **operate all AFCIs in vacant homes**.

In general, this part of the inspection is to determine if power is available to each area of the property, if there are enough receptacles in each area, if lighting is provided in each area and switches work, if receptacles are properly wired and

INSPECTING FIXTURES AND SWITCHES

- Absence of lighting in any area
- Old and missing fixtures
- Switches and fixtures that don't work
- Warm, scorched, loose, damaged, or missing cover plates
- Unsafe practices
- Recessed lights covered by insulation

grounded, and if AFCIs and GFCIs are present where required when the home was originally constructed and operable to protect people in those areas.

Lighting Fixtures and Switches

The NEC provides requirements for lighting fixtures and switches throughout the home, including the following:

- **Adequate amount:** The NEC requires at least one wall-switch-controlled lighting fixture in all rooms; hallways; stairways; utility rooms; basements, crawl spaces, attics that are used for storage or that house mechanical equipment; and garages and at outdoor entrances. Stairways with six or more risers should be switched at both the bottom and top and require three-way switches.

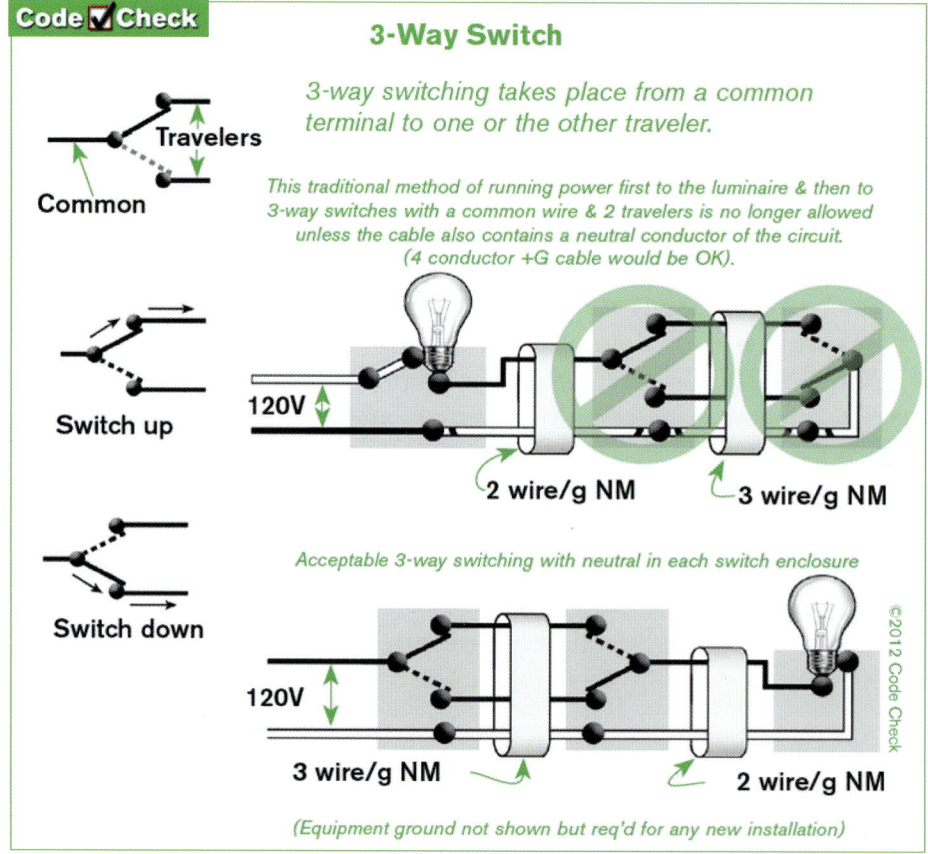

- **Location:** Light switches should be located about 48" from the floor, with switches typically lower in retirement homes (for wheel chair accessibility). Switches for fixtures in the **bathroom** should not be within the plane of the tub or shower areas. Ceiling heat lamps in bathrooms should be beyond the swing of the door. Lighting fixtures in closets should have proper clearances and should not be within 12" of the front edge of closet shelves. A recessed closet light should have a clearance of at least

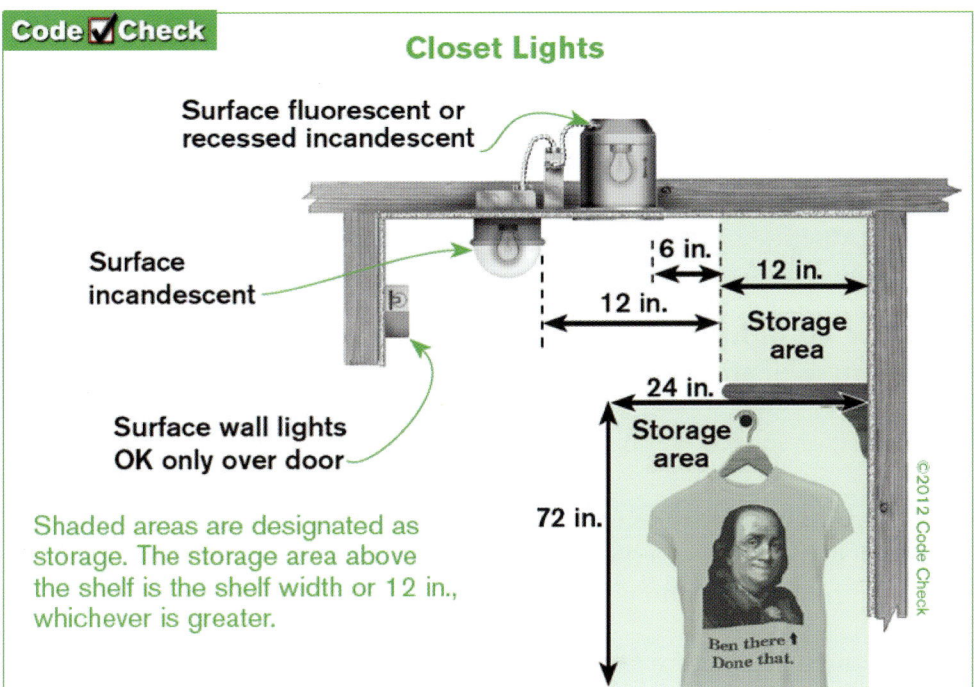

6″ from shelves. In the mid-1990s, NEC rulings banned the use of bare lightbulbs in closets, requiring instead that fully enclosed fixtures be used. Surface-mounted incandescent bulbs should be used only on the wall or ceiling above the door. LED or fluorescent bulbs are a better choice for all applications as they are more efficient and operate much cooler than incandescent bulbs.

- **Safety concerns:** Fixtures in showers and tubs should be listed for damp or wet locations if they are subject to shower spray.

Exterior fixtures also should be properly listed for damp or wet locations.

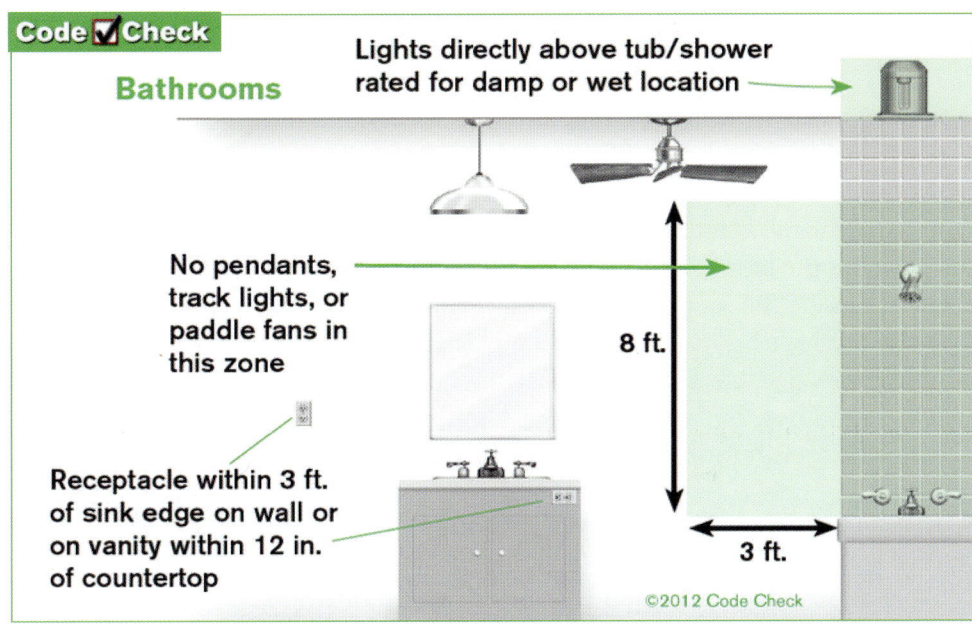

THE ELECTRICAL INSPECTION

These are the steps the home inspector should follow when inspecting lighting fixtures and switches:

1. Check for the **presence** of a wall switch and lighting fixture or connected wall receptacle in each room, hallway, stairwell, attic (only if mechanical equipment is present), basement, crawl space (only if mechanical equipment is present), and garage and at outdoor entrances. Report the absence of lighting in any of these areas.

2. **Operate all lighting switches** and/or dimmers on the interior and exterior to see if they work.

The home inspector should be on the lookout for the following deficiencies:

- **Old or missing fixtures:** The home inspector should recommend that old porcelain light fixtures used with knob-and-tube wiring be replaced. The old cloth and rubber insulation on these fixtures is likely to be brittle and frayed.

    Note if any fixtures have been removed and the wires were not properly terminated and covered.

- **Switches and fixtures that don't work:** For a few decades, the NEC has required that each interior room be equipped with at least one switched receptacle or overhead light. When lights don't go on, it may be that there is no fixture (table lamp) plugged into the corresponding receptacle, a burned out bulb, or a blown fuse. This can be verified when testing receptacles around the room. When you run across one that is dead, flip the switch and see if it becomes energized. It is/was a common practice for electricians to install the receptacle operated by the wall switch in the upside-down orientation (ground hole up) compared with the rest of the receptacles (ground hole down). This way the homeowner can tell which receptacle is operated by the wall switch without having to test every one first. If multiple bulbs are burned out, you should recommend to your client that before taking possession of the house, he or she should have new bulbs installed to verify proper operation of the fixture(s).

    Unresponsive light switches could also indicate a number of other conditions—defective wiring on the circuit or in the switch or fixture, a defective switch mechanism, or poor connections. Whenever the inspector encounters a built-in light fixture with no bulb(s), it is a good idea to use the AC detector to check for power at the fixture's lightbulb socket by turning the switch on and pointing the tester inside the socket. Never assume that the bulb burned out and the homeowner hasn't gotten around to replacing it yet. This testing method is a common practice, but a **bad idea**. If the neutral is not connected the socket will still read hot, but when you put a bulb in it won't work. Just note the absence of a bulb in the fixture and state that it was not tested.

    The home inspector is required to report only that the switch and/or fixture is not working. But if lights flicker or buzz, the cause of the problem is likely a loose connection, a worn-out switch, or improper installation, which can become a shock or fire hazard. The customer should be advised to call an electrician to check and repair the circuit.

- **Overheating at the cover plates:** When you flip on each switch, notice if there is evidence such as heat, scorches, or signs of burning on the wall plate. To be certain, use an infrared thermometer and compare the temperature of the cover plate to others in the house that did not feel warm to the touch. If the suspected switch or cover plate is significantly warmer than others in the house, a problem needs to be corrected. Excessive heat at cover plates should be reported as a **safety hazard** and an electrician recommended to evaluate the problem and make necessary repairs. Keeping in mind of course that dimmers run hotter than standard switches and this is not typically a problem.

Report any **loose, damaged, or missing** cover plates, which might allow a person to come in contact with live electrical wires. A relatively new requirement, 2008 NEC, is the use of tamper-resistant receptacles. These receptacles have spring-loaded shutters that close off the contact openings, or slots, of the receptacles. When a plug is inserted in the receptacle, both springs are compressed and the shutters then open, allowing for the metal prongs to make contact to create an electrical circuit. Because both springs must be compressed at the same time, the shutters do not open when a child attempts to insert an object, such as a paper clip or key, into only one contact opening, and there is no contact with electricity.

Photo #23 *Tamper-resistant receptacles are now required throughout the home.*

- **Unsafe practices:** Report light switches that are within tubs and showers, closet lights that are too close to shelving (less than 12″), bare light bulbs in closets, exterior fixtures that aren't the proper type, and any other unsafe practices you may find.

- **Non-IC lights covered by insulation:** Whenever you find recessed ceiling lights in the top floor of the house, make a note to check it when you get to the attic to see if there is proper clearance around that light. If you don't remind yourself, you may miss lights that are covered with insulation. Tell the customer that he or she or the homeowner should remove the insulation around the fixture or remove the bulb to see if the light should have clearance or if it is rated for an insulated ceiling. The home inspector does not have to dig around or remove bulbs from recessed lights. Simply report that the lights are covered with insulation and that it is a **safety hazard** unless properly rated. The

INSPECTION ORDER

- Exterior service entrance, fixtures, outlets
- Garage wiring and outlets
- Interior power sources, fixtures, outlets
- Attic branch circuit wiring
- Basement main panels, subpanels, branch circuit wiring, outlets

easiest way to check is to remove the bulb and read the sticker on the inside to see if it is an IC or non-IC type.

When non-insulation contact (non-IC) recessed ceiling light fixtures are present on the top floor of the house, they should not be covered with insulation in the attic. A 3″ clearance is required between recessed lights (non-IC) and attic insulation. IC and IC-AT (airtight) lights can be covered with insulation.

Photo #24 *This is an IC-AT recessed light fixture. These are the current energy efficient fixtures used to reduce air leakage to the attic and can be completely buried in insulation.*

NOTE: The home inspector may find unusually shaped rectangular or oval switches for the lighting system. This may be an indication of the presence of a low voltage lighting system. As discussed earlier, this type of lighting system was popular in the 1950s. It used 12- or 24-volt wiring instead of 120-volts, boxes of relays, and one or more switching panels that controlled all the lights in the house. The home inspector should check the presence of light sources in each area and see if the switches work, but he or she does not have to otherwise inspect the system.

WHICH IS WHICH?

These phrases may help you remember outlet wiring:

- Hot—black to brass to the small slot
- Neutral—white to silver to the large slot

Electrical Receptacles

Most receptacles have brass screws on one side to which the live wire (black) is connected. The other side has silver-colored screws to which the neutral (white) wire is connected (these are for CU wire only). These two wires provide a 120-volt circuit to the receptacles. If the receptacle is grounded, the ground wire is connected to a green screw toward the end of the receptacle. If the receptacle has silver screws on both sides, it is a CO/ALR-type receptacle designed for aluminum wiring as discussed previously. If you happen to see them, aluminum wiring is probably in the house as the CO/ALR receptacles are much more expensive than standard ones.

Until the 1960s, most electrical receptacles were **ungrounded**. They had only two slots in them for appliance plugs with two prongs. Some of them were **polarized**—that is, they had a larger neutral slot and a smaller hot slot for polarized appliances with large and small receptacle prongs that could be plugged in correctly. The older types of ungrounded receptacles had slots of the same size, so polarity can't be determined.

Two-slot receptacle junction boxes are not grounded (no ground wire, conduit, or armored cable, a continuous metallic path back to the panel). When these old ungrounded receptacles are replaced, three-slot (grounded) receptacles are typically used (they're cheaper and more readily available). That poses a problem because they are most likely lacking a ground wire. Without testing it, the home inspector cannot tell if a replacement three-prong receptacle is grounded (a little known fact about ungrounded circuits). One of the few code requirements that is not grandfathered due to an original installation exception is the replacement of ungrounded receptacles. If the ungrounded receptacle is located where a GFCI is currently required, it must be upgraded to a GFCI receptacle when it is replaced. You cannot even replace it with another ungrounded receptacle like the one it came with. In most cases, components can be replaced like for like in old houses. That is not the case with ungrounded receptacles.

Beginning in the 1960s, most receptacles were grounded. A ground wire (equipment grounding conductor) provides an alternate path for electricity if something goes wrong with the neutral wire to the receptacle, fixture, or appliance. In actuality, it does not lead directly to the earth, as only the main ground wire out of the main panel goes there. Individual circuit grounds lead back to the neutral busbar in the panel. As a result, any live, unwanted, or stray current is channeled to the grounding system rather than the person touching the receptacle or appliance.

Each modern receptacle has three slots—the large is the neutral, the small is hot, and a little round one for ground. The three-slot grounded receptacles are of value only where appliances with three-prong plugs are used. Appliances such as refrigerators, washers and dryers, microwaves, computers, and power tools are examples. A two-prong plug does not connect to the grounding slot. The reason for this is that the actual name for the ground wire is the equipment grounding conductor. So if the appliance needs it, there are three prongs; if not, there are two prongs.

Another kind of receptacle used today is the split receptacle, also known as a multi-wire circuit. This type of receptacle has two complete 120-volt circuits in a

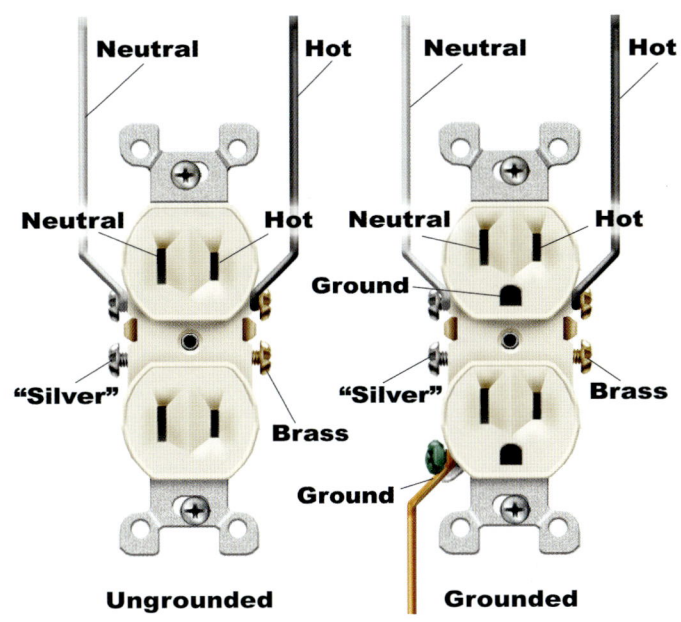

Illustration by Paddy Morrissey

Definitions

A <u>grounded outlet</u> is wired with a ground wire that is connected to the grounding system. A <u>split outlet</u> is wired with two hot wires and one neutral to provide two separate circuits to the outlet in addition to the ground wire for grounding purposes. A <u>GFCI outlet</u> has a monitoring device installed that will trip the circuit when a ground fault is detected. GFCI stands for ground-fault circuit interruptor.

GFCI REQUIREMENTS

- On all outlets within 6' of water
- On garage outlets
- On exterior outlets

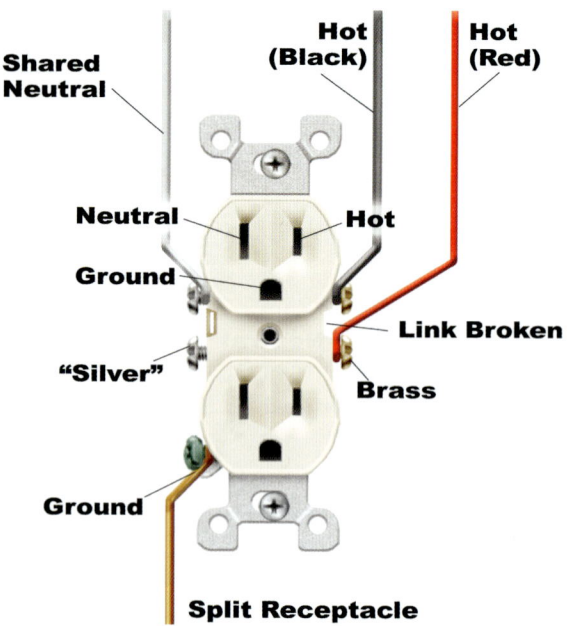

Illustration by Paddy Morrissey

single receptacle. Such receptacles were once common in kitchens where more power was needed, as described earlier.

Another type of receptacle is the **GFCI receptacle**. The GFCI, or ground-fault circuit interrupter, is a monitoring device that compares the amperage of the current flowing to and from the receptacle. A leak (electricity escaping the intended circuit) at the appliance or receptacle is detected and the GFCI will trip about 1/10th second after a ground fault of only 0.005 amps, interrupting the flow of electricity at the circuit. The leak is usually too small to blow a standard 15- or 20-amp fuse or trip a breaker.

A GFCI receptacle protects all downstream receptacles on the same circuit. When the GFCI trips, power is interrupted to all downstream (daisy-chained or linked) receptacles as well. Many GFCI receptacles are designed to be installed with the ground slot facing up. This

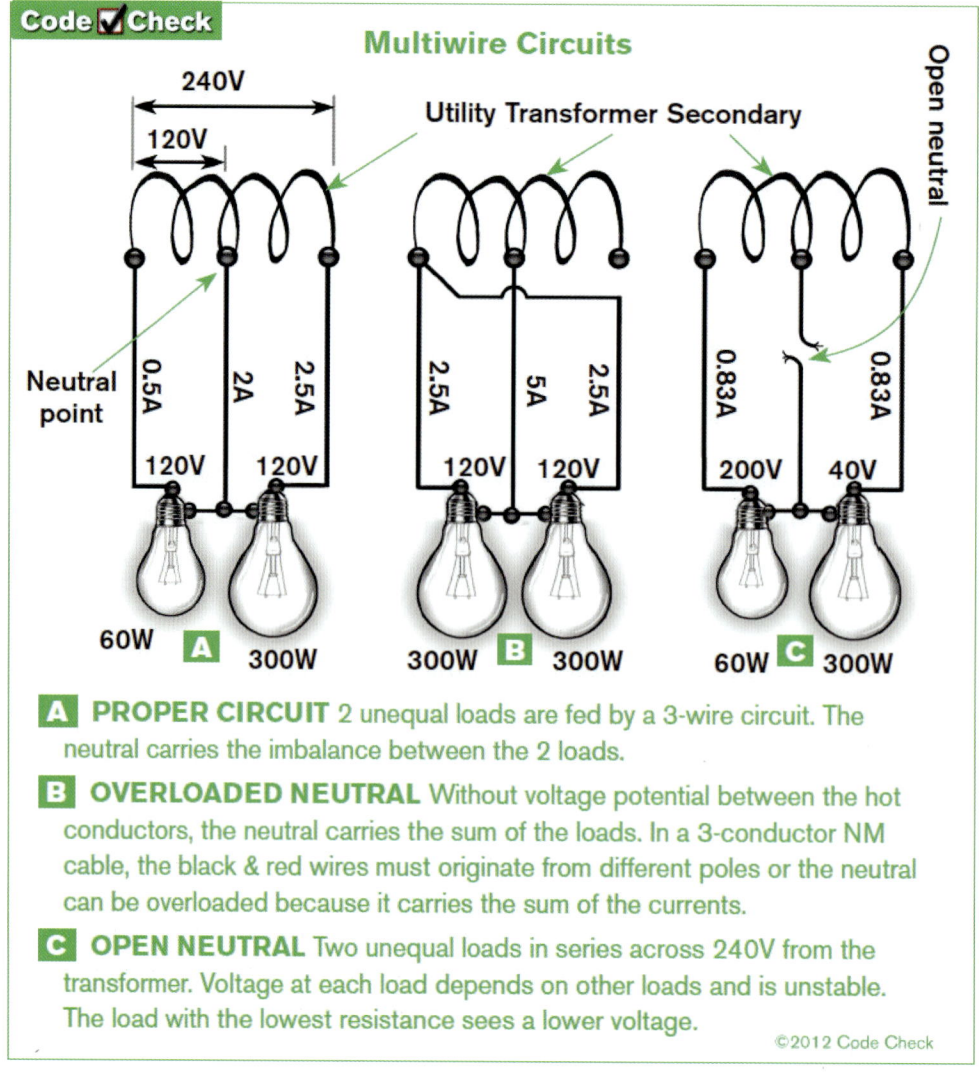

prevents any thin, long metallic objects such as kitchen knives and hairpins from falling onto a partially plugged in appliance's hot and neutral prongs and causing a shock. Do not report this "right or wrong" orientation as a defect.

NOTE: GFCI receptacles are often added to ungrounded circuits in wet locations to provide added protection, and the NEC actually requires this as described above. The receptacle and all linked receptacles on the same circuit should be labeled "No Equipment Ground"; however, the decal stating this is not usually placed on the cover plate.

GFCIs should be tested monthly to make sure they're still in working condition. When the test button on the GFCI is pushed, the reset button should pop out, indicating that the GFCI is working. At this point, the power is interrupted to the receptacle. Power is reinstated by pushing the reset button back in. The same is true for GFCI breakers in the main panels or subpanels. Push the test button, which will cause the breaker to trip. Reset the breaker lever to restore power to the circuit.

The inspector should use a three-pronged GFCI tester in addition to the manual test button on the receptacle or breaker. Use of the tester will tell the inspector if there is proper polarity, grounding, and line and load configuration and whether the power has been properly interrupted by the GFCI.

NOTE: Appliances that could be damaged or cause unreasonable inconvenience if power is lost should not be plugged into GFCI receptacles. GFCIs don't do well on circuits for older motor-driven appliances because they can accidentally trip due to motor surges. These motors tend to trip GFCIs on start-up. A good example is a freezer in the garage. The motor in the compressor of the freezer can easily trip a GFCI, causing the freezer and its contents to thaw and spoil. In addition, computers, security systems, and other large appliances shouldn't be plugged into GFCI protected circuits. This too is changing with the new GFCI technology and requirements. Many appliances are being manufactured to allow for the connection to GFCI-protected circuits even when they have an electric motor. Some of the largest sump pump manufacturers are now requiring that their 120-volt cord and plug–connected pumps be on GFCI-protected circuits. Other requirements include GFCI protection for laundry areas and for dishwashers whether cord and plug–connected or hard-wired.

Regardless of the type of receptacle, improperly wiring the neutral wire to the hot screw and the hot wire to the neutral screw results in reversed polarity. When reversed polarity is encountered, it should be documented as a safety hazard and repairs should be recommended.

In addition, at three-pronged receptacles, when the ground wire is not connected to the receptacle ground screw or there is no ground wire as in an older home, it is called an **open ground**. Reporting requirements are the same as with reversed polarity. Remember, open ground is a condition and ungrounded is a thing. If you take an ungrounded receptacle and install a grounded receptacle in its place, you create a condition called open ground, which is a potential safety issue, whether near water or not.

> **RECEPTACLE LOCATIONS**
> - Every room, basement, garage
> - Every 12' along interior walls and 12" above floor
> - Present in hallways longer than 10'
> - Every 4' along kitchen countertops
> - At least 3' from tub or shower

Be careful, however, not to rely fully on the tester, as there is a commonly used method to make an ungrounded receptacle appear grounded. Without taking the receptacle apart or investing in expensive testing equipment, the inspector has no way to confirm the missing ground. The homeowner's trick is to connect a jumper wire from a neutral screw to the ground screw on the receptacle, giving the appearance (to testing equipment) of an alternate path back to the panel, commonly known as a bootleg ground. Most testers do not test for a true alternate path, just that there is a path back to the source (panel) through the ground slot at the receptacle. There is one exception as a device is available for $300–$400, which will identify this type of false or bootleg ground.

Determining the potential presence of the jumper wire is possible through simple observation. When inspecting an older home, look for evidence of circuit grounds throughout the electrical inspection, specifically at the main panel. If no evidence is found of individual circuit grounds and one or more three-pronged receptacles test correct for a ground, document the evidence (or lack thereof) and recommend that an electrician be called to do more technically exhaustive testing to confirm whether the circuits are in fact grounded.

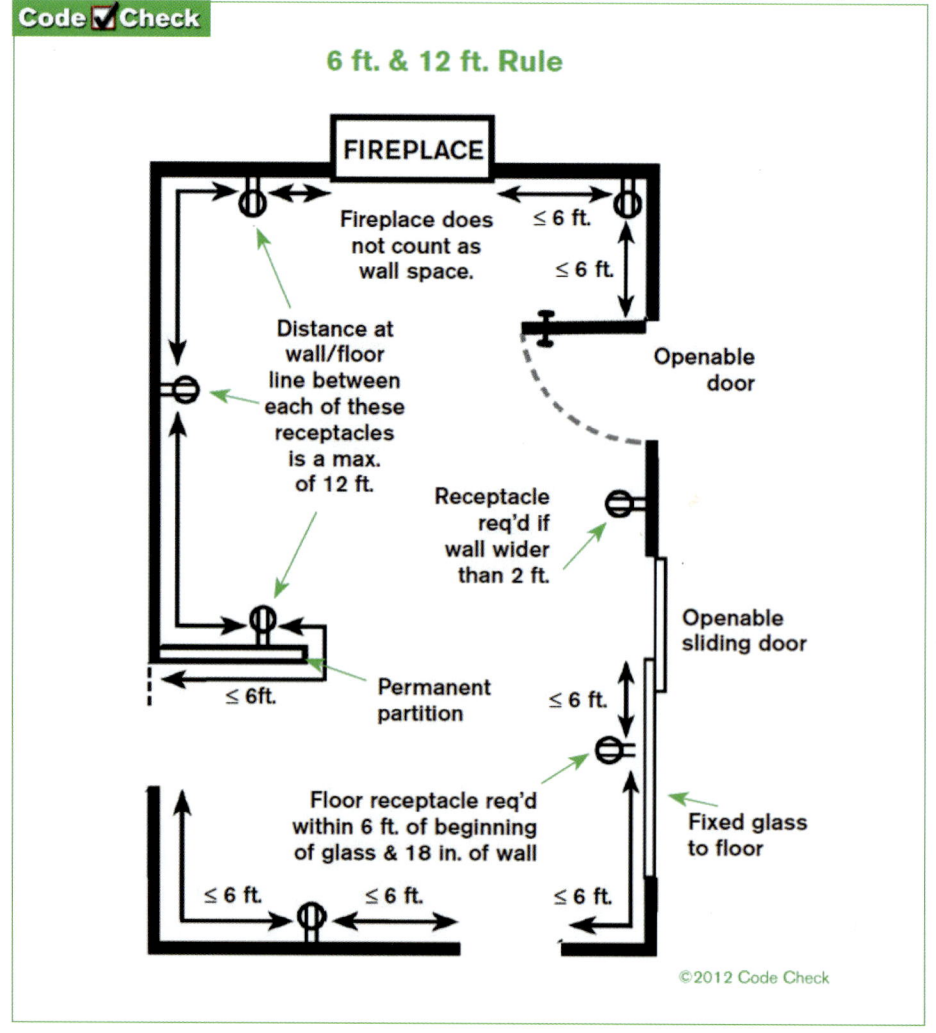

Receptacle Requirements

The NEC requirements for electrical receptacles throughout the home include the following:

- **Grounding:** Today, all new construction requires grounded receptacles. For older homes, the NEC prohibits the use of three-slot receptacles when there is no grounding system. The exception is when you have an ungrounded receptacle in a location that currently requires a GFCI, as explained previously. Recommend that a licensed electrician be consulted to determine the safest method for providing the home with the desired grounded receptacles.

  Location: Receptacles are required every 12′ along interior walls and in hallways that are 10′ or longer. Walls that are at least 2′ feet wide require a receptacle. Wall receptacles are generally set 12″ from the floor, but they should not be present over electrical baseboard heating units. They should be part of the heater itself if one is present.

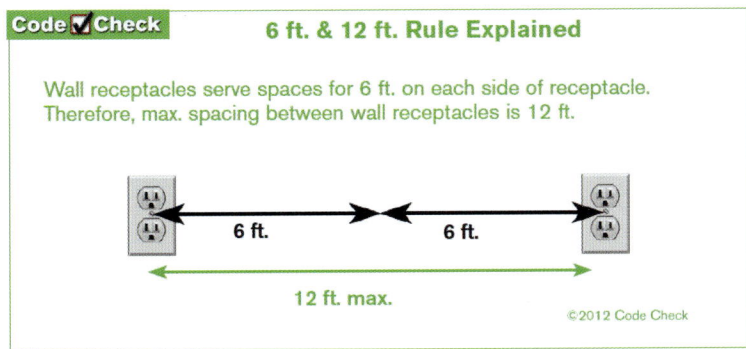

Kitchen countertop receptacles should be spaced no more than 4′ apart. Kitchen receptacles should not be installed flush within (face up) the countertops.

A bathroom receptacle must be near the sink but no more than 3′ from each basin. As in the kitchen, bathroom receptacles should not be installed flush within (face up) the countertops.

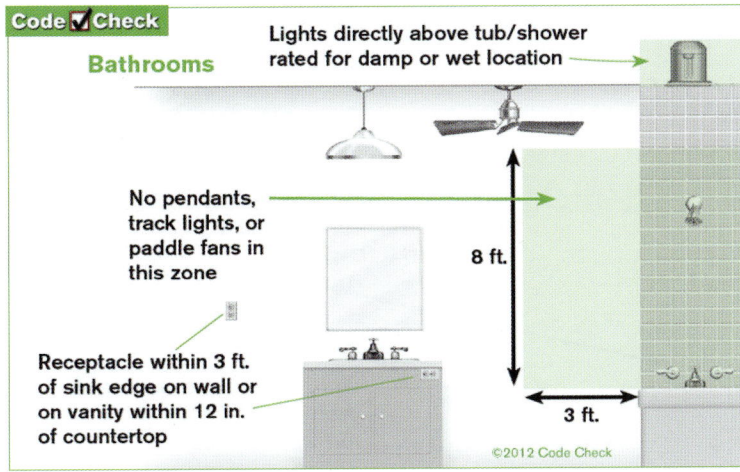

THE ELECTRICAL INSPECTION

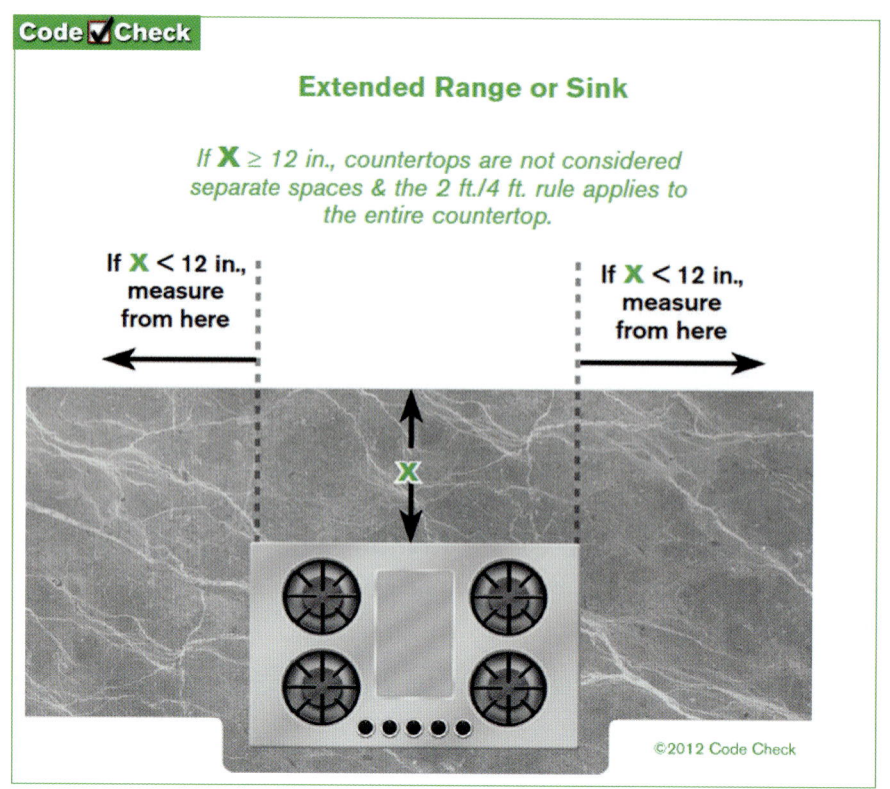

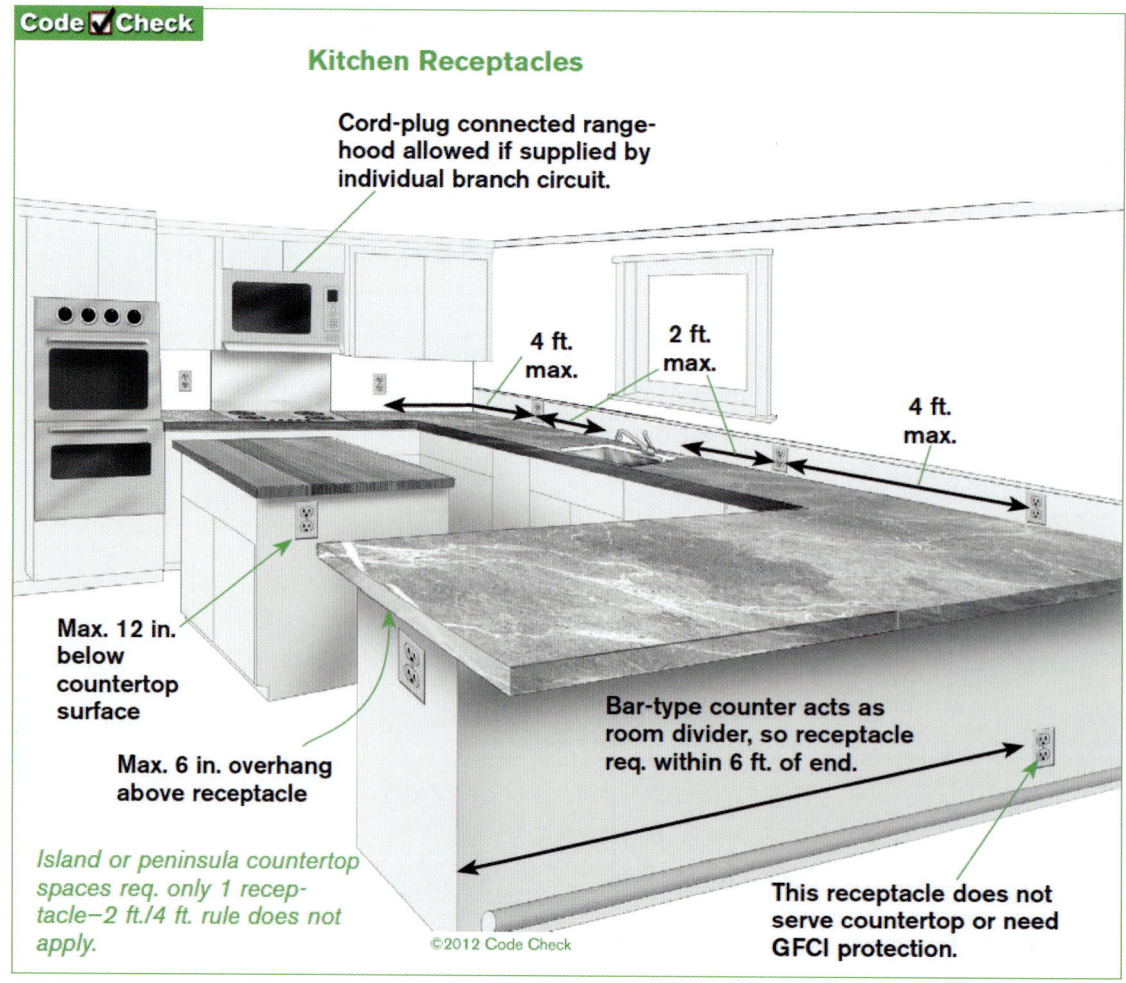

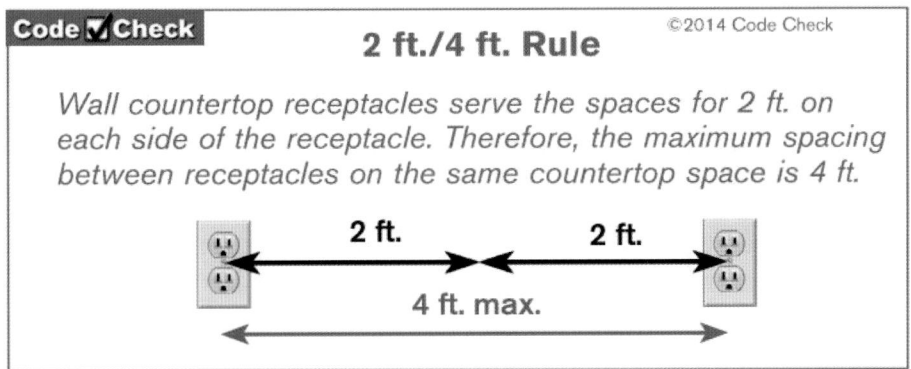

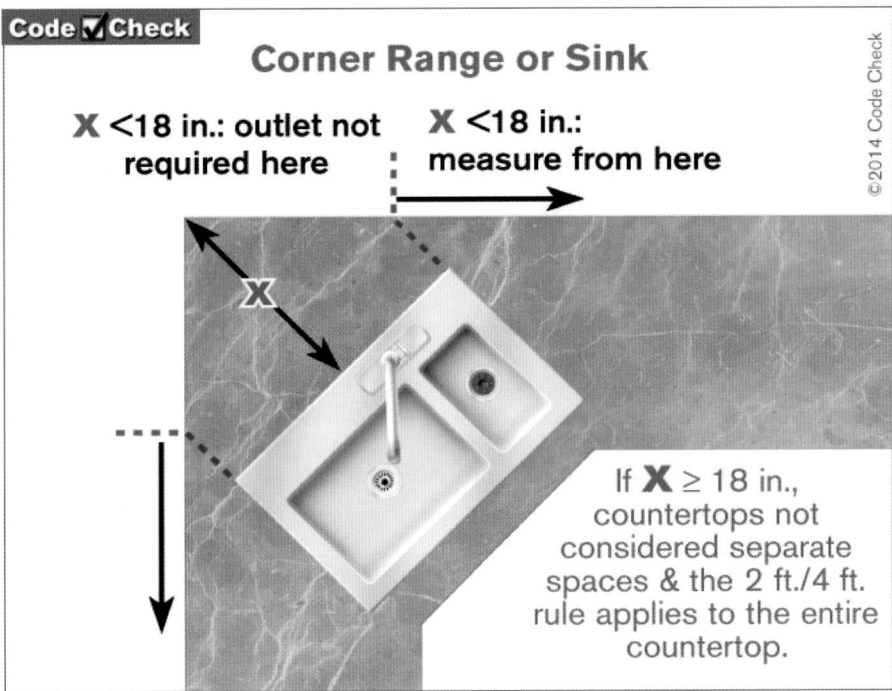

Receptacles are required in every room, including utility rooms, and in the basement, attic, crawl space (if mechanical equipment is present), and garage. The NEC requires receptacles to be flush with the surface of a flammable wall surface or recessed up to 1/4" if the wall surface is nonflammable.

- **Dedicated circuits:** Dedicated circuits are required for large appliances such as dishwashers, refrigerators (not required, but a good idea), freezers, sump pumps, and disposals. The NEC requires at least two dedicated 20-amp small appliance circuits for the kitchen, which the refrigerator may or may not be on. These receptacles must be rated for the amperage of the circuits. GFCIs are not required for some dedicated circuits. As explained above, dishwashers and some sump pumps are required to be on dedicated *and* GFCI-protected circuits.

- **Modern GFCI requirements:** The following require GFCI-protected circuits:

— All exterior receptacles, including garage and accessory buildings

  ■ Except exterior receptacles that are dedicated for snow/ice-melting or similar equipment.

— Crawl spaces (with storage or mechanical equipment) and unfinished basements, except receptacles supplying only permanently installed fire or burglar alarm systems.

— All interior receptacles within 6′ of water such as a wet bar in the living room

— All bathroom receptacles

— Laundry Rooms

— All receptacles serving counters, peninsulas, and islands in the kitchen

— All receptacles servicing aboveground pool pumps and pool lights

— Dedicated receptacles for whirlpool/hydro-massage tub motors

— Dedicated receptacles for exterior hot tubs

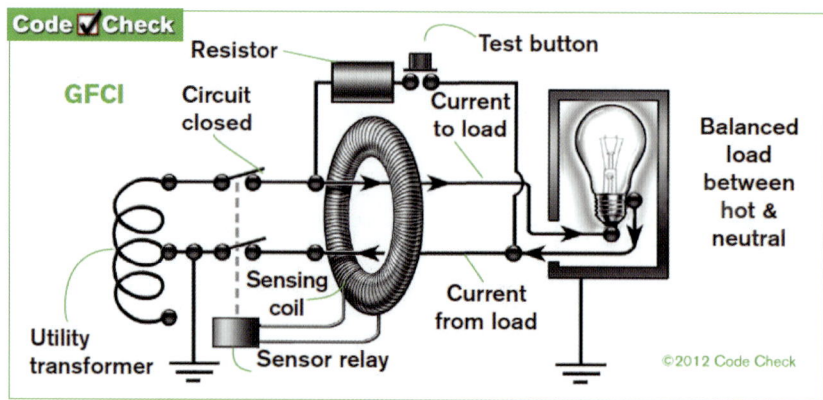

- **Exterior receptacles:** All exterior receptacles are required to be weatherproof. Observe the current condition of the receptacle covers

and receptacles and report any defects. Although outdoor, weatherproof receptacle covers have undergone many changes over the years, do not call older-style weatherproof covers a safety hazard when they are still serving their intended purpose. Recommend that newer weatherproof (wet location) covers be installed as an upgrade.

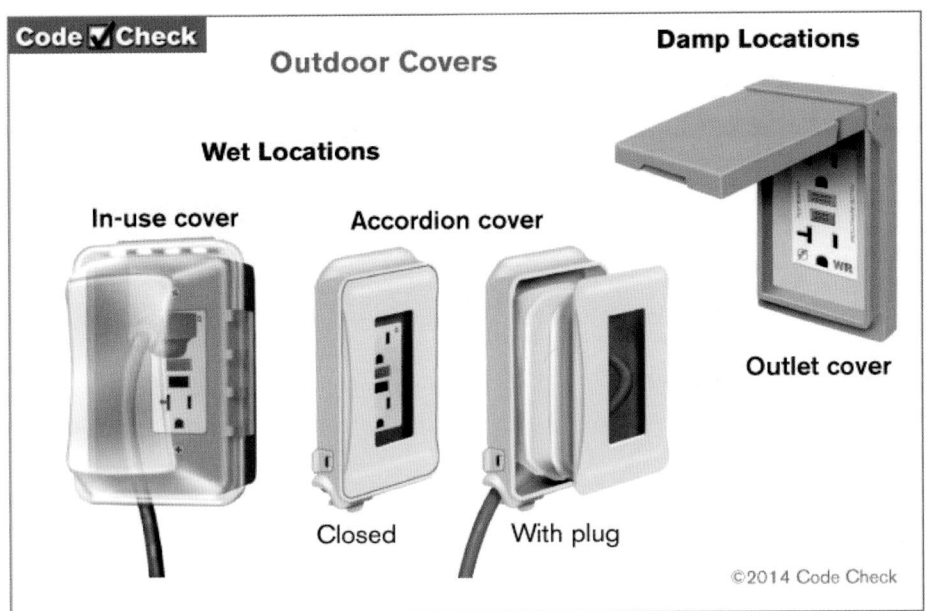

- **AFCI receptacles:** Since 2002 the NEC has required the installation of AFCI protection on all bedroom circuits and has since been added to all other branch circuits in the house. An arc occurs when the electrical path is broken but a path back to the source or ground is close enough for the electricity to "jump" out of the conductor to the desired path. Arcs generate extreme heat (known to exceed 10,000°F) beyond what normally occurs on a circuit, creating a fire hazard. This is what makes an arc welder so effective.

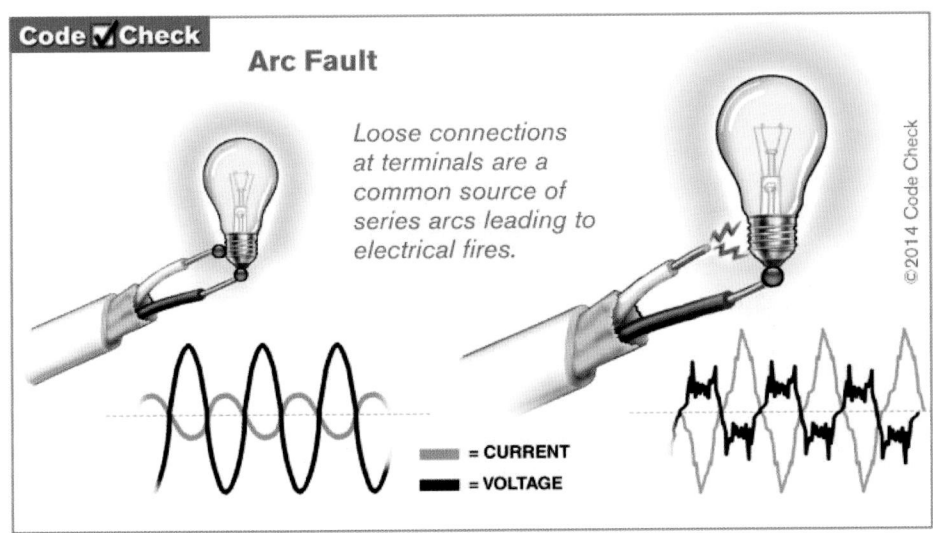

Photo #25 COURTESY OF LEVITON

As of the 2014 NEC, these are the required locations for AFCI and GFCI protected circuits.

AFCI
Family Room
Dining Room
Living Room
Bedroom
Sunroom
Library
Kitchen
Den
Office
Hallways
Closets
Rec Rooms
Laundry Rooms
Similar Areas

GFCI
Kitchen
Bathroom
Garage
Porch
Pool Area
Laundry Rooms

*AFCI technology is also required in college dormitories

An **arc fault** is an unintended arc flowing through an unintended path such as a loose wire in a receptacle arcing in the box when an appliance is plugged in.

The first version of residential "branch-feeder type" **arc fault circuit interrupters** were designed to detect parallel (line-to-line, line-to-neutral, and line-to-ground) arcs posing a danger and similar to a GFCI, these AFCIs were designed to trip the breaker, interrupting power to the circuit. The AFCIs currently required are called "combination-type," and they also detect series arcing (a loose, broken, or otherwise high-resistance segment in a single line), overload protection, and short-circuit protection.

Some motor-driven appliances, light switches, etc., produce small arcs by design. AFCIs can differentiate between designed arcs and hazardous arc faults.

Testing the AFCI is the same as testing a GFCI breaker in the panel box. Simply push the test button and observe whether the breaker trips. This

■ **Parallel**
- Line-to-neutral OR Line-to-ground

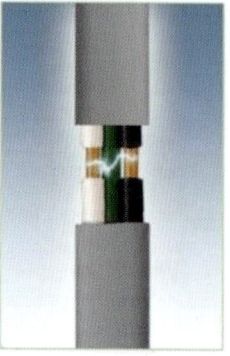

■ **Series**
- In-line

Photo #26 COURTESY OF LEVITON

Parallel and Series Arcing

382 Chapter 5

is the only method approved by most manufacturers; third-party testing devices are not currently approved. Receptacle type AFCI devices are available like GFCI receptacles are. They have their own test and reset buttons.

The various types of arcs (parallel, series, etc.) make it difficult for some manufacturers to design testing equipment capable of simulating the proper arc at the correct amperage to test AFCIs from a receptacle instead of using the test button on the breaker. If you plan to use such a device, research it thoroughly to make sure it is approved for the proper test. Most home inspectors simply push the test button at the AFCI breaker in the panel, as it falls under the definition of a normal homeowner control.

Inspecting the Receptacles

These are the steps the home inspector should follow when inspecting electrical receptacles:

1. Check for the **presence** of at least one receptacle (possibly more) in each room; long hallways; foyers; basement; attics and crawl spaces with storage or mechanical equipment; and garages. Report the absence of receptacles in any of these areas.

2. Check for the **presence of AFCIs and GFCIs** in required areas as noted above and **operate** using attached test buttons **and** your GFCI tester (for GFCIs only) to see if they work. Remember, AFCI and GFCI requirements have increased incrementally since the NEC first required them. Familiarize yourself with the increased requirements. You want to make certain you describe the **absence of an AFCI or GFCI** as a **potential safety hazard only** when it was **required at** the time of **construction**. Otherwise, it is simply a recommended upgrade.

> **INSPECTING RECEPTACLES**
>
> - Insufficient receptacles
> - Warm, scorched, loose, damaged, or missing cover plates
> - Unsafe practices
> - Ungrounded receptacles
> - GFCIs missing or not operating
> - Incorrect wiring

3. Most standards of practice require that a "representative number" of receptacles and switches be tested. The actual definition of *representative number* means at least one in every area where there is more than one. This is so the inspector doesn't have to document the exact location of every inaccessible receptacle hidden behind furniture in an occupied home. Only checking one receptacle and ignoring the rest, however, is not recommended. All too often it is the one receptacle that is not checked that reveals a significant electrical problem requiring expensive repairs. Best practice is to use the GFCI tester and/or neon bulb tester to check **all accessible** receptacles in each room for **current, polarity, open ground, and correct wiring**.

In addition to inspecting the receptacles, the home inspector should check for the following:

- **Insufficient receptacles:** Check for the presence of a receptacle in each room. Be sure to report those room that don't have any receptacles and recommend that additional receptacles or circuits be installed (for example, if only one is present in a bedroom). Many a home inspector has had to pay to wire a room where he or she missed reporting that the room didn't have a power source. Note areas such as basement or garage workshops with extension cord wiring, noting the lack of enough receptacles in the area.

  Also, check the kitchen for extender receptacles (the ones that allow six devices instead of just the two it was designed for) and extension cords that indicate that more receptacles or circuits are needed.

Photo #27 *Extender receptacles are usually a bad idea and indicate the lack of sufficient receptacles.*

Point out to the customer that the homeowner appears to need more receptacles and that the customer should expect the same problem. Keep in mind that many devices are powered with USB cables. Combination receptacle/USB type is an alternative to all of the charger cubes.

Photo #28 COMBINATION RECEPTACLE

These combination type receptacles with both 120v and USB connections are great for all our electronic devices.

- **Overheating at the cover plate:** Feel (or use your infrared thermometer) and look at the receptacle covers for any evidence of overheating such as heat, scorches, or signs of burning. This should be reported as a **safety hazard**, and the home inspector should recommend that an electrician be called to evaluate the situation. Report any loose, damaged, or missing receptacle covers, which might allow a person to come in contact with live wires.

- **Unsafe practices:** Report receptacles that are too close to or within tubs and showers, extension cord wiring, receptacles that are too close to or above electric baseboard heat, and receptacles that are not placed according to NEC rules or just common sense.

- **Ungrounded receptacles:** Some homes have ungrounded receptacles, which isn't a problem in itself. However, the home inspector might find some unsafe conditions at these receptacles, which should be pointed out to the customer. These two-slot receptacles sometimes have a gray **adapter** in them, which has a three-slot receptacle for the appliance plug and two prongs that go into the receptacle. A grounding connection on the adapter (typically a short green wire) is connected under the cover plate screw, supposedly to provide grounding. However, if the junction box is not grounded, the adapter won't be grounded either. Sometimes, people break off the third prong of a three-prong plug and plug it into a two-slot ungrounded receptacle. This shouldn't be done; it's unsafe. The device is no longer protected as the manufacturer had intended, hence the third prong.

Ungrounded three-slot receptacles should have the ground slot filled with an epoxy or a pin designed for this use so that a three-prong plug cannot be used in it or they can be replaced with two-slot receptacles, which are still readily available.

Photo #29 GROUNDING CONNECTION ON ADAPTER

These adapters are no better than an open ground circuit. You should recommend additional grounded circuits if they are needed for computers or electronics.

- **GFCIs missing or not operating:** Check that all required receptacles (garage, bath, exterior, garage, etc.) have GFCIs and report them if they do not. Be careful not to say that they are missing in an older home, which did not have them when the home was built. Make a recommendation for them to be installed as an upgrade. Next, before you test each one for operation, it's a good idea to ask the owner what other rooms are on the same circuit. It's generally okay because computers, electronics, and security systems aren't usually on the same circuits as bathrooms and kitchens. But you might trip the upstairs or hall bathroom receptacle if bathrooms are on the same circuit, which is typical. *Be sure to reset all GFCIs.*

TESTING GFCI OUTLETS

- Test with GFCI tester
- Test with buttons on outlet

> **Personal Note**
>
> *"I've tested GFCIs in several garages that had freezers plugged into them. Very often the GFCI will trip again after the inspection and I'll get a call about spoiled food. And let me tell you, the freezers involved in my inspections always seem to be holding some very exotic and expensive food such as salmon from Norway. Paying to replace food like that can get expensive.*
>
> *Now I always leave the owner a note cautioning him or her to watch the freezer because the GFCI may trip again. I also tell the owner that the freezer shouldn't be plugged into a GFCI outlet. It saves me money."*

Now test each GFCI for operation twice using the following methods:

1. Insert the **GFCI tester** into the receptacle. If the circuit is wired correctly, the correct lights on the tester will be on (depends on your device). Next, **push the button on your tester**. This should trip the GFCI *and* interrupt the circuit, and all lights on your tester will be off. If the lights remain on, the GFCI is not working properly or the circuit is incorrectly wired. If the GFCI worked (tripped), push the reset button on the GFCI receptacle. (Note: Not all GFCI testers have the same light orientation. Be sure to read the directions for your tester.)

2. While your GFCI tester is still plugged into the receptacle, **push the test button on the receptacle** to test it again. If the reset button pops out and the tester lights go off, the GFCI is working and is wired properly. Push the reset button on the GFCI receptacle to reset the circuit.

Photo #30 GFCI RECEPTACLE STICKER

These are the stickers that come in the box when you buy a new GFCI receptacle. Unfortunately, the directions do not say when they should be used. As a result, they are never seen as required.

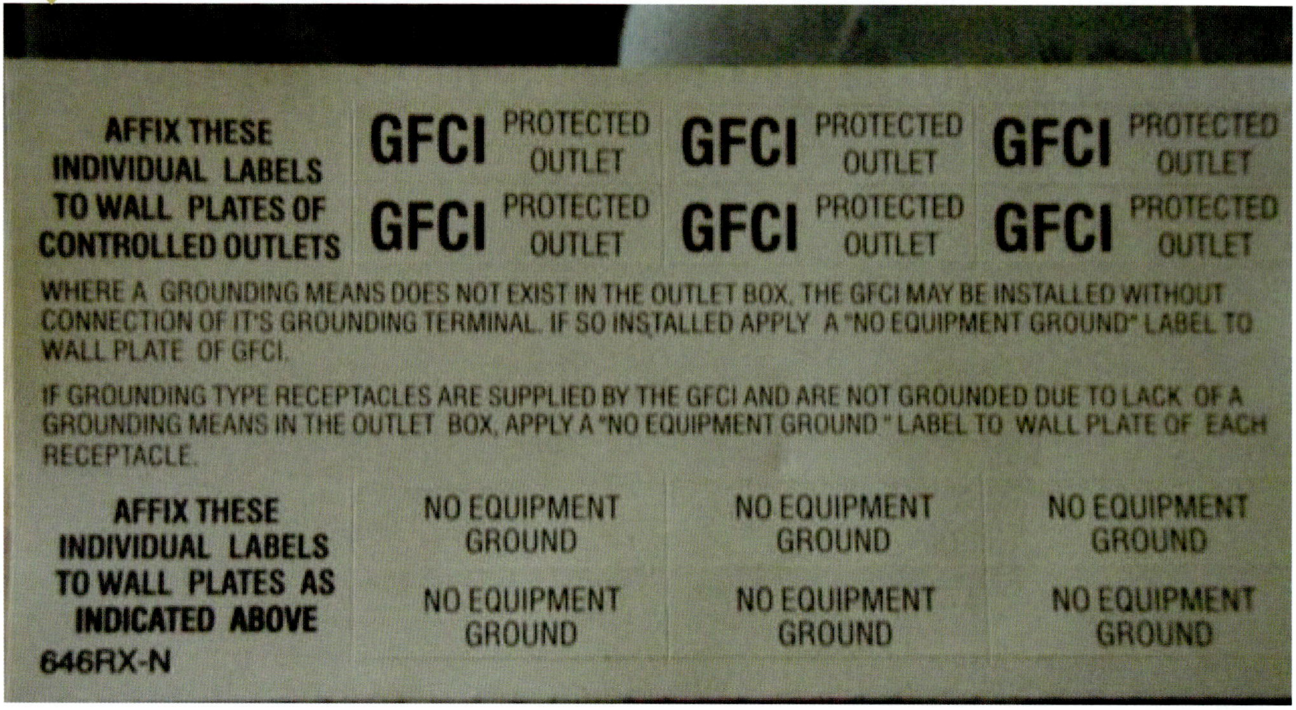

386 Chapter 5

3. If while testing the GFCI receptacle for proper wiring you find an open ground on your device, the testing is somewhat different. Once you have determined that the GFCI is wired without a ground (open ground), you will find that your tester did *not* trip the GFCI. The reason is that your testing device tries to "short" the receptacle to ground, but because it isn't present, it won't trip. Leave your tester in the receptacle and push the test button on the GFCI. It should trip *and* cut the power to your tester. This is operating correctly and is a safe configuration, even without a ground present. What you normally don't see are the stickers or decals that came in the box that say "No Equipment Ground"; these are supposed to be stuck on the receptacle cover plates of those receptacles on that circuit.

4. The last potential problem you may run into while testing a GFCI receptacle is improper wiring. Specifically, the line and load wires have been switched upon installation. If this is the case, your tester will read correctly when it is plugged into the GFCI receptacle. However, when you push the test button on your tester, it will *not* trip the GFCI. It will not trip for a different reason than the open ground scenario above. Basically, the electricity is traveling through the GFCI mechanism in the wrong direction. It should come into the receptacle on the "line" side (from the panel) to feed the circuit. It may stop there if it is the only receptacle on the circuit. But in most cases, the GFCI receptacle feeds or provides power to several other standard receptacles (without GFCI buttons) downstream. This is how you link multiple bathrooms with a single GFCI receptacle or GFCI breaker. This is done by drawing power from the "load" side screws on the GFCI, which feeds the subsequent receptacles downstream in the other bathrooms (or wherever). What happens is that the line and load feeds get switched when installed by a homeowner, which creates a safety issue. Back to testing: it won't trip with your tester, so you leave your tester plugged in and then push the test button on the GFCI. The GFCI will trip, but it will *not* cut the power to the circuit and your tester's lights will remain on. So if you didn't have a tester and you just pushed the test button and it trips and you reset it, it appears to be working correctly. Why would the average person check to see if the power was cut if the test button worked? He or she wouldn't, which is why the manufacturers have come out with several iterations of GFCI receptacles to make them more "idiot proof." The more recent GFCIs came out of the box with the reset button already tripped, and they can't be reset unless the line and load feeds are correct. Brand-new technology in GFCI receptacles does not allow power to the face of the receptacle or to the ones downstream unless properly wired.

Finally, regarding the little lights on brand-new GFCI receptacles, they are called end-of-service life indicators. Think about all of those GFCIs out there since the 1970s. How do we know they will continue to work? The answer is we don't, and they may very well not work at all! That is the reason for the end-of-service lights on new GFCI receptacles. The light indicates that the GFCI mechanism no longer works correctly. The problem is that the lights are not uniform across all manufacturers as to what they do (on or off) and what color they are. You have to know what the light is doing or what the light did before it failed and changed its color.

CAUTION: You may find large appliances such as refrigerators, freezers, and washers plugged into GFCI circuits. Freezers and refrigerators in the garage plugged into GFCI receptacles are a special problem. After the home inspector trips that GFCI, the freezer will have to restart, and the motor surge can trip the GFCI again after the inspection. That means spoiled food and a complaint to the home inspector. If you come across this situation, leave a note for the owners informing them to check that the GFCI didn't trip after the inspection. A trick we learned after buying a couple of freezers full of food is to leave your car keys on top of the freezer and verify that the freezer is running when you retrieve your keys to leave.

- **Incorrect wiring:** See the discussion that follows.

Testing the Receptacles

On pages 375–376, we discussed testing GFCI receptacles for operation. The home inspector should also test:

- All accessible receptacles in each room for current, polarity, and grounding, reporting as a safety hazard receptacles with incorrect wiring, reverse polarity, or open ground.

- Any two-slot receptacles must be tested with the neon bulb tester. This is the small tool with a light attached between two long prongs that can be inserted in the receptacle slots (hot and neutral) and against the cover plate screw to get readings. The table below shows how to test two-slot receptacles with the neon bulb tester.

If it is present, check the receptacle near the main panel for grounding; sometimes this receptacle isn't grounded or GFCI-protected as it should be.

Test **three-slot receptacles** with both the **GFCI tester and the neon bulb tester**. This is a good way to double check for polarity, open ground, and dead outlets. This is more for practice and understanding wiring issues than actually used in the field.

Putting It All Together

This section presented the inspection of the electrical system by components, not by the flow of how the electrical inspection would be performed. Let's review how your inspection really happens.

Definitions

Reverse polarity is where the hot wire is wired to the large slot in an electrical outlet and the neutral wire is wired to the small slot, the opposite of how it should be done. An open ground means that the outlet is not properly grounded. A two-slot outlet may not be grounded, but the three-slot outlet should be grounded.

TESTING OUTLETS

- Correct wiring
- Reverse polarity
- Open ground
- Inoperative

For Beginning Inspectors

This is a good time to buy yourself a GFCI tester and neon bulb tester and get some practice. (Note: Not all GFCI testers have the same light orientation. Be sure to read the directions for your tester.)

Use these tools to test your own outlets first. Then carry the testers with you for several days and test outlets at other people's homes. Be aware that you may be turning off power to important outlets downstream of GFCIs.

Ask first.

TWO-SLOT RECEPTACLES

NEON BULB TESTER OFF = ● ON = ○	CONDITION
● — ○	Correct wiring where hot wire is wired to small slot and neutral wire is wired to large slot.
○ — ●	Reverse polarity where hot wire is wired to large slot and neutral twire is wired to small slot.
● — ●	Inoperative for any number of reasons but basically not providing power to the outlet.
● ○ ●	No ground where checking small and large slots shows that outlet has power, but checking each slot against screw shows no ground.

Illustration by Paddy Morrissey

THREE-SLOT RECEPTACLES

GFCI TESTER OFF = ● ON = ○	NEON BULB TESTER OFF = ● ON = ○	CONDITION
● ○ ○	○ ● ○	Correct wiring where hot wire is wired to small slot and neutral is wired to large slot.
○ ○ ●	○ ● ●	Reverse polarity where hot wire is wired to large slot and neutral twire is wired to small slot.
● ○ ●	● ● ●	Open ground where the outlet is not grounded and no current flows between the upper slots and the grounding slot.
● ● ●	● ● ●	Inoperative for any number of reasons, but basically not providing current or power to the outlet.
○ ○ ○	○ ● ○	Many conditions but usually means there is a weak ground which indicates a leak of current through the outlet.

Illustration by Paddy Morrissey

1. **Exterior electrical:** While inspecting the exterior of the house, you inspect the service entrance, including the mast, masthead, cabling, and meter or main panel or both. You take note of clearances of the service drop and note

> **INSPECTION ORDER**
>
> - Exterior service entrance, fixtures, outlets
> - Garage wiring and outlets
> - Interior power sources, fixtures, outlets
> - Attic branch circuit wiring
> - Basement main panels, subpanels, branch circuit wiring, outlets

the system voltage rating based on the number of service conductors entering the masthead. As you circle the house, you test all exterior receptacles for current, polarity, and open grounds and note the presence of and test all GFCIs. Remember to inspect for weatherproof or wet location enclosures and cover plates at fixtures and receptacles.

2. **Garage:** Watch for handyman or extension cord wiring. Check that surface wiring is enclosed in conduit (protected from physical damage). Note the presence and operation of GFCIs. Check to see if a freezer or refrigerator is plugged into a GFCI receptacle as discussed above.

3. **Interior electrical:** In the kitchen and bathroom and in any other area where receptacles are required, check for the presence and operation of AFCIs and GFCIs, polarity, and open ground. In all other rooms and areas, check accessible receptacles for AFCIs, current, polarity, and grounding. Note the absence of power to any room. Note the proper placement and condition of receptacles and fixtures. Touch cover plates to check for overheating.

4. **Attic area:** Here's where you'll get your first look at branch circuit wiring. Remember to report the existence of knob-and-tube wiring. Watch for wiring and recessed lights buried in insulation (IC/IC-AT versus non-IC) and note open or missing junction boxes (exposed wire splices). Watch for evidence of overheating at connections. Look for proper protection of the wires based on location and attic access.

5. **Basement:** Here, you might find the main panel and subpanels servicing the home. Remove covers if it is safe to do so and examine them to determine system amperage, compatibility of components, grounding, and type of branch circuit wiring. Remember to report the presence of aluminum branch circuit wiring (solid aluminum wiring on 120-volt circuits). Watch for deficiencies at the panels—handyman wiring, tapping before the main, double tapping of fuses or breakers, arcing or burned wiring, melted insulation, and evidence of undersized wiring or oversized breakers/fuses. Trace branch circuit wiring in the basement area and note dedicated circuits to large appliances, junctions boxes, and fixtures and the presence of receptacles. Watch for proper use of conduit and cabling, extension cord wiring, open junction boxes, and so on.

Remember the flow. Start at the main wires, working past the main breaker to the branch circuits, then inspecting the wires. Next, inspect the neutral busbar(s) and grounding system. Finally, inspect the condition of the panel box itself. To avoid having to open it again later, keep the panel open while you document your findings in the report.

Reporting Your Findings

Now let's get back to reporting your findings from the inspection of **fixtures, switches, and receptacles**. Your inspection report should have appropriate places in which to report these findings. You will have an easier time completing your report, if you organize these electrical elements of the inspection by location (exterior, garage, kitchen, bathroom, other rooms, attic, and basement).

In general, you want to be able to record the presence or absence of lighting and power in each area. You should report the presence or absence of AFCIs and/or GFCIs and their operation in areas where you would expect to find them. Also, you should report the results of your tests for reverse polarity and open grounds.

Record your comments on other important findings, as these examples show:

- "Missing cover on junction box on south exterior wall, recommend repair."

- "Recommend GFCIs for garage and bathroom receptacles."

- "Extension cord wiring in attic, recommend repair."

- "Reversed polarity on receptacle near kitchen sink, recommend repair and recommend GFCI protection."

- "Hot cover plate at receptacle on north wall, recommend electrician evaluate."

- "Closet light fixture too close to shelving."

Record the following safety hazards if you find them. Remember, it's a good idea to repeat these on a summary page of your inspection report:

- Reverse polarity or open grounds

- Evidence of overheating at fixtures, switches, and receptacles

- Unsafe practices such as receptacles too close to or within tubs or showers

---

DON'T EVER MISS

- Absence of lighting or power in any room or area
- Switches, fixtures, and outlets that don't work
- Warm, scorched, loose, damaged, or missing cover plates
- Unsafe practices
- Recessed lights covered by insulation
- Reverse polarity or open grounds near water
- GFCIs missing or not operating

CHAPTER 6
THE HEATING INSPECTION

This chapter presents the inspection of the home's heating and cooling systems. We will start with heating, in general. There are two kinds of home heating—central heating and room heating. The home inspection concerns itself with *permanently* installed heating systems, both central and room type. The basic components of central heating systems include the following:

- A **safe compartment** in which to convert fuel or energy to heat. This includes a burner and combustion chamber for converting fossil fuels such as gas, propane, oil, and coal, or solid fuels such as, pellets, wood, and corn to heat, or a chamber containing a resistance coil for converting electrical energy to heat. Fuel oil is popular in certain areas of the United States, mainly in the Northeast and Northwest. At one time, fuel oil was competitively priced, but frequent price fluctuations sometimes make it very expensive. Fuel oil requires an on-site fuel storage tank. Natural gas is a colorless, odorless, flammable gas found beneath the earth's surface. (An odor is added to the gas during processing for easier leak detection.) It is lighter than air and dissipates easily. Propane is a form of liquid petroleum gas. Propane is heavier than air and pools at the lowest point at the floor when it leaks. Unlike natural gas, propane has a natural distinct odor that makes leak detection easier.

- **Combustion air** is required for fuel to burn. The correct amount must be present, and appliances control air intake in various ways, as we will see later. Heat pumps, which may work in conjunction with gas or electric systems, work a bit differently; they transfer heat from one space and release it to another space, in a process called refrigeration. It is much easier and cheaper to move heat than to create it.

> **Chapter Note**
>
> *Pages 393–403 outline the content and scope of the heating inspection. It's an overview of the inspection, including what to observe, what to describe, and what specific actions to take during the inspection.*
>
> *Study these guidelines carefully. These pages also present some special cautions about inspecting the heating system. Please read them and be aware of the potential of harming yourself or damaging the equipment.*

- A **heat exchanger** for transferring heat to air or water. The heat exchanger that transfers heat to air is called a **furnace**; one that transfers heat to water is called a **boiler**. In a heat pump, this function is performed by evaporator and condensing coils using refrigerant.

- For fossil fuel furnaces and boilers, a **disposal system** of flues, smoke pipes, vents, and chimneys is used to remove combustion products from the home.

- A **distribution system** of ducts, pipes, or tubing carries warm air, hot water, or steam throughout the house. Warm air may be conveyed through the distribution system naturally by gravity (convection) or may be pushed by a circulating fan. Hot water can be conveyed by gravity or set in motion by a circulating pump. Mini-split systems are a type of ductless heat pump that blows warm or cold air from cassettes or "heads units," depending on the season, directly into rooms. There are also ducted mini-split systems that have short runs of ducts to adjacent rooms.

Photo #1 DUCTLESS HEAT SYSTEM

Ductless mini-splits or heat pumps are becoming very popular now in new construction and remodel projects. What you see here mounted on the wall is called a head-unit or cassette. It is basically the blower and coil for the system in one tidy box.

- **Heat outlets** such as registers, convectors, or radiators for transferring heat into each room. Some homes have electric radiant heating panels or cables.

- **Temperature and safety controls.** Each heating system requires a thermostat that turns the heat pump, furnace, or boiler on and off to supply heat as needed. And each is designed with automatic (and manual) safety controls that turn off heating equipment when the equipment malfunctions.

A home may be heated room by room entirely with electric baseboards, floor furnaces, wall-mounted area heaters, radiant ceiling cables, or radiant panels. In this case, heat is generated within each room to be heated, not centrally through a distribution system.

6.1 INSPECTION GUIDELINES AND OVERVIEW

These are representative of the various Standards of Practice and state standards that govern the inspection of the interior components of the property.

Most Standards of Practice provide an outline of what is to be inspected and what is to be reported during the inspection of the home's interior living spaces. If licensing, registration, or certification is required in your state, you should follow the state's Standards of Practice. But, of course, not all the details are included in the SOP. There are many other details that will be presented in this chapter.

THE HEATING INSPECTION

- Heating equipment, operating and safety controls
- Combustion air venting
- Combustion product disposal system
- Distribution system
- Heat source per room

HEATING SYSTEM

Observe and/or Report: The act of making a visual examination of a system or component and reporting on its condition.	• Readily openable access panels • Heating and cooling systems • Vent systems, flues, and chimneys • Distribution system(s), ducts, registers, piping, radiators, convectors, etc. • Operation of the system using normal readily accessible control devices
Describe: Report in writing a system or component by type or other observed characteristics to distinguish it from other components used for the same purpose.	• Type of heating system(s) • Type of cooling system(s) • The energy source(s) • Evaporative (swamp) coolers • Type of water supply line • Location of the thermostat
Report deficiencies in:	• Ducts or plenums in contact with earth • Duct systems, chases, vents, registers, absence of insulation in unconditioned space(s), and improper materials • Piping systems, radiators, convectors, etc. • Inoperative units (heating and/or cooling) • Deficiencies in the thermostats • Inappropriate location(s) • Lack of protection from physical damage (bollard or similar) • Burners, burner ignition devices or heating elements, switches, and thermostats that are not a minimum of 18" above the lowest garage floor elevation, unless the unit is listed for garage floor installation • The absence of an opening that allows access to equipment for inspection, service, repair, or replacement without removing permanent construction or building finish

| Report deficiencies in: | - When applicable, a floored passageway service platform that allows access for equipment inspection, service, repair, or replacement
- Mounting and performance of window and wall units
- Performance of heat pumps
- Performance of heating elements (electric strip heat) and condition of conductors
- Gas leaks
- Flame impingement, uplifting flame, improper flame color, or excessive scale buildup
- Absence of a gas shut-off valve within 6' of the appliance
- Absence of a gas appliance connector or one that exceeds 6' in length
- Gas appliance connectors that are concealed within or extended through walls, floors, partitions, ceilings, or appliance housings
- Combustion and dilution air
- Gas shut-off valves
- Access to a gas shutoff valve that prohibits full operation
- Gas appliance connector materials
- Vent pipe, draft hood, draft, proximity to combustibles, vent termination point, and clearances
- Inadequate cooling as demonstrated by its performance
- Noticeable vibration of blowers or fans
- Water or previous evidence in the auxiliary/secondary drain pan
- Condensate drain and auxiliary/secondary pan and drain system including termination
- Primary drain pipe that discharges in a sewer vent
- Missing or deficient refrigerant pipe insulation
- Dirty coils (inside or outside), where accessible
- Outside coil(s) that lack adequate clearances or air circulation or that has deficiencies in the fins, location, levelness, or elevation above grade surfaces
- The presence of active water leaks (swamp cooler)
- The absence of backflow prevention (swamp cooler)
- Damaged duct systems or improper material
- Absence of airflow at accessible supply registers
- Presence of gas piping and sewer vents concealed in ducts, plenums, and chases when visible or indications that their presence exists
- Filters
- Grills or registers and the location of return air openings |
|---|---|

- **Heating equipment:** The home inspector inspects the main heating unit(s) in the home—furnace, boiler, heat pump, or room units—recording the **brand name** of the unit, the **type** of heating unit (for example, forced warm air or gravity hot water), and its **fuel source** (for example, gas, oil, or electricity). The inspector is required to **open readily openable manufacturer's access panels** during the visual inspection and to **operate the heating system using normal operating controls** to check the operation of the heating system. However, the inspector is not required to operate heating systems that are shut down, that don't respond to normal operating controls, or that may cause equipment damage in certain conditions. Most systems can be operated year-round. We will discuss which ones not to operate in the "off" season later in this chapter.

The condition of the unit's fuel source or storage equipment (such as an oil or propane tank or gas meter), outer jacket (cabinet), the burner and combustion chamber, and the visible portions of the heat exchanger are all inspected. This also includes the coils for a heat pump, which are usually accessible. Cracked heat exchangers are reported as a **safety hazard** and as a **major repair** because furnace or boiler replacement is usually recommended. The same applies for a coil clogged with dog hair or dust. It should be reported as a major repair because the coil may need to be cleaned at the very least, if not replaced. The inspector is **required to observe, but not operate, automatic safety controls**.

The home inspector also estimates the unit's age and **remaining useful lifetime**. Several reference books are available to help pinpoint the age of the equipment. We recommend the Carson Dunlop *Technical Reference Guide*. It's important to know whether a furnace or boiler will need to be replaced within the next 5 years and to record that fact in your inspection report. The following chart gives an overview of the life expectancy of various furnaces and boilers.

HEATING SYSTEM	LIFE EXPECTANCY
Gas-fired warm air furnace	15 to 25 years
Oil-fired warm air furnace	20 to 30 years
Electric systems	20 to 25 years
Cast iron boiler	30 to 50 years or more
Steel boiler	30 to 40 years or more
Copper boiler (rare)	10 to 20 years
Circulating pump (hot water)	10 to 15 years
Heat pump (compressor)	12 to 15 years

NOTE: The home inspector is required to inspect **solid fuel heating systems** within the building being inspected, referring to fireplaces, pellet

NOT REQUIRED TO

- Operate heating systems that are shut down, don't respond to controls, or may cause damage if operated
- Operate automatic safety controls
- Observe flue interiors, humidifiers, heat recovery units, or electronic air filters
- Observe the adequacy of or distribution balance of heat supply to each room

stoves, and wood stoves. Fireplaces and wood stoves are presented later in this chapter. As stated in the standards, the home inspector is **not required to ignite or extinguish solid fuel fires or to observe fireplace insert flue connections**.

- **Combustion product disposal system:** For oil and gas-fueled furnaces and boilers, the home inspector inspects chimneys, flues (smoke pipes), and vents for proper installation and safety. If there are abandoned vent openings to the chimney, **inspect** them to verify that they are sealed. The products of combustion are only carbon dioxide and water vapor (CO_2 and H_2O) in complete (100%) combustion. However, most systems do not operate at 100% efficiency, as will be discussed later. Most systems, if not properly maintained, will have incomplete combustion where carbon monoxide (CO) is produced. As we all know, CO can kill you very quickly in

Photo #2 NEWLY INSTALLED THIMBLE

This is a newly installed thimble. You can see the fresh mortar and the shiny new metal of the thimble in the chimney. This is where the combustion appliance(s) will connect there flues or smoke pipes to exhaust their combustion products.

relatively low concentrations. This is why it is very important to verify flue and chimney connections thoroughly. Evidence of combustion products leaking into the home is reported as a **safety hazard**. Draft diverters are examined, and the smoke pipe is checked for the operation of dampers, corrosion, pitch, proper supports, and the seal at the (thimble) chimney. A thimble is a sleeve, typically of sheet metal, passing through the wall of a chimney, used to hold the end of a stovepipe, smoke pipe, or flue (see photo on previous page). The chimney cleanout (if present and accessible) is investigated to determine whether the chimney is blocked with debris from a deteriorating chimney above. The home inspector **is not required to inspect the interior of flues** where they are not accessible.

> **Chapter Note**
>
> *The inspection of fireplaces and wood stoves is presented in the Chapter 7, Interior Inspection.*

- **Heating distribution system:** The inspection of the duct or piping system includes observing the operation and condition of blowers and circulating pumps. Air filters are inspected for warm air systems. Although most standards state that the home inspector is **not required to inspect electronic air filters**, we suggest that you do—carefully, with the proper cautions in mind. It is actually very simple as there is typically a test button on the filter. There will be more discussion on that later. The home inspector checks humidifiers for rust, corrosion, or contamination in the water (a science project growing in the old standing water reservoir type). The inspector also notes their general condition and any effect on other heating equipment but is **not required to inspect the operation or effectiveness of the humidifier**.

  The home inspector checks all visible **ducts and piping** for proper support, dampers, rust, holes, leaking, and insulation. The home inspector checks the condition and operation of all **heat outlets** such as registers, radiators, fan coil units, and convectors.

- **Heat source per room:** A seemingly minor point, but important to customers, is the presence of a heat source in each living area. The home inspector checks for a heat source in each room and records its presence or absence in the inspection report. However, the home inspector is **not required to determine or report on the adequacy of the heat supply to each room**. The inspector should, however, verify that the heat source is functional and not blocked or disconnected or is not a dummy register/radiator. The home inspector also pays attention to the location of air returns with forced-air systems.

Inspection Equipment

Some basic inspection tools are necessary for inspecting the heating system. The home inspector may need a **telescoping inspection mirror** to examine the older style of heat exchangers from all possible angles. The inspection mirror has a long handle and a relatively small mirror face. Also important is a

INSPECTION TOOLS

- Inspection mirror
- Screwdrivers
- Wrenches
- Combustible gas detector
- High-powered flashlight
- Infrared thermometer
- Matches or lighter
- Smoke stick or smoke pencil

high-powered rechargeable flashlight to light up the dark areas while you use the mirror. A **6-in-1, or battery-operated screwdriver,** will come in handy for removing furnace access and electrical panels. You will need a straight blade, Phillips, and 1/4″ and 5/16″ nut-driver bits. However, some panels are bolted on, so it would be a good idea to purchase a **small set of socket wrenches** to keep with your inspection equipment. An infrared **laser thermometer** will come in handy when performing a temperature rise test in gas furnaces and a temperature differential test in cooling systems.

Some inspectors purchase a special **combustible gas detector** to check for unburned fuel (spillage) around the heat exchanger and draft hoods, diverters, and dampers on the flue or smoke pipe. A combustible gas is any gas that, when mixed with air, will burn if ignited, such as methane and propane. Because a combustible gas detector only picks up extremely high concentrations of carbon monoxide (CO), a special CO detector may also be used to determine CO levels.

Carbon monoxide is colorless and odorless, making it difficult to detect. Sufficient amounts of combustion spillage can pose a serious and deadly health risk. At low to moderate levels of exposure, the symptoms can include the following:

- shortness of breath
- mild to severe headaches
- dizziness
- mental confusion
- mild to severe nausea
- fainting

Prolonged exposure to even low levels of carbon monoxide can lead to death.

In this section, we will present techniques for inspecting the heat exchanger that involve observing the flame and visually checking using the inspection mirror and flashlight. This method works for conventional furnaces more than 30 years old, but due to design changes, different techniques must be used on newer mid- and high-efficiency units. For checking around the flue, we'll describe simple tests using **matches, a smoke stick, or a mirror**. Although these tests are acceptable for home inspection, our own home inspectors also use a combustible gas detector, and we recommend that you add it to your list of tools.

Inspection Concerns

In some cases, inspecting the heating equipment can be dangerous. The home inspector should keep three concerns in mind during the inspection of the heating equipment—the customer's safety, the inspector's safety, and damage to the heating equipment. Here are some general rules about the heating inspection that the home inspector should follow:

- **Keep your customer safe.** Of greatest concern during any part of the home inspection is the customer's safety. The home inspector is responsible for the well-being of the customer. The #1 rule of home inspection is to have the customer present during the home inspection, and that means during the heating inspection too.

   However, there is a moment of danger during the heating inspection when you want to pay close attention to where your customer is. That's **when the heating unit is first fired up**, especially with gas-fired furnaces and boilers. With a gas-fired system, there can be too long of a delay before the burner fires while gas is pouring into the combustion chamber. Then when the burner fires, the condition causes a huge flame rollout, shooting a flame a few feet out from the furnace into the room. When firing the unit, both you and your customer should stand to the side. Don't let the customer peer into the chamber at this time. And you shouldn't either.

- **Protect yourself from harm.** Some of the Standards of Practice specifically state observations and actions that the inspector is *not* required to perform. These standards were developed to ensure inspector safety as well as to prevent the inspector from damaging the equipment.

- **Do not disassemble the flue or smoke pipe** during the heating inspection. There is a risk from harmful filth that can be present in the flue and a possibility that the piping can't be reassembled. There are other ways to detect a blocked flue other than taking it apart. You can look through the barometric damper or check the chimney cleanout with your inspection mirror. Corrosion and mineral deposits at the seams are also good indicators of a blockage.

The home inspector will be checking for leaking and corroded humidifiers and their effect on the condition of the furnace and ducts, but is not required to check their operation. **Don't disconnect or disassemble humidifiers** to obtain access to furnace plenums or heat exchangers. Too many inspectors have been cut by sheet metal doing this.

Although some standards say not to inspect **electronic air filters**, we're going to suggest that you do—with caution. An electronic air filter

---

IMPORTANT RULES

- Keep your customer safe.
- Protect yourself from harm.
- Don't cause damage to the equipment.
- Don't operate equipment that has been shut down, that has been switched off, that is improperly vented, that has a suspect chimney, or that indicates an unusually high pressure or temperature.

Section Note

"An instructor here at the American Home Inspectors Training Institute tells how he and a customer were kneeling in front of a gas warm air furnace waiting for it to fire. When the pilot didn't light right away, he knew they were in trouble.

He pushed his customer to the floor away from the furnace and dove to the floor himself. When the pilot ignited, a flame shot out 4 1/2' from the furnace. It would have burned them both. Now he most vigorously cautions all of our students not to do what he did. Always keep yourself and your customer out of the way when firing the furnace."

should not be confused with an electrostatic air filter. An electronic air filter contains a series of fine wire grids that are given an electrostatic charge, which aids the filter in capturing small particles of dust, smoke, and pollen. When the filter is working, it faintly pops and crackles like a bug zapper. The danger to the inspector when testing this type of filter is **electrical shock**. The device has a test button that indicates whether it is working properly. Do not remove the filter; it is very expensive and easily damaged. An electrostatic filter is a filter that, through static electricity, collects dust and small particles in the air.

When inspecting boilers, **don't operate the pressure relief valve** and don't catch your sleeve on one and trip it. The valve will leak after testing and may be difficult or impossible to fix, which may require replacing the valve.

- **Don't cause damage to the equipment.** The home inspector's job is to point out defects in the heating system, not to cause them. **Don't dismantle equipment** other than what you'll be instructed to do in this section—no matter how curious you may be or no matter how many times the customer requests you to. Too many things can go wrong. When you reassemble equipment, it may not work again.

  You'll be inspecting heating units for rust and corrosion, both inside and outside. **Don't scrape at or pick at corrosion** with your screwdriver. This can cause the rust or corrosion to fall away, opening holes in pipes, ducts, burners, and heat exchangers. Simply report the condition. Don't make holes.

  Be careful too with **heating ducts** when inspecting for proper supports. You don't need to hang on them and pull them down to find out if they're not supported properly. With evaporative (swamp) coolers, you may find that ductwork has been significantly damaged by rust.

- **Under certain conditions, don't operate the heating equipment.** Some conditions can cause equipment damage or an unsafe situation in the home. Do *not* turn on equipment that:

  —**Has been shut down.** The system may be shut down for a good reason, such as open piping, unsafe wiring, gas leaks, an unsafe chimney, and fire risks.

  —**Has been switched off.** When a heating system is turned off, talk to the owner or a responsible party and get their permission to turn it on. You may find that it is off for one of the reasons stated above, or you may get permission to turn it back on. That's okay. But always check first, and if there's no one to check with, leave it alone and note it in your report.

  —**Does not appear to be vented properly.** If you notice this condition before firing, don't turn on the equipment. If you've already fired the unit and you observe improper venting or an apparently blocked flue, turn the equipment off promptly.

— **Has a suspect chimney.** For example, you may find an old single whythe (a vertical masonry section that is one unit in thickness), unlined brick chimney with visible damage outside and in the attic. It wouldn't be safe to fire up the heating unit in this case.

— **Has gauges that show unusual pressure or temperature conditions.** If after firing up a boiler, you notice pressure and temperature conditions beyond a safe level, do not let the boiler continue to operate. Turn off the equipment immediately.

— **Has a steam boiler with a water level sight gauge that shows no water.** If the water level is too low in a steam boiler, operating the system can cause the boiler to overheat and crack or worse! Do not operate the system.

> **Section Note**
>
> "One of my inspectors did this inspection for the estate of an old man who had recently died. After studying the furnace and realizing the old man had rerouted exhaust gases back into the furnace, the inspector asked how the man had died. The answer was they didn't really know—old age they thought, his heart just stopped.
>
> 'Try carbon monoxide poisoning,' our inspector said.
>
> He did not fire up that furnace, and he gave a severe warning, reporting the handyman venting as a deadly safety hazard. Of course, nothing was done at that late date to try to determine the old man's cause of death, but we're convinced it was CO poisoning."

6.2 GENERAL INFORMATION

This section will present some general heating terms and concepts the home inspector should be familiar with.

> **Chapter Note**
>
> Pages 403–416 present an introduction to general heating terms, concepts, and types of heating systems.

Thermostats

The main homeowner operating control for a heating system is the thermostat, a temperature-sensitive device that opens and closes a circuit in response to changes in temperature. A thermostat normally operates at low voltage (24 volts). The older thermostats simply start the heating system on a call for heat and turn it off when the thermostat is satisfied.

When the temperature near the thermostat falls below a preset temperature, the contacts within the thermostat close and activate the heating system. When the nearby temperature rises to the preset temperature, the contacts open again and shut it down.

Most older thermostats contain mercury. The contacts are enclosed in glass or have a sealed mercury switch in which a drop of mercury makes and breaks the circuit as it tilts back and forth. When the temperature is cooler, the coil contracts; when the temperature is warmer, it expands.

When the temperature reading that is set on the thermostat falls below a specified degree, the thermostat engages and calls for heat. The coil contracts, tilting the mercury-filled tube that rests on top of the coil to the right. The mercury tube makes contact, providing 24-volt power to an electromechanical switch called a relay. This creates a circuit that signals the furnace to start the heating cycle. Modern thermostats are solid-state electric devices with circuit boards.

Many newer thermostats have **programmable features**. The most basic electronic thermostats can be set to lower the temperature setting automatically at night and raise it again each morning. The latest programmable models can be programmed to raise or lower the temperature multiple times each day, even allowing for different patterns on weekdays and weekends. They can even be connected to Wi-Fi and operated over the Internet via a smart phone or computer. Programmable thermostats operate on a slight delay of about 3 to 5 minutes. If the system does not respond immediately, that does not necessarily indicate a defect. Don't get impatient. Every time you turn the thermostat on or off, you reset the 3- to 5-minute delay!

Most thermostats have a fan control for forced-air systems. Don't be confused. Some older "heat only" thermostats have no fan switch or on/off positions. You just turn it down to 55° or so to turn it off for the summer and up to the proper set point for the winter. This control can be set so that the blower operates automatically when the furnace is on or operates continuously for constant air circulation. The system should always be tested when the fan switch is set to the "Auto" position. Some homeowners put the thermostat fan switch to the "on" position because the fan switch on the furnace itself doesn't work. The furnace will cycle on and appear to work properly. However, if you put the thermostat switch back in the Auto position where it belongs, the furnace will not fire/cycle. This should be reported as a defect and requires repair by a qualified technician.

Some thermostats have an **anticipator**, which anticipates the preset point on the thermostat and turns on the heating system before the preset temperature is reached. This compensates for the lag time between closing the

Photo #3 PROGRAMMABLE THERMOSTATS

Here are a variety of modern programmable thermostats. Many new systems are connected via Wi-Fi and can be controlled remotely with a smart phone.

circuit and delivering the needed heat. The anticipator will also turn off the heating system just before the desired temperature is reached, letting the remaining heat in the combustion chamber bring the temperature up those last few degrees. The anticipator prevents **overshooting**, which occurs when remaining heat in the combustion chamber heats the house higher than the preset temperature after the burner is turned off.

The anticipator, if present, should be calibrated to the particular heating system in the house. If the anticipator is not set correctly, conditions called **short cycling and overshooting** can occur. Short cycling is when the anticipator shuts down the system too soon, so the desired temperature is never reached. Then the heating unit immediately kicks on again, only to shut down too soon again. (There can be additional causes of short cycling.) Remember, it is not the inspector's job to troubleshoot the problem, but to let your client know that a problem exists.

During the inspection of the heating system, the home inspector should **operate each thermostat** to be sure it turns the heating system on and off. But be sure to note the temperature setting before you test the thermostat so that you can return it to the same setting again. A good rule of thumb is to adjust the thermostat up 5° from its current setting. This will allow the system to run long enough to perform your evaluation. Once you are finished, you put it back 5° and you don't need to remember what it was set to in the first place. When inspecting thermostats, watch for the following conditions:

- **Improper location:** Thermostats should be located on interior walls of the home. They should be in locations where factors other than normal home conditions won't unduly affect the temperature in the area. For example, thermostats in cold drafts or too near the front door can turn the heating system on too often. Those located in the path of direct sunshine or fireplace flames won't turn the heating system on often enough.

- **Loose, unlevel:** If an older thermostat is loose or unlevel on the wall, the mercury can open and close the circuit inaccurately, and the setting won't correspond to the actual temperature. This is not a problem with newer digital thermostats. An infrared thermometer can be used to test the actual temperature against the thermostat calibrations. If significant differences are found,

Definitions

A _thermostat_ is a temperature-sensitive device that opens and closes a circuit in response to temperature changes. _Programming features_ on a thermostat can be set to raise or lower temperature settings automatically during certain hours.

An _anticipator_ is a device in a thermostat that turns the heating or cooling system on and off just before preset temperature settings are reached.

Overshooting is a condition when a house is heated or cooled higher or lower than the thermostat is set for.

Short cycling is a condition where the heating/cooling system turns on and off too often.

Section Note

"I once had a problem with a programmable thermostat. Its batteries were low, which I had no way of telling. When I turned off the safety switch to the furnace, the program in the thermostat was lost. The homeowner soon discovered the problem and had to reprogram the thermostat.

When I see this type of thermostat, I tell the homeowners about the low-battery situation and suggest that he or she check whether the program is still functioning after the inspection. That's better than getting a complaint call later."

they should be reported. Customers should be advised that loose or unlevel thermostats should be fixed, or better yet, replaced by a newer programmable model.

> **BE CONSIDERATE**
>
> *Always take note of the <u>temperature setting</u> before you adjust the thermostat for inspection purposes. Then be sure to reset it to the owner's original setting. Remember the 5° rule of thumb.*

- **Not working:** If the heating system doesn't turn on when the thermostat is operated, it may be for any one of several reasons. The system may be turned off. Obviously, if the system doesn't come on, the situation should be further investigated to determine if the problem is with the system or the thermostat. Thermostats can suffer mechanical damage or simply fail. These should be replaced.

> **Section Note**
>
> *"During a home inspection I performed, I turned up the thermostat, but the furnace wouldn't fire. I couldn't figure out why. We called in a heating contractor to take a look at the heating system. When he took off the thermostat cover and scraped nicotine off the contacts, the furnace fired.*
>
> *Thermostats with unprotected contacts can cause problems, especially if there are smokers in the house."*

Zoning

Some homes have zoned heating, where each section or zone of the home is controlled by a separate thermostat. The term **zone control** means different areas of the house are under the control of different thermostats. You may see one thermostat upstairs and one downstairs or multiple thermostats in different parts of the house. Sometimes, zone control is achieved by installing independent furnaces or boilers for upstairs and downstairs heating, each with its own thermostat. Electric baseboard heating and wall- or ceiling-mounted strips will be installed as separate units in each room, controlled by wall thermostats or on the baseboard case itself. The easiest way to understand the setup in a particular house is to count the number of furnaces or boilers and the number of thermostats. If there are more thermostats than systems, it is a zoned system.

A single heating system can be designed for zoned heating. These systems often, but not always, have a "master thermostat." None of the thermostats will switch from heating to cooling unless the master thermostat is first switched to the proper mode. With hot water systems, the boiler can have different circulators or zone control valves to provide heat to different parts of the home.

> **Definitions**
>
> *The <u>master shut-off</u>, also called the <u>safety switch</u>, turns off electricity to the heating system and its controls. The <u>serviceman's switch</u> serves the same purpose as the safety switch and may be the same switch.*

Master Shut-Off

Another normal operating control for central heating systems is a master shut-off or **safety switch** with which to turn off the heating system by hand in the case of an emergency. Safety switches turn off electricity to the furnace or boiler and its controls. When the switch is off, adjusting the thermostat no longer allows the equipment to fire. If the system is missing a master shut-off, recommend to the client that one be installed within sight of the unit. The home inspector may also see an SSU switch, which is a fused disconnect that

Photo #4 SSU SWITCH

This is an SSU switch, which you will periodically find installed. The purpose is to reduce the over current protection down to that of what the appliance requires. There may be a 20-amp circuit protecting the furnace, but it has a maximum rating of 15-amps. The SSU switch would have a 15-amp fuse under the metal cover to properly protect the furnace.

provides overcurrent protection. An example of this is a furnace blower motor that requires 15-amp overcurrent protection that is installed on a 20-amp circuit.

With oil-fired heating equipment, a **remote safety switch** is required, usually at the top of the basement stairs or outside the furnace or boiler room, so that the burner can be turned off without having to approach it. Remote switches often have a red cover plate and are mounted higher on the wall than usual to distinguish them from others. The reason for this is smoke. Oil-fired units can smoke, and if you had to walk through the smoke to shut off the unit, it might be impossible to find and probably unsafe. Turning it off at the top of the stairs or at the entrance to the room is safer, and you can wait until the smoke clears to figure out what the problem is with the unit. Gas-fired systems have safety switches either near the equipment or at a remote location, as is required in some areas of the country. With electric furnaces or boilers, a circuit breaker in a nearby electrical panel or face of the cabinet may serve as the safety switch, but it must still be in the line of sight from the unit.

The home inspector should **test the safety switch** during the inspection of the furnace or boiler. When this master safety switch is turned off, the system and/or burner should stop. Any defective switches should be reported. Some local areas require the boiler's circulating pump or the furnace's fan to remain in operation. The home inspector should find out what his or her local requirements are.

CAUTION: Always be sure that the safety switch is turned back on after an inspection. There are cases of inspectors leaving an empty house without heat during the winter and the condition not being discovered until too late—after plumbing pipes have frozen and burst. One trick is to leave your car keys at the unit. Because you can't leave until you retrieve your keys, you're reminded to turn the unit back on before you go. This trick works well for refrigerators or freezers on GFCI-protected circuits too.

> **CAUTION**
>
> *Always be sure that the <u>safety switch</u> for heating equipment is turned back on after you test it. Check before you leave that the heat is back on, especially if you live in a freezing climate.*

THE HEATING INSPECTION 407

CLEARANCE FROM COMBUSTIBLES

- 6" on top and sides of furnace or boiler
- 24" front for oil-fired furnace or boiler
- 18" front for gas
- Single-wall smoke pipe: 18" for units without draft hoods, 9" for oil with draft hood, 6" for gas
- 3-9" for double-wall smoke pipe
- 1" for Type B gas flue pipe

There is also a **serviceman's switch** within easy reach of the heating unit that serves the same purpose as the safety switch. With gas and electric equipment, the safety switch and the serviceman's switch may be one and the same, although not with oil-fired furnaces and boilers.

Clearances and Codes

When inspecting the heating system, the home inspector should pay attention to the clearances around the heating unit and around exhaust pipes.

Various models of furnaces and boilers may have different **clearance from combustibles** requirements, but typical requirements are at least a 6" clearance above the unit and 0–6" on all sides except the front of the unit. For oil-fired furnaces and boilers, a clearance of 24" is often required between the front of the unit and nearby combustibles, while gas and electric units may require as little as 0". The exhaust

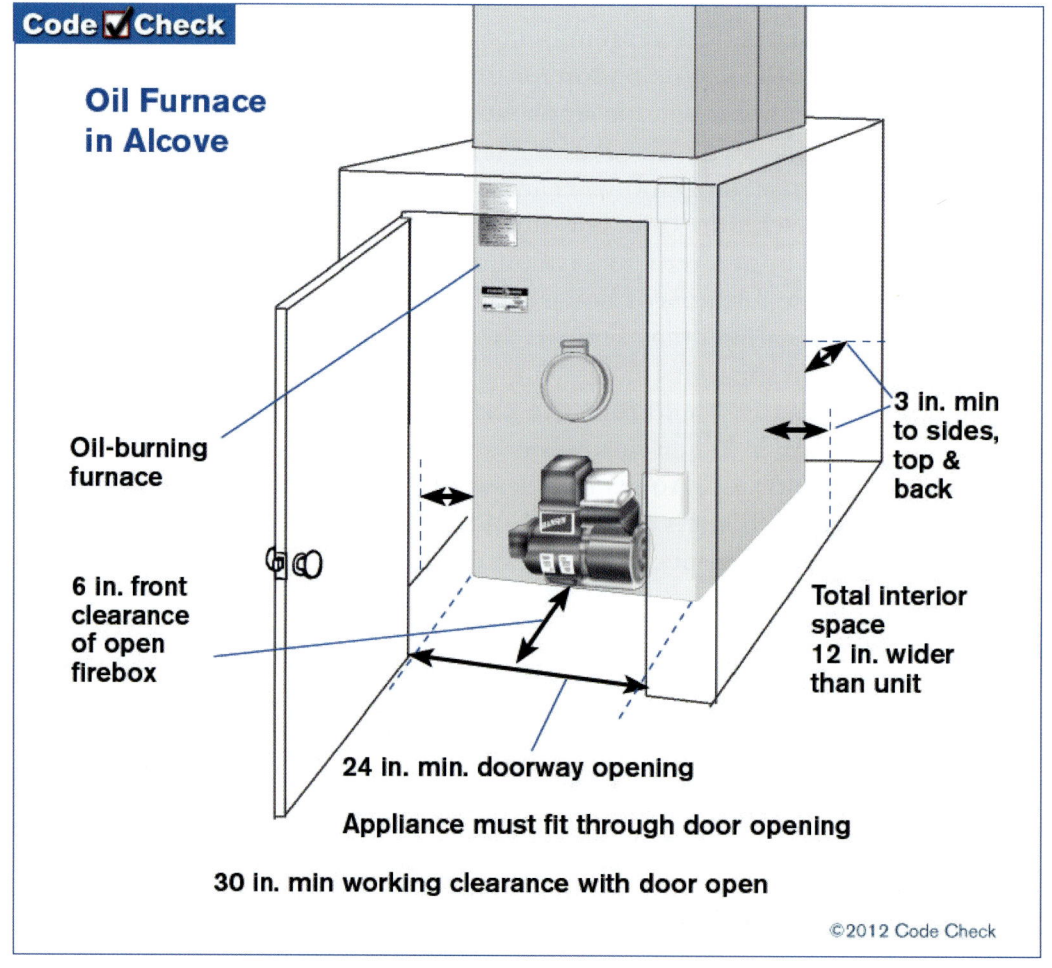

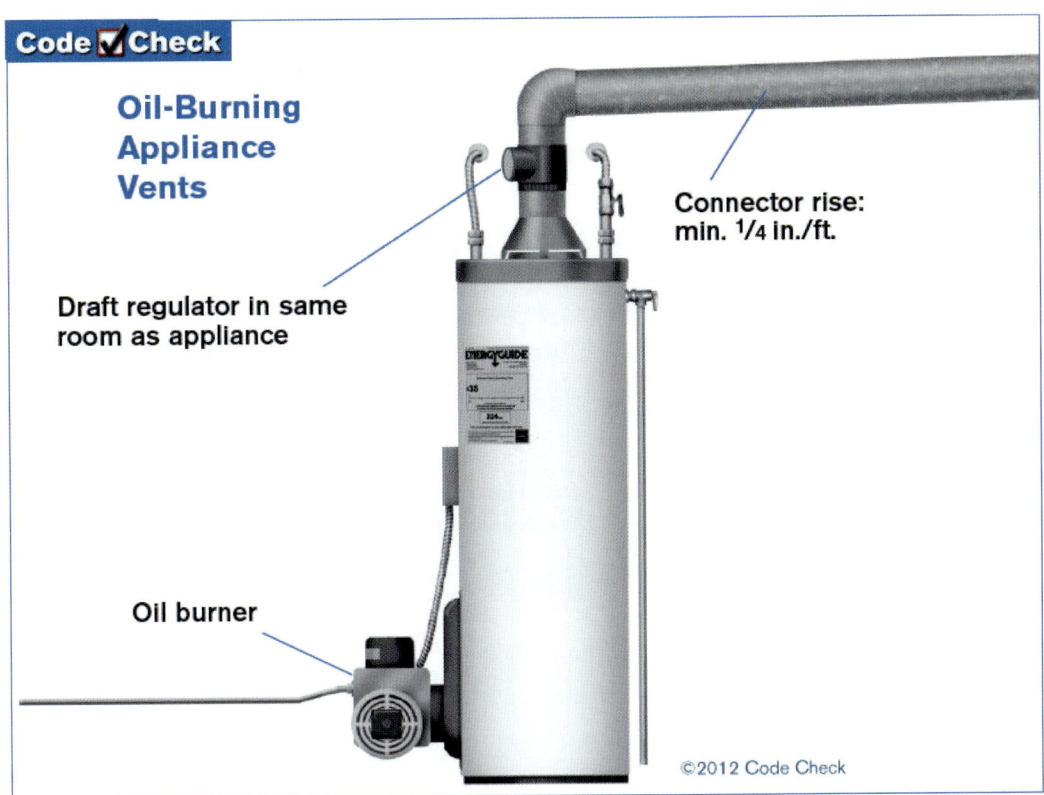

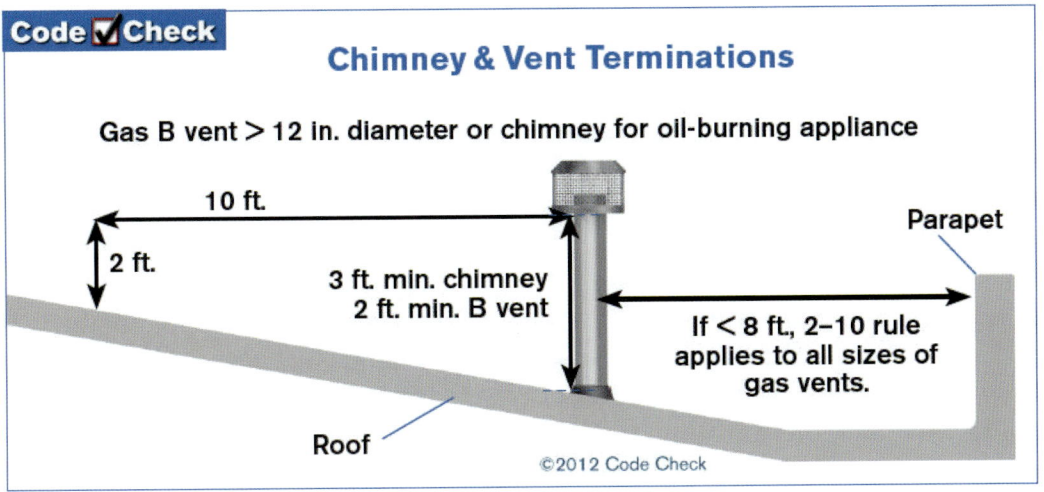

pipe requirements vary too, depending on type of fuel and materials used. The best way to verify proper clearances is to **read the data tag** on the furnace or boiler. It will clearly detail the clearances on the sides and from the draft hood if present. A single-wall metal pipe may require a clearance of up to 18″ for oil furnaces or boilers without a draft hood. With a draft hood, a 9″ clearance is required for oil and a 6″ clearance for gas. Double-wall pipes need clearances of only 3–9″, while a 1″ clearance is enough for gas double-walled "B" vents.

THE HEATING INSPECTION 409

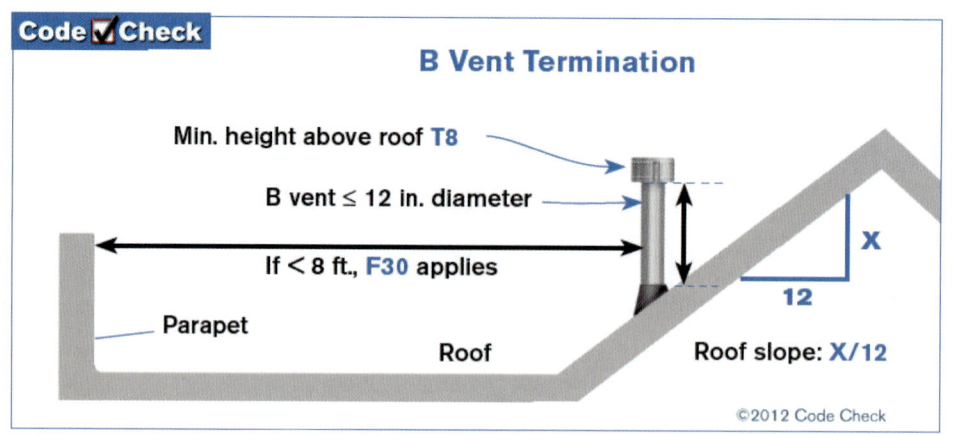

> **Definition**
>
> A *BTU* is a measure of heat output. BTU stands for British Thermal Unit and 1 BTU represents the amount of heat required to raise the temperature of 1 pound of water 1° Fahrenheit.

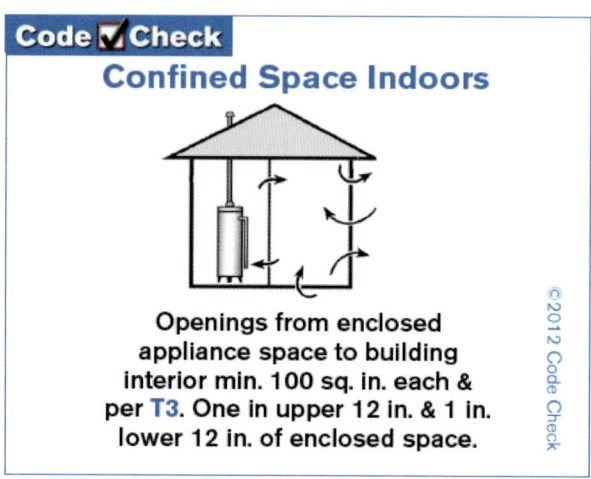

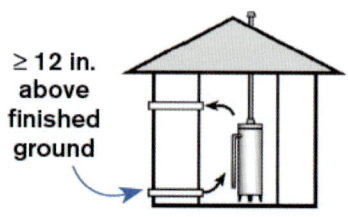

Exhaust or **smoke pipes** should slope upward toward the chimney or termination at a slope of at least 1/4" per foot of length and be well supported. Smoke pipes should be as short as possible. Local codes give requirements about length and the number of elbows (bends) allowed in the run.

Chimney and oil-fired appliance clearances typically follow the 3'-2'-10' rule. That is, the termination of the chimney or oil-fired vent should extend 3' above the roof's surface, and it should be 2' higher than anything within 10' of it, including the ridge, dormers, and parapets. It is slightly different for gas appliances. If the B-vent diameter is less than 12", which most are, then it only has to be 1' above the roof. But if it is less than 8' from a parapet, then the 2/10 rule applies. If a new addition is built that is higher than the existing chimney, the chimney must be extended to meet these requirements. Chimneys not constructed to these standards can experience spillage or back-drafting.

Fossil fuel heating units (oil, propane, or gas-fired, for example) must rely on a supply of combustion and draft (fresh) air for safety. When units are located in **closets or enclosed rooms**, codes require 1 square inch of ventilation per 1000 BTUs of input. (A **BTU** is a British thermal unit. 1 BTU represents the amount of heat required to raise the temperature of 1 pound of water

1° Fahrenheit.) There is, of course, a minimum room size where no additional combustion air is needed. The rule is that you need 50 cubic feet of room volume per 1000 BTU of appliance. So as an example, if you have a 150,000 BTU furnace and a 40,000 BTU water heater side by side, they would need 150 + 40 × 50 = 9500 cubic feet of room volume. Assuming a 10-foot ceiling, that leaves 950 square feet of floor space, or approximately a 30 × 30 room, which is roughly the size of a large two/three-car garage or an unfinished basement. Closet doors should be louvered, and/or rooms should be vented at the top and bottom. Gas or oil-fired furnaces, water heaters, and boilers should not be located in a bedroom, bathroom, or closet, with the exception of a direct-vent type furnace installed according to the manufacturer's specifications. The door to the closet or room should be self-closing and weather-stripped to contain dangerous gases if the system malfunctions. Combustion air for this type of furnace should be drawn from the exterior of the home, but in older homes, it may be drawn from the attic, a crawlspace, or an adjacent room. A note about propane appliances: propane is more than twice as powerful as natural gas. Gas has roughly 1050 BTU/cu ft; propane, 2500 BTU/cu ft.

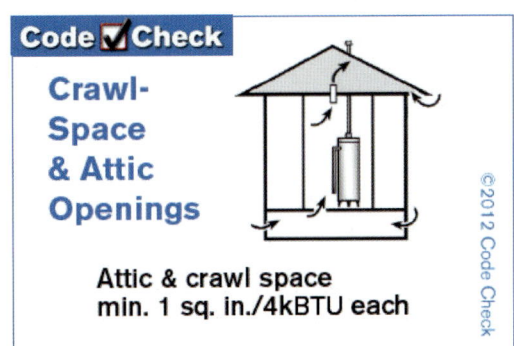

Heat Transfer

The concept of heat transfer refers to moving heat from a warmer object to a cooler object. This happens in three basic ways:

HEAT TRANSFER

- Conduction by physical contact
- Convection by warming air, water, or steam and moving it to a cooler location
- Radiation by radiating energy

- **By conduction:** Some materials are better conductors than others. For example, copper is a better conductor than wood. This explains why the tile floor in the bathroom feels cold while the bath mat feels warm, even though both surfaces are the same temperature. With conduction, heat is transferred from a warmer object to a cooler object by physical contact. An example of conduction is when you touch a hot stove and burn your finger. Most home heating is not accomplished by conduction, with the exception of radiant floor heating systems, which warm your feet as you stand on them.

- **By convection:** Most homes are heated with convection heating. For example, air that is heated expands and become less dense and, therefore, rises. With convection heat transfer, heat is transferred by a fluid such as air, water, or steam that can absorb the heat from a warm location and move it to a cooler location. With forced-air systems, warm air arrives in the living space through **registers**, warming the air in rooms, walls, floors, furniture, and consequently the people in those rooms.

> **Definitions**
>
> *Conduction* is the transfer of heat from a warmer object to a cooler object by physical contact.
>
> *Convection* is the transfer of heat through air, water, or steam that moves heat from a warmer location to a cooler location. Convection heating systems ultimately heat the air in the living space.
>
> *Radiation* is the transfer of heat from a warmer object to a cooler object not in contact with it by radiating heat energy.

When hot water heating systems send hot water to **convectors**, the air in contact with the convectors becomes warmed, and as a result, so do the people in the warm air. A convector is a terminal unit or heat outlet, commonly a baseboard unit, consisting of flat plates, finned plates, or finned pipes over which air passes and is warmed. This is also convective heating.

- **By radiation:** Radiation refers to energy, in the form of heat that moves out in waves from a central point and heats objects in its path. Every object radiates thermal energy. The amount of thermal energy generated is determined by the temperature of the object. With radiation, heat is transferred from a warmer object to a cooler object (or body) that is *not* in physical contact with it. Radiation heat does not warm the air itself. It turns to heat only when the energy is absorbed by the cooler body. An example of radiation heat transfer is when you sit next to a hot stove and the heat is transferred to you from the hot metal.

Hot water and steam heating systems move heated water or steam to metal **radiators** that radiate heat energy in all directions. People in the vicinity absorb the energy, transforming that energy into heat, and are thereby warmed.

To a certain extent, radiators also heat by convection, in that the air in contact with the radiator also is heated.

There are **radiant heating systems** that, in effect, use the entire floor, wall, or ceiling as a radiator. Rooms are warmed by heat energy that radiates from surfaces.

> **HEATING SYSTEMS**
>
> - Gravity warm air
> - Forced warm air
> - Gravity hot water
> - Forced hot water
> - Steam
> - Electric resistance
> - Radiant
> - Heat pump
> - Wood gasification
> - Solar thermal/Radiant floor

Types of Heating Systems

This section will present information on various types of heating systems the home inspector is required to inspect in the course of the heating inspection. The basic types of heating systems are as follows:

- **Gravity warm air:** The gravity warm air furnace heats air, making it less dense and causing it to rise naturally from the furnace through a duct system and circulate throughout the house. Cooler (more dense) air falls through a return duct or opening in the floor. No motorized blowers or fans are used. Fuel can be coal, oil, or gas. Other systems may be fueled by wood pellets, corn, wood, biomass, or other materials.

- **Forced air:** Heat produced by the fuel warms the heat exchanger or refrigerant coil. Air circulation starts when the blower in the furnace or air handler cycles on after the fan switch indicates that the air is sufficiently heated. This air is forced through the ducts and out of the registers in the rooms throughout the home. Return air ducts bring air back to the furnace, completing the cycle. These furnaces are typically fueled by oil, gas, heated refrigerant, or electric coils. Solar energy may also be used. Solar heating systems are not typically part of a home inspections according to most SOPs. It is not a bad idea to become familiar with these systems as they are becoming more common. You want to be able to speak intelligently with your client about their basic operation.

Much progress has been made with forced-air systems in recent years, and **high-efficiency furnaces** (also called **condensing furnaces**) are available that perform up to 98% Annual Fuel Utilization Efficiency (AFUE). This is the number on the yellow Energy Guide label required on new appliances. Condensing furnaces are based on the principle of cooling combustion gases to below their dew point, condensing the vapor and recovering as much **latent heat** as possible. Latent heat is the heat trapped in the water vapor created during the burning of fuel. Remember, CO_2 and H_2O (vapor) are created when fuel is burned. Most condensing

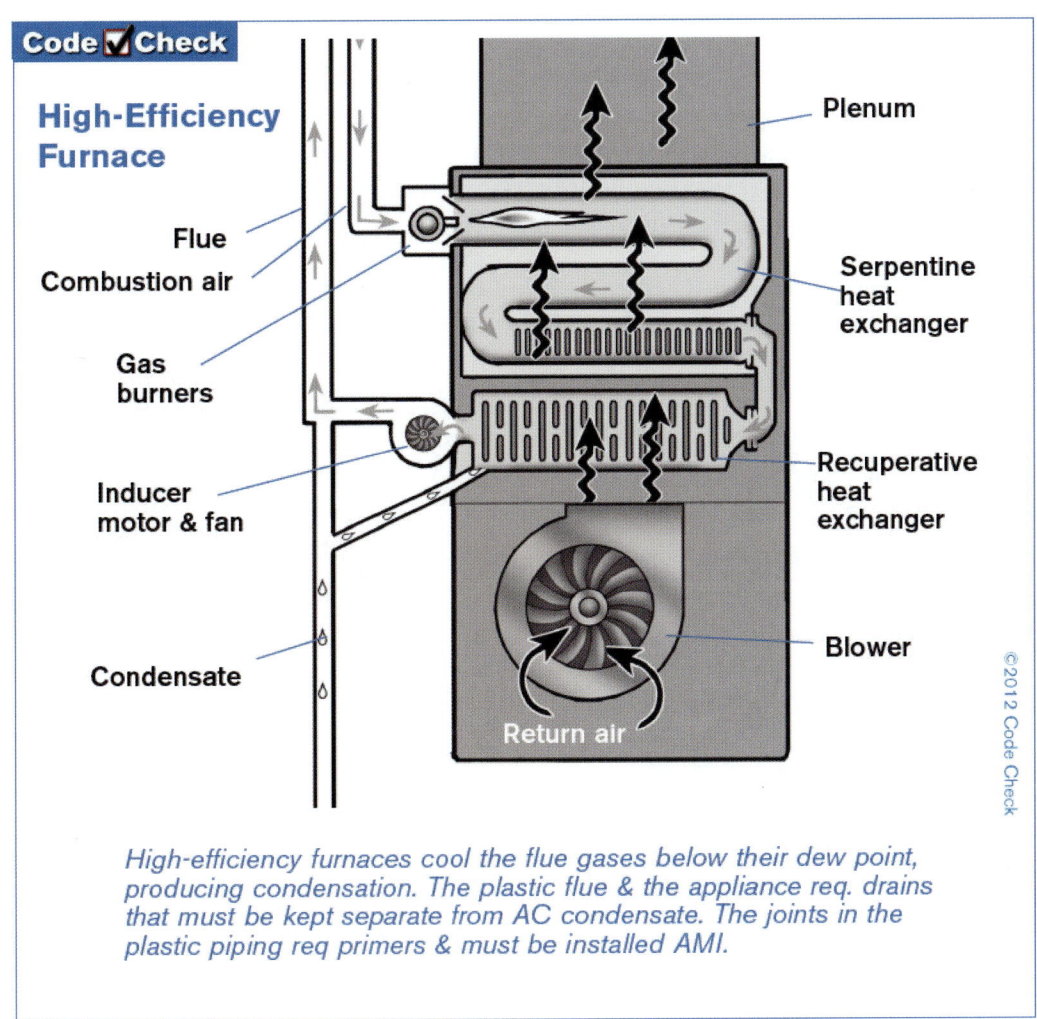

High-efficiency furnaces cool the flue gases below their dew point, producing condensation. The plastic flue & the appliance req. drains that must be kept separate from AC condensate. The joints in the plastic piping req primers & must be installed AMI.

furnaces use outside air for combustion, have two heat exchangers to extract the extra waste heat that would normally go up the flue or chimney, and have a drain to dispose of combustion gas condensate.

- **Gravity hot water:** This system relies on the principle that hot water rises naturally, pushing the cooler water ahead of it, much like the gravity furnace. Once the boiler is fired, hot water starts to move through a pipe system to radiators in each room that give off heat. Cooler water returns to the boiler. Gravity hot water systems are fueled by coal, oil, or gas. This type of boiler is virtually unheard of today.

- **Forced hot water:** This system uses a circulating pump to push hot water through the piping to radiators, convectors, or embedded tubing in the floor in each room. Cooler water returns to the boiler through a second piping system that makes a loop. The system is typically fueled by coal, wood, oil, electricity, or gas. Depending on where you live, newer high-efficiency boilers can achieve 95% efficiency, and innovative technology continues to increase this rate.

- **Steam:** With this system, water is heated in the boiler to produce steam that rises naturally through a piping system to radiators in the house. When cooled, the steam condenses in the pipes and returns as water to the boiler. These units may involve one or two pipes and are heated by gas, oil, wood, or pellets and earlier by coal.

- **Electric resistance heating:** Another method of heating is to have baseboard units or panels on walls or the ceiling in each room. There are also electric resistance heat furnaces, which use electric coils in combination with forced-air systems.

- **Radiant heating:** Radiant heating consists of electric cables, pipes, or tubing buried in floors or ceilings during construction. Electric cables or hot water in the buried pipes heat the surface and radiate heat to the living space. Although electric cables were once popular, many have been abandoned and replaced with other systems. You may still see a thermostat on the wall of every room and wonder what it is for.

Photo #5 RADIANT HEATING THERMOSTAT

This is a typical electric radiant heating thermostat. There would usually be one thermostat per room, so each room is on its own zone as opposed to a central system with a single thermostat.

- **Heat pumps: Air-to-air** heat pumps are essentially air conditioners capable of reversing the flow of refrigerant during the heating season. Technically, a <u>heat pump</u> is a mechanical-compression cycle refrigeration system that can be reversed to heat or cool a controlled space. Installation for this type of system typically consists of two parts: an indoor unit called an air handler and an outdoor unit similar to a central air conditioner, but referred to as a heat pump. A compressor circulates refrigerant that absorbs and releases heat as it travels between the indoor and outdoor units.

  Think of a heat pump as a heat transporter constantly moving heat from one place to another, to where it's needed or not needed, depending on the season. Even in air that seems too cold, heat energy is present. When it's cold outside, a heat pump extracts this outside heat and transfers it inside. When it's warm outside, it reverses direction and acts like an air conditioner, removing heat from the home.

  Note that conventional heat pumps are best for moderate climates, and a supplemental heating source may be needed for lower temperatures in extreme climates. This is not the case for new state of the art Inverter type heat pumps, which work to very low temperatures. This will be discussed later.

  A **geothermal** heat pump or ground source heat pump (GSHP) is a central heating and/or cooling system that transfers heat to or from the ground. It uses the earth as a heat source (in the winter) or a heat sink (in the summer). This design takes advantage of the moderate temperatures in the ground to boost efficiency and reduce the operational costs of heating and cooling systems and may be combined with solar heating to form a geo-solar system with even greater efficiency.

- **Wood gasification:** As wood is burned in the firebox, fresh air is blown downward through the logs and coals. This creates a mixture of hot air and wood gases that are forced through a refractory material where it meets a second jet of super-heated air, creating a torch-like combustion of the retained gases. This process, known as wood gasification, results in almost all the gases being burned with little soot, ash, or creosote residue. This energy is then transferred to a water-jacket heat exchanger and used to heat a home or work environment. Even when the fire burns down, the refractory chamber maintains its temperature; once a heavy-duty draft fan starts, it re-ignites fresh wood.

- **Solar thermal/radiant floor solar heating system:** A radiant floor heating system is often used to provide residential heating. Another option that is perhaps even more plentiful in the housing industry is solar forced-air heating. Both of these systems can be implemented using solar thermal collector systems. While a radiant floor heating system uses solar-heated or gas-heated fluid to heat a space, a forced-air application uses hot air to heat the air space in the home. In order to use solar thermal-heated fluid to heat air for a forced-air heating system, coils of

> **Photo #6 RADIANT FLOOR SOLAR HEATING SYSTEM**
> *Solar thermal, as it's called, can be used to heat the house as well as hot water for taking a shower. We are not required to inspect solar heating systems, but it is a good idea to have basic knowledge of the operating principles.*

tubing carrying the heated fluid are placed in the forced-air path to pick up solar heat and route it to the living space. **Solar air heating** is a solar thermal technology in which the energy from the sun, is captured by an absorbing medium and used to heat air.

6.3 GAS-FIRED SYSTEMS

In this section, we're going to discuss the principles, the components, and the inspection of the natural gas or propane components of gas-fired heating systems, regardless of the type of heating system the burners serve. The study of particular heating systems (warm air, hot water, steam, and so on) begins on page 447.

> **Chapter Note**
>
> *Pages 416–434 present the study and inspection of the gas components of gas-fired heating systems.*

A Word about Efficiencies

Before we discuss the components and inspection of gas-fired heating systems, let's sort out a few terms.

- **Conventional gas systems:** A conventional gas-fired furnace or boiler is the standard type available up to the mid-1970s before improvements began to be made. With these conventional heating

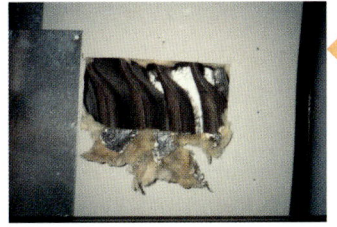

Photo #7 OLDER LENNOX DURACURVE FURNACE

This is an older Lennox Duracurve furnace. The curves of this furnace turned out to be a weak point and cracks were fairly common. A cracked heat exchanger is a safety issue. The problem is you can't see more than maybe 20% of a heat exchanger on a conventional furnace.

Photo #8 INSIDE A HIGH EFFICIENCY FURNACE

This is what's inside of a high efficiency furnace. There are 2 heat exchanger sections, the right-hand tubes and left-hand secondary unit. The secondary heat exchanger is what brings the efficiency up from 80% to 90%+.

Photo #9 INSIDE A HIGH EFFICIENCY FURNACE

This is just a different style of the photo above. Different systems have different designs and configurations.

systems, up to 80% of the heat produced from burning gas stays in the house, while 20% or more goes up the chimney. Another 20% of the warm house air escapes up the chimney when the furnace or boiler isn't operating, and some additional fuel is wasted keeping the pilot burning. So the conventional heating system is said to be between 55% and 65% efficient (AFUE). With conventional systems, house air is used for combustion, the combustion chamber is unsealed, and warm exhaust gases rise naturally up the chimney by convection, commonly called natural draft.

- **Mid-efficiency gas systems:** Beginning in the mid-1970s, some modifications were made to conventional gas-fired furnaces and boilers that increased efficiency to the 78% to 80% AFUE range. One modification is the use of a **motorized vent damper**, which closes when the burners are not in operation, preventing house air (heat) from escaping up the chimney. Another modification is the use of the **induced draft fan** on the exhaust side of the furnace or boiler to pull combustion products through the heat exchanger during operation. The fan, when at rest, reduces heat loss up the flue, much like a damper when the burners are off. Most mid-efficiency systems use an **intermittent pilot** that lights by spark or hot surface igniters only when heat is called for. Another feature is a more convoluted "serpentine" heat exchanger rather than one that is straight. Basically, a mid-efficiency system is a conventional system with the modifications mentioned here.

GAS-FIRED HEATING SYSTEMS

AFUE Ratings

Conventional	55%–65%
Mid-efficiency	80%
High-efficiency	90%–98%

- **High-efficiency gas systems:** The newest gas-fired furnaces and boilers can have an efficiency rating in the 90% to 98% AFUE range; commonly called 90 Plus furnaces. The principle behind these systems, also called condensing furnaces, is to remove so much heat from the water vapor in the exhaust gases that they are reduced to condensation. This is accomplished by having more than one heat exchanger. With high-efficiency units, the condensate is drained through plastic piping or tubing and the cooled gases are exhausted outside through the house roof or wall; no chimney is required.

Other features of high-efficiency units are the use of outside air for combustion air, the presence of induced draft fans, and sealed combustion chambers. In addition, all use electronic ignition rather than a standing pilot.

In general, the home inspector has more access for the inspection of the components in conventional and mid-efficiency gas-fired heating units than with the high-efficiency units. We'll discuss these conventional components in greater detail because they are most likely to be seen due to their access. However, because conventional furnaces are over 30 years old, they are becoming less common as they are replaced with newer higher-efficiency models.

Gas Supply

The gas that fuels the heating system may be **natural gas**, which is drawn from underground fields and purified and blended before being piped to the home by the gas company or utility. **Bottled or LP** (liquefied propane or petroleum) **gas** can be used to fuel heating systems too. LP gas can be a single gas or a mixture such as propane, butane, or isobutane.

Natural gas is distributed to the house in underground pipes at a high pressure of 90 psi (pounds per square inch) or an intermediate pressure of 30 psi. At the house side of the meter, the gas pressure is reduced to **about 0.25 psi (7″ water column)** for home use. There may be a **pressure relief valve or regulator** before the meter to allow pressurized gas to escape. This regulator

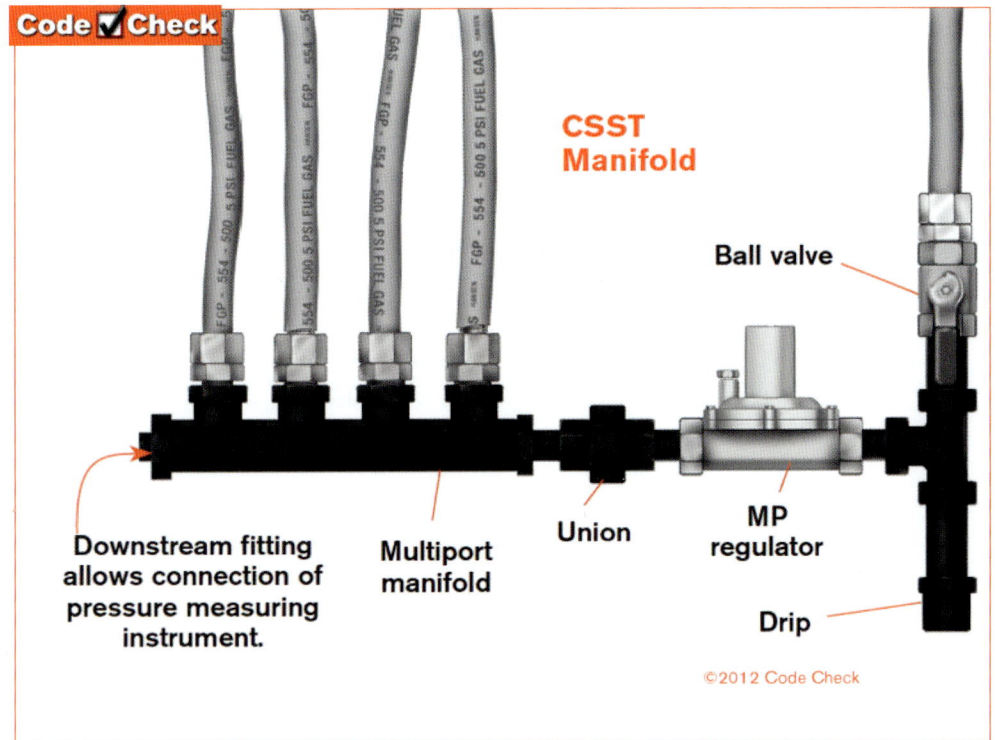

should be on the exterior of the house or vented to the exterior. You may have higher pressures within the house for larger appliances that are fed with CSST and have a regulator at the appliance itself. This allows more BTUs of gas to the appliance without having to run a very large pipe. This is another benefit of using CSST over steel pipe.

The home inspector can check the gas meter to see if it is adequately sized to supply gas to the heating unit and water heater, although it is not commonly done. The meter is rated in cubic feet per hour. **One cubic foot of gas is approximately equal to 1000 BTU**, so a meter rated at 250 cubic feet per hour will supply gas that is the equivalent of 250,000 BTU per hour. The BTU capacity at the meter should be equal to or greater than the sum of the input BTU requirements for the heating system and water heater, along with other devices such as a dryer, gas-log fireplace, and pool heater.

Remember, the gas input rating of an appliance (for example, a 100,000 BTU furnace) is actually 100,000 BTUs per hour that it runs.

Black iron (steel or galvanized) gas piping of 3/4"–1" or more can be used to carry gas from the meter to the heating unit. It runs on the underside of the floor joists and is attached to the joists in a basement or crawl space installation. In a slab-on-grade home, it can be run beneath the slab or more likely through the ceiling space and walls of the home. The piping will be run right beside the heating unit to the level of the burners. Type K and Type L copper may also be used for gas lines.

GAS LINE

- Incoming black iron piping
- Manual turnoff
- Drip leg
- Main gas valves
- Manifold to burner

For Your Information

Check your local codes for what's allowed for gas lines in the home. See if rigid copper, flexible copper, and CSST are permitted.

THE HEATING INSPECTION

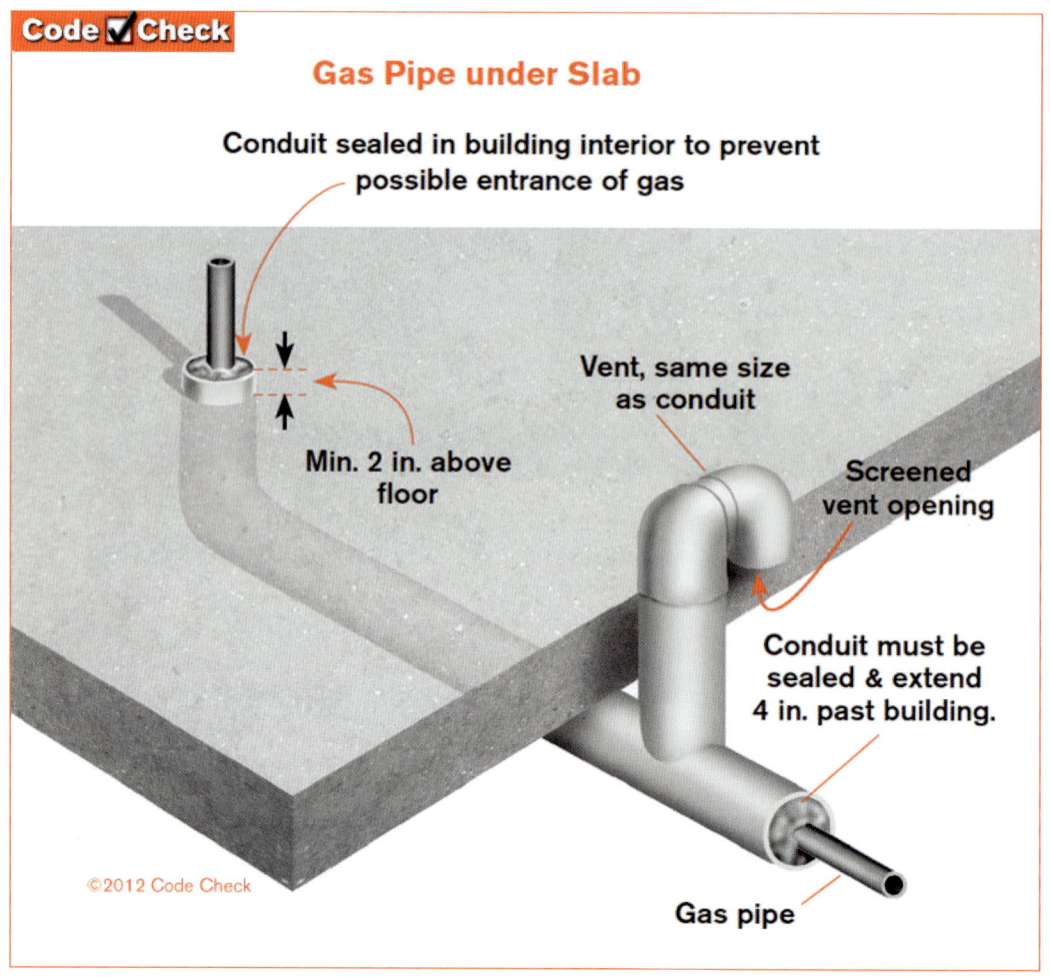

Copper piping may not be permitted for propane or natural gas lines in some communities where the sulfur content is high, which is most of the southwestern United States. In some areas, flexible copper piping may be permitted for natural gas connections between rigid metal lines and appliances. Plastic may not be used indoors. Cast iron or rubber lines are not allowed. Corrugated stainless steel tubing (CSST), a relatively new product (1990s), brings gas from a manifold near the meter to the various gas-fired appliances throughout the house. Exposed gas lines made of any material other than black iron (steel) must be labeled as gas piping with a yellow or black coating or label every 5′. Labels are not required in the same room as the appliance served.

There should be a **manual shut-off valve** in the line at the heating unit so that the gas supply can be turned off, if necessary, for maintenance work or an emergency. Where the gas line turns to meet the heating unit, a **drip leg** (also called a pipe trap) is installed to trap sediment, moisture, and metal chips from the pipeline. (Drip legs may be required depending on the moisture content of the gas and are not necessary in areas with "dry gas.") A sediment trap is usually required for gas-fired furnaces. The gas line feeds into a **combination control** (automatic gas valve and pilot control valve in older systems) that is part of the heating unit. Gas is delivered to the burner through the gas **manifold**.

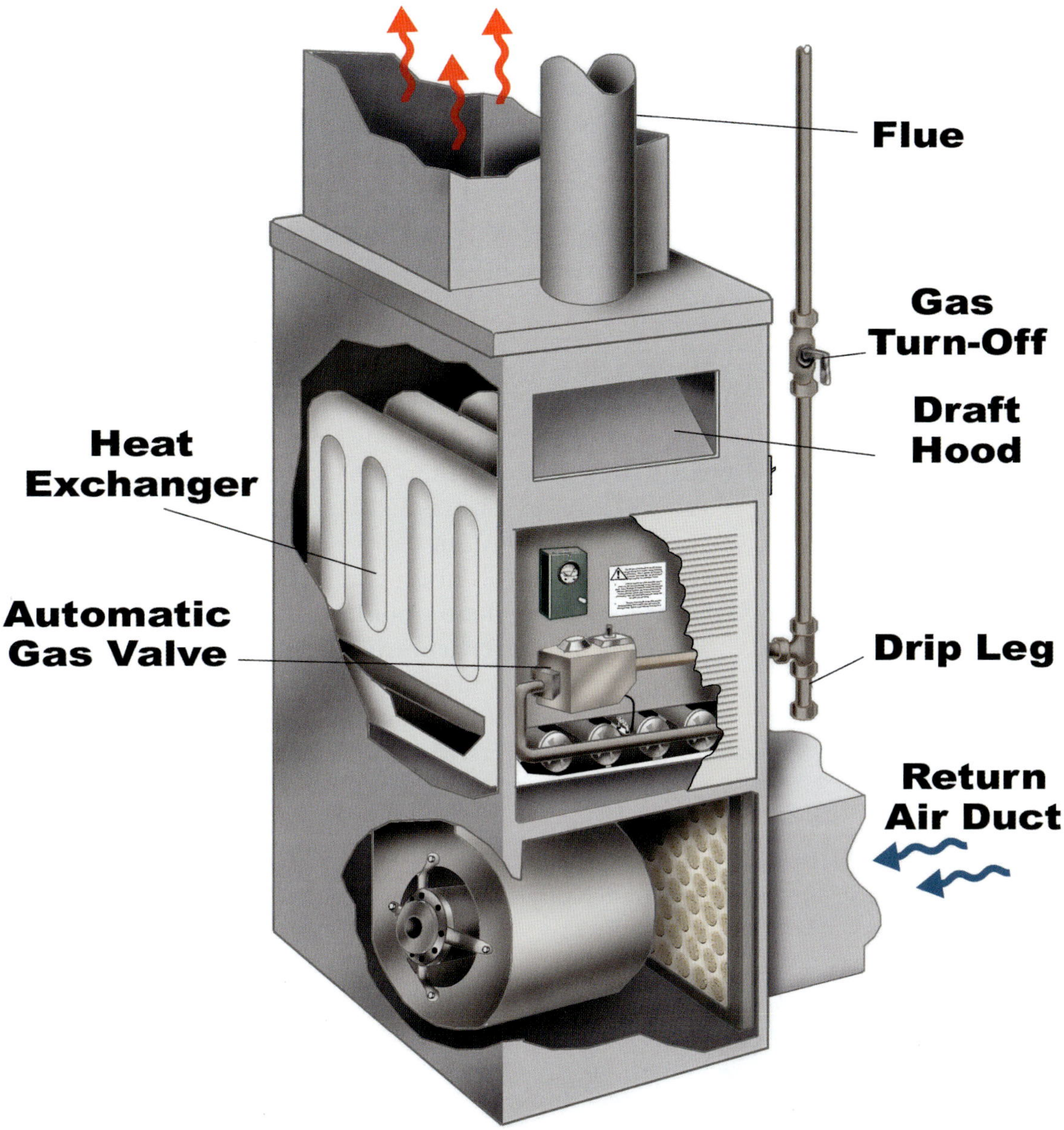

Illustration by Paddy Morrissey

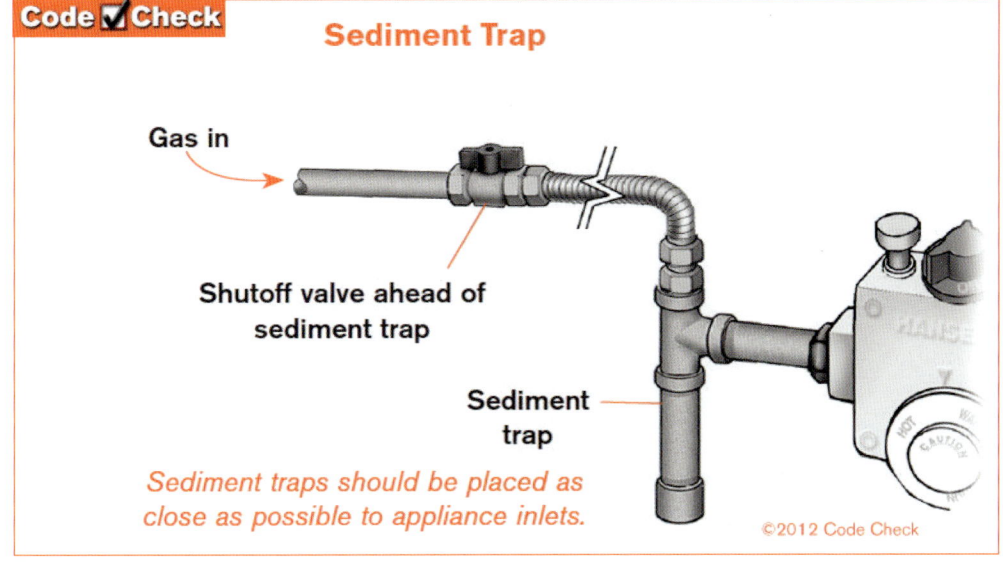

THE HEATING INSPECTION

> **Definitions**
>
> The <u>main automatic gas valve</u> starts and stops the flow of gas to the burners. The <u>pilot control valve</u> starts and stops the flow of gas to the pilot.
>
> A <u>pilot</u> is a small flame that ignites gas at the burners. A <u>standing pilot</u> is one that burns continuously. An <u>intermittent pilot</u> lights only on a call for heat.
>
> A <u>thermocouple</u> is a bimetallic element that senses whether or not the pilot is lighted and controls the pilot control valve, turning off the flow of gas to the pilot when the pilot flame is out.

Gas Controls

The volume and pressure of gas delivered to the burner is controlled by a metering valve. This main control for a gas-fired furnace or boiler is normally a combination control or box-like unit housing the **main automatic gas valve** and the **pilot control valve**.

These are slightly different if you have a mid- or high-efficiency furnace. It may be a two-stage intermittent or hot surface ignition type. It really doesn't matter because you don't do anything to either one during the inspection.

These main controls on the gas-fired system respond to electrical signals from the **thermostat and thermocouple** to start gas flow to the burners when temperatures fall below a preset point and to stop gas flow when temperatures reach a desired level. The controls also respond electrically to a **limit control** on the heating unit to turn off the burners when the unit overheats due to some malfunction if the blower or circulating pump won't turn on. The limit controls, which sense air temperature in furnaces and water temperature in boilers, turn off gas flow to the burners when high temperature limits are reached.

- **The pilot control valve and thermocouple:** Most older gas-fired systems and some mid-efficiency systems have a standing pilot, whose

Photo #10 GAS VALVE OR GAS CONTROL VALVE

This is a typical gas valve or gas control valve. It allows the gas to flow to the burners when the thermostat calls for heat.

purpose is to light the burners when heat is called for and the main gas valve opens. A separate gas line, usually small flexible tubing, runs from the main gas control unit to the pilot.

Conventional gas-fired systems have a **standing pilot**, which means that it burns continuously. The standing pilot uses a safety feature called a **thermocouple** that senses whether the pilot is lighted. The thermocouple is an element made of two dissimilar metals that, when heated by the pilot, completes a circuit to the pilot control valve, keeping it open and letting gas flow from the main gas valve to the burner when called for by the thermostat. If the pilot goes out, the thermocouple cools, breaks the circuit, closes the valve, and stops the flow of gas to the gas valve. When the pilot is out or the thermocouple is bad, the main gas valve will not open and the burner will not ignite.

Customers with standing pilots often ask home inspectors if they should turn off the pilot flame during the summer to save money. In areas where condensation can be a problem, causing rust inside the heat exchanger, the pilot can provide enough warmth to avoid this problem. If condensation is not a problem, the pilot can be turned off. In most places, turning it off for the summer is a good idea. The other issue is whether the thermocouple will work when the pilot is relighted in the fall. Luckily they are very inexpensive devices.

Mid-efficiency gas-fired heating systems may have an **intermittent pilot**, which means that the pilot is lighted only when there is a call for heat. The intermittent pilot is ignited by a spark igniter and uses a thermocouple to verify ignition. Some mid-efficiency and high-efficiency furnaces and boilers may not have pilots at all. To ignite the gas, they use **electronic ignition** with a hot surface igniter or electric spark that is energized when the thermostat calls for heat. A thermocouple-like safety device called a flame sensor will shut down the system if the gas is not ignited, as well as the burners if the burners don't stay lit.

- **Main automatic gas valve:** Normally, the main gas valve is housed in a combination unit with the pilot control valve. This valve starts and stops the flow of gas to the burners and meters the incoming gas stream for constant volume and pressure to the burner. The main gas valve receives feedback from the other control and safety devices (thermostat, limit control, thermocouple, and pilot control valve) to determine whether it is safe or appropriate to allow gas into the combustion chamber.

> **MAIN GAS CONTROLS**
>
> - Main automatic gas valve
> - Pilot control valve

Gas Burners

When inspecting the furnace's heat shield, check to see if it is loose or missing altogether.

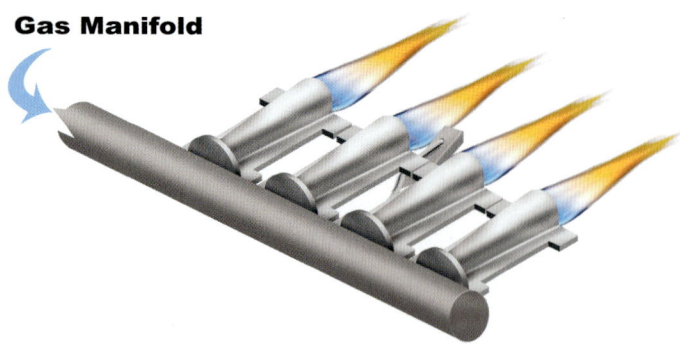

Mono-Port Burners

Illustration by Paddy Morrissey

Definitions

The abbreviation CO stands for carbon monoxide, a life-threatening gas.

Combustion air, also called primary air, is the air required for mixing with fuel gas before the gas is burned.

For Beginning Inspectors

As you begin your study of heating systems, try to view as many different systems as possible. Hands-on experience is an important part of the learning process. Start with conventional gas-fired furnaces and boilers. Ask your friends if you can look at their units and have them fire up the unit so that you can observe the flames. Become familiar with the gas controls, burners, pilot, thermocouple, and so on. Move on to view some of the newer mid-efficiency and high-efficiency models.

For Your Library

It is worthwhile to visit retail heating outlets to see new models. Pick up their pamphlets and start your own files of these heating systems.

A heat shield is the metal cover in front of the heat exchanger chambers and above the burners. It is usually held in place with two small screws. In older style conventional furnaces, it needs to be removed for access to the heat exchanger and burners. Check for rust, holes, or other deterioration. If it is scorched or soot-covered, flames from the burners are making improper contact. If they are found, the above conditions should be included in the inspection report.

The heat exchanger in the conventional and mid-efficiency gas-fired heating system is a semi-sealed firebox, open at the bottom where the gas burners are. Burners in old gas-fired systems were star-shaped or circular. The later conventional systems had **ribbon burners** or tubes, each with a row of small holes, slots, or ports where the gas comes out. **Mono-port** or in-shot burners have a completely different arrangement and operation than ribbon burners. They are like little flame-throwers shooting their flames into the heat exchanger chambers. Unlike the ribbon burner that extends into the heat exchanger, the in-shot burners are mounted outside the heat exchanger. This type of burner is used in both mid- and high-efficiency furnaces and boilers.

Natural gas or propane, if just allowed to flow from the end of a tube, will burn with a yellow, smoky flame containing unburned gas and life-threatening combustion by-products such as carbon monoxide (CO). But gas in a heating system is premixed with air *before* burning so the flame will be primarily blue and the products are mainly carbon dioxide and water vapor. This air, called **combustion or primary air**, is admitted to the burner in conventional systems through an **air shutter** located where the burner tube connects to the manifold. Set screws fit into slots on each tube and are used to adjust the shutters for the ratio of gas and air for proper flame appearance. The shutters are set at the factory or adjusted by the technician who installs the system.

During the inspection of the gas burners, the home inspector can note the condition of the flames above the burner and determine whether the proper mix of gas and combustion air is present by their color. Gas burners can become corroded and their ports clogged, interfering with proper burner operation. The rust comes from the flaking of the heat exchanger above; when the ribbon burners rust, they rust through and the slots become holes. The following conditions will alert the inspector to problems:

Photo #11 MONO-PORT or IN-SHOT TYPE BURNERS

These three burners are called mono-port or in-shot type burners. They are like flamethrowers shooting their flame and heat into the heat exchanger chambers. As you can see, the silver dollar sized holes do not allow for much of an inspection of the heat exchanger.

- **Flames roaring and dancing on the burner:** This condition indicates that the flow (velocity) of the gas/air mixture is greater than the burning rate. It allows unburned gas to escape up the flue and creates CO and waste due to incomplete combustion. Combustion air and/or the gas input rate needs to be adjusted by a qualified technician.

- **Flashback or flames with a blowtorch sound burning inside the burner or near the manifold:** This condition occurs when the flow velocity of the gas/air mixture is lower than the burning rate. This problem also causes CO and waste with soot buildup due to incomplete combustion. Combustion air needs to be reduced or gas flow increased.

- **A bang or pop when the burner shuts down:** This condition may be followed by burning in the burner head. The head is the very beginning of the burner just after the orifice. The flame should project out from the burner and not be in the head area. There may be too much combustion air present, a low gas flow, or a faulty burner.

- **Flames with yellow tips:** This condition is usually caused by a lack of combustion air and can be fixed by increasing its flow, typically into the room. However, it can indicate dirty or clogged burners or a heat exchanger problem. Soot buildup and CO production is the result of this problem.

- **Fluctuating flames:** When the flame varies greatly during burner operation, it can be caused by dirty burners or by erratic gas pressure.

- **Floating flames:** When flames are long and shapeless and seem to float above the burners, it's usually caused by a lack of combustion air. It could

FLAME PATTERNS

- Dancing flames
- Flashback
- Extinction pop
- Yellow flames
- Fluctuating flames
- Floating flames
- Flame rollout
- Disturbance or color change when furnace fan kicks on

indicate an improper air shutter adjustment, dirty burners, or a blocked flue or chimney. The condition is dangerous because flames can roll out of the combustion chamber, causing a fire hazard. The production of CO is always a result of floating flames.

- **Flames rolling out of the combustion chamber:** Flame rollout is the end result of a floating flame condition, indicating that ignited gas is spilling out of the chamber. In addition to being a fire hazard, rollout can scorch other heating components, including wires and safety controls, as well as stored items near the furnace.

- **Flame disturbance or color change when the blower turns on:** In furnaces, a disturbance in flames or changing flame color when the fan is in operation is an indication of a faulty heat exchanger, which is a major defect in the heating system, usually resulting in the furnace being replaced. Flames may lift off the burner, distort, or roll out of the combustion chamber only after the fan turns on.

Definitions

Draft air, also called secondary air, is the air required to insure the discharge of exhaust gases through the flue.

The *draft hood* and *draft diverter* are devices that protect the heating unit from excessive updrafts and chimney downdrafts.

NOTE: In high-efficiency furnaces and boilers, the combustion chamber is usually sealed. In some units, there is a porthole (about a 1″ diameter piece of glass) that the home inspector can look through to verify ignition and flame color. In others, there is no visual access to the combustion chamber. High-efficiency units may have burners in the sealed combustion chamber, or in the case of the pulse furnace, operate by igniting an air/gas mixture released in short pulses directly from a valve instead of a continuously burning flame.

In addition to combustion air, **draft or secondary air** is needed to carry air through the heat exchanger and to discharge the combustion products through the flue. Draft air enters the heat exchanger through the spaces around the burners. Proper ventilation must be available to provide enough combustion and draft air to the heating unit. As mentioned on page 410, gas-fired heating units in confined spaces (less than 50 cu ft of room volume per 1000 BTU of appliance) require additional combustion air venting.

The operation of gas burners requires a small, steady amount of draft air passing through the heat exchanger to ensure that exhaust gases pass up the chimney, but not excessive amounts. The **draft hood** on a boiler and the **draft diverter** on a furnace (see page 1) protect the unit from strong updrafts by allowing room air to be drawn into the flue directly rather than through the combustion chamber. They also protect the unit from downdrafts from the chimney or flue, which could extinguish the pilot flame, by diverting them away from the heating unit. Dilution air should always pass into a hood or diverter, not be flowing out of it. Any spillage from the draft hood or draft diverter during normal operation means a malfunction in the smoke pipe or flue, which could be blocked or possibly too large. Spillage is the term for exhaust gases flowing into the room instead of up the flue or chimney. Most combustion appliances will "spill" for the first 30–60 seconds of operation until the flue pipe warms up and it begins to draft normally. If it continues to "spill" after about a minute, then it is called "back-drafting," which is a **safety hazard** and should be reported as such. This is typically the case when a furnace and water heater share the same flue and the furnace is replaced with a high-efficiency unit that has its own flue going directly outside, not up the chimney. The water heater, by itself, will not draft properly due to the oversized chimney or flue. This can be evidenced by rust and mineral stains (white crust) at the seams of the flue/vent pipe where the water vapor is condensing in the flue before it exits outside at the top. A device called a heat switch, also known as a spillage switch, or roll out safety switch, is a safety device that detects increased heat at the draft hood generated by flue gas spillage. When spillage is detected, the switch deactivates the burner to stop the continued production of combustion products. The heat switch will not allow the burner to restart until the switch has been manually reset. Because exhaust gases can exit through the draft hood or diverter into the home, this condition represents a **safety hazard**.

Photo #12 *The sensor with its wires at the bottom of the draft hood is the spillage switch. It detects heat coming back into the room as a result of the flue being damaged or blocked, a condition called back-drafting.*

Inspecting Gas Components

We're going to talk about inspecting only the gas components of a gas-fired furnace or boiler in this section. These components are similar regardless of what type of heating system they serve. We'll discuss the inspection of different types of furnaces and boilers in detail later in this section. The inspection of the gas components on a heating unit includes checking the following:

- Meter, gas lines, and gas shut-off
- Combustion air
- Flame shield condition
- Burner condition
- Burner ignition
- Flame pattern activity
- Draft hood or draft diverter operation

GAS COMPONENTS

- Meter, gas lines, and gas turnoff
- Combustion air
- Flame shield
- Gas burners
- Draft hood or draft diverter

Follow these procedures to inspect the **gas burners** on a conventional or mid-efficiency gas-fired heating system:

1. **At the heating unit, turn off the unit using the safety switch or serviceman's switch.** You want to turn off the heating unit so that you can safely gain access to the burner area.

2. **Remove the flame shield for inspection.** The burner area may have an outer access panel and/or flame shield that prevents unburned gas from rolling out of the combustion chamber during operation. The interior surface may be inspected for evidence of rollout—scorching and burning. This is not required according to most Standards of Practice. If it is done, it should be attempted only on a conventional furnace, not a mid-efficiency or high-efficiency furnace. The flame shield is typically held in place with two screws.

3. **Examine the burner heads for rust, corrosion, and clogging.** Before the heating unit is fired up, inspect the burners for any signs of rusting and corrosion. Look for mechanical damage to the burners, any displacement, soot, or dirt on the burners that can interfere with normal operation. Note the burner heads or ports for signs of clogging. All of these conditions should be included in your inspection report.

CAUTION: When you discover corrosion, don't use your screwdriver to try to scrape or poke at the corroded areas. You can poke right through the corroded area and make holes. Try not to damage equipment as you inspect it.

4. **Turn the unit on, using the safety switch.** After inspecting the burner components, replace the flame shield and turn on the heating unit using the safety or serviceman's switch so it may fire.

5. **Turn up the thermostat so the heating system fires.** While you are inspecting the living areas of the home, you'll be examining heat registers and radiators and noting the presence of heat sources in each room. Home inspectors usually turn up the thermostat so that the heating system kicks on during this portion of the inspection. However, this depends on the season and whether the unit is already in use. Turning the thermostat up 5° is a good practice because you don't need to remember the previous setting—just turn it back down 5° when you're done. You may also want to confirm that air is coming out of the registers or that the radiators are warming up.

During your inspection, heed these cautions:

— If the gas is turned off to the heating unit or there is a **red tag** on the gas line, do not restart the burner. The red tag, usually from the gas utility, indicates a defect in the system that must be repaired by a qualified technician before it is put back into service.

BURNER PROCEDURES

- Turn off heating unit.
- Remove flame shield and inspect.
- Inspect burners.
- Fire up heating unit.
- Monitor flames.

— If the gas supply is turned off to the furnace or boiler, do not restart the system without talking to the homeowner first. The system may be shut down due to some defect that needs correction. Find out what the circumstances are and get permission from the homeowner to fire up the unit. Better yet, get the homeowner to do it for you.

— Remember to ask your customer to stand aside (you too) when you fire the heating system. Do not stand in front of the burner area, peering into the chamber and waiting for the unit to fire. Move to the side of the heating unit out of harm's way. Flame rollout can occur and endanger both you and your customer.

— If for any reason the pilot goes out during your inspection, follow the directions for relighting it. You should wait 5 minutes before relighting to give unburned gases a chance to dissipate and become diluted. This is especially important when working with an LP gas supply because it is heavier than air, settling to your feet; you don't smell it like you do natural gas; and it takes more time to disperse. *LP gas is extremely explosive!*

When you fire up the heating unit, the gas at the burners should light with a gentle "puh" sound. Watch for any defects in the ignition such as flame rollout, loud noises such as popping and roaring, smoke, or vibration. These are all conditions that require examination and repair by qualified technicians.

- **Observe the flame pattern during operation.** Watch the flames at the burners for those conditions noted on pages 425–426—yellow color, flashback, dancing, fluctuating, floating, rollout, and other distortions.

    If the unit is a forced-air furnace, also monitor the flames after the blower turns on. If the flames' color changes or the blower causes the flames to distort, lift off the burner, or roll out of the combustion chamber, there is a problem with the heat exchanger. (We'll discuss the inspection of the heat exchanger later in this chapter.)

NOTE: In most older furnaces, the blower will operate if the access panel is removed. There should be a safety switch, which when pushed in by the access panel, allows the fan to operate. You can push this switch with your finger to get the fan to operate during your inspection. Make sure the blower door switch hasn't been bypassed, allowing the blower to run with the door missing. This may allow flue gases to be drawn into the house air—an obvious **safety hazard**.

For Beginning Inspectors

If you have a gas-fired heating furnace or boiler, follow these procedures to inspect the gas burners. If not, get permission from friends to examine their burners. Be sure to follow the safety precautions we've mentioned.

Get as much hands-on experience as you can. Pay particular attention to flame patterns so that you can easily recognize defective conditions.

CAUTIONS

Don't stand or allow your customer to stand in front of the heating unit when it's fired up. Both of you should <u>stand to the side</u> out of harm's way.

If you have to relight the pilot during the heating unit inspection, <u>wait 5 minutes</u> for gases to disperse before you relight.

Photo #13 BLOWER DOOR SAFETY SWITCH

This blower door safety switch has been taped over. The purpose of the switch is to prevent the furnace from firing or operating when the blower door is removed. The blower has enough power to suck the flue gases out of the flue pipe and blow them throughout the house ductwork. This is a clear safety issue.

Personal Note

"During one of my inspections, the pilot was out on the furnace. After checking with the owners, I got permission to light the pilot and turn on the furnace. It turns out that the furnace had a malfunctioning gas valve so that gas was released to the burners before the pilot was lighted. When I lighted the pilot, there was a huge flame rollout. Of course, my face was right down there. I burned my forehead and singed my eyebrows.

Please be careful in situations like this one. A burned face is not a good thing to have."

CAUTION

If you detect a <u>strong odor of gas</u> in a home, ask people to leave the house immediately. Call the gas company for help. It is very responsive, usually arriving within 30–60 minutes.

While inspecting the gas components of a furnace or boiler, watch for the following conditions:

- **Gas leaks:** Any strong gas odor in the house should be dealt with immediately. Call the gas company for assistance right away (not a bad idea to have the local utilities' numbers programmed into your phone, just in case) and have the customer and other parties who are present leave the house. Don't take any chances in a serious situation, but don't push the panic button either. A faint odor of gas at pilot lights, especially at old stoves, is common and isn't considered a leak.

  However, the faint odor of gas along piping running to the heating system is an indication of a gas leak. Be especially sensitive to gas leaks at connections/fittings and at the unit itself. These conditions should be reported as a **safety hazard** with the recommendation that the proper personnel be called to correct the situation.

- **Improper LP gas tank location:** National standards dictate the location of LP gas tanks. Because of the explosive nature of LP gas, the tanks should never be located indoors or near a window. In general, they're required to be located at least 10′ from the house. Any violations should be reported as a **safety hazard**.

- **Improper piping or missing shut-off valve:** Follow the gas line from the source (meter in most cases) to the heating unit(s) and report the use of piping materials other than black iron or galvanized steel, Type K or L copper (if permitted in your area), or CSST. Make sure that gas piping is properly labeled as described previously. Watch for improper installation and inadequate piping support. The gas shut-off for the heating unit should be located in the same room as the unit and within reach if overhead.

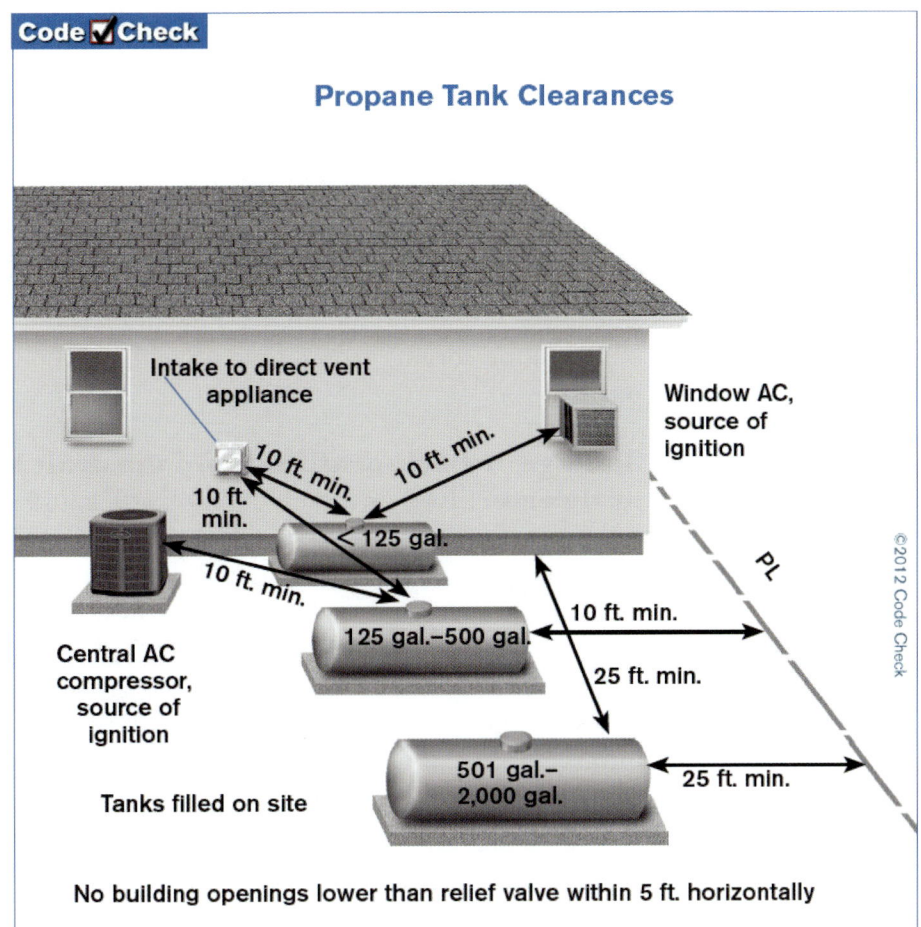

- **Improper vent space:** For those gas-fired systems in confined spaces that use solely house air for combustion air and draft air, make note of whether the heating unit has enough vent space (room volume) to provide the amount of air needed.

- **Missing or scorched flame shield, flame rollout:** Always be sure the flame shield is still in place on a heating unit and report if it's missing. Scorching and burn marks on the flame shield or other components near the combustion chamber should be pointed out to the customer. Explain that **flame rollout** is the cause, a condition caused when unburned gas spills out of the combustion chamber.

- **Dirty, rusted, or corroded burners:** Inspect the burners carefully before firing the furnace or boiler and report these conditions (see pages 443–444). Be sure to note that the system was not tested if the system has been shut down.

- **Evidence of CO production:** Monitor the flames for those conditions that indicate that CO is

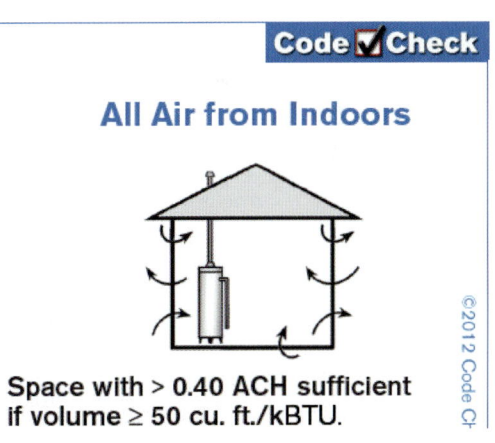

Section Note

"One of my inspectors ran into a situation where there was a gas leak at the furnace connection which he didn't detect before firing the furnace. Upon ignition, the flames rolled out, hit the gas pocket, and blew the furnace cover off. It flew all the way across the basement."

THE HEATING INSPECTION

> **INSPECTING GAS COMPONENTS**
>
> - Gas leaks
> - Improper LP tank location or piping
> - Missing turnoff valve
> - Lack of combustion air space
> - Missing or scorched flame shield
> - Dirty, rusted, or corroded burners
> - CO production
> - Draft spillage
> - Improper clearances and venting

being produced as a result of incomplete combustion—flashback, yellow, floating, or dancing flames. These conditions should be reported as **safety hazards**, and you should recommend that a technician examine the heating unit and correct them (see pages 425–426). Another sign that CO is being produced during combustion is the distinctive smell of **aldehydes**, an odor similar to what you may have smelled in a new mobile home. This smell is the result of the flame cooling when it burns against metal parts.

- **Spillage or back-drafting from the draft hood or diverter:** Light a match or smoke stick and hold it next to the hood or diverter. Move it around the area, waiting to see which way the flame or smoke leans. If the flame or smoke leans in toward the hood or diverter, that's good. But if the flame or smoke leans outward, there may be a down/back-drafting problem and exhaust gases and CO can be released into the home. This should be reported as a **safety hazard**. You can also use an inspection mirror to test for the drafts at the hood or diverter. A fogged up mirror indicates down drafting from the water vapor in combustion products. A combustible gas detector can also be used. Remember, this is detecting the unburned fuel, not CO. It can be used as an indirect method for checking for CO because exhaust gases, regardless of whether CO is present, should not be coming into the house air.

- **Improper clearances and venting:** The home inspector should examine the heating and venting equipment for the proper clearances from combustibles (see pages 408–412), and record any issues in the inspection report. The inspector should examine the flue for proper slope and length, holes, open joints, and corrosion. If the flue (in the room, before the chimney) is longer than 10′ or has more than one elbow, be sure the draft is not affected. If gas appliances vent into a masonry chimney, check the opening where the flue enters the chimney flue for proper sealing with mortar at the "thimble" described earlier. If metal B-vent piping is used, examine it for a tight connection. Any holes or leaks in flues should be recorded as a **safety hazard**. All single-walled piping "vent-connector" or "flue" piping must be mechanically fastened together. Typically three sheet metal screws are used per section to hold the piping together. Duct tape does not qualify as a mechanical connection. B- or L-type vents have interlocking connections that do not require screws.

The condition of the **chimney** should also be inspected. Gas-fired heating systems (except for high-efficiency units that exhaust directly outside) require a chimney or vent for exhausting combustion products.

Type B gas vents or **metal chimneys** are also used for gas-fired units. Masonry chimneys exhausting combustion products from a gas-fired heating system should have a **flue liner**, usually metal, clay, or asbestos cement pipe. Note that the home inspector is not required to inspect the interior of flues where they are not accessible or visible.

A gas appliance flue should not be shared with an oil-fired appliance or fireplace. Note this as a **safety hazard**. However, multiple gas appliances can be vented together and will be discussed later.

The home inspector should check for the presence of a **chimney cleanout** at the base of the chimney. A cleanout leg should be present to catch debris from chimney and flue deterioration. Open the cleanout door carefully, as it may be full of critters, soot, and debris. Use your inspection mirror and flashlight to look up into the interior of the cleanout leg. If a great amount of debris is present, the flue may be blocked. A blocked flue should be reported as a **safety hazard**. Recommend regular cleaning at the cleanout to prevent this unsafe condition.

INSPECTION NOTE

Gas space heaters should be inspected for these same items. Always report any unvented gas space heater as a safety hazard.

All of them produce carbon dioxide, which causes headaches and other symptoms. The malfunctioning ones can produce deadly levels of carbon monoxide.

Section Note

The inspection of the chimney is presented in greater detail in A Chapter 3, Roof Inspection. These details of chimney inspection are not repeated here.

NOTE: For now, we won't discuss how to report your findings about gas burners in your inspection report. This will be covered later in this chapter.

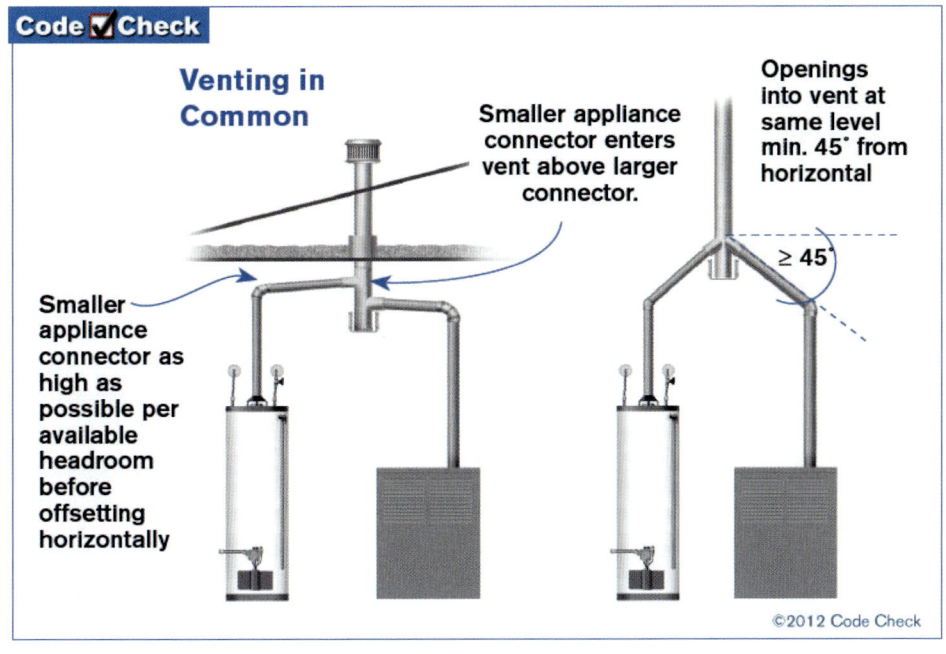

Photo #14 OPEN CLEANOUT DOOR

Always look in the cleanout at the base of a chimney, whether for a fireplace of some type of combustion appliance like a furnace, boiler, or water heater. You want to be sure there are no obstructions and that it has not deteriorated from the combustion gases.

chapter Note

Pages 434–447 show the study and inspection of the oil components of oil-fired heating systems.

6.4 OIL-FIRED SYSTEMS

In this section, we're going to discuss the principles, components, and the inspection of the components of oil-fired heating systems, regardless of the type of heating system the burner serves. The study of particular heating systems (warm air, hot water, steam, and so on) begins on page 447.

Oil Supply

Fuel oil is supplied in commercial grades that vary from #1 to #6—with #1 being the most refined and similar to kerosene and #6 being the least refined and heavy and dark. Home heating systems use #2 fuel oil, which is a clear, yellowish, syrupy liquid like diesel fuel that is specially blended to pump at low winter temperatures.

Fuel oil is delivered to the home and stored in a **steel or nowadays a plastic oil storage tank** buried underground outside or more likely sitting inside the home because the oil is not highly flammable like propane. It does not ignite spontaneously and will extinguish a match dipped into it. Outdoor tanks should be firmly anchored to the home's foundation and should have a corrosion-resistant coating to prolong the life of the tank. There are local codes regarding the size of indoor oil tanks. In general, the indoor tank has a 275-gallon capacity, although some areas allow tanks with a capacity of up to 660 gallons. Tanks must be restrained against (seismic) earthquake movement per local codes.

Metal oil tanks have a lifespan of about 20 years. As the oil level in the tank falls, air in the tank condenses, causing water to sit on the bottom of the tank.

Photo #15 OIL STORAGE TANK VENT AND FILL PIPES

Oil storage tank vent and fill pipes. These are usually very close to the building on the street side of the house. They connect to a tank or tanks in the basement.

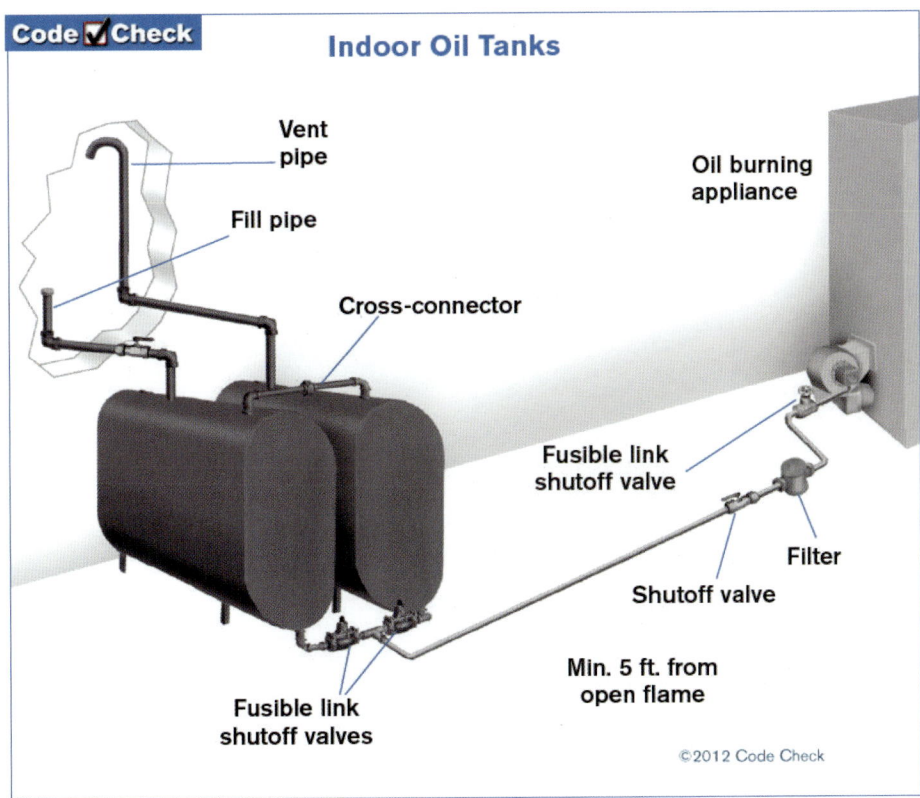

Over time, the tank begins to rust out at the bottom. Be very careful touching an oil tank, as you may dislodge rust and cause a leak. Tanks can be patched or plugged, but eventually the tank must be replaced. Underground storage tanks

> **OIL Components**
>
> - Incoming fill pipe
> - Oil tank
> - Copper supply line to burner
> - Manual oil shut-off
> - Oil filter
> - Return line (optional)
> - Exiting vent pipe

(USTs), especially those over 20 years old, should be tested for leaks. Most parts of the United States and Canada no longer allow buried oil tanks, and they should be removed. A home inspector should advise clients to have the soil tested and to verify if there has been a mandatory removal issued for underground storage tanks (check local requirements).

Indoor tanks have a minimum 1-1/4″ fill and vent pipe that should be pitched toward the tank. The fill and vent pipes should be a minimum of 2′ from any building openings. The fuel supply line may be schedule 40 steel or brass.

Indoor oil tanks must be located at least 5′ from the oil burner. There should be a **manual oil shut-off** and an **oil filter** between the tank and the oil burner. Fuel oil naturally contains small amounts of solid matter that must be filtered out of the supply. The oil filter should be changed annually. The filter may be located on the tank end of the supply line or just before the oil burner at the other end.

The **oil supply line** to the oil burner is minimum 3/8″ OD (outside diameter) Type L copper piping. You may see schedule 40 steel or brass or seamless Cu,

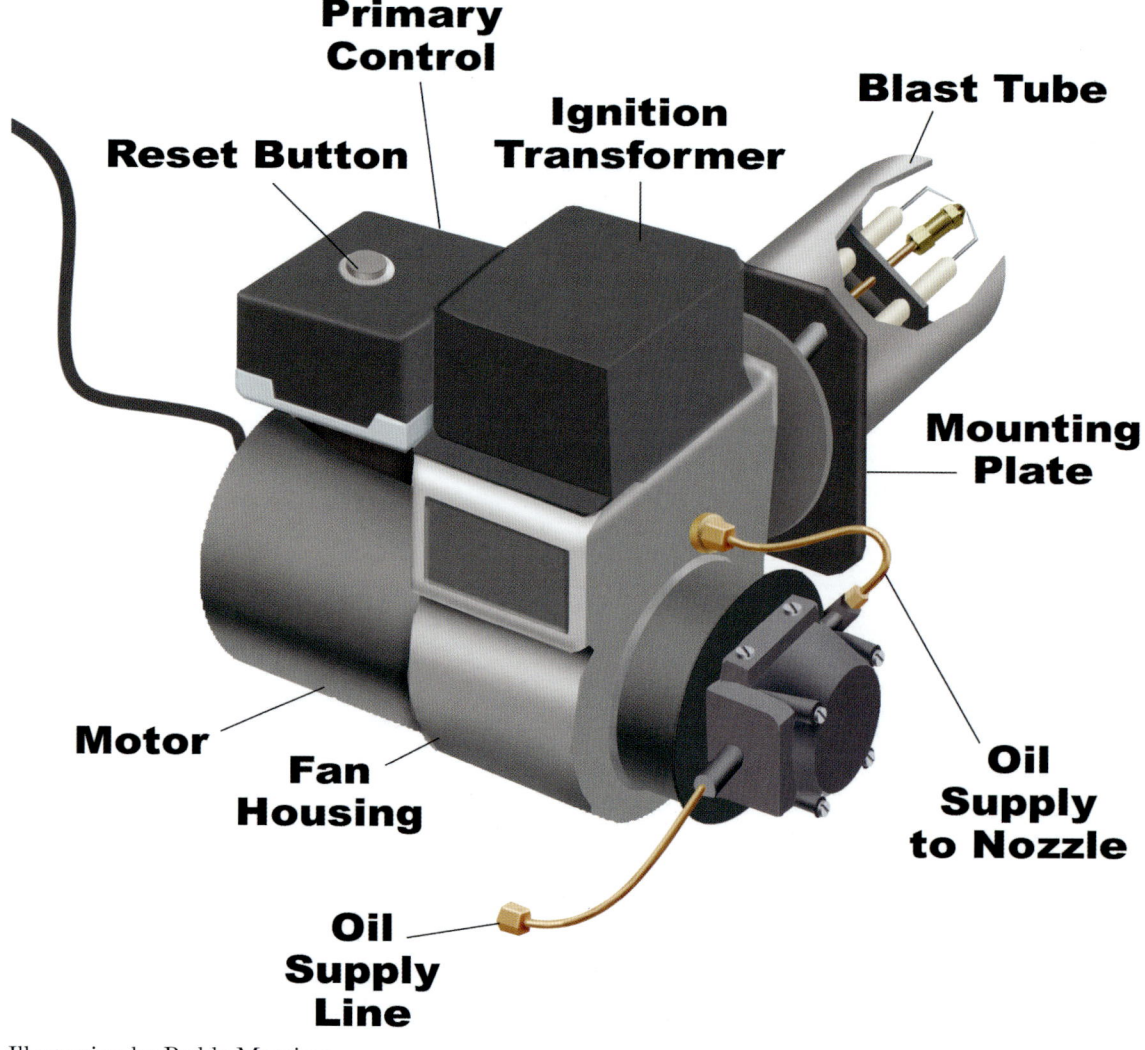

Illustration by Paddy Morrissey

brass, or steel tubing. Often, the supply line is buried in the basement floor, going into the floor just after exiting the oil tank and resurfacing at the oil burner. If the copper piping lies on or just above the floor, it should be protected from mechanical damage, denting, or crimping. If piping is not protected or is already damaged, the home inspector should make a note of that fact in the inspection report.

If oil is fed to the oil burner by gravity, there will be only one line between the tank and the burner. Any excess oil at the oil burner nozzle is fed through a bypass back into the burner. There may be two lines between the tank and the burner—the supply line and a **return line** to return excess oil to the tank. This is usually done if the tank is below the level of the burner or at some distance from the burner.

Oil Controls

The main control for an oil burner is called the **primary control**. This control may be combined in a single unit with the **safety control**. Both controls together are often called the primary control, the primary safety control, or the primary safety relay. We'll use the term *primary control* to mean both.

The primary control to the oil burner responds to electrical signals from the **thermostat** to start the burner motor and to energize the ignition transformer. When the burner starts, oil is sprayed into the combustion chamber, and the ignition transformer ignites the oil spray. If the flame is not established sometime after ignition (15, 30, or 45 seconds), the primary control will turn off the flow of oil to the burner and the burner will shut down. Some primary controls will make a second attempt at ignition, waiting again to verify that ignition has taken place. The primary control responds again to the thermostat when temperature levels are reached to shut down the burner.

The primary control also responds electrically to the **limit control** on the heating unit to shut down the burners when the unit overheats due to some malfunction. The limit controls, which sense air temperature in furnaces and water temperature in boilers, turn off the flow of oil to the burner when high temperatures are reached.

- **Primary control on stack:** Older oil burners have the primary control located in the smoke pipe or exhaust stack on the heating unit. The stack-type primary control, sometimes called a **stack relay**, has a bimetallic coil, or temperature sensor, that extends from the back of the control into the smoke pipe. It verifies the presence of a flame in the combustion chamber by the rise of temperature of the exhaust gases in the smoke pipe. If no heat is sensed after a certain time, the burner will be shut down. The primary control has a **reset button** on it. If the oil burner is shut down after

> **Definition**
>
> The <u>primary control</u> on an oil burner starts and stops the burner in response to thermostat signals and verifies ignition. A primary control may be located on the smoke pipe or on the burner housing.

> **Section Note**
>
> "I remember an incident in our area where the homeowner had left the oil fill pipe in place after converting to a gas heating system. The oil company arrived by mistake and pumped 30 gallons of oil into this fellow's basement before the error was discovered!
>
> And I've read about a case in Minneapolis where the oil company mistakenly pumped 150 gallons into an out-of-use fill pipe, not only filling the basement but contaminating the water supply and saturating the soil in the process. The oil company had to buy the house and remedy the situation."

a failed ignition, the reset button can be pushed *once* to override the control and restart the burner. Pushing it more than once could allow an unsafe accumulation of oil in the combustion chamber.

- **Primary control on burner:** Oil burners in recent years have the primary control located on the oil burner housing. This type of primary control has a cadmium sulfide **photocell** (Flame Safeguard) that sits in this assembly or on the blast tube and "sees" the flame in the combustion chamber to verify ignition. One popular brand of photocell is called a Fire Eye. If the photocell doesn't detect a flame, it will assume that oil is not being ignited and shut down the burner pump. This type of primary control also has a reset button.

Oil Burners

Oil burners consist of **gun-type, pot-type, or rotary-type**. Gun-type burners force oil under pressure with a pump through a nozzle to atomize it into small particles. Pot-type burners rely on gravity to feed the oil, which is vaporized, then burned. Rotary-type burners are also fed by gravity to a rotating disc or cup that throws off the oil into a fine spray using centrifugal force. These oil particles are mixed with air to the proper ratio, then ignited by an electric spark.

The components of the gun-type oil burner are packaged together in a single housing, usually cast aluminum, and are as follows:

Photo #16 GUN-TYPE OIL BURNER

This is a modern gun-type oil burner. Beckett is probably the most common burner you will find on your inspections. It's not a bad idea to go to their website and look at their products to see what is available as well as new products coming to market.

Photo #17 POT-TYPE OIL BURNER

In a pot-type oil burner the fuel oil is vaporized for combustion by heating it from below. The vaporized fuel oil rises vertically where it is burned at the top. These are not very common, and you may never see one, even in markets with fuel oil as the primary source of energy.

- **The primary control**, as described above, may be located on top of the burner housing.

- The **burner motor** is located at one end of the burner housing. Squeaks, grinds, and other noises in the motor are an indication that bearings are wearing out or that the unit needs maintenance.

- A **squirrel cage fan** is located between the motor and the fuel pump. **Air shutters** and shutter adjustment controls are located on the fuel pump side of the fan. The fan forces air into the combustion chamber. Fan openings or slits should be free of dust and debris that may block airflow. The fan should run smoothly without excess noise that could indicate that rotating parts are out of balance, dirty, or worn.

GUN-TYPE OIL BURNER COMPONENTS

- Primary control
- Burner motor
- Fan
- Fuel pump
- Ignition transformer
- Blast tube with nozzle and electrodes

As with gas-fired heating systems, the oil-fired system needs an adequate amount of combustion air. Proper ventilation must be provided. If the heating unit is located in a confined area, vents should be installed at the top and bottom of a doorway into the area, on the wall, or to the exterior.

- The **fuel pump**, located at the other end of the burner housing, connects to the fuel line. Another fuel line runs from the fuel pump to the blast tube. A pump adjustment control is present on the surface of the pump.

THE HEATING INSPECTION

> **Definitions**
>
> The <u>oil burner nozzle</u>, located in the blast tube, shoots out oil particles into the firebox.
>
> <u>Ignition electrodes</u>, also located in the blast tube, work in pairs to provide a spark that ignites the oil.
>
> The <u>flame retention burner</u> has a flame retention ring combustion head that provides increased air pressure, velocity, and rotation for more efficient combustion.

The fuel pump raises oil pressure to 100+ pounds per square inch (psi) and pumps it to the nozzle in the blast tube. A **strainer** in the pump, in addition to the filter in the oil line, removes debris from the fuel so that it does not clog the nozzle.

- The **ignition transformer**, supplying power to the ignition electrodes, is located on top of the oil burner housing.

- The **blast tube**, which extends into the combustion chamber, is mounted on the heating unit by means of a mounting plate and contains the **nozzle** and **ignition electrodes**. Pressurized oil from the oil pump is forced through the nozzle. The resulting oil particles (mist) are mixed with combustion air and forced into the blast tube by the fan. The mixture is ignited by an electric spark between the ignition electrodes, which are powered by the ignition transformer.

  The end of the blast tube normally has a slotted **combustion head** or slotted metal piece through which the air enters the combustion chamber. Newer oil burners, called **flame retention burners**, have a cone-shaped flame retention ring that gives more pressure and rotation to the airstream, providing more efficient combustion. The resulting flame is spherical in shape, is hotter, and does not move far from the end of the blast tube. Older combustion heads cause the flame to be larger, cooler, and shapeless within the chamber and therefore less efficient.

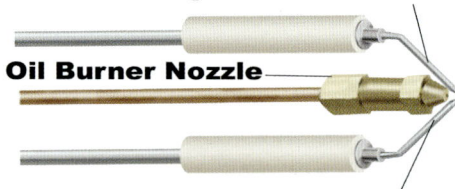
Illustration by Paddy Morrissey

Illustration by Paddy Morrissey

- The **combustion chamber** or firebox for older oil burners is lined with **firebrick**, called refractory, or can have a heavy metal shield. The chamber surrounds the flame and radiates heat back to the flame to help with combustion. This is necessary with oil because of the high flame temperature. If the flame continuously touched the metal heat exchanger, the metal would quickly burn through. Because the burner is a gun that throws a horizontal flame like a torch, the refractory is needed to slow down and redirect the combustion gases toward the heat exchanger. Over time, firebrick can deteriorate to the point that the metal walls of the heating unit are exposed. Flame retention burners can be seen with a combustion chamber lined with a ceramic fiber.

- There should be an **inspection port** (a circle about 3–4″ diameter) at the front of the combustion chamber from which to examine the flames.

The home inspector should be familiar with the following flame conditions:

- **Bright orange flames:** An oil burner flame should be bright yellow orange in older low-pressure burners to yellowish white in high-pressure burners.

- **Sooty flames:** Flames that have sooty or smoky edges are starved for combustion air.

- **White flames:** A pure white flame is an indication of too much combustion air.

- **Blue or red flames:** These color flames also indicate a problem with the burner adjustments. For any circumstance where flames are not bright orange or yellowish white, a specialist should be recommended to adjust the oil pressure, burner, and air-fuel ratio or to replace a faulty or clogged nozzle. Unusual flame activity sometimes indicates a cracked heat exchanger.

> **FLAME CONDITIONS**
>
> - Okay: bright orange, from yellowish orange to yellowish white
> - Not okay: White, blue, or red flames or flames with sooty or smoky edges

> *Definitions*
>
> A <u>barometric damper</u>, located in the smoke pipe above an oil-fired heating system, is a hinged plate that swings open or closed to regulate drafts.
>
> An <u>electronic vent damper</u> automatically opens before the burner starts and closes when exhaust gases cool down.
>
> The <u>bimetallic vent damper</u> expands open when heated and contracts closed when cooled.

The proper draft over the firebox is very important to the efficient operation of an oil burner. Quite a few adjustments can be performed on an oil burner. The amount of air into the blast tube (head air) and the amount of air drawn into the smoke pipe at the damper are very important for efficiency. It is beyond the scope of this course to evaluate operating efficiency or to describe how to perform smoke number tests. A Bacharach True-Spot smoke number test using filter paper and a special device can be used to fine-tune the burn of the fuel oil (based on how clean the oil burn is). What we are looking for is "safe" operation with recommendations for adjustment, tuning, or repair as indicated by the observations made during the inspection. Most oil burners have a **barometric damper** located in the smoke pipe over the heating unit. The barometric damper is a balanced hinged plate in a frame that remains closed or swings open (inward) when pressure inside the flue decreases. The damper allows for a constant draft through the heat exchanger and in the chimney when the system is on. House air is drawn into the exhaust flue, but exhaust gases are not allowed to escape out of the flue. If the damper is missing, taped over, or inoperative, it should be noted in the inspection report.

Another kind of vent damper found is the **bimetallic damper**, which is not electrically driven. It will expand and open when it becomes heated and will contract or close when it becomes cool. We find that these dampers often fail and recommend that they be removed. They are no longer approved for use today. Any automatic damper must have a burner interlock so that the burner will not fire if the damper is closed.

THE HEATING INSPECTION

> **Photo #18 BIMETALLIC DAMPER**
> *Bimetallic dampers will expand and open when it becomes heated and will contract or close when it becomes cool. We find that these dampers often fail, and we recommend that they be removed. They are no longer approved for use today.*

High-Efficiency Oil Systems

High-efficiency (condensing) oil furnaces/boilers condense water vapor produced by combustion and use the resulting heat. This means that the condensate (water) being created must be directed to an appropriate drain just like high-efficiency gas appliances. By capturing this heat, the unit operates more efficiently and uses less fuel. High-efficiency oil burners use a lot of combustion and draft air. The air is provided by a draft fan that brings outside air in a direct pipe that supplies draft air to the oil burner. This is like a gas-fired appliance; the exhaust piping may be plastic, not metal, as well. High-efficiency oil systems are not very common and consequently are very expensive. The efficiency of a furnace is expressed as a percentage of annual fuel utilization efficiency (AFUE). One hundred percent efficiency would mean that all the fuel is used to produce heat, which is not currently possible. The federal government requires furnaces to achieve a minimum AFUE that varies depending on the type of furnace. An oil-fired furnace must achieve an AFUE of 83%. Some high-efficiency condensing systems claim an AFUE of 95% to 98%, but the typical new system is around 86% AFUE.

Inspecting Oil Components

We're going to talk about inspecting only the oil components of an oil-fired boiler or furnace in this section. These components are similar regardless of what type of heating system (water heaters too) they power. We'll discuss the inspection of different types of furnaces and boilers in greater detail later in this section.

Follow these procedures to inspect the operation of the oil burner:

1. **At the heating unit, turn off the unit using the safety switch or serviceman's switch.** You'll want to turn off the heating unit so that you can safely gain access to the combustion chamber.

2. **Open the porthole to the combustion chamber and inspect the chamber lining.** With the system turned off, open this porthole and use your flashlight to inspect the interior of the combustion chamber for firebrick deterioration, collapse, or soot. A badly adjusted oil burner can shoot the oil spray against the far wall of the chamber. This condition cools the oil so that it doesn't burn cleanly and erodes the firebrick. Soot covering the refractory brick can greatly reduce the efficiency and should be cleaned by a qualified technician.

   NOTE: In some cases, you may find an oil-fired system with a porthole partially open as an adjustment to the burner. Sometimes, the porthole is sealed shut. Don't mess with either one. If you can't examine the chamber or view the flame, record that fact in your inspection report.

3. **Close the porthole and turn on the unit using the safety switch.** After inspecting the combustion chamber, fire up the system, heeding these cautions:

   — If the oil supply is turned off to the heating unit, do not start the system without talking to the homeowner first. The heating unit may be shut down due to some defect that needs correction. Find out what the circumstances are and get permission or better yet have the homeowner fire up the unit if he or she is present.

   — If the heating system was in operation before you turned it off and it fails to ignite on restart, you can push the reset button on the primary control **once!** If the unit still won't ignite, don't

---

BURNER PROCEDURES

- Turn off heating unit.
- Open porthole and inspect firebox.
- Fire up the heating unit.
- Observe ignition.
- Monitor flames.
- Inspect front of unit.
- Listen to oil burner.

For Beginning Inspectors

If you have an oil-fired furnace or boiler, follow these procedures to inspect the oil components. If not, find a friend with one and conduct your examination. Be sure to follow the safety precautions we've mentioned.

Section Note

"Oil-fired systems can produce a lot of dirty stuff. Here's an interesting story to show just how much soot was hiding in such a system.

One of our instructors at the American Home Inspectors Training Institute has friends whose oil furnace exploded. So much soot blew out they not only had to replace the furnace and have all the ductwork cleaned, but had to have the furniture professionally cleaned before the place was back to normal."

push the reset button any more as you could cause oil to accumulate in the combustion chamber.

— **Remember to have your customer stand aside** (and you too) when you refire the heating system. Faulty or late ignition can cause too much fuel to ignite at once, resulting in a **puff-back** of flame, smoke, and soot or even a small explosion from the combustion chamber.

4. **Observe ignition.** When you fire the system, watch for any defects such as puff-backs, loud bangs, oil smells, or soot that accompany ignition. These are signs of inadequate maintenance, poor burner adjustments, or some other defect with the burner.

5. **Observe the flames.** The porthole should have a sight glass in it, through which you can look to observe the flames in the combustion chamber.

6. **Examine the front of the heating unit.** While the heating unit is in operation, check the front of its cabinet. Notice any evidence of soot on the front near the porthole and on the burner. Look for any cracks or open joints around the blast tube, mounting plate, and porthole. If you can see flames through cracks and joints, point this out to your customer and recommend that a contractor repair or replace this as needed.

7. **Listen to the oil burner.** There's little the home inspector can do to inspect the oil burner itself. But you can listen to it and report noises such as squeaking or grinding that indicate malfunction. Excess vibrations may mean that mountings are loose.

8. **Verify heat sources throughout home.** While you are inspecting the living areas of the home, you'll be examining heat registers and radiators and noting the presence of heat sources in each room. Home inspectors usually turn up the thermostat so that the heating system kicks on during this portion of the inspection. However, this depends on the season and whether the unit is already in use. Turning the thermostat up 5° each time is a good practice because you don't need to remember the previous setting—just turn it back down 5° when you're done. You may also want to confirm that air is coming out of the registers or that the radiators are warming up.

In general, while inspecting the oil components of a furnace or boiler, the home inspector should watch for the following conditions:

- **Leaking oil tank:** Feel along the bottom of the interior oil tank for leaks. Be careful not to loosen any rust or scale as it may cause a leak. A leaking tank should be replaced or repaired. If the property has an underground tank, let your customers know about it. Some local codes require a leak test for an underground tank before the home can be sold.

For Your Information

Find out what your local codes are regarding oil tanks. A leak test may have to be performed on an underground tank before the home is sold.

- **Improper piping or missing shut-off valve or filter:** Follow the oil line from the tank to the oil burner and report if the oil piping is above the floor and subject to mechanical damage. Copper piping should be protected. Locate the shut-off valve and the oil filter. If either one is missing, report this condition.

- **Improper combustion air:** For oil-fired systems in confined spaces, make note of whether the heating unit has enough venting to provide sufficient combustion air.

- **Oily smoke smells or soot:** An oil burner should operate odor free. Any noticeable odor of oily smoke in the area of the heating unit indicates that the oil burner requires adjustment or repair. A properly functioning oil burner should not produce smoke at the chimney, nor should it produce soot. Check for soot at the top of the chimney, at the firebox porthole, on the refractory inside, at the barometric damper, and in the area near the furnace or boiler. A specialist should be called in to examine and repair/replace components as needed for the oil burner.

- **Deteriorating firebrick or firebox leakage:** Let customers know if you find cracks, broken sections, or holes in the firebox lining. This can be a **safety hazard**, especially if the flames are burning through the firebox walls. Check for cracks and open joints at the firebox. Recommend that such openings be evaluated and repaired by a qualified technician.

- **White, red, blue, or sooty flames:** Anything other than bright orange or yellowish white flames in the firebox are indications of inefficient combustion. They are an indication of an oil burner out of adjustment, a clogged nozzle, improper airflow, or some other malfunction. Customers should be reminded that an oil burner must be **serviced at least annually**. They are not like gas appliances that can be used for years without service and still operate relatively well.

- **Noisy or vibrating oil burner:** These are signs of needed maintenance and should be noted in the inspection report.

- **Spillage from the barometric damper:** An oil burner typically produces carbon monoxide (CO) like any other combustion appliance, so spillage of exhaust gases at the barometric damper is especially dangerous

> **Section Note**
>
> *"I once opened a chimney cleanout door to find the cleanout plugged with soot. The owner asked if I would clean it out for her. Well, I agreed to do it.*
>
> *I put a box under the cleanout door and gave the soot a poke. Stuff kept coming out and coming out. It overflowed the box and kept coming. Soot went all over the place. I wish I hadn't agreed to do it."*

INSPECTING OIL COMPONENTS

- Leaking oil tank
- Improper or unprotected piping
- Missing shut-off or oil filter
- Lack of combustion air venting
- Oily smoke smells or soot
- Deteriorating firebrick or leaking firebox
- Wrong-colored flames
- Noisy or vibrating burner
- Draft spillage
- Improper clearances and venting

and should be considered a **safety hazard**. Report if the damper is missing, broken, or malfunctioning in any way. When the heating unit is in operation, light a match or smoke stick and hold it next to the barometric damper opening in the smoke pipe. If the flame leans in toward the smoke pipe, exhaust is moving up the chimney. If the flame leans outward, it's an indication of a down-drafting problem and CO is potentially being released into the home.

- **Improper clearances and venting:** The home inspector should examine the heating and venting equipment for the proper clearances from combustibles (see pages 408–411 for more information) and record any issues in the inspection report. Examine the smoke pipe for proper slope and length, open joints, and corrosion. If the smoke pipe has a horizontal run longer than 10′ or has more than one elbow, be sure that the draft is not affected. With oil-fired systems, it's especially important to check the junction of the smoke pipe and chimney to be sure it's tightly sealed with mortar at the thimble. Any holes or leaks in the venting systems should be reported as a **safety hazard**.

The condition of the chimney should also be inspected. Oil-fired heating systems require a chimney for exhausting combustion by-products and should have a **flue liner**. The oil burner should not share a flue with a solid-fuel burning appliance or fireplace. If both an oil burner and gas burner share the same flue, the oil burner smoke pipe should enter the flue at a point *below* the flue for a gas burner. The better and most correct orientation is that the smallest BTU appliance should vent above the larger BTU appliance regardless of the fuel being used. This means that the water heater typically vents above the furnace in most homes.

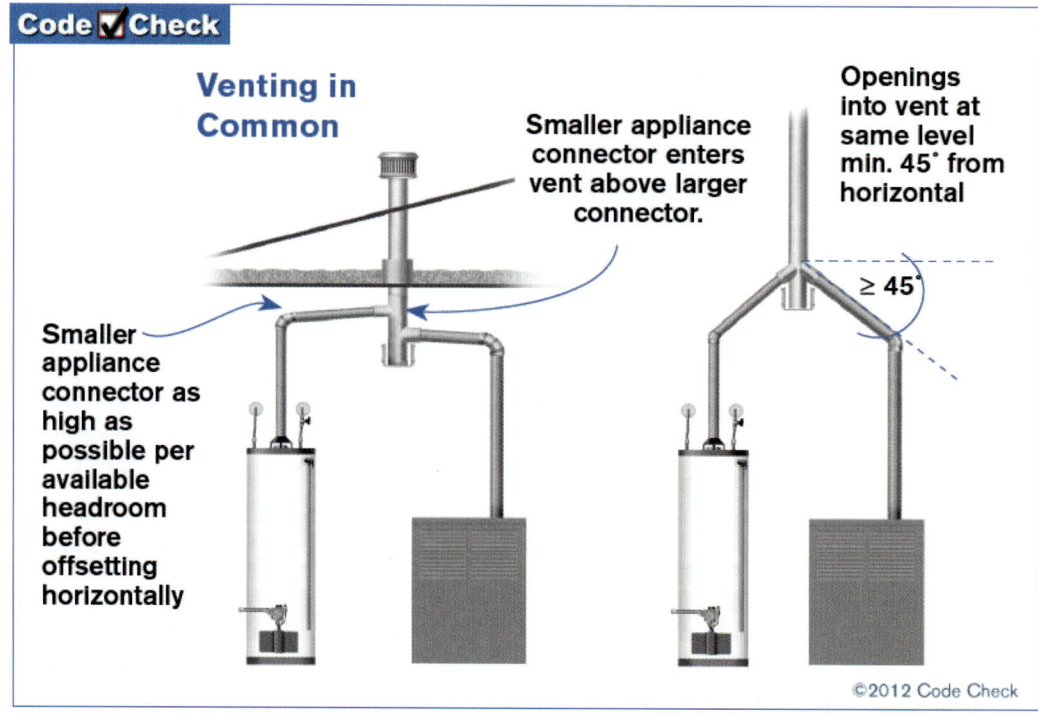

446 Chapter 6

The home inspector should inspect the **chimney cleanout** at the base of the chimney as described on page 433–434.

For now, we won't discuss how to record your findings about oil burners in your inspection report. This will be covered later in this chapter.

6.5 GRAVITY FURNACES

Some people use the term *furnace* or *heater* indiscriminately when talking about any kind of heating system. However, the term *furnace* is used to mean a heating system that heats the home with warm air; the term *boiler* is used when referring to a heating system that heats the home with hot water or steam.

> **Chapter Note**
>
> *Pages 447–451 present the study and inspecting of gravity warm air furnaces.*

Photo #19 *This is a gravity furnace. Note the white covering on the bonnet and ducts. This is most likely asbestos-containing insulation. This is a coal-fired system converted to gas.*

Operation and Distribution

When heated, air expands, becomes lighter, and rises. When cooled, air contracts, becoming heavier and denser, and falls. That's the simple principle behind the **gravity furnace**. Air heated in the furnace rises naturally, carrying warm air to the living areas of the house, and then falls back to the furnace as it cools. This process creates a pattern of air circulation. The gravity furnace has no moving parts. There are no blowers or motors to force the air into the house. The only electrical connections necessary are for the thermostat and burner controls—gas valve (if gas-fired) or oil motor and pump (if oil-fired).

The oldest type of gravity furnace was mounted in a square opening in the floor in the center of the house. Heat rose from a circular opening over a heat exchanger dome. Cool air dropped back to the furnace through the space between the square and circle. The home inspector may find these earliest gravity furnaces still in use, but converted from coal to gas or oil.

The familiar and later type of gravity furnace was called the **octopus furnace** because of the many large supply ducts extending from the top and even larger return duct(s) at the bottom. You may find this type of furnace in older homes, probably converted to gas or oil. They haven't been installed for over well over 80 years. These are the furnace components:

- **Jacket:** Old octopus furnaces are made from heavy-gauge cast iron or steel. Usually located in the center of the basement, this unit is around 4′–6′ in diameter and takes up a great deal of space. The jacket can become scorched, burned, or rusted over time, especially if there is a spillage or back-draft problem. But generally, the construction can last for decades.

- **Fuel burner:** Located at the bottom of the furnace, the combustion chamber on an existing octopus furnace is now most likely to have been modified to accommodate a gas or oil burner.

- **Heat exchanger:** A heat exchanger is a heavy metal box above the combustion chamber that holds and contains the burner flame. In a furnace (of any type), it separates exhaust air from the circulating air that heats the building. The hot gas on one side never comes into direct contact with the circulated house air. If a heat exchanger cracks or rusts through, combustion products will escape through the holes into the house's air supply. This may be a particular problem in gravity furnaces because a cracked heat exchanger allows a natural flow due to convection from the combustion chamber into the house air.

The heat exchanger in an octopus furnace is made of seamed cast iron sections or rings and should be able to be seen and inspected by opening the front access (upper) door. The home inspector should carefully inspect the heat exchanger with a flashlight and an inspection mirror for cracks at seams, rusting, separation, and deterioration. If the heat exchanger fails in an octopus furnace, the whole furnace must be replaced, as would be the case in most furnaces. You would normally make a recommendation for replacement on **any** gravity furnace due to age, obsolescence, and poor efficiency.

> **Definition**
>
> A <u>heat exchanger</u> is a heavy metal box above the combustion chamber that holds and contains the burner flame. In a furnace, it separates exhaust air from the circulating air that heats the house.

- **Bonnet:** The top of the octopus furnace is called the bonnet. Often, this bonnet is covered with plaster reinforced with **asbestos**. The home inspector can recommend that it be repaired or abated by a qualified contractor (asbestos is only dangerous when particles or fibers are released into the air).

- **Supply ducts:** These ducts carry the flow of heated air upward into registers on interior walls or in the floor. Heat distribution in a house heated by a gravity air system is likely to be slow to the far corners of the house. There may be **balancing dampers** in the ducts in the basement to balance the heat supplied to various areas. If there are no dampers, the shortest ducts will get the greatest amounts of warm air.

Supply ducts may be wrapped with asbestos too, usually looking like white or gray paper or canvas and held in place with metal straps at the joints. This insulation can be abated or left in place if in good condition.

- **Return ducts:** Cool air is returned to the furnace when it falls into the return air ducts by a natural draft resulting from the convective air circulation. Return air enters the ducts through very large grills, usually installed in the floor. The home inspector should check the living areas to be sure that return air grills have not been carpeted over or blocked by furniture. The large return ducts enter the furnace at the bottom. Note that the octopus furnace **doesn't have an air filter**. The returning air has so little force that even an air filter could stop its flow.

  You may occasionally find an octopus furnace without return ducts. The return panel at the base of the furnace is left open, and cool air, falling through the grills, drops to the basement and is pulled back into the furnace. This is a dangerous situation. If there is a malfunction or puff-back from the fuel burner or blockage in the flue or chimney, combustion gases can be drawn into the air return duct. Open returns in the basement should be reported as a **safety hazard**.

- **Smoke pipe or flue:** The smoke pipe or flue on the octopus furnace extends from the back of the furnace body to the chimney.

The old gravity furnace can be **updated** to a forced warm air system by installing a blower unit with a filter, fan, and motor assembly. The blower unit is typically installed at the return air duct at the base of the furnace, although it may be found on top of the furnace. Installing a blower on a gravity furnace takes it from being miserably inefficient to terribly inefficient. It is not a recommendation a home inspector should make.

It's important to note that gravity furnaces are still in use because they are very expensive to replace. Asbestos abatement must be performed before the furnace is removed. All of the ductwork must be taken out, and an entirely new furnace and ductwork must be installed.

Inspecting Gravity Furnaces

When inspecting the gravity furnace, the home inspector will be inspecting the following:

- the **furnace** itself, including the fuel burner
- the **distribution ductwork**, supply registers, and returns
- the **venting system** including the flue, chimney, and cleanout

---

GRAVITY FURNACE COMPONENTS

- Cast iron or steel jacket
- Fuel burner, probably converted from coal
- Heat exchanger
- Bonnet, probably asbestos covered
- Supply ducts, may be asbestos wrapped
- Return ducts
- No moving parts, no air filter

For Beginning Inspectors

It would be helpful to locate an old gravity furnace for a practice inspection. Your best bet would be to try older homes in your area (pre-1940s) that may still have the original installation.

INSPECTING GRAVITY FURNACES

- Heat source in each room
- Dirty, loose, missing, covered registers and grills
- Jacket with holes or corrosion
- Cracked heat exchanger
- Presence of asbestos
- Leaking, damaged, loose, or corroded ducts
- Open return in basement

The procedures for inspecting the fuel burner, smoke pipe, chimney, and cleanout were presented earlier (see pages 423–433 for gas burners and pages 438–447 for oil burners). We won't repeat these procedures here.

The home inspector should also inspect the gravity furnace for the following conditions:

- **Lack of heat source in each room:** As the home inspector examines the living spaces of the home, each room should be checked for the presence of a heat source. If no register is present, this should be noted in the inspection report. Turn up the thermostat as you inspect the living area. You can verify whether the heat source is providing heat with your infrared thermometer.

- **Dirty, loose, or missing registers and grills:** Dust and dirt on registers and grills may be from bad housekeeping or from dirty supply ducts because the furnace does not have an air filter. But soot and dark staining on the walls above the registers can indicate a problem with a cracked heat exchanger (especially with an oil burner) that's allowing combustion gases back into the house air supply. This condition should be reported as a **safety hazard**. Also, watch for grills that have been carpeted over (look from the basement to see where the ducts are run and make sure there are registers or returns in those locations in the living areas above) and block airflow. As noted previously, a cracked heat exchanger will allow hot flue gases to seep into the house air, creating a significant safety issue.

- **Defects in furnace jacket:** Inspect the furnace jacket (essentially the cabinet) for any holes, corrosion, or rust that may allow combustion gases to escape into the house. This is especially dangerous with an oil burner. Such holes may be able to be sealed as long as the cause of the problem is dealt with. Scorching or burn marks can indicate areas of possible failure. Staining and soot around the burner indicates spillage and down- or backdrafts.

- **Cracked, rusted, or deteriorated heat exchanger:** After turning the furnace off, open the front access door of the octopus furnace and use your flashlight and inspection mirror to inspect the heat exchanger. If you discover any flaw in the heat exchanger, report it as a major defect and explain the danger of CO escaping into the home from this condition. With the gravity furnace, the only solution to a cracked heat exchanger is furnace replacement.

The visual examination of the heat exchanger does not allow you to see 100% of it, actually only about 25% at best. We recommend that you point this out to the customer and recommend that the unit be evaluated by a furnace technician before closing on the home. This should be marked in your inspection report.

> **Section Note**
>
> *"When I come across an old octopus furnace, I take my time explaining to customers how it works and its level of efficiency. If the unit has no balancing dampers or blower unit added, I know they're not going to be happy with it. And they're going to pay too much for fuel. Asbestos always causes concern too. So it's best to be honest with them."*

Remember that unusual or unstable flame action at the burner, flame rollout and puff-backs, and excessive corrosion around the burner area are probable indications of a faulty heat exchanger. And as mentioned on page 450, soot and staining around the heat registers can also mean that the heat exchanger is in bad shape.

- **Presence of asbestos:** Examine the bonnet for plaster reinforced with asbestos and supply ducts for the presence of asbestos insulation. Explain the options to the customer and note in the inspection report the presence of asbestos-like materials.

- **Leaking, damaged, loose, or corroded ducts:** Inspect the condition of the supply and return ducts and their supports. Because they're likely to be old, look for open joints, rust, and disconnected sections. Be careful about jiggling these ducts. If you cause them to open or fall apart, you're likely to release a lot of dirt into the basement. Check the supply ducts for balancing dampers. Inform your customer about their presence or absence. If they were installed correctly, they need not be adjusted. If they have issues with poor distribution, a technician can adjust them as needed. Gravity furnaces without balancing dampers can be very slow to heat the far reaches of the house.

- **Open return in basement:** The situation where there are no return ducts from the living space back to the furnace can be dangerous. The open return at the base of the furnace can pull CO from a poorly adjusted burner into the home's air supply. In fact, modern local codes now prohibit this setup. With the octopus furnace, the lack of return air ducts and the open return constitute a safety hazard. While a return duct system probably could be installed, a better solution is to replace the entire system.

6.6 FORCED-AIR FURNACES

This chapter will present forced-air furnaces, their components, and the procedures for inspecting them.

Types of Forced-Air Furnaces

There are many types and brands of forced-air furnaces, and each manufacturer has its own unique design and layout. However, all forced-air furnaces have basic components in common. The location of the blower in reference to the rest of the heating components determines whether the furnace is one of several configurations:

- **upflow furnace**—is the traditional furnace described below where the furnace is installed in a vertical orientation and the airflow is "up" with the blower at the bottom of the unit beneath the burner.

- **downflow furnace**—is a furnace that is most commonly installed in a home with a crawl space.

Chapter Note

Pages 451–475 present the study and inspection of forced-air furnaces. It also discusses how to report your findings on furnace inspection.

Section Note

Refer to pages 416–418 for more discussion on the subject of conventional, mid-efficiency, and high-efficiency furnaces.

THE HEATING INSPECTION

The furnace is still installed in a vertical orientation, but the airflow is "down" with the blower at the top of the unit above the burner.

- **horizontal furnace**—is an upflow furnace installed on its side or in a horizontal orientation. Most modern furnaces can be installed vertically or horizontally. You may find a horizontal installation in a crawl space or attic where space is limited.

- **lowboy**—is the name usually associated with an oil-fired furnace where the blower is in the back of the unit behind the burner.

- **highboy**—is the name usually associated with an oil-fired furnace where the blower is at the bottom of the unit beneath the burner. This is the same as an upflow furnace for gas systems.

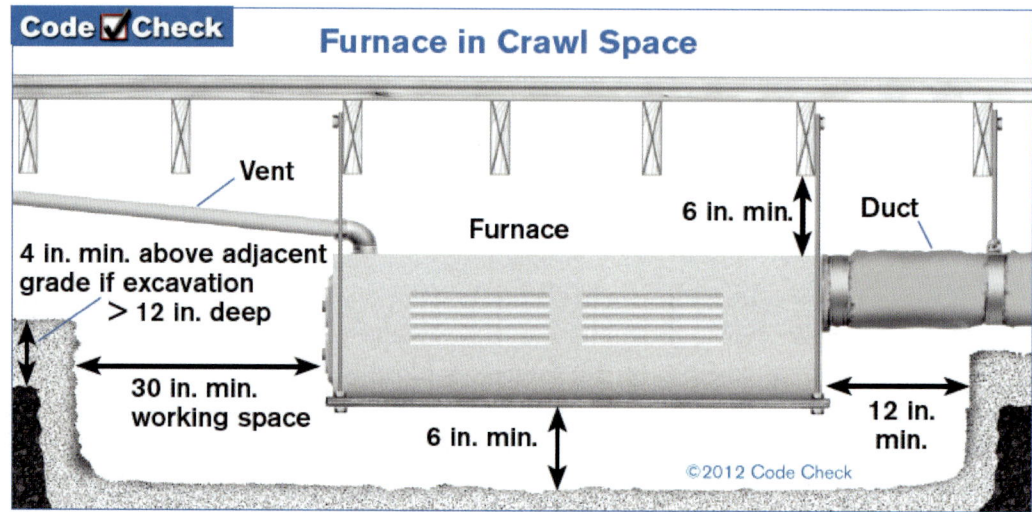

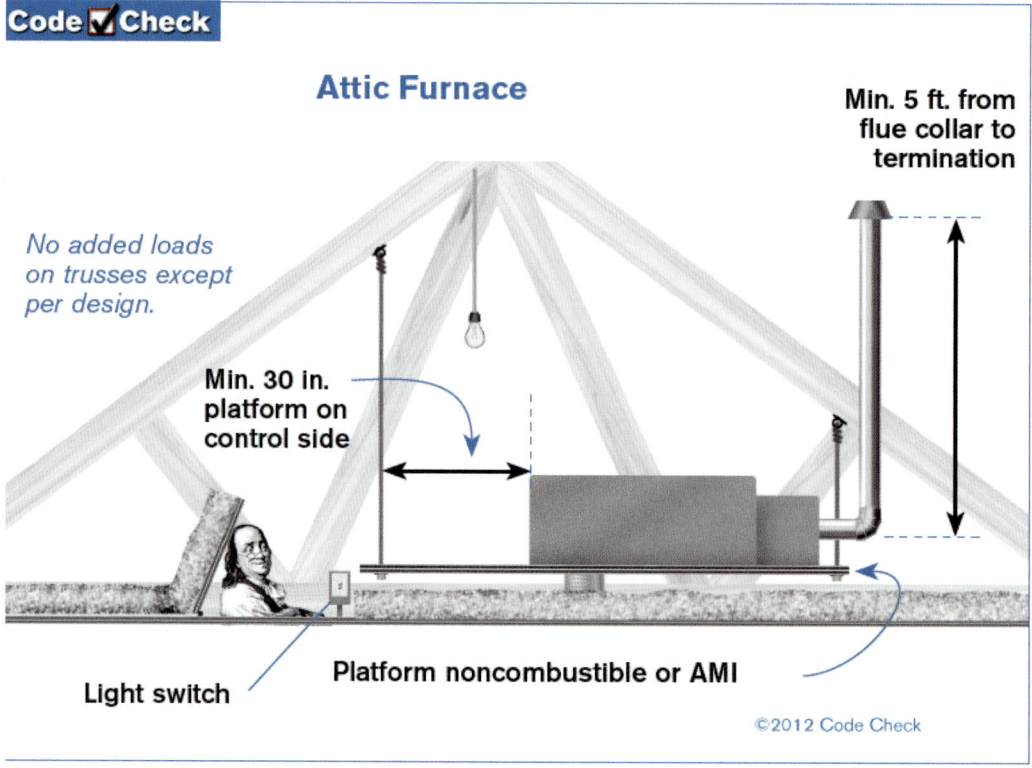

The key to understanding all of these orientations and knowing which is which has to do with the evaporator coil for an air conditioner if one is installed. The evaporator coil will **always** be installed after the heat exchanger as far as the direction of airflow. The reason is that you don't want to cool the air in the evaporator coil and then send it across a metal heat exchanger where condensation can occur and rust out the heat exchanger.

The **conventional gas or oil furnace installed prior to about 1990 typically is configured as an updraft furnace, which** contains these three sections typically arranged this way:

- A **blower unit** containing a fan, a fan motor, and an air filter at the bottom through which return air from the home passes.

- The **burner area** and combustion chamber in the middle where heat is produced. The heat shield is a noncombustible protector that is located in front of the burners. It protects the outer components of the furnace from the heat generated by the burners and from flame rollout if a malfunction occurs.

- The **heat exchanger** at the top through which exhaust gases are vented and surrounding heated air is distributed.

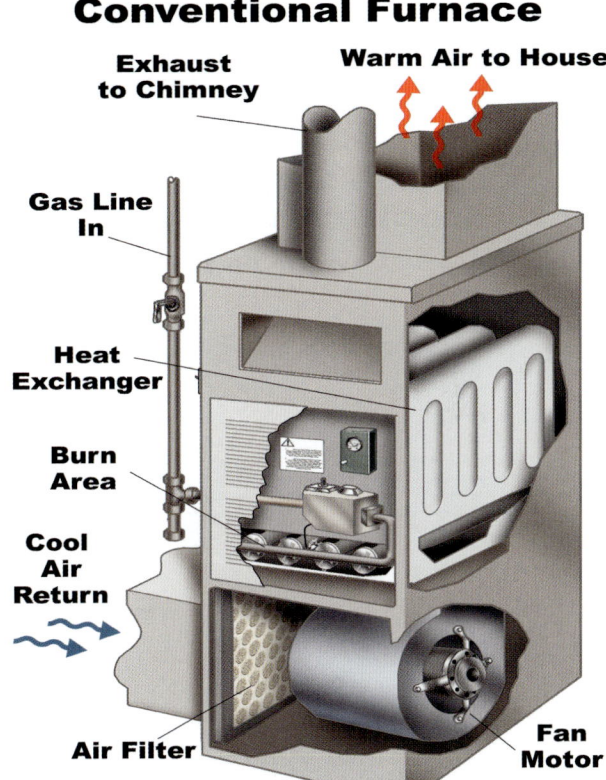

Illustration by Paddy Morrissey

Removing the front access panels on a conventional furnace gives the home inspector a view of the blower and burner areas for inspection. Using a flashlight and mirror, it's possible to examine a portion of the heat exchanger from the burner area, although no heat exchanger is 100% visible. In conventional gas-fired furnaces, only **about 25%**, at best, of the heat exchanger is visible for inspection; in some oil-fired furnaces, you may not be able to see the heat exchanger at all.

Rarely, the home inspector may find some conventional forced-air furnaces with an auxiliary electric heater, called an **electric plenum heater**, installed in the **plenum**, which is the first section of supply duct directly over a furnace from which the main trunk and smaller branch ducts extend out. It's most commonly used with a conventional oil-fired furnace. This auxiliary heater doesn't work at the same time as the primary furnace. It will first try to satisfy the call for heat from the thermostat. When it can't keep up with the heating demand, the plenum heater will switch off. Only then will the furnace turn on.

Some forced-air furnaces are powered solely by electricity, which in most parts of the country is the most

> ### Definitions
>
> The <u>plenum</u> is the first large section of supply duct directly over a furnace from which the main trunk and smaller branch ducts extend out to distribute heat to the house. The evaporator coil of an air conditioner is usually installed in this plenum.
>
> An <u>electric plenum heater</u> is an auxiliary heater, usually added to an oil furnace, that is located in the plenum.

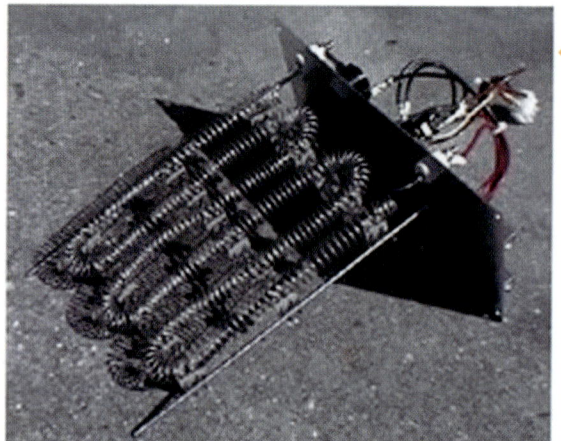

Electric Resistance Coils

Photo #20 *This is an electric heating coil or heat strip. They are usually 5 kW each and can be installed as a single unit or up to three stages.*

Electric Furnace

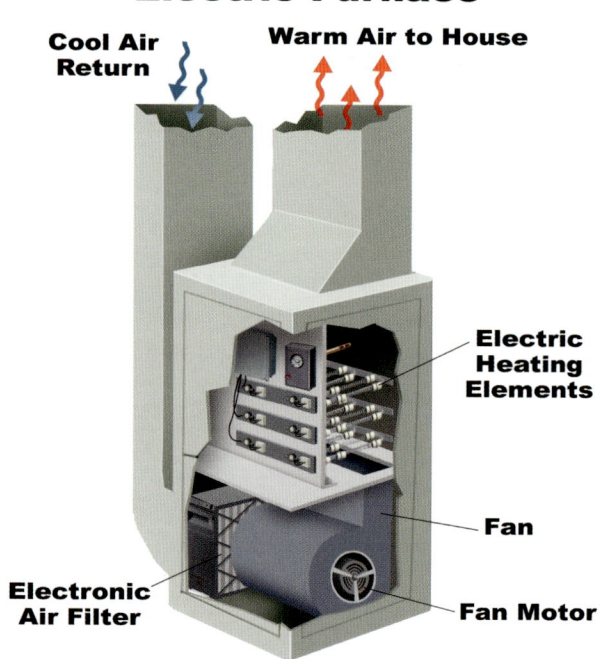

Illustration by Paddy Morrissey

expensive to operate. In **electric furnaces**, there is no combustion. Therefore, there's no need for a burner, heat exchanger, or means of exhausting combustion products. These furnaces have a bank or banks of electric resistance heaters sitting directly in the airstream. The number and size of the heating elements vary depending on the needed heat output, but usually range from one to three sets of 5 kw strips. Air is moved across the heating elements by the blower. The inspection of the electric furnace is quite different from that of an oil or gas furnace. Other than inspecting the filter and fan, the inspection consists largely of examining the electric furnace's operation and the general condition of the electrical wiring. Electric coils either work or they don't.

Older **mid-efficiency gas furnaces** are similar in configuration to the conventional furnaces. They differ with the addition of the **induced draft fan** on the exhaust side of the heat exchanger, which

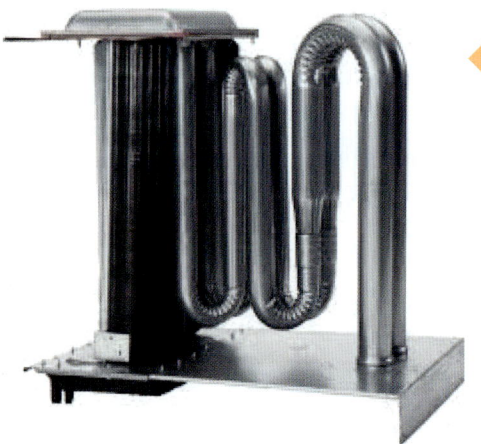

Photo #21 *This is an example of a serpentine heat exchanger. The design allows the hot exhaust gases to remain in the heat exchanger longer, thereby increasing their efficiency.*

is designed to pull combustion products through the serpentine heat exchanger and thus increase efficiency. Most gas-fired units have an **intermittent pilot** that lights only on a call for heat. **Motorized vent dampers**, which close when the unit is not operating to prevent warm air in the house from escaping, may be found on the smoke pipe. Remember, these dampers must have a burner interlock in case the damper doesn't open. Some of these units exhaust hot gases through a metal flue that passes through the house wall or roof rather than the conventional masonry chimney, making the inspection of proper clearances from combustibles very important. The newer mid-efficiency gas furnaces vary considerably from the older generation. They use an induced draft fan, but they have a heat exchanger that is not visible upon inspection because it has a smaller access hole. They also use a hot surface igniter, a mono-port burner system, electronic controls, electronic sensors for fan limit, and flame roll out safety switches. The mid-efficiency furnaces are easily recognized by the metal flue pipes (typically a B vent) used with an induced draft fan.

High-efficiency furnaces, the latest generation of furnaces, vary considerably in configuration from manufacturer to manufacturer. The combustion chamber may be located at the top or middle of the unit, heat exchangers may be located high or low and be totally inaccessible, and other components can be located in different places. In most, there is no visible access to burners except through the site glass or porthole allowing the inspector to confirm ignition and flame color. Depending on what part of the country you're in, you will probably see far more gas units than oil, although oil is still popular in the northeastern and northwestern United States and parts of Canada.

A high-efficiency or **condensing furnace** will have two or even three heat exchangers to extract as much heat as possible from the exhaust gases by condensing the water vapor from combustion. The condensate is discharged to an appropriate drain (floor drain, condensate pump, or sink trap), while the remaining cool gases are forced outside with a forced draft fan through 2–3″ PVC piping through the house wall or roof. High-efficiency furnaces pipe (draw) in outside air to use for combustion air.

Another kind of high-efficiency furnace is the **gas pulse furnace**. This model has an entirely different combustion process. Outside combustion air is mixed with gas in the sealed combustion chamber and ignited by spark plugs, causing the first pulse. The pulse travels down a tailpipe, hits the end of the tailpipe, and sends a shockwave back to the chamber, igniting the next pulse. This begins a self-perpetuating process of shockwaves with 60 to 70 explosions per

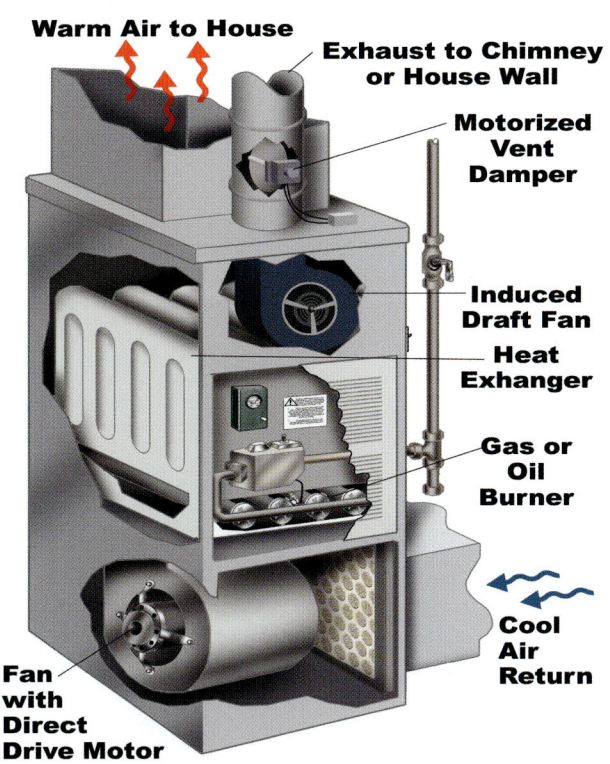

Illustration by Paddy Morrissey

> *Definitions*
>
> An <u>induced draft fan</u> in a furnace pulls combustion by-products through the unit, ensuring a good draft and reducing heat loss.
>
> A <u>motorized vent damper</u>, located in the flue above the furnace, automatically opens and closes to prevent heat loss up the chimney.

Photo #22 HIGH-EFFICIENCY or 90+ FURNACE

This is a high-efficiency or 90+ furnace. You can identify it quickly by the plastic intake and exhaust piping. The plastic piping for the exhaust or flue is to prevent corrosion. Since the exhaust gases are much cooler than a mid-efficiency furnace, the water vapor can start to condense as it travels up the flue and can rust out a metal flue.

second, allowing the blower and spark ignition to be turned off. Hot gases are forced into the heat exchanger where heat is transferred. As with the condensing furnaces, condensate is drained and the remaining cooled exhaust gases are vented to the outside through PVC piping. Some Lennox pulse furnaces installed between 1982 and 1989 had corrosion problems with their heat exchangers. If you come across one of these, it's best to recommend that a qualified heating professional examine the unit. The warranty on the heat exchanger is mostly likely expired. It was lifetime to the original purchaser with proof (a receipt) or 20 years to subsequent owners or owners with no receipt. If you find one of these, recommend replacement as it is past its expected lifetime.

Some forced-air systems use **solar energy** as an energy source (described previously). Solar air heating systems use air collectors to absorb heat that then passes through a heat recovery ventilator or through the air coil of an air-source heat pump. The home inspector cannot be expected to evaluate the performance of solar heating. But components can be inspected for condition—collectors and fans securely fastened and free of deterioration.

NOTE: Central heating that uses a **heat pump** is basically the same as a forced-air furnace with one exception—the heating element is not a gas or oil burner—it's a component of a reverse-cycle air-conditioning system utilizing a

Photo #23 LENNOX PULSE FURNACE

This is the inside of a Lennox Pulse furnace. As you can see it looks nothing like the furnaces discussed so far. It used pulses of gas instead of a continuously burning flame to provide heat to the system. Over time the heat exchangers fatigued and cracked, ultimately requiring replacement.

coil with refrigerant. We'll discuss the heat pump later in this chapter, beginning on page 534.

Furnace Components

Forced-air furnaces share the following components:

- **Furnace controls:** The three main controls on a forced-air furnace are the thermostat, the fan control, and the high-temperature limit control. The **thermostat** was discussed in detail earlier in this chapter (see pages 403–406), so we won't repeat the information here. In forced-air systems, the thermostat turns the burner/system on and off as a result of a call for heat.

- The **fan control** is a temperature-sensitive switch or sensor that turns the furnace fan on and off at preset temperatures. The blower won't turn on until air in the plenum, heated by the burner, reaches a certain point. This varies greatly depending on engineering and whether it's a single-stage, two-stage, or variable speed furnace (about 110°F to 170°F). After the burner turns off, the fan continues running until the air temperature in the plenum falls to the low set point (about 90°F). This ensures that only warm air will be circulated in the house. When the thermostat calls for heat, only the burners should fire. If the fan begins to operate at the same time the burners fire, the fan control is in need of adjustment. In newer furnaces,

FORCED-AIR COMPONENTS

- Furnace controls including fan control and limit control
- Blower unit consisting of a fan wheel and fan motor
- Air filter
- Burner and combustion chamber
- Heat exchanger(s)
- Humidifier (optional)
- Supply and return ducting
- Exhaust system

Definitions

The fan control is a furnace control that turns the fan on and off at preset temperatures. The limit control is another furnace control that turns off the burners if the furnace reaches a preset high temperature. Usually, the fan and limit control are combined in a single switch called the fan/limit switch.

THE HEATING INSPECTION

the limit switch is an electronic sensor connected to a circuit board that is set at around 170°F. This simply shuts down the burners if the heat exchanger overheats. Mid- and high-efficiency furnaces have an induced draft fan that pulls the air through the convoluted (serpentine) heat exchanger. The induced draft fan triggers the igniter, which lights the burner. This in turn causes the blower to activate. The burner shuts off first, followed by the induced draft fan. The blower runs until the heat is bled off from the heat exchanger and the thermostat is met.

The **limit control** is a series of electronic sensors that will turn off the burner if temperatures in the heat exchanger get too hot due to some malfunction in the furnace. The high temperature limit is usually set at about 170°F to 200°F. In older conventional draft furnaces, the limit control also functions as the fan control in a single switch, called the **fan/limit switch**.

NOTE: Some older furnaces (more than 40 to 50 years old) have a manual **summer switch** that allowed the fan to operate independently of the burners. It may be located on the thermostat, mounted next to the safety switch, or housed on the fan control. Homeowners can turn on the fan for air circulation during the summer. This feature is increasingly rare as old units are replaced. This is the same as using the thermostat fan switch on a modern system and placing it to the "on" position instead of the "auto" position. It is also terribly wasteful as most older blowers, permanent split capacitor (PSC) type, are not designed to run 24/7.

- **The blower unit:** All forced-air furnaces have a blower unit containing a **fan wheel and fan motor**. Its purpose is to draw return air back into the furnace, push it through the heat exchanger(s), and send it out through the supply ducts. Most blowers are squirrel cage impellers, where fan blades are on the interior surface of a cylinder that spins in its housing. With a **direct drive fan (by far the most common for the past 30+ years)**, the fan motor is mounted within the fan casing. Older systems have the motor mounted outside the fan casing and drive the fan with a pair of pulleys and a belt.

Photo #24 *This is a standard direct drive Permanent Split Capacitor (PSC) motor that runs at a single speed.*

Photo #25 *This is a belt-driven fan. They are very uncommon in residential systems today. Be sure to check the belt for wear and proper tension, just like on your car.*

Many newer furnaces have a variable speed blower motor, called an electronically commutated motor (ECM), that operates at a variable speed to satisfy the heating needs of the home. It is kind of like having a dimmer switch on the motor, and the electronic controls adjust its speed up or down as needed. If the unit can't meet the heating needs at the lower speed or stage, the blower will ramp up to hit the second speed or stage to meet the home's demand. They are very expensive to replace, with the controller, if not the motor, being the part that fails in most cases.

Photo #26 *This is an ECM motor installed within the blower wheel. These are very expensive variable speed systems that are found on high efficiency heating and a/c systems. You can tell the difference by the large section attached to the end of the motor. There are also several wires in a plastic connector that is unlike a conventional fan motor.*

- **An air filter:** The purpose of the air filter is to remove dust and dirt from the air before it passes into the furnace where it can clog heat exchanger passages, air conditioner coils, ducts, and registers. Inexpensive **air filters** are made of 1″-thick spun fiberglass. They are not very effective and remove only the largest dust particles. Better quality air filters are made of pleated polyester or cotton paper. Like the fiberglass

> **Section Note**
>
> *"Try not to show surprise by the ignorance of some homeowners. I had to keep a straight face while teaching a home maintenance class. When I commented on the furnace air filter, one homeowner said, 'Furnaces have filters?' She'd lived in her current home for 14 years and had never once cleaned or changed the air filter."*

filters, they are disposable. They are able to filter smaller particles but sometimes impede airflow. In many units (depending on your location), filters are mounted between the return air duct and the furnace cabinet at the blower. Newer homes often have a single central return in the hallway wall or ceiling. In better new construction and older homes especially in cold climates, there is a return register in each room with the filter located near the furnace. When inspecting the filter, be sure that it's securely in place, facing the right way for airflow, and clean. Filters should be cleaned or changed, depending on the type, regularly every month or so. Stains around registers can be an indication of a defective filter or leaky ducts as well as other furnace problems such as poorly adjusted burners or a cracked heat exchanger.

An electronic filter contains a series of fine wire grids that are given an electric charge, which aids the filter in capturing small particles. When the filter is working, it faintly pops and crackles like a bug zapper. Electrostatic filters are available to replace ordinary air filters and may be part of a separate unit that sits next to the furnace at the return air duct. The filter may be disposable or permanent (washable). Electronic air filters (not electrostatic) should be cleaned periodically by running them through the dishwasher. Most standards state that home inspectors don't inspect electronic filters because of the danger of shock. However, we suggest that you examine the filter, but do it carefully. There are many types of filters—from the blue or orange inexpensive $0.89 filters to the $18 3M Filtrete™ type. The difference is the particulate size that is captured. The term is MERV for minimum efficiency reporting value. The industry recommendation is a MERV 8–11, which is a typical pleated paper filter for a couple of dollars each. The 3M type filters have a MERV in the range of 13–16, and the cheapest about MERV 1–4 rating.

- Burner area and combustion chamber: See pages 423–433 for information on gas burners and pages 438–447 for information on oil burners. Electric furnaces, of course, will not have a burner or combustion area. Instead, you'll find a bank of heating elements.

- **The heat exchanger:** This is the most critical component of a forced-air heating system. The heat exchanger in modern furnaces is made from sheet metal, usually aluminized steel or stainless steel. It sits above or below the draft fan and is open to the combustion chamber and burner, transferring heat from burning fuel to the air that circulates through the house. The hot gas inside the heat exchanger never comes into contact with the air circulated in the home.

If a heat exchanger cracks or rusts through, combustion products will escape through the holes into the home's air supply. **Cracks** can occur at

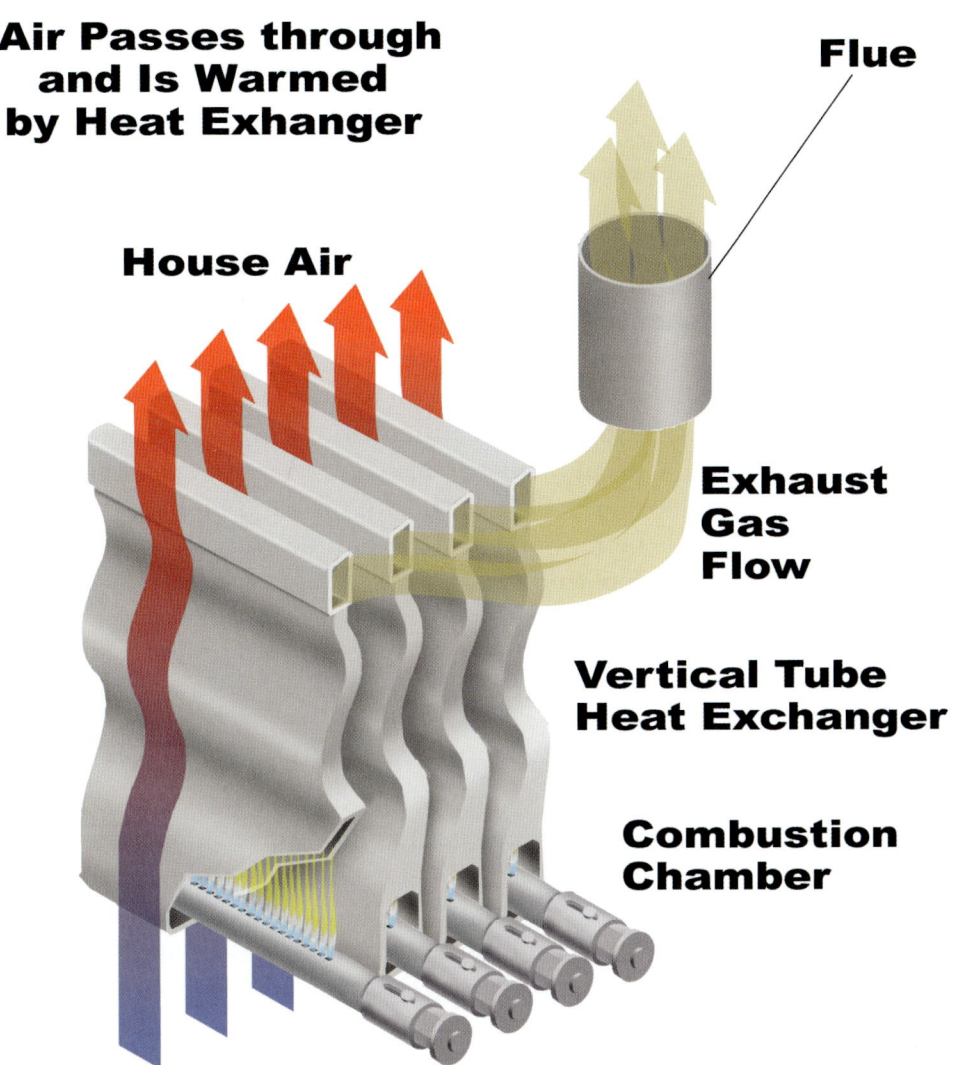

Air Passes through and Is Warmed by Heat Exhanger

House Air

Flue

Exhaust Gas Flow

Vertical Tube Heat Exchanger

Combustion Chamber

Illustration by Paddy Morrissey

Photo #27 *This heat exchanger is rusted to the right side. This is nothing that can be seen during and inspection. This is why heat exchangers are excluded from the SOP.*

sharp corners and at welded seams due to metal fatigue, and once started, they will grow because of the continual expansion and contraction of the metal. **Corrosion and rust** from too much condensation or water in the furnace can cause holes in the heat exchanger. If the burner and combustion area is rusted, corroded, and flaking, chances are the heat

Definitions

Relative humidity is the ratio of the amount of water vapor in the air at a specific temperature to the maximum amount the air could hold at that temperature, expressed as a percentage.

Dry-bulb temperature refers to the temperature of air as measured by a conventional thermometer.

Wet-bulb temperature is measured with a device called a hygrometer, designed to measure the temperature in a way that reflects the cooling properties of evaporating water.

Section Note

"One of my inspectors found water dripping out of the ductwork in a house. He couldn't figure out what was going on. It looked like a plumbing leak, but he wasn't sure.

We were having a few weeks of hot weather that spring. The inspector realized that the homeowner had turned on the central air-conditioning without turning off the humidifier, which was condensing like crazy. He turned off the humidifier and the dripping stopped."

exchanger is too. Because faulty heat exchangers are virtually impossible to repair cost effectively, the furnace must be replaced.

- **Humidifiers:** The home inspector may find a humidifier added to a forced-air furnace. The purpose of the humidifier is to add moisture to the circulating air when the furnace is operating. Humidifiers may be mounted in the return duct or in the supply plenum. Those located over the heat exchanger can damage the heat exchanger if they leak, causing rusting and corrosion. Leaky humidifiers can also harbor mold and other microbes that may cause health problems; the leak should be repaired and the unit thoroughly cleaned or replaced.

There are several types of humidifiers. The **drum or reservoir humidifier** is located in the return duct with a bypass to the supply plenum. The **evaporative humidifier** can be found on the supply plenum with a tray of evaporative pads inside the plenum. This type is likely to develop leaks over the heat exchanger. Other kinds are cascade, atomizing, and steam-generating. The most common humidifier in newer furnaces is the **flow-through humidifier**, in which the water flows through the humidifier and drains out. The flow-through humidifier may be mounted to the return air duct and connected to the hot air supply from the furnace with a humidifier supply takeoff duct. The natural pressure differential between the supply and return sides of the furnace diverts some heated air to the humidifier, where the warm air absorbs the moisture. You may also see the humidifier mounted directly on the hot air supply duct with no supply takeoff duct.

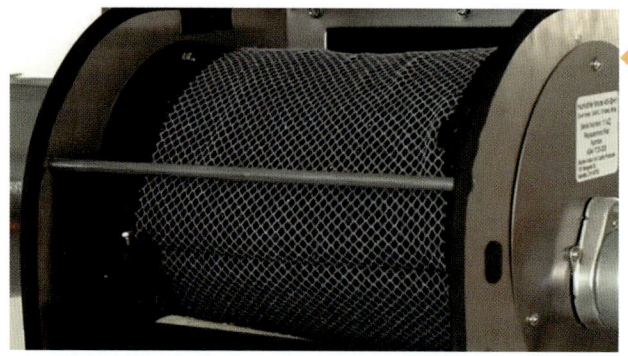

Photo #28 *Older style drum humidifier. This type of unit relies on a reservoir of water and a foam wheel that rotates. These usually turn out to be great science projects with many things growing in the stagnant water.*

Photo #29 FLOW-THROUGH HUMIDIFIER
Flow-through humidifiers work much better and stay cleaner longer than the drum humidifiers do. They do, however, waste quite a bit more water than the drum type.

The home inspector is not required to inspect the humidifier. However, you should make sure the humidifier is connected to a water and power supply. Be sure to check the humidifier for its general condition and leakage and for potential or actual damage to furnace components.

- **Supply and return ducts:** Heated air is blown through the furnace to room registers through supply ducts. Cool air is gathered in return grill(s) for redelivery back to the furnace. There are two basic types of distribution systems. The **extended plenum (or trunk) system** (shown on page 464) consists of the plenum mounted on the furnace, a large extended supply duct (the main trunk), and branch ducts that deliver heat to registers in each room. Registers for outside rooms are normally located along a perimeter or exterior wall. Return grill(s), which are typically located on walls opposite the heat registers, bring cool air back to the furnace through return ducts.

  High-velocity systems are usually seen as a retrofit in an old house. Typically installed in an attic, they use small high-pressure ducts and nozzles instead of traditional large ducts and registers. These systems cool the house, but have a smaller footprint and easier duct runs. Because high-velocity systems do not require large registers, they can easily blend in with existing décor. The systems are also highly efficient because less heat is lost through the shorter, narrower ducts.

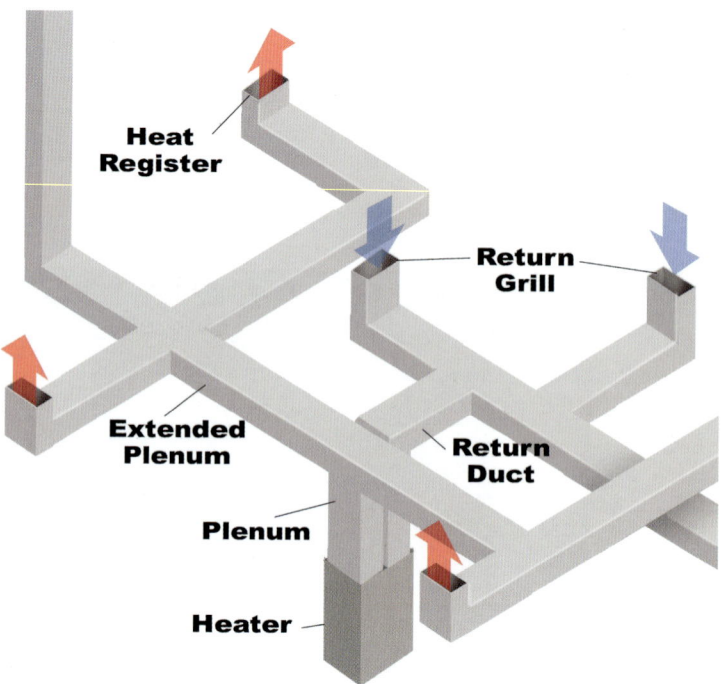

Illustration by Paddy Morrissey

Another type of distribution system is called the **radial system**, where each supply duct takes off directly from the furnace to individual room registers. In this system, which is common in gravity furnaces, there is no main supply duct. A variation on the radial system is the **perimeter loop arrangement**, common in most slab-on-grade houses, where one duct encircles the entire perimeter of the house and feeder ducts run from each side of the house back to the furnace.

Supply and return ducts may be made of sheet metal, fiberglass, plastic, duct board, or glass-reinforced plastic sheets, drywall, or wood (return only). In any case, ducts should be airtight, properly supported, and free of damage such as corrosion or water damage. Ducts should be insulated in cold areas, where they pass through an unheated attic, basement, or crawl space, for example. Current energy efficiency codes no longer allow building cavities or chases to be used for return ducting. The codes have never allowed for supply ducting to use building cavities. The most common cavities used are the floor joist bays in a basement or crawl space where sheet metal or foil-covered cardboard enclose the bay as a return duct back to the furnace. Now ALL ducts, both supply and return, must be ducted to and from the furnace or air handler.

> **CAUTION**
>
> *There should be <u>no open return</u> in the basement. Leaking combustion air from the furnace could be drawn into the home's air supply.*

For noise control and to reduce vibration, there may be a **canvas fabric or rubberized plastic collar** between the main supply duct and the furnace. The vibration-dampening collar should be in good condition—not torn or not having open sections. Some fabrics used in older systems, pre-1975, contained asbestos, and the customer should be warned about that. Supply ducts may have **balancing duct dampers** used to equalize the volume of air in the branch ducts. If the distribution system is zoned, where supply and return ducts are divided into separate loops, the flow of heated air is controlled by **motorized zone dampers**. In this case, an individual thermostat for each zone causes its motorized damper to open and close.

The presence and placement of **return grills** is important for good air circulation. Each system has specific requirements to produce optimal airflow. Furnace operation requires that air returning to the furnace through return ducts be unrestricted. An HVAC technician can perform a test called a total external static pressure (TESP) test. This easily verifies whether the return ductwork is restricted or undersized. This test is beyond the scope of a home inspection. If additional efficiency testing is thought to be necessary, it would be performed by an Energy Auditor or Building Science professional. Therefore, each area of the house that has a heat register <u>should</u> also have a return grill. For rooms without a return grill, doors are often undercut (about 3/4″ – 1″ of clearance above carpets) to improve airflow, but this gap is inadequate to provide optimal results. Ideally, there should be no **open return** in the basement because leaking combustion air from the furnace may be drawn into the home's air supply.

> *Definitions*
>
> A <u>balancing duct damper</u>, located in the branch supply ducts, equalizes the flow of warm air to the house.
>
> A <u>motorized duct damper</u>, located in zoned supply ducts, controls the flow of warm air to zones within the house.

NOTE: Supply and return ducts in older slab-on-grade homes are normally buried in or beneath the concrete slab, making inspection of them impossible for the home inspector. Ducts in the concrete can collapse or leak and rust out, causing a restriction in airflow. The inspector should pay attention to airflow at registers and grills to verify that airflow is not restricted (they work or they don't; we are not quantifying the performance). Customers should be informed that the inspector cannot inspect the ducts themselves.

- **Exhaust system:** As discussed earlier, conventional forced-air systems have a conventional smoke pipe connected to the chimney, a B vent (a double-walled metal pipe used to vent gas-fired appliances), or an L vent (a double-walled metal pipe used to vent oil-fired appliances). High-efficiency furnaces exhaust cooled gases in plastic piping through the house wall or roof and drain condensate to the floor drain or other appropriate location. The type of piping varies depending on the manufacturer. Types include PVC, ABS, and proprietary materials from various manufacturers. A couple of types are known to be defective: Plexvent, Plexvent II, and Ultravent. They were part of a 1989 CPSC recall. The reimbursement for replacement ended May 1, 2009. The pipes are plastic and either gray or black in color. Typically, stickers had been placed on the pipes identifying them as such. All piping should be inspected for its condition.

> *Section Note*
>
> Check your local codes on this issue of whether an open return is allowed in the basement within 10′ of the furnace. It's not allowed in many areas.

Photo #30 *The pipes are plastic and either gray or black in color. There were typically stickers on the pipes identifying them as such. All piping should be inspected for its condition and probable need of replacement.*

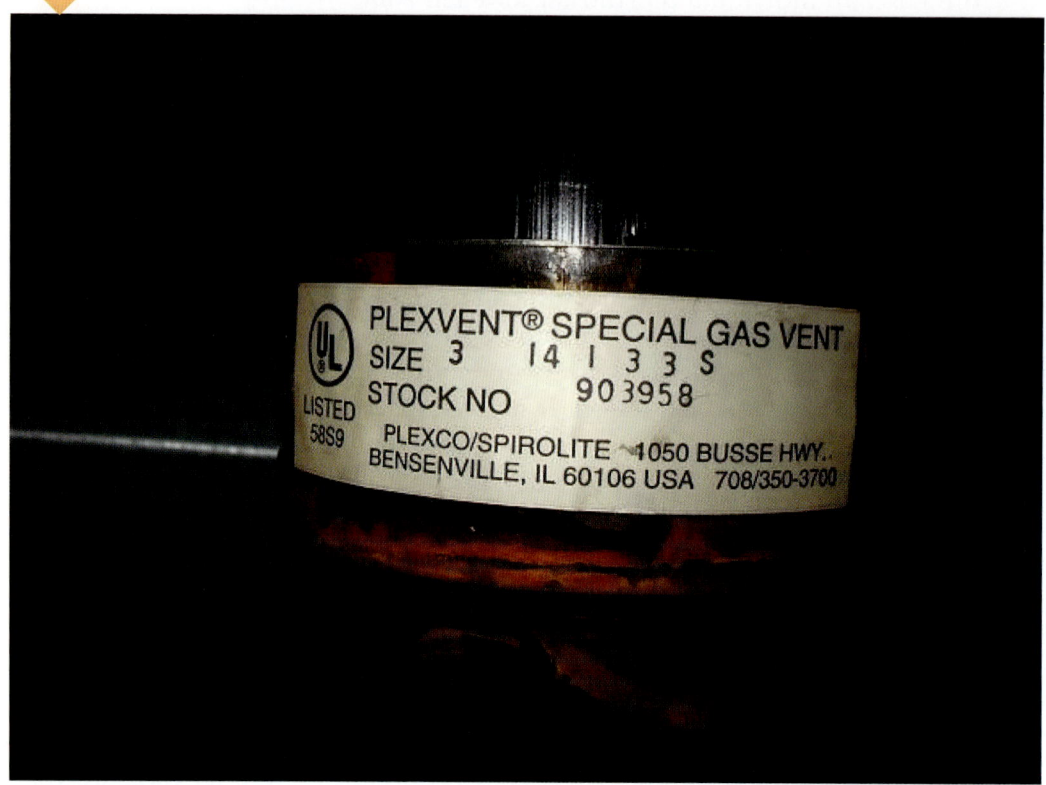

For Beginning Inspectors

Visit your friends and inspect as many forced-air furnaces as possible. For each furnace, go through the whole procedure as outlined in these pages.

Inspecting Forced-Air Furnaces

The home inspector will inspect the **furnace**, its **distribution system**, and its **venting system**. Note that the procedures for inspecting the fuel burner, smoke pipe or flue, chimney, and cleanout were presented earlier in this chapter (see page 423 for gas burners and page 438 for oil burners). We won't repeat these procedures here. The home inspector should also inspect the forced-air furnace for the following conditions:

- **Lack of heat source in each room:** As you inspect each room in the house, note whether a heat source is present and be sure to report if there is no heat source. After you've turned up the thermostat, you can hold a tissue in front of each heat register to check the flow of air from the register into the room. Lack of airflow can indicate a restriction or disconnection in the supply ducts, damaged or crushed supply ducts, a fan problem, or some other furnace malfunction. A tissue held against the return air grill will test the pull of air back to the furnace—the tissue should be sucked against the grill. A more accurate test is to use an infrared laser thermometer. The inspector "shoots" the register with an infrared laser thermometer to be sure that air is coming out, by measuring the temperature of the grill, which

Photo #31 DATA TAG

The manufacturer's data tag has a lot of useful information. The temperature rise and age of the equipment are probably the two most important. On this tag the temperature rise is 25-55 degrees. That means that the air coming out of the supply registers should be 25-55 degrees hotter than it went in at the return.

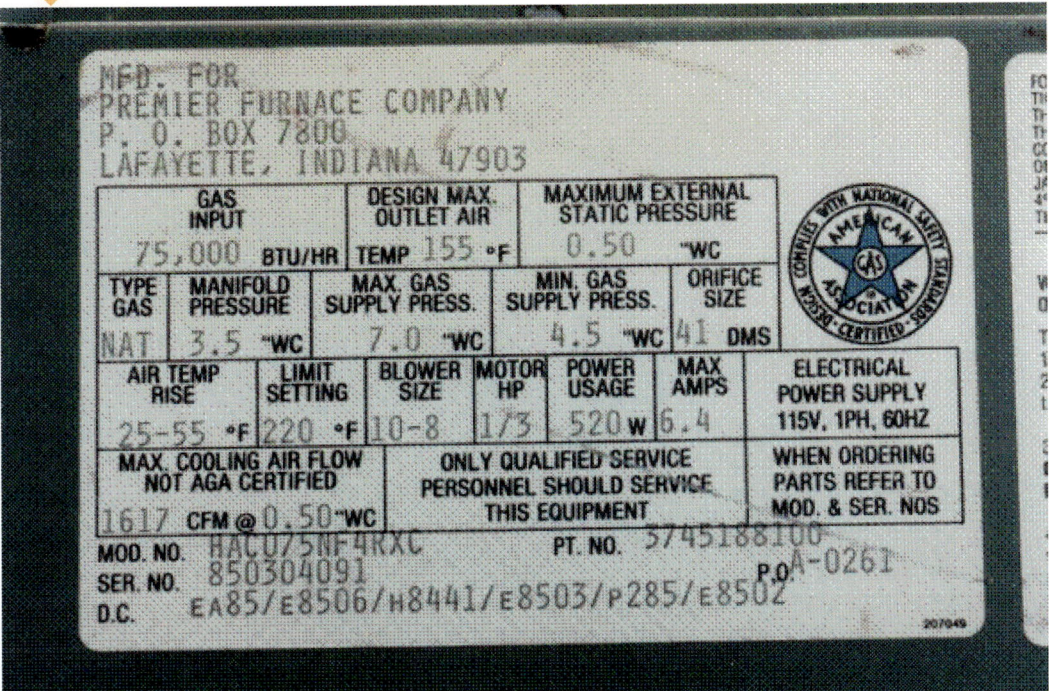

will be representative of the air flowing across it. The laser is also used to determine the proper temperature rise in furnaces and the temperature differential in air conditioners and heat pumps. The temperature rise is dictated by the manufacturer and is listed on the furnace's data tag. The inspector "shoots" the supply and return registers to determine if the difference falls within the temperature rise listed on the data tag.

- **Dirty, loose, or missing registers or grills:** As you inspect registers, note if there is soot and dark staining on the walls above or beside them. This condition can indicate a cracked heat exchanger that is sending combustion products into the home, which is a **safety hazard**. If return grills are not present in each room, check the doors to see if there's adequate airflow under them.

- **Defects in the furnace cabinet:** Examine the outside of the furnace cabinet for damage, holes, corrosion, or rust. Scorch and burn marks in the area of the heat exchanger can indicate a heat exchanger problem. Staining and soot around the burner indicates spillage and downdrafts.

> **Section Note**
>
> *"I always stress making a note in the inspection report about the absence of a heat source in each room. It seems a small thing, but customers get angry when they discover a room without a heat register after they move in. If you miss this point, you'll only end up paying to have a heat source put in. I've paid for some myself."*

- **Cracked, rusted, or corroded heat exchanger:** After turning off the furnace, remove the access panels and examine as much of the heat exchanger as possible. While inspecting the heat exchanger is beyond the scope of most Standards of Practice, we recommend that you examine as much of it as you can. (You may not have access to the heat exchanger in an oil furnace or a mid- or high-efficiency furnace). Use your flashlight and inspection mirror to inspect the heat exchanger for cracks and/or corrosion. Be particularly careful about looking at welded areas and curves. Some manufacturers' models have had a history of faulty heat exchangers and other problems, including corrosion in some of the earlier high-efficiency models due to condensation. A cracked or faulty heat exchanger can be indicated by the following items, and the home inspector should look for each one. Each situation should be reported as a **safety hazard**, and the home inspector should **recommend evaluation by a**

Photo #32 BURN MARKS ON A GAS FURNACE

We are looking up under or in to the draft hood at the top of the furnace. The two oval holes at the bottom of the photo are the top or end of the heat exchanger chambers. The round hole at the top is the flue pipe going to the exterior. The significant rust must be noted and a technician recommended.

furnace technician before closing. The customer should be informed that the only cost-effective cure for a cracked heat exchanger may be replacing the furnace.

- — **Scorch and burn marks on the furnace jacket**

- — **Staining around registers or on front of furnace:** Staining here or on walls next to the room registers can indicate a problem heat exchanger.

- — **Visible cracks**

- — **Corrosion, rust, or scaling on or below the heat exchanger**

- — **Unusual flame activity:** As described earlier for gas and oil burners (pages 425, 426, 441), unusual flame action can mean problems with the heat exchanger.

- **Faulty temperature rise:** You can perform a "temperature rise" test on the furnace. This is an optional test that may be performed during the heating **or** cooling season. You should run a gas or oil furnace at any time during the year. It will not damage the appliance. The appliance that you can't operate when it's hot outside is the heat pump in the heating mode. You may upset the homeowner by running the furnace when he or she has the air-conditioning on, but it will not damage the equipment. Use your thermometer to check the temperature of the supply air and the temperature of the return air. This test should be performed by punching a hole (with an awl) in the supply and return plenums and inserting a thermometer. This is NOT what we as home inspectors do because this is destructive. We test at the nearest supply and return register or at the filter slot right at the furnace if accessible. The furnace data plate (see page 467) will state the furnace's **temperature rise range (25° to 55° in example tag)**, between hot supply air and cold return air. For example, supply air may be at 120° and return air at 70°, making the difference within the 25° to 55° range (120 − 70 = 50). A temperature rise that is too small means there is an airflow issue, generally that the fan speed is set too high. The air does not contact the heat exchanger long enough to heat up adequately. A temperature

> **Section Note**
>
> *"I had inspected a furnace and found no holes in the heat exchanger. Later, when a heating contractor came in to service and evaluate it, he pulled out the burners and created a 1/2" hole in the heat exchanger. He told my customer that I should have found this.*
>
> *The customer called me, hopping mad. I went back to look at the furnace and knew I hadn't missed that hole. I had to face down the heating contractor until he finally admitted that he had done it."*

> **Section Note**
>
> *"I was inspecting a badly corroded Lennox G-12 furnace. The burners were so clogged up, the flames were hardly coming out. I knew immediately that the furnace needed replacement. However, I continued in my inspection and inspected the entire furnace. Even when you know the furnace is a write-off, complete the inspection. That's what customers paid for, and they'll be upset if you stop right away."*

> **Section Note**
>
> *Inform your customer that only about 25%, at best, of the heat exchanger in a conventional gas furnace is visible for inspection. In oil-fired and mid- and high-efficiency gas units, you may not be able to see the heat exchanger at all. The furnace should be evaluated by a qualified furnace technician.*

rise that is too high indicates the opposite: not enough airflow, generally an obstruction such as a blocked air-conditioning coil or a very dirty filter, or the fan speed is set too low. It is beyond the scope of the inspection for you to determine the reason behind the improper temperature rise.

- **Dirty, damaged, noisy, or malfunctioning blower:** Examine the fan before you fire up the system, looking for signs of damage, missing blades, and dirt. After the furnace is fired up, listen to the fan as it turns on. Noises and excessive vibrations can indicate loose bearings or mountings, a worn belt, dirty blades, or misalignment.

- **Dirty or missing air filter:** Dirty air filters can impede the flow of air into the furnace and allow the plenum to get hot enough to turn off the furnace (hits the high limit) in a pattern of short cycling. Always check filters regularly.

  CAUTION: If you find an **electronic air filter**, turn off the master furnace switch, which will usually turn off power to the filter too. Wait about 30 seconds to let the static charge dissipate before pulling the filter out for inspection, if you choose to. Otherwise, you're in for a shock, literally.

- **Presence of asbestos:** If an older furnace has a fabric vibration dampening collar between the furnace and the plenum, it might contain asbestos. The home inspector won't be able to say with any certainty if asbestos is present, but customers should be warned about the possibility. Insulated ducts should be examined for asbestos as well. Duct insulation containing asbestos doesn't necessarily have to be removed. White cloth or fabric type duct wrap on pre-1975 systems is a sign that asbestos may be present.

- **Dirty or leaking humidifier:** The home inspector is not required to inspect the humidifier for operation, but should check for its potential damaging effect on other furnace components.

- **Leaking, damaged, loose, disconnected, or corroded ducts:** Examine visible supply and return ductwork for condition, noting any open joints, corrosion, and loose supports.

- **Open return in basement:** Report the presence of an open return in the basement, which is prohibited by modern building codes. CO from the furnace can be sucked into the home's air supply. This situation should be reported as a **safety hazard**.

- **Missing or malfunctioning dampers:** Malfunctioning balancing dampers can be discovered by the airflow being diminished at the registers where airflow and warmth would be impeded. Motorized zone damper operation can be verified by operating each zone's thermostat (one at a time) and checking airflow. Be careful with houses that have multiple zones, whether furnaces or boilers. Always check them one zone at a time. Turn off all thermostats in the house;

> **Section Note**
>
> *"An inspector I know (not on my staff, fortunately) forgot to turn the furnace back on after an inspection. The house happened to be unoccupied. When the owners returned, they found the plumbing pipes frozen and burst. Of course, the inspector had to pay for the damage and repair—a very expensive mistake."*

then turn them on one at a time and see what happens. Verify that all parts of the house are heated and that all components appear to operate. Note that zone dampers don't close completely, so there will be some airflow when the damper is closed.

CAUTION: When you finish your furnace inspection, be sure to turn the furnace back on and return the thermostats to their original settings (remember the 5° rule). Leaving the furnace off in an empty house in winter can be a major mistake for the home inspector.

Reporting Your Findings

When you're inspecting the heating system, have your client present. It's a smart practice. When the client comes with you, you have an opportunity to fully explain the inspection and point out findings. Customer knowledge is a big step toward the prevention of complaint calls later.

Keep a running dialogue going with the client. Not everyone is familiar with furnace operation, and he or she may not understand what you're doing and the significance of your findings. Because furnace defects can be a serious safety hazard to the home's occupants, you want to be sure that the customer understands what you're saying. So **keep it simple**, but do talk about it. And pay attention to whether the client understands.

> **IMPORTANT POINT**
>
> *Always review your inspection report with the customer after the inspection. Helping the customer understand what your findings are prevents lawsuits later.*

During the inspection, be sure to explain the following:

- **What you're inspecting**—the burners, the heat exchanger, the fan, the ductwork, the smoke pipe, and so on.

- **What you're looking for**—rust, corrosion, gas leaks, downdrafts, dirty filters, cracks in the heat exchanger, and so on.

- **What you're doing**—testing airflow and return with a laser; turning off the furnace to inspect the burners; testing the draft diverter with a match, mirror, or smoke tube; inspecting the heat exchanger; and so on.

- **What you're finding**—signs of a lack of combustion air, cracks in the firebox, a leaking humidifier, a filled chimney cleanout and blocked chimney flue, and so on.

- **Suggestions about dealing with the findings**—cleaning the burners, changing the air filter, replacing the entire furnace, having a furnace technician evaluate the heat exchanger, having the oil burner serviced, and so on. But use caution, don't make uneducated guesses about how repairs should be made. Talk about what you could not inspect and why (unit turned off, disconnected, or not accessible, etc.).

Be sure to review the inspection report with your client after the inspection. Even though you've been careful to provide information during the inspection, often the client will forget some or all of what you've said. Go through the inspection report

> **DON'T EVER MISS**
>
> - Heat source in each room
> - Burner problems
> - Evidence of CO production
> - Gas or oil leaks, oil odors, and smoke
> - Holes, cracks, or rusting in heat exchanger
> - Missing filters
> - Upgrade or problem furnaces
> - Improper clearances
> - Spillage from draft hood or diverter or damper
> - Improper venting and holes in vent pipes

page by page, pointing out where you've marked certain findings. This is especially important with technical systems such as heating, where the client may not understand thoroughly. The review gives you another chance to check his or her understanding. Point out where you've indicated major repairs, safety hazards, and items requiring replacement in the near future.

Filling in Your Report

Every home inspector needs an inspection report. A **written report** is the work product of the home inspection, and every home inspector is expected to deliver one to the customer after the inspection. Inspection reports vary a great deal in the industry. Some home inspection companies develop their own version; others use state required formats (Texas), home inspection software, apps, or formats provided by training companies such as AHIT. Some are considered to be excellent, while others are not very good. A workable and easy-to-use inspection report is important for a home inspector. Of greater importance are its thoroughness, accuracy, and helpfulness to the customer. Whatever reporting format you choose, make sure it presents your findings in a clear, professional manner such that it reduces your liability and client dissatisfaction.

The **Don't Ever Miss** list is a reminder of those specific findings you should include in your inspection report. We list these items based on years of experience performing home inspections. Missing them can result in complaint calls and possible lawsuits. Here is an overview of what to report on during the inspection of the furnace:

- **Furnace information:** Record the brand name, model, and serial number of the furnace. This should be located on the data plate on the furnace, although you may not be able to find all this information on an old gravity furnace. Identify the type of furnace (gravity or forced-air) and the type of fuel used. To determine the age of the equipment, check the ANSI number, which can be found on all combustion equipment made in approximately the last 30 years. The date is coded and allows you to figure out the age within 3 to 4 years. Using a reference book such as the Carson Dunlop *Technical Reference Guide* is very helpful for determining the age of most furnaces, boilers, air conditioners, heat pumps, and water heaters.

- **Operation:** Note in your report whether the furnace fired and make a special note if the furnace was not operating. If you performed a temperature rise test, you might want to report if the differential was within the range of the manufacturer's data tag.

- **Heat exchanger:** Note whether you were able to inspect the heat exchanger. Report any defects found, such as rusting and corrosion and visible cracks. It's a good idea to give the heat exchanger an overall rating. Here's a suggestion on how to do that:

Photo #33 FURNACE INFORMATION DATA PLATE

This tag is a bit easier to tell the age as it states that it was made 4/95. We can verify that a couple of ways. First with the Carson Dunlop Technical Reference Guide, which tells us that K in the serial number is 1995 and that 17 is the seventeenth week, which would fall in April. Another way is to use the ANSI number (top right) and use the formula previously discussed. An ANSI number of 1993 means the device was made between 1993 and 1997. Lastly, the temperature rise is 35-65 degrees.

THE HEATING INSPECTION

> **OLDER FURNACES**
>
> *For furnaces over 17 years old, in your inspection report, always note them as items <u>probably requiring replacement within the next 5 years</u>. The furnace will be reaching the end of its lifetime in about 5 years.*

— Use **satisfactory** only if you've found no defects in the heat exchanger or no signs of defects *and* the furnace is not past its lifetime.

— Use **marginal** if it is operational, but beyond its normal life expectancy. They should anticipate having to replace the system within the next 5 years.

— Use **poor** if you've found cracks or holes in the heat exchanger *or* you've found any of the other signs that indicate a cracked heat exchanger. Again, recommend that a technician evaluate the furnace before closing if you rate it as poor.

- **Other components:** Report on the condition of the furnace cabinet, burner, filter, blower, vent (flue) pipes, and distribution ducts and registers. Note defects such as oil burners that need servicing, fan motors with loose worn bearings that make a squealing sound, dirty filters, and open joints in vent pipes.

- **Recommending an evaluation:** The home inspector should always recommend that a qualified technician be called in to evaluate the furnace if the following conditions are found. Be sure to make a note of your recommendation in the inspection report.

    — If you rate the condition of the heat exchanger as marginal or poor

    — If the furnace didn't fire

> **Section Note**
>
> *The American Home Inspectors Training Institute offers both manual and computerized reports. These reports include an inspection agreement, complete reporting pages, and helpful customer information. If you're interested in purchasing the <u>Home Inspection Report</u>, please contact us at 1-800-441-9411.*

- **Major defect or repair:** If the furnace needs replacement because of a cracked heat exchanger, because it is well beyond its life expectancy, or because it's not operating, identify the condition as a major defect or repair in your report. Another major repair to list is the lack of return ducts in a gravity furnace.

- **Safety hazards:** Never miss reporting any safety hazards you've found. It's a good idea to report them on the furnace page of your report and then summarize them on a summary page. For the inspection of the furnace, don't miss these safety hazards:

    — Cracked, rusted, or deteriorating heat exchanger

    — Evidence of CO production (if a CO detector is used)

    — Spillage, improper venting, holes in vent pipes

— Improper clearances

— Gas or oil leaks and improper location of an LP gas tank

— An open return in the unfinished portion of the basement

— Blocked flue

6.7 HOT WATER BOILERS

Although the term *boiler* is used to describe the heating unit, the water in the hot water heating system boiler is not actually brought to the boiling point. The water in a hot water system is heated to about 160°F to 185°F (water boils at 212°F).

> **Chapter Note**
>
> *Pages 475–493 present the study and inspection of hot water heating systems.*

Types of Hot Water Systems

A hot water heating system heats a home and its occupants by a combination of convection, conduction, and radiation. That is, water is heated in a boiler and moves through pipes to radiators, convectors, or embedded tubing throughout the house, transferring heat with it. The water cools and returns to the boiler to be reheated and recirculated. This pattern of water circulation and recirculation is the basic principle of hot water systems. A hot water system is completely filled with water.

- **Gravity hot water systems:** The earliest hot water systems from the late 1800s, which are no longer installed, are called gravity systems. When heated, water expands and becomes less dense so that it rises. Because the system is filled with water, the rising hot water pushes the cooler water in the piping ahead of it. This starts a simple cycle of circulation through a gravity system by convection.

    Piping in the old gravity hot water systems is about 3″ in diameter; modern hot water systems use piping that is smaller—about 1″ in diameter.
    A gravity system has no moving parts.

    Water expands as it's heated, and a gravity system, like all hot water boilers, has an **expansion tank** to accommodate this expansion. Most often, the expansion tank in a gravity system is open to the atmosphere. That means when there's too much water in the system, the tank will overflow to an **overflow pipe** that is routed outside or to a basement drain. This is called an **open system**. Water in an open system is not under pressure. The expansion tank is located above the highest

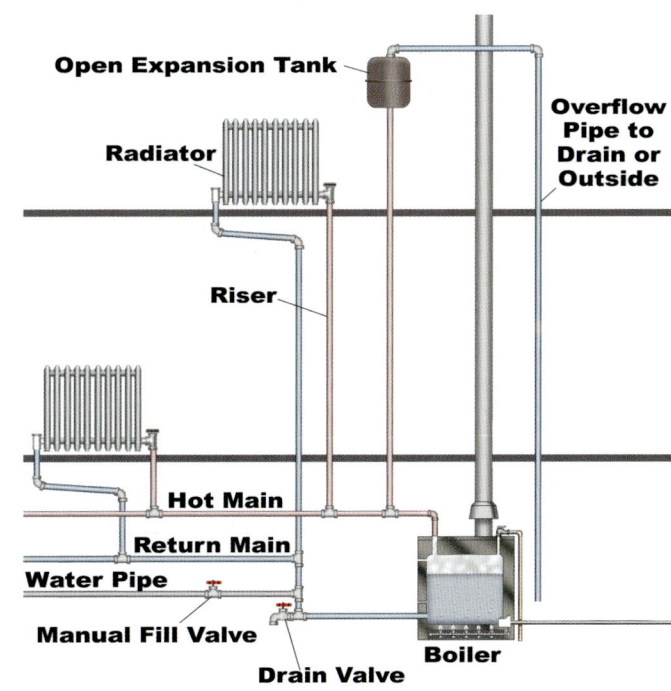

Illustration by Paddy Morrissey

> **Definitions**
>
> In a <u>hot water heating system</u>, water heated in a boiler is transmitted through pipes to radiators. Heated water rises naturally in a <u>gravity hot water system</u>. Water is circulated in a <u>forced hot water system</u> by a circulating pump.
>
> An <u>expansion tank</u> in a <u>hot water system</u> provides space for water to expand into. An <u>open system</u> has an expansion tank open to the atmosphere and located above the highest radiator. A <u>closed system</u> has a sealed expansion tank located just above the boiler.

radiator in the home, typically in the attic, and has a sight glass to show water level. When water in the gravity hot water system is low, water is added manually through the **manual fill valve** (when the boiler is cold).

Gravity hot water heating systems are obsolete but may still be found in operation in very old homes. The old boiler is typically made of cast iron and is 2 to 6 times larger than the new modern boilers. Their heating efficiency is very low. Old cast iron radiators are usually found with these systems. A radiator control valve at one end of the radiator regulates water flow—and therefore heat to the radiator and therefore the room.

- **Forced hot water systems:** A forced hot water heating system is also called a **hydronic** system. It can be In this system, water circulation doesn't depend on convection processes as in a gravity system. Here, water is moved through the piping system by the action of the pump.

A forced hot water system is a **closed system**, meaning that it has a **closed expansion tank**. This tank is partially filled with trapped air that compresses to accommodate the expansion of heated water (much like on a modern water heater). The tank is located near and just above the level of the boiler.

In a closed system, the water everywhere in the system is under pressure. The pressure is about **12 psi** (pounds per square inch) in the typical two-story home. This is based on the principle that 1 psi of pressure is required to lift water 2.31′ of height. Therefore, it takes over 8 psi to lift water the required 19′ in a two-story home. Add a few extra pounds to maintain pressure in the upper-floor radiators, and the total pressure required would be about 12 psi. (Three-story homes would require 17 psi; four stories, 22 psi; and five stories, 26 psi.)

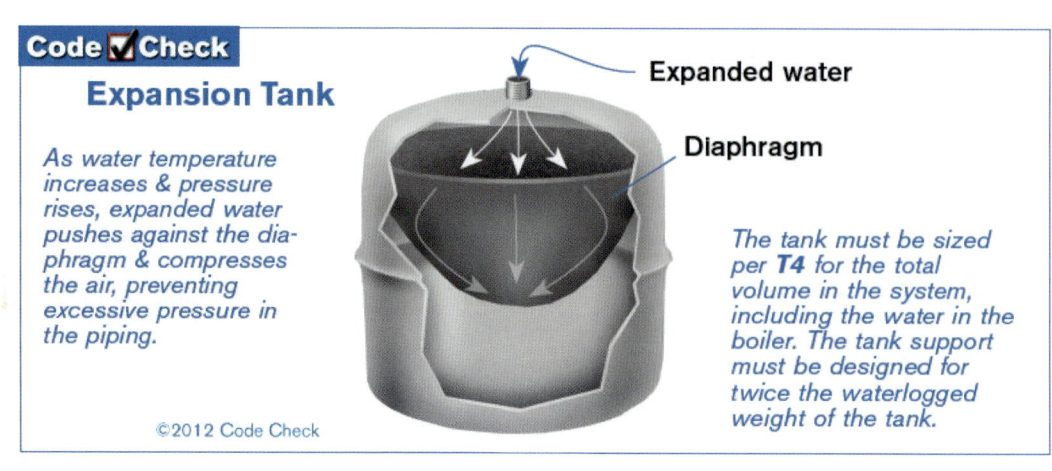

Code ✓ Check

Expansion Tank

As water temperature increases & pressure rises, expanded water pushes against the diaphragm & compresses the air, preventing excessive pressure in the piping.

©2012 Code Check

— Expanded water

— Diaphragm

The tank must be sized per **T4** for the total volume in the system, including the water in the boiler. The tank support must be designed for twice the waterlogged weight of the tank.

476 Chapter 6

This internal system pressure is maintained by an **automatic fill valve** that adds incoming (city or well) water to the system to keep it at the required level within the system, which maintains the pressure. A **pressure relief valve** discharges water from the system when pressure reaches a dangerous level. A **pressure-reducing valve** reduces the higher pressure of (city or well) water in the plumbing system before it enters the boiler. In newer systems, the automatic fill valve and the pressure-reducing valve are a single component.

> **HOT WATER SYSTEMS**
>
> - Gravity hot water (open system)
> - Forced hot water (closed system)
>   — One-pipe system
>   — Two-pipe system
>   — Radiant system

Photo #34 CONVECTOR OR BASEBOARD HEAT

This is a convector or baseboard heat. The hot water from the boiler circulates through the copper tubing and the aluminum fins radiate the heat into the room by convection as the cooler air near the floor warms as it passes by.

THE HEATING INSPECTION

The newer forced hot water systems use embedded tubing, baseboard, or freestanding **convectors** instead of the old radiators. Embedded tubing is very common in higher-end homes. Plastic tubing, typically PEX, is laid on the floor/deck and buried in concrete or Gyp-Crete. Convectors have a copper water tube running through them. Attached to the tube are a number of fins or metal plates that heat the air passing through the convector.

- **Two-pipe systems:** A forced hot water heating system may have separate piping that runs to and from the boiler. Heated water is delivered to convectors or radiators through the hot main and risers; cooler water is returned to the boiler through the return piping. This is called a direct return system. Although this system is more costly to install, it allows for **zoned heating**. Zoned heating is accomplished with the addition of zone valves to a single pump or multiple circulating pumps or even with multiple boilers in larger homes.

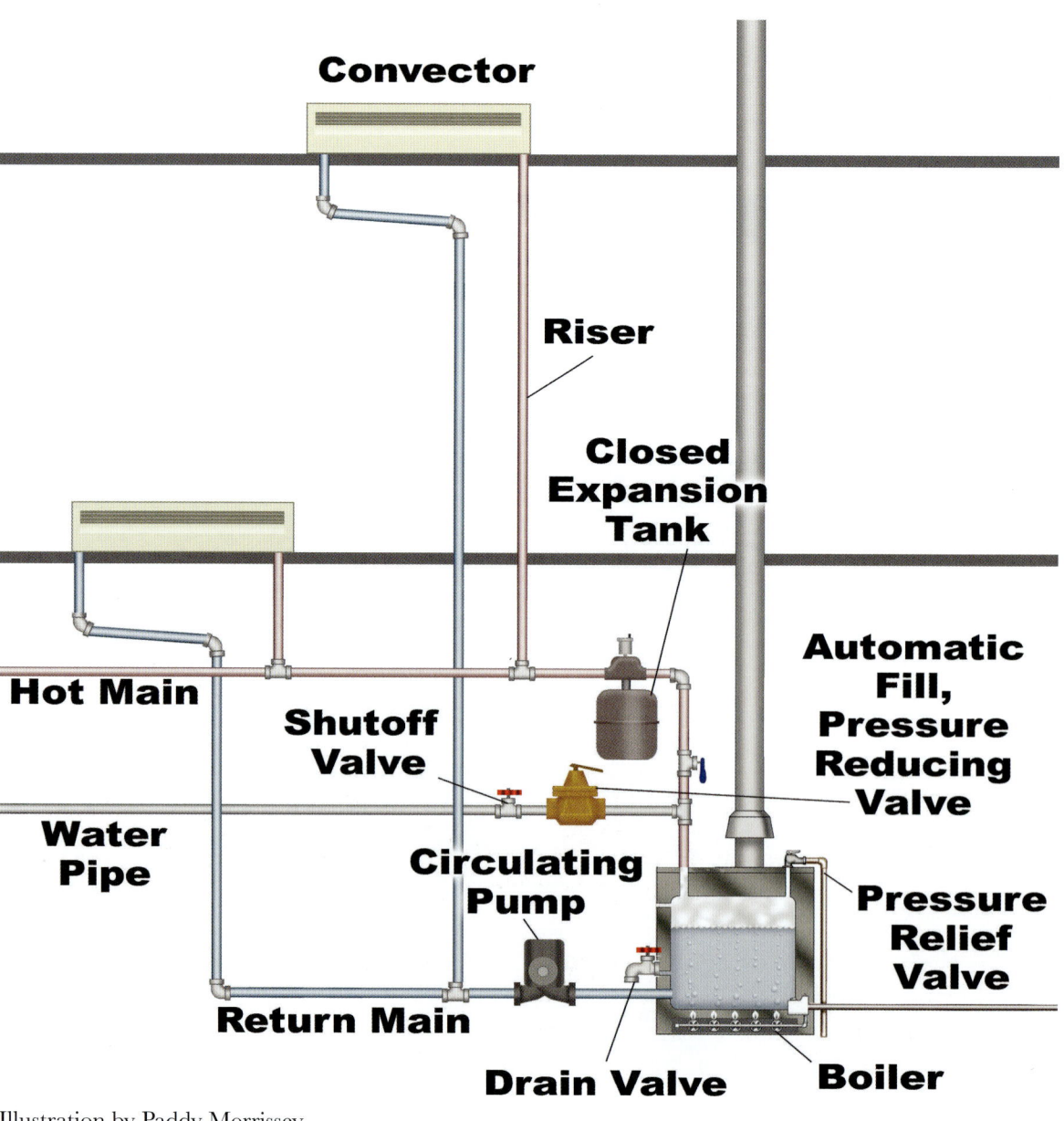

Illustration by Paddy Morrissey

- **One-pipe systems:** Forced hot water systems may have only a single piping run. The **series loop** is one continuous piping run that incorporates the radiators or baseboard convectors into the run. Closing off one convector in the run shuts off the heat supply to the whole loop. Another approach with a one-pipe system is to have the convectors attached to the run with risers, allowing each one to be controlled without affecting water flow in the loop. With either approach, the convectors at the end of the run receive cooler water than those at the beginning of the run. To compensate for this, convectors are usually smaller near the boiler and larger at the end of the run.

Photo #35 *This is a very large zoned system. As you can see there are nine circulating pumps (red and black pumps in middle) and nine zone controls (gray boxes at bottom). Note the blue expansion tank to the right, and you can just see the draft hood on the right edge of the photo.*

- **Radiant floor heating:** In many new hot water systems, water is circulated through continuous rows of tubing, which are buried in the wall, floor, or ceiling. The tubing heats the floor, wall, or ceiling, which radiates the heat to the room. Older radiant panels used black steel or galvanized steel pipes. Today, pipes are more likely to be copper or plastic tubing (PEX). This system can be zoned to supply heat to different sections of the home. The home inspector may find radiant hot water systems in slab-on-grade homes, where the piping is buried in the concrete slab. Many new homes have

Definitions

A <u>one-pipe hot water</u> system uses a single piping run for moving water to and from the boiler. A <u>two-pipe</u> system has separate supply and return piping runs. <u>Radiant floor heating</u> is a hot water system consisting of continuous piping laid out in rows that are buried in the floor or ceiling.

Photo #36 RADIANT FLOOR HEATING SYSTEM

Typical radiant floor heating system utilizing a hot water boiler and PEX tubing. This white tubing will be embedded in concrete to provide thermal mass for the system to maintain constant temperatures within the room.

THE HEATING INSPECTION

> **Photo #37 RADIANT HOT WATER SYSTEM**
> *This is the same radiant hot water system as the system in the floor, but wall-mounted.*

radiant floor heating where the tubing is buried in concrete on a framed deck or the basement slab is heated too.

For human comfort, water temperatures in radiant hot water heating are kept lower than in other types of hot water heating systems. The temperature of the water ranges from about 85° for floor installations to between 115° and 120° for ceiling or wall installations.

Types of Hydronic Boilers

Just like forced-air furnaces, there are generations of hot water boilers from the older units to the newest high-tech units. The conventional forced hot water, or hydronic, boiler has these basic components:

- The **burner area** and combustion chamber, located at the bottom of the boiler.

- The **heat exchanger** above the burner from which exhaust gases are vented and the surrounding water is heated and then distributed to the home.

- The **circulating pump**, which sits outside the boiler on the return pipe, is used to move water through the heating system.

- On the outside of the boiler is a **pressure relief valve** that provides an escape for hot water if pressure

> **TYPES OF HOT WATER BOILERS**
>
> - Conventional gas or oil
> - Electric boilers
> - Mid-efficiency gas or oil
> - High-efficiency condensing boilers

> **Photo #38 MANIFOLD FOR DISTRIBUTION OF WATER**
> *This the manifold for the distribution of the water throughout the home. Each pair of tubes is generally a zone, one supply and one return. This would be located behind an access panel when the home is finished.*

increases beyond allowable limits. Piping must have proper extension to within 18″ of the floor, which is different from that of water heaters, which is within 6″ of the floor. There is also a combination **temperature, pressure gauge** showing readings of boiler conditions.

- A coil, called the **tankless coil**, may be inserted in the boiler to heat water for domestic use.

Removing the access panel on the burner side of the boiler will give the home inspector access to the burner area and the heat exchanger casing. But in a boiler, usually, very little of the heat exchanger is visible and cannot be inspected directly. The good thing about boiler heat exchanger issues is that they leak water, and it is usually easy to determine if the heat exchanger is leaking.

Some forced hot water boilers are powered by electricity. The **electric boiler** operates similar to the electric water heater. Electric resistance coils, insulated from the water, are inserted through the boiler wall and made watertight. The heating elements are energized in sequence to prevent an electrical overload. When the thermostat is satisfied, the elements and the circulating pump are turned off. Smaller electric boilers may be used to heat add-on rooms or additions.

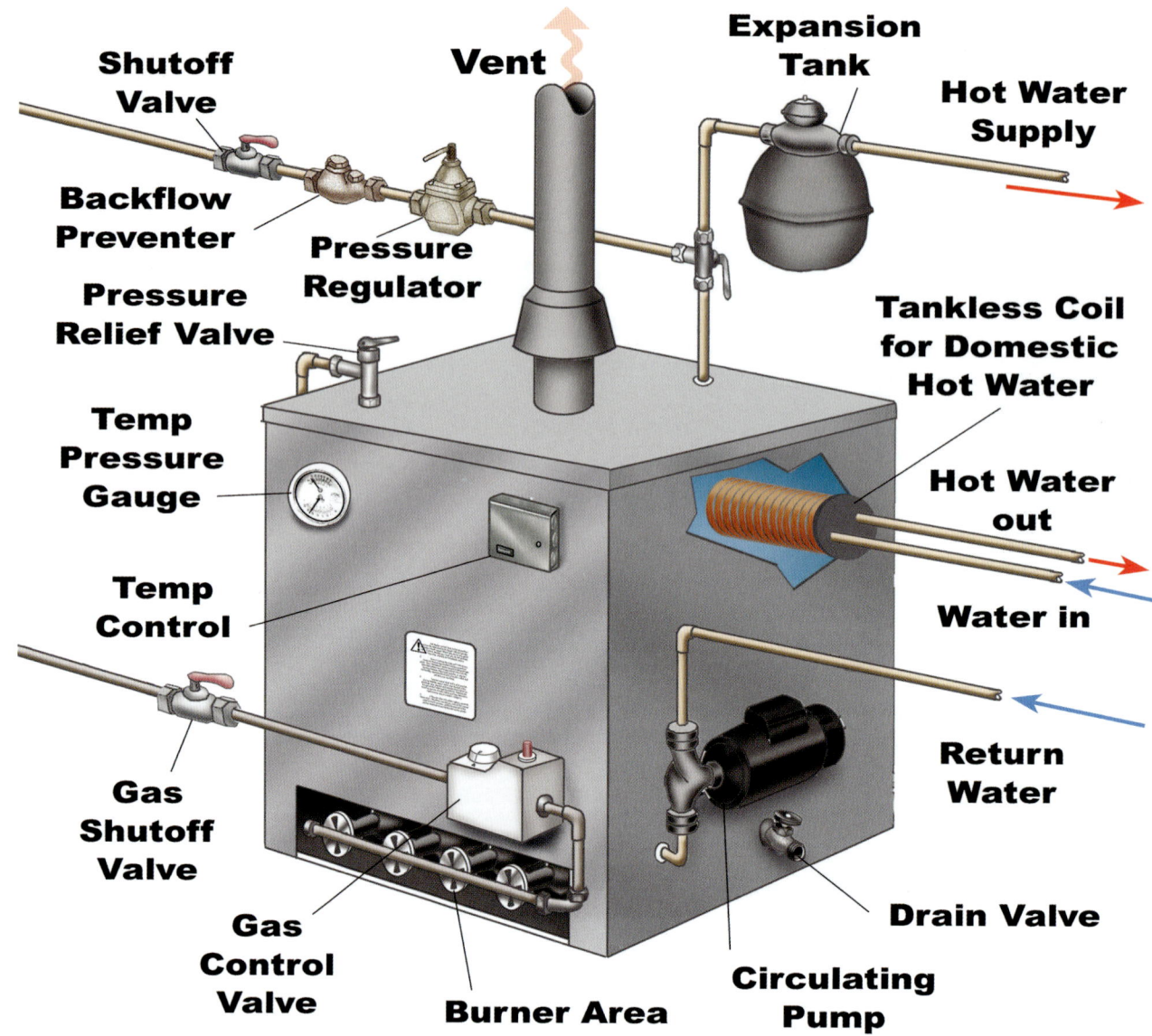

Illustration by Paddy Morrissey

The **mid-efficiency boilers** that came on the market in the mid-1970s marked improvements in much the same way furnaces were improved at that time. They're basically conventional boilers with the addition of **an induced draft fan** to pull combustion gases through the unit and thus increase efficiency. **Motorized vent dampers** were also added to prevent warm air from escaping up the chimney when the boiler was off. As mentioned earlier, these must have a burner interlock in case the damper fails to open.

High-efficiency boilers can perform at 95+% efficiency. Usually, they are gas-fired, although condensing oil boilers are occasionally seen. They vary in configuration from manufacturer to manufacturer. **Condensing boilers** have two or more heat exchangers like furnaces to extract as much heat as possible from the exhaust gases, causing the water vapor in the exhaust gas to condense. The condensate is drained to an appropriate drain,

CONVERSIONS

You may find old gravity systems converted to forced hot water and coal boilers updated to oil or gas. All aspects of the old setup must be compatible with the new heating system.

482   Chapter 6

while the remaining cool gases are forced with an induced draft fan through 2–3″ plastic piping, typically PVC to the outside through the house wall or roof.

Boiler Components

Forced hot water, or hydronic, boilers have the following components:

- **Boiler controls:** The **thermostat** is one of the main operating controls of a hot water heating system. In addition to the thermostat, there are a number of operating and safety controls.

In newer boilers, because the heat exchanger is smaller and more efficient, the thermostat activates the burner and circulating pump simultaneously. In some boilers, however, the pump can be manually set to run constantly during the heating season. In older systems, when there is a call for heat, the thermostat activates the burner only. A separate **pump control** with a temperature-sensitive **aquastat** turns on the pump when the water temperature reaches a preset level of about 120°. Some systems have a **modulating aquastat** that senses outdoor temperatures and turns on the pump at varying water temperatures. The lower the outside temperature, the higher the circulating water temperature.

If the hot water boiler is also used as a source of domestic hot water, then the thermostat will control only the circulating pump. The burner is controlled by an aquastat that senses water temperature. In such systems, a flow-control valve prevents hot water from rising into the distribution piping when heat is not called for in the house.

A hot water boiler has a safety device called the **limit control**, which will turn off the burner if temperatures get too high. If water was allowed to boil in a hot water system, expanding steam could burst pipes and damage the boiler. Therefore, the limit control is set at about 200° below the boiling point of water.

Another safety control on the boiler is the **pressure relief valve**. This valve prevents pressure within the system from exceeding a dangerous level (usually set at 28 psi to 30 psi).

BOILER CONTROLS

- Thermostat
- Pump control
- Limit control
- Pressure relief valve
- Pressure-reducing valve
- Backflow preventer
- Automatic fill valve
- Low water cutoff

Definitions

The *pump control* turns on the circulating pump at a signal from the thermostat upon a call for heat or from an aquastat at a certain preset temperature.

The *limit control* turns off the burners if the water reaches a preset high temperature.

An *aquastat* is a temperature-sensitive device, immersed in water to detect water temperature, that activates the circulating pump. A *modulating aquastat* senses outdoor temperature and changes circulating water temperature requirements accordingly.

A *pressure relief valve* will discharge water from a boiler if pressure approaches dangerous limits.

The *pressure-reducing valve* reduces water pressure in the (city water) plumbing line to acceptable boiler pressure. An *automatic fill valve* adds water to the boiler if pressures fall below the required pressure.

A *check valve* or *back-flow prevention* device is also present to keep dirty boiler water from entering the house drinking water.

A *low water cutoff* shuts off the boiler when water levels fall.

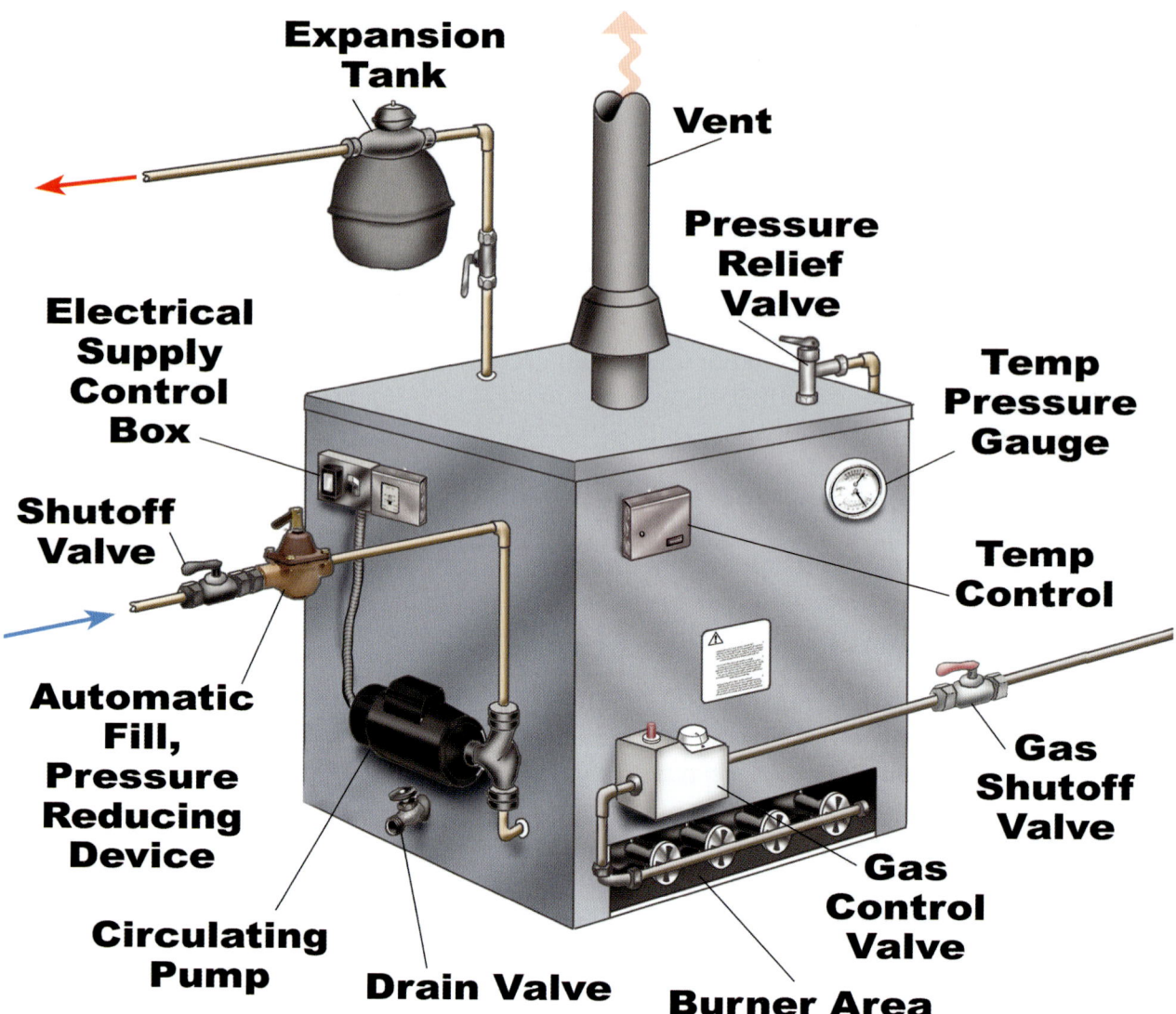

Illustration by Paddy Morrissey

Because the water discharged from a pressure relief valve is very hot, an extension should be attached to it to discharge within 18″ of the floor. This extension should not be threaded at the bottom or be capped. Another safety control found on some larger boilers is the **low water cutoff**. This device will shut down the burners if there isn't enough water in the system. There are other controls on the plumbing line to the boiler. A **pressure-reducing valve** will automatically reduce the pressure on incoming (city or well) water to the right level for the heating system from about 65 psi to 12 psi for a typical home. The **automatic fill valve**, part of the same unit as the pressure-reducing valve, adds water to the system if pressure falls below 12 psi. In the newest systems, this unit will also be equipped with a **backflow preventer** that prevents water from the heating system from backing up into the house water system.

All hot water boilers have a **temperature/pressure gauge** either in a combination gauge or as a pressure gauge in addition to a pencil-type thermometer. The pressure shown is the actual working pressure of the system. If this pressure exceeds 30 psi and the relief valve is not discharging, you should err on the conservative side and turn off the boiler. You may also have a bad pressure gauge or pressure relief valve. It is not our job to troubleshoot the reason for the malfunction. Just record it in your report and recommend a technician repair as needed.

- **Zone controls:** In zoned heating, where supply piping is divided into separate loops, each zone (room) has its own thermostat. The thermostat first turns on the burner on a call for heat. Then it activates either the zone's circulating pump (if each zone has one) or the zone's **zone valve** (if there's only one circulating pump). The zone valves are electrically operated.

- **The circulating pump:** On a hydronic or forced hot water boiler, the circulating pump, located in the return piping, pushes the water through the boiler and piping system. Depending on the type of boiler, the pump is designed to operate constantly, intermittently only when heat is called for, or at certain preset water temperatures. Constant operation can be controlled by a manual on/off switch, set to "on" during the heating season and "off" during the summer.

- **Burner area and combustion chamber:** See pages 423–433 for information on gas burners and pages 438–447 for information on oil burners. Electric boilers, of course, do not have a burner or combustion chamber area. Instead, you'll find a bank of heating elements.

- **Heat exchanger:** The boiler heat exchanger is not typically visible for inspection. The heat exchanger can be made of cast iron, copper, or steel. It allows the heat from the burner to pass through it while it heats the water on the other side of the heat exchanger. A boiler may be a **dry base boiler**, where the heat exchanger is set above the combustion chamber, normally seen in gas-fired boilers with vertical tube cast iron heat exchangers.

> **For Beginning Inspectors**
>
> *It's time to see some boilers. For older systems, try any friends who live in older homes. You may even find an old gravity system. For newer systems, try a heating showroom or distributor and get someone to show you the new models. Because there's variation from model to model, try to locate and identify boiler controls.*

A **wet base boiler** is constructed so that water in the heat exchanger surrounds the combustion chamber. A wet base horizontal tube steel heat exchanger is primarily used with oil-fired boilers. The same danger that exists with forced-air heat exchangers, where combustion products can enter the home's air supply, does not exist with boiler heat exchangers. If a heat exchanger develops holes from rusting or corrosion, water will leak into the combustion chamber. The home inspector can spot a cracked or rusted heat exchanger by the presence of water damage or significant rust in the burner area. A heat exchanger may be repaired in rare cases, but most often the boiler must be replaced.

- **Expansion tank:** An expansion tank provides space for heated water to expand into. As mentioned earlier, the **open expansion tank** for a

Photo #39 BOILERS

These are very high-tech and high-efficiency boilers. There are many types of boilers available. If they are common in your area, you should visit a local supplier or HVAC shop for information.

FORCED HOT WATER COMPONENTS

- Boiler controls including:
  - Limit control
  - Pump control
  - Pressure-relief valve
  - Pressure-reducing valve
  - Automatic fill valve
  - Low water cutoff
  - Backflow prevention device
- Zone valves, if zoned
- Circulating pump
- Burner and combustion chamber
- Heat exchanger
- Expansion tank
- Distribution piping
- Radiators or convectors
- Exhaust system

gravity hot water system will be located above the highest radiator, most likely in the attic or closet. These tanks have an overflow pipe that discharge excess water to the outside, sometimes onto the roof, or to a floor drain in the basement.

A forced hot water system has a **closed expansion tank** that is partially filled with air. When water is heated, it expands in the closed system, the air in the tank is compressed. The tank is located above the level of the boiler so that air cannot get into the supply piping. (Any air trapped in the circulating water is removed by a trap at the top of the boiler that the homeowner should bleed off manually from time to time.)

One type of expansion tank has water and air in contact with each other. As the water absorbs the air over time, the tank can become **waterlogged**. Newer tanks have a diaphragm or rubber bladder between water and air to prevent air absorption, although there can be problems with the diaphragm causing a waterlogged condition. A waterlogged expansion tank causes the pressure relief valve on the boiler to discharge whenever the boiler fires due to the increased pressure. The expansion tank should be drained and air put back in or replaced, depending on the type.

- **Distribution piping:** Supply and return lines for a forced hot water heating system should be well supported and free of leaks. Pipes passing

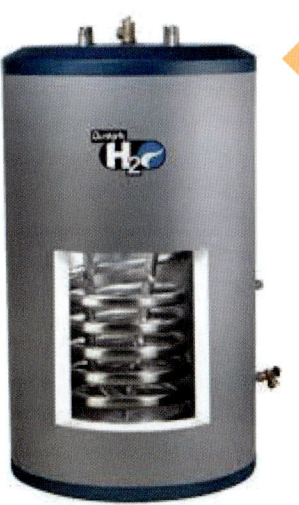

Photo #40 INDIRECT WATER HEATER

This is an indirect water heater. The water circulating inside the coil comes from a boiler. The water in the tank around the coil is heated for household needs, like showering.

through unheated areas such as crawl spaces and attics should be insulated. See pages 478–480 for information on the various distribution layouts, such as one-pipe and two-pipe systems and zoned systems.

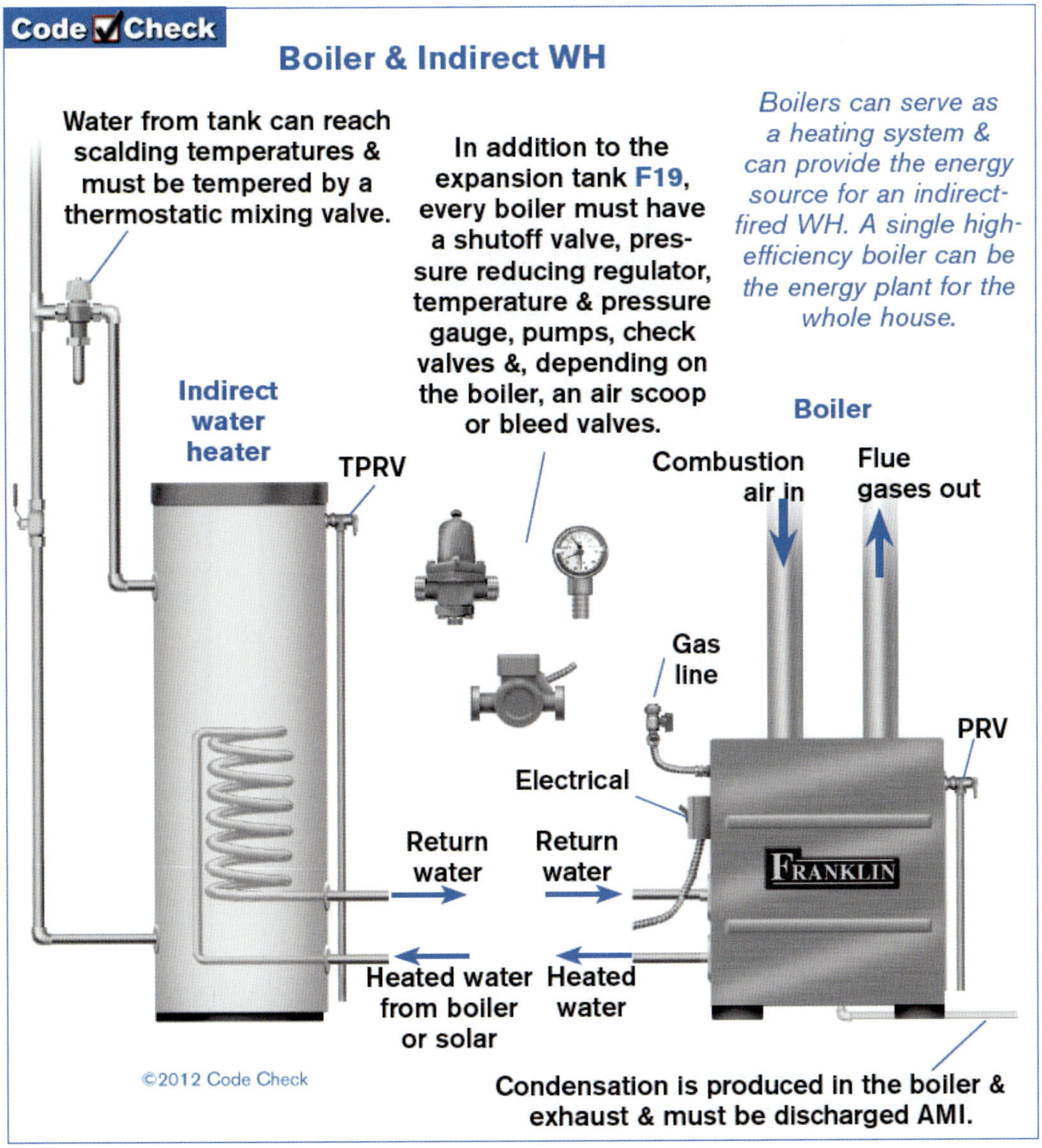

Code Check: Boiler & Indirect WH

Water from tank can reach scalding temperatures & must be tempered by a thermostatic mixing valve.

In addition to the expansion tank **F19**, every boiler must have a shutoff valve, pressure reducing regulator, temperature & pressure gauge, pumps, check valves &, depending on the boiler, an air scoop or bleed valves.

Boilers can serve as a heating system & can provide the energy source for an indirect-fired WH. A single high-efficiency boiler can be the energy plant for the whole house.

Indirect water heater — TPRV

Boiler — Combustion air in — Flue gases out — Gas line — Electrical — PRV

Return water / Return water

Heated water from boiler or solar / Heated water

Condensation is produced in the boiler & exhaust & must be discharged AMI.

©2012 Code Check

THE HEATING INSPECTION   487

With **radiant panel heating**, the pipes can leak into the floor or ceiling. Such leaks are difficult to locate and expensive to repair. Repairs require the floor or ceiling to be opened, which can be very costly. A break in the piping can leak for a long time before it's discovered. One sign of a problem can be that the automatic fill valve is sending a constant stream of water to the system. The valve will be cold to the touch, and there will be an audible noise at the valve. High water usage (water bill) can also be an indicator.

- **Radiators and convectors:** Cast iron radiators allow water to pass through, heating the metal and radiating heat in all directions. A control valve on many systems at one end of the radiator can be shut off to prohibit water flow through the radiator. Old valves may not shut off completely or will leak if adjusted. A small bleed valve is located near the top of the radiator, allowing trapped air to be removed periodically.

Convectors have a water tube through them. Attached to the tube are a number of fins that heat up and heat the air passing through the convector. **Baseboard convectors** are normally copper tubes and aluminum fins. A sheet metal housing with openings and vanes above and below the pipe help increase airflow. The baseboard convector should be installed high enough above the carpeting to allow airflow. Some control of heat to the room is normally achieved by closing a vane to restrict airflow through the convector.

- **Exhaust system:** As discussed, gas and oil-fired heating units must have an exhaust system to rid the unit of combustion products. Old gravity and conventional forced hot water boilers exhaust through the chimney, B-vent, smoke pipe, or flue, while the high-efficiency boilers exhaust cooled combustion gases in PVC piping through the house wall or roof and drain condensate to the floor drain or other appropriate drain. All exhaust piping should be inspected for condition and proper venting.

Inspecting Hot Water Boilers

When inspecting the gravity and forced hot water boiler, the home inspector will be inspecting the following:

- The **boiler** itself, including the burner

- The **distribution piping** and radiators, or convectors

- The **venting system**, including the smoke pipe, flue, chimney, and cleanout

The procedures for inspecting the burner, smoke pipe, chimney, and cleanout were presented earlier in this chapter (see pages 423–433 for gas burners and pages 438–447 for oil burners). We won't repeat those procedures here.

The home inspector should also inspect the hot water boiler for the following conditions:

- **Lack of heat source in each room:** Again, as you inspect the home interior, turn up the thermostat, check for a heat source in each room, and check that it is functioning. Radiators should be located on exterior walls, preferably under windows. Sometimes, these old radiators may not be working or are disconnected. Feel each one for the presence of heat, or preferably, use your infrared thermometer. For zoned heating, turn up each thermostat, one at a time, and verify heat in each zone.

- **Leaking radiators and convectors:** As you check the heat source in each room, examine each radiator to see if its control valve is leaking, but **do not operate this valve**. Note if the air bleed valve has been painted shut, which often happens. Point out that the valve should be kept in operating condition. Examine convectors for general condition too, reporting if their fins are dirty, if carpeting restricts airflow through the convector, and if any leaking is present.

- **Leaking radiant panels:** If you determine that the home is heated with hot water radiant panels in the floor or ceiling, keep an eye out for any leaking as you move through the living area.

- **Defects in the boiler jacket:** Inspect the outside of the boiler jacket for leaking, damage, holes, corrosion, or rust. Carefully check the boiler for leaks and dripping. Excessive rusting or staining in an area can indicate a leak on the inside. A leaking boiler may be able to be repaired, but it will probably have to be replaced. Leaking should be reported as a **major defect**. Scorching or burning can indicate a problem with the combustion chamber. Staining and soot around the burner indicates spillage and back-drafting.

> **CAUTION**
>
> *If the temperature pressure gauge shows readings <u>above 30 psi or 200°</u> for a forced hot water boiler in a typical home, turn off the boiler immediately.*

- **Temperature or pressure too high or low:** Read the temperature pressure gauge while the boiler is still operating. Note if the temperature is too high for safe operation (over 200°F) and if the pressure in the boiler is too high (over 30 psi) or too low (under 12 psi for a typical home). If the temperature or pressure readings are over these indicated levels, *turn off the boiler immediately* and report the condition as a **safety hazard**. Inform the homeowner to have the boiler inspected by a qualified technician before refiring the unit. The problem may manifest as a faulty pressure relief valve that is discharging water. Pressures above normal may signal a waterlogged expansion tank. During your reading, note if the gauge itself is broken, cracked, and so on.

- **Leaking, corroded, or missing pressure relief valve:** Inspect the relief valve, which should be located on top of or on the side near the top of the boiler, not along the piping away from the boiler. **Do not operate this valve.** The valve should be free of corrosion and should not leak. Missing pressure relief valves should be reported as a **safety hazard**. Leaking or corroded valves should be replaced.

> **INSPECTING FORCED HOT WATER BOILERS**
>
> - Lack of heat source in each room
> - Leaking radiators, convectors, or radiant panels
> - Jacket defects
> - Temperature or pressure too high or low
> - Leaking, corroded, or missing relief valve or extension
> - Problem heat exchanger
> - Pump dripping or not working
> - Waterlogged or leaking expansion tank
> - Leaking zone valves
> - Leaking or poorly supported piping
> - Unusual noises

Check that the extension is present and properly installed. The extension pipe diameter should not downsize as it goes down the boiler. Check that the extension ends within 18″ from the floor and is not threaded or capped at the end. Improper extensions should be reported as a **safety hazard**. If there's evidence that water has been discharging frequently from the relief valve, it may be an indication of a waterlogged expansion tank. High pressures build up each time the boiler is fired, causing the relief valve to discharge water.

- **Cracked or rusted heat exchanger:** Use the safety or serviceman's switch to turn off the boiler. Then remove the access panel on the burner side of the boiler. The heat exchanger may not be visible for inspection, but as you examine the burner area, note if there is any evidence of leaking from the heat exchanger onto this area. There will be signs of rusting, corrosion, flaking metal, or water seepage and even dripping water. This condition should be reported as a **major defect** in the boiler. Suggest that a qualified service technician examine the boiler and point out to customers that the boiler will probably have to be replaced.

- **Dripping or malfunctioning circulating pump:** After checking the interior of the boiler, fire it back up to proceed with your inspection of the burners. At this time, you'll be able to determine if the thermostat turns on the pump and burners simultaneously. The pump should not be leaking or dripping, which is a sign of worn seals. Listen to the pump for noises that can indicate worn bearings. Note if the pump appears to be over- or under-oiled. Circulating pumps only last 10 to 15 years and then have to be replaced. Report if the pump is not operating at all.

- **Buzzing or arcing electrical work:** As the boiler operates, listen to the electrical wiring for any signs of buzzing or arcing. Report if any of the control boxes on the boilers are missing their covers—they should be covered.

- **Leaking or loose tankless coil:** If the boiler has a tankless coil insertion to produce domestic hot water, examine it to see if it is leaking or if nuts or bolts connecting it to the boiler are loose. Another type of domestic hot water system you may see is the **sidearm heater**, which is a tankless coil in a separate gravity-fed piping loop at one side of and above the boiler. The tankless coil should have its own pressure relief valve. You may also see an indirect water heater. This is where the boiler water circulates and heats the water in what looks like a standard water heater tank.

- **Waterlogged or leaking expansion tank:** As the boiler refires and continues to operate, note if pressure is quickly building to the point where the relief valve discharges. This is an indication that the expansion tank is waterlogged. Even newer diaphragm tanks can become waterlogged due to damage of the diaphragm. Inform the client of this condition and recommend that the expansion tank be checked and have air put back in. Check the exterior of the tank for leaks as well.

- **Leaking zone valves:** If the heating system is zoned and has zone valves rather than separate circulating pumps, check the zone valves for leaks and drips.

- **Leaking or poorly supported piping:** Examine visible piping for leaks. Make a note of loose, broken, corroded, or missing supports. Check to see if piping is insulated in unheated areas, and if the insulation contains asbestos-like materials, point that out to the client. Suggest that asbestos-like material be tested and possibly removed if in poor condition.

- **Noise in the heating system:** Finally, listen for noises. Water circulation in hydronic systems should be virtually silent. Noisy water circulation indicates air in the pipes that should be bled off. Squeaks in the pipes just after water begins to circulate indicate thermal expansion of the pipes and a rubbing against supports and framing. Support hangers can be oiled or lined to eliminate this problem.

CAUTION: When you finish your boiler inspection, turn the boiler back on and return thermostat settings to their original settings. Leaving an empty house without heat in the winter can be a major mistake for the home inspector.

Reporting Your Findings

Talk to your client while you're inspecting the boiler, but have the client stand back as you fire it. Always consider yourself responsible for your client's safety.

Explain to your client what you were inspecting at the boiler and what you found. Take time to answer any questions. Remember that clients may not understand what they see at the boiler and are counting on you to make sense of it for them. Be sure to stress any safety hazards you find and tell the customers that you will indicate safety hazards in the inspection report. Suggest that customers review the report again on their own.

When reporting on the inspection of the hot water boiler, be sure to include the following for gravity and forced hot water boilers, gas and oil-fired:

WHAT'S THE SYSTEM?

If a hot water boiler has no circulating pump, you've found an old gravity hot water heating system. If it also has a water level site gauge, then you've found a steam boiler.

For Beginning Inspectors

Get out there and inspect some hydronic boilers. Follow the procedures as instructed in these pages, being careful not to operate those valves we've said not to operate. Don't forget to inspect the burner, vent piping, chimney, and cleanout (see earlier pages on gas and oil burners for procedures). If your friends are willing, let them pretend to be your customers so that you can practice your communication skills.

> **OLDER BOILERS AND CIRCULATING PUMPS**
>
> *In your inspection report, note these items as <u>requiring replacement within the next 5 years</u>. They will be reaching the end of their lifetime in 5 years.*
>
> - *Cast iron and steel boilers over 30 years old*
> - *Copper boilers over 10 years old*
> - *Circulating pumps over 10 years old*

- **Boiler information:** Record the brand name, model, and serial number of the boiler. This should be located on the data plate on the boiler, although it may be missing from an old gravity system. Identify the type of boiler (gravity or forced hot water) and the type of fuel used. Report the approximate age of the boiler by checking the ANSI number as previously described.

- **Operation:** Note in your report if the boiler fired and make a special note if the boiler wasn't operating.

- **Heat exchanger:** Note that the heat exchanger is not visible for inspection. But report any evidence of defects found, such as leaking and rusting and corrosion in the burner area. Give the heat exchanger an overall rating because the boiler will most likely have to be replaced if heat exchanger problems exist. Here's a rating system:

  — Use **satisfactory** if you've found no signs of leaking from the heat exchanger into the burner area *and* the boiler is not past its lifetime.

  — Use **marginal** if you've found some minor signs of a problem *or* the boiler is past its lifetime. Recommend that a qualified technician evaluate the boiler if you find the boiler marginal.

  — Use **poor** if you've found definite and extensive signs of a defective or leaking heat exchanger. Recommend a technician if you rated the boiler as poor.

> **DON'T EVER MISS**
>
> - Heat source in each room
> - Burner problems
> - Gas leaks, oil odors, and smoke
> - Leaking boilers
> - Dangerous temperature or pressure readings
> - Missing relief valve or improper extension
> - Defective and leaking heat exchanger
> - Improper clearances
> - Inadequate combustion air venting
> - Spillage from draft hood or diverter or damper
> - Improper venting and holes in vent pipes

- **Other components:** Record your findings on the condition of the boiler jacket, burner, circulating pump, gauges and valves, piping and expansion tank, radiators or convectors, and venting systems. Write up the defects you've found, such as a leaking pressure relief valve, a waterlogged expansion tank, a pump that needs oil, and oil burners that need adjustment.

- **Major defects and repairs:** Boiler conditions that are of particular concern include a faulty heat exchanger, a leaking boiler, a boiler operating with temperatures or pressures too high, or a boiler that is not operating. These conditions should be noted in your inspection report as a major defect or repair.

- **Safety hazards:** All safety hazards found during the inspection of a hot water boiler should be noted in the inspection report.

— Gas or oil leaks

— Improper clearances

— Spillage, improper venting, and holes in vent pipes

— Boiler temperature or pressure readings that are too high

— Missing pressure relief valve or improper extension

NOTE: We stress the importance of accurate and detailed reporting because of the high-ticket liability the home inspector has regarding the heating system. If you miss reporting findings listed in the Don't Ever Miss list, you'll hear about it later in the form of a complaint call. The home inspector who misses these details in the inspection report will only have to pay later—perhaps for a whole new boiler.

6.8 STEAM BOILERS

A steam boiler is similar to a hot water boiler in many ways, although there are some basic and important differences.

Steam Systems

When water is heated to the boiling point (212° at sea level), it changes to steam, which contains heat. Steam rises through a large diameter piping system to radiators in the home, pushing air ahead of it. When heat is given up at the radiator, the steam condenses back into water (condensate), which returns through the same piping or a second system of piping to the boiler. Air valves on the radiators and/or vents on the return piping allow air to escape. This is a **gravity system**! Steam systems are no longer typically installed as a new installation, although the home inspector may see replacement boilers and new parts installed to keep an old steam system in operation.

Steam boilers operate with the boiler **3/4 full of water**. The rest of the boiler and the piping system are filled with air when the boiler is at rest. Pressure within the boiler is much lower than that of hot water systems, only from about **0.5 psi to 3 psi** as opposed to 12 psi in hot water boilers.

- **One-pipe system:** A one-pipe steam system (shown on the next page) has a single pipe attached to each radiator. Steam flows into the radiator through this pipe, and condensate returns down the same pipe. Radiators have a **supply valve** that can

> **Section Note**
>
> *"No, I don't have any stories about boilers blowing up. My inspectors know to turn off the boiler if gauge readings are too high and the pressure relief valve is not discharging. They've learned to be careful, as I hope you will."*

> **Chapter Note**
>
> *Pages 493–500 present the study and inspection of steam boilers.*

> **Definitions**
>
> *In a gravity steam heating system, water boiled in a boiler changes to steam, which rises naturally through pipes to radiators and condensate drains back to the boiler.*
>
> *A one-pipe steam system has a single pipe to and from each radiator. A two-pipe system has two pipes at each radiator with separate return piping.*
>
> *A Hartford loop is a loop of return piping that turns upward to connect to the equalizer just below the water level, preventing water from flowing out of the boiler in case of a leak in the return piping. The equalizer is piping from the top of the boiler to the bottom that balances pressure above and below the water line.*

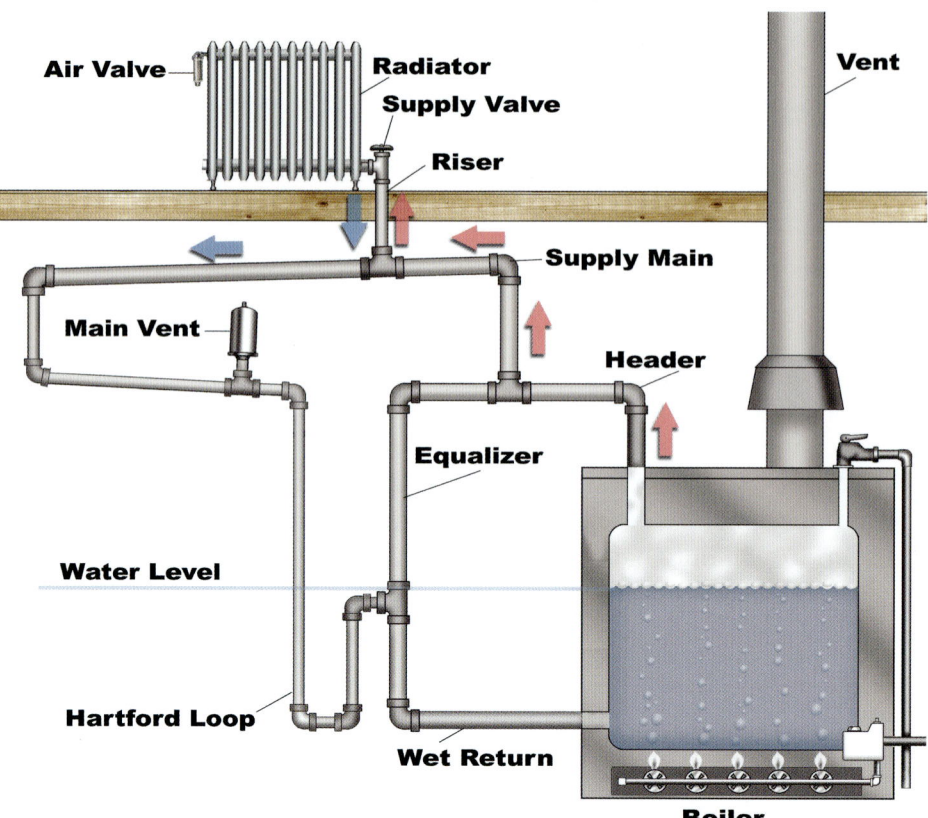

One-Pipe Steam System

Illustration by Paddy Morrissey

be turned fully off or fully on for heat supply. They also have an **air valve** to vent air at the radiator.

- **Two-pipe system:** Radiators in a two-pipe system (shown on the next page) have two pipes, one at each end, to receive steam and to return condensate to the return piping. These radiators also have a supply valve for controlling steam flow, which in a two-pipe system can be set partially open or closed to control heat. Two-pipe radiators don't have an air valve. Instead, the return piping has a **steam trap**, which allows air and condensate to pass in the return piping but closes on steam contact. The air is vented through the **main vent**.

The piping in both one-pipe and two-pipe systems must slope downward about 1″ for every 10–20′ of length. That way, condensate anywhere in the distribution piping will flow back to the boiler.

A system is called a **dry return** if the return piping joins the boiler above the boiler water level. A **wet return** joins the boiler below the water level. When a wet return is used, a **Hartford (as in the insurance company) loop** should be present. The purpose of the Hartford loop is to prevent water from draining out of the boiler in case of a leak in the return line. Water will drain only until it reaches the level of the top of the Hartford loop. A connection between the header at the top of the boiler and the return at the bottom of the boiler is called an **equalizer**. Its purpose is to prevent rising steam from forcing boiler water back up the returns. The equalizer ensures that pressures above and below the water line are the same.

Two-Pipe Steam System

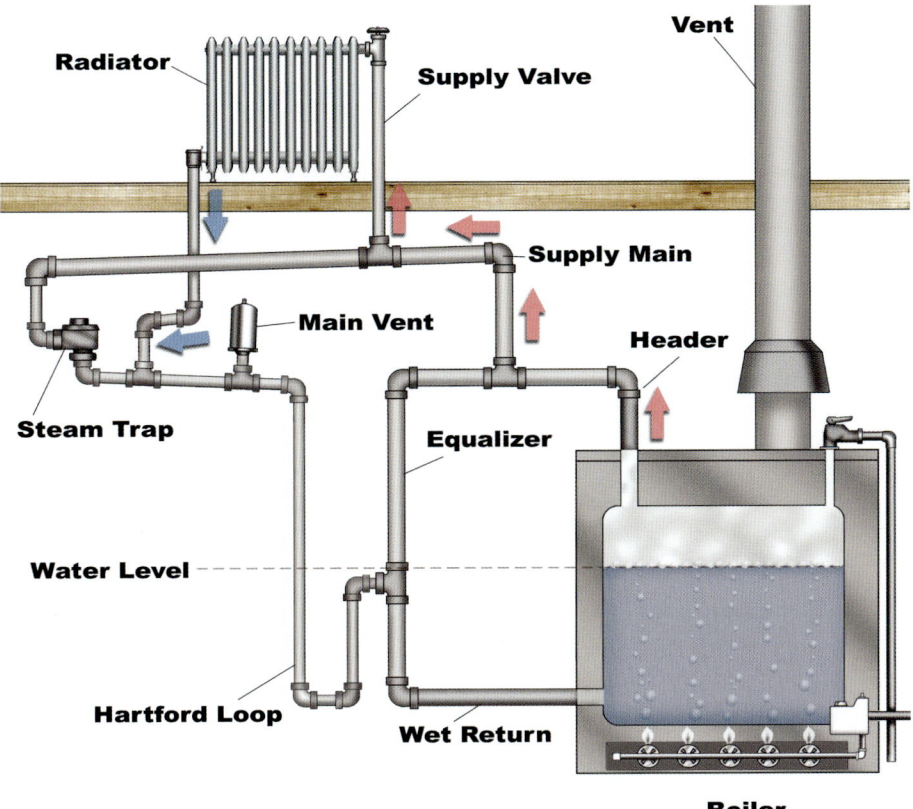

Illustration by Paddy Morrissey

There are variations on the gravity steam system—the **vapor steam system** and a two-pipe system. No air is allowed in this system, and no air needs to be released. Vapor system radiators have a vacuum air valve that prevents air from entering the system.

Steam Boiler Controls and Gauges

A gravity steam heating system is simple and does not require motors or electrical connections other than those for the thermostat and the burner controls. These are the basic controls on a steam boiler:

- **Basic operating controls:** With a steam boiler, the **thermostat** turns on the burners after a call for heat. As steam rises through the system, pressure begins to rise. When operating pressure reaches between 2 psi and 3 psi, a **pressure-sensitive switch** on the boiler turns off the burners. Some steam boilers are operated with a heat timer instead of a thermostat. The heat timer turns on the burner for a preset number of minutes on the hour or half hour.

- **Limit control:** A steam boiler has a safety device called the high pressure limit control that will turn off the burners if pressure within the

> **BOILER CONTROLS AND GAUGES**
>
> - Thermostat
> - Limit control
> - Pressure relief valve
> - Temperature, pressure gauge
> - Low water cutoff
> - Water level sight gauge
> - Water fill valve

THE HEATING INSPECTION

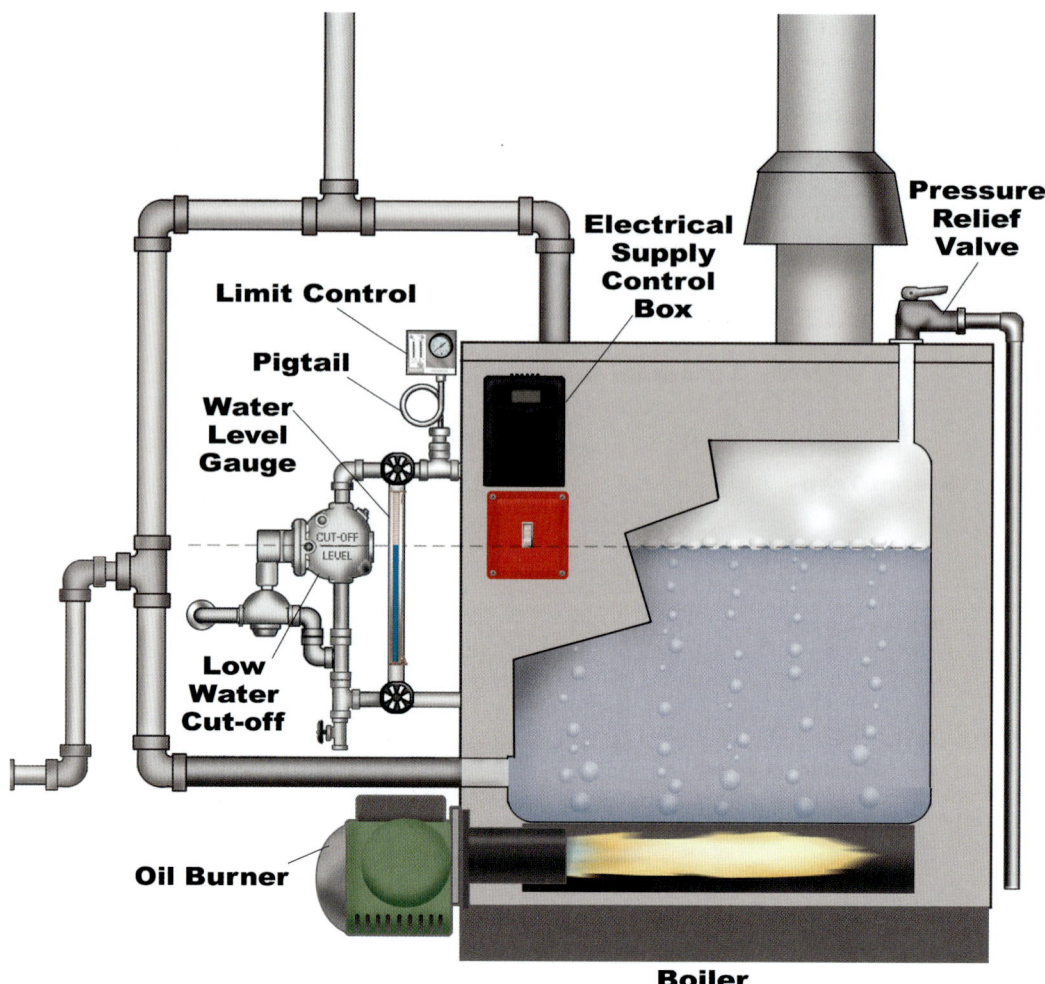

Illustration by Paddy Morrissey

system reaches a preset pressure limit of **5 psi**. This control is connected to the boiler with a pigtail pipe (one that has a curl in it). The loop of the pigtail has water in it to prevent the corrosive action of the steam from affecting the control.

- **Pressure relief valve:** Another safety control is the pressure relief valve that prevents pressure from building to a dangerous level in the boiler. If pressures reach a preset high limit of **15 psi**, the valve will discharge. There should be an extension from the valve to within 18" of the floor.

- **Temperature, pressure gauge:** The boiler will have a gauge showing temperature and pressure readings for the system. If the gauge shows a pressure reading of 15 psi and the relief valve is not discharging, the boiler should be turned off.

- **Low water cutoff:** This safety control shuts down the burner when the level of water in the boiler drops below the designed level. The low water cutoff may be in the boiler or mounted on the outside. The external unit, located in a triangular housing, has a float that drops when the water level falls and turns off the burner. It also has a **blow-off valve** at the bottom. This valve should be opened once a month to remove accumulated silt and mud from the unit, which could block the float from dropping.

- **Water level sight gauge:** Steam boilers have a glass tube sight gauge that shows the water level in the boiler. Water levels should vary from 1/2 to 3/4 full—highest when the boiler is cold and slightly lower when the system is up to pressure and steaming. If the gauge is filled with water or water comes out when the top valve on the glass is opened, the system has too much water. If water is not visible in the glass and no water comes out when the bottom valve on the glass is opened, the system has too little water.

- **Water fill valve:** Some steam boilers have an **automatic** fill valve that will feed water to the boiler to maintain water levels. This automatic valve may be in a combination unit with the low water cutoff. However, many steam boilers have a **manual** fill valve that must be opened to introduce more water to the system.

> ### Hot Water and Steam Settings
>
> A _steam boiler_ has an operating pressure of _0.5 to 3 psi_. A pressure limit control turns off the burners at about _5 psi_. Its relief valve discharges at _15 psi_.
>
> A _hot water boiler_ has an operating pressure at about _12 psi_. A temperature limit control turns off the burners at about _200°_. Its pressure relief valve discharges at _30 psi_.

> ### Photo #41 WATER LEVEL SIGHT GAUGE
>
> _The water level sight gauge indicates how much water is inside the boiler. Be careful with identification as you may find a boiler with a water level site gauge that is no longer a steam system. The key is to look for a circulating pump._

THE HEATING INSPECTION

> **For Beginning Inspectors**
>
> *If you have friends who own older homes that have steam boilers, by all means take the time to inspect the boilers. Don't be surprised if you find new replacement parts brought in to keep an old steam system going.*

> **INSPECTING STEAM BOILERS**
>
> - Improperly sloped or noisy piping
> - Pressure that is too high
> - Inappropriate or fluctuating water levels
> - Rusty or dirty water
> - Malfunctioning low water cutoff
> - Missing Hartford loop

Inspecting Steam Boilers

We're not going to repeat all the procedures for inspecting boilers here, just those items that set steam boilers apart from hot water boilers. See these pages for other items to be inspected:

- Thermostats and clearances from combustibles: pages 403–416
- Gas and oil burners: pages 423–433 and 438–447
- Boilers: pages 488–491

The home inspector should watch for the following conditions with steam boilers:

- **Improperly sloped or noisy piping:** As shown in the illustrations on page 495, all steam systems should have sloping piping to allow condensate to run back to the boiler. An acceptable slope is 1" for every 10–20' of piping. If the slope is wrong (sags) and condensate pools in the piping, you'll hear a loud bang or knock as steam hits it at the start of each heating cycle. Inappropriate water levels, clogged air valves on one-pipe system radiators (sometimes painted closed by the homeowner), or a malfunctioning steam vent on two-pipe systems can also cause loud banging sounds.

- **Pressure too high:** While the boiler is operating, watch the temperature, pressure gauge. Operating pressures should be within the 0.5 psi to 5 psi range. If the pressure reading is 15 psi or more, *turn off the boiler immediately* and report the condition as a **safety hazard**. Be sure to inform the homeowner to have the boiler inspected by a qualified technician before refiring the unit. The cause of the problem may be a faulty pressure relief valve that should be discharging water. During your reading, note if the gauge itself is broken, cracked, and so on.

- **Inappropriate or fluctuating water levels:** The home inspector should pay close attention to the water level sight gauge. CAUTION: If no water is visible in the sight gauge, *do not fire up the system*, or if it has already been fired, *turn it off*. Without the appropriate water levels, the boiler can crack as it fires and overheat. The low water cutoff should not be allowing the burners to fire if the water level is too low. A gauge filled to the top indicates too much water in the system. With too much water, it's possible to flood the entire system with water, including the piping and the radiators. Both of these conditions should be reported.

The water level in the sight gauge should not fluctuate wildly during boiler operation. As stated earlier, water levels should vary only between 1/2 and 3/4 full—highest when the boiler is cold and lowest when the system is up to pressure and steaming. Rapidly fluctuating water levels can indicate that there is excessive dirt buildup in the boiler or that the boiler is operating at an excessive output. The condition should be checked by a qualified technician.

The glass gauge may show a longtime water level, no matter where the level is at the time of inspection. A high water level and a low rust line in the gauge may indicate that the system is constantly refilling due to a leaky return.

> **WHAT'S THE SYSTEM?**
>
> *If a boiler has an operating water level sight gauge, you've found a steam boiler. (But watch out. Some steam systems can be converted to hot water without removing the old sight gauge. The key is the added circulating pump.)*

- **Rusty water:** A steam system should be cleaned every few years to remove accumulated rust and mud buildup. Excessive buildup can be seen as rusty or dirty water in the sight gauge. Inform the customer that the system should be flushed by a qualified technician.

  Sometimes, water within the system has been treated to dissolve buildup. It may also be treated with a leak stopper whose granules slowly deposit and plug leaks in the system. If the water in the glass gauge sparkles, a leak stopper may have been added. If you suspect the water may have been treated, let the customer know that it should be tested periodically.

- **Malfunctioning low water cutoff:** During the inspection, you may test the blow-off valve on the low water cutoff. You want to be sure that it will turn off the burner when the water level in the chamber falls. The blow-off valve should be opened once a month to remove silt and mud that can stop the cutoff from operating properly, but some homeowners never do this.

  While the system is operating, open the blow-off valve. Put a bucket under it and stand back. Rusty, dirty water can spray out, staining your clothes and shoes. And if the valve hasn't been opened for years, mud can come out. As the low water cutoff chamber empties, the burners should shut off. If the burners do not shut off, the unit should be repaired or replaced. Be sure to close the blow-off valve again after this test. This is by no means required by any of the SOPs, but it is certainly a good idea.

- **Missing Hartford loop:** If the boiler has a wet return (return piping entering the boiler below the water line), there should be a Hartford loop as described on page 493. The Hartford loop prevents water from draining out of the boiler in case of a leak in the return line. Recommend installing a Hartford loop if the wet return doesn't have one.

REMEMBER: When you finish your boiler inspection, be sure to turn the boiler back on and return thermostats to their original settings.

> **Chapter Note**
>
> *Pages 500–503 present electric heating and other less common types of heating systems.*

> **DON'T EVER MISS**
>
> - Pressure that is too high
> - Low water levels
> - Dirt buildup
> - Malfunctioning low water cutoff
> - Plus all the don't ever misses listed for boilers on page 492

Reporting Your Findings

Follow the directions given on pages 492–493 for reporting your findings for boiler inspections in your inspection report. Be sure to report the type of heating system as a steam boiler.

Pay attention to earlier instructions for reporting major repairs, safety hazards, and items requiring replacement as stated on page 492. These items refer to steam boilers too.

6.9 OTHER HEATING SYSTEMS

A home may be heated with systems other than gravity or forced-air furnaces and gravity hot water, forced hot water, and steam boilers.

Electric Heating

Electricity is a clean energy source, but it is usually more expensive to use than gas, propane, or oil. Furnaces and boilers may be powered by electricity, which was already discussed on pages 453 and 482. There are other ways electricity can be used to heat the home:

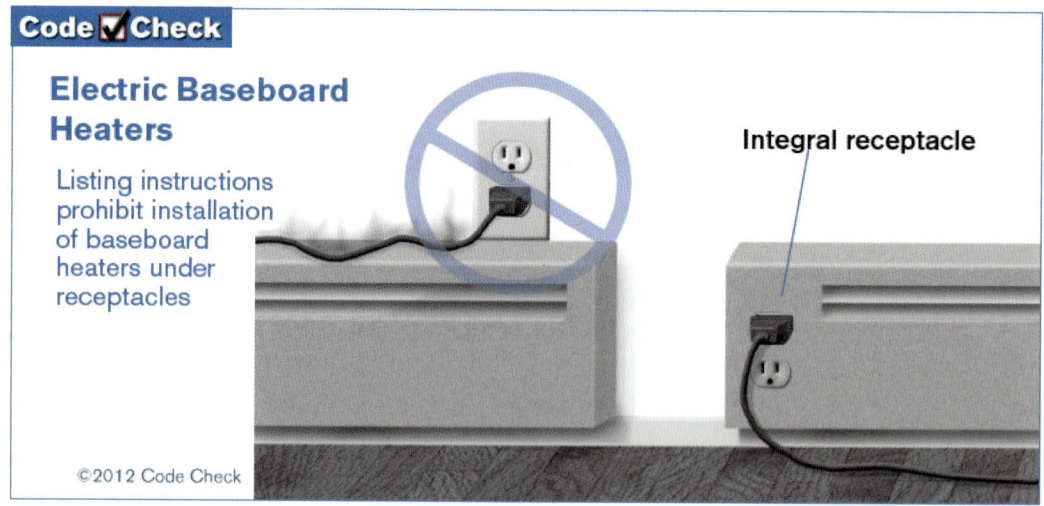

- **Resistance heating:** Electric baseboard convectors, wall-mounted strips, or floor inserts may be used to heat the home, but this method is not to be considered a central heating system. Each resistance unit in the house, one per room most likely, operates as a separate heating source. Each resistance heater has its own manual thermostat, either located on the unit or mounted on the wall. The wall-mounted strips and floor inserts sometimes have a fan to circulate the warm air. Most baseboard heaters use gravity and convection to circulate the heat produced by the system.

Resistance heaters can get very hot, so their clearance from combustibles is important. Curtains and draperies should be kept 8″ above the heaters or 3″ away and 1″ above the floor if they are hanging in front of the heaters.

There should be no receptacles above the heaters, although built-in or integral receptacles with heaters are acceptable.

- **Radiant heating:** Similar in concept to hot water radiant heating, electric radiant heating consists of electrical cables embedded in ceilings or floors during construction. The cables heat the surface, radiating heat into the room. Each room has a separate control. If the distribution wiring breaks, it can be difficult if not impossible to locate the problem. Most often, when electrical radiant heating fails, the system is abandoned and replaced with electric baseboard heaters or a central system.

- **Heat pumps:** Electric-powered, a heat pump is a reverse-cycle air-conditioning system. In the air-to-air heat pump, heat is removed from the house air and moved to the outside using the refrigerant as the transport media when in the air-conditioning mode. In the heating mode, heat is captured outdoors and brought inside and released. This will be discussed more fully later in this chapter beginning on page 534.

Other Heating Systems

The home inspector may find **combination heating systems**. For example, one zone of the home may have forced-air heat while another may still use a gravity hot water system. Any combination may be possible. In a case like this, both systems must be inspected.

There are also **hydro-air systems** (see next page for diagram) that combine hot water and forced air. The way this type of system operates is that hot water is heated in a boiler or water heater and sent to a hot water heat exchanger coil in a blower unit (air handler). The hot water coil heats the air, which is blown through it and into the home through normal supply ducts.

You may come across many other systems. Pellet stoves, corn burning stoves or boilers, wood burning boilers, and wood furnaces with a back-up fuel are all used in various parts of the country. They have many of the same components as a normal furnace. Inspect these heating units one component at a time.

Floor and Wall Furnaces

Depending on the age of the home and your local climate, you may find floor or wall furnaces. They are just like the other furnaces described except that they do not have a fan or ductwork. The wall or floor furnace is a metal box with a burner in it. They are usually poorly maintained and prone to produce CO. There are specific clearance requirements for both types as they get very hot. They work using convection

ELECTRIC HEATING

- Furnaces and boilers
- Baseboard, wall, or floor resistance heating
- Ceiling or floor radiant panel heating
- Heat pumps

Section Note

Wall Furnaces—Usually found in warmer climates, smaller homes, or cottages or installed in added rooms. Older units may be unsafe. Do Not attempt to light the pilot. Clearances are 12" from a door, 6" from a wall, and 18" from a ceiling.

Floor Furnaces—The floor furnace is similar to the wall furnace, except that it is suspended between floor joists. Lift the grille, if possible, and look for deterioration.

Hydronics

Hydronic heating can be distributed through baseboard convectors, duct heaters, or in-slab radiant heating in either slab-on-grade construction or raised floors. Each zone will have its own thermostat & typically its own circulation pump or zone valve. Return lines will typically have manifolds that combine various sections of hydronic tubing.

Hydronic Duct Heater

Hydronic Tubing in Slab

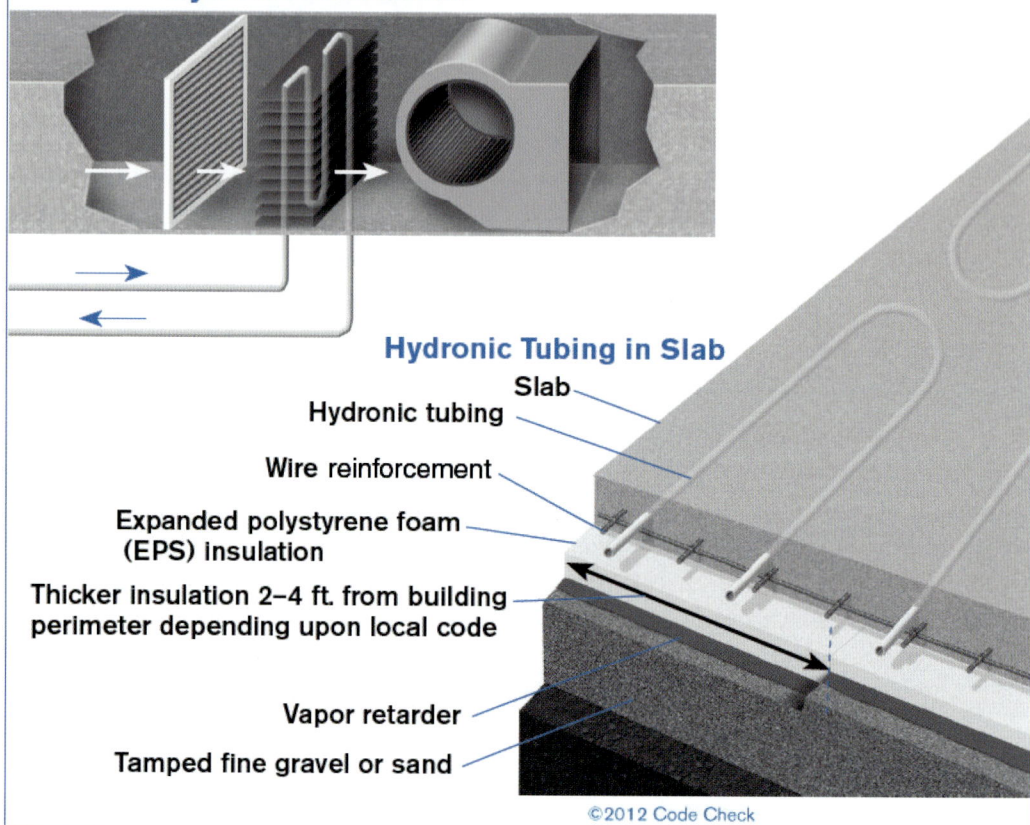

- Slab
- Hydronic tubing
- Wire reinforcement
- Expanded polystyrene foam (EPS) insulation
- Thicker insulation 2–4 ft. from building perimeter depending upon local code
- Vapor retarder
- Tamped fine gravel or sand

©2012 Code Check

Wall Furnace Clearances

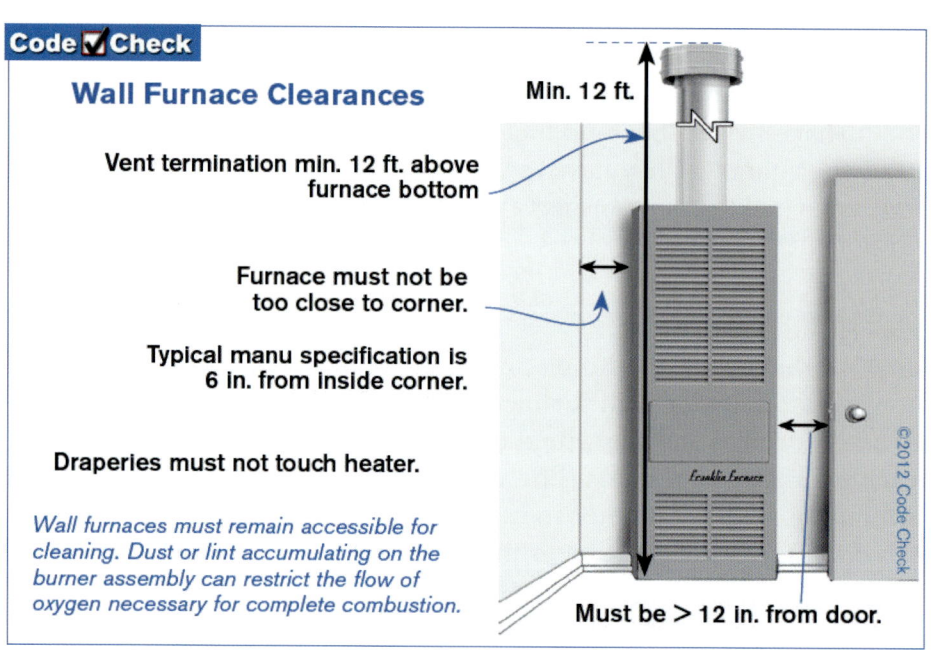

Vent termination min. 12 ft. above furnace bottom

Furnace must not be too close to corner.

Typical manu specification is 6 in. from inside corner.

Draperies must not touch heater.

Wall furnaces must remain accessible for cleaning. Dust or lint accumulating on the burner assembly can restrict the flow of oxygen necessary for complete combustion.

Min. 12 ft.

Must be > 12 in. from door.

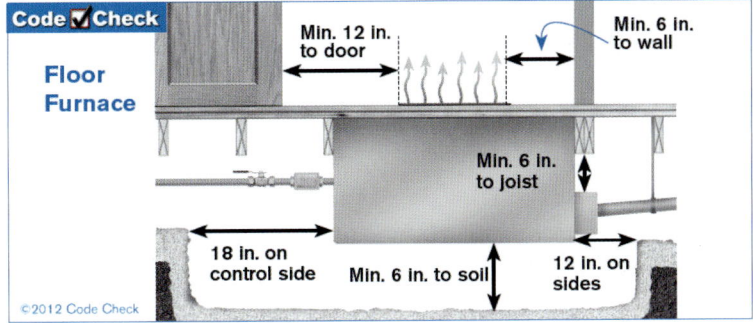

as discussed for the gravity furnace. They are still readily available and in use in warmer climates where minimal heat is needed in the winter. They should almost always be recommended for cleaning and repair by a technician.

The home inspector should not be upset when coming across a heating system that he or she hasn't seen before. Take the time to examine the system and try to figure out how it operates. Many times, unfamiliar systems will have familiar components that you've seen before. Don't be afraid to let customers know that you've found an uncommon system and that you may not be able to tell them everything they need to know about it. It's best to be honest with customers up front. Suggest that a qualified technician inspect the system.

6.10 THE COOLING INSPECTION
This section will present information on central air conditioning and heat pump systems.

Inspection Guidelines and Overview
These are the Standards of Practice that govern the inspection of the home's cooling system, and by that, we mean central air-conditioning. However, many states' SOPs require the inspection of non-central air-conditioning, which now include mini-split systems, but most do not require the inspection of window units. Please study your Standards of Practice carefully.

> **For Your Library**
>
> *The Carson Dunlop Technical Reference Guide is a good tool to have for determining year of manufacture and remaining lifetime. Add it to your library. Call 800-441-9411 to get information on ordering.*

COOLING SYSTEM

Observe and/or Report: The act of making a visual examination of a system or component and reporting on its condition.	• Readily openable access panels • Heating and cooling systems • Vent systems, flues, and chimneys • Distribution system(s), ducts, piping, radiators, convectors, etc. • Operate the system using normal readily accessible control devices
Describe: Report in writing a system or component by its type (or other observed characteristics) to distinguish it from other components used for the same purpose.	• Type of heating system(s) • Type of cooling system(s) • Energy source(s) • Evaporative (swamp) coolers • Type of water supply line • Location of the thermostat

The standards provide an outline of what is to be inspected and what is to be reported during the cooling inspection. Here's more of an overview:

> **Chapter Note**
>
> *Pages 503–509 outline the content and scope of the cooling inspection. It's an overview of the inspection, including what to observe, what to describe, and what specific actions to take during the inspection. Study these guidelines carefully. This section also mentions some special rules about when and when not to operate the cooling system.*

- **Cooling equipment source:** The inspector is required to open readily openable manufacturer's access panels during the visual inspection and to operate the cooling system using normal operating controls.

  The home inspector is not required to operate the air-conditioning system when weather conditions don't permit. A general rule for home inspectors is not to turn on the cooling system if the current outside temperature is less than 60° at the time of the inspection or dropped below about 50° the night before, although it's fine to operate the system if the temperature has warmed up during the day. Also, the home inspector is not required to operate the cooling system if the system is shut down, has not yet been operating this season, or the circuit breaker for the unit is turned off.

> **THE COOLING INSPECTION**
>
> - Cooling equipment and operating controls
> - Distribution system
> - Cool-air source per room

  The condition of the compressor, condenser, evaporator, air handler/furnace, and connections are inspected. The inspector examines each, looking for defective operation, dirt, noise, and leaking. The inspector also determines the age of the cooling unit (inside and outside components) and its remaining useful lifetime. The Carson Dunlop *Technical Reference Guide* is useful for this purpose. Most cooling systems, primarily the compressor, last about 8 to 12 years. In the South and Southwest, where these systems are used more frequently, the lifetime is closer to 8 to 10 years. Any central air-conditioning compressor over 10 years old should be reported as an item that may need replacement within 5 years.

  The home inspector is not required to inspect non-central air conditioners such as window units, but is typically required to inspect wall units and mini-split or ductless heat pump systems.

- **Distribution system:** The cooling system's distribution system may be and most likely is the same as that for the forced-air furnace, including the blower, filter, and ductwork. In many cases, air-conditioning has been added to a heating system and the ductwork is not properly sized for this use. This is especially true of new high-efficiency air-conditioning and heat pump units. The ductwork may need to be improved (enlarged) or replaced. These items are normally inspected as part of the heating inspection. But for independent, stand-alone cooling units, which are often found in homes with boilers, the home inspector inspects the ductwork, condensate drain piping, air handler, air filters, and other items for their condition. Defects such as restricted airflow, (damaged or crushed ducts), loose ducts, and vibrations are reported.

- **Cooling source per room:** An easy part of the inspection, but an important one, is to check for the presence of a cool-air source in each room. This may not be an issue in many parts of the country, but in areas of the South, Southwest, and Southeast, air-conditioning is essential and virtually all homes have it. The inspector records the presence or absence of these cooling sources in the inspection report. However, the inspector is **not required to observe the uniformity or adequacy of the cool-air supply to each room**.

> **NOT REQUIRED TO**
> - Operate cooling systems when weather conditions or other circumstances may cause equipment damage
> - Observe non-central air conditioners (window units)
> - Observe the adequacy of cool-air supply to each room

NOTE: Effective January 1, 2015, residential cooling units sold must be rated 14 SEER for replacement systems and 15 SEER for new construction on a phase in basis. SEER stands for Seasonal Energy Efficiency Ratio, the method used to judge how efficiently an air conditioner performs. The previous standard was 13. The higher the SEER number, the greater the energy efficiency. This number will be increasing over time just as the AFUE is for heating devices.

The 14 SEER requirement does not mean that a cooling system must be replaced now. But when it is, installing a unit rated 14 SEER (preferably 17 SEER or higher) provides maximum efficiency. Today's most efficient units achieve a SEER rating in the upper-20s to lower 30s.

The Refrigerant Cycle

An air-conditioning system has four basic components: the **compressor**, a **condenser**, an **evaporator**, and an **expansion device**. These components are connected in a sealed system. The sealed system contains a **refrigerant** that changes from liquid to gas and back to liquid as it flows through the system. The refrigerant in older home cooling systems is a chlorofluorocarbon, commonly called **Freon**. Newer, more environmentally friendly refrigerants are being produced. Carrier Corp. has trademarked a version of R-410A as **Puron™**, much like, R-22 or Freon has been for decades. The system also includes a means of removing heat from the condenser and a means of circulating air across the evaporator coil and throughout the house.

The operating principles behind the refrigerant cycle in an air cooling system are as follows:

> **WHAT COOLING COMPONENTS DO**
> - Compressor pressurizes gas, which heats up.
> - Condenser removes heat from gas, which condenses to liquid.
> - Expansion device depressurizes liquid, which cools down.
> - Evaporator causes liquid to absorb heat from air, which changes the liquid to gas.

1. **Gas heats up as its pressure is raised.** The **compressor** increases the pressure of the refrigerant when it is in its gas state. This causes its temperature to rise so that it is capable of giving off heat.

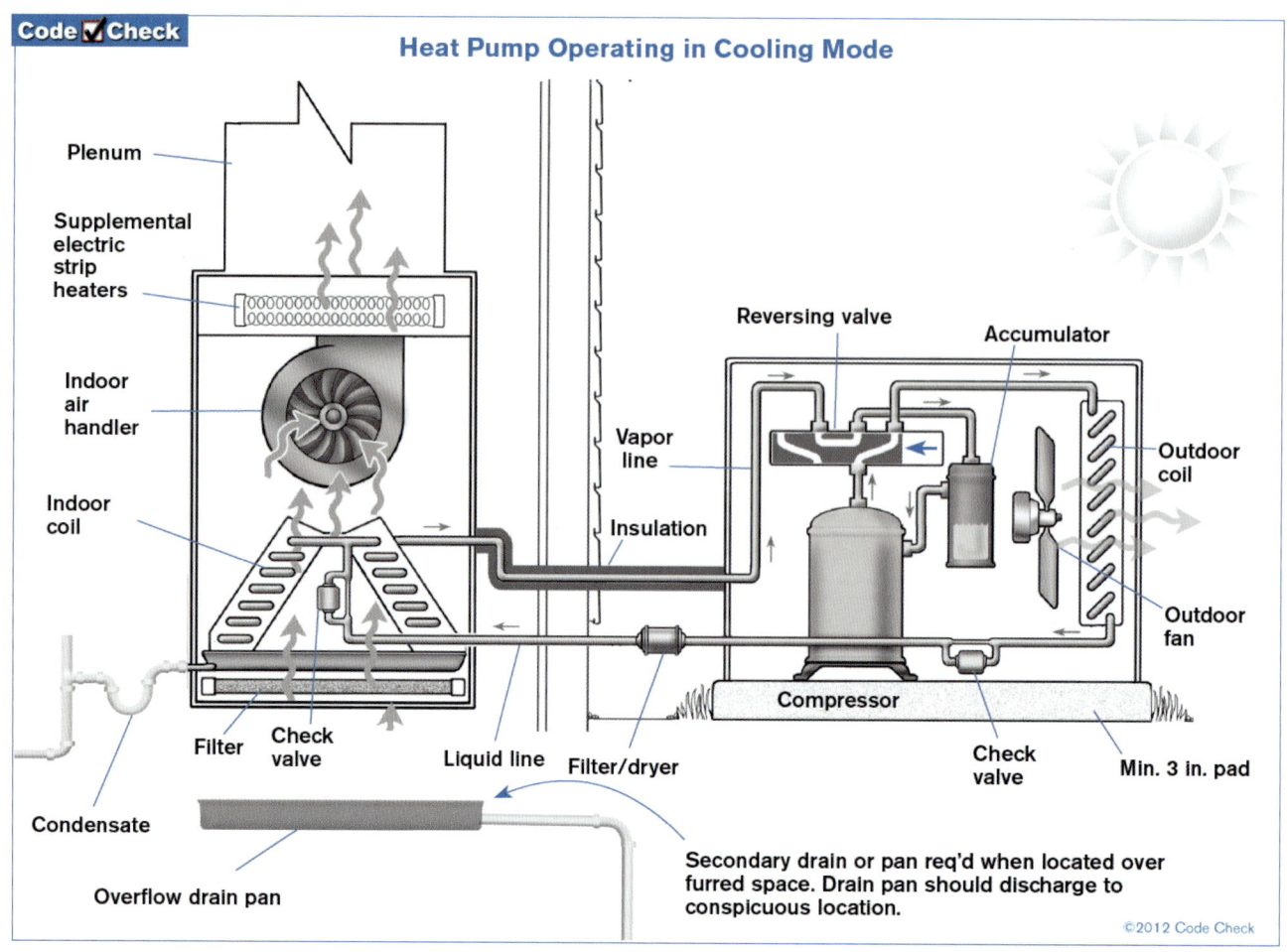

2. **Heat is removed from the gas, causing the gas to become a liquid.** As the high-temperature pressurized gas moves through the **condensing coils**, heat is removed by means of a fan (air-cooled) or by means of water (water-cooled). In a geothermal system, heat is removed by the water and is then transferred to the soil, a lake, a well, or another cool place. When heat is removed, the gas condenses to a hot liquid that is under a high pressure.

3. **Liquid cools as its pressure drops.** The high-pressure liquid passes through an **expansion device**, or pressure-reducing device (thermostatic expansion valve TXV), causing its temperature to drop.

4. **The liquid absorbs heat and turns back into a gas.** The liquid refrigerant passes through the **evaporator coil(s)** and absorbs heat from the house air passing over the coil, thereby cooling the house air. A fan circulates the cool air

Illustration by Paddy Morrissey

506 Chapter 6

throughout the house. As the liquid absorbs heat, it turns back into a cool, low-pressure gas and the process begins again. The illustrations on the previous page show a refrigerant cycle in air-conditioning mode. In a heat pump or geothermal system in heating mode, the refrigerant is reversed so that it runs "backwards."

Inspection Concerns

The main concern the home inspector should have during the inspection of the cooling system is not to damage the equipment. Operating the system under certain conditions can cause damage to the compressor. The following rules should be followed to avoid doing harm to the unit. First, **do not operate** the cooling equipment if:

- **The outside temperature is less than 60°** or the temperature dropped below 50° the night before the inspection. Most manufacturers suggest this 50° to 60° range for safe operation. For a **heat pump**, the unit should not be operated in a cooling mode if the temperature is **less than 60°** or in a heating mode if the temperature is over 70°. (We'll talk more about heat pumps later in this chapter.) The home inspector will inspect the heat pump in either its cooling mode or its heating mode, not both unless the temperature is between 60° and 70°, in which case you can test either or both modes. Although it is recommended to test in one mode, if it works in one mode, it should work in the other mode unless there is a problem with the reversing valve. If the unit is already operating in the cooling mode, you will inspect its cooling mode. If the unit is already in the heating mode, you will inspect its heating mode.

- **The unit is shut down at its main power source.** Ask the homeowner why the system is off and then decide whether it is safe to operate the equipment without damaging it. *It may not be.* In either case, ask the homeowner to turn it on if he or she wants it tested.

> **DO NOT OPERATE AIR CONDITIONER**
> - If outside temperature is under 60° or if under 50° the night before
> - If system is shut down
> - If system hasn't been operated this season
>
> **RECOMMEND UNIT BE SERVICED**
> - If compressor or condenser fan doesn't start
> - If compressor groans and squeals
> - If compressor short-cycles
> - If any part doesn't work

The compressor's motor, safety devices, and oil lubricant are sealed in a shell. When the system is off, the oil absorbs the refrigerant so that it no longer protects the moving parts. In cold climates, some compressors have a heater (at the base of the compressor) to maintain a high enough temperature to prevent this absorption. However, if the circuit breaker is turned off to the cooling equipment, it's also off to the heater. If you start up a cold system, you can cause damage because the oil will no longer be able to lubricate properly. The system's power supply should be turned on for **24 hours before startup** to allow the heater (if present) time to perform its work. Some home inspectors finding this condition will turn on the power and come back the next day to inspect the cooling system. Or you may want to call the day before the inspection to have the power turned on.

- **The unit hasn't been operated this season.** For the same reasons given above, be careful about operating the cooling equipment if it hasn't yet been used this season. Check first to see that the power has been on to the unit for at least 24 hours and that the heater is operating, if present. If the power is still off, follow the directions given above.

NOTE: If you've just inspected the furnace and the cooling system's evaporator coil is located in the furnace plenum, wait 5 minutes after the blower stops to give the plenum time to cool down before starting the air-conditioning unit.

The other concern of the home inspector while inspecting the cooling system is when to turn off the system if something appears to be going wrong. There are certain signs that the equipment is malfunctioning. The home inspector **should recommend servicing** if during its operation:

> **Section Note**
>
> *"I don't mean to scare you with these warnings, but it is important not to start or continue to operate air-conditioning equipment if there's a chance you may damage it. If the basic rules as laid out on these pages are followed, you should be all right."*

- **The condenser fan or the compressor goes on but not both.** The condenser fan and the compressor should both start upon a call for cool air at the thermostat. The exception is when a heat pump goes through the defrost cycle. If only one of them goes on, it may be that you've activated a time delay on the compressor. Some compressors have a time delay of 2–7 minutes. Wait to see if the compressor will start up before you decide if there's a problem. If the compressor doesn't start, something is wrong with the equipment, in which case the system should not be allowed to continue operation.

- **The compressor groans or squeals.** The compressor should run smoothly, so any unusual or loud noises indicate a problem. The equipment should be turned off and examined by a service technician.

- **The compressor short-cycles.** The compressor should go off and on in response to the thermostat, not on and off repeatedly. Depending on the outdoor temperature, the compressor should run from about 8 to 20 minutes at a time. The hotter it is outside, the longer the run time should be. Short cycling indicates a problem, and the unit should be shut down.

- **Any part of the cooling system is not operating.** If during your inspection of the cooling system you notice any part of it not operating even though the power is on, shut down the system before damage is done.

If you don't operate the air-conditioning or heat pump system for any of the reasons given above or have to turn off the system once started, share your reasons with the client. Explain the situation and why the unit can't be inspected. If you live and work in a northern climate, you don't have the opportunity to inspect the cooling system during the winter and a good deal of the spring and fall. Clients usually understand the situation. They would rather have the system inspected later than to have damaged equipment. This is a good time to recommend that your client (the buyer) purchase a home warranty policy. When you don't operate the system due to some malfunction, you should recommend that the system be checked by a qualified serviceperson to find the problem.

A Word about Cooling Capacity

It's possible but not easy to tell if a cooling system has the correct capacity for the house it serves. However, the inspector is not required to judge the adequacy of the cooling capacity or report this fact to customers. The information given here is for your knowledge.

> **RATINGS IN TONS**
>
> *A ton of air-conditioning will provide 12,000 BTUs of cooling per hour. The amount of cooling capacity required varies depending on the region of the country.*

Cooling systems may be rated in **either BTUs or tons**. A ton of air-conditioning will provide 12,000 BTUs of cooling an hour. (When referring to cooling capacity, 1 BTU equals the amount of heat that must be absorbed to *lower* the temperature of 1 pound of water 1° Fahrenheit.)

Many people use a rule of thumb to estimate the size of equipment necessary, usually that 1 ton of cooling capacity is needed per a given square footage. This calculation usually gives **incorrect** results. The Air Conditioning Contractors of America (ACCA) puts out a publication known as the Manual J that offers formulas for accurately determining how much cooling capacity is required. Most contractors now use Manual J software to perform calculations. Only an air-conditioning professional can make an accurate determination of needed cooling capacity. Do not get into a discussion with your client regarding the adequacy or size of the cooling or heating systems.

Another reason home inspectors are not required to determine the adequacy of cooling power is that it's difficult to determine the tonnage or BTU rating for the cooling system. Manufacturers tend to state "nominal" tonnage or BTU ratings within the model number of the unit. However, because they use so many different codes, it's hard to know what the numbers mean. For example, in a Trane unit, the first digit in a certain model number indicates tonnage—3XXX indicates 3 tons. But numbers in a Lennox unit indicate BTU—HSX-311 indicates 31,100 BTUs. Fortunately most manufacturers encode the tonnage in the middle of the model number. The middle group of numbers is usually divisible by 12. A Goodman model number may be CK-36-1AB. The 36 is 3 tons (36 divided by 12). Web searches may provide some information, or you may consult reference guides such as the Carson Dunlop *Technical Reference Guide*. Keep in mind that home inspectors are not required to determine the adequacy or size of the cooling supply and that it is **not recorded** in the inspection report.

> **Chapter Note**
>
> *Pages 510–529 present the study and inspection of air-cooled air-conditioning.*

> **COMPONENTS**
>
> - Outdoor unit with the compressor, condenser coils, and fan
> - Lines for gas refrigerant and liquid refrigerant
> - Indoor plenum unit or air handler with an expansion device, the evaporator coil(s), condensate tray, and condensate line
> - Furnace components

6.11 AIR-COOLED AIR-CONDITIONING

Air-cooled air-conditioning or air-cooled heat pump systems can work in **conjunction with a forced-air furnace**, where the furnace blower and duct system are used by the cooling system too. Air-cooled systems may also operate as **stand-alone units** (if the house has a boiler or electric baseboard heat, for example, not a furnace) with its own air handler and its own ductwork.

The Furnace-Related Cooling System

This type of cooling system (split system) has two main components. An **outdoor component**, which houses the compressor, the condenser coil, and a fan. The refrigerant in a gaseous state is compressed by the **compressor**. As the gas runs through a **condenser coil**, heat is removed from the gas by a **fan** that draws outside air across the coils. Then the gas loses heat and condenses to a hot, high-pressure liquid state.

The liquid refrigerant is sent inside the house to the **indoor component**, an evaporator coil, which sits in the plenum directly above the furnace in a vertical orientation, beside the furnace in a horizontal orientation, or in an air handler on a stand-alone system. Here, an **expansion device** (TXV) reduces pressure on the liquid, which cools it down. The liquid flows through the **evaporator coil(s)**, where it absorbs heat from the house air flowing through the plenum. This cools the air, which the blower circulates through the house using the furnace or air handler ductwork. As the liquid refrigerant picks up heat, it turns back into a gas. The cool, low-pressure gas returns to the outdoor unit. The evaporator coil sits above a **condensate tray** or pan that catches condensate (humidity removed from the air) that forms on the outside of the very cold evaporator coil(s). Condensate is drained through a **condensate line** to a condensate pump or floor drain in basement units or to the exterior or a sink trap in units mounted in an attic, a crawl space, or a closet.

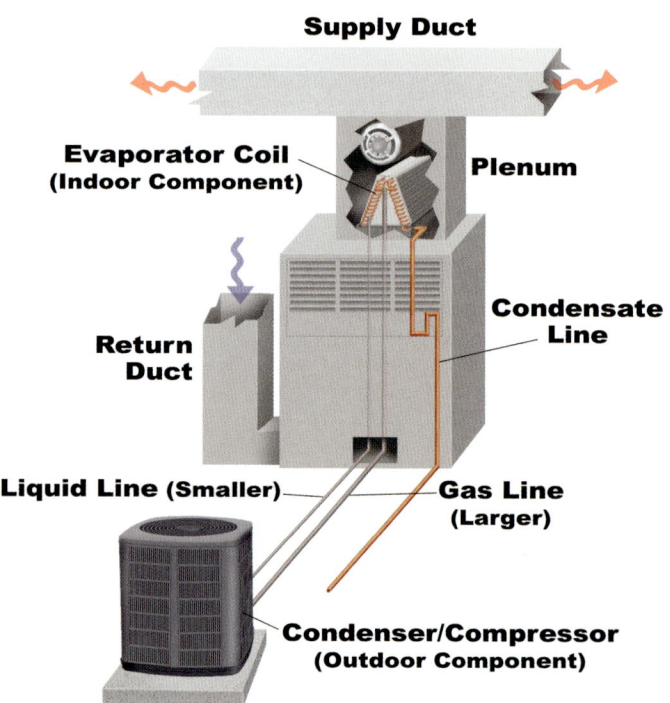

Illustration by Paddy Morrissey

Here is a more detailed explanation of the components of an air-cooled air-conditioning or heat pump system that works in conjunction with the forced-air furnace:

- **Outdoor unit:** The outdoor cabinet houses the compressor, the condenser, and the fan. It is a large box-like or cylindrical unit with louvered or exposed (coil visible) sides. There should be at least **12″ of side clearance** (all four sides) from foliage, fences, walls, or obstructions and **4–6′ above it**. The cabinet should be located where there is a minimum of direct sunshine because the cooler the air flowing over the condenser, the more efficient the refrigerant cycle. The cabinet should be **level**, mounted on a concrete or prefabricated plastic pad, and high enough to be out of the way of snow (heat pumps). A tilt of 10° or greater can damage the compressor and put strain on the refrigerant lines. In hurricane-prone areas, the cabinet must be securely fastened to the building, ground, or roof.

CLEARANCES
• 12″ on all sides of the outdoor cabinet
• 4–6′ above the outdoor cabinet

OUTDOOR COMPONENTS
• Outdoor cabinet
• Compressor
• Condenser
• Condenser fan
• Disconnect switch

  There should be an **exterior electrical disconnect within sight of** the outdoor cabinet so that the unit can be turned off for maintenance or service. If no disconnect is present, recommend that one be installed. This is a **safety hazard** for the technician servicing the unit, not the homeowner. The unit is on a 240-volt circuit with fuses or a circuit breaker protecting it. During the off-season, the circuit breaker on air-conditioning units should be turned off to prevent any inadvertent action at the thermostat from starting the cooling system. Because heat pumps provide both heating and cooling, its breaker must remain on at all times for normal use.

- **The compressor:** The compressor is the heart of the cooling or heat pump system and its most expensive component, costing about 50% of the entire system. It typically lasts from 10 to 15 years (perhaps 8 to 10 years in the South and Southwest). When the compressor wears out and has to be replaced, it may be more cost effective to put in a new air-conditioning system depending on efficiency, refrigerant used, and age (see 14 SEER note on page 505). Newer high-efficiency air-conditioning and heat pump units may have dual compressors or variable capacity cooling so that the compressor can adjust its output for energy savings and homeowner comfort.

  The **function** of the compressor is to move the refrigerant through the system and to compress refrigerant gas until it becomes a high-pressure, high-temperature gas capable of giving off heat. Low-pressure gas is drawn to the compressor through the low-pressure refrigerant (suction) line from the evaporator coil, and high-pressure gas is delivered from the compressor to the condenser coil.

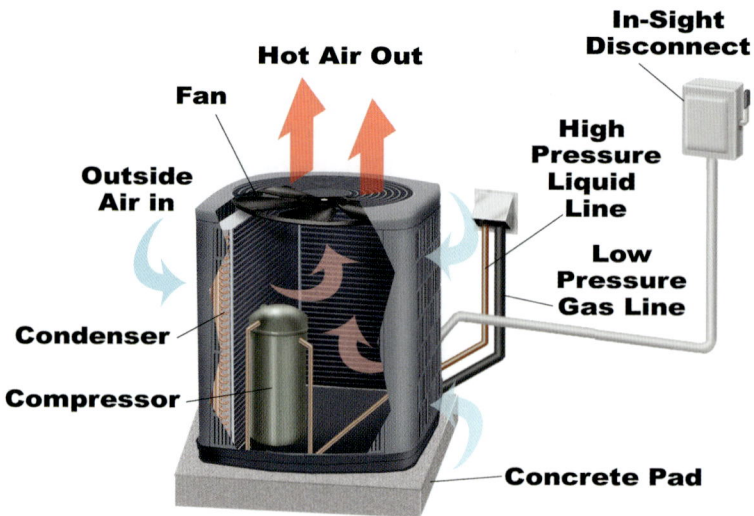

Illustration by Paddy Morrissey

> **Definition**
>
> The <u>compressor</u> moves the refrigerant through a cooling system and pressurizes the refrigerant gas in order to raise its temperature.

The compressor is a **sealed unit** with a motor, safety devices, and an oil lubricant. Compressors are typically one of two types: reciprocating or scroll. By far, scroll compressors are most common today. (It's not possible for the home inspector to inspect the compressor other than to determine whether it is operating.) When the cooling system is shut down, the oil slowly absorbs the refrigerant and no longer is able to protect the moving parts of the compressor. To prevent this condition, some compressors in cold climates have a **heating element** that keeps the oil free of refrigerant. The heater will continue to work as long as the power supply to the system is not turned off.

Before restarting the cooling system at the beginning of the season, power should be turned on **24 hours before startup** to allow the heater (if present) time to heat the oil. Also, remember that the outside temperature should be **above 60°** at the time of startup and not have fallen below 50° the night before. Starting the system under the wrong conditions can severely damage the compressor.

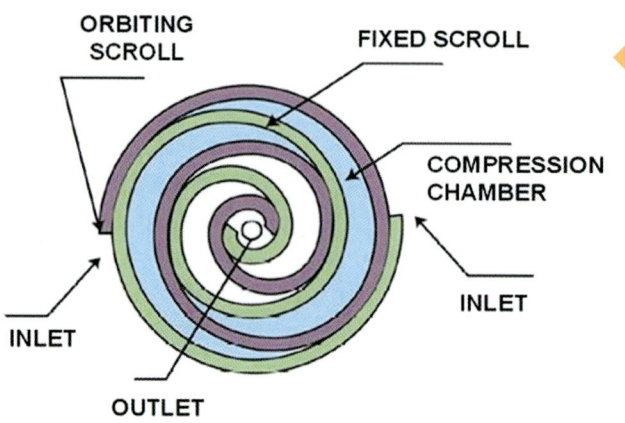

Photo #42 *This is a digram of the interior of a scroll type compressor. YouTube has great animations that show exactly how they work. They basically compress the refrigerant toward the center and out to the evaporator coil.*

512 Chapter 6

The compressor turns on and off in response to the thermostat. Upon a call for cool air at the thermostat, both the compressor and the fan in the outdoor unit should start up. The compressor should run smoothly and quietly, without going on and off repeatedly.

- **The condenser:** The condenser is a passive, non-mechanical device. It consists of a copper or aluminum coil of thin wall tubing covered with fins to increase its surface area. The function of the condenser is that of a **heat exchanger**. Outside air is pulled over the condenser fins, transferring heat from the high-pressure refrigerant gas inside the condenser to the air (or in a water cooled system, the water). This causes the high-pressure refrigerant gas to condense to a hot liquid. The condenser fins should be kept clean, unobstructed, and free of damage. Be sure to note the presence of a dryer vent nearby, as this will cause the coil to become clogged with lint over time.

- **The condenser fan:** The fan in the outdoor cabinet moves air through the condenser coils. Outside air is pulled through the cabinet to help cool the refrigerant in the condenser. Hot air is expelled back to the outdoors. Fans may be placed vertically or horizontally in the cabinet. They should be kept clean and not be damaged.

- **Refrigerant lines:** Two copper lines move the refrigerant through the cooling system. The **low-pressure line** (fat one) carries the cool low-pressure refrigerant gas from the evaporator to the compressor (from inside to outside). It should be insulated to prevent condensation from forming in the building cavities, attic, crawl space, or basement ceiling space. When the system is operating properly, the low-pressure line should be cool to the touch (it may be sweating but should not have frost or ice on it). The **high-pressure line** (thin one) carries the hot high-pressure refrigerant liquid from the condenser to the evaporator (from outside to inside). This line feels warm or hot.

- **Indoor unit:** The indoor unit that works in conjunction with the furnace sits in the plenum above the furnace in a vertical orientation or beside it in a horizontal orientation. Its components include the evaporator coil, the expansion device, the condensate tray, and the condensate lines.

- **The evaporator:** The evaporator coil is like the condenser coil in configuration in that it has copper or aluminum tubing to which thin fins

---

REFRIGERANT LINES

- The larger line carries low-pressure gas from inside to outside. It should be cool to the touch.
- The smaller line carries high-pressure liquid from outside to inside. It should be warm to the touch.

Definitions

The <u>condenser</u> in a cooling system is a coil through which the refrigerant gas flows, releasing heat to the air and becoming a liquid.

<u>Refrigerant lines</u> are copper tubing that carry refrigerant in both gas and liquid states through a cooling system.

Definition

The <u>evaporator</u> in a cooling system is a coil through which the refrigerant liquid flows, absorbing heat from the air and becoming a gas.

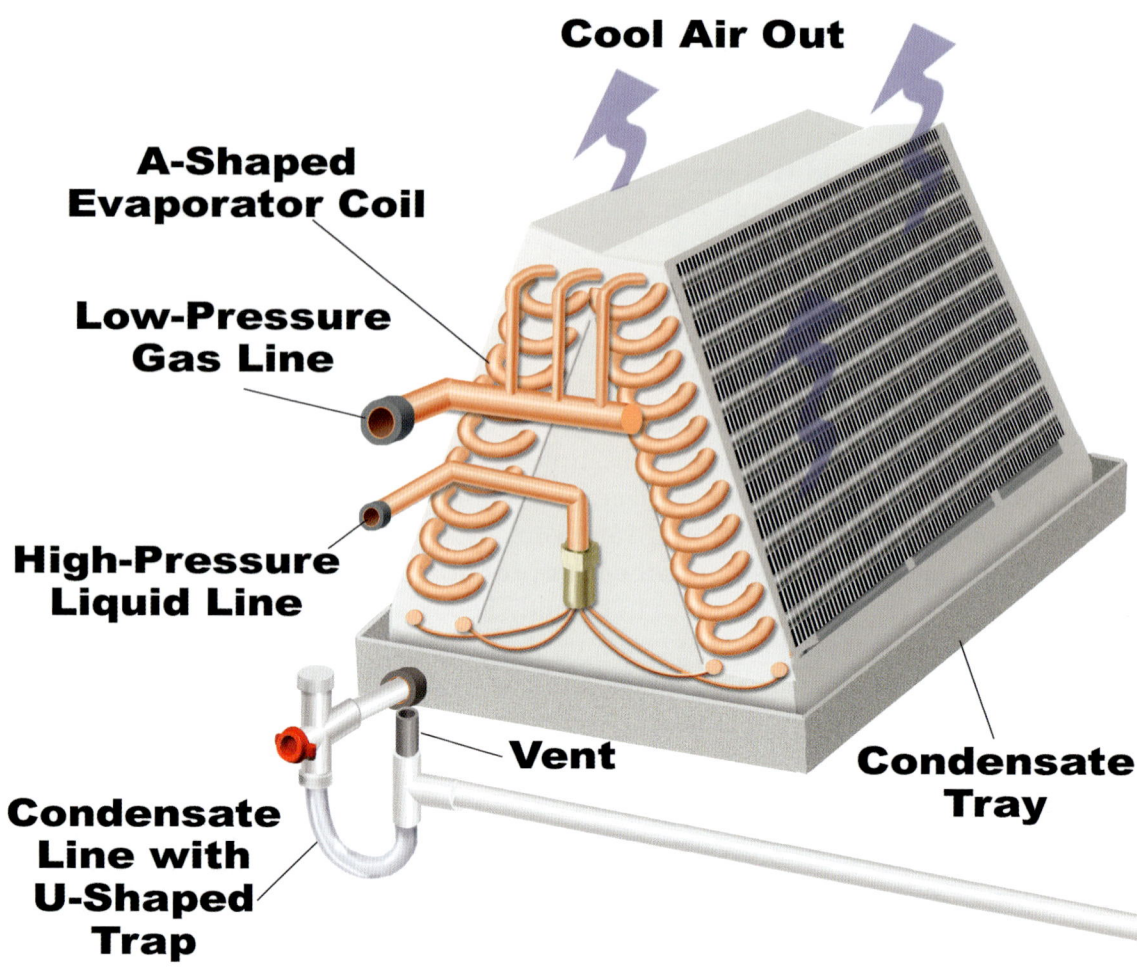

Illustration by Paddy Morrissey

are attached. A common evaporator coil is called an **A-coil** because of its shape with the double plates of coils connected at the top. They also may be slab coils (flat) or N-shaped coils. The liquid refrigerant first flows through an **expansion device** to drop its temperature and then flows through the evaporator coils as the blower moves air across them. The liquid absorbs heat from the warm air and cools the tubing and fins, which likewise cools the air in the house. The cool air is circulated through the house through the furnace ductwork. The air is also dehumidified in the process. As the refrigerant absorbs this heat, it changes back to a low-pressure gas.

When the evaporator coil(s) sit in the plenum, they're not typically visible to the home inspector, but you'll know they're there because of the refrigerant lines at the plenum. It is usually completely visible in the case of an air handler for a stand-alone system or heat pump.

The **temperature differential or split** of the air before and after the evaporator should be between 14° and 22° depending on what part of the country you're in. In warm, humid climates, a colder coil is needed to remove humidity, whereas a hot dry climate calls for a warmer coil. This is accomplished by the amount of air flowing across the coil. The slower the airflow, the better the dehumidification. The faster the airflow the less dehumidification. So, in hot humid climates like South Carolina the airflow will be moving across the coil slower resulting in a colder coil and better dehumidification. While in a hot arid climate like Phoenix, the airflow is faster as there is very little humidity to be removed from the air. In South Carolina you would like a supply vs. return differential of about 20° and in Phoenix it might be closer to 15°. There are a large number of variables that we as home inspectors will not be able to determine so in general a difference (supply vs. return) should be about 14° to 22°. If the air on the outlet side is too warm, it can be the result of too little refrigerant in the system, too much air passing over the evaporator, or too high fan speeds. If the outlet air is too cold, it can be the result of a dirty filter, clogged evaporator coils, ice on the coils, or too low fan speed.

> **INDOOR COMPONENTS**
> - The expansion device
> - The evaporator coils
> - The condensate tray
> - The condensate lines
> - The furnace fan, filter, and ductwork

- **Furnace fan, filter, and ductwork:** Older furnaces were equipped with single-speed fans, not adequate for use with a cooling system unless it's modified for multiple speeds to increase airflow for the cooling system. Frosting or icing coils are an indication that airflow isn't adequate or that the unit is low on refrigerant. The furnace air filter should be changed every month or two during the heating and cooling seasons to keep the blower and evaporator fins clean.

> *For Beginning Inspectors*
>
> *Get out there and start looking at central air-conditioning. The most common type will probably be the air-cooled unit that works in conjunction with the furnace. So get plenty of practice identifying its parts as described on these pages. If other types of cooling systems are popular in your area, start your study by seeing as many of these as possible.*

The cooling system uses the same furnace ductwork for distributing cool air through the house. More duct capacity is needed to circulate cool air than warm air. The heavier cool air, blown at greater speeds, drags along the ducts with more friction. If a home has small 4″ round branch heating ducts, it's likely that the cooling performance of the air conditioner will be reduced. These undersized ducts can whistle and vibrate as the cool air is forced through them at higher speeds.

Ideally, air-conditioning registers should be located in or near the ceiling but that's not how furnace ductwork is normally installed. However, some homes with furnaces have **high-low registers**. In this system, high registers for cooling and low registers for heating are present in each room. These combination register systems must be balanced by the register dampers at each change of season.

Any ductwork in the attic or crawl space must be insulated to reduce the effect on the cooling system of high summer temperatures in these areas. Obviously the same is true for the ductwork in the winter with cold temperatures because it is the same ductwork used all year.

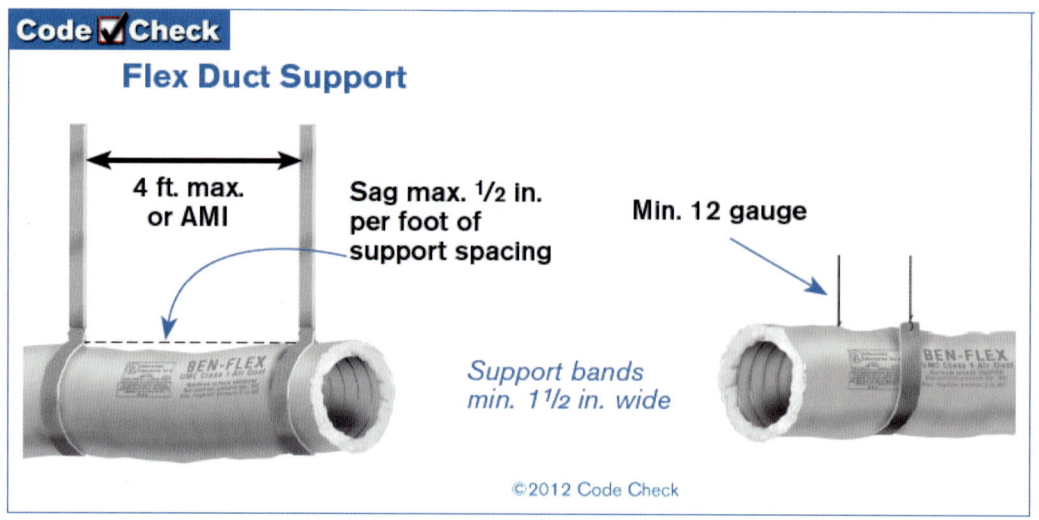

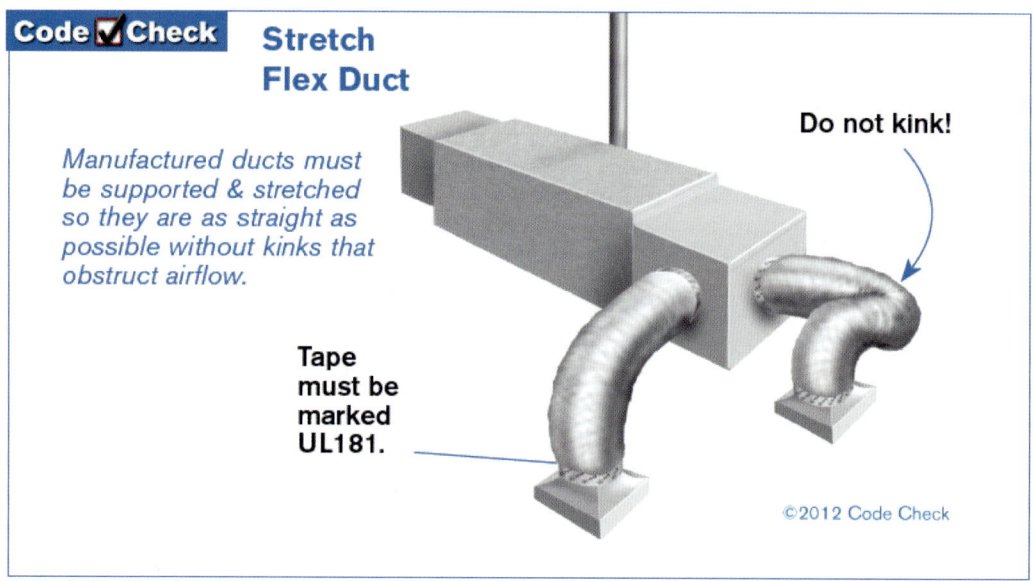

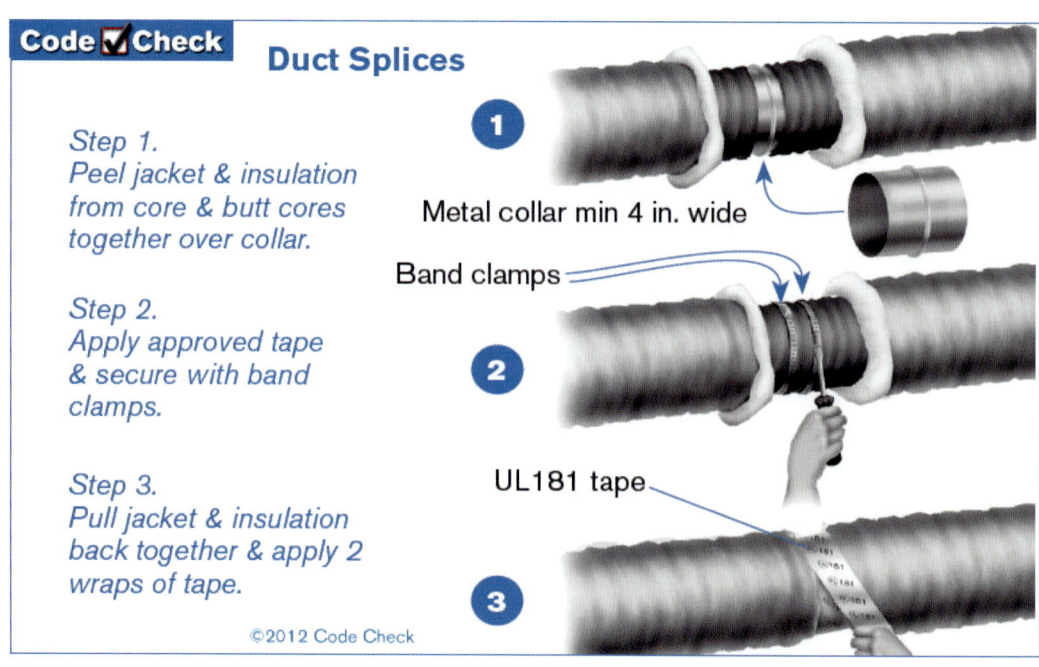

NOTE: When the furnace has a **humidifier** with a bypass from its location in the return duct to the plenum, air flows through the bypass to the plenum. During the cooling season, a damper in the bypass should be closed. If no damper is present, air flowing through the bypass can affect the air conditioner's efficiency and may ice up the evaporator coils.

- **The condensate pan:** When household air passes over the evaporator, condensation forms on the coils. This condensation is collected in a condensate tray under the coil where it can be removed. This tray should be free of leaks, cracks, rust, and obstructions (debris, sludge, etc.) so that water can drain properly. Some of the old air-conditioning systems had tin pans that rusted out after years of use. Because of the coil's position above the furnace heat exchanger, leaks or water overflowing from the condensate tray can drip onto the furnace heat exchanger. Worse yet is when the system is installed in the attic above a finished ceiling. If it leaks, clogs, or overflows, the ceiling below will be damaged. This being a potential problem, there must be a secondary means of collecting and disposing of the condensate created.

- **The condensate line:** The condensate drain line should be insulated to prevent sweating (in humid climates) and have a trap and a vent in it to prevent cool air from escaping through the pipe. The line should run to a floor drain, to a nearby sink, through the foundation and on to ground outside the house, or as appropriate for your region. Condensate is not drinkable, and it should not be allowed to enter the domestic water supply. You may find the line terminating in a hole in the slab or floor, allowing the condensate to drain into the ground under the slab or in the crawl space. This is **not** an acceptable practice. As mentioned above, where the system is installed in a location where finish materials can be damaged, a secondary means of condensate collection and disposal is required. This applies not only to attics, but also to closets and even basements if the floor drain is not immediately adjacent to the furnace or air handler. The least costly choice is for there to be two separate lines

Photo #43 *The condensate drain line should have a trap and a vent just like any plumbing fixture. If you think of the condensate pan as a sink, then it makes more sense as to why you would need a vent and a trap. It may NOT connect to a plumbing vent pipe in the attic, trapped or otherwise.*

THE HEATING INSPECTION

Photo #44 As you can see in the photo there are three fittings for the condensate line to attach to. The one the PVC pipe is connected to is the primary for the vertical orientation of the unit. The black circle to the left is the secondary fitting for the vertical orientation or the primary fitting for the horizontal orientation, which is not being used. The top circle is the secondary fitting for the horizontal orientation. Inside the unit are two pans. One runs horizontal across the bottom in this, the vertical orientation. The other pan is on the left side of the cabinet, as shown, to collect condensate if the unit were in its horizontal orientation.

attached to the condensate tray or pan within which the evaporator coil sits. These two lines are attached to fittings where one is slightly higher than the other. This is so that when the pan or line clogs as the water level in the pan rises, it will begin to flow out of the second higher fitting, which has its own condensate line that terminates to a "conspicuous" location. The second option is to use a secondary pan installed beneath the entire evaporator coil section and plenum. This will catch any condensate that overflows because the primary pan was clogged or the primary pan leaked or rusted through. The third option is to use a float switch (see photo on next page). This is best used for vertical installation because a secondary pan is not possible. A float switch is installed in either the primary or secondary line right at the main pan.

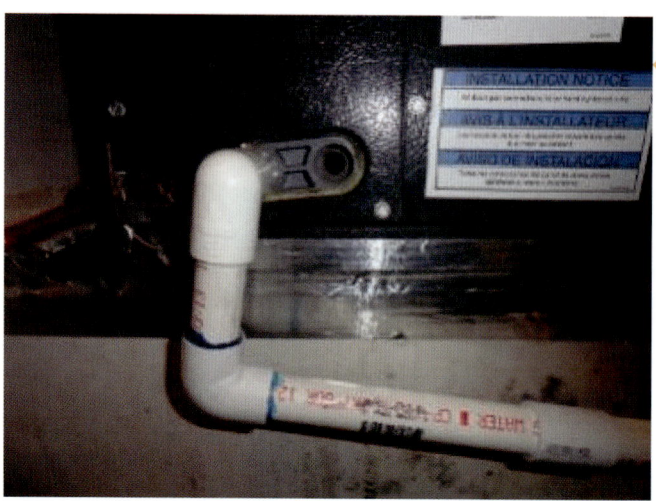

Photo #45 CONDENSATE DRAIN LINE

Condensate drain lines must terminate someplace where the water will not damage anything. This could be a floor drain, sink trap, or the side of the house. You can see the secondary drain hole open beside the primary. This is a bad idea. If the primary line clogs, the water will flow out that hole and damage the drywall-covered platform it sits on.

If the line clogs and the water level rises, the float will shut down the air-conditioning so that no more condensate can be created. You can use any combination of these as long as you have the means to catch the primary and secondary condensate in areas with finished materials that could be damaged.

Photo #46 PAN BENEATH EVAPORATOR COIL AND PLENUM

This system is close to correct. We have a primary line and a secondary pan. The primary line is not correct as the vent is both on the wrong side of the trap and it's capped.

Photo #47 FLOAT SWITCH

In a modern proper installation, whether vertical or horizontally installed, the secondary condensate drain should be utilized. The float-switch as seen here is the cheapest and probably best method of protecting finish materials in a house. The float-switch will shut the a/c off when the condensate level rises to an unsafe level in the pan. It's that simple. A/C off and no more condensate. Homeowner calls the HVAC technician to blow out the lines and clear the line.

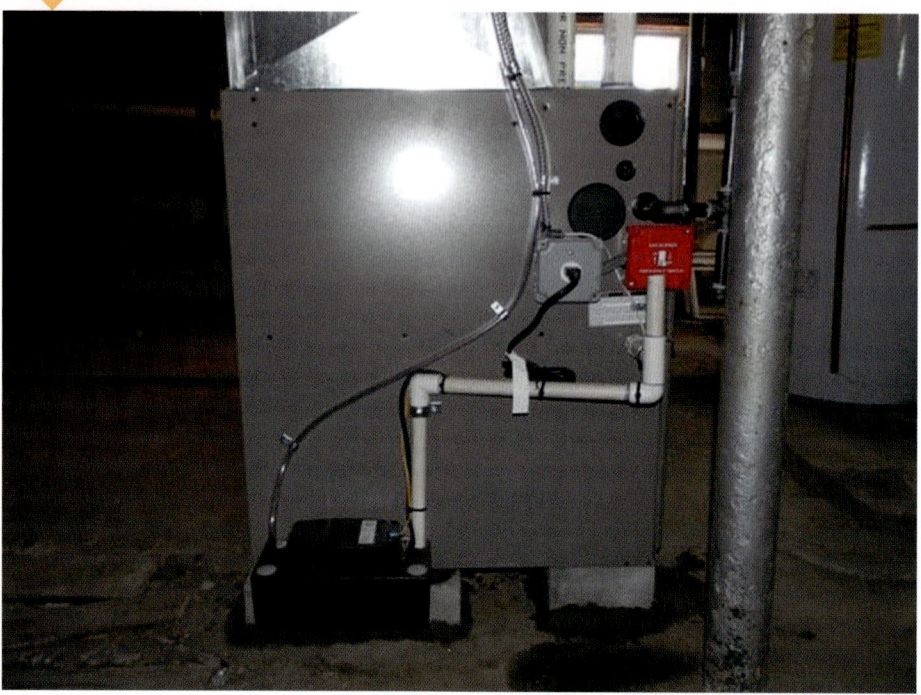

Photo #48 *Condensate pumps can be used in locations where the condensate can't drain to a safe place by gravity. They should be interconnected with the unit's thermostat wiring in case the pump fails. They work just like the float-switch mentioned previously. They can be connected to both a/c and high-efficiency furnaces, which both produce condensate.*

Occasionally, you may find the condensate line discharging into a small rectangular box next to the furnace. This box contains a **condensate (lift) pump** that pumps the condensate to a level where it can be sent to a desired location. The pump has a float control that activates the pump when water reaches a preset level. It should be connected to the unit's thermostat wiring to prevent operation of the air-conditioning unit if the pump fails. This prevents condensate from overflowing on the floor and potentially damaging finish materials.

The Stand-Alone Air-Cooled Unit

When a home doesn't have a forced-air furnace and is heated by electric baseboard, hot water, or steam, central air-conditioning must operate independent of the heating system. A mini-split or ductless air conditioner or heat pump may be installed to cool a large portion of the main living area and not every room. These stand-alone air-conditioning or heat pump systems are identical in operation to air-cooled system described earlier. They have the identical components outdoors in the compressor/condenser cabinet, but the inside components are contained in an **air handler** or cassette/head unit.

STAND-ALONE SYSTEM

If there's no furnace, the indoor unit for an air-cooled system contains its own fan, filter, and ductwork.

520   Chapter 6

Photo #49 *This is the other half of the system from the very beginning of the chapter on page 394. The compressor as well as the condensing coil are inside of the unit.*

Photo #50 MINI-SPLIT HEAT PUMP

This is the head unit for the mini-split unit. It is typically mounted high on the wall or in the ceiling in some units. It is usually controlled by a hand-held remote control.

They consist of the evaporator coils, a blower, its own air filter, a condensate tray and line, and connections to its own supply and return ductwork (if present). There are also high-velocity systems that operate a bit differently, but the inspection is still the same.

Photo #51 *This is a high velocity system and is generally found as a standalone system in a house with a boiler. Since there is no ducting used for a boiler, an entire new system has to be installed. These systems can be installed in tight quarters where conventional ductwork won't fit.*

Here are some special considerations for attic or closet installations for stand-alone units:

- **Condensate drainage:** As described above, this applies to all systems, stand-alone or otherwise. Its condensate line should have a trap and vent in it at the air handler. When units are attic- or closet-mounted, there is concern that a cracked or clogged condensate tray or line can leak and damage the ceiling or finish materials below. Most pans have a fitting for an **auxiliary condensate line** just above the main line fitting. If the main tray and line become clogged, the level of condensate will rise and be drawn off by the auxiliary drain. If an auxiliary line fitting is missing, the whole cabinet, including the condensate tray, should sit above an **auxiliary condensate drip pan** with its own drain line as a backup.

The condensate lines should drain through the lower portion of the roof to a gutter or through the exterior wall to the outside. The secondary or auxiliary line should discharge in a **conspicuous** location, typically above a window or door; if the secondary line is dripping water, it's a clue that the primary line may be clogged. The lines should not terminate into the plumbing vent stack. Most local codes do not permit this because of the possibility of sewer gas backing up into the airflow through the fan unit and entering the house.

Photo #52 AIR HANDLER

This is a typical air handler or fan coil unit for a heat pump. You will notice right away that the blower and coil are reversed from the normal a/c furnace configuration. The top compartment may or may not have electric heat strips installed as it depends on the local climate where it's installed.

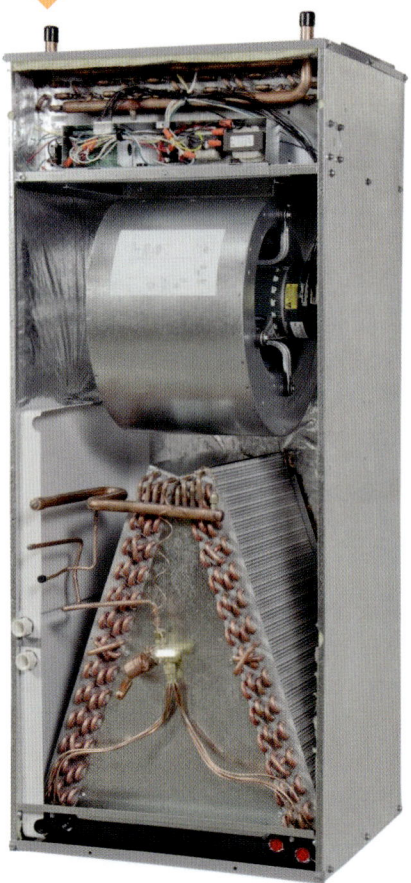

NOTE: The condensate tray line and the auxiliary drain line should be two completely separate lines. It defeats the purpose if the lines are joined. Optionally, a float switch may be interconnected to the thermostat wiring in the same way as the condensate pump mentioned earlier.

- **Ductwork:** Because a home without a forced-air system won't have ductwork for moving air through the home, a stand-alone air-cooled system must have its own ductwork installed. In the case of mini-splits or ductless heat pumps, as the name implies, there are no ducts. The system blows air into the room from the cassette or head unit hanging on the wall.

> **Definitions**
>
> A <u>stand-alone air-cooled air-conditioning system</u> has an outdoor compressor/condenser unit and an independent indoor evaporator unit with its own fan, filter, and ductwork. It does not work in conjunction with a forced warm air furnace.
>
> An <u>auxiliary condensate drip pan</u> is used with an attic- or closet-mounted stand-alone unit as a backup against leaks in the main condensate tray and line.

High-velocity systems have small round, flexible, insulated ductwork. The air velocity is increased to allow enough airflow through the small ducts. Instead of conventional-style heating registers being used, discharge nozzles are mounted in ceilings to blow in cool air. A large return grill is often mounted in the ceiling on the top floor, but it can be placed anywhere. If it is a standard system and not a high-velocity type, the ductwork will be comparable to that found with the forced-air furnace. The only difference is that if the ductwork is located in the attic, it will be insulated to R-6 or R-8 in a modern system. There are also ducts made with duct board, which is a compressed fiberglass material with a foil covering.

Inspecting Air-Cooled Systems

During the inspection of the air-conditioning or heat pump system, the home inspector should identify the **type** of system and determine its **age** and

> **Photo #53 INSULATED FLEX DUCTING**
>
> *This is commonly known as insulated flex ducting. It can be uninsulated as well and just called flex ducting. The R-values range from 4.2 to 6.0 to 8.0. The straighter the runs are the better they are, and we already talked about supports.*

Photo #54 DUCTBOARD

This is Duct-board and it comes in 4' × 10' sheets. They are cut and made into plenums and ducts. The material is supposed to be sealed together with FSK tape and not foil tape. Be sure to check manufacturer's specifications. It can NOT be used outdoors. It has an R-value of 4.3 depending on manufacturer.

DO NOT OPERATE

- If outside temperature is under 60° or under 50° the night before.
- If system is shut down.
- If system hasn't been operated this season.

RECOMMEND UNIT BE SERVICED

- If compressor or condenser fan doesn't start.
- If compressor groans and squeals.
- If compressor short cycles.
- If any part doesn't work.

remaining useful lifetime based on the information in the *Technical Reference Guide*. The inspector should make a determination as to **whether to operate** the system. The inspection should include examining the following air-conditioning components:

- Outdoor cabinet
- Refrigerant lines
- Indoor unit (evaporator coil in furnace plenum or in air handler)
- Condensate drain system
- Ductwork

These procedures should be followed when inspecting the cooling system:

1. **Examine the compressor/condenser unit.** Begin your examination of the cooling system by starting with the outdoor unit while performing the exterior inspection of the home. Note the presence of an electrical disconnect, clearances (airflow) around the unit, the condition of the cabinet, condensing coil fins, and fan blades. Also, note whether the cabinet is level and whether the refrigerant lines are kinked or damaged. Many condensing coils have hail damage or damage from children bending the soft aluminum fins. In either case, this reduces airflow and efficiency. A technician can straighten the fins with a "fin comb."
2. **Determine if you'll turn on the unit.** It's always a good idea to know what the temperature was the night before the inspection.

Then when you're outside the home during the inspection, take note of the current temperature. When you're examining the outdoor unit, note if the disconnect switch is turned off, indicating that the system is shut down. Talk to the homeowner, if present, and find out why the system is off and if it can be turned on, by the owner, without damage. Remember that if the unit hasn't been operated this season, it should have its power on 24 hours before the inspection to prevent potential damage to the compressor.

3. **Turn on the equipment.** If you've decided to go ahead and turn on the equipment, lower the thermostat (same 5° mentioned before) while you're inspecting the interior of the house. Listen for any problems with the air-conditioning as the system starts up. Shut off the equipment if the compressor and condenser fan don't start up within 3 to 5 minutes depending on the delay programmed into the thermostat or if you hear problem noises or if any parts aren't functioning.

4. **Let the equipment run for 15 minutes.** Continue with other aspects of the interior inspection and let the system operate for 10 to 15 minutes depending on whether it was already in use when you arrived. As the cooling system comes up to speed, check registers and return grills for airflow. If the system is part of a forced-air furnace you do not need to verify airflow twice as the blower and ductwork are the same for both systems. If it is a stand-alone system, you will need to check for airflow using your infrared thermometer as previously discussed. Check visible ductwork if you have not already done so.

5. **Go outside once more to check the outdoor unit.** While the system is still operating, check the outdoor unit once more. Check fan operation and feel for warm to hot air blowing out of the unit. Feel the refrigerant lines for an indication of any problems—the larger line should feel cold but not be covered with ice, and the smaller line should feel warm to hot.

6. **Examine the indoor unit.** Allow the cooling system to continue operating while you listen to the indoor evaporator unit. Check the temperature of air before and after the coil for appropriate differential (nearest supply and return registers). Note any excessive vibrations, fan motor problems, condensate leaking, functioning condensate lift pump, and so on.

7. **Turn off the cooling system.** Finally, turn off the system by returning the thermostat to its original setting, up 5°. Then inspect the indoor unit more closely by checking the condition of the cabinet for rusting and corrosion; the presence and condition of the air filter (if at unit),

> **Section Note**
>
> *"Don't ever let a customer talk you into turning on an air conditioner that you know should not be operated. Sometimes the customer can be quite convincing. But don't do it.*
>
> *If the temperature is too low or the system hasn't been operated yet, you can cause a lot of damage to the compressor. And, of course, you'd be the one to have to replace it—no matter who wanted you to try it. Explain your reasons to the customer and suggest that someone be called in to examine the unit at the appropriate time."*

mounting (if an attic unit), and condition of the condensate tray, line(s) pump, etc.

Watch for the following conditions during the inspection of the air cooled air-conditioning system:

- **Obstructed or tilted outdoor unit:** Check the outdoor unit to be sure the proper clearances at the sides and tops are met. Check that the unit is level and explain why a tilt of only 10° can be harmful to the compressor and the refrigerant lines. Be sure to report unlevel compressor/condenser units in your inspection report. Excessive settlement of the pad under the unit can cause refrigerant lines to kink or fracture and lose refrigerant.

- **Missing exterior disconnect:** There should be an electrical box near the outside cabinet so that the system can be turned off at this point and will not respond to the thermostat during the off season. This is a precaution against someone turning down the thermostat at the wrong time, starting the compressor and damaging it.

- **Electrical wiring:** Check the condition of the low voltage wiring to ensure that it is not deteriorating and is not in need of repair or replacement. Make sure the line voltage (240v) wiring is in appropriate flexible conduit and rated for exterior use. Also, take a look to see that the wiring is protected from mechanical damage as it enters the condenser unit or disconnect.

- **Damaged, dirty, leaking, corroded, or rusted equipment:** Check all the outdoor and indoor components of the cooling or heat pump system (you most likely will not be able to see the evaporator coils above the furnace in the plenum). Cabinets and all operating components should be kept clean and free from dust, lint, tree fluff, rust, and corrosion. Look for and report dirty, rusted, or clogged coils or broken fins; broken or bent blades on the condenser fan; any evidence of leaking components; and damaged and leaking refrigerant and condensate lines.

    Take special care when inspecting condensate trays in the plenum because leaking above the heat exchanger can have dire consequences on the condition of the furnace heat exchanger. If you find leaking from the tray into the furnace, take that into consideration during your inspection of the heat exchanger.

- **Missing or dirty air filter:** If you find the air filter missing, you can bet that the evaporator coil will be dirty and clogged and that the system isn't operating properly. If this is your determination, recommend that a technician clean and service the unit/coil. Air filters are very important to the smooth operation of a cooling system. Any restriction in airflow will greatly reduce the efficiency, even more so than for the heating system. Remind customers that filters should be cleaned or replaced about every month or two during the heating and cooling seasons.

- **Noisy, vibrating, or malfunctioning equipment or loose mountings:** Examine as much of the equipment you have access to for these conditions. The compressor, condenser fan, inside blower unit, and condensate pump (if present) should all operate smoothly without excessive noise and vibration. Explain to customers the seriousness of some of the defects you may find. For example, a noisy or short cycling compressor represents a serious problem, loss of efficiency, and an expensive repair, while a dirty or vibrating condenser fan can be repaired easily. A serviceperson should be called in to examine any compressor problems. Vibrations can be caused by loose mountings or dirty imbalanced parts rather than faulty equipment.

- **Frost or icing:** Any sign of frost or ice buildup on the evaporator coils or the refrigerant lines is an indication that the system isn't operating properly. It's usually the result of insufficient airflow through the coil or not enough refrigerant in the system. This should be reported in the inspection report.

> **INSPECTING AIR-COOLED COOLING SYSTEMS**
>
> - Missing disconnect
> - Obstructed or tilted outdoor unit
> - Damaged, dirty, leaking, corroded, rusted, noisy, vibrating, or malfunctioning equipment
> - Missing or dirty air filter
> - Extreme temperature differential
> - Frost or icing
> - Improper condensate drainage
> - Improper ductwork
> - Lack of cooling source in each room

- **Too high or too low temperature differential:** You can note temperature differentials in the cooling system in three ways—temperature differences in airflow in and out of the outdoor unit, in temperature between the larger and smaller refrigerant lines, and in airflow in and out of the evaporator coil.

A simple check for system operation is to feel if the air blown out of the outdoor unit is considerably warmer than the outside air. You can also feel the refrigerant lines—the larger line should feel cold, and the smaller

> **Photo #55 FILTER DRIER**
>
> *Filter-driers may or may not have a site-glass to view the refrigerant. The arrow on the label indicates the direction of flow. These are both for a/c systems as the arrow only points in one direction. You will see on a heat pump the arrow has two points pointing in both directions. We don't do anything with these devices. Just know what they are and what they do.*

line should feel warm. If the larger line is not cold, the system is probably low on refrigerant. The refrigerant level can be checked through the sight glass on the line, if present. If bubbles are visible, it's an indication that the refrigerant level is low. It may also be connected to the filter drier, a device that filters particulate and removes moisture from the liquid refrigerant.

At the evaporator coil, the home inspector should determine if there's a **proper temperature differential of 14° to 22°** between the return and supply side of the evaporator coils. Practically speaking, this is done at the nearest supply and return registers or filter slot. Too low a differential (less than 14°) can indicate that the unit is low on refrigerant, has a bad compressor, or is too old to transfer heat properly. Too high (greater than 22°) can indicate restricted airflow from a dirty evaporator coil or air filter or a malfunctioning fan. An extreme temperature differential should be reported in your inspection report.

> **REMINDER**
>
> *After the inspection of the air-conditioning system, return thermostat settings to their original settings.*

> **DON'T EVER MISS**
>
> - Lack of cooling source in each room
> - Extreme temperature differential
> - Rusted or leaking condensate trays over heat exchangers
> - Damaged, leaking, corroded, rusty, noisy, or vibrating equipment
> - Missing air filter

- **Improper condensate drainage:** Closely examine the condensate tray and condensate lines for their condition, watching for corrosion, rusting, or leaking. Note if a trap and vent are present in the line. Report any improper drainage, such as draining the condensate into a hole in the slab, into the crawl space, or into a plumbing vent. For attic or closet installations, note the absence of an auxiliary drip pan under the air handler and/or the absence of a separate auxiliary drain or float switch.

- **Leaking, damaged, loose, or corroded ducts:** Examine the visible ductwork for its condition, noting any open joints, corrosion, loose supports, disconnected or crushed sections, missing insulation, or any condition that impedes airflow.

- **Lack of cooling source in each room:** If a cool-air source is missing in a room, note its absence in the inspection report. This is similar to reporting heat sources. Customers will be calling later wanting you to install a cool-air outlet in any rooms you missed on the report.

Reporting Your Findings

During the cooling inspection, be sure to continue to communicate with your customer about your findings. Often, customers don't understand why you aren't testing the cooling equipment in the winter. Explain your reasons for not operating the system without giving a boring technical lecture, but say enough to help customers understand how equipment can be damaged if the system is started at the wrong time or under the wrong conditions. Customers may not fully understand how the air conditioner works, but they should be able to understand that you are taking measures to not damage the equipment.

If a home has a central air conditioner and you find a room that is missing a cool-air register, make a note of it in your inspection report on the appropriate page for the kitchen, the bathrooms, and any other room. Missing a cooling source in a room can cause as much trouble later as missing a heating source.

When reporting on the inspection of the air-conditioning system, be sure to report on the condition of the following:

- **Outdoor unit:** Your inspection report might be organized so that the air-conditioning outdoor unit (compressor and condenser) is reported with other exterior items. Record the brand name, model, serial number and type of cooling (air or water) of the unit. Indicate the fuel source (gas or electric). Just a note about gas air conditioners: they are very uncommon residentially, but you may run across one in a high-end large home or estate. We do not do anything with them. You should do a bit of online searching to see what one looks like just in case. You should also give the condition of the outdoor unit an overall rating of satisfactory, marginal, or poor, noting its age and defects such as a tilted unit, obstructions to the unit, rusted components, broken fan blades, a noisy compressor, and so on. Make a note indicating whether an electrical disconnect is present.

> **OLDER AIR CONDITIONERS**
>
> *Note air conditioners over 10 years old as <u>items requiring repair or replacement within the next 5 years</u> in your inspection report. The compressor will be reaching the end of its lifetime within 5 years.*

- **Indoor unit:** You may be reporting information about the indoor unit on a different page of your report. In any case, report on the type of air-conditioning system you find. Report on findings you may have, such as a leaking condensate tray or a missing air filter.

- **Operation:** First, be sure to distinguish between an air-conditioning system you haven't operated and one that isn't operating due to malfunction. Be clear about reporting this. In other words, note if the unit was or wasn't started due to outside conditions (too cold outside). It's a good idea to write the reason you didn't turn it on (outside temperature too low or power not on for 24 hours, for example). If you tried to start the air conditioner and it didn't run, note that. Report on whether the operating temperature differential was within range.

- **Major defects and repairs:** If the air-conditioning system is not in operating condition, report it as a major defect. Serious compressor problems represent a major repair expense.

> *Chapter Note*
>
> *Pages 529–539 present information on other types of cooling systems, including the water-cooled system, the gas chiller, and the evaporator cooler. The heat pump, another method of cooling, is presented on page 534.*

6.12 OTHER COOLING SYSTEMS

In this section, other types of air-conditioning systems will be presented.

Water-Cooled Air-Conditioning

The difference between air-cooled air-conditioning and water-cooled air-conditioning is in the **condenser**. All other aspects of the two types of systems are the same. A water-cooled system condenser uses water from many different sources (a well, lake, or pond; a recirculated ground-loop; or direct exchange with the refrigerant lines themselves), which absorbs heat from the refrigerant. The condenser has a water jacket surrounding the refrigerant coil. The surrounding water cools the refrigerant gas and changes it to a liquid, serving the same purpose as the condenser in an air-cooled system.

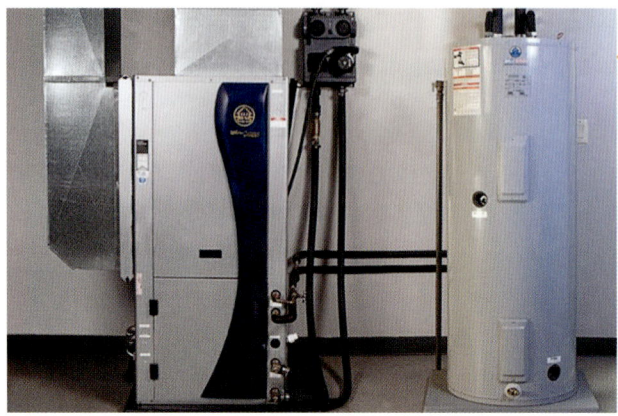

Photo #56 *This is a water-cooled heat pump system with an integrated domestic hot water tank. You can see the water lines coming in/out from the top middle of the photo. The other set of water lines going to the water heater are to heat/preheat the domestic hot water. Check out www.waterfurnace.com for more information on these systems.*

Because a water-cooled system doesn't depend on outside air, the compressor/condenser unit is located inside. The compressor/condenser unit is usually combined in one box with the evaporator and located near or in the same box as the air handler. Because the system doesn't need long refrigerant lines connecting the compressor/condenser with the evaporator, it needs less refrigerant.

An open loop water-cooled system (with domestic/city water) is considered wasteful because warm water from the condenser must be continually discharged and replaced with cooler domestic water. This discharged water is not drinkable and is typically discharged to a floor drain or the lawn. In some areas, local codes prohibit discharge into the public sewer or private septic system, which would be quickly overwhelmed. In fact, they may prohibit the use of open loop water-cooled air conditioners entirely. The use of wells and ponds or lakes are a better reusable source of water. You should check your local codes.

In larger commercial installations of a water-cooled air-conditioning system, discharge water may be sent to a **cooling tower** on the roof. The water is cooled in the tower by the use of high-volume fans and is recycled to the condenser. This water must be treated to prevent scale buildup in the piping and to keep bacteria and yeasts from growing in it. (Legionnaire's disease is often a result of contaminated recycled cooling tower water.) Although rare, a home may have a cooling tower, but the home inspector is not required to inspect it other than for leaking.

CAUTION: A water-cooled system must have water flowing to the condenser when the system is operating; otherwise, severe damage can result to the unit. If possible, the home inspector should check that the water supply valve to the unit is open before starting the system. Also, heed the warnings about not operating the system if its main power source is turned off. It could have been turned off due to a malfunction with the system. Check with the homeowner first.

When inspecting the water-cooled system, the home inspector should inspect all equipment (including the condenser) as presented on pages 524–529. Following are additional conditions the home inspector should look for with a water-cooled air-conditioning system:

- **Leaks:** Check inlet and outlet piping and the condenser water jacket for leaking. Notice any signs of corrosion or rusting from the effect of leaking.

- **Improper discharge:** Try to determine where warm water from the condenser is being discharged or recycled. If the method used is in violation of local codes, record that information in the inspection report.

- **Extreme temperature differential:** Feel the inlet and outlet piping at the condenser for a temperature difference. If the difference is too high, it's an indication that too little water is flowing into the condenser (a smaller amount of water absorbs more heat). It should be warm to the touch. If it's too hot to touch, something is wrong and must be noted.

- **Short cycling compressor:** One of the reasons the compressor in a water-cooled system may short-cycle is that the water pressure may be too high or too low.

> **For Your Information**
>
> *Check your local codes on whether open loop water-cooled systems are permitted and on the acceptable means of discharging warm water from the system.*

The Gas Chiller

Gas chillers operate on the same principles as the refrigerant cycle used in conventional air-conditioning systems. If you have a propane refrigerator in your RV or cabin, then you know how a gas chiller works. The basic differences between these systems are as follows:

- Ammonia or lithium bromide is used as the refrigerant instead of Freon or Puron.

- Heat is used to drive the system instead of a compressor where natural gas or propane is used to produce the heat required.

The operating principles behind the refrigerant cycle in the gas chiller are the following:

1. A **generator** heats a solution of liquid ammonia or bromine, changing it to a high-temperature, high-pressure gas.

2. A **condenser** air cools the ammonia gas to a high-pressure liquid state. A **flow restrictor** between the condenser and evaporator reduces the pressure and the temperature of the liquid ammonia.

3. The liquid ammonia in the **evaporator tank** absorbs heat from water piped through the tank. Water from a coil over the furnace that has been

warmed by household air enters the tank. Cooled water is sent back to the coil to cool the household air. As the liquid ammonia absorbs heat from the water, it changes back into a low-pressure gas.

4. An **absorber** mixes the ammonia gas with a solution of hot liquid ammonia and is air-cooled until the gas is absorbed into the solution. A high-pressure pump sends the liquid ammonia back to the generator.

The gas chiller is usually used only in large commercial installations and is not often seen in residential homes. Some smaller home-use chillers have been introduced but have not been very successful. It's rare that the home inspector will come across one.

EVAPORATIVE COOLER

The evaporative (Swamp) cooler works in dry climates. It uses the evaporation process to cool and moisturize the air for home cooling.

The Evaporative (Swamp) Cooler

Most air-conditioning systems take in warm, moist air and produce cool, dry air. The evaporative cooler works differently, taking in warm, dry air and producing cool, moist air. That's why it's used only in dry climates such as the Southwest, as well as parts of Colorado, Utah, California, Texas, Nevada, Idaho, and eastern Washington State.

The evaporator cooler consists of a sheet metal or plastic cabinet containing the following:

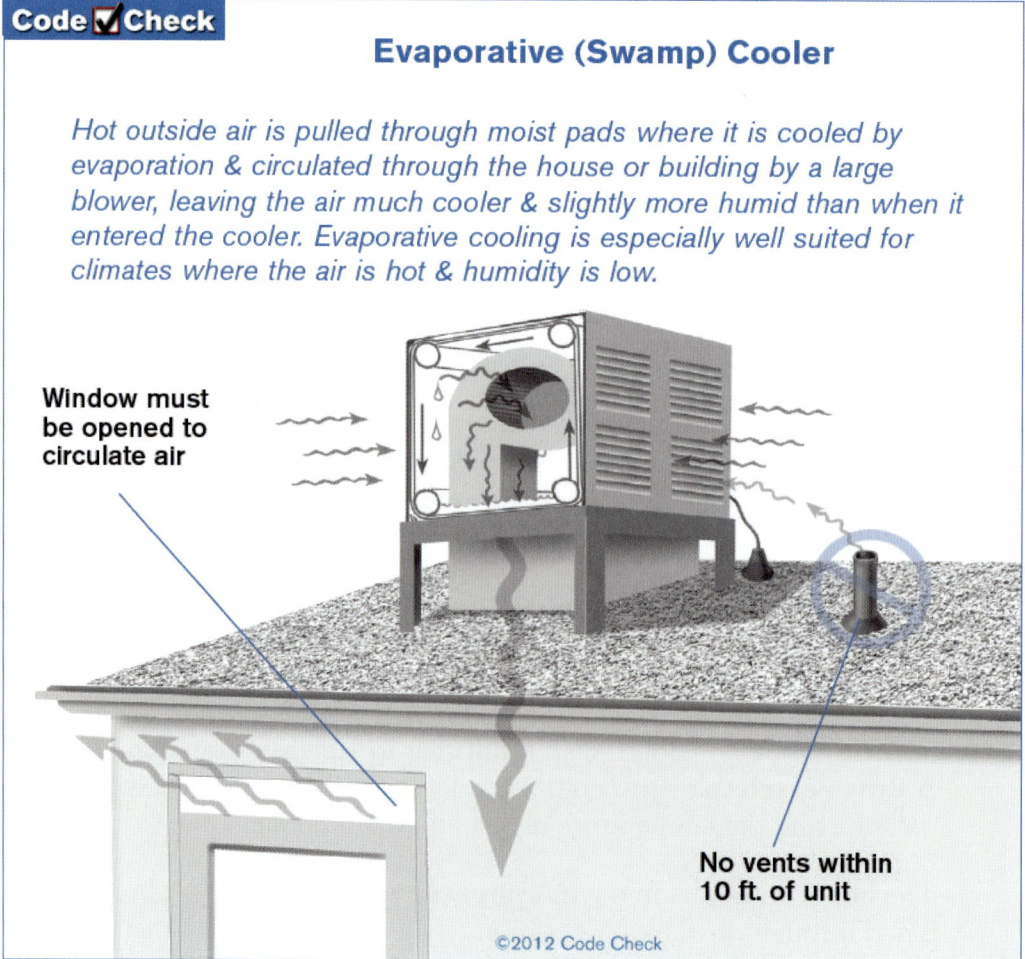

Chapter 6

- A high-volume, two-speed **blower unit** to draw in outside air, pass it through the cooler pad to cool it, and circulate the cooled air through the duct system and ultimately back outside, carrying the heat with it. Inspect the blower unit (fan, motor, and belt) for proper operation—listen for sounds or vibrations indicating loose mountings, loose belt, or worn bearings.

- The **pad type** cooler has **pads** that hold water that evaporates as the warm outside air passes over it. As the water evaporates, it absorbs heat from the house air and thus cools it. Pads should be cleaned or replaced regularly to prevent the buildup of salts, algae, bacteria, and yeasts. Inspect the pads to see if they need to be cleaned or replaced.

- A **rotary type** cooler has a **drum** made of absorbent foam screening material that rotates through a tank of water, and the air passes over the top of the drum, causing the water to evaporate.

> **Chapter Note**
>
> *Pages 534–539 present the study and inspection of heat pumps for heating and air-conditioning.*

- **Water supply:** Each type of evaporative cooler has connections to the home's domestic water supply to keep water flowing into the cooler. Coolers have a **pump** to draw water out of a reservoir to keep the pads wet. Water level in the tray or reservoir is maintained with a float valve that adds water when required.

The main item to watch for when inspecting the evaporative cooler is rusting and leaking of the various parts. If the unit is mounted on the ground, it should be properly secured and be a minimum of 3″ above the ground. There should be a disconnect in sight of the unit. With a swamp cooler, there should be backflow protection on the water supply. The unit may have an internal air gap, which is permissible. There should be a 10′ horizontal clearance to plumbing vents or gas appliance vents or flues. When the unit is in operation, windows and doors must be left ajar to allow the humidified air to absorb the heat from within the house and then move it outdoors through the opened windows and doors. Alternately, Up-Dux are installed for this purpose. An Up-Dux is a ceiling vent that allows the air to pass through the attic and out the roof vents. When the evaporative cooler is on, air pressure automatically opens the Up-Dux dampers, and gravity closes the dampers when the cooler is off. A sliding damper (cookie sheet) or barometric damper is installed so that when the user switches from evaporative cooling to central air-conditioning or heating, the user doesn't end up air-conditioning or heating the outside.

Mini-Splits or Ductless Heat Pumps

Mini-splits are ducted or ductless systems that are very popular in Europe and Asia. Like conventional systems, they locate the compressor and condenser outside the house. Unlike these systems, the mini-split does not require an evaporator in the attic or basement. Instead of bulky ductwork, the system uses copper tubing that transports refrigerant to wall-mounted blowers (head units or cassettes) in each room. They usually heat or cool a single room. Multiple "head units" may

Reversing Valve in Heating Mode

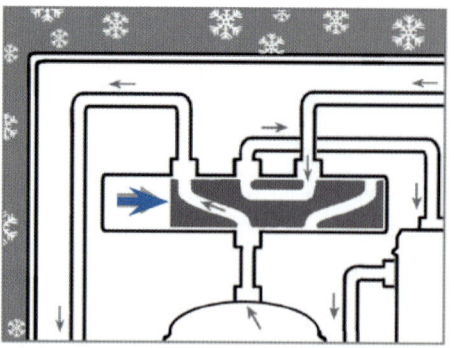

Heat pumps can be used for both heating & cooling.

A **reversing valve** determines the direction of refrigerant flow.

In **heating mode,** the outdoor coil extracts heat from the atmosphere & the indoor coil gives up that heat to the interior space.

When the outdoor temperature is below the balance point, supplementary electric strip heaters are activated in the indoor air handler.

In **cooling mode,** the system operates as in **F2**.

©2012 Code Check

be added for other rooms, but this is less common and less efficient. In winter, the system can be reversed (heating mode) to absorb heat from outdoor air and move it into the house.

6.13 THE HEAT PUMP

A heat pump is a year-round system that operates as an air conditioner in the hot season and a heating system in the cold season. It's basically a **reverse-cycle air conditioner**. When operating in its heating mode, the evaporator and the condenser switch functions. The evaporator becomes the condenser, releasing warm air for the home, and the condenser becomes the evaporator, absorbing heat from outdoors. This is accomplished by the addition of a **reversing valve** that changes the direction of the refrigerant process.

Air-to-Air Heat Pumps

An air-to-air heat pump is a reverse-cycle air-cooled air conditioner. The illustration on the next page shows its operation in the cooling mode, which is identical to a standard air conditioner. Notice the position of the reversing valve. Here, it sends the returning low-pressure gas in a loop up and then down to the compressor. High-pressure gas leaving the compressor is routed by the valve to the condenser.

In the winter, the cycle is reversed by changing the position of the reversing valve. The refrigerant actually flows in the opposite direction. Only the function of the coils changes.

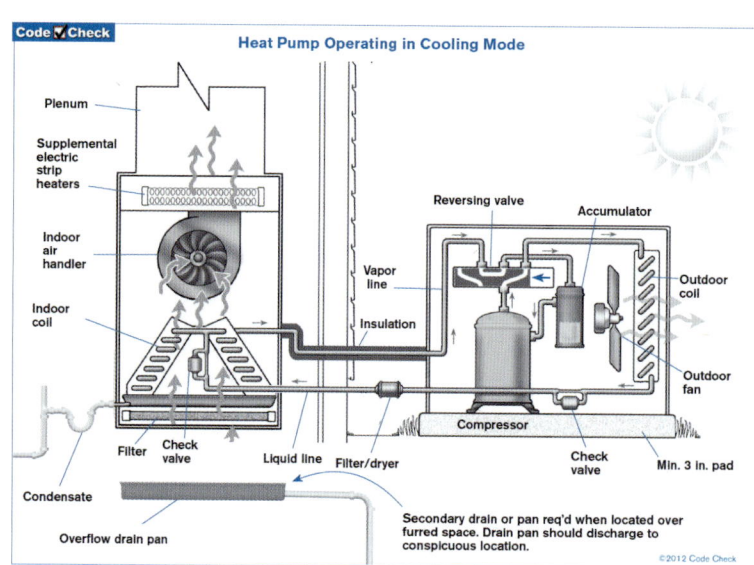

1. The high-pressure refrigerant gas leaves the **compressor** and is routed by the reversing valve to the inside coil that now acts as a condenser.

2. In the **condenser**, which is located in the furnace plenum or in a stand-alone unit or air handler, heat is removed from the pressurized gas by means of the blower that blows cool house air over it, thereby warming it. When the heat is removed from the gas, it condenses to a warm liquid that is under high pressure.

> **THE WINTER CYCLE**
>
> *In winter, the reversing valve in the air-to-air heat pump reverses the flow of refrigerant, and the indoor and outdoor coils switch functions. The evaporator becomes the condenser and vice versa.*

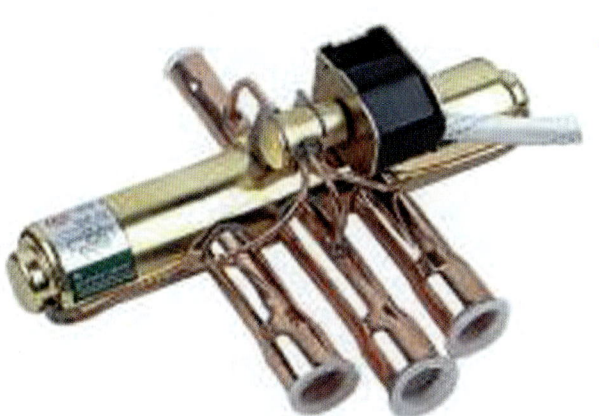

Photo #57 *This is a reversing valve. It is the device that makes it a heat pump instead of an air conditioner. You must check for the presence or absence of a reversing valve.*

3. The high-pressure liquid passes through the outside **expansion device** to reduce its pressure, causing its temperature to drop. (Note that the expansion device is the same as the one inside for cooling mode or in an air conditioner). This liquid passes through the outside coil that now acts as an evaporator.

4. The **evaporator**, located in the outdoor cabinet, absorbs heat as outside air is drawn over the coils, changing the refrigerant back into a low-pressure gas. Remember, even though it is cold outside, the air temperature is warmer than the refrigerant is and will absorb heat. Older style and old technology heat pumps were good down to about 30°F. The new inverter or variable speed compressors will provide heat down to temperatures as low as 5°F. They can actually work to lower temperatures, but their efficiency falls off rather quickly.

The air-to-air heat pump typically has the same indoor and outdoor components as the air-cooled air conditioner. This is the typical **split system** where the compressor, reversing valve, outdoor coil, and fan are in the outdoor cabinet and the indoor unit consists of the inside coil, condensate tray, and condensate line (in addition to the filter and fan if it's a stand-alone unit). You may also find the inside and outside components all in one "box" on the roof or ground. This is called a package unit or single package unit. Everything is the same, just all in one box. These types of units are very common in commercial buildings, condos, and apartments. Residentially they may be roof-mounted in warmer climates. The

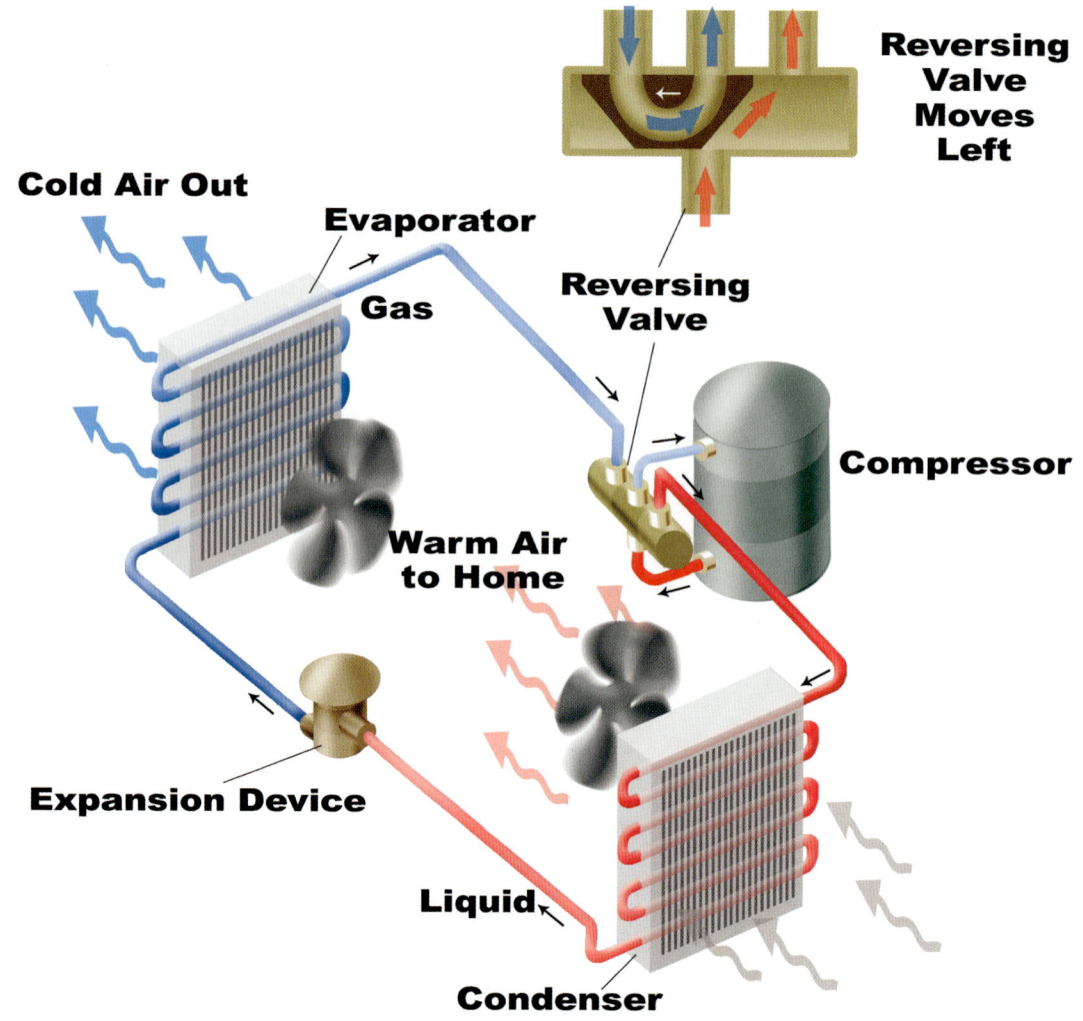

Illustration by Paddy Morrissey

> **CAUTION**
>
> *Run the heat pump in only one mode during the inspection—the cooling mode if over 70° and the heating mode if under 60°.*

home inspector may find these variations, but the function of all the components remains the same.

The heat pump has its limitations. When the outside temperature falls too low, the outdoor coil loses its ability to collect heat from the outside air and is no longer able to produce enough heat to heat the home. At a preset temperature (known as the **balance point setting**), the compressor unit automatically shuts down and the furnace (or some other means of auxiliary heating such as electric resistance heaters) takes over the job of heating the home. The balance point setting varies depending on the home's heating load and the capacity of the heat pump.

One issue with heat pumps during the heating season is that the exterior coil may frost over at temperatures below 37°F. In this situation, the heat pump briefly reverses to cooling mode (90 seconds of each hour) to defrost the exterior coil. While inspecting a heat pump in the winter, you may see a large puddle of water at the base of the unit on the pad. This water came from the frost that melted during the defrost cycle.

NOTE: There are also **ground source** and **water source** heat pumps that operate the same as water-cooled air conditioners described above. These systems use pipes or tubing buried in the earth below the frost line or located in a body of water such as a lake to collect and dissipate heat depending on the operating mode (heating or cooling). In general, more heat is available to be collected from the ground in winter months than with air-to-air units, but installation costs run much higher. A good resource is one of the largest manufacturers of ground source heat pumps, Water Furnace International, Inc. Its website explains all aspects of heat pumps and, specifically, ground source or geothermal heat pumps.

Inspecting Air-to-Air Heat Pumps

The home inspector needs to inspect the operation of the heat pump in only one of its modes. The equipment is the same as an air conditioner, and any defects to be found will become apparent in either mode—heating or cooling (with the exception of a stuck reversing valve). If the heat pump runs in one mode, it will run in the other. In fact, running the heat pump in the wrong mode in the wrong season can result in damage to the compressor.

If the heat pump is currently operating as a cooling system, then inspect it in its cooling mode. If the heat pump is operating as a heating system, then inspect it in its heating mode. The key is the outside temperature at the time of the inspection; if the temperature is **over 70°**, test it in the cooling mode, and if the temperature is **under 60°**, test it in its heating mode. Strictly speaking, if the outdoor temperature is between 60° and 70°, you could run one or the other or both modes without damaging the equipment. We recommend that you operate it in the mode in use at the time of the inspection, just to be safe.

When inspecting the heat pump in either mode, follow the instructions given earlier in this chapter for inspecting air-cooled air conditioners, both plenum and stand-alone units (pages 524–529). The inspection is basically the same because the components of the systems are similar and have similar problems. There are only a few points to be made:

- Where **snowfall** is heavy, the base of the outdoor heat pump cabinet should sit 6–8″ off the ground. This is accomplished with a stand, feet, or by wall-mounting the unit above grade. Wall mounting is more common for mini-split systems.

- Heat pumps are usually **sized** for the highest load of the house, not necessarily just the heating load. If they're sized for heating, they'll have too much cooling power or vice versa. This of course depends on what the local climate is and which load is more important—cooling in Phoenix or heating in Minneapolis.

> **OLDER HEAT PUMPS**
>
> *For any heat pump over 10–15 years old, report it as an <u>item requiring repair or replacement within the next 5 years</u> in your inspection report. The unit will be reaching the end of its useful lifetime within 5 years.*

> **Photo #58 WALL-MOUNT HEAT PUMPS**
> *It is very common to see mini-split systems mounted on wall brackets. You may also find conventional heat pumps on brackets too in areas with snow fall. The snow may block the coil and reduce efficiency, so they may be mounted above the ground on stands or platforms.*

- **Thermostats** for heat pumps and auxiliary or emergency heaters sometimes confuse homeowners. They may constantly turn on the auxiliary heaters before the heat pump normally shuts off (remember balance point setting). Modern thermostats should be wired to prevent overriding the compressor and allowing the auxiliary heat to operate when outdoor temperatures are warm enough to allow the compressor to heat the home efficiently. Older units may turn the auxiliary heat on prematurely or can be overridden by the homeowner, which is wasteful and expensive to operate.

- In heating mode, for standard heat pump systems (not the inverter type), the **temperature differential** when testing performance should be about half the outside temperature. The refrigerant can absorb about half the available heat. For example, if the outdoor temperature is 60°, the refrigerant can absorb 30°. The refrigerant itself is about 20°. As the outdoor temperature approaches 20°, there is little temperature differential and therefore less and less heat to capture.

The procedure for testing for proper operation of the heat pump in heat mode is as follows:

1. Measure the outdoor temperature just prior to testing, divide by 2, and record. Example, If it's 40° outside record 40 divided by 2 = 20°.

2. Measure the temperatures at the supply and return registers as previously described.

3. Take the difference between the supply and return temperatures and compare to the temperature in step one above.

- Again, the amount of heat a heat pump puts out at the registers in the heat mode (not inverter type systems) should be equal to 1/2 of the outside temperature. For example, the supply register temperature is 90° and the return temperature is 65° the difference is 25°. Now if the outdoor temperature was 50° the heat pump would be performing correctly as the difference of the supply and return temperatures would be equal to half of the outdoor temperature. This is just like testing the furnace or air conditioner, only we use different values. These numbers are approximate as the age and efficiency of the unit tested will indicate numbers that are slightly higher or lower than this example.

- In climates where it sometimes gets very cold, heat pumps have auxiliary or emergency heating capacity. You may even find a gas furnace combined with a heat pump. The heat pump will provide heat during the warmer portions of the winter, and the gas furnace will provide heat when it gets really cold. The system automatically switches between systems depending on the outside temperature. The inverter type heat pumps provide a steady output of heat (at registers) of about 100° down to a certain temperature depending on the manufacturer. Many new inverter type systems (Google it) can put out a 40° temperature rise down to a 0°F outdoor temperature.

- **Defrost cycle:** Moisture can build up on the outside coil during the heating cycle. In cold weather (37° and below for most units), moisture will condense into frost. A defrost cycle occurs approximately every 60 to 90 minutes and lasts approximately 30 to 90 seconds.

Reporting Your Findings

When reporting on the inspection of the heat pump, you'll fill in the sections of your report for both the air-conditioning systems (condensing coil and evaporator coil sections) and the heating system (air handler or furnace). Indicate in both sections that the type of system is a heat pump. Refer to earlier pages in this chapter for reporting on heating and cooling systems. Be sure to report your findings on the following:

- Brand name, model, and serial number of the units
- Condition of the heat pump components
- Its operation
- Any conditions that might warrant a major defect or repair

CHAPTER 7
THE INTERIOR INSPECTION

This chapter presents an overview of the inspection of the interior of the home.

7.1 INSPECTION GUIDELINES AND OVERVIEW

These are representative of the various standards of practice and state standards that govern the inspection of the interior components of the property.

Most standards of practice provide an outline of what is to be inspected and what is to be reported during the inspection of the home's interior living spaces. If licensing, registration, or certification is required in your state, you should follow the state's standards of practice. But, of course, not all the details are included in the SOP. There are many other details that will be presented in this chapter.

> **Chapter Note**
>
> *Pages 541–549 lay out the content and scope of the interior inspection. It's an overview of the inspection, including what to observe and what specific actions to take during the inspection. Study the guidelines carefully.*
>
> *For convenience, we've included the inspection of fireplaces and wood stoves in the interior inspection.*

INTERIOR SYSTEM

Observe and/or Report: The act of making a visual examination of a system or component and reporting on its condition.	• Visible indications used to render the opinion of adverse (structural) performance
	   ○ binding, out-of-square, non-latching doors
	   ○ sloping floors
	   ○ window, wall, floor, or ceiling cracks or separations
	• Installed and accessible smoke and carbon monoxide alarms
	• Orientation of hot and cold faucet controls
	• Installed mechanical drain stops (pop-ups)
	• Walls, ceilings, and floors
	• Steps, stairways, and railings
	• Countertops and installed cabinets
	• Doors and windows
	• Garage vehicle doors and garage vehicle door operators
	• Installed ovens, ranges, surface cooking appliances, microwave ovens, dishwashers, and food waste grinders by using normal operating controls to activate the primary function

Report deficiencies in:	• Deteriorated materials
	• Foundation components such as beams, joists, bridging, blocking, piers, posts, pilings, columns, sills, or subfloor
	• Exposed or damaged reinforcement
	• Crawl space drainage that is not performing
	• Evidence of water penetration
	• Performance of doors and hardware
	• The absence of or deficiencies in fire separation between the garage and the living space and between the garage and its attic
	• The absence of performing emergency escape and rescue openings in all sleeping rooms
	• A solid wood door less than 1-3/8" thick, a solid or honeycomb core steel door less than 1-3/8" thick, or a 20-minute fire-rated door between the residence and an attached garage
	• Weather stripping, gaskets, or other air barrier materials
	• The condition and performance of garage doors and hardware
	• The condition and performance of windows and components
	• Insulated windows that are obviously fogged or that display other evidence of broken seals
	• Deficiencies in glazing, weather stripping, and glazing compound in windows and doors
	• The absence of safety glass in hazardous locations
	• Spacing between intermediate balusters, spindles, or rails for steps, stairways, guards, and railings that permit passage of an object greater than 4" in diameter, except that on the open side of the staircase treads, spheres less than 4-3/8" in diameter may pass through the guard rail balusters or spindles
	• Deficiencies in steps, stairways, landings, guardrails, and handrails
	• The absence of ground-fault circuit interrupter protection in:
	○ bathroom receptacles
	○ garage receptacles
	○ outdoor receptacles
	○ crawl space receptacles
	○ unfinished basement receptacles
	○ kitchen countertop receptacles
	○ receptacles that are located within 6' of the outside edge of a sink
	○ the failure of operation of ground-fault circuit interrupter protection devices
	○ missing or damaged receptacle, switch, or junction box covers
	• Improper use of extension cords

Report deficiencies in:	• The absence of smoke detectors/alarms:
	    ○ in each sleeping room
	    ○ outside each separate sleeping area in the immediate vicinity of the sleeping rooms
	    ○ in the living space of each story of the dwelling
	• The absence of airflow at accessible supply registers
	• HVAC filters
	• Grills or registers
	• The location of return air openings
	• Commodes/water closets, fixtures, showers, tubs, and enclosures
	• Commodes/water closets that were damaged, had loose connections to the floor, were leaking, or had tank components that did not operate
	• The presence of active leaks
	• The absence of:
	    ○ fixture shut-off valves
	    ○ dielectric unions, when applicable
	    ○ backflow devices, anti-siphon devices, or air gaps at the flow end of fixtures
	• The performance of fixtures and faucets not connected to an appliance
	• The performance of water supply, as determined by viewing functional flow in two fixtures operated simultaneously
	• Fixture drain performance
	• Orientation of hot and cold faucet controls
	• Installed mechanical drain stops (pop-ups)
	• Commodes/water closets, fixtures, showers, tubs, and enclosures
	• Commodes/water closets that were damaged, had loose connections to the floor, were leaking, or had tank components that did not operate
	• Hydromassage therapy equipment
	    ○ Inoperative units
	    ○ The presence of active leaks
	    ○ Deficiencies in components and performance
	    ○ Missing and damaged components
	    ○ The absence of an opening that would allow access to equipment for inspection, service, repair, or replacement without removing permanent construction or building finish
	    ○ The absence or failure of operation of ground-fault circuit interrupter protection devices
	• Appliances:
	    ○ Dishwashers
	        • inoperative units
	        • deficiencies in performance or mounting
	        • rusted, missing, or damaged components
	        • the presence of active water leaks
	        • the absence of backflow prevention (loop or air-gap)

Report deficiencies in:	○ Food waste disposers
	   • inoperative units
	   • deficiencies in performance or mounting
	   • missing or damaged components
	   • the presence of active water leaks
	○ Range hoods and exhaust systems
	   • inoperative units
	   • deficiencies in performance or mounting
	   • missing or damaged components
	   • ducts that do not terminate outside the building if the unit is not of a recirculating type or configuration
	   • improper duct material
	○ Electric or gas ranges, cooktops, and ovens
	   • inoperative units
	   • missing or damaged components
	   • combustible material within 30" above the cooktop burners
	   • absence of an anti-tip device, if applicable
	   • gas leaks
	   • the absence of a gas shut-off valve within 6' of the appliance
	   • the absence of a gas appliance connector or one that exceeds 6' in length
	   • gas appliance connectors that are concealed within or extended through walls, floors, partitions, ceilings, or appliance housings
	   • thermostat accuracy (within 25° at a setting of 350°F)
	   • mounting and performance
	   • gas shut-off valves
	   • access to a gas shut-off valve that prohibits full operation
	   • gas appliance connector materials
	○ Microwave ovens
	   • inoperative units
	   • deficiencies in performance or mounting
	   • missing or damaged components
	○ Mechanical exhaust systems and bathroom heaters
	   • inoperative units
	   • deficiencies in performance or mounting
	   • missing or damaged components
	   • ducts that do not terminate outside the building
	   • a gas heater that is not vented to the exterior of the building unless the unit is listed as an unvented type

Report deficiencies in:	○ Garage door operators
	• inoperative units
	• deficiencies in performance or mounting
	• missing or damaged components
	• installed photoelectric sensors located more than 6" above the garage floor
	• door locks or side ropes that have not been removed or disabled
	○ Dryer exhaust systems
	• missing or damaged components
	• the absence of a dryer exhaust system when provisions are present for a dryer
	• ducts that do not terminate to the outside of the building
	• screened terminations
	• ducts that are not made of metal with a smooth interior finish

Although most standards include the inspection of fireplaces, solid wood stoves, and fuel-burning appliances as part of the heating inspection, we consider them to be part of the interior inspection. The table on page 584 reviews the guidelines regarding these items.

Virtually every space in the living area is inspected, including all rooms, closets, foyers, hallways, and stairwells. It should be noted that the home inspector will be checking plumbing fixtures and faucets, the electrical switches and receptacles, and the presence of heat and/or cooling sources in each room during the interior inspection. These items were presented in great detail in other chapters. We'll repeat some of that information in these pages as a reminder.

INSPECTING INTERIORS

- Walls, ceilings, and floors
- Interior stairways and balconies
- Counters and cabinets
- Doors and windows
- Fireplaces and wood stoves

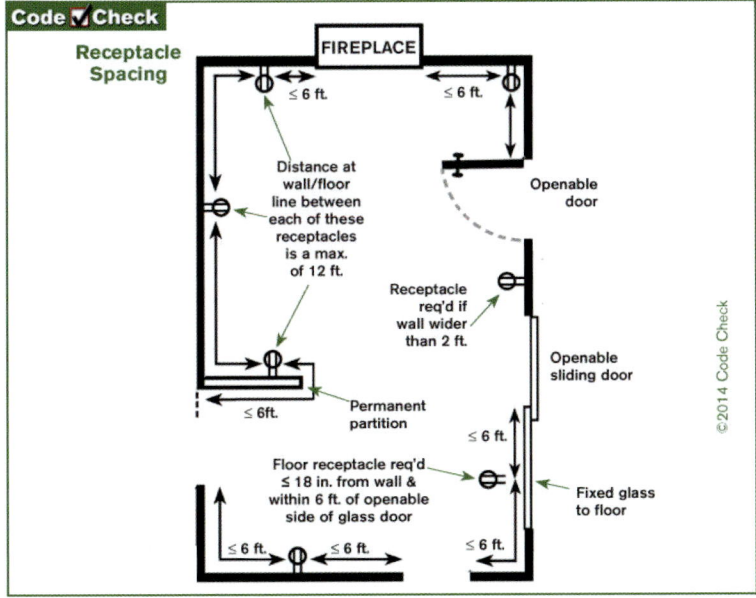

THE INTERIOR INSPECTION

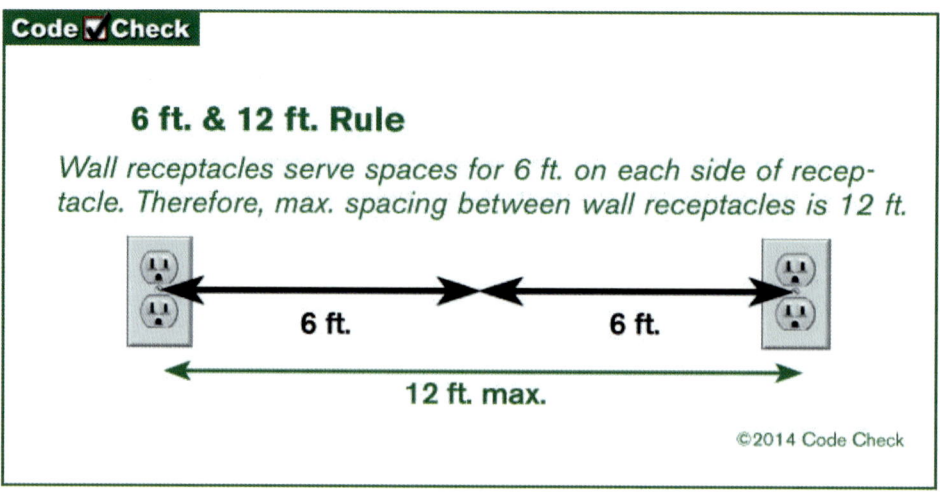

> **Section Note**
>
> *"The interior inspection gives you an excellent opportunity to establish a good relationship with your customers. Now you'll be talking about things that everyone understands, such as the condition of ceilings and windows. Take advantage of it."*

Here is an overview of the additional aspects of the interior inspection:

- **Walls, ceilings, and floors:** The home inspector examines the condition of walls and ceilings in all rooms and finished spaces, noting defects in the plaster, drywall, or other facings, and watches for cracking and evidence of leaking, which are often caused by defects in other systems, such as the structure roofing and plumbing. Floors are examined to determine if they're level, show evidence of structural problems, and show signs of deterioration. Particular attention is paid to evidence of leaking and wood rot in the kitchen and bathrooms, where plumbing is present. The inspector must watch for and report signs of **water penetration** into the building and any signs of abnormal or harmful condensation on building components.

  The home inspector also inspects **separation walls and ceilings** between a dwelling unit and an attached garage or other dwelling unit (condo, townhouse, etc.) for proper construction, wall and ceiling coverings, and safety requirements.

  Note that the inspector is **not required to observe paint, wallpaper, and other finish treatments on the interior walls, ceilings, and floors or to examine carpeting**. In general, the home inspector does not comment on decorative touches in a home. These issues are subjective and a matter of taste and play no role in the home inspection.

- **Interior stairways and balconies:** All interior steps, stairways, balconies, and railings are inspected for condition and safety hazards. The inspector examines treads and risers for proper dimensions, headroom, proper lighting at stairways, and general condition.

- **Counters and cabinets:** The kitchen of the home is thoroughly inspected, including the condition of the countertops and built-in

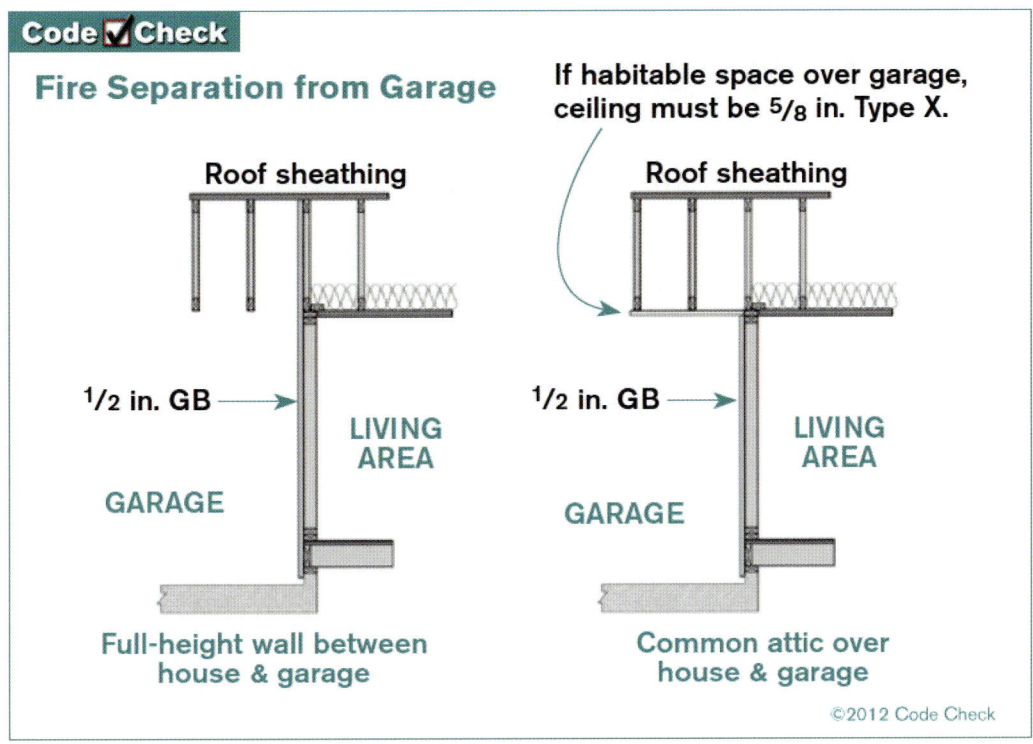

cabinets. Cabinet doors are opened to examine operation and any hidden defects that may be hiding inside, especially defects such as leaking plumbing and wood rot found underneath the sink. Drawers are pulled out and checked for smooth operation. Recent changes to leading standards of practice now require the inspector to examine some household appliances. Installed appliances, such as ovens, ranges, surface cooking appliances, microwave ovens, dishwashers, and food waste grinders must be inspected by using normal operating controls to activate their primary function. We'll outline the procedures that you should follow to test the operation of these appliances, as well as exhaust fans

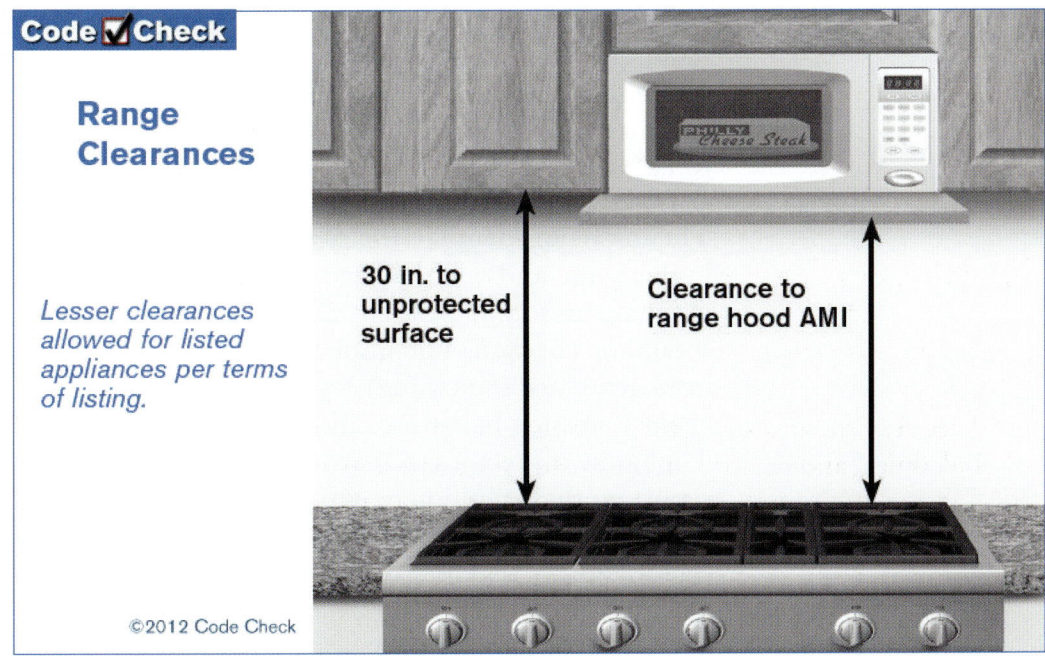

THE INTERIOR INSPECTION 547

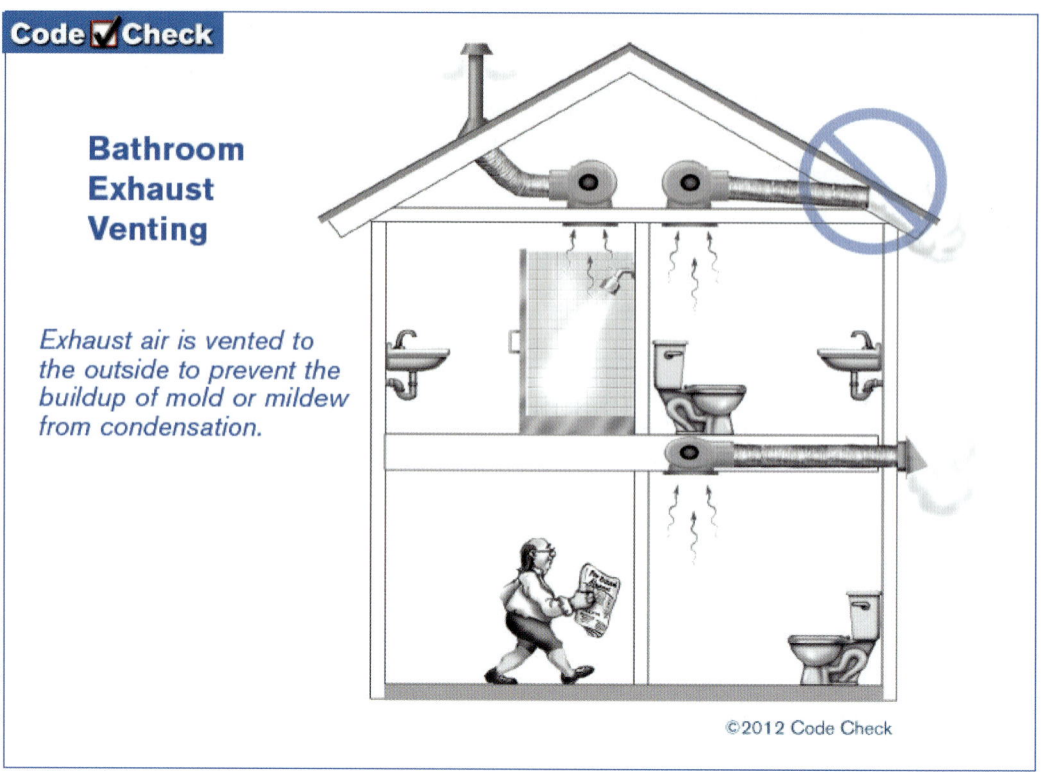

in the kitchen and bathroom. Even if your SOP doesn't require testing, these are simple tests to perform and are helpful to the customer.

> **Section Note**
>
> *"Just because the interior inspection seems so much easier than other aspects of the home inspection doesn't mean that you can slack off during it.*
>
> *First, the interior inspection can provide clues to major problems in the home's structure, in water penetration, and in other systems. You wouldn't want to miss those clues.*
>
> *Second, there can be many small defects in the interior that you don't want to miss. You'll only have to pay for them later when customers discover your oversights."*

- **Doors and windows:** The inspector operates doors in the home to find defects such as defective or missing hardware, deteriorating finishes, improper or poor installation, and water penetration around windows and doors to the exterior.

- **Separation doors** between the dwelling and the garage are examined for fire resistance and safety requirements. These requirements have changed over the years, were removed, and then were reinstated in various jurisdictions. You will have to determine what is/has been required in your market.

- The inspector identifies the type of windows present in the home and opens all accessible windows to check operation. If possible, all accessible windows should be checked. The inspector watches for leaking insulated glass (something of particular concern to clients), missing hardware, and rotted sills and sashes. The home inspector is not required to observe or report on the condition or suitability of draperies, blinds, shutters, or other window treatments. Window treatments are a matter of interior decoration and beyond the scope of the home inspection. Besides, the home inspector's tastes aren't necessarily better than anyone else's—and they could be a lot worse.

- **Fireplaces and fireplace stoves:** Although considered to be part of the heating inspection, this includes the inspection of fireplaces and wood stoves. The home inspector will identify the *type* of fireplace and give the fireplace a visual examination to check the condition of its hearth extension, mantel, firebox, and damper. The inspector is *not required to ignite or extinguish a fire*. When the **flue** can be seen with a flashlight and inspection mirror and it's accessible, the inspector examines it for rust, cracking, and creosote or soot buildup. However, this is not always possible, and most standards state that the inspector is *not required to inspect the interior of the flues that are not readily accessible*.

  Some fireplaces have a **metal insert**, which is a fireplace stove inserted in the existing masonry fireplace. These inserts may sit completely or partially in the firebox. There can be problems with the connection between a metal insert and the flue, but it's virtually impossible to inspect this connection. Therefore, guidelines state that the home inspector is *not required to observe fireplace insert flue connections*. An easy way to see if the insert flue was properly installed is to look at the top of the chimney for a liner protruding from the clay flue tile. This typically would have been installed when the insert was installed.

Most standards of practice mention one more item. They state that the home inspector does not have to inspect **recreational facilities**.

Inspection Tools

The home inspector needs a powerful rechargeable flashlight (LED or incandescent) during the interior inspection to light dark areas and to **sidelight** ceilings and walls when looking for defects. An **inspection mirror** will come in handy when inspecting the interior of fireplaces. For inspecting electrical receptacles in each room, use a **GFCI tester** and/or **neon bulb tester**, which can be purchased at any hardware store.

7.2 WALLS AND CEILINGS

Wall and ceiling facings are materials such as plaster or drywall that are applied directly to wall studs, trusses, furring strips, and ceiling joists. Wall and ceiling coverings are materials such as paint, wallpaper, and other coatings; plywood paneling; and acoustic tiles that line or finish the facings.

> **Chapter Note**
>
> *Pages 549–559 present the study and inspection of interior walls and ceilings.*

Plaster Facing

Plaster is a dry powder made largely from **gypsum** (sulfate of calcium), which forms a paste when wet. Other aggregates such as sand, asbestos, horsehair, or lime can be present in plaster to provide stability, strength, and workability.

Wet plaster is applied in layers, forming a durable wall and ceiling facing. It may be used on solid walls such as brick and concrete block or on wood-framed walls. On a framed wall, it was originally applied in three layers to a 1″ wide by 1/4″ thick wood lath or to a wire mesh nailed to the studs. A scratch coat was applied first, which formed the so-called *key* to anchor it to the lath. A second layer called the brown coat was applied and then a final layer or finish coat. By

Gypsum Lath Board

Wire Lath

Illustration by Paddy Morrissey

the 1930s, plaster began to be applied to a **gypsum board lath**, which is a premanufactured plaster sheet covered with paper, usually 16″ by 48″ in size. In the 1950s, a new type of gypsum lath was used, called "button board" as it has numerous holes in it about the size of a nickel that allow the plaster to "key" in and stay in place. The gypsum board lath was sometimes reinforced with a *wire lath* at corners and door frames. Then one or two layers of plaster were applied. It is currently used only in certain parts of the country or in high-end homes. A product called Blue Board is used, which has a special coated paper to accept the skim coat of plaster.

Plaster is first applied with a trowel to the ceiling, then the walls. The plaster facing does not extend to the floor, and the space left is normally covered with a baseboard molding. Plaster can be used on arches and other curved or irregular surfaces.

When inspecting plaster walls and ceilings, the home inspector should watch for the following defects:

- **Deteriorating plaster:** When plaster is soaked with water, its structure is altered and it becomes powdery, causing it to lose its cohesion and strength. Plaster in this condition cannot be re-hardened and must be replaced or covered over with a new facing such as drywall. The home inspector may find powdery areas with no sign of water currently present, but the cause of these areas is definitely water damage.

> ### *Definitions*
>
> A *facing* is the material applied directly to studs and joists to form walls and ceilings.
>
> *Plaster* is a powder made of gypsum and other aggregates that form a paste when wet and a durable surface when applied and dried. *Gypsum* is a common mineral that also is called sulfate of calcium.
>
> *Lath* refers to strips of wood, wire mesh, or gypsum board that are attached to studs, truss chords, and ceiling joists, forming a base for plaster to adhere to.

> ### BULGES
>
> - Sidelight ceilings and walls to locate sags and bulges.
> - You can confirm plaster detachment by tapping and hearing a dull thud.
> - You can confirm lath detachment by pushing and sensing movement.
> - *Be gentle*. Don't bring down the plaster.

Deterioration of plaster walls and ceilings can be caused by the condition of the plaster itself. If the original application of the plaster was faulty (from improper additives, extreme temperatures, poor drying, or too much reworking), the finish coat can shrink or lose its adhesion. Extended cold temperatures in an unoccupied house and dampness can cause the lime in the brown coat to disintegrate, resulting in the finish coat cracking, pulling away, and falling off.

Always inspect plaster walls for water stains, old or fresh, and investigate the source of those stains. Stains if they are active or fresh are currently wet as verified by a moisture meter. Water may be entering the home through the roof, siding, or windows due to a plumbing leak or a leak from an air conditioner condensate line, or it may be

For Beginning Inspectors

A home inspector needs a good, powerful flashlight for his or her work. It might be a surprise that you'll use a flashlight in the daytime to light ceilings and walls, but you will.

Get out your flashlight now and sidelight some ceilings and walls in your own home. Lighting the surfaces from the side will cast a shadow behind any protruding or sagging areas that you'll miss with the naked eye. Try it.

Photo #1 WATER STAINS

Water stains from a bathroom above. Always note stains, patches, or mismatched paint.

the result of excessive condensation. Be suspicious of patched areas where repairs have been made.

- **Loose, bulging, or sagging areas:** Use your flashlight when inspecting plaster walls and ceilings, even in the daytime. Shine a flashlight parallel to the walls and ceilings to create shadows that will reveal any irregularities or deformations.

A bulge or sag can indicate that the plaster has become completely detached from the lath (lost its key or anchor). This can happen when the plaster deteriorates or when expansion and contraction of the lath forces it loose. If you tap a bulge with the end of a screwdriver and hear a dull thud rather than a crisp sound, it's an indication that the plaster has become detached. Don't tap too hard on a ceiling because detached plaster is weak and can fall.

A bulge or sag can also indicate **detachment of the lath itself**. This can be caused by rusted and pulled lath nails. As nails pull out, the weight carried by the remaining nails can become too much to bear. Over time, a large area can become loose and collapse. Lath detachment can be determined by pushing against the bulge, trying to see if there is a space behind the plaster and therefore is not bonded any more. Don't push at the plaster too vigorously.

> **INSPECTING PLASTER**
>
> - Deterioration and water damage
> - Loose, bulging, or sagging areas
> - Cracks

> **Section Note**
>
> *For information on cracks in the framing and foundation, see Chapter 1, on the inspection of the structure.*

- **Cracks:** Be sure to note any cracks you find in plaster walls and ceilings, even if you can't correctly diagnose their causes (remember that plaster was last installed in about 1960). Plaster can show cracks due to some fault in the plaster, normal stress the framing exerts on the plaster, or abnormal movement in the structure of the house. In general, if narrow cracks exist without separation, the cause is not structural. But cracks wider than 1/4" or those with displacement at each side are probably due to structural problems.

Displacement is a condition where the sides of the crack are not flush (that is, when one side is offset from the other).

A fine **network of cracks** in the plaster is normally a sign that the original plaster application was faulty, as noted previously, where the finish coat can shrink and crack. There may be cracks in the plaster at the **intersection of different backing materials** such as brick and lath due to their different expansion and contraction rates. Plaster can also crack from the **expansion and contraction of the framework** when there are wide temperature swings or there is excessive humidity in the home. In this case, plaster over gypsum board may show cracks at the perimeter of the boards. A solution to these types of nonthreatening cracks is to cover them with flexible patching materials or wall coverings instead of filling them.

Cracks that signal **structural problems** should be further investigated to try to determine their source. The following are some examples:

— Cracks on interior walls can be caused by insufficient support to the wall and a resulting sag to the wall. Interior walls that are parallel to the supporting floor structure should be carried on double or triple joists.

— Angled wall cracks can be an indication of settlement of the framing or the foundation.

— Ceiling and wall cracks around open stairways can indicate normal stress at these points. More serious cracking with displacement indicates lack of proper structural support in the stairway framing.

— Second-floor ceilings can crack when stressed by a knee wall in the attic.

— **Truss uplift** is when the bottom chord of a roof truss bows upward during the cold months and returns to its position during the warmer months. Truss uplift can carry the ceiling with it, causing cracking to appear at the junction of the ceiling and walls. A solution to this condition is to conceal the crack with a crown molding; it is only a cosmetic issue.

— Aging ceiling joists can sag enough to cause the ceiling plaster to crack from the stress. These cracks can run the length of the house along each side of the main girder in the middle of the joist span.

— Tiny cracks from the corners of exterior doors and windows are an indication of expansion and contraction of the lintel or header.

Section Note

"One of my inspectors came across an old plaster dining room ceiling that had a considerable sag to it. The sag was greatest at the center of the room, but the entire ceiling was sloped toward the center. It was the worst case of detachment he'd ever seen.

He explained that the whole thing was in danger of collapsing and that he was not going to touch it.

Then he issued a stern safety warning in the report. When someone came in later to examine it, the ceiling came down in one great crash.

I'm glad the inspector used his judgment and refused to touch the ceiling. Both he and his customer could have been badly injured. You've got to be careful."

Drywall

Drywall, which is basically the same material as plaster, came into use in the 1960s and is still used today. It's also called plasterboard, wallboard, and Sheetrock. Drywall comes in large 1/4"– 5/8" thick sheets 4' wide and up to 14' long and is made of a gypsum mixture covered with a treated paper. The edges are slightly recessed so that joints can be finished. New paperless drywall is available that is covered with a variety of materials, such as fiberglass. Mold growth is reduced on these panels compared to those covered with paper.

Drywall was formerly nailed to the framing, although these days it is usually screwed **and** glued to the wall studs, ceiling joists, and furring strips. **Joint cement**, which is a plaster-like paste, and a tape made of paper or fiberglass is applied to provide a level, seamless surface. Special techniques are used to finish the edges as shown in the illustration to the right.

Definitions

Drywall, which is a premanufactured plaster sheet covered with paper, is used as a wall and ceiling facing.

Joint cement is a plaster-like paste used to seal the joints between sheets of drywall.

THE INTERIOR INSPECTION

Photo #2 DRYWALL

This is typical of drywall installation. Seams are taped and mudded. Nail or screw heads are mudded. The green material in the bathroom is called Greenboard. It is for damp locations only and should not be used in areas like a tub surround or shower.

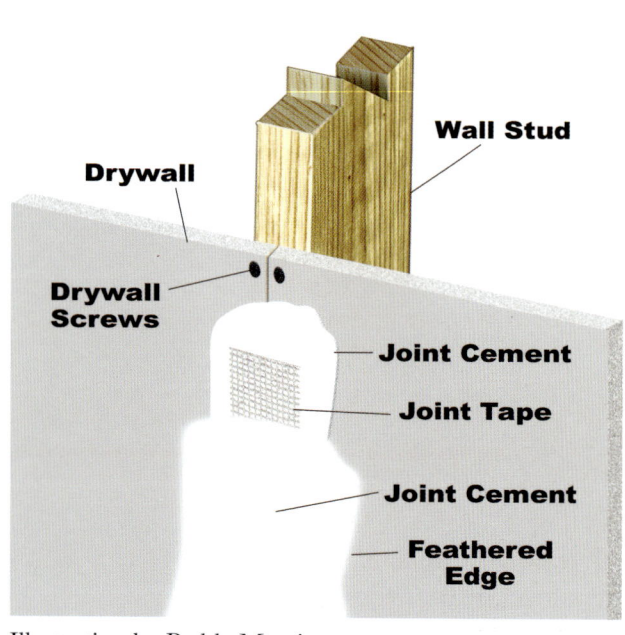

Illustration by Paddy Morrissey

Drywall is also used for **separation walls and ceilings** between the garage and the living area, as required for fire safety. In some areas, a single sheet of 1/2" drywall is allowed, although other areas require fire-rated 5/8" drywall to be used. The inspector is only required to ensure that an intact wall separation is present.

The home inspector should watch for the following problems with drywall:

- **Deterioration:** Drywall can deteriorate due to water damage just as plaster does. Try to determine the source of the water stains. Sections of deteriorating drywall can be replaced. Tape at the seams of drywall can become loose if the drywall is exposed to water damage, if the drywall is in an unconditioned space, if there is too much dampness, or if the original installation was poorly done.

- **Nail pops:** These are bulges in the drywall where the nails are backing out of the studs, ceiling joists, or truss chords. Nail pops are usually due to the expansion and contraction or shrinkage of the framing. But they can also indicate inadequate bracing in the frame. In extreme cases, the joint cement and tape can pop off and expose the nails. Assuming there are no structural problems, nails can be reset to solve the problem. If the drywall is too heavy, **dimples** can form around concealed nails. If you push up against the drywall near a dimpled area and you sense a little movement, it can indicate that nailing during the installation of the drywall could have weakened it in this area. It may also mean that too few nails were used.

> **INSPECTING DRYWALL**
> - Deterioration and water damage
> - Nail pops
> - Loose or sagging areas
> - Cracks

- **Loose or sagging areas:** If the drywall on a ceiling is less than 1/2" thick, it can sag, especially on trusses with 2-foot centers. So can damp drywall, which becomes heavier as it picks up moisture, or poorly nailed drywall.

Photo #3 DRYWALL DETERIORATION DUE TO WATER DAMAGE

More staining due to leakage from the bathroom above. Always start at the top of the home and work your way down to understand what was above the stain(s). Was it the roof, bathroom, air conditioner, etc.?

> **For Beginning Inspectors**
>
> *If you have an opportunity to visit construction sites where homes are being built, arrange to stop by during the installation of drywall. Being able to see how joints are finished can be an aid in determining what can go wrong with them later.*

> **FACINGS**
>
> - Plaster
> - Drywall
> - Wood planking and paneling
> - Plywood
> - Fabricated boards and panels

- **Cracks:** Joint cracks in a drywall facing can be the result of expansion and contraction of the framing or from structural movement. The home inspector should distinguish between joint cracks and visible joint seams, which may just be the result of poor workmanship when the drywall was installed. Drywall sheets can crack from structural stresses. It's not uncommon to see the small cracks from the corners of exterior doors and windows from a shrinking header.

NOTE: Drywall may have been installed over a plaster wall or ceiling to cover the deteriorating plaster. Drywall must be firmly attached through the plaster to wall studs or ceiling joists, not to the plaster or lath itself. Otherwise, the old plaster can further detach itself and cause the drywall to sag under its weight.

Other Facings

Other materials used for wall and ceiling facings are listed here:

- **Wood planks and paneling:** Facings may be tongue and groove planking, which is also called matchboard. This was common in older homes and may still be seen on closet walls and even some ceilings. Today, you might see planking in family rooms. Solid wood paneling or raised panels may be used in high-quality homes.

- **Plywood:** Thicker plywood in veneered finishes or unfinished can be used as a facing fastened directly to the wall studs without a backing. Plywood as thin as 1/16"–1/8" without a backing would be too soft and wavy to be used as a facing but may be nailed or glued over an existing plaster or drywall base. If you find a plywood-covered wall, push against it to determine if there is anything behind it.

- **Fabricated boards and panels:** Wood, chips, and fibers can be used to manufacture various types of boards and panels that can be used as facings for walls and ceilings. Masonite is an example. In some cases, the joints between boards or panels are covered with a wooden lath, usually on walls but on ceilings too to complete the pattern.

A Word about Structure

When inspecting interior walls and ceilings, the home inspector's main concern should always be to detect any sign of **structural problems** hiding behind the surfaces. Facings can show stress that indicates settlement or movement of the structure or problems with the framing

> **STRUCTURE**
>
> *Pay attention to walls and ceilings for signs of structural problems.*
>
> *Investigate further and report your findings.*

such as inadequate or damaged supporting members. Investigate further. And always report these conditions or suspect conditions if you can't determine the exact cause.

Wall and Ceiling Coverings

As noted earlier, wall and ceiling **coverings** are materials such as paint, wallpaper, and other coatings, plywood, and acoustic tiles that line or finish the facings. The home inspector is not required to inspect the finishes on interior walls and ceilings, but it doesn't hurt to be able to point out particular problems with these finishes and to have helpful information for the customer. The home inspector should pay attention to any defects noted on the surface of walls and ceilings and distinguish between problems with the coverings themselves and other findings that should be reported, such as water damage, deteriorating plaster, and so on.

Some wall and ceiling coverings are listed here:

> **LEAD PAINT**
>
> There _could be_ lead paint in homes built before 1978. There _most likely_ is lead paint in homes built before 1950.

> **Definition**
>
> _Kalsomine_ is a mixture of glue, pigment, and water that was once used as a finish on plaster ceilings.

- **Paint:** Plaster, drywall, and plywood should be cleaned and primed before painting (or applying wallpaper). The primer fills pores, seals off constituents in the facing that may harm the paint, and provides a surface for good adhesion.

  Try not to mistake problems in a plaster surface with problems with the paint. **Peeling or flaking paint** usually indicates that no primer was applied. An old plaster ceiling may be peeling because of a hidden layer of **kalsomine**. This was a mixture of glue, water, and pigment that was applied to ceilings and lasted until the glue deteriorated. Kalsomine should have been washed off with warm water and sponges before painting. To repair this condition, the ceiling needs to be scraped back to the powdery kalsomine layer and then washed before repainting.

  Sometimes, chemicals in the plaster can damage the paint, causing a localized or spotty discoloring. Other stains that bleed into new paint usually indicate that the facing was not properly cleaned or that a previous water stain bled through. Using an oil-based paint over wallpaper can dissolve the ink in the wallpaper, which bleeds through into the paint. Using a water-based paint over wallpaper can loosen the glue.

  SAFETY CONCERN: Customers may ask about **lead in paint**. The home inspector is not qualified or required to test for the presence of lead, but this information may prove helpful if customers ask. Lead was used for pigmentation and as a drying agent in oil-based paints until the early 1950s. It was then used only as a

> **COVERINGS**
>
> - Paint
> - Wallpaper
> - Stains, varnish, shellac, and wax
> - Decorative plywood
> - Texturing
> - Ceiling tiles

drying agent in both flat and gloss oil-based paints until 1978, when the standard was changed to allow no more than 0.06% lead by weight in residential paint. Lead was generally not used in latex paints. So there *may be* leaded paint in homes built before 1978. And there *most likely is* leaded paint in homes built before 1950.

Lead affects the central nervous system by slowing development and is especially dangerous to children under the age of 6. Lead can be ingested or breathed in as paint dust. Most commonly, young children get paint dust on their fingers by touching surfaces where the paint is peeling, then putting their fingers in their mouths. Depending on applicable federal regulations, lead paint may be encapsulated with fresh paint, polyurethane, vinyl wallpaper, and so on. In some areas, more stringent state or local regulations apply. Lead paint should be removed by trained professionals for safety reasons and to avoid contaminating the entire house.

- **Wallpaper:** The home inspector should sidelight wallpapered walls to see if the paper is hiding defects in the walls underneath. Uneven areas should be tapped to test for detachment. Keep an eye out for loose wallpaper that can indicate water damage or failing wallpaper glue. Such areas should be pointed out to your customer because repairs would be needed. Point out wallpaper that's been painted over, as it is very difficult and somewhat expensive to remove.

- **Stains, varnish, shellac, and wax:** Natural wood planking or paneling is normally finished with a coating that doesn't hide the wood. An indoor wood stain is a colorant designed to bring out the grain or to even out the color, but it's not a finish and should be protected by varnish, shellac, or wax. Varnish is oil based and can't be easily removed after cure. Shellac is a natural product dissolved in alcohol and can be washed off with alcohol or diluted ammonia. Wax can be applied to protect a stain or over varnish or shellac. Wax must be removed before a new finish is applied.

- **Plywood:** Thin decorative plywood may be installed over the wall facing as a covering. Push against the plywood to see if it has a proper backing. A plywood covering can be sidelighted to spot areas that are loose.

- **Texturing:** Walls and ceilings may have a textured finish achieved by adding sand or other agents to conventional finishes. Texturing of the finish coat of plaster may be done manually with a trowel. Some popcorn ceilings installed through the early 1970s may contain asbestos. **Stippling** (also called **knock-down**) is a texturing process where a stipple finish is sprayed over drywall, then troweled flat.

> **Section Note**
>
> *"Don't overlook ceilings in closets. One of my inspectors noticed that a drywall ceiling in a downstairs closet had been covered with wood. That's almost certainly a sign that there's been leaking from above. It's a common way for homeowners to cover up the damage to the ceiling.*
>
> *When the inspector found an upstairs bathroom above the closet, he investigated closely and found a rotted floor beneath the toilet. There had been extensive water damage."*

- **Acoustic tiles:** Acoustic tiles, popular as a ceiling finish since the 1950s, are typically made of fiberboard, but can be made of fiberglass, cork, or mineral particles. They may be plastic coated. Earlier tiles were a foot square. These tiles can be nailed or glued to strapping, installed over a plaster ceiling, or hung in a grid of metal moldings. The acoustic tiles in drop ceilings or suspended ceilings are larger. Note that installing a hung ceiling lowers the ceiling by 2″–3″.

Trim

Most rooms have interior trim, including **baseboards**, at the intersection of walls and floors, and **casings** around windows and doors. Baseboards can be made of wood, plastic, and even tile or marble. There may be **crown moldings** at the intersection of walls and ceilings. The home inspector should inspect all the trim and note any missing, loose, cracked, broken, or water-stained pieces.

7.3 FLOORS

This section presents information on the construction and inspection of floors in the home.

> **Chapter Note**
>
> *Pages 559–567 present procedures for inspecting the flooring and floor finishes in the home.*

Construction

Most homes have a two-layer floor consisting of a subfloor and a finish floor above it. The subfloor may be softwood tongue and groove planking, laid either perpendicular or diagonally to the joists. Today, most homes use **5/8′–3/4′ thick plywood, oriented strand board (OSB), or particle board sheets** for subflooring. These sheets are laid perpendicular or diagonally to the joists. If the subfloor is laid perpendicular, the hardwood finish floor is installed parallel to the joists. If the subfloor is on the diagonal, the finish floor is laid either perpendicular or parallel to the joists.

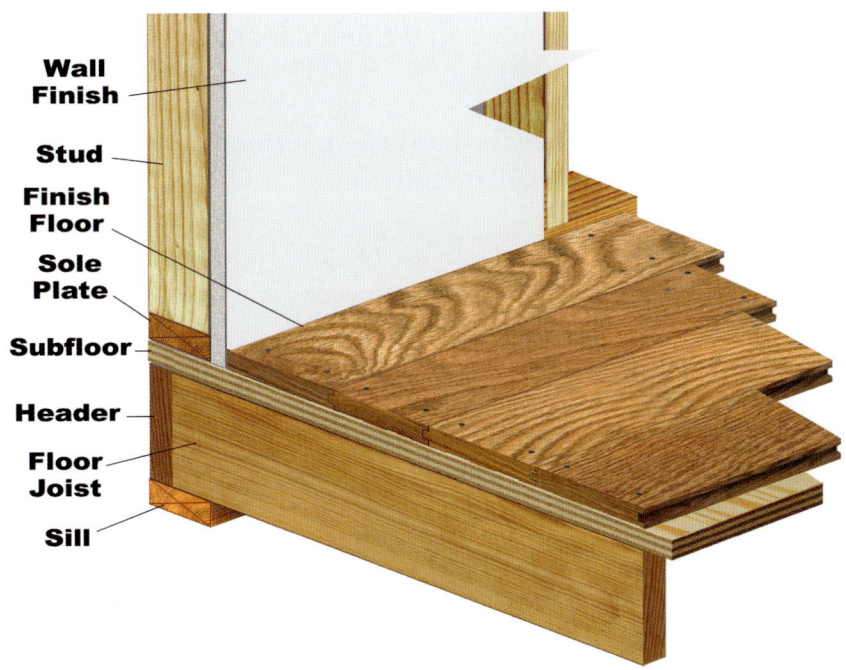

Illustration by Paddy Morrissey

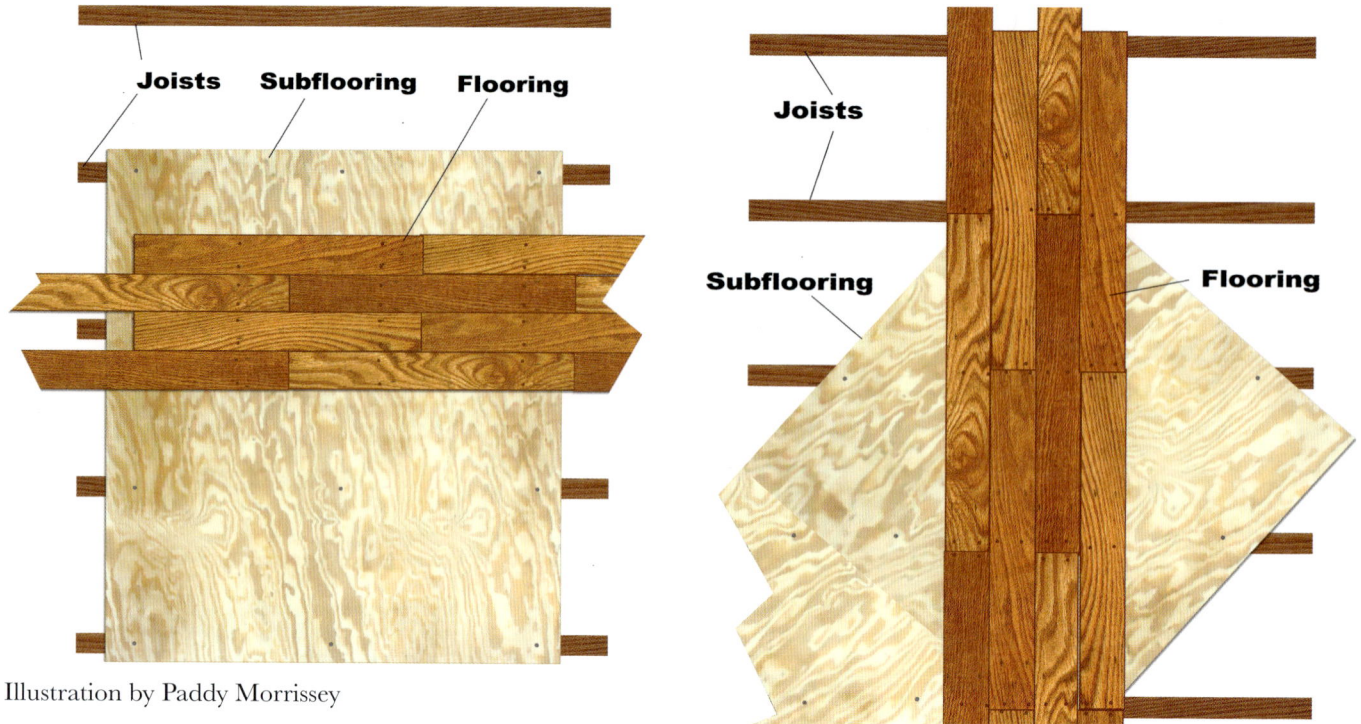

Illustration by Paddy Morrissey

The meeting edges of the plywood or particle board sheets are nailed to the joists. A structural adhesive is usually applied to the joists to add strength to the connection. Finish flooring is applied over the plywood. The home inspector should inspect two-layer flooring from above and below where possible. In some cases, older hardwood floors were put in without a subfloor. You'll want to check from below first before you assume that a subfloor is present.

In slab-on-grade construction, the finish flooring is laid over a poured concrete slab that is generally 3.5"–4" thick for a floating slab and much thicker for a monolithic or post-tensioned slab. Because the slab is not visible, the home inspector must learn to detect slab settlement, cracking, shifting, and water penetration through the slab by the evidence shown in the finish flooring.

Wood Finish Flooring

Wood finish flooring in a home may be hardwood, softwood, engineered wood, or laminate and may be left exposed or covered over.

- **Hardwood flooring** is usually made of oak, although other dense woods such as beech, birch, hard pine, maple, pecan, and walnut are used.

- In a **tongue and groove floor** laid over a subfloor, the hardwood boards are normally 3/8"–3/4" thick and 1-3/4"–3" wide, but may be thicker and wider in higher-quality homes. The boards are laid over the subflooring as shown in the drawings on page 556. In tongue and groove flooring, the top edge of each board is slightly wider than the lower edge. When boards are toe-nailed in place, the top edges fit tight with no nails showing and the lower edges have a small gap.

Where hardwood flooring is laid without a subfloor, boards should be at least 1/2" thick and 2-1/2" wide to provide the needed strength and support. A hardwood floor may be made of **planks**, which are simply boards more than 3″ wide.

Another style of hardwood flooring is **parquet**. This type of floor consists of 6″ squares, each made up of six 1″ strips of wood. The squares are laid at right angles to each other. Originally, these strips were cut and laid on the job, but modern parquet squares are preassembled and glued to a plywood backing. The squares are then nailed or glued to the subfloor.

- **Softwood floors** are commonly pine, but may be fir or cedar. When softwood is used as a finish flooring, 1″ thick by 4″ wide tongue and groove boards are used.

> **WOOD FLOORS**
> - Hardwood tongue and groove and planks
> - Hardwood parquet
> - Softwood tongue and groove and planks
> - Softwood subfloor exposed

Softwood in 1 × 4 or 1 × 6 planks was often used as the **subfloor** under hardwood floors. These planks were spaced with a slight gap and nailed through directly to the joists. Softwood tongue and groove planks were also used as a subfloor under linoleum and other kitchen floor coverings. In this case, the top surface was smooth. Sometimes, an underlayment of 1/4″ plywood was added between the softwood subfloor and the linoleum or other covering.

Several years ago, it became fashionable to expose the original pine subfloor in the kitchen. Because the surface is soft and it's hard to keep spills out of the joints, this is not an ideal kitchen floor. Homeowners usually use polyurethane finishes to seal the joints.

Buckling floor boards are caused by dampness and humidity, which cause the wood to swell across the grain and buckle upward if there is no room to expand sideways. When moisture gets trapped between the flooring and the subflooring, the finish floor can be lifted as each layer expands, warps, and buckles.

A concrete slab may have hardwood flooring glued over it. Pieces of flooring can pop up if the glue is broken down by moisture in the concrete.

- **Engineered wood flooring** is made from layers of wood glued together with the grain running in different directions. It is available in three-ply (layers) and five-ply. Depending on the veneer's (top layer) thickness, it can be sanded and refinished. Engineered wood floors are more dimensionally stable compared with solid wood, meaning that they expand and contract less in response to changes in temperature and humidity. Therefore, they are especially suited for use in kitchens, bathrooms, basements, and utility rooms.

- **Wood laminate flooring** is made with layers that are fused together during a lamination process of heat and pressure. As a result, this flooring product has enhanced strength and stability that give it a highly realistic look of hardwood flooring. Wood laminate flooring is comprised of the following layers:

- **Top Layer:** Finished to protect from fading, abrasions, wear, and stains.
- **Visual Layer:** Highly detailed and realistic photograph to give the natural look and texture of real wood.
- **Core Layer:** Made from a high-density fiberboard that provides strength and stability.
- **Bottom Layer:** Uses a melamine backer to provide stability.

- **Synthetic plastic laminates** are not wood at all. They consist of a fiberboard center sandwiched between plastic laminate layers. The "wood grain" look comes from a photograph laminated to the surface.

- **Floating floors** may be laminate or engineered wood. An underlayment of thin sheets of cork or foam is first laid over the subfloor. The strips of wood are made with tongue and groove edges that fit together snugly. Adhesive may be applied to the edges of the flooring, or they may snap together, but the floor is not glued to the underlayment. The tongue and groove planks may be attached to each other but not to the floor. Some systems interlock and require no adhesive at all. Pergo is one of the most widely known brands, but there are many others.

Sanding of wood floors can get rid of stains and mechanical damage, but there are limitations to the amount of sanding that can be done to hardwood and softwood floors. Although a 3/4" hardwood floor can be sanded several times, a 3/8" floor can be sanded only once. A softwood floor should only be sanded once and not to less than 5/8" in thickness when there is no subfloor.

The home inspector should pay attention to the condition of the finish flooring. Water can do extensive damage to wood floors, causing boards and parquet squares to **warp, twist, and cup**. Water stains on wood floors may indicate **wood rot**.

Flooring Tiles

Flooring tiles made of natural materials such as stone, marble, or fired clay can be laid in mortar over a stiff subfloor or a concrete slab. Different kinds of tiles include the following:

- **Ceramic or porcelain tiles** are hard-fired clay tiles that can be glazed or unglazed. They come in various sizes from 1"–24" squares and are from 1/4"–1/2" thick. They're commonly used in kitchens, bathrooms, and entryways where water resistance is important, but may be found anywhere in the house. The most common problems with these floors are cracked tiles due to flexible subflooring and grout deterioration that allows water to seep through the finish floor and damage the wood subfloor underneath.

> **Section Note**
>
> "I've seen some exposed softwood subfloors in kitchens where the polyurethane finish needs to be reapplied. The finish doesn't last forever, and joints open up again, collecting whatever drops and spills on the floor. I usually warn customers about this so that another coat can be applied to prevent water damage."

> **Definition**
>
> <u>Terrazzo</u> is a mix of marble chips and concrete that is laid in squares bordered by lead beading. It is ground and polished for a smooth and durable floor covering.

The tiles are laid in a mortar base or adhesive over a concrete floor or a stronger-than-normal subfloor. The tiles are spaced so that grout can be added between the tiles. A water-resistant material or building paper should be laid over the subfloor before mortar is added.

- **Slate, stone, and marble tiles** are, of course, natural materials cut to size for use in the home. Their installation is similar to that of ceramic tiles. Because of the weight of the tiles, a concern is that the underlying flooring system is not strong enough to support the tiles without sagging or is not rigid enough to eliminate the flex in the floor. Common problems are cracked tiles, deteriorating grout, and staining on marble and other types of stone.

- **Terrazzo** is a material made of marble chips set in concrete. The mix is laid in squares bordered by lead beading, ground, and then polished for a smooth finish. These types of floors are often found in public buildings such as schools and hospitals, less often in homes.

Floor Coverings

A variety of other floor coverings are available for installation over a subfloor or even over a finished hardwood floor if the homeowner wishes.

- **Carpeting** is most often laid over a subfloor or a layer of unfinished plywood, but it can be laid over hardwood floors if the homeowner wishes, which is typical of older homes. The home inspector is not required to report on the condition or quality of the carpeting, and customers should be told that. However, you should watch for signs of any problems with the floor underneath and signs of water damage. If carpets have ridges, tears, or wrinkles that cause a trip hazard, you can suggest that the carpet be stretched tight or repaired by a carpet professional.

> **COVERINGS**
> - Carpeting
> - Linoleum sheets
> - Vinyl sheets and tiles
> - Rubber and asphalt

Don't make any assumptions about what's under the carpeting. Even if you find hardwood floors in a bedroom closet, don't assume that the bedroom is hiding hardwood floors under the carpeting. If the customer wants to know, have the owner stipulate in writing what's under the carpeting or request that he or she lift the carpeting to find out, but don't guess.

- **Resilient floor coverings** include a range of tiles and sheet goods that can be laid as a floor finish.

Linoleum is a sheet product made of organic materials and drying oils laid on a cloth backing. Rubber tiles and tiles made from asphalt with inorganic fillers were the first water-resistant products made for bathrooms. They were later replaced by plastic floor coverings such as solid vinyl, vinyl-asbestos, and vinyl-faced sheets and tiles.

These coverings are laid over the subfloor and typically an underlayment of 1/4" plywood to create a flat, smooth surface. Plastic sheets and tiles are laid with adhesives that hold them to the underlayment. Some tiles are available with a peel-and-stick adhesive already applied. Resilient floor coverings may experience the following problems:

- **Cracking and tearing** in sheets can occur from stress when the underlayment or subfloor is not tightly fastened and the floor is free to move.

- **Irregularities** in the surface of sheets can occur if the surface underneath isn't smooth. Any gaps or joints in the underlayment can become visible in the covering. When there's water damage in the subfloor and underlayment, warping and delamination can cause the covering to lift. Any ridges or humps in the covering will eventually wear out from foot traffic.

- **Snapping and crackling sounds** that come from the sheet as you walk over it is a sign that the adhesive is defective.

- **Loose sheets and tiles** can occur when moisture penetrates to the adhesive layer, causing the adhesive to lose its bond.

> **For Beginning Inspectors**
>
> *From now on, wherever you go, think about the floors you're walking on. Identify the type of finish or covering, notice its condition, think about the construction underneath, and notice any signs of structural problems.*

Concrete Floors

Concrete floors are generally found in garages and basements, as well as in slab-on-grade construction. They are usually covered with another finish flooring material, but you may see concrete as a finish floor throughout the house. The concrete is often stained, stamped, or engraved using the same techniques seen in some driveways and patios. Interior concrete floors are prone to the same problems as any concrete, including cracking.

Inspecting Floors

The first aspect of floor inspection is to determine whether the condition of the floors indicates any **structural problems** in the home. Be sure to inspect floors from above and below, where possible, to investigate the cause of structural problems. The following conditions may be seen:

- **Sloping floors:** An unlevel floor has a continuous slope in one direction. This can be caused by foundation settlement pulling the floor lower at the outer edges of the house. If floors slope inward toward partitions, the condition can be caused when the interior walls shrink more than the outer wood framing and pull the floors down with them. In floating slab-on-grade construction, where the slab is not attached to or resting on the foundation, a settling slab can pull interior walls down with it.

Floors should be level. If they're not, it should be noted in your inspection report. Some home inspectors carry a marble or ball bearing with them to roll on the floor or use a four foot level to confirm a slope. If you find sloping floors, investigate the cause, but don't guess if you're not sure.

- **Uneven floors:** An uneven floor has highs and lows in it, but not a continuous slope. A **hollow** can be caused by the failure of a single joist. When a hollow is present in the floor along an interior wall, it may be that the partition is built between the joists. If the hollow appears on either side of a doorway, it's an indication of poor support for the studs on either side of the opening.

  A **ridge** in an upstairs floor may be caused by a downstairs partition built parallel to a joist. There may be a **bulge** in the floor over a support column, indicating that the column is moving up or the house is moving down. There could be a warped or broken joist or an improperly fastened girder under the bulge. Another cause of a bulge can be from an overloaded cantilevered joist, where the joist's interior end is being forced upward.

- **Sagging floors:** This is where there is a low area in the middle of a room. This may be due to poor support in the floor structure. When there are heavy loads such as waterbeds, refrigerators, or pianos, the supporting structures may not be able to hold the load and floors can sag. More support is needed. If an upstairs floor is sagging, check the ceiling below. If it's sagging too, the problem should be looked at by a qualified professional.

- **Deflecting floors:** Floors can have too much upward and downward movement. **Bouncy floors** are usually due to weakness in the joists or a lack of proper bridging. **Soft or springy floors** can indicate a problem between the subfloor and joists—poor support of the subfloor by the joists because of poor nailing or loss of connection.

  Spongy floors can be caused by warped subflooring. Improper spanning also causes the above problems. Sometimes, concrete slabs are covered by a raised wood floor, commonly called a sleeper, which may be covered with carpeting or resilient flooring or tile. If the floor is spongy or soft when you walk on it, it could be caused by rotted wood in the floor framing where water has seeped between the slab and the raised floor. It could also be the result of insect damage, or the wood framing may not be properly spanned.

- **Noisy floors: Squeaks** in flooring are caused by a poor connection between the subfloor and the joists. Weight on the floor pushes the subfloor down to the joist, and the resulting squeak is caused by nails sliding in and

> **INSPECTING FLOORS FOR STRUCTURAL PROBLEMS**
>
> - Sloping floors
> - Uneven floors
> - Sagging floors
> - Deflecting floors
> - Noisy floors
> - Open joints at walls

out. You may notice **drumming and rattling** sounds from the floor as you walk across it. These sounds are associated with the joists, not the subfloor. Low-frequency sounds are caused by weak, flexible floor joists. Higher frequencies are the result of stiffness in the joists.

- **Slab settlement and cracking:** In slab-on-grade construction, watch for open joints between the floor and the walls. If the concrete slab settles, it can sink without pulling down walls with it and leave open spaces between the floor and the interior walls. The walls should be shimmed so that they have the proper support and continue to provide support for structures above them. If the slab settles and there is no damage to the foundation, this condition is not a serious structural problem as long as the walls are supported. However, if there are also signs of foundation cracking and settlement, a structural engineer should be called to evaluate the situation.

> **Section Note**
>
> *"Homeowners wanting to sell their homes are notoriously clever about covering up defects. One of my inspectors found a new built-in window seat in a room. Everything seemed fine.*
>
> *However, the inspection from underneath revealed a totally rotted subfloor in that area. The owner was trying to hide the problem.*
>
> *Don't be misled by new carpeting in bathrooms either. I can't tell you how many times I've seen that trick. A good home inspector will never miss rotted flooring around tubs, showers, and toilets."*

Inspect the surface of floors over slabs, especially at the edges of the floor, for any indication of **cracks** in the slab. The slab can shrink during cure and pull away from the foundation, leaving cracking along the floor edge. Watch for water damage from moisture coming up through cracks in the slab. Slab cracks may not be easy to notice through the finish flooring. You may be able to feel them underfoot as you walk on the floor, and you may be able to see evidence of them if you sidelight the floor with a flashlight.

The second aspect of the floor inspection is to inspect the **condition of the finish flooring or floor covering**. First, identify the type of floor covering. Inspect from below, if possible, to determine the type of subfloor. Generally, the floor construction as seen from the basement or crawl space is the same throughout the house. Determine if the flooring is put in over a concrete slab. Then watch for the following defects:

- **Water damage and wood rot:** Always look at flooring for water stains or softness, indicating water damage and wood rot to the underlayment and subfloor. And always report it when you find it. Be sure to check for wood rot around plumbing in the kitchen and the bathrooms. Don't depend on your eyes alone. Test areas by pushing at them with your foot or get down and press against them with your hands. Another area that should be checked for wood rot is on exterior walls that have an **outside deck or balcony**. When the floor joists extend through the exterior wall to support the deck or balcony (called cantilevering), water can seep in. Check along the outer edge of the floor in this area for wood rot.

- **Trip hazards:** Point out trip hazards to customers, including loose floor boards and tiles, torn or raised sheet floor covering, and loose metal or plastic moldings used as transition pieces between different floor finishes. Trip hazards are easy to notice, repairs are generally easy, and customers appreciate having them brought to their attention. Carpeting can also be a trip hazard if it is torn, loose, or wrinkled.

NOTE: When eyeing the carpeting, be sure to note if carpeting is blocking a heat register or return air register. With hot water convectors or electric baseboard heaters, note if carpeting is blocking airflow.

> **INSPECTING FLOOR COVERINGS**
>
> - Water damage and wood rot
> - Trip hazards
> - Loose, warped, or buckled wood flooring
> - Loose, torn, or cracked sheet covering
> - Loose, damaged, or missing tiles

- **Loose, warped, or buckled wood flooring:** Warping, twisting, cupping, or buckling of floor boards are the result of moisture—leakage onto the floor or the subfloor, or dampness and high humidity—and from being laid too tightly. Try to determine the cause.

- **Loose, torn, or cracked sheet covering:** Inspect linoleum and vinyl sheet goods for any irregularities. Report if you find these defects in resilient sheet coverings. (See page 564.)

- **Loose, damaged, or missing tiles:** Walk over tile floors, both natural and manmade, feeling for any tiles that are loose. With grouted tile floors, inspect the grout and report if the grout is broken or missing or is otherwise poorly installed, which could allow water to get through to the subfloor.

7.4 WINDOWS AND DOORS

During the exterior inspection, windows and exterior doors are inspected from the outside. Now the home inspector is required to inspect and operate interior doors and windows from the inside.

> *Chapter Note*
>
> *Pages 567–578 present information about the inspection of interior windows and doors.*

Window Components

The components showing on the interior of the window are the following:

- **The sash** (upper and lower in the traditional single- or double-hung window) is the framework that holds the glass or other glazing material. The top and bottom pieces of the sash are called **rails**; the sides are called **stiles**. The sash is the portion of the window that moves up or down, slides side to side, swings out or in, or remains stationary depending on the type of window. The sash can be made of wood, aluminum, steel, vinyl, or fiberglass.

- **Glazing** refers to the glass, plastic, acrylic, or polycarbonate within the sash. Each layer of glass or other material is called a pane. Glazing maybe a **single pane, double pane, or even triple pane**. Glazing is held in the sash by putty, glazing compound, or rubber gaskets.

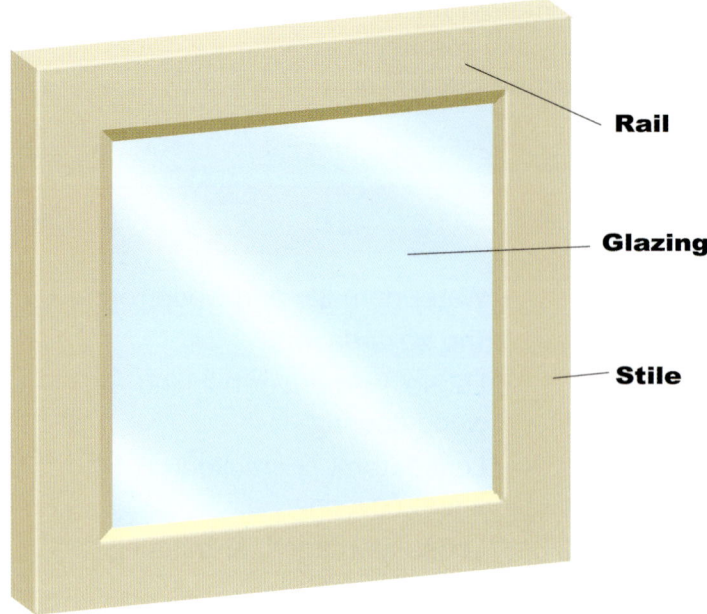

Illustration by Paddy Morrissey

- **Double panes** are windows consisting of two panes of glass sealed with an air space between them. In higher-end windows, it may have Argon gas, which has only recently become popular in areas other than the cold northern areas. The multiple pane or insulated windows are commonly called insulated glass units (IGU) or Thermopanes™ (which is a trade name).

- **Triple panes** may be three layers of glass or two outer layers of glass with a plastic layer between them. There are a number of ratings that come with new windows. The overall efficiency of a window is called the U-value or U-factor. This is an efficiency determined by the National Fenestration Rating Council (NFRC) so consumers can compare various brands of windows apples to apples. The other common rating that is very important in sunny climates is the Solar Heat Gain Coefficient (SHGC). This has to do with the coatings on the glass that reflects heat and UV rays, from the sun in the south and from the interior in cold climates. The coatings are known as low-e. For both the U-value and the SHGC the lower the number the better. When multiple-pane windows are cracked or the seal is broken between layers of glass, air and moisture leak into the layers. Leaking multiple panes will discolor and should be reported. This is, however, typically just a cosmetic issue as the loss of efficiency is minimal with the exception of Argon filled windows. Most SOPs do not require commenting on failed seals. (Even though not required by most SOPs, many homeowners want to know this due to the cost of replacement.)

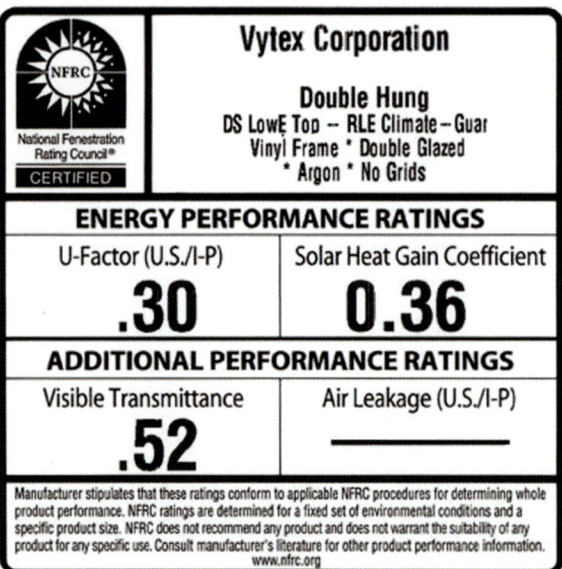

Photo #4 *NFRC label showing the window efficiency.*

568   Chapter 7

- **Muntins** are a grid of crosspieces of wood, metal, plastic, or lead that hold small panes of glass in a multiple-light window. Snap-in muntins made of wood or plastic can be applied over a larger pane to imitate true muntins.

  Glazing can be **transparent** (clear) or **translucent** (obscured, opaque, or cloudy) by design. **Safety glazing** includes tempered or heat-treated glass, which shatters into small, smooth-edged cubes upon impact. Laminated glass, **often found in hurricane-prone areas** (also with or without safety glazing), has a plastic inner layer between panes to hold broken pieces of glass when the pane cracks

Illustration by Paddy Morrissey

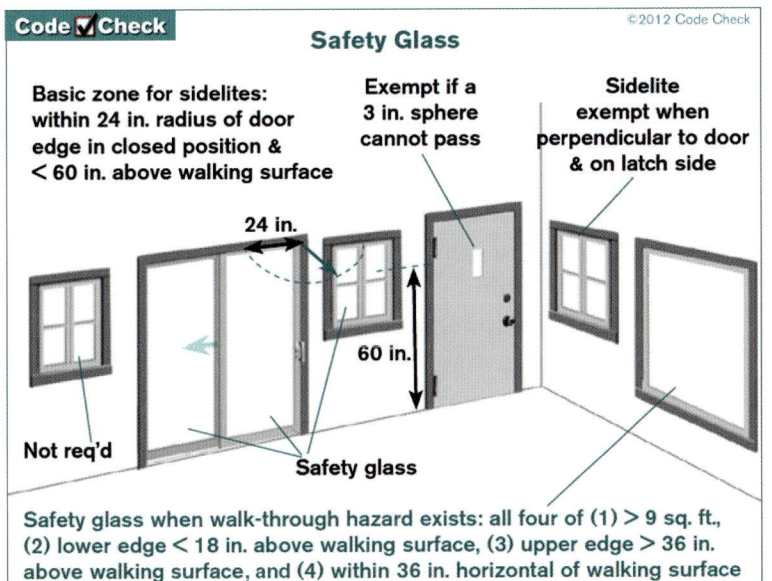

Definitions

The <u>window frame</u>, which surrounds and holds the sash, is made up of a top piece called the <u>head</u>, side pieces called <u>jambs</u>, and a bottom piece or <u>sill</u>. The <u>window casing</u> covers the edge of the frame where it meets the wall.

  or shatters, much like a car windshield. Some windows have a wire mesh embedded between the lights for security reasons, but this does not protect against injury if the glass is broken. As a matter of fact wire mesh glass is considered dangerous as someone who went through a wired glass window would be severely cut by the wire mesh. This should be noted as a safety hazard.

- The window frame surrounds the sash and holds it in place. The frame can be made of wood, aluminum, steel, vinyl, or fiberglass. The top piece of frame is called the **head**, the sides of the frame are called the **jambs**, and the bottom piece is called the **sill**. The sill is shaped to be a seat for the sash and to provide weather resistance. The sill can be shallow

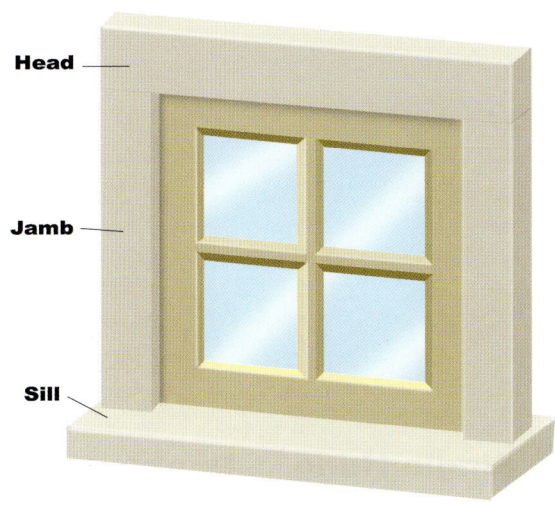

The Frame

Illustration by Paddy Morrissey

THE INTERIOR INSPECTION

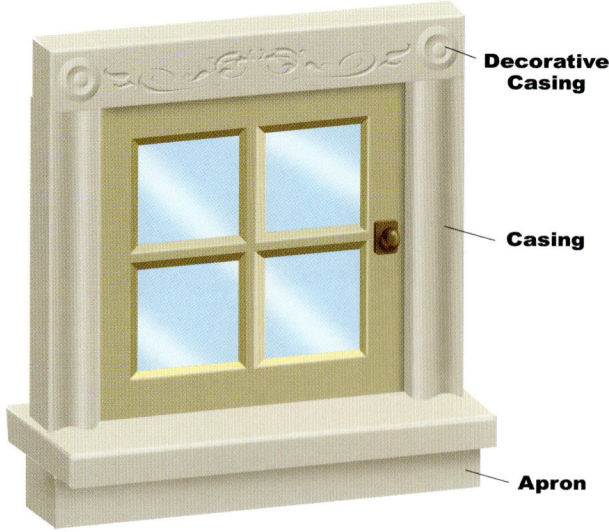

Interior Casing

Illustration by Paddy Morrissey

WINDOW TYPES

- Single and double hung
- Casement
- Awning and hopper
- Fixed-pane picture windows
- Multiple pane
- Jalousie

Single Hung   Double Hung

Illustration by Paddy Morrissey

or deep like the traditional window sill on which you can set a flowerpot and can extend beyond the casings on each side. Not all styles of windows have an extending sill as part of their makeup.

- **The casing**, or outermost element of the window, covers the edge of the window frame where it meets the wall. Actually, there may or may not be interior casing around the frame. When casings are present, they vary greatly, sometimes providing decorative touches to the window.

Types of Windows

The home inspector should identify the type of windows present in the home. Many styles are available, as shown here:

- **Single- and double-hung windows:** This type of window has two sashes. The top sash is on the exterior; the bottom sash is on the interior. In the single-hung window, the bottom sash moves up and down in the frame. The double-hung window allows both sashes to move, although you'll often find that the top sash is painted or nailed/screwed in place. Early windows were held open (up) in the frame with a counterweight system. A sash cord at each side of the sash goes over a pulley at the top. A counterweight at the end of the cord inside the wall cavity holds the window in place. Newer types use springs, spiral balances, or coiled steel tape concealed in the side of the sash to serve the same purpose.

Double-hung windows may be made of wood, metal, vinyl, or a combination. Glazing may be single, double, or triple panes held in place with putty, glazing compound, rubber, or plastic.

These windows should be opened fully during the inspection to test the operation of the sash counterbalance mechanism. The sash cord or other type of mechanism may be broken or missing. The sashes may not move at all or may move too freely in their frame. They may not be held in place once opened. When the window is closed, check that the lock holding the sashes in position is operating and holding the sashes tightly to prevent air and moisture infiltration and for security.

Some newer double-hung windows can be pivoted at the bottom so that the sashes can be rotated inward to clean the outside. This should be demonstrated during the inspection. Be very careful as it is easy to break the plastic clip in the mechanism.

Older double-hung windows often came with storms and screens permanently mounted in two- or three-channel metal or plastic frames. If the system is two-channel, the sash must be removed to change the storm and screen panels. In a three-channel system, also called a triple track or self-storing, the screen can be pushed up out of the way. When inspecting these types of double-hung windows look at the sills. The lower edge of the storm frame should be caulked to the sill, but should have drain or weep holes to allow rainwater to run out. Often, the weep holes are blocked and you'll see rotted sills and evidence that excess water has leaked into the house.

- **Casement:** The casement window is hinged at one side and opens inward or outward, but generally outward. It opens by means of an operating crank usually located at the bottom of the window.

Locks or latches on the side opposite the hinges pull the sash tight when closed. The windows can be made of wood, metal, vinyl, or a combination, and can have single, double, or triple panes. Outward-opening casement windows have provisions for a screen to be installed on the interior of the window frame.

When inspecting casement windows, open the latches and turn the crank to fully open the window. The crank mechanism can be worn, or the gears may be stripped. Hinges can become corroded. Note if the sash is warped and whether it can close and lock tightly against air and water infiltration. The old metal-framed casement windows can rack and warp, making it difficult to close them tightly. Problems should be pointed out to the customer and reported.

> **Section Note**
>
> *Your community may have local codes requiring safety glazing of a particular type or in a certain location in the home. You should be aware of these local regulations.*

Casement

Illustration by Paddy Morrissey

Awning

Hopper

Illustration by Paddy Morrissey

Slider

Illustration by Paddy Morrissey

> **Section Note**
>
> *"Don't be surprised to find casement windows with cranks that don't work well. One of my inspectors came across one where the gears were entirely stripped. The owner opened the window by pushing it out and closed it by going outside and forcing it closed. Some people can adapt to anything."*

> **FOR SAFETY**
>
> - Fire safety: There should be one window per room with at least a 20" wide opening and a 24" tall opening and the sill no more than 44" above the floor.
> - Stair safety: Windows on stairs should be at least 36" from the floor. If the windows are lower than that, they should have guards or grills to stop someone from falling through.

- **Awning windows and hoppers:** These are also hinged windows. The awning window is hinged at the top and opens outward. The hopper window, often found in basements, is hinged at the bottom and typically opens inward. Both may have a crank operator as a means of opening them. They are in other ways similar to the casement window and have the same types of problems. Inspection procedures are similar to the casement window.

- **Horizontal sliders:** In a slider window, the sash moves horizontally in the frame. The slider can have sashes of wood, metal, fiberglass, or vinyl with bearings or rollers in the sash or frame for easy operation. Glazing can be single, double, or triple pane. Sliders should be tested for smooth operation.

  Some sliders are of very low quality. They are simply a pane of glass with a handle or knob attached to the surface of the glass and move in a metal or wood track. They are almost never tight and consequently allow air and water in, making them useless for any climate.

- **Fixed-pane windows:** This is a window that doesn't open and close and consists of a large fixed light of glass. The term for this type of window is a picture window. Remember, inspect insulated glass windows for a lost seal between the panes. A leaking thermal-pane window may have condensation between the panes or permanent clouding or discoloration. Don't ever miss reporting a leaking seal. *Keep in mind that a leaking dual-pane window seal is cosmetic in nature. The energy efficiency lost due to a failed seal has been proven to be negligible. The issue is the expense. People don't want fogged or cloudy windows, and glass is expensive.* Picture windows with a single pane of glass often have damage on the sill from condensation on the inside surface of the window that flows down onto the sill.

- **Jalousie:** This window contains narrow strips of glass in a device that allows the strips to move together, lifting outward from the bottom. When inspecting the jalousie window, the inspector should test its operation, paying attention to whether the glass strips close tightly again. Any damage to the strips should be noted. Be careful to observe that the small metal tabs holding the glass in their frames are present before you relieve tension on the assembly. The pieces of glass can fall out as they may have been held in place only by the pressure of the crank mechanism.

Jalousie

Illustration by Paddy Morrissey

Inspecting Windows

During the interior inspection, most standards require the home inspector to do the following:

- **Look at all accessible** of windows during the inspection.

- **Operate all accessible** of windows during the inspection.

- Report on the **condition** of windows when problems exist.

We recommend that you test and/or operate all accessible windows in the home. Watch for and report the following window defects found during the interior inspection:

- **Rotted or damaged sashes, frames, and casings:** Examine each window for any damage to the sashes, frames, and casings. Note if any of the framing is out of square or plumb (visually). Windows pulled out of square can be an indication of some movement in the wall, especially if it's a load-bearing wall. Sashes can come apart at the joints. This often happens when people lift the sash by the top rail rather than pull it up with the hardware or recess at the bottom. The same is true for horizontal sliders where people pull rather than push the sash closed. Watch for wood rot, rust, or corrosion on all components. Steel casement windows can rust out, and the sashes can rack. Check any **muntins** present for damage and looseness.

> **INSPECTING WINDOWS**
>
> - Rotted or damaged sashes, frames, and casings
> - Rotted or damaged sills
> - Deteriorating paint or finishes (inside and outside)
> - Cracked, broken, or leaking glazing
> - Loose, damaged, or missing putty
> - Faulty operation
> - Missing or damaged storm and/or screen

THE INTERIOR INSPECTION 573

> **Section Note**
>
> *The inspection of windows from the exterior is covered in Chapter 2. Only the inside components are inspected during the interior inspection.*

> **BE CAREFUL**
>
> *With double-hung windows, always hold the top sash as you lift up on the bottom sash. It can be painful to have the top sash drop and catch your fingers or, worse, crack the glass.*

- **Rotted or damaged sills:** The sill is probably the most vulnerable part of the framing, and wooden sills often have wood rot. A properly installed window has a sill that tilts toward the exterior for drainage. With self-storing windows, be sure to check the sill carefully. The drain holes should not be caulked over or clogged. Check the wall below the window for water damage to see if water has been leaking in over the sill.

- **Deteriorating paint or finish:** Examine all wooden window components to see if new paint or refinishing is necessary. Windows take a lot of wear and tear, and homeowners don't always pay enough attention to deteriorating paint and other finishes. Note if windows that should open have been painted shut. This may be a safety issue, especially in bedrooms.

- **Cracked, broken, or leaking glazing:** Identify the type of glazing present, if possible. Determine whether the glazing is single pane, double pane, triple pane, and so on. Inspect the glazing for any cracks, breaks, and damage such as BB holes. Don't miss any fogged multi-pane windows, which can be detected by condensation or discoloration between the panes. A lost seal can't easily be fixed, so replacement often is the only option if the view is seriously impaired.

- **Loose, damaged, or missing gaskets or seals:** Always check around the window for the condition of putty and glazing compound, gaskets, and seals. Take time with multiple-pane windows to check around each pane for muntins that are loose.

- **Faulty operation:** The home inspector is not required to operate every window, only a representative number (one per room) in the house. However, be sure to operate any windows that you suspect don't work properly. A good inspector will operate all accessible windows, not just one per room.

  With double-hung windows, look for broken/missing sash cords; inoperable locks; loose, broken, or missing hardware; windows that are painted shut, that are screwed or nailed shut, that stick, that won't hold their position; and so on. With casement awning and hopper windows, report corroded cranks, missing crank handles, and cranks that don't work or are stripped.

- **Missing storm and/or screen:** In self-storing storm and screen systems, check that the storm and screen are present. The storm could have been broken and never replaced. For casement windows, note the presence of a storm or screen on the interior (depending on the season),

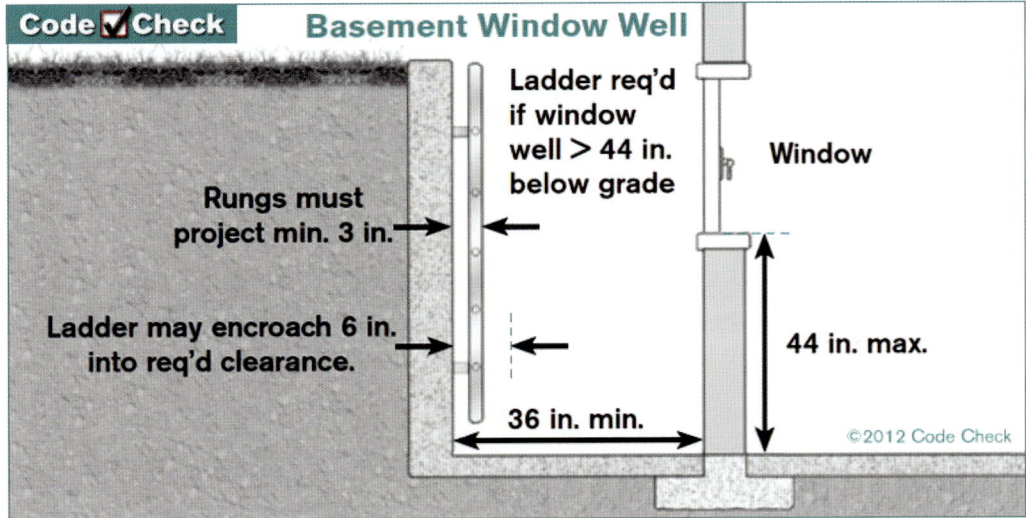

and for the portion not installed, ask the owner if it's available. Note its condition if possible.

- **Egress windows and window wells:** If a room is used as a bedroom, fire safety codes usually require that it have a means of egress (exit) directly outside. In practice, this usually means a window. The window must be large enough and the sill low enough to allow a person to climb out or more accurately, a fireman to crawl in in case of emergency. The sill must be no higher than 44"

Section Note

"One of my inspectors was mystified when he noticed a window sill tilted in toward the room. Then he realized that the window had been installed backward. Obviously, that was reported."

Photo #5 WINDOW WELLS

Egress window wells for basement bedrooms. This is a window with a ladder inside of the corrugated metal retaining walls for escape or egress as shown in the diagram above.

THE INTERIOR INSPECTION 575

above the floor. In addition, the opening must be at least 20″ wide and 24″ tall. The opening may be no less than 5.0 square feet for windows located at grade and no less than 5.7 square feet for windows above grade (second story and higher). There are also specific requirements for basements and bedrooms in basements (see diagram on previous page).

DOORS

- Flush solid
- Flush hollow core
- Paneled
- Louvered
- Pocket
- Bifold

Interior Doors

Doors inside the home can be of several types, such as flush, louvered, or paneled or with glass lights. They may be hinged, folding, or sliding and made of wood, metal, plastic, or composition.

- **Flush doors** are built of veneers glued to a solid or hollow core. The **hollow core door** is made of a honeycomb or patterned cardboard core that is framed in solid rails along the top and bottom and solid stiles along the sides. A piece of wood is located in the knob area for boring out to fit the knob and latch. The construction is covered with a thin outer ply of paint or finish grade veneer.

These doors are light in weight and not very good as sound barriers. Hollow core doors are fairly easily damaged, and it isn't uncommon to see holes in them from overactive kids. The doors can delaminate if the glue doesn't hold.

Hollow core doors are the most common type used inside homes today and are suitable for interior use except for the fire-rated door required between the living area and the garage (which should be 1-3/8″ solid core wood, truly fire-rated, or steel).

- **Panel doors** are made of solid components. The rails and stiles (top, bottom, and sides) are grooved in such a way as to hold an inset raised or flush panel. In wood panel doors, the different shrinking rates can cause the panels to crack along the grain. There are plastic molded panel doors that look like real wood. They may also contain glass as in French doors.

- **Louvered doors** have wood, plastic, or cloth slats in a frame. They may be used as room dividers or in closets and bathrooms.

- **Pocket doors** are designed to slide into the walls. Door hardware is concealed in the edge that is exposed at the wall opening.

- **Bifold doors** are designed with hinges in the middle to allow one section of the door to be folded back on the other before the door is swung to the side.

- **Closet doors** can be flush, paneled, or louvered. There may be a single hinged door, a set of hinged pairs, bifold, or doors suspended on tracks so they slide past one another.

In general, interior doors should have the proper **clearances** for a threshold or carpeting and floor coverings. If there isn't a return air opening in each room, the clearance below doors should be at least 3/4″ to allow for airflow.

Interior doors may or may not have **locking capability**. If they do, check that the lock mechanism works. Knob locks generally have a hole in the outer knob so that a probe can be inserted to unlock the mechanism. Some knob locks are keyed for additional privacy and security. Keyed knob locks usually have a push button or another means of disabling the lock function. By the way, try the knobs before you enter a room. You don't want to close a door that has a missing knob on the inside and then locks on you so that you can't get out of the room. Verify that the doorknobs are installed in the correct orientation and lock to the interior of the room, not the hallway. You may find a number of bedrooms that have the knobs reversed, which is a safety issue that must be noted.

> **SAFETY CONCERN**
>
> *The passage door between the living area and garage should be <u>fire-rated</u> and be a 1-3/8″ solid core wood or steel clad door.*

Inspecting Doors

The home inspector should visually examine all interior doors and operate a representative number of them, including opening and closing and checking hardware. A good home inspector will operate all of the interior doors. Watch for the following conditions when inspecting each door:

> **Section Note**
>
> *Exterior doors, including entryway doors and garage doors, are inspected during the exterior inspection. These inspection procedures will not be repeated here.*

- **Poor operation:** Open the doors and check their operation. Doors should hang in their frames with a clearance of about 1/8″ on the top and sides with 3/4″ at the bottom. Something is wrong if they rub, stick, don't close, hang out of square, or are not level. Try to determine what is going on. The door may have swelled from a high moisture content during the summer months, hinges can be loose, or there may be a structural problem in the framing or wall. Stop moldings are nailed on the inside of the frame to hold hinged doors in position when they are closed. If the stop moldings are not close enough, the doors can rattle. Check to see if a doorstop is present behind the door. If not, note if the wall is damaged where the doorknob strikes it. Be sure to recommend stops if they're not present and damage is visible.

  Operate closet doors too. If closet doors are on a track, check that the small floor guides are in place so that one door doesn't swing in and out from its track and bang against or damage the other.

- **Cracked, broken, or damaged components:** Examine the casings, frame, and door itself for condition. Check casings and frame to see if they are out of square, are loose, have loose joints, or are damaged. Inspect the door on both sides for defects such as warping, delaminating plies, holes or dents, cracked panels, scratches, and so on. These deficiencies should be reported.

> **INSPECTING DOORS**
>
> - Poor operation
> - Cracked, broken, or damaged components
> - Loose, broken, or missing hardware

The home inspector may find a hollow core door that's been cut down to size to fit a smaller frame. Often when this is done, the top or bottom rail may be cut away (because they're not very wide to begin with). This is not an acceptable method because the strength of the door is seriously impaired. If overcut, it will typically wobble when it is moved. Instead, a door should be ordered to the size of the frame.

If an interior door has glazing or requires safety glass, be sure to inspect the condition of the glazing and report any cracks or breaks. Check the condition of the putty holding the lights in place. With interior French doors with muntins, observe whether any muntins are loose, cracked, or broken.

- **Loose, broken, or missing hardware:** If you haven't checked the hardware and weather stripping on the entryway doors, do so now. Work the locks, including the dead bolts, to be sure everything is functioning properly. For paired entryway doors with top and bottom slide bolts, check that the bolts extend far enough up into the head and down into the threshold. Test knob locks on interior doors and see if the latch extends into the strike plate. Check that hinges, strike plate, and knob assembly are screwed tight and that all parts are present. Hinge pins are often missing. A note about safety is to report the presence of double-keyed dead bolts at entry doors. These are doors that require a key to unlock the door from the inside too. This may pose a safety hazard in an emergency if the key is not present. Be sure to note this in your report.

> **Section Note**
>
> *"Always look behind doors. One of my inspectors didn't, and he missed an electrical subpanel behind a bedroom door."*

ABOUT REPORTING: Instructions for using your inspection report to report your findings of window and door defects will be presented later in this chapter. See page 594 for reporting general window findings and pages 594–613 for reporting room-by-room inspection of windows and doors.

7.5 STAIRS AND BALCONIES

Included in the interior inspection is the examination of all steps, stairways, and balconies in the home.

Inspecting Stairways

The home inspector should inspect all interior steps and stairways in the home. Over the years, codes have changed across the country regarding handrail requirements, dimensions of risers and treads, and other aspects of stairways. You should check with your local building requirements for information.

> **GENERAL RULE**
>
> *Stairs should be uniform. There should be no more than a 3/8" variation in riser height for the entire staircase, not step to step.*
>
> *Check your local requirements.*

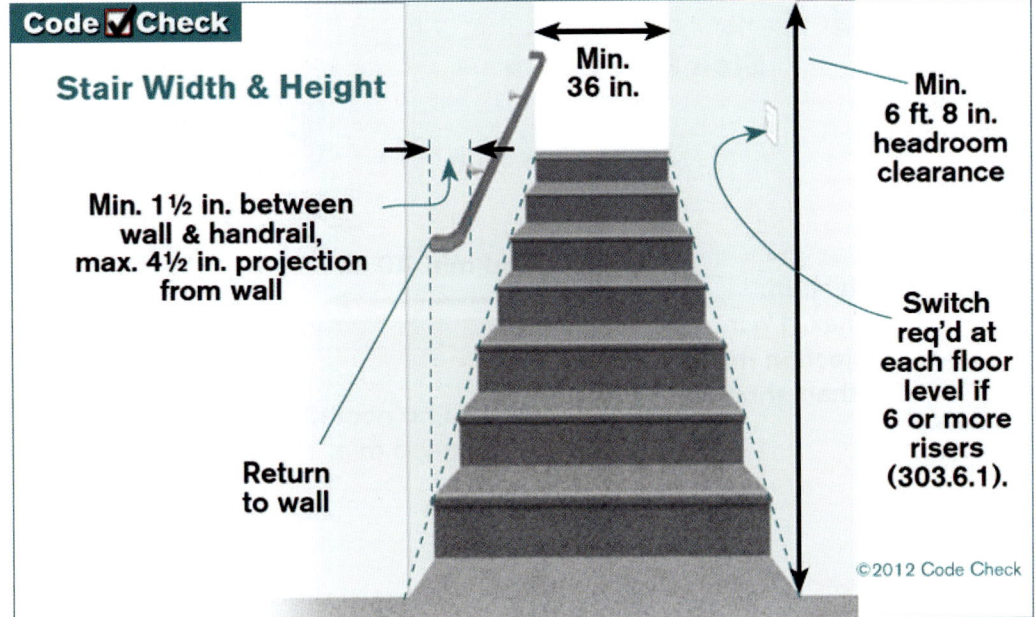

When inspecting interior or exterior stairways, the home inspector should inspect the following stairway components and dimensions:

- **Stringers:** The stairway is supported on long diagonal supports called stringers, which are fastened at both ends to joists, headers, and the floor in the framework. If the stairway abuts a wall, the stringer can be fastened to the wall studs. A stairway can have one, two, or three or more stringers depending on their width. Stringers are made of wood or metal, but most often wood. Inspect the stringers for cracks, warping, and deterioration of any sort. Watch for any evidence that stringers have shifted or pulled away from the treads or framing.

- **Risers and treads: Risers** are the vertical portion of the stairs. Risers should all be the same height, generally from 7"–8" high. Some stairways were/are constructed with **open risers**, in which the vertical portion below each step is left open (generally not permitted and considered unsafe). The riser opening is much like a baluster; a 4" sphere may not pass through the opening. The treads are the horizontal surface of the stairs. They should be of even depth, generally from 9"–11" deep, including an inch or so for the **nosing**, or extension of the tread over the riser.

Inspect risers and treads for uniform height and depth. Unexpected changes between steps can be dangerous and should be reported as a **safety hazard**. Be sure that risers and treads are securely fastened and undamaged. Loose or seriously worn

> **Chapter Note**
>
> *Pages 578–584 present the study and inspection of stairs and balconies.*

> **Section Note**
>
> *Check your local regulations and requirements for interior stairways*

THE INTERIOR INSPECTION

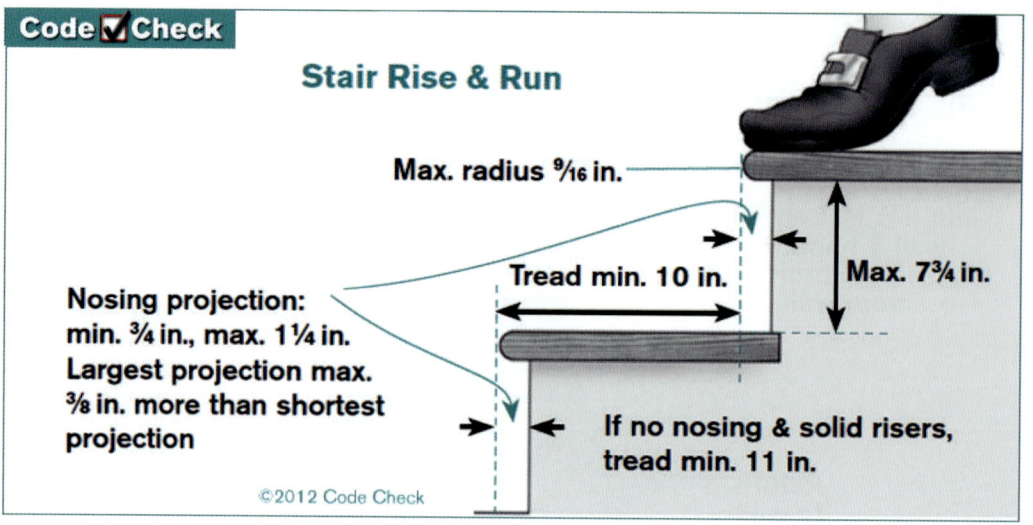

INSPECTING STAIRS

- Cracked, warped, damaged, or shifted stringers
- Uneven, poorly supported, loose, or damaged treads and risers
- Loose, broken, or missing handrails and balusters
- Balusters too far apart
- Improper width or headroom
- Windows too low or unprotected

treads presenting a trip hazard should be recommended for repair and reported as a **safety hazard**.

NOTE: Interior stairs with open risers can pose a safety hazard to families with young children. Small children may crawl through the opening between treads and fall through.

- **Handrails and balusters:** A stairway should have a handrail supported by balusters on each open side. With stairs built against a wall, the wall side should also have a handrail, which can be fastened to hangers nailed or screwed to the studs. The handrail should be at least 1-1/4″–2″ in diameter and have enough clearance from the wall to permit a good grip. The handrail must return to the wall at the top and bottom to prevent catching something on the open ends. A recommended height is from 34″–38″ above the stairs. Balusters should be a maximum of 4″ apart to prevent small children from falling through. Loose, broken, or missing handrails as well as loose, broken, or missing balusters and balusters that are spaced too far apart should be reported as safety hazards. Keep in mind that older homes typically have larger baluster spacing, and they may pose a safety hazard. In most cases, they aren't "fixable" without great difficulty or expense. Point out the potential safety issue and let the buyer know that temporary safety measures can be employed while their children are small/young.

- **Headroom:** Stairs should be at least 36″ wide and should have 6′8″ of headroom above the imaginary line strung from nosing to nosing, top to bottom of stairs. The home inspector is likely to find that basement and attic stairs, if present, won't meet these dimensions. (Note that the inspection of the basement staircase is considered part of the basement inspection of the home, covered in greater detail in Chapter 01.)

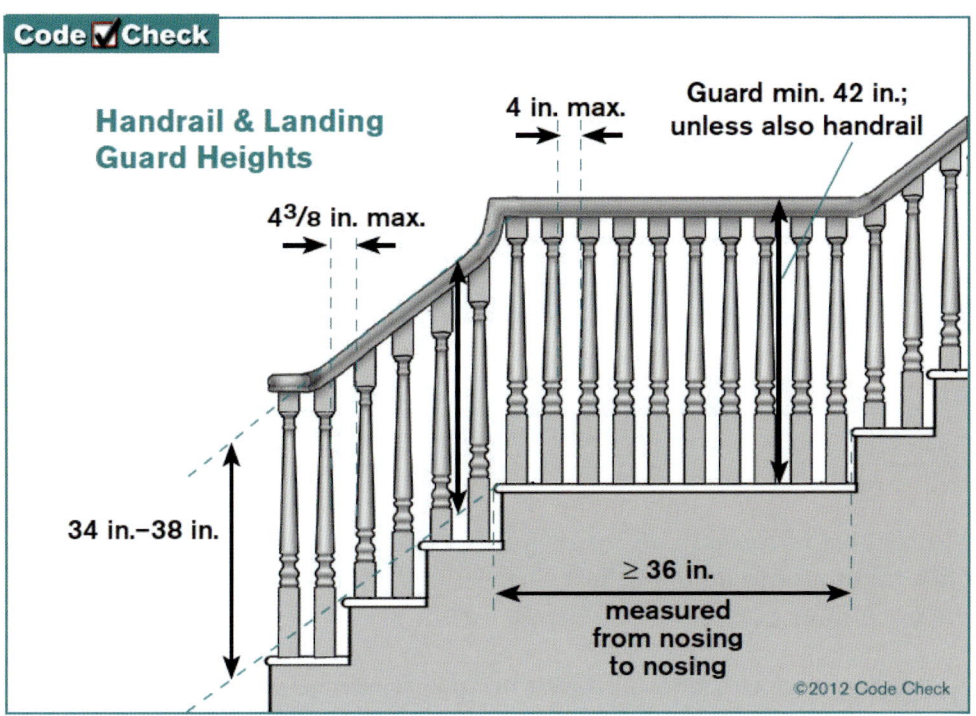

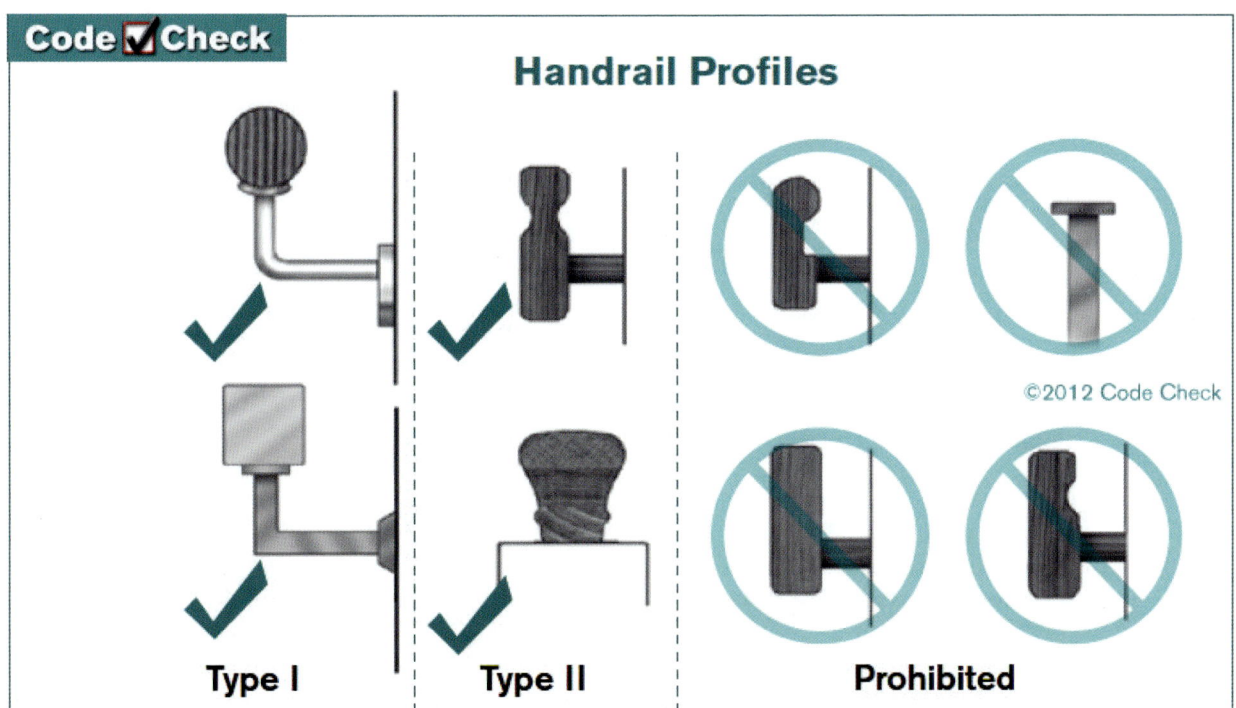

- **Doors and windows:** If there is a door at the top of the stairs, it should open away from the stairs. If the door opens toward the stairs, there should be a minimum 36" deep landing present so that someone coming up the stairs can't be pushed down when the door opens.

Glass adjacent to stairways, landings, and ramps within 36" horizontally of a walking surface must be safety glass. The glass may be protected with a 1-1/2" guard that is 34"–38" above the walking surface.

THE INTERIOR INSPECTION

> **STAIR SAFETY HAZARDS**
>
> - Uneven or loose risers and treads
> - Loose or missing handrails
> - Balusters too far apart
> - Window too low or unprotected

- **Winders:** When stairways curve or make a turn, pie-shaped treads called winders may be used. Although winders were commonly used in the past, their use is no longer considered as safe as straight stairs. Ideally, there should be a flat landing at a turn. Codes vary as to how narrow the tread of the winder can be. In general, the tread depth should be equal to that of the straight treads at a distance of 12″ from the narrow end of the 10″ tread depth at the walk line (6″ minimum).

- Spiral staircases are built entirely with winders. But some local codes don't permit spiral staircases as the only means of getting from one floor to another. Minimum width is 26″, all treads must be identical, minimum headroom is 6′6″, minimum tread depth is 7.5″ at 12″ inches from the center post, and the maximum riser must be a height of 9.5″.

  The home inspector doesn't have to report winders as a safety hazard unless their condition is bad. But their presence should be pointed out to the client.

- **Lack of lighting:** Stairways should be well lit. Those with six risers or more should have three-way light switches at the bottom and top of the stairs. (Unfinished basement stairs don't require this.)

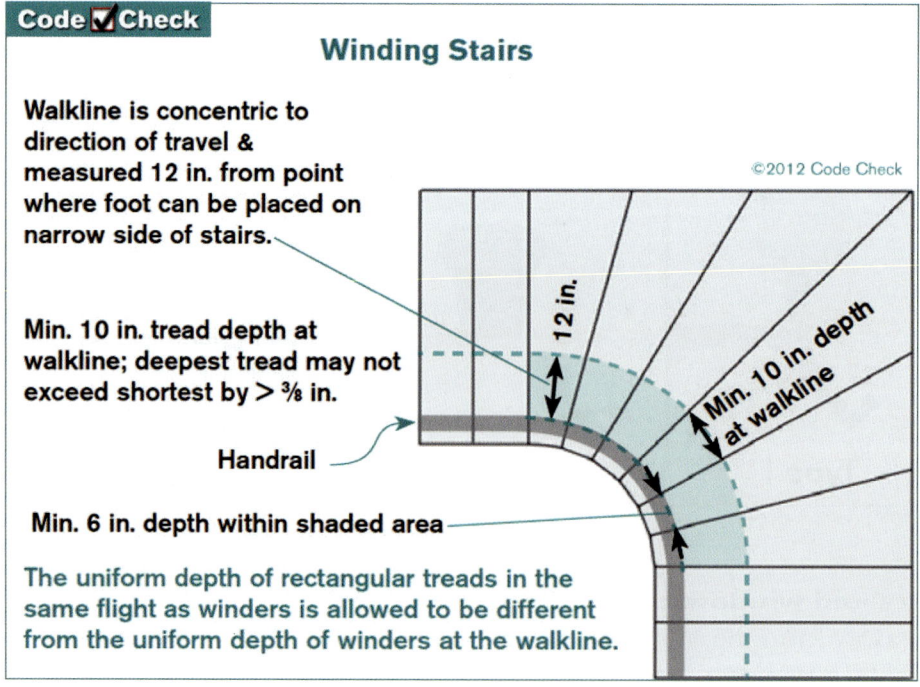

Inspecting Balconies

Interior balconies extend from a wall over a living area with no visible connection to the floor below. The balcony can be supported on cantilevered floor joists or on joists or girders spanning two bearing walls. Some balconies have supports such as cables, chains, rods, or wood that support the balcony from above or from a back wall.

Like staircases, balconies should have a handrail (or more correctly a guardrail and balusters) at the most 4″ apart to protect the safety of people on the balcony. Guard rails should be present whenever there is a height difference from the balcony to the floor below of greater than 30″. The guardrail must be at least 36″ high. Inspect balconies very carefully. The flooring should be undamaged. The whole structure should be securely fastened and sturdy. Walk out to the edge and test the structure for bounce. If you notice any shaking, sagging, or tilting, the balcony should be reported as a **safety hazard**. Give the guardrail a shake and touch the balusters to see if any of them can be shaken or moved. Any that are loose or damaged could allow someone to fall through and should be reported as a **safety hazard**.

Pay attention to and report any structural irregularities. When the joists are cantilevered, the downward load

For Beginning Inspectors

Take notice of any interior stairways and balconies you see. As a mental exercise, try to determine how they're constructed, what members are providing support, and what might cause the structure to become unsafe.

PAY ATTENTION TO

- Structural irregularities
- Shaking, sagging, or tilting
- Loose or damaged handrail and balusters

Photo #6 INTERIOR BALCONIES

Verify that spacing between balusters is within the 4″ requirement. Also note, even though technically allowed, if the railing assembly is climbable. Small children can climb up and over a "legitimate" railing assembly and injure themselves.

THE INTERIOR INSPECTION

at the unsupported end of the joist is reflected by an upward load on the joist at an equal distance from the support point. If the joist is overloaded at its cantilevered end and is pushed downward, there can be a bulge in the floor at the other end of the joist (middle of room). Or the joist can crush or crack where it's supported by the wall below. Sometimes, the uncantilevered portion of the room can be overloaded, causing the balcony to rise.

ABOUT REPORTING: Instructions for using your inspection report to report your findings of stairway and balcony defects are presented on page 594.

7.6 FIREPLACES AND FUEL-BURNING APPLIANCES

> *Chapter Note*
>
> *Pages 584–595 present the study and inspection of fireplaces and wood stoves.*

Fireplaces today exist for the pleasure of having a comforting fire, not for heating efficiency. Conventional wood-burning fireplaces lose more heat up the chimney than they provide. Because they use warm house air for combustion, they actually take heat from the house. The use of glass doors on the fireplace and the use of outside air for combustion helps to reduce heat loss. A fireplace stove (commonly called a wood-burning stove), of course, can be an efficient heat source. If you live in a market with a lot of wood burning stoves or fireplace inserts, it would be in your best interest to review *NFPA 211, Standard for Chimneys, Fireplaces, Vents, and Solid Fuel-Burning Appliances*. It is a relatively short standard with all of the details needed for a proper inspection of these devices.

FIREPLACES	
Observe and/or Report: The act of making a visual examination of a system or component and reporting on its condition.	• Fuel-burning fireplaces, fireplace stoves, and fireplace inserts • Fuel-burning accessories installed in fireplaces • Dampers by opening and closing them, if readily accessible and manually operable • Chimneys and vent systems
Describe: Report in writing a system or component by its type, or other observed characteristics, to distinguish it from other components used for the same purpose.	• Fuel-burning fireplaces, fireplace stoves, and fireplace inserts • Fuel-burning accessories installed in fireplaces • Chimneys and vent systems
Report as deficient deficiencies in:	• Presence of built-up creosote in accessible areas of the firebox and flue • The presence of combustible materials in near proximity to the firebox opening • The absence of fire-blocking at the attic penetration of the chimney flue, where accessible • Damper, lintel, hearth, hearth extension, and firebox • Gas valve and location • Circulating fan • Combustion air vents • Cleanouts not made of metal, pre-cast cement, or other noncombustible material

The inspector is not required to:	• Verify the integrity of the flue • Perform a chimney smoke test • Determine the adequacy of the draft • Inspect interiors of vent systems, flues, and chimneys that are not readily accessible • Seals and gaskets • Ignite or extinguish fires • Automatic fuel feed devices • Mantles and fireplace surrounds • Inspect fuel-burning fireplaces and appliances located outside the inspected structure(s) • Move fireplace inserts and stoves or firebox contents • Operate gas fireplace(s) or light pilot flames

EPA-Certified Stoves

Newer EPA-certified stoves with stricter emission standards allow primary air to enter the stove through a long, thin slit across the top of the firebox. This creates a better mixture of oxygen with the fuel load for a more efficient primary combustion. Instead of letting the combustible gases emitted by the fuel load escape up the flue, the gases are burned through a catalytic combustor or a non-catalytic secondary combustion air system. A **catalytic combustor** is a ceramic round, square, or rectangular insert with numerous small channels, or tubes, running through it. Applied to the ceramic surface is a layer of a catalytic chemical, generally platinum or palladium. When sufficient temperatures are reached, this chemical coating reacts with smoke passing through the channels, reducing the smoke's ignition temperature and burning the smoke. As smoke passes through the combustor and is burned, it creates heat instead of pollution. The chemical coating is not burned or consumed in the process.

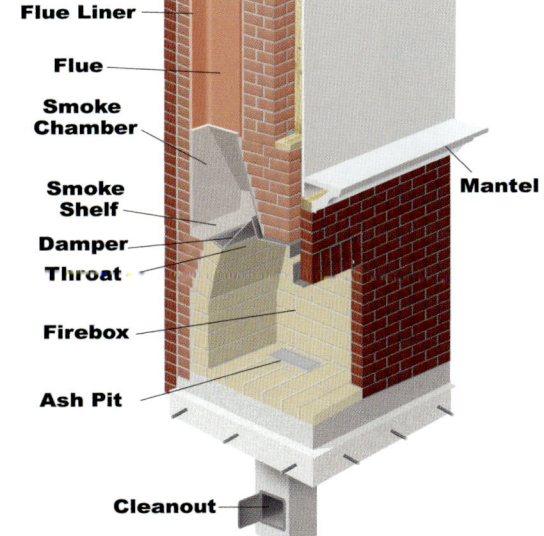

Illustration by Paddy Morrissey

Non-catalytic stoves (called non-cat stoves) maximize combustion efficiency by providing a secondary combustion air system. Smoke and gases emitted by the fuel load are burned by the injection of secondary air into the stove. These stoves have a set of perforated stainless steel tubes (or a perforated baffle or another similar device) across the top of the firebox. These tubes introduce air across the top that mixes with the combustible gases rising from the fuel load, maximizing the combustion of the gases.

The Masonry Fireplace

The conventional masonry fireplace is built with a foundation and footing system as shown in the illustration. The floor of the fireplace is called the **hearth**, which is typically poured concrete about 4″ thick. The hearth is required to extend out in front of the fireplace by 16″–20″ and at least 8″–12″, and is typically covered with at least 1″ of firebrick, stone, slate, or tile. The extension depth depends on the size of the fireplace opening. There's often a hole in the rear of the hearth

> **Definitions**
>
> A <u>hearth</u> is the floor of the fireplace. The <u>firebox</u> is the open chamber in which the fire burns. The top of the firebox is called the <u>throat</u>. A <u>damper</u> is a metal plate that closes the throat when the fireplace is not in use.
>
> <u>Firebrick</u> is a special brick designed to withstand high temperatures.

> **Definitions**
>
> The <u>smoke shelf</u> above a fireplace interferes with and interrupts chimney downdrafts.
>
> The <u>smoke chamber</u> is the area between the damper and the flue that guides smoke toward the flue.
>
> <u>Combustion air</u> is the air necessary to allow for the proper ignition and burning of the fuel.

leading to an **ash pit and cleanout** in the basement below or to an exterior wall so that ashes can be removed easily.

The **firebox** is the open chamber in which the fire burns. Proper function depends on the relationship between the dimension of the opening and the dimension of the firebox. These measurements can vary according to design. For example a Rumford fireplace is a completely different design than is typical, having a much shallower firebox. The firebox walls are usually firebrick but may be made of stone or concrete block with a firebrick liner. Firebricks are mortared with a thin **refractory mortar**. The firebox back wall is often angled toward the front.

At the top of the firebox is the **throat**, which is fitted with a metal **damper** that can be closed when the fireplace isn't being used. The throat should be offset from the centerline of the flue, either to the front or to the back. (The illustration on the previous page shows the throat offset toward the front.) The base of the offset is called the **smoke shelf**, which provides deflection of downdrafts, snow, and rain. The **smoke chamber** is the area between the damper and the flue. Its sloping wall helps to direct smoke up to the chimney. Smoke chambers should have a smooth parging or stucco finish to encourage the flow of smoke.

The chimney for a conventional fireplace is typically made of the same material as the fireplace. At one time, the chimney was unlined, but since about 1950, a **flue liner** is required. The liner is usually 5/8″ thick terra cotta tiles that come in sections from 2′–3′ long. Fireplaces should not share a flue with any other appliance, especially another fireplace.

There should not be combustible materials within 6″ of the sides of the opening. An example is wood trim. Any combustible material above the opening that sticks out more than 1-1/2″, such as a wooden mantel shelf, should have a clearance of 12″.

Because fireplaces use warm inside air to burn wood, they wastefully draw warm air from the house. One method of making the fireplace more efficient is to bring in **outside combustion air**. Most local codes require it. Outside air is brought in through 4″ venting from the outside to the floor or wall of the firebox where a damper may control the airflow.

Other devices are used to make fireplaces more efficient. Some fireplaces have **blowers and fans** designed to increase the amount of warm air projected into the room. Special grates and hollow tubes are other devices used for the same purpose.

NOTE: Some masonry fireplaces have a **metal firebox** of steel plating. The metal firebox is kept 1/2″–1″ away from the masonry, and the gap is filled with non-combustible insulation. If the gap isn't provided, the metal can buckle and the masonry can crack. Don't confuse a metal firebox in a masonry fireplace with zero clearance or with manufactured or prefabricated fireplaces as well as fireplace inserts mentioned on the following pages.

Other Types of Fireplaces

The home inspector will come across other types of fireplaces during the course of his or her inspections:

> **FIREPLACES**
> - Conventional masonry
> - Gas burning
> - Coal burning
> - Zero clearance
> - Fireplace inserts
> - Decorative

- **Gas fireplaces:** Gas fireplaces were popular around the turn of the 20th century. They're recognizable by their very small fireboxes and decorative borders of marble, cast iron, or ceramic tiles. These old fireplaces **cannot** be used to burn wood without making significant improvements. Today, there are natural gas fireplaces on the market, and you may find masonry wood-burning fireplaces converted to gas. The new gas-only models can't be used to burn wood either.

- **Coal fireplaces:** These were also popular around the turn of the 20th century. You can usually identify an old coal-burning fireplace by the narrow and shallow firebox and the cast iron grate with a pull-out drawer in the bottom to remove the ashes. Some units have heavy slotted covers to put over the opening. In general, it's not a good idea to use a coal fireplace for burning wood, although an examination of the system by a specialist may indicate that everything is in order to burn wood. But recommend the examination in any case.

- **Zero clearance or factory-built fireplaces:** Since the 1970s, different types of factory-built or zero clearance metal fireplaces have become available. These are highly engineered units that can be wall-mounted or freestanding. A damper is sometimes present, but there is no smoke shelf. Some models have glass doors or a fixed glass panel. The units are connected to a metal flue and often a wood-framed chimney chase. They're very light and can be installed without a special foundation. One type of prefabricated unit is called a Heatilator™, which has inlet grills for cool room air intake and outlet grills above the firebox for heated air release to the room. The wall of the room with the grills can be covered with plaster or drywall. Most if not all of the new installations are for gas logs only due to pollution issues with burning wood in metropolitan areas.

Home inspectors have reported many problems with these prefabricated units, including corrosion, cracked fireboxes, open flue joints, broken hangers, and displaced metal flues. They also have a limited life-span of about 20 years, which is not commonly known.

> **DON'T GET SLOPPY**
>
> *Never skip a fireplace without inspecting the inside. You'll be sorry if you give the fireplace a good rating only to realize later that it's just a roughed-in opening or a decorative fireplace. You'll also be out the money it will cost to install a real one for your customer.*

- **Fireplace inserts:** An insert is really a fireplace stove with a door on the front. This insert may sit completely or partially in a conventional masonry fireplace's firebox and is connected to the fireplace flue or has its own. (Inserts are not allowed in

Photo #7 ZERO CLEARANCE FIREPLACES

This is the backside of a factory-built fireplace. As you can see the "zero-clearance" term is quite deceiving as there is actually a clearance required for proper installation.

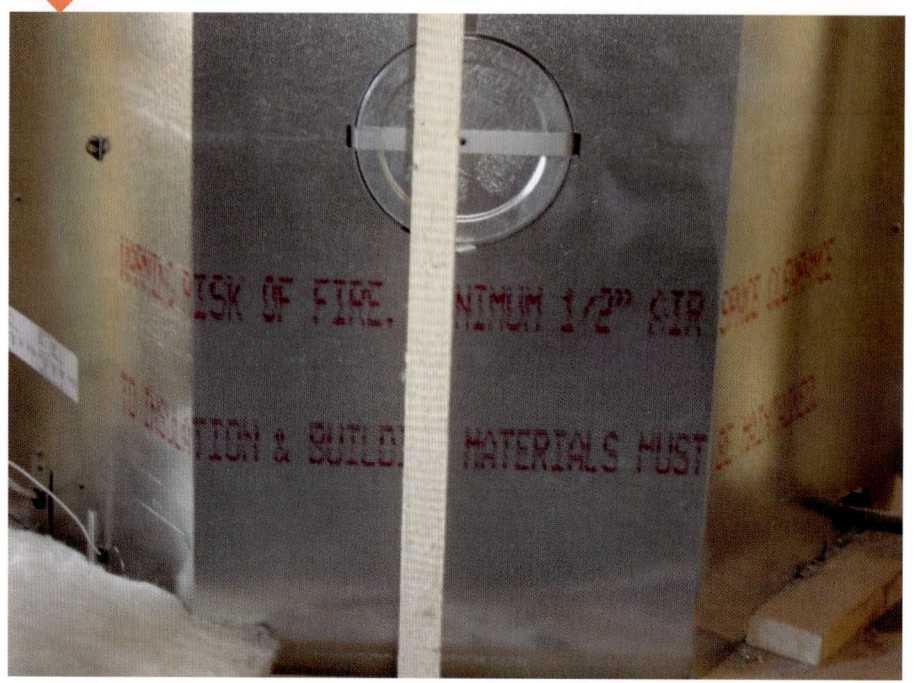

Photo #8 FIREPLACE INSERTS

The front side of the same fireplace with its sealed glass front and gas logs installed. The louvered section below the firebox is where the gas valve, igniter, and controls are located. It usually tilts down from the top edge for access.

zero clearance fireplaces.) Most guidelines state that the inspector does **not have to inspect the fireplace insert flue connections due to its inaccessibility**. Customers should be informed of this. There have been serious chimney fire problems due to bad connections with the insert and flue, but it's impossible to see without removing the insert (the insert has to be removed to inspect it properly in any case). Always recommend that a specialist come to remove and inspect a fireplace insert. Another problem with inserts is that it's difficult to clean the chimney, allowing dangerous levels of soot and creosote buildup. In many cases these inserts must have a sleeved metal flue pipe running within the original clay liner. While outside on the roof inspecting the chimney you may see this metal piping emerging from the original flue with its own cap/cover assembly.

- **Decorative fireplaces:** From about 1920 to 1940, non-functioning, decorative fireplaces were popular. They have also made a comeback in certain parts of the country today. Although these fireplaces look real, they're not and there's no chimney associated with the fireplace. This is why it's so important *never to get sloppy* during an inspection and overlook a fireplace. Imagine reporting that a fireplace is operational only to have your customer discover later that besides not working, it isn't even a real fireplace.

- **Roughed-in fireplaces:** Sometimes, an opening has been left with a connection to the chimney intended to provide the space for a fireplace to be installed at a later date. Most local codes require the area to be sealed off. It's not uncommon for homeowners to try to use them without a firebox and damper system present. Generally, it would cost a substantial amount to have the real fireplace installed.

- **Ventless fireplaces:** Ventless fireplaces are freestanding units that do not require a chimney or flue to exhaust combustion gases to the outside. They may be fueled by propane, natural gas, alcohol-based gels, or electricity. They rely on indoor air for combustion and exhaust a low level of harmful combustion gases into the room, making a chimney or flue unnecessary. Models that use propane or natural gas must be connected to a supply line, limiting where they can be installed. Ventless fireplaces have been available since the early 1980s, and some older models have a reputation for being poorly made and unhealthy, as they may allow a buildup of carbon monoxide and moisture in the home. Newer models must meet federal standards and many have a built-in carbon monoxide detector and oxygen detector to shut off the fireplace if carbon monoxide levels become too high or oxygen levels become too low. Electric or gel-fueled models don't have this problem, as they do not produce emissions of any great quantity. All ventless fireplaces produce heat, although gas and propane models are more effective in this regard than electric or gel-fueled units.

Inspecting Fireplaces

You do not have to ignite or extinguish a fire in the fireplace during the fireplace inspection, but you are required to inspect the following aspects of the fireplace:

> **FIREPLACE FIRES**
>
> *The home inspector <u>does not have to light or put out a fire in the fireplace</u>. If a fire is already going, inform the customer that the fireplace inspection will be limited.*

- **The damper** for its operation and condition

- **The firebox lining** for the condition of the firebrick and mortar or steel and other materials

- **The flue** for its condition (cracked or rusted) and the state of soot and creosote coverage, if possible

- **The facing** around the fireplace for evidence of smoking, indicating a possible drafting issue

- **Clearances** from combustibles

Begin the fireplace inspection by examining the front of the fireplace. When you start the fireplace inspection, look over the basics and watch for the following conditions:

Photo #9 *A factory-built fireplace. Note the panels instead of true firebrick. The rear panel is cracked down the middle. Fireplace is full of ash and should be noted as it limits your view.*

- **Discolored, deteriorating, or loose facing:** Look at the facing just above the firebox. If this area has a dark or black tint or discoloration, it usually indicates that the fireplace releases smoke into the house. A fireplace can smoke for several reasons:

  — **Soot and creosote buildup in the flue.**

  — **Poor construction of the fireplace system.** For example, the chimney may be too short or too close to something at its termination on the roof, the flue may be too small, the firebox may be poorly shaped, there may not be a smoke shelf, and so on.

  — **Downdrafting** from winds affecting chimney operation. This can usually be corrected by installing a chimney cap on the chimney or a rain cap on the flue.

  — A **negative pressure condition** within the home. Some modern homes are sealed so tightly that running a clothes dryer or exhaust fans and using the fireplace can depressurize the home. This condition pulls air down the chimney and causes backdrafting or smoking.

For Beginning Inspectors

If you know people with fireplaces, stop in to have a look. Bring a strong flashlight and your inspection mirror and perform an inspection for them.

Check the facing brick for cracking and mortar condition. Watch for any sign that the facing is loose or moving. The whole facing may move due to a weak floor system that can't support the masonry.

- **Undersized or poorly supported hearth:** The hearth should extend out at least 16"–20" and extend 8"–12" on either side of the fireplace depending on the size of the fireplace opening. If you find an undersized hearth extension, point it out to the customer with a caution that sparks and coals can fall out. We recommend putting a fireproof rug in front of an undersized hearth. (Note that some factory-built units don't have a hearth extension and are required to; others have undersized hearth extensions.) Fireplace hearths that sit above floor level should be checked to see if they're properly supported and not tilting or cracking.

- **Improper clearances:** Check that decorative wooden surrounds are 6" from the fireplace opening and that mantel shelves are at least 12" above the opening. Inspect the condition of wood near the opening. Wood can dry out and char from repeated heatings and will combust at a much lower temperature. Check the mantel shelf by grabbing hold of it and nudging it slightly to make sure it is securely attached. But be careful—sometimes you can grab one and it'll be so loose that it falls right off the wall.

The next step in the inspection is to inspect the inside of the fireplace. Inspect the firebox for the following conditions:

- **Cracked, broken, deteriorating, or buckling lining:** First identify the type of lining that's present, such as firebrick or metal. Then use your flashlight to carefully inspect firebrick for cracks, breaks, and any disintegration. Check the mortar for any loose, broken, or missing sections. Evaluate metal fireboxes for buckling sections and open joints. Open sections in the firebricks or metal could start a fire and should be reported as a **safety hazard** with a recommendation that repairs be made.

    NOTE: Modern factory-built fireplaces have precast panels that look like firebricks. They are prone to cracking with a lot of use and are easily replaced.

- **Broken, missing, or malfunctioning damper:** Reach in and operate the damper. It

> **Section Note**
>
> *"If you find a fireplace insert, take the time to talk about it with the customer. You don't have to inspect the flue connection, but it's helpful that customers understand why. Inform them about annual cleaning and recommend that they have a specialist remove, clean, and evaluate the insert. That's good advice. Many fires have been caused by these inserts from poor flue connections or metal flues that weren't installed to go up to the top of the chimney."*

INSPECTING FIREPLACES

- Discolored, loose, or deteriorating facing
- Undersized or poorly supported hearth and hearth extensions
- Improper clearances
- Deteriorating lining and mortar
- Broken, missing, or malfunctioning damper
- Blower not operating
- Dirty flue, open joints, and displaced flues

should open completely and close tightly. Use your flashlight to check if the damper is rusted through, broken, or obstructed in some way. Some older fireplaces may not have a damper, which should be reported with the recommendation that one be installed. A common retrofit installation is a damper installed at the top of the flue instead of the throat and smoke chamber being rebuilt.

- **Blower not operating:** If the fireplace has a built-in blower or fan, check it to see if it operates even though it is not required.

- **Dirty flue:** You may or may not be able to see up into the flue, depending on the amount of offset. But try to get your inspection mirror up past the damper and shine your flashlight on it to see what you can. A flue with more than 1/8" of soot and creosote should be cleaned, and any obstructions such as a bird nest should be removed. If you can't examine the flue or very much of it, you should recommend that the **flue be evaluated and cleaned** by a specialist. Fireplace flues should be cleaned on an annual basis, depending on use, to eliminate the potential of chimney fires. Some experts suggest cleaning by a professional chimney sweep once for every 1 to 1-1/2 cords of hardwood burned.

Most standards state that the home inspector does not have to examine the fireplace flue. That standard was included largely because it's so often impossible to do or to do in any significant way. However, we suggest that you make some attempt to look up into the flue, reporting any defective conditions. If the flue is not visible, report that in your inspection report.

NOTE: Also, with factory-built fireplaces and any fireplace with a gas log set, the damper must be removed or at least blocked open to prevent asphyxiation because there is no smoke with a gas-log fireplace.

Fuel-Burning Appliances

Fuel-burning fireplace stoves include those that burn wood, pellets, corn, or other fuels, although they are often referred to collectively as wood stoves. Inspecting fireplace stoves involves checking clearances and examining the condition of the stove, smoke pipe, chimney, and flue requirements.

The heavy fireplace stove should be firmly mounted on a concrete floor or on a protective pad over a wood floor. Stove doors should close tightly, and the stove box should be without cracks or open joints. The wood stove may have a metal or lined masonry chimney, and under no circumstances should it share a flue with another appliance. A wood stove sharing a flue with another appliance is considered a **safety hazard**. Depending on age and efficiency, the wood stove can produce a great amount of soot and creosote. The flue must be cleaned regularly.

Wood stoves may be listed by the Underwriters Laboratories (UL) and are said to be **UL rated**. Installation clearances are set out in these listings and are typically those shown in the diagrams on the next page.

CAUTION: Don't report a wood stove as being safe if you don't know. Sometimes, metal chimneys pass through walls and ceilings and you can't see them to determine if the proper clearances are met. Suggest that a chimney or wood stove specialist evaluate the safety of the flue.

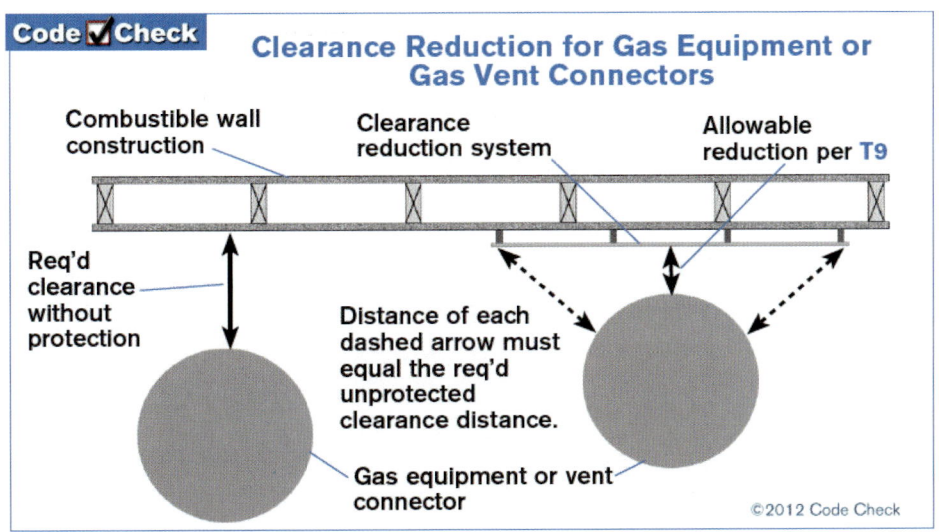

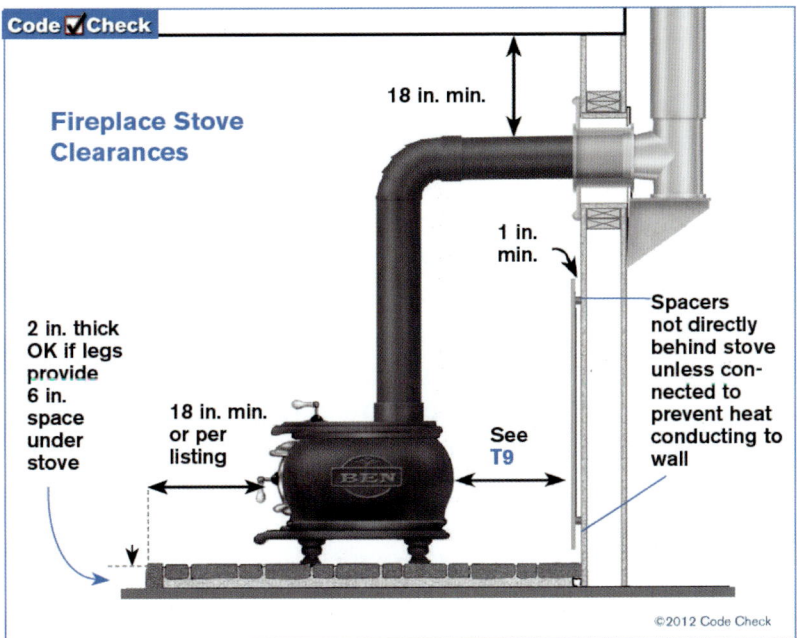

Reporting Your Findings

We're going to catch up on how to report some of the interior items that have been presented in this chapter thus far, including windows, stairways, balconies, and fireplaces.

The four components of a home inspection are **examination**, **analysis**, **communication**, and a **written report**. Remember that you should continue to communicate with your customer even if you're inspecting "simple" items such as windows. Customers still need to hear what's going on, and what you consider to be an easy or well-known subject may not be familiar to the customer. Don't assume what the customer does and doesn't know. Keep a steady flow of conversation going. Often, it's the small tips that customers will remember best. As you perform the interior inspection, talk to your customer, explaining:

- **What you're inspecting**—the ceiling, walls, floors, window sill, door hardware, fireplace damper, etc.

> **KEEP TALKING**
>
> *Don't go silent during the interior inspection just because the items being inspected are everyday things. Customers still want to know what's going on.*

> **Report Available**
>
> *The American Home Inspectors Training Institute provides both manual and computerized reports. These reports include an inspection agreement, complete reporting pages, and helpful customer information.*
>
> *If you're interested in purchasing the <u>InspectIt Report Software</u>, please call us at 1-800-441-9411*

- **What you're looking for**—water damage, sagging plaster, rotted wood, cracked firebrick, uneven stair treads, and so on.

- **What you're doing**—side lighting the ceiling to find bulges, listening to floor noises, testing the balcony for stability, and so on.

- **What you're finding**—nail pops in the drywall, weak floor joists, a leaking dual-pane window, a loose stairway handrail, a dirty fireplace flue, and so on.

- **Suggestions about dealing with the findings**—replacing a section of drywall, refinishing the window framing, having a specialist remove and check a fireplace insert, and so on. But be careful not to make uneducated guesses about how repairs should be made.

Filling in Your Report

Every home inspector needs an inspection report. A **written report** is the work product of the home inspection, and every home inspector is expected to deliver one to the customer after the inspection. Inspection reports vary a great deal in the industry. Some home inspection companies develop their own version; others use state required formats (Texas), home inspection software, apps, or formats provided by training companies such as AHIT. Some are considered to be excellent, while others are not very good. A workable and easy-to-use inspection report is important for a home inspector. Of greater importance are its thoroughness, accuracy, and helpfulness to the customer. Whatever reporting format you choose, make sure it presents your findings in a clear, professional manner such that it reduces your liability and client dissatisfaction.

The **Don't Ever Miss** list is a reminder of those specific findings you should include in your inspection report. We list these items based on years of experience performing home inspections. Missing them can result in complaint calls and possible lawsuits. Here is an overview of what to report on during the inspection of the foundation:

- **General window overview:** You should have an area in your inspection report for recording general window information. That's the place to record the window materials (wood, vinyl, metal, etc.) and the types of windows (casement, double-hung, etc.) you've found in the house. Be sure to record any evidence of any insulated glass windows that are leaking in the home. Make a note of cracked glass and missing putty or cracked/broken seals/gaskets too.

- **Stairs and balconies:** State the condition of the stairs and interior balconies using a satisfactory, marginal, poor designation if you wish. Note defects that you've found and don't forget to include safety hazards such as missing railings, balusters too far apart, and unstable balconies.

- **Fireplaces:** First identify the type of fireplace (masonry, wood-burning, gas, insert, etc.). If there's more than one, identify each and give its location. If you've tested the built-in blower, don't forget to mention that and indicate whether it's operating. We suggest that if you haven't seen much or any of the flue that you write *Recommend having flue cleaned and evaluated* just to be on the safe side. Note other defects you've found. Pay special attention to any safety hazards and be sure to indicate if the fireplace is roughed in and is not a real fireplace.

- **Fireplace stoves:** If you've found a fireplace stove and you've inspected it, be sure to record your findings in your inspection report.
- **Safety hazards:** Never overlook reporting safety hazards. It's a good idea to record them on the page of the inspection report dealing with the item and then listing them again on a summary page of your report.
  — Uneven or loose risers and treads on stairs
  — Loose or missing guardrails and handrails, balusters too far apart, or instability of stairs and balconies
  — Cracked lining in fireplaces and fireplace stoves, improper clearances, open joints in a metal firebox, flues shared with the furnace, and so on.

7.7 ROOM-BY-ROOM INSPECTION

The interior inspection includes the careful inspection of each room in the home. The table below gives an overview of what must be inspected in each room. Some items, such as the heating, electrical, and plumbing aspects relating to these rooms, will be reviewed in these pages only briefly.

> **DON'T EVER MISS**
> - Windows: rotted framing, broken or leaking insulated glass, loose putty, not operating
> - Stairs: Damaged stringer, treads, and risers, loose or missing handrails, balusters too far apart, windows unprotected
> - Balconies: Loose or missing guardrails, balusters too far apart, instability
> - Fireplaces: Smoky condition, improper clearances, deteriorating lining and mortar, broken or missing damper, and dirty flue
> - Fireplace stoves: Improper clearances, sharing flue with another appliance

> *Chapter Note*
>
> *Pages 595–613 present an overview of the interior inspection of the house, room by room.*

ROOM-BY-ROOM INSPECTION OVERVIEW

Kitchen	Bathroom	Other Rooms
• Ceiling, walls, floor • Doors and windows • Heat source • Electrical: fixtures, switches, receptacles • Countertops and cabinets • Plumbing: sink, faucets, pipes, water flow, and drainage • Appliances and exhaust fan	• Ceiling, walls, floor • Doors and windows • Shower, sink, and tub surrounds • Heat source • Electrical: fixtures, switches, receptacles • Plumbing: sink, tub, shower, toilet, faucets, pipes, water flow, and drainage • Exhaust fan	• Ceiling, walls, floor • Doors and windows • Heat source • Electrical: fixtures, switches, receptacles

It's important to develop a **routine** for conducting the inspection in each room so that nothing is overlooked. The routine may be inspecting certain items in order—for example, first the ceiling, walls, and floor, then the windows and doors, then electrical, and so on. Another approach is to start by inspecting the door and then proceeding around the room clockwise or counterclockwise, examining walls, windows, heat registers, receptacles, and so on, as you pass by. The important thing is to do it the same way every time and not miss anything.

Electrical Review

During the interior inspection, the home inspector will examine the **electrical components** in each room. The inspector should determine if power and lighting are available to each area, if there are enough receptacles and they're properly wired and grounded, and if GFCIs are present to protect people in areas near water. The home inspector is required to:

- Operate all accessible **lighting fixtures and switches** throughout the home.

- Check for the **presence of receptacles** in each room and in long hallways.

- Check all accessible receptacles room by room for **current**.

- Check receptacles for **polarity and grounding**.

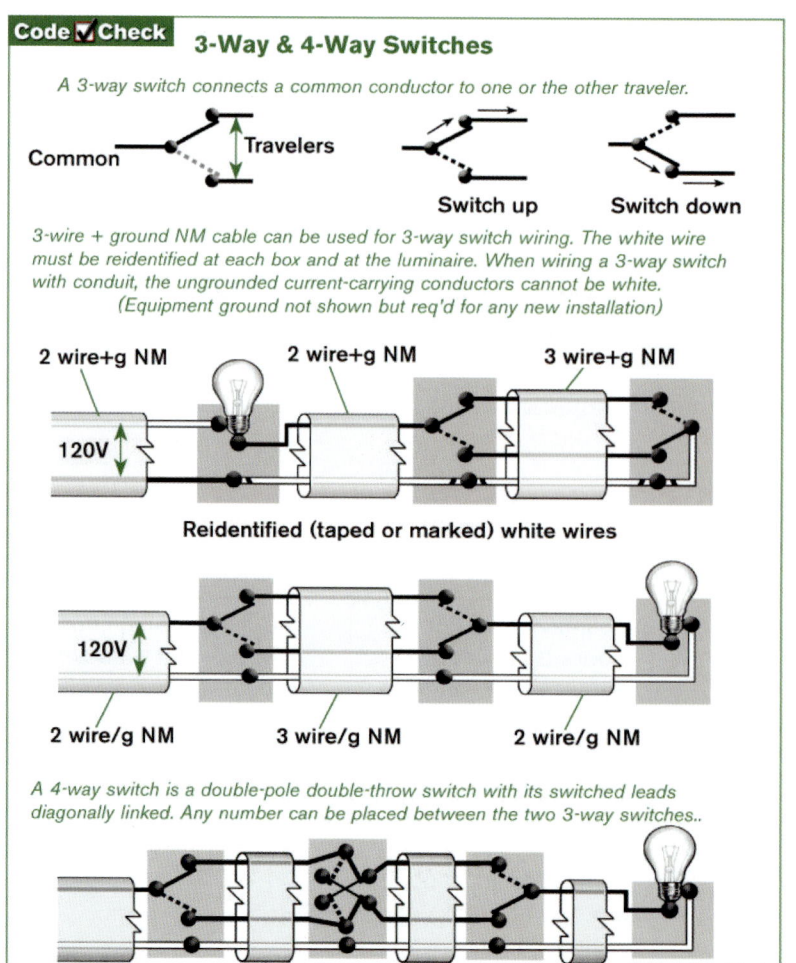

Photo #10 *These stickers should be on all GFCI protected receptacles. It may not have the test and reset buttons, but it could still be GFCI protected by a breaker or another receptacle.*

- Check for the **presence of GFCIs** where required and **check and test all GFCIs**.

- Look for electrical **defects and violations**.

AFCIs (arc fault circuit interrupters) are designed to protect against fires. You may see arcing when you unplug an appliance quickly and a spark is visible. Electrical arcs also occur when an electrical wire in the wall is damaged. Unchecked, arcing can quickly start a fire. An AFCI device detects arcing and shuts down the receptacle before any damage can occur. AFCIs have been required in all bedrooms in homes built since 2002. In 2014, the requirement was expanded to all living areas of new homes, they are mandatory pretty much throughout the entire home for all 120v 15- and 20-amp circuits. AFCI testers are available, but they may not be approved for the testing of the device. Inspectors should only use the test button on the breaker to see if an AFCI device is working properly, which is the method the AFCI breaker manufacturers recommend. Keep in mind that many of the homes that you will be testing with AFCI breakers are for bedrooms. Many homes have the bedrooms turned into home offices. Be sure to take a look around the house to see if computers or other high-tech equipment are in use before you push the AFCI test button. This is especially true for portions of the country that have the main panel on the exterior of the home or in the garage where you have not yet inspected the interior of the home. Most inspectors only test AFCI circuits if the home is vacant to avoid any problems with cutting the power to electronic devices.

To sum it all up, when you inspect a room, first turn on installed lighting fixtures and/or the ceiling fan. Then check for receptacles and test them for current. In the kitchen, bathroom, laundry room, and unfinished basement, check the receptacles for the presence of GFCIs. Then test the GFCI receptacles twice for operation using the following methods:

1. Insert the **GFCI tester** into the receptacle. If the circuit is correctly wired, the appropriate lights on the tester will be on. Then **push the button** on

> **A Practical Guide to Inspecting**
>
> *Chapter 5 presents complete information on the electrical inspection. The information presented here includes only a small portion relating to room by room inspection.*

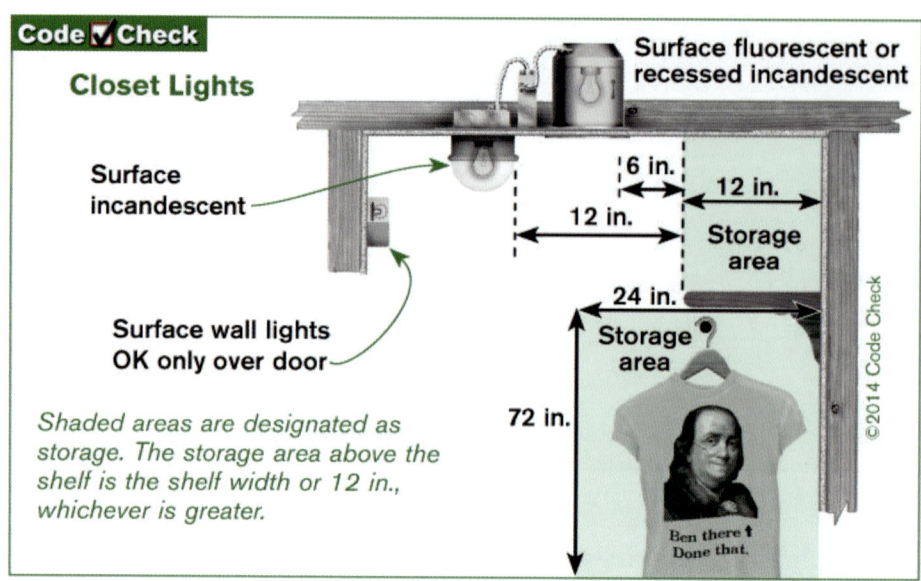

Definitions

A <u>GFCI</u> is a ground fault circuit interrupter that trips after a ground fault is detected, stopping the flow of electricity in a circuit. The purpose is for electrocution hazard protection.

An <u>AFCI</u> is an arc fault circuit interrupter that trips to prevent fires due to arcing.

Section Note

"I've tested GFCIs in several garages that had freezers plugged into them. Very often, the GFCI will trip again after the inspection and I'll get a call about spoiled food. And let me tell you, the freezers involved in my inspections always seem to be holding some very exotic and expensive food, such as salmon from Norway. Paying to replace food like that can get expensive.

Now I always leave the owner a note cautioning him or her to watch the freezer because the GFCI may trip again. I also tell the owner that the freezer shouldn't be plugged into a GFCI receptacle. It saves me money."

the tester. This should trip the GFCI and interrupt the circuit, and all lights on the tester will be off. If the lights remain on, either the GFCI is not working or the circuit is incorrectly wired. If the GFCI worked, push the reset button on the GFCI receptacle.

2. Next, push the **test button on the** receptacle, while leaving the tester plugged into the receptacle, to test it again. If the reset button pops out and the lights on your tester go out, the GFCI is working. Push the reset button on the GFCI receptacle to reset the circuit.

CAUTION: You may find large appliances such as refrigerators, freezers, or washers plugged into GFCI circuits when they probably shouldn't be. Freezers and refrigerators in the garage plugged into GFCI receptacles are a special problem. After the home inspector trips that GFCI, the freezer will have to restart and the motor surge may trip the GFCI again after the inspection. That means spoiled food and a complaint to the home inspector. If you come across this situation, leave a note for the owners, telling them to check that the GFCI hasn't tripped again after the inspection. A good practice is to leave your car keys on top of the fridge/freezer so that when you leave, you open the door, check that the light comes on, take your keys, and leave knowing that it worked when you left.

Any **two-slot (ungrounded) receptacles** will have to be tested with the **neon bulb tester**. This is a small tool with a light attached between two long prongs (see page 601) that can be inserted in the

Code Check
GFCIs

TWO-SLOT RECEPTACLES

NEON BULB TESTER OFF = ● ON = ○	CONDITION
(● outlet ○)	Correct wiring where hot wire is wired to small slot and neutral wire is wired to large slot.
(○ outlet ●)	Reverse polarity where hot wire is wired to large slot and neutral twire is wired to small slot.
(● outlet ●)	Inoperative for any number of reasons but basically not providing power to the outlet.
(● outlet ● with ○ top)	No ground where checking small and large slots shows that outlet has power, but checking each slot against screw shows no ground.

Illustration by Paddy Morrissey

receptacle slots and against the cover plate screw to get readings. The table below shows how to test two-slot receptacles with the neon bulb tester.

You may want to test **three-slot receptacles** with both the **GFCI tester and the neon bulb tester**. This is a double check of polarity, open ground, and inoperative receptacles.

Be sure to test all **receptacles** for polarity and open grounding. Receptacles near water with these problems can be especially dangerous and should be reported as a **safety hazard**.

Don't miss noting the absence of power to any area or checking all accessible receptacles per room, including other rooms such as the utility room, mudroom, and laundry room.

Definitions

<u>Reverse polarity</u> is where the hot wire is wired to the large slot in an electrical receptacle and the neutral wire is wired to the small slot, the opposite of how it should be done.

An <u>ungrounded receptacle</u> means that it is not grounded. A two-slot receptacle may not be grounded, whereas the three-slot outlet should be grounded.

For Beginning Inspectors

This is a good time to buy yourself a GFCI tester and neon bulb tester and get some practice.

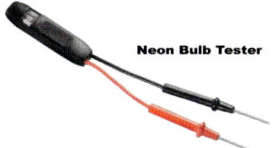
Neon Bulb Tester

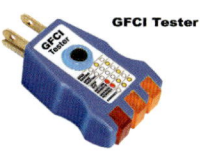
GFCI Tester

Use these tools to test your own receptacles first. Then carry the testers with you for several days and test receptacles at other people's homes. Always be aware that you may be turning off power to important receptacles downstream of GFCIs. Ask first.

THE INTERIOR INSPECTION

THREE-SLOT RECEPTACLES			
GFCI TESTER OFF = ● ON = ○	**NEON BULB TESTER** OFF = ● ON = ○		**CONDITION**
● ○ ○			Correct wiring where hot wire is wired to small slot and neutral is wired to large slot.
○ ○ ●			Reverse polarity where hot wire is wired to large slot and neutral twire is wired to small slot.
● ○ ●			Open ground where the outlet is not grounded and no current flows between the upper slots and the grounding slot.
● ● ●			Inoperative for any number of reasons, but basically not providing current or power to the outlet.
○ ○ ○			Many conditions but usually means there is a weak ground which indicates a leak of current through the outlet.

Illustration by Paddy Morrissey

TESTING RECEPTACLES

- Correct wiring
- Reverse polarity
- Open ground
- Inoperative

PLUMBING IN KITCHEN AND BATHROOMS

- Turn on all faucets.
- Check for hot water.
- Check for functional flow and drainage.
- Check visible piping.
- Flush each toilet.
- Examine all fixtures for condition.
- Look for leaks.

Definitions

The <u>functional flow and drainage</u> is a reasonable flow at the highest fixture in a dwelling when another fixture is operated simultaneously.

A <u>drain</u> is functional when it empties in a reasonable amount of time and does not overflow when another fixture is operated simultaneously.

Plumbing and Heating Review

During the interior inspection, the home inspector will also examine the **plumbing components**. In general, the inspector will determine if plumbing fixtures and faucets are in good condition, if functional water flow and drainage are acceptable, and if there are any leaks in the plumbing system or damage as a results of those leaks. The home inspector is required to:

- **Operate all plumbing fixtures** in the home, turning on each faucet in sinks, tubs, and showers, and flushing each toilet.

- Check for the **presence of hot water** at hot water faucets (left-hand faucet).

- Check faucets for condition and **functional flow**.

- Inspect all fixtures for condition and **functional drainage**.

- Check visible **piping and traps** under sinks for proper venting, P-traps, or S-traps.

- Look for evidence of **leaks** in the plumbing, old or new. Remember, old leaks are noted as stains and new leaks are wet as determined using a moisture meter or noting that liquid water is present.

> **HEAT OR COOLING IN EACH ROOM**
>
> - Adjust the thermostat.
> - Check for heat or cooling source.
> - Examine condition of heating registers.
> - Confirm heat or cooling.

In summary, the home inspector runs the water at the kitchen sink, checks water flow (volume) and drainage, checks the faucet and sink condition, and inspects the trap(s) underneath. In the bathroom, each fixture, including the toilet, is inspected for condition. Functional flow can be tested by turning on sink and tub faucets and then flushing the toilet. The inspector checks the sink, shower, and tub for condition and drainage. The toilet is inspected for operation. The tank is not required to be inspected, but it is a good idea to do so as many people have repaired the flush chain linkage improperly, using various items such as paper clips, which clearly are not approved for plumbing.

The home inspector will also inspect certain **heating/cooling components** during the interior inspection. The inspector should manipulate thermostats to turn on the heating or cooling system while in the living area and then observe heating or cooling in each room. Registers, radiators, and convectors are inspected, and the presence of heat or cooling is confirmed. The inspector is required to:

- Adjust the **thermostat** to start the heating or cooling system.

- Observe the presence of the **heat or cooling source** in each room. (A register, vent, radiator, baseboard heater, etc.)

- Inspect the **condition and operation** of registers and returns, radiators, and convectors, confirming heat or cooling.

This test can be performed easily by using your infrared thermometer to verify that something is coming out of the register or the radiator is warming up. You are not testing for balance or adequacy, just whether it functions as a heating/cooling source.

Note that complete information on the inspection of the plumbing and HVAC systems is presented in other chapters. The information presented in this chapter on the interior inspection is only a small portion related to room-by-room inspection.

Laundry Room

The washer and dryer are not typically tested during a home inspection. The connections for the washing machine water should be evaluated for corrosion and leakage. The standards state specifically that you are not required to test the washing machine hookups (except for Texas if the washer is not present). The electrical receptacles for the washer and 120v gas dryer should be dedicated, and nothing should be sharing them. If there are other receptacles in the room, they should be GFCI-protected. If there is a standard electric 240v dryer, we do not do anything with it. If there is a gas connection for the dryer, whether in use or not, be sure to check for damage or for the presence of any gas leaking. If there is a laundry tub or slop sink, it should be tested like any other sink; fill it, drain it, and check for leaks.

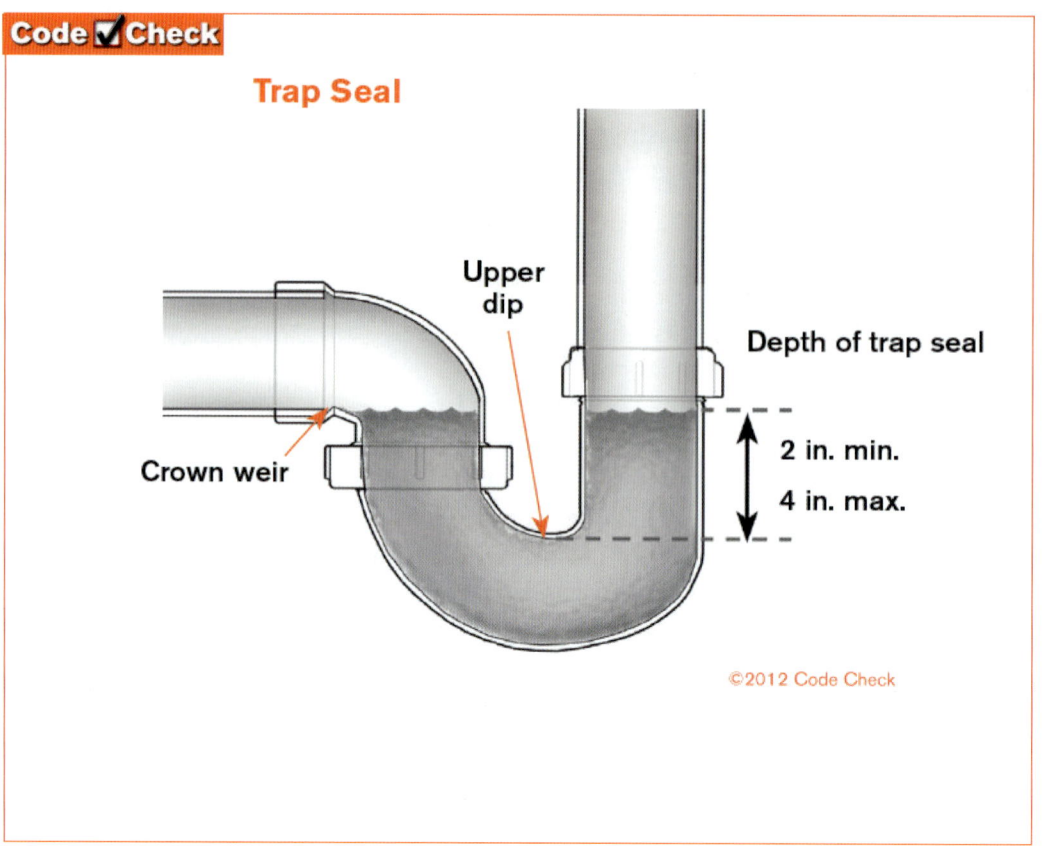

AROUND THE KITCHEN

Develop a routine for inspecting the kitchen and follow it religiously. Set it up so that you don't forget any of the inspection items on your list.

Inspecting the Kitchen

Inspecting the kitchen in the proper order can save time. Filling the sinks, turning on the stove/oven, and starting the dishwasher should be done first. The other items can be addressed while you wait for the preceding items to finish their operation.

- **Installed kitchen lighting:** It's a good idea to start the inspection of any room by trying the light switch by the door. Get into the habit of flipping the switch upon entry and leave them on making use of the available light.

- **The sink:** Check the sink for general condition, including cracks, rust, and other damage. Turn on the water at the sink and test first for hot water, always toward the left or the left-hand handle. Evaluate the faucet for leaking and examine its condition. Put the stopper in the sink(s) and fill it/them with 3″–4″ of water; then remove the stopper(s) to determine functional drainage. If there's a garbage disposal, turn it on while the sink is draining to confirm its operation. While the water continues to drain, look under the sink for any signs of water leaking.

- **Appliances:** According to many standards, you must now test the operation of the dishwasher, garbage disposal, kitchen stove/oven, refrigerator (built-in), microwave, and any exhaust fans or hoods present.

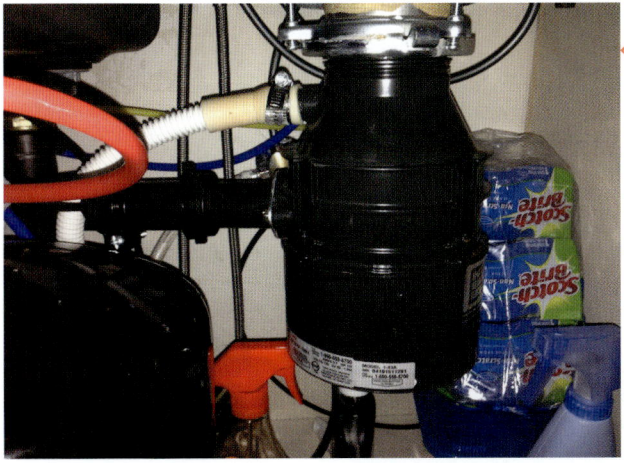

Photo #11 *This is a typical garbage disposal or food waste disposer. Note the cream/white hose on the left from the dishwasher. It doesn't look looped, but it is as it should be, but is out of the photo to the left.*

Photo #12 *This is a standalone gas cooktop, which is not part of a stove. You test it by turning on each of the burners to verify proper operation.*

- **Kitchen cooktop/stove/oven:** To inspect the burners, turn them on one at a time to see if each one works, then all at once for electric ranges. Try both the bake and broiler elements in each oven to be sure they heat up. Check the oven door (or doors) to see if the spring works and the oven door doesn't fall open. The stove should have an anti-tip device that should be tested. We suggest that you don't get involved with testing the timer, self-cleaning function, clock, or lights. These are minor points.

  CAUTION: Remember to turn off the burners and oven(s) when you're finished. Some ranges have a microwave as the top oven. You can test a microwave by putting a cup of water (always bring a coffee mug) in it for 60 seconds. The water should be very hot to boiling after 1 minute.

- **Dishwasher:** It's always a good idea to ask the homeowner (if present) if the dishwasher works and is hooked up. Always look inside before you test the dishwasher. You never know what may be stored in there (sometimes stuffed teddy bears). You won't have to run the dishwasher through the longest cycle. A short cycle should be enough to determine whether the sprayers work and the motor runs. Check to be sure it doesn't leak on the floor or under the sink. If the discharge hose is connected to the sink drain,

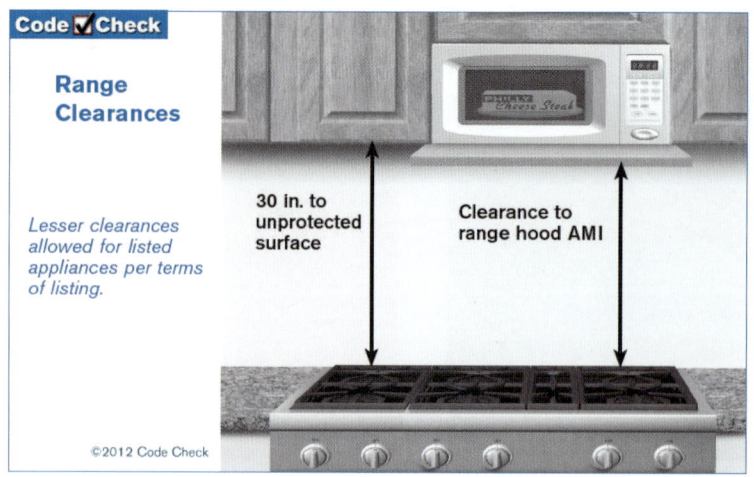

Photo #13 *There may be other things in the cabinet that are not part of the inspection such as this water filtration or reverse osmosis (RO) system. Just check it for leaks and note its presence.*

it should be water-tight and looped or have an air-gap installed so that sink water doesn't drain into the dishwasher when the sink is drained.

- **Refrigerator:** This is a fairly cursory inspection, just enough to make sure the refrigerator is operating. Open the freezer door and feel packages in the freezer to see if they're frozen solid. Open the refrigerator door and leave it open until you hear the motor kick in. Check the gaskets around the door. Using your coffee mug, fill it with water and/or ice from the fridge door. If it works, don't report anything; if it doesn't, make a note in your report. Then use this cup full of water for your microwave test.

- **Exhaust fan:** Test exhaust fans for operation. They may be present on the range hood, on the microwave, or on an exterior wall. Be sure that ductwork for any fans exhausts to the exterior. (You would have noticed its discharge during your exterior and/or roofing inspection and would notice it later in your attic inspection.) Exhaust fans may also be of a recirculating type, as is the case with most microwave ovens. A hood vented to the exterior is only **required** with "open-top" broilers (the Jenn-Air® type cooktops that you can cook steaks or burgers on), both gas and electric.

Photo #13 *This doesn't even look like an exhaust fan when it's slid back under the cabinets. Don't overlook items like this. You pull it out and it turns on automatically.*

- **Ceiling fan:** To inspect a ceiling fan in a kitchen or any other room, first touch the fan to see if it's securely attached to the ceiling (odds are if you can touch it, it might be too low to the ground). Don't turn it on if it feels loose. Run the fan and check if it wobbles, squeals, or vibrates too much in its mounting.

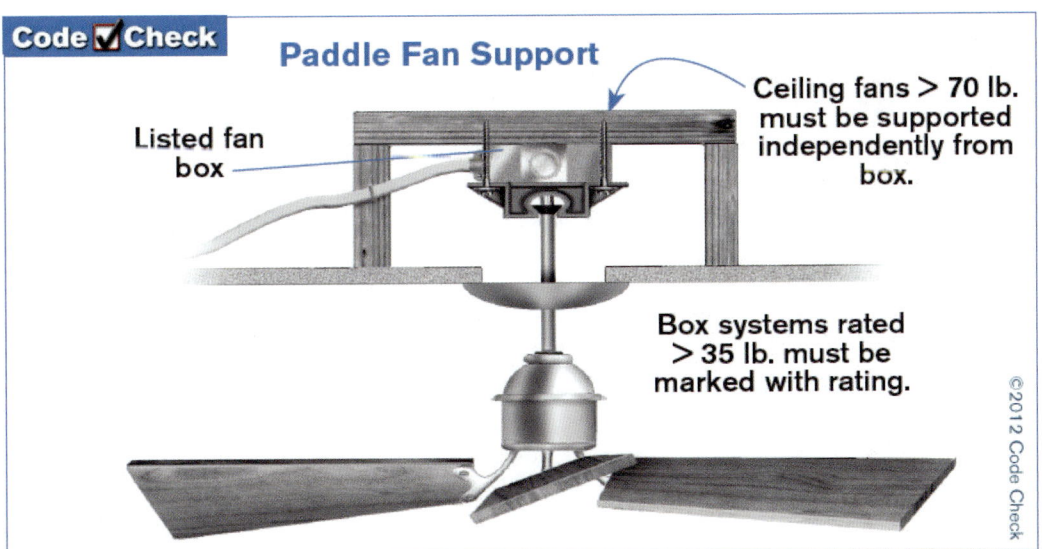

- **Countertops and receptacles:** Whatever material is used for the countertops, it should be unbroken, be tightly fastened, and not have surface damage such as large scratches, dents, burn marks, cracks, or holes. Some homeowners will arrange items on the countertop to cover up damage, so it's a good idea to move things around to double check. Lean on the edge of the counter to see if the counter is secured to the base cabinet. Islands in particular are often loose. You can discover any looseness of laminates

For Beginning Inspectors

Get out your flashlight, GFCI tester, and neon bulb tester.

Perform a complete inspection of your own kitchen as outlined here. Repeat the inspection in a different order until you find one that makes sense to you.

THE INTERIOR INSPECTION

SELECTED APPLIANCES

- Dishwasher
- Kitchen stove
- Refrigerator
- Exhaust fan
- Microwave
- Ceiling fan

by pressing down on the surface. Look around the sink for any evidence of wood rot (the particle board underneath swells when wet). Examine tile countertop finishes for any damaged or missing grout. The home inspector should be able to give an overall rating of satisfactory, marginal, or poor as to countertop condition. It's not necessary to write up every scratch in your inspection report, but you should mention them in your conversation with the customer. As you're checking out the countertops, pay attention to the receptacles at that level. All kitchen countertop receptacles should be GFCI protected.

- **Kitchen cabinets:** Next, turn your attention to the kitchen cabinets. Open all cabinets, which should open easily, close tightly, and have secured hinges. Notice if interior shelves and partitions are in good shape or are damaged or missing. Open and close each drawer.

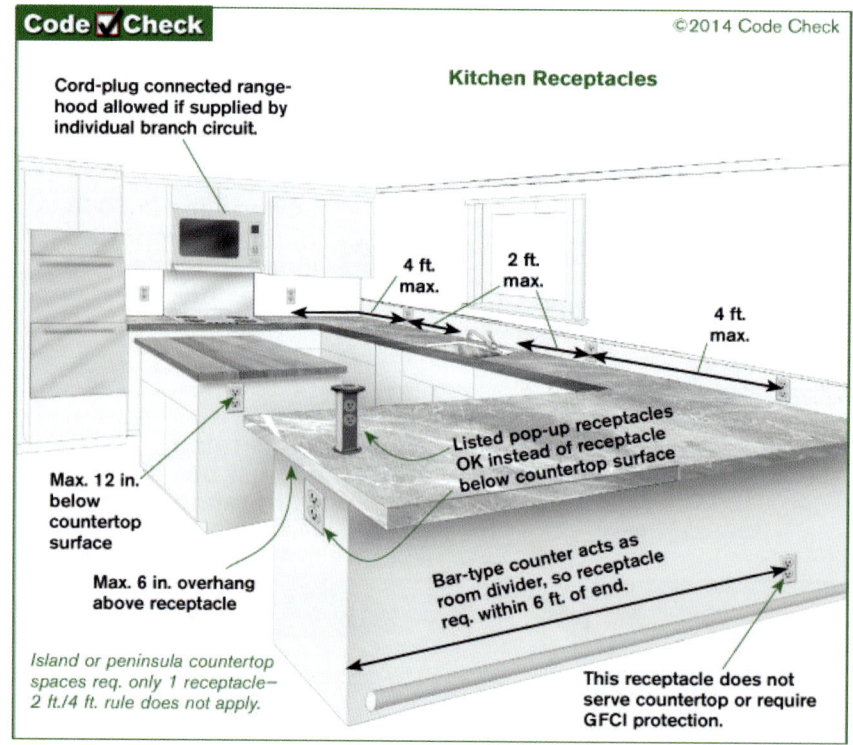

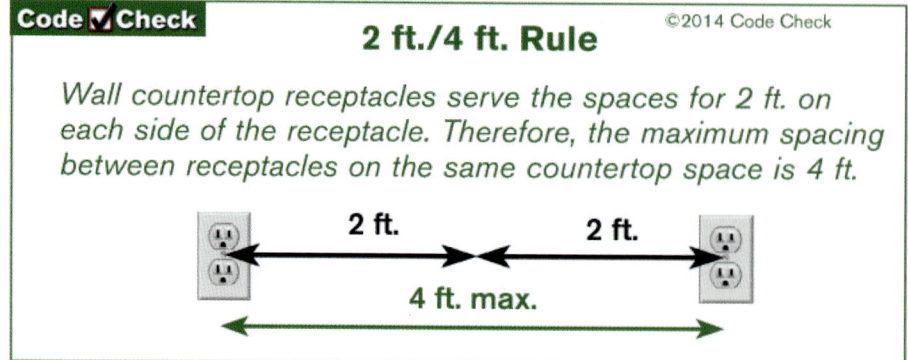

606   Chapter 7

- **Kitchen perimeter and ceiling:** Circle the perimeter of the kitchen, examining the walls, windows, and doors as you go. Sometimes, the window at the sink is forgotten, and it may be neglected because of its position. Use your flashlight to sidelight walls and take the time to sidelight the ceiling from several locations in the room to locate any bulges, sags, or deterioration of the facing. When checking each wall, notice the presence of a heat or cooling source (register, radiator, or convector). Also, notice the presence of receptacles other than countertop receptacles. Test the wall receptacles for current.

- **Floors:** As you make your circle around the room, you should look for any problems with the floor at the junction with the walls, at doorways, beneath windows, and so on. Then walk back and forth across the room and check it carefully for structural problems, squeaks and bouncy areas, deterioration, or looseness in the finish flooring or covering. Also look for evidence of water damage or wood rot. Check for evidence of rotted subflooring where water damage is likely to occur, such as in front of the sink and dishwasher. Keep the floor in mind as you look under the sink and inside cabinets.

Section Note

"One of my inspectors turned on a dishwasher in a brand-new home without checking first. To be honest, there was no one in the home to ask about it. Well, the dishwasher went through its cycle all right, but decided to drain its contents out under the sink and onto the kitchen floor.

The discharge hose hadn't been hooked up under the sink.

Of course, the inspector cleaned up the mess."

Inspecting the Bathroom

Again, the home inspector should develop a routine for inspecting the bathroom and not vary from the routine. It's important not to miss any of the items to be inspected. We've suggested one option here:

IN THE BATHROOM

<u>Leaks and water damage, wood rot, and metal shower pans.</u> Don't miss them. Ever. Examine bathrooms from below whenever possible.

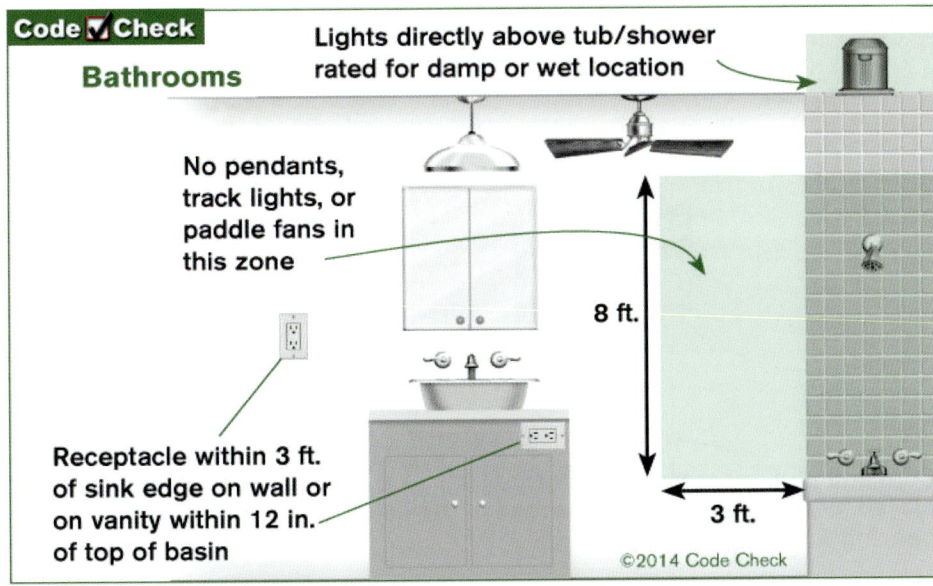

THE INTERIOR INSPECTION

- **Installed bathroom lighting:** Try the light switch by the door when you enter the room.

- **Walls, windows, door, and ceiling:** You should begin by filling the sink and tub, just as when inspecting the kitchen, and do the rest of the inspection while waiting for them to fill. Before focusing on the toughest bathroom items, inspect the walls and ceiling.

  If a first-floor bathroom sits directly under a second-floor bathroom, pay attention to the ceiling for any signs of leakage from above. As you inspect walls, test towel racks, toilet paper holders, and tub grips for secure attachment to the wall. Notice if there is a **heat source** in the bathroom. Be sure to report the absence of heat in the bathroom unless it is completely within the house with no exterior walls.

  Bathroom windows can have water damage because of their proximity to the tub or shower. Sometimes, homeowners have plastic curtains on bathtub windows that, if not opened often enough, can cause sills and sashes to rot and mildew. Make sure the door to the bathroom operates freely, latches, and locks. Check any other doors present (for example, linen closets). Be sure to inspect the back as well as the front of the door. Check to see if the doorstop is in place to protect the wall behind the door.

- **The floor:** Always inspect the bathroom floor carefully. Look for deterioration of the floor and subfloor around the edges of the room; under the sink; and around the toilet, tub, and shower. Push against flooring with the toe of your shoe or get down on your hands and knees to push against and gently probe flooring, especially around the toilet and tub. You don't want to miss wood rot and water damage. With plastic

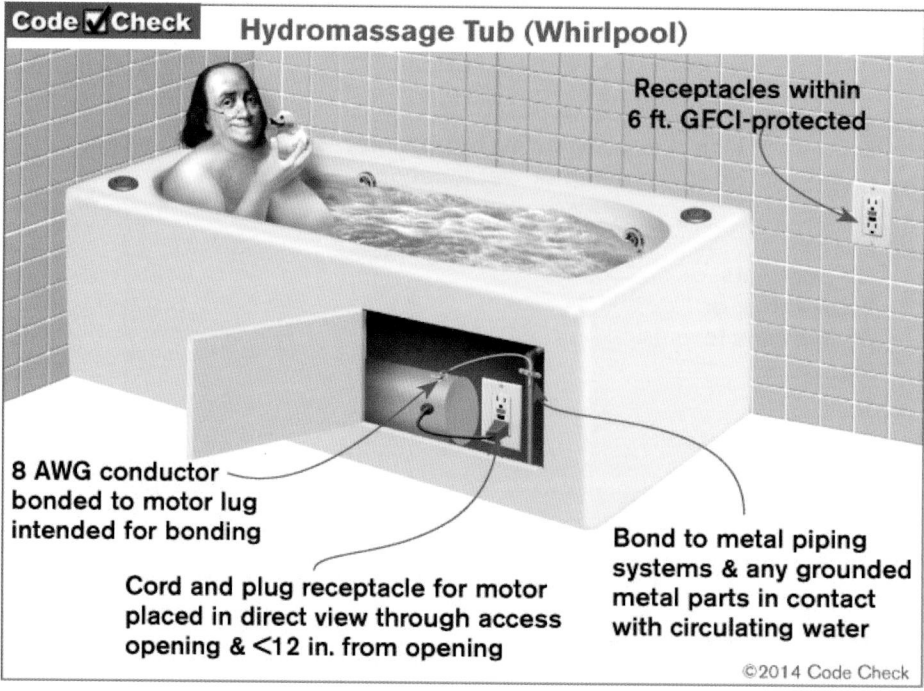

resilient floor coverings, check for deterioration of the sheet or tiles and loose adhesive. With ceramic and other types of tile, examine the condition of the grout. Broken or missing grout lets water into the subflooring. Water can also get through the floor if it rises over the sanitary base around the edges. Grout at the edges of the floor isn't enough to stop water, and the sanitary base should be present. You need a special tile or molding for the floor wall joint. If a floor is carpeted, be suspicious that it's covering a problem. Lift the carpet at a corner, if possible, to check the floor underneath.

- **Receptacles:** Test bathroom receptacles for polarity and grounding. Check for the presence of a GFCI receptacle and test those that are present. Just because they don't have the test buttons present doesn't necessarily mean they aren't GFCI protected. They may be linked to another bathroom or a breaker in the main panel. Test all of them with your GFCI tester's test button.

- **The lavatory:** Check the lavatory (sink) for general condition, including cracks, nicks, and other damage. Run the water and check for the presence of hot water, always on the left as you use the fixture. Check functional flow by turning on the lavatory and tub faucets and then flushing the toilet. Be sure to open the cabinet below the lavatory and inspect the piping, trap, and floor inside.

- **The toilet:** Flush the toilet at least twice during your inspection to test its operation. Examine the tank lid and bowl for any signs of cracks, damage, and leaking. Check to see if the toilet is tightly secured to the floor. Straddle the bowl, hold it between your knees, and gently rock it back and forth to do this. Or you can bend down and gently lift the bowl to test for looseness. A loose or cracked bowl should be reported.

- **Bidets:** Long popular in Europe, bidets are becoming more common in North American homes. A bidet is used for personal hygiene. It looks like a toilet without a lid and has hot and cold water and a stopper like a sink. It is actually a sink. Hot and cold water lines should be connected in the same manner as the lavatory, except that they should be equipped with a vacuum breaker or an anti-siphon device to prevent a cross connection. Check to see that it's secured to the floor and that the water flow and drainage are adequate. Test the spray nozzle as well as the rinse position on the diverter valve.

- **Tub and shower:** Examine tubs, shower stalls, and tub and shower combinations for the condition of the fixtures and faucets. Look for

> **HOMEOWNER TRICKS**
>
> - Covering bathroom floor problems with carpeting.
> - Not using the shower for a while before the home inspection to hide leaking.
> - Misrepresenting the age of the home. (Check for date under toilet tank lid or under pedestal sink.)
> - Arranging items on countertops to cover up damage.
> - Boarding over closet ceilings to hide water damage.
> - The list goes on.

leaking. Some older showers had a ceramic tile floor laid over a **metal shower pan**, which was made of lead or tin. These metal shower pans are notorious for leaking, and if it isn't leaking now, it will soon. Never miss reporting the presence of a metal shower pan if identified (as seen from below in a crawl space or basement).

You should suspect that a metal shower pan is present in an older home (1950s) if the floor of the shower is laid with the very small ceramic tiles, as that was the style with these pans.

> ### For Beginning Inspectors
>
> *Get out your flashlight, GFCI tester, and neon (in older homes) bulb tester again and head for the bathroom for a complete inspection. After doing your own bathroom, bother your friends again and practice inspecting as many bathrooms as you can. Be careful in older homes that had "tubs" but did not have shower heads. That big window was not a problem when it was a tub, but when someone added a shower head, you have leakage issues into the walls.*

If you can't tell whether the shower pan is leaking, you can block the shower drain, using a specific stopper for this purpose, and let water fill the bottom of the shower. Then uncover the drain and try to observe leaking from under the shower, if possible. In any case, observe the shower from underneath and look for evidence of leaking. You can often see the corrosion and leaking around the shower drain, and water will have done a great deal of damage to the floor and underlying wood structure. The wall around the tub, or surround as it's called, must be inspected too. Ceramic tile used to be applied with cement mortar pressed against wire mesh, which was called setting it in **mud (is still popular with high-end houses)**. That makes for a heavy wall requiring strong framing. The wall was water-resistant as long as the grout lasted and the reinforced wall didn't crack. Tiles were applied to plywood or green gypsum board (green board) with water-resistant adhesives for a lighter wall. Check the tile for condition and for broken and missing grout. Ceramic tile surrounds are vulnerable to leaking at the junction of the tub and the tiles where caulking may be inadequate. Water see page is common around the escutcheons (trim ring at faucet and handles). Use your screwdriver to tap against tiles to test for looseness—loose tile makes a crackling noise, whereas tight tile rings. Pushing against the tiles that yield can indicate loose tiles or deterioration of the plaster, drywall, or backing. Inform customers that tile work should be repaired and open joints regrouted or caulked to prevent water damage to the wood framing and ceiling below.

NOTE: Doors on showers and tubs, as well as windows and modern glass surrounds, should be safety glass or plastic rather than regular glass so that the bather can't be injured by falling against them. This also prevents injury if something were to break the window from outside.

- **Exhaust fan:** First check that the fan has its own switch. You may find some fans wired to the light switch so that they go on every time the light does. This is wasteful, and you might want to suggest rewiring it. Turn on the bathroom exhaust fan to see if it works. Noisy fans are caused by dirty or distorted blades. Be sure that vent piping exhausts to the exterior and not to the attic or crawl space.

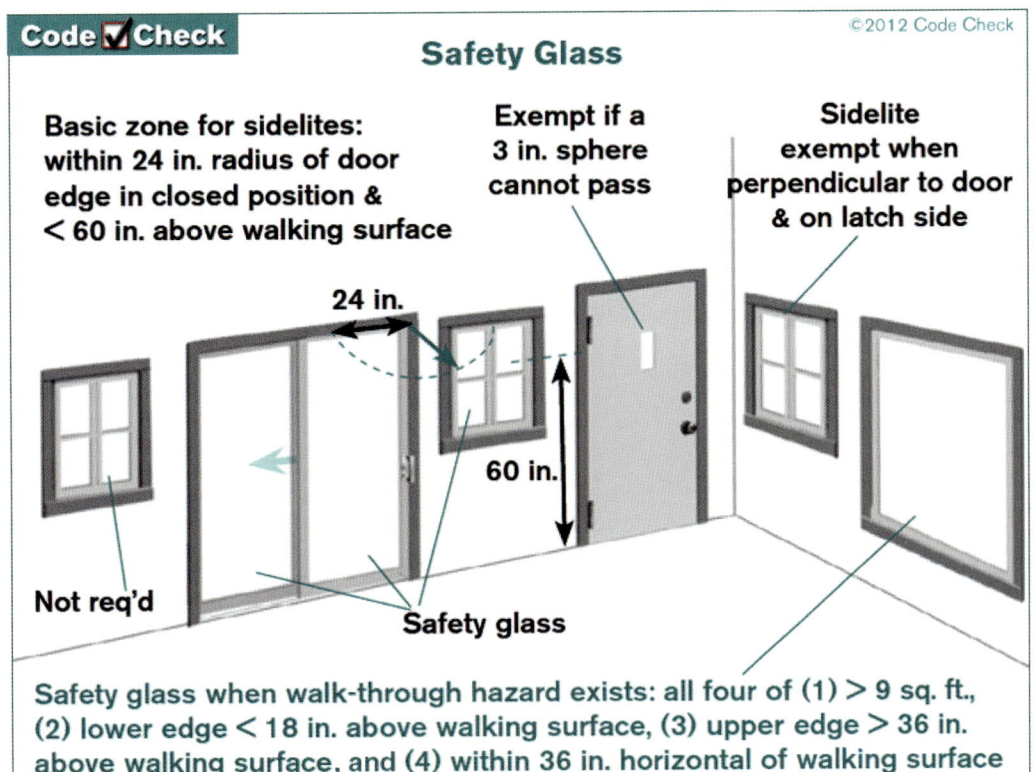

Inspecting Other Rooms

Routine is important too in examining the other rooms in the house, and you may approach bedrooms differently from family rooms. Give the walls, ceiling, and floor in each room a good inspection. Remember to look for a heat source in each room and to perform the necessary electrical tests on selected lights, fans, and receptacles. Operate accessible windows and don't forget to look behind doors in every case. As you conclude your interior inspection, remember to inspect foyers and hallways and any closets in them, including closets under stairs.

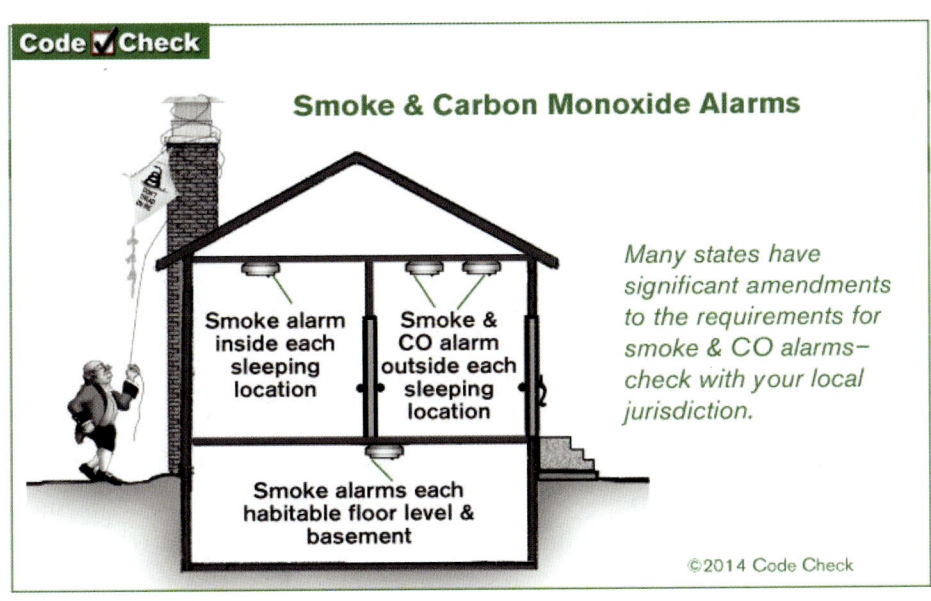

During your inspection, check for the presence of smoke and carbon monoxide alarms in the home. Test each one for operation, holding the button down long enough to determine if they are interconnected as they should be in a newer home. Advise customers that there should be a smoke alarms on each level of the home and in each bedroom and its hallway at the very least (many more will be in a new home) and that each one should be tested once a month. Smoke alarms have a life expectancy of only 7 to10 years, so those old yellowed ones should most likely be replaced.

A WORD ABOUT CEILING STAINS: Always report any sign of water damage or leaking in a ceiling. And when you find staining, try to figure out what's causing it.

DON'T EVER MISS

- Missing power, lighting, or heat source in any room
- Water damage, wood rot, and water stains, old or new
- Ceiling, wall, and floor conditions indicating structural problems
- Loose, cracked, or damaged ceiling and wall facings
- Electrical safety hazards
- Metal shower pans
- Plumbing leaks
- Fans not exhausted outside

Reporting Your Findings

Your inspection report should have a separate page used to record your findings on the kitchen. Separate pages or sections should be devoted to the bathroom(s), preferably a section for each bathroom in the house. Smaller sections should be available for each of the other rooms, such as the living room and bedrooms.

Here is an overview of how to report your findings on the room-by-room interior inspection:

- **Kitchen:** Report your findings on the condition of the ceiling, walls, and floors in the kitchen. Note defects such as ceiling and wall cracks, sloping and uneven floors, wood rot, and signs of leaking. Note the presence or absence of a heat source. Write your findings with regard to the condition of the countertops and cabinets, noting if any hardware is missing or broken or any structures are loose or detached. Write your remarks about the doors and windows in the kitchen. It's a good idea to report on windows in general and for each room. Record your findings about the plumbing situation in the kitchen and laundry room. Rate the functional flow and drainage at the sink as adequate or poor. Then record the results of testing receptacles in the kitchen. Remember to classify reverse polarity and an open ground as a **safety hazard**. We suggest that you recommend GFCIs if they're missing.

  It helps to have a list of appliances in your report with a checklist so that you can indicate if the appliance was present, was tested, and is operating.

- **Bathroom:** As with the kitchen, record your findings for walls, ceilings, floors, doors, and windows in the bathroom. Note the presence or absence of a heat source. Rate the functional flow and drainage at the bathroom fixtures as adequate or poor. Then record the results of testing receptacles and the presence of GFCIs in the bathroom. If the room has a ventilation fan, indicate if you've operated it and whether it's operating.

It helps in filling in the bathroom report when each fixture is listed on the page with a checklist for rating faucets, pipes, fixture condition, and so on. Note defects such as faucets are leaking, tub/shower needs caulking, and tile needs grout or caulk in corners and at dissimilar materials (tub/wall joints, loose toilet bowl, and so on).

- **Other rooms:** Begin by identifying which room you're reporting your findings on. Record your findings for the walls, ceiling, floor, windows, doors, heat source, and electrical situation for each room. Don't miss mentioning any water stains from leaks, rotted flooring, and other conditions stated in the Don't Ever Miss list.

7.8 THE INSULATION AND VENTILATION INSPECTION

In this chapter, you'll learn about the guidelines for the insulation and ventilation inspection.

> **Section Note**
>
> *Ice dams occur when heat from the attic melts snow on the roof and the water flows down the roof and refreezes at the eaves. The water freezes because the gutters and eaves (overhangs) are not heated. As the ice builds up, melting and refreezing water backs up under the shingles and seeps into the structure through seams in the roof sheathing, gaps around plumbing stacks, and nail holes. This ice buildup settles in the gutters and under roof shingles, causing roof damage. As the ice dams melt, water leaks into the house, damaging the walls and ceilings.*
>
> *Proper attic insulation and ventilation as well as a waterproof shingle underlayment applied to the roof deck can prevent ice dams from forming.*

> **Photo #14 INSULATION AND VENTILATION**
>
> *If you live in a cold climate, then you know what this is all about. Ice-damming is a significant problem in freezing climates. The lack of insulation and/or poor attic ventilation both contribute to ice-damming.*

> **Chapter Note**
>
> *Pages 613–616 lay out the content and scope of the insulation and ventilation inspection. It's an overview of the inspection, including what to observe, what to describe, and what specific actions not to take. Study them carefully.*

Inspection Guidelines and Overview

These are representative of the various standards of practice and state standards that govern the inspection of the interior components of the property.

Most standards of practice provide an outline of what is to be inspected and what is to be reported during the inspection of the home's interior living spaces. If licensing, registration, or certification is required in your state, you should follow the state's standards of practice. But, of course, not all the details are included in the SOP. There are many other details that will be presented in this chapter.

INSULATION AND VENTILATION SYSTEMS

Observe and/or Report: The act of making a visual examination of a system or component and reporting on its condition.	• Ventilation of attics and foundation areas • Insulation and vapor retarders where visible • Kitchen, bathroom, laundry, and similar exhaust systems • Clothes dryer exhaust system(s) • Presence of water penetration and/or condensation
Describe: Report in writing a system or component by its type, or other observed characteristics, to distinguish it from other components used for the same purpose.	• Approximate average depth and type of attic insulation(s) • Vapor retarders in accessible unfinished spaces • Absence of insulation in unfinished spaces at conditioned surfaces • Attic and crawl space ventilation
Report as deficient deficiencies in:	• Crawl space ventilation that is not performing • Attic ventilation that is not performing • Missing insulation, at conditioned surfaces • Attic ventilators • Range hoods and exhaust system ducts/vents that do not terminate outside the building, if the unit is not of a re-circulating type or configuration • Absence of proper duct/vent material
The inspector is not required to:	• Operate powered ventilators • Provide an exhaustive list of locations of deficiencies and water penetrations • Damaged duct systems or improper material • Damaged or missing duct insulation • Traverse attic load-bearing components that are concealed by insulation or by other materials • Activate/operate thermostatically controlled fans • Break or otherwise damage the surface finish or seal on or around access panels and covers • Determine the adequacy of ventilation

Most standards of practice provide a good outline of what is to be inspected and reported during the inspection of the insulation and ventilation in the home. Not all details are included in this chart. These details will be presented in the following sections.

For the inspection of **unfinished spaces** (attics and crawl spaces, for example), most requirements in the standards of practice for the structural inspection state that the home inspector is required to make every effort to get into and inspect these unfinished spaces. And for his or her own protection, the home inspector should report on how access was gained and from where he or she inspected the spaces. Reporting in this way lets customers know that some defects may not be found if access is limited. This is important for the inspection of insulation and ventilation as well as the other aspects of crawl space and attic inspection.

> **REQUIRED TO**
>
> - Enter crawl spaces and attics, where possible.
> - Report the method used to observe crawl spaces and attics.

- *The home inspector is required to enter underfloor crawl spaces and attic spaces except when access is obstructed, when entry could damage property, or when dangerous or adverse situations are suspected.*

- *The home inspector is required to report the method used to observe underfloor crawl spaces and attics.*

The insulation and ventilation inspection consists of inspecting the following:

- **Insulation and vapor retarder:** For the most part, insulation and vapor retarders are only visible in unfinished areas such as attics and crawl spaces. The home inspector is expected to examine these areas for insulation and to report its **presence and location**; identify the **type** of insulation; inspect its condition and installation; and determine if the insulation is adequate, which in most cases, is not and the inspector will want to recommend additional insulation. The inspector also attempts to determine the presence or absence of a vapor barrier on the warm in winter side of the interior insulation. This does not apply to the entire country. In certain warm humid climates like the southeastern United States, Florida, and the Gulf Coast installation may differ. Check local requirements. Keep in mind that the primary purpose and use of vapor retarders is/was to prevent condensation within wall cavities in *cold* climates. That being the case, the home inspector may not see vapor retarders in warmer drier portions of the country.

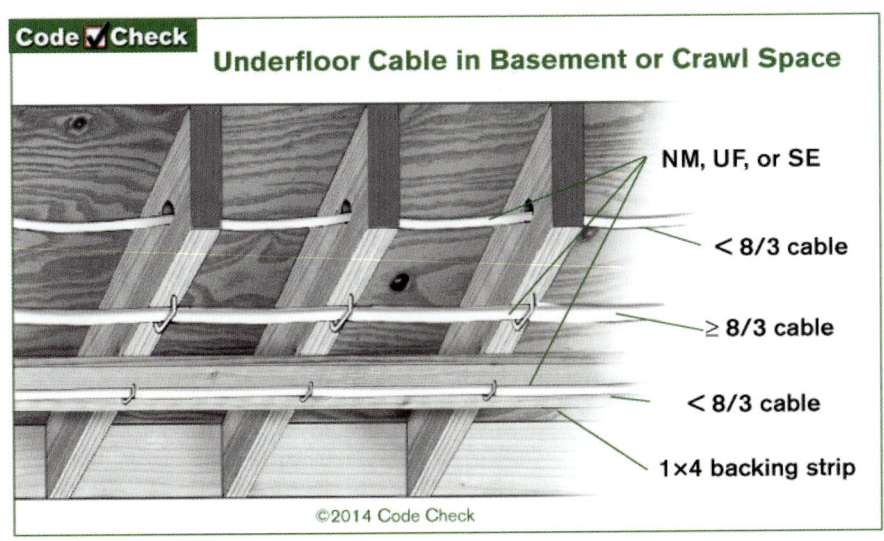

THE INTERIOR INSPECTION

Note that the home inspector is **not required to report on concealed insulation and vapor retarders**. This instruction refers to insulation in exterior walls that is not visible (although we'll suggest a method to help get an idea of exterior wall insulation) and vapor retarders that may be hidden above or below insulation, as in the crawl space or attic.

Where foam board insulation is used, it should be covered with a non-combustible material. The home inspector reports any exposed foam board insulation within the living space as a **fire hazard**.

In unheated areas, the home inspector also checks plumbing pipes, heating ductwork, and venting system piping for the presence or lack of insulation.

THE INSPECTION

- Visible insulation and vapor retarders
- Attic and foundation ventilation
- Exhaust venting
- The attic

Illustration by Paddy Morrissey

- **Attic and foundation ventilation:** The home inspector examines the attic and foundation areas for proper ventilation in the form of roof or soffit and crawl space perimeter wall venting. The types of roof vents are identified. The home inspector determines if vents are **performing** and are not blocked by insulation or painted over. Much attention is paid to **condensation**, especially in cold climates in the winter and warm humid climates in the summer, and **deterioration of structural members**, both of which are the result of poor ventilation and/or lack of insulation. The adequacy of ventilation is based on such indications. Ventilating fans are also examined.

- **Venting systems:** Kitchen, bathroom, and laundry venting systems must be vented to the outside. During the insulation and ventilation inspection, the home inspector makes sure that house vents do not exhaust into the attic, garage, or crawl space and contribute to a moisture problem.

- **The attic:** For convenience, we've included the inspection of the attic along with the insulation and ventilation inspection. This chapter presents the entire attic inspection, which is covered in pieces in other sections. The full attic inspection includes examining the roof and floor structure, the chimney chase, insulation, roof vents, plumbing pipes, exhaust venting, and electrical features. The home inspector examines the attic for any evidence of leaking and/or condensation and determines the adequacy of insulation and ventilation.

7.9 INSULATION

At one time in our history, little attention was paid to insulation because fuel was inexpensive. The use of insulation in homes started when fuel costs increased. Insulation slows the rate of heat loss from a house. Whenever there is a difference in temperature between the interior and exterior of structures such as walls, floors, and ceilings, air currents form to move heat from the warm side to the cold side of these structures. The air spaces between tiny fibers or foam bubbles in insulation slow down the movement of these air currents and consequently reduce heat loss.

Types of Insulation

Different types of insulation have different capacities to resist heat transfer. Insulation is given an **R-value**, which is a number used by the industry to represent the **amount of heat resistance per inch of thickness**. The higher the R-value, the greater the resistance. The U.S. Department of Energy recommends an **R-value**, or total heat resistance, for insulation in various locations in the home. For example, an R-value of at least 49 is recommended in attics in northern climates. A type of insulation with an R-value of 2.9/inch would require a thickness of about 13″ to meet an R-value of 38.

$$\text{R-value per inch} \times \text{number of inches} = \text{R-value}$$

Some common insulation products are produced in **batts (rolls or sheets) and blown-in varieties**. Insulating batts are manufactured in lengths of 4′ and 8′ and in thicknesses of 3-1/2″–12″. Blankets are available in large sheets (for example, a blanket in thickness from 1-1/2″–3″.) Widths of batts are 15″ or 23″ to fit between studs and joists at spacing of 16″ and 24″. The insulating wool-like material in batts and blankets is made up of thin manufactured fibers created from glass or mineral waste such as sand, rock, and slag.

- **Fiberglass batt and blanket insulation** is made of threads of glass covered with a coating that binds the fibers in place. The insulation may be white or dyed a distinctive color (such as pink or yellow) by the manufacturer. Fiberglass insulation in the form of batts and blankets has an R-value of 3 to 3-1/2 per inch depending on manufacturer (requiring about 12″–12-1/2″ of attic insulation to achieve an R-38 rating). It is resistant to moisture, mildew, fungus, and vermin. Most types of fiberglass insulation are non-combustible. You'll often see 3-1/2″ fiberglass batts in the attics of **older homes**, installed when the home was built. The paper facing on the insulation stated the

---

TYPES OF INSULATION

- Batts and blankets
- Loose fill/blown-in
- Rigid board
- Spray applied foam

Chapter Note

Pages 617–632 present the study and inspection of insulation in the home.

Definitions

The R-value is a number that represents an insulation material's resistance to heat flow per inch of thickness. An R-rating is the total heat resistance for a given thickness of insulation.

BATTS AND BLANKETS

- Fiberglass
- Rock wool

R-rating of the insulation as R-11 (3.1 R-value × 3-1/2″ thickness). Insulation requirements have changed in recent years. This amount of fiberglass batt insulation wouldn't meet the requirements for attic insulation today. Modern insulation is high-density fiberglass with up to an R-15 value for 2 × 4 walls and R-21 for 2 × 6 walls.

> **Definitions**
>
> *Rock wool* is an insulating fibrous material made by blowing steam through molten rock or slag.
>
> *Kraft paper* is a water-resistant, asphalt-impregnated paper that can be used as a vapor barrier.
>
> *Loose fill* insulation is a loose material such as fiberglass, rock wool, or cellulose that is poured or blown in place between wall studs and attic joists.

- **Rock mineral/wool batt and blanket insulation** is made from fibers created by blowing steam through molten rock or mineral waste. Rock wool is typically dark gray in color. Mineral wool is a tan color. In batt and blanket form, its R-value is 3.7/inch (requiring only 10-1/2″ of attic insulation for R-38), slightly better than fiberglass. This type of insulation is resistant to rot and has good resistance to fire.

Batt and blanket insulation may be faced on neither side, one side, or both sides with plain paper, treated kraft paper, or plastic or metal foil. **Kraft paper** is an asphalt-impregnated paper that is water-resistant enough to serve as a vapor retarder. Metal foil on batts and blankets will reflect heat if the foil side faces a free air space. You may be familiar with foil-faced insulation on ductwork and piping, where the insulation faces open space. Of course, if foil facing is covered with or is touching drywall, its heat reflective properties are lost.

CAUTION: During installation, when the fibers in batt and blanket insulation can become airborne, the tiny fibers can be a skin and eye irritant or can be breathed in. Glass fibers may be more irritating than mineral fibers, but once the insulation is in place, there is no hazard. However, the home inspector may loosen glass or mineral fibers if the insulation is handled during an inspection. Some inspectors wear a dust mask and a disposable jumpsuit for protection.

Another form of insulation is called **loose fill or blown-in**. Loose-fill insulation is normally supplied in bags or bales and can be poured or blown into wall cavities or in horizontal spaces such as between ceiling joists in the attic. Loose-fill fiberglass insulation is generally less efficient inch for inch than batt or blanket insulation. Moreover, the older types of insulation in walls can pack down or settle over time due to vibrations of road traffic, wind, and activity in the home, leaving uninsulated space at the top of the wall cavity. This is no longer the case today. Loose fill insulation may be made of the following materials:

> **LOOSE FILL**
>
> - Fiberglass
> - Rock wool
> - Cellulose
> - Vermiculite

- **Fiberglass loose-fill insulation** is made of the same glass threads as batt and blanket insulation, but the threads are not glued together so they can be blown in. The R-value of fiberglass loose fill is 2.5–3.0 per inch (requiring about 15″ to meet recommendations for an R-value of 38 in attic installations). Fiberglass as loose fill is less efficient per inch than in batts and blankets for most brands.

INSULATION TYPE	R-VALUE/ INCH (AVERAGE)	R-11	R-13	R-15	R-19
FG Batts (Low/High Density)	3.1 to 4.3	3.5	3.5	3.5	5.5
Blown-in FG	2.2 to 2.5				
Mineral Wool Batts (Rock & Slag)	3.7		3.5	4.1	5.1
Cellulose	3.6 to 3.8		3.5	4.1	5.1
Plastic Fiber Insulation (PET)	3.8 to 4.3			3.7	4.7
Cotton Insulation (Blue Jeans)	3.4			4.4	5.6
Straw Bale	2.4 to 3.0				
Polystyrene	3.8 to 5	2.5	3.0	3.4	4.3
Polyisocyanurate	5.6 to 8	1.6	1.9	2.2	2.8
Polyurethane	5.5 to 6.5	1.8	2.2	2.5	3.2
Vermiculite & Perlite	2.4	4.6	5.4	6.3	7.9
UFFI	4.6	2.4	2.8	3.3	4.1
AirKrete	3.9	2.8	3.3	3.8	4.9
Phenolic Foam	4.8	2.3	2.7	3.1	4.0

- **Rock wool loose-fill insulation** is essentially the same material as that used in batts and blankets. However, its R-value is less as a loose fill—only 2.9/inch (requiring 13″ for an R-38 value in the attic).

- **Cellulose loose-fill insulation** can be blown into wall cavities or horizontal attic spaces. It's made of shredded recycled newspaper or wood fibers treated with a fire retardant. Cellulose loose fill is usually gray in color and feels like lint. Old cellulose is yellowish orange, almost like sawdust in older homes. Its R-value is 3.7/inch (requiring only 10-1/4″ for an R-38 value in the attic), a higher value than either fiberglass or rock wool. But cellulose **had** a greater tendency to settle in wall cavities of older homes.

The fire-retardant chemicals used in treating cellulose are in either granular or liquid form. The fire retardant may not perform over time. Granules can eventually sink to the bottom of the loose fill. Liquid applications remain water soluble and

For Beginning Inspectors

The best way to learn how to identify different types of insulation products is to see them. Identification of the type of insulation is required during the home inspection. Visit home centers to see what's available. Talk to builders to find out what is being used in construction in your area. And take a look at as many attics as you can.

Section Note

Find out the recommended R-ratings for your area of the country.

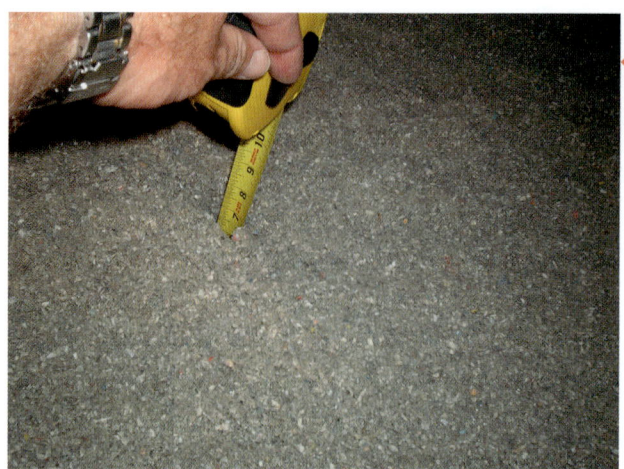

Photo #15 *Cellulose insulation being measured. It looks like about 7" of insulation or about R-26, (7" × 3.7/in = 25.9).*

RIGID INSULATION

- Fiberglass
- Polystyrene, extruded or bead board
- Urethane

can be leached out if the insulation becomes wet. Both conditions render the insulation vulnerable to fire. That's why the home inspector should carefully inspect electrical conditions in an attic filled with cellulose insulation. Junction boxes must be covered, and non-IC lights should not be covered with any insulation. Cellulose easily absorbs water. If cellulose loose fill in the attic becomes waterlogged from condensation or a roof leak, the fire-retardant chemicals can have a corrosive effect on the metal gussets of attic trusses and on electrical armored cable and pipes in contact with it.

Photo #16 IC-AT RECESSED LIGHT FIXTURE

This is an IC-AT recessed light fixture. Remember, IC means that it can be buried in insulation and AT means that it is the more energy efficient, air-tight type.

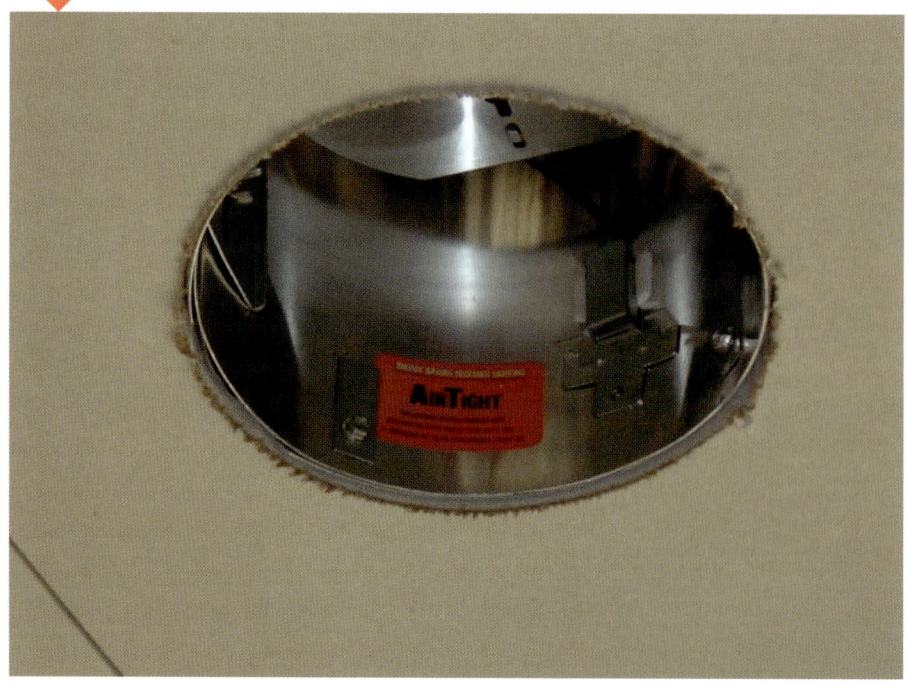

- **Vermiculite loose fill insulation** is a silicate mineral that is heated and expanded. As loose fill, its small particles are rectangular in shape. Vermiculite is fireproof and resistant to rot and mildew, although it does absorb moisture. It may also have asbestos in it. Vermiculite's R-value is 2.4/inch (requiring about 15.8″ for an R-38 value in the attic). There is currently a Trust set up for the vermiculite brand Zonolite. You may want to do a Google search for the details on this trust and the restitution available to homeowners who have it in their attics. Another natural loose-fill insulation is **perlite**, which is made from volcanic rock. Both of these insulations tend to be more expensive than others. They were commonly used in the 1950s.

> **Definitions**
>
> *Cellulose* is a loose-fill insulation made of recycled newspaper or wood fibers treated with a fire retardant.
>
> *Vermiculite* is a silicate mineral.
>
> *Polystyrene and urethane* are plastic foams that can be formed into rigid boards used in insulating foundations, exterior walls, and roofs. Urethane is also available in less rigid forms and as a spray-applied insulation.

Rigid board insulation can be used on foundation and masonry walls, under vinyl and aluminum siding, and under roofs. It comes in widths of 24″ and 48″ and can be made from fiberglass; wood fiberboard; or foamed plastics such as polystyrene, Polyisocyanurate, or urethane. Rigid foamed insulation is often installed on the exterior of a foundation during construction.

- **Fiberglass rigid board**, with an R-value of 4/inch, is commonly used for insulating the exterior of foundation walls. On the exterior, it also serves as a drainage layer around a basement.

- **Polystyrene rigid board insulation** is a plastic foam formed into boards. Two kinds of polystyrene are used—**extruded polystyrene**, where the foam is produced by extrusion, and **bead board**, where the foam is produced by expanding and then fusing granular pellets. They have R-values of 3.8/inch to 5.0/inch depending on the type. Both are used for exterior or interior foundation insulation, under slabs, under sidings, and on roofs. Polystyrene can burn easily and rapidly once it is ignited and then melts, spreading fire with the molten flow. Therefore, rigid polystyrene boards used in interior living spaces must not be left exposed. Any exposed polystyrene boards found in living spaces during a home inspection should be reported as a **safety hazard**.

- **Urethane Polyiso rigid board insulation** is made with a foam that has bubbles filled with chlorofluorocarbon gas and is cream/off-white in color. Its R-value is high at 6-8/inch, which provides good insulation. However, urethane boards also pose a fire hazard if they're left exposed in a home, and they give off toxic fumes in a fire.

> **SITE-FOAMED**
>
> - UFFI
> - Urethane
> - AirKrete

Urethane foams can be produced in less rigid forms from limp to spongy. This softer urethane insulation may be used in a home to seal openings

> **Definitions**
>
> <u>Site-foamed insulation</u>, made of various syrups (polyol) and reactants (MDI), is mixed on the site and foamed in place.
>
> <u>UFFI</u> (urea formaldehyde foam insulation) is a site-foamed insulation that was used in the 1970s and early 1980s, but was not used after about 1983. UFFI released formaldehyde gas into the home during the curing process and under conditions of high temperatures and humidity.
>
> <u>AirKrete</u> is a site-foamed insulation made of a mixture of a cement containing syrup and air.

> **ASBESTOS INSULATION**
>
> Be careful when inspecting any insulation you suspect contains asbestos. <u>Don't disturb it</u>. It's dangerous when asbestos fibers are released into the air and breathed in.

between the foundation and sill or at wall penetrations. It is recognizable by its yellow-orange color and shiny, wet appearance.

Another type of insulation is spray-applied **site-foamed insulation** or foamed-in-place insulation. As the name implies, this type of insulation is produced at the site. The insulating material in a syrup form (polyol) is mixed with a reactant catalyst (MDI), and a foam is created that can be poured or sprayed into structural cavities.

- **Urea formaldehyde foam insulation** (abbreviated UFFI), used in the 1970s and early 1980s, was produced on-site from a syrup mixed with formaldehyde as the catalyst. It was discovered that UFFI released formaldehyde gas into the home during the first year or so after installation and under high temperatures and moist conditions. The foam itself is a good insulator, identifiable by its light color, soft foamy appearance, frail crumbly structure, and habit of squeezing out of openings like soap lather. UFFI is also resistant to fire, rot, and fungus.

  UFFI is suspected of being a **health hazard**. The American Cancer Society considers formaldehyde a potential carcinogen. The use of UFFI was banned in 1983, although the government reversed itself a few years later. But UFFI is still not installed today due to the stigma associated with it. If the home inspector finds or suspects old UFFI insulation in a home built in the 1970s or early 1980s, it has probably already released all of its formaldehyde. The customer should be informed of the finding and told that its presence is most likely no longer a health concern.

- **Urethane foam**, as described earlier, can be mixed on site, then poured or sprayed to foam in place. Again, as a plastic foam, urethane site-foamed insulation must be covered.

- **AirKrete** is a form of site-foamed insulation made of a cement containing syrup that is foamed with air and poured into cavities as a non-flexible insulator. It provides a good alternative to the plastic foams because it doesn't burn or produce toxic fumes. However, it is not water-resistant and may cause structural rot if poured into wall cavities that become wet.

Asbestos in Insulation

Asbestos is a mineral fiber found in rocks. There are different kinds of asbestos fibers, all of which are fire-resistant and not easily destroyed or degraded by natural processes. The mere presence of asbestos in building materials and home products is not necessarily a **health risk**. The danger occurs when asbestos fibers are released from the material to the air and breathed in. There are two classifications of asbestos products: friable and non-friable. The EPA defines a friable material as one that can be reduced to powder with hand pressure. Pipe insulation (white powdery type) is considered friable. An example of a non-friable material is vinyl asbestos tile (VAT). Once inhaled, asbestos fibers can become lodged in tissue for a long time, and cancer of the lung can develop after many years of exposure. Experts say that no level of exposure to asbestos fibers is totally safe.

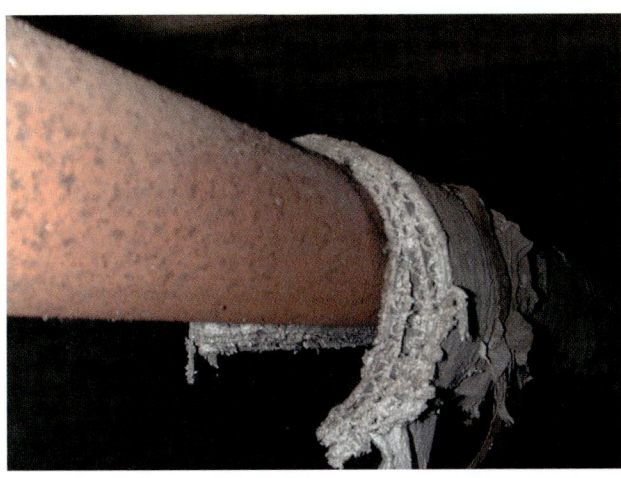

Photo #17 *This is asbestos-containing pipe insulation in poor condition. This is very typical in old houses with steam or hot water boilers. Write it up as a possible asbestos material and recommend testing.*

The **Environmental Protection Agency** (EPA) has placed restrictions and bans on the use of asbestos in home products since the late 1970s. For asbestos already in the home, the EPA recommends removal of the asbestos product by a qualified asbestos-removal contractor to an approved disposal site, or encapsulation of any undamaged asbestos left in place in the home. The process of removal is dangerous because that's when the fibers are disturbed and can be released to the air.

Asbestos is used in products because of its strength, its good thermal and acoustic insulating properties, its use as a binder, and its fire resistance. It was used in many materials, including asbestos-cement siding and roofing, vinyl floor coverings, textured paints, patching compounds, plaster, drywall, pipe insulation, ceiling tiles, adhesives, and roofing mastic. Because the EPA didn't begin ruling on the issue until the 1970s, asbestos can still be found in homes built before 1980. Asbestos in insulation includes the following:

- **Wall and attic insulation:** Generally, asbestos fibers were used as loose-fill insulation in homes built from the 1930s through the 1950s. The fill is likely to look fibrous or powdery (some of it looks like kitty litter). Some vermiculite insulation contained asbestos fibers (Google Zonolite Trust). It's difficult to know for certain whether insulation contains asbestos, and the home inspector should not engage in guessing. If asbestos is suspected, it should be reported and possibly submitted for testing by a local laboratory, keeping in mind that specific sampling protocols are in place to confirm or deny the asbestos content of various materials.

- **Water pipe and heating duct insulation:** A common pipe and duct insulation called AirCell® contains asbestos and looks like corrugated cardboard when viewed from the end. This insulation, if deteriorating or damaged, is one of the most common causes of asbestos fibers being released into the home. Removal by qualified disposal technicians is expensive.

- **Plaster reinforced with asbestos:** Plaster mixed with asbestos was used to insulate boiler and furnace parts, supply ducts, and hot water/steam piping (especially at elbows and tees). A plaster covering was used on the bonnets of old gravity furnaces. When you see it, you can be almost certain that asbestos is present, based on the practices used years ago.

- **Millboard:** Made of asbestos and gypsum, millboard can be found as a protective insulator on the walls and floors near a wood stove. Millboard was often mounted inside boiler and furnace cabinets as well.

Tell customers that the identification of asbestos in the home is beyond the scope of the home inspection and that home inspectors are not trained to identify asbestos. You're really not trained! You can make a fairly good guess with pipe and duct wrapping and plaster with asbestos in it, but you can never be certain. Positive identification can be made only by sending samples to a qualified laboratory for testing. Inform the customer whenever asbestos insulation is suspected in the home. Even when you're sure you've found asbestos insulation, it's best to report that although you're fairly certain it contains asbestos, a sample should be sent to a lab for confirmation.

> **ASBESTOS IDENTIFICATION**
>
> *The home inspector is not trained to identify asbestos in the home. You can report that asbestos is suspected, but <u>don't give a definite opinion</u>.*
>
> *Positive identification can be done only through a laboratory.*

Insulating the Home

Insulation should be installed around the heated living space in the home. In cold climates, insulation should be installed with the **vapor retarder** against the warm in winter side of the living space. The vapor barrier is a thin sheet of material such as polyethylene film, aluminum (foil), or kraft paper that is vapor-resistant. This retarder

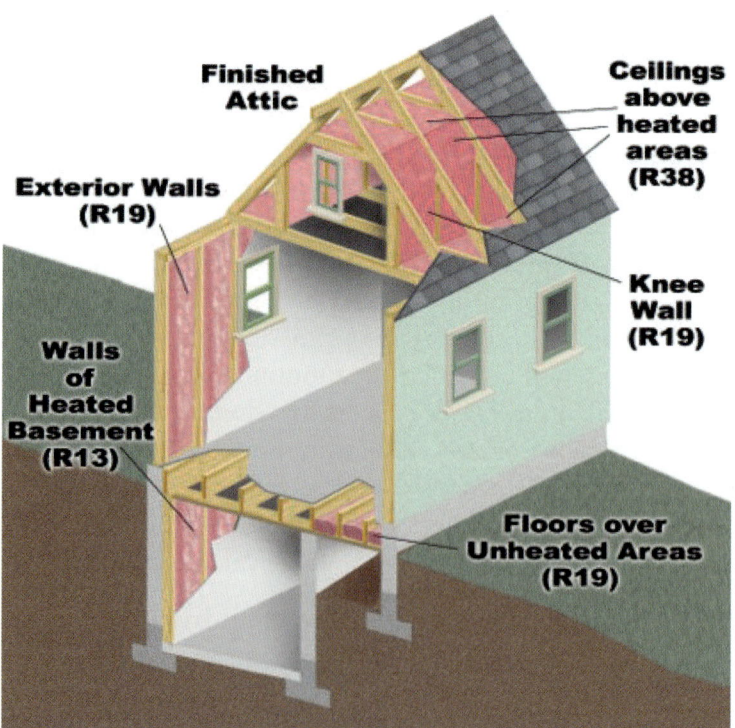

Illustration by Paddy Morrissey

may be a separate sheet, but some insulations have a vapor retarder facing. Most closed-cell spray-applied foam insulations do not require a separate vapor retarder, whereas most open-cell foams do. The purpose of the vapor retarder is to prevent structural damage due to the condensation of moisture from the home that would normally travel from the warm sides to the cold sides of the ceiling below the attic, floors above unheated spaces, and exterior walls. The improper installation of insulation and the vapor barrier can actually promote condensation and result in structural damage.

The areas shown below should be insulated.

- **Floors over unheated areas:** If the basement or crawl space is not heated, then the floor above the area should be insulated with the vapor barrier against the floor, as shown below. An R-rating of at least R-19 is recommended. Floors above a porch or over an unheated garage should also be insulated. It's not unusual to find crawl space insulation installed with the vapor barrier down, but that's not correct.

- **Ceilings below unheated areas:** The floor of an unheated attic should be insulated, not the attic walls and rafters. However, in new construction, you may see the underside of the roof insulated with spray-applied foam or cellulose beneath netting and no ventilation, making the unfinished attic part of the house. Homeowners don't always understand this and insulate the rafters, thinking an unfinished attic should be warm. The vapor barrier should be installed against the ceiling or warm side of the space.

The home inspector may note improper installation in the attic, such as faced insulation installed retarder side up. And there should be, at most, one vapor barrier. Sometimes, faced insulation is added over existing insulation, adding a second vapor barrier. If two layers exist, each with a vapor barrier, the top barrier should be slit open to allow moisture movement. Recommendations are R-49 of insulation in northern and mountainous states and a minimum of R-30 in the south.

INSULATED AREAS

- Floors over unheated areas
- Ceilings below unheated areas
- Roof slope and knee walls
- Exterior walls
- Pipes and ducts in unheated areas
- Walls in heated crawl spaces and basements

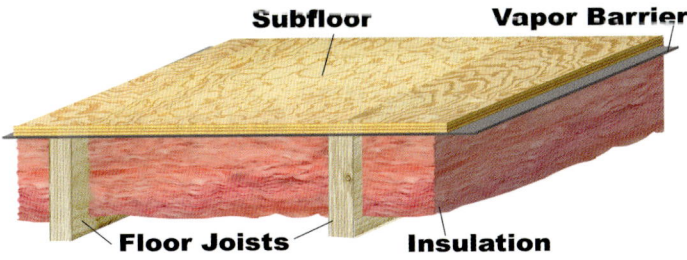

Illustration by Paddy Morrissey

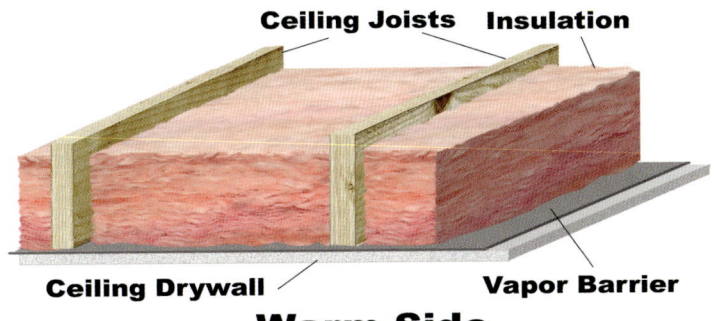

Illustration by Paddy Morrissey

- **The roof slope and knee walls:** If the attic is a heated, finished space, then insulation should be installed on the back of the knee walls, on top of the ceiling, and on the underside of the roof slope. (When the roof slope is insulated, space must be left behind the insulation for ventilation.) An R-rating of R-30 to R-49 is recommended for slopes and ceilings, with R-19 for knee walls.

A **flat roof** above a heated space and the **cathedral roof** should both have insulation. The installation of a vapor barrier and the proper ventilation between the insulation and roof surface is essential in both cases. Both roof types are subject to rot if ventilation is inadequate or blocked.

Illustration by Paddy Morrissey

- **Exterior walls:** Insulation should be placed between wall studs as batts or blankets or blown in, or exterior continuous foam board should be used. A minimum R-13 is required in the warmest parts of the country, whereas R-25 is required in the coldest areas. This is based on the 2015 IRC. The vapor barrier should be installed on the inside of the home just behind the drywall. Where plastic foam insulation is used, either site-foamed or rigid board, it must be covered for fire safety.

- **Pipes and ducts in unheated areas:** When the basement and especially a crawl space is not heated, all plumbing piping and heating ducts should be wrapped in insulation. A minimum R-rating of R-3 is recommended for pipes, which is only an inch or so of insulation, depending on which type is used. R-8 is recommended for heating ducts. Exhaust vents/ducts in unheated areas should also be insulated to prevent condensation from forming.

- **Interior walls of heated basement or crawl space:** Many areas of the country do not require insulation on the walls of heated basements. Rigid board insulation may be applied directly to the walls (but must be covered with drywall), or wall studs can be provided to fill with batt insulation and finished with drywall if desired. If the crawl space is to be heated and cooled, then insulation should be installed on the crawl space walls and the crawl space should NOT be vented. Insulation in these areas should be at least R-19.

- **Exterior basement walls:** The exterior of the basement may be insulated with rigid board insulation that acts as an insulator and drains water to a perimeter drain tile system. Insulation should extend down the entire wall below grade. The insulations should be in the R-15 to R-19 range.

In summary, for the following areas of the home, these are the R-ratings currently recommended in new construction by the U.S. Department of Energy:

- **R-3:** For plumbing piping in unheated areas

- **R-8:** For heating ducts in unheated areas

- **R-13 to R-25:** For exterior framed walls and R-19 for crawl space and basement walls, if crawl space or basement is heated

- **R-21:** For floors over unheated spaces and knee walls; R-30 for roof slopes

- **R-30:** For ceilings below attics, generally for most southern states

- **R-49:** For ceilings below attics, generally for most northern and mountainous states

> **For Beginning Inspectors**
>
> *It should be obvious that a home inspector needs to measure the thickness of insulation to determine its R-rating. Find a ruler or tape measure and inspect whatever insulation is visible in your home. Identify the type of insulation; then multiply its R-value by the number of inches to get its total R-rating. Compare your findings with the latest recommendations as listed here. Perhaps more insulation should be added.*

The chart below shows the R-values of various types of insulation covered in this section, along with the thickness required to meet recommended R-ratings. For example, for fiberglass batts to meet a recommended R-rating of R-19 for floors over unheated spaces, a 6″ thickness is required.

R-VALUES AND AMOUNT OF INSULATION REQUIRED

Insulation Types	R-Value	R-13	R-19	R-30	R-38
Batts, Blankets					
Fiberglass	3.1/inch	4″	6″	9.5″	12.5″
Rock wool	3.7/inch	3.5″	5″	8″	10.5″
Loose Fill					
Fiberglass	2.2/inch	6″	8.5″	13.5″	17.5″
Rock wool	2.9/inch	4.5″	6.5″	10.5″	13″
Cellulose	3.6/inch	3.5″	5.5″	8.5″	10.5″
Vermiculite	2.1/inch	6″	9″	14.5″	18″
Rigid Board					
Fiberglass	4/inch	3″	5″	7.5″	9.5″
Polystyrene					
Extruded	3.9/inch	3.5″	5″	7.5″	9.5″
Bead board	3.6/inch	3.5″	5.5″	8.5″	10.5″
Urethane	6/inch	2″	3″	5″	6.5″
Site-Foamed					
UFFI	4.2/inch	3″	4.5″	7″	9″
Urethane	6/inch	2″	3″	5″	6.5″
Airkrete	4/inch	3″	5″	7.5″	9.5″

Amounts of insulation in chart are rounded to the nearest half inch.

Inspecting the Insulation

The home inspector is required to inspect visible insulation within the home, making every effort to gain access to the unfinished areas (attic and crawl spaces) of the home to do so. During the insulation inspection, the inspector's job is to:

- Identify the type of insulation found.

- Measure the average insulation thickness and give an opinion on its adequacy; recommend additional insulation if it is not to current standards.

- State where insulation is missing at conditioned surfaces. (Required)

- Inspect the condition of the insulation (compressed, displaced, missing, damaged).

- Note any deficiencies in the installation of the insulation. Remember, insulation must be touching the surface it is supposed to be insulating. It can't be floating in midair or strung across ceiling joists or truss chords.

- Confirm the presence of a vapor retarder and its proper orientation, if possible.

During the insulation inspection, the home inspector should watch for the following conditions:

> **INSULATION INSPECTION**
> - Identify the type found.
> - Note the average thickness.
> - Note its condition and installation.
> - Locate the vapor barrier.

> **Code ☑ Check**
> **Air Flow through Soffit**
> Air communicates through soffit to attic or ceiling space above.
> ©2012 Code Check

- **Inadequate amount or missing insulation:** Checking the adequacy of the insulation in the attic and other unfinished areas requires measuring it. Inform customers that additional insulation can be installed over the old (with the exception of vermiculite, which should be removed first). The R-ratings of existing and new insulation can be added—for example, if 6" of existing fiberglass batt insulation in the attic has a rating of R-19 and another 6" is added, then the total R-rating would be R-38 (19 + 19). Remind customers that the new insulation should be unfaced (no vapor retarder).

The home inspector is not required to report on **concealed insulation**, and your customer should be made to understand this. But try to look at the insulation. If the attic floor is covered with planking or decking, look for any loose boards that can be lifted so that you can see the insulation underneath. You can also try to examine the insulation in an **exterior wall** by removing an electrical receptacle or light switch cover plate and looking into the space with a flashlight. Or you can use a wooden or plastic probe such as a chopstick or a plastic crochet hook to probe into the area, but be careful when working around electricity. You may not be able to see any insulation in the wall, but don't report it missing if you don't know.

Sometimes, the electrician pulled the insulation away from the receptacle, and you just can't see it. Make sure customers understand.

Examine plumbing pipes and heating ducts in unheated areas such as the attic and crawl space. They should be insulated. If they aren't, report them as a deficiency and recommend insulating or replacing as necessary.

- **Missing vapor barrier:** When you measure the insulation, try to determine if a vapor retarder is present.

> **INSPECTING INSULATION**
>
> - Inadequate amount or missing
> - Missing vapor barrier
> - Improper installation
> - Torn, loose, or damaged insulation
> - Damp or wet insulation
> - Presence of asbestos
> - Exposed plastic insulation

Photo #18 *This is an example of a typical warning label on faced fiberglass batt insulation.*

Identify the type of vapor retarder present (whether kraft paper, foil, or a plastic film) and see if it faces the right way (against the warm side). If you can't determine whether the vapor barrier is there, report it as not visible.

- **Improper installation:** Check insulation for problem installation such as the following examples:

  — **Vapor barrier upside-down.**

  — **Between attic rafters.** When the attic is intended to be an unheated area, homeowners often mistakenly insulate between the rafters (underside of roof) instead of the floor. This lets heat escape from the house into the attic and out of the vents. In a finished attic, look behind the knee wall, if possible, to determine how insulation is installed. It should be located on the attic floor and on the back side of the knee wall, not between the rafters.

  — **Gaps.** Watch for gaps in installation. A considerable amount of the insulation's effectiveness is lost when it doesn't completely cover a surface. Gaps may be left around openings for plumbing pipes, electrical work, ductwork, chases, and exhaust vents in the attic floor.

THE INTERIOR INSPECTION

INSTALLATION PROBLEMS

- Vapor barrier reversed
- Between rafters
- Gaps
- Too close to recessed lights
- Blocking vents

— **Too close to recessed lights.** When certain recessed ceiling fixtures (non-IC) are present on the top floor of the house, they should not be covered with insulation in the attic. A clearance of 3″ is required between the recessed lights (non-IC type) and attic insulation. Newer lights may be rated for "insulation contact," meaning that they can be buried in insulation. They will be labeled IC or IC-AT. If you come across recessed fixtures buried in the insulation, you don't have to dig through the insulation to determine if the light is rated to be covered. However, the customer should be warned that the problem needs to be fixed at a later date as this situation could represent a fire hazard.

— **Blocking vents.** Insulation should never block vents because it would interfere with proper ventilation and lessen the effectiveness of the insulation by "wind-washing" the insulation.

Section Note

"It's fairly common to find insulation improperly installed when there's an attic bedroom.

Try to get a look behind the knee wall—there's usually a door to a storage area somewhere in the room. It's not uncommon to find the insulation between the rafters behind the wall. I always suggest that the rafter insulation be removed and used on the back of the knee wall and on the floor."

COMMUNICATING

If the customer hasn't seen the insulation in the attic or crawl space, talk about what you saw in there or take photos. <u>You are their eyes</u>, so take the time to describe your findings. And make sure the customer understands.

- **Torn, loose, or damaged insulation:** Watch for any damage to insulation. Insulation in the floor above unheated areas can become loose and begin to fall. Insulation on pipes can be damaged. These cases should be reported. Damaged insulation no longer does its job of providing heat resistance.

- **Damp or wet insulation:** Check insulation for dampness and wetness or for clumps of cellulose insulation, especially in the attic. A localized wet spot or clumping can be an indication of a roof leak. If the insulation is consistently damp throughout the attic, there's most likely a problem with the ventilation in the attic.

- **Presence of asbestos:** As noted on pages 622–624, you may find insulation containing asbestos.

- **Exposed foam board insulation:** Report any exposed foam (polystyrene or urethane) insulation in the living area as a **safety hazard**. Look for it in garages and basements. Inform customers that such insulation should be covered.

Reporting Your Findings

When you're inspecting the insulation, you must make every effort to investigate the attic and other unheated areas where it's possible to gain access. Of course, your customer isn't going to be in these areas with you. When you come out of these spaces, communicate your findings with the customer. Discuss what you were looking for and explain what you found. Because the customer hasn't seen the area firsthand, you might want to take photos. Take your time in describing the following:

- **What you were inspecting**—the insulation on the floor, ceiling, walls, pipes, ducts, and so on.

- **What you were looking for**—improper installation, any damage to the installation, presence of asbestos, and so on.

- **What you were doing**—seeing what type of insulation was present, measuring the insulation, looking for the vapor barrier, and so on.

- **What you found**—inadequate amount of insulation, blocked soffit vents, double vapor barrier, and so on.

- **Suggestions about dealing with the findings**—taking insulation from between the rafters and putting on the attic floor, slicing open vapor barrier of added insulation, removing/abating asbestos insulation on pipes, and so on. But don't make uneducated guesses about how to remedy any situation.

> **Section Note**
>
> "You can give insulation an R-rating based on its R-value and thickness. But you should let customers know that the R-rating is meaningful only if the insulation is intact. When insulation is damaged or falling down, it's not going to meet the R-rating. I always let my customer know that the R-rating works only when the insulation is in good shape."

Filling in Your Report

Every home inspector needs an inspection report. A **written report** is the work product of the home inspection, and every home inspector is expected to deliver one to the customer after the inspection. Inspection reports vary a great deal in the industry. Some home inspection companies develop their own version; others use state required formats (Texas), home inspection software, apps, or formats provided by training companies such as AHIT. Some are considered to be excellent, while others are not very good. A workable and easy-to-use inspection report is important for a home inspector. Of greater importance are its thoroughness, accuracy, and helpfulness to the customer. Whatever reporting format you choose, make sure it presents your findings in a clear, professional manner such that it reduces your liability and client dissatisfaction.

The **Don't Ever Miss** list is a reminder of those specific findings you should include in your inspection report. We list these items based on years of experience performing home inspections. Missing them can result in complaint calls and possible lawsuits. Here is an overview of what to report on during the inspection of the insulation:

- **Attic:** First identify the type of insulation you found, such as fiberglass, cellulose, rock wool, and so on. It's also a good idea to record where the insulation was installed in the attic—between the rafters, on the walls,

> **DON'T EVER MISS**
>
> - Improperly installed insulation
> - Missing vapor barriers
> - Exposed plastic insulation
> - Suspected asbestos
> - Buried recessed light fixtures

or on the floor. Report the condition of the insulation, noting any problems with installation, blocked vents, the presence of old UFFI insulation, and so on. Don't miss reporting buried recessed light fixtures as a potential **safety hazard**.

We suggest that you record the **thickness of the insulation** and rate it according to your own system. You might want to use adequate or not adequate. We also suggest that you write the R-value of the insulation. When you review this information with your customer, you can explain what the R-value finding is and what it should be in the attic (R-30 to R-49). You can also tell the customer how much insulation, if any, should be added to meet the recommended rating.

Note whether a vapor retarder is present and identify the type found. Note whether it's installed properly.

- **Crawl space:** First note if insulation is present. If it is, identify the type of insulation found and where it's installed (under the floor structure or on the walls). Record its thickness and R-rating. Note any defects such as improper installation. Note the presence or absence of a vapor barrier. Regarding heating ducts and plumbing pipes, note whether they should be insulated and whether insulation is present. Don't miss reporting suspected asbestos insulation on plumbing and heating pipes.

- **Exterior walls:** If you've had the opportunity to inspect wall insulation, record your findings in your inspection report. You might want to write general comments such as "Wall insulation appears adequate" or "Could not confirm wall insulation during inspection."

- **Garage/Basement:** Again, identify the type of insulation present. Be sure to note exposed plastic rigid board or kraft paper facing insulation as a safety hazard in your report.

> **Chapter Note**
>
> *Pages 632–643 present the study and inspection of the home's ventilation.*

7.10 VENTILATION

The purpose of ventilation is often misunderstood by homeowners who might think it only has to do with cooling the home. The true purpose of the ventilation process is **to remove warm air from the attic in the winter**. With unlimited available moisture in a closed space, wood becomes saturated, causing it to rot and deteriorate. Ventilation, by allowing air to move past the framing in the attic, replaces damp air with dry air to reduce this problem.

Crawl Space Ventilation

When the soil under a crawl space is not covered, it continually releases moisture. It is recommended that the dirt or gravel floor of the crawl space be covered with a **vapor** retarder to prevent moisture from the soil being released into the crawl space. This is turning out to not be the case. Another current crawl space configuration is sealed, insulated, and conditioned (heated/cooled) not vented to the exterior as has been done for decades. The moisture in the crawl space, it has been found in many parts of the country, actually comes from the outdoor air through the wall vents into the crawl space, not from the soil as was originally thought. Be sure to consult local code requirements for current practices in your area. Vapor barriers used to be polyethylene sheeting, roofing paper, blacktopping, or concrete. Current vapor retarders must be a Class 1 type with 6″ overlaps sealed or taped and 6″ lapped and sealed to the foundation wall, as well as an approved type of mechanical ventilation. Even with a vapor retarder, the crawl space air contains moisture that can condense on the framing or be released into the home. Proper ventilation prevents this from happening.

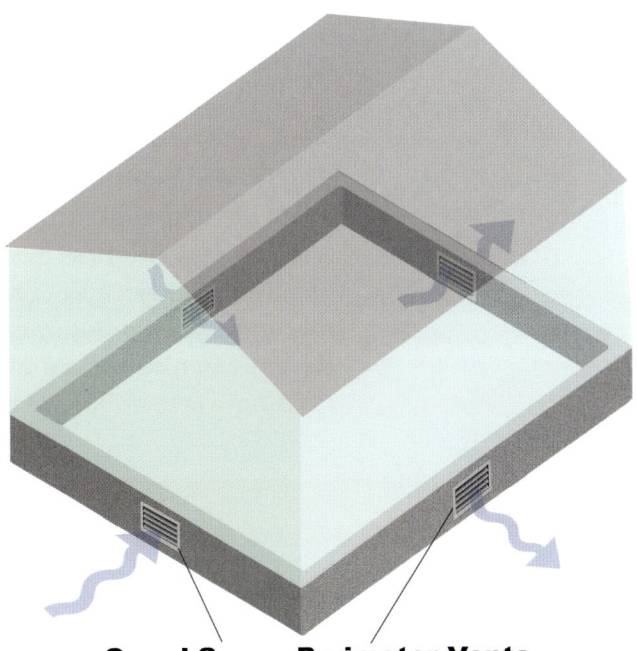

Crawl Space Perimeter Vents
Illustration by Paddy Morrissey

Perimeter vents are required in a crawl space to keep the moisture from rising into the home. Ideally, there should be vents in all four walls, one at each corner, within 3′ of the corner to provide cross ventilation. The amount of venting depends on the size of the crawl space and whether it has a vapor barrier on the floor.

- With a vapor retarder, 1 square foot of free vent is needed for every 1500 square feet of floor area.

- Without a vapor retarder, 1 square foot of free vent is needed for every 150 square feet of floor area.

> **CRAWL SPACE VENTS**
>
> - One on each wall or at least on opposite walls
> - With vapor barrier on floor, 1 sq. ft. of free vent for every 1500 sq. ft. of floor area
> - Without vapor barrier, 1 sq. ft. of free vent for every 150 sq. ft. of floor area

The home inspector is responsible only for noting the presence of proper vents in the crawl space, not for their use by homeowners.

Moisture can enter the crawl space another way. Warm humid air from the house or outside naturally migrates to the cooler crawl space. That's why the floor over the crawl space is typically insulated. A vapor barrier should be laid against the warm side of the floor with the insulation on the crawl space side (fuzzy side down). The vapor barrier can't stop all the moist warm air from entering the crawl space. That is why air-sealing the penetrations in the deck/floor should be sealed to prevent the air movement into the crawl space. The cold side of the insulation needs to be ventilated to remove the moist air that does get through. The perimeter vent system provides the ventilation needed to remove moisture trapped in the insulation.

The results of poor crawl space ventilation can be spotted in the staining, discoloration, and rotting of the structural members including the sill, wooden columns and joists, and subfloor. We've seen homes where the subfloor above a crawl space has rotted away. In one case, the ventilation was so poor that the sill had completely rotted and the house had settled down to the foundation. That house had an uncovered soil floor, and no perimeter venting was present.

A Word about Radon

The home inspector may come across special ventilation techniques in the crawl space or basement or other methods used to remove radon from a home. Radon is a colorless, odorless gas that occurs naturally when uranium in soil and rocks breaks down. Because air pressure in the home is usually lower than the pressure in the soil, a house can act like a vacuum and draw radon gas into the home. Radon can also be found in well water and can be released into the home through running water at faucets or showers.

Radon, a radioactive gas, is the number two cause of lung cancer behind cigarette smoking. It is estimated that 1 out of 15 homes in the country have elevated radon levels. The EPA and the Surgeon General recommend that all homes be tested for radon levels. It is further recommended that homes with a radon level of **4 or more pCi/L** (picocuries of gas per liter of air) use a radon mitigation technique to reduce that level. Homeowners with a reading between 2 and 4 pCi/L should consider using a radon reduction technique.

For homes with crawl spaces, the radon reduction technique that may be used is to ventilate the crawl space with or without the use of fans. Another approach is **sub-slab** or **submembrane depressurization**, which involves covering the soil in the crawl space with a heavy plastic sheet (or if already covered with concrete) and using a vent pipe and fan to draw the radon from under the plastic sheeting or slab. Other techniques are available with basement or slab-on-grade homes, costing from $500 to $2,500 to remove radon that enters the home through the soil. Methods used when water is the source of radon in the home are more expensive.

A general home inspection does not include inspecting the home for radon. However, most home inspectors become qualified (and licensed in some states) to add radon inspection to the list of services they offer. You might want to check out the National Radon Proficiency Program (NRPP) for more information on certification and licensing requirements. Radon testing is done by placing special canisters or continuous monitors in the home for a period of time. These devices, which detect radon in the air, must be sent to a qualified laboratory where the radon concentrations can be determined or may be read on-site in the case of continuous monitors.

> **Definitions**
>
> <u>Radon</u> is a gas occurring naturally from the breakdown of uranium in the soil, rocks, and water. The abbreviation <u>pCi/L</u> is a measurement that stands for picocuries of gas per liter of air—the way radon is measured.

> **ATTIC VENTS**
>
> - Vent area split for cross ventilation
> - 1 sq. ft. of free vent for every 300 sq. ft. of floor area if evenly distributed or if a vapor retarder is present
> - Twice the amount of vent area if louvers are present

Attic Ventilation

The attic area also requires ventilation. Warm moist air from the house naturally tries to move into the attic due to stack effect. The vapor barrier laid along with the insulation on the attic floor plays a large role in preventing warm moist air from entering the attic, but it can't stop it completely. In new construction, the ceiling penetrations are sealed to prevent this movement of air into the attic. The vapor retarder is there to stop vapor diffusion. Air leakage is the far greater culprit with regard to moisture

Photo #19 EXHAUST FANS

Here is new construction in Michigan where the two round vents are exhaust fans and the louvered vent to the left is the soffit vent. Now where do you think the warm moist air coming from the bath exhaust fans will go? Probably right back up into the attic at the soffit vent intake. This is a terrible configuration. Even if you wanted to vent the bath fans through the soffit, make sure they are far enough away from the soffit vents so as not to cause a problem.

movement into the attic. The moist air that does get into the attic must be removed to prevent moisture buildup in the attic. This is done through ventilation.

Attic vents are required in the attic to release moisture from the area. Generally, 1 square foot of net vent is required for every 300 square feet of attic floor area. This assumes that half of the venting is from the eaves or soffits and the other half is from the ridge, roof, or gable ends. This ratio is also acceptable if the attic has an approved vapor retarder installed. This requirement is often not met. If it is not evenly distributed between the upper and lower portions of the attic or if no vapor retarder is present, you need twice as much ventilation, or 2 square feet per 300 square feet of attic floor. It should be noted that louvers and screening typically block airflow by about 50%, meaning that when louvers or screening are present, twice the visible vent area is required. The vent area should be split for air movement in and out. A single vent does little to move the air. A soffit and ridge combo is best.

> **Section Note**
>
> *"Few homeowners really understand the principles of attic ventilation. I've seen many cases where the owner's actions contribute to moisture buildup in the attic. Blocking vents and covering them in winter to save heat are among the top mistakes.*
>
> *I like to take the time to teach customers to be concerned about good ventilation first and heat loss second."*

THE INTERIOR INSPECTION

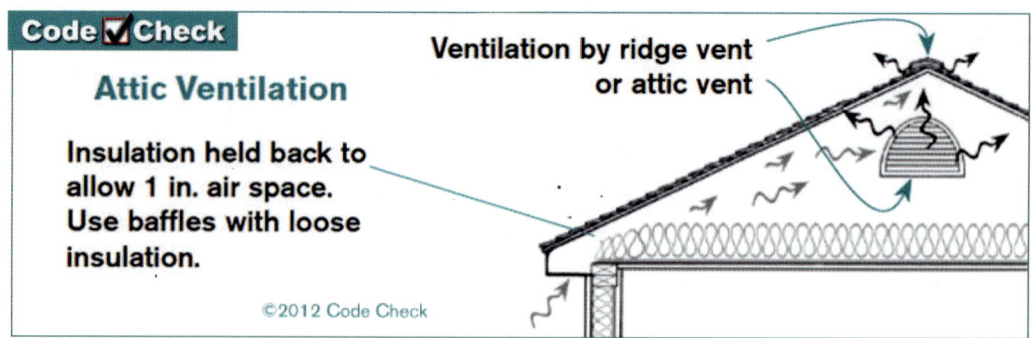

Wind Parallel to Vents

Wind Perpendicular to Vents

Illustration by Paddy Morrissey

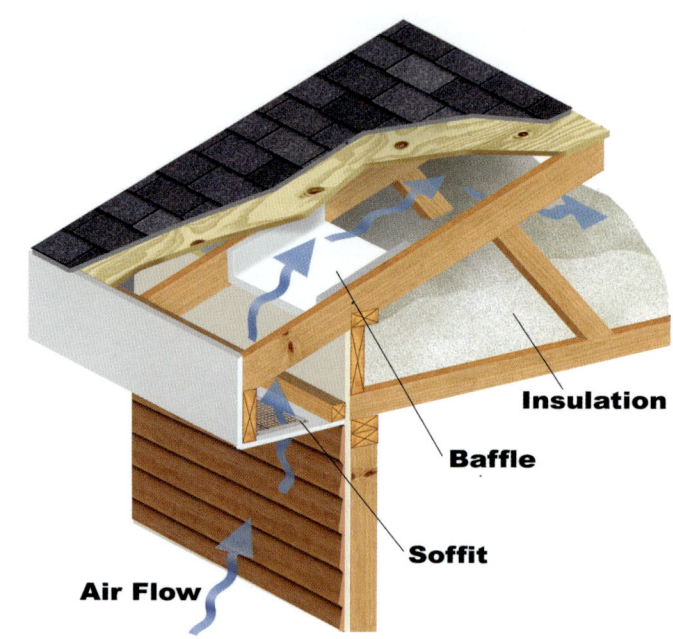

Illustration by Paddy Morrissey

ATTIC VENTILATION

- Gable vents
- Soffit vents
- Ridge vents
- Roof-top vents
- Turbine vents
- Power ventilator

Gable vents, located at the gable ends of the roof, are most effective when the wind is blowing parallel to the roof ridge so that air can move directly through the attic from end to end. They are less effective when the wind is blowing perpendicular to the ridge. In that case, smaller air currents can occur at each end of the attic without a direct pass through the attic, and therefore, little to no ventilation occurs.

Gable vents should be unobstructed and louvers undamaged. Some homeowners cover the gable vents during the winter months in the mistaken belief that this will save heat in the house. Covering the gable vents in the winter is far more likely to allow moisture buildup in the attic and cause damage to the structural members. When inspecting the attic, watch for gable covers or plastic sheets near the gable vents. Advise customers not to cover any vents in the winter.

The home may have **soffit vents** or eaves located in the soffit under the eaves along each side of the roof. Air movement flows into the soffit vents, up

Photo #20 GABLE VENTS

Be sure to verify if the vents are actually vents. Notice anything unusual about the way these gable end louvers are installed? If it were a true vent with a hole in the gable wall, the vent would be flashed and sealed differently. This is just a nailed-on louvered grill for decoration.

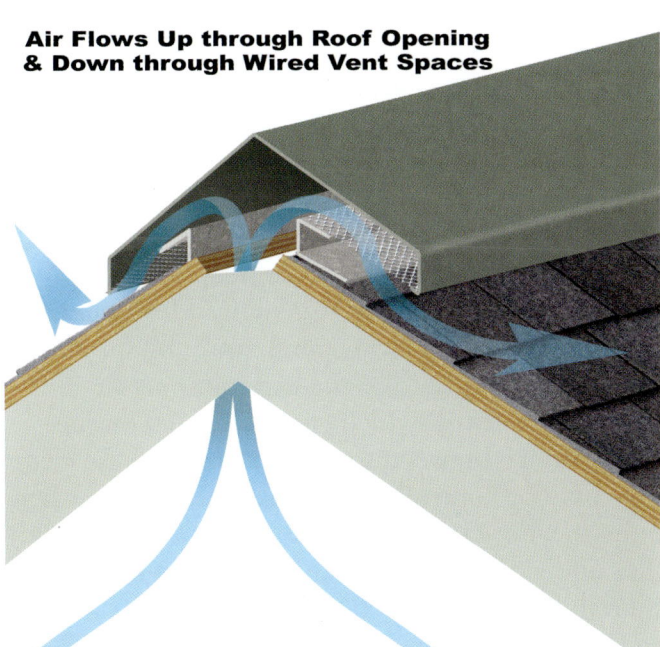

Illustration by Paddy Morrissey

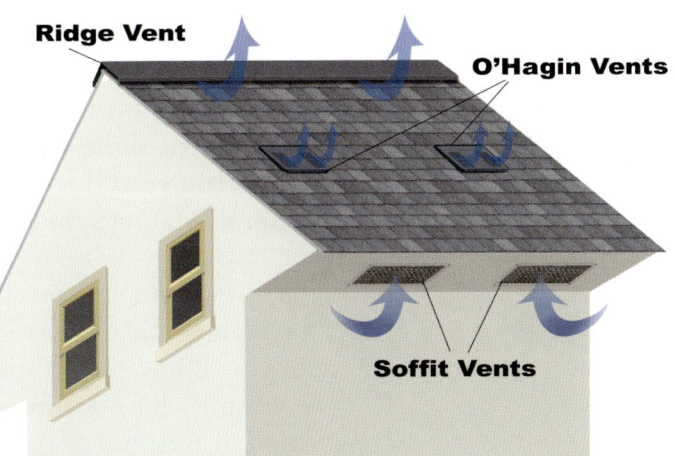

Illustration by Paddy Morrissey

through the attic, and out the roof or ridge vents. When soffit vents are present, care must be taken to prevent the attic insulation from blocking the air passages at the lower edge of the rafters. A baffle should be in place to hold the insulation away from the air passage area. Some attics, especially flat roofs, have only soffit vents.

The **ridge vent**, which typically runs the length of the roof ridge, has an open vent area on its underside to move air from the attic.

Section Note

"I did an inspection where the homeowner had a misting system in his attic to tend to his marijuana plants. The moisture may have been healthy for the plants, but not the attic. No ventilation system on earth could have stopped the delamination and wood rot present in that attic. The word stupid comes to mind, doesn't it?"

Photo #21 O'HAGIN VENTS

This is the underside of an O'Hagin vent. The oval hole is covered by a screened cover to prevent critters and insects from getting in the attic. The vent cover on the roof is designed to follow the contours of the roof covering used. They are available for asphalt shingles, clay, and concrete tiles too.

The most effective method of ventilating the attic is the **combination ridge vent and soffit vents**. This allows air to enter from the soffit area and move up through the attic to the roof ridge, providing good ventilation.

A home may have vents in the face of the roof for releasing air from the attic. A new variety of these are called O'Hagin vents.

A **turbine vent**, located on the roof face, is an air-powered series of vanes on a central rotating spindle. Turbine vents work only when the wind is blowing. On still days, they do no more than a regular roof vent. Some people wire the turbine, preventing it from spinning due to the bearings squealing. This essentially creates a large hole in the roof as the turbine sheds water in the rain by spinning and flinging the water off the vanes. Always make sure the turbine spins.

Some attics have **a power ventilator (fan)**, which can be located on the gable end of the attic or on the roof surface between the roof rafters. These electrically or solar-powered ventilators may be controlled by a manual switch, a thermostat, or a humidistat. Usually, the thermostat is set to activate the ventilator fan when the attic temperature reaches about 100°. In theory, the power ventilator is installed for summer use only, when the ventilator's actions remove hot air from the attic and reduce the heat load. It is possible to add a humidistat that controls the fan based on the humidity in the attic. This is very effective in cold climates.

The home inspector should try to operate the power ventilator during the inspection. Check to see that a gable-mounted ventilator doesn't cut down on the free vent space required for the attic. And make sure there is sufficient vent area in the whole attic so that the ventilator is not starved for air during its operation. It has been shown that they are not properly sized and can actually suck the heated/cooled air out of the house. There is also the issue of the electricity used to operate them, which exceeds the benefit of removing the heat in the summer.

The home inspector may see a large fan mounted in the upper hall ceiling. This is a **whole house fan** with an intake from the house. It is designed to change house air every few minutes or so. A whole house fan may also be mounted in the gable, where house air will be drawn up into the attic through a self-closing louver in the hall ceiling. The whole house fan needs to have an appropriate free area for intake and exhaust. The whole house fan is not a power ventilator. They should be covered and insulated for the off season so that heated house air doesn't go into the attic. Older style whole house fans are terribly inefficient in the off season (winter). Newer fans come with insulated covers that are opened when the fan cycles on and off, making them very efficient year-round.

A homeowner may take precautions with ventilation and do everything possible to eliminate warm moist air from the attic, but then make mistakes about other mechanical **venting systems** in the home. Kitchen and bathroom exhaust fans and the plumbing vent stack should always vent to the outside. Often, the exhaust venting passes through the attic. There may be deterioration of the piping and ducting or open joints that allow warm air to escape into the attic, contributing to moisture buildup.

In worst-case scenarios, home venting systems exhaust directly into the attic. This should never be done. The home inspector should report any exhaust vents terminating in the attic, crawl space, or garage and advise customers to remedy the situation. It's not uncommon to see a bathroom vent exhausting into the attic. When that occurs, the extra moisture drawn into the attic causes plywood sheathing to delaminate. Oriented strand board (OSB) roof sheathing will begin to crumble and may turn black from excess moisture and ultimately to mulch.

The results of poor attic ventilation can be very serious and costly to repair. Moisture buildup in the attic can cause rusting of nails and gussets in trusses, delamination of the roof sheathing, and rotting of the wood structural members. Repairing the situation can be costly and should be classified as a major repair.

> **Section Note**
>
> *"One of my inspectors put his foot through a cathedral ceiling.*
>
> *He'd been careful when first getting on the roof and had tested several steps. Finding no signs of a weakened condition, he decided the roof was all right and he got overconfident. His next vigorous step plunged him right through the ceiling.*
>
> *Don't assume that the roof is in the same condition throughout. Small spots of deteriorating sheathing may be present."*

Vaulted Cathedral and Flat Roofs

Ventilation in cathedral or vaulted ceilings and flat roofs is a special concern, and they're often inadequately ventilated. It is not unusual for the home inspector to find the roof over a cathedral ceiling to be weakened by delaminated sheathing due to poor ventilation and minimal insulation. Special care must be taken to test each step during the roof inspection over a vaulted or cathedral ceiling.

Code Check — Wood Structural Panel Grade Mark

©2012 Code Check

- Panel rating "Structural 1" denotes max. performance.
- Span rating — Max. span (in.) between supports when used for sheathing: Roof/Floor
- Thickness of panel
- Durability rating
- Veneer rating

APA RATED SHEATHING STRUCTURAL I
32/16 15/32 INCH
SIZED FOR SPACING
EXPOSURE 1
000
PS 1-83 C-D
NER-QA397 PRP-108

THE INTERIOR INSPECTION

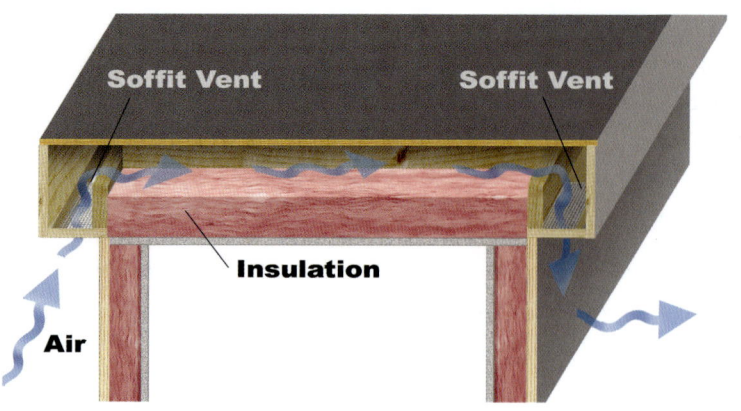

Illustration by Paddy Morrissey

As noted on page 625, there must be adequate ventilation space between the insulation and the roof sheathing in the cathedral ceiling. Cathedral ceilings should have soffit vents and a ridge vent to move the air through this space. There should also be vents at both ends (top and bottom) of **each** rafter bay.

A flat roof cavity may not be insulated, and many were not intended to be. When insulation is added, the problem of proper ventilation arises. One approach is the use of continuous soffit vents at both edges of the roof, as shown in the illustration of the flat roof on page 639.

Another approach is to install wooden strapping members over the roof joists to create a deeper space under the roof. The insulation rests between the roof joists, and the roof sheathing is then installed on top of the strapping. This leaves a ventilating space between the two. In some cases, a vapor retarder and rigid board insulation are installed over the roof sheathing in an attempt to insulate the roof. No ventilating space is present.

Whatever the means of ventilating cathedral ceilings and insulated flat roofs, these areas remain susceptible to moisture buildup. Even if problems are not present, customers should be cautioned to watch them carefully for new problems that may arise.

> **INSPECTING VENTILATION**
>
> - Evidence of poor ventilation
> - Inadequate ventilation
> - Blocked, covered, or damaged vents
> - Inoperable ventilator
> - Improper exhaust venting

Inspecting the Ventilation

The ventilation inspection takes place primarily on the roof, in the attic, and in the crawl space. The home inspector must do the following during the inspection:

- Identify the type and location of vents.

- Report on the condition of vents.

- Judge the adequacy of ventilation by its performance.

- Check power ventilators to see if they operate.

The home inspector should watch for the following conditions during the inspection of ventilation in the home:

- **Evidence of poor ventilation:** Reading the signs of poor ventilation is the first consideration during the inspection.

  In the attic, delaminated roof sheathing is a sign, as is rust on roofing nails and truss gusset plates. Rotting structural members may be a sign of poor ventilation, although rot may be present from a localized roof leak.

Frost on roofing nails in winter indicates condensation of moisture in the attic air, also a sign of poor ventilation. Feel the insulation. Consistently damp or wet insulation means that the insulation and attic aren't being properly ventilated.

In the crawl space, delamination of the plywood subflooring indicates poor ventilation. Another sign can be moisture-laden insulation falling from the floor over the crawl space, typically due to condensation.

- **Inadequate ventilation:** The home inspector should confirm the presence of adequate free vent area. This can be done by a rough estimate. Remember the attic requirements—**1 square foot of free vent for every 300 square feet of attic floor for most homes**. For example, if the attic is roughly 30′ by 40′, or 1200 square feet, there should be 4 square feet of free vent (1200 ÷ 300) or 8 square feet if louvers are present. You can do similar calculations for the crawl space, using the requirements stated earlier.

Another judgment of ventilation adequacy is the number and location of vents. Remember, there should be split vents in the attic and perimeter vents on opposite walls near corners in the crawl space. Of course,

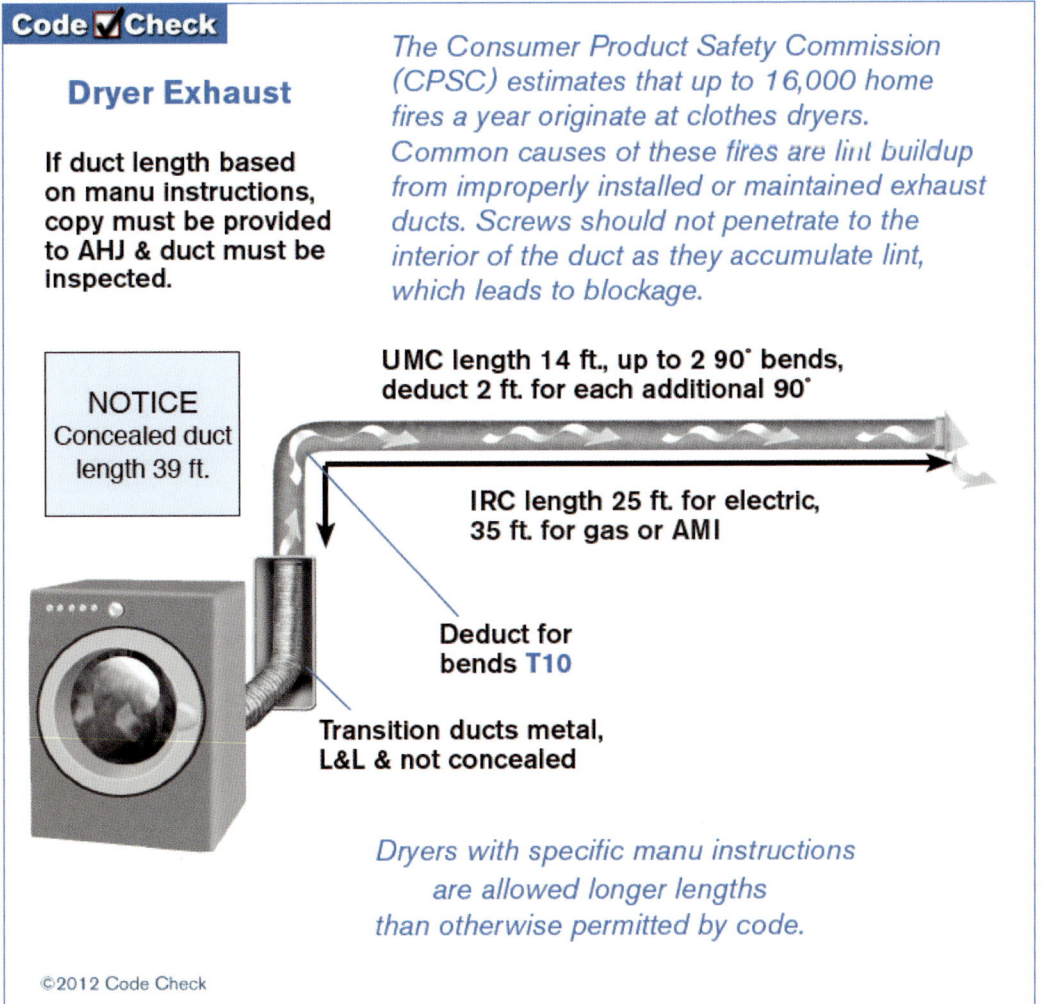

adequacy and performance can be judged by the condition of the structural members in the attic and crawl space. If vents are too few or they're too small AND there is evidence of a problem, advise customers of what is required to improve ventilation.

- **Blocked, covered, or damaged vents:** Examine the condition of the vents. Make sure vents are not blocked with insulation or painted over, especially soffit vents Baffles should be installed to prevent the insulation from blocking the soffit vents.

Photo #22 *Baffles can be made from cardboard, plastic or foam. The purpose is to hold the insulation back away from the roof deck to allow air to pass from the soffit vent to the upper ridge or gable vents.*

In general, vents should be in good condition and not obstructed with debris or animal nests. Dirty or painted screening can cut down on or stop the operation of the vent. Point out any broken or missing louvers. Watch for gable vents that are covered with plastic or wood or for turbine vents that are covered with canvas or plastic bags in an effort to save heat. Keep an eye out in summer when these covers may be set aside and advise customers to throw them out and not use them during the winter.

- **Inoperable power ventilator:** Try the power ventilator to see if it's working. Also check to see if a gable-mounted power ventilator is cutting down on the amount of free vent area required in the attic.

- **Improper exhaust venting:** Locate kitchen and bathroom exhaust vents, dryer vents, and the plumbing vent stack in the attic area to be sure they exhaust through the roof. Also pay attention to their condition—holes in the vent piping and open joints will throw moist air into the attic. Roof leaks onto plumbing vents can cause holes from corrosion.

Reporting Your Findings

Reporting on ventilation depends a great deal on how your inspection report is laid out. Roof vents may be reported on your roof page, for example, while attic conditions are on the attic page. In any case, be sure to cover these basic areas in your reporting:

- **Roof vents:** You'll be noting the type of attic and roof vents during the inspection of the roof and exterior of the home. First identify the type of vents present, such as soffit vents, ridge venting, roof-top vents, gable vents, turbine, and power ventilators. Indicate the different kinds you found. Note their condition and record specific defects such as broken louvers in gable vents, broken roof-top vents, vents covered by insulation or boarded up for the season, and so on.

- **Attic:** We suggest that you use a special area for recording evidence of **moisture or condensation** in the attic. By the way, it's important to indicate whether the attic is finished and you couldn't see behind the finished walls/ceiling to determine if condensation is present. Make use of the terms not visible *and* not accessible in this situation. Record the results of poor ventilation, noting any deterioration in the sheathing and roof framing.

> **DON'T EVER MISS**
> - Signs of inadequate ventilation
> - Blocked soffit vents
> - Exhaust venting terminating in attic

Note whether fans and plumbing vents are exhausted to the attic or through the roof. Record the condition of such items, noting defects such as holes and open joints in vent piping. Don't forget to record if a power ventilator is not operating.

- **Crawl space:** First note whether perimeter vents are present. Then write your findings, including situations where vents are blocked or not enough vents are used, keeping in mind the condition of the structure. A lot of old crawl spaces don't meet current requirements but don't show any signs of a problem.

7.11 INSPECTING THE ATTIC

Throughout this chapter, we've presented most of what you need to know about attic inspection in bits and pieces. This chapter will put the attic inspection all together for you.

The following items are included in the attic inspection:

- The access
- Structural members
- Evidence of water penetration and condensation
- Insulation and vapor retarder
- Vents and ventilation
- Chimney chase
- Electrical safety
- Exhaust venting
- Condition of and access to equipment such as furnaces, air handlers, fans, and so on.

> **Section Note**
>
> *Perform a complete inspection of your own (or a friend's) attic, paying attention to the order in which you do it. Try to develop a routine that helps you not miss anything.*

> **Chapter Note**
>
> *Pages 643–650 present a summary of the attic inspection.*

Always report the means of access to the attic, whether it's the attic stairs, pull-down stairs, or a scuttle hole in the ceiling. And always report whether attic access is limited in any way. Some attic spaces may be too small to get into and move around in, and the attic inspection may have to be done by standing on a ladder in the hall, garage, or closet. Whatever the case, be sure to accurately describe the **methods used** to observe the attic. Let your customers know that existing defects may not be found when access is limited. This is for your own protection.

Make every attempt to get across the entire length of the attic during the inspection, but be careful where you walk. Some attics have plank floors, some a plank walkway or catwalk down the center, and others only exposed ceiling joists or truss chords. Whatever you do, don't step between the ceiling joists. Your foot will go right through the ceiling. Watch out too when walking on planks that aren't nailed down. Lighting is likely to be insufficient in the attic, so take your flashlight with you. And as mentioned earlier, if you are susceptible to respiratory ailments, you might want to wear a dust mask to protect yourself from insulation fibers and years of dust accumulation.

The order of attic inspection is up to the home inspector. It's wise to develop a routine so that nothing is missed. Some home inspectors make one slow trip up and down the attic, examining all aspects at the same time. Others examine the roof structure first, then concentrate on insulation, ventilation, the chimney, and so on, in turn.

ATTIC ACCESS

- Formal stairway
- Pull-down stairs
- Scuttle

The Access

Start the attic inspection by examining the entryway to the attic. **Formal stairs** may be present with a door at the bottom. Examine them as you would any other staircase for the condition of risers and treads, secure handrails, and proper lighting. Stairs that open directly into the attic space should have a secure guardrail along the stairwell. When the stairway opens into the attic in this way, it should be considered part of the attic space requiring insulation. Heat from the house should not be allowed to enter the stairwell. Try to determine if the door at the bottom is properly sealed/weather-stripped and closes tightly and if there is insulation under the stairs and along the stairway walls. (For stairway inspection, see pages 574–580.)

Be careful when you open the **pull-down stairway**. If the cables are broken or the counterweights are detached or they are not properly fastened to the framing, the stairs may come down too quickly or just fall down. Before you climb the stairs, examine the stairway for loose/broken treads, split/cracked stringers, and loose or missing fasteners. Be sure to note improper installation of the pull-down stairs. They should generally be attached to the framing with 16d nails or lag bolts, NOT drywall screws. Make a note in your report of whatever you find and use your own ladder to gain access to the attic. If there are no provisions to insulate this type of stairway, such as a cover or insulated box over the opening, suggest to customers that they add insulation here. Even a sheet of plywood with insulation on the back side over the opening would cut down on conditioned air entering the attic.

The entry to the attic may be a simple **scuttle or hatch, a 2 × 2 square of drywall,** in a hall ceiling or closet, and you'll probably need a ladder to get in. Note if the hatch cover fits securely to prevent conditioned air from entering the attic. Again, if insulation isn't present on the attic side of the hatch cover, you can

Photo #23 *A typical set of pull-down stairs installed with drywall screws. These screws will shear or snap off and the stairs will come crashing down. 16d or lag screws are required by most manufacturers.*

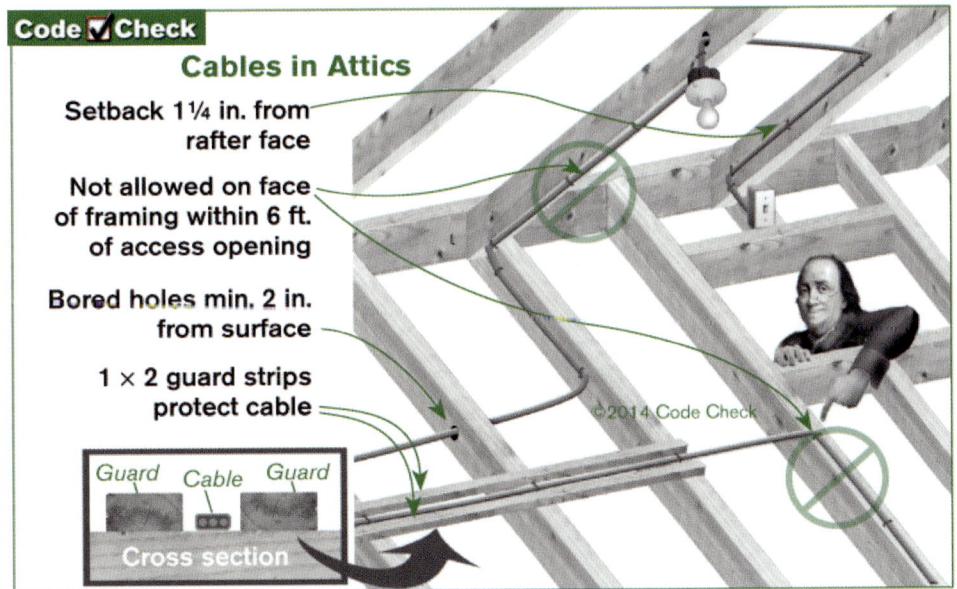

suggest to customers that insulation be added. Several inches (4"–6") of foam glued to the back works much better than a fiberglass batt stapled to the drywall square. There should also be a curb or dam around the access hole so that loose or blown-in insulation doesn't fall each time the attic is accessed.

Once you gain access to the attic, take a moment to examine the area before you go charging in. Determine if the lighting is adequate (required if mechanical equipment is present in the attic), if conditions are safe, whether you'll be able to access the entire space, and so on. Check the floor so that you know how to get from one end to the other. And make a note of what's in the attic, such as chimneys, exhaust venting, furnaces or air handlers that you don't want to miss. It's wise to get yourself organized before you begin the inspection.

Structure Review

During the attic inspection, the home inspector will inspect the **roof structure** of the home, including the following structural members:

ATTIC STRUCTURE

- Cracked, bowing, or twisting rafters
- Rafter spread and sidewall separation
- Sags in the roof
- Delaminated plywood
- Loose truss fastenings; bowing trusses; cracked, cut, or missing members
- Deterioration of structural members
- Water penetration

- Rafters, collar ties, purlins, and knee walls
- Lateral bracing
- Roof sheathing
- Ceiling structure

Check down the rafters for any cracks, warping, and sagging. Be sure rafters are securely fastened to all other framing members—ridge, top plate, and joist connections and supporting structures. Rafters should be reinforced if they're supporting heavy equipment on the roof and should not be cut for any reason. Watch for **rafter spread**, a condition where the roof load bearing on the rafters forces them outward. Check the ridge board for cracking and twisting. If collar ties or purlins are present, inspect them for buckling and secure nailing to the rafters.

If **roof trusses** are present, watch for any cracked, cut, or missing truss members and check gussets for secure attachment. Be sure that lateral bracing is present along the diagonal webs of the truss if it's required. (Usually, a brightly colored tag on the truss states whether this is required.) Another condition that can be present is **truss uplift**, a phenomenon where the bottom chord of a roof truss bows upward during the cold months and returns to normal position during the warmer months. Often, it will carry the ceiling with it, and you can see cracks at the ceiling-wall intersection in the rooms below.

Inspect the roof sheathing and check for sags, warping, and buckling of the panels or boards. Check that nails and H-clips (if present) are in place and holding. Report any indication of delamination of the plywood sheathing. In older homes 1× planking was typically used, so look for cracked or split boards and knots that have cracked.

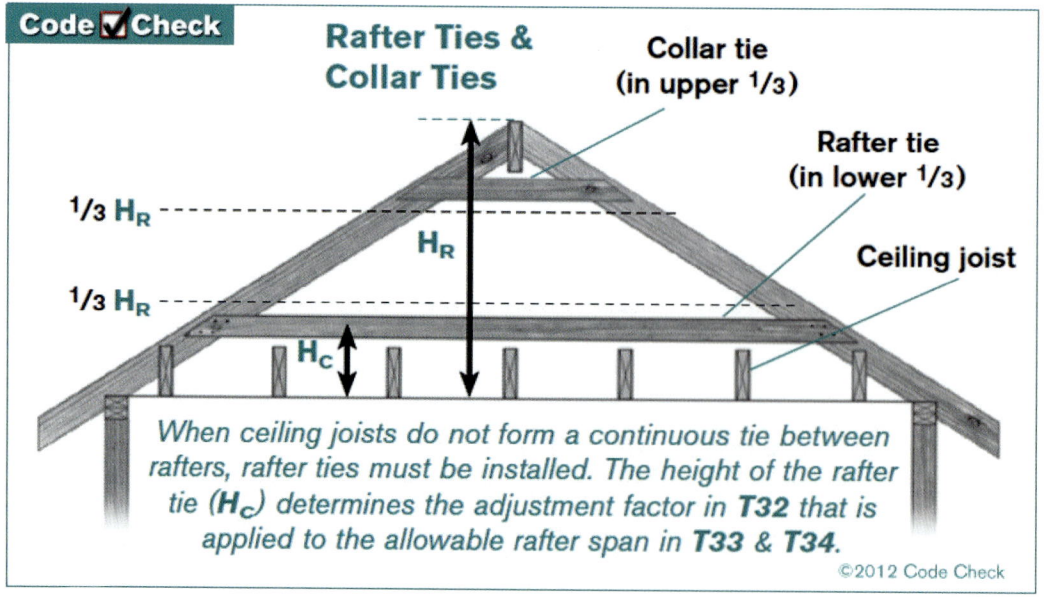

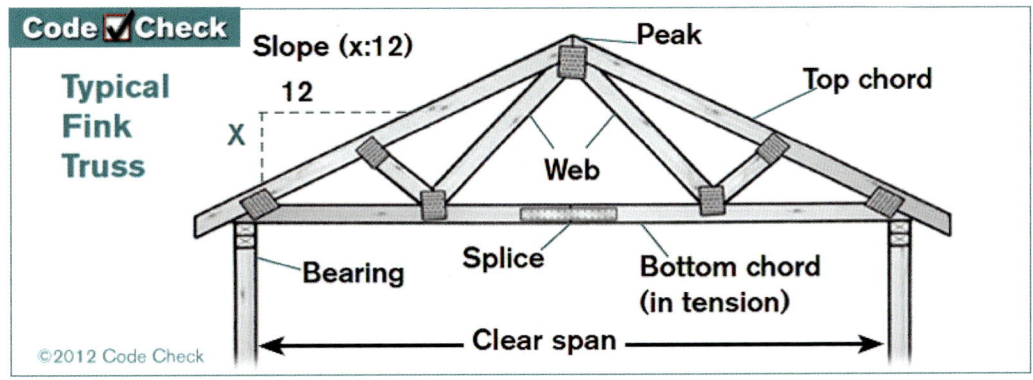

OSB will turn to mulch over time with excessive attic moisture or continuous leaking of the roof covering. As you inspect structural members, watch for any signs of water penetration, condensation, or deterioration in any of the members.

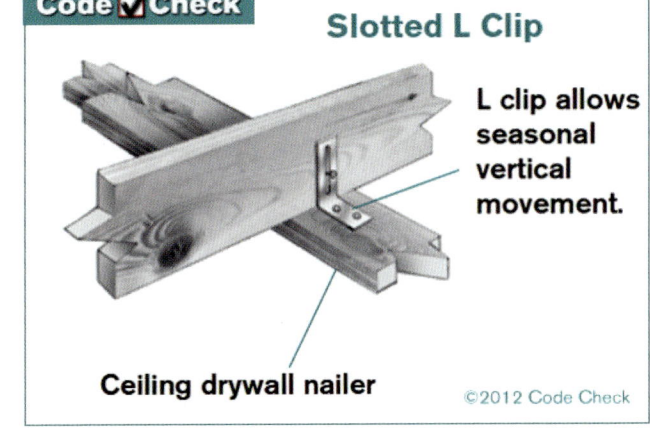

Water Penetration
The home inspector should examine the attic for any evidence of water leaking into the house. Examine the sheathing and rafters for any signs of deterioration from water penetrating through the roof surface. Inspect the chimney to see if there is any deterioration in the mortar and bricks from leaking flashings or moisture condensing in an unlined chimney. Check carefully around other roof openings such as vents and piping to be sure they are water-tight.

Insulation
Inspect the attic insulation as instructed on pages 613–632. First, identify the type of insulation; then estimate the depth in inches. Check for proper installation and look for gaps, blocked vents, and so on. Feel the insulation for dampness and determine the condition of the insulation. Try to locate a vapor retarder against the warm side of the house. If foam rigid insulation is present and exposed in the living areas, report it as a **safety hazard**. Advise customers to cover the rigid insulation for fire safety.

Ventilation
Inspect the attic ventilation as instructed on pages 632–643. Locate and identify the type of vents. Check the vents for condition and blockage. Watch for any vents that are covered over completely in the winter. Watch for improper venting of plumbing and house exhaust fans.

The Chimney
Check the chimney chase in the attic for condition and signs of leaking at the roof penetration. In a **masonry**

> **Personal Note**
>
> *"I found the children's swimming pool in the attic during one of my inspections. When I came down from the attic, I told my customers I had good news and bad news. I told them they had an indoor pool, but they had to use it in the attic. Otherwise, the roof leak would wreck the ceiling.*
>
> *Be sure to investigate all of the attic and everything in it. I could have so easily dismissed this pool, thinking it was just being stored up there. Be suspicious about buckets and basins sitting in the attic."*

THE INTERIOR INSPECTION

> **Section Note**
>
> *For more information on chimney inspection, see Chapter 03.*

chimney, check the mortar and bricks for condition. If the chimney is not lined (has no separate flue), any cracked or missing bricks or missing mortar means that carbon monoxide gases, soot, creosote, and sparks may be escaping directly into the attic. This should be reported as a **safety hazard**.

Metal chimneys passing through the attic must be isolated from the floor and roof framing with approved fittings. Metal chimneys must have at least a 2″ clearance from combustibles, and the home inspector may find this clearance open in the attic floor. This is a **fire hazard**, as a fire starting in the basement can move right up the chimney into the attic. An appropriate fitting around this clearance opening should be a noncombustible material such as sheet metal. Inspect a metal chimney for corrosion, rusting, and open or loose joints. Look for soot or creosote buildup around the joints. Any discoloration indicates that smoke and carbon monoxide gases are leaking into the attic. Report any open or leaking joints as a **safety hazard**.

> **ATTIC ELECTRICAL**
>
> - Uncovered or missing junction boxes
> - Damaged or brittle knob-and-tube wiring
> - Wiring buried under insulation
> - Extension cord wiring
> - Recessed lights covered by insulation

Electrical Safety

The home inspector's main concern with the electrical wiring in the attic is whether it poses any safety hazards, not that it is code-compliant.

Carefully inspect the visible wiring, junction boxes, fans, and light fixtures in the attic. The home inspector should watch for and report the following **safety hazards**:

- **Uncovered or missing junction boxes:** We've seen uncovered junction boxes half buried in the insulation and even splices with no junction boxes. These practices are terribly unsafe and must be reported and remedied.

- **Brittle and damaged knob-and-tube wiring:** Knob-and-tube wiring is old wiring that can become damaged or brittle after years of overheating. Check out the wiring and the connections for condition. This wiring should never be buried under the insulation because of the likelihood of it being damaged in some way. It's a definite safety hazard and is prohibited by the NEC. When knob-and-tube wiring is present, check out any light fixtures or switches present where connections are likely to be poor. We always suggest that these old fixtures and connections with cloth-insulated wire be replaced for safety's sake.

> **Section Note**
>
> *For more information on inspecting the electrical system, see Chapter 05.*

- **Extension-cord wiring:** The NEC forbids the use of extension cords as part of the permanent wiring in a home. This is especially dangerous in the attic, where extension cords are taking the place of proper wiring to light the attic. Report the use of extension cords as a safety hazard.

- **Recessed lights covered with insulation:** Unless a recessed ceiling light fixture is rated for an insulated ceiling (IC), there should be a 3″

clearance between the fixture and the insulation. It's easy to tell if the light is rated. The home inspector is not required to dig out the light to check, but should advise the customer to do so and provide proper clearance if the light is not properly rated. The inspector should report the fixture as a safety hazard if it's covered with insulation.

You'll be a hero if you find safety hazards in the attic. Some homeowners never go into the attic to look, and dangerous situations can be sitting there waiting for something to happen.

Equipment in the Attic

The home inspector will inspect fans and power ventilators and any heating and cooling equipment located in the attic. There must be a catwalk from the access hole to the mechanical equipment as well as an overhead light and electrical receptacle if mechanical equipment is present. If these are not present, recommend that they be installed. If an air handler or furnace is present, care should be taken to inspect the condition of the condensate tray and auxiliary drip pan for any signs of corrosion, rusting, or leaking into the attic.

Reporting Your Findings

When you report on your inspection of the attic, begin by noting how you accessed the attic. Be specific. Record whether you inspected it from the scuttle, the pull-down

> **Section Note**
>
> *"One of my inspectors found a situation of immediate danger when he saw knob-and-tube wiring sparking onto old cellulose insulation in an attic. He told the homeowner and the realtor on the spot, suggesting that they call an electrician immediately. He was a hero, although the homeowner chose not to listen to his warnings. The home burned down a week later!"*

> **DON'T EVER MISS**
>
> - Deteriorating structural members
> - Water penetration
> - Improperly installed insulation
> - Signs of inadequate ventilation
> - Deteriorating chimney
> - Electrical safety hazards

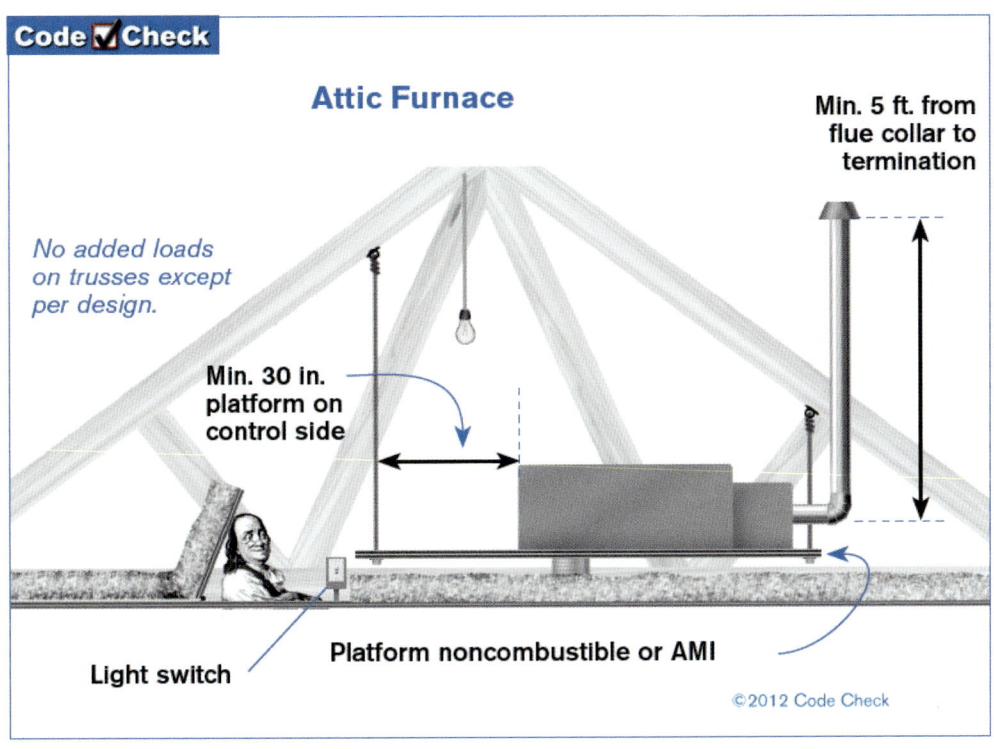

Code Check — Attic Furnace
- No added loads on trusses except per design.
- Min. 30 in. platform on control side
- Min. 5 ft. from flue collar to termination
- Light switch
- Platform noncombustible or AMI

©2012 Code Check

THE INTERIOR INSPECTION 649

stairs, or the stairs, or whether you got into the attic and viewed all of it or were not able to view it at all. This is for your own protection. Serious defects can be present under the roof that you're not able to see. Be sure that your report clearly states this.

We've already discussed reporting on the insulation and ventilation inspection of the attic. Here's what is left to report on:

- **Roof structure:** Identify structures as rafters or trusses and note their condition in your report. Then identify the sheathing material and its condition. Make a note of any defects such as loose gusset plates on trusses, cracked rafters, and other structural problems you observed.

- **Chimney:** Report on the chimney chase as viewed from the attic, noting missing bricks or mortar as a safety hazard.

- **Water penetration:** Don't miss recording roof leaks. Make a point of distinguishing between old and fresh water stains if you like (use a moisture meter to distinguish between the two), but don't overlook writing about water stains just because they're old. You probably can't determine whether the roof is still leaking.

- **Electrical:** Always record your findings of electrical safety hazards as indicated on pages 647–648. If you've reported these safety hazards on the attic page, it's a good idea to repeat them on a summary page of your report.

GLOSSARY

ABS
An abbreviation for acrylonitrile butadiene styrene, a black plastic piping used in DWV piping. Uses mechanical glued no-hub joints.

A-coil
A type of evaporator coil in a cooling system that consists of double plates of coils connected at the top, forming an "A" shape.

Acoustic tiles
Ceiling tiles made of fiberboard, fiberglass, cork, or mineral particles.

Adapter
A device with a 3-slot receptacle for an appliance plug and a 2-prong plug for inserting into a 2-slot receptacle.

Adequate flow
Whether there is enough water volume flowing, which is measured in gallons per minute.

Aerobic bacteria
Bacteria that live in an oxygen-rich environment and break down solid waste matter.

Air-cooled air-conditioning
A cooling system where heat is removed from the refrigerant by means of a fan blowing air over the condenser.

Air gap
A "gap of air" between the fixture and the sink or tub it is filling or draining to.

AirKrete
A site-foamed insulation made of a mixture of cement containing syrup and air.

AL
An abbreviation for the metal aluminum and indicating that breakers or other components are approved for use with aluminum wiring.

Alligatoring
A process in which the solvent in paint evaporates too quickly, leaving residual solvent in the paint and causing wrinkling or cracking of the surface.

Alternating current
An electrical current, used in homes, in which electrons move back and forth at a frequency of 60 cycles per second.

Aluminum siding
Horizontal planks of aluminum with a baked-on enamel surface, used as a wall cladding.

Ampacity
The number of amps that can safely pass through a given conductor.

Amperage
The unit of measure for current.

Amperage rating
In home inspection, the size of service supplied to a home. For example, a 100-amp or 200-amp service.

Amps
The unit of measure for current.

Anchor post
In a tieback, the wooden post that connects to a wooden retaining wall and extends back into the soil.

Angled crack
A diagonal foundation crack caused when the upload and download on the foundation offset each other.

Anode rod
In a water heater, a rod, usually magnesium or aluminum, that gives up ions before the steel tank does, thus protecting the tank.

Anticipator
A device on a thermostat that turns a heating system on or off just before temperature settings are reached.

Anti-oxidant compound
A grayish paste applied to aluminum wiring connections to prevent aluminum oxide from forming.

Anti-siphon device
See *Backflow preventer*.

Aquastat
A temperature-sensitive device in a boiler that is immersed in water to detect temperature changes in water, thereby activating the circulating pump.

Aquifer
A water-bearing strata of permeable rock, sand, or gravel in the earth.

Arc fault
An unintended arc flowing through an unintended path such as a loose wire in a receptacle arcing in the box when an appliance is plugged in.

Artesian well
A well whose aquifer has enough pressure to bring water to the surface without a pump.

Asbestos
A mineral fiber found in rocks and used in home products including insulation. The EPA considers asbestos fibers to be a health hazard.

Asbestos cement shingles
A mixture of Portland cement and asbestos fibers in shingle form that is used as a roof covering.

Asbestos cement siding
A mixture of portland cement and asbestos fibers in shingle form, used as a wall cladding.

Asphalt composition siding
Asphalt-impregnated felted mats coated with an asphalt formation and covered with a granular material, used in shingle form as a wall cladding.

Asphalt shingles
Asphalt-impregnated felted mats coated with an asphalt formation and covered with a granular material that are used in shingle form as a roof covering.

Automatic fill valve
A valve on the plumbing line to a boiler that adds water to the system.

Auxiliary condensate line
Drain piping from an air conditioning system in addition to the main condensate line.

Awning window
A window hinged at the top to open outward.

Backflow preventer
A device such as an anti-siphon device or vacuum breaker that prevents water from being siphoned from a contaminated source into the supply system.

Balancing duct damper
A damper located in the branch supply ducts that equalizes the flow of warm air from the furnace to the house.

Balcony
A platform protruding from the house that is not supported by the ground.

Balloon framing
A construction method where long vertical studs and corner posts run from the foundation to the roof and the floors are hung on the wall frame.

Balusters
The vertical poles that support the railing of a staircase.

Barometric damper
A hinged plate located in the smoke pipe above an oil-fired heating system which swings open or closed to regulate drafts.

Baseboard
    A trim piece used at the intersection of the wall and floor.

Battens
    Narrow strips of wood placed over joints in vertical wood plank siding to seal the joints.

Batts
    Pre-cut lengths of fibrous insulation manufactured to fit between studs and joists and made of cellulose, fiberglass, or rock wool.

Bay windows
    Three windows set at angles with each other in a bay that protrudes from the structure.

Bead board
    Rigid board polystyrene insulation produced by expanding and fusing granular pellets.

Beams
    See *Girders*.

Below grade
    Below the surface of the ground.

Bending
    In terms of structure, the movement of a structural member out of its original position without shearing as a result of forces applied to the member.

Beveled
    Clapboards that are tapered planks rather than perfectly rectangular in cut.

Bifold door
    A two-section door hinged in the middle to allow one section to fold back on the other before the door is swung to the side.

Bi-metallic vent damper
    A damper in a smoke pipe that expands open when exhaust gases heat up and contracts closed when gases cool.

Bitumen
    Petroleum asphalt or coal tar.

Blankets
    Continuous rolls of fibrous insulation manufactured to fit between studs and joists and made of cellulose, fiberglass, or rock wool.

Blast tube
    The component of an oil burner that holds the nozzle and ignition electrodes and extends into the combustion chamber.

Bleeder
    Piping that runs from exterior drain tile under or through the footings to interior tile and to the sump pump.

Blocking
    A bracing method using a brace of wood between joists that is the same depth as the joists giving stiffness to the joists.

Boiler
    A heating unit that heats the home with hot water or steam distributed through pipes.

Bonding
    Electrically connecting two or more conductive items together and to the grounding system.

Bow
    A vertical curve in a wall, where the wall has an outward curve from top to bottom.

Bow windows
    More than three windows set at angles with each other in a bay that protrudes from the structure.

Box bay
    Bay windows where the windows are set in a bay at right angles to each other.

Branch circuit wiring
    That portion of the electrical system that runs from the electrical panel to outlets, switches, and fixtures in the home.

Branch lines
    Water supply pipes that carry water from risers to fixtures and faucets in the house.

Brass

An alloy of copper and zinc.

Brazed

The use of silver solder in the soldering process.

Breaker

See *Circuit breaker*.

Brick ties

Accordion-style metal fasteners used to attach a brick veneer to the wood framework of a house.

Brick veneer

A wall construction method in which an outer layer of bricks is attached to the wood framework of the house using brick ties.

Bridging

A bracing method using a 2 × 4 brace of wood between joists giving stiffness to the joists. Cross bridging uses diagonal 1 × 3s between joists.

British thermal unit

A unit of measure of heat output, representing the amount of heat required to raise or lower the temperature of 1 pound of water 1° Fahrenheit. Abbreviation *BTU*.

Building paper

A paper installed between plank sheathing and wall cladding that acts as a water repellent.

Built-in gutters

A trough built as part of the roof at the rafter ends, normally made of wood lined with metal.

Built-up roofing

Alternating layers of impregnated felt and hot bitumen topped with a weather-resistant coat of bitumen that is used as a roof covering. Usually topped with gravel, slag, or a layer of roll roofing.

Bulge

A combination of both bow and sweep in a wall.

Busbar

A conductor bar that provides connections and power for fuses and breakers and thus to circuits.

Butterfly roof

A roof style with two opposite slopes sloping inward toward the center of the roof.

BX cable

A metal armored cable used in branch circuit wiring which carried only a hot and neutral wire until the 1950s, but now also carries a ground wire.

Cantilever

An extension of the floor structure that depends on the strength of the unsupported portion of the girder or joists to carry the load of the structure.

Carbon monoxide

A life-threatening gas and combustion byproduct. Abbreviation *CO*.

Casement window

A window hinged at one side to open outward.

Casing

A wood piece covering the edge of a window or door frame where it meets the wall cladding.

Caulking

A waterproof material used to seal joints at interfaces between building components, used with some wall claddings.

Cavity wall

A masonry wall with a dead air space left between inner and outer layers of masonry.

Cellulose insulation

An insulating material made of shredded recycled newspaper or wood fibers treated with a fire retardant and used as loose fill.

Centrifugal pump

A motorized pump that lifts water from a well by means of a paddle wheel driven by a motor. Used in jet and submersible pumps.

Ceramic tiles

Hard-fired clay tiles that can be glazed or unglazed and used as a floor covering.

Cesspool

    A masonry-lined hole used to hold and break down solid materials from the home's waste system before releasing them into the ground through porous masonry.

Chalking

    A process in which ultraviolet radiation causes the vehicle in exterior house paint to break down and pigment particles to be released.

Chase

    See *Chimney chase*.

Check valve

    On a sanitary pump, a valve that prevents waste from the sewer line from backing up into the crock.

Checking

    In wood plank siding, a crack or split along the grain as a result of cupping.

Chemical corrosion

    Corrosion that occurs when metals react with oxygen, carbon dioxide, or salts in water, using metal atoms to form new compounds.

Chimney cap

    A concrete covering for the top of the chimney chase.

Chimney chase

    The outer construction that encloses the flue.

Chimney flashing

    Metal or roll roofing flashings used in the joint between the chimney and roof to prevent water penetration.

Chimney flue

    The channel that carries gases, fumes, and smoke from heating units and fireplaces.

Chinking

    A mortar made of clay, sand, and other binders such as animal hair used to fill the gaps between logs in a log home.

Chord

    An outside member of a truss, horizontal or on an angle.

Cinderblock

    A block made of slag from steel making or railroad cinders that were used in home construction.

Circuit

    A complete path of an electric current.

Circuit breaker

    An overload protection device that opens a circuit and stops the flow of electricity when the circuit overloads.

Circulating pump

    The pump that circulates water in a hot water heating system.

Cistern

    A reservoir, tank, or container for storing or holding water or other liquid

Clapboard

    Overlapping, horizontal wood plank siding made from either rectangular planks or tapered planks.

Cleanout

    A plug-sealed extension at the sewer outlet that is unplugged when work needs to be performed on the sewer lines.

Clear

    In wood shingles or shakes, wood with no knots or wormholes.

Closed cornice

    Trim and moldings at the eave with both a vertical fascia board and a horizontal soffit.

Closed system

    A hot water system with a sealed expansion tank located just above the boiler.

Closed valley

    A valley where the roof covering continues over the valley and the flashing is not visible.

CO/ALR

    A rating indicating that breakers, connectors, switches, and outlets are approved for use with aluminum branch circuit wiring.

Coated steel
   Steel sheeting coated with tin, antimony, lead, or nickel alloys and used as a roof covering.

Collar ties
   Horizontal structural members of the roof that connect opposite pairs of rafters together to prevent rafter sag and rafter spread.

Columns
   Vertical supports that carry the weight of the structure from the girders to the ground, transmitting weight to the footings.

Combustion air
   The air required for mixing with fuel such as oil or gas before the fuel is burned.

Combustion chamber
   The chamber in a furnace or boiler in which fuel is burned. Called a firebox in older oil burners.

Composition board
   Planks or sheets of compressed wood fibers with weather resistant binders, used as a wall cladding.

Compound wall
   A solid masonry wall built of two different materials.

Compression
   A stress that pushes on a structural member tending to make that member reduce its size.

Compressor
   The component of a cooling system that moves refrigerant and pressurizes the refrigerant gas in order to raise its temperature.

Concrete block
   A block made of crushed stone, Portland cement, builder's sand, and water used in construction, especially foundation walls.

Concrete masonry unit (CMU)
   Various kinds of hollow-core blocks used in foundation construction.

Condensate line
   Drain piping from an air-conditioning system to dispose of condensation.

Condensate tray
   A tray under an air-conditioning unit to collect condensation.

Condenser
   A coil in a cooling system through which the refrigerant gas flows that removes heat from the gas, condensing it into liquid form.

Condensing units
   See *High-efficiencies*.

Conduction
   The transfer of heat from a warmer object to a cooler object by physical contact.

Conductor
   A material that offers a low resistance to an electric current flowing through it. Also, the wire used in the home's electrical system as in the grounding conductor, service conductor, and so on.

Conduit
   A metal cable, rigid or flexible, used in branch circuit wiring, which can carry two hot wires, a neutral, and a ground wire.

Convection
   The transfer of heat through air, water, or steam that moves heat from a warmer location to a cooler location.

Convectors
   Heat outlets in the home consisting of finned plates or pipes that deliver hot water from a boiler and warm the air passing over them.

Conventional heating systems
   Generally refers to furnaces and boilers manufactured before the mid 1970s which had low operating efficiencies.

COPALUM
   Special crimp connectors that are used in connecting aluminum branch circuit wiring to copper at each receptacle, switch, and junction.

Copper-clad aluminum
   An electrical conductor composed of an inner aluminum core and outer copper cladding

Copper pigtailing
> A wire nut method used in connecting aluminum branch circuit wiring to copper at each receptacle, switch, and junction.

Cornice
> The trim and moldings at the eave line.

Cornice molding
> A trim piece used at the intersection of the wall and ceiling.

Counter flashing
> A second layer of flashing that covers a bottom layer of flashing where roof and wall meet.

Course
> Each row of siding material.

CPVC
> An abbreviation for chlorinated polyvinyl chloride, a white or beige plastic piping used in supply piping. Joints are solvent-welded.

Crawl space
> The unfinished area between the house floor and the ground.

Crazing
> A condition in a paint surface where the new layer of paint shrinks while drying causing a net-like pattern of cross cracking.

Creosote
> A by-product of a wood burning fire.

Cricket
> A small peaked roof perpendicular to the main roof slope constructed at the high side of a chimney.

Cross bridging
> See *Bridging*.

Cross connection
> A condition where water from the DWV system can be siphoned back into the supply system.

Cupola
> A small, rounded structure built on top of a roof; it is normally used to ventilate attics.

Cupping
> In wood plank siding, a warp across the grain of the board.

Current
> The flow of electricity that results when the electromotive force is applied across a given resistance. Also called amperage, is measured in amps.

Damper
> In a fireplace, a metal plate that closes the throat when the fireplace is not in use.

Dead load
> The weight of a structure itself, its sheathing and wall coverings, and other integral components.

Deadman
> In a tieback, a cross piece spiked to the anchor post at the end in the soil, used to anchor a wooden retaining wall to the soil.

Deck
> An independent structure or platform that is attached to the house.

Decorative fireplace
> A false fireplace designed to imitate the look of a real fireplace.

Dedicated circuit
> A circuit provided for the sole use of a large appliance such as the refrigerator or dishwasher.

Deep wells
> A well in which the water level is at a depth exceeding 25 feet, beyond which the ordinary suction pump does not operate satisfactorily.

Delamination
> A deterioration process during which the layers in the laminated plywood panel begin to separate.

Desulfovibrio bacteria
> Bacteria that live in hot water in the presence of magnesium, causing hot water to smell like rotten eggs. Can contaminate water heaters.

Detachment
 With veneer or stucco wall cladding, the separation of the siding material from its attachment to the house.

Dielectric connector
 A type of connector used between two dissimilar metal pipes that prevents metal-to-metal contact between the pipes and stops the flow of electricity along the pipes.

Dip tube
 In a water heater, the tube that sends cold water to the bottom of the tank.

Dormer
 A structure built out from the roof slope having its own roof and walls.

Double course
 An application of wood shingles or shakes where an undercourse, not exposed to the weather, is covered completely by a top course.

Double hung window
 A window with two sashes which both move.

Double tapping
 Adding wires at fuses or breakers for the purpose of adding more circuits to the electrical system. Not allowed, except with breakers approved for double tapping.

Downspout
 The vertical piping connected to gutters that carries rainwater from the roof to the ground.

Draft air
 The air required to insure discharge of exhaust gas from a heating system through the flue.

Draft diverter
 A device built into a furnace that protects the heating system from excessive updrafts and chimney downdrafts.

Draft hood
 A device on top of a boiler that protects the heating system from excessive updrafts and chimney downdrafts.

Drain pipes
 Any discharge pipes in the DWV system.

Drain tile
 Flexible, perforated plastic piping used in footing drains.

Drain valve
 On a water heater, a valve at the base of the tank used to drain water.

Drain, waste, and vent system (DWV)
 Piping that carries water and waste from the home's fixtures to the sewer or septic system.

Drip edge
 A flashing laid at the eaves and rakes to direct water flow into the gutters or off the roof.

Drip loop
 Slack in electrical wires at the masthead which prevents water from running into the conduit.

Drum trap
 A canister-shaped unvented trap used under fixtures such as bathtubs and laundry sinks.

Dry base boiler
 A boiler with the heat exchanger set above the combustion chamber.

Dry laid
 A stone foundation laid stone upon stone without mortar or footings.

Dry vent
 A vent in the home's DWV system that carries only air and water vapor.

Drywall
 A manufactured gypsum sheet covered with paper and used as a wall and ceiling facing.

Drywell
 A buried gravel pit that accumulates water and allows it to seep into the ground slowly.

DWV
 See *Drain, waste, and vent system*.

Eave
 The overhang or lower portion of the roof that extends beyond the outer wall.

Edge grain
> A cut of wood taken at right angles to the rings of a tree.

Efflorescence
> The white mineral deposit left after water passes through the foundation wall bringing dissolved salts from the wall material. It appears on the interior wall after the water has evaporated.

Electric plenum heater
> An auxiliary heater, usually added to an oil-fired furnace, located in the plenum.

Electric resistance room heating
> Baseboard convectors, wall mounted strips, or floor inserts that each operate as a separate heating plant.

Electrical meter
> The meter provided by the utility company that measures home electrical use in watts.

Electrolytic corrosion
> Corrosion that occurs when two dissimilar metals are connected to each other in water containing dissolved salts, releasing metal ions and causing a current to flow.

Electromotive force
> The force that drives a current of electrons through a given resistance. Electromotive force, also called voltage, is measured in volts.

Electronic vent damper
> A damper in a smoke pipe that automatically opens before the burner starts and closes when exhaust gases cool down.

Equalizer
> A loop of piping running from the top of a steam boiler to the bottom that balances pressure above and below the water line in the boiler.

Evaporator
> A coil in a cooling system through which refrigerant flows that causes the refrigerant liquid to absorb heat which changes the liquid to a gas.

Evaporative cooler
> A cooling system that uses the evaporation process to cool and moisturize the air for home cooling, typically in dry climates.

Expansion device
> A device in a cooling system through which refrigerant liquid flows that depressurizes the liquid and cools it down.

Expansion tank
> A tank in a hot water heating system that provides space for water to expand into. Tanks may be open or closed.

Extruded polystyrene insulation
> Rigid board insulation produced by extrusion.

Facing
> The material applied directly to studs and joists to form walls and ceilings.

Fan control
> A temperature-sensitive switch that turns the furnace fan off and on at preset high temperatures.

Fan/limit switch
> A furnace control combining both a fan control and a limit control.

Fan safety switch
> A switch on a furnace that prevents the fan from operating when the access panel is removed.

Fascia
> A flat trim board fastened to the outer edge of the roof rafters.

Faucet
> A device used to turn water on and off at a delivery point, and operates with a washer, a cartridge, a ball, a valve, or an O-ring mechanism.

Felt paper
> An underlayment laid on roof sheathing under the roof covering.

Fiberglass insulation
> An insulating material made of threads of glass covered with a coating that binds the fibers in place and used as batts, blankets, loose fill, and rigid board.

Fiberglass shingles
> Mats of glass fibers covered with bitumen and a granular material and used in shingle form as a roof covering.

Finish flooring
> The flooring applied over the subfloor that provides the finish floor for the home.

Fink truss
> A triangular roof truss with W-shaped interior webbing.

Firebox
> In a fireplace, the open chamber in which the fire burns.

Firebrick
> A special brick designed to withstand high temperatures.

Fireplace insert
> A metal stove with a door that is totally or partially inserted into a fireplace.

Firewall
> A fire resistant wall used where garage walls abut the house, preventing the spread of fire.

Fish-mouthing
> A condition with asphalt shingles where the center portion of the tabs curl upward due to overheating.

Fixed-pane window
> A window that does not open or close.

Fixture
> Any sink, tub, shower, and toilet to which water is delivered in the home.

Flame retention burner
> An oil burner with a flame retention ring that provides for more efficient combustion.

Flame retention ring
> On an oil burner, a cone-shaped, slotted head on the blast tube that provides pressure, velocity, and rotation to the air stream.

Flame rollout
> A condition in a gas burner where the flames burn outside the combustion chamber.

Flashing
> Sheet metal used at interfaces between building components to prevent water penetration.

Flat roof
> A variation of a shed roof with a very small slope, less than 2/12.

Floating slab
> Where an independent slab does not rest on the foundation wall.

Floor truss
> An engineered, prefabricated rectangular floor framing component.

Flue
> A channel in a chimney or combustion appliance for conveying flame, exhaust gases, and smoke to the exterior.

Flue liner
> A material that lines the chimney, usually terra cotta tiles.

Flue pipe
> The exhaust pipe running from a gas water heater to the chimney.

Flush door
> A door made of veneer glued to a solid or hollow core.

Flux
> A material used in the soldering process that eliminates chemical contamination.

Footing drain
> A drainage system laid around the perimeter of a foundation below the level of the slab which drains water from the soil to another location.

Footings
> The bases on which the foundation rests which support and distribute the weight of the structure to the soil.

Forced-air heating system
> A system in which air heated in a furnace is circulated by means of a blower unit through ductwork to registers in the house.

Forced hot water heating system
> A system in which water heated in a boiler is circulated by means of a circulating pump through pipes to radiators or convectors throughout the house. Also called a hydronic system.

Foundation
> The part of the structure that supports it, transmits its weight from above-grade walls to the footings, and protects it from effects of soil pressure.

Frost line
> The depth of penetration of frost into the ground, normally about 4′ below grade in cold climates.

Functional drainage
> A determination of whether water drains fast enough and completely.

Functional flow
> A determination of whether water flows with enough pressure and volume.

Furnace
> A heating unit that heats the home with warm air distributed through ductwork.

Fuse
> An overload protection device that melts and opens a circuit when the circuit overloads. May be cartridge or screw-in types. Type D fuses are time delay, type P is sensitive to heat buildup between the fuse and fuse holder, types S and C prevent the wrong size fuse fitting into the fuse holder.

Gable roof
> A roof style made up of two equal and opposite slopes that meet to form a ridge.

Gable vent
> A vent located at the gable ends of the roof.

Galvanic corrosion
> See *Electrolytic corrosion*.

Galvanized steel
> Steel sheeting covered with zinc and used as a roof covering.

Gambrel roof
> A roof style with a double slope on each side where the bottommost slope is the steepest.

Gas chiller
> A cooling system that uses ammonia as a refrigerant and uses heat to drive the refrigerant cycle.

Gas manifold
> In a gas burner, the gas line that delivers gas to the burners.

GFCI
> An abbreviation for a ground fault circuit interrupter, a monitoring device that will trip after a ground fault is detected, stopping the flow of electricity in a circuit.

GFCI receptacle
> A receptacle which has a monitoring device that will trip the circuit when a ground fault is detected.

GFCI tester
> A testing device used to test the operation of GFCI receptacles and three-slot receptacles for polarity and grounding.

Girders
> Horizontal load-bearing members of a floor system that carry the weight of the floor and wall loads to the foundation and columns. Also called beams.

Glazing
> The window pane made of glass or other material.

GPM
> An abbreviation for gallons per minute, a measurement of water flow.

Grade
> The slope of the land at the building site.

Grade beams
> Poured reinforced concrete beams that rest on grade, just in the ground, or on piers.

Grading
> The slope of the land around the house.

Gravity hot water heating system
> A system in which water heated in a boiler rises naturally through pipes to radiators in the house.

Gravity steam heating system
> A system in which water boiled in a boiler changes to steam which rises naturally through pipes to radiators and condensate drains back to the boiler.

Gravity heating system
A system in which air heated in the furnace rises naturally through ductwork without the aid of a blower unit. Also called an octopus furnace.

Gray water
Drainage from all portions of the house plumbing other than the toilet, which is called black water.

Ground-level gutter
A concrete trough in the ground that catches rainwater runoff from the roof and carries it away from the house.

Grounded receptacle
A receptacle wired with a ground wire that is connected to the grounding system.

Grounding
The process of electrically connecting electrically conductive items to the earth by which means excess electrical current is absorbed into the ground.

Grounding conductor
The wire used to ground the home's electrical system.

Grounding system
The means by which a home's electrical system is grounded, typically by connecting a ground wire to plumbing pipes, a concrete encased electrode, or to metal rods buried in the earth.

Gusset plate
A piece of wood placed over partial bearing joists and nailed into the joists to hold them in place. In a truss, metal or wood connectors that hold members of the truss together.

Gutter
A metal, plastic, or wood trough attached to the roof at the eaves to collect rainwater and carry it away from the roof.

Gypsum
A common mineral, also called sulfate of calcium, used in plaster.

Hardwood
Woods such as oak, beech, birch, hard pine, maple, pecan, and walnut.

Hartford loop
A loop of return piping that turns downward to connect to the equalizer just below the water level, preventing water from flowing out of a steam boiler in case of a leak in return piping.

Head
The top piece in a window frame.

Header
A horizontal framing member that carries the load above a window or door opening. Also called a lintel.

Header joist
The perimeter joist nailed to the sill. Also called the rim joist.

Header rows
Rows of bricks turned small end out to act as ties to hold a brick wall together.

Hearth
The floor of the fireplace, usually poured concrete about 4″ thick.

Heartwood
The wood taken from the inner core of a tree.

Heat exchanger
A heavy metal hood above the combustion chamber that holds and contains the burner flame. In a furnace, it separates exhaust air from the circulating air that heats the house. In a boiler, it separates exhaust air from the circulating water.

Heat pump
A reverse-cycle air conditioner that operates as both a cooling and heating system by reversing the flow of refrigerant.

Heating chamber
In a gas water heater, the chamber where the gas is burned.

Heating elements
In an electric water heater, the upper and lower electrical heating units.

High-efficiencies

Gas and oil furnaces and boilers with an operating efficiency in the 90+% range. Units typically have two or more heat exchangers, reducing exhaust gas temperatures low enough to condense. Also called condensing units.

Hip roof

A roof style with a slope on all four sides, either meeting in a peak or a ridge line.

Hollow core door

A door with a honeycomb or patterned cardboard core framed in solid rails and jambs and covered with a veneer.

Hopper window

A window hinged at the bottom to open inward.

Horizontal crack

A horizontal foundation crack often caused by pressure being applied by soil outside the foundation.

Hose bib

A faucet on the exterior of the home.

Hot wire

An electrically charged wire, carrying a charge of 120 volts in home circuits.

Howe truss

A triangular roof truss that incorporates vertical webbing into its configuration.

House main

See *Service pipe*.

House trap

A large U-shaped fitting with capped heads found where the home waste lines join the public sewer.

Hub

Enlarged end of a pipe which is made to provide a connection into which the end of the joining *pipe* will fit.

Humidifier

A device added to a furnace that adds moisture to the circulating air.

Hydronic boiler

A boiler used in a forced hot water heating system.

Ice damming

A phenomenon that occurs when melting snow refreezes at the eaves and traps water from snow melting from the upper part of the roof.

ID

An abbreviation for inside diameter, referring to pipe measurements.

Ignition electrodes

On an oil burner, a pair of electrical elements located in the blast tube to provide a spark that ignites the oil.

Induced draft fan

A fan that pulls combustion products through a furnace or boiler, ensuring a good draft and reducing heat loss.

Insulator

A material that offers a high resistance to an electric current flowing through it.

Interlayment

Roofing felt installed between courses of wood shakes.

Intermittent pilot

A pilot which lights only on a call for heat.

J channel

A manufactured component of an aluminum or vinyl siding system which has a curved channel that the planks fit into. Used around window and door openings to make a weather tight seal.

Jalousie window

A window with narrow strips of glass that move together, lifting out from the bottom as the window opens.

Jambs

The side pieces in a window frame.

Jet pump

A motorized pump that recirculates pressurized water into a well and pushes water to the surface by means of a centrifugal pump and jet assembly.

Joint cement

A plaster-like paste used to seal the joints between sheets of drywall.

Joists

Horizontal members of a floor system that carry the weight of the floor to the foundation, girders, or load-bearing walls.

Junction box

A covered metal box used to protect connections or junctions in an electrical circuit.

Kalsomine

A mixture of glue, pigment, and water that was once used as a finish on plaster ceilings.

Knee wall

Supporting wall running from the ceiling joists to rafters to prevent rafter sag.

Knob-and-tube wiring

Old branch circuit wiring using ceramic knobs to secure wire to surfaces and tubes to pass wires through framing members.

Knockout

The fuse holder. An open knockout is one without a fuse in it.

Kraft paper

A water-resistant, asphalt-impregnated paper that can be used as a vapor barrier.

Laminated glass

A multiple light glazing with a sticky plastic inner light that holds broken pieces of glass together when the glass breaks.

Laps

Strips of roll roofing.

Lath

Strips of wood, wire mesh, or gypsum board attached to studs and joists to form a base for plaster to adhere to.

Leach field

See *Seepage field*.

Ledger

A framing member installed for the purpose of attaching floor joists. Typical method of attachment for decks.

Ledger strips

Lengths of wood nailed along the bottom edge of a girder to provide support for joists.

Light

Each pane of glass making up a window.

Limit control

A control that turns off the burners in a furnace when circulating air reaches a preset high temperature or in a boiler when water reaches a preset high temperature (forced hot water) or pressure reaches a preset high pressure (steam).

Lintel

A horizontal steel member that carries the masonry components above an opening, such as a door or window.

Live load

The weight of the home's occupants, the furnishings of the home, and other weight the structure must support.

Load

A light or appliance that uses electricity on a circuit.

Loose-fill insulation

A loose insulating material poured or blown into place between wall studs and attic joists and made of fiberglass, rock wool, cellulose, or vermiculite.

Louvered door

A door with plastic, wood, or cloth slats in a frame.

Low water cut-off

A safety control on a boiler that shuts off the burner when the water level falls below the required amount for the system.

Low voltage system

A lighting system featuring boxes of relays, unusual switches, and one or more switching panels.

LP gas

Liquefied propane or petroleum gas used as a fuel source. Can also be a mixture of propane, butane, or iso-butane.

Macerating toilets
Often used in basements due to their ability to pump waste (liquids and solids) straight up.

Main automatic gas valve
A device on a furnace or boiler that starts and stops the flow of gas to the burners.

Main disconnect
Fuse(s) or breaker(s) that alone or together stop the entire flow of electricity to the home. Located at the meter, in a service box, or in the main panel.

Main overload protection device
See *Main disconnect*.

Main panel
A metal box holding overload protection devices and/or disconnects for the home's electrical circuits.

Main shut-off valve
A valve that turns off the water supply to the house.

Main vent
A plumbing vent to which vent piping from each fixture is attached; it maintains the DWV system at atmospheric pressure so that gravity can clear the waste pipes.

Mansard roof
A variation on the hip roof with steeply sloping sides and a top portion that is flat or meets in a peak or a ridge.

Manual turn-off
A valve that turns off the fuel supply to a heating unit.

Master shut-off
A device that turns off electricity to the heating system and its controls. Also called a safety switch or serviceman's switch.

Masthead
A device used to provide a weatherproof connection between electrical supply lines and a building's service entrance box.

Mechanical vent
A device installed for venting purposes in an unvented location. Does not vent to the outside. Also called an air admittance valve.

Metal insert
A fireplace stove inserted in the existing masonry fireplace.

Metal shower pan
A shower pan made of lead or tin that is notorious for leaking.

Mid-efficiencies
Gas and oil furnaces and boilers with an operating efficiency in the 80% range. Units typically have an induced draft fan and motorized vent dampers.

Mildew
A fungus that can live on and in paint.

Millboard
An insulating material made of asbestos and gypsum.

Modulating aquastat
A device in a hot water boiler that senses outdoor temperature and changes circulating water temperature requirements accordingly.

Moisture permeable
A surface that allows moisture to pass through it.

Monolithic slab-on-grade
Construction where the slab and the foundation are poured as one piece.

Mortar
A mixture of a binder (lime, masonry cement, Portland cement), an aggregate (sand), and water. Used to bond masonry units such as concrete blocks, stones, and bricks together.

Mortise and tenon connections
Joining joists to girders where a mortise (hole) in the girder accepts the tenon (a projecting end) of the joist.

Motorized duct damper
A damper located in zoned supply ducts that controls the flow of warm airfrom a furnace to zones within the house.

Motorized vent damper
A damper located in the smoke pipe above a furnace or boiler that opens and closes automatically to prevent heat loss up the chimney.

Multi-pane window
   A window with small pieces of glass set into wood or lead muntins.

Multiple lights
   Glazing consisting of two or three layers of glass or other material.

Multiple tapping
   See *Double tapping* and *Tapping before the main*.

Muntins
   A grid of cross pieces of wood or lead that hold small panes of glass in a multi-pane window.

Nail pops
   A condition where nails cause bulges in drywall when they back out of the studs.

National Electrical Code (NEC)
   A national standard for electrical installations published by the National Fire Protection Association.

Neon bulb tester
   A testing device used to test two-slot and three-slot receptacles for polarity and grounding.

Neutral busbar
   A conductor bar that provides connections for the main neutral and ground wires and the ground and neutral wires from each branch circuit.

Neutral wire
   A wire with no electrical charge (where equal and opposite currents cancel each other out) that provides a return path for electricity in a circuit.

No-hub joints
   A type of joint between two sections of pipe made with a sleeve that is securely clamped to both pipe sections. Commonly known by the brand Fernco.

Nosing
   The extension of the tread over a riser on a staircase.

Octopus furnace
   See *Gravity heating system*.

Ohms
   The unit of measure for resistance.

Oil burner nozzle
   A device located in the blast tube which shoots out oil particles into the firebox.

One-pipe system
   A hot water or steam heating system with a single piping run to and from the boiler and the radiators or convectors.

Open ground
   Where a grounded type receptacle is not grounded.

Open return
   In the basement, an opening in the furnace or return ducts for collecting return air. Most often prohibited.

Open system
   A hot water system that has an expansion tank open to the atmosphere and located above the highest radiator in the home.

Open valley
   A valley where the roof covering stops short of the valley and the flashing is visible.

Operating controls
   On a gas water heater, a control unit with a thermostat and gas controls.

Outlet
   An electrical connecting device providing receptacles into which appliances can be plugged for power.

Overflow
   An auxiliary drain in bathtubs and some sinks.

Overfusing
   Using a fuse on a circuit that is larger than the wire's capacity. Not allowed.

Overhead door
   A garage vehicle door made of hinged panels that "bend" along overhead tracks as the door is opened. May be manually or automatically opened.

Overload protection device
　　A fuse or breaker which will break the circuit when it overloads.

Overshooting
　　A condition when a house is heated higher than the thermostat is set for.

Palmer valve
　　A hinged valve in the floor drain that allows water from the drain tile system to flow through the floor drain into the sewer.

Panel door
　　A solid door where the rails and stiles are grooved in such a way to hold an inset panel.

Parapet
　　A low wall running along the edge of a flat roof.

Parquet
　　A finish floor composed of 6″ squares made up of six 1″ strips of wood laid at right angles to each other.

Patio
　　A flat, paved area abutting the house.

PB
　　An abbreviation for polybutylene, a blue or gray plastic piping used in supply piping. Uses press-on fittings on joints.

pCi/L
　　An abbreviation for picocuries of gas per liter of air, the way radon is measured.

PE
　　An abbreviation for polyethylene, a plastic piping sometimes used in public water systems.

Pedestal-style pump
　　Motor mounted on a shaft sitting above the water level.

Perlite
　　An insulating material made of volcanic rock and used as loose fill.

Picture window
　　A large fixed-pane window.

Piers
　　Columns supporting a structure that are built on footings in a hole below the frost line.

Pigment
　　The color particles in paint.

Pilaster
　　A masonry column built against a wall to help absorb the horizontal load and stiffen the wall.

Piles
　　Columns supporting a structure that are driven into the ground to reach soil of bearing strength.

Pilot
　　The small flame that ignites gas in a gas burner.

Piston pump
　　A motorized pump that lifts water from a well with a series of pistons. Also called a reciprocating pump.

Pitch pocket
　　A circular metal box surrounding the plumbing stack, filled with a plaster of paris material, topped with tar or bitumen, and used as stack flashing.

Pitting
　　Disintegration of the surface of the driveway material caused by poor quality materials or installation, acid spills, or the use of a de-icing salt.

Pivot window
　　A window that pivots open from a center hinge.

Plaster
　　A powder made of gypsum and other aggregates that forms a paste when wet and a durable surface when applied and dried; used as a wall and ceiling facing.

Platform framing
　　A construction method where the stories of the house are constructed one on top of each other.

Plenum
　　The first large section of supply or return duct directly before or after a furnace from which smaller ducts branch out to or from the house.

Ply
A layer of roof covering.

Plywood
A building material made of three or more layers of wood sheets joined with glue.

Plywood siding
Plywood sheets, some with a decorative or grooved outer surface, used as a wall cladding.

Pocket door
A door designed to slide sideways for concealment in a wall.

Polarized receptacle
A receptacle with a large neutral slot and a smaller hot slot for plugging in appliances with large and small prongs.

Polystyrene foam boards
A plastic rigid board insulation used as a wall insulator. Must be covered for fire safety.

Polystyrene insulation
A plastic foam insulation manufactured as rigid boards.

Porch
A roofed extension of the house that is built as a part of the house.

Porch columns
Vertical members that support the porch roof and the floor system.

Post and beam
An old construction method in which a small number of posts and beams carry the weight of the structure to a plank flooring.

Poured concrete
In a foundation wall, concrete poured into forms that are removed after the concrete has set, thereby forming a wall.

Power
The work produced by the flow of current through a given resistance. Power is measured in watts, kilowatts, and BTUs.

Power ventilator
An electrically powered ventilator located at the gable end of the roof or on the roof surface between rafters.

Pressure gauge
On a pressure tank, a gauge that shows the pressure reading of the tank.

Pressure reducing valve
A valve on the water supply line to a boiler that reduces water pressure to an acceptable boiler pressure.

Pressure relief valve
A valve on a boiler that will discharge water from the boiler if pressure approaches dangerous limits.

Pressure switch
On a pressure tank, a switch that automatically starts and stops the well pump at preset pressures.

Pressure tank
A storage tank that holds well water under pressure by being partially filled with air.

Pressure-treated wood
Wood impregnated with chemical preservatives that protect the wood from termites and fungi that cause rot.

Primary control
A control on a oil burner that starts and stops the burner in response to thermostat signals, and verifies ignition. May be located on the smoke pipe or burner housing.

PSI
An abbreviation for pounds per square inch, a measurement of water pressure.

P-trap
A P-shaped trap commonly used today below fixtures and usually vented.

Puffback
In an oil burner, a condition where smoke, soot, or flames escape from the combustion chamber.

Pull-out fuse block
A handled block containing cartridge fuses that can be pulled out to stop the flow of electricity.

Pump control
> A control on a boiler that turns on the circulating pump at a signal from the thermostat upon a call for heat or from an aquastat at a certain preset temperature.

Pump house
> A separate building constructed for the purpose of housing well equipment.

PVC
> An abbreviation for polyvinyl chloride, a white plastic piping used in DWV piping. Uses mechanical solvent-welded no-hub joints.

Racking
> A condition where a structure leans in such a way that the angles it forms with the foundation are no longer 90°.

Radiant heating
> A system consisting of continuous piping from the boiler or electric cables laid out in rows buried in the floor or ceiling, thereby heating a room by radiation.

Radiation
> The transfer of heat from a warmer object to a cooler object not in contact with it by radiating heat energy.

Radiators
> Heat outlets made of heavy metal piping that deliver hot water or steam from the boiler and radiate heat into the room.

Radon
> A gas that occurs naturally when uranium in the soil and rocks breaks down. The EPA considers radon to be a health hazard.

Rafter spread
> A condition where the roof load bearing on the rafters forces them outward.

Rafters
> Structural members of a pitched roof that support the roof covering and transmit roof loads to bearing walls and beams below.

Rail
> The top or bottom piece in a window sash.

Rain cap
> A metal cap attached to the top of the chimney flue allowing gases to escape but preventing rain from entering the flue.

Rake
> The overhang at the gable end of the roof.

Reciprocating pump
> See *Piston pump*.

Recreational facilities
> Spas; saunas; steam baths; swimming pools; exercise, entertainment, athletic, playground, and other similar equipment; and associated accessories.

Refrigerant
> The gas in a cooling system that changes between a gas and liquid state, commonly called Freon or Puron.

Refrigerant lines
> The copper piping that moves the refrigerant in both gas and liquid states through a cooling system.

Registers
> Heat outlets in the home that deliver warm air from the furnace.

Relief valve
> On a water heater, a valve that releases water when temperature or pressure is too high.

Relief valve extension
> Discharge piping from the relief valve on a water heater to the floor.

Resilient floor coverings
> A range of tiles and sheet goods laid as a finish floor, including linoleum, rubber tiles, and various vinyl sheets and tiles.

Resistance
> The opposition offered by a material when a current passes through it. Resistance is measured in units called ohms.

Resting slab
> Where a slab is laid to rest on top of a conventional foundation.

Retaining wall

    A wall constructed to hold back soil.

Return ducts

    Ducts that deliver air from the home back to the furnace or air conditioner.

Reverse grading

    A condition where the land around the house slopes toward the foundation.

Reverse polarity

    Where the hot wire is wired to the large slot in an electrical outlet and the neutral wire is wired to the small slot, the opposite of how it should be done.

Reverse trap toilet

    A two-piece (tank and bowl) toilet with a larger wetted area than earlier models.

Reversing valve

    A valve in a heat pump that changes the direction of the refrigerant.

Ribbon slate

    Slate shingles with a ribbon of color in them.

Ridge

    The horizontal intersection of two sloping roof surfaces.

Ridge board

    A horizontal framing board at the peak of the roof to which rafters are attached.

Ridge cover

    Protective flashing laid across the ridge and finished with shingles or roll roofing to protect the ridge from water penetration.

Ridge vent

    A vent located on the roof ridge, running the length of the ridge.

Rigid board insulation

    Wide rigid boards of insulation used on foundations and walls and made of fiberglass, wood fiberboard, or foamed plastics.

Rigid metal conduit

    See *Conduit*.

Rise

    The vertical height of the roof.

Riser

    The vertical portion of a step in a stairway.

Risers

    Water supply pipes that carry water vertically up through the house.

Rock wool

    An insulating fibrous material made by blowing steam through molten rock or slag and used as batts, blankets, or loose fill.

Roll roofing

    An asphalt-impregnated felted mat of fibers coated with asphalt formations, covered with a granular material, and used in strips as a roof covering.

Romex cable

    A non-metallic sheathed cable used in branch circuit wiring which carries a hot, a neutral, and a ground wire.

Roof covering

    The outer layer of shingles, tiles, or other materials used to protect the roof from water penetration.

Roof truss

    An engineered, prefabricated geometric roof framing component.

Roughed-in fireplace

    An opening left with a connection to the chimney intended to provide the space for a fireplace to be installed later.

Run

    The horizontal length of the roof from the eave to the center point.

R-value

    A number that represents an insulation material's resistance to heat flow per inch of thickness.

Safety glazing
Glass is a breakable material, which when broken into smaller sharp pieces often called shards can cause serious injury. Safety glazing material, usually tempered glass or laminated glass, reduces the risk of injury.

Safety reverse feature
A mechanism on an automatic overhead door that will reverse the movement of the door if it encounters an obstacle when closing.

Safety switch
See *Master shut-off*.

Sanitary pump
A sealed crock located in the basement floor that contains an electric pump and pumps gray water from fixtures into the sewer line or drywell.

Sash
The framework in a window that holds the glass or other material.

Scarfed joint
A joint used in plywood siding where edges of abutting sheets are angle cut to fit snugly and prevent water penetration.

Scissors truss
A roof truss used in vaulted or cathedral ceilings.

Scuppers
An outlet in the side of a building for draining water.

Seepage field
Underground porous concrete drain tiles that receive liquid discharge from a septic system for seepage into the ground.

Self-flashed valley
A valley where the roof covering continues over the valley but there is no flashing underneath.

Self-storing window
A double hung window with a storm and screen permanently mounted in a three-channel metal or plastic frame.

Separation walls
Walls between the garage and living area that must be covered with drywall for fire resistance. Also called firewalls.

Septic tank
A watertight underground tank of concrete, steel, or fiberglass into which household waste is held and broken down for release to a seepage field.

Service box
A metal box, separate from the main panel, that contains the main disconnect.

Service conductors
The wires bringing electricity to the home.

Service drop
Overhead wires bringing the electrical service to the home.

Service entrance
The portion of a home's electrical system from the utility pole to the home's main disconnect.

Service lateral
Underground wires bringing the electrical service to the home.

Service pipe
The pipe that brings water from its public or private source into the house.

Serviceman's switch
See *Master shut-off*.

Setback feature
A feature on a thermostat that can be set to automatically lower temperature settings during certain hours.

Sewage ejector pump
Consists of an electric pump along with its sump or crock. Also known as a solid waste pump or an ejector pump or a lift pump because it can pass solids up to 2″ in diameter through the pump.

Shallow Wells

A water well, generally dug up by hand or by machinery

Shear

A stress resulting from forces being applied upon a structural member from opposite directions. Can cause the member to crack, split, or completely separate.

Sheathing

Sheets of plywood or wood planking used to cover the roof frame.

Shed roof

A roof style with a single slope slanting in one direction.

Shiplap

A style of milled plank used in plank siding that is laid close enough to appear to be butted.

Shoe

The curved section at the bottom of the downspout that directs water away from the house.

Short cycling

A condition where the heating or cooling system turns on and off too often.

Sidelight

Shining a flashlight parallel to the wall or ceiling to bring out defects, sags, or bows that wouldn't be visible shining the flashlight directly on the wall or ceiling.

Siding

See *Wall cladding*.

Sill

The bottom piece in a window frame. Also, the 2 × 4 or 2 × 6 laid flat and anchored to the foundation, providing a pad for the framing system.

Single bus panel

An electrical panel with a single pair of busbars for either 120-volt or 240-volt circuits.

Single course

An application of wood shingles or shakes where each course is exposed to the weather.

Single hung window

A window with two sashes, only one of which moves.

Single ply

One layer of roof covering.

Single-ply membrane

A modified asphalt, plastic, or rubber membrane laid in adhesives or mechanically fastened that is used as a roof covering.

Siphon jet toilet

A reverse trap toilet with a quiet flush.

Siphon vortex toilet

A late model one-piece toilet with a large wetted area and a silent flush.

Site-foamed insulation

Insulation made of syrups and reactants mixed at the building site and foamed in place.

Slab floor

A poured concrete floor, as in a garage, that rests directly on the ground.

Slab-on-grade

A poured concrete slab that rests directly on the ground.

Slate shingles

Sedimentary rock in shingle form that is used as a roof covering.

Slider window

A window with a sash that moves horizontally.

Slope

The ratio of a roof's rise to its run. Normally expressed with the measure of the rise over a run of 12′. A slope of 3/12 is stated as "three in twelve."

Smoke chamber

In a fireplace, the area between the damper and the flue that guides smoke toward the flue.

Smoke shelf

In a fireplace, the base of the offset between the damper and the flue that interferes with and interrupts chimney downdrafts.

Snow shovel
In roofing, a metal finger-like claw installed with slate roofing to hold snow and ice in place until it melts.

Soffit
The horizontal board laid on the underside of the eave.

Soffit vent
A vent located in the soffit along each side of the roof.

Softwood
Woods such as pine, fir, and cedar.

Soil pipes
Waste pipes that carry waste from toilets in the home.

Soil stack
The main vertical waste pipe fed by all other waste pipes that carries waste to the sewer to the septic system.

Soldering
The process of using flux and a soft solder to make a joint in copper piping.

Sole plate
In platform framing, the horizontal framing member nailed to the deck, rim-joist, and floor joists at the outer edge of the structure.

Solid brick wall
A wall construction where three layers of brick are used to construct a solid wall with no wood framing.

Solid waste pump
A sealed tank in the basement floor that contains an electric pump that pumps toilet waste up to the sewer line.

Solvent
The third constituent in paint that evaporates after the paint is applied. Also called the thinner.

Spalling
The crumbling and falling away of the surface of bricks, blocks, or concrete.

Span
The distance center to center between two like framing members such as floor joists.

Spillage
A condition where combustion by-products spill out of a heating unit's exhaust system.

Split bus panel
An electrical panel with two or more pairs of busbars. The upper busbar is for 240-volt circuits, one of which provides power to the lower busbar. The lower busbar is for 120-volt circuits.

Split receptacle
A receptacle wired with two hot wires and a neutral, which provide two separate circuits to the receptacle, plus the ground wire for grounding purposes.

Square
The amount of roofing material used to cover 100 square feet of roof surface.

Stack relay
A oil burner primary control that is located on the smoke pipe.

Stacks
Vertical piping in the DWV system.

Standalone air-conditioning system
A cooling system with a compressor/condenser unit and an evaporator unit with its own fan, filter, and ductwork. Does not work in conjunction with a furnace.

Standing pilot
A pilot flame that burns continuously.

Standpipe
An outdoor elevated water reservoir.

Starter course
Shingles or shakes laid under the first course of shingles at the edge of the roof.

Step crack
An angled crack appearing along the block joints in a concrete block foundation.

Step flashing
Short lengths of overlapped flashing to form a continuous sloping flashing that is used parallel to the slope of the roof.

Stile
　　The side piece in a window sash.

Stippling
　　A texturing process where a stipple finish is sprayed over drywall.

Stop molding
　　A bottom framing piece in a door frame that stops the movement of the door.

S-trap
　　An S-Shaped unvented trap once used under plumbing fixtures.

Stringer
　　The side supporting member that supports a stairway.

Structure
　　A home's skeleton, including its foundation and footings, roof, and framework.

Stucco
　　A water resistant, plaster-like material made of sand, cement, and water, applied and used as a wall cladding. May have an acrylic finish.

Subflooring
　　Horizontal sheets or planks that transfer the load of the home's furnishings and people to the floor joists.

Submersible pump
　　A motorized pump that sits in the well and pushes water to the surface by means of a motor and centrifugal pump.

Subpanel
　　A panel connected to a main panel for the purpose of providing more circuits and better distribution of electricity to the home.

Sump pump
　　A pit located in the basement floor that contains an electric pump that pumps water from the perimeter drain system away from the house.

Supply ducts
　　Ducts that deliver warm air from a furnace to the home or deliver cool air from a cooling system to the home.

Supply system
　　Distribution piping from the source of water supply to the home's fixtures and faucets.

Supported slab
　　Where the edges of a slab rest on a ledge at the top of the foundation wall.

Surround
　　The wall around the bathtub that is made of ceramic tile or a premolded fiberglass.

Sweep
　　A horizontal curve in a wall, where the wall has an outward curve from side to side.

Tab
　　In a shingle roof, each shingle.

Tankless coil
　　A coil inserted into a boiler to heat water for domestic use.

Tapping before the main
　　Adding wires before or at the main disconnect for the purpose of providing more circuits to the electrical service. Not allowed.

Temperature, pressure gauge
　　A gauge on a boiler that shows the current operating temperature and pressure in the boiler.

Tempered glass
　　Glass that shatters into small, smooth edged cubes when it breaks.

Tension
　　A stress that pulls at a structural member tending to make that member increase in size.

Terne metal
　　A copper containing steel alloy sheet covered with an 80% lead and 20% tin plating and used as a roof covering.

Terrazzo
　　A mix of marble chips and concrete laid in squares bordered by lead beading and polished smooth and used as a floor covering.

Texturing

Adding sand or other agents to a conventional finish on a wall or ceiling. Also a design put in the finish coat of plaster done manually with a trowel.

Thermocouple

A bimetallic element that senses whether or not the pilot is lighted and controls the pilot control valve, turning off the flow of gas to the pilot when the pilot flame is out.

Thermostat

A temperature-sensitive device that opens and closes a circuit in response to temperature changes in the air, thereby activating a heating or cooling system.

Thinner

See *Solvent*.

Three-phase

A 120/240-volt service with four conductors in a home.

Throat

In a fireplace, the top of the firebox.

Tieback

A heavy wooden post and cross piece used to anchor a wooden retaining wall to the soil behind it.

Tile

Concrete or clay flat, curved, or corrugated shaped forms that are used as a roof covering.

T-lock shingles

A rare style of interlocking asphalt shingles.

Tongue and groove floor

Boards with the top edge of each board wider than the lower. When nailed in place, the top edges fit snug with no gaps.

Top plate

In platform framing, the horizontal framing member nailed to the wall studs at the top of each story.

Trap

A device that holds water in the plumbing system and prevents the backflow of gases.

Tread

The horizontal portion of a step on a stairway.

Trim

The pieces added to the exterior siding that protect the framework from water penetration.

Truss

An engineered, prefabricated framing member used in floor and roof construction.

Truss uplift

A phenomenon where the bottom chord of a truss bows upward during the cold months and returns to its normal position during the warmer months.

Turbine vent

A vent with air-powered vanes on a central rotating spindle and located on the roof face.

Turn-off valves

Valves in the water supply system that allow water to be turned off to certain locations in the house.

Type D fuse

Typically used for electrical devices such as an AC unit.

Type P fuse

Has an added safety feature in that it is also sensitive to heat buildup between the fuse and the fuse holder.

Type S and C fuses

A mechanism designed to fit into a screw shell socket to determine whether the fuse is blown. Available in 15, 20, and 30 amperes.

UFFI

An abbreviation for urea formaldehyde foam insulation, which is made of an insulating material in a syrup form and a reactant to create a site-foamed insulation.

Underground feed (UF)

Cable used underground.

Underlayment

Roofing felt laid in a single layer between the roof sheathing and the roof covering.

Unlined flue
　　A chimney where the chase serves as the flue.

Upheaval
　　A condition where sections of a driveway rise due to poor construction, an insufficient base, or tree roots and stones moving under the surface.

Urethane insulation
　　A plastic foam insulation manufactured as rigid boards or foamed in place at the building site.

Vacuum breaker
　　See *Backflow preventer*.

Valley
　　The trough formed by the junction of two sloping sides of the roof.

Valley flashing
　　Metal or roll roofing flashing laid in a valley to protect the junction from water penetration.

Vapor barrier
　　A type of waterproof sheeting used to prevent the passage of moisture through a surface.

Vault
　　An elevated indoor water reservoir, often located in the attic, from which water flows by gravity.

V-crack
　　A crack that increases in width along its path.

Vehicle
　　The film-forming compound in paint.

Veneer
　　See *Brick veneer*.

Vent pipes
　　Pipes that carry gases and pressure that builds up in the DWV system.

Vent stack
　　Main vertical vent pipe fed by all other vent pipes that exhausts through the roof.

Vent system
　　All vent pipes in the home, exhausting above the roof.

Vermiculite
　　An insulating material made from heated and expanded mica and used as loose fill.

Vertical crack
　　A vertical foundation crack often caused by settlement of the structure.

Vinyl siding
　　Horizontal polyvinyl chloride planks, used as a wall cladding.

Voltage
　　See *Electromotive force*.

Voltage rating
　　In home inspection, the size of volt service supplied to the home. For example, a 120-volt or 240-volt service.

Volts
　　The unit of measure for electromotive force.

Wall cladding
　　A siding or covering for the exterior of the house that protects the framework of the structure.

Wall sheathing
　　Sheets of plywood or wood planking used to cover the wall framework of the structure.

Wall studs
　　Vertical wall framing members.

Washdown toilet
　　An older model two-piece (tank and bowl) toilet with a large bulge in front of the bowl and a small wetted area.

Water cooled air conditioning
　　A cooling system where heat is removed from the refrigerant by means of water surrounding the condenser.

Water hammer
　　Happens when water flow is shut off suddenly and a shock wave is sent back toward the supply end. It happens because flowing water has momentum.

Water heater

A household appliance consisting of a gas or electric heating unit under a tank in which water is heated and stored.

Water level sight gauge

A glass tube showing water level in a steam boiler.

Waterlogged

Filled or soaked with water as to be heavy or hard to manage

Water meter

A device for measuring and registering the quantity of water that passes through a pipe or other outlet.

Water pressure

The push behind the water flow.

Watts

The unit of measure of power. One watt is equal to 3.4 BTUs.

Web

An interior member of a truss.

Weep holes

Openings in the bottom row of brick in a veneer wall providing an exit for water accumulating behind the veneer.

Well

A deep hole made in the ground through which water can be removed.

Well pit

A masonry chamber with a hatch cover and a floor below the frost line.

Well pump

Made to draw water from the well and push and/or pull it through the house piping system with enough force to provide an adequate flow.

Wet base boiler

A boiler where the heat exchanger surrounds the combustion chamber.

Wet vent

Provides ventilation from two fixtures on the same floor where the upper fixture (a sink) shares the same pipe as a lower fixture (a shower).

Whole house fan

A fan with an intake from the house designed to change house air every minute or so. Can be gable-mounted with a self-closing louver in an upper hall ceiling.

Winders

Pie-shaped treads used when staircases curve or make a turn.

Window frame

The framing that surrounds and holds the sash.

Wire mesh

A mesh attached to the wall sheathing and studs used to anchor a stucco base coat to the wall.

Wood plank siding

Rectangular wood planks, installed vertically or horizontally as a wall cladding.

Wood shakes

Thick, rough, uneven shingles that are handsplit, split and sawn on one side, or sawn on both sides, used as a wall cladding.

Wood shingles

Shingles that are sawn and are of uniform thickness, used as a wall cladding.

Wood stove

An insulated freestanding metal wood burning unit with a door.

Yankee gutters

Planks nailed to the roof surface to prevent rainwater from escaping from the roof in areas such as over doorways.

Yield or draw-down test

Test the pumping capacity of a well.

Zero clearance fireplace
A prefabricated insulated metal fireplace unit that can be wall-mounted or freestanding.

Zone control
Where different areas of the home are under the control of different thermostats.

INDEX

Above-grade construction
    Brick veneer 69-70
    Inspection 62-73
    Log homes 68-69
    Post and beam 68
    Reporting 74
    Solid masonry 71-73
    Wood framing 63-67
    Standards of practice 2-3
    Structural Insulated Panels (SIPs) 67
Acoustic tiles 559
Air cooled air conditioning
    Concerns 399-403
    Cooling 510-520
    Furnace-related components 510-520
    Heating 512
    Inspection 524-529
    Reporting 529-530
    Standalone components 520-524
AirKrete insulation 622
Aluminum siding 103
Aluminum wiring 350, 351, 353, 364
Amperage rating 320-323, 329
Arc-Fault Circuit Interrupter (AFCI) 349
Asbestos 622-624
Asbestos cement shingles 181-183
Asbestos cement siding 106
Asphalt composition siding 105
Asphalt shingles 167-171
Attic
    Access 644, 645
    Chimney 647-648
    Electrical 648-649
    Equipment 649
    Inspection 644-649
    Insulation 647
    Reporting 649-650
    Structure 645-647
    Ventilation 632-642, 647
    Vents 634-639
    Water penetration 647
Attic moisture 88
Awning window 121, 572

Balconies
    Construction 582, 583
    Inspection 134, 582-584
    Reporting 139, 140, 593, 594
Balloon framing 65, 81

Basement
    Drainage 39-40
    Floors 42
    Insulation 624, 626
    Inspection 35-49
    Overview 4
    Penetrations 35-39
    Reporting 49-52
    Stairs 41-43
    Supporting structures 43-46
    Water penetration 35-39
Bathroom
    Inspection 607-610
    Overview 595
    Plumbing 600-601
    Receptacles 609
    Reporting 612
    Walls, ceiling, floor 607, 608
Batt, blanket insulation 617, 618
Bifold door 576
Block foundation 15-16
Branch circuit wiring
    Aluminum 350, 351
    BX cable 356, 357
    Conduit 355, 356
    Inspection 355-360
    Knob-and-tube 356, 357, 359, 361
    MC 357
    NEC 357-360
    Overview 355
    Reporting 366-367
    Romex 353, 356
Breakers
    Main disconnect 324-325
    Main panel 326-328
    Reporting 353
Brick foundation 20
Brick veneer 69, 70
Brick veneer wall 112-114
Built-up roofing 173-175

Cantilevers 78, 79
Casement window 121, 571
Cathedral roof
    Insulation 626
    Ventilation 639, 640
Ceilings (see Walls and ceilings)
Cellulose insulation 619

Chimney
    Chase 201-204
    Clearances 200-201
    Construction 199
    Cricket 195, 197
    Flashings 195-196
    Flue 204-205
    Inspection 198-207, 648-649
    Reporting 206-207
Circuits
    Amperage 315, 316
    Household 314
    Multi-wire 357
    Voltage 314, 316
Clearances and codes
    Chimney 409
    Combustion air 408
Codes
    Plastic piping 238-239
    Relief valve extensions 273
    Septic systems 252, 254
    S-traps 254, 256
    Water heater exhaust 275
    Water heater location 275
    Wells 224
Collar ties 82
Columns 5, 43-44
Composition board siding 101
Concerns
    Equipment 308-310
    Fixtures, switches 369-370
    Flow 355, 356
    Main panel 339-340
    Overview 301, 304-307
    Reporting 336-337, 352-354, 366, 391
    Service entrance 304, 305, 316
Controls, gauges, valves
    Aquastat 483
    Automatic fill valve 484, 496
    Back-flow preventer 484
    Basic operating controls 495
    Exterior disconnect 511
    Fan control 457
    Fan/limit switch 458
    Fan safety switch 428
    Limit control 422, 437, 458, 483, 495
    Low water cut-off 483, 496

Main gas valve 423
Manual turn-off 420, 436
Master shut-off 406-408
Pilot control valve 422
Pressure reducing valve 483
Pressure relief valve 483, 496
Primary control 437, 438
Pump control 483
Reversing valve 534
Temperature, pressure gauge 484
Thermostat 403-406
Water fill valve 497
Water level sight gauge 497
Zone valve 485
Cooling capacity 508
Cooling Inspection
    Capacity 509
    Concerns 507-509
    Overview 503-505
    Refrigerant Cycle 505-507
Cooling system discharge
    Flue liner 433
    From combustibles 408, 410
    Gas lines 420, 422
    LP gas tank 430
    Oil pipes and tank 434
    Open return 448, 451, 465
    Outdoor compressor 510
    Remote safety switch 406
Corrosion 234, 235
Cracks 25-27
Crawl space
    Access 54
    Floor 54-57
    Inspection 54-57
    Insulation 57, 626
    Reporting 58-59
    Structures 58
    Ventilation 55-57, 632, 633
Cricket 195, 197
Cross connections 247-249

Dampers
    Balancing 448, 465
    Barometric 441
    Bimetallic vent 441
    Electronic vent 443
    Motorized duct 465
    Motorized vent 418, 455, 482
Decks
    Inspection 133, 134
    Reporting 139, 140
Decorative fireplace 589
Doors
    Bifold 576
    Closet 576
    Flush 576

Hollow core 576
Inspection 125-127, 577, 578
Louvered 576
Panel 576
Passage door 142
Pocket 576
Reporting 128, 593, 594
Types 576, 577
Vehicle door 147-149
Dormer 207
Double hung window 120, 121, 570, 571
Downspouts 210-212
Drainage
    Downspouts 210-211
    Flat roof 211-212
    Gutters 208-210
    Inspection 207-212
    Reporting 212
    Sanitary pumps 267, 268
    Sump pumps 267
Drip edge flashing 194
Driveways
    Inspection 135
    Reporting 139
Drywall 553-556
DWV system
    Drainage pumps 267-268
    Functional drainage 267, 269
    Inspection 260-264
    Overview 251
    Piping materials 257-260
    Reporting 268-271
    Septic systems 252, 254
    Venting system 254-257

Electrical
    AFCI 597
    Attic 113
    Bathroom 609
    GFCI tester 9, 597-598
    Neon bulb tester 9, 598
    Inspection review 597-599
    Kitchen 607
    Reporting 612
    Testing GFCI's 598
    Testing outlets 598
    Electric heating 500-501
Electromotive force 311-312
EPA-Certified Stoves 585
    Evaporator cooler 532-534
Exterior Insulation and Finish System (EIFS) 110-111
Exterior wall insulation 626

Faucets types 288-289
    Inspection 289-290
    Reporting 296

Sinks, tub, showers 290-292
    Toilets 293-295
Fiberglass insulation 617-619
Fiberglass shingles 167
Fireplaces
    Coal 587
    Decorative 589
    EPA-Certified 585
    Fuel-Burning 592
    Gas 587
    Insert 549, 587, 589
    Inspection 589-592
    Masonry 585, 586
    Overview 584-585
    Reporting 593, 594
    Roughed-in 589
    Ventless 589
    Zero clearance 587
Fixed-pane window 121, 572
Fixtures and faucets 289-295
Fixtures and switches 367-390
    Inspection 367-390
    NEC 368
    Reporting 391
Flashings
    Chimney 195-196
    Drip edge 194
    Inspection 189-198
    Penetration 196-197
    Reporting 198
    Ridge and hip 189, 190
    Roof-to-wall 192-193
    Sloped roof-to-flat-roof 194
    Valley flashing 190-192
Flat roof 162, 211-212
    Insulation 626
    Ventilation 639, 640
Floors
    Basement 42
    Bathroom 608
    Concrete 564
    Construction 559, 560
    Crawl space 53
    Finish flooring 560-562
    Hardwood 560
    Inspection 564-567
    Interior 59-62
    Kitchen 607
    Reporting 593
    Resilient 563, 564
    Softwood 561
    Terrazzo 563
    Tiles 562
Floor and Wall Furnace 501-503
Flue 204-205
Footing drains 12-13
Footings 10-12

Forced warm air furnace
    Components 457-465
    Concerns 399-403
    Controls 457
    Description 476-478
    Inspection 466-471
    Reporting 471-475
    Types 451-456
Foundations 3
    Block 15-16
    Brick 20
    Cracks 25-27
    Footing drains 12-13
    Footings 10-12
    Inspection 24-32
    Reporting 34
    Types 10-20
    Walls 14
    Wood 20-21
Functional drainage 267, 269
Functional flow 289-290
Fuses
    Main disconnect 323, 324
    Main panel 347-350
    Reporting 353

Gable roof 161
Gable vent 636
Gambrel roof 161
Garage
    Floor 145-146
    Passage door 142
    Inspection 140-144
    Reporting 148, 149
    Safety concerns 144, 145
    Siding, trim 141
    Structure 144
    Vehicle door 147-149
    Windows and Doors 142
Gas chiller 531-532
Gas-fired systems
    Burners 423-427
    Concerns 399-403
    Controls 422-423
    Conventional 416, 417
    Gas supply 418-420
    High efficiency 418
    Inspecting 427-433
    Mid-efficiency 417-418
    Reporting 471-475, 491, 492
Gas piping 296-300
GFCI 597, 598
    Main panel 347, 349, 350
    NEC 360
    Outlets 372-376
    Tester 307, 308, 350, 375
Girders 46, 49-50

Glazing 122, 567, 568
Grade beams 21-22
Grading
    Inspection 136-138
    Reporting 139, 140
Gravity hot water boiler
    Concerns 399-403
    Description 475-476
Gravity warm air furnace
    Components 447-449
    Concerns 399-403
    Inspection 449-451
    Operation and Distribution 447-449
    Reporting 471-475
Grounding
    Outlets 344-346
    System 329-336

Heat pump
    Air-to-Air 534-537
    Components 537-537
    Inspection 537-539
    Operation 534-537
    Reporting 539
Heat Systems
    Electric resistance 414
    Forced air 413, 485
    Forced hot water 414, 476
    Forced warm air 460, 466
    Gravity hot water 414
    Gravity warm air 412
    Heat Pump 415
    One Pipe 479
    Radiant 414
    Radiant floor 415, 479
    Reporting 471-475, 491-493, 491
    Steam 414
    Two Pipe 478
Heat Transfer 411-412
Heating review 600, 601
High efficiencies
    Boilers 480-483
    Furnaces 413-414, 455
    Gas 416-418
Hip flashing 189-190
Hip roof 161
Hollow core door 576
Hopper window 121, 571
Hose bibs 244, 251,
Hot water boiler
    Components 483-488
    Concerns 399-403
    Controls 483-484
    Description 475-491
    Inspection 488-491
    Reporting 491-493
    Types 475-480

Hot water system
    Components 272-276
    Electric 282-284
    Gas 277-281
    Inspection 271-288
    Reporting 288
Hydrolic Biolers
    Components 483-488
    Types 480-483
Humidifier 462, 516

Inspection
    Air cooled cooling 503-505
    Above-grade construction 62-67
    Around the House, 128-136
    Attic 644-649
    Balconies 134, 607-611
    Basement 35-52
    Boilers 488-491
    Branch circuit wiring 355-360
    Chimney 198-206
    Concerns 157-160, 400-403, 507-509
    Crawl space 53-57
    Decks 133, 134
    Doors 125-127, 577, 578
    Drainage 207-212
    DWV system 260-264
    Electrical 597-599
    Equipment 156-157, 308, 399-400
    Fireplace overview 545
    Fireplaces 589-592
    Fixtures and faucets 216, 289-290
    Fixtures, Switches, and Receptacles 367-391
    Flashings 189-198
    Floor 54, 145-146, 564-567
    Flow 289, 290
    Flue 204-205
    Forced air 466
    Forced hot water 488-491
    Forced warm air 466-471
    Foundation 24-32
    Fuses and Breakers 346-350
    Garage and Carport 140-148
    Gas burner 427-433
    Gas Piping 296-300
    Grading 136-138
    Heating 600
    Heat pump 537-539
    Hot water system 277-288
    Inside 30-32
    Insulation 614-616, 627-630
    Insulation overview 614-616
    Interior framing 74-78
    Interior overview 541-545
    Kitchen 602-607
    Knob-and-Tube Wiring 361-362

Index 681

Modern Wiring 362-363
Oil burner 443-447
Other rooms 611-612
Outside 28-30
Overview 1, 3-5, 91-94, 150-156,
   213-218, 395-399, 503
Patios 135
Plumbing 600, 602
Porches 132-133
Private Water Supply 229-232
Reporting 34, 62, 74, 116, 128, 139,
   148, 187-188, 198, 206, 232-233,
   250, 251, 268-271, 288, 296,
   471-475, 491-493, 528-529,
   593-594, 612
Retaining walls 138, 139
Roof covering 166-189
Roof structure 80-90
Room-by-room 595, 611
Rules 46-51
Sidewalks 135, 139
Slabs 60
Slab-on-grade 23, 60, 61
Stairs 578-582
Standards 2-3, 91, 151, 213-218,
   304, 395-396, 503, 541-545
Steam boiler 493-499
Steps, stoops 129-131
Structure 144, 145
Trim 141
Vegetation 136
Ventilation 640-642
Ventilation overview 614-616
Walls and ceilings 549-559
Walks and Driveways 135
Wall cladding 92-94
Water service piping 240-245
Water service entrance 218-219
Water supply piping 234-249
Windows 142, 573-576
Wiring 350-352
Wood stove 589
Insulated Concrete Forms 17-18
Insulation
   AirKrete 622
   Asbestos 622-624
   Attic 624, 625
   Basement 626
   Batts and blankets 617
   Cathedral roof 626
   Cellulose 619
   Crawl space 626
   Exterior wall 626
   Fiberglass 617-618, 620
   Flat roof 626
   Home 624-627
   Inspection 614-616, 627-630

   Installment 624-627
   Kraft paper 618
   Loose fill 618
   Polystyrene 621
   Reporting 630-631
   Rigid board 620
   Rock wool 618, 619
   R-ratings 618
   R-values 617
   Site-foamed 622
   Types 617-622
   UFFI 622
   Urethane 621, 622
   Vermiculite 620
Interior framing
   Cantilevers 78, 79
   Floors 60-62
   Structural framing 78
Internal stresses 8-10

Jalousie window 121, 573
Joists 47-51, 79, 83

Kitchen
   Appliances 602-605
   Cabinets 603
   Countertops 605
   Inspection 602-607
   Overview 595
   Plumbing 600, 601
   Receptables 605
   Reporting 611
   Walls, ceiling, floor 607, 608
Knob-and-tube wiring 361-362

Laundry Room 601
Lead 557
Lightning rods 206
Log homes 68-69
Loose fill insulation 618-620
Low voltage system 306, 372

Main disconnect 324, 325
Main panel
   Breakers, fuses 326-328
   Inspection 345-352
   Location 340
   NEC 340
   Reporting 352-354
   Safety 339, 340
   Subpanels 343-344
   Types 341-343
   Wiring 350-352
Mansard roof 161
Masonry fireplace 585, 586
Masthead 308, 316, 318
Metal roofing 183-185

Metal siding 103-105
Meter 319-320
Mid efficiencies
   Boilers 482
   Furnaces 454-455
   Gas 416-418
   Mini-Split Heat Pump 534
Modern Wiring 362-363
Movement 7-8
Multiple pane window 572

National Electrical Code
   Branch circuit wiring 355
   Bushings 357
   Covered Junction boxes 359
   Description 302
   Fixtures, switches 368
   Grounding 333
   Main disconnect 324
   Main panel 340
   Outlets 375
   Service entrance 317, 318
   Surface 358
   Wood framing 358

Oil-fired systems
   Burners 438-441
   Concerns 399-403
   Controls 437-438
   Inspection 443-447
   Oil supply 434-437
   Reporting 471-475, 491-493
   High-Efficiency Systems 442
Outlets
   GFCI testing 349
   Ground testing 373, 377
   Inspection 383-388
   NEC 375

Paint 114-116, 557
Parapet 198
Patios
   Inspection 135
   Reporting 139, 140
Penetration flashing 196-197
Perimeter vent 633
Piers 21
Piles 21
Piping materials
   ABS 239, 259, 260
   Brass 236-237, 258-259
   Cast iron 257, 258
   Copper 219, 235, 236, 237, 238, 259
   CPVC 239
   Galvanized steel 237, 258
   Lead 237, 240, 259
   PB 220, 239, 240

PEX 239
Plastic 238-239, 259
PVC 259, 280, 290
Pivot window 121
Plaster 550-552
Platform framing 63, 65, 81
Plumbing review 600, 601
Plywood siding 100-111
Pocket door 576
Polystyrene insulation 621
Porches
   Inspection 132-133
   Reporting 139, 140
Post and beam 68
Poured concrete foundation 16-17
Power 310
Power ventilator 638
Precast Concrete Walls 18
Private water supply 223-229
   Inspection 229-232
Public water supply 219-223

Radon 634
Rafters 80-84
Rafter spread 166
Receptacles
   Electrical 372-376
   Inspecting 383-388
   Reporting 391
   Requirements 377-383
   Testing 388
Refrigerant cycle 505, 506
Resilient floor coverings 563, 564
Resistance 311, 312
Retaining walls
   Inspection 138, 139
   Reporting 139, 140
   Types 138, 139
Reverse polarity 388
   Reporting 391
   Types 388-389
Ridge 82
Ridge flashing 189, 190
Ridge vent 637, 638
Rigid board insulation 620
Rock wool insulation 618, 619
Roll roofing 171-173
Roofs
   Enemies 162-164
   Expected lifetime 162, 183
   Rafter spread 166
   Ridge 165
   Slope 168, 179, 181
   Structure 165, 166, 197-198, 205
   Terms 160
   Truss uplift 166
   Types 161, 162

Roof coverings
   Asbestos cement shingles 159, 181-183
   Asphalt shingles 167-171
   Built-up 173-175
   Concerns 157-160
   Fiberglass shingles 167
   Inspection 166-189
   Metal 183-184
   Reporting 187-188
   Roll roofing 171-173
   Single ply membranes 186-187
   Slate 181-183
   Sprayed Polyurethane Foam 185
   Tile 179-181
   Wood shingles and shakes 175-179
Roof drainage
   Downspouts 210-212
   Flat roof 194, 197, 207
   Gutters 208-210
   Inspection 207-212
   Reporting 212
Roof structure
   Attic moisture 88
   Framing members 80-84
   Inspection 80-90
   Reporting 90
   Water penetration 88
Roof-top vent 637
Roof-to-wall flashing 192-193
Room-by-room inspection 595, 611-612
Roughed-in fireplace 589
R-ratings 618, 626, 627
R-values 617, 626, 627

Sanitary pumps 218, 270, 296
Self-storing window 570, 571
Septic systems 252, 254
Service drop 317-318
Service entrance
   Amperage rating 321-324
   Conductors 319
   Grounding 316, 328
   Inspection 316-325
   Main disconnect 316, 324
   Meter 319-321
   NEC 325
   Overview 316
   Reporting 337-338
   Service drop 317-318
   Voltage 318-319
Sheathing 87
Shed roof 162
Showers 290-292
Sidewalks
   Inspection 135-136
   Reporting 139, 140
Siding (see wall cladding)

Single hung window 120
Single ply membranes 186-187
Sinks 290-292
Site-foamed insulation 622
Skylights 206
Slab-on-grade
   Construction 23-24
   Inspection 60-62
   Reporting 62
Slate 181-183
Slate shingles 114
Slider window 121, 572
Sloped roof-to-flat-roof flashing 194
Soffits/Eaves 166
Soffit vent 638
Solar systems 206
Solid masonry walls 71-73, 111-112
Sprayed Polyurethane Foam 185
Stairs
   Components 579-582
   Inspection 578-580
   Reporting 593, 594
Standards of Practice 2-3, 91, 151, 213-218
Steam boiler
   Concerns 399-403
   Controls and gauges 495-497
   Inspection 498-500
   Reporting 500
   Systems 493-495
Steps, stoops
   Inspection 129-131
   Reporting 140
Stairs 53
Stone masonry foundation 18-19
Structure
   Above-grade 62-67
   Basement 35-53
   Concerns 58
   Foundations 10-18
   Insulated Panels 22, 67
   Interior framing 74-78
   Roof 80-90
Stucco siding 108-110
Subpanels 343-344
Sump pumps 53, 267

Tankless coil 286
Terrazzo 563
Thermal-pane window 572
Thermostat 403-406
Tiles 179-181
   Acoustic 559
   Flooring 562
Toilets 293-294
Trim 141, 559
Truss uplift 166
Trusses 84-87

Turbine vent 638
Tubs 290-293

UFFI insulation 622
Urethane insulation 621, 622

Valley flashing 190-192
Valves and devices
   Anti-siphon device 244, 249
   Check valve 267
   Drain valve 274
   Drum trap 256
   Gas turn-off 278
   Main shut-off 218
   Mechanical vent 269
   Pressure gauge 224, 228
   Pressure reducing valve 220
   Pressure switch 224, 228
   P-trap 255, 256
   Relief valve 231, 273
   S-trap 256
   Turn-off valve 272
   Vacuum breaker 248, 249
Vegetation
   Inspection 136
   Reporting 140, 141
Ventilation 55-57, 79
   Attic 634-639
   Cathedral roof 639, 640
   Crawl space 632-633
   Flat roof 639, 640
   Inspection 640-642
   Radon 634
   Reporting 642, 643
Venting system 254-256
Vents
   Attic 635
   Gable 636
   Perimeter 633
   Power ventilator 638
   Ridge 637, 638
   Roof-top 639
   Soffit 638
   Turbine 638
Vermiculite insulation 620
Vinyl siding 105

Wall cladding
   Asbestos cement 106
   Asphalt composition 105
   Brick and stone facings 114
   Brick veneer 112-114
   Composition board 101
   Exterior Insulation and Finish System (EIFS) 110-111
   Fiber Cement Siding 107
   Flashings 113
   Inspection 94-116, 118
   Metal 103-105
   Paint 114-116
   Plywood 100-101
   Reporting 116-117
   Slate shingles 114
   Solid masonry 111-112
   Stucco 108-109
   Vinyl 105
   Wall sheathing 95, 97
   Wood plank 97-100
   Wood shingles, shakes 102
Walls and Ceilings
   Acoustic tiles 559
   Bathroom 608
   Coverings 557-559
   Drywall 553-556
   Fabricated board 556
   Facings 556
   Inspection 549-559
   Kitchen 607
   Plaster 549-553
   Plywood 556, 558
   Reporting 593, 594
   Structure 556
   Trim 559
Wood planks, paneling 556
Waste disposal 252-254
Water cooled air conditioning 530-531
Water Distribution Piping 234-251
   Corrosion 234, 235
   Types of 236-240
Water heaters
   Electric 282-284
   Gas 277-281
   Other 286-288
   Oil-Fired, 284-286
   Reporting 288
Water penetration 35-39, 88
Water service entrance
   Inspection 219-234
   Piping materials 219-221
   Private supply 223-229
   Public supply 219-223
   Pump components 224
   Types of well pumps 225-227
   Reporting 232-233
Water supply piping
   Corrosion 234, 235
   Cross connections 247-249
   Functional flow 245-247
   Hose bibs 244, 251
   Inspection 240-245
   Overview 236
   Piping materials 236-245
   Reporting 250, 251
Weight 6
Well pumps
   Inspecting 229-232
   Jet 225, 227
   Piston 225
   Submersible 226
Wind and water 8
Windows
   Awning 572
   Casement 571
   Components 567-570
   Construction 121-123
   Double hung 570, 571
   Fixed-pane 572
   Garage 143
   Glazing 123, 567
   Hopper 572
   Inspection 123-125, 573-576
   Jalousie 573
   Multiple pane 570
   Reporting 148, 593, 594
   Self-storing 571
   Single hung 570
   Slider 572
   Thermal-pane 572
   Types 120-123, 570-573
Wiring
   Aluminum 364-366
   Amperage 315, 316
   Branch circuit 306, 350, 353, 355
   BX cable 357
   Conduit 319, 337, 353, 355, 390
   Damaged 350-351
   Gauges 337, 344, 364
   Grounding conductor 331
   Handyman 352
   Hot 314, 318, 334
   Incompatible 350
   Knob-and-tube 356, 361
   Main panel 350-352
   Modern 362-363
   MC 357
   NEC 357-360
   Neutral 314
   Outlets 383-388
   Reporting 352, 366
   Romex 353, 356
   Service conductors 319
Wood foundation 20-21
Wood framing 63-79
Wood plank siding 97-100
Wood shingles, shakes 102-103, 175-179
Wood stoves
   Inspection 592
   Reporting 593, 594

Zero clearance fireplace 588
Zoning 406